Pearson New International Edition

Modern Physics
Randy Harris
Second Edition

Pearson Education Limited
Edinburgh Gate
Harlow
Essex CM20 2JE
England and Associated Companies throughout the world

Visit us on the World Wide Web at: www.pearsoned.co.uk

© Pearson Education Limited 2014

 ISBN 10: 1-292-02326-0
ISBN 13: 978-1-292-02326-7

British Library Cataloguing-in-Publication Data
A catalogue record for this book is available from the British Library

Table of Contents

The Dawn of a New Age

Chapter Outline

1   Troubling Questions
2   A Glimpse of the New World

Introductory classical physics covers a body of knowledge that can explain a vast amount of what goes on around us, from the everyday to the abstract. Why does a bicycle go forward when the rider pushes downward on a pedal? What forms can energy take, and if it is conserved, why can't we reuse indefinitely? How do waves propagate energy and information without any matter moving from source to receiver? What are electric and magnetic fields?

However, early in the 20th century, revolutionary ideas arose that shook classical physics to its foundation. Even the most basic and "obvious" truths about space and time and the nature of the matter around us came under assault. In this chapter, we discuss several telling signs that something was wrong with the classical picture, then we survey the path ahead. (Certain topics from classical physics are particularly important to modern physics. A review of these topics is available on the companion website.)

1 Troubling Questions

The core topics of classical physics are mechanics, electromagnetism, and thermodynamics. Let us take a look at some of the problems that loomed in these areas at the dawn of the modern age.

Classical mechanics attained a cohesive form in the late 1600s with the work of Sir Isaac Newton. Triumphant in explaining the behaviors of macroscopic objects at ordinary speeds, Newton's work reigned unchallenged for centuries. As convincing as anything were its successes in celestial applications. When the orbit of the planet Uranus was found to deviate slightly from what Newton's laws predicted it should be, the instinctive response was to attribute the deviation not to any failure of those laws but rather to some unseen heavenly body. Newton's laws predicted its location, and Neptune was later found right where it should be. After such satisfying confirmation, it was natural to expect further examples. Mercury's orbit is somewhat elliptical, but the ellipse is not retraced again and again. It precesses—that is, its points of maximum radius advance slightly with each orbit about the Sun. Newton's laws predicted one rate of precession; actual observation differed. The discrepancy was again thought to be due to an unseen planet, but in this case, none could be found.

Maturing in the mid-19th century with James Clerk Maxwell's completion and integration of the laws of Gauss, Ampere, and Faraday, electromagnetism has been extremely successful. It superbly explains the physics behind telephonic communication and electrical power supply, which had become commonplace by the end of the 19th century, and it continues to prove its validity in countless applications to this day. Early on, however, doubts were raised about the theory's prediction of waves of electromagnetic radiation. For one thing, the lack of explicit reference to a medium of propagation seemed to put light in a special category among wave phenomena. Another problem had to do with the energy expected in electromagnetic radiation exchanged with matter. Charges in the matter should jiggle around at rates dependent on the temperature, producing and absorbing electromagnetic energy as they do. A standard wave calculation predicted that the electromagnetic intensity nearby should be infinite! Yet another perplexing question concerned the ability of light to eject electrons from a metal, known as the photoelectric effect. In the classical view, a light wave is simply a pair of self-propagating electric and magnetic fields spread diffusely through some region of space. If light encounters an electron in a metal, these fields should be able to transfer energy to the electron and knock it out of the metal. Light of low intensity might require considerable time to deposit enough energy, but a high intensity should knock electrons out at a high rate and—owing to its stronger electric and magnetic fields—should eject them with greater kinetic energy. In fact, even very low-intensity light can eject electrons immediately, and the kinetic energy of an ejected electron is completely independent of the light's intensity. The frequency of the light seemed to be the deciding factor, and classical electromagnetism could not explain why.

By the end of the 19th century, statistical thermodynamics had become one of the cornerstones of physics. Its laws had been established, and correct predictions were being made. A major step forward was the formulation of the equipartition theorem. This says that each independent degree of freedom possessed by a particle in a thermodynamic system should manifest $\frac{1}{2}k_BT$ of energy on average, where k_B is the Boltzmann constant and T is the temperature. There are three dimensions of translational freedom, leading to the famous formula for the average translational kinetic energy of a particle: $\frac{3}{2}k_BT$. In a solid, each atom has three additional degrees of freedom due to elastic potential energy in each dimension. With six total degrees of freedom per atom, the equipartition theorem predicts that a solid should have a heat capacity—energy per degree per mole—of $3k_BN_{Av}$, where N_{Av} is Avogadro's number. This prediction supported an early empirical observation that many solids seem to have a heat capacity very near this value. However, even solids that adhered to the prediction at ordinary temperatures deviated noticeably at low temperatures, where the heat capacity seemed to drop off toward zero. To classical statistical physics, this was thoroughly baffling.

Perhaps attracting more scrutiny than any other classically inexplicable phenomenon at the turn of the 20th century was the subject of atomic spectra. Atoms emit only certain wavelengths of light. Why? With the discovery of the electron by J. J. Thomson in 1898, hopes of explaining spectra rose—for a small charged particle somehow jiggling around in an atom should emit electromagnetic radiation. Neither the proton nor the atomic nucleus was yet known, and Thomson's model of the atom assumed that its electrons were embedded in a uniform sea of positive charge. No plausible oscillations of the electrons in this model could explain the observations. About a dozen years later, the work of Ernest Rutherford and his students produced the now-familiar model of electrons orbiting a positive nucleus. Although the quantum age had by then begun, Rutherford's nuclear model was still classical, and it actually compounded the mystery. An orbiting electron would be accelerating continuously, and any time a charged particle accelerates, it radiates electromagnetic energy. The nuclear atom should be unstable, with the electron spiralling into the nucleus! Perhaps not surprisingly, this model also failed to explain the spectral evidence. Some of its basic elements survived, but it was to be profoundly altered by the new paradigm.

2 A Glimpse of the New World

Much of modern physics rests on two basic ideas: First, space and time are not the absolutes they might seem to be. Second, things we might think of as particles may behave as waves, and vice versa. Although these ideas are now accepted as fundamental to physics, they initially met with considerable opposition.

The main reason they remained hidden for so long is that they involve behaviors not easily observed. And the reason they were not universally welcomed is that they often seem counterintuitive. These two reasons are related. A behavior certainly would not be counterintuitive if it were subject to simple observation. By the same token, we cannot justifiably claim to possess intuition about a phenomenon we cannot observe. Loosely speaking, modern physics is the study of the small and the fast, but no one has ever actually seen an individual atom nor has anyone ever traveled at a significant fraction of the speed of light relative to Earth. We must be careful not to apply preexisting notions based on experience to situations in which we have no experience.

The branch of modern physics dealing with space and time is special relativity. Although it is often said to be the physics that applies when objects or frames of reference are moving at very high speed, this is rather misleading, for it makes relativity sound like a special case. Relativity agrees with classical physics at low speeds, but it also succeeds at speeds comparable to that of light, where classical physics fails. Thus, classical mechanics is the special case. Of the many startling claims of special relativity, one is particularly helpful as an introduction and preparation for the challenges ahead: If passengers on a (very) high-speed train confirm that clocks at the front and back of their train strike noon simultaneously, observers on the ground will confirm that these clocks do not strike noon simultaneously. This discrepancy is very small at ordinary speeds, but it is *not* an optical illusion.

The other main branch of modern physics is quantum mechanics, which has its own challenging notions. In classical mechanics and electromagnetism, we treat the electron as a particle, but in small confines, it behaves as a diffuse wave. It does not have a specific location! All we can know are probabilities of finding the electron *if* an attempt were made to do so, and the probabilities are related to the amplitude of the wave. These claims are met with amusement and disbelief by some people, but upon them rest major areas of science, such as chemistry, modern electronics, materials science, modern optics (lasers), nuclear physics, and a host of others. We say that quantum mechanics applies in the realm of very small confines, not usually open to casual scrutiny, but as in the case of relativity, this is somewhat inaccurate. Quantum mechanics is correct for small and large and converges to the special case of classical mechanics in the limit of large things.

It is natural to ask how classical mechanics can be a special case of two different things. The figure schematically depicts the realms of applicability of the different theories. The special relativity we study in this text is valid only for large things. It is not correct quantum mechanically. Similarly, the quantum mechanics we study is, with a few noted exceptions, not relativistically correct; rather, it is valid only for slow-moving things. Classical physics is the region where these two overlap. The region conspicuously missed by both regions is the realm of the small and fast. This is the focus of high-energy physics—the search for the fundamental structure of the universe.

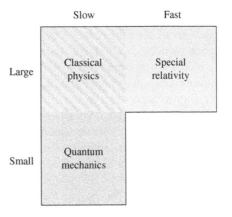

Classical physics is tremendously successful in its realm, but modern physics is truly an eye-opener. On to the new world!

Waves and Particles I: Electromagnetic Radiation Behaving as Particles

Chapter Outline

We now begin our investigation of quantum mechanics. In some sense, quantum mechanics is the study of small things—so small that it is essentially impossible to observe them without affecting their very behavior. For example, the simplest way of observing an object is to look at it. But to do that, light must be bounced off it, and light carries energy, some of which will unavoidably be transferred to the object. Ordinarily, the effect is inconsequential, but if the object is very small, such as a single electron, it might be significant. Thus, we shouldn't be too surprised that the behavior might vary, depending on how the observation is made.

A cornerstone of quantum mechanics is **wave-particle duality**: Things may behave as waves or as discrete particles, depending on the situation. The "situation" might be imposed by a deliberate experiment or governed simply by the dimensions of the region where the thing is confined. Two of the most important things we study are massive objects and electromagnetic radiation. In classical situations, our observations reveal electromagnetic radiation behaving as waves and massive objects as discrete particles. We now look at the nonclassical side of the coin. In this chapter, we study the complementary topic—electromagnetic radiation behaving as a collection of discrete particles. We begin with a brief look at the discovery that sparked the quantum revolution.

Figure 1 Radiation exits a cavity through a hole, which behaves as a blackbody.

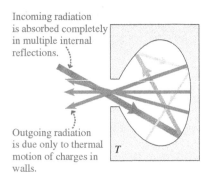

Incoming radiation is absorbed completely in multiple internal reflections.

Outgoing radiation is due only to thermal motion of charges in walls.

T

1 Blackbody Radiation: A New Fundamental Constant

The quantum age dawned with the work of Max Planck in the year 1900. Planck was trying to find a theory that would explain **blackbody radiation**. All materials emit electromagnetic radiation, because they contain charged particles that jiggle around, and an accelerating charge radiates electromagnetic energy. The amount of energy radiated depends on the average energy of the motion, which, in turn, depends on the temperature. For example, coals radiate invisible infrared energy even when cold, but when heated, they emit more radiation, much of it in the red end of the spectrum. They visibly glow "red hot." Most materials, however, also *reflect* electromagnetic energy. A **blackbody** is defined to be any object from which electromagnetic radiation emanates solely due to the thermal motion of its charges. Any radiation that *strikes* it must be absorbed rather than reflected, hence the name. (The term must not be taken too literally. The Sun's surface, from which reflection is insignificant, is a blackbody.)

While coal is a good approximation, fabricating a true blackbody might seem problematic. Imagine, however, an object with an interior cavity and a small hole connecting it to the exterior, depicted in Figure 1. Any radiation entering the hole would reflect from the cavity's inner surface many times, losing energy to the object at each reflection. Essentially none would reflect back directly through the hole. On the other hand, all areas of the inner surface contain charges in thermal motion, constantly absorbing electromagnetic energy and reradiating it as they jiggle around. They will furthermore be in equilibrium with the electromagnetic energy in the cavity—the charges and the radiation will have the same temperature, *T*. The portion of the radiation leaking out of the small hole will be characteristic of this temperature, so the *hole* behaves as a blackbody of temperature *T*.

Experiment demonstrates that the energy emitted by a blackbody, or equivalently a cavity, is small at low frequency, reaches a maximum, then falls again toward zero thereafter. This is illustrated by the experimental curve in Figure 2, which plots electromagnetic energy *dU* per frequency range *df*, known as **spectral energy density**. Classical *theory*, on the other hand, differed. If the electromagnetic radiation in a cavity behaves strictly as sinusoidally oscillating *waves* of arbitrary amplitude, the average energy of a wave of any given frequency should be $k_\mathrm{B}T$. Multiplying this by a factor that accounts for the *number* of different waves per frequency range *df* in volume *V*, the classical prediction for spectral energy density is

$$\frac{dU}{df} = k_\mathrm{B}T \times \frac{8\pi V}{c^3} f^2 \qquad \text{Spectral energy density via classical wave theory}$$

Something is certainly wrong here, for as Figure 2 shows, this parabolic function diverges as *f* increases without bound. If true, all materials would radiate infinite power.

Figure 2 Experiment shows that as frequency increases, the blackbody spectral energy density reaches a maximum, then falls off. Classical wave theory predicts a divergence.

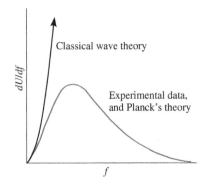

Classical wave theory

Experimental data, and Planck's theory

dU/df

f

Planck found that he could match the experimental data with a curious assumption: The energy at frequency f is somehow restricted to $E = nhf$, where n is an integer and h is a constant. The specific error in classical wave theory is in the average energy of a given wave, which is obtained by integrating over an assumed continuum of possible energy values. Under Planck's assumption, these values are discrete, so *the integral becomes a sum*, with a notably different result. Replacing the $k_B T$ of wave theory with Planck's result, the spectral energy density becomes

$$\frac{dU}{df} = \frac{hf}{e^{hf/k_B T} - 1} \times \frac{8\pi V}{c^3} f^2 \qquad (1)$$

Planck's spectral energy density

which fits the experimental curve perfectly.

The value Planck quoted for h, the now famous **Planck's constant**, was 6.63×10^{-34} J·s. Naturally, it was the value that matched his formula to the experimental curve. While it is tempting to question why he couldn't derive it, the fact that it was even *possible* to match the curve was significant. Although varying h would change the energy density's magnitude at all frequencies, it would not alter its shape. Had there been no merit in Planck's assumption, it would have been the most bizarre coincidence for that shape to match the experimental curve. With hindsight, we now realize that Planck's constant *cannot* be derived, for it is one of nature's fundamental constants (e.g., the universal gravitational constant G), all of which are a matter of experimental observation. For the discovery, Planck was awarded the 1918 Nobel Prize.

Planck's constant
$h = 6.63 \times 10^{-34}$ J·s

Planck's spectral energy density is the crucial link between temperature and electromagnetic radiation. Interestingly, although the assumption $E = nhf$, on which Planck based his formula, might suggest electromagnetic radiation behaving as an integral number of particles of energy hf, Planck hesitated at the new frontier—others carried the revolution forward. Let us take a look at the next major step.

2 The Photoelectric Effect

Classically, electromagnetic radiation is a wave. The energy it carries is diffuse, distributed continuously along a broad wave front, and its intensity—energy per unit time per unit area—is proportional to E_0^2, where E_0 is the amplitude of the electric field oscillations. In the 1880s, Heinrich Hertz demonstrated that a light beam directed at the surface of a metal could liberate electrons. This is called the **photoelectric effect**—light producing a flow of electricity—and is depicted in Figure 3. It was also known that a certain amount of energy is required simply to free an electron. The electron is bound to the metal; pulling it loose takes energy; and any surplus becomes the freed electron's kinetic energy. The minimum energy required to free an electron, the **work function** ϕ, is a characteristic of the particular metal. Table 1 lists some values (subject to variation, depending on impurities and other factors).

If light were strictly a wave, this effect should have several specific traits. First, if light of one wavelength is able to eject electrons, then light of any wavelength should be able to do it. Independent of the wavelength, the rate at which energy arrives (the intensity)—and therefore the rate at which electrons

Figure 3 The photoelectric effect: Light liberating an electron from a metal surface.

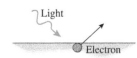

TABLE 1

Metal	Work Function ϕ (in eV)
Cesium	1.9
Potassium	2.2
Sodium	2.3
Magnesium	3.7
Zinc	4.3
Chromium	4.4
Tungsten	4.5

are ejected—could be made arbitrarily large simply by increasing E_0. Second, if the intensity is low, then even though electrons might still be ejected, a measurable time lag should arise. Because a wave is diffuse, considerable time might be needed for enough energy to accumulate in the electron's vicinity. (See Exercise 16.) Finally, at any given frequency, if the intensity is increased, the departing electrons should be more energetic. A stronger electric field should produce a larger acceleration.

Imagine the experimenter's surprise when weak light of 500 nm wavelength ejects electrons from sodium, with no time lag, while light of 600 nm wavelength cannot, even at *many times* the intensity. Moreover, the energy of the electrons liberated by the 500 nm light is completely independent of the intensity. Classically, this cannot be explained!

In 1905, Albert Einstein proposed the following explanation: The light is behaving as a collection of particles, called **photons**, each with energy given by

Energy of a photon

$$E = hf \tag{2}$$

where h is Planck's constant. A given electron is ejected by a *single* photon, with the photon transferring all its energy to the electron and then disappearing—multiple photons very rarely gang up on one electron. If the light's frequency is too low, such that the photon energy hf is less than the work function ϕ, then there is simply insufficient energy in any given photon to free an electron. *So none are freed, no matter how high the intensity;* no matter how abundant the photons. (The photon energy becomes internal energy or reflected light.) However, if the frequency is high enough, such that $hf > \phi$, then electrons can be ejected. The kinetic energy given to the electron would then be the difference between the photon's energy and the energy ϕ required to free the electron from the metal.

Photoelectric effect

$$KE_{max} = hf - \phi \tag{3}$$

The subscript "max" arises because ϕ is the energy needed to free the *least* strongly bound electrons. Others may also be freed, but less of the photon's energy would then be left for kinetic energy.

Einstein's interpretation of the photoelectric effect explains not only the observation that a certain minimum frequency is required but also the other classically unexpected results. If a single photon—a *particle of concentrated energy* rather than a diffuse wave—does have enough energy, ejection should be immediate, with no time lag. Also, the electron's kinetic energy should depend only on the energy of the single photon—the frequency—not on how many strike the metal per unit time (the intensity). In all respects, Einstein's explanation agrees with the experimental evidence, and the achievement earned him the 1921 Nobel Prize in physics.

EXAMPLE 1

Light of 380 nm wavelength is directed at a metal electrode. To determine the energy of electrons ejected, an opposing electrostatic potential difference is established between it and another electrode, as shown in Figure 4. The current of photoelectrons from one to the other is stopped completely when the potential difference is

1.10 V. Determine (a) the work function of the metal and (b) the maximum-wavelength light that can eject electrons from this metal.

SOLUTION

(a) In the region between the electrodes, the electrons lose kinetic energy as they gain potential energy. If a potential energy difference of $qV = (1.6 \times 10^{-19}\,\text{C})$ $(1.10\,\text{V}) = 1.76 \times 10^{-19}\,\text{J} = 1.10\,\text{eV}$ is the most they can surmount, their kinetic energy leaving the first electrode must be no larger than 1.10 eV. The potential difference that barely stops the flow is known as the **stopping potential**. Using equation (3),

$$1.76 \times 10^{-19}\,\text{J} = (6.63 \times 10^{-34}\,\text{J}\cdot\text{s})\left(\frac{3 \times 10^8\,\text{m/s}}{380 \times 10^{-9}\,\text{m}}\right) - \phi$$

$$\Rightarrow \phi = 3.47 \times 10^{-19}\,\text{J} = 2.17\,\text{eV}$$

(b) If the wavelength of the light were increased to λ', the frequency—and thus the photon energy—would decrease. The limit for ejecting electrons is when an incoming photon has only enough energy to free an electron from the metal, with none left for kinetic energy. Again using equation (3),

$$0 = hf' - \phi = (6.63 \times 10^{-34}\,\text{J}\cdot\text{s})\left(\frac{3 \times 10^8\,\text{m/s}}{\lambda'}\right) - 3.47 \times 10^{-19}\,\text{J}$$

$$\Rightarrow \lambda' = 573\,\text{nm}$$

Wavelengths longer than 573 nm have insufficient energy per photon, so no photoelectrons are produced. The maximum wavelength for which electrons are freed is called the **threshold wavelength**, and the corresponding minimum frequency is the **threshold frequency**.

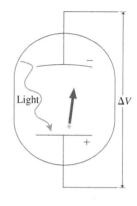

Figure 4 Current between the electrodes stops when the opposing potential energy difference equals the maximum kinetic energy of the photoelectrons.

The central point in Einstein's explanation of the photoelectric effect is that electromagnetic radiation appears to be behaving as a collection of *particles*, each with a discrete energy. Something that is discrete, as opposed to continuous, is said to be **quantized**. In the photoelectric effect, the energy in light is quantized.

EXAMPLE 2

How many photons per second emanate from a 10 mW 633 nm laser?

SOLUTION

For each photon,

$$E = hf = h\frac{c}{\lambda} = (6.63 \times 10^{-34}\,\text{J}\cdot\text{s})\left(\frac{3 \times 10^8\,\text{m/s}}{633 \times 10^{-9}\,\text{m}}\right) = 3.14 \times 10^{-19}\,\text{J}$$

To find number of particles per unit time, we divide energy per unit time by energy per particle:

$$\frac{\text{number of particles}}{\text{time}} = \frac{10 \times 10^{-3}\,\text{J/s}}{3.14 \times 10^{-19}\,\text{J/particle}} = 3.18 \times 10^{16}\,\text{particles/s}$$

Clearly, photons are rather "small," and it is easy to see how a light beam could appear continuous.

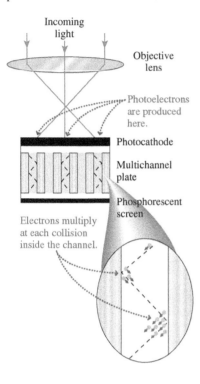

Figure 5 In a night vision device, a light image becomes an image of free electrons, amplified in a multichannel plate and then revealed on a screen.

Incoming light

Objective lens

Photoelectrons are produced here.

Photocathode

Multichannel plate

Phosphorescent screen

Electrons multiply at each collision inside the channel.

$hc = 1240\,\text{eV} \cdot \text{nm}$

The photoelectric effect has long been used in simple light sensors, where light intensity registers as a photocurrent, but it is also used in more sophisticated ways. Let us take a look at one.

REAL-WORLD EXAMPLE NIGHT VISION

By "replacing" a photon with an electron, whose charge makes it easier to "amplify," the photoelectric effect is a common front end on optical imaging systems. One example is the night vision device (NVD). A typical NVD is shown schematically in Figure 5. An objective lens focuses an optical image onto a thin piece of material, called a photocathode, where the photoelectric effect transforms it into an image of freed electrons. Naturally, the dimmer the light, the fewer the photoelectrons. Amplification is accomplished via a microchannel plate. This element has hundreds of thousands of channels per square centimeter. An electron entering a channel at one end, driven through by a potential difference, knocks off other electrons at each collision with the channel walls, emerging at the other end with about 10,000 fellow electrons. (Macroscopic objects that work this way are known as photomultiplier tubes and are widely used in astronomy and particle physics, as well as in medical imaging.) This greatly amplified signal then strikes a phosphorescent screen to produce the final visible image in the phosphor's characteristic color.

Optimizing photocathode materials is front-line research, but we can easily grasp one of the basic constraints.

Applying the Physics

(a) If we wish a light-sensing device relying on the photoelectric effect to be sensitive to the entire visible spectrum (400–700 nm), explain why zinc would be a poor choice of photocathode. See Table 1. (b) A common photocathode containing the alkali metals cesium, potassium, and sodium has a very low effective work function of about 1.4 eV. What wavelengths can it "see"?

SOLUTION

(a) Zinc has a work function of 4.3 eV. Example 1 showed that a material with a *lower* work function has a threshold wavelength of 573 nm. Thus, wavelengths in the orange and red end of the spectrum would not liberate any photoelectrons. Zinc would "see" even less of the visible spectrum.

(b) The work function equals the energy of the longest-wavelength photon that can free an electron. Before finding this wavelength, we note that it is quite common to express wavelengths in nanometers and energies in electronvolts, so a value for the product hc in these units is very convenient. Exercise 27 shows that it is 1240 eV · nm. Thus,

$$E = \frac{hc}{\lambda} \rightarrow 1.4\,\text{eV} = \frac{1240\,\text{eV} \cdot \text{nm}}{\lambda}$$

$$\Rightarrow \quad \lambda = 886\,\text{nm}$$

This material can see all wavelengths in the visible spectrum and well into the infrared.

3 The Production of X-Rays

We use the name **X-rays** for electromagnetic radiation whose wavelengths are in the 10^{-2} nm to 10 nm region of the spectrum. The name was coined by Wilhelm Röentgen, who first studied the radiation. Among other things, he

Figure 6 X-rays are produced when electrons "boiled" off a hot filament are accelerated into a metal target.

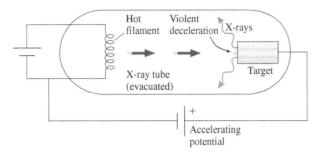

found that X-rays could expose photographic film after passing through a solid object, such as a human being. For his work, he received the first Nobel Prize in physics in 1901. Nowadays, X-rays are an important tool in many areas of research, but their production also gives key evidence of electromagnetic radiation's particle nature.

As shown in Figure 6, X-rays can be produced by smashing high-speed electrons into a metal target. When they hit, these violently decelerating charges produce much radiation, called **bremsstrahlung**, a German word meaning "braking radiation." The fact that electromagnetic radiation can be produced this way is not surprising from the classical perspective, but if it is strictly a wave, we might expect it to cover the entire spectrum. Although the total energy is limited by the number of electrons arriving per unit time, there is no reason waves shouldn't emerge with some amplitude at all wavelengths. But this isn't what happens.

Figure 7 depicts the spectrum produced when electrons of kinetic energy 25 keV strike a molybdenum target. A broad range is apparent,[1] but none of wavelength less than $\lambda_c = 0.050$ nm. This is called the **cutoff wavelength**, and there is no classical explanation for so sharp a termination of the spectrum.

The nonclassical explanation is that electromagnetic radiation of a given frequency simply cannot be of arbitrarily small amplitude. If the radiation is quantized, the minimum energy allowed at frequency f is hf, a *single photon*. We cannot produce half a photon, so if multiple electrons do not combine their energies into a single photon, no photon could ever be produced of energy greater than the kinetic energy of a single electron. Is this the case? Setting the kinetic energy of an incoming electron equal to the energy of one photon,

Figure 7 The X-ray spectrum produced when 25 keV electrons strike a molybdenum target.

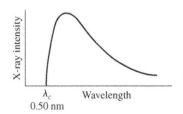

$$25 \times 10^3 \text{ eV} = \frac{hc}{\lambda} = \frac{1240 \text{ eV} \cdot \text{nm}}{\lambda}$$
$$\Rightarrow \lambda = 0.050 \text{ nm}$$

This is fairly convincing evidence. Electrons apparently do not combine their energies.

[1]Not shown are characteristic X-ray spikes due to interactions specific to the elements in the target material rather than simple deceleration.

4 The Compton Effect

We now consider yet another phenomenon that couldn't be explained by the classical view of electromagnetic radiation as strictly waves, one that uncovers another important property of photons. The situation is the scattering of electromagnetic radiation from free stationary electrons. According to classical electromagnetic wave theory, the electrons would oscillate and therefore reradiate, or "scatter," electromagnetic energy in all directions *initially at the same frequency as the incoming radiation.*

Arthur Holly Compton, investigating this phenomenon with X-rays and using carbon atoms as the source of electrons, found that some radiation scattered backward immediately with a wavelength significantly longer than that of the incoming X-rays. (The electrons involved are initially bound to carbon atoms, but so weakly as to be effectively free. See Exercise 30.) Compton's explanation treated the X-rays as a collection of photons, each with a discrete energy but also with another property we usually associate with a particle—momentum. Signs point this way from two directions:

1. According to special relativity, an object with zero mass should have momentum related to its energy by

$$E = pc$$

2. According to classical electromagnetic wave theory, electromagnetic waves do carry momentum. However, for a diffuse wave, we speak of momentum *density*, which is related to the energy density by

$$\frac{\text{energy}}{\text{volume}} = \frac{\text{momentum}}{\text{volume}} \times c$$

With two such compatible clues, it seems reasonable that the momentum of a photon might be given by

$$p = \frac{E}{c} = \frac{hf}{c} = \frac{h}{\lambda}$$

Is this true? Compton provided the first experimental evidence. Let us set the stage.

A Two-Particle Collision

In the particle view of electromagnetic radiation, the interaction of X-rays and electrons is simply a collection of separate two-particle collisions between photon and electron, for which we may now express momentum and energy conservation. As shown in Figure 8, we assume that an X-ray photon of wavelength λ strikes a stationary electron, and afterward, the electron scatters

Figure 8 Momentum and energy when a photon strikes a free electron.

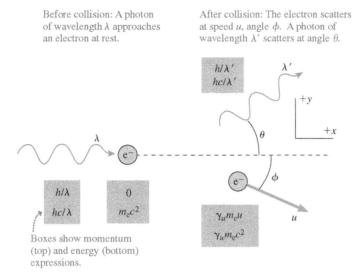

Before collision: A photon of wavelength λ approaches an electron at rest.

After collision: The electron scatters at speed u, angle ϕ. A photon of wavelength λ' scatters at angle θ.

Boxes show momentum (top) and energy (bottom) expressions.

at speed u and angle ϕ, while a scattered photon of wavelength λ' departs at θ. Using hc/λ for the photon energy (more convenient than the equivalent hf), we have

Momentum conserved:

$$x\text{-component:} \quad \frac{h}{\lambda} = \frac{h}{\lambda'}\cos\theta + \gamma_u m_e u \cos\phi \tag{4}$$

$$y\text{-component:} \quad 0 = \frac{h}{\lambda'}\sin\theta - \gamma_u m_e u \sin\phi \tag{5}$$

Energy conserved:

$$h\frac{c}{\lambda} + m_e c^2 = h\frac{c}{\lambda'} + \gamma_u m_e c^2 \tag{6}$$

As it happens, the electron often moves very fast after the collision, so we must use the relativistically correct expressions for its momentum and energy. The photon expressions are already correct; *non*relativistic ones do not exist for things that always move at c.

Equations (4) to (6) have been found to agree completely with experimental observations when a photon collides with a free electron. All tests since Compton's original work have reaffirmed the conclusion: The momentum of a photon is given by

$$p = \frac{h}{\lambda} \tag{7}$$

Momentum of a photon

13

The Compton effect's most striking departure from classical expectation is the large and immediate wavelength shift in the scattered radiation. We clarify this by eliminating the electron speed u and scattering angle ϕ from among equations (4) to (6). (The somewhat lengthy algebra is left to Exercise 38.) What remains is

Compton effect

$$\lambda' - \lambda = \frac{h}{m_e c}(1 - \cos\theta) \qquad (8)$$

The difference in wavelength between the incident and scattered photons depends only on the angle of scatter, a discovery that won for Compton the 1927 Nobel Prize. We see also that the scattered photon is always of longer wavelength than the incident. Its energy is always less, which makes sense, for kinetic energy is given to the electron. In particular, the maximum increase in wavelength is for backward scatter of the photon, $\theta = 180°$, because a "head-on" collision imparts the maximum possible energy to the electron. (*Note:* In Compton's experiment, some radiation of the incident wavelength *was* scattered at all angles, because some X-rays effectively interact with a much heavier mass—the whole atom—giving a negligible wavelength shift. See Exercise 33.)

EXAMPLE 3

An X-ray photon of 0.0500 nm wavelength strikes a free, stationary electron, and the scattered photon departs at 90° from the initial photon direction. Determine the momenta of the incident photon, the scattered photon, and the electron.

SOLUTION

For the incident photon,

$$p_{\text{incident}} = \frac{h}{\lambda} = \frac{6.63 \times 10^{-34}\,\text{J}\cdot\text{s}}{0.05 \times 10^{-9}\,\text{m}} = 1.33 \times 10^{-23}\,\text{kg}\cdot\text{m/s}$$

We may solve (8) for the scattered photon's wavelength.

$$\lambda' - 0.0500 \times 10^{-9}\,\text{m} = \frac{6.63 \times 10^{-34}\,\text{J}\cdot\text{s}}{(9.11 \times 10^{-31}\,\text{kg})(3 \times 10^8\,\text{m/s})}(1 - \cos 90°)$$

$$\Rightarrow \lambda' = 0.0524\,\text{nm}$$

Thus,

$$p' = \frac{h}{\lambda'} = \frac{6.63 \times 10^{-34}\,\text{J}\cdot\text{s}}{0.0524 \times 10^{-9}\,\text{m}} = 1.26 \times 10^{-23}\,\text{kg}\cdot\text{m/s}$$

For the electron's direction, we use equations (4) and (5).

$$\frac{h}{\lambda} = \frac{h}{\lambda'}\cos 90° + \gamma_u m_e u \cos\phi \quad \rightarrow \quad \frac{h}{0.0500\,\text{nm}} = \gamma_u m_e u \cos\phi$$

$$0 = \frac{h}{\lambda'}\sin 90° - \gamma_u m_e u \sin\phi \quad \rightarrow \quad \frac{h}{0.0524\,\text{nm}} = \gamma_u m_e u \sin\phi$$

Dividing the bottom equation (y) by the top (x), $\gamma_u m_e u$ cancels.

$$\frac{0.0500}{0.0524} = \tan \phi \implies \phi = 43.6°$$

Reinserting in either gives the magnitude of the electron's momentum.

$$0 = \frac{6.63 \times 10^{-34}\,\mathrm{J \cdot s}}{0.0524 \times 10^{-9}\,\mathrm{m}} \sin 90° - \gamma_u m_e u \sin 43.6°$$

$$\implies \gamma_u m_e u = 1.83 \times 10^{-23}\,\mathrm{kg \cdot m/s}$$

Thus,

$p_e = 1.83 \times 10^{-23}$ kg·m/s at 43.6° from direction of incident photon.

The vector momentum addition is shown in Figure 9. Even though massless, X-rays are very energetic particles. The electron is "bumped" to 2×10^7 m/s, nearly one-tenth the speed of light.

If treating X-rays as a collection of photons predicts so well what we experimentally observe, why is the *wave* theory of electromagnetic radiation still around? The answer is deceptively simple: The behavior of electromagnetic radiation is just as wave theory predicts, *if* the wavelength is long. Particle and wave behaviors converge at long wavelengths. Of course, this "answer" raises a thornier question: Can a line be drawn between wave and particle? This issue we take up in Section 6. For now, we simply note that if instead of a 0.0500 nm wavelength X-ray, we "hit" the electron in Example 3 with visible light of 500 nm wavelength, the wavelength *change* predicted by equation (8) would be the same as before. The *percent* change, rather than the approximate 5% in the example, would be only 0.0005%. Without great precision, the scattered radiation would seem to be the same wavelength as the incident—the prediction of classical wave theory.

Here we have one example of the **correspondence principle**. This principle, which should be viewed as a guideline rather than a quantitative "law" of physics, states that a nonclassical theory should agree with the previous classical one in the appropriate limit. For example, special relativity is a nonclassical theory that agrees with classical mechanics in the limit of small velocities. To this we add that the nonclassical particle theory of electromagnetic radiation agrees with classical wave theory in the limit of long wavelengths. As the wavelength of a beam of electromagnetic radiation is increased, the energy per photon decreases. A given intensity would then comprise a larger number of less-energetic photons and would begin to exhibit the behavior we expect of a continuous wave. (Occurring only for *short* wavelengths, the photoelectric effect might appear to violate the principle, but no "classical expectation" is really valid, because electron binding in solids is fundamentally quantum mechanical.)

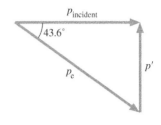

Figure 9 Momentum conservation in photon-electron collision.

In connection with the correspondence principle, it is often said that classical behavior follows in the limit that h goes to zero. It is true that photon energies and momenta tend to be small because h is so small. If h were indeed zero, E and p (i.e., hf and h/λ) would be zero, and light would never behave as a granular collection of particles. However, Planck's constant is a fundamental *constant* of nature—the constant associated with quantum phenomena—and as such, never "goes" anywhere. Thus, it is better to say that classical behavior follows in the limit of long wavelengths.

An Inelastic Collision

The photon-electron collision in the Compton effect is necessarily elastic. Because the mass/internal energy of fundamental particles like the electron cannot change, neither can the system's kinetic energy. In fact, we may rearrange the energy-conservation equation (6) as $E = E' + (\gamma_u - 1) m_e c^2$. Photons have only kinetic energy (no mass/internal energy), so this is a statement of *kinetic* energy conservation. (*Note:* The electron kinetic energy is the relativistically correct form.) Let us reinforce our grasp of the conservation laws by considering a system in which mass *is* subject to change.

EXAMPLE 4

A neutron and proton bound together by the "strong force" is called a **deuteron**. It is the nucleus of the hydrogen isotope **deuterium**, also known as "heavy hydrogen." A helium nucleus is two protons and two neutrons bound together by the same force. Suppose a very energetic photon strikes a helium nucleus and breaks it into two deuterons, each departing at $0.6c$, as depicted in Figure 10. The photon vanishes in the process. (a) What was the photon's energy? (b) In what directions do the deuterons depart? (The mass of a deuteron is 2.01355 u, and of a helium nucleus, 4.00151 u, where 1 u $= 1.66 \times 10^{-27}$ kg.)

SOLUTION

(a) Let us use a subscript He for helium and D for a deuteron. Before the collision, we have a photon and a stationary helium nucleus. Afterward, we have two deuterons moving at $0.6c$. Energy is conserved:

$$h\frac{c}{\lambda} + m_{He}c^2 = 2 \times \gamma_{0.6c}\, m_D c^2$$

Noting that $\gamma_{0.6c} = 1.25$, we have

$$
\begin{aligned}
h\frac{c}{\lambda} &= c^2(2 \times 1.25\, m_D - m_{He}) \\
&= c^2[2 \times 1.25(2.01355\text{ u}) - 4.00151\text{ u}] \\
&= c^2(1.0324\text{ u}) \\
&= (3 \times 10^8\text{ m/s})^2(1.0324\text{ u} \times 1.66 \times 10^{-27}\text{ kg/u}) \\
&= 1.54 \times 10^{-10}\text{ J} \cong 1\text{ GeV}
\end{aligned}
$$

Figure 10 A photon disintegrates a nucleus.

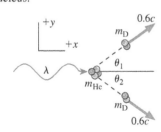

An energetic photon, indeed! This exceeds the entire mass-energy of a proton, $(1.67 \times 10^{27}\,\text{kg})(3 \times 10^8\,\text{m/s})^2 = 1.5 \times 10^{-10}\,\text{J}$. In the collision we are analyzing, almost all the photon's energy goes into kinetic energy of the deuterons; the system's final mass (4.0271) is only slightly higher than the initial (4.00151).

(b) Directions arise only in the vector momentum-conservation equations. Conserving p_y, which is initially 0, would merely tell us that θ_1 must equal θ_2, as symmetry demands. This, in turn, tells us that the deuterons have equal p_x. Thus

$$p_x \text{ conserved:} \quad \frac{h}{\lambda} = 2 \times (\gamma_{0.6c} m_\text{D}\, 0.6c) \cos \theta$$

Multiplying by c and again using $\gamma_{0.6c} = 1.25$ enables us to use our earlier result on the left side.

$$\frac{hc}{\lambda} = 1.5 m_\text{D} c^2 \cos \theta$$
$$1.54 \times 10^{-10}\,\text{J} = 1.5(2.01355 \times 1.66 \times 10^{-27}\,\text{kg})(3 \times 10^8\,\text{m/s})^2 \cos \theta$$
$$\Rightarrow \theta = 70°$$

5 Pair Production

The photoelectric effect and the Compton effect are two important ways in which electromagnetic radiation interacts as a particle with matter. We now discuss a third.

In 1932, a revolutionary new particle was discovered. Carl D. Anderson (Nobel Prize, 1936) was studying the effects of cosmic rays, energetic particles bombarding Earth, when he noticed something behaving like an electron but of positive charge. It curved the right amount but the "wrong" way in a magnetic field. This *posi*tively charged elec*tron* was termed the **positron**. We now know that high-energy photons are constantly creating positrons all around us (fortunately not in dangerous numbers) through **pair production**. This process can be revealed, as depicted in Figure 11, by a **bubble chamber** detector immersed in a magnetic field, in which charged particles leave visible trails of bubbles as they curve. From apparently nothing, there suddenly appear two charged particles deflecting in opposite directions. The energy to produce the massive electron-positron pair comes from a high-energy photon, which, being uncharged, leaves no trail. Charge is conserved because the total charge of the pair is zero. Figure 12 shows actual bubble chamber trails of two electron-positron pairs.

The revolutionary aspect of the positron is that it is antimatter. For the positron, life is short and its end dramatic. It quickly finds an electron—any will do—and after a brief quantum dance, they annihilate together: erased, their entire energy suddenly transformed to two photons. The process, **pair annihilation**, is addressed in Exercises 41 and 42.

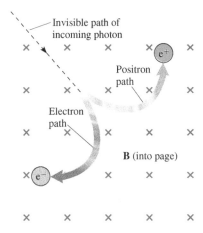

Figure 11 In pair production, a gamma-ray photon becomes an electron, which curves one way in a magnetic field, and a positron, which curves the other way.

Figure 12 Bubble chamber trails showing electron-positron pair production. Photons, uncharged and invisible, are incident from the top. The lower, slowly diverging arcs are one pair. The electron and positron in the upper pair have less energy and spiral faster because much of the photon energy goes to a freed atomic electron (the straighter trail).

EXAMPLE 5

Calculate the energy and wavelength of the least energetic photon capable of producing an electron-positron pair.

SOLUTION

The photon's energy goes to the massive particles as mass/internal energy plus kinetic. The least energetic one must still create the particles but would leave them no kinetic energy. Thus, the photon energy must equal twice the particle mass energy.

$$2m_ec^2 = 2(9.11 \times 10^{-31} \, \text{kg})(3 \times 10^8 \, \text{m/s})^2$$

$$= 1.64 \times 10^{-13} \, \text{J} \cong 1 \, \text{MeV}$$

Knowing the photon's energy, we may solve for its wavelength.

$$h\frac{c}{\lambda} = 2m_ec^2 \implies \lambda = \frac{hc}{2m_ec^2}$$

$$= \frac{(6.63 \times 10^{-34} \, \text{J} \cdot \text{s})(3 \times 10^8 \, \text{m/s})}{1.64 \times 10^{-13} \, \text{J}}$$

$$= 1.21 \times 10^{-12} \, \text{m}$$

The term often used for electromagnetic radiation of wavelength shorter than the X-ray range is **gamma rays**. Here, a gamma-ray photon becomes an electron-positron pair.

Judging from the example, it might seem that pair production isn't really a way in which electromagnetic radiation *interacts* with existing matter, but rather a way of *producing* matter. It does involve an interaction, however, for a photon cannot become an electron-positron pair in a vacuum. Conspicuously missing from the example was any consideration of momentum. Momentum isn't conserved if a (moving) photon becomes two stationary massive particles. Even if the photon were more energetic, allowing the pair some kinetic energy after their creation, momentum could not be conserved. We can always choose to consider the process from a reference frame where the newly created particles have opposite velocities. The final momentum would again be zero, but we would still have a nonzero initial momentum—a single photon. Impossible!

What actually happens is that the gamma ray passes by a massive particle, such as an atomic nucleus; they interact via the electromagnetic force; and then a pair is created and some momentum is transferred to the nucleus. Although momentum can't be conserved without it, the nucleus isn't affected much—it "steals" little energy. To show this, suppose we add to the situation in Example 5 a stationary lead nucleus of mass 3.5×10^{-25} kg, to which the photon transfers all its momentum. The speed of the nucleus would be

$$v = \frac{p_{\text{photon}}}{m_{\text{nucleus}}} = \frac{h/\lambda}{m_{\text{nucleus}}} = \frac{6.63 \times 10^{-34} \, \text{J} \cdot \text{s}/1.21 \times 10^{-12} \, \text{m}}{3.5 \times 10^{-25} \, \text{kg}} \cong 1600 \, \text{m/s}$$

Its kinetic energy would be approximately 4×10^{-19} J, or about 6 orders of magnitude less than the total energy involved in the process. Thus, we see that the nucleus can indeed ensure momentum conservation without significantly affecting the energy.

The preceding discussion raises a point that crops up often in physics. Whenever "small" particles interact with "large" ones, the small ones tend to have nearly all the kinetic energy. Why? The kinetic energy of a nonrelativistic particle may be written as $p^2/2m$, so if the interacting particles have comparable momenta (numerator), then a particle with a much larger mass (denominator) will have a much smaller kinetic energy. The rule also tends to hold when massless and massive particles interact, with the massless one filling the small role. For instance, when an atom emits a photon, the recoiling atom and photon have equal momenta, but almost all the kinetic energy goes to the photon.

6 Is It a Wave or a Particle?

This may be the most perplexing question for the student of quantum mechanics. The simplest answer is that "it" has no predetermined nature. The observation itself—whether the experimenter bounces light off "it," places something in its path, or interacts with it in any way—determines whether "it" will exhibit a wave or a particle nature. Much of what we discuss here applies not only to electromagnetic radiation but also to massive objects. To cover case, let us refer simply to "the phenomenon."

The Wavelength and the Experiment

We advance the answer a step further with a rough criterion: The behavior a phenomenon exhibits depends on how its wavelength λ compares with the "relevant dimensions" of the experimental apparatus, which we represent simply as D. All phenomena may, in principle, be described by a **wave function**. The familiar sinusoidal functions for the electric and magnetic fields in a plane wave of light are one example. A massive object might also be described by a sinusoidal wave function. If its wavelength is much smaller than D, the phenomenon will exhibit a particle behavior; if comparable to or larger than D, it will exhibit a wave behavior.

Figure 13 depicts how the behavior a phenomenon exhibits might depend on a relevant dimension of the apparatus. The boaters are conducting an experiment—blindfolded. If the wavelength of the approaching disturbance (the phenomenon) is larger than D, the width of the boat, these experimenters will certainly proclaim it a wave, because the boat is small enough to respond to its crests and troughs separately. But if the wavelength is much smaller than D, the boat responds to the whole thing at once, and the experimenters might conclude that a particle, not a diffuse wave, has struck. By the same logic, passengers on an immense ocean liner would see even the top disturbance as a

Figure 13 An "experiment" in which a disturbance behaves as a wave or a particle, depending on the relative size of the wavelength and the relevant dimension D of the apparatus.

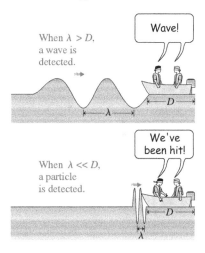

When $\lambda > D$, a wave is detected.

Wave!

We've been hit!

When $\lambda \ll D$, a particle is detected.

$\lambda \ll D$: particle

$\lambda \gtrsim D$: wave

particle, because $\lambda \ll D$, while ants floating on a popcorn kernel would see the bottom one as a wave, because $\lambda > D$.

A simple application of the criterion to electromagnetic radiation is the case of light passing through a single slit. To see the obvious wave phenomenon of diffraction, the slit width must be narrower than or comparable to the wavelength. If it is much greater, the wave passes straight through, as would particles.

Useful though the criterion may be, it is dangerous to view wave-particle duality too rigidly, as wave *versus* particle. The natures are not incompatible but complementary, just two faces of the same phenomenon. We can't fully explain the behavior of a given phenomenon by either nature alone, and there is a close relationship between the two natures. The famous $E = hf$ and $p = h/\lambda$, which *quantitatively* link the particle properties E and p to the wave properties f and λ, are one part of the relationship. We now discuss another.

A Double-Slit Experiment

There is no more direct way to see the link between wave and particle natures than the double-slit experiment. Suppose light is directed at a double slit and is thereafter detected on photographic film beyond the slits. At high intensities, we observe a typical interference pattern, the intensity varying from a maximum (constructive) at the center of the film, to zero (destructive), then back to a maximum, and so on. The light is exhibiting the wave nature we attribute to it classically. Particles don't interfere or cancel; waves do.

Now suppose the intensity is greatly reduced, so that a pattern is no longer visible on the screen. The film still registers the arrival of light, but sporadically at scattered locations. Apparently, the light is being detected one photon—one *particle*—at a time. Figure 14 shows the result if the film registers an arrival with a spot. Although the locations of the spots at first seem almost completely unpredictable, we eventually begin to discern a regular pattern. Understanding the link between wave and particle rests on two key observations: First, the exact location where the next photon will be found evidently can't be known, but logically, the probability of detecting it in a given region should be proportional to the density of spots there—high where density is high, low where density is low. Therefore, if the density of spots assumes a pattern, the *probability* assumes a pattern. Second, careful study reveals that the density of spots in a region is directly proportional to what wave theory (physical optics) predicts should be the relative intensity in that region, which is, in turn, proportional to the square of the amplitude of the electromagnetic wave. In particular, no photons are ever detected at the locations where wave theory says there should be points of destructive interference. *Although the light is being detected one particle at a time, its wave nature is still apparent.*

Combining the two observations, we conclude that because both are proportional to the density of spots, there is a proportionality between the probability of detecting the particle and the square of the amplitude of the wave. This connection between particle and wave natures is a cornerstone of quantum mechanics:

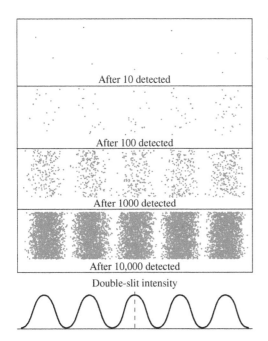

Figure 14 Photons producing a double-slit interference pattern—one *particle* at a time.

After 10 detected

After 100 detected

After 1000 detected

After 10,000 detected

Double-slit intensity

When a phenomenon is detected as *particles*, we cannot predict with certainty where a given particle will be found. The most we can determine is a probability of finding it in a given region, which is proportional to the square of the amplitude of the associated *wave* in that region.

$$\text{probability of finding } particle \text{ in a region} \propto \left(\text{amplitude of } wave \text{ in that region}\right)^2$$

To clarify the nomenclature, if the wave in question is the electromagnetic field, its "associated particle" is the photon. Equivalently, if the particle in question is the photon, its "associated wave," its alter ego, is the electromagnetic field. In electricity and magnetism, we learn that electromagnetic fields exert forces on charges, and we now claim that they also measure the probability of finding the associated particle—the photon. We point this out partly to prepare the reader for a possible shock: The wave associated with a massive object is indeed a measure of the probability of finding the particle, but it doesn't appear to have any other side to its personality.

EXAMPLE 6

Light of wavelength 633 nm is directed at a double slit, and the interference pattern is viewed on a screen. The intensity at the center of the pattern is 4.0 W/m². (a) At what rate are photons detected at the pattern's center? (b) At what rate are photons detected at the first interference minimum? (c) At what rate are photons detected at a point on the screen where the waves from the two sources are out of phase by one-third of a cycle? (*Note:* From physical optics, the double-slit intensity varies according to $I = I_0 \cos^2(\frac{1}{2}\phi)$, where ϕ is the phase difference between the waves from the two slits and I_0 is the intensity when $\phi = 0$, that is, at the center of the pattern.)

SOLUTION

(a) Each photon has energy

$$h\frac{c}{\lambda} = (6.63 \times 10^{-34}\,\text{J} \cdot \text{s})\frac{3 \times 10^8\,\text{m/s}}{633 \times 10^{-9}\,\text{m}} = 3.14 \times 10^{-19}\,\text{J}$$

We must therefore have

$$\frac{4.0\,\text{J/s} \cdot \text{m}^2}{3.14 \times 10^{-19}\,\text{J/photon}} = 1.27 \times 10^{19}\,\text{photons/s} \cdot \text{m}^2$$

(b) The first interference minimum is a point of destructive interference, because the difference in distances traveled to the screen creates a phase difference of π (one-half cycle) between the waves from the two sources. If the net wave (electric field) is zero, its square is zero and so is the intensity. No photons are detected here.

(c) Somewhere between the center of the pattern and the first minimum, the waves will be out of phase by one-third cycle: $\phi = \frac{1}{3}2\pi$. We know that I_0 is 4.0 W/m^2, so we have

$$I = (4.0\,\text{W/m}^2)\cos^2[\tfrac{1}{2}(\tfrac{1}{3}2\pi)] = 1.0\,\text{W/m}^2$$

Because this is one-fourth the value at the center, the probability of detecting photons here is one-fourth as large, so only one-fourth as many will be detected per unit time per unit area around this point.

$$3.18 \times 10^{18}\,\text{photons/s} \cdot \text{m}^2$$

Although we detect *particles*, the probability of their detection is governed by the behavior of the associated electromagnetic wave.

Finally, we address a point central to quantum mechanics. In the double slit, it is not proper to ask, "Through which slit did the 17th photon pass?" We haven't allowed for this, and by altering the experiment so as to observe a particle passing through a slit—an experiment in itself, requiring some interaction with light in one slit alone—we would alter the very behavior we wish to observe. Because interference requires two coherent waves, the pattern would be disturbed. We can't have it both ways. Wavelike interference can only be observed by allowing each "particle" to behave as a wave—*passing through both slits simultaneously.*

Is it a wave or a particle? It may behave as either, depending on the situation, but the two natures are inextricably related.

PROGRESS AND APPLICATIONS

Ejecting Electrons with X-Rays Section 2 discusses the photoelectric effect in which photons roughly in the visible wavelength range eject the least tightly bound electrons in a metal. Logically, shorter-wavelength, more-energetic photons should be able to free electrons that are more tightly bound. Today this effect is being exploited to reveal much about how electrons are bound to atoms in materials and how the atoms themselves are arranged. At the forefront of the work is the University of California's Advanced Light Source (ALS). The "light" in this case is X-rays whose wavelength can be tuned from 0.1 nm to 100 nm. To produce the powerful beam needed, the simple method of smashing electrons into a target gives way to a stream of electrons circulating in a synchrotron. Any charged particle emits electromagnetic radiation when it accelerates, and at the ALS, special magnets, called undulators, wiggle the circulating electrons so as to produce a very bright narrow beam of X-rays. When the beam is directed at a sample, photoelectrons are produced. Studying their kinetic *energies* when free, known as **photoelectron spectroscopy**, tells us about their energies when bound in the material, and studying their motion when free tells us about their locations when bound and, thus, the locations of the atoms. The latter technique is termed **photoelectron diffraction**. The diffraction isn't that of the X-rays but of photoelectrons. As noted in Section 6, objects with mass also exhibit wave-particle duality, and these photoelectrons behave as waves of such short wavelengths as to provide a very high-resolution picture of the atomic landscape from which they were ejected.

A New Way to Produce X-Rays   Because of their penetrating abilities, X-rays have found a great host of uses in learning what is inside things without breaking them open, probing everything from human bodies to construction materials to superconductors. While the century-old tried-and-true method of Section 3 is still the leader, the conventional X-ray machine, with its hot filament sealed in a tube, is rather unwieldy, and the tube's lifetime is often short. The huge and growing field of nanotechnology—applications in which some crucial element is measured in nanometers—may provide a new method. In work conducted at the University of North Carolina, carbon nanotubes are allied with the quantum-mechanical effect of "field emission" to produce a beam of X-rays strong enough to replace the conventional X-ray machine in several uses. A nanotube is a regular meshwork of carbon atoms, forming a cylinder of only about 1 nm radius, and is closely related to many other all-carbon structures discovered in the 1980s. These continue to surprise us with new, remarkable properties and are a very hot topic of physics research. In the X-ray source application, bundles of nanotubes are deposited in a thin layer on a metal disk. Electrons are coaxed from the layer toward a target not by heating a filament, which wastes power and produces electrical noise, but by field emission, a room-temperature way of producing a flow of electrons that relies on the quantum-mechanical effect of tunneling. The resolution of the new technique is excellent, and another potential advantage is faster response time for tracking moving objects. (See Yue et al., *Applied Physics Letters*, 8 July 2002.)

Medical Imaging with Positrons   As noted in Section 5, once a positron is produced, it soon engages in pair annihilation, simultaneously yielding *two* photons of a characteristic energy (see Exercise 42). This trait is exploited in an increasingly common medical imaging procedure known as positron emission tomography (PET).

A tracer material containing a radioisotope that emits positrons at a safely low rate is introduced into the patient via the bloodstream, where it collects in certain tissues. The patient is then placed inside a machine surrounded by a ring of detectors that "look" for photons of the characteristic energy. A positron emitted by the tracer—after no more than about a millimeter of bouncing around—finds an electron with which to annihilate. Each pair is nearly stationary when annihilation occurs, so the two photons created in a given annihilation move in opposite directions. When two photons are detected *simultaneously*, pair annihilation must have occurred along the line connecting the two detectors. Many intersecting lines indicate a high density of annihilations at a point—a concentration of the tracer—in the two-dimensional "slice" of the patient viewed by the detector ring. As the ring passes along the patient's body, looking at each slice, a three-dimensional image of density versus position emerges. Figure 15 shows (a) the basic layout of a PET machine and (b) an actual image.

Figure 15 Positron emission tomography. (a) A tracer emits a positron that annihilates with a nearby electron, yielding two photons that place the annihilation along a line between the detectors. Many lines combine to produce a two-dimensional image of a slice. (b) Multiple slices produce a three-dimensional image—in this case, showing high tracer uptake in the liver and kidneys.

(a)

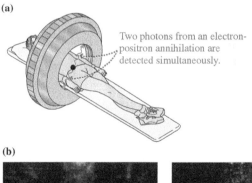

Two photons from an electron-positron annihilation are detected simultaneously.

(b)

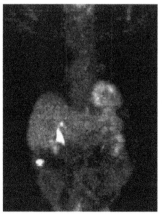
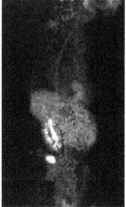

Chapter Summary

Electromagnetic radiation behaves in some situations as a collection of particles—photons—having the particlelike properties of discrete energy and momentum, which are related to the wave properties of frequency and wavelength:

$$E = hf \qquad (2)$$

$$p = \frac{h}{\lambda} \qquad (7)$$

where h is Planck's constant, 6.63×10^{-34} J · s. Electromagnetic radiation is more likely to exhibit a particle nature when the wavelength is small compared with the relevant dimensions of the experimental apparatus. For a given intensity, a short wavelength corresponds to a large energy per particle and a correspondingly small particle flux—number per unit time per unit area. The radiation is thus relatively particlelike. For long wavelengths, it is more likely to behave as a continuous wave.

Electromagnetic radiation may exhibit its particle nature in several ways. In the photoelectric effect, a photon gives up a discrete amount of energy to an electron in a metal. In the Compton effect, a short-wavelength photon scatters from an essentially free electron, and both electron and photon obey the usual conservation laws for particles with discrete momentum and energy. In pair production, these conservation laws are also obeyed as a high-energy photon disappears, transferring its discrete energy to a pair of massive particles.

When electromagnetic radiation is detected as particles, it is uncertain where a given photon will be found. The most that can be determined is a probability of finding it in a given region, which is proportional to the square of the amplitude of the associated wave—the oscillating electromagnetic field—in that region.

* indicates advanced questions

Conceptual Questions

1. Consider two separate objects of unequal temperature. What would you do with them and what would have to happen thereafter to enable them to reach the same common temperature? Use this idea to explain why the electromagnetic radiation enclosed in a cavity has a temperature that is the same as that of the cavity walls.

2. The charge on a piece of metal can be "watched" fairly easily by connecting it to an electroscope, a device with thin leaves that repel when a net charge is present. You place a large excess negative charge on a piece of metal, then separately shine light sources of two pure but different colors at it. The first source is extremely bright, but the electroscope shows no change in the net charge. The second source is feeble, but the charge disappears. Appealing to as few fundamental claims as possible, explain to your friend what evidence this provides for the particle nature of light.

3. You are conducting a photoelectric effect experiment by shining light of 500 nm wavelength at a piece of metal and determining the stopping potential. If, unbeknownst to you, your 500 nm light source actually contained a small amount of ultraviolet light, would it throw off your results by a small amount or by quite a bit? Explain.

4. Suppose we produce X-rays not by smashing *electrons* into targets but by smashing protons, which are far more massive. If the same accelerating potential difference were used for both, how would the cutoff wavelengths of the two X-ray spectra compare? Explain.

5. In the Compton effect, we choose the electron to be at the origin and the initial photon's direction of motion to be in the $+x$ direction. (a) We may also choose the xy-plane so that it contains the velocities of the outgoing electron and photon. Why? (b) The incoming photon's wavelength λ is assumed to be known. The unknowns after the collision are the outgoing photon's wavelength and direction, λ' and θ, and the speed and direction of the electron, u_e and ϕ. With only three equations—two components of momentum conservation and one of energy—we can't find all four. Equation (8) gives λ' *in terms of θ*. Our lack of knowledge of θ *after* the collision is directly related to a lack of knowledge of something *before* the collision. What is it? (Imagine the two objects are hard spheres.) (c) Is it reasonable to suppose that we *could* know this? Explain.

6. An isolated atom can emit a photon, and the atom's internal energy drops. In fact, the process has a name: spontaneous emission. Can an isolated electron emit a photon? Why or why not?

7. We analyze the photoelectric effect using photon energy alone. Why isn't the photon momentum a consideration? (It may help to reread the discussion of momentum and energy in connection with pair production.)

8. A ball rebounds elastically from the floor. What does this situation share with the ideas of momentum conservation discussed in connection with pair production?

9. A low-intensity beam of light is sent toward a narrow single slit. On the far side, individual flashes are seen sporadically at detectors over a broad area that is orders of magnitude wider than the slit width. What aspects of the experiment suggest a wave nature for light, and what aspects suggest a particle nature?

10. A coherent beam of light strikes a single slit and produces a spread-out diffraction pattern beyond. The number of photons detected per unit time at a detector in the very center of the pattern is X. Now two more slits are opened nearby, the same width as the original, equally spaced on either side of it, and equally well

illuminated by the beam. How many photons will be detected per unit time at the center detector now? Why?

Exercises

Section 1

11. For small z, e^z is approximately $1 + z$. (a) Use this to show that Planck's spectral energy density (1) agrees with the result of classical wave theory in the limit of small frequencies. (b) Show that, whereas the classical formula diverges at high frequencies—the so-called **ultraviolet catastrophe** of this theory—Planck's formula approaches 0.

12. At what wavelength does the human body emit the maximum electromagnetic radiation? Use Wien's law from Exercise 14 and assume a skin temperature of 70°F.

13. Equation (1) expresses Planck's spectral energy density as an energy per range df of frequencies. Quite often, it is more convenient to express it as an energy per range $d\lambda$ of wavelengths. By differentiating $f = c/\lambda$, we find that $df = -c/\lambda^2\, d\lambda$. Ignoring the minus sign (we are interested only in relating the magnitudes of the ranges df and $d\lambda$), show that, in terms of wavelength, Planck's formula is

$$\frac{dU}{d\lambda} = \frac{8\pi Vhc}{e^{hc/\lambda k_B T} - 1}\frac{1}{\lambda^5}$$

14. According to **Wien's law**, the wavelength λ_{max} of maximum thermal emission of electromagnetic energy from a body of temperature T obeys

$$\lambda_{max}T = 2.898 \times 10^{-3}\ \text{m} \cdot \text{K}$$

Show that this law follows from the spectral energy density $dU/d\lambda$ obtained in Exercise 13. Obtain an expression that, when solved, would yield the wavelength at which this function is maximum. The transcendental equation cannot be solved exactly, so it is enough to show that $\lambda = 2.898 \times 10^{-3}$ m · K/T solves it to a reasonable degree of precision.

15. The electromagnetic intensity of all wavelengths thermally radiated by a body of temperature T is given by

$$I = \sigma T^4 \text{ where } \sigma = 5.67 \times 10^{-8}\ \text{W/m}^2 \cdot \text{K}^4$$

This is the **Stefan-Boltzmann law**. To derive it, show that the total energy of the radiation in a volume V at temperature T is $U = 8\pi^5 k_B^4 VT^4/15h^3c^3$, by integrating Planck's spectral energy density over all frequencies. Note that

$$\int_0^\infty \frac{x^3}{e^x - 1}dx = \frac{\pi^4}{15}$$

Intensity, or power per unit area, is then the product of energy per unit volume and distance per unit time. But because intensity is a flow in a given direction away

from the blackbody, c is not the correct speed. For radiation moving uniformly in all directions, the average *component* of velocity in a given direction is $\frac{1}{4}c$.

Section 2

16. In the photoelectric effect, photoelectrons begin leaving the surface at essentially the instant that light is introduced. If light behaved as a diffuse wave and an electron at the surface of a material could be assumed localized to roughly the area of an atom, it would take far longer. Estimate the time lag, assuming a work function of 4 eV, an atomic radius of approximately 0.1 nm, and a reasonable light intensity of 0.01 W/m^2.

17. Light of 300 nm wavelength strikes a metal plate, and photoelectrons are produced moving as fast as 0.002c. (a) What is the work function of the metal? (b) What is the threshold wavelength for this metal?

18. What is the stopping potential when 250 nm light strikes a zinc plate?

19. What wavelength of light is necessary to produce photoelectrons of speed 2×10^6 m/s with a magnesium target?

20. What is the wavelength of a 2.0 mW laser from which 6×10^{15} photons emanate every second?

21. A 940 kHz radio station broadcasts 40 kW of power. How many photons emanate from the transmitting antenna every second?

22. To expose photographic film, photons of light dissociate silver bromide (AgBr) molecules, which requires an energy of 1.2 eV. What limit does this impose on the wavelengths that may be recorded by photographic film?

23. Light of wavelength 590 nm is barely able to eject electrons from a metal plate. What would be the speed of the fastest electrons ejected by light of one-third the wavelength?

24. With light of wavelength 520 nm, photoelectrons are ejected from a metal surface with a maximum speed of 1.78×10^5 m/s. (a) What wavelength would be needed to give a maximum speed of 4.81×10^5 m/s? (b) Can you guess what metal it is?

25. You are an early 20th-century experimental physicist and do not know the value of Planck's constant. By a suitable plot of the following data, and using Einstein's explanation of the photoelectric effect (KE = $hf - \phi$, where h is *not* known), determine Planck's constant.

Wavelength of Light (nm)	Stopping Potential (V)
550	0.060
500	0.286
450	0.563
400	0.908

26. A sodium vapor light emits 10 W of light energy. Its wavelength is 589 nm, and it spreads in all directions. How many photons pass through your pupil, diameter 4 mm, in 1 s if you stand 10 m from the light?

27. Using the high-precision values of h, c, and e, show that the product hc can be expressed as 1240 eV · nm.

Section 3

28. A television picture tube accelerates electrons through a potential difference of 30,000 V. Find the minimum wavelength to be expected in X-rays produced in this tube. (Picture tubes incorporate shielding to control X-ray emission.)

29. When a beam of monoenergetic electrons is directed at a tungsten target, X-rays are produced with wavelengths no shorter than 0.062 nm. How fast are the electrons in the beam moving?

Section 4

30. A typical ionization energy—the energy needed to remove an electron—for the elements is 10 eV. Explain why the energy binding the electron to its atom can be ignored in Compton scattering involving an X-ray photon with wavelength about one-tenth of a nanometer.

31. A 0.057 nm X-ray photon "bounces off" an initially stationary electron and scatters with a wavelength of 0.061 nm. Find the directions of scatter of (a) the photon and (b) the electron.

32. A 0.065 nm X-ray source is directed at a sample of carbon. Determine the maximum speed of scattered electrons.

33. Compton used X-rays of 0.071 nm wavelength. Some of carbon's electrons are too tightly bound to be stripped away by these X-rays, which accordingly interact essentially with the atom as a whole. In effect, m_e in equation (8) is replaced by carbon's atomic mass. Show that this explains why some X-rays of the incident wavelength were scattered at all angles.

* 34. An X-ray source of unknown wavelength is directed at a carbon sample. An electron is scattered with a speed of 4.5×10^7 m/s at an angle of 60°. Determine the wavelength of the X-ray source.

35. Determine the wavelength of an X-ray photon that can impart, at most, 80 keV of kinetic energy to a free electron.

36. A photon scatters off of a free electron. (a) What is the maximum possible change in wavelength? (b) Suppose a photon scatters off of a free proton. What is the maximum possible change in wavelength now? (c) Which more clearly demonstrates the particle nature of electromagnetic radiation—collision with an electron or collision with a proton?

37. Verify that the formula $\Delta KE = -\Delta mc^2$ applies in Example 4.

* 38. From equations (4) to (6) obtain equation (8). It is easiest to start by eliminating ϕ between equations (4) and (5), using $\cos^2 \phi + \sin^2 \phi = 1$. The electron speed u may then be eliminated between the remaining equations.

* 39. Show that the angles of scatter of the photon and electron in the Compton effect are related by the following formula:

$$\cot \frac{\theta}{2} = \left(1 + \frac{h}{mc\lambda} \right) \tan \phi$$

Section 5

40. A gamma-ray photon changes into a proton-antiproton pair. Ignoring momentum conservation, what must have been the wavelength of the photon (a) if the pair is stationary after creation, and (b) if each moves off at 0.6c, perpendicular to the motion of the photon? (c) Assume that these interactions occur as the photon encounters a lead plate and that a lead nucleus participates in momentum conservation. In each case, what fraction of the photon's energy must be absorbed by a lead nucleus?

41. A stationary muon μ^- annihilates with a stationary antimuon μ^+ (same mass, 1.88×10^{-28} kg, but opposite charge). The two disappear, replaced by electromagnetic radiation. (a) Why is it not possible for a single photon to result? (b) Suppose two photons result. Describe their possible directions of motion and wavelengths.

42. In positron emission tomography (PET), discussed in Progress and Applications, an electron and positron annihilate, and two photons of a characteristic energy are detected (see also Exercise 41). What is this energy, and what is the corresponding wavelength? The pair can be assumed to be essentially stationary before annihilation.

43. As shown in Section 5, a lead nucleus can ensure momentum conservation in electron-positron pair production without affecting the energy balance. But roughly what is the limit on the mass of such a "detached participant"? Assume again that it acquires all the momentum of the photon, whose wavelength is 1.21×10^{-12} m, but the energy it "steals" is less insignificant, 0.01% of the photon's energy. What is the mass of this less-detached participant?

Section 6

44. A beam of 500 nm light strikes a barrier in which there is a narrow single slit. At the very center of a screen beyond the single slit, 10^{12} photons are detected per square millimeter per second. (a) What is the intensity of the light at the center of the screen? (b) A second slit is now added very close to the first. How many photons will be detected per square millimeter per second at the center of the screen now?

45. Electromagnetic "waves" strike a single slit of 1 μm width. Determine the *angular full width* (angle from first minimum on one side of the center to first minimum on the other) in degrees of the central diffraction maximum if the waves are (a) visible light of wavelength 500 nm and (b) X-rays of wavelength 0.05 nm. (c) Which more clearly demonstrates a wave nature?

46. A bedrock topic in quantum mechanics is the uncertainty principle. It is discussed mostly for massive objects, but the idea also applies to light: Increasing certainty in knowledge of photon position implies increasing *un*certainty in knowledge of its momentum, and vice versa. A single-slit pattern that is developed (like the double-slit pattern of Section 6) one photon at a time provides a good example. Depicted in the accompanying figure, the pattern shows that photons emerging from a narrow slit are spread all over; a photon's *x*-component of momentum can be any value over a broad range and is thus uncertain. On the other hand, the *x*-coordinate of *position* of an emerging photon covers a fairly small range, for w is small. Using the single-slit diffraction formula $n\lambda = w \sin \theta$, show that the range of likely values of p_x, which is roughly $p \sin \theta$, is inversely proportional to the range w of likely position values. Thus, an inherent wave nature implies that the precisions with which the particle properties of position and momentum can be known are inversely proportional.

Comprehensive Exercises

47. A photon has the same momentum as an electron moving at 10^6 m/s. (a) Determine the photon's wavelength. (b) What is the ratio of the kinetic energies of the two? (*Note:* A photon is *all* kinetic energy.)

48. A photon and an object of mass m have the same momentum p.

   (a) Assuming that the massive object is moving slowly, so that nonrelativistic formulas are valid, find in terms of m, p, and c the ratio of the massive object's kinetic energy to the photon's kinetic energy, and argue that it is small.

   (b) Find the same ratio found in part (a), but using relativistically correct formulas for the massive object. (*Note:* $E^2 = p^2c^2 + m^2c^4$ may be helpful.)

   (c) Show that the low-speed limit of the ratio of part (b) agrees with part (a) and that the high-speed limit is 1.

   (d) Show that at *very* high speed, the kinetic energy of a massive object approaches pc.

49. Radiant energy from the Sun arrives at Earth with an intensity of 1.5 kW/m^2. Making the rough approximation that all photons are absorbed, find (a) the radiation pressure and (b) the total force experienced by Earth due to this "solar wind."

50. A flashlight beam produces 2.5 W of electromagnetic radiation in a narrow beam. Although the light it produces is white (all visible wavelengths), make the simplifying assumption that the wavelength is 550 nm, the middle of the visible spectrum. (a) How many photons per second emanate from the flashlight? (b) What force would the beam exert on a "perfect" mirror (i.e., one that reflects all light completely)?

51. The average intensity of an electromagnetic wave is $\frac{1}{2}\varepsilon_0 c E_0^2$, where E_0 is the amplitude of the electric-field portion of the wave. Find a general expression for the photon flux j (measured in photons/s · m^2) in terms of E_0 and wavelength λ.

52. Show that the laws of momentum and energy conservation forbid the complete *absorption* of a photon by a free electron. (*Note:* This is not the photoelectric effect. In the photoelectric effect, the electron is not free; the metal participates in momentum and energy conservation.)

53. An electron moving to the left at $0.8c$ collides with an incoming photon moving to the right. After the collision, the electron is moving to the right at $0.6c$ and an outgoing photon moves to the left. What was the wavelength of the incoming photon?

54. An object moving to the right at $0.8c$ is struck head-on by a photon of wavelength λ moving to the left. The

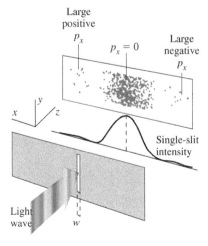

Large
positive
p_x

$p_x = 0$

Large
negative
p_x

x y z

Single-slit
intensity

Light
wave w

object absorbs the photon (i.e., the photon disappears) and is afterward moving to the right at $0.6c$. (a) Determine the ratio of the object's mass after the collision to its mass before the collision. (*Note:* The object is not a "fundamental particle," and its mass is therefore subject to change.) (b) Does kinetic energy increase or decrease?

55. Photons from space are bombarding your laboratory and smashing massive objects to pieces! Your detectors indicate that two fragments, each of mass m_0, depart such a collision moving at $0.6c$ at $60°$ to the photon's original direction of motion. In terms of m_0, what are the energy of the cosmic-ray photon and the mass M of the particle being struck (assumed initially stationary)?

Answers to Selected Exercises

17. 3.12 eV, 399 nm
19. 82.4 nm
21. 6.42×10^{31} photons per sec
23. 1.22×10^6 m/s
29. 8.15×10^7 m/s
31. 130.5°, 23.9°
35. 0.00659 nm
41. (b) opposite, 1.18×10^{-14} m

43. 9.1×10^{-27} kg
45. 60°, 5.73×10^{-3} degrees, visible light
47. 7.38×10^{-10} m, 600
49. 5×10^{-6} Pa, 6.37×10^8 N
51. $\frac{1}{2}\varepsilon_0 E^2 \lambda/h$
53. 2.91×10^{-12} m
55. $\frac{3}{4}m_0 c^2$, $\frac{7}{4}m_0$

Credits

12: LBNL/Photo Researchers; **(both):** Positron Emission Tomography Department, NIH Clinical Center, National Institutes of Health

Waves and Particles II: Matter Behaving as Waves

Chapter Outline

1   A Double-Slit Experiment
2   Properties of Matter Waves
3   The Free-Particle Schrödinger Equation
4   The Uncertainty Principle
5   The Not-Unseen Observer
◎ 6   The Bohr Model of the Atom
▲ 7   Mathematical Basis of the Uncertainly Principle—
      The Fourier Transform

Electromagnetic radiation, classically a wave, has a particle nature. We now begin our study of the complementary and fascinating truth that matter, classically particlelike, has a wave nature. Although a challenging notion, it is the key to understanding behaviors in the submicroscopic world, and thus it lies at the heart of much of modern science.

To force light to show its wave nature, we need an apparatus with a dimension comparable to its wavelength. For instance, light of 0.6 μm wavelength, such as a sodium streetlight, seems to pass straight through a 1 m wide doorway but visibly diffracts when passing through a 1 μm aperture—which isn't hard to make. The wave nature of *matter* would seem a much less foreign concept if we could obtain similar evidence so easily, but we can't, and the reason is that the wavelength of **matter waves**, as a rule, is even smaller than that of light—much smaller. Before we begin our quantitative study of this "hidden" nature, it may be helpful to point out perhaps the most widely known idea in science that rests directly on it: Electrons orbiting atoms can have only certain energies. Why? The atom confines its electrons to *very* small dimensions, in which case their wave nature should predominate. We know from studying waves and sound that when a wave is confined, as on a stretched string or in an organ pipe, only certain discrete standing waves are possible. Why are only certain energies allowed in the atom? The electrons, confined to dimensions less than a 1 nm, are behaving as standing waves.

Being diffuse, waves are analyzed differently from discrete particles. In classical mechanics, objects are particles, and the equations governing their behavior—kinematic equations, $\mathbf{F} = d\mathbf{p}/dt$, and so forth—are relatively simple. Waves, on the other hand, obey equations involving more sophisticated

From Chapter 4 of *Modern Physics*, Second Edition. Randy Harris. Copyright © 2008 by Pearson Education, Inc.
Published by Pearson Addison-Wesley. All rights reserved.

calculus. For instance, waves on a string obey the "wave equation," a partial differential equation in position and time, and light obeys Maxwell's equations, similarly involving calculus with both position and time variables. The distinction between particle and wave natures also governs what questions we ask. For particles, it is often, "Where is it going? When will it get there?" For waves, we ask, "What is its amplitude? What is its wavelength? How spread out is it? Where is it zero?"

We consider these questions soon, and afterward we introduce the Schrödinger equation, the equation obeyed by matter waves. First, however, is the Big Question: Just what is a matter wave, and how do we know it even exists? Nothing illustrates the point better than the double-slit experiment.

1 A Double-Slit Experiment

Imagine a beam of monoenergetic electrons[1] striking a barrier with a slit, beyond which is a screen that registers each electron's arrival by producing a small flash. When the slit is "wide," as shown at the top of Figure 1, the beam passes straight through and produces—electron by electron—a stripe on the screen essentially the same width as the slit. But with a narrow slit, we find electrons registering sporadically *over the entire screen*. Although this spreading alone is hard to reconcile with the notion of electrons as strictly particles, if we add a second slit, the conclusion is inescapable.

Suppose, then, that we add a second narrow slit. Again, with either slit open alone, electrons are detected sooner or later at *all* points on the screen. But when both are open together, we see certain places, where electrons *had been detected* with either slit open separately, where electrons are now never detected. Opening a second "door" decreases to zero the number of electrons arriving per unit time at specific, regularly spaced locations on the screen, even at such low intensity that they must pass through one at a time! This is impossible to explain if electrons are simply particles passing through one slit or the other. A particle passing through one slit would not suddenly have reason to avoid specific locations on the screen just because another slit had been opened elsewhere. On the contrary, this is destructive interference. Because interference requires multiple coherent waves, *each* electron must be behaving as a wave passing through *both* slits at once.

Figure 2 shows how the electron flashes accumulate with both slits open, and Figure 3 shows the final pattern in an actual electron double-slit experiment. Figure 2 should look familiar—it is the double-slit photon-detection pattern of Figure 14. The point is that both electromagnetic radiation and massive objects exhibit the same kind of wave-particle duality. Associated with the particle of light (photon) is a wave of oscillating electromagnetic field. We must now accept that there is also a wave associated with a massive particle. So what is analogous to light's electromagnetic fields? In a matter wave, what is oscillating?

To identify at least one property of this wave, we return to the same two observations we made about light: (1) Although it is apparently impossible to say where the next electron will be detected, the probability that it will be

Figure 1 Intensity patterns when an electron beam strikes various slits.

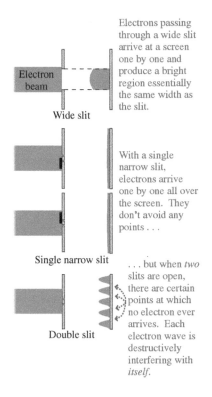

Electrons passing through a wide slit arrive at a screen one by one and produce a bright region essentially the same width as the slit.

Wide slit

With a single narrow slit, electrons arrive one by one all over the screen. They don't avoid any points . . .

Single narrow slit

. . . but when *two* slits are open, there are certain points at which no electron ever arrives. Each electron wave is destructively interfering with *itself*.

Double slit

[1]The electron is our preferred massive object of study because of its relatively small mass. As we will soon see, this makes its wavelength not too small, so its wave nature is more easily revealed.

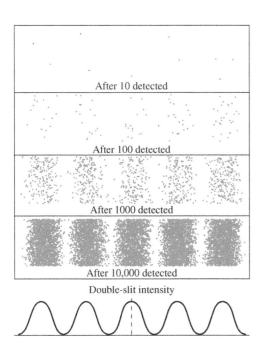

After 10 detected

After 100 detected

After 1000 detected

After 10,000 detected

Double-slit intensity

Figure 2 Electrons producing a double-slit interference pattern—one particle at a time.

found in a given region should be proportional to the density of spots there. (2) If we concede that coherent waves of equal amplitude emerge from the two slits, we would expect an interference pattern. In particular, we would expect the amplitude at the pattern's center, where the interference is constructive, to be twice what it would be if only one slit were open, and the square of the amplitude, proportional to intensity, should be four times as large. And what does the experiment show? It shows a density of spots that is four times larger at the center with both open than with either alone. In fact, for the entire pattern, there is a proportionality between the density of spots and the intensity—the square of the wave—arising from the standard analysis of the double slit. Combining these observations—that the probability of finding the particle and the square of the wave's amplitude are proportional to the same thing (the density of spots)—we reach the same conclusion as for light:

Figure 3 Actual double-slit pattern produced by electrons.

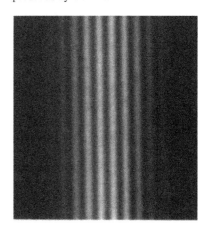

> When a phenomenon is detected as *particles*, we cannot predict with certainty where a given particle will be found. The most we can determine is a probability of finding it in a given region, which is proportional to the square of the amplitude of the associated *wave* in that region.
>
> $$\text{probability of finding } particle \text{ in a region} \propto \left(\text{amplitude of } wave \text{ in that region} \right)^2$$

Although electromagnetic radiation and massive objects share this fundamental wave-particle relationship, matter waves differ in an important way: They cannot be directly detected. Electric and magnetic fields can be isolated and caused to exert forces on objects—we can directly detect them. But we haven't found any analogous way to directly detect matter waves. No one has ever "seen" one. So how do we answer the question, What is oscillating? Apparently, we have only a single candidate—*probability* is oscillating.[2]

Matter Wave Interference: Evidence

The double slit is conceptually the simplest experiment for verifying matter wave interference, but unfortunately it isn't easy to do. The first evidence that matter has a wave nature was obtained by Clinton J. Davisson and Lester H. Germer in 1927. Investigating properties of metal surfaces by observing how a nickel crystal scatters a beam of electrons, Davisson and Germer were surprised to find that the electrons seemed to scatter preferentially at only certain discrete angles. Particles should not do this.

Microscopically, a crystal is an arrangement of regularly spaced atoms. If a wave is incident, each atom reflects the wave in all directions. In essence, each becomes a point source of waves. These sources produce an interference pattern, just as do the multiple slits of a diffraction grating, with sharp interference maxima separated by broad regions of low intensity. In the Davisson-Germer experiment, whose apparatus is shown in Figure 4, the experimental detection rate versus angle agrees perfectly with a theoretical prediction (see Exercise 23) based on the assumption that each electron behaves as a diffuse wave reflecting from many atoms and *interfering with itself*.

The key to the experiment's success in revealing the electron's wave nature is that the relevant dimension of the apparatus, the atomic spacing, is very small. A crystal is thus an excellent testbed to verify a wave nature. But nowadays, it is the other way around—the electron's wave nature, taken for granted, is exploited to learn about the crystal. In essence, the diffraction pattern maps out the microscopic geometry. Figure 5 is a good

[2]A common misconception is that the electron's *mass* is oscillating, perhaps that bits of it somehow jiggle back and forth. The wave isn't the particle. Mass doesn't oscillate in a matter wave any more than photons oscillate in an electromagnetic wave. It may be helpful to view both phenomena consistently as essentially waves of oscillating probability, addressing other possible traits only as the need arises.

Figure 4 Davisson and Germer's original electron diffraction apparatus, showing the mechanism for varying a sample's angle.

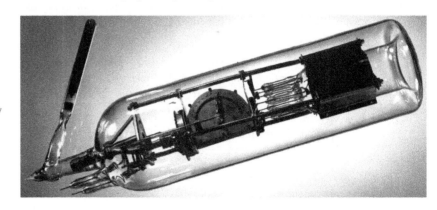

example. Produced by electrons diffracting from a single grain of aluminum-manganese alloy, it reveals atoms arranged in a five-sided geometry. (Actually, such a geometry came as a surprise when first seen in the 1980s, and study of "quasicrystals" with such symmetries has been quite active ever since.)

The Bragg Law

In a crystal, matter waves often penetrate to many atomic planes deeper than the surface, and the most commonly used quantitative relationship for constructive interference, which we now obtain, thus requires a bit more work than for a simple grating. Suppose, as depicted in Figure 6, a beam is directed at an angle θ with respect to a surface atomic plane, and the detector is positioned to receive waves reflecting at the same angle with the plane. An atom in the top plane reflects a small portion of the wave, ray 1, which scatters in all directions. But much of the wave penetrates deeper, so an atom in the second atomic plane also scatters a portion in all directions. As shown in the figure, ray 2 has $2d \sin \theta$ farther to travel than ray 1 to reach the detector, where d is the spacing between atomic planes. Ray 3 travels the same distance farther than ray 2, and so on with each deeper atomic plane. With the incident beam and detector at equal angles, the waves scattering from any atoms in the *same* plane—for instance, rays 1 and 4—always have the same distance to travel from source to detector. So we view interference only between atomic planes at different

Figure 5 Interference pattern of electron waves diffracted by aluminum manganese alloy.

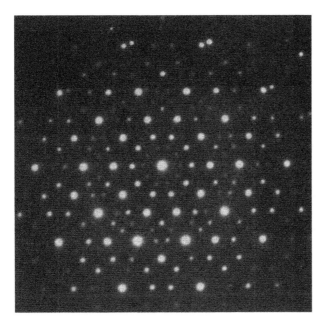

Figure 6 Diffraction of a beam from multiple atomic planes.

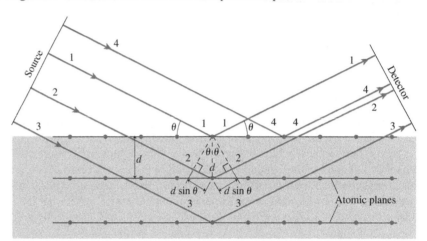

depths in the crystal—very nice! Constructive interference occurs at angles where

$$2d \sin \theta = m\lambda \tag{1}$$

This is known as the **Bragg law**, for father-son team W. H. Bragg and W. L. Bragg, who won the 1915 Nobel Prize for their diffraction work. Their source wasn't electrons, however—it was X-rays. But the same equation applies, because a wave is a wave. We noted in Section 4 that X-rays may behave as particles where longer-wavelength visible light would behave as waves. The spacing d of atomic planes in a crystal is so small that even X-rays behave as waves. Anything will be wavelike in small enough dimensions, and diffraction patterns have been produced by beams of neutrons and even whole atoms. Of course, to exploit interference condition (1) in the case of matter waves—to determine an actual plane spacing d—we would need the wavelength. So let us now turn to the quantitative properties of matter waves.

2 Properties of Matter Waves

What properties characterize a wave? It should have a wavelength, a frequency, and a speed. It should also have an amplitude that varies with position and time. The generic term for the function giving the amplitude is **wave function**. Because what actually oscillates depends on the kind of wave, we use different symbols for the wave functions of different kinds of waves. For a transverse wave on a string, we often use the symbol $y(x, t)$. The string's transverse displacement y varies as a function of the position x along the string and time t. For an electromagnetic plane wave moving along the x-axis, we have two wave functions, $\mathbf{E}(x, t)$ and $\mathbf{B}(x, t)$, which describe how the oscillating electric and magnetic fields vary with position and time. For a matter wave, the symbol we choose for the wave function is $\Psi(x, t)$. Strictly speaking, it should be referred to as the **probability amplitude**, for it is the amplitude of the wave that (when squared) tells us probability. In practice, however, we usually just call it the wave function. In the next section, we will encounter the "wave equation" that this wave function must obey. But first let us study some properties and behaviors that don't require us to have an explicit formula for the wave function.

Matter wave function: $\Psi(x, t)$
Probability amplitude

Wavelength

In our discussions so far, wavelength seems to play the pivotal role. What is it? In 1924, Louis de Broglie submitted the following hypothesis: The wavelength of the matter wave associated with a massive object depends on its momentum p and is given by

$$\lambda = \frac{h}{p} \tag{2}$$

Wavelength of matter wave

This relationship has been confirmed beyond any doubt, even for relativistic speeds, by experiments such as crystal diffraction, in which the momentum of the electrons in a beam is known, and analysis of the pattern establishes the wavelength. The contribution won for de Broglie the 1929 Nobel Prize, and in recognition, we often refer to the wavelength of a matter wave as the **de Broglie wavelength**. *This relationship between wavelength and momentum is universal*—true for all phenomena.

EXAMPLE 1

If moving at 900 m/s, what would be the wavelength of (a) an electron and (b) a 25,000 kg airplane? (c) Which is more likely to exhibit a wave nature?

SOLUTION

(a) $\lambda_{\text{electron}} = \dfrac{6.63 \times 10^{-34}\,\text{J} \cdot \text{s}}{(9.11 \times 10^{-31}\,\text{kg})(900\,\text{m/s})} = 8.1 \times 10^{-7}\,\text{m}$

(b) $\lambda_{\text{airplane}} = \dfrac{6.63 \times 10^{-34}\,\text{J} \cdot \text{s}}{(25,000\,\text{kg})(900\,\text{m/s})} = 2.9 \times 10^{-41}\,\text{m}$

(c) An apparatus with a relevant dimension on the micrometer scale might coax the electron to show its wave side. Actually, this is very slow as electron speeds go, so considerably smaller dimensions are usually needed. The airplane's wavelength, however, is a good 25 orders of magnitude smaller than the atomic nucleus ($\sim 10^{-15}$ m). Although "composite" objects much bigger than electrons—whole atoms, for instance—have been shown to behave in experiments as simple waves with a wavelength obeying equation (2), where p is the object's center-of-mass momentum, in no conceivable experiment would something so big as an airplane ever behave as a wave.

In ordinary situations, the wavelengths of matter waves are short enough to ensure particlelike behavior, because Planck's constant is so small. However, as an object's momentum approaches zero, wouldn't its wavelength become arbitrarily large? We might draw the unsettling conclusion that any stationary object should behave as a wave. We shall face this predicament in Example 5, but the upshot is that it is hard to be sure that something is indeed stationary.

With our quantitative grasp of wavelength, let us return to the simplest example of interference.

EXAMPLE 2

Suppose a beam of electrons moving at 3×10^6 m/s strikes a barrier that has two narrow slits separated by 0.020 μm, beyond which are electron detectors.[3] At the center detector, directly in the path the beam would follow if unobstructed, 100 electrons per second are detected. As the detector angle varies, the number per unit time varies in a typical double-slit pattern between the maximum of 100 s^{-1} and the minimum of 0. The first minimum occurs at detector X, an angle θ_X from the center. (a) Find θ_X. (b) How many electrons would be detected per second at the center detector if one of the slits were blocked? (c) How many would be detected per second at the center detector and at detector X if one slit were narrowed so that it *alone* would give a count rate 36% of its original value?

SOLUTION

(a) At detector X, the first point of destructive interference, the wave from one slit has $\frac{1}{2} \lambda$ farther to travel than the wave from the other. From physical optics, we know that the difference in distances traveled by the two waves in a double-slit experiment is $d \sin \theta$, where d is the slit separation. Thus,

$$d \sin\theta_X = \frac{1}{2} \lambda$$

According to de Broglie's hypothesis, equation (2),

$$\lambda = \frac{h}{p} = \frac{6.63 \times 10^{-34}\,\text{J}\cdot\text{s}}{(9.11 \times 10^{-31}\,\text{kg})(3 \times 10^6\,\text{m/s})} = 2.43 \times 10^{-10}\,\text{m}$$

[3]As noted earlier, it is hard to do the electron double slit. In fact, the first success, shown in Figure 3, didn't come until the 1960s—and even then, it required a few tricks. The problem is that the smallest achievable slit separations are still much larger than the electron wavelength, even if the electron moves rather slowly, as assumed in Example 2.

Reinserting,

$$(0.020 \times 10^{-6}\,\text{m})\sin\theta_X = \frac{1}{2}(2.43 \times 10^{-10}\,\text{m}) \implies \theta_X = 0.35°$$

(b) With both slits open, the detection rate is $100\,\text{s}^{-1}$. This is proportional to the particle detection probability and, thus, to the *square of the amplitude of the matter wave*, the total wave arriving from both slits.

$$|\Psi_T|^2 \propto 100\,\text{s}^{-1} \implies |\Psi_T| \propto 10$$

(*Note:* To avoid distractions, we omit the units on Ψ. As discussed in Exercise 29, including them would merely introduce a proportionality constant that would cancel in the end.) The waves from the slits add equally at this point of constructive interference, so the amplitude of either wave alone must be half the total.

$$|\Psi_1| \propto 5 \implies |\Psi_1|^2 \propto 25\,\text{s}^{-1}$$

The electron detection rate would be $25\,\text{s}^{-1}$ at the center detector. Note that without a second slit/wave to interfere, 25 electrons per second would arrive at *all* detectors. With two slits, twice as many *should* be detected each second, but only *on average*. At points of constructive interference, 100 are detected per second, and at points of destructive interference, none. The average *is* 50, but its distribution in such a pattern cannot be understood by a strict particle view.

(c) If only the single narrowed slit were open, all detectors would register a detection rate 0.36 times $25\,\text{s}^{-1}$, or $9\,\text{s}^{-1}$:

$$|\Psi_1'|^2 = 0.36 \times |\Psi_1|^2 \propto 0.36 \times 25\,\text{s}^{-1} = 9\,\text{s}^{-1}$$

The amplitude of the wave follows:

$$|\Psi_1'|^2 \propto 9\,\text{s}^{-1} \implies |\Psi_1'| \propto 3$$

This is 60% of the original amplitude. Sensibly, an amplitude only 60% of the original implies a *square* of the amplitude of only 36%.

With both slits open, we have two waves of different amplitudes, one proportional to 5 (original) and one to 3 (narrowed). At the center detector, where they *add* constructively, the total amplitude is proportional to $5 + 3$:

$$|\Psi_T'|_{\text{constr}} \propto 8 \implies |\Psi_T'|^2_{\text{constr}} \propto 64\,\text{s}^{-1}$$

At detector X, where the waves are 180° out of phase, the interference would no longer be totally destructive—their amplitudes aren't equal. Still, they *subtract*, so the total amplitude would be proportional to $5 - 3$:

$$|\Psi_T'|_{\text{destr}} \propto 2 \implies |\Psi_T'|^2_{\text{destr}} \propto 4\,\text{s}^{-1}$$

Figure 7 Electron detection rate versus angle for equal-width slits, unequal-width slits, and one slit.

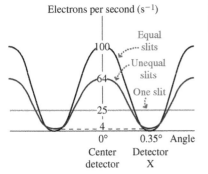

The average is $\frac{1}{2}(64 \text{ s}^{-1} + 4 \text{ s}^{-1}) = 34 \text{ s}^{-1}$, which is the sum of the 9 s^{-1} and 25 s^{-1} expected from each slit alone. But to find the probability, or detection rate, at a location, we do not add the *probabilities* from each slit. Probabilities are always positive, so they can't cancel. Rather, we add the *waves*, which may add constructively or destructively, to find the total wave, and then square that to find the probability.

Figure 7 shows how the electron detection rate in Example 2 varies with angle for the equal-width, one-slit, and unequal-width cases. Note that, except for part (a), Example 2 could have involved light. We would simply replace the term *matter wave* with "electric field" and *electron detection rate* or *probability* with "light intensity." We have analyzed electron behavior via standard wave theory.

Having gained some quantitative feel for matter waves, let us take a look at producing and using a matter wave beam.

EXAMPLE 3

To put the wave nature of electrons to use, an accelerating potential is often the start. Obtain a formula for the potential difference V required to give a particle of mass m and charge q a wavelength of λ. Assume that the potential difference is insufficient to accelerate the particle to relativistic speeds.

SOLUTION

The accelerating potential gives the electron kinetic energy, and velocity is related to the wavelength via the de Broglie formula.

$$qV = \frac{1}{2}mv^2 \qquad v = \frac{p}{m} = \frac{h}{m\lambda}$$

Eliminating v between the two gives

$$V = \frac{h^2}{2mq\lambda^2}$$

We see that a shorter wavelength requires a higher accelerating potential. As noted in Section 1, the electron's small wavelength is now routinely exploited. This result is an important element.

REAL-WORLD EXAMPLE USEFUL WAVELENGTHS AND ACCELERATING POTENTIAL

The **transmission electron microscope (TEM)** is a workhorse in biological sciences and several other fields. The TEM replaces the optical microscope's illuminating light beam with a beam of electrons accelerated through a potential difference, while magnetic "lenses" take the place of glass ones, as depicted schematically in Figure 8. After passing through the sample and a series of "lenses," the electron beam produces an image on a screen. As we learn in optics, a microscope's resolution is limited by diffraction; features smaller than the wavelength are blurred. Light has wavelengths measured in hundreds of nanometers. The TEM's electrons have much shorter wavelength, diffract less, and thus reveal much finer detail.

In **low-energy electron diffraction (LEED)**, another application relying on an accelerating potential, the fact that electrons diffract as waves is, as the name suggests, the whole point. Like the Davisson-Germer experiment, LEED reflects an electron beam from a crystal. By using "low" accelerating potentials, electrons in LEED don't penetrate far, and the resulting diffraction peaks reveal the geometrical structure of the atoms on the surface. Let us take a look at the accelerating potentials in these applications.

Applying the Physics

(a) To produce a good diffraction pattern in a technique like LEED, an incident beam should have a wavelength comparable to the separation between the "slits"—the atoms that scatter the beam. A typical atomic spacing in a crystal is 0.2 nm. Approximately what potential difference is appropriate? (b) The accelerating potential in a particular TEM is 50 kV. If this were the only factor governing resolution, how small a detail could be seen?

SOLUTION

(a) Using the relationship derived in Example 3, we have

$$V = \frac{(6.63 \times 10^{-34}\,\text{J}\cdot\text{s})^2}{2(9.11 \times 10^{-31}\,\text{kg})(1.6 \times 10^{-19}\,\text{C})(0.2 \times 10^{-9}\,\text{m})^2} = 38\ \text{V}$$

Accelerating voltages in LEED are typically 20–200 V, so our estimate is quite good.

(b) By the same formula, the accelerating potential determines the wavelength

$$50 \times 10^3\ \text{V} = \frac{(6.63 \times 10^{-34}\,\text{J}\cdot\text{s})^2}{2(9.11 \times 10^{-31}\,\text{kg})(1.6 \times 10^{-19}\,\text{kg})\lambda^2}$$

$$\Rightarrow \lambda = 0.0055\ \text{nm}$$

We conclude that such fast electrons, much less wavelike than in the LEED application, could, in principle, resolve details of about 0.01 nm. As it turns out, aberrations in the magnetic lenses limit even the best TEMs, which use nearly 10 times this accelerating potential, to resolutions no finer than about 0.1 nm. Still, this is far better than the approximate 100 nm limit of optical microscopes.

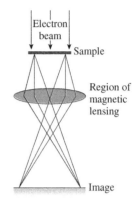

Figure 8 In an electron microscope, electrons replace light rays and magnetic fields replace lenses.

Frequency

Interference patterns give clear evidence for the wavelength of matter waves. The evidence for the frequency isn't so direct, but again, the relationship is the same as for electromagnetic radiation:

$$f = \frac{E}{h} \tag{3}$$

Frequency of matter waves

It is often more convenient to express equations (2) and (3) in terms of the **wave number** and **angular frequency**, defined as follows:

$$k \equiv \frac{2\pi}{\lambda} \qquad\qquad \omega \equiv \frac{2\pi}{T}$$

Wave number   Angular frequency

Note that wave number is a "spatial frequency." Just as angular frequency ω is inversely proportional to the temporal period T, k is inversely proportional to the spatial period λ. Another very convenient definition is

$$\hbar \equiv \frac{h}{2\pi} = 1.055 \times 10^{-34}\ \text{J} \cdot \text{s}$$

With these definitions, we express the fundamental wave-particle relationships as

Fundamental wave-particle relationships

$$p = \frac{h}{\lambda} = \hbar k \qquad\qquad\qquad (4)$$

$$E = hf = \hbar\omega \qquad\qquad\qquad (5)$$

Velocity

We have left matter wave velocity for last because we simply won't use it much, but it is worthwhile to see why. The famous $v = f\lambda$ does correctly give the *wave* speed. Using equations (4) and (5), it is

$$v_{\text{wave}} = f\lambda = \frac{E}{h}\frac{h}{p} = \frac{E}{p}$$

However, this may or may not be the speed of the *particle*. We saw that massless particles, such as photons, move at c, and their *particle* properties E and p are related by $E = pc$. The above relationship then confirms that electromagnetic *waves* also move at c. Matter waves would move at c if $E = pc$ also held for massive particles—but it doesn't. They would at least move at the *particle* speed if E were equal to pv_{particle}, but this too is not the case. (Exercise 31 discusses the point further.)

Wave and particle velocities, known respectively as phase and group velocities. The main point here is that the formula $v = f\lambda$ is of rather limited use for massive particles, because v is neither the speed of the particle nor the speed of light. The usual relationships between *strictly* particle properties ($p = mv$, $\text{KE} = \frac{1}{2}mv^2$, etc.) are fine, and equations (4) and (5) are universal. But for massive particles, E is not hc/λ nor $hv_{\text{particle}}/\lambda$, and p is neither hf/c nor hf/v_{particle} (Exercise 32 focuses on the correct way to relate energy to wavelength and momentum to frequency.)

3 The Free-Particle Schrödinger Equation

How do we determine the wave function $\Psi(x, t)$ of a matter wave? In one sense, all types of waves are the same. For each, there is an underlying **wave equation**, of which the **wave function** (don't confuse these terms!) must be a solution. Let us look at two familiar cases.

Waves on a String

For transverse waves on a stretched string, the wave equation is

$$v^2 \frac{\partial^2 y(x, t)}{\partial x^2} = \frac{\partial^2 y(x, t)}{\partial t^2}$$

where v is the wave speed. The wave function is the solution $y(x, t)$, which gives the string's transverse amplitude as a function of position and time. All wave equations ultimately rest on fundamental laws, and this one comes (after some clever adaptations) from $\mathbf{F}_{net} = m\mathbf{a}$. A basic sinusoidal solution of this wave equation, illustrated in Figure 9, is the wave function

$$y(x, t) = A \sin(kx - \omega t) \quad \text{where} \quad \frac{\omega}{k} = v$$

Figure 9 A wave disturbance on a string.

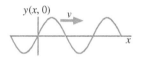

Electromagnetic Waves

The fundamental laws governing electromagnetic phenomena are Maxwell's equations. In vacuum, where charges and currents are absent, they are

$$\oint \mathbf{E} \cdot \mathbf{dA} = 0 \quad \text{(6a)} \qquad \oint \mathbf{B} \cdot \mathbf{dA} = 0 \quad \text{(6b)}$$

$$\oint \mathbf{E} \cdot \mathbf{dl} = -\frac{\partial}{\partial t} \int \mathbf{B} \cdot \mathbf{dA} \quad \text{(6c)} \qquad \oint \mathbf{B} \cdot \mathbf{dl} = \frac{1}{c^2} \frac{\partial}{\partial t} \int \mathbf{E} \cdot \mathbf{dA} \quad \text{(6d)}$$

Although we omit the details, these, like $\mathbf{F}_{net} = m\mathbf{a}$, can be rearranged into wave equations—one for $\mathbf{E}$, one for $\mathbf{B}$—involving partial derivatives in space and time. A primary difference is that electromagnetic waves *by nature* have *two* parts, $\mathbf{E}$ and $\mathbf{B}$. The basic sinusoidal solution/wave function in this case is a **plane wave**. By definition, a plane wave moves in one direction and has a constant amplitude—it doesn't spread out. Figure 10 depicts a plane wave moving in the x direction, and the solutions of Maxwell's equations that describe it are

$$\mathbf{E}(x, t) = A \sin(kx - \omega t)\hat{\mathbf{y}}$$
$$\mathbf{B}(x, t) = \frac{1}{c} A \sin(kx - \omega t)\hat{\mathbf{z}} \qquad \text{where} \quad \frac{\omega}{k} = c \quad \text{(7)}$$

Figure 10 An electromagnetic plane wave.

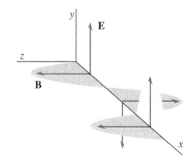

Matter Waves

The wave equation obeyed by matter waves is the **Schrödinger equation**. In this chapter, we consider only the special case of free particles. In the absence of external forces, the Schrödinger equation is

Schrödinger equation
(free particle)

$$-\frac{\hbar^2}{2m}\frac{\partial^2 \Psi(x, t)}{\partial x^2} = i\hbar\frac{\partial \Psi(x, t)}{\partial t} \tag{8}$$

This equation can trouble beginning students of quantum mechanics on two accounts: First, because its form is certainly not intuitively obvious, we might hope for a derivation from first principles. However, there simply is no more basic physical principle on which it is built. Its acceptance as, in essence, a "law" rests on its rendering correct predictions—probabilities of finding particles, for instance. Although we can't derive it, we will soon argue that at least it has a plausible foundation.

The second concern is that the Schrödinger equation is complex, involving i; that is, $\sqrt{-1}$. It might be incorrectly concluded that a matter wave is not "real." Unfortunately, this would also seem to fit perfectly with the point we made earlier: The wave function is not directly observable. (Why should it be, since it isn't real anyway?) The reason for the i is not that matter waves are unreal, but that they can't be represented by a single real function. Like electromagnetic waves, they, by nature, have two parts, and a complex function, carrying twice the information of a real one, enables us to handle them together. In analyzing an electromagnetic wave, we could treat **E** and **B** as a single complex unit by including an i (see Exercise 35), without making either field "unreal." We don't do this, because **E** and **B** have different personalities, and we like to keep them separate. But we haven't found similar reasons to keep the two parts of a matter wave separate, so we use a single complex function. It is simply a matter of convenience (see Exercise 34).

It may be convenient, but can we *physically interpret* a complex wave function? At the risk of sounding impertinent, there is no need, for the wave function itself cannot be physically detected. What *is* open to experimental scrutiny is the wave function's "square," which is a real, nonnegative quantity: the probability density.

Probability Density

We have noted that for all phenomena, the probability of detecting the particle is proportional to the square of the wave's amplitude. But what does this mean if the wave has two parts, an **E** and a **B**, or real and imaginary parts of $\Psi(x, t)$? For electromagnetic waves, experiment verifies that the probability is proportional to $E^2 + (cB)^2$, which, not coincidentally, is proportional to the total electromagnetic intensity. Adding the squares seems to be the natural way.

Experiment verifies the same for matter waves—add the squares of the real and imaginary parts.

$$[\text{Re } \Psi(x, t)]^2 + [\text{Im } \Psi(x, t)]^2 = \Psi^*(x, t)\Psi(x, t) = |\Psi(x, t)|^2$$

where $\Psi(x, t) = \text{Re } \Psi(x, t) + i \text{ Im } \Psi(x, t)$. Note that Ψ^* signifies the complex conjugate of Ψ and, conveniently, gives the expression the appearance of a simple square. Fortunately, we will usually work with just a single real wave function, a piece of the full complex one, and when we say "the square of the wave function," it is a simple square. But when we do use the full complex function, this expression is understood to mean the product of the function and its complex conjugate.

Until now, we have been careful to say that the probability and square of the wave's amplitude are proportional. Suppose we look for the particle in a region of width δ surrounding a certain point. For a given wave amplitude, there is a given probability of finding the particle there. But if δ is so small that the wave's amplitude is essentially constant around that region, then the probability of finding the particle in a region of width 2δ must be twice as large. Thus, the square of the wave function's amplitude must give a probability *per unit length* In three dimensions, it is probability *per unit volume*. The generic term for probability per unit length or volume is **probability density**.

$$\text{probability density} = |\Psi(x, t)|^2 \tag{9}$$

The Plane Wave

Let us now reveal the foundation of the free-particle Schrödinger equation by considering its most basic solution. A plane-wave solution is the **complex exponential**

$$\Psi(x, t) = A e^{i(kx - \omega t)} \tag{10}$$

where A is a constant. To verify that this is a solution of equation (8), the question is

$$-\frac{\hbar^2}{2m} \frac{\partial^2 A e^{i(kx - \omega t)}}{\partial x^2} \overset{?}{=} i\hbar \frac{\partial A e^{i(kx - \omega t)}}{\partial t}$$

Taking the partial derivatives on both sides, we have

$$-\frac{\hbar^2}{2m} (ik)^2 A e^{i(kx - \omega t)} = i\hbar(-i\omega) A e^{i(kx - \omega t)}$$

and canceling,

$$\frac{\hbar^2 k^2}{2m} = \hbar\omega \tag{11a}$$

That the functional dependence on position and time cancels means that function (10) obeys the Schrödinger equation for all values of x and t, provided only that k and ω are related as in condition (11a). It is left as an exercise to show that the more familiar $A\sin(kx - \omega t)$ and $A\cos(kx - \omega t)$—applicable to waves on a string, for example—simply don't work the same way. They are not solutions. It is true by the Euler formula that $Ae^{i(kx - \omega t)}$ is equivalent to $A\cos(kx - \omega t) + iA\sin(kx - \omega t)$, so there is a similarity. But the complex exponential has two parts, and they are out of phase by one-quarter cycle.

The requirement that (11a) must hold is the key to seeing how the Schrödinger *wave* equation relates to the classical physics of *particles*. We hope that it isn't at odds with the fundamental wave-particle relationships, $p = \hbar k$ and $E = \hbar\omega$. What happens if we insert them? Condition (11a) becomes

$$\frac{p^2}{2m} = E \tag{11b}$$

Given that $p^2/2m = (mv)^2/2m = \frac{1}{2}mv^2$, this merely says that the particle's kinetic energy must equal its total energy, which is the classical truth, because a free particle has no potential energy. Thus, *the Schrödinger equation is related to a classical accounting of energy.*

Although the wave function isn't physically detectable, Figure 11, which plots $Ae^{i(kx - \omega t)}$ at $t = 0$, provides some insight into the mathematical nature of a plane wave. The real part of Ψ is a cosine, the imaginary part a sine, and the two parts are out of phase in such a way that the *magnitude is constant*—it varies neither in position nor in time. The direct calculation of the probability density agrees:

$$|\Psi(x,\,t)|^2 = \Psi^*(x,\,t)\Psi(x,\,t) = \left[Ae^{-i(kx - \omega t)}\right]\left[Ae^{+i(kx - \omega t)}\right] = A^2$$

or

$$|\Psi(x,\,t)| = A$$

That the probability per unit length is constant means that if we were to look for it, *a particle represented by a plane wave would be equally likely to be found anywhere.*

Obviously, a plane wave is not very realistic, but it is still quite useful. In physical optics, we speak of plane waves of light, because they are often a sufficiently good approximation of the actual wave. The same is true of matter waves. But the plane wave's importance goes even deeper, for a more general wave can be treated as an algebraic sum of plane waves—they are easily analyzed "building blocks." We will make use of this fact at several points later in the text. Let us now turn to a topic where we need not know the actual $\Psi(x, t)$. It is one of the most profound ideas in all of physics.

Figure 11 A plane matter wave: The real and imaginary parts of $Ae^{i(kx - \omega t)}$, plotted at $t = 0$.

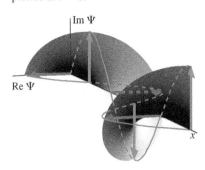

4 The Uncertainty Principle

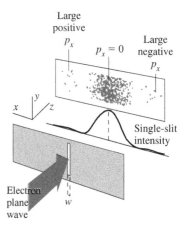

Figure 12 Single-slit diffraction of an electron plane wave.

The mere fact that a phenomenon has a wave nature implies inherent uncertainties in its particle properties. For example, passing through a single slit causes an electromagnetic plane wave to spread out, so it must also cause uncertainty in the momenta of the particles (photons) detected afterward. The same must apply to an electron plane wave. Figure 12 depicts a single-slit pattern developed (like the earlier double slit) one electron at a time. The x-component of momentum of an electron after passing through is obviously uncertain.

What we mean by "uncertainty" in momentum is that if the experiment is repeated many times *identically*, the momentum detected after passing through the slit still varies over a range of values. But how do we quantify it? Suppose that the p_x-values we record fall within the range -1 kg·m/s to $+1$ kg·m/s, except for one at $+50$ kg·m/s. What value do we assign to the uncertainty? 1 kg·m/s? 25 kg·m/s? 51 kg·m/s?

The definition of uncertainty is an arbitrary choice, but it obviously should measure how far deviations are from the mean (average) value. In physics, we define it as **standard deviation**. For example, suppose repeated experiments are carried out to determine a quantity Q, where Q might represent position x, a component of momentum p_x, or any other measurable quantity. The value Q_1 is obtained n_1 times, the value Q_2 is obtained n_2 times, and so on. We find the **mean** $\overline{Q}$ by multiplying a particular value Q_i by the number of times it is obtained, n_i, summing over all values, then dividing by the total number of times for all values.

$$\overline{Q} = \frac{\sum_i Q_i n_i}{\sum_i n_i} \tag{12}$$

The standard deviation ΔQ is defined as the square root of the mean of the squares of the values' deviations from the mean (explaining its alternative name, root-mean-square deviation). Here we merely present the formula that goes with the words:

$$\Delta Q = \sqrt{\frac{\sum_i (Q_i - \overline{Q})^2 n_i}{\sum_i n_i}} \tag{13}$$

This definition is very well suited to its role. It is the most tractable one that is zero *if and only if* there is only one value ever obtained, which would automatically be $\overline{Q}$, and when values do vary, it gets larger as they become more spread out.

Although it is important to know that uncertainty has a logical definition, as we continue to investigate the uncertainty principle in this section, we won't actually *use* the definition. The point is that when we say, for instance, that there is "an uncertainty in the electrons' momentum," we aren't speaking of something nebulous but a specific value following from a concrete definition.

So let us return to the single slit. As Figure 12 shows, there is an uncertainty in the x-component of momentum of electrons detected beyond the slit, for which the symbol is Δp_x. (The symbol Δ often means "change," but not here. Here it means uncertainty, or standard deviation.) On the other hand, were we to conduct a different experiment, designed to establish the position of electrons exiting the slit, there would be an uncertainty in this quantity, too—Δx. The electron wave front is spread over the entire width w, so there would be a probability of finding the particle anywhere in this range, and the narrower the slit, the smaller would be this uncertainty. Above all, there is a link between the uncertainties in p_x and x. Because the width of a diffraction pattern, related to Δp_x, is inversely proportional to the slit width, related to Δx, *the uncertainties are inversely proportional.*

$$\Delta p_x \propto \frac{1}{\Delta x}$$

Figure 13 As a wave becomes more compact, its overall wavelength and momentum are less well defined.

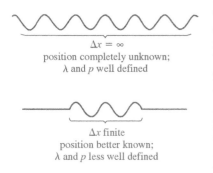

$\Delta x = \infty$
position completely unknown;
λ and p well defined

Δx finite
position better known;
λ and p less well defined

Δx small
position even better known;
λ and p even less well defined

Although we have used the familiar single slit as a vehicle, the particular experiment is not to "blame" for the conclusion. Regardless of the circumstances, it is an inescapable consequence of matter's wave nature—whether obvious or not—that increased precision in the knowledge of position implies decreased precision in the knowledge of momentum and vice versa. Figure 13 illustrates a simplified, qualitative argument. The top wave is infinite and regular. While there is no doubt of its wavelength, there would be a probability of finding the particle at places along the entire infinite x-axis. Wavelength and, thus, momentum h/λ are certain ($\Delta p = 0$), but essentially nothing is known about the particle's position ($\Delta x = \infty$). The center wave is regular over only a finite region. The cost of obtaining a wave for which the particle's probable whereabouts are narrowed down ($\Delta x \neq \infty$) is that the wave is not regular everywhere. In any fair way of taking into account all of space, the wavelength cannot be said to be simply λ, so neither can we claim that the momentum is precisely h/λ ($\Delta p \neq 0$). The bottom wave gives an even better known position, but only by further restricting the region over which the wave is regular. Accordingly, it is even less fair to say that the wavelength of this wave as a whole is λ, so Δp is larger still. The relationship between Δp and Δx is developed quantitatively in Section 7. Here we concern ourselves only with the conclusion, known as the **uncertainty principle**, and its ramifications.

Momentum-position uncertainty
principle

Because of a particle's wave nature, it is theoretically impossible to know precisely both its position along an axis and its momentum component along that axis; Δx and Δp_x cannot be zero simultaneously. There is a strict theoretical lower limit on their product:

$$\Delta p_x \Delta x \geq \frac{\hbar}{2} \tag{14}$$

Often referred to as the Heisenberg uncertainty principle, for its discoverer Werner Heisenberg (Nobel Prize 1932), it is a shocking revelation. There is a *theoretical limit* on the precision with which some familiar quantities can be known simultaneously. If we know a particle's position *exactly*, we can know *nothing* about its momentum ($\Delta x = 0 \Rightarrow \Delta p_x = \infty$). If momentum is known exactly, position is completely unknown. The plane wave is a good example of the latter case. This fundamental matter wave has a wavelength perfectly regular throughout space, giving it a perfectly precise momentum, but it represents a particle equally likely to be found anywhere. A property in which there is no uncertainty is said to be **well defined**. For the plane wave, momentum is well defined ($\Delta p_x = 0$), but position couldn't be more *un*defined ($\Delta x = \infty$).

Don't be troubled by the inequality in (14)—there is no uncertainty about the uncertainty principle. The $\geq$ reflects the simple fact that there is a particular wave shape, called a **Gaussian**, also known as a bell curve, for which the product of uncertainties is a minimum. Figure 14 shows a Gaussian wave form, a constant C times a "Gaussian factor" $e^{-(x/2\varepsilon)^2}$ where ε is a constant. It is maximum at $x = 0$, falls off toward 0 symmetrically as x becomes large, and the rate of fall-off depends on ε. If ε is large, the wave form is broad, falling off very slowly; whereas if ε is small, the wave form is narrow. We leave the actual calculation of uncertainties from wave functions until later, but it shouldn't be surprising that the position uncertainty Δx is proportional to ε. It is also true that Δp is *inversely* proportional to ε, and it is only for a particle whose matter wave function is of this form that the product of the two uncertainties is the minimum theoretically possible, $\frac{1}{2}\hbar$. For any other shape, simultaneous knowledge of the two is less precise: $\Delta p_x \Delta x > \frac{1}{2}\hbar$.

The whole idea behind the uncertainty principle is rather upsetting to a student of classical physics. Classically, we claim that we can calculate a particle's position and velocity for all time via $\mathbf{F} = m\mathbf{a}$ and kinematics. We need only know the forces acting and the initial position and velocity. But now we see that even starting such a calculation is problematic, for precise knowledge of position and velocity simultaneously is impossible. Fortunately, as we soon see, the uncertainty principle is of little consequence for "large" things.

On the other hand, it is of great consequence for the small things we study in quantum mechanics. As we saw in Example 1, while wavelengths of macroscopic objects are ridiculously small, an electron might well have a wavelength measured in nanometers or larger. Undoubtedly, it would behave as a particle in a situation where distances are measured in meters, as in a television's cathode-ray tube. But it should definitely show its wave side when confined in a system measured in fractions of a nanometer. Such a system is the atom, probably the most logical test of quantum mechanics, and the simplest atom is hydrogen—essentially an electron orbiting a stationary proton. In such small confines, the electron must be treated not as an orbiting particle but as a bound three-dimensional wave surrounding the proton. Because the wave is spread diffusely, the probability of finding the electron is spread diffusely. Our knowledge of the atom's approximate size sets a rather small *maximum* possible value for the position uncertainty, and there is, correspondingly, a rather large *minimum* theoretical uncertainty in momentum.

Figure 14 A Gaussian wave form, $\Delta x \, \Delta p = \frac{1}{2}\hbar$.

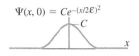

$$\Psi(x, 0) = Ce^{-(x/2\varepsilon)^2}$$

EXAMPLE 4

The hydrogen atom is known to be about 0.1 nm in radius. That is, the electron's orbit, whatever may be its shape, extends to about this far from the proton. Accordingly, the uncertainty in the electron's position is no larger than about 0.1 nm. What is the minimum theoretical uncertainty in its velocity?

SOLUTION

An electron in an atom moves in three dimensions, but considering components of motion along just one of the axes should give us a pretty good approximation.

$$\Delta p_x \Delta x \geq \frac{\hbar}{2} \quad \rightarrow \quad \Delta p_x(0.1 \times 10^{-9}\,\text{m}) \geq \frac{1.055 \times 10^{-34}\,\text{J} \cdot \text{s}}{2}$$

$$\Rightarrow \quad \Delta p_x \geq 5.3 \times 10^{-25}\,\text{kg} \cdot \text{m/s}$$

Now using $p = mv$,

$$\Delta v_x = \frac{\Delta p_x}{m} \geq \frac{5.3 \times 10^{-25}\,\text{kg} \cdot \text{m/s}}{9.11 \times 10^{-31}\,\text{kg}} = 5.8 \times 10^5\,\text{m/s}$$

From Example 4, we conclude that an experiment designed to determine the hydrogen electron's speed, if repeated identically, must produce a range of values covering more than $\frac{1}{10}\%$ of c. In fact, careful study of the hydrogen atom reveals slight relativistic effects. Actually, the theoretical minimum Δp_x of $5.3 \times 10^{-25}\,\text{kg} \cdot \text{m/s}$ would apply only if the wave function were a Gaussian, which it is not, so the true uncertainty is somewhat larger. But to be too concerned with this point is to overlook much of the power of the uncertainty principle. It governs all phenomena, for all have an underlying wave nature, and it may be used for order-of-magnitude calculations *in complete ignorance* of the wave function. We shall see just how useful this can be in Example 6, which gives us an excellent estimate of the hydrogen electron's *energy*. First, let us revisit the problem of reconciling the uncertainty principle with classical mechanics.

The Classical Limit

The uncertainty principle places no significant limitation on the use of classical mechanics in classical situations. In the following example, we justify this claim and also confront our earlier predicament: A stationary object, with a corresponding infinite wavelength, should behave as a wave.

EXAMPLE 5

By simple visual inspection, we can establish the location of an object within an uncertainty of about 550 nm, the wavelength of visible light. Suppose the object is a 1 mg grain of sand, apparently stationary. (a) What is the minimum uncertainty in its velocity, and if moving at this speed, how long would it take to travel the smallest distance perceivable, about 1 μm? (b) A wavelength of 1 nm would be small enough to ensure particle behavior in everyday circumstances. How fast would the grain of sand have to move to have such a wavelength?

SOLUTION

(a) $$\Delta p_x \Delta x \geq \frac{\hbar}{2} \rightarrow \Delta p_x \left(5.5 \times 10^{-7}\,\text{m}\right) \geq \frac{1.055 \times 10^{-34}\,\text{J} \cdot \text{s}}{2}$$

$$\Rightarrow \quad \Delta p_x \geq 9.59 \times 10^{-29}\,\text{kg} \cdot \text{m/s}$$

In essence, Δp_x is small because $\hbar$ is small.

$$\Delta v = \frac{\Delta p}{m} \geq \frac{9.59 \times 10^{-29}\,\text{kg} \cdot \text{m/s}}{10^{-6}\,\text{kg}} = 9.59 \times 10^{-23}\,\text{m/s}$$

In Example 4, the electron's velocity uncertainty was nearly relativistic. It is a relief to find it so much smaller here. Large mass is the reason. Quantum-mechanically speaking, a grain of sand is huge.

$$t = \frac{\text{distance}}{\text{speed}} = \frac{10^{-6}\,\text{m}}{9.59 \times 10^{-23}\,\text{m/s}} = 1.04 \times 10^{16}\,\text{s}$$

$$= 3.3 \text{ million centuries}$$

Clearly, we can know both the position and the velocity of this object precisely enough to apply classical mechanics.

(b) Using the de Broglie formula,

$$v = \frac{p}{m} = \frac{h/\lambda}{m} = \frac{6.63 \times 10^{-34}\,\text{J} \cdot \text{s}}{(10^{-6}\,\text{kg})(10^{-9}\,\text{m})} = 6.63 \times 10^{-19}\,\text{m/s}$$

Part (a) calculates the *theoretical* minimum velocity uncertainty—more precise knowledge of v is impossible—but measurements in classical situations don't even come close to such a ridiculously small speed. Here we see that even a (classically) tiny object could appear absolutely stationary yet have a wavelength so short as to behave particlelike for all classical purposes.

A Practical Application

The uncertainty principle alone explains a behavior for which classical arguments fail. Classically, there is no lower limit on the energy a small particle may have as it orbits a large body. For instance, a satellite may be positioned at any distance from a planet and, if given the proper velocity, maintain a circular orbit. The smaller the orbit radius, the lower would be the energy, though there is a *practical* lower limit in which the satellite simply rests on the planet's surface. By analogy, if an electron orbits a proton in a hydrogen atom, there should be no lower limit on the energy it may have. But there *is* a minimum energy, called the ground-state energy, and it is inconsistent with the electron simply resting on the proton. The electron's wave nature—specifically, the inverse relationship between its momentum and position uncertainties—is the answer to the mystery.

Figure 15 If p_x has nonzero mean, a typical value of p_x differs considerably from Δp_x, but if the mean is zero, a typical value cannot be much larger than Δp_x.

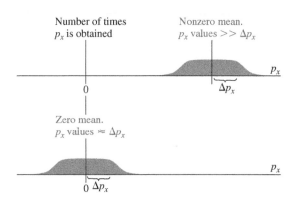

Before we show this, we discuss a point that bears on various applications of the uncertainty principle: If the mean of a quantity is *zero*, then the *uncertainty* in the quantity and *typical values* of the quantity are comparable. If the mean is nonzero, this need not hold. For instance, a position mean of 100.0 m with an uncertainty of 0.1 m implies typical position values in the range of 99.9 m to 100.1 m—obviously not comparable to 0.1 m. However, the same uncertainty with a mean of zero would imply positions between -0.1 m and $+0.1$ m (or 0 and 0.1 m, if negative values aren't allowed), which *are* comparable to the uncertainty.

Figure 15 illustrates the point in the context of momentum. The top diagram shows results of a hypothetical experiment in which measured p_x values have a mean that is large and positive. Essentially all p_x values are much larger than Δp_x. The bottom diagram shows a case with the same Δp_x but a mean of zero. Any p_x value within about Δp_x of the mean is likely. The chance of its being $10\Delta p_x$ is clearly quite small, and even the chance of its being within, say, $\frac{1}{10}\Delta p_x$ of zero is rather small. Therefore, the mostly likely values of p_x are those roughly the same order of magnitude as Δp_x.

EXAMPLE 6

An electron is held in orbit about a proton by electrostatic attraction. Its total mechanical energy is the sum of its kinetic energy and the electrostatic potential energy between charges $+e$ and $-e$ that are a distance r apart.

$$E = \frac{1}{2}mv^2 + \frac{1}{4\pi\varepsilon_0}\frac{(+e)(-e)}{r}$$

(a) If the electron behaves as a classical particle, it must obey $F = ma$. Assuming a circular orbit, apply $F = ma$ to eliminate v in favor of r in the energy expression, and demonstrate that the energy has no minimum.

(b) Suppose now that the electron behaves as an orbiting wave. The energy expression decreases as both position r and momentum mv approach zero. Assume that each is very small and thus comparable to its respective uncertainty: $r \approx \Delta r$ and $p \approx \Delta p$. The uncertainty principle then implies that $pr \approx \hbar$. Use this to eliminate v in favor of r in the energy expression.

(c) Sketch on the same axes the energy expressions from parts (a) and (b) versus r.

(d) Find the minimum possible energy for the orbiting electron wave and the corresponding value of r.

SOLUTION

(a) Coulomb's law gives us the electrostatic force, and the acceleration of a particle in circular motion is v^2/r.

$$F = ma \quad \rightarrow \quad \frac{1}{4\pi\varepsilon_0}\frac{e^2}{r^2} = m\frac{v^2}{r} \quad \Rightarrow \quad v^2 = \frac{e^2}{4\pi\varepsilon_0 mr}$$

Thus,

$$E_{\substack{\text{classical} \\ \text{particle}}} = \frac{1}{2}m\left(\frac{e^2}{4\pi\varepsilon_0 mr}\right) - \frac{1}{4\pi\varepsilon_0}\frac{e^2}{r} = \underbrace{\frac{e^2}{8\pi\varepsilon_0 r}}_{\text{Kinetic}} - \underbrace{\frac{e^2}{4\pi\varepsilon_0 r}}_{\text{Potential}} = -\frac{e^2}{8\pi\varepsilon_0 r}$$

We see that the negative potential energy is of greater magnitude than the positive kinetic, and the total strictly decreases (becomes more negative) as r decreases. There is no minimum energy.

(b) Assuming $pr = \hbar$, we have $p = \hbar/r$ or $v = \hbar/mr$. Thus,

$$E_{\substack{\text{matter} \\ \text{wave}}} = \frac{1}{2}m\left(\frac{\hbar}{mr}\right)^2 - \frac{1}{4\pi\varepsilon_0}\frac{e^2}{r} = \frac{\hbar^2}{2mr^2} - \frac{e^2}{4\pi\varepsilon_0 r}$$

Now, as r decreases and the wave becomes more compact, likely values of the speed increase inversely, and so must the kinetic energy.

(c) The two plots are shown in Figure 16. While the energy of a classical particle decreases monotonically as r decreases, the energy of the matter wave reaches a minimum and then increases.

(d) To find the minimum, we set the derivative to 0.

$$\frac{dE_{\substack{\text{matter} \\ \text{wave}}}}{dr} = -\frac{\hbar^2}{mr^3} + \frac{e^2}{4\pi\varepsilon_0 r^2} = 0$$

$$\Rightarrow \quad r = \frac{4\pi\varepsilon_0\hbar^2}{me^2} = \frac{4\pi(8.85\times10^{-12}\,\text{N}\cdot\text{m}^2/\text{C}^2)(1.055\times10^{-34}\,\text{J}\cdot\text{s})^2}{(9.11\times10^{-31}\,\text{kg})(1.6\times10^{-19}\,\text{C})^2}$$

$$= 5.3\times10^{-11}\,\text{m}$$

Reinserting,

$$E_{\substack{\text{matter} \\ \text{wave}}} = \frac{\hbar^2}{2m}\left(\frac{me^2}{4\pi\varepsilon_0\hbar^2}\right)^2 - \frac{e^2}{4\pi\varepsilon_0}\left(\frac{me^2}{4\pi\varepsilon_0\hbar^2}\right) = -\frac{me^4}{32\pi^2\,\varepsilon_0^2\hbar^2}$$

$$= -\frac{(9.11\times10^{-31}\,\text{kg})(1.6\times10^{-19}\,\text{C})^4}{32\pi^2(8.85\times10^{-12}\,\text{N}\cdot\text{m}^2/\text{C}^2)^2(1.055\times10^{-34}\,\text{J}\cdot\text{s})^2}$$

$$= -2.2\times10^{-18}\,\text{J} = -13.6\,\text{eV}$$

Figure 16   As the radius of an orbiting matter wave approaches zero, its momentum uncertainty and, thus, kinetic energy approach infinity.

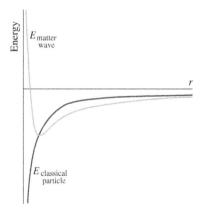

This value happens to equal the experimentally verified minimum energy, and the radius is also the correct most probable radius at which to find the electron (which *doesn't* rest on the proton, whose radius is 10,000 times smaller). That they agree *so closely* is an accident—we have made many approximations—but it is no accident that they are of the correct order of magnitude. The uncertainty principle is a powerful tool.

The Uncertainty Principle in Three Dimensions

The qualitative idea behind the uncertainty principle is the same in multiple dimensions as in one. The more compact the wave along a given axis, the less well we can specify the wavelength and therefore the momentum component *along that axis*. The result is a logical generalization of the one-dimensional result:

$$\Delta p_x \Delta x \geq \frac{\hbar}{2} \qquad \Delta p_y \Delta y \geq \frac{\hbar}{2} \qquad \Delta p_z \Delta z \geq \frac{\hbar}{2}$$

Note that the dimensions are independent. The single-slit pattern of Figure 12 bears this out. Passing through the slit, narrow along x only, produces a large uncertainty in p_x, indicated by the subsequent detections being spread over a large region of the screen. In the y-direction, the aperture is wide, so less is known about this component of position, and there is correspondingly little spreading of the pattern in that dimension. Thus, Δp_y and Δx can be small simultaneously.

The Energy-Time Uncertainty Principle

The momentum-position uncertainty relation is, at heart, a mathematical relationship. A width in space is inversely proportional to a "width" in the spatial frequency $k = 2\pi/\lambda$ (see Section 7). It is the fundamental wave-particle physics, $p = \hbar k$, that takes it the final step. The same math relates a width in time to a width in the *temporal* frequency $\omega = 2\pi/T$. With $E = \hbar\omega$, the corresponding physical consequence is

Energy-time uncertainty principle

$$\Delta E \, \Delta t \geq \frac{\hbar}{2} \qquad\qquad (15)$$

How do we interpret this? If a state, or even a particle, exists for only a limited span of time, its energy is uncertain. One example is the fleeting life of certain exotic subatomic particles. Their lifetimes can be quite short—less than 10^{-20} seconds—and this leads to considerable uncertainty in their mass/energy. Another example is the state temporarily occupied by an electron as it jumps down through energy levels in an atom. Because the state is occupied for a finite time interval Δt, its energy is uncertain by an amount ΔE inversely related to Δt, which in turn gives rise to an uncertainty in the energy of the photon produced when the electron drops down. This effect contributes to the broadening of atomic spectral lines (see Exercise 72).

5 The Not-Unseen Observer

Let us spend a little time summarizing the limitations that quantum mechanics places on our knowledge. If the forces are known, the Schrödinger equation may, in principle, be solved for the wave function of a massive object, which contains all information that can be known. But this isn't everything we might expect classically. The uncertainty principle, for instance, says that a wave function of simultaneously precise momentum and position is a theoretical impossibility. It follows that any experiment or measurement that precisely determines position must result in a state in which nothing is known about the momentum and vice versa.

Suppose we carry out an experiment on a particle, experiment A, applying external forces in such a way as to determine both its position and its momentum as precisely as possible, such that $\Delta x\, \Delta p = \hbar/2$. Assume, for the sake of discussion, that Δx is 100 μm, and call the wave function Ψ_A. We have found the wave function, but we aren't satisfied, for we haven't really "found" the particle—its "location." All we have is this mysterious probability amplitude.

We conduct another experiment, experiment B, in which the particle registers its presence at a detector at a definite location. We rejoice—we have found the particle. However, there are no "point detectors." If the detector's width is smaller than the 100 μm position uncertainty in Ψ_A, then we have indeed narrowed down the possible locations, but we haven't established a location with complete certainty. Yes, we have reduced the uncertainty in position, but if this is so, experiment B has changed the wave function. At the very least, it has increased Δp.

If we repeated this pair of experiments many times—experiment A to establish the initial wave function Ψ_A and experiment B to "find" the particle—experiment B would find it at various locations within the 100 μm uncertainty of wave function Ψ_A, and the number detected at a given location would be proportional to $|\Psi_A|^2$. In essence, we would simply verify that $|\Psi_A|^2$ is proportional to the probability of finding the particle after experiment A. But because experiment B changes the wave function, we can't "watch"—repeatedly find—the *same* particle while preserving a single wave function Ψ_A.

The double-slit experiment, depicted in Figure 17, is a good example of these ideas. In effect, the slits are an experiment A, establishing an initial wave function Ψ_A beyond them, and experiment B is the detection of a particle at

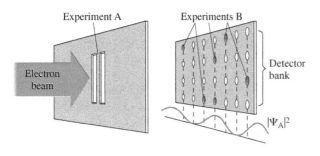

Figure 17 Experiment A establishes Ψ_A, which repeated experiments B verify.

the screen. By sending in a beam of particles one at a time, we are carrying out experiment A then experiment B repeatedly. Where Ψ_A is large, experiment B registers particles in abundance; where Ψ_A is zero, experiment B registers no particles. We cannot conduct an intermediate experiment, determining which slit a given particle passes through, and yet hope to observe the interference pattern exhibited by Ψ_A, for this intermediate experiment would itself alter the wave function. (A recent confirmation is discussed in Progress and Applications.) To observe interference at the screen, we must allow each particle's wave function to pass through both slits simultaneously—otherwise there would not be two coherent waves to interfere.

The discussion raises an interesting point: If we cannot know the location of a particle *until* we actually look for it, it is hard to justify the claim that it even *has* a location before we look for it. Early in the quantum age, many eminent physicists, most notably Albert Einstein himself, asserted that theories of wave-particle duality must be incomplete, that some modification is needed to allow "real" quantities, such as position, to have definite values at all times. However, the modern consensus, known as the **Copenhagen interpretation**, is that until an experiment actually localizes it, a particle simply does not have a location.

In summary, rather than the classical ideas of position and velocity, quantum mechanics allows us to know only probabilities and corresponding uncertainties based on the most recent observation of the "particle," and a determination of one property is liable to alter another. (*Note:* There is a way to precisely determine an uncertain property without in any way upsetting the particle. It involves "entangled" particles.

⊙ P T I O N A L   6 The Bohr Model of the Atom

It is instructive to take a look at an early attempt to solve the mysteries of the atom. This work, for which Niels Bohr won the 1922 Nobel Prize, is known as the **Bohr model of the atom**, or simply the Bohr atom.

When the fundamental workings of something are so obscure as to defy formulation of a comprehensive theory, we construct a model. We observe that a system behaves in a certain way, and the model is a simplified theory that tries to explain the behavior. If it agrees with further experimental observation, we cautiously take it as evidence that its basic assumptions are valid, and we move forward. If, on the other hand, the model's predictions are at odds with further experiment, the model must be changed. Still, we learn something worthwhile: At least one of the model's assumptions is invalid.

The Bohr model predicted that the electron orbiting the proton in a hydrogen atom may take on only certain, discrete energies, and the predicted values agreed with the experimental evidence. Combining simple quantum principles with classical physics, it is based on (1) the classical second law of motion, applied to an electron assumed to be held in circular orbit by its electrostatic attraction to a proton, as shown in Figure 18; (2) a classical expression for the energy of the orbiting electron; and (3) a postulate involving the quantization of the electron's angular momentum.

Figure 18   A classical picture of an electron orbiting a proton.

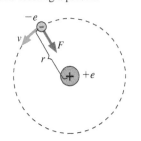

The classical second law of motion sets the Coulomb force between electron and proton equal to the mass times the centripetal acceleration for circular motion:

$$\frac{1}{4\pi\varepsilon_0}\frac{e^2}{r^2} = m\frac{v^2}{r} \quad \text{or} \quad v^2 = \frac{e^2}{4\pi\varepsilon_0 m}\frac{1}{r} \tag{16}$$

The work of combining this with the classical expression for energy was done in Example 6. The result is

$$E_{\substack{\text{classical} \\ \text{particle}}} = -\frac{e^2}{8\pi\varepsilon_0 r} \tag{17}$$

It is negative because the negative potential energy exceeds the positive kinetic. In this classical expression, energy varies continuously, for r may take on any of a continuum of values.

Now we add Bohr's main postulate: The electron's angular momentum L may take on only the values

$$L = n\hbar \qquad \text{where } n = 1, 2, 3, \dots$$

Because $L = mvr$ in a circular orbit, this condition may also be written

$$mvr = n\hbar \qquad n = 1, 2, 3, \dots \tag{18}$$

Figure 19 illustrates a plausible basis for Bohr's postulate. If we assume that the orbiting electron behaves as a wave wrapped around a circle and that it must meet itself smoothly, so that the circumference is an integral number of wavelengths, then $\lambda = h/p$ implies that the product mvr may take on only the values $n\hbar$.

Between equations (16) and (18), we may eliminate v and obtain a condition restricting r only to certain values.

$$r = \frac{(4\pi\varepsilon_0)\hbar^2}{me^2}n^2 \qquad n = 1, 2, 3, \dots \tag{19}$$

or

$$r = a_0 n^2 \qquad \text{where } a_0 \equiv \frac{(4\pi\varepsilon_0)\hbar^2}{me^2} = 0.0529 \text{ nm}$$

According to Bohr's theory, the electron orbits at certain radii that are multiples of the **Bohr radius** a_0. Energy, in turn, is also quantized. Inserting equation (19) into (17),

$$E = -\frac{me^4}{2(4\pi\varepsilon_0)^2\hbar^2}\frac{1}{n^2} = -13.6 \text{ eV}\frac{1}{n^2} \qquad n = 1, 2, 3, \dots \tag{20}$$

The allowed values of the electron's energy depend on the integer n, known as the **principal quantum number**. As noted, these agree with the experimental evidence.

Figure 19 Fitting whole waves around a circumference.

$2\pi r = 1\lambda$

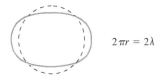

$2\pi r = 2\lambda$

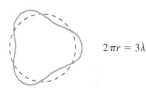

$2\pi r = 3\lambda$

$2\pi r = n\lambda$ but $\lambda = \dfrac{h}{p} = \dfrac{h}{mv}$

Thus $2\pi r = n\dfrac{h}{mv}$

$mvr = n\dfrac{h}{2\pi}$

$L = n\hbar$

Bohr model radii for hydrogen

Bohr model energies for hydrogen

The Bohr model of the atom is an excellent example of working with the knowledge at hand—the Schrödinger equation hadn't even been developed yet! However, it *is* flawed. Although orbiting electrons are *most likely* to be found at certain distances from the proton, they must really be treated as diffuse waves spread over a broad range of radii. This casts doubt on (19), which, in turn, calls into question the model's predicted energies. Furthermore, in reality, orbiting electron waves have not only *rotational* kinetic energy, due to motion about the origin, but also *radial* kinetic energy due to motion toward and away from the origin.

A D V A N C E D   7   Mathematical Basis of the Uncertainty Principle—The Fourier Transform

The uncertainty principle rests on a mathematical relationship completely independent of any physical application: The more spatially compact a wave is, the less well its wavelength may be specified.

To begin, consider the left-hand plots in Figure 20, which show periodic functions of position. All repeat within the same interval along the x-axis, indicated by λ_1. The top waveform is a pure sinusoidal wave. The other

Figure 20 Three functions of the same fundamental wavelength but different spectral (harmonic) contents.

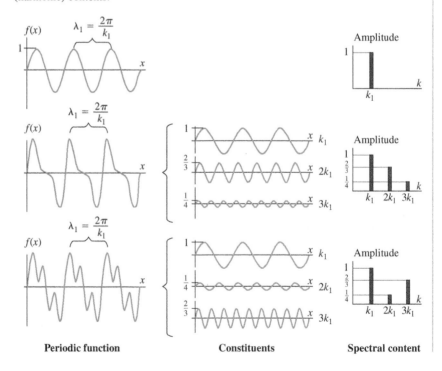

Periodic function   Constituents   Spectral content

two are not pure, but they are algebraic sums of pure waveforms of different wavelengths, as shown in the figure's center plots. These sums have the same fundamental (longest) wavelength as the top waveform, plus differing amounts of wavelengths half as long and one-third as long. Waveforms rich in such harmonics are common in musical instruments. A wave on a guitar string, for example, consists of a large amplitude of the fundamental wavelength, coexisting with shorter-wavelength harmonics of various amplitudes. The important point here is that a complicated periodic waveform can often be treated as an algebraic sum of pure sine waves of different wavelengths. To know the amplitudes of the different wavelengths is to know the waveform's "spectral content," and these are the right-hand plots in Figure 20. Such plots may be familiar, for they are what the graphic equalizer on a stereo displays, with big spikes at one end when the bass is loud and at the other when the treble is loud. And what does this have to do with the uncertainty principle? Making a wave very compact makes it a sum of pure waves covering a huge range of wavelengths, and this means a huge range of *momenta*.

For what follows, it is more convenient to refer to wave number than to wavelength. Don't forget its definition, $k = 2\pi/\lambda$, and that it is a spatial frequency. For instance, if λ were 1.0 m, k would be 2π m^{-1}, a whole cycle (radians is understood) per meter; if λ is 0.5 m, k is 4π m^{-1}, two cycles per meter. As a simple but useful example of its convenience, the harmonics shown in Figure 20 have wavelengths obeying $\lambda_n = \lambda_1/n$. The corresponding wave numbers are $2\pi/(\lambda_1/n) = n\,2\pi/\lambda_1$, integral multiples of the fundamental wave number. It is usually more convenient to speak of something that can be integral *multiples* of a basic value than a basic value *over* an integer.

Now, adding pure sine waves whose wave numbers are multiples of a fundamental wave number always yields a *periodic* function. But what of a nonperiodic waveform? A wave *pulse*, like that shown in Figure 21, is of great interest in quantum mechanics, for it approximates a well-localized particle. It isn't periodic, but can it be considered as a sum of pure sine waves? The answer is yes, but not if the sum is restricted to multiples of a fundamental wave number.

Figure 22 shows why. Waveform (a) is a pure sine wave whose wave number is the pulse's *apparent* wave number k_0. Obviously, it is a poor approximation of the pulse. Waveform (b), a sum of just three sine waves of different amplitudes and wave numbers, does considerably better. Waveforms (c) and (d) add wave numbers more densely spaced and covering a greater range above and below k_0, and here we begin to see a trend. The periodic "impostors" retreat from our desired waveform. We can eliminate them completely only by including an *infinite* number of waves in the sum. We will soon see how we knew what amplitudes and wave numbers to add together. But, as illustrated by waveform (e), the main point is this: A nonperiodic wave can be treated as a sum of sine waves of different amplitudes covering a *continuous* range of wave numbers. It isn't a sum, but an integral.[4]

In quantum mechanics, our basic function is the pure sinusoidal plane wave describing a free particle, given in equation (10): $\Psi(x, t) = A e^{i(kx - \omega t)}$. We aren't interested here in how things behave in time, so we choose the convenient time of zero. Thus, our "building block" is e^{ikx}. Now we claim that any

Figure 21   A wave pulse.

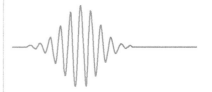

[4]In some sense, an integral over k is like a sum over all multiples of a fundamental wave number that is infinitesimal, dk. Its infinite wavelength allows the wave's overall period to be infinite. A pulse *never* repeats.

Figure 22   Building a single isolated pulse from pure sine waves requires a continuum of wave numbers.

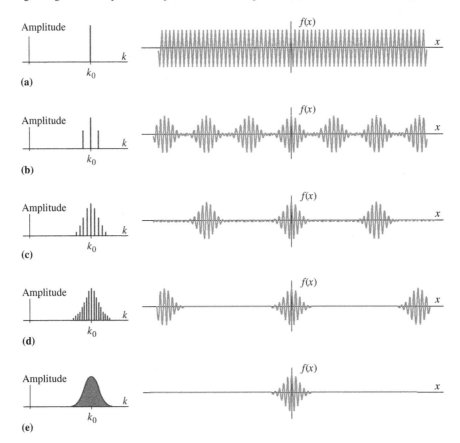

general, nonperiodic wave function $\psi(x)$ can be expressed as a sum/integral of these building blocks over the continuum of wave numbers:[5]

Function $\psi(x)$ as a sum of plane waves of amplitude $A(k)$

$$\psi(x) = \int\limits_{-\infty}^{+\infty} A(k)\, e^{ikx}\, dk \tag{21}$$

The amplitude $A(k)$ of the plane wave is naturally a function of k, for it tells us how much of each different wave number goes into the sum. As we will soon see, it is the key to the whole idea. Although we can't, of course, pull it out of the integral, the equation can be "solved" for $A(k)$. The result is

Fourier transform $A(k)$ of function $\psi(x)$

$$A(k) = \frac{1}{2\pi} \int\limits_{-\infty}^{+\infty} \psi(x)\, e^{-ikx}\, dx \tag{22}$$

[5]It is conventional to use $\Psi(x, t)$ when time is a factor, and $\psi(x)$ otherwise.

The proper name for $A(k)$ is the **Fourier transform** of the function $\psi(x)$. Fourier analysis is the technique of treating general functions as sums of basic ones, and the word *transform* suggests doing something with a function, such as throwing $\psi(x)$ in an integral with e^{ikx} and obtaining something else, $A(k)$, related to that function—which is what we're doing. Before applying it, two points are worth reiterating. First, although the building block e^{ikx} is not as easy to visualize as a real sinusoidal function, it is just two such functions linked in a special way, $\cos(kx) + i \sin(kx)$. Second, equation (21) defines $A(k)$ as the amplitude of each building block, which means that, although continuous, it is really the same quantity shown in the "amplitude" plots in Figures 20 and 22. Now let us use equation (22) to see what it really tells us.

Gaussian Wave Packet

A plausible wave function for a reasonably well-localized particle is the **Gaussian wave packet**:

$$\psi(x) = Ce^{-(x/2\varepsilon)^2} e^{ik_0 x} \tag{23}$$

Let us inspect this one piece at a time. The C is just a constant setting the function's "height" and related to the total probability, which doesn't concern us much here. The $e^{-(x/2\varepsilon)^2}$ is what qualifies the whole function as "Gaussian." As noted in Section 4, it is a maximum at $x = 0$ and falls off on either side. The fall-off is fast when ε is large and slow when it is small. In other words, the width of the bell curve is proportional to ε. Multiplying the Gaussian factor is $e^{ik_0 x}$, a plane wave of wave number k_0. A Gaussian is just a bump, but multiplying it by this sinusoidal function gives the product an oscillatory character. Figure 23 shows the real part of the product. From the $\cos(kx_0)$—the real part of $e^{ik_0 x}$—it gets its wavelength $\lambda = 2\pi/k_0$, and from the Gaussian factor, its fall-off. Figure 24 represents the entire complex Gaussian wave packet in the same way that Figure 11 does a pure plane wave. The difference here is that our plane wave is modulated by the Gaussian factor. This certainly looks more particlelike than a plane wave alone, but what else does this imply?

To answer this, we calculate $A(k)$. Using (22),

$$A(k) = \frac{1}{2\pi} \int\limits_{-\infty}^{+\infty} Ce^{-(x/2\varepsilon)^2} e^{ik_0 x} e^{-ikx}\, dx$$

$$= \frac{C}{2\pi} \int\limits_{-\infty}^{+\infty} e^{-(1/4\varepsilon^2)x^2 + i(k_0 - k)x}\, dx$$

The integral is a standard form, known not coincidentally as a **Gaussian integral**,

$$\int\limits_{-\infty}^{+\infty} e^{-az^2 + bz}\, dz = \sqrt{\frac{\pi}{a}} e^{b^2/4a}$$

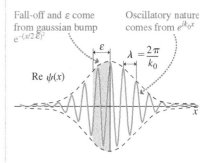

Figure 23 The real part of a Gaussian matter wave packet.

Fall-off and ε come from gaussian bump $e^{-(x/2\varepsilon)^2}$

Oscillatory nature comes from $e^{ik_0 x}$

ε

$\lambda = \dfrac{2\pi}{k_0}$

Re $\psi(x)$

x

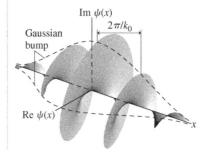

Figure 24 A Gaussian wave packet: A plane wave $Ce^{ik_0 x}$ of wavelength $2\pi/k_0$, modulated by a Gaussian bump, $e^{-(x/2\varepsilon)^2}$.

Im $\psi(x)$

$2\pi/k_0$

Gaussian bump

Re $\psi(x)$

x

Figure 25 The Fourier transform $A(k)$ of a Gaussian wave packet.

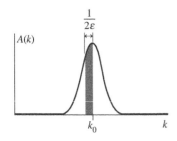

We have $a = 1/(4\varepsilon^2)$ and $b = i(k_0 - k)$, so

$$A(k) = \frac{C}{2\pi} e^{-\varepsilon^2(k-k_0)^2} \sqrt{4\varepsilon^2\pi} \qquad (24)$$

Now we reach the pivotal question: What does $A(k)$ tell us? It is plotted in Figure 25, confirming what we see in the formula itself—that $A(k)$ also happens to be a Gaussian function (which explains the shape chosen for the "amplitudes" in Figure 22). This one, however, is a function of k and is centered at $k = k_0$. Equation (21) says that we can create our Gaussian $\psi(x)$ by adding pure e^{ikx} plane waves, each multiplied by the coefficient $A(k)$ given in (24). We conclude that in this sum, we would need large amplitudes of plane waves whose wave number is near k_0 and smaller amplitudes for other wave numbers. Furthermore, as ε gets small, $\psi(x)$ gets narrow, but $A(k)$ gets wide, for ε is in the *numerator* of the Gaussian's argument in $A(k)$ and in the *denominator* in $\psi(x)$. *The width of $\psi(x)$ is inversely proportional to the width of $A(k)$.* (Why the width of $A(k)$ is shown as $1/(2\varepsilon)$ rather than just $1/\varepsilon$ we address a bit later.)

Figure 26 plots $A(k)$ and the real part of $\psi(x)$ for different ε values. When ε is very large, the Gaussian factor in $\psi(x)$ falls off slowly, and $\psi(x)$ is

Figure 26 The spatial width of $\psi(x)$ is inversely proportional to the wave number width of $A(k)$.

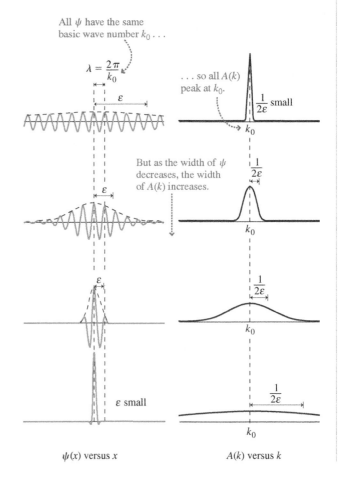

essentially just a pure plane wave e^{ik_0x}. The $A(k)$ plot says exactly the same thing. It says that the "sum" in (21) is just a single plane wave of wave number k_0. At the other extreme, when ε is very small, $\psi(x)$ is compact, but $A(k)$ is correspondingly very broad. We conclude that making a wave function $\psi(x)$ more compact makes its range of wavelengths less compact and vice versa.

As to the physics, we know that $p = \hbar k$, so a function consisting of a range of wave numbers consists of a range of momenta—a momentum measurement might obtain any of them. The inverse relationship between the spatial width of a function and the "width" of its wave numbers (the width in k) thus implies an inverse relationship between Δx and Δp. This is the uncertainty principle.

The Inverse Relationship

The Gaussian wave packet is a very important special case, but Fourier analysis confirms the uncertainty principle in all cases. Before summarizing the general conclusions, let us take a look at another special case, which shows how the Fourier transform underlies some rather familiar physics.

EXAMPLE 7

We introduced the uncertainty principle in connection with the single slit. Assume, as in Figure 12, that the slit is along the x direction, that it is of width w, and that as far as that direction alone goes, the probability amplitude $\psi(x)$ is just a constant C ending at the slit's edges, giving the simple function shown in Figure 27. Find and plot $A(k)$, and interpret your result.

SOLUTION

To investigate this function via equation (22), we insert C and integrate only between $-w/2$ and $+w/2$, for $\psi(x)$ is 0 everywhere else.

$$A(k) = \frac{1}{2\pi} \int_{-w/2}^{+w/2} Ce^{-ikx}\, dx = \frac{1}{2\pi} \int_{-w/2}^{+w/2} C[\cos(kx) + i\sin(kx)]dx$$

The imaginary part disappears, the integral of an odd function (sine) over an interval symmetric about the origin. Carrying out the remaining integral,

$$A(k) = \frac{C}{2\pi} \frac{\sin(+kw/2) - \sin(-kw/2)}{k} = \frac{C}{\pi} \frac{\sin(kw/2)}{k} \qquad (25)$$

Figure 28 plots $A(k)$, and its appearance is conspicuous. Evidently, there are certain wave numbers, when $A(k) = 0$, not "present" at all in $\psi(x)$. Wave number is related to momentum, and in the case we consider here, it is the x-component of momentum—the "sideways" momentum. With certain values missing, there should be certain angles where particles are never detected—diffraction minima! In fact, squaring $A(k)$ gives exactly the same function that describes single-slit intensity. We already know that a diffraction pattern gets wide as w gets narrow, but the easiest way to see it from result (25) is that the first minimum is where $kw/2 = \pi$ or $k = 2\pi/w$. As w gets small, the k-value where this feature occurs gets larger—the pattern spreads out. That the width of $A(k)$ is inversely proportional to the width w again confirms that the momentum uncertainty is inversely proportional to the position uncertainty.

Figure 27 The simple probability amplitude of a single slit.

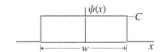

Figure 28 The Fourier transform $A(k)$ of the single-slit function.

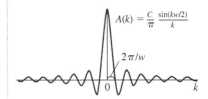

At this point it is certainly justified to ask whether this inverse relationship is merely a mathematical peculiarity of the functions we have chosen to consider. Absolutely not! It always holds. As other examples in the end-of-chapter exercises verify, a more compact wave is necessarily one of less well-defined wave number. In Section 4, we observed that the Gaussian $\psi(x)$ is special, the one for which the product of the widths is minimum. Reexamining the arguments of the Gaussians in (23) and (24), for $\psi(x)$, we have $[x/(2\cdot\varepsilon)]^2$, and for $A(k)$, we have $[\varepsilon(k-k_0)]^2 = [(k-k_0)/(2\cdot\frac{1}{2\varepsilon})]^2$. We see that where ε appears in $\psi(x)$, $\frac{1}{2}$ appears in $A(k)$. We will find that the factor appearing here in a Gaussian isn't just a measure of the width but is, in fact, the defined uncertainty, the standard deviation of the function. Thus, for a Gaussian function, $\Delta x = \varepsilon$, $\Delta k = \frac{1}{2\varepsilon}$, and the product $\Delta x \Delta k$ is $\frac{1}{2}$. Although we won't go into the proof, it is true that for any other mathematical function, the product is larger, so that in general

$$\Delta k\, \Delta x \geq \frac{1}{2} \tag{26}$$

Adding in the physics then gives the famous result:

$$\left.\begin{array}{ll}\text{math:} & \Delta k\, \Delta x \geq \frac{1}{2} \\ \text{physics:} & p = \hbar k\end{array}\right\} \rightarrow \Delta p_x \Delta x \geq \frac{\hbar}{2}$$

As a mathematical procedure, equation (22) takes a function of x and returns a function of k, or 2π over the *spatial* period. Replacing x by t, it would take a function of t and return a function of 2π over the *temporal* period T, which is ω. In other words, the Fourier transform of a general function $f(t)$ would be $A(\omega)$. Replacing the corresponding quantities in (26), we may write

$$\Delta \omega\, \Delta t \geq \frac{1}{2} \tag{27}$$

Combining this with $E = \hbar\omega$ then gives the energy-time uncertainty principle.

$$\left.\begin{array}{ll}\text{math:} & \Delta \omega\, \Delta t \geq \frac{1}{2} \\ \text{physics:} & E = \hbar\omega\end{array}\right\} \rightarrow \Delta E \Delta t \geq \frac{\hbar}{2}$$

It is worthwhile to mention some nomenclature that in a very simple way distills the basic idea behind the Fourier transform. Figures 20, 22, 23, and 27 show various functions of position x. We say that they represent the function in the spatial domain. Each one has a corresponding plot versus k that describes the same phenomenon, the "amplitude" plots of Figures 20 and 22, and the $A(k)$ plots in Figures 25 and 28. All these are said to be in the wave number domain. They convey the same information, just in a different way—as functions of the spatial frequency k rather than x. For a wavelike function of time rather than position, we would say that a plot of $f(t)$ versus t is in the time domain, and a plot of its Fourier transform, a function of ω, would be in the frequency domain. See Progress and Applications for an example of this nomenclature dealing with recent Nobel Prize–winning physics and accompanied by a plot that looks suspiciously like some in this section.

The Fourier transform is an indispensable tool in many areas of modern technology—quantum optics (lasers), signal transmission, acoustics, and metrology (fundamental measurements). One example is the problem of transmitting a laser pulse $f(t)$ whose duration Δt is short. Regardless of the intended "central" frequency ω_0, the Fourier transform $A(\omega)$ reveals that the pulse really contains a range of frequencies $\Delta\omega$ around ω_0. Though the central frequency has the largest amplitude, others, intended or not, are present. Moreover, because $\Delta\omega \propto 1/\Delta t$, the shorter the pulse, the greater the range of frequencies that must be transmitted to accurately reproduce it. If any are left out, the pulse is distorted. A similar situation arises in transmitting any signal that is not a pure sine wave. Any modulation or higher-harmonic detail superimposed on a pure sine wave—as radio superimposes voice upon a "carrier frequency"—results in a signal comprising a range of frequencies within a nonzero "bandwidth" of the central one. Both transmitter and receiver must be able to process the entire range to reproduce the complex signal faithfully.

PROGRESS AND APPLICATIONS

Keeping an Eye on the Double Slit Verification of even the bedrock ideas of quantum mechanics, still a quite active pursuit, contributes in important ways to our understanding. We claim that if in a double-slit experiment we were to watch whether a particle passed through one slit or the other, we would destroy the interference pattern—formation of the pattern requires the particle to pass through both. Using a double-path electron interferometer, effectively equivalent to an electron double slit, scientists have confirmed it (E. Buks, et al., *Nature,* 26 February 1998, pp. 871–874). In the standard double slit, a path difference to different locations causes a phase difference, which in turn gives constructive or destructive interference. In this experiment, electrons may take two different paths to a single collection location, but the phase relationship is altered by the asymmetric influence of a magnetic field—varying the field varies the interference. One path is essentially free, while the other passes through a tiny "quantum dot" serving as an electron weigh station coupled to a detector. When the detector sensitivity is set very low, thus concealing any knowledge of a passing electron, the interference pattern is clear. As the detector's sensitivity is increased, the pattern's visibility diminishes—the important phase relationship is lost.

Quantum Information As technology marches on, the realities and peculiarities of quantum mechanics assume an increasingly important role. What could once be essentially ignored, in areas ranging from communication to basic standards of measurement, is becoming a central idea. In the past decade or two, the topic of **quantum information** has exploded. In essence, the term acknowledges that we are now becoming able to manipulate much of the tenuous information that quantum mechanics allows us to know—not classical notions like particle position and velocity, but the quantum state. A promising application is in the field of **quantum computing**. The heart of today's digital computing is the data bit, which can be in either one of two states, usually a 0 or 1. A dynamical analog would be a classical particle that must be in either one room or another, but not both. A quantum particle, however, can be in any of an infinite number of superpositions/sums of two quantum states. A simple example would be the superposition $\Psi = a\,\Psi_1 + b\,\Psi_2$, where Ψ_1 and Ψ_2 are Gaussian functions whose isolated bumps are far apart, and a and b are arbitrary constants governing the probabilities of being found at one bump or the other. This more flexible bit of information is known as a **qubit**. Qubits can be combined to carry vastly more information than the same number of standard data bits, giving hope of massive parallel processing that may revolutionize information handling in the years to come. Many two-state systems have been studied to serve as a qubit—for instance, two different energy states of a bound electron and two photon spin states.

Working with the Uncertainty Principle The uncertainty principle ties together uncertainties in position and momentum, but it has considerably wider application. The physical world exhibits many pairs of quantities, known as conjugate quantities, that are inherently linked in the same way. To know one quantity exactly is to be completely ignorant of its conjugate. Conversely, if one quantity is known, an inadvertent "observation" of its conjugate will disturb that knowledge. Conjugate quantities having to do with light, such as phase and photon number, are of great current interest. Light in which fluctuations in one aspect have been reduced at the cost of uncontrolled fluctuations in its conjugate is known as **squeezed light**. With certain unusually smooth characteristics, squeezed light promises to enhance high-speed communication, optical imaging, studies of delicate atom processes, and many other technologies. Avoiding run-ins with the uncertainty principle is also at the root of interest in so-called **quantum-nondemolition (QND)** measurements. Using QND techniques, a recent experiment was able to detect the same photon repeatedly without losing it, which is the usual fate of a photon actually "seen" (G. Nogues, et al., *Nature,* 15 July 1999, pp. 239–242). Progress in QND should aid the advance of quantum computing, as well as gravitation. Gravitational waves are predicted to exist, but they are so weak that quantum fluctuations tend to obscure their observation.

Tight Control in Time and Frequency As our desire for ever higher precision in scrutinizing the physical universe increases, new techniques must be developed. A great advance, earning the 2005 Nobel Prize for John L. Hall and Theodore W. Hänsch, was the development of the **optical frequency comb technique**, which provides an excellent example of Fourier analysis. A laser can be made to produce many closely spaced frequencies at the same time. (Exercise 80 discusses a simple case.) The upper right plot in Figure 29 depicts their varying amplitudes in the "frequency domain"—that is, plotted versus frequency. Picturing them in the "time domain" produces a seemingly unrelated plot, but it is really the same information, expressed in a form more useful for understanding the application. In this view, the sum over frequencies gives a pulse, but regularly repeated, and the separation between the pulses is inversely proportional to the spacing of the frequencies. Compare these two plots with the plots in Figure 22, which show exactly this relationship, differing only in that position replaces time, and wave number replaces (temporal) frequency. Moreover, the broader the range of laser frequencies/modes included, the narrower the pulse, which is the idea expressed in equation (27). The lower plots in Figure 29 reveal that an offset in the starting point of the regularly spaced lines, though not changing the separation of the pulses, leads to the little peaks within each being somewhat out of phase. A major achievement of Hall and Hänsch was to stabilize this phase relationship, contributing to extremely precise control of the light. The host of applications is large and expanding, from global positioning systems (GPS) and astronomical observations to studies of matter/antimatter asymmetries and drift in fundamental constants.

Figure 29 Short-pulse laser light in the time and frequency domain.

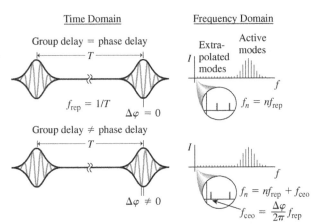

Chapter Summary

Just as electromagnetic radiation—classically a wave—may behave as particles, a massive object—classically a discrete particle—may behave as a wave. Its wave number and angular frequency are given by the fundamental wave-particle relationships:

$$p = \frac{h}{\lambda} = \hbar k \qquad (4)$$

$$E = hf = \hbar\omega \qquad (5)$$

A matter wave function is represented by $\Psi(x, t)$, and obeys the Schrödinger equation, which is based on energy and for a free particle is

$$-\frac{\hbar^2}{2m}\frac{\partial^2 \Psi(x, t)}{\partial x^2} = i\hbar\frac{\partial \Psi(x, t)}{\partial t} \qquad (8)$$

The square of the wave function's absolute value gives the probability per unit length of finding the particle:

$$\text{probability density} = |\Psi(x, t)|^2 \qquad (9)$$

Owing to a particle's underlying wave nature, its momentum and position cannot be precisely known simultaneously. There is a theoretical lower limit on the product of the uncertainties:

$$\Delta p_x \, \Delta x \geq \frac{\hbar}{2} \qquad (14)$$

This is known as the uncertainty principle and is a consequence of $p = \hbar k$ and the mathematical properties of waves. A wave function for which momentum is known precisely ($\Delta p = 0$) is one for which the position is completely unknown ($\Delta x = \infty$); the probability density is spread throughout space. Conversely, a wave function for which the position is known precisely is one for which the momentum is completely unknown.

---

* indicates advanced questions

Conceptual Questions

1. Experiments effectively equivalent to the electron double slit have been conducted in different, novel ways, producing obvious maxima and minima. Often the point is stressed that the intensity is *extremely* low. Why is this fact emphasized so much? How low is low enough to make the point?

2. Generally speaking, why is the wave nature of matter so counterintuitive?

3. In Figure 6, rays are shown scattering off atoms that are lined up in columns, with the atoms in one atomic plane exactly above those in the plane below. Actually, the atoms in different planes are usually *not* aligned this way. They might, for instance, be aligned as in the accompanying figure. Does this affect the validity of the Bragg law (1)? Explain your answer.

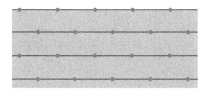

4. All other things being equal, which would be more likely to exhibit its wave nature—a proton or an electron—and why? By making something *unequal*, how could you "compensate," so as to make one as wavelike as the other?

5. Incandescent lightbulbs heat up a filament "white hot," producing light of all wavelengths that has little to do with the filament's composition. Gas vapor bulbs, such as sodium and mercury streetlights, produce colors that do depend on the gas in the bulb. Viewed with a diffraction grating (even a simple CD!), whereas the incandescent spectrum is continuous, that of a gas vapor (or fluorescent) bulb has characteristic lines. How is this indirect evidence of the wave nature of orbiting electrons?

6. An electron beam strikes a barrier with a single narrow slit, and the electron flux—number of electrons per unit time per unit area—detected at the very center of the resulting intensity pattern is F_1. Next, two more identical slits are opened, equidistant on either side of the first and equally "illuminated" by the beam. What will be the flux at the very center now? Does your answer imply that more than three times as many electrons pass through three slits than through one? Why or why not?

7. If a particle's position uncertainty is zero, what can be said of its momentum uncertainty? If a particle's position uncertainty is infinite, what can be said of its momentum uncertainty?

8. When we refer to a "bound" particle, we usually mean one for which there is no probability of finding it outside some finite confines. Could a bound particle be perfectly dead stationary, meaning a well-defined velocity of zero? Why or why not?

9. A classmate studies Figures 12 and 17, then claims that when a spot appears, its location simultaneously establishes the particle's x-component of momentum, according to the angle from center, and its position (i.e., at the spot). How do you answer this claim?

10. Starting with the assumption that a general wave function may be treated as an algebraic sum of sinusoidal functions of various wave numbers, explain concisely why there is an uncertainty principle.

Exercises

Section 1

11. A beam of electrons strikes a barrier with two narrow but equal-width slits. A screen is located beyond the barrier, and electrons are detected as they strike the screen. The "center" of the screen is the point equidistant from the slits. When either slit alone is open, 10 electrons arrive per second in a very small region at the center of the screen. When both slits are open, how many electrons will arrive per second in the same region at the center of the screen?

12. Analyzing crystal diffraction is intimately tied to the various different geometries in which the atoms can be arranged in three dimensions and upon their differing effectiveness in reflecting waves. To grasp some of the considerations without too much trouble, consider the simple square arrangement of identical atoms shown in the figure. In diagram (a), waves are incident at angle θ

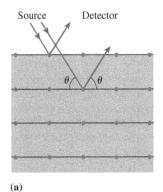

(a)

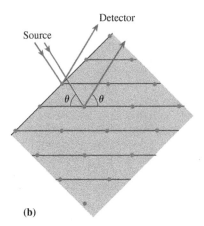

(b)

with the crystal face and are detected at the same angle with the atomic plane. In diagram (b), the crystal has been rotated 45° counterclockwise, and waves are now incident upon planes comprising *different sets of atoms*. If in the orientation of diagram (b), constructive interference is noted only at an angle $\theta = 40°$, at what angle(s) will constructive interference be found in the orientation of diagram (a)? (*Note:* The spacing between *atoms* is the same in each diagram.)

13. The setup depicted in Figure 6 is used in a diffraction experiment using X-rays of 0.26 nm wavelength. Constructive interference is noticed at angles of 23.0° and 51.4°, but none between. What is the spacing d of atomic planes?

14. A beam of electrons strikes a crystal at an angle θ with the atomic planes, reflects off many atomic planes below the surface, and then passes into a detector also making angle θ with the atomic planes. (a) If the minimum θ giving constructive interference is 35°, what is the ratio λ/d, where d is the spacing between atomic planes? (b) At what other angles θ, if any, would constructive interference occur?

Section 2

15. How slow would an electron have to be traveling for its wavelength to be at least 1 μm?

16. A Bragg diffraction experiment is conducted using a beam of electrons accelerated through a 1.0 kV potential difference. (a) If the spacing between atomic planes in the crystal is 0.1 nm, at what angles with respect to the planes will diffraction maxima be observed? (b) If a beam of X-rays produces diffraction maxima at the same angles as the electron beam, what is the X-ray photon energy?

17. Determine the Compton wavelength of the electron, defined to be the wavelength it would have if its momentum were $m_e c$.

18. A particle is "thermal" if it is in equilibrium with its surroundings—its average kinetic energy would be $\frac{3}{2} k_B T$. Show that the wavelength of a thermal particle is given by

$$\lambda = \frac{h}{\sqrt{3 m k_B T}}$$

19. The average kinetic energy of a particle at temperature T is $\frac{3}{2} k_B T$. (a) What is the wavelength of a room-temperature (22°C) electron? (b) Of a room-temperature proton? (c) In what circumstances should each behave as a wave?

20. What is the wavelength of a neutron of kinetic energy 1 MeV? Of kinetic energy 20 eV? (The difference is important for fission of uranium, as a neutron will be

more easily absorbed when its wavelength is very large compared with the dimensions of the uranium nucleus, ~15 fm. In effect, a neutron of long wavelength behaves more like a diffuse wave than like a localized particle.)

21. (a) What is the range of possible wavelengths for a neutron corresponding to a range of speeds from "thermal" at 300 K (see Exercise 18) to $0.01c$? (b) Repeat part (a), but with reference to an electron. (c) For this range of speeds, what range of dimensions D would reveal the wave nature of a neutron? Of an electron?

22. Roughly speaking, for what range of wavelengths would we need to treat an electron relativistically, and what would be the corresponding range of accelerating potentials? Explain your assumptions.

23. Atoms in a crystal form atomic planes at many different angles with respect to the surface. The accompanying figure shows the behaviors of representative incident and scattered waves in the Davisson-Germer experiment. A beam of electrons accelerated through 54 V is directed normally at a nickel surface, and strong reflection is detected only at an angle ϕ of 50°. Using the Bragg law, show that this implies a spacing D of nickel atoms on the surface in agreement with the known value of 0.22 nm.

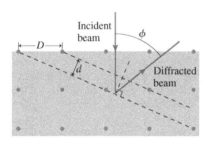

24. The Moon orbits Earth at a radius of 3.84×10^8 m. To do so as a classical particle, its wavelength should be small. But small relative to what? Being a rough measure of the region where it is confined, the orbit radius is certainly a relevant dimension against which to compare the wavelength. Compare the two. Does the Moon indeed orbit as a classical particle? ($m_{Earth} = 5.98 \times 10^{24}$ kg and $m_{Moon} = 7.35 \times 10^{22}$ kg)

25. In the hydrogen atom, the electron's orbit, not necessarily circular, extends to a distance of about an angstrom (1 Å = 0.1 nm) from the proton. If it is to move about as a compact classical particle in the region where it is confined, the electron's wavelength had better *always* be much smaller than an angstrom. Here we investigate how large might be the electron's wavelength. If orbiting as a particle, its speed at 1 Å could be no faster than that for *circular* orbit at that radius. Why? Find the corresponding wavelength and compare it to 1 Å. Can the atom be treated classically?

26. A beam of electrons of 25 eV kinetic energy is directed at a single slit of 2.0 μm width, then detected at a screen 4 m beyond the slit. How far from a point directly in the line of the beam is the first location where no electrons are ever detected?

27. Electrons are accelerated through a 20 V potential difference, producing a monoenergetic beam. This is directed at a double-slit apparatus of 0.010 mm slit separation. A bank of electron detectors is 10 m beyond the double slit. With slit 1 alone open, 100 electrons per second are detected at all detectors. With slit 2 alone open, 900 electrons per second are detected at all detectors. Now both slits are open.

   (a) The first minimum in the electron count occurs at detector X. How far is it from the center of the interference pattern?
   (b) How many electrons per second will be detected at the center detector?
   (c) How many electrons per second will be detected at detector X?

28. A beam of particles, each of mass m and (nonrelativistic) speed v, strikes a barrier in which there are two narrow slits and beyond which is a bank of detectors. With slit 1 alone open, 100 particles are detected per second at all detectors. Now slit 2 is also opened. An interference pattern is noted in which the first minimum, 36 particles per second, occurs at an angle of 30° from the initial direction of motion of the beam.

   (a) How far apart are the slits?
   (b) How many particles would be detected (at all detectors) per second with slit 2 alone open?
   (c) There are multiple answers to part (b). For each, how many particles would be detected at the center detector with both slits open?

29. In Example 2, neither $|\Psi|^2$ nor $|\Psi|$ are given units— only proportionalities are used. Here we verify that the results are unaffected. The actual values given in the example are particle detection rates, in particles/second, or s^{-1}. For this quantity, let us use the symbol R. It is true that the particle detection rate and the probability density will be proportional, so we may write $|\Psi|^2 = bR$, where b is the proportionality constant. (a) What must be the units of b? (b) What is $|\Psi_T|$ at the center detector (interference maximum) in terms of the example's given detection rate and b? (c) What would be $|\Psi_1|$, $|\Psi_1|^2$, and the detection rate R at the center detector with one of the slits blocked?

30. Calculate the ratio of (a) energy to momentum for a photon, (b) kinetic energy to momentum for a relativistic massive object of speed u, and (c) total energy to

momentum for a relativistic massive object. (d) There is a qualitative difference between the ratio in part (a) and the other two. What is it? (e) What are the ratios of kinetic and total energy to momentum for an *extremely* relativistic massive object, for which $u \cong c$? What about the qualitative difference now?

31. Classically and nonrelativistically, we say that the energy E of a massive free particle is just its kinetic energy. (a) With this assumption, show that the classical particle velocity $v_{particle}$ is $2E/p$. (b) Show that this velocity and that of the matter wave differ by a factor of 2. (c) In reality, a massive object also has internal energy, no matter how slowly it moves, and its total energy E is γmc^2, where $\gamma \equiv 1/\sqrt{1 - (v_{particle}/c)^2}$. Show that $v_{particle}$ is pc^2/E and that v_{wave} is $c^2/v_{particle}$. Is there anything wrong with v_{wave}?

32. Nonrelativistically, the energy E of a free massive particle is just kinetic energy, and its momentum p is, of course, mv. Combining these with fundamental relationships (4) and (5), derive a formula relating (a) particle momentum p to matter wave frequency f and (b) particle energy E to the wavelength λ of a matter wave.

Section 3

33. In Section 3, it is shown that $\Psi(x, t) = Ae^{i(kx - \omega t)}$ satisfies the free-particle Schrödinger equation for all x and t, provided only that the constants are related by $(\hbar k)^2/2m = \hbar\omega$. Show that when the function $\Psi(x, t) = A\cos(kx - \omega t)$ is plugged into the Schrödinger equation, the result cannot possibly hold for all values of x and t, no matter how the constants may be related.

34. Because we have found no way to formulate quantum mechanics based on a single real wave function, we have a choice to make. In Section 3, it is said that our choice of using complex numbers is a convenient one. Show that the free-particle Schrödinger equation (8) is equivalent to two *real* equations involving two *real* functions, as follows:

$$\frac{\hbar^2}{2m}\frac{\partial^2 \Psi_1(x, t)}{\partial x^2} = \hbar\frac{\partial \Psi_2(x, t)}{\partial t} \quad \text{and}$$

$$-\frac{\hbar^2}{2m}\frac{\partial^2 \Psi_2(x, t)}{\partial x^2} = \hbar\frac{\partial \Psi_1(x, t)}{\partial t}$$

where $\Psi(x, t)$ is by definition $\Psi_1(x, t) + i\Psi_2(x, t)$. How is the complex approach chosen in Section 3 more convenient than the alternative posed here?

* 35. In Section 3, we claim that in analyzing electromagnetic waves, we could handle the fields **E** and **B**

together with complex numbers. Show that if we define an "electromagnetic field" $\mathbf{G} \equiv \mathbf{E} + ic\mathbf{B}$, then the two of Maxwell's equations that link **E** and **B**, (6c) and (6d), become just one:

$$\oint \mathbf{G} \cdot \mathbf{dl} = \frac{i}{c}\frac{\partial}{\partial t}\int \mathbf{G} \cdot \mathbf{dA}$$

Electromagnetic waves would have to obey this complex equation. Does this change of approach make **E** and/or **B** complex? (Remember how a complex number is defined.)

36. An electron moves along the x-axis with a well-defined momentum of 5×10^{-25} kg·m/s. Write an expression describing the matter wave associated with this electron. Include numerical values where appropriate.

37. A free particle is represented by the plane wave function $\Psi(x, t) = A\exp[i(1.58 \times 10^{12}\, x - 7.91 \times 10^{16}\, t)]$, where SI units are understood. What are the particle's momentum, kinetic energy, and mass? (*Note:* In nonrelativistic quantum mechanics, we ignore mass/internal energy, so the frequency is related to kinetic energy alone.)

Section 4

38. (a) Experiment X is carried out nine times identically, and the value 5 is obtained all nine times. Calculate the mean by definition (12), then the standard deviation by definition (13). (b) Experiment Y is carried out nine times identically, and the integers 1 through 9 are each obtained once. Repeat the calculations of part (a) for this experiment. (c) For nine repetitions of experiment Z, the tally is that 1, 5, and 9 are each obtained three times. Repeat the calculations. (d) Explain any differences between the results in parts (b) and (c). Is standard deviation a reasonable measure of spread?

39. Verify the claim made in Section 4 that if all results of a repeated experiment are equal, the standard deviation, equation (13), will be 0.

40. A visual inspection of an ant of mass 0.5 mg verifies that it is within an uncertainty of 0.7 μm of a given point, apparently stationary. How fast might the ant actually be moving?

41. The uncertainty in the position of a baseball of mass 0.145 kg is 1 μm. What is the minimum uncertainty in its speed?

42. A mosquito of mass 0.15 mg is found to be flying at a speed of 50 cm/s within an uncertainty of 0.5 mm/s. (a) How precisely may its position be known? (b) Does this inherent uncertainty present any hindrance to the application of classical mechanics?

43. The position of a neutron in a nucleus is known within an uncertainty of ~5×10^{-15} m. At what speeds might we expect to find it moving?

44. To how small a region must an electron be confined for borderline relativistic speeds—say, $0.05c$—to become reasonably likely? On the basis of this, would you expect relativistic effects to be prominent for hydrogen's electron, which has an orbit radius near 10^{-10} m? For a lead atom "inner-shell" electron of orbit radius 10^{-12} m?

45. A 65 kg man walks at 1 m/s, known to within an uncertainty (unrealistically small) of 1 μm/h. (a) Compare the minimum uncertainty in his position to his actual physical dimension in his direction of motion, 25 cm from front to back. (b) Is it sensible to apply the uncertainty principle to the man?

46. One of the cornerstones of quantum mechanics is that bound particles cannot be stationary—even at zero absolute temperature! A "bound" particle is one that is confined in some finite region of space, as is an atom in a solid. There is a nonzero lower limit on the kinetic energy of such a particle. Suppose a particle is confined in one dimension to a region of width L. Obtain an approximate formula for its minimum kinetic energy.

47. An electron in an atom can "jump down" from a higher energy level to a lower one, then to a lower one still. The energy the atom thus loses at each jump goes to a photon. Typically, an electron might occupy a level for a nanosecond. What uncertainty in the electron's energy does this imply?

48. The ρ^0 is a subatomic particle of fleeting existence. Data tables don't usually quote its lifetime. Rather, they quote a "width," meaning energy uncertainty, of about 150 MeV. Roughly what is its lifetime?

49. A crack between two walls is 10 cm wide. What is the angular width of the central diffraction maximum when (a) an electron moving at 50 m/s passes through? (b) A baseball of mass 0.145 kg and speed 50 m/s passes through? (c) In each case, an uncertainty in momentum is introduced by the "experiment" (i.e., passing through the slit). Specifically, what aspect of the momentum becomes uncertain, and how does this uncertainty compare with the initial momentum of each?

50. If things really do have a dual wave-particle nature, then if the wave spreads, the probability of finding the particle should spread *proportionally*, independent of the degree of spreading, mass, speed, and even Planck's constant. Imagine that a beam of particles of mass m and speed v, moving in the x direction, passes through a single slit of width w. Show that the angle θ_1 at which the first diffraction minimum would be found ($n\lambda = w \sin \theta_n$, from physical optics) is proportional to the angle at which the particle would likely be deflected $\theta \cong \Delta p_y / p$,

and that the proportionality factor is a pure number, independent of $m, v, w,$ and h. (Assume small angles: $\sin \theta \cong \tan \theta \cong \theta$.)

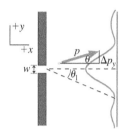

51. In Exercise 45, the case is made that the position uncertainty for a typical macroscopic object is generally so much smaller than its actual physical dimensions that applying the uncertainty principle would be absurd. Here we gain some idea of how small an object would have to be before quantum mechanics might rear its head. The density of aluminum, 2.7×10^3 kg/m³, is typical of solids and liquids around us. Suppose we could narrow down the velocity of an aluminum sphere to within an uncertainty of 1 μm per decade. How small would it have to be for its position uncertainty to be at least as large as $\frac{1}{10}\%$ of its radius?

52. A particle is connected to a spring and undergoes one-dimensional motion.

(a) Write an expression for the total (kinetic plus potential) energy of the particle in terms of its position x, its mass m, its momentum p, and the force constant κ of the spring.

(b) Now treat the particle as a wave. Assume that the product of the uncertainties in position and momentum is governed by an uncertainty relation $\Delta p \Delta x \approx \frac{1}{2}\hbar$. Also assume that because x is, on average, 0, the uncertainty Δx is roughly equal to a typical value of $|x|$. Similarly, assume that $\Delta p \cong |p|$. Eliminate p in favor of x in the energy expression.

(c) Find the minimum possible energy for the wave.

53. The energy of a particle of mass m bound by an unusual spring is $p^2/2m + bx^4$.

(a) Classically, it can have zero energy. Quantum mechanically, however, though both x and p are "on average" zero, its energy cannot be zero. Why?

(b) Roughly speaking, Δx is a typical value of the particle's position. Making a reasonable assumption about a typical value of its momentum, find the particle's minimum possible energy.

Section 6

54. The allowed electron energies predicted by the Bohr model of the hydrogen atom are correct. (a) Determine the three lowest. (b) The electron can "jump" from a higher to a lower energy, with a photon carrying away the energy difference. From the three energies found in part (a), determine three possible wavelengths of light emitted by a hydrogen atom.

55. Verify that equation (19) follows from (16) and (18).

56. What is the density of a solid? Although the *mass* densities of solids vary greatly, the *number* densities (in mol/m^3) vary surprisingly little. The value, of course, hinges on the separation between the atoms—but where does a theoretical prediction start? The electron in hydrogen must be treated not as a particle orbiting at a strict radius, as in the Bohr atom, but as a diffuse orbiting wave. Given a diffuse probability, identically repeated experiments dedicated to "finding" the electron would obtain a range of values—with a mean and standard deviation (i.e., uncertainty). Nevertheless, the allowed radii predicted by the Bohr model are very close to the true mean values.

(a) Assuming that atoms are packed into a solid typically j Bohr radii apart, what would be the number of moles per cubic meter?

(b) Compare this with the typical mole density in a solid of 10^5 mol/m^3. What would be the value of j?

57. In the Bohr model of the hydrogen atom, the electron can have only certain velocities. Obtain a formula for the allowed velocities, then obtain a numerical value for the highest speed possible.

Section 7

58. The top two plots in the accompanying diagram show a Gaussian wave function $\psi(x)$ and its Fourier transform $A(k)$. (a) How does the $\psi(x)$ plot demonstrate that the particle's momentum is roughly $(10^9 \text{ m}^{-1}) h$? (b) How does the $A(k)$ plot demonstrate the same thing? (c) If you measured the particle's momentum, $(10^9 \text{ m}^{-1}) h$ would be a likely value. Would $(0.9 \times 10^9 \text{ m}^{-1}) h$ be a likely value? Would $(1.1 \times 10^9 \text{ m}^{-1}) h$? Would $(0.5 \times 10^9 \text{ m}^{-1}) h$? (d) The bottom plots show two different Gaussian wave functions. Make sketches of their corresponding Fourier transforms.

59. The diagram shows the Fourier transform $A(k)$ of a Gaussian wave function $\psi(x)$ that represents a reasonably well-localized particle. (a) Determine approximate quantitative values for the wave function's wavelength and for the particle's position uncertainty. (b) Can you determine the particle's approximate position? Why or why not?

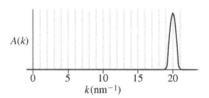

60. A 1 ns pulse of electromagnetic waves would be 30 cm long. (a) Consider such a pulse of 633 nm wavelength laser light. Find its central wave number and the range of wave numbers it comprises. (b) Repeat part (a), but for a 1 ns pulse of 100 MHz radio waves.

61. If a laser pulse is of short enough duration, it becomes rather superfluous to refer to its specific color. How short a duration must a light pulse be for its range of frequencies to cover the entire visible spectrum? (The visible spectrum covers frequencies of ~4.5 to 7.5×10^{14} Hz.)

62. What is the range of frequencies in a 1 ns pulse of (a) 1060 nm infrared laser light and (b) 100 MHz radio waves? (c) For which is the "uncertainty" in frequency, relative to its approximate value, larger?

63. A 1 fs pulse of laser light would be 0.3 μm long. What is the range of wavelengths in a 0.3 μm long pulse of (approximately) 600 nm laser light? (1 fs = 10^{-15} s.)

64. Equation (21) expresses a function $\psi(x)$ as a sum of plane waves, each with a coefficient $A(k)$. Equation (22) finds the coefficients from the given function $\psi(x)$. The equations aren't independent statements; in fact, one is the inverse of the other. Equation (22) gives $A(k)$ when $\psi(x)$ is known, and (21) does the reverse. Example 7 calculates $A(k)$ from a specific $\psi(x)$. Show that when this $A(k)$ is inserted into (21), the original $\psi(x)$ is returned. Use the Euler formula and the symmetry properties of odd and even functions to

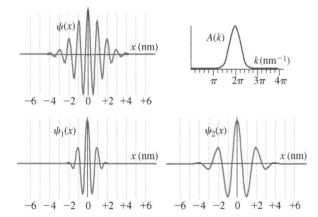

simplify your work. (Nonetheless, you will probably have to look up the final integral in a table of integrals.)

65. Determine the Fourier transform $A(k)$ of the oscillatory function $f(x)$ and interpret the result.

$$f(x) = \begin{cases} e^{ik_0x} & -\frac{1}{2}L \leq x \leq +\frac{1}{2}L \\ 0 & |x| > \frac{1}{2}L \end{cases}$$

66. Determine the Fourier transform $A(k)$ of the oscillatory function $f(x)$ and interpret the result. (The identity $\cos(k_0x) = \frac{1}{2}(e^{+ik_0x} + e^{-ik_0x})$ may be useful.)

$$f(x) = \begin{cases} \cos(k_0x) & -\frac{1}{2}L \leq x \leq +\frac{1}{2}L \\ 0 & |x| > \frac{1}{2}L \end{cases}$$

67. A particle is described by

$$\psi(x) = \begin{cases} C & |x| \leq +\frac{1}{2}w \\ 0 & |x| > \frac{1}{2}w \end{cases}$$

What momenta can never be measured?

68. A function $f(\alpha)$ is nonzero only in the region of width 2δ centered at $\alpha = 0$.

$$f(\alpha) = \begin{cases} C & |\alpha| \leq \delta \\ 0 & |\alpha| > \delta \end{cases}$$

where C is a constant.

(a) Find and plot versus β the Fourier transform $A(\beta)$ of this function.

(b) The function $f(\alpha)$ might represent a pulse occupying either finite distance (α = position) or finite time (α = time). Comment on the wave number spectrum if α is position and on the frequency spectrum if α is time. Specifically address the dependence of the width of the spectrum on δ.

69. A signal is described by the function

$$D(t) = Ce^{-|t|/\tau}$$

(a) Calculate the Fourier transform $A(\omega)$. Sketch and interpret your result.

(b) How are $D(t)$ and $A(\omega)$ affected by a change in τ?

* **70.** Consider the following function:

$$f(x) = \begin{cases} Ce^{+\alpha x} & -\infty < x < 0 \\ Be^{-\alpha x} & 0 \leq x < +\infty \end{cases}$$

(a) Sketch this function. (Without loss of generality, assume that C is greater than B.) Calculate the Fourier transform $A(k)$.

(b) Show that for large k, $A(k)$ is proportional to $1/k$.

(c) In general, $f(x)$ is not continuous. Under what condition will it be, and how does $A(k)$ behave at large values of k if this condition holds?

(d) How does a discontinuity in a function affect the Fourier transform for large values of k?

Comprehensive Exercises

71. (a) Find the wavelength of a proton whose kinetic energy is equal to its internal energy. (b) The proton is usually regarded as being roughly of radius 10^{-15} m. Would this proton behave as a wave or as a particle?

72. According to the energy-time uncertainty principle, the lifetime Δt of a state and the uncertainty ΔE in its energy are inversely proportional. Hydrogen's 656 nm red spectral line is the result of an electron making a transition "downward" from a quantum state whose lifetime is about 10^{-8} s.

(a) What inherent uncertainty in the energy of the emitted photon does this imply? (*Note:* Unfortunately, we might use the symbol ΔE for the energy difference—i.e., the energy of the photon—but here it means the *uncertainty* in that energy difference.)

(b) To what range in wavelengths does this correspond? (As noted in Exercise 2.57, the uncertainty principle is one contributor to the broadening of spectral lines.)

(c) Obtain a general formula relating $\Delta\lambda$ to Δt.

* **73.** The proton and electron had been identified by 1920, but the neutron wasn't found until 1932. Meanwhile, the atom was a mystery. Helium, for example, has a mass about four times the proton mass but a charge only twice that of the proton. Of course, we now know that its nucleus is two protons and two neutrons of about the same mass. But before the neutron's discovery, it was suggested that the nucleus contained four protons plus two electrons, accounting for the mass (electrons are "light") and the total charge. Quantum mechanics makes this hypothesis untenable. A *confined* electron is a *standing* wave. The fundamental standing wave on a string satisfies $L = \frac{1}{2}\lambda$, and the "length of the string" in the nucleus is its diameter, $2R_{nuc}$, so the electron's wavelength could be no longer than about $4R_{nuc}$. Assuming a typical nuclear radius of 4×10^{-15} m, determine the kinetic energy of an electron standing wave confined in the nucleus. (Is it moving "slow" or "fast"?) The charge of a typical nucleus is $+20e$, so the electrostatic potential energy of an electron at its edge would be $-(1/4\pi\varepsilon_0)20e^2/R_{nuc}$ (it would be slightly lower at the center). To escape, the electron needs enough energy to get far away, where the potential energy is 0. Show that it definitely would escape.

Computational Exercises

74. Here we study the plots of Figures 20 and 22.

(a) Plot the point (1,1). Plot the function $f(x) = 1 \sin(\frac{2\pi}{1}x)$ from $x = 0$ to $x = 3$.

(b) Plot the points $(1,1)$, $(2, \frac{2}{3})$, and $(3, \frac{1}{4})$, then plot
$f(x) = 1 \sin(\frac{2\pi}{1}x) + \frac{2}{3} \sin(2\,\frac{2\pi}{1}x) + \frac{1}{4}\sin(3\,\frac{2\pi}{1}x)$
from $x = 0$ to $x = 3$.

(c) Can you produce the other plots in Figure 20?

(d) Plot the points $(5 + \frac{n}{4}, \exp(-2.25[(5 + \frac{n}{4}) - 5]^2))$, where n goes from -4 to $+4$ in integral steps (9 points). Then plot from $x = -40$ to $x = +40$ the function with nine terms, each of the form $\exp(-2.25[(5 + \frac{n}{4}) - 5]^2) \cos[(5 + \frac{n}{4})x]$, where n goes from -4 to $+4$ in integral steps.

(e) Can you produce the other plots in Figure 22?

75. Equation (25) gives a Fourier transform of a particular function. If equation (21) is correct, then multiplying this amplitude $A(k)$ times e^{ikx} and integrating over all k from $-\infty$ to $+\infty$ should return that particular function. Actually, because $A(k)$ is an even function of k, multiplying it by the imaginary part of e^{ikx} (i.e., $i \sin kx$) would produce an integrand that is an odd function of k, which would integrate to 0. Therefore, it is only necessary to multiply $A(k)$ by the real part, $\cos kx$.

(a) Define $f(x)$ to be the integral of this $A(k)$ times $\cos kx$, with these provisions: For simplicity, define C to be 1 and w to be 2. Although the integral from $-\infty$ to $+\infty$ can be done exactly (or looked up in a table of integrals), it isn't a very easy one. To see what is really happening, it is better to use a numerical integration routine on a computer. So, define $f(x)$ as the numerical integral, with limits on k from -200 to 200. (You may need to tweak the limits just a bit to avoid $k = 0$, where the function is really finite but may not appear so to your computer.) Afterward, plot $f(x)$ as a function of x from -3 to $+3$. What do you see, and why?

(b) Change w to 3, then plot $f(x)$ and discuss the result.

(c) Restrict the range of k in the numerical integration to -50 to $+50$. What happens? Can you explain qualitatively why?

76. Here we demonstrate that a continuum of waves is required to produce an isolated triangular peak.

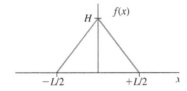

Depicted in the accompanying diagram, the function is described by

$$f(x) = \begin{cases} H - (2H/L)|x| & |x| < L/2 \\ 0 & |x| > L/2 \end{cases}$$

and its Fourier transform is

$$A(k) = \frac{2H}{\pi k^2 L}(1 - \cos(kL/2))$$

We will apply equation (21) in steps to see how well the initial $f(x)$ can be reproduced by a sum. Because $A(k)$ is an even function of k, if we write e^{ikx} in equation (21) as $\cos(kx) + i \sin(kx)$, the imaginary part of the integral disappears, for the integrand is an odd function of k. The remaining integrand is an even function, so equation (21) becomes:

$$f(x) = 2 \int_0^{+\infty} A(k) \cos(kx)dk$$

(a) First, by direct use of equation (22), show that the given Fourier transform is indeed correct.

(b) Now, defining H and L to be 1 for convenience, evaluate $A(k)$ at values of $k = n(2\pi/L)$, where n is 0, 1, and 2. Then plot the sum of $2A(k)\cos(kx)$ over these three k values from $x = -4$ to $x = +4$. (You may have to displace your function along the k-axis a bit, perhaps to 10^{-6}. $A(k)$ is finite there, but your computer may not think so.)

(c) Repeat part (b), but let n run through all integers from 0 to 16.

(d) Repeat part (c), but let n run through all *half* integers from 0 to 16 (i.e., 0, 0.5, 1, 1.5, ...).

(e) Repeat part (d), but for all quarter integers from 0 to 16.

(f) Finally, repeat part (e) for sixteenths of an integer.

(g) Your plots may be about right, but something is missing. Multiply the total functions you plotted in parts (e) and (f) by $2\pi/4$ and $2\pi/16$, respectively. How does this fix things, and why?

(h) How do your results show that to produce an isolated pulse, a continuum of wave numbers is required?

Answers to Selected Exercises

11. 40
13. 0.333 nm
15. 728 m/s
17. 2.43×10^{-12} m
19. (a) 6.29 nm; (b) 0.147 nm
21. (a) 1.46×10^{-10} m to 1.32×10^{-13} m;
(b) 6.23×10^{-9} m to 2.43×10^{-10} m
23. 2.2×10^{-10} m
25. cannot be treated classically
27. (a) 0.14 mm; (b) 1600; (c) 400
29. (a) s/m; (b) $10 \ s^{-1/2}\sqrt{b}$; (c) $5 \ s^{-1/2}\sqrt{b}$, $(25 \ s^{-1})b$, $25 \ s^{-1}$
37. 1.67×10^{-22} kg·m/s, 8.35×10^{-18} J, 1.67×10^{-27} kg
41. 3.6×10^{-28} m/s
43. 6.3×10^{6} m/s
45. $\Delta x \sim 10^{-26} \times 25$ cm

47. 5.3×10^{-26} J
49. (a) $0.0167°$; (b) 1.05×10^{-31} degrees $= 1.83 \times 10^{-33}$ rad
51. $r < 10^{-5}$ m
53. (b) $\frac{3}{2}\sqrt[3]{\hbar^4 b/2m^2}$
57. $e^2(4\pi\varepsilon_0)\hbar n$, 2.2×10^6 m/s
59. (a) 0.314 nm, 0.5 nm
61. 0.3 fs
63. 95 nm
65. $\frac{1}{2\pi}\frac{\sin[(k_0-k)\frac{1}{2}L]}{(k_0-k)\frac{1}{2}L}$
67. $2n\pi\hbar/w$
69. $\frac{C\tau}{2\pi}\frac{2}{1+(\omega\tau)^2}$
71. 7.64×10^{-16} m, particle

Credits

Photograph Credits

3: From Claus Johnson, Dietrich Brandt, Stanley Hirschio, *Am J Phys*, 42 (1974): 4–11, fig 8; **4:** Ernest Orlando Lawrence, Berkeley National Laboratory; **5:** D. Schechtman, et al., *Phys Rev Letters*, 53 (1984)

Art Credits

29: Courtesy of the Royal Swedish Academy of Sciences

Special Relativity

Chapter Outline

Special relativity is the theory governing physical phenomena when one object or reference frame moves relative to another at a speed comparable to that of light: $c = 3 \times 10^8$ m/s. At such high speeds, classical Newtonian mechanics has been found to be inadequate, and seemingly obvious truths about space, time, and energy are profoundly altered. It is very important to bear in mind that essentially all speeds with which we have experience are "low" speeds, much less than c. Spacecraft, for instance, travel no faster than a mere 25,000 mi/h, or about 10^4 m/s. At such speeds, relativistic effects are imperceptibly small, and classical mechanics is satisfactory. Because we have no experience with high speeds, we really have no reliable intuition by which to judge the predictions of special relativity. Startling though these predictions are, it cannot be said that they are contrary to observation and therefore incorrect.

Given the high speed required, it is little wonder that special relativity emerged so late—there was no obvious evidence of its effects. Its discovery by Albert Einstein in 1905 was brought on by advances in the field of electromagnetism in the mid-19th century. Even so, Einstein's theory—a work of genius—was a tremendous leap forward and ran counter to many cherished beliefs. Not surprisingly, detractors abounded. With technological advances in the years since its discovery, however, the experimental evidence of its validity has mounted, until no serious opposition remains.

1 Basic Ideas

An important concept in special relativity is that of an inertial frame of reference, or simply **inertial frame**. By definition, this is a frame of reference in which an object experiencing zero net force—a free object—moves at constant velocity. In classical physics, this is any *frame* moving at constant velocity.

Consider, for example, an object floating freely in space. Any observer moving at constant velocity, perhaps gliding by in an unpowered spacecraft, would determine the object's velocity to be constant (its actual value dependent on the spacecraft's velocity) and would thus be in an inertial frame. An observer in an accelerating rocket would see the object's velocity changing relative to him- or herself, so the rocket would not be an inertial frame.

Einstein's fundamental postulates of special relativity can be stated as follows:

1. The form of each physical law is the same in all inertial frames.
2. Light moves at the same speed relative to all observers.

According to the first postulate, an experiment should proceed identically in a spacecraft floating at rest relative to Earth as in a spacecraft moving at a constant 1,000,000 m/s relative to Earth. No amount of experimentation could prove that a given inertial frame is actually moving. Consider a simple example: If a man standing on the ground drops a ball from shoulder height, it lands at his feet a certain span of time later. If he is inside a high-speed train moving horizontally at a constant 100 m/s and drops the ball, it lands at his feet after the same span of time. In each case, his observation agrees with a law of the same form, $\mathbf{F} = m\mathbf{a}$, without taking into account any motion relative to anything else. The physical behaviors are identical. In fact, were it not for giveaways like bumps, noise, windows, and so forth, the man simply could not prove that his frame is in motion relative to Earth. Since he has no evidence that it is *he* who moves, he can justifiably claim that he is stationary, and it is *Earth* that moves. According to Einstein's first postulate, then, it is impossible to prove that any one frame is truly in motion or that any frame is truly at rest. We say that there is no universal rest frame relative to which all motion might be measured. No motion is absolute—all is relative.

Einstein's first postulate seems quite reasonable when applied to simple mechanical examples like the man on the train. But Einstein's second postulate can be very troubling. Imagine that Anna, a track star, runs to the right at $0.2c$ relative to Bob, who is standing still, as depicted in Figure 1. Anna carries a flashlight and shines it in the direction in which she is running. According to Einstein's second postulate, Anna must determine that the beam moves at c relative to herself, and Bob must also determine that the beam moves at c *relative to himself*. A student of classical physics is often tempted to claim either that the beam moves at $1.0c$ relative to Anna and $1.2c$ relative to Bob or that it moves at $1.0c$ relative to Bob and $0.8c$ relative to Anna. The underlying assumption is that we may add the velocity of the beam relative to Anna to the velocity of Anna relative to Bob to obtain the velocity of the beam relative to Bob. We will see later that this classical assumption about adding velocities is invalid. In any case, the two claims are incompatible. Therefore, we face the question, Relative to what or whom does light move at c? Besides the observer—that is, besides Einstein's answer—there are only two alternatives: the source and a medium.

As to the first alternative, Maxwell's equations, which govern all electromagnetic phenomena, predict that light propagates at a speed independent of the speed of the source. All experiments in which light from high-speed sources has been timed agree. The second alternative calls for a bit more thought.

Figure 1 Anna and Bob watch a light beam.

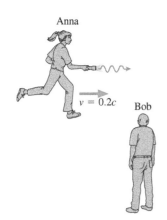

Anna

$v = 0.2c$

Bob

Mechanical waves require a medium whose deformation is communicated from one point to another via intermolecular forces, resulting in a propagating wave. The speed of the wave depends on properties of the medium, not on the motion of source or observer. An explosion causes pressure variations in the air around it. This "deformation" propagates outward as a sound wave at a speed dependent only on properties of the medium—air. It is reasonable to suppose that the propagation of light also requires a medium, and early scientists chose the name **ether**. What air is to sound, ether would be to light. Thus, light would always move at speed c *relative to the ether*, independent of the motion of source or observer. Furthermore, since light travels throughout the universe, ether would have to permeate space. We might even go so far as to proclaim ether the universal rest frame—the one thing really at rest, relative to which the motions of all other things could be judged.

Let us return to Anna running with the flashlight. We now accept that because Anna is the source, her motion has no effect on the speed of the light. To claim that the beam moves at c relative to Bob is to claim that the ether is at rest with respect to Bob and that Anna would see the light moving away from herself at $0.8c$. By analogy, were Anna to shout while running through still air at $0.2v_s$, where v_s is the speed of sound in air, the sound in front of Anna would be moving away at $0.8v_s$, while moving at $1.0v_s$ relative to Bob. On the other hand, to claim that the light beam moves at c relative to Anna is to claim that the ether moves with Anna and would therefore carry the light away from Bob at $1.2c$. Again by analogy, if the air happened to be stationary relative to Anna and thus blowing at $0.2v_s$ relative to Bob, the sound of Anna's shout would move at $1.0v_s$ relative to Anna and $1.2v_s$ relative to Bob.

If ether exists, we might expect it to be detectable. Certainly, it is not as apparent as air. But by considering how we might prove the existence of air, we will see how we might do the same for ether. Even if observers cannot feel the wind at their faces, they can determine the speed at which air moves by timing echoes. Suppose the air is moving at v_{air} relative to the stationary Bob, as in Figure 2. Bob shouts and listens for the echo from an obstacle downwind, a distance L away. The sound moves at $v_s + v_{air}$ relative to Bob as it travels downwind, arriving at the obstacle after a time $L/(v_s + v_{air})$. After reflecting, the sound returns at $v_s - v_{air}$ and arrives back at Bob's location after an additional time $L/(v_s - v_{air})$. If we add these and find a common denominator, we obtain a total time of $2v_sL/(v_s^2 - v_{air}^2)$. Bob could calculate the speed v_{air} relative to himself knowing only the speed v_s of sound in air, the distance L, and the round-trip time.

The first experiments that attempted to determine the speed of ether relative to Earth involved timing round-trips of light beams. The most famous, the **Michelson-Morley experiment** used the interference of light taking round-trips in perpendicular directions. All such experiments have failed to find a nonzero speed. Curiously, ether does not appear to be moving relative to Earth. Maybe this is true. But Earth orbits the Sun. Why should ether orbit with Earth? To salvage the belief in ether, some scientists suggested that perhaps moving objects like Earth drag ether along with them. The results of experiments over many years showed no evidence of such an ability; indeed, the belief in ether was further shaken with each new

Figure 2 The round-trip time for sound depends on the motion of its medium, air.

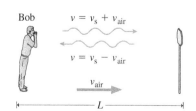

failed attempt to find it. There being no *evidence* of ether's existence, another possibility is that it does not exist. This is the prevailing belief: Light does not require a medium.

Were ether to exist, then *only* in a frame stationary relative to the ether would light move at c in all directions. In any other frame, light would move away from an observer at different speeds in different directions, like a shout on a windy day. Maxwell's equations predict that light will move at c, independent of direction. If ether existed, this could only be true in the one frame stationary relative to the ether, and Maxwell's equations would have to be of a different form in all other frames. Einstein's first postulate would not be met. Perhaps it is possible to patch up Maxwell's equations to include the effects of a frame's motion through ether, to generalize them so that those we now accept are a special case of a form correct for all frames. However, with no evidence of ether's existence, Einstein's second postulate is as plausible a solution to the "problem" as any. In essence, it is a proclamation that Maxwell's equations *as we now have them* are correct in all frames. Consequently, light moves at c in all directions relative to an observer, regardless of the observer's frame of reference.

Still, the reader may find the postulate unpalatable. Even though Anna and Bob move at $0.2c$ relative to one another, each must determine a beam of light to be moving at c relative to him- or herself. Is something wrong with our concepts of distance and time or with the laws of mechanics? The answer is full of irony. Originally, no one doubted the laws of mechanics. It was the laws of electromagnetism that were thought to be in error, because they predicted the same speed for light moving in all directions without reference to a medium. But with Einstein's postulate that Maxwell's equations are correct in all frames, we find that it is the laws of mechanics that must be reevaluated. Classical notions of space and time must be discarded.

In special relativity, distance and time become inextricably related. Accordingly, the following definition is indispensable:

> An **event** is anything with a location in space and a time.

The birth of a child is a single event, occurring at a certain time and at a certain location. The regular eruptions of an ancient geyser constitute a *collection* of events, all with the same location but different times. In taking a snapshot of a friend, we record a collection of events, all with the same time but different locations.

Let us now discuss the startling consequences of Einstein's postulates. As we do, we will often refer to observers Anna and Bob. Understanding special relativity is hopeless if we can't keep straight *who* is doing the observing, and assigning names is the easiest way to do so.

2 Consequences of Einstein's Postulates

The consequences we now discuss are provocative. Distance and time intervals are no longer what our limited intuition tells us they should be. We will quantify these claims later, but to gain the best grasp of their origin and meaning, we begin with a qualitative discussion.

Consequence I: Relative Simultaneity

Anna is riding on a railroad flatcar that is moving east at speed v, as depicted in Figure 3. In each hand, she holds a flashbulb, which she causes to flash at precisely the same instant. Bob is standing on the ground, watching Anna pass. We have two events—the flashes—with different locations. According to postulate 2, Anna will see both light beams move at c *relative to herself*, despite the fact that she moves relative to Earth. The flashes occur at the same distance from Anna, as Figure 4(a) shows, so the beams arrive simultaneously. This arrival is a single event, with a single location—her head—and a single time.

According to postulate 2, Bob must also see both beams travel at c relative to himself. But according to Bob, Anna moves some distance to the east while the light beams travel, as Figure 4(b) shows, so the beam from the west flashbulb has farther to go. If Bob were to agree that the beams originated simultaneously, he would conclude that the beam from the east flashbulb will reach Anna first. This is a contradiction. A single event, the arrival of two light beams at the same time at a single location—Anna's head—either occurs or it doesn't. Though Anna and Bob might not agree on its location or its time, they must agree on whether it occurs at all. So long as we accept Einstein's postulate, there is only one way out of the contradiction. If Bob is to agree that the beams *arrive* at Anna simultaneously, that the single final event even occurs, he must determine that the beams from the flashbulbs do not *originate* simultaneously—that these *two* events do not occur at the same time. In fact, he must determine that the west flashbulb goes off first, because light from it has farther to go and the beams move at the same speed. Later we will use the Lorentz transformation equations to quantify the time interval according to Bob and to verify that the west flashbulb flashes first. Though the discrepancy in times is extremely small at ordinary speeds, the effect is real.

> Two events at different locations that are simultaneous in one frame of reference will not be simultaneous in a frame of reference moving relative to the first.

Before moving on, we emphasize a vital point: The preceding arguments had *nothing at all* to do with Bob's specific location in his frame or the time it takes light to reach his eyes. The issue here is *not* which beam reaches *Bob* first, which does depend on where he stands, but rather which *begins* first, which has nothing to do with where he stands. Attempting to blame the effect on optical illusions is the comfortable yet incorrect way out of accepting a counterintuitive notion. The truth is more challenging. Bob could be standing right next to one flashbulb when it flashes and have an assistant, Bob Jr., standing next to the other flashbulb when it flashes. Each records the time of his flash and neither has to wait for the light to reach his eyes. *They record different times.* Anna, in her frame, causes the bulbs to flash simultaneously, but Bob and Bob Jr., from their frame, determine that she causes the bulbs to flash at different times.

Later in the chapter, we will occasionally refer to Anna or Bob "seeing" something. However, our interest will invariably be where and when events

Figure 3 Anna and Bob watch two lights flash.

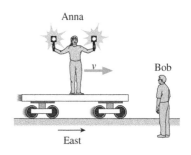

Figure 4 Anna sees beams moving equal distances at c. Bob sees beams moving at c, but one has farther to travel to reach the moving Anna.

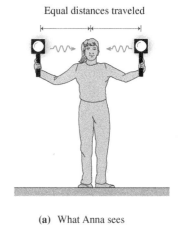

Equal distances traveled

(a) What Anna sees

Different distances traveled

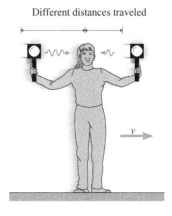

(b) What Bob sees

Figure 5 Bob watches Anna with her flashlight.

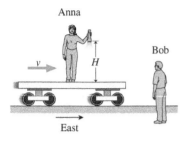

Anna

Bob

v

H

East

Figure 6 According to Bob, the beam moves farther but at the *same* speed. His time interval must be longer.

(a) What Anna sees

v

(b) What Bob sees

actually occur, unobscured by delays in light reaching the observer's eyes. Therefore, "seeing" an event will always be taken to mean what would be seen by an observer *in Anna's or Bob's frame* who happens to be right on the spot to see it. We might imagine Anna and Bob each on a very long train, and each has an army of assistants on his or her train poised to record times of events that occur right at their particular locations. For the time being, we will explicitly refer to additional observers in each frame (Amy and Bob Jr.) who stand ready to confirm the claims.

Consequence II: Time Dilation

Figure 5 shows Anna again on her flatcar moving east and Bob standing on the ground. Anna now holds a flashlight and directs the beam to a mirror at her feet. As illustrated in Figure 6, the beam reflects back to the flashlight *at the same location* in Anna's frame, covering a total distance 2*H*. The total time is 2*H*/*c*. Bob, on the other hand, sees a moving flatcar. The beam reflects at a point east of where it originated and returns to the flashlight at a point still farther to the east. Moving diagonally, the beam travels a total distance *greater* than 2*H*. By postulate 2, Bob must see the beam move at *c* (not faster), so Bob will have to wait a total time *greater* than 2*H*/*c*. We have two events—the creation of the light beam and its arrival back at the flashlight—occurring at the same location in Anna's frame, and the time that passes in Bob's frame is longer. (We will see later why we emphasize the events being at the same location in one frame. Here we simply note that if there is such a frame, it is special. The events would occur at different locations in *all* other frames.)

> Two events occurring at the same location in one frame will be separated by a longer time interval in a frame moving relative to the first.

Again, although the effect is not noticeable at ordinary speeds, it is real. Suppose Anna brushes her teeth. It takes her 30 s by her watch. Bob, watching from the outside, is precisely beside Anna when she starts brushing her teeth. Bob records this time—call it noon. Bob Jr., standing on the ground east of Bob, is beside Anna when she finishes. Bob Jr. will record a time of *more* than 30 s after noon. According to Bob and Bob Jr. and all others in Bob's frame of reference, Anna is brushing her teeth slowly, doing all things slowly, aging slowly.

Note that all that is required for this and other relativistic effects to occur is *relative* motion. Anna is moving relative to Bob, but Bob is moving relative to Anna. Thus, Anna must see Bob brushing his teeth slowly and aging slowly. The reader may suspect a paradox. How can each see the other aging more slowly than themselves? Understanding this effect is intimately tied to the principle that simultaneity is not absolute, as we will see in Example 4.

Consequence III: Length Contraction

Anna and Bob occupy their usual frames, but, as we see in Figure 7, Bob now holds a plank in an east-west orientation. He could determine the length of the plank by finding the time interval between two events: Anna passing one end of the plank, and Anna passing the other. The length of the plank would be the time between these events multiplied by Anna's velocity relative to Bob. Though Anna sees a *moving* plank, she could determine its length by finding the time interval between the same two events: first one end of the plank passing herself, then the other end passing her. The plank's length is the time between these events multiplied by the plank's velocity relative to Anna. Now, the two events occur in the same place in Anna's frame of reference—specifically, Anna's very location. (According to Bob, the plank is stationary, so its ends are at different locations.) Our discussion of time dilation then tells us that the time interval in Anna's frame will be less than Bob's. Taking less time to pass, the plank is shorter according to Anna than it is according to Bob. The effect, an object occupying less space when moving than when stationary, is called **length contraction**. Later we will quantify this effect without basing it on time dilation. But no matter how we approach it, we must use a method of assigning a length to an object while it is actually *moving*. Distance = speed × time is as good as any. If a train moving at 10 m/s passes by in 100 s, its length is unquestionably 1000 m.

The same warning applies to this effect as to the two previous effects: It is a grave mistake to dismiss length contraction as an optical illusion caused by delays in light traveling to the observer from the moving object. The effect is real. Suppose the plank is of length L according to Bob, who holds it. If in Anna's frame, Anna and her assistant Amy each happen to be aligned with an end of the passing plank *at precisely the same time*, then in their frame, Anna and Amy will be a distance apart *less than L*.

> The length of an object in a frame through which the object moves is smaller than its length in the frame in which it is at rest.

Again, all that is required is relative motion. If Anna on her flatcar were holding a plank of length L, it would occupy a distance less than L according to observers in Bob's frame of reference, because Anna's plank moves relative to Bob.

We now consider a question that in one form or another is a common source of consternation for the beginning student of special relativity. In so doing, we will begin to see the interdependence of the consequences. What appear to be paradoxes are usually just examples of applying one consequence of special relativity and ignoring the others. They are a package deal, and we must buy the whole package.

Anna has developed a revolutionary new plane capable of attaining speeds near that of light. It is 40 m long when parked on the runway. Bob has a 20 m long airplane hangar with open doorways at each end, as in Figure 8(a). Anna, a young and daring type, takes off, accelerates to high speed, then swoops through the hangar. At a high enough speed, Anna's plane fits entirely within the hangar all at once according to Bob, occupying only 20 m as shown in Figure 8(b). In other words, Bob sees the tail of Anna's plane at one doorway at precisely noon on his watch, while Bob Jr. sees the plane's nose at the other doorway also precisely at noon. Now consider Anna's perspective. Anna is at rest relative to her plane and thus sees its length as 40 m. She sees the

Figure 7 Bob holds a plank, which is moving relative to Anna.

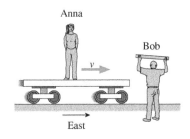

Figure 8 Whether one object fits inside another depends on the observer's frame of reference.

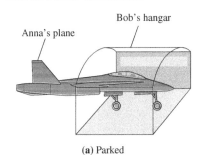

(a) Parked

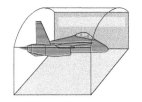

(b) According to Bob

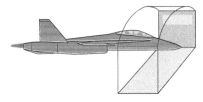

(c) According to Anna

hangar as moving relative to herself. It must occupy less space in Anna's frame than it does in Bob's frame, in which it is at rest. Thus, Anna will see the hangar as only 10 m long. As Figure 8(c) shows, her 40 m plane cannot possibly fit in all at once.

How can we resolve this apparent paradox? Here is the connection: The two events—the two ends of the plane at the two doorways—occur *simultaneously* according to Bob, so they cannot be simultaneous according to Anna. In fact, Anna observes that her plane's nose reaches the doorway through which it exits *before* its tail enters the other doorway. According to Anna, the plane need not and does not fit in the hangar all at once. The whole idea of "all at once" is a question of simultaneity, which depends on the frame.

A question often asked is, What would happen if the plane were to be stopped suddenly—will it fit in or not? We note first that no object can be stopped without force being applied to it somewhere, and a sudden stopping of the plane would be a violent process certain to deform the object in either frame. A mechanism in Bob's hangar reaches out and grabs Anna's plane, exerting sufficient force at many points on the plane to stop it essentially all at once (zero stopping distance would require infinite force). But simultaneous stopping of the different points of the plane in Bob's frame cannot be simultaneous in Anna's. Anna sees the nose stop first. Meanwhile, the other points are still moving, getting closer to the front, reducing the overall length. The last point to stop is the tail. When it is all over, the plane will have been squashed until it fits entirely within the hangar. Now in the same reference frame, Bob and Anna would agree that it fits, and that the experiment was a harrowing set of events.

Evidence of Relativistic Effects

The most famous early evidence supporting special relativity involved the behavior of muons. Muons are comparatively rare subatomic particles that are created when cosmic rays strike the upper atmosphere. It is well known that the muon is unstable. It will spontaneously decay—turn into something different—after a period of time. The time elapsing before decay varies from muon to muon, but the average is known to be 2.2 μs in a frame in which muons are at rest. Given the altitude at which the muons are produced and the speed at which they are found to travel thereafter, a classical calculation indicates that essentially none should reach Earth's surface—but many do!

The explanation involves either time dilation or length contraction, depending on the observer. To demonstrate this, suppose that Bob stands on Earth and watches a clock glued to a muon. Anna flies with the muon.

1. Bob observes events—ticks of a clock—that occur at the same place in the muon's (Anna's) frame. Due to time dilation, these events must take more time as measured by Bob's clock than by the muon's. On average, 2.2 μs will elapse before the muon decays in the frame in which it is at rest (Anna's frame), so Bob's watch must register more than 2.2 μs. If, according to Bob, the muons survive longer before decaying—they age less rapidly—they will indeed reach Earth's surface in greater abundance.

2. Anna, on the other hand, says that it is Earth and its atmosphere that move. Due to length contraction, the distance between the upper atmosphere and the surface will be smaller in Anna's frame than in the frame in which they are at rest (Bob's frame). If, according to Anna and her muon traveling companions, the distance that passes by is shorter, then more muons will survive to meet the surface.

The muon detection rate at Earth's surface predicted by special relativity is in excellent agreement with the experimental findings. We will return to the muon problem after introducing the relationships that will enable us to treat it quantitatively.

3 The Lorentz Transformation Equations

The Lorentz transformation equations are the fundamental equations relating position and time in one inertial frame to position and time in another. They are a modification of classical relationships, but accommodating Einstein's postulates. We will begin with the classical relationships. First, however, we introduce conventions used throughout the chapter.

In relating observations in one frame to those in another, we refer to two representative frames: frame S and frame S'. As illustrated in Figure 9, frame S' moves at speed v in the positive x direction relative to frame S. Viewed from frame S', frame S moves in the *negative x'* direction. (The x- and x'-axes are collinear and are shown otherwise only for clarity.) We reserve the symbol v *exclusively* for the relative speed between the two frames. The symbol u will be used for the velocity of an object moving relative to a frame. Quantities such as position, velocity, and time have different values in different frames. In frame S', these would be denoted by x', u', and t', while in frame S, they would be x, u, and t. Lastly, we define the instant at which the two origins pass as time zero in both frames.

Classical Galilean Relativity

Once again, Anna is on her flatcar moving at speed v relative to Bob, who stands on the ground, as depicted in Figure 10. We choose to the right as being positive, so Anna's frame of reference is frame S', and Bob's is frame S. At time zero, Anna releases an object from the origin of her frame, and it flies eastward at constant speed u' relative to herself. According to Anna in frame S', the object's position is $x' = u't$. *Classically*, time is time, so there is no reason to use separate t and t'. Relative to Bob in frame S, the object's position is denoted by x (no prime) and is the sum of the distances from Anna to the object and from Bob to Anna: $x = u't + vt$, or $x = x' + vt$. Together with our assumption that $t' = t$, we have equations relating position and time in one frame to position and time in another:

$$x' = x - vt \qquad t' = t \qquad (1)$$

Classical transformation

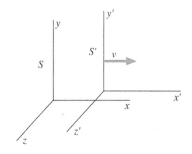

Figure 9 Two reference frames: Frame S' moves at velocity $+v$ relative to S, and frame S moves at $-v$ relative to S'.

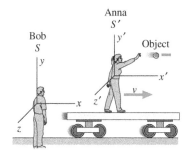

Figure 10 The velocity of an object depends on the frame of reference.

We say that equations (1) are a **transformation** between frames S and S'. If the object beeped regularly, we could find the locations of these events in frame S' from their locations in frame S. Furthermore, the velocity of an object is the time derivative of its position, and applying this definition to the transformation gives us a result familiar from classical mechanics: $u' = dx'/dt' = d(x - vt)/dt = u - v$.

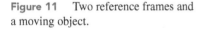

$$u' = u - v \qquad (2)$$

The object's velocity according to Anna in frame S' differs from its velocity according to Bob in frame S.

That position and velocity have different values in different frames of reference is sensible, and it seems natural that an object's position relative to a moving frame could be expressed as a function of its position relative to the ground, the speed of the frame, and the elapsed time. But the assumption that time is absolute, *also quite natural*, dooms classical relativity. Equation (2), for instance, is at odds with Einstein's second postulate, for it says that if the object that Anna released were a light signal, such that $u' = c$, its speed u according to Bob would be $c + v$.

Special Relativity

Our path to the Lorentz transformation equations begins with the application of Einstein's postulates to a very familiar law of physics: A free object moves at constant velocity. Figure 11 shows the essentials. We assume that at time zero the object was at the point where the origins coincided. With no net external force, it must travel at constant velocity; its position must be a linear function of time in both frames.

$$x' = u't' \qquad x = ut \qquad (3)$$

Avoiding unnecessary assumptions, we allow that a given event in the object's life may occur at different locations *and times* in the two frames. As before, suppose that the object beeps regularly. We seek a relationship that would give us the x' and t' of each such event in frame S' from its x and t in frame S. At this point, our only guidelines are that constant velocity in one frame—position being a linear function of time—should imply constant velocity in the other. As it turns out, this implies a fairly simple relationship: (x', t') must be related to (x, t) by a **linear transformation**.

Figure 11 Two reference frames and a moving object.

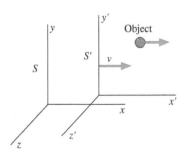

$$x' = Ax + Bt \qquad t' = Cx + Dt \qquad (4)$$

where A, B, C, and D are constants. It is left as an exercise to verify from equations (4) that if x/t is constant, then x'/t' is constant. The main point is that for a free object to move at constant velocity in all frames, we require only that the transformation be linear. It is not required that time be absolute—that $t = t'$.

To determine the constants A, B, C, and D, we need to consider only three special cases of motion.

1. If the object were fixed at the origin of frame S', it would move at speed v relative to frame S, so equations (3) would become $x' = 0$ and $x = vt$. Inserting these in the first of equations (4), we obtain

$$B = -Av \qquad (5)$$

2. If the object were fixed at the frame S origin, it would have a velocity of $-v$ according to someone in frame S', so equations (3) would be $x' = -vt'$ and $x = 0$. Inserting these in (4) gives

$$D = -\frac{B}{v} \qquad \text{or} \qquad D = A \qquad (6)$$

    (The algebra that yields this equation and equation (8) below is left to Exercise 18.) Thus far, we have merely set up two frames with relative motion. We have not invoked anything particularly "relativistic." With our third special case comes the crucial element.

3. If the object were a beam of light, Einstein's second postulate demands that its speed be c in both frames. Equations (3) become

$$x' = ct' \qquad x = ct \qquad (7)$$

Inserting these in (4) and using (5) and (6) gives

$$C = -\frac{v}{c^2}A \qquad (8)$$

With B, C, and D now in terms of A, we may write equations (4) as

$$x' = A(x - vt) \qquad t' = A\left(-\frac{v}{c^2}x + t\right) \qquad (9)$$

We can deduce A by a fairly simple argument if we first solve equations (9) for x and t.

$$x = \frac{1}{A\left(1 - \frac{v^2}{c^2}\right)}(x' + vt') \qquad t = \frac{1}{A\left(1 - \frac{v^2}{c^2}\right)}\left(+\frac{v}{c^2}x' + t'\right) \qquad (10)$$

The only difference between the frames is that S' moves at $+v$ relative to frame S, while S moves at $-v$ relative to S'. It follows that (9) and (10) have to be identical except for the sign of v, and this simply requires that their leading coefficients be equal.

$$\frac{1}{A\left(1 - \dfrac{v^2}{c^2}\right)} = A \quad \text{or} \quad A = \frac{1}{\sqrt{1 - \dfrac{v^2}{c^2}}} \equiv \gamma_v \qquad (11)$$

This factor is ubiquitous in special relativity, so it is given a special symbol: γ_v. As we shall see, this is often *the* measure of the departure of relativistic expectations from classical ones. It increases continuously from essentially 1 at small speeds toward infinity as v approaches c.

$$\gamma_v \equiv \frac{1}{\sqrt{1 - \dfrac{v^2}{c^2}}} \geq 1$$

Finally, inserting (11) into (9) and (10), we have the Lorentz transformation equations.

Lorentz transformation equations

$$x' = \gamma_v(x - vt) \qquad (12a) \qquad t' = \gamma_v\left(-\frac{v}{c^2}x + t\right) \qquad (12b)$$

$$x = \gamma_v(x' + vt') \qquad (13a) \qquad t = \gamma_v\left(+\frac{v}{c^2}x' + t'\right) \qquad (13b)$$

Note that equations (12) and (13) are actually equivalent but simply solved for different quantities. We include both merely for convenience. It is fairly easily argued that spatial coordinates perpendicular to the direction of relative motion are the same in both frames (see Exercise 19). Thus,

$$y' = y \qquad z' = z \qquad (14)$$

Distances perpendicular to the direction of relative motion are not subject to length contraction.

When $v \ll c$, which is known as the **classical limit**, γ_v is essentially 1, and the terms in equations (12) and (13) involving v/c^2 are usually negligible. (Exercise 44 discusses an exception.) In this limit, the equations reduce to the classical transformation of (1). Classical physics is valid in the realm of small speeds.

Consequences Revisited

Now we are ready to quantify the claims of Section 2. Each consequence involved intervals between a *pair* of events—either spatial intervals or time intervals or both. Let event 1 have position and time (x_1, t_1) in frame S and (x_1', t_1') in frame S'. Event 2 has positions and times (x_2, t_2) and (x_2', t_2'). If we insert (x_1, t_1) and (x_1', t_1') into equation (12a) and separately insert (x_2, t_2) and (x_2', t_2') into that equation and then subtract the two equations, we obtain

$$x_2' - x_1' = \gamma_v\left[(x_2 - x_1) - v(t_2 - t_1)\right]$$

We could evaluate any of the Lorentz transformation equations for a pair of events in the same way. The point is that equations (12) and (13) can be used directly for a pair of events just as for a single event.

The first consequence of Einstein's postulates, dealing with relative simultaneity, we quantify in an example.

EXAMPLE 1

Anna is on a flatcar moving east at $0.6c$ relative to Bob, as shown in Figure 12. She holds a flashbulb in each hand and causes them to flash simultaneously. Anna's hands are 2 m apart and her arms are oriented in an east-west direction. According to Bob, which flashbulb flashes first and by how much?

SOLUTION

Let Anna's frame be S' and Bob's S. Event 1 is the east flash and event 2 the west flash. According to Anna, the two events occur simultaneously, so $t_2' - t_1' = 0$, and they are a distance apart $x_2' - x_1' = -2$ m. To find the time interval according to Bob, we use (13b).

$$t_2 - t_1 = \gamma_v\left[+\frac{v}{c^2}(x_2' - x_1') + (t_2' - t_1')\right]$$

$$= \frac{1}{\sqrt{1 - \frac{(0.6c)^2}{c^2}}}\left[\frac{0.6c}{c^2}(-2\text{ m}) + 0\right] = 1.25\frac{-0.6 \times 2\text{ m}}{3 \times 10^8\text{ m/s}} = -5\text{ ns}$$

Event 2 has the smaller (earlier) time. That is, the west bulb flashes 5 ns earlier than the east bulb. Note that if we calculated t_2 and t_1 separately, from $x_2' = -1$ m and $x_1' = +1$ m, we would obtain -2.5 ns and $+2.5$ ns, respectively. According to Bob, the west bulb flashes before the origins cross, while the east one flashes after.

Time Dilation

Consider the situation of Figure 13. Two events—ticks of a clock—occur *at the same location* in frame S', so that $x_2' = x_1'$. Evaluating (13b) for this pair of events, the term with $x_2' - x_1'$ would drop out, leaving $t_2 - t_1 = \gamma_v(t_2' - t_1')$, or, in more compact notation, $\Delta t = \gamma_v\Delta t'$. The special term **proper time** is used for the time that elapses in the frame in which events all occur at the same location. In the case we have considered here, that frame is S', but it need not be in general, so we choose the distinctive symbol Δt_0.

$$\Delta t = \gamma_v\,\Delta t_0 \qquad (15)$$

The time interval Δt that passes between two events in another frame is longer by the factor γ_v than the interval Δt_0 in the frame in which the events occur at the same location.

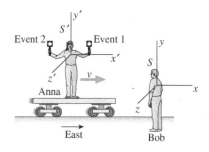

Figure 12 Bob viewing two events that occur simultaneously according to Anna.

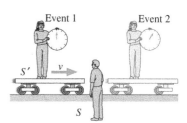

Figure 13 Two events, ticks of a clock, at the same location in frame S'.

Special Relativity

For any series of related events, such as ticks of a clock or beats of a heart, there is always a frame where events occur at the same place, or a frame that follows the events around. For instance, a duck may dive and turn as it quacks in flight, but in the duck's frame of reference, the quacks all occur at the same location. Section 10 shows that observers in all other frames will agree on the time that they see elapsing in this special frame, although each sees a different time pass on their own clock. We might have guessed this, though, because the alternative makes no sense. Imagine the time passing on Bob's bathroom clock as he brushes his teeth depending on who happens to be observing him from a passing spaceship! The point is that relativity never causes us to feel as though we are moving in slow motion. We each feel normal in our own frame, no matter who else might be watching.

Length Contraction

Consider Figure 14. To establish the length of an object fixed in frame S' and thus moving relative to himself, Bob observes its ends *at the same time* in his frame. These two observations are events for which $t_2 = t_1$. If we evaluate (12a) for these events, $t_2 - t_1$ drops out, leaving $x_2' - x_1' = \gamma_v(x_2 - x_1)$, or $L = L'/\gamma_v$.[1] The length of an object in the frame in which it is at rest—its rest frame—is given the symbol L_0 and is known as **proper length**.

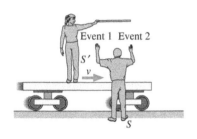

Figure 14 Bob sees a moving object. Its length is the distance between its ends at the same instant in *his* frame.

$$L = \frac{L_0}{\gamma_v} \qquad (16)$$

The length L of a moving object is shorter by the factor γ_v than its length L_0 in the frame in which it is at rest.

As in the case of time dilation, no matter what frame we occupy or who else might be watching, we never feel contracted. We never move relative to ourselves. It is only observers in other frames who will determine that an object occupies less space than normal.

Fitting It All Together

Now let us take another look at the muon problem.

EXAMPLE 2

A muon is created in the atmosphere 3 km above Earth's surface, heading downward at speed $0.98c$. It survives $2.2\ \mu s$ in its own frame of reference before decaying. (a) Classically, how far would the muon travel before decaying, and how much longer than $2.2\ \mu s$ would it have to survive to reach the surface? (b) Relativistically, according to an observer on Earth, how long will the muon survive before decaying? Will it reach the surface? (c) Relativistically, according to the muon, what is the distance from the point in the atmosphere where the muon is created to Earth's surface, and how much time will it take this distance to pass the muon?

[1]Of course, Anna in frame S' won't agree that Bob's observations are simultaneous, but she does at least agree that they are made *at the ends of the object*, a distance apart equal to the length of the object fixed in her frame.

SOLUTION

(a) The muon would travel $d = vt = (0.98 \times 3 \times 10^8 \text{ m/s})(2.2 \times 10^{-6} \text{ s}) = 647$ m. To travel 3 km would require

$$t = \frac{d}{v} = \frac{3 \times 10^3 \text{ m}}{0.98 \times 3 \times 10^8 \text{ m/s}} = 10.2 \ \mu s$$

It would have to live 8 μs longer. It shouldn't reach the surface, for the distance is about five times too far, or equivalently, the muon survives only about one-fifth the required time.

(b) To do any relativistically correct calculation, we need γ_v.

$$\gamma_v = \frac{1}{\sqrt{1 - \dfrac{v^2}{c^2}}} = \frac{1}{\sqrt{1 - \dfrac{(0.98)^2 c^2}{c^2}}} = 5.03$$

Now a warning is in order. Having found the ubiquitous γ_v, we may find correct time and space intervals, but plugging in blindly to a time-dilation or length-contraction formula will give the wrong answer 50% of the time. It should be reasoned beforehand whether the interval sought is larger or smaller than the known interval. An observer on Earth "sees" 2.2 μs elapse on the muon's wristwatch, ticking at the same location in the muon's frame, so *more* time must elapse on the observer's own clock. We must multiply (not divide) 2.2 μs by 5.03. Of course, equation (15) agrees. It comes with the condition that Δt_0 is the interval in the frame where the events occur at the same location. Thus, Δt_0 must be the 2.2 μs in the frame of the muon, which watches things that conveniently pass by its very own location, and Δt must be the interval in the Earth observer's frame, in which the upper atmosphere and Earth's surface are definitely different locations.

$$\Delta t = \gamma_v \, \Delta t_0 = 5.03 \times 2.2 \ \mu s = 11.1 \ \mu s$$

From the classical perspective, the muon would have to survive at least 10.2 μs to reach the ground. That calculation was valid because the speed, distance, and time involved were all according to the *same* (Earth) observer. The trap to avoid is using a distance according to an observer in one frame and a time according to an observer in a different frame. Similarly, we can find a distance according to an Earth observer if we use the lifetime of the muon as computed in the Earth frame. At 0.98c, the muon could travel $(0.98 \times 3 \times 10^8 \text{ m/s})$ $(11.1 \times 10^{-6} \text{ s}) = 3.25$ km. According to the Earth observer, the muon survives 11.1 μs and could travel 3.25 km, allowing it to reach the surface.

(c) The muon sees a moving "object," specifically the region of atmosphere between the point where it is born and Earth's surface. These points are 3 km apart according to an Earth observer, but according to the muon, they are closer together. We should expect to divide 3 km by 5.03. The equation $L = L_0/\gamma_v$ agrees. It is Earth's frame in which this object is at rest, so L_0 is 3 km.

$$L = \frac{L_0}{\gamma_v} = \frac{3 \text{ km}}{5.03} = 597 \text{ m}$$

Length contraction is real. According to the muon, this object moving at $0.98c$ occupies only 597 m. Consequently, it will pass by in only

$$t = \frac{L}{v} = \frac{597 \text{ m}}{0.98 \times 3 \times 10^8 \text{ m/s}} = 2.03 \text{ } \mu s$$

The muon, which by its own wristwatch survives 2.2 μs, will meet the ground after 2.03 μs.

It is worth noting that according to the Earth observer, the muon could have been created at an altitude as high as 3.25 km and still strike the surface, although just barely. If it had been created at this height, the muon would have seen an "object" 3.25 km/5.03 = 647 m long, which would pass by in exactly 2.2 μs (i.e., 647 m/$0.98c$). The muon would agree that it barely survives to meet the surface. Both observers must agree on this! A collision between a muon and Earth is a single event. If an event occurs in one frame, it must occur in all frames. However, the explanations may differ. The observer on Earth says that time dilation is responsible, while the muon argues that it is length contraction. Exercises 33 and 34 address the fact that the muon lifetime actually varies, leading to the number of muons decaying exponentially with time, although still at a rate that is inexplicable without relativity.

EXAMPLE 3

A proposed plane would carry intercontinental travelers at speeds many times those of today's fastest airliners. Imagine that such a plane is 50 m long (when parked) and cruises at 6000 m/s (13,400 mi/h, or about Mach 18). At precisely noon, it passes over Los Angeles, and an observer on the ground with exceptional eyesight peers through its window. He sees that the clock inside also reads precisely noon. (a) How long is the moving plane according to this observer? (b) Later, a ground observer in Seattle, 1600 km north, checks the plane's clock as it passes overhead. By how much does the reading differ from that on her watch?

SOLUTION

(a) The ground observer in Los Angeles must see a length shorter than the plane's proper length of 50 m.

$$L = \frac{L_0}{\gamma_v} = 50 \text{ m} \sqrt{1 - \left(\frac{6 \times 10^3}{3 \times 10^8}\right)^2} = 50 \text{ m} \left(1 - 4 \times 10^{-10}\right)^{1/2}$$

Here we have a situation that often arises when v is much less than c. The quantity in parentheses differs from 1 by only a tiny amount. Raising it to any power requires either a calculator of great precision or some kind of approximation. The binomial approximation given in the margin (a truncated power series) works well. To use it here, we replace x with -4×10^{-10} and a with $\frac{1}{2}$.

$$L = 50 \text{ m} \left[1 + (-4 \times 10^{-10})\right]^{1/2}$$

$$\cong 50 \text{ m} \left[1 + \frac{1}{2}(-4 \times 10^{-10})\right] = 50 \text{ m} - 10^{-8} \text{ m}$$

Binomial approximation:

When $|x| \ll 1$: $(1 + x)^a \cong 1 + ax$

The plane would occupy 10 nm less space than it does at rest.

(b) The ground observers watch a single clock ticking off events *at the same location* in the plane's frame, so this clock registers the proper time Δt_0, and the time passing on their own watches is the longer Δt. We calculate Δt in the usual classical way, because both it and the 1600 km are according to the same (ground) observers.

$$\Delta t = \frac{\Delta x}{v} = \frac{1600 \times 10^3 \text{ m}}{6000 \text{ m/s}} = 267 \text{ s} \quad \text{(L.A. to Seattle in 4.4 min!)}$$

$$\Delta t_0 = \frac{\Delta t}{\gamma_v} = 267 \text{ s} \sqrt{1 - \left(\frac{6 \times 10^3}{3 \times 10^8}\right)^2}$$

Again using the approximation,

$$\Delta t_0 = 267 \text{ s}\left[1 + (-4 \times 10^{-10})\right]^{1/2} \cong 267 \text{ s}\left[1 + \frac{1}{2}(-4 \times 10^{-10})\right]$$

$$= 267 \text{ s} - 5.3 \times 10^{-8} \text{ s}$$

The plane's clock will read 53 ns earlier than the Seattle observer's watch. We see that even at speeds very high by ordinary standards, relativistic effects are quite small.

Now let us confront the perplexing question of two observers each seeing the other aging more slowly and contracted along the direction of relative motion. Before we do, we note an important point: When two observers pass, although their wristwatches will, in general, read different values, they will agree on what those values are. For instance, if Anna sees Bob's wristwatch read 8 when he passes, while hers reads 11, then Bob sees Anna's wristwatch read 11 when she passes, while his reads 8.

EXAMPLE 4

Anna and Bob are on identical spaceships of length $\ell = 12\sqrt{3}$ m $\cong$ 21 m. (The weird length value makes other values nice.) Anna's spaceship (frame S') moves to the right relative to Bob's (frame S). Clocks are attached to each ship at its center, its front, and its tail. Figure 15 shows what Bob sees at $t = 0$. The clocks at the ship's tails are aligned, Anna's tail-end clock reads 0, and the clock at the front of Anna's spaceship is precisely aligned with the clock at the center of Bob's. (a) How fast is Anna moving? (b) At $t = 0$, what do Anna's clocks read according to Bob? (c) Show that the ships' centers will be aligned 20 ns later, according to Bob. (d) Find the readings on Anna's clocks when Bob's read 20 ns, 40 ns, and 60 ns. (e) Find pairs of events showing time dilation and length contraction from *Anna's* perspective.

Figure 15 How Anna's passing ship appears to Bob.

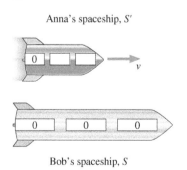

Anna's spaceship, S'

Bob's spaceship, S

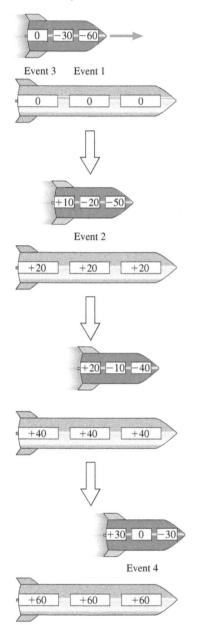

Figure 16 According to Bob, Anna's clocks are unsynchronized, and they advance slowly.

Event 3   Event 1

Event 2

Event 4

(a) Bob sees the length of Anna's ship contracted. It is only half as long as his identical one, so γ_v must be 2.

$$\frac{1}{\sqrt{1 - \dfrac{v^2}{c^2}}} = 2 \quad \Rightarrow \quad v = \frac{\sqrt{3}}{2}c$$

(b) When Anna's front clock ticks, it is an event that announces t' at that clock's location in her frame. We wish to know this t' when $t = 0$, so we suppose that at $t = 0$, someone in Bob's frame, say Bob Jr., is right on the spot to see Anna's front clock, $x = \frac{1}{2}\ell$. Knowing the coordinates (x, t) of this tick/event in frame S, we can find its time in S' via (12b),

$$t' = 2\left[-\frac{(\sqrt{3}/2)c}{c^2}\left(\frac{1}{2}12\sqrt{3}\text{ m}\right) + 0 \right]$$

$$= -\frac{(3/2)12\text{ m}}{3 \times 10^8\text{ m/s}} = -60\text{ ns}$$

Again, we are not studying optical illusions. This is *the time* at this location in Anna's frame, and Bob Jr. is there to confirm it. (*Note:* The time-dilation and length-contraction formulas are fine for pairs of events, but if a *single* event is the question, then the Lorentz transformation equations are the answer.) For Anna's center clock, Bob would rely on an assistant at $x = \frac{1}{4}\ell$ making an observation at $t = 0$. Equation (12b) then yields $t' = -30$ ns. The top diagram in Figure 16 shows Bob's observations at $t = 0$. (We refer to the numbered events later.) Anna's clocks don't strike 0 simultaneously according to Bob, and they shouldn't, for they *do* strike 0 simultaneously according to Anna.

(c) Bob sees the center of Anna's ship move $\frac{1}{4}\ell$. The time according to him, distance over speed, is thus

$$\Delta t = \frac{(1/4)(12\sqrt{3}\text{ m})}{(\sqrt{3}/2)(3 \times 10^8\text{ m/s})} = 20\text{ ns}$$

(d) To find the readings Bob and his assistants see on Anna's clocks at $t = 20$ ns, we could use (12b) again, but the faster way is time dilation. Bob must see Anna's clock advancing half as fast as his own ($\gamma_v = 2$). For every 20 ns on his clocks, each of Anna's must be seen to advance 10 ns. Figure 16 shows the results.

(e) Figure 16 makes length contraction and time dilation obvious according to Bob, but it also shows Anna observing these effects. At the passing of clocks labeled as event 1 and event 2, observers in Anna's frame at $t' = -60$ ns and $t' = -20$ ns—that is, 40 ns apart in their frame—look at the *same* clock in

Bob's frame and see it advance only 20 ns. This is time dilation. (To verify time dilation, Anna and her assistants would never make the mistake of viewing *different* clocks in Bob's frame, for Anna says that Bob's clocks are unsynchronized.) At events 3 and 4, observers at the same $t' = 0$ instant in Anna's frame and only half her ship's length apart see the very ends of Bob's ship. It is contracted to half as long.

Figure 17 shows Anna's complementary view of the events in Example 4. Comparing with Figure 16, we see that, as noted earlier, at every event where two clocks pass (not just the four labeled), Anna and Bob agree on those clocks' readings. The important point is this: It is the fact that simultaneity of events is not absolute that allows each observer to see the other's clocks running slower than his or her own and the other's distances contracted. Figures 16 and 17 reveal other interesting points. For instance, events 2 and 3 occur in a different *order* in the two frames.

Using identical passing ships again, Figure 18 clarifies Einstein's second postulate. In this case, the ships' centers are the frame origins. (Exercise 29 verifies that the events satisfy the Lorentz transformation equations.) A burst of light occurs at the origins just as they cross. The pulse then spreads in all directions. Although Bob sees the pulse reach the ends of Anna's moving ship at different times, it reaches the ends of his stationary ship simultaneously at 40 ns. He sees the pulse spreading symmetrically from his origin. Now consider Anna's view: Judging by the times we see in her frame, she sees the pulse reach the ends of her ship simultaneously and also at 40 ns. Each sees the pulse spreading symmetrically at the same speed from the center of his or her own ship.

EXAMPLE 5

People on Earth know that it takes light 40 years to reach Planet X from Earth. Anna has just been born. Can she get to Planet X by the time she is 30 years old? If so, what speed is required? (*Note:* The distance light travels in a year is called a light-year, and the symbol is 1 ly. It happens to be 9.5×10^{15} m, but it is easier not to use the conversion here.)

SOLUTION

It might seem that to be 40 ly from Earth by the time she is 30, Anna would have to travel faster than c. But Planet X is 40 ly away according to an *Earth* observer— Bob, of course. To Anna in her spaceship moving at v relative to Earth, the Earth–Planet X "object" will be shorter.

$$L = \frac{40 \text{ ly}}{\gamma_v}$$

As v approaches c, the distance approaches 0. The conclusion is provocative. Anna may go as far as she likes in as little time as she pleases by merely traveling at a

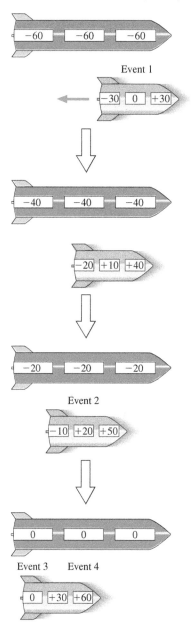

Figure 17 Anna sees Bob's ship contracted and his clocks running slowly.

Special Relativity

Figure 18 A light pulse appears to spread the same distance in all directions in the same time according to both observers.

Anna

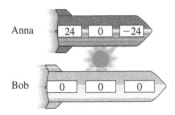

Bob

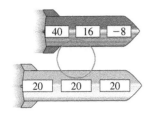

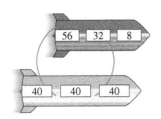

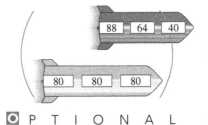

sufficiently large fraction of c.[2] Here, the "object" must pass by in 30 yr of Anna's time. Using distance and time according to her,

$$\text{speed} = \frac{\text{distance}}{\text{time}} \quad \rightarrow \quad v = \frac{40 \text{ ly}/\gamma_v}{30 \text{ yr}}$$

Dividing by c, we have

$$\frac{v}{c} = \frac{40 \text{ ly}}{30 \text{ yr} \cdot c} \sqrt{1 - \frac{v^2}{c^2}} = \frac{40}{30} \sqrt{1 - \frac{v^2}{c^2}}$$

We have used the fact that 30 yr times c is 30 ly. Squaring both sides and solving for v yields

$$v = 0.8c$$

It is helpful to confirm that everything fits together in Example 5. As the reader may easily verify, for $v = 0.8c$, $\gamma_v = \frac{5}{3}$. According to Anna, the Earth–Planet X object is only 40 ly $\div \frac{5}{3} = 24$ ly long. At $0.8c$, it would pass in only 30 years. But how can Anna reach Planet X in 30 years when it takes light 40 years? We must be careful about who is doing the observing. According to Bob, light does take 40 years, but Anna takes even longer, for she moves at only $0.8c$. Bob says that Anna takes $\Delta t_B = 40 \text{ ly}/0.8c = 50$ yr to reach Planet X. Still, he must agree that Anna is only 30 years old when she gets there. Whereas Anna's explanation is length contraction, Bob's is time dilation. He watches a clock fixed in Anna's frame register Δt_A, and the interval Δt_B on his own is longer.

$$\Delta t_B = \gamma_v \Delta t_A \quad \rightarrow \quad 50 \text{ yr} = \frac{5}{3}\Delta t_A \quad \Rightarrow \quad \Delta t_A = 30 \text{ yr}$$

A question to ponder: Because Anna moves relative to the Earth–Planet X system, though still at a speed less than c, she sees a distance shorter than 40 light-years, requiring less than 40 years to pass by. What must light "see"?

O P T I O N A L   4 The Twin Paradox

Simply stated, the twin paradox is as follows: If one of two twins stays on Earth while the other travels away at high speed, and they each see the other aging more slowly, then when the traveling twin returns, each twin would claim that the other is younger. Impossible! Two people cannot sit down together in a room and each see that the other is many years younger.

But there is no paradox. The crucial factor overlooked is that in order for the twins to get back together and discuss their beliefs, one of them must *accelerate*. In so doing, the accelerating twin must change reference frames, from one heading away from Earth to one heading toward it. An observer always in the same inertial frame will determine that a moving clock is running

---

[2]Acceleration does affect times, but it depends on the observers' separation (Exercise 49) and is negligible when Anna and Bob are close together. On the other hand, too rapid an acceleration would be fatal. We can simplify things by assuming that Anna is born on board a moving ship just as it passes Earth.

slowly by the usual time-dilation formula, even if that clock accelerates. At any instant, the proper speed to use in γ_v would be the instantaneous speed. In the twin paradox, the observations of the twin who remains on Earth (approximately inertial) are the reliable ones. But if an *observer* accelerates, we cannot apply time dilation so simply. Consider a case where Bob remains on Earth and Anna (Bob's fraternal twin sister) makes the round trip away and back. When Anna accelerates *toward* Bob, she moves to a different inertial frame in which the truth is that Bob is *absolutely* older, regardless of any difference in aging *rates*. It is the asymmetry caused by Anna's acceleration that allows her to agree with ever-reliable Bob when she gets back—that Bob is older.

Anna and Bob—and Carl

Let us examine the twin paradox in the context of Example 5. As we know, Earth-bound Bob waits 50 years by his own clock for Anna to reach Planet X but agrees with Anna that she is 30 years old when she gets there. For $v = 0.8c$, $\gamma_v = \frac{5}{3}$, and 50 yr $\div \frac{5}{3} = 30$ yr. But according to Anna, *Bob* is moving. In the 30 years passing on her watch as the Earth–Planet X object goes by, she must claim that Bob ages only 30 yr $\div \frac{5}{3} = 18$ yr. Thus, when Anna reaches Planet X, Bob says, "I'm 50 years old, and Anna is 30," and Anna says, "I'm 30 years old, and Bob is 18."

Thus far, we have no paradox. None of this is contrary to our experience, for no one has ever done this. As shown in Figure 19, what *would* be a paradox is if Anna were to return to Earth and meet Bob, with Bob saying, "I'm 100, you're 60," and Anna saying, "I'm 60, you're 36."

To resolve the paradox, we introduce another observer, Carl, who happens to be in a ship heading toward Earth at 0.8c and passing Planet X just as Anna does. Carl is in an inertial frame—always has been and always will be. When Carl passes Earth, Bob will unarguably be 100 years old, because Bob waits 50 years for Anna to reach Planet X and will wait another 50 for Carl to arrive. Now Carl will age 30 years in flight and must say that Bob ages less. Carl sees Bob moving at the same relative *speed* that Anna does, so Carl must also determine that Bob ages 18 years. If Bob is 100 when Carl gets to Earth and Bob aged 18 years during the flight, then Bob must be 82 years old, according to Carl, when Carl passes Planet X. This is truth in Carl's frame!

To return, Anna must accelerate; that is, she must change from one inertial frame to another. (It makes no difference whether her *speed* could be kept constant. An inertial frame has constant *velocity*.) So far, we have not considered how this might affect Anna's perceptions, but Carl doesn't accelerate, so we can rely on his observations. Figure 20 demonstrates the main point. Anna jumps from one frame, where Bob is 18 years old, to another, where Carl informs her that Bob is 82 years old. Although on the return leg of the journey, Anna does determine that Bob is aging more slowly than herself, it is too late. Bob's huge forward leap in age (according to Anna) has settled the matter. As Figure 21 illustrates, Bob will be much older than Anna when they reunite.

Two questions may still haunt the reader: (1) How is it possible that when Anna and Carl are both at Planet X, Anna says Bob is 18 years old, while Carl says Bob is 82 years old? (2) Can Carl tell Anna about Bob's future? Suppose

Figure 19   A paradox.

Figure 20   Anna changes frames.

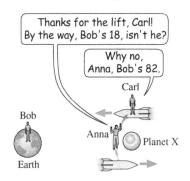

Figure 21 Paradox resolved.

Bob sends a light signal from Earth toward Planet X so that it arrives at the precise instant Anna and Carl pass Planet X. If according to Bob it takes light 40 years to reach Planet X and it takes Anna 50 years, then Bob had better send this signal when he is 10 years old. Let the light signal be an image of Bob blowing out candles at his 10th birthday party. When this signal reaches Planet X, both Anna and Carl will see an image of Bob as a 10 year old. Each will have intercepted all earlier signals, so they will have knowledge of Bob's prior activities, but none beyond that. The answer to question 2 is, No, because neither has actually seen any of Bob's life after his 10th birthday.

However, we don't answer the question "What is Bob's age?" by saying, "The age he appears to be in the light signal that just arrived." Neither Anna nor Carl will say that Bob is 10 years old when they reach Planet X, because each realizes that Bob will have aged while the light traveled. But Anna and Carl are scrupulous record keepers. From their observations, they can calculate what Bob's age must be when they pass Planet X, and the conclusions they reach differ markedly. Let us investigate this and, in so doing, answer question 1.

Figure 22 shows how each of the three observers sees the situation as Bob's light signal leaves Earth. As we showed earlier, Anna sees the distance between Earth and Planet X as 24 ly. She sees the light signal and Planet X both moving, and the separation between them is decreasing at a rate of $1.8c$. (This value is a relative velocity according to a third party, Anna. She doesn't

Figure 22 A light beam traveling from Earth to Planet X according to three different observers.

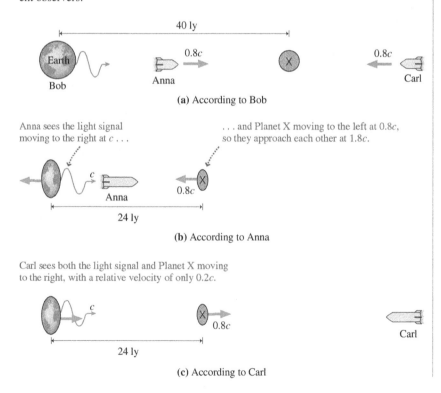

say that something moves faster than c relative to herself. The point is further addressed in Section 6.) Thus, only $24 \text{ ly}/1.8c = 13\frac{1}{3}$ yr passes for Anna as this light signal travels. If $13\frac{1}{3}$ years go by on her clock, then the time interval she determines to have passed on Bob's moving clock is smaller: $\Delta t_{\text{B}} = 13\frac{1}{3} \text{ yr} \div \frac{5}{3} = 8$ yr. Anna concludes that when she reaches Planet X, Bob is $10 \text{ yr} + 8 \text{ yr} = 18$ yr. Carl, on the other hand, must also see a separation between Earth and Planet X of 24 ly, but he sees the light signal catching up to the moving Planet X at a rate of only $0.2c$. According to Carl, the time for the signal to reach Planet X is $24 \text{ ly}/0.2c = 120$ yr. He too knows that less time will have passed on Bob's moving clock, and so he judges that it marked off $\Delta t_{\text{B}} = 120 \text{ yr} \div \frac{5}{3} = 72$ yr. Added to the 10-year age indicated by the arriving light, Carl deduces that when he is at Planet X, Bob is 82 years old.

It is interesting to note that if Carl jumps to Anna's ship, accelerating *away* from Bob, Bob is 82 years old before the jump and only 18 years old after. Nothing ominous happens, however, for Bob is far away, and *no one* around Planet X knows anything about his life beyond its first 10 years.

The Light Signals Solution

We conclude our discussion of the twin paradox with an alternative route to the same conclusion in Anna's round-trip to Planet X.

Figure 23 shows Anna's journey from Bob's point of view. Anna travels away at a speed/slope less than c, then reverses course and returns at the same speed. To keep each other fully informed, Anna and Bob, by prearrangement, send out light signals at 10-year intervals. The signals Bob sends away from Earth have slope $+c$. If he sends one every 10 years, the first—Bob at his 10th birthday party—will not reach the speedy Anna until she reaches Planet X, when she is 30 years old. The signals Anna sends back toward Earth have slope $-c$. So long as no one changes reference frames, symmetry demands that Bob also receive his first signal from Anna when he is 30 years old, and it must show Anna as a 10 year old. Each *actually sees* images of the other aging only one-third as much as themselves. Immediately upon turning around, Anna begins to receive signals from Bob much more frequently. Every $3\frac{1}{3}$ years of her return trip she sees a new image of Bob another 10 years older. The images she now sees show

Figure 23 According to Bob, Anna moves at constant speed/slope away from Earth, then toward Earth. They regularly exchange light signals, all of which have slope of magnitude c.

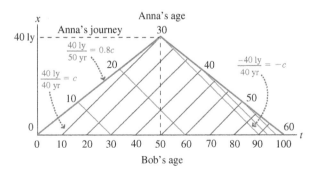

Bob aging three times as rapidly as herself. As soon as Bob begins to receive signals that Anna sends on her return trip, he too receives one every $3\frac{1}{3}$ years and sees Anna aging three times as rapidly as himself. But here is the asymmetry: While Anna begins to see Bob aging more rapidly at the *midpoint* of her journey, the instant she changes frames, Bob has to wait 90 years (50 years for Anna to reach Planet X and another 40 for the light from there to reach Earth). Now there is only another 10 years left. Anna sees Bob age one-third as fast for 30 years and three times as fast for 30 years $[(30 \text{ yr} \times \frac{1}{3}) + (30 \text{ yr} \times 3) = 100 \text{ yr}]$. Bob sees Anna age one-third as fast for 90 years and three times as fast for only 10 $[(90 \text{ yr} \times \frac{1}{3}) + (10 \text{ yr} \times 3) = 60 \text{ yr}]$. When it is all over, Bob has received 6 signals, confirming that Anna has aged 60 years, and Anna has received 10, proving that poor Bob has aged 100 years.

The danger in this kind of solution to the twin paradox is that it emphasizes what is *seen* rather than what is actually happening. During neither leg of the journey would the observers claim the other is aging only one-third as rapidly as themselves. As we know, γ_v is $\frac{5}{3}$, not 3. And certainly neither observer would make the mistake of saying that the other is aging *more* rapidly (as long as the observer is not accelerating). Both realize that what they actually see is a combination of time dilation and the effect of their rapidly increasing or decreasing separation. The Doppler effect, discussed in Section 5, takes both of these factors into account. It shows that the rate at which signals would actually be received is decreased by the factor $\sqrt{(1 - v/c)/(1 + v/c)}$ when the source is moving away and increased by $\sqrt{(1 + v/c)/(1 - v/c)}$ when the source approaches. For a speed $0.8c$, these are, respectively, $\frac{1}{3}$ and 3. The light signals approach to the twin paradox is straightforward. One twin need only count the light signals he or she sees to determine the age of the other twin—and seeing is believing. But it does skirt the point that the asymmetry is introduced instantly when the traveling twin changes frames.

5   The Doppler Effect

Just as for sound, if a light source moves relative to an observer, the frequency received by the observer need not be that emitted by the source. The effects are not identical, however. Sound requires a medium, while light does not. Moreover, in the case of light, we are usually interested in relative speeds comparable to c, in which case the time interval between the *production* (not simply arrival) of consecutive wave fronts in the observer's frame is not the same as in the source's.

In Figure 24, an observer stands at the origin of frame S. A light source moves at an angle θ with respect to the line connecting the observer and the source and emits a frequency f_{source} in the frame in which it is at rest (frame S'). It emits consecutive wave fronts at point 1 and point 2. Let us call the time between the *production* of these fronts in the observer's frame Δt_{p}. The fronts would *arrive* at the observer separated by this time interval were it not for the motion of the source. In Figure 24, the source is getting farther away, and the time interval between the arrivals, Δt_{a}, will be larger than Δt_{p} by the time it takes the second front to travel the extra distance, $v\Delta t_{\text{p}} \cos \theta$. (This result

Figure 24 A light source moves at angle θ with respect to the line connecting it and the observer. The wavefront emitted at point 2 has farther to travel to the observer than the wavefront emitted at point 1.

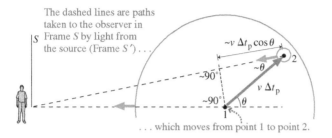

The dashed lines are paths taken to the observer in Frame S by light from the source (Frame S') . . .

. . . which moves from point 1 to point 2.

assumes that the lines connecting points 1 and 2 to the observer are nearly parallel. Since one period of light is about 10^{-14} s, the source would not move far.) Dividing by c gives the time to travel the extra distance, so the time between the arrivals of the two fronts is

$$\Delta t_{\rm a} = \Delta t_{\rm p} + \frac{v}{c}\Delta t_{\rm p}\cos\theta = \Delta t_{\rm p}\left(1 + \frac{v}{c}\cos\theta\right)$$

The observed period is $\Delta t_{\rm a}$. If classical physics were applicable, $\Delta t_{\rm p}$ would be the source period, and we could merely invert the equation to relate observed frequency to source frequency. However, the source period $T_{\rm source}$ is the time interval between the production of the consecutive wave fronts *in frame S'*. The fronts are produced at the same place in frame S', so the time interval between their production in frame of reference S is longer: $\Delta t_{\rm p} = \gamma_v T_{\rm source}$.

$$\Delta t_{\rm a} = \gamma_v T_{\rm source}\left(1 + \frac{v}{c}\cos\theta\right) = T_{\rm source}\frac{1 + \frac{v}{c}\cos\theta}{\sqrt{1 - \frac{v^2}{c^2}}}$$

The observed frequency is $1/\Delta t_{\rm a}$, and the source frequency is $1/T_{\rm source}$. Inverting thus gives

$$f_{\rm obs} = f_{\rm source}\frac{\sqrt{1 - \frac{v^2}{c^2}}}{1 + \frac{v}{c}\cos\theta} \qquad (17) \quad \text{Doppler effect}$$

Again, this accounts for two factors: (1) Consecutive wave fronts produced by the source have different distances to travel to the observer (as in the classical Doppler effect in sound), and (2) time dilation.

If the source moves away from the observer, $\theta = 0$.

$$f_{obs} = f_{source} \frac{\sqrt{1 - \dfrac{v^2}{c^2}}}{1 + \dfrac{v}{c}} = f_{source} \frac{\sqrt{\left(1 - \dfrac{v}{c}\right)\left(1 + \dfrac{v}{c}\right)}}{\sqrt{\left(1 + \dfrac{v}{c}\right)\left(1 + \dfrac{v}{c}\right)}} = f_{source}\left(\frac{1 - \dfrac{v}{c}}{1 + \dfrac{v}{c}}\right)^{\frac{1}{2}} \quad (18)$$

The observed frequency is smaller than the source frequency, implying a longer period and wavelength than in the source frame. One of the important clues that the universe is expanding is the **redshift** in the light from distant stars. All the wavelengths coming from them are shifted toward the red (longer wavelength) end of the spectrum. In recent years, numerous redshifts greater than 5 and one as large as 10 have been reported. If the observed wavelength is 10 times the source wavelength, the source is moving *very* fast.

It is left as an exercise to verify that if the source moves *toward* the observer ($\theta = 180°$), then f_{obs} is given merely by switching the sign of v in equation (18). In this case, the observed frequency is higher and the period and wavelength shorter than in the source frame—the light is blueshifted. Time dilation alone would lead to a *longer* period, because an observer of a moving source says that its charges are oscillating slower than they do in the source frame. The observed period is actually smaller, so we conclude that the time-dilation effect is outweighed by the decreasing source-observer separation.

If the source gets neither closer to nor farther from the observer ($\theta = 90°$), equation (17) becomes $f_{obs} = f_{source}\sqrt{1 - v^2/c^2}$. This lower frequency is called the transverse redshift. In the classical treatment of sound, there is no shift if the separation does not change. The sole reason here is time dilation. A simple example would be a source circling an observer. Waves all have the same distance to travel to the observer, but they are produced by charges that, according to the observer, are oscillating slowly.

EXAMPLE 6

The wavelengths observed from a star are four times their ordinary values. How fast is the star receding from Earth?

SOLUTION

A longer wavelength corresponds to a smaller frequency. Thus, $f_{obs} = \dfrac{1}{4}f_{source}$.

$$f_{obs} = f_{source}\left(\frac{1 - \dfrac{v}{c}}{1 + \dfrac{v}{c}}\right)^{\frac{1}{2}} \quad \rightarrow \quad \frac{1}{4}f_{source} = f_{source}\left(\frac{1 - \dfrac{v}{c}}{1 + \dfrac{v}{c}}\right)^{\frac{1}{2}}$$

or

$$\frac{1}{4}\sqrt{1 + \frac{v}{c}} = \sqrt{1 - \frac{v}{c}}$$

Squaring and solving,

$$\frac{v}{c} = \frac{1 - (1/4)^2}{1 + (1/4)^2} = 0.882c$$

6 Velocity Transformation

With a firm grasp on position and time, we may now relate velocity in different frames. We know that the classical transformation $u' = u - v$ is wrong. The correct one is a straightforward application of the Lorentz transformation equations. We begin by considering an object moving along the x-axis. By definition, the velocity of an object in frame S' is the differential displacement in that frame divided by the differential time interval in that frame.

$$u' \equiv \frac{dx'}{dt'}$$

We may use equations (12) to relate the infinitesimal changes dx' and dt' in frame S' to those in frame S, dx and dt.

$$u' = \frac{\gamma_v(dx - v\,dt)}{\gamma_v\left(-\dfrac{v}{c^2}dx + dt\right)}$$

Canceling γ_v, then dividing numerator and denominator by dt, we obtain

$$u' = \frac{\dfrac{dx}{dt} - v}{-\dfrac{v}{c^2}\dfrac{dx}{dt} + 1}$$

By definition, dx/dt is u, the velocity of the object in frame S, so that

$$u' = \frac{u - v}{1 - \dfrac{uv}{c^2}} \quad \text{(19a)} \qquad \text{and} \qquad u = \frac{u' + v}{1 + \dfrac{u'v}{c^2}} \quad \text{(19b)}$$

Equation (19b) is simply (19a) solved for u, but its form is no surprise. Just as for the Lorentz transformation, simply changing the sign of v adapts the relationship to the other frame. If velocities are small compared with c, the denominators are essentially 1, reproducing the classical velocity transformation, $u' = u - v$.

Figure 25 A spaceship and a meteorite moving relative to Earth.

EXAMPLE 7

A spaceship is traveling away from Earth at $0.8c$, as shown in Figure 25. Farther out, a meteorite is traveling toward Earth at $0.6c$. Both velocities are according to an observer on Earth. According to an observer on the spaceship, what is the velocity of the meteorite (relative to herself)?

SOLUTION

Equations (19) involve a velocity u of an object according to frame S, a velocity u' of that object according to frame S', and a relative velocity v between frames. The object here is the meteorite, so the two reference frames are Earth and the spaceship. The choice of which frame to designate as S' is arbitrary, but once made, everything else follows. Let us choose Earth as frame S and the spaceship as frame S'. By convention, S' moves in the positive direction relative to S, so velocities away from Earth must be taken as positive. We know that the object's velocity u according to an observer on Earth in frame S is $-0.6c$ and that v is $0.8c$. We seek the object's velocity u' according to the spaceship frame S'. Inserting in equation (19a) gives

$$u' = \frac{-0.6c - 0.8c}{1 - \frac{(-0.6c)(0.8c)}{c^2}} \quad \Rightarrow \quad u' = \frac{-1.4c}{1.48} = -0.946c$$

Not surprisingly, the meteorite travels in the negative direction, toward Earth, according to an observer on the spaceship. Applying classical arguments, we would predict a relative velocity between ship and meteorite of $-1.4c$ (the numerator), but we see that the value is actually less than c.

A bit of valid classical physics should be noted. The meteorite's speed relative to the spaceship is indeed $1.4c$, *according to an observer on Earth*. If Bob on Earth sees a spaceship moving away at $0.8c = 2.4 \times 10^8$ m/s and the meteorite moving toward Earth at $0.6c = 1.8 \times 10^8$ m/s, the two are surely getting 4.2×10^8 m closer every second. This logic is sound because all three of these velocities are according to the same (Earth) observer. To calculate such a quantity, the relativistic velocity transformation is not appropriate, for it relates velocities according to *different* observers. But the $1.4c$ is not an example of something moving relative to an *observer* at a speed greater than c. It is the meteorite's speed *according* to the Earth observer but *relative* to the spaceship. The speed $0.946c$ is also the meteorite's speed relative to the spaceship but according to the spaceship. Because in special relativity we are not usually interested in a relative velocity between two objects according to a third party, when we say simply "the velocity of B relative to A," it is understood to mean according to A.

Provided that v and u (or u') are less than c, the value of u' (or u) given by equations (19) is always strictly less than c. No observer will ever see something moving relative to himself faster than c. On the other hand, if the "object" were a light beam moving at c in one frame, equations (19) would show its speed to be c in the other frame, independent of v, as Einstein's postulates demand. The proofs of these claims are left as exercises.

We complete the relativistic velocity transformation by considering velocity components perpendicular to the axis of relative motion. By definition, the

y-component of velocity in frame S' involves the displacement along the y'-axis and the time in that frame.

$$u'_y \equiv \frac{dy'}{dt'}$$

Using $y' = y$ and equation (12b) to rewrite the denominator, we have

$$u'_y = \frac{dy}{\gamma_v \left(-\dfrac{v}{c^2} dx + dt\right)}$$

Dividing by dt and rearranging,

$$u'_y = \frac{\dfrac{dy}{dt}}{\gamma_v \left(-\dfrac{v}{c^2}\dfrac{dx}{dt} + 1\right)} = \frac{u_y}{\gamma_v \left(1 - \dfrac{u_x v}{c^2}\right)}$$

The corresponding equation relating z-components follows identically. Thus,

$$u'_x = \frac{u_x - v}{1 - \dfrac{u_x v}{c^2}} \qquad (20a)$$

Relativistic velocity transformation

$$u'_y = \frac{u_y}{\gamma_v \left(1 - \dfrac{u_x v}{c^2}\right)} \qquad (20b) \qquad u'_z = \frac{u_z}{\gamma_v \left(1 - \dfrac{u_x v}{c^2}\right)} \qquad (20c)$$

As always, solving explicitly or merely switching the sign of v would give (u_x, u_y, u_z) in terms of $\left(u'_x, u'_y, u'_z\right)$.

7 Momentum and Energy

We now come to some of the most fascinating and momentous discoveries in the history of science. In a sense, we are at a familiar juncture. In classical physics, once we learn to *describe* motion, via position and its time derivatives, we study what *governs* motion. The second law of motion is usually the initial focus, but we soon find that the more fundamental and often more useful law for a system of particles is $\mathbf{F}_{\text{net external}} = d\mathbf{P}_{\text{total}}/dt$, where $\mathbf{P}_{\text{total}}$ is the system's total momentum. This tells us that if the system is isolated from external forces, the total momentum is conserved.

$$\mathbf{P}_{\text{total}} = \sum_i \mathbf{p}_i = \text{constant} \quad (\text{isolated system})$$

Classically, the momentum of an individual particle is $m\mathbf{u}$. (Again, we use $\mathbf{u}$ for the velocity of a particle because v is reserved for the relative velocity between two frames.) Why should the conserved property we call momentum be given by the simple formula $m\mathbf{u}$? It has several things going for it. Its conservation is experimentally verified—a must!—at least at low speeds. And it is reasonable that the vector property that is transferred but not lost as one object collides with another should depend on mass and velocity. But it has another interesting property. Classically, if the sum of $m\mathbf{u}$ for all particles in an isolated system is conserved in one frame of reference, then it is automatically conserved in another. We show this via the classical velocity transformation. Restricting our attention to one-dimensional motion for now, we see that

$$P'_{\text{total}} = \sum_i m_i u'_i = \sum_i m_i (u_i - v) = \sum_i m_i u_i - \sum_i m_i v$$

or

$$P'_{\text{total}} = P_{\text{total}} - v \sum_i m_i \tag{21}$$

Given that the system's total mass does not change and that v is constant, P_{total} and P'_{total} differ by a constant. If one does not change, the other cannot.

But the classical velocity transformation is wrong. Let us see what happens when we apply the relativistic transformation.

Figure 26 A collision seen in two different frames of reference.

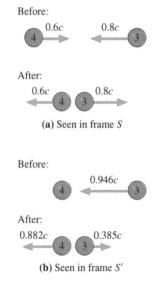

(a) Seen in frame S

(b) Seen in frame S'

EXAMPLE 8

Consider the collision shown in Figure 26(a) between particles of mass 3 and 4 (in arbitrary units). If momentum is given by $p = mu$, the total momentum in frame S before the collision is 0, because the particles' individual momenta are equal and opposite. They also add to 0 after the collision, so the total momentum is conserved. Using the relativistically correct velocity transformation, find the four velocities in frame S', moving to the right at $0.6c$, and show that $\sum_i m_i u'_i$ is *not* conserved.

SOLUTION

We apply equation (19a) four times, using $v = 0.6c$ and the four u values given in Figure 26(a).

$$\text{Before:} \quad \frac{0.6c - 0.6c}{1 - \dfrac{(0.6c)(0.6c)}{c^2}} = 0 \qquad \frac{-0.8c - 0.6c}{1 - \dfrac{(-0.8c)(0.6c)}{c^2}} = -0.946c$$

$$\text{After:} \quad \frac{-0.6c - 0.6c}{1 - \dfrac{(-0.6c)(0.6c)}{c^2}} = -0.882c \qquad \frac{0.8c - 0.6c}{1 - \dfrac{(0.8c)(0.6c)}{c^2}} = 0.385c$$

Figure 26(b) illustrates the collision in frame S' with these velocities.

$$\text{Before: } \sum_i m_i u_i' = 4(0) + 3(-0.946c) = -2.84c$$

$$\text{After: } \sum_i m_i u_i' = 4(-0.882c) + 3(0.385c) = -2.38c$$

According to Einstein's first postulate, a law of physics should hold in all frames. Example 8 thus gives us theoretical grounds for rejecting the classical momentum formula. Perhaps it shouldn't be surprising that it also fails the experimental test. At high speeds, $\sum_i m_i u_i$ is not conserved·in *any* frame. (Neither "after picture" in Example 8 is correct.) Theoretically and experimentally, $m\mathbf{u}$ is wrong.

The classical momentum $m\mathbf{u}$ and the classical velocity transformation combine to give equation (21), which says that the total momenta in the two frames differ by a constant. Relativistically, things are not so easy, but the "complication" leads to one of the most stunning claims of Einstein's theory. Using the relativistic velocity transformation, it can be shown that there is *no* candidate for a relativistic momentum—no function of m and $\mathbf{u}$—for which the total momenta in two frames would differ by a constant. The difference would invariably have some functional dependence on the particle velocities u_i, which may vary as the particles interact. Therefore, the only way momentum conservation can be salvaged is if this other function of the particle velocities is also conserved. The requirement that momentum conservation must hold in all frames implies that *momentum conservation is tied to conservation of some other property.*

Obtaining the correct momentum formula and "other property" by theoretical reasoning is rather messy. We will take a shortcut to the other property by simply accepting the correct momentum as a given. Supported by experimental evidence of its conservation at all speeds, the relativistically correct expression for momentum is

$$\mathbf{p} = \gamma_u m\mathbf{u} \quad \text{where} \quad \gamma_u \equiv \frac{1}{\sqrt{1 - \dfrac{u^2}{c^2}}} \qquad (22) \qquad \text{Momentum}$$

Note that u is $\sqrt{u_x^2 + u_y^2 + u_z^2}$ in three dimensions and that (22) reduces to the classical momentum at ordinary speeds, where $\gamma_u \cong 1$.

The algebraic details leading to the equation that follows are left to Exercise 68. We are most interested in the result. Seeking something analogous to classical relationship (21), if we apply the relativistic velocity transformation (19) to our new relativistic momentum (22) summed over the system, we arrive at

$$\sum_i \gamma_{u_i'} m_i u_i' = \gamma_v \sum_i \gamma_{u_i} m_i u_i - v\gamma_v \sum_i \gamma_{u_i} m_i \qquad (23)$$

or

$$P'_{\text{total}} = \gamma_v P_{\text{total}} - v\gamma_v \sum_i \gamma_{u_i} m_i$$

If it is true that P and P' are both constant/conserved, then $\sum_i \gamma_{u_i} m_i$ must also be constant. What could it be? What besides momentum must be conserved in an isolated system? There is only one ready candidate: *total* energy. It cannot be just kinetic energy, because kinetic energy need not be conserved. The quantity $\gamma_{u_i} m_i$ must somehow account for the total energy of particle i, including both kinetic *and internal* energies. Actually, as it stands, it has units of mass, but if we multiply it by the universal constant c^2, we obtain units of energy: $\text{kg} \cdot \text{m}^2/\text{s}^2$. (The motivation may seem a bit weak, but we soon see how it fits in.) Thus,

Total energy of an object moving at speed u

$$E = \gamma_u mc^2 \tag{24}$$

This claim follows directly from Einstein's postulates, through the Lorentz transformation, the requirement that the same law hold in all frames, and so on. It must not be underestimated. Nowhere in classical physics is the claim made that there is a simple way, if any at all, to determine the total energy of an object. The idea is revolutionary.

The most striking consequence is that mass measures energy. If an object is stationary, its total energy is mc^2. This includes all *internal* energy in whatever form it might take.

Internal energy of an object

$$E_{\text{internal}} = mc^2 \tag{25}$$

Classically or relativistically, kinetic energy is the energy associated simply with the motion of an object. If we subtract from the energy of a moving object the (internal) energy it would have at rest, we have kinetic energy.

Kinetic energy

$$\text{KE} = \text{energy moving} - \text{energy at rest}$$
$$= \gamma_u mc^2 - mc^2 = (\gamma_u - 1)mc^2 \tag{26}$$

We begin to see the plausibility and consistency of Einstein's claim by considering the total energy of a slow-moving object. Using the binomial approximation,

$$\gamma_u mc^2 = \left(1 - \frac{u^2}{c_2}\right)^{-\frac{1}{2}} mc^2 \cong \left[1 + \left(-\frac{1}{2}\right)\left(-\frac{u^2}{c^2}\right)\right] mc^2$$

$$= mc^2 + \frac{1}{2}mu^2 \quad (u \ll c)$$

This fits perfectly. If u is zero, then the total energy is simply the internal energy mc^2, and if u is nonzero, the total energy exceeds the internal energy by the classical kinetic energy. Now consider the simple case of a completely

Figure 27   A completely inelastic collision. Kinetic energy is converted to internal energy.

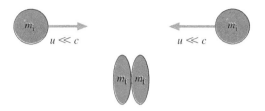

Figure 27   A completely inelastic collision. Kinetic energy is converted to internal energy.

inelastic head-on collision between two slow-moving objects of the same mass and speed, illustrated in Figure 27. Momentum conservation requires that the objects be stationary after the collision. By symmetry, neither object would exchange net energy with the other. Therefore, conservation of total energy requires that for each object,

$$\left(mc^2 + \frac{1}{2} mu^2 \right)_{\text{final}} = \left(mc^2 + \frac{1}{2} mu^2 \right)_{\text{initial}}$$

But $u_{\text{f}} = 0$, so

$$m_{\text{f}}c^2 = m_{\text{i}}c^2 + \frac{1}{2} m_{\text{i}}u_{\text{i}}^2$$

This says that the final mass/internal energy exceeds the initial mass/internal energy by the "lost" kinetic energy. This is in perfect harmony with the classical explanation that lost kinetic energy becomes internal thermal energy.

Einstein's momentum and energy formulas (22), (24), and (26) are plotted in Figure 28. The momentum formula agrees with the classical linear one at low speeds but diverges as u approaches c. In this limit, the kinetic energy and total energy also diverge. For this reason alone, it should not be possible to accelerate a massive object to the speed of light. Infinite energy would be required.

Figure 28   The variation of momentum, energy, and kinetic energy as an object's speed varies from 0 to c. The classical momentum and kinetic energy formulas are shown for comparison.

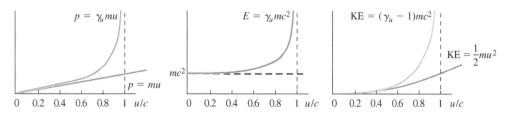

Mass and Energy

According to equation (25), the energy of an object at rest depends solely on its mass. For example, heating—adding energy to—an object at rest increases its mass; cooling decreases it. These changes are immeasurably small in ordinary circumstances because c^2 is a very large number. A mass change of 1 kg corresponds to an energy difference of 9×10^{16} J, which is more than enough to put the Empire State Building in a low orbit about Earth. However, we cannot simply make mass disappear arbitrarily. Generally speaking, exchange of energy requires a force.

Chemical reactions involve the electrostatic force, which is attractive between the positive nucleus and orbiting electrons and repulsive between the electrons themselves. The electrons rearrange themselves, resulting in a change in the *internal* kinetic and electrostatic potential energies. In an exothermic reaction, energy is lost to the surroundings, reducing the internal energy of the sample and therefore its mass. For example, as two hydrogen atoms unite to form a molecule, the lowering of electrostatic potential energy results in approximately 7×10^{-19} J being given off. Using $\Delta E = \Delta mc^2$, we see that the mass decreases by about 8×10^{-36} kg. This is only about one-billionth of the molecular mass. Understandably, such small changes went unnoticed for centuries.

Nuclear reactions, on the other hand, are much more energetic for the simple reason that they involve a much stronger force, aptly named the strong force. For now, we note only that it is an attractive force shared by all constituents of the nucleus—neutrons and protons alike. (It must be strong, for it is what prevents the nucleus from flying apart. It overwhelms the electrostatic repulsion between protons.) When a proton and neutron unite to form a deuterium, or heavy hydrogen, nucleus, the lowering of the energy associated with the strong force gives off about 4×10^{-13} J to the surroundings. The corresponding mass decrease is 4×10^{-30} kg, roughly 1/1000 of the nuclear mass. Thus, the fractional change in mass is about 6 orders of magnitude larger than in a typical chemical reaction. Pound for pound, nuclear reactions are much more energetic.

When discussing how the mass of an object may change, it is important to bear in mind that mass measures the internal energy of the whole system of particles. Consider a simple object: a helium balloon. If the balloon is heated, its internal thermal energy will increase and so will its mass. But what of the individual helium atoms? Their masses do not increase, because their internal energies have not changed. The mass of the balloon as a whole has increased because its individual constituents have gained *kinetic* energy, which is *internal* to the system. It may seem odd that a system can gain mass without its constituents gaining mass, but *mass* is not conserved; *energy* is, and mass measures its internal forms. On the other hand, the mass of an object is not dependent on its *overall* motion relative to an observer.[3] If we throw the balloon at speed u, its overall kinetic energy would increase, but its *internal* energy would not be affected, so neither would its mass. The mass of an object is the same when viewed from any reference frame. (Section 10 has a more formal discussion.)

[3]Some introductory texts talk of so-called relativistic mass: $M_{rel} = \gamma_u m$. The notion is unnecessary and, worse yet, leads to confusing interpretations. Quoting Einstein himself, "It is not good to introduce the concept of the mass $M = m/\sqrt{1 - v^2/c^2}$ of a moving body for which no clear definition can be given. It is better to introduce no other mass concept than the 'rest mass' m. Instead of introducing M, it is better to mention the expression for the momentum and energy of a body in motion." In other words, all we need are $p = \gamma_u mu$ and $E = \gamma_u mc^2$.

In physics, we often speak of fundamental particles. A fundamental particle is one that is not composed of other particles. Most objects we study are not fundamental. As we know, an atom is composed of electrons and a nucleus. Nuclei, in turn, comprise neutrons and protons, and even neutrons and protons are combinations of more-basic particles. Nevertheless, there is widespread belief that certain particles are fundamental. The electron appears to be of this class. As far as we know, the electron has *no internal structure*. It has mass (internal energy without internal structure!), but with nothing inside to jiggle around more rapidly and thus absorb heat or any other form of energy, this mass is not subject to change. Immutable properties that characterize a fundamental particle are known as intrinsic properties. Charge is one such property. **Intrinsic mass** is another.

Momentum and Energy Applied

Let us solidify our grasp of the principles with several examples.

EXAMPLE 9

The kinetic energy of a proton is half its internal energy. (a) What is the proton's speed? (b) What is its total energy? (c) Determine the potential difference V through which the proton would have to be accelerated to attain this speed.

SOLUTION

(a) Kinetic energy is $(\gamma_u - 1)mc^2$ and internal energy is mc^2.

$$(\gamma_u - 1)m_pc^2 = \frac{1}{2}m_pc^2 \implies \gamma_u = 1.5$$

$$\frac{1}{\sqrt{1 - (u/c)^2}} = 1.5 \implies u = 0.745c$$

We see that for an object's kinetic energy to be a significant fraction of its internal energy, the object must be moving very fast. Internal energy dwarfs kinetic energy for slow objects.

(b) The total energy of the proton is the sum of its kinetic and internal energies.

$$E = (\gamma_u - 1)mc^2 + mc^2 = \gamma_u m_p c^2$$

$$= 1.5(1.67 \times 10^{-27}\,\text{kg})(3 \times 10^8\,\text{m/s})^2$$

$$= 2.25 \times 10^{-10}\,\text{J} = 1409\,\text{MeV}$$

(c) Classically or relativistically, the kinetic energy gained by a charged particle is equal in magnitude to the potential energy change as it is accelerated through a potential difference.

$$\text{KE} = |q\,\Delta V|$$
$$(\gamma_u - 1)mc^2 = |q\,\Delta V|$$
$$(1.5 - 1)(1.67 \times 10^{-27}\,\text{kg})(3 \times 10^8\,\text{m/s})^2 = (1.6 \times 10^{-19}\,\text{C})\,|\Delta V|$$
$$\implies \Delta V = 470\,\text{MV}$$

Had we used the classical kinetic energy formula with the same speed, $0.745c$, we would have obtained $\Delta V = 291$ MV. Kinetic energy increases very rapidly as speed approaches c, and a much larger potential difference is required than would be expected classically.

Let us now apply the relativistic conservation laws.

EXAMPLE 10

Object 1, of mass $9m_0$ and heading east at $0.8c$, collides with object 2, of mass $12m_0$ and moving west at $0.6c$. The two stick together. Find the mass and speed of the resulting combined object. (*Note:* m_0 is an arbitrary mass unit.)

SOLUTION

Let us define the positive x direction as east. The reader is encouraged to verify that if we were to use the classical formula, the objects' momenta before the collision would be equal and opposite, so the total would be 0—that is, the final object would be at rest.

Relativistically, we must not assume that mass is constant, which would be to assume that the system's internal energy is constant. Because the collision is completely inelastic, kinetic energy will be lost, so we should expect the internal energy to increase. With both mass and speed unknown, the single momentum-conservation equation is insufficient to solve the problem, but we have a powerful new tool: an expression for the total energy possessed by an object, and total energy must be conserved. In what follows we use a subscript f for the final combined object, and we make use of the fact that $\gamma_{0.8c} = \frac{5}{3}$ and $\gamma_{0.6c} = \frac{5}{4}$.

Momentum $(\gamma_u mu)$ conserved: $\gamma_{u_1} m_1 u_1 + \gamma_{u_2} m_2 u_2 = \gamma_{u_f} m_f u_f$

$$\frac{5}{3} 9m_0(0.8c) - \frac{5}{4} 12m_0(0.6c) = \frac{1}{\sqrt{1 - (u_f/c)^2}} m_f u_f$$

$$3m_0 c = \frac{1}{\sqrt{1 - (u_f/c)^2}} m_f u_f$$

As noted, the classical formula would imply that the final object should be at rest. We see that it will be moving.

Energy $(\gamma_u mc^2)$ conserved: $\gamma_{u_1} m_1 c^2 + \gamma_{u_2} m_2 c^2 = \gamma_{u_f} m_f c^2$

$$\frac{5}{3} 9m_0 c^2 + \frac{5}{4} 12m_0 c^2 = \frac{1}{\sqrt{1 - (u_f/c)^2}} m_f c^2$$

$$30m_0 c^2 = \frac{1}{\sqrt{1 - (u_f/c)^2}} m_f c^2$$

We have two equations in two unknowns. Dividing the momentum equation by the energy equation gives

$$\frac{3m_0 c}{30m_0 c^2} = \frac{u_f}{c^2} \implies u_f = 0.100c$$

Reinserting in either equation yields $m_f = 29.85m_0$. The initial mass was $21m_0$, so the mass/internal energy does indeed increase.

A calculation of total kinetic energy before and after the collision in Example 10 verifies that kinetic energy has decreased. Using equation (26),

$$KE_f - KE_i = (\gamma_{0.1c} - 1)29.85m_0c^2 - \left[\left(\tfrac{5}{3} - 1\right)9m_0c^2 + \left(\tfrac{5}{4} - 1\right)12m_0c^2\right]$$

$$= -8.85m_0c^2$$

The kinetic energy change is exactly $-\Delta mc^2$ (i.e., $21 - 29.85 = -8.85$). Kinetic energy is converted into increased thermal energy, which registers as increased mass. In fact, this relationship must hold for any number of particles colliding or breaking apart (see Exercise 96). If the total energy is conserved as particles interact, then the changes in internal energy and kinetic energy must be opposite.

$$\Delta KE = -\Delta mc^2 \qquad\qquad (27)$$

EXAMPLE 11

The nucleus of a beryllium atom has a mass of 8.003111 u, where u is an **atomic mass unit**: 1.66×10^{-27} kg. This nucleus is known to spontaneously fission (break up) into two identical pieces, each of mass 4.001506 u. Assuming the nucleus to be initially at rest, at what speed will its fission fragments move, and how much kinetic energy is released? (*Note:* The masses are given to fairly high precision because, as we see, the initial and final differ only slightly.)

SOLUTION

Relativistically or classically, if a stationary object breaks into two equal fragments, momentum conservation requires that the fragments move oppositely at equal speed. We could use equation (27) to find KE_f and then the speed, but let us simply apply energy conservation. Using a Be subscript for the beryllium and 1 and 2 for the fragments, we have

$$m_{Be}c^2 = \gamma_1 m_1 c^2 + \gamma_2 m_2 c^2 = 2\gamma_u mc^2$$

$$\gamma_u = \frac{m_{Be}}{2m} = \frac{8.003111 \text{ u}}{2(4.001506 \text{ u})} = 1.000012$$

$$\frac{1}{\sqrt{1 - (u/c)^2}} = 1.000012 \implies u = 0.005c$$

For the energy released, equation (27) gives

$$\Delta KE = -\Delta mc^2 = -(2 \times 4.001506 \text{ u} - 8.003111 \text{ u})(1.66 \times 10^{-27} \text{ kg/u})c^2$$

$$= 1.5 \times 10^{-14} \text{ J} \cong 93 \text{ keV}$$

This is in good agreement with the experimentally measured value.

It may puzzle the reader that none of the recent examples has involved a second reference frame—a pattern has been broken. But views from different frames are not so much the interest here as is the fact that momentum and energy *in any frame* depend on mass and speed in ways different from the classical. The fascinating point is that it is the claim that conservation laws must be the same in all frames that led to this discovery.

Before we move on, we note a general formula that relates the energy, momentum, and mass of a particle. It is left as an exercise to show that the speed u can be eliminated between $E = \gamma_u mc^2$ and $p = \gamma_u mu$, yielding

$$E^2 = p^2c^2 + m^2c^4 \tag{28}$$

Because this relationship is independent of the speed, it is often very convenient, and we will use it at various points in the text.

The Particle Accelerator

Einstein's famous mass-energy equivalence is central to the purpose of **particle accelerators**. These immense scientific apparatus speed up particles to nearly the speed of light. They are the tools of high-energy physics, which seeks to identify the fundamental building blocks of the universe. The electron is the most familiar fundamental particle, but many others have been found. Still others are, at present, mere theoretical predictions. Often, these undiscovered particles are expected to be fairly heavy. But how do we create mass? As Example 10 demonstrated, Einstein's mass-energy relationship is the key. If particles collide inelastically, kinetic energy decreases and mass/internal energy increases. In high-energy physics, we smash familiar particles like protons and electrons together at very high speeds to make available a large initial kinetic energy from which to create massive new particles. The greater the mass expected of a particle, the greater must be the initial kinetic energy.

It is instructive to contrast two common types of particle accelerator. In a stationary-target accelerator, a moving particle is smashed into a stationary particle. In a collider (short for colliding beams apparatus), the two particles smashed together are both moving toward a head-on collision. To produce the maximum mass with the minimum input of energy, the collider is preferable. Why? Consider two identical particles. If both are moving at speed u in opposite directions, the total momentum is zero. Therefore, if they stick together, the final particle must be at rest. *All* the initial kinetic energy is converted to mass. If, on the other hand, one particle is moving and one is stationary, the initial total momentum is nonzero, so the final particle must be moving. Some kinetic energy is necessarily left over after the collision, not available to become mass. Although the simple example of a completely inelastic collision is not realistic, the underlying principle holds no matter what may result from the collision. In a collider, the final kinetic energy is a minimum and the final mass a maximum. Exercise 93 compares the two accelerator types quantitatively.

Massless Particles

Experimental evidence indicates that there are particles for which $E = pc$. When these particles interact with other objects, the momentum and energy they carry are found to obey this relationship within experimental uncertainty. Comparing with (28), there is only one possible conclusion: They have no mass.

$$E = pc \quad (m = 0)$$

But shouldn't particles that move about and transfer momentum to other things have mass? There is no theoretical requirement. That applying $\mathbf{F} = m\mathbf{a}$ problematic does not prove that $m = 0$ is impossible. It may simply indicate that this classical law is inapplicable to massless particles. The topic of the most well-known massless particle: the particle of light, or **photon**. No experiment has ever demonstrated a mass for the photon. If it is not zero, it is immeasurably small. In fact, the assumption that it is zero is central to our accepted theories of electromagnetic radiation.

Special relativity tells us some important things about the photon (and about other massless particles). First, having no mass, photons have no internal energy. Their energy is all kinetic. Second, if m is zero, the only way $p = \gamma_u m u$ and $E = \gamma_u mc^2$ can be *non*zero is for the speed u to be c, in which case both formulas are undefined products of infinity and zero. It is true that all photons move at c, from the instant of their creation to the instant of their disappearance. However, the expressions for p and E *are* indeterminate. So what *does* determine the momentum and energy of a photon?

8 General Relativity and a First Look at Cosmology

It might be said that special relativity begins with Einstein's deceptively simple postulate that the speed of light is the same in all frames. General relativity, a more general theory (sensibly), begins with another "simple" postulate: Inertial mass and gravitational mass are the same. In introductory physics, we learn Newton's universal law of gravitation. The force between objects of mass m and M separated by r is $F = GMm/r^2$, where G is the universal gravitational constant. Taking m to be an object near Earth's surface, with M and r being Earth's mass and radius, the force on m is

$$F_{\text{grav}} = \frac{GM_{\text{Earth}}}{r_{\text{Earth}}^2} m \cong 9.8 \text{ m/s}^2 \times m$$

In introductory mechanics, we also learn the second law of motion. The acceleration of an object of mass m is proportional to the net force on the object and inversely proportional to m.

$$\mathbf{a} = \mathbf{F}_{\text{net}} \frac{1}{m}$$

On the face of it, these two properties of the mass m are entirely different. There is no fundamental reason why the property governing how hard gravity pulls on an object should have anything to do with the property governing the object's reluctance to accelerate when a net force is applied. Accordingly, it might be safer to use an m_g, signifying a gravitational property, in the first equation and an m_i, for an inertial property, in the second.

Figure 29 The floor pushes upward on Bob, who is at rest on Earth. The floor must also push "upward" on Anna, whose frame accelerates at g in gravity-free space.

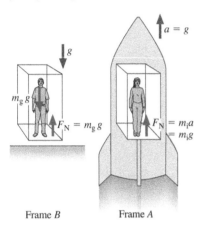

Frame B Frame A

$$F_{\text{grav}} = 9.8 \text{ m/s}^2 \times m_g \qquad a = F_{\text{net}}\frac{1}{m_i}$$

Now consider what happens when an object is dropped from shoulder height. In this case, the net force is simply the gravitational force. Thus,

$$a = (9.8 \text{ m/s}^2 \times m_g)\frac{1}{m_i} = 9.8 \text{ m/s}^2 \frac{m_g}{m_i}$$

If m_g and m_i were truly different properties, there is no reason why we could not have one object with $m_i = 1.1m_g$ and another with $m_i = 0.9m_g$, in which case they would accelerate at different rates. This is certainly not what we expect. In fact, the equivalence of m_g and m_i has been experimentally verified to better than 1 part in 10^{12}. Although we tend to take it for granted, their equality has an important consequence: It should be impossible to determine whether we are in an inertial frame permeated by a uniform gravitational field or in a frame in which there is no field but which accelerates at a constant rate.

Suppose Bob stands in a closet on Earth, frame B, as depicted in Figure 29. He is in a frame of reference that is inertial and in which there is a uniform gravitational field of $g = 9.8 \text{ m/s}^2$ downward. (This is a good approximation, although Earth rotates and the field at its surface is not perfectly uniform.) Anna is in an identical closet, frame A, but out in space, far from any gravitational fields. By means of a rocket engine, Anna's closet is accelerating in a straight line at 9.8 m/s^2. For Bob to remain stationary, the floor must push upward on his feet with a force whose magnitude equals the downward force, $F_N = m_g \times 9.8 \text{ m/s}^2$. For Anna to accelerate along with her rocket-powered closet, the floor must push "upward" on her feet with a force sufficient to give her an acceleration of 9.8 m/s^2. By the second law of motion, this is $F_N = m_i \times 9.8 \text{ m/s}^2$. If m_g and m_i are equal, the forces are equal and would provide no clue to distinguish whether an observer is in frame A or frame B. The normal force is only the simplest indicator. The fact is that no mechanical experiment could distinguish the frames. In the linearly accelerating frame A, all things appear to be affected by a downward force just as they are in frame B. The floor must push "up" on objects, and "dropped" objects appear to accelerate downward (because, once let go, they do not accelerate along with the frame). All effects could be attributed to an "inertial force" of $-m_i\mathbf{a}$ opposite the acceleration, as depicted in Figure 30. Provided that m_i equals m_g, this force would mimic a gravitational force $m_g\mathbf{g}$ in all respects.

Figure 30 In both the inertial frame with gravity and the accelerating frame without, a downward force appears to act.

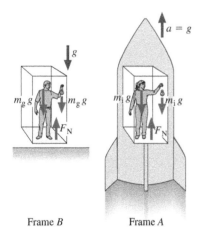

Frame B Frame A

By the same token, no mechanical experiment would be able to distinguish a frame that is accelerating in free fall in a uniform gravitational field from one that is inertial and without a gravitational field. As Figure 31 shows, an observer in the inertial frame would see all objects floating or moving at constant velocity, because no forces act. An observer in the free-falling frame would also see objects seemingly moving at constant velocity (though all would actually be accelerating with the frame), because the gravitational force $m_g\mathbf{g}$ is exactly canceled by the inertial force $-m_i\mathbf{a}$.

Figure 31 Things seem the same in a frame that is free falling due to gravity as in a frame floating without gravity.

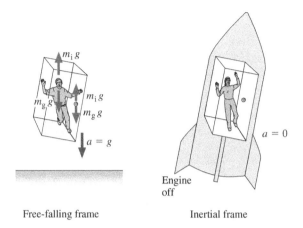

Free-falling frame   Inertial frame

The Principle of Equivalence

Einstein's customary leap forward was to postulate that *all* physical phenomena, not just mechanical ones, occur identically in a frame accelerating in gravitational free fall as in an inertial frame without gravity. No experiment could distinguish the frames. Accordingly, he generalized the concept of an inertial frame by defining a *locally* inertial frame: one that is falling freely in a gravitational field. (It is "local" because it must be small enough that nonuniformities in the field are negligible, giving the same acceleration for objects within it. Also note that this definition includes ordinary gravity-free inertial frames as a special case.) We may now state Einstein's fundamental postulate of general relativity, known as the **principle of equivalence**.

> The form of each physical law is the same in all locally inertial frames.

Principle of equivalence

This postulate is only the basis of general relativity. Just as the Lorentz transformation equations follow from the postulates of special relativity, a mathematical framework follows from this postulate. Unfortunately, general relativity theory is too sophisticated to discuss quantitatively here. It involves the mathematics of tensors and differential geometry. Nevertheless, some of its astonishing predictions can be understood qualitatively just from the principle of equivalence. Three have attracted particular attention: (1) gravitational redshift, (2) the deflection of light by the sun, and (3) the precession of the perihelion of Mercury.

Gravitational Redshift and Time Dilation

According to the principle of equivalence, light emitted at one point in a gravitational field will have a different frequency if observed at a different point. We see this by analyzing not a fixed light source and observer in a gravitational field g, but the equivalent case of a source and observer in a frame without gravity but accelerating at g. In Figure 32(a), a source in an accelerating frame emits a wave front when the frame has zero speed. Anna, a distance H "above" the source, observes the wave front after a time H/c. But by this time she is moving "upward" at speed $v = gH/c$. Thus, the light is observed in a frame that moves at velocity gH/c *away* from the frame in which it was emitted. According to Anna, the light will be redshifted. Provided that g and H are not too large, v will be small, and we may apply the binomial approximation to the Doppler formula (18).

$$
f_{obs} = f_{source}\left(\frac{1 - \dfrac{v}{c}}{1 + \dfrac{v}{c}}\right)^{\frac{1}{2}} = f_{source}\left(1 - \frac{v}{c}\right)^{\frac{1}{2}}\left(1 + \frac{v}{c}\right)^{-\frac{1}{2}}
$$

$$
\cong f_{source}\left(1 - \frac{1}{2}\frac{v}{c}\right)\left(1 - \frac{1}{2}\frac{v}{c}\right)
$$

$$
\cong f_{source}\left(1 - \frac{v}{c}\right)
$$

Figure 32 In (a), a wave front travels from source to observer in an accelerating frame without gravity. Because the observer's velocity at reception of the front differs from the source's velocity at emission, there is a Doppler shift in frequency. Thus, there must be a frequency difference in (b), the equivalent stationary frame with gravity.

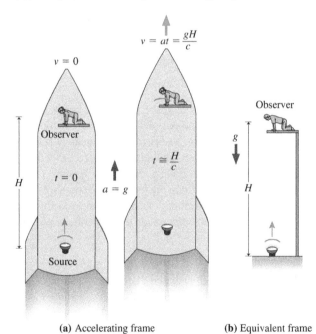

(a) Accelerating frame   (b) Equivalent frame

In the last step, we have discarded the v^2/c^2 term. Thus

$$f_{\text{obs}} \cong f_{\text{source}}\left(1 - \frac{gH}{c^2}\right) \tag{29}$$

Einstein's postulate is that a gravity-free frame accelerating at g is equivalent to a fixed frame in a gravitational field g. Thus, equation (29) must also apply in the frame as shown in Figure 32(b). As light moves upward, its frequency must become smaller and its wavelength longer, as illustrated in Figure 33. We reach a truly fascinating conclusion: This is a time-dilation effect, but it has nothing to do with relative motion between the source and observer frames. Consider 600 nm light, which has a frequency of 5×10^{14} Hz. As one second passes at the source, 5×10^{14} wave fronts are emitted. It might be said that 5×10^{14} distinct events have passed in the life of the source. But in a given second, Bob receives fewer wave fronts, because he observes a smaller frequency. To witness all 5×10^{14} events in the source's life, Bob has to wait more than one second. Relative to Bob, the source, deeper in the gravitational field, is aging slowly. In fact, the time passing at the lower point must be less than the time passing at the higher point by the same factor that appears in equation (29).

$$\Delta t_{\text{lower}} \cong \Delta t_{\text{higher}}\left(1 - \frac{gH}{c^2}\right) \tag{30}$$

Does time really pass more slowly on Earth's surface than at some altitude above? The weakness of most gravitational fields ($gH/c^2 \ll 1$) makes gravitational time dilation a small effect. But today's high-precision clocks, whose time bases are atomic oscillations of extremely short period, can reveal it.

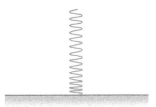

Figure 33 A light beam's wavelength grows longer and its frequency decreases as it rises in a gravitational field.

REAL-WORLD EXAMPLE RELATIVITY AND THE GLOBAL POSITIONING SYSTEM

Signals from GPS satellites can locate objects on Earth's surface easily within a few meters, but this requires great precision in timekeeping. Each satellite sends a time signal, and an error of just 10 ns would translate, at light's great speed, to a distance error of 3 m. This requirement has thrust into the mainstream of modern technology a topic previously of concern to only a few physicists and astronomers.

Special relativity tells us that a satellite moving relative to Earth's surface will run slowly. General relativity tells us that a clock runs slower when it is deeper in a gravitational field, so gravitational time dilation will cause a satellite's clock to run faster than a clock at ground level. Equation (30) gives the simplest case of a uniform field. In Earth's nonuniform field, the corresponding relationship (see Exercise 98) is

$$\Delta t_{\text{Earth}} \cong \Delta t_{\text{satellite}}\left[1 - \frac{1}{c^2}\left(\frac{GM}{r_{\text{Earth}}} - \frac{GM}{r_{\text{satellite}}}\right)\right] \tag{31}$$

where M is Earth's mass and r is the distance from the *center* of the Earth. This is more similar to equation (30) than it might first appear. The factor gH in (30) looks like a change in gravitational potential energy divided by mass; that is, mgH/m. Equation (31) is the same, only it uses the form for gravitational potential energy that is appropriate when positions are not confined to the region very near Earth's surface: $U(r) = -GMm/r$.

Applying the Physics

A GPS satellite orbits at an altitude of 2.0×10^7 m and a speed of 3.9×10^3 m/s. Earth's radius is 6.4×10^6 m, and a point at its equator has tangential speed of 460 m/s. (a) By approximately what fraction must the time be adjusted to account for both regular/speed-dependent and gravitational time dilation? (b) If unaccounted for, how soon would the time be in error by 10 ns?

SOLUTION

(a) For regular time dilation, we need the satellite's speed relative to a point on Earth's surface. Of course, different points on a rotating globe move at different speeds, and a receiver might also be in motion. However, even Earth's equatorial speed is much smaller than the satellite's speed, so using just the satellite's speed will give us a good approximation. Thus, for a clock ticking on board the satellite, we have

$$\Delta t_{\text{Earth}} = \frac{\Delta t_{\text{satellite}}}{\sqrt{1 - \left(\frac{3.9 \times 10^3}{3 \times 10^8}\right)^2}} = \left(1 - 1.7 \times 10^{-10}\right)^{-1/2} \Delta t_{\text{satellite}}$$

$$\Delta t_{\text{Earth}} \cong \left(1 + 8.5 \times 10^{-11}\right) \Delta t_{\text{satellite}}$$

For the gravitational effect, we add Earth's radius to the orbit *altitude*, and note that $GM_{\text{Earth}} = (6.67 \times 10^{-11} \text{ N} \cdot \text{m}^2/\text{kg}^2)(5.98 \times 10^{24} \text{ kg}) = 4.0 \times 10^{14} \text{ m}^3/\text{s}^2$. Thus,

$$\Delta t_{\text{Earth}} \cong \Delta t_{\text{satellite}}\left[1 - \frac{4.0 \times 10^{14} \text{ m}^3/\text{s}^2}{(3 \times 10^8 \text{ m/s})^2}\left(\frac{1}{6.4 \times 10^6 \text{ m}} - \frac{1}{2.64 \times 10^7 \text{ m}}\right)\right]$$

$$\cong \Delta t_{\text{satellite}}\left(1 - 5.26 \times 10^{-10}\right)$$

The gravitational effect makes the satellite's time slightly larger. Its clock runs a tiny bit *faster* than a surface clock. The speed-dependent effect makes the satellite's clock run *slower*, but by an even tinier amount. Adding the fractional changes for each, we have

$$\frac{\Delta t_{\text{Earth}} - \Delta t_{\text{satellite}}}{\Delta t_{\text{satellite}}} \cong -5.26 \times 10^{-10} + 8.5 \times 10^{-11}$$

$$= -4.4 \times 10^{-10}$$

(b) Inserting a discrepancy of 10 ns,

$$\left|\frac{10 \times 10^{-9} \text{ s}}{\Delta t_{\text{satellite}}}\right| \cong \left|4.4 \times 10^{-10}\right|$$

$$\Delta t_{\text{satellite}} = 23 \text{ s}$$

We see that in a very short time, enough error would accumulate to make the system useless.

In practice, clocks aboard GPS satellites are preset to a frequency that accounts for the gravitational effect relative to Earth's surface, as it depends only on the known orbit radius. Velocities and elevations of receivers vary, and accounting for these effects requires real-time calculations in the receiving unit.

If a gravitational field somehow warps time intervals, even when there is no relative motion, why shouldn't it warp space intervals? Indeed, one of the tenets of general relativity is that a massive heavenly body warps space-time nearby. Representing warped space-time in three dimensions is difficult. It is easier in two dimensions, in which space is area. Figure 34 shows a massive heavenly body disturbing the regularity of a two-dimensional space. Inhabitants of this two-dimensional universe *expect* all cells to be of equal area. We outside observers can see that the cells near the heavenly body are really larger, but only from our extradimensional viewpoint. Similarly, the warpage of real three-dimensional space is not apparent to human beings. We are creatures of our space of three dimensions and cannot stand back to view our universe on *four*-dimensional axes. Nevertheless, even reduced-dimensional views such as Figure 34 provide a qualitative understanding of some effects of general relativity, as we will soon see.

The fact that gravity can cause a redshift is just one sign of a more basic truth: Gravity affects light. As we know, light has no mass; its energy is all kinetic. So it must be that gravity pulls on forms of energy other than mass/internal energy. As light moves away from Earth, its kinetic energy must decrease as potential energy increases. But this leads to the question, How can we use Newton's universal law of gravitation, $F = GMm/r^2$, to account for the effect of gravity without an m for light? The answer is that this law is really a

Figure 34   A two-dimensional representation of a massive object warping space.

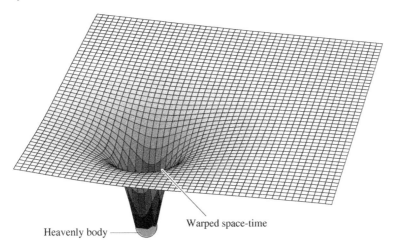

Warped space-time

Heavenly body

special case, correct only when the gravitational field is very weak. In this limit, the effect on light is negligible, and there is no need to consider an *m*. For a strong field, however, general relativity comes into play, and Newton's law is replaced by a different view—warped space-time. The variation of light's frequency near a massive heavenly body is viewed as a natural result of its passage through a region where the regularity of space and time is disturbed.

Deflection of Light by the Sun

We have seen that gravity "pulls" on light moving directly away from a heavenly body. But what if the light is traveling laterally—does it curve? It must! As shown in Figure 35, a laterally moving light beam would appear to curve toward the floor in Anna's rocket-powered closet, so it must curve toward the floor in Bob's Earth-bound closet.

Again, we don't try to reconcile the curvature with Newton's law of gravitation. Rather, the light simply moves in the most natural way given the warped space-time through which it passes. A guiding classical principle still applies: Light always takes the minimum time to travel from one point to another. Figure 36 shows two possible paths of a light beam originating at one point in space, passing through the warped space-time near a large heavenly body, then observed at another point. The darker path follows what inhabitants of the flat, two-dimensional space might believe is a straight line—one of the lines in a grid that would be regular if space were not warped. Smugly observing from our extradimensional perspective, however, we see that the other path is shorter. This is the path the light actually takes, so an observer with a "flat perspective" sees a beam that appeared to curve as it passed near the heavenly body and thus seems to have originated at a different point in space.

Figure 35   A light beam curving in an accelerating frame without gravity and in the equivalent stationary frame with gravity.

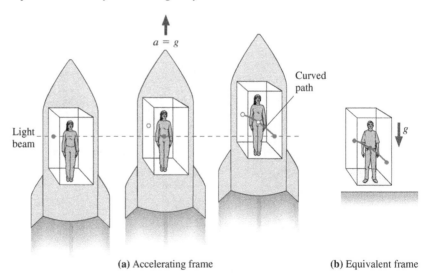

(a) Accelerating frame   **(b)** Equivalent frame

Figure 36   A light beam takes the shortest path, which to inhabitants of warped space does not appear straight.

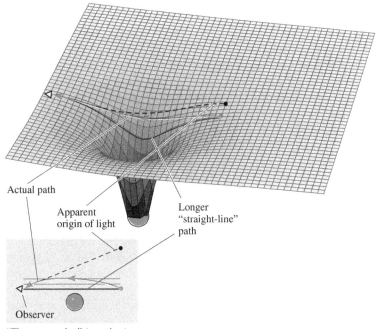

Actual path

Apparent
origin of light

Longer
"straight-line"
path

Observer

"Flat perspective" (top view)

Our Sun doesn't warp space much. Its gravitational redshift, for example, is only about 2 parts in a million. To have any hope of seeing deflection of light by the Sun, observations have to be made of light rays passing very close to it, where its field is strongest. This light, of course, comes from other stars. Their positions should appear to shift slightly as the Sun passes between them and Earth. The problem is that light passing so close is usually obscured by the brightness of the Sun. Therefore, the best time to make an observation is when the Sun is "darkened"—during a solar eclipse. An observation during an eclipse in 1919, shortly after Einstein formulated his theory, showed a deflection of about 2 s of arc for light barely grazing the Sun. Agreement with the prediction of general relativity was excellent, and Einstein was instantly famous. Progress and Applications discusses the bending of light applied to cosmology in the phenomenon of **gravitational lensing**.

Precession of the Perihelion of Mercury

The orbits of the planets about the Sun are not exactly circular, but slightly elliptical. At one point in its orbit, called aphelion, a planet will be slightly farther than average from the Sun, and at another, called perihelion, slightly closer. As long as a system is simply one object orbiting another, it is a direct prediction of classical Newtonian gravitation that the same path in space is retraced indefinitely. Influences of other heavenly bodies will cause the orbit to precess. The points of aphelion and perihelion progressively creep around

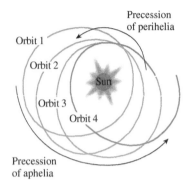

Figure 37   An orbit precessing about the Sun.

Precession of perihelia

Orbit 1

Orbit 2

Sun

Orbit 3

Orbit 4

Precession of aphelia

in a circular fashion, as depicted in Figure 37. Mercury's orbit precesses due to the perturbing effects of the other planets, and Newtonian theory can predict what the precession rate should be. But much to the consternation of early astronomers, the predicted rate did not agree precisely with observation. The problem was that Newton's law of gravitation is correct only for a weak gravitational field. If any planet deviates from the classical expectation, it should be Mercury, for it orbits where the Sun's field is strongest. Using general relativity, a correction to the classically expected precession rate of Mercury may be calculated. The result of 43 s of arc per century is in good agreement with observation.

Cosmology

Cosmology is the study of the behaviors of heavenly bodies. It is invariably coupled to gravitation because gravity is the dominant interaction, being the one fundamental force in nature that is both long range and only attractive. The nuclear forces (the strong and the weak) are negligible at distances beyond about 10^{-15} m, and the remaining force, the electromagnetic, is largely canceled out for electrically neutral objects. Much of cosmology can be understood through classical Newtonian gravitation, but some behaviors require general relativity.

Stellar collapse describes the fate of individual stars. Early in a star's life, the enormous gravitational attraction of its mass is balanced by its tendency to expand due to the constant generation of energy (via nuclear fusion). The radius remains constant. When the star's fuel begins to burn out, gravity gets the upper hand and gravitational collapse begins. If the star is not much more massive than our Sun, the result is a **white dwarf**, and then ultimately a cold, dead chunk of matter typically no larger than Earth. For stars several times the Sun's mass, the extra gravitational pressure is able to force protons and electrons to combine, forming neutrons and tiny particles known as **neutrinos** The neutrinos carry away a huge amount of energy in a cataclysmic explosion known as a supernova. What remains is a cold **neutron star** of fantastic density, about 10^{13} times that of lead, with a typical radius of only tens of kilometers. For even larger stars, there is a third possible fate: becoming a **black hole**.

One of the most startling features of general relativity is that space can have singularities; that is, discontinuities or divergences. A singularity occurs when a body of mass M becomes so compact that its radius drops below the **Schwarzschild radius**, $r_S = 2GM/c^2$. The singularity would be separate from the universe as we know it. It would simply be a silent hole in space. Moreover, its gravitational field would be so strong that not even light could leave it, thus the name *black* hole. (Exercise 101 discusses a crude derivation of the Schwarzschild radius from this assumption.) The presence of a black hole would be betrayed almost alone by its external gravitational effects and its ability to gobble up things from the outside. A black hole has an **event horizon**. Things outside can go in, but once inside the event horizon, there is no way out. An unlucky trespasser gets a one-way ticket to the singularity. It should be noted that not even the atomic nucleus—trillions of times denser than ordinary solids—comes close to qualifying as a black hole. A typical nuclear diameter is 10^{-15} m, but its Schwarzschild radius would be roughly 10^{-52} m. With so few external signs, obtaining conclusive evidence of black holes is not easy. Nevertheless, most cosmologists accept not only that they exist, but also that they are a fairly common feature of the centers of galaxies.

As far as the universe as a whole is concerned, the most basic observation is that it is expanding, and it appears to have been doing so ever since a **Big Bang**, an explosion of an unimaginably hot and dense collection of relativistic particles. In this chapter, we look at its expansion since the formation of galaxies. (We refer to galaxies because they move more or less independently. Stars do not, for they orbit each other in galaxies. Actually, many galaxies orbit in groups or clusters, but the word *galaxy* will serve our purpose.) If objects were to begin moving away from an origin at the same time, each maintaining its original speed, they would later be spread out according to their speeds. After 1 unit of time, those moving at a speed of 1 would be 1 unit away, those moving at a speed of 2 would be 2 units away, and so forth. Perhaps surprisingly, this would also appear to be the case no matter which object/galaxy served as the observer's frame of reference (see Exercise 102). Thus, if the universe did begin with a big bang, an observer in any given galaxy would see a proportionality between the distance to another galaxy and its speed.

This is just what we observe. The evidence comes from the Doppler shifts in the light spectra from distant galaxies. The farther a galaxy is from Earth, the greater the redshift in its spectrum, implying a greater recessional speed. We find that the speed increases linearly with distance.

$$v = H_0 r$$

This relationship is known as Hubble's law, and the constant H_0 as the **Hubble constant**. Because an object moving a distance r at constant speed v would travel for a time r/v, and because this is the same constant $1/H_0$ for all galaxies, $1/H_0$ is often referred to as the age of the universe. The evidence suggests a value between 10 and 20 billion years.

The Hubble constant is not known with great precision, mostly because it is hard to determine distances to faraway galaxies. But even if distances could be known precisely, a guess at the age of the universe based on the Hubble constant is approximate at best, for the expansion rate is not constant. Galaxies have not moved out independently at constant velocity, because they all feel the gravitational attraction of the universe as a whole. This alone would suggest that the expansion rate is decreasing. Even so, the rate of its decrease would depend on the total amount of mass/energy in the universe. Analogies to escape velocity in classical physics are very helpful. A projectile launched from a planet at a certain speed would escape if the planet were of very low density but would return to a very dense planet. There would be a critical density at which it would barely escape; there is similarly a critical density for the universe.

Present evidence suggests that the universe is very close to critical, but the cause is still in question. Luminous matter such as stars, the easiest to document, accounts for only 0.4% of critical density. Theories regarding the production of mass in the early universe suggest that nonluminous ordinary matter (protons, neutrons, and electrons) should total about 5% of critical density. This **dark matter** would be in the form of diffuse gases as well as dark stars—white dwarfs, neutron stars, and black holes. However, studies of the orbital motions of galaxies in clusters indicate that there is much more matter that isn't ordinary—about 30% of critical density. On this, speculation abounds, with kinds of particles predicted but never actually observed being high on the list. But even this leaves more than 60% of critical density missing. A prime candidate to supply the deficit is a term Einstein originally tacked on to his theory of general relativity in an effort to explain a *stable* universe, but then discarded when expansion was discovered. It has now regained favor. Known as the **cosmological constant**, it is a mysterious energy density that would permeate the universe but not dissipate as the universe expands. It could explain not only the near critical density but also recent data indicating that the expansion rate of the universe is actually *increasing*.

Cosmology obviously has many interesting open questions.

O P T I O N A L 9 The Light Barrier

In the 1940s, it was widely claimed that no airplane could be made to exceed the speed of sound—the attempt would end in disintegration. Many doubted this claim of a "sound barrier," for it had no theoretical support. Here we discuss a different barrier and a claim that is supported by Lorentz transformation equations: *No information may travel faster than the speed of light.*

In Figure 38, Bob is at the origin of frame S, and Anna is at the origin of frame S', in a spaceship moving in the $+x$ direction at speed $v < c$ relative to Bob. At time zero, just as the origins cross, Bob has an original thought. In a spasm of inspiration, he seizes upon the perfect finale to the symphony he had been composing. This event—event 1—has position and time $x_1 = 0$, $t_1 = 0$. Bob wishes to share his newly completed symphony with others as soon as

Figure 38 Bob has an original thought.

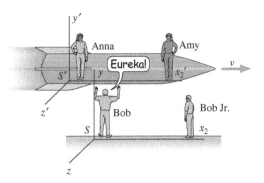

possible. He sends the completed symphony—the "information"—to Bob Jr., standing at x_2, via the fastest method available. If the information moves at speed u_0 by this method, its arrival at Bob Jr.—event 2—occurs at time

$$t_2 = \frac{x_2}{u_0}$$

Anna's assistant Amy is riding near the front of Anna's spaceship and happens to be precisely aligned with Bob Jr. when he receives the information. Bob Jr. instantly communicates the information to Amy. Occurring at the same location and time, the arrival of the information at Bob Jr.'s location and its communication to Amy is a single event (again, event 2). From its position and time in Bob's frame, equations (12) give its position (Amy's location) and time in Anna's.

$$
\begin{aligned}
x_2' &= \gamma_v\left(x_2 - v\frac{x_2}{u_0}\right) = \gamma_v\left(1 - \frac{v}{u_0}\right)x_2 \\
t_2' &= \gamma_v\left(-\frac{v}{c^2}x_2 + \frac{x_2}{u_0}\right) = \gamma_v\left(-\frac{v}{c^2} + \frac{1}{u_0}\right)x_2
\end{aligned}
\tag{32}
$$

As soon as Amy receives the information, she sends it to Anna, also via the fastest method. In Anna's frame, the time that passes as the information travels from x_2' (Amy's location) to the origin of S' (Anna's location) is x_2'/u_0. It leaves Amy at t_2', so it arrives at the origin—event 3—at time

$$t_3' = t_2' + \frac{x_2'}{u_0}$$

Now substituting from (32),

$$
\begin{aligned}
t_3' &= \left[\gamma_v\left(-\frac{v}{c^2} + \frac{1}{u_0}\right)x_2\right] + \frac{1}{u_0}\left[\gamma_v\left(1 - \frac{v}{u_0}\right)x_2\right] \\
&= \gamma_v x_2 \frac{2}{u_0}\left[1 - \frac{v}{c}\left(\frac{u_0}{2c} + \frac{c}{2u_0}\right)\right]
\end{aligned}
\tag{33}
$$

If u_0 is less than c, then t_3' is positive, and all is well. But for any $u_0 > c$, there is a $v < c$ for which t_3' is *negative*. (See Exercise 103.) Recall that event 3 is the symphony reaching Anna at the origin of frame S' and that the origins, Anna and Bob, pass at time zero on both clocks. Anna would be whistling the completed symphony *before* she passes Bob, who, by assumption, conceives of it at the instant of passing. This violates the principle of cause and effect.

Figure 39   Causes (events of the past) reside in the past light-cone, while effects (events of the future) reside in the future light-cone.

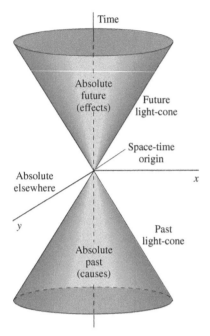

Figure 39   Causes (events of the past) reside in the past light-cone, while effects (events of the future) reside in the future light-cone.

If we accept that cause must precede effect, then superluminal information transfer is forbidden.

The issue of cause and effect leads us back to a point raised in connection with Example 4: Events may occur in a different order in different frames. If this is true, might cause precede effect in one frame but effect precede cause in another? Such a thing would certainly be mind-boggling, but the Lorentz transformation equations do not allow it. Events can be reversed, but not if they are causally related (see Exercise 104).

Figure 39 illustrates potentially causal events. The focus is an event at the space-time origin. All events that may have been a cause of this event—events of the **absolute past**—are confined within the **past light-cone**, whose slope is the speed of light. For instance, an event on the time axis—at the *spatial* origin—at $t < 0$ could certainly have been a cause of the event at the space-time origin at $t = 0$, and so could events spatially not too far from that axis. An event on the surface of the past light-cone, a distance $\Delta x = c\, \Delta t$ away, could have been a cause only if information from it were communicated to the space-time origin at the speed of light. Thus, events in the past but *outside* the past light-cone are too far away to be causally related. This region is known as the **absolute elsewhere**. At time zero, it constricts to a single point, because no event anywhere else can have an instantaneous effect on the event at the space-time origin. The meaning of the **future light-cone** is complementary. It contains all events that are not too far away to be affected by the event at the space-time origin—events of the **absolute future**. Naturally, it spreads spatially as time progresses.

🅐 D V A N C E D   10 The Fourth Dimension

In this section, we will see more clearly why we speak of space-time as though time were no different from the three spatial dimensions. We also study other aspects of the four-dimensional nature of special relativity.

Recall from Section 3 that for a free object to move at constant velocity in different frames, we require a linear transformation. The logical generalization of equations (4) to three spatial dimensions is

$$x' = A_{11}x + A_{12}y + A_{13}z + A_{14}t$$
$$y' = A_{21}x + A_{22}y + A_{23}z + A_{24}t$$
$$z' = A_{31}x + A_{32}y + A_{33}z + A_{34}t$$
$$t' = A_{41}x + A_{42}y + A_{43}z + A_{44}t$$

We again assume that the relative motion between frames is along the x and x' axes. This would allow us to proceed as in Section 3 without any explicitly four-dimensional appearances, but keeping all four equations provides better insight. From equations (12) through (14), we see that most of the A constants are 0 and the Lorentz transformation equations may thus be written as

$$
\begin{aligned}
x' &= \gamma_v\left(x - \frac{v}{c}ct\right) \\
y' &= y \\
z' &= z \\
ct' &= \gamma_v\left(ct - \frac{v}{c}x\right)
\end{aligned}
\qquad \text{or} \qquad
\begin{bmatrix} x' \\ y' \\ z' \\ ct' \end{bmatrix} =
\begin{bmatrix}
\gamma_v & 0 & 0 & -\gamma_v\dfrac{v}{c} \\
0 & 1 & 0 & 0 \\
0 & 0 & 1 & 0 \\
-\gamma_v\dfrac{v}{c} & 0 & 0 & \gamma_v
\end{bmatrix}
\begin{bmatrix} x \\ y \\ z \\ ct \end{bmatrix}
\qquad (34)
$$

The first and fourth equations differ only in the exchange of ct' for x' and ct for x. Mixing with position as it does, time must be treated, in a real sense, as a fourth dimension. We refer to the three spatial dimensions together with time as a **four-vector**. The matrix form of (34) emphasizes the four-dimensional nature of space-time and is often a convenient way of using the equations all at once, as we see in the following example.

EXAMPLE 12

For the situation in Example 4, (a) determine the Lorentz transformation matrix from Bob's frame to Anna's frame, then (b) using matrix multiplication, verify the initial ($t = 0$) time on Anna's front clock.

SOLUTION

(a) We have $v/c = \sqrt{3}/2$ and $\gamma_v = 2$, so the Lorentz transformation matrix in (34) is

$$
\begin{bmatrix}
2 & 0 & 0 & -\sqrt{3} \\
0 & 1 & 0 & 0 \\
0 & 0 & 1 & 0 \\
-\sqrt{3} & 0 & 0 & 2
\end{bmatrix}
$$

(b) A $t = 0$ in Bob's frame, Bob Jr., at $x = \frac{1}{2}\ell = 6\sqrt{3}\,\text{m}$, sees Anna's front clock tick.

$$
\begin{bmatrix} x' \\ y' \\ z' \\ ct' \end{bmatrix} =
\begin{bmatrix}
2 & 0 & 0 & -\sqrt{3} \\
0 & 1 & 0 & 0 \\
0 & 0 & 1 & 0 \\
-\sqrt{3} & 0 & 0 & 2
\end{bmatrix}
\begin{bmatrix} 6\sqrt{3}\,\text{m} \\ 0 \\ 0 \\ 0 \end{bmatrix} =
\begin{bmatrix} 12\sqrt{3}\,\text{m} \\ 0 \\ 0 \\ -18\,\text{m} \end{bmatrix}
$$

The time on Anna's front clock is $t' = (-18\,\text{m})/c = -60$ ns. Note that we also obtain its location in Anna's frame.

Four-Vectors

In special relativity, certain quantities that are classically vectors acquire a fourth component; they become four-vectors. By definition, any four quantities (A_x, A_y, A_z, A_t) that transform from one frame to another via a Lorentz transformation constitute a four-vector. We already have one example: the position-time four-vector (x, y, z, ct).

An important characteristic of four-vectors is that each has a related quantity that is the same for observers in all frames. Following the form of (34), the Lorentz transformation equations for an arbitrary four-vector are

$$A'_x = \gamma_v\left(A_x - \frac{v}{c}A_t\right) \quad A'_y = A_y \quad A'_z = A_z \quad A'_t = \gamma_v\left(A_t - \frac{v}{c}A_x\right) \tag{35}$$

It is left as an exercise to show from these relationships that

$$A'^2_t - (A'^2_x + A'^2_y + A'^2_z) = A^2_t - (A^2_x + A^2_y + A^2_z) \tag{36}$$

On both sides, we see the sum of the squares of the spatial components subtracted from the square of the "time component." Whatever may be the physical nature of this calculation's result, it is obviously the same in frame S as in frame S'. Such a quantity is called an **invariant**. Identifying $A^2_x + A^2_y + A^2_z$ with the square of the three-component vector portion of A, we may write

$$A'^2_t - \mathbf{A}' \cdot \mathbf{A}' = A^2_t - \mathbf{A} \cdot \mathbf{A} = \text{invariant associated with } A$$

Let us investigate the invariant related to the four-vector $A = (x, y, z, ct)$. We know that a *difference* between events also obeys the Lorentz transformation equations. Thus

$$A^2_t - \mathbf{A} \cdot \mathbf{A} = (c\Delta t)^2 - (\Delta x^2 + \Delta y^2 + \Delta z^2)$$

Because this is the same in all frames, we may find its value in the most convenient: the frame in which the events occur at the origin. In this frame, $A^2_t - \mathbf{A} \cdot \mathbf{A}$ is simply $(c\Delta t)^2$, where Δt is the time interval in that frame. Perhaps the events are the heartbeats of a space traveler at the origin of frame S. An observer in frame S' would see these events at varying spatial coordinates and separated by longer time intervals, due to time dilation, but would agree on the number of heartbeats. This confirms what we argued earlier: The proper time for series of events in a given frame does not depend on who is watching from another frame.

Momentum-Energy Four-Vector

We have encountered another four-vector, though a little work is needed to see it. Equation (23) relates momenta in two frames summed over all particles, but it is also true for a single object.

$$\gamma_{u'}mu' = \gamma_v\gamma_u mu - v\gamma_v\gamma_u m$$

Using $p_x = \gamma_u mu_x$ and $E = \gamma_u mc^2$, we may write this as

$$p_x' = \gamma_v\left[p_x - \frac{v}{c}\left(\frac{E}{c}\right)\right] \qquad (37)$$

Invoking the identity $\gamma_{u'} = (1 - u_x v/c^2)\gamma_v\gamma_u$, which follows from the relativistic velocity transformation (see Exercise 67), we can relate energy in frame S' to quantities in frame S.

$$\gamma_{u'}mc^2 = \left[\left(1 - \frac{u_x v}{c^2}\right)\gamma_v\gamma_u\right]mc^2 = \gamma_v\left[(\gamma_u mc^2) - v(\gamma_u mu_x)\right]$$

or

$$E' = \gamma_v(E - vp_x)$$

Dividing this by c and placing it and (37) beside the position-time Lorentz transformation equations, we see a great similarity.

$$x' = \gamma_v\left[x - \frac{v}{c}(ct)\right] \qquad p_x' = \gamma_v\left[p_x - \frac{v}{c}\left(\frac{E}{c}\right)\right]$$

$$\qquad (38)$$

$$ct' = \gamma_v\left[(ct) - \frac{v}{c}x\right] \qquad \frac{E'}{c} = \gamma_v\left[\left(\frac{E}{c}\right) - \frac{v}{c}p_x\right]$$

The relationship between p_x and E is virtually identical to that between x and t. It is also true that $p_y' = p_y$ and $p_z' = p_z$ (see Exercise 109). Thus, p_x, p_y, p_z, and E/c obey a Lorentz transformation and constitute a four-vector, just as do x, y, z, and ct. As time (ct for proper units) must be considered an essential part of the position-time four-vector, or four-space, energy (E/c) is an essential part of the four-momentum.

And what is the invariant associated with four-momentum? For the case $A = (p_x, p_y, p_z, E/c)$, we have

$$A_t^2 - \mathbf{A}\cdot\mathbf{A} = (E/c)^2 - p^2$$

If we choose S to be the frame in which the object is at rest, the momentum is 0 and the energy is simply mc^2. The invariant is m^2c^2, where m is the mass in the rest frame of the object. Observers in all frames agree on the mass/internal energy of an object.

Special Relativity Stands Up to the Test Classical mechanics was confirmed centuries ago—or so we thought. With modern technology, there has been no pause in the scrutiny of special relativity. The possibility of violations of its fundamental postulates, proposed by new theories of fundamental forces, have redoubled interest. In 2002, a team of researchers at the Universities of Konstanz and Düsseldorf in Germany confirmed the constancy of the speed of light to a high degree of precision. Their apparatus was a modern twist on the Michelson-Morley interferometer, consisting of perpendicular cavities made of a very stable sapphire crystal and kept at a temperature of 4 K to reduce thermal noise. They monitored the interference as Earth revolved about the Sun, taking their laboratory from one frame to another moving relative to the first at about 60 km/s. At such a low speed, the effect of the frame motion was expected to be small, but they ruled out effects almost 5 orders of magnitude smaller. Even the icon $E = mc^2$ receives regular attention. A team of scientists from universities and labs in several countries recently measured the mass change when a nucleus captures a neutron to become a different nucleus and then emits electromagnetic radiation (*Nature*, 22–29 December 2005, 1096–1097). The emitted electromagnetic energy was found to equal the change in mc^2 of the neutron and nuclei within 0.00004%. Einstein's claims seem to be holding up quite well.

Gravitational Lenses: Applying the Bending of Light
If a gravitational field can bend light, then light should be able to travel from source to observer by *multiple* paths around a massive object. Indeed this happens, and it is known as gravitational lensing. Figure 40 is a superb example. Taken by the Hubble Space Telescope, it shows multiple images of the same galaxy. The massive "object" in this case is a cluster of galaxies, which produce the bright spots at the center of the image.

Gravitational lensing is an indispensable tool in cosmology nowadays. One application is in sorting out the redshift associated with the expansion of the universe. Objects with large redshifts can be seen lensed by objects with smaller redshifts, confirming that the more-distant object is moving faster. Another application is to gauge the mass distribution of a galaxy cluster; the mass density must be greatest where the lensing effect is most pronounced. Because all mass, not just luminous mass, contributes to the effect, gravitational lensing is also one of the most important techniques in the search for dark matter. Not only can the presence of dark matter be inferred in galaxy clusters, but also light from a distant star can be perceptibly

Figure 40 Gravitational lensing. The bright spots in the middle are part of a galaxy cluster. The loop-shaped formations at 4, 8, 9, and 10 o'clock are images of the same distant galaxy whose light has reached Earth by curving in different directions around the cluster.

magnified when a dark star passes between it and Earth. This effect is known a microlensing.

Waves of Gravity? Some forefront theories make predictions that meet with considerable skepticism. General relativity makes a prediction that almost no one doubts but which has thus far defied all attempts at direct measurement: gravitational waves. A charged object when accelerated emits electromagnetic radiation that propagates outward in a wavelike fashion. In a similar phenomenon, the warping of space caused by accelerating massive objects should propagate as waves. However, these disturbances are expected to be very faint in most systems, because gravity is a weak force. (Everyone has seen static electricity stick things together, but the only gravitational force apparent to the senses involves Earth, which is of immense mass.) Indirect evidence was obtained in the 1970s, when a system of two mutually orbiting pulsars was found to be losing energy at a rate predicted by general relativity and attributable to gravitational waves (Nobel Prize, 1993, Hulse & Taylor). However, direct detection is still elusive. In the vanguard of the search is the Laser Interferometer

Gravitational-Wave Observatory (LIGO). This facility has two locations separated by nearly 2000 miles to discriminate between local effects and those from a broad wave reaching Earth. Such a wave should cause slight variations in length along different arms of the interferometers. Among the hopes are confirmation that gravitational waves move at c and that they are transverse in a way that agrees with the distinctive angular momentum they are predicted to carry. It is also hoped to detect the lively radiation that should accompany colliding black holes, which would further validate the theory of general relativity.

Chapter Summary

There is no evidence for the *absolute* motion of any inertial frame of reference. All motion is relative. Arguing that an experiment should proceed identically in any frame, irrespective of its motion relative to any other, Albert Einstein postulated that the laws of physics must be the same in all inertial frames. In particular, Maxwell's equations, which yield the speed of light c, are the same. Therefore, light will move at c relative to an observer in any inertial frame.

A direct result of Einstein's postulates is that an event's position and time in one frame will, in general, be different from its position and time in another. The equations relating these positions and times are the Lorentz transformation equations.

$$x' = \gamma_v(x - vt) \tag{12a}$$

$$t' = \gamma_v\left(-\frac{v}{c^2}x + t\right) \tag{12b}$$

Following from these equations are important consequences of Einstein's postulates: time dilation, in which an observer in an inertial frame determines time to pass more slowly on a moving clock than on his or her own; length contraction, in which a moving object is shorter along the direction of relative motion than it is in the frame in which it is at rest; and relative simultaneity, in which two events simultaneous in one frame are separated by a nonzero time interval in another.

The demand that momentum conservation hold in all frames leads to the relativistically correct expression for momentum and an expression, absent in classical physics, for the total energy of a moving object.

$$\mathbf{p} = \gamma_u m\mathbf{u} \tag{22}$$

$$E = \gamma_u mc^2 \tag{24}$$

The laws governing momentum and energy conservation are inextricably related.

Einstein generalized the concept of an inertial frame to include a frame that is falling freely in a gravitational field. No experiment could distinguish the two frames. This view led to the idea of a gravitational field warping space-time and explains the effect of gravity on light.

The speed of light is an absolute upper limit on the speed at which information may move relative to an observer.

---

* indicates advanced questions

Conceptual Questions

1. Explain to your friend, who is willing to accept that light moves at the same speed in any frame, why clocks on a passing train are not synchronized. If it helps, assume that Anna is at the middle of the train.
2. A friend says, "It makes no sense that Anna could turn on lights in her hands simultaneously in her frame but that they don't turn on simultaneously in another—she decides to do it, and it's done." By considering the tractable, if somewhat unrealistic, situation of Anna's thought being communicated to her hands by light signals, answer this objection.
3. The Lorentz transformation equations have x and t and x' and t'. Why no v and v'?
4. You are gliding over Earth's surface at a high speed, carrying your high-precision clock. At points X and Y on the ground are similar clocks, synchronized in the ground frame of reference. As you pass over clock X, it and your clock both read 0. (a) According to you, do

clocks X and Y advance slower or faster than yours? (b) When you pass over clock Y, does it read the same time, an earlier time, or a later time than yours? (Make sure your answer agrees with what ground observers should see.) (c) Reconcile any seeming contradictions between your answers to parts (a) and (b).

5. A thin plate has a round hole whose diameter in its rest frame is D. The plate is parallel to the ground and moving upward, in the $+y$ direction, relative to the ground. A thin round disk whose diameter in *its* rest frame is D is also parallel to the ground but moving in the $+x$ direction relative to it. In the frame of the ground, the plate and disk are on course so that the centers of the hole and disk will at some point coincide. The disk is contracted, but the hole in the plate is not, so the disk will pass through the hole. Now consider the frame of the disk. The disk is of diameter D, but the hole is contracted. Can the disk pass through the hole, and if so, how?

6. In the twin paradox situation, a fellow student objects to the argument that Anna's acceleration is the root of the asymmetry. "All motion is relative! Anna is accelerating relative to Bob, but Bob is accelerating relative to Anna." Answer this objection.

7. Does the asymmetric aging of an Earth-bound observer and his twin who travels away and back demand "relativistic speed"? (Overlook the fact that each has a limited life span.)

8. You are floating in space when you notice a flying saucer circling you. Each time it passes in front of you, you note the reading on its clock. Do you see its clock advancing faster or slower than your wristwatch? Does the space alien see your wristwatch advancing faster or slower than his clock? Explain.

9. The Doppler effect formula involves two speeds, v and c. The Doppler formula for sound involves three speeds (source, listener, and sound). Why a different number?

10. A relativity enthusiast says, "If $E = mc^2$ and energy is conserved, then mass is conserved." How do you answer?

11. Can a single object of mass 4 explode into two objects each of mass greater than 2? Explain your reasoning.

12. Can two moving objects of mass 2 and 3 stick together and form a single object of mass less than 5? Explain your reasoning.

13. Two objects isolated from the rest of the universe collide and stick together. Does the system's final kinetic energy depend on the frame of reference in which it is viewed? Does the system's *change* in kinetic energy depend on the frame in which it is viewed? Explain your answers.

14. Particles of light have no mass. Does the Sun's mass change as a result of all the light it emits? Explain.

15. You are strapped into a rear-facing seat at the middle of a long bus accelerating from rest at about 10 m/s² (a rather violent acceleration for a bus). As the back of the bus passes a warning sign alongside the street, a red light of precisely 650 nm wavelength on the sign turns on. Do you see this precise 650 nm wavelength? Does your friend sitting at the front of the bus see the wavelength you see? How could the same observations be produced with the bus and sign stationary?

16. In a television picture tube, a beam of electrons is sent from the back to the front (screen) by an electron gun. When an electron strikes the screen, it causes a phosphor to glow briefly. To produce an image across the entire screen, the beam is electrically deflected up and down and left and right. The beam may sweep from left to right at a speed greater than c. Why is this not a violation of the claim that no information may travel faster than the speed of light?

Exercises

Section 3

17. Appearing in the time-dilation and length-contraction formulas, γ_v is a reasonable measure of the size of relativistic effects. Roughly speaking, at what speed would observations deviate from classical expectations by 1%?

18. Verify that the special case $x' = -vt'$, $x = 0$ leads to equation (6) when inserted in linear transformations (4) and that special case $x' = ct'$, $x = ct$ in turn leads to (8).

19. If an object actually occupies less space physically when moving, it cannot depend on the direction we *define* as positive. As we know, an object aligned with the direction of relative motion is contracted whether it is fixed in frame S and viewed from S', or the other way around. Use this idea to argue that distances along the y- and y'-axes cannot differ at all. Consider a post of length L_0 fixed in frame S, jutting up from the origin along the $+y$-axis, with a saw at the top poised to slice off anything extending any higher in the passing frame S'. Also consider an identical post fixed in frame S'. What happens when the origins cross?

20. Through a window in Carl's spaceship, passing at $0.5c$, you watch Carl doing an important physics calculation. By your watch it takes him 1 min. How much time did Carl spend on his calculation?

21. According to an observer on Earth, a spacecraft whizzing by at $0.6c$ is 35 m long. What is the length of the spacecraft according to passengers on board?

22. According to Bob on Earth, Planet Y (uninhabited) is 5 ly away. Anna is in a spaceship moving away from

Earth at 0.8c. She is bound for Planet Y to study its geology. Unfortunately, Planet Y explodes. According to Bob, this occurred 2 yr after Anna passed Earth. (Bob, of course, has to wait a while for the light from the explosion to arrive, but he reaches his conclusion by "working backward.") Call the passing of Anna and Bob time zero for both. (a) According to Anna, how far away is Planet Y when it explodes? (b) At what time does it explode?

23. Anna is on a railroad flatcar moving at 0.6c relative to Bob. (Their clocks read 0 as Anna's center of mass passes Bob's.) Anna's arm is outstretched in the direction the flatcar moves, and in her hand is a flash-bulb. According to the wristwatch on Anna's hand, the flashbulb goes off at 100 ns. The time of this event according to Bob differs by 27 ns. (a) Is it earlier or later than 100 ns? (b) How long is Anna's arm (i.e., from her hand to her center of mass)?

24. A pole-vaulter holds a 16 ft. pole. A barn has doors at both ends, 10 ft. apart. The pole-vaulter on the outside of the barn begins running toward one of the open barn doors, holding the pole level in the direction he's running. When passing through the barn, the pole fits (barely) entirely within the barn all at once. (a) How fast is the pole-vaulter running? (b) According to whom—the pole-vaulter or an observer stationary in the barn—does the pole fit in all at once? (c) According to the other person, which occurs first, the front end of the pole leaving the barn or the back end entering, and (d) what is the time interval between these two events?

25. Anna and Bob are in identical spaceships, each 100 m long. The diagram shows Bob's view as Anna's ship passes at 0.8c. Just as the backs of the ships pass one another, both clocks there read 0. At the instant shown, Bob Jr., on board Bob's ship, is aligned with the very front of Anna's ship. He peers through a window in Anna's ship and looks at the clock. (a) In relation to his own ship, where is Bob Jr.? (b) What does the clock he sees read?

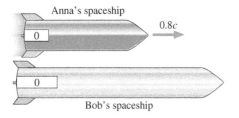

Anna's spaceship

0.8c

Bob's spaceship

26. Bob is watching Anna fly by in her new high-speed plane, which Anna knows to be 60 m in length. As a greeting, Anna turns on two lights simultaneously, one at the front and one at the tail. According to Bob, the lights come on at different times, 40 ns apart. (a) Which comes on first? (b) How fast is the plane moving?

27. Bob and Bob Jr. stand at open doorways at opposite ends of an airplane hangar 25 m long. Anna owns a spaceship, 40 m long as it sits on the runway. Anna takes off in her spaceship, then swoops through the hangar at constant velocity. At precisely time zero on both Bob's clock and Anna's, Bob sees Anna at the front of her spaceship reach his doorway. At time zero on his clock, Bob Jr. sees the tail of Anna's spaceship at his doorway. (a) How fast is Anna's spaceship moving? (b) What will Anna's clock read when she sees the tail of her spaceship at the doorway where Bob Jr. is standing? (c) How far will Anna say the front of her spaceship is from Bob at this time?

28. The diagram shows Bob's view of the passing of two identical spaceships, Anna's and his own, where $\gamma_v =$ The length of either spaceship in its rest frame is L_0 What are the readings on Anna's two unlabeled clocks?

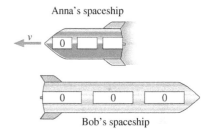

Anna's spaceship

v

Bob's spaceship

* 29. Refer to Figure 18. (a) How long is a spaceship? (b) At what speed do the ships move relative to one another? (c) Show that Anna's times are in accord with the Lorentz transformation equations. (d) Sketch a set of diagrams showing Anna's complementary view of the passing of the ships. Include times in both frames.

30. You are in a bus traveling on a straight road at 20 m/s. As you pass a gas station, your clock and a clock in the station read precisely 0. You pass another gas station 900 m farther down the road. (In the frame of reference of the gas stations, all gas station clocks are synchronized.) (a) As you pass the second station, do you find its clock to be ahead of, or behind your own clock, and (b) by how much?

31. A spaceship travels at 0.8c. As this spaceship covers the 4000 km from coast to coast, by how much will the time interval registered on an onboard clock differ from the time interval measured on the ground?

32. You are on a high-speed train, traveling at a decent clip: $0.8c$. On the ground are two signal stations 5 km apart, each with a status-reporting sign, which always give simultaneous reports. At precisely noon on the train's clocks, the conductor at the front of the train passes one station and sees a sign reading "All Clear," and another employee at the back passes the other station and sees a sign reading "Severe Electrical Storms Reported! Slow to $0.1c$!" (a) How long is the train? (b) Should it slow down? (c) Suppose that both reporting signs display the time very precisely, updated every microsecond. By how much would the two observed time readings differ, if at all?

33. A famous experiment detected 527 muons per hour at the top of Mt. Washington, New Hampshire, elevation 1910 m. At sea level, the same equipment detected 395 muons per hour. A discriminator selected for muons whose speed was between $0.9950c$ and $0.9954c$. Given that the mean lifetime τ of a muon in a frame in which it is at rest is 2.2 μs and that in this frame the number of muons decays exponentially with time according to $N = N_0 e^{-t/\tau}$, show that the results obtained in the experiment are sensible.

34. In the frame in which they are at rest, the number of muons at time t is given by

$$N = N_0 e^{-t/\tau}$$

where N_0 is the number at $t = 0$ and τ is the mean lifetime 2.2 μs. (a) If muons are produced at a height of 4.0 km, heading toward the ground at $0.93c$, what fraction will survive to reach the ground? (b) What fraction would reach the ground if classical mechanics were valid?

35. A supersonic plane travels at 420 m/s. As this plane passes two markers a distance of 4.2 km apart on the ground, how will the time interval registered on a very precise clock onboard the plane differ from 10 s?

36. How fast must a plane 50 m long travel to be found by observers on the ground to be 0.10 nm shorter than 50 m?

37. According to Bob, on Earth, it is 20 ly to Planet Y. Anna has just passed Earth, moving at a constant speed v in a spaceship. When Anna passes Planet Y, she is 20 years older than when she passed Earth. Calculate v.

38. A plank, fixed to a sled at rest in frame S, is of length L_0 and makes an angle of θ_0 with the x-axis. Later, the sled zooms through frame S at a constant speed v parallel to the x-axis. Show that according to an observer who remains at rest in frame S, the length of the plank is now

$$L = L_0 \sqrt{1 - \frac{v^2}{c^2} \cos \theta_0}$$

and the angle it makes with the x-axis is

$$\theta = \tan^{-1}(\gamma_v \tan \theta_0)$$

* 39. Bob, in frame S, is observing the moving plank of Exercise 38. He quickly fabricates a wall, fixed in his frame, that has a hole of length L and that is slanted at angle θ, such that the plank will completely fill the hole as it passes through. This occurs at the instant $t = 0$. According to Anna, moving with the plank, the plank is of course not of length L, but of length L_0. Moreover, because Bob's wall moves relative to her, Anna sees a hole that is less than L in length; a plank longer than L is headed toward a hole shorter than L. Can the plank pass through the hole according to Anna? If so, at what time(s)? Explain.

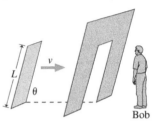

Bob

40. An experimenter determines that a particle created at one end of the laboratory apparatus moved at $0.94c$ and survived for 0.032 μs, decaying just as it reached the other end. (a) According to the experimenter, how far did the particle move? (b) In its own frame of reference, how long did the particle survive? (c) According to the particle, what was the length of the laboratory apparatus?

41. A muon has a mean lifetime of 2.2 μs in its rest frame. Suppose muons are traveling at $0.92c$ relative to Earth. What is the mean distance a muon will travel as measured by an observer on Earth?

42. A pion is an elementary particle that, on average, disintegrates 2.6×10^{-8} s after creation in a frame at rest relative to the pion. An experimenter finds that pions created in the laboratory travel 13 m on average before disintegrating. How fast are the pions traveling through the lab?

* 43. Anna and Bob have identical spaceships 60 m long. The diagram shows Bob's observations of Anna's ship, which passes at a speed of $c/\sqrt{2}$. Clocks at the back of both ships read 0 just as they pass. Bob is at the center of his ship and at $t = 0$ on his wristwatch peers at a second clock on Anna's ship.

(a) What does this clock read?
(b) Later, the back of Anna's ship passes Bob. At what time does this occur according to Bob?

(c) What will observers in Bob's frame see on Anna's two clocks at this time?

(d) Identify two events that show time dilation and two that show length contraction *according to Anna*.

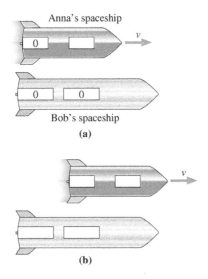

Anna's spaceship

Bob's spaceship

(a)

(b)

44. Demonstrate that equations (12) and (13) become the classical transformation equations (1) when $v \ll c$, except when applied to events *very* far away, in which case time is still not absolute.

Section 4

45. Planet W is 12 ly from Earth. Anna and Bob are both 20 yr old. Anna travels to Planet W at $0.6c$, quickly turns around, and returns to Earth at $0.6c$. How old will Anna and Bob be when Anna gets back?

46. Anna and Bob are both born just as Anna's spaceship passes Earth at $0.9c$. According to Bob on Earth, Planet Z is a fixed 30 ly away. As Anna passes Planet Z on her continuing outward journey, what will be (a) Bob's age according to Bob, (b) Bob's age according to Anna, (c) Anna's age according to Anna, and (d) Anna's age according to Bob?

47. Consider Anna, Bob, and Carl in the twin paradox. (a) According to Anna, when Planet X passes her, clocks on Planet X and Earth tick simultaneously. Using the Lorentz transformation equations, calculate the time interval between these two events in the Earth-Planet X frame. (b) According to Carl, when Planet X passes, clocks on Planet X and Earth tick simultaneously. What is the time interval between these events in the Earth-Planet X frame? (c) What does the clock on Planet X

read when Carl and Anna reach it? Show how your results from parts (a) and (b) agree with Figure 20.

* **48.** You stand at the center of your 100 m spaceship and watch Anna's identical ship pass at $0.6c$. At $t = 0$ on your wristwatch, Anna, at the center of her ship, is directly across from you and her wristwatch also reads 0.

(a) A friend on your ship, 24 m from you in a direction toward the tail of Anna's passing ship, looks at a clock directly across from him on Anna's ship. What does it read?

(b) Your friend now steps onto Anna's ship. By this very act, he moves from a frame where Anna is one age to a frame where she is another. What is the difference in these ages? Explain. (*Hint:* Your friend moves to Anna's frame, where the time is whatever the clock at the location reads.)

(c) Answer parts (a) and (b) for a friend 24 m from you but in a direction toward the front of Anna's passing ship.

(d) What happens to the reading on a clock when you accelerate toward it? Away from it?

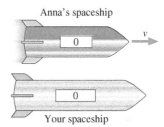

Anna's spaceship

Your spaceship

* **49.** From a standstill, you begin jogging at 5 m/s directly toward the galaxy Centaurus A, which is on the horizon 2×10^{23} m away.

(a) There is a clock in Centaurus A. According to you, how will readings on this clock differ before and after you begin jogging? (*Remember:* You change frames.)

(b) The planet Neptune is between Earth and Centaurus A, 4.5×10^9 m from Earth. How much would readings on a clock there differ?

(c) What would be the time differences if you had instead begun jogging in the opposite direction?

(d) What do these results tell you about the observations of a traveling twin who accelerates toward his Earth-bound twin? How do these observations depend on the distance between the twins?

50. A meterstick is glued to the wall with its 100 cm end farther to the right, in the positive direction. It has a clock at its center and one on each end. You walk by

the meterstick in the positive direction at speed v.
(a) When you reach the center clock, it reads 0. What do the other two read at this instant in your frame. (b) You instantly reverse direction. The clock at the center is still reading 0 and so is yours. What do the others read? (c) How does this relate to the twin paradox?

Section 5

51. Show that for a source moving toward an observer, equation (17) becomes

$$f_{obs} = f_{source}\sqrt{\frac{1 + v/c}{1 - v/c}}$$

52. By what factor would a star's characteristic wavelengths of light be shifted if it were moving away from Earth at $0.9c$?

53. At rest, a light source emits 532 nm light. (a) As it moves along the line connecting it and Earth, observers on Earth see 412 nm. What is the source's velocity (magnitude and direction)? (b) Were it to move in the opposite direction at the same speed, what wavelength would be seen? (c) Were it to circle Earth at the same speed, what wavelength would be seen?

54. The light from galaxy NGC 221 consists of a recognizable spectrum of wavelengths. However, all are shifted toward the shorter-wavelength end of the spectrum. In particular, the calcium "line" ordinarily observed at 396.85 nm is observed at 396.58 nm. Is this galaxy moving toward or away from Earth? At what speed?

55. A space probe has a powerful light beacon that emits 500 nm light in its own rest frame. Relative to Earth, the space probe is moving at $0.8c$. An observer on Earth is viewing the light arriving from the distant beacon and detects a wavelength of 500 nm. Is this possible? Explain.

56. With reckless disregard for safety and the law, you set your high-performance rocket cycle on course to streak through an intersection at top speed. Approaching the intersection, you *observe* green (540 nm) light from the traffic signal. After passing through, you look back to *observe* red (650 nm) light. Actually, the traffic signal never changed color—it didn't have time! What is the top speed of your rocket cycle, and what was the color of the traffic signal (according to an appalled bystander)?

57. For reasons having to do with quantum mechanics, a given kind of atom can emit only certain wavelengths of light. These spectral lines serve as a "fingerprint." For instance, hydrogen's only visible spectral lines are 656, 486, 434, and 410 nm. If spectral lines were of absolutely precise wavelength, they would be very difficult to discern. Fortunately, two factors broaden them: the uncertainty principle and Doppler broadening. Atoms in a gas are in motion, so some light will arrive that was emitted by atoms moving toward the observer and some from atoms moving away. Thus, the light reaching the observer will cover a range of wavelengths. (a) Making the assumption that atoms move no faster than their rms speed—given by $v_{rms} = \sqrt{2k_B T/m}$, where k_B is the Boltzmann constant—obtain a formula for the range of wavelengths in terms of the wavelength λ of the spectral line, the atomic mass m, and the temperature T. (*Note:* $v_{rms} \ll c$.) (b) Evaluate this range for the 656 nm hydrogen spectral line, assuming a temperature of 5×10^4 K.

58. To catch speeders, a police radar gun detects the beat frequency between the signal it emits and that which reflects off a moving vehicle. What would be the beat frequency for an emitted signal of 900 MHz reflected from a car moving at 30 m/s?

Section 6

59. Bob is on Earth. Anna is on a spacecraft moving away from Earth at $0.6c$. At some point in Anna's outward travel, Bob fires a projectile loaded with supplies out to Anna's ship. Relative to Bob, the projectile moves at $0.8c$. (a) How fast does the projectile move relative to Anna? (b) Bob also sends a light signal, "Greetings from Earth," out to Anna's ship. How fast does the light signal move relative to Anna?

60. According to Anna, on Earth, Bob is on a spaceship moving at $0.8c$ toward Earth, and Carl, a little farther out, is on a spaceship moving at $0.9c$ toward Earth. (a) According to Bob, how fast and in what direction is Carl moving relative to himself (Bob)? (b) According to Bob, how fast is Carl moving relative to Earth?

61. Prove that if v and u' are less than c, it is impossible for a speed u greater than c to result from equation (19b). [*Hint:* The product $(c - u')(c - v)$ is positive.]

62. In a particle collider experiment, particle 1 is moving to the right at $0.99c$ and particle 2 to the left at $0.99c$, both relative to the laboratory. What is the relative velocity of the two particles according to (an observer moving with) particle 2?

63. A light beam moves in the xy-plane and has an x-component of velocity of u_x. (a) In terms of u_x and c, what is its y-component? (b) Using equations (20a) and (20b), calculate its velocity components in a frame moving in the x direction at speed $v = u_x$, and comment on your result.

64. A light beam moves at an angle θ with the x-axis as seen from frame S. Using the relativistic velocity

transformation, find the components of its velocity when viewed from frame S'. From these, verify explicitly that its speed is c.

65. You fire a light signal at 60° north of west. (a) Find the velocity components of this signal according to an observer moving eastward relative to you at half the speed of light. From them, determine the magnitude and direction of the light signal's velocity according to this other observer. (b) Find the components according to a different observer, moving westward relative to you at half the speed of light.

66. At $t = 0$, a bright beacon at the origin flashes, sending light uniformly in all directions. Anna is moving at speed v in the $+x$ direction relative to the beacon and passes through the origin at $t = 0$. (a) Show that according to Anna, the only light with a positive x'-component is that which in the beacon's reference frame is within an angle $\theta = \cos^{-1}(v/c)$ of the $+x$-axis. (b) What are the limits of θ as v approaches 0 and as it approaches c? (c) The phenomenon is called the headlight effect. Why?

* 67. Using equations (20), show that

$$\gamma_{u'} = \left(1 - \frac{u_x v}{c^2}\right)\gamma_v \gamma_u$$

Section 7

68. By applying the relativistic velocity transformation to the left side of equation (23) and using the algebraic identity derived in Exercise 67, verify equation (23).

69. What is the ratio of the relativistically correct expression for momentum to the classical expression? Under what condition does the deviation become significant?

70. What are the momentum, energy, and kinetic energy of a proton moving at $0.8c$?

71. What would be the internal energy, kinetic energy, and total energy of a 1 kg block moving at $0.8c$?

72. By how much (in picograms) does the mass of 1 mol of ice at 0°C differ from that of 1 mol of water at 0°C?

73. A spring has a force constant of 18 N/m. If it is compressed 50 cm from its equilibrium length, how much mass will it have gained?

74. A typical household uses 500 kWh of energy in 1 month. How much mass is converted to produce this energy?

75. Determine the momentum of an electron moving (a) at speed 2.4×10^4 m/s (about three times escape velocity) and (b) at speed 2.4×10^8 m/s. (c) In each case, by how much is the classical formula in error?

76. In the collision shown, energy is conserved, because both objects have the same speed and mass after as

before the collision. Since the collision merely reverses the velocities, the final (total) momentum is opposite the initial. Thus, momentum can be conserved only if it is zero.

(a) Using the relativistically correct expression for momentum, show that the total momentum is zero—that momentum is conserved. (Masses are in arbitrary units.)

(b) Using the relativistic velocity transformation, find the four velocities in a frame moving to the right at $0.6c$.

(c) Verify that momentum is conserved in the new frame.

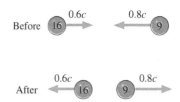

77. Is it possible for the momentum of an object to be mc? If not, why not? If so, under what condition?

78. Show that the relativistic expression for kinetic energy $(\gamma_u - 1)mc^2$ is equivalent to the classical $\frac{1}{2}mu^2$ when $u \ll c$.

79. At Earth's location, the intensity of sunlight is 1.5 kW/m². If no energy escaped Earth, by how much would Earth's mass increase in 1 day?

80. The weight of the Empire State Building is 365 kilotons. Show that the complete conversion of 1 kg of mass would provide sufficient energy to put this rather large object in a low Earth orbit (orbit radius ≅ Earth's radius).

81. Radiant energy from the Sun, approximately 1.5×10 away, arrives at Earth with an intensity of 1.5 kW/m At what rate is mass being converted in the Sun to produce this radiant energy?

82. (a) A high-explosive material employing chemical reactions has an explosive yield of 10^6 J/kg, measured in joules of energy released per kilogram of material. By what fraction does its mass change when it explodes? (b) What is the explosive yield of a material that produces energy via *nuclear* reactions in which its mass decreases by 1 part in 10,000?

83. How fast must an object be moving for its kinetic energy to equal its internal energy?

84. How much work must be done to accelerate an electron (a) from $0.3c$ to $0.6c$ and (b) from $0.6c$ to $0.9c$?

85. An electron accelerated from rest through a potential difference V acquires a speed of $0.9998c$. Find the value of V.

86. What is the momentum of a proton accelerated through 1 gigavolt (GV)?

87. A proton is accelerated from rest through a potential difference of 500 MV. (a) What is its speed? (b) Classical mechanics indicates that quadrupling the potential difference would double the speed. Were a classical analysis valid, what speed would result from a 2000 MV potential difference? (c) What speed actually results?

88. A particle of mass m_0 moves through the lab at 0.6c. Suddenly it explodes into two fragments. Fragment 1, mass $0.66m_0$, moves at 0.8c in the same direction the original particle had been moving. Determine the velocity (magnitude and direction) and mass of fragment 2.

89. The boron-14 nucleus (mass: 14.02266 u) "beta decays," spontaneously becoming an electron (mass: 0.00055 u) and a carbon-14 nucleus (mass: 13.99995 u). What will be the speeds and kinetic energies of the carbon-14 nucleus and the electron? (*Note:* A neutrino is also produced. We consider the case in which its momentum and energy are negligible. Also, because the carbon-14 nucleus is much more massive than the electron, it recoils "slowly"; $\gamma_u \cong 1$.)

90. A 3.000 u object moving to the right through a laboratory at 0.8c collides with a 4.000 u object moving to the left through the laboratory at 0.6c. Afterward, there are two objects, one of which is a 6.000 u mass at rest.
(a) What are the mass and speed of the other object?
(b) Determine the change in kinetic energy in this collision.

91. A 10 kg object is moving to the right at 0.6c. It explodes into two pieces, one of mass m_1 moving left at 0.6c and one of mass m_2 moving right at 0.8c. (a) Find m_1 and m_2. (b) Find the change in kinetic energy in this explosion.

92. Particle 1, of mass m_1, moving at 0.8c relative to the lab, collides head-on with particle 2, of mass m_2, moving at 0.6c relative to the lab. Afterward, there is a single stationary object. Find, in terms of m_1, (a) m_2; (b) the mass of the final stationary object; and (c) the change in kinetic energy in this collision.

93. Consider the collisions of two identical particles, each of mass m_0. In experiment A, a particle moving at 0.9c strikes a stationary particle.

(a) What is the total kinetic energy before the collision?

(b) In experiment B, both particles are moving at a speed u (relative to the lab), directly toward one another. If the total kinetic energy before the collision in experiment B is the same as that in experiment A, what is u?

(c) In both experiments, the particles stick together. Find the mass of the resulting single particle in

each experiment. In which is more of the initial kinetic energy converted to mass?

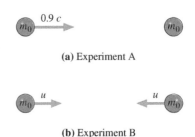

(a) Experiment A

(b) Experiment B

94. A kaon (denoted K^0) is an unstable particle of mass 8.87×10^{-28} kg. One of the means by which it decays is by spontaneous creation of two pions, a π^+ and a π^-. The decay process may be represented as

$$K^0 \to \pi^+ + \pi^-$$

Both the π^+ and π^- have mass 2.49×10^{-28} kg. Suppose that a kaon moving in the $+x$ direction decays by this process, with the π^+ moving off at speed 0.9c and the π^- at 0.8c. (a) What was the speed of the kaon before decay? (b) In what directions do the pions move after the decay?

95. In the frame of reference shown, a stationary particle of mass m_0 explodes into two identical particles of mass m moving in opposite directions at 0.6c. Momentum is obviously conserved in this frame. Verify explicitly that it is conserved in a frame of reference moving to the right at 0.6c.

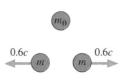

96. Write out the total energy of a collection of interacting massive objects, break each term into internal and kinetic parts, and show that equation (27) follows.

97. Show that $E^2 = p^2c^2 + m^2c^4$ follows from expressions (22) and (24) for momentum and energy in terms of m and u.

Section 8

98. Equation (30) is an approximation correct only if the gravitational time-dilation effect is small. In this exercise, it is also assumed to be small, but we still

allow for a nonuniform gravitational field. We start with (29), based on the Doppler effect in the accelerating frame. Consider two elevations, the lower at r_1 and the upper at $r_1 + dr$. Equation (29) becomes

$$\frac{f(r_1 + dr)}{f(r_1)} = \left(1 - \frac{g(r_1)dr}{c^2}\right)$$

Similarly, if we consider elevations $r_1 + dr$ and $r_1 + 2dr$, we have

$$\frac{f(r_1 + 2dr)}{f(r_1 + dr)} = \left(1 - \frac{g(r_1 + dr)dr}{c^2}\right)$$

We continue the process, incrementing r by dr, until we reach r_2.

$$\frac{f(r_2)}{f(r_2 - dr)} = \left(1 - \frac{g(r_2 - dr)dr}{c^2}\right)$$

Now imagine multiplying the left sides of all the equations and setting the product equal to the product of all the right sides. (a) Argue that the left side of the product is simply $f(r_2)/f(r_1)$. (b) Assuming that the term $g\,dr/c^2$ in each individual equation is very small, so that products of such terms can be ignored, argue that the right side of the product is

$$1 - \frac{1}{c^2}\int g(r)dr$$

(c) Deduce $g(r)$ from Newton's universal law of gravitation, then argue that equation (31) follows from the result, just as (30) does from (29).

99. According to an observer at Earth's equator, by how much would his clock and one on a satellite in geosynchronous orbit differ in one day? (Geosynchronous orbit means an orbit period of one day—always in the same place in the sky.)

100. If it is fundamental to nature that a given mass has a critical radius at which something extraordinary happens (i.e., a black hole forms), we might guess that this radius should depend only on the mass and fundamental constants of nature. Assuming that $r_{critical}$ depends only on M, G, and c, show that dimensional analysis gives the equation for the Schwarzschild radius to within a multiplicative constant.

101. A projectile is a distance r from the center of a heavenly body and is heading directly away. Classically, if the sum of its kinetic and potential energies is positive,

it will escape the gravitational pull of the body, but if negative, it cannot escape. Now imagine that the projectile is a pulse of light of energy E. Since light has no internal energy, E is also the kinetic energy of the light pulse. Suppose that the gravitational potential energy of the light pulse is given by Newton's classical formula, $U = -(GMm/r)$, where M is the mass of the heavenly body and m is an "effective mass" of the light pulse. Assume that this effective mass is given by $m = E/c$.

Show that the critical radius for which light could not escape the gravitational pull of a heavenly body is within a factor of 2 of the Schwarzschild radius given in the chapter. (This kind of "semiclassical" approach to general relativity is sometimes useful but always vague. To be reliable, predictions must be based from beginning to end on the logical, but unfortunately complex, fundamental equations of general relativity.)

102. Suppose particles begin moving in one dimension away from the origin at $t = 0$ with the following velocities: 0, ± 1, ± 2, ± 3 m/s, and so on. (a) After 1 s, how will the velocities of the particles depend on distance from the origin? (b) Now consider an observer on one of the moving particles *not* at the origin. How will the *relative* velocities of the other particles depend on distance from the observer?

Section 9

103. Here we verify the conditions under which t_3' in equation (33) will be negative. (a) Show that $t_3' < 0$ is equivalent to the following:

$$\frac{v}{c} > \frac{u_0}{c}\frac{2}{1 + u_0^2/c^2}$$

(b) By construction, v cannot exceed u_0, for if it did, the information could not catch up with Amy at event 2. Use this to argue that if $u_0 < c$, then t_3' must be positive for whatever value v is allowed to have. (c) Using the fact that $(x - 1)^2 \geq 0$, show that the right side of the expression in part (a) never exceeds 1. This confirms that when $u_0 > c$, v need not exceed c to produce a negative t_3'.

104. From the Lorentz transformation equations, show that if time intervals between two events, Δt and $\Delta t'$, in two frames are of opposite sign, then the events are too far apart in either frame for light to travel from one to the other. Argue that therefore they cannot be causally related.

Section 10

105. (a) Determine the Lorentz transformation matrix giving position and time in frame S' from those in frame S in the classical limit $v \ll c$. (b) Show that it yields equations (1).

106. For the situation given in Exercise 22, find the Lorentz transformation matrix from Bob's frame to Anna's frame, then solve the problem via matrix multiplication.

107. Show that equation (36) follows from the arbitrary four-vector Lorentz transformation equations (35).

108. A 1 kg object moves at $0.8c$ relative to Earth. (a) Calculate the momentum and energy of the object. (b) Determine the Lorentz transformation matrix from Earth's frame to the object's frame. (c) Find the momentum and energy of the object in the new frame via matrix multiplication.

109. From $\mathbf{p} = \gamma_u m\mathbf{u}$ (i.e., $p_x = \gamma_u mu_x$, $p_y = \gamma_u mu_y$, and $p_z = \gamma_u mu_z$), the relativistic velocity transformation (20), and the identity $\gamma_{u'} = (1 - u_x v/c^2)\gamma_v \gamma_u$, show that $p_y' = p_y$ and $p_z' = p_z$.

110. Equations (38) relate momentum and total energy in two frames. Show that they make sense in the nonrelativistic limit.

111. An object of mass $3m_0$ moves to the right at $0.8c$. (a) Calculate its momentum and energy. (b) Using the relativistic velocity transformation, determine its velocity in a new frame of reference moving to the right at $0.5c$, then use this to determine the object's momentum and energy in the new frame. (c) Verify that equations (38) are satisfied.

112. Equations (38) show that the four-momentum of a particle obeys a Lorentz transformation. If we sum momentum and energy over all particles in a system, we see that the *total* momentum and energy also constitute a four-vector. It follows that $(E_{\text{total}}/c)^2 - P_{\text{total}}^2$ is the same quantity in any frame of reference. Depending on what is known, this can be a quicker route to solving problems than writing out momentum and energy conservation equations. In the laboratory frame, a particle of mass m and energy E_i collides with another particle of mass m initially stationary, forming a single object of mass M. (a) Determine the frame of reference where the *after*-collision situation is as simple as possible, then determine the invariant in that frame. (b) Calculate the invariant *before* the collision in the *laboratory* frame in terms of E_i and m. (You will need to use $E_i^2/c^2 - p^2 = m^2c^2$ for the initially moving particle to eliminate its momentum.) Obtain an expression for M in terms of m and E_i. (c) Write out momentum and energy conservation equations in the laboratory frame, using u_i for the speed of the initially moving particle and u_f for the speed of the final combined particle. Show that they give the same result for M in terms of m and E_i. (*Note:* The identity $\gamma_u^2 u^2 = \gamma_u^2 c^2 - c^2$ will be very handy.)

Comprehensive Exercises

*__113.__ Derive the following expressions for the components of acceleration of an object, a_x' and a_y', in frame S' in terms of its components of acceleration and velocity in frame S.

$$a_x' = \frac{a_x}{\gamma_v^3 \left(1 - \dfrac{u_x v}{c^2}\right)^3}$$

$$a_y' = \frac{a_y}{\gamma_v^2 \left(1 - \dfrac{u_x v}{c^2}\right)^2} + \frac{a_x \dfrac{u_y v}{c^2}}{\gamma_v^2 \left(1 - \dfrac{u_x v}{c^2}\right)^3}$$

114. (a) Determine the Lorentz transformation matrix giving position and time in frame S' from those in frame S for the case $v = 0.5c$. (b) If frame S'' moves at $0.5c$ relative to frame S', the Lorentz transformation matrix is the same as the previous one. Find the product of the two matrices, which gives x'' and t'' from x and t. (c) To what single speed does the transformation correspond? Explain this result.

*__115.__ A point charge $+q$ rests halfway between two steady streams of positive charge of equal charge per unit length λ, moving opposite directions and each at $c/3$ relative to point charge. With equal electric forces on the point charge, it would remain at rest. Consider the situation from a frame moving right at $c/3$. (a) Find the charge per unit length of each stream in this frame. (b) Calculate the electric force and the magnetic force on the point charge in this frame, and explain why they must be related the way they are. (Recall that the electric field of a line of charge is $\lambda/2\pi\varepsilon_0 r$, that the magnetic field of a long wire is $\mu_0 I/2\pi r$, and that the magnetic force is $q\mathbf{v} \times \mathbf{B}$. You will also need to relate λ and the current I.)

116. Classically, the net work done on an initially stationary object equals the final kinetic energy of the object. Verify that this also holds relativistically. Consider only one-dimensional motion. It will be helpful to use the expression for p as a function of u in the following:

$$W = \int F\, dx = \int \frac{dp}{dt} dx = \int \frac{dx}{dt} dp = \int u\, dp$$

117. Both classically and relativistically, the force on an object is what causes a time rate of change of its momentum: $F = dp/dt$.

Special Relativity

(a) Using the relativistically correct expression for momentum, show that

$$F = \gamma_u^3 m \frac{du}{dt}$$

(b) Under what condition does the classical equation $F = ma$ hold?

(c) Assuming a constant force and that the speed is zero at $t = 0$, separate t and u, then integrate to show that

$$u = \frac{1}{\sqrt{1 + (Ft/mc)^2}} \frac{F}{m} t$$

(d) Plot u versus t. What happens to the velocity of an object when a constant force is applied for an indefinite length of time?

118. A rocket maintains a constant thrust F, giving it an acceleration of g (i.e., 9.8 m/s^2). (a) If classical physics were valid, how long would it take for the rocket's speed to reach $0.99c$? (b) Using the result of Exercise 117(c), how long will it really take to reach $0.99c$?

119. Exercise 117 gives the speed u of an object accelerated under a constant force. Show that the distance it travels is given by

$$x = \frac{mc^2}{F}\left[\sqrt{1 + \left(\frac{Ft}{mc}\right)^2} - 1\right]$$

120. In Example 5, we noted that Anna could go wherever she wished in as little time as desired by going fast enough to length-contract the distance to an arbitrarily small value. This overlooks a physiological limitation. Accelerations greater than about 30g are fatal, and there are serious concerns about the effects of prolonged accelerations greater than 1g. Here we see how far a person could go under a constant acceleration of 1g, producing a comfortable artificial gravity.

(a) Though traveler Anna accelerates, Bob, being on near-inertial Earth, is a reliable observer and will see less time go by on Anna's clock (dt') than on his own (dt). Thus, $dt' = (1/\gamma_u)dt$, where u is Anna's instantaneous speed relative to Bob. Using the result of Exercise 117(c), with g replacing F/m, substitute for u, then integrate to show that

$$t = \frac{c}{g}\sinh\frac{gt'}{c}$$

(b) How much time goes by for observers on Earth as they "see" Anna age 20 years?

(c) Using the result of Exercise 119, show that when Anna has aged a time t', she is a distance from Earth (according to Earth observers) of

$$x = \frac{c^2}{g}\left(\cosh\frac{gt'}{c} - 1\right)$$

(d) If Anna accelerates away from Earth while aging 20 years and then slows to a stop while aging another 20, how far away from Earth will she end up, and how much time will have passed on Earth?

Computational Exercise

121. In an inertial frame without gravity, the fastest-running clock is a stationary one. In a freely falling frame, it should be a clock accelerating with the frame. All observers agree on the proper time passing on a clock, so observers on Earth should find that the path actually followed by an object/clock that is subject only to gravity is one that maximizes the proper time from starting point to ending point. Here we verify that this is true. Assuming $v \ll c$, regular (speed-dependent) time dilation tells us that the time interval $d\tau$ we see on a moving clock is related to our interval dt on Earth's surface by

$$d\tau = dt\left(1 - \frac{v^2}{c^2}\right)^{1/2} \cong dt\left(1 - \frac{1}{2}\frac{v^2}{c^2}\right)$$

Equation (30) tells us that the time $d\tau$ passing on a clock ticking higher in the gravitational field is larger than the time dt on the surface according to

$$d\tau \cong dt\left(1 - \frac{gH}{c^2}\right)^{-1} \cong dt\left(1 + \frac{gH}{c^2}\right)$$

Taking both effects into account at once, we have

$$d\tau \cong dt\left(1 + \frac{gH}{c^2} - \frac{1}{2}\frac{v^2}{c^2}\right)$$

or

$$d\tau - dt \cong \left(\frac{gH}{c^2} - \frac{1}{2}\frac{v^2}{c^2}\right)dt$$

Adding/integrating these deviations over a finite time interval yields

$$\Delta\tau - \Delta t \cong \int \frac{gH}{c^2}\,dt + \int \frac{-v^2}{2c^2}\,dt$$

This is how much the proper time on the moving object exceeds that on Earth's surface. Were it merely to float above the surface at zero speed, its clock would run faster, outpacing the ground clock. Were it to move at ground level, its time would fall behind a stationary clock. Consider motion described by $H(t) = k(t - t^b)$. No matter what k and b might be, the object would be at ground level at $t = 0$ and $t = 1$, so we can vary these parameters and see what effect it has on the moving clock's proper time, while still getting to the same ending point at the same time. (a) Insert the assumed

$H(t)$ and its derivative $v(t)$ into the given integrals, then carry out the indefinite integration to obtain two functions whose sum gives $\Delta\tau - \Delta t$ as a function of t. (b) Write a program, in which k and b can be easily varied, that will plot the two functions and their sum versus time together on one set of axes, and $H(t)$ and $v(t)$ on another, and that will also print out the total value of $\Delta\tau - \Delta t$ when $t = 1$. Use 9.8 m/s^2 for g. (c) Plot all functions from $t = 0$ to $t = 1$ for the following special cases: $(k, b) = (0, 1)$, $(7, 3)$, $(-7, 3)$, $(20, 4)$, $(1, 20)$, and $(0.2, 20)$. (d) Discuss the "height effect" and "speed effect" for each of the special cases of part (c). (e) From your understanding of classical mechanics, determine what k and b must be for a real particle leaving the ground at $t = 0$ and returning at $t = 1$. Run your program for this case, then vary k and b independently by small amounts. Discuss your findings.

Answers to Selected Exercises

17. 0.14c

21. 43.75 m

23. later, 0.8 m

25. 60 m, 2.67×10^{-7} s

27. $v/c = 0.781$, 1.04×10^{-7} s, 24.375 m

29. 24 m, $v/c = 0.6$

31. 0.0067 s behind

35. 9.8 ps earlier

37. $c/\sqrt{2}$

39. it must; top passes through $(v/c^2)L_0 \cos\theta_0$ earlier

41. 1549 m

43. (a) -100 ns; (b) 141 ns; (c) 100 ns, zero

45. Bob is 60 yr, Anna is 52 yr

47. (a) 32 yr; (b) 32 yr

49. (a) jumps ahead 128 days; (b) 250 ns; (c) behind by same amounts

53. (a) toward, $v/c = 0.25$; (b) 687 nm; (c) 549 nm

55. yes

57. $2\dfrac{\sqrt{3k_BT/m}}{c}\lambda$, 0.15 nm

59. 0.385c, c

63. (a) $\sqrt{c^2 - u_x^2}$; (b) $(0, c)$

65. (a) $(-0.8c, 0.6c)$; (b) $(0, c)$

71. 9×10^{16} J, 6×10^{16} J, 1.5×10^{17} J

73. 2.5×10^{-17} kg

75. (a) 2.19×10^{-26} kg · m/s; (b) 3.64×10^{-22} kg · m/s; (c) 3×10^{-7}% low, 40% low

77. $c/\sqrt{2}$

79. 1.83×10^5 kg/day

81. 4.71×10^9 kg/s

83. $\dfrac{\sqrt{3}}{2}c$

85. 25.1 MV

87. (a) 0.759c; (b) 2.07c; (c) 0.948c

89. $u_e = 0.99971c$, $u_C = -1.62 \times 10^{-3}\,c$, 20.6 MeV, 17.1 keV

91. $m_2 = 6.43$ kg, $m_1 = 1.43$ kg, 1.93×10^{17} J

93. (a) $1.29m_0c^2$; (b) 0.795c; (c) $2.57m_0$, $3.29m_0$, exp. B

99. ~48 μs

105. $\begin{bmatrix} 1 & 0 & 0 & -v/c \\ 0 & 1 & 0 & 0 \\ 0 & 0 & 1 & 0 \\ -v/c & 0 & 0 & 1 \end{bmatrix}$

111. (a) $4m_0c$ and $5m_0c^2$; (b) $\sqrt{3}m_0c$ and $2\sqrt{3}m_0c^2$

115. (a) $\lambda\sqrt{8}/3$ and $5\lambda\sqrt{8}/12$; (b) both $\sqrt{8}q\lambda/24\pi\varepsilon_0 r$

Credits

40: W. N. Colley (U. Virginia) & E. Turner (Princeton), J. A. Tyson (UC Davis), HST, NASA

Bound States: Simple Cases

Chapter Outline

To make quantum mechanics useful in real applications, we must have a way to account for the effects of external forces—the interaction of our object of study with its surroundings. We begin the chapter by adapting the Schrödinger equation to include these effects. Afterward, we study applications to **bound states**. A bound state is one in which a particle's motion is restricted by an external force to a finite region of space. A mass on a spring, subject only to a Hooke's law restoring force, is an example of a bound state. No matter how much energy we give the mass, the spring invariably causes the mass to oscillate between finite extremes of travel, called turning points. A ball rolling over an isolated bump is subject to a force that changes its speed temporarily, but if friction were negligible, the ball would thereafter roll at constant speed indefinitely—it wouldn't be bound. It may seem backward to study the behavior of particles bound by external forces before studying presumably simpler unbound states, but the study of bound states turns out to be the simplest framework for grasping most of the basic ideas of quantum mechanics.

The standard problems we consider may seem oversimplified and unrealistic, and thus of little applicability, but understanding them is crucial for two reasons. First, as in all of science, we must understand the simple to have any hope of understanding the complicated, and much is to be learned about the nature of quantum mechanics by studying the so-called simple cases. Second, most real applications confronting scientists cannot be solved exactly. They are either too complicated mathematically or plagued by incomplete knowledge of the interactions or (most often) both. A simple, tractable model is required, and some of the most frequently used models are the one-dimensional cases we study here.

1 The Schrödinger Equation

We discussed the Schrödinger equation in the absence of external forces:

$$-\frac{\hbar^2}{2m}\frac{\partial^2 \Psi(x,t)}{\partial x^2} = i\hbar\frac{\partial \Psi(x,t)}{\partial t} \tag{1}$$

By substitution, we verified that the plane wave $\Psi(x,t) = Ae^{i(kx-\omega t)}$ is a solution:

$$-\frac{\hbar^2}{2m}(ik)^2 Ae^{i(kx-\omega t)} = i\hbar(-i\omega)Ae^{i(kx-\omega t)}$$

or

$$\frac{\hbar^2 k^2}{2m}\Psi(x,t) = \hbar\omega\Psi(x,t)$$

Using $p = \hbar k$ and $E = \hbar\omega$ and noting that $p^2/2m$ is just another way of writing $\frac{1}{2}mv^2$, this becomes

$$\frac{p^2}{2m}\Psi(x,t) = E\Psi(x,t) \quad \rightarrow \quad \text{KE}\,\Psi(x,t) = E\Psi(x,t)$$

We concluded that the Schrödinger equation is based on energy accounting—without external interactions, the energy E is just kinetic. A plausible way to generalize the equation to include the effects of an external force is merely to tack on the potential energy associated with that force. We learn in classical mechanics that it isn't even *possible* to define a potential energy for *non*conservative forces, such as friction, so our generalization is good only for conservative forces, such as the electrostatic force. Adding potential energy,

$$(\text{KE} + U(x))\,\Psi(x,t) = E\,\Psi(x,t)$$

Thus, we might guess that the appropriate partial differential equation to replace (1) should be

$$-\frac{\hbar^2}{2m}\frac{\partial^2 \Psi(x,t)}{\partial x^2} + U(x)\Psi(x,t) = i\hbar\frac{\partial \Psi(x,t)}{\partial t} \tag{2}$$

Time-dependent Schrödinger equation

[1]This is the general form of the Schrödinger equation, so the "time-dependent" qualifier could be omitted. We include it to help distinguish it from the forthcoming special case: the time-*in*dependent form.

This **time-dependent Schrödinger equation**[1] has passed the experimental test, so we accept it as the correct law obeyed by a matter wave. To determine the behavior of a particle in classical mechanics, we solve $\mathbf{F} = m\,d^2\mathbf{r}/dt^2$ for

$r(t)$, given knowledge of the net external force on the particle. The analogous task in quantum mechanics is to solve the Schrödinger equation for $\Psi(x, t)$, given knowledge of the potential energy $U(x)$.

2 Stationary States

The first step in solving (2) is to use a standard mathematical technique: **separation of variables**. We assume that the wave function may be expressed as a product of a spatial part and a temporal part.

$$\Psi(x, t) = \psi(x)\,\phi(t) \tag{3}$$

Why? For one thing, it allows us to break a differential equation with two independent variables, x and t, into simpler equations for position and time separately. More important, although it does indeed reduce the generality of our solution, we shall see that these "special" solutions are the ones of greatest interest. Inserting (3) into (2) and then factoring out terms constant with respect to the partial derivatives, we have

$$-\frac{\hbar^2}{2m}\phi(t)\frac{\partial^2\psi(x)}{\partial x^2} + U(x)\psi(x)\phi(t) = i\hbar\psi(x)\frac{\partial\phi(t)}{\partial t}$$

The next step in separation of variables is to divide both sides by the product $\psi(x)\phi(t)$.

$$-\frac{\hbar^2}{2m}\frac{1}{\psi(x)}\frac{\partial^2\psi(x)}{\partial x^2} + U(x) = i\hbar\frac{1}{\phi(t)}\frac{\partial\phi(t)}{\partial t} \tag{4}$$

The left side depends solely on position, the right solely on time—the variables are separate. The final step in the process is a simple but subtle deduction. Position and time are both independent variables. For example, the familiar traveling wave on a string is an oscillatory function of position at any given time, but it is also an oscillatory function of time at any given position, so a full description requires both x and t, which take on values independently. Suppose equation (4) holds when $x = x_1$ and $t = t_1$. What about $\{x, t\} = \{x_1, t_2\}$? The left side would not change, *so the right side cannot*, no matter what t_2 might be. In other words, the right side cannot vary with t. Similarly, the left side cannot vary with x. Our subtle deduction: Both sides are constant. Let us use a C for this **separation constant**.

$$-\frac{\hbar^2}{2m}\frac{1}{\psi(x)}\frac{d^2\psi(x)}{dx^2} + U(x) = i\hbar\frac{1}{\phi(t)}\frac{d\phi(t)}{dt} = C \tag{5}$$

In general, the potential energy could be a function of time, $U(x, t)$, and the technique we have used here would fail. The variables would not be separate.

However, we will consider only cases in which the potential energy is time independent. Accordingly, we have two separate, ordinary differential equations, linked together by the separation constant C—one involving the spatial part of the wave function, and the other the temporal. We take them one at a time.

The Temporal Part, ϕ (t)

The "temporal half" of (5) is

$$i\hbar \frac{1}{\phi(t)} \frac{d\phi(t)}{dt} = C \qquad \text{or} \qquad \frac{d\phi(t)}{dt} = \frac{iC}{\hbar} \phi(t) \tag{6}$$

This qualifies as a first-order differential equation because it involves only a first derivative of the function. We treat it like any other constant. We take what will be our usual route of merely presenting the result of the mathematical solution, then moving on to the physics. The solution of (6) is

Temporal part of $\Psi(x, t)$

$$\phi(t) = e^{-i(C/\hbar)t} \tag{7}$$

In one sense, this is a method of solving the differential equation. In fact, it is the physicist's favorite method: Guess, then see if it works. That this function does satisfy equation (6) is left as a quick exercise for the reader. As to the physics, if we use the Euler formula to rewrite it as $e^{-i(C/\hbar)t} = \cos[(C/\hbar)t] - i\sin[(C/\hbar)t]$, we see that each part is a pure sinusoidal function whose frequency ω (the coefficient of t) is $C/\hbar$. A pure *frequency* implies, through the fundamental relationship $E = \hbar\omega$, a pure, well-defined *energy*. Therefore,

$$C = \hbar\omega = E$$

In separating variables, we focus on those solutions whose energy is well defined, and the separation constant is that energy. This claim may seem a bit weak, but as we now see, it fits perfectly into the resolution of one of the most perplexing inconsistencies in classical physics.

According to assumption (3), the total wave function is now

$$\Psi(x,t) = \psi(x)e^{-i(E/\hbar)t} \tag{8}$$

Note that we haven't even begun to consider the particle's interactions with its surroundings through the potential energy $U(x)$, so $\psi(x)$ is still general. Nonetheless, let us calculate the probability density.

$$\Psi^*(x,t)\Psi(x,t) = \left[\psi^*(x)e^{+i(E/\hbar)t}\right]\left[\psi(x)e^{-i(E/\hbar)t}\right] = \psi^*(x)\psi(x) \tag{9}$$

Its time dependence disappears! Probability density is subject to experimental scrutiny, but the wave function itself is not. So we see that for wave functions of form (8), the whereabouts of the "particle" do not change with time in any *observable* way. Accordingly, they are called **stationary states**. This is a pivotal idea in physics. Classically, an electron—a charged *particle*—orbiting in an atom should constantly lose energy in the form of electromagnetic radiation. The atom should be unstable. Quantum mechanically, the electron is not an accelerating charged particle, but rather a stationary "cloud." If its probability density is constant, its charge density is constant, so it *shouldn't* radiate energy—its energy can be a well-defined constant. Quantum mechanics explains the stability of the atom!

The Spatial Part, $\psi(x)$

Turning now to the "spatial half" of equation (5), if we replace C by E and multiply both sides by $\psi(x)$, we obtain the **time-independent Schrödinger equation**.

$$-\frac{\hbar^2}{2m}\frac{d^2\psi(x)}{dx^2} + U(x)\psi(x) = E\psi(x) \tag{10}$$

Time-independent Schrödinger equation

This is as far as we can go without the potential energy, and $U(x)$ is indeed what distinguishes one application from another, just as the net force does classically. Conveniently, the temporal part of the wave function $\phi(t)$ has "absorbed" the i from the time-dependent form (2), leaving only real coefficients in the time-independent form (10). We will refer to $\phi(t)$ when necessary, but we have obtained it once and for all—it is *always* $e^{-(iE/\hbar)t}$—so most of the rest of the chapter we devote to studying the spatial wave functions $\psi(x)$ that follow from considering different potential energies. (*Note:* The spatial wave function $\psi(x)$ is often termed simply "the wave function," as is $\Psi(x, t)$, but the ambiguity rarely causes trouble.) Unfortunately, the functions $U(x)$ for which (10) has a simple solution are few, and this dictates what we regard as a simple case.

3 Physical Conditions: Well-Behaved Functions

Each simple case we consider has its own wave functions $\psi(x)$ describing the particle, but certain physical, as opposed to mathematical, conditions must be met in all cases. For one thing, the total probability of finding the particle must be 1. Perhaps the particle is an electron. Whether or not it has a definite location, it has a definite charge with a strict value—we cannot have half a fundamental charge. The procedure by which we ensure that the wave function gives a unit probability is called **normalization.** Another requirement is that a wave function be **smooth**.

Normalization

To be physically acceptable, a wave function must be normalizable. If the probability per unit distance $|\Psi(x, t)|^2$ is multiplied by a small distance dx and then summed over all space, the result must be 1.

$$\int\limits_{\text{all space}} |\Psi(x,t)|^2 dx = 1 \tag{11}$$

We might liken the probability to a feather pillow: It can be squashed flat, fluffed into a rounded form, or compressed to a small volume, but even though the density and extent may vary, the total amount of feathers is fixed.

One consequence of this condition is that the wave function itself can't diverge, meaning that it can't become infinite. A second consequence, addressed in Exercise 19, is that although the wave function might extend over all of infinite space, it must fall to 0 faster than $|x|^{-1/2}$ as $x \to \pm\infty$; otherwise, probability integral (11) would diverge. (Actually, there is an "exotic" exception to each consequence. See Comprehensive Exercise 73 for an interesting discussion.)

Smoothness

To be physically acceptable, a wave function must be smooth. There are two aspects to smoothness: continuity of the wave function and continuity of its derivative. Never may the wave function itself be discontinuous. Not only would this be contrary to what we expect of wavelike phenomena, but it would also represent a particle of infinite kinetic energy. Figure 1 shows a wave with an abrupt deviation. Near the deviation, it resembles a wave of very short wavelength, which implies very large momentum. If we measured the momentum, we might obtain a very large value. In the extreme limit, where the abrupt deviation becomes a discontinuity, the "short wavelength" becomes zero wavelength, implying *infinite* momentum and kinetic energy. This is physically unacceptable. A different route to the same conclusion is through the mathematical form of the Schrödinger equation itself. Its kinetic energy term, the far-left term in (10), has a second derivative of $\psi(x)$ with respect to position. If the wave function had a discontinuity, its first derivative would be infinite at the point of discontinuity, and its second derivative would be a weird sequence of plus and minus infinities. We simply cannot make physical sense of such a pathological function.

With one exception, the first derivative, or slope, of the wave function must also be continuous. If the first derivative is continuous, the second derivative—and thus the kinetic energy—is finite, which must hold if the potential energy $U(x)$ and total energy E are both finite, for the Schrödinger equation is based on these three energies adding up. The exception arises if we *do* allow the potential energy to jump to infinity at any point along the x-axis, for then the restriction against the kinetic energy being infinite at that point fails. Obviously, infinite potential energy is not completely realistic, but the notion of a solid wall or barrier is a useful one. In confining a particle to some region of

Figure 1 An abrupt jump acts like a very short wavelength.

space, we often imagine that it is confined between "walls" that are stout enough to prevent its escape, no matter how much kinetic energy it has. If we assume that a wall exerts a strong repulsive force—electrostatic, for instance—then the particle encountering the wall will lose kinetic energy rapidly, gaining electrostatic potential energy. The strongest wall would be one where the potential energy abruptly jumps to an arbitrarily large value; a particle of any speed would instantly rebound. In this idealized but useful case of walls of infinite potential energy, the wave function's derivative/slope need not be continuous at the walls. (In fact, though we omit the justification, it *won't* be continuous there.)

4 A Review of Classical Bound States

Before we consider our first simple case of a quantum-mechanical bound particle, let us briefly review the physics of *classical* bound particles. In classical mechanics, we learn that when nonconservative forces are absent, total mechanical energy, $E = KE + U$, is conserved. Plots of energy versus position show this clearly. Figure 2 gives the simple example of a mass on a spring of spring constant κ. The spring's potential energy is $\frac{1}{2}\kappa x^2$, a parabolic plot. The total mechanical energy never varies from whatever value is initially given to the system—it is a horizontal line. The kinetic energy is the "distance" above the potential energy parabola but below the total energy line. These "heights" are labeled for arbitrary values of x and E. Increasing E would increase the amplitude A of the motion, but at any finite E, the mass is bound within the region $-A \leq x \leq +A$.

Now suppose that at the arbitrary x-value shown in Figure 2, the mass is moving to the right. Its kinetic energy is large compared with the potential, but as it moves, potential increases as kinetic decreases—it slows down. When the

Figure 2 Energy versus position for a mass connected to a spring.

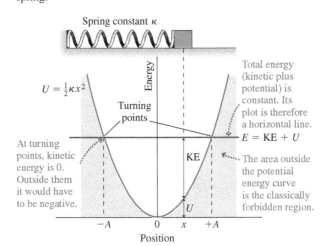

mass reaches the point $x = +A$, the energy is all potential and the kinetic energy is 0. This is a **turning point**. The mass is stationary, but there is a force on it to the left, so it must return toward the origin. It cannot proceed to values of x larger than $+A$. If it did, the potential energy would, of course, be larger, but since the total must be constant, the kinetic energy would have to be negative. Because for any given E, the mass is confined to values of x "inside" the potential energy plot, the shaded region outside is known as the **classically forbidden region**.

Figure 3 shows a different system in which bound states are possible. Atom 1 is fixed at the origin, while atom 2 moves in response to their shared electrostatic interaction. We won't study the origin of this potential energy. We simply note that atoms, due to their dispersed orbiting electrons and compact positive nuclei, do not attract or repel as simple point charges. The potential energy is positive and large for small interatomic separation x, and has a minimum value that is negative, then asymptotically approaches 0 from the negative side as $x \rightarrow \infty$. At small values of x, atom 2 is strongly repelled by atom 1 ($F = -dU/dx > 0$), and at large x, it is attracted ($-dU/dx < 0$). Accordingly, a bound, oscillatory state—a diatomic molecule—is possible, but it depends on the total energy. If the total energy is negative,[2] labeled E_{bound}, atom 2 will be bound, oscillating between turning points x_a and x_b. If the total energy is positive, labeled $E_{unbound}$, atom 2 has only a single turning point. Were atom 2 moving toward atom 1, it would momentarily stop at this point, then move away, never to return. Although the potential energy does increase as x becomes very large, so that atom 2 slows due to the attractive force as it moves off, there is no outer turning point where the potential energy rises to meet the total energy. This situation differs from the simple mass on a spring, for which there is no total energy large enough for the mass to be unbound, because the

[2]Energy may be negative due to the usual freedom to choose zero potential energy. We choose it at $x = \infty$. Although this makes the *potential* energy negative for some values of x, *kinetic* energy is still positive between x_a and x_b, as it must be. The choice conveniently divides bound from unbound states simply according to the sign of the total energy.

Figure 3 Energy versus position for the interatomic force between a large atom fixed at the origin and a small one free to move.

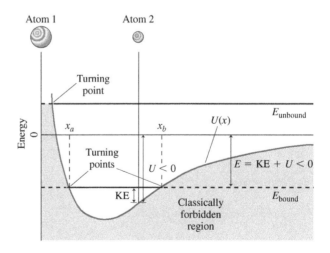

harmonic-oscillator potential energy $\frac{1}{2}\kappa x^2$ increases forever in both directions. In summary, a bound state results when a particle is "caught" between two turning points, where the potential energy rises to meet the total energy.

It is worthwhile to take a brief look ahead. In common with classical bound states, quantum-mechanical bound states have constant total energy, shared between kinetic and potential. But in quantum mechanics, we don't speak of a particle's position at a given time—a classical notion. Rather, we seek the wave function $\Psi(x, t)$. We will soon find that in quantum mechanics, bound states are *standing waves*. Accordingly, just as there are only certain discrete standing waves possible for waves on a string stretched between fixed ends, there are only certain discrete states possible for a matter wave bound by a potential energy. Figure 4 shows the first four possible standing waves obtained in a quantum-mechanical treatment of the harmonic oscillator, plotted on four horizontal axes whose heights correspond to their respective energies. (We will use this way of representing both matter waves and their energies on the same plot throughout the text.) Different energies are possible, but not all energies. The "fundamental" (one antinode) standing wave is the lowest in energy; the "second harmonic" (two antinodes) is next; and so forth.

Besides being restricted to only certain energies, the standing waves of quantum-mechanical bound states differ from the classical case in another intriguing way. Whereas a classical particle is restricted to locations "inside" the potential energy plot, wave functions for quantum-mechanical bound states often extend beyond the classical turning points—into the classically forbidden region. Consequently, there is a probability of finding the particle where, classically, it cannot be!

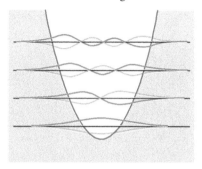

Figure 4 In quantum mechanics, bound states are standing waves.

5 Case 1: Particle in a Box—The Infinite Well

The situation in which the particle-confining potential energy $U(x)$ allows the simplest solution of the time-independent Schrödinger equation is the so-called **particle in a box**, or **infinite well**, in which a particle is confined between insurmountable, infinitely rigid walls. Classically, it would simply bounce back and forth, but our quantum-mechanical solution of the Schrödinger equation will be standing waves.

The forces exerted by ordinary walls of wood or brick are complicated. We choose to confine an electron of charge $q = -e$ between simple "walls" of electrostatic potential energy. Batteries are connected to two parallel plate capacitors, whose centers are separated by a distance L. An electron moves in the region between them, as shown in the center diagram of Figure 5.[3] Small holes allow the electron entry. The batteries' positive terminals are connected to the inside plates; so once inside a capacitor, the electron experiences an electrostatic force back the way it came. (Remember that the force on a *negative* charge is *opposite* the electric field.) Because ideally the electric field is confined to the space within each capacitor, the electron would move at constant speed and kinetic energy everywhere else. Correspondingly, the electrostatic potential and the electron's potential energy are *constants* everywhere except for in the space within each capacitor. Defining the batteries' positive

---

[3]We use the familiar capacitor to discuss potential energy, but in practical applications, such as semiconductor "quantum dots," the electrostatic walls are on the atomic scale, much thinner than any "real" capacitor.

Figure 5 Confining a particle.

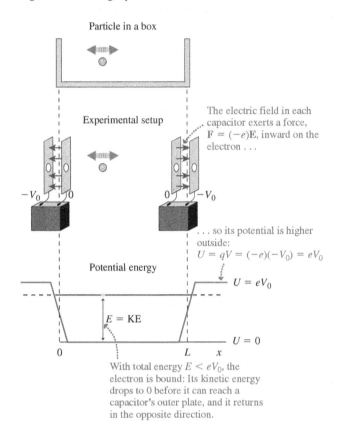

Particle in a box

Experimental setup

The electric field in each capacitor exerts a force, $\mathbf{F} = (-e)\mathbf{E}$, inward on the electron . . .

$-V_0$ 0

0    $-V_0$

. . . so its potential is higher outside:
$U = qV = (-e)(-V_0) = eV_0$

$U = eV_0$

Potential energy

$E = \mathrm{KE}$

$U = 0$

0   L x

With total energy $E < eV_0$, the electron is bound: Its kinetic energy drops to 0 before it can reach a capacitor's outer plate, and it returns in the opposite direction.

terminals as $V = 0$ and their negative terminals as $V = -V_0$, the electron's potential energy ($U = qV$) would be 0 when between the capacitors and $U_0 = eV_0$ when outside the capacitors on either side. The potential energy is shown at the bottom of Figure 5.

Now suppose the electron is between the capacitors, with kinetic energy greater than eV_0. Once it reaches the entry hole of a capacitor, it would slow down, but because its energy is higher than the barrier, it would pass completely through, never to return. On the other hand, if its kinetic energy were less than eV_0, it could not escape. Its kinetic energy would fall to 0 before it reached the capacitor's negative plate, so it would return the way it came. It is such a bound state that we consider.

We will see in Section 6 what difficulties arise in trying to solve the Schrödinger equation without further simplification of our model. Indeed, it cannot be solved "in closed form" (without computational approximation techniques, discussed in Section 10). We arrive at a problem that *is* solvable by making two changes. First, to avoid the complication of addressing the electron's behavior in the small space within each capacitor, we assume the capacitors to be of negligible width, so that the potential changes abruptly. Second, we imagine that the capacitors are charged to infinite potential, that the walls are infinitely high. Exactly why this admittedly unrealistic assumption simplifies the math we defer to Section 6. Here we simply exploit the conclusion: The wave function cannot extend beyond an *infinitely* high potential energy barrier—it must be 0 outside the "walls." With these two changes, the potential energy function of Figure 5 becomes the abruptly changing and infinitely high $U(x)$ shown in Figure 6, the famous **infinite well** potential energy. The reader may be a bit uneasy with this severe, rather unphysical function, but it doesn't really give unphysical results. The results are, in fact, simply the limiting case of those given by more realistic potential energy functions as their shapes approach that of the infinite well.

If, as we have noted, the wave function must be 0 *outside* infinite walls, our solution of the Schrödinger equation now reduces to finding what functions satisfy it in the region *between* the walls and then ensuring that the overall wave function is continuous. In the region between the walls, the potential energy $U(x)$ has been chosen to be 0, so the time-independent Schrödinger equation (10) becomes

$$-\frac{\hbar^2}{2m}\frac{d^2\psi(x)}{dx^2} = E\psi(x)$$

Rearranging, we obtain

$$\frac{d^2\psi(x)}{dx^2} = -\frac{2mE}{\hbar^2}\psi(x) \qquad \text{or} \qquad \frac{d^2\psi(x)}{dx^2} = -k^2\psi(x) \qquad (12)$$

where, for convenience, we have made the definition

$$k \equiv \sqrt{\frac{2mE}{\hbar^2}} \qquad (13)$$

Equation (12) demands that the second derivative of $\psi(x)$ be proportional to $\psi(x)$, and, importantly, the proportionality constant is negative. So what is $\psi(x)$? As we did to obtain solution (7) from (6), we adopt the method of guessing the answer, then checking that it solves the equation. What function has a second derivative that is a negative constant times itself? Any sinusoidal function.[4] Let us try sine. To yield the k^2 in (12), we need a k in the argument.

$$\psi(x) = A \sin kx \qquad (14)$$

The reader is encouraged to plug in and verify that (14) satisfies (12), no matter what may be the value of multiplicative constant A. Other sinusoidal functions, such as cosine, would satisfy (12) mathematically, but one of our *physical* requirements rules them out.

The wave function must be continuous. It is 0 outside, so the wave function inside the well must fall to 0 at the walls. At the left wall, $x = 0$, (14) already satisfies the condition, as $\cos kx$ or any other function that is really just

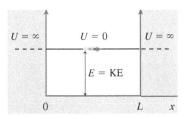

Figure 6 An infinite well.

[4]Recall a similar classical mechanics problem: a mass on a spring of force constant κ. The famous $F = ma$ becomes $-\kappa x = ma$, or $-\kappa x = m\,d^2x/dt^2$. Here too a function is proportional to its second derivative, with a negative proportionality constant, and we know that $x(t)$ must be sinusoidal.

a sine displaced along the *x*-axis would not. But what of the right wall, $x = L$? Demanding that $\psi(x)$ be 0 there gives

$$A \sin kL = 0$$

Now we have a problem: The constant *A* must not be 0. If it were, the entire wave function would be 0. There would be zero probability, no particle. The only way the wave function as a whole can be continuous and yet nonzero is if the following condition holds:

$$kL = n\pi \qquad (15)$$

where *n* is an integer.

With this step we have "solved the Schrödinger equation." That is, we have found the physically acceptable wave function $\psi(x)$ for the given potential energy $U(x)$. But more important, the final, seemingly innocuous condition (15) heralds one of the most fascinating predictions of quantum mechanics, for it implies that the particle's energy is quantized. Using equation (13),

$$\sqrt{\frac{2mE}{\hbar^2}}\, L = n\pi \;\Rightarrow\; E = \frac{n^2\pi^2\hbar^2}{2mL^2}$$

The particle's energy is not arbitrary. *It must be one of these discrete values.* The wave functions have a suspiciously familiar appearance. Inserting $kL = n\pi$ into (14), we obtain for each integer *n*—that is, for each energy—a corresponding wave function.

$$\psi_n(x) = A \sin\frac{n\pi x}{L} \qquad (0 < x < L)$$

The wave functions are of typical standing-wave form. *Quantum mechanically, bound states are standing waves.*

To complete our solution, we ensure that the allowed wave functions are normalized. Whatever may be the value of *n*, the total probability of finding the particle must be 1, and this requirement fixes the value of the arbitrary constant *A*. Inserting our newly found wave function into normalization condition (11), we have

$$\int\limits_{\text{all space}} |\Psi(x,t)|^2 dx = \int\limits_{-\infty}^{+\infty} |\psi(x)|^2 dx = \int\limits_{0}^{L} \left(A \sin\frac{n\pi x}{L}\right)^2 dx = 1$$

Note that, as we will often do, we have used equation (9), which shows that for a stationary state, the wave function's temporal part "drops out" of the probability density. Furthermore, although the spatial part here and in every other case in this chapter is real, we will continue to use $|\psi(x)|^2$ or $\psi^*(x)\psi(x)$ rather than $\psi^2(x)$, so as not to get into bad habits that might cause trouble later. The integral $\int_0^L \sin^2[(n\pi/L)x]\,dx$ equals $L/2$, independent of n, so that

$$A^2 \frac{L}{2} = 1 \quad \Rightarrow \quad A = \sqrt{\frac{2}{L}}$$

Thus, we have the normalized, continuous wave functions representing the allowed states of a particle in an infinite well and their corresponding energies.

$$\psi_n(x) = \begin{cases} \sqrt{\dfrac{2}{L}} \sin \dfrac{n\pi x}{L} & 0 < x < L \\ 0 & x < 0, x > L \end{cases} \qquad E_n = \frac{n^2 \pi^2 \hbar^2}{2mL^2} \qquad (16)$$

Let us look more closely at our results. Figure 7 shows the four lowest-energy wave functions $\psi(x)$ plotted on horizontal axes whose heights are proportional to the respective energies E_n (ratios 1:4:9:16). Because the temporal parts of the wave functions oscillate in time—the reason for the faint inverted wave at each level—the functions are in many ways typical standing waves.[5] In fact, the quantum energy levels may be obtained solely from *classical* standing-wave conditions combined with $p = \hbar k$: Wavelengths of standing waves are given by $\lambda_n = 2L/n$ and wave numbers by $k_n = 2\pi/\lambda = \pi n/L$, so that

$$E = \text{KE} = \frac{p^2}{2m} = \frac{(\hbar k)^2}{2m} = \frac{\hbar^2 \pi^2 n^2}{2mL^2}$$

Figure 8 shows the corresponding probability densities, $|\psi(x)|^2$, and we clearly see one of the hallmarks of standing waves: nodes, where the probability density is 0. But how, we might ask, can the particle get from one place in the well to another if there is no possibility of it ever being found at a point in between? The answer is basic to quantum mechanics. It is a wave, not a particle. We know that a standing wave may be thought of as two waves passing one another in opposite directions, and while bouncing back and forth, they form nodes where the displacement is always 0. As a wave phenomenon, nodes shouldn't surprise us, and we cannot demand that the "particle" behave as a classical particle. In particular, we can't watch it, for the photons we would need to bounce off it would introduce potential energies that we have ignored in our solution of the Schrödinger equation. The assumed simplicity of the situation prevents our having detailed knowledge of the particle's behavior. But this is no weird special case; lack of knowledge of precise whereabouts is a fact in *all* the real situations to which quantum mechanics is applied. We cannot, for example, say exactly what an electron orbiting a nucleus is doing. Given these unavoidable limitations in the microscopic

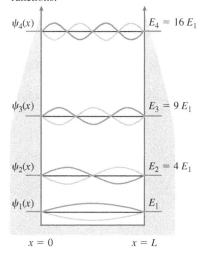

Figure 7 Infinite well wave functions.

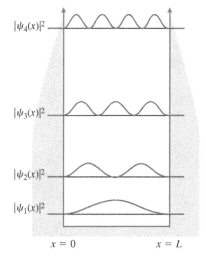

Figure 8 Infinite well probability densities.

[5]Whereas standing waves on a string are periodically flat, quantum-mechanical standing waves never are. Total probability must never vanish. The time-varying function multiplying $\psi(x)$ isn't sine or cosine, as for waves on a string, but rather is $\phi(t) = e^{-i\omega t}$, which is never 0. When Re $\Psi(x, t)$ is 0, Im $\Psi(x, t)$ is maximum, and vice versa. We might visualize a quantum-mechanical standing wave as a sine wave spinning about the x-axis in the Re-Im plane.

world, the predictions of quantum mechanics have succeeded, while those of classical physics have failed. Sight unseen, the "particle" is a wave.

The standing wave of minimum energy is known as the **ground state** and its energy as the **ground-state energy**. It is in the ground state that quantum-mechanical behavior deviates most from the classical expectation. Most important, the kinetic energy is not 0. *A bound particle cannot be stationary.* This would violate the uncertainty principle, for having a position uncertainty comparable to L and a momentum identically 0 is impossible. Another deviation from the classical is that in its ground state, the particle is most likely to be found near the center. Classically, if we were to "turn on the lights" suddenly and catch the particle somewhere in the course of its constant-speed back-and-forth motion, it is equally likely to be found anywhere within the well. On the other hand, the correspondence principle says there should be a limit in which the particle behaves classically. This limit is at the "other end"—large n. Larger n correspond to shorter wavelengths ($\lambda_n = 2L/n$), and the shorter the wavelength, the more particlelike and classical the behavior should be. As we see in Figure 8, the larger the n, the more evenly the probability of finding the particle is spread over the well—the classical expectation.

Before we apply what we have learned, we reiterate that the wave function tells us probabilities of finding the particle at various locations. The integral of the probability density (prob/length) over *all* space is the total probability of 1. So to determine the probability of finding the particle in some restricted region of interest, we simply integrate over that region.

EXAMPLE 1

An electron is confined in an infinite well, in the ground state with an energy of $0.10 \, \text{eV}$. (a) What is the well's length? (b) What is the probability that the electron would be found in the left-hand third of the well? (c) What would be its next higher allowed energy? (d) If the electron's confines were roomier, $L = 1.0 \, \text{mm}$, while its energy remained $0.10 \, \text{eV}$, what would be the probability of finding it in the well's left-hand third, and what would be the minimum possible fractional increase in its energy?

SOLUTION

(a) In the ground state, $n = 1$. Inserting values in energy expression (16), we obtain

$$0.10 \times 1.6 \times 10^{-19} \, \text{J} = \frac{1^2 \pi^2 (1.055 \times 10^{-34} \, \text{J} \cdot \text{s})^2}{2(9.11 \times 10^{-31} \, \text{kg}) L^2} \implies L = 1.94 \, \text{nm}$$

(b) The probability density is $|\psi(x)|^2$.

$$|\psi_n(x)|^2 = \left(\sqrt{\frac{2}{L}} \sin \frac{n\pi x}{L} \right)^2 = \frac{2}{L} \sin^2 \frac{n\pi x}{L}$$

As noted above, we sum this over the region of interest, $x = 0$ to $x = L/3$.

$$\text{probability} = \int \frac{\text{probability}}{\text{length}} \, dx = \int |\psi_n(x)|^2 \, dx = \frac{2}{L} \int_0^{L/3} \sin^2 \left(\frac{n\pi x}{L} \right) dx$$

$$= \frac{2}{L}\left[\frac{x}{2} - L\frac{\sin(2n\pi x/L)}{4n\pi}\right]\Bigg|_0^{L/3} = \frac{2}{L}\left[\frac{L}{6} - L\frac{\sin(2n\pi/3)}{4n\pi}\right]$$

$$= \frac{1}{3} - \frac{1}{2n\pi}\sin\frac{2n\pi}{3}$$

Thus, for an electron in the $n = 1$ state,

$$\text{probability} = \frac{1}{3} - \frac{1}{2\pi}\sin\frac{2\pi}{3} = \frac{1}{3} - 0.137 = 0.196$$

The probability is less than the classical expectation of one-third, and it agrees with the probability density plots of Figure 8. In the ground state, $|\psi(x)|^2$ is largest in the center and smaller near the walls. In fact, the probability of finding the electron in the *center* third must be $1 - 2 \times 0.196 = 0.609$.

(c) The energies are proportional to n^2, so the $n = 2$ state is 0.40 eV, four times the ground-state energy.

(d) To evaluate the integral, we need n.

$$0.10 \times 1.6 \times 10^{-19}\,\text{J} = \frac{n^2\pi^2(1.055 \times 10^{-34}\,\text{J}\cdot\text{s})^2}{2(9.11 \times 10^{-31}\,\text{kg})(0.001\,\text{m})^2} \quad \Rightarrow \quad n = 5.2 \times 10^5$$

We can use our previous result, simply substituting the new value.

$$\text{probability} = \frac{1}{3} - \frac{1}{2(5.2 \times 10^5)\pi}\sin\frac{2(5.2 \times 10^5)\pi}{3}$$

Whatever may be the precise value of n, the probability is essentially one-third.

The smallest possible increase from the nth state would be to $n + 1$. Noting that nothing else changes, so that other factors cancel top and bottom, we have

$$\text{fractional change} = \frac{E_{\text{final}} - E_{\text{initial}}}{E_{\text{initial}}} = \frac{(n + 1)^2 - n^2}{n^2} = \frac{2}{n} + \frac{1}{n^2}$$

Because n is so large, we can ignore the $1/n^2$.

$$\text{fractional change} \cong \frac{2}{n} = \frac{2}{5.2 \times 10^5} \cong 4 \times 10^{-6}$$

Even though a 0.10 eV electron is quite slow by classical standards, we see here that when occupying macroscopic accommodations measured in millimeters, it is a very high energy state quantum-mechanically speaking. Its probability density is a blur—a million nodes and antinodes evenly spread over the box—and its "energy spectrum" would appear continuous.

The famous evidence shown in Figure 9 may help dispel some lingering doubts about quantum-mechanical bound states. Electrons on the surface of a piece of copper are bound within a circular "corral" of roughly 14 nm diameter, formed by 48 iron atoms (the spikes at the perimeter). Though more complicated than our simple one-dimensional cases, the result is qualitatively the

Figure 9 Electron standing wave bound in a quantum corral.

same. We see a clear pattern of concentric antinodes—a two-dimensional standing wave. The image was produced by a scanning tunneling electron microscope. Notably, it represents a probability density, not a wave function, and is the combined result of many electron detections. It isn't watching a given electron.

Let us now take a look at one of the most important characteristics of the quantum well, its discrete energy jumps, and the most conspicuous evidence of these jumps: the distinctive wavelengths of photons they produce.

EXAMPLE 2

Suppose an electron is trapped in a quantum well 5 nm wide with walls that are high enough for the infinite well to be a good approximation. (a) The electron makes a transition down to its ground state from the next-lowest state, giving energy to a photon. What are the photon's energy and wavelength? (b) How would photon wavelengths produced in other transitions compare? Longer? Shorter? Both?

SOLUTION

(a) Energy is conserved. What the electron loses must go to the photon. Thus, the photon energy is the difference between the electron's energies.

$$E_{photon} = \frac{2^2\pi^2\hbar^2}{2mL^2} - \frac{1^2\pi^2\hbar^2}{2mL^2} = \frac{3\pi^2\hbar^2}{2mL^2}$$

$$= \frac{3\pi^2(1.055 \times 10^{-34}\,\text{J}\cdot\text{s})^2}{2(9.11 \times 10^{-31}\,\text{kg})(5 \times 10^{-9}\,\text{m})^2} = 7.23 \times 10^{-21}\,\text{J} = 0.045\,\text{eV}$$

Accordingly,

$$E = \frac{hc}{\lambda} \quad \Rightarrow \quad \lambda = \frac{(3 \times 10^8\,\text{m/s})(6.63 \times 10^{-34}\,\text{J}\cdot\text{s})}{7.23 \times 10^{-21}\,\text{J}} = 27.5\,\mu\text{m}$$

(b) As we see in Figure 7, the energies get farther apart. No two are as close as the ground state and $n = 2$, so transitions between other levels would produce higher-energy, shorter-wavelength photons. The characteristic of having a maximum wavelength would help to distinguish this system from others—the hydrogen atom, for instance, in which higher quantum energy levels actually get closer together. Spectral "fingerprints" are indispensable windows on the inner workings of quantum systems.

REAL-WORLD EXAMPLE THE QUANTUM WELL LASER

Many new optoelectronic devices—such as light sources and their counterpart, light sensors—depend on the precision and adaptability of the electron's discrete energy levels in a quantum well, in conjunction with the properties of semiconducting materials. In a semiconductor, many electrons, called conduction electrons, move about rather freely, much as they do in a conductor, with energies near a level that, for convenience, we define as 0. Ordinarily, their energy cannot drop *below* 0. However, buried at deeper energies are valence electrons that are more tightly bound to the semiconductor atoms. If one of these is missing—known as a *hole*—a conduction electron can drop down to fill the hole, a process depicted in Figure 10a. This is the source of light in the diode laser and the nonlaser light-emitting diode (LED). A typical energy jump down into the hole is about 1.50 eV, which gives a photon wavelength of about 830 nm. Because the conduction electrons are *not* bound in small dimensions, they behave much like classical particles that can take on a continuum of energies, which hampers the establishment of "lasing" action; that is, the production of many photons of essentially identical wavelength.

The quantum well laser embeds an extremely thin layer of one kind of semiconductor between thicker layers of another kind. The interfaces between the materials constitute electrostatic walls, and the thin layer is the quantum well, shown in Figure 10b. Not only does the well make the energy of the upper level in the electron's downward transition more precise, but it also increases the energy going to the photon by the difference between the quantum well's ground state and 0, which can be tuned according to the well width—a very nice feature.

Applying the Physics

Given a 3 nm wide quantum well in Figure 10b, what is the wavelength of the emitted photon?

SOLUTION

The energy of the $n = 1$ state is

$$E_1 = \frac{\pi^2(1.055 \times 10^{-34}\,\text{J} \cdot \text{s})^2}{2(9.11 \times 10^{-31}\,\text{kg})(3 \times 10^{-9}\,\text{m})^2} = 6.7 \times 10^{-21}\,\text{J} = 0.042\,\text{eV}$$

Adding this to the energy difference, 1.50 eV, from the zero level down to the valence level, the new photon energy would be 1.54 eV, or 2.46×10^{-19} J.

$$E = \frac{hc}{\lambda} \quad \Rightarrow \quad \lambda = \frac{(3 \times 10^8\,\text{m/s})(6.63 \times 10^{-34}\,\text{J} \cdot \text{s})}{2.46 \times 10^{-19}\,\text{J}} = 807\,\text{nm}$$

The model we have discussed here shows how characteristics of the quantum well are exploited, but it does oversimplify. In reality, the electrons in the semiconductor, due to their interactions with the semiconducting material, behave as though their mass is smaller, which would increase E_1 and thus the photon energy. Moreover, the holes in the valence states are in the same physical region as the conduction electrons, so they too get trapped in the quantum well and thus also assume quantized energies. In fact, more effort is now going into lasers based not on the quantum well but on the quantum dot (discussed in Progress and Applications) in which electrons are bound in all three dimensions.

Another factor overlooked in our treatment of the quantum well laser is that the well really isn't deep enough for the infinite well energies to be an especially good approximation. What do we do if it isn't infinite?

Figure 10 (a) Conduction electrons dropping down to fill valence holes in a semiconductor, and (b) electrons in precise quantum well states dropping down.

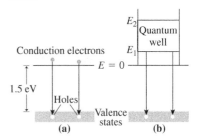

159

Figure 11 Finite well potential energy.

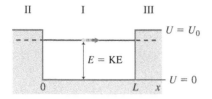

6 Case 2: The Finite Well

Our second simple case, the **finite well**, involves a more realistic potential energy function than the infinite well, so it is a more accurate model in many circumstances. As the name suggests, we simply drop the assumption that the "height" of the potential energy walls is infinite. The price we pay for this, however, is that we can no longer solve the Schrödinger equation completely for the wave functions and energies. At some point, we must resort to computational approximation techniques, known as a numerical solution. But there is much to be learned about basic quantum mechanics from the finite well before facing this difficulty.

First, the potential energy function that defines the finite well, depicted in Figure 11, is given by

$$U(x) = \begin{cases} 0 & 0 < x < L \\ U_0 & x < 0, x > L \end{cases} \tag{17}$$

It still jumps abruptly at the walls but to a value U_0 that is finite. Because it *is* finite, a particle could be given enough total energy to escape ($E > U_0$), but we restrict our attention to bound states where $E < U_0$. On the other hand, though the *potential energy* is finite, the lingering, somewhat unrealistic assumption of an abrupt jump means that the *force, $F = -dU/dx$*, remains infinite at the walls, so a classical particle bouncing off the wall would still do so instantly.

For easier reference, we rewrite the time-independent Schrödinger equation (10) as

$$\frac{d^2\psi(x)}{dx^2} = \frac{2m(U(x) - E)}{\hbar^2}\psi(x) \tag{18}$$

As before, we have a proportionality between $\psi(x)$ and its second derivative, but the proportionality constant varies as we move from one region to another region in which $U(x)$ is a different constant value. The sign of the constant is crucial. In the region between $x = 0$ and $x = L$, where we have defined $U(x)$ to be 0, the constant is negative—$\psi(x)$ and its second derivative must be of opposite sign. Inescapably, this describes an oscillatory, wavelike function. As shown in Figure 12, if $\psi(x)$ is always concave down when positive and concave up when negative, it must continually return to the axis. Thus, when E is greater than the *local* value of U, $\psi(x)$ is oscillatory, as it is inside the infinite well. But now we must also be concerned with the regions outside the well, where $U(x)$ is defined as U_0 and is greater then E. The proportionality constant in these regions is positive, so $\psi(x)$ and its second derivative must be of the *same* sign. Oscillatory functions like sine do not meet this criterion, but exponential functions do. It is left as an exercise

Figure 12 The behavior of a wave function depends on which is larger—E or U.

Here $E > U$, so $U - E$ is negative, and ψ and $d^2\psi/dx^2$ have opposite signs. Because ψ is always concave down when it is positive and concave up when it is negative, it must oscillate in this region.

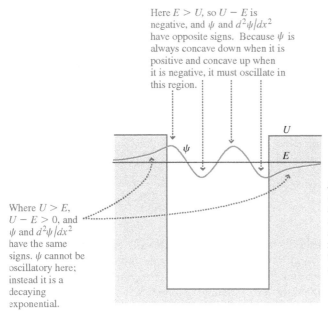

U

ψ

E

Where $U > E$, $U - E > 0$, and ψ and $d^2\psi/dx^2$ have the same signs. ψ cannot be oscillatory here; instead it is a decaying exponential.

Note: Although $\psi(x)$ and $U(x)$ plots are shown together, they are different entities, so neither their relative heights nor their intersections are meaningful.

to verify that when $U(x)$ is simply U_0, equation (18) is satisfied by a function of the form

$$\psi(x) = Ae^{\pm \alpha x} \quad \text{where} \quad \alpha \equiv \sqrt{\frac{2m(U_0 - E)}{\hbar^2}} \qquad (19)$$

But $\psi(x)$ was 0 outside the *infinite* well—why do we worry about these classically forbidden regions now? The answer is that besides the troubling notion of negative kinetic energy (which we return to later), we have no reason to exclude the wave function there. Exponential functions are smooth, and they don't *have to* diverge. So long as we assume $e^{-\alpha x}$ to the right of the well, where $x > 0$, and $e^{+\alpha x}$ on the left, where $x < 0$, both sides would be *decaying* exponentials outside. Thus, they fit our physical conditions outside the well, and in fact, we would never be able to satisfy the smoothness requirement at the well boundaries/walls if we *did* exclude them. Then why *was* $\psi(x)$ zero outside the infinite well? It is a limiting case. The limit $U_0 \to \infty$ implies that $\alpha \to \infty$. The decaying exponentials fall off infinitely rapidly outside an infinite well.

The wave function depicted in Figure 12 clearly shows the difference in character between the region inside the well ($U < E$), where $\psi(x)$ is oscillatory, and those outside ($U > E$), where it exponentially decays. Because it satisfies the Schrödinger equation, does not diverge, and is smooth everywhere, it is physically acceptable. So where does energy *quantization* come in?

Figure 13 shows an acceptable finite well standing wave with its "exponential tails" in the classically forbidden region, while above and below it are *mathematical* solutions of the Schrödinger equation for slightly higher and lower energies. As we know, solutions inside the well are sinusoidal, such as $\sin kx$. But from equation (13), the wave number k is $\sqrt{2mE}/\hbar$, so a

Figure 13 Unless the energy is just right, a solution of the Schrödinger equation will diverge at infinity.

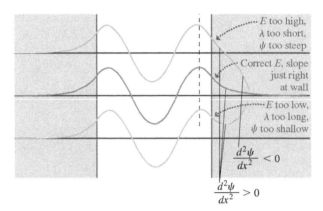

higher E implies a shorter wavelength. At the left wall, each of the three functions is an exponential smoothly meeting a sinusoidal function, but their slightly different wavelengths cause them to be progressively more out of step as they approach the right wall. The middle one hits the wall at just the right angle to join smoothly with a simple *decaying* exponential. Mathematically, an exponential that increases with x is also a solution, as the $\pm$ in equation (19) tells us, and the higher and lower energies, hitting at the wrong angle, can be made smooth only by adding such a function. This increasing exponential causes $\psi(x)$ to diverge as $x \to \infty$, so these solutions are physically unacceptable. Although these "bad" solutions do obey the Schrödinger equation in the classically forbidden region—their second derivatives are always the same sign as $\psi(x)$—their curvatures are just wrong. We could nail down $\psi(x)$ on the *right* side, but then the *left* side would misbehave. In fact, there is no way around the problem. Wave functions of only certain energies can satisfy the smoothness conditions without diverging at one end or both. Energy is quantized.

At this point, those interested in a detailed solution of the finite well to the point of obtaining the energy quantization condition should refer to A Closer Look: Solving the Finite Well.

A Closer Look ## Solving the Finite Well

The potential energy given in equation (17) and Figure 11 divides our one-dimensional space into three distinct regions: region I, $0 < x < L$, where $U(x)$ is, by definition, 0; region II, $x < 0$, where $U(x)$ is the constant U_0; and region III, $x > L$, where $U(x)$ is also U_0. When the potential energy changes abruptly from one region to another, we solve the Schrödinger equation for $\psi(x)$ piecewise, meaning independently in each region. Then, by adjusting the arbitrary constants accompanying each $\psi(x)$, we ensure that the wave function, as a whole, obeys the physical requirements of smoothness and normalization. We begin our methodical approach with region I.

Region I, 0 < x < L

In equation (12), we already have the Schrödinger equation for this region of zero potential energy.

$$\frac{d^2\psi(x)}{dx^2} = -k^2\psi(x) \qquad \text{where} \qquad k \equiv \sqrt{\frac{2mE}{\hbar^2}}$$

Previously, we argued that $\sin kx$ satisfies this differential equation and that it fits the requirement of being 0 at the left wall, matching the zero wave function outside the well. But in the finite well case, the wave function is *not* 0 outside the well, so $\sin kx$ alone cannot be correct. A more general solution of such a second-order (involving the second derivative) differential equation will have two arbitrary constants, essentially constants of integration. It is common to express these constants as multiplicative coefficients of two independent functions that are summed. The general solution that goes along with these words is

$$\psi(x) = A \sin(kx) + B \cos(kx)$$

Rather than knowing the mathematical reasons for why this should be the general solution of (12), it is much more important for our purposes simply to be confident that it *is* a solution, no matter what the values of arbitrary constants A and B might be. Verification is left as an exercise. This function is certainly smooth, and it diverges nowhere, so it obeys our physical requirements. But to be certain that the wave function for all space is similarly well behaved, we must consider the other regions.

Region II, x < 0

Here, $U(x) = U_0$, so the time-independent Schrödinger equation (18) becomes

$$\frac{d^2\psi(x)}{dx^2} = \frac{2m(U_0 - E)}{\hbar^2}\psi(x)$$

Or, rearranging

$$\frac{d^2\psi(x)}{dx^2} = \alpha^2\psi(x) \quad \text{where} \quad \alpha = \sqrt{\frac{2m(U_0 - E)}{\hbar^2}} \quad (20)$$

By construction $U_0 > E$, so the proportionality constant between $\psi(x)$ and its second derivative is now positive, which implies an exponential function. There are actually two such functions, differing by a sign in the argument, and the general solution is the sum, each multiplied by an arbitrary multiplicative constant.

$$\psi(x) = Ce^{+\alpha x} + De^{-\alpha x}$$

Sine and cosine are physically acceptable in their region, region I. Are these exponentials physically acceptable in region II? Both are smooth, but no matter what the value of U_0, $e^{-\alpha x}$ diverges as $x \to -\infty$. Therefore, although it is correct mathematically, the requirement that the wave function be normalizable makes this term physically unacceptable. *D must be 0.* Note that we have no similar reason to throw out $Ce^{+\alpha x}$, for though it does diverge as $x \to +\infty$, region II covers only negative values of x, where this function is never infinite.

Region III, x > L

Because $U(x)$ is the same, the mathematical solution of the Schrödinger equation is the same here as in region II. Thus,

$$\psi(x) = Fe^{+\alpha x} + Ge^{-\alpha x}$$

But now the physically unacceptable term is $e^{+\alpha x}$, which diverges as $x \to +\infty$ for any value of U_0. F must be 0.

Altogether, we have

$$\psi(x) = \begin{cases} Ce^{+\alpha x} & x < 0 \\ A\sin(kx) + B\cos(kx) & 0 < x < L \quad (21) \\ Ge^{-\alpha x} & x > L \end{cases}$$

where

$$k \equiv \sqrt{\frac{2mE}{\hbar^2}} \quad \text{and} \quad \alpha \equiv \sqrt{\frac{2m(U_0 - E)}{\hbar^2}}$$

Having thrown out divergent terms, our $\psi(x)$ is normalizable, and its pieces are *separately* smooth. All that remains is to ensure that they obey the smoothness requirements at the boundaries where the regions meet. Regions II and I meet at $x = 0$, and regions I and III meet at $x = L$. Smoothness requires that $\psi(x)$ and its derivative be continuous at these two boundaries, which gives us four conditions. (In the infinite well, we had only two—continuity of $\psi(x)$ at the boundaries—because the condition on the derivative doesn't apply when $U(x)$ is infinite, as noted in Section 3.)

$\psi(x)$ **continuous at $x = 0$:** $\psi_{\text{II}}(0) = \psi_{\text{I}}(0)$

$$Ce^{+\alpha 0} = A\sin(k0) + B\cos(k0) \Rightarrow \boxed{C = B}$$

$$\frac{d\psi(x)}{dx} \text{ continuous at } x = 0: \frac{d\psi_{\text{II}}}{dx}\bigg|_{x=0} = \frac{d\psi_{\text{I}}}{dx}\bigg|_{x=0}$$

$$\alpha Ce^{+\alpha 0} = kA\cos(k0) - kB\sin(k0) \Rightarrow \boxed{\alpha C = kA}$$

$\psi(x)$ **continuous at $x = L$:** $\psi_{\text{I}}(L) = \psi_{\text{III}}(L)$

$$\boxed{A\sin(kL) + B\cos(kL) = Ge^{-\alpha L}}$$

$$\frac{d\psi(x)}{dx} \text{ continuous at } x = L: \frac{d\psi_{\text{I}}}{dx}\bigg|_{x=L} = \frac{d\psi_{\text{III}}}{dx}\bigg|_{x=L}$$

$$\boxed{kA\cos(kL) - kB\sin(kL) = -\alpha Ge^{-\alpha L}}$$

Although it certainly isn't obvious yet, these four conditions lead to the same qualitative conclusion as the continuity conditions did for the infinite well: quantization of the particle's energy. Showing it involves some algebraic gymnastics.

From the first two boxed results, we have $A = \alpha C/k$ and $B = C$. Inserting these in the last two results gives

$$\frac{\alpha}{k}C\sin(kL) + C\cos(kL) = Ge^{-\alpha L}$$

$$k\frac{\alpha}{k}C\cos(kL) - kC\sin(kL) = -\alpha Ge^{-\alpha L}$$

Dividing the last equation by $-\alpha$, the right sides become equal. Thus,

$$\frac{\alpha}{k}C\sin(kL) + C\cos(kL) = -C\cos(kL) + \frac{k}{\alpha}C\sin(kL)$$

Finally, the remaining arbitrary constant C cancels, and dividing both sides by $\sin kL$ and rearranging a bit, we have

$$2\cot kL = \frac{k}{\alpha} - \frac{\alpha}{k} \qquad (22)$$

Although not very attractive, this is, in fact, an energy quantization condition. From equations (13) and (20), we know that k and α depend on E and U_0, and for a given well depth U_0, equation (22) holds for only certain discrete values of E.

Unfortunately, this is where our solution without approximation ends, for it is a so-called transcendental equation and cannot be solved by pencil-and-paper techniques. One revealing limit can be seen fairly easily, however. The limit $U_0 \rightarrow \infty$ implies that $\alpha \rightarrow \infty$, and equation (22) then becomes $\cot kL = -\infty$. This, in turn, requires that $kL = n\pi$, which is precisely condition (15) from the infinite well. The infinite well is indeed a limiting case of the finite well.

Graphing is one way to see how equation (22) implies energy quantization. It is left as an exercise to show that after inserting the definitions of k and α from equations (13) and (20) and carrying out some algebra, we can at least isolate U_0 in equation (22):

$$U_0 = \begin{cases} \dfrac{\hbar^2 k^2}{2m}\sec^2\dfrac{kL}{2} & (n-1)\pi < kL < n\pi \quad n = 1, 3, 5, \ldots \\[2ex] \dfrac{\hbar^2 k^2}{2m}\csc^2\dfrac{kL}{2} & (n-1)\pi < kL < n\pi \quad n = 2, 4, 6, \ldots \end{cases}$$

$$(23)$$

Figure 14 plots the right side of (23) as a function of k. A plot of the left side would simply be a horizontal line at U_0, the depth of the well, so we see that allowed values of k are intersections of the right side plot with a horizontal well depth line. *Of primary importance is that they cross at only certain points*—equation (23) holds for only certain discrete values of k, with corresponding discrete values of E ($\equiv \hbar^2 k^2/2m$). A representative U_0 line is shown. Intersecting four curves, it represents a potential well with four allowed values of k, and so four energy levels. Apparently, even the shallowest U_0 line would intersect the leftmost curve—a finite well always has at least one bound state, one standing wave. As the potential well becomes deeper, the U_0 line would intersect more curves, and the number of allowed values of k and E would increase; the well would "hold" more bound states. However, the number of discrete energy levels is finite for any finite U_0. See Exercises 42 and 48 for further investigation of quantization condition (22) and Figure 14. Finally, without exact values for E, and thus k and α, we cannot obtain exact wave functions, but it is possible to go further than equation (21), eliminating all but one arbitrary constant, which multiplies the whole wave function and thus allows it to be normalized. See Exercise 46.

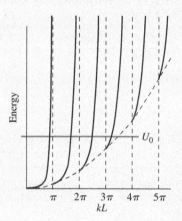

Figure 14 Allowed wave numbers in the finite well: intersections of curves with horizontal well-depth line.

Let us now compare the finite and infinite wells. Figure 15 shows allowed wave functions and probability densities for both wells, where, as usual, each horizontal axis is at a height proportional to that state's energy. Because all bound-state situations involve standing waves, certain characteristics are the same: Energy is quantized, and there is a ground state of minimum total energy in which the kinetic energy is not 0—a "fundamental" standing wave with some maximum wavelength limited by the well's width. But what of the differences?

Figure 15 Wave functions, probability densities, and energies in the finite and infinite wells.

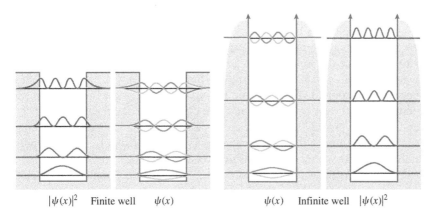

$|\psi(x)|^2$ Finite well $\psi(x)$ $\psi(x)$ Infinite well $|\psi(x)|^2$

Perhaps the most remarkable difference is that finite well wave functions penetrate the classically forbidden region. Although exponentially decaying, they are not 0, so there is a probability of finding the particle outside the well. In these regions, the total energy E is less than the potential U_0. Apparently, the kinetic energy is negative. To a classical physicist, this would be nonsense.

The measure of how far $\psi(x)$ extends into the classically forbidden region is the parameter α. Using an absolute value on x to handle either side, the exponentially decaying wave function outside the well has the form

$$\psi(x) \propto e^{-\alpha|x|}$$

The exponential decays by a fraction $1/e$ at the point where $\alpha|x| = 1$, corresponding to a distance from the wall of $|x| = 1/\alpha$. This distance is known as the **penetration depth** and is given the symbol δ.

$$\delta \equiv \frac{1}{\alpha} = \frac{\hbar}{\sqrt{2m(U_0 - E)}} \tag{24}$$

Penetration depth

This says that the penetration should become deeper as the energy E nears the value of the confining potential U_0, which Figure 15 bears out.

On hearing that a particle may be found where it "cannot be," with negative kinetic energy, many students hunger for proof. Although tunneling phenomena provide unmistakable evidence of matter waves passing through classically forbidden regions, actually detecting a particle with negative kinetic energy is problematic. Position and momentum can't be determined simultaneously. To detect a particle in the classically forbidden region, the experiment would need a position uncertainty no larger than $\sim\delta$, the interval in which the probability is significant. (We wouldn't want our experiment to have a much larger uncertainty—certainty not comparable to L—for we might then be detecting a particle actually *inside* the well.) This very experiment would introduce a momentum uncertainty no *smaller* than $\sim\hbar/\delta$. Because KE $= p^2/2m$, this would imply kinetic energy uncertainty no smaller than $\sim\hbar^2/2m\delta^2$. But according to (24), this in turn is $U_0 - E$, or the magnitude of the (negative) kinetic energy. Thus, no experiment could be certain that the particle it finds has negative kinetic energy.

Furthermore, we must be careful in interpreting the penetration of the classically forbidden region. We cannot conclude that a particle is constantly passing outside the well and then going back inside. Once outside, where the potential energy doesn't change and the force is thus 0, what reason would it have to turn around? More to the point, we can't watch a quantum-mechanical particle undisturbed anyway. We must be content with the meager knowledge that there is a probability of finding the particle outside the well *if* an attempt were made to find it there. If no attempt is made, we simply have an undisturbed standing wave that happens to extend beyond the walls.

Matter wave penetration into the classically forbidden region has an electromagnetic analog. When light waves undergo total internal reflection at an interface between two media, no sinusoidal wave propagates into the second medium. All energy is reflected. But there is an oscillating electromagnetic field that decays exponentially with distance from the interface. Furthermore, if the second medium is thin enough that the field doesn't decay too much within, a significant amount of light intensity will get through. If light waves can do this, it shouldn't surprise us that matter waves might be able to escape through a thin wall. This is the phenomenon of quantum-mechanical tunneling.

Related to penetration of the classically forbidden region is another important distinction between the finite and infinite wells. As Figure 15 shows, the energy levels in a finite well are lower than those of an infinite well of equal width. This is true simply because the wave functions in the finite well do *not* stop abruptly at the walls. We noted previously that the penetration depth is greatest for the highest energy, and to meet smoothly such a gradually sloping exponential outside, the wave functions *inside* must be nearly horizontal at the wall. As we see, this implies a longer wavelength inside the well than for the corresponding infinite well function, and so a smaller k and E. At the other extreme, in the ground state, the penetration of the finite well's classically forbidden region is small enough that the wave function inside must already be nearly 0 at the wall, so its wavelength is only slightly longer than in the infinite well ground state, and its energy only slightly lower.

7 Case 3: The Simple Harmonic Oscillator

Of our simple cases, the harmonic oscillator is the most realistic. Once again, the potential energy defines the problem. The harmonic oscillator potential energy is $U(x) = \frac{1}{2}\kappa x^2$, where κ is the spring constant, as depicted in Figure 16. This case is more realistic because $U(x)$ is a continuous function. Moreover, it is a good approximation of the actual potential energy whenever particles undergo small oscillations about an equilibrium position. In the immediate vicinity of a local minimum, all continuous potential energy functions "look" parabolic; that is, there is a parabola that closely approximates the function about its local minimum. The bond between two atoms in a diatomic molecule is a

Figure 16 Classical oscillator: mass on a spring.

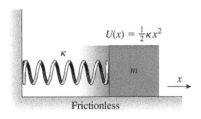

$U(x) = \frac{1}{2}\kappa x^2$

κ

m

x

Frictionless

good example. Figure 17 shows the potential energy shared by two atoms in a diatomic molecule, plotted versus their separation x. The force is strongly repulsive (large slope) for small separations and weakly attractive (small slope) at large separations, but in the immediate vicinity of the equilibrium separation x_0, $U(x)$ is nearly parabolic. Therefore, the lowest energy vibrations about the stable equilibrium point will be essentially those of a simple harmonic oscillator.

Inserting the harmonic oscillator potential energy, the time-independent Schrödinger equation is

$$-\frac{\hbar^2}{2m}\frac{d^2\psi(x)}{dx^2} + \frac{1}{2}\kappa x^2\psi(x) = E\psi(x) \qquad (25)$$

This is one of the few cases that can be solved exactly—without numerical methods—for the wave functions and corresponding quantized energies. Unfortunately, it is still rather complicated. We leave the exact, methodical solution to a higher-level course, but the arguments that energy should be quantized are similar to those for the finite well. In that case, requiring smoothness at the points where $U(x)$ jumps would demand that, for almost all values of E, we include in the wave function $\psi(x)$ exponentials that diverge as $|x| \to \infty$. For only certain, discrete values of E does $\psi(x)$ have a simple decay to 0 outside. The

Figure 17 For small oscillations about a point of stable equilibrium, all potential energies resemble a parabola—a simple harmonic oscillator.

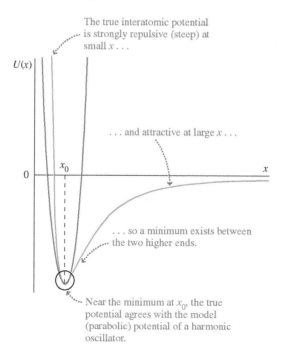

The true interatomic potential is strongly repulsive (steep) at small x . . .

. . . and attractive at large x . . .

$U(x)$

0

x_0

x

. . . so a minimum exists between the two higher ends.

Near the minimum at x_0, the true potential agrees with the model (parabolic) potential of a harmonic oscillator.

same is true here, except that starting with a nice, smooth potential energy in the first place, the mathematical solutions are automatically smooth. Still, for only certain E values is the curvature outside just right so that they settle down to 0 at both extremes, and these are the quantized energies. (See Section 10 for a discussion of a simple computer technique that demonstrates these behaviors.)

Although we won't solve the Schrödinger equation for the oscillator case, we gain a bit more experience with it by turning the question around. Rather than solving (25) for $\psi(x)$, suppose we find a function of a certain form that works. How far can we go with it?

EXAMPLE 3

For a simple harmonic oscillator of spring constant κ and mass m, one solution of the Schrödinger equation is of the form $\psi(x) = Ae^{-ax^2}$, a Gaussian centered at the origin. Determine the energy and the properly normalized wave function in this state.

SOLUTION

The given $\psi(x)$ must be a solution of (25).

$$-\frac{\hbar^2}{2m}\frac{d^2Ae^{-ax^2}}{dx^2} + \frac{1}{2}\kappa x^2 Ae^{-ax^2} = EAe^{-ax^2}$$

The multiplicative constant cancels. Carrying out the differentiation,

$$-\frac{\hbar^2}{2m}(-2a + 4a^2x^2)e^{-ax^2} + \frac{1}{2}\kappa x^2 e^{-ax^2} = Ee^{-ax^2}$$

The exponential now also cancels, and after rearranging a bit, we have

$$\left(\frac{\hbar^2 a}{m} - E\right) - \left(\frac{2\hbar^2 a^2}{m} - \frac{1}{2}\kappa\right)x^2 = 0$$

This can be made to hold for all values of x by adjusting a so that the coefficient of x^2 is 0. This, in turn, tells us E, because the term in parentheses on the far left must also be 0. Note that it is no accident that the conditions to be met are fairly simple. Were the function not actually a solution, we would have quite a mess at this point.

$$\frac{2\hbar^2 a^2}{m} = \frac{1}{2}\kappa \implies a = \frac{\sqrt{m\kappa}}{2\hbar} \qquad \text{so that} \qquad E = \frac{\hbar^2 a}{m} = \frac{\hbar}{2}\sqrt{\frac{\kappa}{m}}$$

To properly normalize the wave function, we calculate the total probability.

$$\int_{-\infty}^{+\infty} |\psi(x)|^2\, dx = \int_{-\infty}^{+\infty} (Ae^{-ax^2})^2\, dx = A^2 \int_{-\infty}^{+\infty} e^{-2ax^2}\, dx = A^2 \sqrt{\frac{\pi}{2a}}$$

The integral table has been used to evaluate the **Gaussian integral**. Setting this equal to 1, we obtain the normalization constant.

$$A = \left(\frac{2a}{\pi}\right)^{1/4} = \left(\frac{2\sqrt{m\kappa}/2\hbar}{\pi}\right)^{1/4} = \left(\frac{m\kappa}{\pi^2\hbar^2}\right)^{1/8}$$

Thus,

$$E = \frac{\hbar}{2}\sqrt{\frac{\kappa}{m}} \qquad \text{and} \qquad \psi(x) = \left(\frac{m\kappa}{\pi^2\hbar^2}\right)^{1/8} e^{-(\sqrt{m\kappa}/2\hbar)x^2}$$

The rigorous solution of (25) shows that the allowed energies of the harmonic oscillator are given by

$$E = (n + \tfrac{1}{2})\hbar\omega_0 \quad (n = 0, 1, 2, 3, \dots) \quad \text{where } \omega_0 \equiv \sqrt{\frac{\kappa}{m}} \quad (26)$$

Harmonic oscillator energies

Note that the energies are equally spaced, an important characteristic of many oscillating systems.[6] (Exercise 53 obtains a very close result by a simplified, yet instructive, approach.) For each energy, there is a unique wave function, several of which are given in Table 1 Each is the product of a normalization constant, a Gaussian factor, and one of a set of related functions known as the Hermite polynomials, given the symbol $H_n(bx)$. From the table and equation (26), we see that the simple Gaussian considered in the example is the ground state.

Several wave functions and probability densities are plotted on the energy-level diagram of Figure 18. Because the potential energy "walls" aren't infinite, all wave functions penetrate into the classically forbidden region. Also, as in the infinite and finite wells, an oscillator in its ground state is most likely to be found at the center. Classically, an oscillator is most likely to be found where its speed is smallest—at the extremes of its travel. But once again, we see that as the particle energy becomes large, the predictions of quantum mechanics and those of classical mechanics converge. For large n, the probability density is largest near the classical turning points.

Figure 18 Wave functions, probability densities, and energies of a harmonic oscillator.

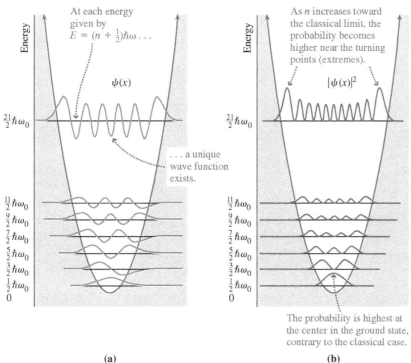

(a)

(b)

The probability is highest at the center in the ground state, contrary to the classical case.

TABLE 1 Harmonic oscillator solutions

n	$\psi_n(x)$
0	$\left(\dfrac{b}{\sqrt{\pi}}\right)^{1/2} e^{-\frac{1}{2}b^2x^2}$
1	$\left(\dfrac{b}{2\sqrt{\pi}}\right)^{1/2} (2bx)e^{-\frac{1}{2}b^2x^2}$
2	$\left(\dfrac{b}{8\sqrt{\pi}}\right)^{1/2} (4b^2x^2 - 2)e^{-\frac{1}{2}b^2x^2}$
3	$\left(\dfrac{b}{48\sqrt{\pi}}\right)^{1/2} (8b^3x^3 - 12bx)e^{-\frac{1}{2}b^2x^2}$
n	$\left(\dfrac{b}{2^n n! \sqrt{\pi}}\right)^{1/2} H_n(bx)e^{-\frac{1}{2}b^2x^2}$

Note: $b \equiv (m\kappa/\hbar^2)^{1/4}$

[6]That n is allowed to be 0 is not cause for alarm. It doesn't correspond to zero *kinetic* energy, so it doesn't violate the uncertainty principle. We could equivalently say $E_n = \left(n - \dfrac{1}{2}\right)\hbar\omega_0$, with n being any positive integer. Also, ω_0 is the angular frequency of the classical harmonic oscillator, *not* a wave function frequency, as in $e^{-i\omega t}$.

REAL-WORLD EXAMPLE THERMAL BEHAVIOR OF A DIATOMIC GAS

In introductory thermodynamics, we learn that different kinds of gases have different molar heat capacities. Monatomic gases have one value, essentially independent of the element, while diatomic gases seem to cluster around a few different values. Theoretical arguments say that these values correspond to translational motion of the molecule as a whole, rotation of the molecule, and vibration due to the interatomic "spring." For the common diatomic gases N_2, O_2, and H_2, the actual values at room temperature agree quite well with the arguments—but only if the atoms don't vibrate.

The answer to this classically puzzling situation is that oscillator energies are quantized. In collisions, translational and vibrational energy can be exchanged, and if there were more energy in translation than in vibration, we might expect the exchange to tend to equalize them. However, a quantum oscillator cannot drop below its ground state, and if the translational energy is insufficient to bump it up to the next allowed energy, its vibrational energy will never change. Heat capacity is a change in energy per unit change in temperature. If over some range of temperatures the oscillators never budge from their ground states, vibrational motion will contribute nothing to the heat capacity.

Before taking a quantitative look, we address a rather minor point here, but one that we will use in a more general form later: When *two* particles share a mutual force but neither is fixed, the relative motion can be analyzed as though one particle is fixed (effectively infinite mass) while the other moves about it under the influence of the mutual force. We need only use the proper effective mass for the moving particle. When the particles are *equal* mass, this "reduced mass" is half the mass of either particle. (The more general case is discussed in Comprehensive Exercise 7.80.) Now let us explain the lack of vibration in a diatomic molecule.

Applying the Physics

The effective spring constant of the H_2 molecule is 573 N/m. Should vibrational energy contribute to hydrogen's heat capacity at room temperature?

SOLUTION

According to equation (26), allowed oscillator energies are separated by $\hbar\omega_0$. Using a reduced mass of half the hydrogen mass, the classical angular frequency of vibration is

$$\omega_0 = \sqrt{\frac{\kappa}{m}} = \sqrt{\frac{573 \text{ N/m}}{\frac{1}{2} \times 1.67 \times 10^{-27} \text{ kg}}} = 8.28 \times 10^{14} \text{ rad/s}$$

Thus, to jump from one vibrational state to another requires an energy input of

$$\Delta E = (1.055 \times 10^{-34} \text{ J} \cdot \text{s})(8.28 \times 10^{14} \text{ rad/s}) = 8.74 \times 10^{-20} \text{ J}$$

The average translational kinetic energy of a gas particle is $\frac{3}{2}k_B T$, where k_B is the Boltzmann constant. At a room temperature of 300 K, this is

$$\frac{1}{2}(1.38 \times 10^{-23} \text{ J/K})(300 \text{ K}) = 6.2 \times 10^{-21} \text{ J}$$

As we see, the energy needed for the vibrational jump is more than 10 times what translational energy can provide. Crude though this estimate may seem, it is no coincidence that hydrogen's heat capacity, which is fairly constant around room temperature, begins an unmistakable increase in the range of *thousands* of kelvin.

Not only do individual molecules have "springs," but at low temperatures, essentially all materials form solids, and solids are full of oscillators. An important consequence of the ground state's nonzero kinetic energy is that even at absolute zero temperature, motion doesn't stop. To cool a collection of oscillating particles to absolute zero, we would remove all energy *possible*. But the result would not be a state of zero motion. It would only be one in which all oscillators are in their ground states. Still there is *something* that would be zero: entropy. In such a state, there could be no random, disordered distribution of energy. It is as ordered as it can be.

8 Expectation Values, Uncertainties, and Operators

With a good grasp of the basic bound systems, we now discuss other important elements of quantum mechanics. Quantum mechanically, we can't know all that we might hope to know, but in addition to simple probabilities, another very useful thing we can determine is an **expectation value**.

Mathematically, an expectation value is an average. The probability *per unit length* is $|\psi(x)|^2$, so we may write

probability of being found in the interval dx around $x = |\psi(x)|^2\, dx$

As we know, if we sum/integrate this probability over all space, we must get 1 (normalization). The standard prescription for an average is to multiply this probability of finding the particles at x by the actual value x, *then* integrate over all space. The symbol for the average, known as an expectation value, is an overscore bar:

$$\bar{x} \equiv \int\limits_{\text{all space}} x|\psi(x)|^2\, dx \qquad (27)$$

The term *expectation value* is carefully chosen. To refer to (27) as the "average value" of the position would be to suggest that the particle always *has* a position, contrary to the modern view of quantum mechanics. Moreover, a small particle cannot be watched without altering its state, so it would be impossible to verify an average position in any case. The expectation value is the value we would obtain if we were to begin with a particle in state A, do an experiment to "find" the particle, *begin again* with a particle in state A, find it, and so on, repeating the identical experiment many times and averaging the locations. Note that the expectation value of x is a numerical value, not an explicit function of x, because the integral has been taken over that variable.

By the same logic, the expectation value of the square of the position is

$$\overline{x^2} \equiv \int\limits_{\text{all space}} x^2|\psi(x)|^2\, dx$$

Our interest in the square is that it is part of how we choose to define uncertainty. In quantum mechanics, we define uncertainty as standard deviation, which, in the case of position x, is given by

$$\Delta x \equiv \sqrt{\int_{\text{all space}} (x - \bar{x})^2 |\psi(x)|^2 \, dx} \qquad (28)$$

This is the square root of the mean of the squares of the deviations of x from its expectation value—the rms deviation. It is the simplest quantity that is 0 if and only if x *never* deviates from its expectation value and that increases as deviations increase. We see this more clearly by rewriting it as

$$\Delta x \equiv \sqrt{\int_{\text{all space}} [(x - \bar{x})\psi(x)]^2 dx} \qquad (29)$$

The integral can be 0 only if the *integrand* is everywhere 0, for the integrand is nonnegative. But what does this require? Imagine a wave function $\psi(x)$ that is centered on the value $x = x_0$ and that falls off symmetrically on both sides. Clearly, its expectation value $\bar{x}$ would be x_0. But for the integrand in (29) to be 0, $\psi(x)$ itself would have to be 0 everywhere except at the single point $x = \bar{x} = x_0$, where multiplication by $x - \bar{x}$ would cause the integrand to be 0. The wave function would have to be an infinitesimally narrow spike. (See Section 11 for further discussion of this peculiar function.) Thus, equation (29) is 0 if and only if there is just a single point where the particle might be found, it is *non*zero for any spread out (nonspiky) function, and it increases as $\psi(x)$ becomes broader—a good definition of uncertainty.

It is usually easier to calculate uncertainty by putting it in a slightly different form. Noting that $\bar{x}$ is a value, not a function of x, we may write (28) as

$$\Delta x = \sqrt{\int_{\text{all space}} (x^2 - 2x\bar{x} + \bar{x}^2)|\psi(x)|^2 \, dx}$$

$$= \sqrt{\int x^2 |\psi(x)|^2 \, dx - 2\bar{x} \int x|\psi(x)|^2 dx + \bar{x}^2 \int |\psi(x)|^2 dx}$$

The first integral is the expectation value of x^2, the second the expectation value of x, and the third, due to normalization, simply 1. Thus,

$$\Delta x = \sqrt{\bar{x^2} - 2\bar{x}\,\bar{x} + \bar{x}^2} = \sqrt{\bar{x^2} - \bar{x}^2} \qquad (30)$$

Although it is no longer obvious that the quantity in the radical is positive, this form is usually more convenient. It also makes it clear that to calculate uncertainty/standard deviation, we need only two pieces of information: the average of the square and the square of the average.

EXAMPLE 4

An electron is in a state given by the wave function

$$\psi(x) = Ae^{-[(x-b)/2\varepsilon]^2}$$

Determine (a) the value of A, (b) the expectation value of the position, and (c) the uncertainty in position.

SOLUTION

(a) We determine the arbitrary constant A via normalization.

$$\int_{\text{all space}} |\psi(x)|^2\,dx = \int_{-\infty}^{+\infty} \left(Ae^{-[(x-b)/2\varepsilon)]^2}\right)^2 dx$$

$$= A^2 \int_{-\infty}^{+\infty} e^{-(x-b)^2/2\varepsilon^2}\,dx = 1$$

This is a standard Gaussian integral. With $a \equiv 1/(2\varepsilon^2)$, its value is $\sqrt{2\pi\varepsilon^2}$.

$$A^2\sqrt{2\pi\varepsilon^2} = 1 \quad \Rightarrow \quad A = \frac{1}{\sqrt{\varepsilon}(2\pi)^{1/4}}$$

(b) Inserting in (27),

$$\bar{x} = \int_{\text{all space}} x|\psi(x)|^2\,dx = A^2 \int_{-\infty}^{+\infty} x\,e^{-(x-b)^2/2\varepsilon^2}\,dx$$

This is also a Gaussian integral, whose value is $b\sqrt{2\pi\varepsilon^2}$. Thus,

$$\bar{x} = A^2 b\sqrt{2\pi\varepsilon^2} = \left(\frac{1}{\sqrt{\varepsilon}(2\pi)^{1/4}}\right)^2 b\sqrt{2\pi\varepsilon^2} = b$$

The result makes sense, for the function is symmetric about the point $x = b$.

(c) According to (30), we need to calculate $\overline{x^2}$.

$$\overline{x^2} = \int_{\text{all space}} x|\psi(x)|^2\,dx = A^2 \int_{-\infty}^{+\infty} x^2\,e^{-(x-b)^2/2\varepsilon^2}\,dx$$

Again we have a Gaussian integral, evaluating to $(\varepsilon^2 + b^2)\sqrt{2\pi\varepsilon^2}$.

$$\overline{x^2} = \left(\frac{1}{\sqrt{\varepsilon}(2\pi)^{1/4}}\right)^2 (\varepsilon^2 + b^2)\sqrt{2\pi\varepsilon^2} = \varepsilon^2 + b^2$$

Now inserting in (30),

$$\Delta x = \sqrt{(\varepsilon^2 + b^2) - b^2} = \varepsilon$$

Example 4 proves that the factor multiplying the 2 in the denominator of the exponent's argument is not just a measure of the wave function's width but is, in fact, the uncertainty as we define it—the standard deviation. Another feature of the Gaussian wave function also becomes clearer. Rewriting $\psi(x)$ in terms of $\bar{x}$ and Δx rather than b and ε, we have

$$\psi(x) = \frac{1}{\sqrt{\Delta x}(2\pi)^{1/4}} e^{-[(x-\bar{x})/2\Delta x]^2}$$

As the width Δx of $\psi(x)$ becomes small, its maximum value, the exponential's coefficient, becomes large. This must be the case if the total probability is to remain fixed.

We may calculate the expectation value of any function of position in the same way as for x and x^2.

$$\overline{f(x)} \equiv \int_{\text{all space}} f(x)|\psi(x)|^2 \, dx$$

But here we must be careful in interpreting the result. The expectation value of the function is *not*, in general, the function evaluated at the point $\bar{x}$—that is, $\overline{f(x)} \neq f(\bar{x})$. Consider a simple counterexample: the potential energy function $U(x) = \frac{1}{2}\kappa x^2$ for a mass on a spring. By symmetry, the expectation value of the position is 0; $\bar{x} = 0$. At this point in space, the potential energy, $U(\bar{x})$, is also 0. But $\overline{U(x)}$ is an average of potential energy values times probabilities at *all* locations. Because the particle's position x varies and the potential energy is nonnegative, this average potential energy is certainly not 0: $\overline{U(x)} \neq U(\bar{x})$.

Now let us generalize to quantities other than position. We use the name **observable** for any property that can be measured, such as position, momentum, energy, or angular momentum. Using the generic symbol Q to cover any observable, the general form for calculating an expectation value is

Expectation value

$$\overline{Q} = \int_{\text{all space}} \Psi^*(x, t)\hat{Q}\Psi(x, t) \, dx \qquad (31)$$

This recipe is a given, simply part of the basic apparatus of quantum mechanics. The symbol $\hat{Q}$ is the **operator** associated with observable Q, and for each observable, there is a unique operator. For position, it is simply x. But in many cases, $\hat{Q}$ is a differential operator, taking a derivative of the function to its right. Consequently, its location in the probability integral isn't arbitrary—it *must* be between $\Psi^*(x, t)$ and $\Psi(x, t)$, the function on which it operates.

Although it is reasonable that x is the proper operator to put in the probability integral to calculate the expectation value of position, it isn't at all obvious what we would use for any other observable. Derivations can involve subtle arguments and sophisticated math. The momentum operator is a good

TABLE 2 Basic operators

Observable	Momentum	Position	Energy
Operator	$\hat{p} = -i\hbar \dfrac{\partial}{\partial x}$	$\hat{x} = x$	$\hat{E} = i\hbar \dfrac{\partial}{\partial t}$

example. Because we are concerned mostly with its use, we simply present the result. For momentum, the operator—which when put in the proper location in the probability integral gives the expectation value—is

$$\hat{p} = -i\hbar \frac{\partial}{\partial x}$$

Momentum operator

Strange though this operator may appear, we soon see that it gives very sensible results.

Functions of an operator are also allowed. For example, we obtain the operator for kinetic energy as follows:

$$\text{KE} = \frac{p^2}{2m} \quad \rightarrow \quad \hat{\text{KE}} = \frac{1}{2m}\hat{p}^2 = \frac{1}{2m}\left(-i\hbar\frac{\partial}{\partial x}\right)\left(-i\hbar\frac{\partial}{\partial x}\right) = \frac{-\hbar^2}{2m}\frac{\partial^2}{\partial^2 x}$$

If not basic themselves, most quantum-mechanical operators are combinations of those for the basic dynamical properties: momentum, position, and energy. In Table 2, we complete the list of basic operators by adding that for total (as opposed to kinetic) energy. Note that, with operators in hand, we may write the Schrödinger equation (2) in a form clearly illustrating its foundation—energy:

$$\hat{\text{KE}}\Psi(x, t) + \hat{U}(x)\Psi(x, t) = \hat{E}\Psi(x, t)$$

Our general method for calculating expectation values also enables us to generalize the definition of uncertainty to arbitrary observables.

$$\Delta Q = \sqrt{\overline{Q^2} - \overline{Q}^2} \tag{32}$$

Uncertainty

Using the infinite well as a model system, let us calculate some uncertainties and see if they accord with the uncertainty principle.

EXAMPLE 5

For a particle in the ground state of an infinite well, find (a) Δx, (b) Δp, and (c) the product $\Delta x \, \Delta p$.

SOLUTION

(a) Equations (30) and (32) agree that to calculate uncertainty, we need the expectation value of the square and the square of the expectation value. Equation (31) is the general form for expectation value, so we can certainly use it to find $\bar{x}$. But a considerable simplification is that, as in equation (9), the temporal part of Ψ drops out (because the product $e^{+i\omega t} e^{-i\omega t}$ is 1). Thus, the expectation value of position relies on the spatial part $\psi(x)$ alone.

$$\bar{x} = \int_{\text{all space}} \psi^*(x)x\psi(x)dx$$

Note that we have put the "operator" where (31) says it should be. Because x isn't a differential operator, it doesn't matter where it is in the integral, but it is a good habit to follow the pattern. In the ground state, $\psi_1(x) = \sqrt{2/L}\sin(\pi x/L)$ inside the box, and is 0 elsewhere, so "all space" reduces to 0 to L.

$$\bar{x} = \int_0^L \left(\sqrt{\frac{2}{L}}\sin\frac{\pi x}{L}\right)x\left(\sqrt{\frac{2}{L}}\sin\frac{\pi x}{L}\right)dx = \frac{2}{L}\int_0^L x\sin^2\left(\frac{\pi x}{L}\right)dx$$

$$= \frac{2}{L}\int_0^L x\frac{1-\cos(2\pi x/L)}{2}dx = \frac{2}{L}\left(\frac{L^2}{4} - \frac{1}{2}\int_0^L x\cos\left(\frac{2\pi x}{L}\right)dx\right)$$

Integration by parts reveals the remaining integral to be 0. Therefore,

$$\bar{x} = \frac{1}{2}L$$

This expectation value is certainly expected. Even classically, the average of the positions we would find if we were to repeatedly turn on the lights and catch the particle in its back-and-forth motion is the center of the box.

$$\overline{x^2} = \int_0^L \left(\sqrt{\frac{2}{L}}\sin\frac{\pi x}{L}\right)x^2\left(\sqrt{\frac{2}{L}}\sin\frac{\pi x}{L}\right)dx = \frac{2}{L}\int_0^L x^2\sin^2\left(\frac{\pi x}{L}\right)dx$$

$$= \frac{2}{L}\int_0^L x^2\frac{1-\cos(2\pi x/L)}{2}dx = \frac{2}{L}\left(\frac{L^3}{6} - \frac{1}{2}\int_0^L x^2\cos\left(\frac{2\pi x}{L}\right)dx\right)$$

After integration by parts of the remaining integral, we have

$$\overline{x^2} = \frac{2}{L}\left(\frac{L^3}{6} - \frac{L^3}{4\pi^2}\right) = L^2\left(\frac{1}{3} - \frac{1}{2\pi^2}\right)$$

Now using the general form (32),

$$\Delta x = \sqrt{\overline{x^2} - \bar{x}^2} = \sqrt{L^2\left(\frac{1}{3} - \frac{1}{2\pi^2}\right) - \left(\frac{1}{2}L\right)^2} = 0.181L$$

The result doesn't mean that the particle may never be found farther than $0.181L$ from the center. Standard deviation is a statistical definition. Although it increases as values become more spread out from the average, it doesn't encompass all possible values. Logically, the spread increases in proportion to the width of the box.

(b) Again using (31), but here being particularly careful about placement in the integrand, we have

$$\bar{p} = \int_{\text{all space}} \psi^*(x)\,\hat{p}\,\psi(x)dx$$

Inserting the momentum operator and $\psi(x)$ gives

$$\bar{p} = \int\limits_0^L \left(\sqrt{\frac{2}{L}}\,\sin\frac{\pi x}{L}\right)\left(-i\hbar\frac{\partial}{\partial x}\right)\left(\sqrt{\frac{2}{L}}\,\sin\frac{\pi x}{L}\right)dx$$

$$= \int\limits_0^L \left(\sqrt{\frac{2}{L}}\,\sin\frac{\pi x}{L}\right)(-i\hbar)\frac{\pi}{L}\left(\sqrt{\frac{2}{L}}\,\cos\frac{\pi x}{L}\right)dx$$

$$= -i\hbar\frac{2\pi}{L^2}\int\limits_0^L \sin\left(\frac{\pi x}{L}\right)\cos\left(\frac{\pi x}{L}\right)dx$$

The remaining integral happens to be 0, so $\bar{p} = 0$. Quantum mechanical or not, the fact that the particle is *bound* demands that it should be equally likely to be found traveling to the right as to the left. Because momentum is a *vector*, the "average" must be 0.

$$\overline{p^2} = \int\limits_{\text{all space}} \psi^*(x)\,\hat{p}^2\psi(x)dx$$

$$= \int\limits_0^L \left(\sqrt{\frac{2}{L}}\,\sin\frac{\pi x}{L}\right)\left(-\hbar^2\frac{\partial^2}{\partial x^2}\right)\left(\sqrt{\frac{2}{L}}\,\sin\frac{\pi x}{L}\right)dx$$

$$= \int\limits_0^L \left(\sqrt{\frac{2}{L}}\,\sin\frac{\pi x}{L}\right)(-\hbar^2)\frac{\partial^2}{\partial x^2}\left(\sqrt{\frac{2}{L}}\,\sin\frac{\pi x}{L}\right)dx$$

$$= \int\limits_0^L \left(\sqrt{\frac{2}{L}}\,\sin\frac{\pi x}{L}\right)(-\hbar^2)\left(\frac{-\pi^2}{L^2}\right)\left(\sqrt{\frac{2}{L}}\,\sin\frac{\pi x}{L}\right)dx$$

$$= \frac{\pi^2\hbar^2}{L^2}\int\limits_0^L \left(\sqrt{\frac{2}{L}}\,\sin\frac{\pi x}{L}\right)^2 dx$$

The integrand is just $|\psi(x)|^2$, so the remaining integral is merely the total probability, which is 1.

$$\overline{p^2} = \frac{\pi^2\hbar^2}{L^2}$$

Now inserting into general form (32),

$$\Delta p = \sqrt{\overline{p^2} - \bar{p}^2} = \sqrt{\frac{\pi^2\hbar^2}{L^2} - 0} = \frac{\pi\hbar}{L}$$

The uncertainty is nonzero—but it must be! Although the average of this vector is 0, the particle may at least be found moving in different directions, which demands a nonzero momentum uncertainty.

(c) The product of the uncertainties is

$$\Delta x\, \Delta p = 0.181L\frac{\pi\hbar}{L} = 0.568\hbar$$

Here we have a nice example of the harmony of the quantum mechanics we've studied thus far. According to the uncertainty principle, $\Delta x\, \Delta p \geq \frac{1}{2}\hbar$. This fits perfectly! While the momentum uncertainty decreases with increasing L, because longer wavelength implies less kinetic energy, the position uncertainty increases, for the wave is more spread out, and the product is independent of L. The reason the product isn't *equal to* $\frac{1}{2}\hbar$ is simply that $\psi(x)$ isn't a Gaussian, the function with the minimum possible product.

It is left as an exercise to show that in the infinite well, both Δx and Δp increase with increasing n. Thus, the ground state is the least uncertain combination of position and momentum. It is also an exercise to show that Δx approaches the classical value $L/\sqrt{12}$ as $n \to \infty$. In agreement with the correspondence principle, quantum-mechanical predictions approach the classical as n becomes large.

OPTIONAL 9 Nonstationary States

In separating variables to solve the Schrödinger equation, we restrict our attention to stationary states, in which the energy is well defined and the probability density $\Psi^*\Psi$ is independent of time. A quick look at a more general case gives us important insight into the process of jumping from one stationary state to another.

A bound particle, as we know, will have quantized energy. Let us refer to its allowed energies as $E_1, E_2, E_3, \ldots$ and the corresponding solutions of the time-independent Schrödinger equation as $\psi_1, \psi_2, \psi_3, \ldots$. The total wave function in stationary state n is given by equation (8).

$$\Psi_n(x, t) = \psi_n(x)e^{-i(E_n/\hbar)t}$$

Now consider a sum of two such solutions, but of different energies.

$$\Psi(x, t) = \psi_n(x)e^{-i(E_n/\hbar)t} + \psi_m(x)e^{-i(E_m/\hbar)t} \tag{33}$$

Because the Schrödinger equation is a *linear* differential equation, any sum of solutions is also a solution. Each individual function is a solution of the time-*dependent* Schrödinger equation, so their sum is also a solution. But neither is a solution of the time-*independent* Schrödinger equation *of the other*, and because n and m involve different values of E, the sum does not have a well-defined energy. (For a quick formal proof, based on the ideas discussed in Section 11, see Exercise 67.) Solution (33) also lacks the other important characteristic we expect of a stationary state. Its probability density varies with time.

$$\Psi^*(x, t)\Psi(x, t)$$
$$= \left[\psi_n(x)e^{+i(E_n/\hbar)t} + \psi_m(x)e^{+i(E_m/\hbar)t}\right]\left[\psi_n(x)e^{-i(E_n/\hbar)t} + \psi_m(x)e^{-i(E_m/\hbar)t}\right]$$
$$= \psi_n^2(x) + \psi_m^2(x) + 2\psi_n(x)\psi_m(x)\cos\left(\frac{E_n - E_m}{\hbar}t\right) \tag{34}$$

(*Note:* For simplicity we have assumed the spatial functions to be real and have dispensed with absolute value signs.) We see that the variation is a periodic function of time, of angular frequency $(E_n - E_m)/\hbar$.

The wave function given in (33) may be thought of as crudely representing a transitional state between two stationary states. Perhaps it represents an electron in an infinite well as it jumps down from a high to a low energy state—the nth to the mth. During the transition, its wave function and energy are combinations of those of the initial and final states. On the other hand, if energy is to be conserved, something else must be happening, for a system cannot by itself start with one energy and end with another. As discussed in Example 2, the "something else" is quite often the production of a photon. Initially, the electron is in a stationary state of well-defined energy E_n. It then enters a transitional phase, during which a photon is being generated and the electron's energy is not well defined. Finally, the electron is in a stationary state of well-defined energy E_m, and a photon of energy $E_n - E_m$ emerges. Energy is conserved. A detailed study of the photon's generation wouldn't be appropriate here, but our crude picture contains the key feature: In a *non*stationary state, probability density does vary with time, and if the particle making the transition is charged, its charge density should vary with time, so electromagnetic radiation *should* result.

Is the association of charge density with probability density valid? Classically, the hydrogen atom should be unstable, with the orbiting electron accelerating and therefore radiating away its energy into electromagnetic waves. The quantum-mechanical explanation of the atom's stability is that the electron is in a stationary state, so its probability density and charge density do not vary with time in any way. If no charge accelerates, no radiation is generated. This alone would make the association of the two densities plausible. What we have found here further strengthens the case. To generate a photon of energy $E_n - E_m$, *charge* must oscillate at angular frequency $\omega = (E_n - E_m)/\hbar$, and the transitional state *probability* density (34) oscillates at exactly this frequency.

10 The Computer Approach   O P T I O N A L

The Schrödinger equation is exactly solvable for only certain simple potential energy functions. We now study an instructive technique to find physically acceptable wave functions and corresponding quantized energies by computer. Although not exact, they may, in principle, be obtained to an arbitrarily high degree of precision. In short, we begin with a guess for $\psi(x)$ in some small starting region of the x-axis, then we find its values point by point as we move away by imposing the fact that $\psi(x)$ must obey the Schrödinger equation. But how?

We first observe that by the definition of a derivative, evaluating df/dx at two points Δx apart gives

$$\frac{df}{dx}\bigg|_x = \lim_{\Delta x \to 0} \frac{f(x + \Delta x) - f(x)}{\Delta x} \quad \text{and} \quad \frac{df}{dx}\bigg|_{x - \Delta x} = \lim_{\Delta x \to 0} \frac{f(x) - f(x - \Delta x)}{\Delta x}$$

By the same definition, if we take a difference between these two, divide by Δx, then let Δx approach 0, we have the derivative of the derivative—the second derivative.

$$\frac{d^2 f}{dx^2} = \lim_{\Delta x \to 0} \frac{\lim_{\Delta x \to 0}\left(\dfrac{f(x + \Delta x) - f(x)}{\Delta x}\right) - \lim_{\Delta x \to 0}\left(\dfrac{f(x) - f(x - \Delta x)}{\Delta x}\right)}{\Delta x}$$

$$= \lim_{\Delta x \to 0} \frac{f(x + \Delta x) - 2f(x) + f(x - \Delta x)}{\Delta x^2}$$

Before putting this to use, we note that the numerator would be identically 0 if $f(x)$ were a *linear* function—a straight line—because its value at x would be the average of its values on either side, $(f(x + \Delta x) + f(x - \Delta x))/2$. Thus, this "finite difference" form of the second derivative is indeed nonzero only if $f(x)$ has a curvature at the point x. Now, after replacing f by ψ and dropping the limit symbol, we insert it in the time-independent Schrödinger equation.

$$-\frac{\hbar^2}{2m} \frac{\psi(x + \Delta x) - 2\psi(x) + \psi(x - \Delta x)}{\Delta x^2} + U(x)\psi(x) = E\psi(x)$$

Rearranging a bit, we have

$$\psi(x + \Delta x) = 2\psi(x) - \psi(x - \Delta x) + \frac{2m\Delta x^2(U(x) - E)}{\hbar^2}\psi(x) \qquad (35)$$

This is the form of the Schrödinger equation that a computer can use.

And what must we give the computer? Of course, $U(x)$ must be specified, as well as the particle's mass m. Then we must choose a certain energy E to test. After that, equation (35) simply says that to find ψ at the point $x + \Delta x$, the computer need only know its values at two earlier points, $\psi(x)$ and $\psi(x - \Delta x)$. But it can then find ψ at the point $x + 2\Delta x$, because it now knows its values at the two earlier points, $\psi(x + \Delta x)$ and $\psi(x)$. The process continues until the computer finds ψ at all points Δx apart along the entire x-axis.

But where do those first two values of ψ come from, and why do we need *two* anyway? We need two because the Schrödinger equation is a *second*-order differential equation, involving a second derivative. For example, the first-order equation $df(x)/dx = -bf(x)$ has solution $f(x) = Ae^{-bx}$, where A is an arbitrary constant, essentially a constant of integration. Solutions to second-order equations, besides being harder to obtain, have two arbitrary constants. The constants may be specified in different ways—ways that don't appear equivalent—but in any case, they determine the solution for all space. In an "analytical" solution to a differential equation (see A Closer Look: Solving the Finite Well), they usually appear as multiplicative constants in front of two independent functions. In our present "numerical" solution, we take them to be the values of the solution at a starting point and a point next to it. In effect, by specifying these, we specify the "height" of the solution at a starting point and its slope—how it changes or doesn't change—at that point. From there, the numerical solution simply charts $\psi(x)$ according to the curvature imposed by the Schrödinger equation. By an essentially equivalent route, we may also plot $\psi(x)$ in the negative direction from the starting points. The $\psi(x)$ that results is automatically as smooth as the point-by-point solution allows, so the only remaining physical condition of concern is normalizability. It must not diverge, and this is the key to applying the procedure and spotting the answers.

Given $U(x)$ and m, we choose a Δx small enough that $\psi(x)$ should change only a little from one point to another, a small fraction of what we might guess to be a typical wavelength. Then we choose an energy E to test. In almost all cases, what we find is that for *any* initial $\psi(x)$ at the starting point, no matter how we choose the slope there—whether $\psi(x + \Delta x)$ is greater than, less than, or equal to $\psi(x)$—the point-by-point solution diverges as x goes to $+\infty$, $-\infty$, or both. We *can* choose the initial slope just right so that $\psi(x)$ dies nicely to 0 at one end, but this uses up the arbitrariness of the slope, and $\psi(x)$ still diverges at the other end. We conclude that this E is "wrong" and move on to another. At only certain values of E, we find that for *any* initial $\psi(x)$ at the starting point (unless the starting point is by chance actually a node), we can choose a slope there such that $\psi(x)$ dies to 0 at one end, *and it automatically does so at the other, too*. These are the allowed, quantized energies. Note that because this works for any initial value $\psi(x)$ at the starting point, we still have freedom to choose this value. This doesn't change the character or shape of $\psi(x)$, but merely its "vertical" size. In fact, it simply allows us to normalize it. In concise terms, once a correct energy is found, the two arbitrary constants allow us to fit the **boundary conditions** that $\psi(x)$ go to 0 at both ends, which uses up one constant, and to normalize the function, using up the other.

It might seem that the computer approach would take forever, as there are infinitely many possible energies and infinitely many slopes to try at each. It turns out that the divergence of $\psi(x)$ changes drastically as the trial E passes through a "real" value, so we can zero in relatively fast. Moreover, if the potential energy function is symmetric, it greatly simplifies choosing slopes. Several end-of-chapter exercises apply the approach to the finite well, the harmonic oscillator, and other cases.

A D V A N C E D   11   Well-Defined Observables: Eigenvalues

A well-defined observable is one for which the uncertainty is zero; that is, one for which an experiment designed to measure that observable can obtain only a single value. There is a mathematical tool that allows us to determine easily whether a wave function describes a state for which a given observable is well defined. Before introducing it, however, let us consider what functions we might *expect* to have well-defined values of the basic observables.

Momentum: We met the basic quantum-mechanical plane wave, the complex exponential e^{ikx}. Being a simple sinusoidal function of pure wavelength and spread equally over all space, giving an infinite position uncertainty, it is the prototype function of well-defined momentum.

Energy: In Section 2, we asserted that the temporal part of the wave function, $e^{-i\omega t}$, has a pure frequency and thus a well-defined energy.

Position: A wave function of well-defined position would allow no probability of finding the particle anywhere but at a single point. Calling this point x_0, $\psi(x)$ would have to be 0 everywhere but at x_0. We give this peculiar wave function the special symbol $\psi_{x_0}(x)$. It is crudely pictured in Figure 19.

Now the mathematical tool:

> **Definition:** Given an operator $\hat{Q}$, the function $f(x)$ is an **eigenfunction** of the operator if and only if the operator acting on the function yields a constant times the same function.
>
> $$\hat{Q} \qquad f(x) \qquad = \qquad \lambda \qquad f(x)$$
>
> **Operator Eigenfunction**   **Eigenvalue Eigenfunction**
>
> The constant λ is said to be an **eigenvalue** of the operator. In general, an operator will have multiple eigenvalues and corresponding eigenfunctions meeting the condition.

This tool's utility in quantum mechanics is as follows:

> A wave function Ψ is one for which observable Q is well defined—for which there is no uncertainty in the outcome of a measurement of Q—if and only if it is an eigenfunction of the operator $\hat{Q}$, and the eigenvalue is the well-defined value of the observable.
>
> $$Q \text{ is well defined} \quad \Leftrightarrow \quad \Delta Q = 0 \quad \Leftrightarrow \quad \hat{Q}\Psi = \overline{Q}\Psi$$

Note that $\overline{Q}$ is in the place of the eigenvalue, which is correct, for $\overline{Q}$ *is* a constant, and if there is indeed no uncertainty in the observable's value,

Figure 19 A function for which position is well defined.

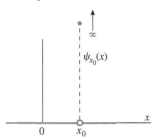

the mean and that single value are necessarily one and the same. Before discussing the proof of this claim, let us see if it agrees with our earlier expectations.

Momentum: If the function e^{ikx} is one of well-defined momentum ($\Delta p = 0$), it should be an eigenfunction of the momentum operator.

$$\hat{p}e^{ikx} = -i\hbar\frac{\partial}{\partial x}e^{ikx} = \hbar k e^{ikx}$$

It is, and the eigenvalue is indeed the well-defined momentum, $p = \hbar k$. Other functions don't behave this way. Example 6 identifies several "failures."

Energy: Similarly, $e^{-i\omega t}$ should be an eigenfunction of the energy operator.

$$\hat{E}e^{-i\omega t} = i\hbar\frac{\partial}{\partial t}e^{-i\omega t} = \hbar\omega e^{-i\omega t}$$

This works the same way, telling us that E is a well-defined $\hbar\omega$.

Position: Given the weird nature of the function depicted in Figure 19, this one is a bit tricky.[7] Still, the question is

$$x\psi_{x_0}(x) \overset{?}{=} x_0\psi_{x_0}(x)$$

Because the function $\psi_{x_0}(x)$ is 0 everywhere but at x_0, both sides of the equation are 0 at all these points. At the only other point, $x = x_0$, the variable x multiplying $\psi_{x_0}(x)$ on the left side is (trivially) x_0, the same as the value on the right. The equation holds, and this peculiar function is the only one for which it does. It is *the* function describing a well-defined position.

To prove that $\hat{Q}\Psi = \overline{Q}\Psi \Rightarrow \Delta Q = 0$ is not difficult. Starting with a calculation of $\overline{Q^2}$ and *assuming* that $\hat{Q}\Psi = \overline{Q}\Psi$ does hold,

$$\overline{Q^2} = \int\limits_{\text{all space}} \Psi*\hat{Q}^2\Psi dx = \int\limits_{\text{all space}} \Psi*\hat{Q}(\hat{Q}\Psi)dx$$

$$= \int\limits_{\text{all space}} \Psi*\hat{Q}(\overline{Q}\Psi)dx = \overline{Q}\int\limits_{\text{all space}} \Psi*\hat{Q}\Psi dx = \overline{Q}^2$$

Thus, $\Delta Q = \sqrt{\overline{Q^2} - \overline{Q}^2} = 0$. A general proof of the reverse—$\Delta Q = 0 \Rightarrow \hat{Q}\Psi = \overline{Q}\Psi$—involves math too lengthy to present here. It may, however, be verified fairly easily for the momentum operator. This is left as an exercise.

[7]The reader may quail at this glib discussion of an obviously pathological function. Things must be much more precisely defined before mathematicians are happy. However, precise justifications do exist. For better or for worse, physicists often charge forward without much attention to them.

EXAMPLE 6

Which of the following wave functions have a well-defined momentum? For those that do, what is its value? (a) $Ae^{-(x/2\varepsilon)^2}$, (b) $A\cos k_0 x$, (c) $A[\cos(k_0 x) - i\sin(k_0 x)]$, (d) $A[\cos(k_0 x) - \sin(k_0 x)]$.

SOLUTION

(a) $\hat{p}\,\psi(x) = -i\hbar\dfrac{\partial}{\partial x}Ae^{-(x/2\varepsilon)^2} = (-i\hbar)\,Ae^{-(x/2\varepsilon)^2}\left(\dfrac{-x}{2\varepsilon^2}\right)$

This is not a constant times $Ae^{-(x/2\varepsilon)^2}$, so the momentum of this wave function is not well defined. Of course, we wouldn't expect a Gaussian "bump" like this to have zero Δp, for Δx is not infinite.

(b) $-i\hbar\dfrac{\partial}{\partial x}A\cos k_0 x = i\hbar k_0 A\sin k_0 x$

Again, because this is not a constant times $A\cos k_0 x$, the momentum is not well defined. It may seem odd that an infinitely long cosine function doesn't have a well-defined momentum, as it would seem to have a well-defined wavelength. The answer is basic to quantum mechanics and reflected in the form of the momentum operator. The fundamental plane waves are not sines or cosines, but complex exponentials. Only they have well-defined momenta.

(c) $-i\hbar\dfrac{\partial}{\partial x}A\big[\cos(k_0 x) - i\sin(k_0 x)\big] = -i\hbar k_0 A\big[-\sin(k_0 x) - i\cos(k_0 x)\big]$

$$= -\hbar k_0 A\big[-i\sin(k_0 x) + \cos(k_0 x)\big]$$

This is $-\hbar k_0$ times the original function. The multiplicative constant, the eigenvalue, is the well-defined value of the observable, so the momentum is a well-defined $-\hbar k_0$. In fact, this function is $Ae^{-ik_0 x}$. Because the momentum is negative, we see that this complex exponential represents a particle moving in the negative direction; whereas for $Ae^{+ik_0 x}$, it moves in the positive.[8] This further demonstrates why $A\cos k_0 x$ does *not* have a well-defined momentum. Writing it as $\cos k_0 x = \frac{1}{2}(e^{+ik_0 x} + e^{-ik_0 x})$, we see that it is really equal parts of two waves of opposite momentum. Its momentum expectation value would be 0, but the particle could be found moving in either direction. The same arguments apply to the sine functions of the infinite well.

(d) $-i\hbar\dfrac{\partial}{\partial x}A\big[\cos(k_0 x) - \sin(k_0 x)\big] = i\hbar k_0 A\big[\sin(k_0 x) + \cos(k_0 x)\big]$

Momentum is not well defined. The "missing" i is crucial.

[8]An electromagnetic wave's direction of motion may be seen from a "snapshot." It is the direction of $\mathbf{E}\times\mathbf{B}$. If we shift $\mathbf{E}$ relative to $\mathbf{B}$ by 180°, we have a wave moving in the opposite direction. Similarly, by shifting the real part of a positive-moving matter wave 180° relative to the imaginary, an e^{+ikx} becomes an e^{-ikx}, giving a negative-moving wave.

Categorizing wave functions as eigenfunctions of operators has many applications. It is widely used in more advanced analysis, such as matrix quantum mechanics. Probably its most useful application, though, is the one we have highlighted: It is the simplest way of determining whether a function has a well-defined value of a given observable.

PROGRESS AND APPLICATIONS

Quantum Wells as Light Sources   With advances in fabricating microscopic structures in recent decades, the physics of quantum wells has assumed a major role in modern technology. The well consists of electrostatic barriers in semiconductor crystals (or, in some cases, carbon nanotubes), and the usual captives are the electron and its semiconductor alter ego, the hole. If the particle's quarters confine it in only one dimension, leaving it essentially free in two others, we call it a **quantum well**. If the particle is confined in two dimensions and free in one, it is in a **quantum wire**. When confined in all dimensions, it is in a **quantum dot**. All three are being studied for a host of applications, but the dot is particularly attractive because, meeting standing- wave conditions along all axes, its levels are the most tightly controlled.

In many ways, a quantum dot is like a designer atom. Both have quantized energies, but quantum dots are more flexible in that they can be tailored to the specific application by varying their size. Among the most promising applications of quantum dots is as a medium for producing laser light. Most lasers rely on transitions between electron energy levels specific to the material—gas lasers on levels in the gas atoms, and traditional solid state lasers on fairly broad energy "bands" in the semiconductor material. But the energy levels in a quantum dot are more easily controlled, for they also depend on the simple geometry of the wells. As we find for a particle in a box, a smaller L implies higher energies. Many early difficulties in producing uniform dots have been overcome. A major advance was the development of a "self-assembly" method in the 1990s, in which stresses in a growing crystal spontaneously form pyramid-shaped dots of regular size and distribution. Numerous layers can be used, and when placed between mirrors to produce a resonant cavity, as depicted in Figure 20, the many dots fill the same role as atoms in other lasers. When they mature, quantum dot lasers should offer not only a convenient way to choose a frequency anywhere in the visible band but also a small and efficient package well suited to the increasing use of light that is anticipated in communication and computer design.

Figure 21 shows two samples produced by a team at Sandia National Laboratories, that feature an interesting and seemingly opposite application of quantum dots: efficient generation of normal *white* light. Although far more efficient than the old standard incandescent, today's fluorescent bulb, besides being rather bulky, is still typically less than 50% efficient. Solid-state light sources—lacking evacuated chambers, transformers, and hot filaments—are already used in many low-power applications, but they may one day replace the standard lightbulb as the transistor did its vacuum tube predecessor. Coupled with the efficient LED, the quantum dot is a contender. In several different approaches being studied, ultraviolet light from an LED striking quantum dots has been converted to a broad spectrum of wavelengths by the interplay between the geometric properties of the dots and the chemical properties of the material of which they are made. Efficiencies are already better than standard fluorescent bulbs.

Detecting DNA with a Quantum Dot   The tunability of allowed energies in quantum dots has gained many applications in biology and medicine. In one, shown in Figure 22, a quantum dot is the heart of a very sensitive detector of DNA. First, two special molecules are introduced—a "capture probe" and a "reporter probe"—which, when encountering a DNA molecule, form a three-molecule sandwich. The quantum dot is the crucial indicator that the sandwich has formed and thus that DNA is present. It is clothed in special molecules with an affinity for the *capture* probe. If the sandwich forms, this attraction brings into close proximity the quantum dot and the *reporter* probe, which only then are

Figure 21 Light from glowing quantum dots.

Figure 20 Quantum dots forming a laser.

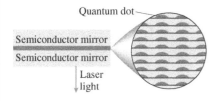

Quantum dot

Semiconductor mirror
Semiconductor mirror

Laser
light

able to "talk" by a process known as fluorescence resonance energy transfer (FRET). In this clever process, a photon of one energy excites a "donor"—the quantum dot, or QD, in the figure—which transfers a portion of the energy by a non-light-producing resonant interaction to a nearby "acceptor"—the Cy5—which then deexcites, producing its own distinctive photon of longer wavelength. Molecular-based materials that talk in this unmistakable way—absorbing one wavelength, exchanging energy, emitting another—without some kind of garbling are not easy to find. The versatile quantum dot can be tuned to the specific application and provides a nice solution.

Halos in the Classically Forbidden Region Wave functions of bound particles usually extend into the classically forbidden region, sometimes very far. One example is the heavy-hydrogen nucleus—a neutron and proton bound together by their shared "strong force"—in which the particles are more likely to be found in the classically forbidden region than in the classically allowed region. Cases where penetration is unusually high continue to attract quite a bit of attention, and the outlying wave function tails are referred to as **halos**. Although electrons form halos in atoms, and atoms form halos in molecules, the most commonly studied halos are in certain nuclei, where an excess of neutrons forms the halo. For instance, the common helium-4 nucleus binds two protons and two neutrons in a very tight unit, but helium-6, depicted in Figure 23, adds two more neutrons, which haunt regions quite far from the nuclear core. Forces in the atomic nucleus are very complicated, and halos provide an important view in helping unravel the mysteries.

Figure 22 A quantum dot DNA nanosensor. Sandwiched DNA sticks to a quantum dot (QD). "Excitation" energy excites the dot and emerges, after FRET, as the emission (Cy5) photon.

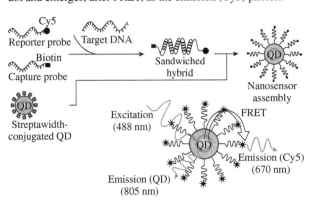

Figure 23 A two-neutron halo around helium.

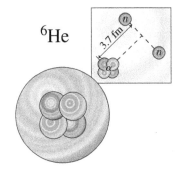

Chapter Summary

To understand the quantum-mechanical behavior of a massive object, it is necessary to know the wave function $\Psi(x, t)$, a solution of the Schrödinger equation, which, in the presence of potential energy $U(x)$, is

$$-\frac{\hbar^2}{2m}\frac{\partial^2}{\partial x^2}\Psi(x, t) + U(x)\Psi(x, t) = i\hbar\frac{\partial}{\partial t}\Psi(x, t) \qquad (2)$$

Solving the Schrödinger equation for $\Psi(x,t)$ is roughly analogous to the classical procedure of solving $\mathbf{F} = m\, d^2\mathbf{r}/dt^2$ for $\mathbf{r}(t)$.

Separation of variables yields the time-independent Schrödinger equation

$$-\frac{\hbar^2}{2m}\frac{d^2\psi(x)}{dx^2} + U(x)\psi(x) = E\psi(x) \qquad (10)$$

The wave function $\Psi(x, t)$ becomes $\psi(x)e^{-i(E/\hbar)t}$. Known as a stationary state, its energy E is well defined, and its probability density does not vary with time.

A quantum-mechanical treatment is required in small systems whenever the dimensions are comparable to or less than the wavelength of $\Psi(x, t)$. Such a system cannot be constantly watched to keep track of position, momentum, and so on, because an observer would have to interact with it somehow, disturbing the very behavior being observed. If no attempt is made to find it, a massive object in a small system behaves not as a particle but as a wave.

When a massive object is bound, only certain wave functions satisfy the physical conditions of smoothness and normalizability, and they form standing waves. This is the root of energy quantization, in which energy is restricted to a certain discrete set of allowed values, each with corresponding wave function. In all bound cases, the minimum-energy state has nonzero kinetic energy—if a particle is bound, it cannot be absolutely stationary. Three simple cases of bound particles, often used as models of more complicated systems, are the finite well, for which a numerical solution is needed to obtain energies and wave functions; the harmonic oscillator, whose energies are

$$E = (n + \tfrac{1}{2})\hbar\omega_0 \quad \text{where} \quad \omega_0 \equiv \sqrt{\frac{\kappa}{m}} \qquad (26)$$

and the infinite well, or particle in a box, whose energies and wave functions are

$$\psi_n(x) = \sqrt{\frac{2}{L}}\sin\frac{n\pi x}{L} \quad 0 < x < L \quad E_n = \frac{n^2\pi^2\hbar^2}{2mL^2} \qquad (16)$$

In the limit of large energies, the predictions of quantum mechanics and classical mechanics converge.

Observations are governed by probabilities. An experiment yielding a value for an observable such as position or momentum would in general yield a different value if repeated identically. The experiment cannot be simply a later observation of the same system, as any observation disturbs it. The result of many identical repetitions would produce an average, known as an expectation value, and a standard deviation, which quantum mechanics chooses as its definition of uncertainty. They may be calculated from the wave function via

$$\overline{Q} = \int\limits_{\text{all space}} \Psi^*(x, t)\hat{Q}\Psi(x, t)dx \qquad (31)$$

and

$$\Delta Q = \sqrt{\overline{Q^2} - \overline{Q}^2} \qquad (32)$$

where $\hat{Q}$ is the operator associated with the observable.

A bound particle may make a transition between one stationary state and another, at which time its probability density *does* vary in time; it oscillates. When a charged particle drops to a lower energy state, the oscillation frequency of its charge density is just right to generate a photon that carries away the energy difference.

---

* indicates advanced questions

Conceptual Questions

1. Quantization is an important characteristic of systems in which a particle is bound in a small region. Why "small," and why "bound"?

2. A student of classical physics says, "A charged particle, like an electron orbiting in a simple atom, shouldn't have only certain stable energies; in fact, it should lose energy by electromagnetic radiation until the atom collapses." Answer these two complaints qualitatively, appealing to as few fundamental claims of quantum mechanics as possible.

3. The term *interaction* is sometimes used interchangeably with *force*, and other times interchangeably with *potential energy*. Although force and potential energy certainly aren't the same thing, what justification is there for using the same term to cover both?

4. Explain to your friend, who is skeptical about energy quantization, the simple evidence provided by distinct colors you see when you hold a CD (serving as a diffraction grating) near a fluorescent light. It may be helpful to contrast this evidence with the spectrum produced by an incandescent light, which relies on heating a filament to produce a rather nonspecific blackbody spectrum.

5. Just what is stationary in a stationary state? The particle? Something else?

6. When is the temporal part of the wave function 0? Why is this important?

7. We say that the ground state for the particle in a box has nonzero energy. What goes wrong with ψ in equation (16) if $n = 0$?

8. Equation (16) gives infinite well energies. Because equation (22) cannot be solved in closed form, there is no similar compact formula for finite well energies. Still, many conclusions can be drawn without one. Argue on largely qualitative grounds that if the walls of a finite well are moved closer together but not changed in height, then the well must progressively hold fewer bound states. (Make a clear connection between the width of the well and the height of the walls.)

9. A *half*-infinite well has an infinitely high wall at the origin and one of finite height U_0 at $x = L$. Like the finite well, the number of allowed states is limited. Assume that it has two states, of energy E_1 and E_2, where E_2 is not much below U_0. Make a sketch of the potential energy, then add plausible sketches of the two allowed wave functions on separate horizontal axes whose heights are E_1 and E_2.

10. Consider a particle in the ground state of a finite well. Describe the changes in its wave function and energy as the walls are made progressively higher (U_0 is increased) until essentially infinite.

11. A particle is subject to a potential energy that has an essentially infinitely high wall at the origin, like the infinite well, but for positive values of x is of the form $U(x) = -b/x$, where b is a constant. (a) Sketch this potential energy. (b) How much energy could a classical particle have and still be bound by such a potential energy? (c) Add to your sketch a plot of E for a bound particle and indicate the outer classical turning point (the inner being the origin). (d) Assuming that a quantum-mechanical description is in order, sketch a plausible ground-state wave function, making sure that your function's second derivative is of the proper sign when $U(x)$ is less than E and when it is greater.

12. Simple models are very useful. Consider the twin finite wells shown in the figure, at first with a tiny separation, then with increasingly distant separations. In all cases, the four lowest allowed wave functions are plotted on axes proportional to their energies. We see that they pass through the classically forbidden region between the wells, and we also see a trend. When the wells are very close, the four functions and energies are what we might expect of a single finite well, but as they move apart, pairs of functions converge to intermediate energies. (a) The energies of the second and fourth

states decrease. Based on changing wavelength alone, argue that this is reasonable. (b) The energies of the first and third states *increase*. Why? (*Hint:* Study how the behavior required in the classically forbidden region affects these two relative to the others.) (c) The distant-wells case might represent two distant atoms. If each atom had one electron, what advantage is there in bringing the atoms closer to form a molecule? (*Note:* Two electrons can have the same wave function.)

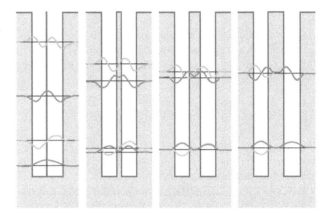

13. In the harmonic oscillator wave functions of Figure 18, there is variation in wavelength from the middle to the extremes of the classically allowed region, most noticeable in the higher-n functions. Why does it vary as it does?

14. Summarize the similarities and differences between the three simple bound cases considered in this chapter.

15. Consider a particle bound in an infinite well, where the potential inside is not constant but a linearly varying function. Suppose the particle is in a fairly high energy state, so that its wave function stretches across the entire well; that is, it isn't caught in the "low spot." Decide how, if at all, its wavelength should vary. Then sketch a plausible wave function.

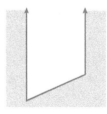

16. The quantized energy levels in the infinite well get farther apart as n increases, but in the harmonic oscillator they are equally spaced. (a) Explain the difference by considering the distance "between the walls" in each case and how it depends on the particle's energy.

(b) A very important bound system, the hydrogen atom, has energy levels that actually get closer together as n increases. How do you think the separation between the potential energy "walls" in this system varies relative to the other two? Explain.

17. In several bound systems, the quantum-mechanically allowed energies depend on a single quantum number. We found in Section 5 that the energy levels in an infinite well are given by $E_n = a_1 n^2$, where $n = 1, 2, 3, \ldots$ and a_1 is a constant. (Actually, we know what a_1 is, but it would only distract us here.) Section 7 showed that for a harmonic oscillator, they are $E_n = a_2(n - \frac{1}{2})$, where $n = 1, 2, 3, \ldots$. (Using an $n - \frac{1}{2}$ with n strictly positive is equivalent to $n + \frac{1}{2}$ with n nonnegative.) Finally, for a hydrogen atom, a bound system $E_n = -a_3/n^2$, where $n = 1, 2, 3, \ldots$. Consider particles making downward transitions between the quantized energy levels, each transition producing a photon. For each of these three systems, is there a minimum photon wavelength? A maximum? It might be helpful to make sketches of the relative heights of the energy levels in each case.

18. Quantum-mechanical stationary states are of the general form $\Psi(x, t) = \psi(x) e^{-i\omega t}$. For the basic plane wave, this is $\Psi(x, t) = A e^{ikx} e^{-i\omega t} = A e^{i(kx - \omega t)}$, and for a particle in a box, it is $\Psi(x, t) = A \sin(kx) e^{-i\omega t}$. Although both are sinusoidal, we claim that the plane wave alone is the prototype function whose momentum is pure—a well-defined value in one direction. Reinforcing the claim is the fact that the plane wave alone lacks features that we expect to see only when, effectively, waves are moving in both directions. What features are these, and, considering the probability densities, are they indeed present for a particle in a box and absent for a plane wave?

Exercises

Section 3

19. Under what circumstance does the integral $\int_{x_0}^{\infty} x^b dx$ diverge? Use this to argue that a physically acceptable wave function must fall to 0 faster than $|x|^{-1/2}$ does as x gets large.

Section 4

20. A comet in an extremely elliptical orbit about a star has, of course, a maximum orbit radius. By comparison, its minimum orbit radius may be nearly 0. Make plots of the potential energy and a plausible total energy E versus radius on the same set of axes. Identify the classical turning points on your plot.

21. A classical particle confined to the positive x-axis experiences a force whose potential energy is

$$U(x) = \frac{1}{x^2} - \frac{2}{x} + 1 \quad \text{(SI units)}$$

(a) By finding its minimum value and determining its behaviors at $x = 0$ and $x = +\infty$, sketch this potential energy.

(b) Suppose the particle has an energy of 0.5 J. Find any turning points. Would the particle be bound?

(c) Suppose the particle has an energy of 2.0 J. Find any turning points. Would the particle be bound?

Section 5

22. A study of classical waves tells us that a standing wave can be expressed as a sum of two traveling waves. Quantum-mechanical traveling waves, are of the form $\Psi(x, t) = A e^{i(kx - \omega t)}$. Show that the infinite well's standing-wave function can be expressed as a sum of two traveling waves.

23. Write out the total wave function $\Psi(x, t)$ for an electron in the $n = 3$ state of a 10 nm wide infinite well. Other than the symbols x and t, the function should include only numerical values.

24. An electron in the $n = 4$ state of a 5 nm wide infinite well makes a transition to the ground state, giving off energy in the form of a photon. What is the photon's wavelength?

25. An electron is trapped in a quantum well (practically infinite). If the lowest-energy transition is to produce a photon of 450 nm wavelength, what should be the well's width?

26. Because protons and neutrons are similar in mass, size, and certain other characteristics, a collective term, *nucleons,* has been coined that encompasses both of these constituents of the atomic nucleus. In many nuclei, nucleons are confined (by the strong force) to dimensions of roughly 15 femtometers. Photons emitted by nuclei as the nucleons drop to lower energy levels are known as gamma particles. Their energies are typically in the MeV range. Why does this make sense?

27. Where would a particle in the first excited state (first above ground) of an infinite well mostly likely be found?

28. What is the probability that a particle in the first excited ($n = 2$) state of an infinite well would be found in the middle third of the well? How does this compare with the classical expectation? Why?

29. A tiny 1 µg particle is in a 1 cm wide enclosure and takes a year to bounce from one end to the other and back. (a) How many nodes are there in its enclosure? (b) How would your answer change if the particle were more massive or moving faster?

* **30.** A particle is bound by a potential energy of the form

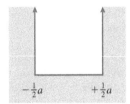

$$U(x) = \begin{cases} 0 & |x| < \frac{1}{2}a, \\ \infty & |x| > \frac{1}{2}a \end{cases}$$

This differs from the infinite well of Section 5 in being symmetric about $x = 0$, which implies that the probability densities must also be symmetric. Noting that either sine *or* cosine would fit this requirement and could be made continuous with the zero wave function outside the well, determine the allowed energies and corresponding normalized wave functions for this potential well.

Section 6

31. Verify that solution (19) satisfies the Schrödinger equation in form (18).

32. A finite potential energy function $U(x)$ allows $\psi(x)$, the solution of the time-independent Schrödinger equation, to penetrate the classically forbidden region. Without assuming any particular function for $U(x)$, show that $\psi(x)$ must have an inflection point at any value of x where it enters a classically forbidden region.

33. Verify that $A \sin(kx) + B \cos(kx)$ is a solution of equation (12).

34. A 50 eV electron is trapped between electrostatic walls 200 eV high. How far does its wave function extend beyond the walls?

35. An electron is trapped in a finite well. How "far" (in eV) is it from being free if the penetration length of its wave function into the classically forbidden region is 1 nm?

36. Whereas an infinite well has an infinite number of bound states, a finite well does not. By relating the well height U_0 to the kinetic energy and the kinetic energy (through λ) to n and L, show that the number of bound states is given roughly by $\sqrt{8mL^2 U_0/h^2}$. (Assume that the number is large.)

37. The deeper the finite well, the more states it holds. In fact, a new state, the nth, is added when the well's depth U_0 reaches $h^2(n-1)^2/8mL^2$. (a) Argue that this should be the case based only on $k = \sqrt{2mE/\hbar^2}$, the shape of the wave inside, and the degree of penetration of the classically forbidden region expected for a state whose energy E is only negligibly below U_0. (b) How many states would be found up to this same "height" in an *infinite* well.

Exercises 38–41 refer to a particle of mass m trapped in a half-infinite well, with potential energy given by

$$U(x) = \begin{cases} \infty & x \le 0 \\ 0 & 0 < x < L \\ U_0 & x \ge L \end{cases}$$

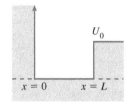

38. Advance an argument based on $p = h/\lambda$ that there is no bound state in a half-infinite well unless U_0 is at least $h^2/32mL^2$. (*Hint:* What is the maximum wavelength possible within the well?)

39. A finite well always has at least one bound state. Why does the argument of Exercise 38 fail in the case of a finite well?

* **40.** Write solutions to the Schrödinger equation appropriate in the various regions, impose required continuity conditions, and obtain the energy quantization condition:

$$\sqrt{E} \cot\left(\frac{\sqrt{2mE}}{\hbar}L\right) = -\sqrt{U_0 - E}$$

* **41.** Using the result of Exercise 40 and a computer or calculator able to solve (transcendental) equations, find the two bound-state energies for a well in which $U_0 = 4(\pi^2\hbar^2/2mL^2)$.

* **42.** By largely qualitative arguments, Exercise 37 shows that a finite well can hold an nth state only if its depth U_0 is at least $h^2(n-1)^2/8mL^2$. Show that this result also follows from equation (23) and the accompanying Figure 14.

* **43.** Obtain expression (23) from equation (22). Using $\cos\theta = \cos^2(\frac{1}{2}\theta) - \sin^2(\frac{1}{2}\theta)$ and $\sin\theta = 2\sin(\frac{1}{2}\theta)\cos(\frac{1}{2}\theta)$, first convert the argument of the cotangent from kL to $\frac{1}{2}kL$. Next, put the resulting equation in quadratic form, and then factor. Note that α is positive by definition.

* **44.** Using equation (23), find the energy of a particle confined to a finite well whose walls are half the height of the ground-state infinite well energy, E_1. (A calculator or computer able to solve equations numerically may be used, but this happens to be a case where an exact answer can be deduced without too much trouble.)

* **45.** There are mathematical solutions to the Schrödinger equation for the finite well for *any* energy, and in fact, they can be made smooth everywhere. Guided by A Closer Look: Solving the Finite Well, show this as follows:

    (a) Don't throw out any mathematical solutions. That is, in region II ($x < 0$), assume that $\psi(x) = Ce^{+\alpha x} + De^{-\alpha x}$, and in region III ($x > L$), assume that $\psi(x) = Fe^{+\alpha x} + Ge^{-\alpha x}$. Write the smoothness conditions.

    (b) In Section 6, the smoothness conditions were combined to eliminate A, B, and G in favor of C. In the remaining equation, C canceled, leaving an equation involving only k and α, solvable for only certain values of E. Why can't this be done here?

    (c) Our solution is smooth. What is still wrong with it physically?

    (d) Show that

$$D = \frac{1}{2}\left(B - \frac{k}{\alpha}A\right) \quad \text{and}$$

$$F = \frac{1}{2}e^{-\alpha L}\left[\left(A - B\frac{k}{\alpha}\right)\sin(kL) + \left(A\frac{k}{\alpha} + B\right)\cos(kL)\right]$$

and that setting these offending coefficients to 0 reproduces quantization condition (22).

* **46.** It is possible to take the finite well wave functions further than (21) without approximation, eliminating all but one normalization constant C. First, use the continuity/smoothness conditions to eliminate A, B, and G in favor of C in (21). Then make the change of variables $z \equiv x - L/2$ and use the trigonometric relations $\sin(a + b) = \sin(a)\cos(b) + \cos(a)\sin(b)$ and $\cos(a + b) = \cos(a)\cos(b) - \sin(a)\sin(b)$ on the functions in region I, $-L/2 < z < +L/2$. The change of variables shifts the problem so that it is symmetric about $z = 0$, which requires that the probability density be symmetric and thus that $\psi(z)$ be either an odd or even function of z. By comparing the region II and region III functions, argue that this in turn demands that $(\alpha/k)\sin(kL) + \cos(kL)$ must be either $+1$ (even) or -1 (odd). Next, show that these conditions can be expressed, respectively, as $\alpha/k = \tan(kL/2)$ and $\alpha/k = -\cot(kL/2)$. Finally, plug these separately back into the region I solutions and show that

$$\psi(z) = C \times \begin{cases} e^{+\alpha(z+\frac{1}{2}L)} & z < -\frac{1}{2}L \\ \dfrac{\cos kz}{\cos(\frac{1}{2}kL)} & -\frac{1}{2}L < z < +\frac{1}{2}L \\ e^{-\alpha(z-\frac{1}{2}L)} & z > +\frac{1}{2}L \end{cases}$$

or

$$\psi(z) = C \times \begin{cases} e^{+\alpha(z+\frac{1}{2}L)} & z < -\frac{1}{2}L \\ \dfrac{-\sin kz}{\sin(\frac{1}{2}kL)} & -\frac{1}{2}L < z < +\frac{1}{2}L \\ -e^{-\alpha(z-\frac{1}{2}L)} & z > +\frac{1}{2}L \end{cases}$$

Note that C is now a standard multiplicative normalization constant. Setting the integral of $|\psi(z)|^2$ over all space to 1 would give it in terms of k and α, but because we can't solve (22) exactly for k (or E), neither can we obtain an exact value for C.

* **47.** Consider the delta well potential energy:

$$U(x) = \begin{cases} 0 & x \neq 0 \\ -\infty & x = 0 \end{cases}$$

Although not completely realistic, this potential energy is often a convenient approximation to a *very* strong, *very* narrow attractive potential energy well. It has only one allowed bound-state wave function, and because the top of the well is defined as $U = 0$, the corresponding bound-state energy is negative. Call its value $-E_0$.

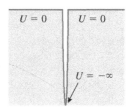

191

(a) Applying the usual arguments and required continuity conditions (need it be smooth?), show that the wave function is given by

$$\psi(x) = \left(\frac{2mE_0}{\hbar^2}\right)^{1/4} e^{-\left(\sqrt{2mE_0}/\hbar\right)|x|}$$

(b) Sketch $\psi(x)$ and $U(x)$ on the same diagram. Does this wave function exhibit the expected behavior in the classically forbidden region?

* **48.** Figure 15 shows the allowed wave functions for a finite well whose depth U_0 was chosen to be $6\pi^2\hbar^2/mL^2$. (a) Insert this value in equation (23), then, using a calculator or computer, solve for the allowed values of kL, of which there are four. (b) Using $k = \sqrt{2mE}/\hbar$, find the corresponding values of E. Do they appear to agree with Figure 15? (c) Show that the chosen U_0 value implies that $\alpha = \sqrt{(12\pi^2/L^2) - k^2}$. (d) Defining L and C to be 1 for convenience, plug your kL and α values into the wave function given in Exercise 46, then plot the results. (*Note:* Your first and third kL values should correspond to even functions of z, thus using the form with $\cos kz$, while the second and fourth correspond to odd functions.) Do the plots also agree with Figure 15?

Section 7

49. For the harmonic oscillator potential energy, $U = \frac{1}{2}\kappa x^2$, the ground-state wave function is $\psi(x) = Ae^{-\left(\sqrt{m\kappa/2\hbar}\right)x^2}$, and its energy is $\frac{1}{2}\hbar\sqrt{\kappa/m}$.

(a) Find the classical turning points for a particle with this energy.

(b) The Schrödinger equation says that $\psi(x)$ and its second derivative should be of the opposite sign when $E > U$ and of the same sign when $E < U$. These two regions are divided by the classical turning points. Verify the relationship between $\psi(x)$ and its second derivative for the ground-state oscillator wave function. (*Hint:* Look for the inflection points.)

50. A 2 kg block oscillates with an amplitude of 10 cm on a spring of force constant 120 N/m. (a) In which quantum state is the block? (b) The block has a slight electric charge and drops to a lower energy level by generating a photon. What is the minimum energy decrease possible, and what would be the corresponding fractional change in energy?

51. Air is mostly N_2, diatomic nitrogen, with an effective spring constant of 2.3×10^3 N/m, and an effective oscillating mass of half the atomic mass. For roughly what temperatures should vibration contribute to its heat capacity?

52. To a good approximation, the hydrogen chloride molecule, HCl, behaves vibrationally as a quantum harmonic oscillator of spring constant 480 N/m and with effective oscillating mass just that of the lighter atom, hydrogen. If it were in its ground vibrational state, what wavelength photon would be just right to bump this molecule up to its next-higher vibrational energy state?

53. In Section 5, it was shown that the infinite well energies follow simply from $\lambda = h/p$; the formula for kinetic energy, $p^2/2m$; and a famous standing-wave condition, $\lambda = 2L/n$. The arguments are perfectly valid when the potential energy is 0 (inside the well) and L is strictly constant, but they can also be useful in other cases. The length L allowed the wave should be roughly the distance between the classical turning points, where there is no kinetic energy left. Apply these arguments to the oscillator potential energy, $U(x) = \frac{1}{2}\kappa x^2$. Find the location x of the classical turning point in terms of E; use *twice* this distance for L; then insert this into the infinite well energy formula, so that E appears on both sides. Thus far, the procedure really only deals with kinetic energy. Assume, as is true for a classical oscillator, that there is as much potential energy, on average, as kinetic energy. What do you obtain for the quantized energies?

54. The potential energy shared by two atoms in a diatomic molecule, depicted in Figure 17, is often approximated by the fairly simple function $U(x) = (a/x^{12}) - (b/x^6)$, where constants a and b depend on the atoms involved. In Section 7, it is said that near its minimum value, it can be approximated by an even simpler function—it should "look like" a parabola.

(a) In terms of a and b, find the minimum potential energy $U(x_0)$ and the separation x_0 at which it occurs.

(b) The parabolic approximation $U_p(x) = U(x_0) + \frac{1}{2}\kappa(x - x_0)^2$ has the same minimum value at x_0 and the same first derivative there (i.e., 0). Its second derivative is κ, the spring constant of this Hooke's law potential energy. In terms of a and b, what is the spring constant of $U(x)$?

Section 8

55. Classically, if a particle is not observed, the probability per unit length of finding it in a box is a constant $1/L$ along the entire length of the box. With this, show that the classical expectation value of the position is $\frac{1}{2}L$, that the expectation value of the square of the position is $\frac{1}{3}L^2$, and that the uncertainty in position is $L/\sqrt{12}$.

56. Show that the uncertainty in a particle's position in an infinite well in the general case of arbitrary n is given by

$$L\sqrt{\frac{1}{12} - \frac{1}{2n^2\pi^2}}$$

Discuss the dependence. In what circumstance does it agree with the classical uncertainty of $L/\sqrt{12}$ discussed in Exercise 55?

57. Show that the uncertainty in a particle's momentum in an infinite well in the general case of arbitrary n is given by $n\pi\hbar/L$.

58. What is the product of the uncertainties determined in Exercises 56 and 57? Discuss the result.

59. Determine the expectation value of the position of a harmonic oscillator in its ground state.

60. Show that the uncertainty in the position of a ground-state harmonic oscillator is $(1/\sqrt{2})(\hbar^2/m\kappa)^{1/4}$.

61. Show that the uncertainty in the momentum of a ground-state harmonic oscillator is $(\sqrt{\hbar/2})(m\kappa)^{1/4}$.

62. What is the product of the uncertainties determined in Exercises 60 and 61? Explain.

63. Repeat Exercises 60–62 for the first excited ($n = 1$) state of a harmonic oscillator.

64. If a particle in a stationary state is *bound*, the expectation value of its momentum must be 0. (a) In words, why? (b) Prove it. Starting from the general expression (31) with $\hat{p}$ in place of $\hat{Q}$, integrate by parts, then argue that the result is identically 0. Be careful that your argument is somehow based on the particle being *bound*; a free particle certainly may have a nonzero momentum. (*Note:* Without loss of generality, $\psi(x)$ may be chosen to be real.)

Section 9

65. In equation (33), the two solutions are added in equal amounts. Show that if we instead added different percentages of the two solutions, it would not change the important conclusion related to the oscillation frequency of the charge density.

* **66.** Consider a wave function that is a combination of two different infinite well stationary states, the nth and the mth.

$$\Psi(x, t) = \frac{1}{\sqrt{2}}\Psi_n(x)e^{-i(E_n/\hbar)t} + \frac{1}{\sqrt{2}}\Psi_m(x)e^{-i(E_m/\hbar)t}$$

(a) Show that $\Psi(x, t)$ is properly normalized.

(b) Show that the expectation value of the energy is the average of the two energies: $\overline{E} = \frac{1}{2}(E_n + E_m)$. (*Be careful:* The temporal part of the wave function definitely does *not* drop out.)

(c) Show that the expectation value of the square of the energy is given by

$$\overline{E^2} = \frac{1}{2}(E_n^2 + E_m^2)$$

(d) Determine the uncertainty in the energy.

Section 10

See the Computational Exercises section.

Section 11

67. Prove that the transitional-state wave function (33) does not have a well-defined energy.

68. To describe a matter wave, does the function $A\sin(kx)\cos(\omega t)$ have a well-defined energy? Explain.

69. Does the wave function $\psi(x) = A(e^{+ikx} + e^{-ikx})$ have a well-defined momentum? Explain.

70. The operator for angular momentum about the z-axis in spherical polar coordinates is $-i\hbar(\partial/\partial\phi)$. Find a function $f(\phi)$ that would have a well-defined z-component of angular momentum.

71. Show that $\Delta p = 0 \Rightarrow \hat{p}\psi(x) = \overline{p}\psi(x)$. That is, verify that unless the wave function is an eigenfunction of the momentum operator, there will be a nonzero uncertainty in momentum. Start by showing that the quantity

$$\int_{\text{all space}} \psi^*(x)(\hat{p} - \overline{p})^2\psi(x)dx$$

is $(\Delta p)^2$. Then, using the differential operator form of $\hat{p}$ and integration by parts, show that it is also

$$\int_{\text{all space}} [(\hat{p} - \overline{p})\psi(x)]^*[(\hat{p} - \overline{p})\psi(x)]dx$$

(*Note:* Because momentum is real, $\overline{p}$ is real.) Together these show that if Δp is 0, then the preceding quantity must be 0. However, the integral of the complex square of a function (the quantity in brackets) can only be 0 if the function is identically 0, so the assertion is proved.

Comprehensive Exercises

72. In a study of heat transfer, we find that for a solid rod, there is a relationship between the second derivative of the temperature with respect to position along the rod and the first with respect to time. (A *linear* temperature change with position would imply as much heat flowing into a region as out, so the temperature there would not change with time.)

$$\frac{\partial^2 T(x, t)}{\partial x^2} = b\frac{\partial T(x, t)}{\partial t}$$

(a) Separate variables. That is, assume a solution that is a product of a function of x and a function of t,

193

plug it in, then divide by it. Obtain two ordinary differential equations.

(b) Consider a fairly simple, if somewhat unrealistic, case. Suppose the temperature is 0 at $x = 0$ and $x = L$, and positive in between. Write down the simplest function of x that (1) fits these conditions and (2) obeys the differential equation involving x. Does your choice determine the value, including sign, of some constant?

(c) Obtain the full $T(x, t)$ for this case.

73. In Section 3, we learned that to be normalizable, a wave function (1) must not itself diverge and (2) must fall to 0 faster than $|x|^{-1/2}$ as x gets large. Nevertheless, we find two functions that slightly violate these requirements very useful. Consider the quantum mechanical plane wave $Ae^{i(kx-\omega t)}$ and the weird function $\psi_{x_0}(x)$ pictured in Figure 19, which we here call by its proper name, the Dirac delta function. (a) Which of the two normalizability requirements is violated by the plane wave, and which by the Dirac delta function? (b) Normalization of the plane wave could be accomplished if it were simply truncated, restricted to the region $-b < x < +b$, being identically 0 outside. What would then be the relationship between b and A, and what would happen to A as b approaches infinity? (c) Rather than an infinitely tall and narrow spike like the Dirac delta function, consider a function that is 0 everywhere except the narrow region $-\varepsilon < x < +\varepsilon$, where its value is a constant B. This too could be normalized. What would be the relationship between ε and B, and what would happen to B as ε approaches 0? (What we get is not exactly the Dirac delta function, but the distinction involves comparing infinities, a dangerous business that we will avoid.) (d) As we see, the two "exceptional" functions may be viewed as limits of normalizable ones. In those limits, they are also complementary to each other in terms of their position and momentum uncertainties. Without getting into calculations, describe how they are complementary.

74. The figure shows a potential energy function. (a) How much energy could a classical particle have and still be

bound? (b) Where would an unbound particle have its maximum kinetic energy? (c) For what range of energies might a classical particle be bound in either of two different regions? (d) Do you think that a quantum-mechanical particle with energy in the range referred to in part (c) would be bound in one region or the other? Explain.

75. Consider a particle of mass m and energy E in a region where the potential energy is a constant U_0, greater than E, and the region extends to $x = +\infty$. (a) Guess a physically acceptable solution of the Schrödinger equation in this region and demonstrate that it is a solution. (b) The region noted in part (a) extends from $x = +1$ nm to $+\infty$. To the left of $x = 1$ nm, the particle's wave function is $D \cos(10^9 \text{ m}^{-1}x)$. Is $U(x)$ also greater than E here? (c) The particle's mass m is 10^{-30} kg. By how much (in eV) does U_0, the potential energy prevailing from x = 1 nm to $+\infty$, exceed the particle's energy?

76. Exercise 53 outlines a procedure for predicting how the quantum-mechanically allowed energies for a harmonic oscillator should depend on a quantum number. In essence, allowed kinetic energies are the particle-in-a-box energies, except the length L is replaced by the distance between classical turning points, expressed in terms of E. Apply this procedure to a potential energy of the form $U(x) = -b/x$, where b is a constant. Assume that at the origin there is an infinitely high wall, making it one turning point, and determine the other turning point in terms of E. For the average potential energy, use its value at halfway between the turning points, again in terms of E. Find an expression for the allowed energies in terms of m, b, and n. (Although three-dimensional, the hydrogen atom potential energy is of this form, and the allowed energy levels depend on a quantum number exactly as this simple model predicts.)

77. The harmonic oscillator potential energy is proportional to x^2, and the energy levels are equally spaced: $E_n \propto (n + \frac{1}{2})$. The energy levels in the infinite well become farther apart as energy increases: $E_n \propto n^2$. Because the function $\lim_{b \to \infty} |x/L|^b$ is 0 for $|x| < L$ and infinitely large for $|x| > L$, the infinite well potential energy may be thought of as proportional to $|x|^\infty$.

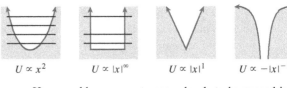

$U \propto x^2$ \qquad $U \propto |x|^\infty$ \qquad $U \propto |x|^1$ \qquad $U \propto -|x|^{-1}$

How would you expect energy levels to be spaced in a potential well that is (a) proportional to $|x|^1$ and (b) proportional to $-|x|^{-1}$? For the harmonic oscillator and infinite well, the number of bound-state energies is infinite, and arbitrarily large bound-state energies are possible.

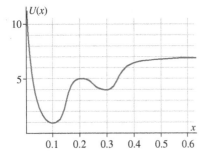

Are these characteristics shared (c) by the $|x|^1$ well and (d) by the $-|x|^{-1}$ well?

Exercises 78–88 refer to a particle of mass m described by the wave function

$$\psi(x) = \begin{cases} 2\sqrt{a^3}\, x\, e^{-ax} & x > 0 \\ 0 & x < 0 \end{cases}$$

78. Verify that the normalization constant $2\sqrt{a^3}$ is correct.

79. Sketch the wave function. Is it smooth?

80. Determine the particle's most probable position.

81. What is the probability that the particle would be found between $x = 0$ and $x = 1/a$?

82. Calculate the expectation value of the position of the particle.

83. Calculate the uncertainty in the particle's position.

84. Determine the expectation value of the momentum of the particle. Explain.

85. Calculate the uncertainty in the particle's momentum.

86. What is the product of Δx and Δp (obtained in Exercises 83 and 85)? How does it compare with the minimum theoretically possible? Explain.

87. The particle has $E = 0$. (a) Show that the potential energy for $x > 0$ is given by

$$U(x) = -\frac{\hbar^2 a}{m}\frac{1}{x} + \frac{\hbar^2 a^2}{2m}$$

(b) What is the potential energy for $x < 0$?

88. The potential energy in the case where the particle has $E = 0$ is given in Exercise 87. (a) On the same axes, sketch the wave function and the potential energy. (b) What is the probability that the particle would be found in the classically forbidden region?

89. Consider the differential equation $d^2f(x)/dx^2 = bf(x)$. (a) Suppose that $f_1(x)$ and $f_2(x)$ are solutions. That is,

$$\frac{d^2 f_1(x)}{dx^2} = bf_1(x) \quad \text{and} \quad \frac{d^2 f_2(x)}{dx^2} = bf_2(x)$$

Show that the equation also holds when the linear combination $A_1 f_1(x) + A_2 f_2(x)$ is inserted. (b) Suppose that $f_3(x)$ and $f_4(x)$ are solutions of $d^2f(x)/dx^2 = bf^2(x)$. Is $A_3 f_3(x) + A_4 f_4(x)$ a solution? Justify your answer.

Exercises 90–92 refer to a particle described by the wave function

$$\psi(x) = \sqrt{\frac{2}{\pi}}\, a^{3/2}\, \frac{1}{x^2 + a^2}$$

90. Show that the normalization constant is correct.

* **91.** Calculate the uncertainty in the particle's position.

* **92.** (a) Taking the particle's total energy to be 0, find the potential energy. (b) On the same axes, sketch the wave function and the potential energy. (c) To what region would the particle be restricted classically?

93. A particle is described by the wave function

$$\psi(x) = \frac{\sqrt{2/\pi}}{x^2 - x + 1.25}$$

(a) Show that the normalization constant $\sqrt{2/\pi}$ is correct.

(b) A measurement of the position of the particle is to be made. At what location is it most probable that the particle would be found?

(c) What is the probability per unit length of finding the particle at this location?

Exercises 94–97 refer to a bound particle of mass m described by the wave function

$$\psi(x) = A x e^{-x^2/2b^2}$$

94. Sketch $\psi(x)$. Would you expect this wave function to be the ground state? Why or why not?

95. What is the most probable location at which to find the particle?

96. Given that the particle's total energy E is 0, show that the potential energy is $U(x) = \dfrac{\hbar^2}{2mb^4}x^2 - \dfrac{3\hbar^2}{2mb^2}$

97. For a total energy of 0, the potential energy is given in Exercise 96. (a) Given these, to what region of the x-axis would a *classical* particle be restricted? Is the quantum-mechanical particle similarly restricted? (b) Write an expression for the probability that the (quantum-mechanical) particle would be found in the classically forbidden region, leaving it in the form of an integral. (The integral cannot be evaluated in closed form.)

98. A harmonic oscillator has its minimum possible energy. What is the probability of finding it in the classically forbidden region? (*Note:* At some point, a computer or calculator able to do numerical integration will be needed.)

Computational Exercises

Guidelines for application of equation (35). With length, time, and mass at our disposal, we choose our units so that the particle mass m and the value of $\hbar$ are both 1. Now, let x be a point Δx to the right of the origin. Equation (35) becomes

$$\psi(2\Delta x) = 2\psi(\Delta x) - \psi(0) + 2(\Delta x)^2(U(\Delta x) - E)\psi(\Delta x)$$

After choosing initial values $\psi(0)$ and $\psi(\Delta x)$, and assuming U is known and a value for Δx selected, we need only pick an E, and $\psi(2\Delta x)$ can be found. Thereafter, taking x to be a point $2\Delta x$ to the right of the origin, we have

$$\psi(3\Delta x) = 2\psi(2\Delta x) - \psi(\Delta x) + 2(\Delta x)^2(U(2\Delta x) - E)\psi(2\Delta x)$$

and the process can be repeated indefinitely. Choosing $\psi(0)$ and $\psi(\Delta x)$ is simplified if $U(x)$ is symmetric about $x = 0$, for this implies a symmetric probability density, which in turn requires that $\psi(x)$ be either an even or odd function of x. An odd function is 0 at the origin, so $\psi(0)$ must be 0. Since the slope is, in general, nonzero, $\psi(\Delta x)$ must be nonzero, and we define it to be 1 (affecting only the vertical scale of ψ overall). An even function, on the other hand, has 0 slope at the origin, so $\psi(0)$ and $\psi(\Delta x)$ must be of equal value, which we can define to be 1.

99. **Finite Well:** The goal here is to find the energies for a finite well whose width L is 4 and whose depth U_0 is 5 in the simple system of units discussed above. To exploit symmetry, assume that the finite well extends not from $x = 0$ to $x = 4$, but from $x = -2$ to $x = +2$. For $U(x)$, the function 2.5*sign(x^2 − 4) + 2.5 can be adapted to almost any computer. (a) Plot this $U(x)$. (b) For Δx, use 0.001. Now, following the above guidelines on choosing $\psi(0)$ and $\psi(\Delta x)$, test both odd and even functions at different trial values of E by finding ψ at all positive multiples of Δx out to $x = 4$ and plotting the results. Note that because of the functions' symmetries, there is no need to plot negative values of x. Find four allowed energies. (c) What tells you that an energy is correct? (d) Using the definitions of k and α, the finite well energy quantization condition, given in equation (22), can be written

$$2\cot\left(\frac{L\sqrt{2mE}}{\hbar}\right) = \sqrt{\frac{E}{U_0 - E}} - \sqrt{\frac{U_0 - E}{E}}$$

It can't be solved exactly, but do your values satisfy it reasonably well?

100. **Harmonic Oscillator:** The harmonic oscillator can be solved exactly for the quantized energies, and here we

compare those results with a numerical approach. Along with the values of m and $\hbar$ discussed above, we choose our units so that the spring constant κ is also 1. The potential energy function $U(x)$ is then simply $\frac{1}{2}x^2$. For Δx, use 0.001. (a) Following the above guidelines on choosing $\psi(0)$ and $\psi(\Delta x)$, test both odd and even functions at different trial values of E by finding ψ at all positive multiples of Δx out to $x = 4$ and plotting the results. Note that because of the functions' symmetries, there is no need to plot negative values of x. Find four allowed energies. (b) What tells you that an energy is correct? (c) Compare your results with the exact values given in equation (26).

101. **Half-Infinite Well:** A half-infinite well has an infinitely high wall at the origin and one of finite height U_0 at $x = L$. Like the finite well, it cannot be solved exactly. Here we find energies numerically for one whose width L is 2 and whose depth U_0 is 5 in the simple system of units discussed in the above guidelines. The half-infinite well potential energy isn't symmetric about $x = 0$, but part of the symmetric-case discussion still applies. Because the left wall is infinite, $\psi(x)$ must be 0 for $x \leq 0$, so $\psi(0)$ must be 0. Assuming a nonzero slope there, we can define $\psi(\Delta x)$ to be 1. (In essence, we are keeping only the conditions that apply to odd functions, which must be 0 at the origin.) For $U(x)$, the function 2.5*sign($x − 2$) + 2.5 can be adapted to almost any computer and is correct for positive x, which is all that matters. (a) Using 0.001 for Δx, test different trial values of E by finding ψ at all multiples of Δx out to $x = 4$ and plotting the results. Find two allowed energies. (b) What tells you that an energy is correct? (c) The "unsolvable" energy quantization condition for a half-infinite well is given in Exercise 40. Do your values satisfy it reasonably well?

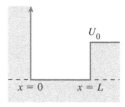

196

Answers to Selected Exercises

21. $2 \pm \sqrt{2}$, yes, $\sqrt{2} - 1$, no

23. $1.41 \times 10^4 \text{ m}^{-1/2} \sin(9.42 \times 10^8 \text{ m}^{-1}x)e^{-i(5.14 \times 10^{13} s^{-1})t}$

25. 0.64 nm

27. $L/4$ or $3L/4$

29. 2×10^{13}

35. 0.038 eV

45. $C + D = B$, $\alpha(C - D) = kA$, $A \sin kL + B \cos kL = Fe^{\alpha L} + Ge^{-\alpha L}$, $k(A \cos kL - B \sin kL) = \alpha(Fe^{\alpha L} - Ge^{-\alpha L})$

49. $\pm\left(\dfrac{\hbar^2}{m\kappa}\right)^{1/4}$

53. $\dfrac{1}{\sqrt{8}}n\pi\hbar\sqrt{\kappa/m}$

59. zero

63. $\sqrt{\dfrac{3}{2}}\left(\dfrac{\hbar^2}{m\kappa}\right)^{1/4}, \sqrt{\dfrac{3\hbar}{2}}(m\kappa)^{1/4}, \dfrac{3}{2}\hbar$

73. (a) plane wave (2), Dirac delta (1); (b) $A = 1/\sqrt{2b}$; (c) $B = 1/\sqrt{2\varepsilon}$

75. (b) no; (c) 1.35×10^{-20} J

77. (a) and (b) closer together; (c) Yes; (d) energy cannot be arbitrarily high, infinite number of states still possible

81. 0.323

83. $0.866/a$

85. $a\hbar$

89. (b) no

91. a

93. (b) $\frac{1}{2}$; (c) 0.637

95. $\pm b$

97. (a) $-b\sqrt{3} < x < +b\sqrt{3}$, no

Credits

Photograph Credits

9: IBM; **21:** Sandia Corporation

Art Credits

22: Courtesy of *Nature* magazine; **23:** Courtesy of Dr. L. B. Wang

Unbound States: Steps, Tunneling, and Particle-Wave Propagation

Chapter Outline

Common to all topics in this chapter is the absence of a force capable of confining a particle to a region of space. Because the particle isn't bound, standing waves do not form, and energy is not quantized. Nevertheless, the surprising behaviors we discuss are further evidence of an inherent wave nature. Among other things, we find that a particle may be turned back by a force when classical mechanics says it should proceed, and it may prevail against a force where classical physics says it should be turned back. We begin in Section 1 by studying the effects of very simple forces on plane waves, followed in Section 2 by an introduction to the fascinating idea of quantum-mechanical tunneling. In Section 3, we study some applications of tunneling, such as the classically baffling phenomenon of radioactive alpha decay. The chapter ends with a section devoted to understanding the richer behavior of not-so-simple, but more realistic, free-particle wave functions, clarifying the relationship between the wave function and the motion of the particle.

1 The Potential Step

The first obstacle we place in the path of our free particles is simply an abrupt increase in the potential energy—a **potential step**. Just as a light wave striking a glass plate divides—some transmitted, some reflected—so does a matter wave divide when it encounters an abrupt change in conditions. This doesn't mean that a massive particle divides, any more than a photon divides in the case of light. But because in either case the wave is related to the probability of finding the particle, the division of the wave governs the probability of a given incident particle—photon or massive object—being transmitted or reflected.

To say anything about this, however, we must be able to distinguish between particles moving one way and those moving the other, and to do this we must be careful about the wave functions we use. The plane-wave solution of the free-particle Schrödinger equation:

$$\Psi(x, t) = A e^{+ikx - i\omega t} \qquad \text{right-moving}$$

This represents a particle whose momentum is in the positive x-direction. It is an unrealistic function for a single particle in the sense that, although its momentum is well defined, the position uncertainty is infinite—the particle is equally likely to be found anywhere. However, in the cases we consider here, we will use it to represent a steady *beam* of particles all moving in the positive direction, with A related to the *number* (rather than probability) per unit distance. By replacing k $(=p/\hbar)$ by $-k$, we represent a beam with momentum in the negative x-direction.

$$\Psi(x, t) = A e^{-ikx - i\omega t} \qquad \text{left-moving}$$

Right-moving: e^{+ikx}
Left-moving: e^{-ikx}

Because we will concentrate on stationary states, in which the same $e^{-i\omega t}$ appears in all $\Psi(x, t)$, the spatial parts are our main concern: $\psi(x) = e^{+ikx}$ moves right and $\psi(x) = e^{-ikx}$ moves left.

Facing complex spatial wave functions after an entire chapter on bound states in which they were real, a brief digression is helpful. Here we consider particles that move freely before encountering a force. Between the walls in the infinite and finite wells, the potential energy was 0, so a "particle" would also move freely. But there we used $\sin kx$ and $\cos kx$, while here we use e^{+ikx} and e^{-ikx}. Why? The time-independent Schrödinger equation for $U = 0$ is

$$\frac{d^2\psi(x)}{dx^2} = -\frac{2mE}{\hbar^2}\psi(x) = -k^2\psi(x) \qquad \text{where} \qquad k \equiv \sqrt{\frac{2mE}{\hbar^2}} \qquad (1)$$

All four functions—$\sin kx$, $\cos kx$, e^{+ikx}, and e^{-ikx}—satisfy the equation. Each is a sinusoidal wavelike function whose second derivative is opposite the function itself. In the *bound* systems, we could have started off with e^{+ikx} and e^{-ikx}, but $\sin kx$ and $\cos kx$ satisfy the physical requirements and are, in fact, sums and differences of the right- and left-moving e^{+ikx} and e^{-ikx} (see Exercise 13), just as we expect for a *standing* wave. Complex exponentials would have been an unnecessary detour. In an unbound system, however, where we need to keep directions of motion separate, they are the correct choice.

$E > U_0$

Now consider free particles encountering a potential step. In Figure 1, a representative electron moves to the right in a region of zero potential energy, until it encounters a very narrow region, where it experiences a large force opposite its direction of motion—a backward "kick." Passing through, its potential energy jumps abruptly to U_0 and stays there. Because a force is a *change* in potential energy $(F = -dU/dx)$, the narrow region near $x = 0$ is the

Figure 1 A free electron encounters a potential step that is classically surmountable.

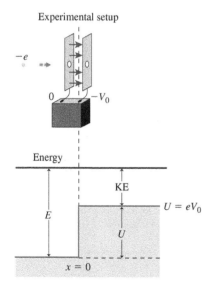

Experimental setup

Energy

only place where the electron experiences a force. The potential energy is given by

$$U(x) = \begin{cases} 0 & x < 0 \\ U_0 & x > 0 \end{cases}$$

Let us start with the case in which an incident particle has kinetic energy E greater than the potential energy jump, as Figure 1 shows. Classically, it should merely slow down abruptly at $x = 0$, its kinetic energy dropping as potential energy jumps, then proceed at constant reduced speed. There is no classical turning point where its kinetic energy falls to 0 and at which the force would cause a reversal of its motion. The particle would not rebound.

But classical physics won't do. To understand the behavior of something as small as an electron, we must apply quantum mechanics. In the region to the left of the step, $x < 0$, we will have a right-moving incident wave, and we allow for a left-moving reflected wave. Each solution of (1) is still a solution if it includes an arbitrary multiplicative constant, which will eventually tell us how they compare; so for the incident wave, we use Ae^{+ikx}, and for the reflected wave, Be^{-ikx}. In the region to the right of the step, $x > 0$, where $U = U_0$, the Schrödinger equation is

$$\frac{d^2\psi(x)}{dx^2} = -\frac{2m(E - U_0)}{\hbar^2}\psi(x) \tag{2}$$

Note that because E exceeds U_0, $\psi(x)$ and its second derivative are still of opposite sign, as in (1), so the same functions work here as when U is 0. The only difference is the coefficient of $\psi(x)$, making it convenient to rewrite (2) as

$$\frac{d^2\psi(x)}{dx^2} = -k'^2\psi(x) \qquad \text{where} \qquad k' \equiv \sqrt{\frac{2m(E - U_0)}{\hbar^2}} \tag{3}$$

The mathematical solutions here differ only in having k' in place of k. To again distinguish directions, we choose the pair of functions $e^{+ik'x}$ and $e^{-ik'x}$. However, we have a physical reason to throw out one of these. Beyond $x = 0$, there is no change in potential energy—no force to reflect anything moving to the right. Because there can thus be nothing moving to the *left* in this region, $e^{-ik'x}$ is physically inapplicable. Altogether, then, for $x < 0$, we have incident (inc) and reflected (refl) waves, and for $x > 0$, we have only a right-moving transmitted (trans) wave.

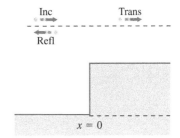

Figure 2 Incident particles may be reflected or transmitted.

$$\psi_{x<0}(x) = Ae^{+ikx} + Be^{-ikx} \qquad \psi_{x>0}(x) = Ce^{+ik'x} \tag{4}$$
$$\textbf{Inc} \qquad \textbf{Refl} \qquad\qquad\qquad \textbf{Trans}$$

Figure 2 represents these various parts schematically.

The square of Ae^{+ikx} is proportional to the number of particles per unit distance on the left of the step and moving to the right—incident particles.

201

The square of any complex exponential is 1 ($e^{+iz} \times e^{-iz} = 1$), so this density is particularly simple: A^*A. (Remember that, in general, when we "square" a wave function, we mean the complex square—the function times its complex conjugate. Also, with complex spatial wave functions, we must allow for complex coefficients.) The corresponding quantity for reflected particles—on the left of the step and moving to the left—is B^*B, and for transmitted particles, it is C^*C.

$$|\psi|^2_{\text{inc}} = A^*A \qquad |\psi|^2_{\text{refl}} = B^*B \qquad |\psi|^2_{\text{trans}} = C^*C \qquad (5)$$

It is worth reiterating that because $E > U_0$, it would be absurd to allow for reflection of a classical particle. But a light wave divides whenever it encounters a different medium, giving us some precedent. In fact, without allowing for reflection in our matter wave, we simply could not satisfy the smoothness requirement.

The wave function and its derivative must be continuous at the point where the two regions meet. These conditions are

$$\psi_{x<0}(0) = \psi_{x>0}(0): Ae^{+ik0} + Be^{-ik0} = Ce^{+ik'0}$$
$$\text{or} \qquad A + B = C$$
$$\left.\frac{d\psi_{x<0}}{dx}\right|_{x=0} = \left.\frac{d\psi_{x>0}}{dx}\right|_{x=0} : ikAe^{+ik0} - ikBe^{-ik0} = ik'Ce^{+ik'0} \qquad (6)$$
$$\text{or} \qquad k(A - B) = k'C$$

In the case of a bound particle, imposing the physical requirements leads to quantization. However, no restriction on the value of k (hence, E) arises from conditions (6). Because no particle is bound, we don't have the conditions at *two* ends that would inevitably lead to a standing wave. An incident particle may have any energy.

What conditions (6) give us are reflection and transmission probabilities. We calculate these from ratios of numbers per unit time in the corresponding beams:

$$\frac{\text{number}}{\text{time}} = \frac{\text{number}}{\text{distance}}\frac{\text{distance}}{\text{time}} \propto |\psi|^2 v$$

Using $v = p/m = \hbar k/m \propto k$ to express this in terms of k, we have

$$\frac{\text{number}}{\text{time}} \propto |\psi|^2 k$$

The transmission probability, given the symbol T, is thus

$$T = \frac{\dfrac{\text{number transmitted}}{\text{time}}}{\dfrac{\text{number incident}}{\text{time}}} = \frac{|\psi|^2_{\text{trans}} k_{x>0}}{|\psi|^2_{\text{inc}} k_{x<0}} = \frac{C^*C}{A^*A}\frac{k'}{k}$$

and the reflection probability R is

$$R = \frac{\dfrac{\text{number reflected}}{\text{time}}}{\dfrac{\text{number incident}}{\text{time}}} = \frac{|\psi|^2_{\text{refl}} k_{x<0}}{|\psi|^2_{\text{inc}} k_{x<0}} = \frac{B^*B}{A^*A}$$

Now, eliminating B from conditions (6) yields $C = [2k/(k + k')]A$, and eliminating C yields $B = [(k - k')/(k + k')]A$. Thus,

$$T = \frac{[2k/(k + k')]A^*[2k/(k + k')]A}{A^*A} \frac{k'}{k} = \frac{4kk'}{(k + k')^2}$$

and

$$R = \frac{[(k - k')/(k + k')]A^*[(k - k')/(k + k')]A}{A^*A} = \frac{(k - k')^2}{(k + k')^2}$$

We could have deduced one probability from the other, for the total number of particles had better be conserved, so the transmission and reflection probabilities *must* add to 1. Verifying that they do is left as an exercise.

Finally, we express the probabilities in terms of U_0 and E. Using the definitions of k and k', we have

$$T = 4\frac{\sqrt{E(E - U_0)}}{\left(\sqrt{E} + \sqrt{E - U_0}\right)^2} \qquad R = \frac{\left(\sqrt{E} - \sqrt{E - U_0}\right)^2}{\left(\sqrt{E} + \sqrt{E - U_0}\right)^2} \qquad (7)$$

Notably, expressions (7) are essentially identical to those giving reflected and transmitted intensities of a light wave normally incident on the interface between two media. Those for light differ only in that $\sqrt{E}$ and $\sqrt{E - U_0}$, proportional to the speeds in the two regions, are replaced by the speeds c/n, where n is the medium's refractive index. The behaviors are completely analogous. The most important point here is that, contrary to the classical expectation, the reflection probability is nonzero.

EXAMPLE 1

An electron of kinetic energy 5 eV encounters a 2 eV potential step. What is the probability that it will be reflected?

SOLUTION

Its total energy is its initial kinetic energy, because it starts where $U = 0$, and U_0 is given to be 2 eV.

$$R = \frac{\left(\sqrt{5} - \sqrt{5 - 2}\right)^2}{\left(\sqrt{5} + \sqrt{5 - 2}\right)^2} = 0.016$$

Something about Example 1 might seem troubling. Planck's constant is nowhere to be found in expressions (7). Apparently, the probability obtained would apply just as well to a bowling ball with a kinetic energy of 50 J encountering a potential jump of 20 J. But never would we expect to see the bowling ball reflect. It is a classical case, and it should simply slow down to a kinetic energy of 30 J. What's wrong?

We have assumed that the potential energy jumps abruptly in an infinitesimal region at the origin. This is a valid approximation as long as the region where it actually changes is much narrower than the wavelength of the incident particle. *Subatomic* particles have rather small momenta and thus long wavelengths, so circumstances in which the assumption is valid are common. As we have come to expect, wave behavior prevails because the wavelength is large compared with the relevant dimension of the apparatus—the step's abrupt jump. But a calculation of the wavelength of a moving *macroscopic* object, gives a ridiculously small value, far less than nuclear dimensions. Our simple assumptions and analysis fail in such cases.

A common misconception is that a particle may reflect at a potential jump simply because the potential energy *increases*, but it may do so even if the potential energy *drops*. A force *in a particle's direction of motion* may cause it to reflect. Reflection and transmission probabilities for a potential drop follow from the same analysis, merely replacing U_0 by $-U_0$, and in particular, the reflection probability for a drop is *not* zero (see Exercise 15). The conclusion really shouldn't be too surprising, given that, with E greater than the potential energy at all points, reflection is at odds with classical mechanics *in either case*. The analogous behavior of light is again helpful. Just as any increase *or* decrease in refractive index causes partial reflection of a light wave, *any* change in potential energy results in partial reflection of a matter wave.

$E < U_0$

Now let us consider what happens when particles encounter a potential step whose height U_0 is greater than the particle energy. As shown in Figure 3, the situation is the same as before, but the potential jump is higher. An electron behaving classically would slow to a stop somewhere in the tiny region around the origin, then reverse its direction. It certainly should reflect.

The analysis actually differs very little. For $x < 0$, we will still have two solutions representing incident and reflected waves. For $x > 0$, however, things have changed. The Schrödinger equation is

$$\frac{d^2\psi(x)}{dx^2} = \frac{2m(U_0 - E)}{\hbar^2}\psi(x) \tag{8}$$

This is equation (2) slightly rearranged simply to better suit it to a case where $E < U_0$. Now $\psi(x)$ and its second derivative are of the *same* sign—a crucial distinction. Oscillatory functions don't satisfy this condition, but exponentials do. In more compact form,

$$\frac{d^2\psi(x)}{dx^2} = \alpha^2\psi(x) \qquad \text{where } \alpha \equiv \sqrt{\frac{2m(U_0 - E)}{\hbar^2}} \tag{9}$$

Figure 3 A classically insurmountable potential step.

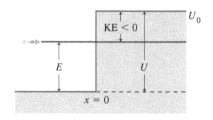

Two functions work:

$$\psi(x) = e^{+\alpha x} \quad \text{and} \quad \psi(x) = e^{-\alpha x} \tag{10}$$

However, the region to the right of the step extends forever, so we must throw out $e^{+\alpha x}$, for it diverges as $x \to +\infty$. Thus, in place of (4), we now have

$$\psi_{x<0}(x) = Ae^{+ikx} + Be^{-ikx} \qquad \psi_{x>0}(x) = Ce^{-\alpha x}$$
$$\textbf{Inc} \qquad \textbf{Refl}$$

(The conspicuous absence of a "Trans" label we address soon.) The smoothness conditions analogous to (6) become

$$\psi_{x<0}(0) = \psi_{x>0}(0): Ae^{+ik0} + Be^{-ik0} = Ce^{-\alpha 0}$$
$$\text{or} \qquad A + B = C$$

$$\left.\frac{d\psi_{x<0}}{dx}\right|_{x=0} = \left.\frac{d\psi_{x>0}}{dx}\right|_{x=0} : ikAe^{+ik0} - ikBe^{-ik0} = -\alpha Ce^{-\alpha 0}$$
$$\text{or} \qquad k(A - B) = -\alpha C$$

It might seem that a full calculation of reflection and transmission probabilities R and T should follow, but a close look at the magnitude of B answers many questions. Eliminating C between the smoothness conditions gives $B = -[(\alpha + ik)/(\alpha - ik)]A$.

$$|B| = \sqrt{B^*B} = \sqrt{\left(-\frac{\alpha + ik}{\alpha - ik}A\right)^*\left(-\frac{\alpha + ik}{\alpha - ik}A\right)}$$
$$= \sqrt{\left(\frac{\alpha - ik}{\alpha + ik}A^*\right)\left(\frac{\alpha + ik}{\alpha - ik}A\right)} = \sqrt{A^*A} = |A|$$

The magnitudes of B and A are equal. (B merely points in a different "direction" in the complex plane.) It follows that

$$R = \frac{B^*B}{A^*A} = 1$$

Because R and T must add to 1, it would seem that the transmission probability is 0. Indeed, it is. If a particle were transmitted, it should continue moving to the right at constant speed indefinitely, since it experiences no force beyond $x = 0$. But the wave function falls exponentially to 0 beyond the step; nothing survives to be found infinitely far away. Although it doesn't do so abruptly at $x = 0$, the incoming wave does reflect completely. Inferring T from R is the best way to determine it, because it isn't proper to *calculate* a transmission probability from C^*C. Our ratios involve the number *per unit time*, $|\psi|^2 v$, but in the region $x > 0$, the speed v is not "real" (KE $= \frac{1}{2}mv^2$ is negative). Because no number per unit time can be specified, neither can a transmission probability.

On the other hand, a calculation of number *per unit distance* is still justified. The quantity $|\psi|^2$ is still real, and because the wave penetrates the step, there is a probability of finding electrons on the "wrong" side of the step. But it can't be concluded that *particles* are constantly getting through to $x > 0$,

Figure 4 Reflection and transmission probabilities for a potential step.

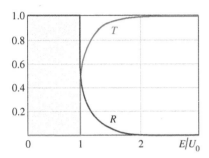

then going back through to $x < 0$, for there is no force beyond the step that could reflect anything. We simply accept that as long as no attempt is made to find a particle, we merely have an undisturbed wave that, though it reflects completely, happens to penetrate the classically forbidden step. The "penetration depth" is the same as where the wave function outside the finite well was also simply a dying exponential.

$$\delta = \frac{1}{\alpha} = \frac{\hbar}{\sqrt{2m(U_0 - E)}}$$

The closer E is to U_0, the greater is δ, and the slower the decay of the wave function. In any case, the wave function is very small for $x \gg \delta$.

As always, electromagnetic waves show analogous behavior. Just as a $U_0 > E$ step completely reflects massive particles, a smooth metal surface completely reflects light—making it a good mirror. The light wave doesn't propagate through the metal, and no photons are transmitted, but there is an electromagnetic field within the metal, oscillating with time and decaying exponentially with depth. For an electromagnetic wave, the penetration depth is often called skin depth.

Figure 4 shows reflection and transmission probabilities plotted versus E/U_0 for a potential step. If E is less than U_0, the wave is totally reflected. When E exceeds U_0, the reflection probability falls rapidly with increasing E.

2 The Potential Barrier and Tunneling

Tunneling is one of the most important and startling ideas in quantum mechanics. The simplest situation is a **potential barrier**, a potential energy jump that is only temporary. If a particle's energy is less than the barrier's "height," it should not get through—classically.

E > U₀

Let us first consider the case where E is greater than the barrier height U_0. As shown in Figure 5, at $x = 0$, the potential energy jumps up, giving the particle a "kick" in the backward direction, and at $x = L$, it drops back to 0, giving it a forward kick.

$$U(x) = \begin{cases} 0 & x < 0, x > L \\ U_0 & 0 < x < L \end{cases}$$

Figure 5 A classically surmountable potential barrier.

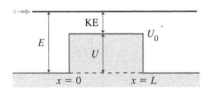

Classically, the particle shouldn't reflect; it should merely slow down between $x = 0$ and $x = L$, then return to its previous speed. Let us see what quantum mechanics has to say.

In the region $x < 0$, we should again have our incident and reflected waves. Between $x = 0$ and $x = L$, the situation is exactly as it was to the right of the potential step when E was greater than U_0. Thus, Schrödinger equation (3) applies just as before, giving the same mathematical solutions: $e^{+ik'x}$ and

$e^{-ik'x}$. In the case of the simple step, we threw out the left-moving $e^{-ik'x}$, for there was nothing beyond $x = 0$ able to reflect a wave. Now there is—the potential drop at $x = L$. Therefore we cannot justifiably throw out this solution. Finally, in the region $x > L$, where the potential energy is again 0, the Schrödinger equation is the same as for $x < 0$, as are its mathematical solutions, e^{+ikx} and e^{-ikx}. But here we do throw one out, e^{-ikx}, for nothing moves to the left in *this* region. Altogether, we have

$$\psi_{x<0}(x) = Ae^{+ikx} + Be^{-ikx} \qquad \psi_{x>L}(x) = Fe^{+ikx}$$
$$\textbf{Inc} \qquad \textbf{Refl} \qquad\qquad\qquad \textbf{Trans} \qquad (11)$$
$$\psi_{0<x<L}(x) = Ce^{+ik'x} + De^{-ik'x}$$

The smoothness requirements at the two points where regions meet are

$$\psi_{x<0}(0) = \psi_{0<x<L}(0): Ae^{+ik0} + Be^{-ik0} = Ce^{+ik'0} + De^{-ik'0}$$
$$\text{or} \qquad \boxed{A + B = C + D}$$
$$\left.\frac{d\psi_{x<0}}{dx}\right|_{x=0} = \left.\frac{d\psi_{0<x<L}}{dx}\right|_{x=0} : ikAe^{+ik0} - ikBe^{-ik0} = ik'Ce^{+ik'0} - ik'De^{-ik'0}$$
$$\text{or} \qquad \boxed{k(A - B) = k'(C - D)}$$
$$\psi_{0<x<L}(L) = \psi_{x>0}(L): \boxed{Ce^{+ik'L} + De^{-ik'L} = Fe^{ikL}}$$
$$\left.\frac{d\psi_{0<x<L}}{dx}\right|_{x=L} = \left.\frac{d\psi_{x>L}}{dx}\right|_{x=L} : \boxed{ik'(Ce^{+ik'L} - De^{-ik'L}) = ikFe^{ikL}}$$

As before, these give us the reflection and transmission probabilities, but now "transmission" is finding a right-moving particle in the region $x > L$. Thus,

$$R = \frac{B^*B}{A^*A} \qquad T = \frac{|\psi|^2_{\text{trans}}\, k}{|\psi|^2_{\text{inc}}\, k} = \frac{F^*F}{A^*A}$$

Between the four conditions boxed above, we can eliminate C and D, then solve for B and F in terms of A. The algebraic details are left as an exercise.

$$R = \frac{\sin^2(k'L)}{\sin^2(k'L) + 4\dfrac{k'^2k^2}{(k^2 - k'^2)^2}} \qquad T = \frac{4\dfrac{k'^2k^2}{(k^2 - k'^2)^2}}{\sin^2(k'L) + 4\dfrac{k'^2k^2}{(k^2 - k'^2)^2}} \qquad (12)$$

Finally, using the definitions of k and k', we obtain

$$R = \frac{\sin^2\left[\sqrt{2m(E - U_0)}\,L/\hbar\right]}{\sin^2\left[\sqrt{2m(E - U_0)}\,L/\hbar\right] + 4(E/U_0)\left[(E/U_0) - 1\right]}$$

$$T = \frac{4(E/U_0)\left[(E/U_0) - 1\right]}{\sin^2\left[\sqrt{2m(E - U_0)}\,L/\hbar\right] + 4(E/U_0)\left[(E/U_0) - 1\right]} \qquad (13)$$

As they should, R and T add to 1, and just as in the $E > U_0$ potential step, reflection is possible, contrary to the classical expectation.

Obviously, with the width L now a factor, the probabilities for a barrier are more complicated than those for a step, but this richer detail admits an interesting phenomenon: **resonant transmission**. Although both probabilities are in general nonzero, the numerator of R involves a sine. When this is 0, there is no reflection. The condition is

$$\frac{\sqrt{2m(E - U_0)}}{\hbar}L = n\pi \quad \text{or} \quad E = U_0 + \frac{n^2\pi^2\hbar^2}{2mL^2} \tag{14}$$

This is not energy quantization. Incident particles may be sent in with any energy, but resonant (complete) transmission occurs at only certain energies. A familiar behavior in light (yet again!) is completely analogous. Nonreflective coatings exploit the same wave properties. If the width and refractive index are chosen properly, a thin film will pass light without reflection. In both applications, reflections within the film ("over" the barrier) precisely cancel the wave reflected from the first interface. As always, it is important to remember that waves, not particles, interfere. A particle—photon or massive—encountering an obstacle may later be detected as a *particle*, having been either reflected or transmitted, but the process involves a probability that comes only from the *wave* function.

$E < U_0$—Tunneling

A particle may escape confinement that classical mechanics says it cannot escape. This is tunneling, a fascinating phenomenon whose application we discuss in the next section. Here we analyze it in the simplest case, for which we have already laid the groundwork. Shown in Figure 6, the situation is a potential barrier with $E < U_0$. A classical particle would rebound at first encounter, $x = 0$.

The solutions of the Schrödinger equation in the regions outside the barrier, $x < 0$ and $x > L$, are identical to the $E > U_0$ barrier. Things are different between 0 and L, which before was classically allowed and is now classically forbidden, but the solutions in this circumstance are the ones we discussed in connection with the $E < U_0$ potential *step*. The Schrödinger equation is again (8), and the mathematical solutions are $e^{+\alpha x}$ and $e^{-\alpha x}$. In the case of the step, we threw out $e^{+\alpha x}$, because it diverges as $x \to +\infty$. The barrier does *not* extend to infinity, so we have no reason to throw it out. The solutions altogether are thus:

Figure 6 Tunneling.

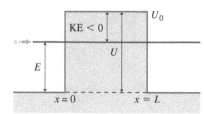

$$\psi_{x<0}(x) = Ae^{+ikx} + Be^{-ikx} \qquad \psi_{x>L}(x) = Fe^{+ikx}$$
$$\textbf{Inc} \qquad \textbf{Refl} \qquad\qquad\qquad \textbf{Trans} \tag{15}$$
$$\psi_{0<x<L}(x) = Ce^{+\alpha x} + De^{-\alpha x}$$

The solutions inside the barrier may still seem troubling, because α is real. Comparing with the other regions, we might say that the wave number and momentum are imaginary. In a way, this fits, for the kinetic energy inside the barrier is, after all, negative. In any case, there is no "real" momentum inside the barrier, and the two functions do not represent right- and left-moving particles. Still, both are needed to ensure smoothness.

It is left as an exercise to obtain the smoothness conditions, from which we find the reflection and transmission probabilities. (Exercise 28 shows that they can actually be deduced by a simple replacement.)

$$R = \frac{\sinh^2\left[\sqrt{2m(U_0 - E)}\,L/\hbar\right]}{\sinh^2\left[\sqrt{2m(U_0 - E)}\,L/\hbar\right] + 4(E/U_0)(1 - E/U_0)}$$

$$T = \frac{4(E/U_0)(1 - E/U_0)}{\sinh^2\left[\sqrt{2m(U_0 - E)}\,L/\hbar\right] + 4(E/U_0)(1 - E/U_0)}$$

(16)

Both are, in general, nonzero—a particle can escape through a barrier that it can't surmount classically. It is important to grasp that it can do this *not* due to some mysterious fluctuation in its energy, allowing it to go "over the top." On the contrary, from the start, we assumed a stationary state, in which energy is well defined. *The particle never has sufficient energy to surmount the barrier.* Instead, it "tunnels" through, and the principles of quantum mechanics demand that there be such a possibility. The solution to the left of the barrier is some combination of incident and reflected waves, of positive and negative momentum. At $x = 0$, it smoothly joins a function inside the barrier that tends to die off (the C in the exponentially increasing $Ce^{+\alpha x}$ being usually quite small). And at $x = L$, this smoothly joins a transmitted wave of positive momentum. There is no physically acceptable solution that is identically zero beyond the barrier.

Figure 7 shows wave functions (real part) for particles of different energies incident on a barrier from the left. Note that the wavelengths decrease as kinetic energy increases. At energy E_1, the exponential decay within the barrier is rapid, and little transmission occurs. At E_2, barely below the barrier height, the wave decays less rapidly, leaving a larger transmitted "tail." Energy E_3 is above the barrier, but we see evidence of significant reflection—the wave is of smaller amplitude to the right of the barrier than to the left. Also, the wavelength is longer when it is "over" the barrier, because the speed is smaller there. Energy E_4 happens to be the first transmission resonance—the wave on the right is of precisely the same amplitude as on the left. Note that the barrier's width is $\frac{1}{2}\lambda$. Not coincidentally, this is just the condition we would expect for maximum transmission of a light wave through a thin film surrounded by air. At E_5, though not a transmission resonance, little reflection occurs—the amplitude on the right is only slightly less than on the left.

Figure 8 shows reflection and transmission probabilities for all energies incident on the same barrier as in Figure 7, with the above energies E_1 to E_5 indicated by dashed lines. Although reflection dominates for $E < U_0$ and transmission for $E > U_0$, both occur at all energies except transmission resonances. In the limit $L \to \infty$, the barrier becomes a step and Figure 8 becomes Figure 4.

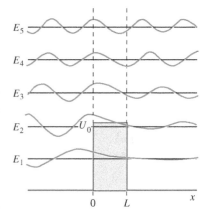

Figure 7 Wave functions for particles of different energies incident from the left on a potential barrier.

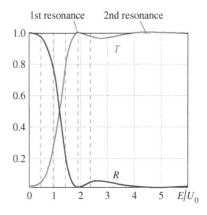

Figure 8 Reflection and transmission probabilities for a potential barrier.

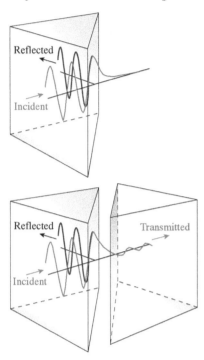

Figure 9 Frustrated total internal reflection—an electromagnetic analog of quantum-mechanical tunneling.

The inevitable electromagnetic analog to tunneling is light striking a thin metal film. If the film is thin enough, the exponentially decaying electromagnetic field within the metal will still be significant at the far side of the film, and some fraction of the incident intensity will emerge. A half-silvered mirror operates on this principle. Another analog to tunneling is the phenomenon of frustrated total internal reflection, represented schematically in Figure 9. In the top diagram, an electromagnetic wave traveling through a prism strikes the interface with the outside air, which is of lower refractive index. The incident angle exceeds the critical angle, so the wave is totally internally reflected. But though there is no light per se transmitted into the air, there is a time-varying, exponentially decaying electromagnetic field in the space beyond. To this point, the behavior is analogous to the $E < U_0$ potential step, except that the incident and reflected waves move in perpendicular directions. If a second prism is brought near, so that the decaying field is intercepted before it falls off too much, the step is effectively replaced by a narrow barrier (the air-space), and the internal reflection is no longer total—it is "frustrated." The incident wave is partially transmitted, and the narrower the barrier, the greater the transmission.

Tunneling Through Wide Barriers

In many applications, the transmission probability for tunneling is very small. Inside the barrier, the exponentially increasing component $Ce^{+\alpha x}$ is negligible, so $\psi(x)$ is essentially just $De^{-\alpha x}$, or $De^{-x/\delta}$, where $\delta \equiv 1/\alpha$. If $L \gg \delta$, very little of the wave survives to $x = L$. The condition for a "wide" barrier is thus

$$\frac{L}{\delta} = \alpha L = \frac{\sqrt{2m(U_0 - E)}}{\hbar}L \gg 1 \qquad (17)$$

We see that the barrier is "wide" if L is large, or E is much less than U_0, or both.

It is left as an exercise to show that if (17) holds, then the transmission probability of (16) assumes the simpler form

$$T \cong 16\frac{E}{U_0}\left(1 - \frac{E}{U_0}\right)e^{-2L\sqrt{2m(U_0-E)}/\hbar} \qquad (18)$$

EXAMPLE 2

An electron encounters a barrier of height 5.0 eV and width 1.6 nm. What is the transmission probability if its energy is (a) 2.0 eV? (b) 3.0 eV?

SOLUTION

First, we see if condition (17) holds.
    For 2.0 eV,

$$\frac{L}{\delta} = \frac{\sqrt{2(9.11 \times 10^{-31}\,\text{kg})(5.0 - 2.0)(1.6 \times 10^{-19}\,\text{J})}}{1.055 \times 10^{-34}\,\text{J} \cdot \text{s}}1.6 \times 10^{-9}\,\text{m} = 14.2$$

For 3.0 eV,

$$\frac{L}{\delta} = \frac{\sqrt{2(9.11 \times 10^{-31}\,\text{kg})(5.0 - 3.0)(1.6 \times 10^{-19}\,\text{J})}}{1.055 \times 10^{-34}\,\text{J} \cdot \text{s}}\,1.6 \times 10^{-9}\text{m} = 11.6$$

In both cases, the barrier is wide, many times the penetration depth. Now, having just calculated the arguments of the exponential in (18), we have

$$T_{2\text{eV}} = 16\frac{2}{5}\left(1 - \frac{2}{5}\right)e^{-2\times 14.2} \cong 2 \times 10^{-12}$$

$$T_{3\text{eV}} = 16\frac{3}{5}\left(1 - \frac{3}{5}\right)e^{-2\times 11.6} \cong 3 \times 10^{-10}$$

The example illustrates an important point. When transmission probabilities are very small, they vary quite sharply with energy. Both probabilities are small, but a modest 50% increase in particle energy gives a transmission probability more than 100 times larger. This sensitivity is due to the exponential dependence in (18), and the smaller the probability, the more pronounced the variation (see Exercise 33).

Finally, although the transmission probability for a *single* tunneling event may be quite small, in many real situations, barriers are constantly bombarded at extremely high rates, which can still translate to a significant flux of escaping particles. An alpha particle *almost* trapped in an atomic nucleus may get 10^{20} chances to tunnel out every second!

3 Alpha Decay and Other Applications

Imagine: Bob is standing on ground that is flat except for an isolated hill. As shown in Figure 10, Anna wishes to roll a large ball over the hill to Bob. The ball would have a gravitational potential energy of 900 J if perched atop the hill. Anna rolls the ball, which loses no mechanical energy as it travels; friction is negligible. When the ball reaches Bob, its kinetic energy is 200 J. Impossible! The ball's total mechanical energy at the top of the hill must have been *at least* 900 J—its potential energy at that point—and this should have added to its kinetic energy as it rolled down. Classically, the ball can have no less than 900 J of kinetic energy when it reaches Bob. For the ball to arrive with a kinetic energy of 200 J, its kinetic energy as it passed over (through?) the hill would have had to be *negative* 700 J.

Something quite like this occurs in the radioactive process known as **alpha decay**. Certain atomic nuclei are known to be unstable—they eliminate excess energy by spontaneously emitting a high-energy particle. The energy carried away by the particle leaves the remaining nucleus in a lower-energy, more stable state. The original nucleus is usually called the "parent nucleus," and the nucleus remaining after decay the "daughter nucleus." One of the particles that may be emitted is two protons and two neutrons stuck together tightly, known as an **alpha particle**. An example is the alpha decay of uranium-238, depicted in Figure 11. A uranium-238 nucleus contains 92 protons and 146 neutrons, for a total of 238 "nucleons." After emitting an alpha particle,

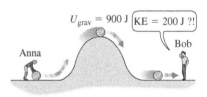

Figure 10 How did that happen?

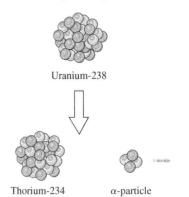

Figure 11 Alpha decay.

Uranium-238

Thorium-234   α-particle

what remains is a nucleus of 90 protons (92 − 2) and 144 neutrons (146 − 2), or 234 nucleons: thorium-234. Both being positively charged, the thorium nucleus and the alpha particle repel one another. As the alpha particle moves away from the thorium, electrostatic potential energy is converted to kinetic, and the alpha particle speeds up. However, experiment reveals a "deficiency" in the final kinetic energy. Let us calculate the minimum energy we might *classically* expect the alpha particle to have.

To understand alpha decay, we need to introduce a few ideas belonging to nuclear physics. The constituents of the nucleus are held together not by electrostatic force, for this alone would violently scatter the positively charged protons, but by the altogether different **strong force**. All nucleons, both protons and neutrons, are found to attract one another via this particularly strong force, but only when very close together. It may be said that they attract each other only when in contact. Thus, the nucleus may be viewed crudely as a collection of nucleons stuck as close together as possible in an approximately spherical arrangement. Now, as depicted in the potential energy curve of Figure 12, an alpha particle far outside the radius of a large nucleus would experience only the electrostatic repulsion from the protons inside, so its electrostatic potential energy would *increase* if it were brought closer. Upon reaching the surface, however, the attractive strong force would be overwhelming and lead to a rapidly *decreasing* potential energy. Accordingly, the alpha particle would be at a point of maximum potential energy when at the nuclear surface.[1]

Scattering experiments—a refined term for throwing things at each other and watching how they rebound—have determined nuclear radii fairly accurately, and the radius of the thorium-234 nucleus is approximately 7.4×10^{-15} m. At the surface of a thorium nucleus (90 protons), an alpha particle (2 protons) would thus have an electrostatic potential energy of

$$U_{\text{elec}} = \frac{q_1 q_2}{4\pi\varepsilon_0 r} = \frac{(2 \times 1.6 \times 10^{-19}\,\text{C})(90 \times 1.6 \times 10^{-19}\,\text{C})}{4\pi(8.85 \times 10^{-12}\,\text{C}^2/\text{N}\cdot\text{m}^2)(7.4 \times 10^{-15}\,\text{m})}$$
$$= 5.6 \times 10^{-12}\,\text{J} = 35\,\text{MeV}$$

When a uranium nucleus alpha-decays, the alpha particle at the surface of the daughter thorium nucleus would have 35 MeV of electrostatic potential energy and would speed up as it is repelled away. Classically, the kinetic energy can be no less than 0 at the nuclear surface, so it can be no less than 35 MeV when very far away, where the potential is negligible. An alpha particle with less than 35 MeV of kinetic energy should never be found. The experimental truth is that an alpha particle emitted from uranium-238 and detected far from the thorium-234 daughter nucleus has a kinetic energy of only 4.3 MeV. Quantum mechanics provides the answer: The alpha particle never has to possess 35 MeV of energy.

The horizontal gray line for E in Figure 12 represents the true situation. Initially, an alpha particle moves relatively freely within the uranium nucleus, pulled equally in all directions by the 234 other nucleons. As it approaches the barrier at the surface, however, the other nucleons exert a net force on it back toward the center. Although the alpha particle doesn't have enough energy to surmount this barrier, it may quantum-mechanically tunnel.

[1]The behavior of a molecule in a water drop is similar. It attracts all others, so energy is needed to bring it to the surface. Thus, the drop's lowest energy is when its surface area is a minimum, which is the basis of surface tension. The aptly named and successful "liquid drop model" of the nucleus assumes that nucleons behave like molecules in a liquid drop.

Figure 12 To escape the nucleus, an alpha particle must tunnel.

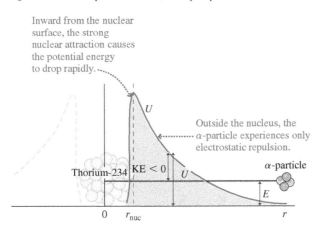

Inward from the nuclear surface, the strong nuclear attraction causes the potential energy to drop rapidly.

Outside the nucleus, the α-particle experiences only electrostatic repulsion.

α-particle

Thorium-234   KE < 0

U

U

E

0 r_{nuc} r

A calculation of the transmission probability for our multifarious potential energy is too involved to present here. But calculated **decay rates** (decays per second) agree well with experimentally determined values. In simplified form, the calculation is as follows:

$$\frac{\text{number of decays}}{\text{time}} = \frac{\text{number of times } \alpha \text{ strikes barrier}}{\text{time}}$$
$$\times \text{ transmission probability}$$

$$= \frac{\text{one strike}}{\text{time to cross diameter}} \times T$$

$$= \frac{1}{\text{diameter of nucleus/speed}} \times T$$

$$= \frac{v}{2r_{\text{nuc}}} T$$

Of course, once the alpha particle escapes, alpha decay of the original nucleus is no longer possible, because the element has changed (e.g., uranium becomes thorium). So referring to a number per unit time for a single nucleus is nonsense. But with the huge number of nuclei in even a macroscopically small sample of radioactive material, simply multiplying by the total number yields a proper average decay rate. As noted, agreement with experiment is very good, but we must not overlook the simple fact that the probabilistic nature of alpha decay is evidence of its quantum-mechanical basis. Watching individual nuclei, we would find great variation in the time required for decay, and this is exactly what we expect if the decay is governed by quantum-mechanical probabilities.

Example 2 provided the key to understanding another classical mystery of alpha decay. Most alpha particles have energies E in the 4–9 MeV range, yet their decay rates differ by more than 20 orders of magnitude, as shown in Table 1. The probability of the alpha particle tunneling in a single encounter with the nuclear surface is very small, and as we found in Example 2, when this is true, transmission probabilities are extremely sensitive to the value of E.

TABLE 1 Energies and decay times in α decay

α-emitting nucleus	α-particle energy (MeV)	Mean time to decay
Po-212	8.8	4.4×10^{-7} seconds
Rn-220	6.3	79 seconds
Ra-224	5.7	5.3 days
Ra-226	4.8	2300 years
U-238	4.3	6.5×10^9 years

In conclusion, according to classical physics, alpha decay—in the unexpected low energy of alpha particles, in its probabilistic nature, and in the vast range of decay rates—would be completely baffling. Its explanation is a triumph of quantum mechanics.

The Tunnel Diode

Figure 13 Tunnel diode.

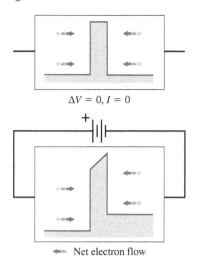

$\Delta V = 0, I = 0$

Net electron flow

A tunnel diode is an electronic circuit element whose response to applied voltages is unusual and very fast. In a narrow region between the device's two ends (leads), there is a change in the material's physical properties that prevents simple conduction of electrons from one end to the other. In essence, the electrons at the ends are separated by an electrostatic potential barrier they can't classically surmount, crudely depicted in Figure 13. By design, however, the barrier is fairly thin, and significant tunneling occurs. With no applied voltage, it occurs equally in both directions—there is no *net* flow. When a potential difference is applied, the situation becomes asymmetric. Right and left tunneling rates differ, and a net current flows.

The tunnel diode may seem to have little utility, as an applied voltage will induce current flow in many materials. But one of its distinctive features is *how* the current varies with voltage. It doesn't steadily increase as applied voltage is increased; at some points, it decreases. Moreover, changing the applied voltage changes the transmission rates almost instantly, and quick response is very desirable at high frequencies. The more common devices that control current via changing voltage rely on relatively slow thermal diffusion of the charge carriers. Although its early promise as a high-frequency switch in integrated circuits has dimmed, the tunnel diode has found use in a variety of modern electronic circuits. A more complex device, the *resonant* tunneling diode, is discussed in Progress and Applications.

SQUIDS

A **tunnel junction**, two conductors separated by an insulating barrier, is a key element in many electronic devices, and when the insulator separates two *superconductors*, it is known as a **Josephson junction**, through which electrons tunnel in pairs. The Josephson junction is at the heart of devices known as SQUIDs (superconducting quantum interference devices). The insulator serves as a weak link between the charges' motions on the two sides, coupling them together as would a weak spring connecting two pendula. As illustrated in Figure 14, with this kind of coupling, energy/current flow is intimately dependent on the phase relationship between the things that oscillate on the two sides—pendula or charge-carrier wave functions—and there may be constructive or destructive interference. In the case of charges separated by the weak link in a SQUID, the phase relationship is also a very sensitive function of any nearby magnetic field. Depicted in Figure 15, a SQUID is, in essence, a loop with two Josephson junctions. Interference caused by small changes in the magnetic flux passing through it produces easily detected changes in the current I. SQUIDs can detect extremely small magnetic fields, such as those produced by the human heart and brain.

Field Emission

As we know, to remove an electron from a given kind of metal requires a certain minimum amount of energy: the work function ϕ. In effect, the metal's electrons reside in a potential well, due to their attraction to the positive ions, and they are "reflected" at its walls by a potential step they cannot surmount, as shown in Figure 16(a). Owing to the random thermal distribution of speeds, at any given temperature, a small fraction of the electrons have sufficient kinetic energy to escape the metal. Those that do escape participate in an equilibrium exchange of electrons with the surrounding space. Heating a metal filament to enhance this effect, known as

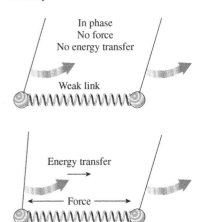

Figure 14 The effect of one oscillator on another depends on the phase relationship.

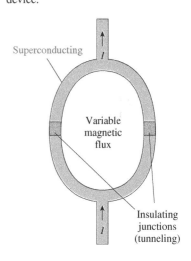

Figure 15 Elements of a SQUID—superconducting quantum interference device.

Figure 16 Electrons in a metal (a) behave as though in a finite well. An electric field (b) alters the "wall," so that tunneling may occur.

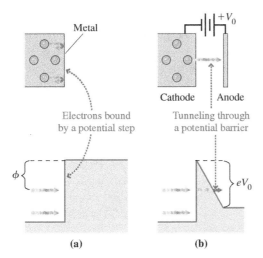

215

Figure 17 One pixel of a field emission display. Applying a positive bias turns on any of the three different colors of subpixel.

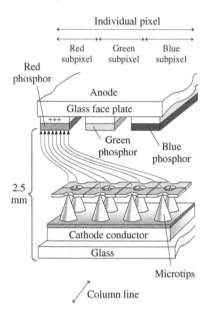

Figure 18 Schematic diagram of an STM in operation.

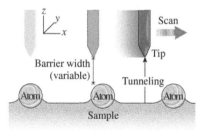

Figure 19 A missing atom, as seen by an STM.

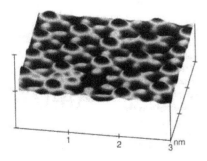

thermionic emission, has long been used as a source for electron beams, such as those in the conventional cathode-ray tubes used in televisions and X-ray machines.

But there is another way to coax electrons from their potential well. If a positive electrode is brought nearby, the potential step may effectively be changed to a potential barrier. In Figure 16(b), the positive electrode modifies the potential energy function "seen" by the electrons—lowering it outside the metal. (*Remember:* Negatively charged electrons are at low potential *energy* where the *potential* is high.) Now electrons moving too slowly to surmount the work function barrier may tunnel. The technique can be used to generate an electron beam and is known as **field emission**, after the electric field in the region of changing potential energy between metal and electrode. In many applications, it is preferable to thermionic emission, for heating a metal filament not only wastes power but often produces considerable electrical noise.

Field emission is the heart of an alternative kind of flat-screen display in active development, the aptly named field emission display (FED), depicted in Figure 17. Its potential advantages over the traditional liquid crystal displays commonly used in laptop computers include wider viewing angle and quicker response.

The Scanning Tunneling Microscope

Tunneling probability is very sensitive to barrier width, and nothing puts this to better use than the **scanning tunneling microscope** (STM), whose initial design won the 1986 Nobel Prize in physics (Binnig and Rohrer). In this device, a slender metal tip is positioned near the sample under study. Because tip and sample are not actually in contact, the free electrons in each cannot pass between them in the usual classical way—a potential barrier intervenes. However, in the STM, the separation is made small enough that significant quantum-mechanical tunneling occurs. Variation in the tip-sample separation smaller than typical atomic dimensions translates to easily measurable changes in tunneling current. Thus, as the tip of a tunneling microscope is scanned laterally over a sample's surface, as shown in Figure 18, it is able to "see" individual atoms. Furthermore, calling the tunneling direction the z and the scan direction the x, by repeating the scan with the tip displaced slightly in the y-direction, an entire "topological map" of the sample's surface can be generated. Phenomenal results have been obtained. Figure 19 shows a lone atom missing from a pattern of iodine atoms adsorbed on a platinum surface. The hexagonal geometry that characterizes the iodine bonding is quite clear.

The STM ranks as one of the most indispensable tools in modern technology. Its uses are already legion, including studies of the geometry and composition of an endless list of surfaces; locating important biological molecular groups such as the fundamental building blocks of DNA; mapping microscopic vortices in superconductors; nudging atoms from one point on a surface to another. And no end is in sight.

The metal tip of an STM has a work function, and the same is true of samples we might study with an STM. The two work functions are not, in general, equal, and in the STM, a potential difference is applied between tip and sample, giving a slope to the potential energy function felt by electrons moving between them. Nevertheless, by treating the space between tip and sample as a simple rectangular barrier whose "height" above the electron energy is typical of a work function, we can understand why the tunneling current should vary in a detectable way, even for the extremely small variations in tip-sample separations "seen" by an STM.

Applying the Physics

Electrons in an STM tunnel between sample and tip. Using a typical metallic work function of 4 eV for $U_0 - E$, about how much would the tip-sample separation have to change to produce a 10% decrease in tunneling current? Use the wide-barrier approximation.

SOLUTION

In equation (18), only L changes. Thus,

$$\frac{T_f}{T_i} = \frac{e^{-2L_f\sqrt{2m(U_0-E)}/\hbar}}{e^{-2L_i\sqrt{2m(U_0-E)}/\hbar}} = e^{-2\Delta L\sqrt{2m(U_0-E)}/\hbar}$$

The tunneling *current* will vary as the tunneling probability varies. Setting the ratio to 0.9 and taking logs on both sides gives

$$\ln(0.9) = -2\Delta L\frac{\sqrt{2(9.11 \times 10^{-31}\,\text{kg})(4 \times 1.6 \times 10^{-19}\,\text{J})}}{1.055 \times 10^{-34}\,\text{J}\cdot\text{s}}$$

$$\Rightarrow \Delta L = 5 \times 10^{-12}\,\text{m} = 0.005\,\text{nm}$$

Atomic radii are on the order of 0.1 nm. In practice, the resolution of even the best STM doesn't exceed about 0.01 nm, but our estimate certainly suggests that this remarkable device should be able to "see" atoms. As an alternative to translating a varying current to an image of varying height, STMs often sense the tip location needed to keep the tunneling current *constant*, and the motion of the tip thus tracks the height of the sample.

4 Particle-Wave Propagation

Thus far, our study of unbound states has concentrated on the effect of simple forces on plane waves. A plane wave is not the most realistic matter wave for a single particle. To represent a reasonably compact moving particle, a traveling wave pulse is much better. It is broad in one region and essentially 0 elsewhere. But the behavior of a pulse is considerably more complicated, even with *no* steps or barriers, so we will have plenty to keep us busy as we restrict our attention to pulses moving in vacuum or in homogeneous media.

A wave pulse may be treated as a sum of plane waves, and to understand the behavior of the whole, we consider the behavior of its parts. Each constituent plane wave moves at its own speed, or phase velocity, giving rise to two important consequences: (1) The speed of the region where the probability density is largest—the speed of the particle, or group velocity—may differ distinctly from the speeds of the constituent plane waves; and (2) an initially well-localized wave pulse will spread out with time, known as dispersion, as its constituents get progressively out of step.

Phase and Group Velocities

Figure 20 Wave group: The crests and envelope move at different speeds.

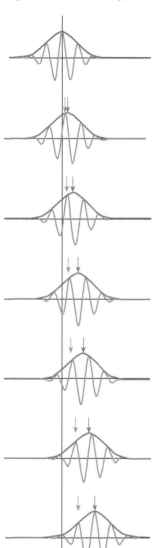

Figure 20 shows a traveling wave pulse, which we associate with a traveling particle, at several successive times. Regarded as a sum of plane waves, we refer to it as a **wave group**. The light red arrows indicate the motion of a particular crest. The thin red outline traces the "envelope" of the wave group, a shape that moves with the group and defines the maximum possible displacement at each point. The dark red arrows indicate the motion of the envelope, which clearly does not move at the same speed as the crests. The speed of the envelope is known as the **group velocity**. If we are interested in knowing when the particle is likely to arrive at some destination, it is the speed of the envelope, where the probability is large—group velocity—that is of interest. The speed at which an individual crest moves—**phase velocity**—is rather unimportant. Nevertheless, an understanding of the group's motion comes only through study of its parts. Let us begin with the simplest possible wave group.

A Simple Wave Group

Consider a wave group consisting of just two plane waves of equal amplitude A. Using the form

$$\Psi(x, t) = Ae^{i(k_1 x - \omega_1 t)} + Ae^{i(k_2 x - \omega_2 t)}$$

(*Note:* Despite the i and the use of Ψ, the main ideas in this section apply to all wave phenomena, including electromagnetic radiation.) We wish our group to have reasonably well-defined wave number and frequency, so we choose k and ω values that deviate by only very small amounts dk and $d\omega$ above and below central values k_0 and ω_0.

$$k_1 = k_0 + dk \qquad k_2 = k_0 - dk$$
$$\omega_1 = \omega_0 + d\omega \qquad \omega_2 = \omega_0 - d\omega$$

Thus,

$$\Psi(x, t) = Ae^{i[(k_0 + dk)x - (\omega_0 + d\omega)t]} + Ae^{i[(k_0 - dk)x - (\omega_0 - d\omega)t]}$$

Factoring out common terms leaves

$$\Psi(x, t) = Ae^{i(k_0 x - \omega_0 t)}\left(e^{+i[(dk)x - (d\omega)t]} + e^{-i[(dk)x - (d\omega)t]}\right)$$

Now, using the Euler formula, we obtain a form essentially identical to that of a classical beat frequency. The *sum* of two sinusoidals becomes a *product* of two whose wave numbers and frequencies are vastly different.

$$\Psi(x, t) = Ae^{i(k_0x - \omega_0 t)} 2 \cos[(dk)x - (d\omega)t] \tag{19}$$

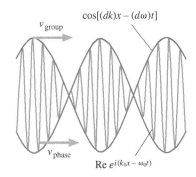

Figure 21 Simple wave group.

We have a complex exponential that moves at speed ω_0/k_0, the phase velocity appropriate to the central values k_0 and ω_0, modulated by a cosine function that moves at speed $d\omega/dk$. As shown in Figure 21, it is the latter term that defines the envelope—the group velocity is $d\omega/dk$. We see this more clearly by computing the probability density.

$$\Psi^*(x, t)\Psi(x, t) = 4A^2 \cos^2[(dk)x - (d\omega)t] \tag{20}$$

The phase velocity disappears. Because a particle must move as the probability of finding it moves, we expect the speed of the particle to be best represented by the speed of $|\Psi|^2$, $d\omega/dk$. Our surprising conclusion is that the group/particle velocity doesn't depend on the actual central values ω_0 and k_0, but rather on *how ω varies with k* from one constituent wave to another.

Although this simple wave group exhibits an important feature—that the probability density moves at speed $d\omega/dk$—it isn't very particlelike. It is periodic, as is any *finite* sum of periodic functions. So let us now turn to a more particlelike case in which the probability density isn't spread out all over space.

A Particlelike Wave

The most general way of expressing a wave group is

$$\Psi(x, t) = \int_{-\infty}^{+\infty} A(k)e^{i(kx - \omega t)} dk \tag{21}$$

This is a sum of plane waves of all different wave numbers, each multiplied by its particular amplitude $A(k)$, and each including its time dependence. Position x and time t are the usual independent parameters, and we will address $A(k)$ soon, but where do we get ω? This is a central question, and the answer is that it can be considered a function of k, for each phenomenon has built into it a relationship between ω and k, or equivalently between E and p. Consider two familiar cases: electromagnetic (EM) waves and matter waves. We see that for plane-wave solutions to Maxwell's equations in vacuum, $\omega = ck$, equivalent to $E = cp$. For plane-wave solutions to the free-particle Schrödinger equation, $\omega = \hbar k^2/2m$, equivalent to $E = p^2/2m$. A relationship expressing frequency as a function of wave number is known as a **dispersion relation**.

$$\text{EM wave dispersion relation: } \omega(k) = ck \tag{22}$$

$$\text{Matter wave dispersion relation: } \omega(k) = \frac{\hbar k^2}{2m} \tag{23}$$

Before looking closer at the group behavior, consider the phase velocity in these two cases. By definition, phase velocity is just the standard formula for the velocity of a plane wave.

Phase velocity

$$v_{\text{phase}} = \lambda f = \frac{\omega}{k} \tag{24}$$

Thus,

$$\text{EM waves: } v_{\text{phase}} = \frac{\omega}{k} = c \tag{25}$$

$$\text{Matter waves: } v_{\text{phase}} = \frac{\omega}{k} = \frac{\hbar k}{2m} \tag{26}$$

Whereas electromagnetic plane waves, unsurprisingly, all move through vacuum at the same speed c, matter plane waves of different wave number move at different speeds. Here is where the distinction between phase and group velocities arises. Our main object of study is a wave group whose wave numbers cover a range of values centered on k_0. In the case of matter waves, the phase velocity corresponding to this central wave number would be $\hbar k_0/2m = p_0/2m = v_0/2$, which doesn't equal the velocity v_0 of the particle. However, the phase velocity is not the important one. (This is quite a relief, for as we soon see, it can exceed c!) The wave function (19) for the two-wave group bears this out. Its complex exponential moves at the central, or average, phase velocity ω_0/k_0, but that part of the wave function disappears in the probability density, which is what really corresponds to the particle's motion and moves at a different velocity. Does this also hold in a more general group?

As written, wave group (21) is general, but almost always we are interested in a wave function of a particular shape, and one of the most commonly considered shapes is a Gaussian wave packet—a single bump. At $t = 0$, we desire our wave function to be of the form

$$\Psi(x, 0) = C\, e^{-(x/2\varepsilon)^2}\, e^{ik_0 x} \tag{27}$$

Note that this is a right-moving plane wave multiplied by a Gaussian bump that falls off away from the origin. Because of the Gaussian factor, it is not infinitely broad ($\Delta x \neq \infty$), so its momentum is not perfectly well defined. However, the oscillatory complex exponential gives it an approximate wave number of k_0 and thus momentum of $\hbar k_0$. In fact, its real part, involving $\cos k_0 x$, would resemble the top/starting wave in Figure 20. The way we ensure that integral (21) agrees with (27) at $t = 0$ is by the proper choice of $A(k)$. Here we simply study the result. For the wave function given at $t = 0$ by (27), equation (21) gives the wave function at arbitrary time t, and its probability density is

$$|\Psi(x, t)|^2 = \frac{C^2}{\sqrt{1 + D^2t^2/4\varepsilon^4}} \exp\left[\frac{-(x - st)^2}{2\varepsilon^2(1 + D^2t^2/4\varepsilon^4)}\right] \quad (28)$$

$$\text{where } s \equiv \left.\frac{d\omega(k)}{dk}\right|_{k_0} \quad \text{and} \quad D \equiv \left.\frac{d^2\omega(k)}{dk^2}\right|_{k_0} \quad (29)$$

Given the many factors in (28), it is worthwhile noting first that it is correct at $t = 0$. It reduces to

$$|\Psi(x, 0)|^2 = C^2\, e^{-x^2/2\varepsilon^2}$$

which is indeed the complex square of (27). So what does it do as t progresses? Taking it one piece at a time, consider a case where $D = 0$.

$$D = 0: \ |\Psi(x, t)|^2 = C^2\, e^{-(x-st)^2/2\varepsilon^2} \quad (30)$$

This is just a pulse "sliding" along the x-axis at speed s, and given the definition of s in (29), we see that this is the same result as for our earlier two-wave group.

$$v_{\text{group}} = s = \left.\frac{d\omega(k)}{dk}\right|_{k_0} \quad (31) \qquad \text{Group velocity}$$

Note that nonzero D wouldn't change this conclusion. As we soon find out, D governs not the speed of the probability density, but how much it spreads in time.

Let us calculate the group velocity for the familiar cases. From equations (22) and (23),

$$\text{EM waves: } v_{\text{group}} = \frac{d\omega(k)}{dk} = \left.\frac{d}{dk}\, ck\right|_{k_0} = c \quad (32)$$

$$\text{Matter waves: } v_{\text{group}} = \frac{d\omega(k)}{dk} = \left.\frac{d}{dk}\frac{\hbar k^2}{2m}\right|_{k_0} = \frac{\hbar k_0}{m} \quad (33)$$

The group velocity of an electromagnetic pulse in vacuum is c, because all of its constituent waves share that phase velocity—they must move as one. Equation (26) told us that a matter wave's constituent plane waves move at different speeds, but group velocity (33) is just what we expect it to be: $\hbar k_0/m = p_0/m = v_0$, the velocity of the *particle*. No matter what may be the

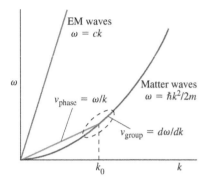

Figure 22 Dispersion relations for EM and matter waves. The phase velocity is the slope of a line from the origin, while the group velocity is the slope of the tangent line.

phase velocity of constituent waves, the region of high probability moves at the speed we expect of the associated particle.

How do our results relate to Figure 20? As noted in connection with equation (27), the wave function starts out looking just like the top plot in the figure. As time progresses, its little crests do indeed move at a phase velocity different from the speed of the envelope. But these features disappear in the probability density (28), leaving just the envelope, a smooth pulse moving at the group/particle velocity.

Figure 22 illustrates the relationships between the phase and group velocities for our familiar cases of EM waves in vacuum and free-particle matter waves. The two plots are dispersion relations (22) and (23). The dashed oval on the matter-wave plot represents the range of wave numbers and frequencies in a group—a continuum, but still a restricted range. The slope of the line from the origin to the central wave number is the phase velocity of the plane wave whose wave number is k_0. Lines to other points in the range, of course, have different slopes, or different phase velocities, but none of these is the velocity of the probability density—the group/particle velocity. As we have shown, this velocity is the *slope of the curve* at k_0. We found that the phase velocity of the central wave was $v_0/2$ and the group velocity was v_0, and the diagram clearly shows that the group velocity exceeds the phase velocity. The electromagnetic plot is comparatively easy to interpret. No specific range is indicated, but it is clear that the phase velocities are all the same and must equal the group velocity.

The interested reader is encouraged to take a look at Computational Exercise 59. Using a simple sum of real cosine functions in place of equation (21), it obtains plots, suitable for animation, that resemble those in Figure 20 and that clarify phase and group velocities and their dependence on the dispersion relation.

An Electromagnetic Pulse, and a Surprise

Let us consider the behavior of an electromagnetic wave pulse traveling through a medium where plane waves of different frequencies move at different speeds.

EXAMPLE 3

For waves in the region of the electromagnetic spectrum used for **GPS** (global positioning system) signals, the interaction between the electromagnetic fields and Earth's ionosphere leads to a refractive index that varies according to

$$n(\omega) = \sqrt{1 - \frac{b}{\omega^2}}$$

where ω is angular frequency and b is a constant. (a) Find the dispersion relation. (b) For a pulse of central frequency ω_0, determine the phase and group velocities. (The reader may quail at seeing a refractive index less than 1, for it implies a phase velocity greater than c. We confront the seeming violation of special relativity afterward.)

SOLUTION

(a) By definition, the refractive index of a material is the ratio of the speed of light in vacuum to the speed of a pure electromagnetic plane wave in the material— that is, to the phase velocity.

$$n = \frac{c}{v_{\text{phase}}} \quad \Rightarrow \quad v_{\text{phase}} = \frac{c}{\sqrt{1 - b/\omega^2}}$$

But the speed of a plane wave is also ω/k, so that

$$\frac{\omega}{k} = \frac{c}{\sqrt{1 - b/\omega^2}}$$

Solving for ω, we obtain the dispersion relation.

$$\omega(k) = \sqrt{b + (kc)^2} \tag{34}$$

(b) Using (31),

$$v_{\text{group}} = \left. \frac{d\omega(k)}{dk} \right|_{k_0} = \frac{k_0 c^2}{\sqrt{b + (k_0 c)^2}}$$

We now reexpress this in terms of the given ω_0. Using (34), we obtain

$$\omega_0 = \sqrt{b + (k_0 c)^2} \quad \Rightarrow \quad k_0 = \frac{1}{c} \sqrt{\omega_0^2 - b}$$

Thus,

$$v_{\text{group}} = \frac{c\sqrt{\omega_0^2 - b}}{\omega_0} = c\sqrt{1 - b/\omega_0^2}$$

Finally, evaluating the phase velocity also at the central frequency, we have

$$v_{\text{phase}} = \frac{c}{\sqrt{1 - b/\omega_0^2}} \qquad v_{\text{group}} = c\sqrt{1 - b/\omega_0^2}$$

The example seems to make a very unpalatable claim: The pulse's group velocity is okay, but its phase velocity is greater than c. We don't have to look far for this "problem" to recur. When mass/internal energy is taken into account, the same holds true for matter waves, even in vacuum (see Exercise 44).

Is special relativity violated? It is true that any individual plane wave may travel faster than c. But a pure plane wave—of infinite extent in space and infinite duration in time—cannot transmit *information*. It doesn't vary in any significant way, in a way capable of conveying information from one place to another. On the contrary, to transmit any intelligence, the wave must be modulated in some way, perhaps varying amplitude or frequency or simply turning it on and off. When modulated, it is no longer a single plane wave, but becomes a combination of plane waves—a wave group. The information travels at the group velocity, which is less than c. Under somewhat exceptional conditions, which have understandably garnered considerable attention (see Progress and Applications), even group velocity may exceed c, but this requires further rethinking of what it means to transmit information, and in no case has a violation of special relativity been suggested.

Dispersion

Not only can differences in the phase velocities cause a wave group to move at a speed quite different from its constituents, but it can also lead to the phenomenon of **dispersion**, the spreading of a wave pulse. Dispersion arises whenever the dispersion relation is nonlinear; that is, when D in equation (29)—the *second* derivative of ω with respect to k—is nonzero. Probability density (30) assumes $D = 0$, and it describes a Gaussian pulse simply sliding along the x-axis, undeformed, at the group velocity. However, when D is nonzero, we have to go back to probability density (28). In the denominator of the exponential's argument, D causes the moving Gaussian to become broader, ultimately a constant of 1. In the factor multiplying the exponential, it causes the probability density as a whole to decrease, so the pulse flattens out. Thus, the probability of finding the particle spreads over an ever larger region, while the probability per unit length diminishes. Governing this behavior, D is called the **dispersion coefficient**.

Dispersion would occur for the GPS pulse in Example 3, because the dispersion relation (34) for the medium is nonlinear; for the same reason, it occurs for a matter wave *even in vacuum*. As shown in Exercise 48, probability density (28) becomes

$$|\Psi(x, t)|^2 = \frac{C^2}{\sqrt{1 + \hbar^2 t^2/4m^2\varepsilon^4}}\exp\left[\frac{-(x - st)^2}{2\varepsilon^2(1 + \hbar^2 t^2/4m^2\varepsilon^4)}\right] \quad (35)$$

Note that because the factor $\hbar^2 t^2/4m^2\varepsilon^4$, which causes the spreading, is proportional to ε^{-4}, the narrower the pulse's initial width, the more rapidly it spreads in time. Exercise 49 investigates the phenomenon.

It is worth reiterating that our wave group is a solution of the free-particle Schrödinger equation, just as is a single plane wave, but unlike the plane wave, it is a good description of a well-localized particle. Figure 23 shows the time evolution of the probability density of a moving free particle. Dispersion invariably leads to increasing uncertainty in a particle's position.

Figure 23 Dispersion causes a matter wave to spread.

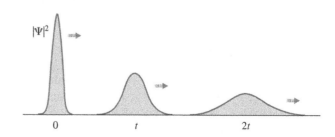

PROGRESS AND APPLICATIONS

Resonant Tunneling Diode Photon Detector

Applications of tunneling in modern electronics are multiplying rapidly nowadays. One holding great promise, developed by scientists at Toshiba Research Europe and Cambridge University, exploits tunneling characteristics along with those of the ubiquitous quantum dot (J. C. Blakesley, et al., Physical Review Letters, February 18, 2005). As shown in Figure 24, the device is a diode with *two* barriers that electrons must tunnel through, separated by a classically allowed region. Perhaps not surprisingly, the behavior exhibits features of both the $E < U_0$ and $E > U_0$ barriers. Tunneling through the barriers shows resonances that correspond to discrete energy levels in the intervening well. (Exercises 39, 40, and 56 investigate **resonant tunneling**.) As we know, even very small changes can alter tunneling probabilities—and thus currents—drastically, and in this device, a single photon causes the change. It creates a hole (a state missing an electron) that becomes trapped and alters the tunneling rate via the electrostatic influence of its positive charge. Devices able to detect single photons would be very useful in applications ranging from quantum communication to medical imaging, and this one appears to recognize single photons with considerably greater reliability than other methods.

STM Marches On   The STM continues to make news. In a splendid development of the standard technique, researchers at the Colorado School of Mines have added a new dimension. In the standard STM image, electrons of the highest energies in a conducting sample dominate the scene, often obscuring the behavior of lower-energy ones. To filter among them, the new technique uses a tip made of a specially cleaved semiconducting crystal. Whereas a metal tip cannot "look" for specific energies, the semiconductor tip, with its bands of allowed energies, can sift the tunneling current according to electron energy by varying the tip-to-sample bias voltage. Figure 25 shows on the left a view of a silicon surface produced by standard techniques, with 12 atoms prominent within the diamond. Six other atoms, differing in both location and energy due to the different nature of their bonding, are essentially invisible. When the new technique is applied to look for these energies, as shown on the right, it is the other atoms that disappear. (P. Sutter, et al., Physical Review Letters, April 25, 2003.)

It is not only the eyesight of the STM that continues to improve. We often wish to grasp and manipulate microscopic objects, and the atomic-scale dexterity of the STM is increasingly answering the call. Researchers at the University of Berlin have employed an STM to carry out a chemical reaction with single molecules. As shown in Figure 26, an STM is used as a source of electrons (a) to loosen an iodine from iodobenzene, leaving a phenyl (b). The iodine is coaxed to a convenient, out-of-the-way location (c) by van der Waals interactions and chemical forces between it and the tip. By the same

Figure 24 In a quantum dot resonant tunneling diode, electrons tunnel from the emitter through two barriers. A photon promotes an electron and the hole left behind, trapped in a quantum dot, alters the tunneling probability.

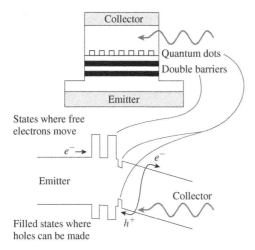

Figure 25 An STM with X-ray vision.

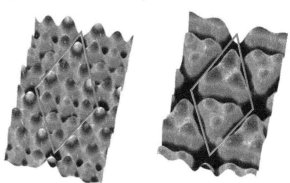

Figure 26 Single-molecule surgery via STM.

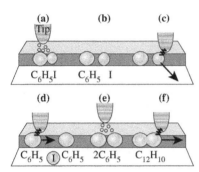

forces, the phenyl is slid over (d) to another phenyl, then, with excitation provided by another shot of tunneling electrons (e), the two are "welded" into a biphenyl molecule (f). (Saw-Wai Hla, et al., Physical Review Letters, September 25, 2000.)

Many Speeds of Light   The group velocity of light has become quite a hot topic in recent years, as new experimental techniques are probing all extremes. In the late 1990s, light's group velocity was slowed to less than 1 m/s by sending it into a rather exotic medium, a Bose-Einstein condensate, in which the refractive index increases abruptly. Other methods of slowing light pulses to pedestrian speeds are also being studied. Light of such slow group velocity may lead to new light switches or other optoelectronic devices. It may also prove applicable to nonlinear optics, in which a medium doesn't respond linearly to the electromagnetic field. This effect is exploited, among other things, to double laser frequencies. Presently, nonlinear optics requires high-power lasers, but slow light may provide a low-power alternative.

The ability to slow light has recently led to a further twist. In several experiments carried out at Harvard, MIT, and the Air Force Research Laboratory, using both gaseous and solid media, the group velocity of a light pulse has been slowed greatly as it interacts with the media, at which point a separate laser signal begins a transformation of its information from light to atomic spin states, as depicted in Figure 27, and ending in a final "image" frozen in the spin states, known as a polariton. A later laser signal retrieves the light pulse on demand with little distortion. This ability to "stop" a light pulse may prove

very important to the processing and storage of quantum information.

At the other extreme, several experiments in the past decade or so have demonstrated a group velocity for light greater than c. The effect occurs in media at frequency ranges characterized by anomalous dispersion, in which the refractive index, contrary to its usual behavior, decreases with frequency. Whenever something—such as phase velocity—appears to move at superluminal speeds, the first question is always whether it can be used to transmit information. In all cases, the answer has been no. Some feature of a pulse may seem to travel through a region faster than light could through a vacuum; it may even seem to emerge before the apparently corresponding feature in the incident pulse enters. But its information is encoded in complex ways, and even the "front edge" of an incident pulse carries information about the whole, so the arrival of any feature is not really the question. When anomalous dispersion prevails, it is common to speak of a "signal velocity" distinct from the group velocity, and never has this been found to exceed c.

Figure 27 A light pulse "stopped" and restored.

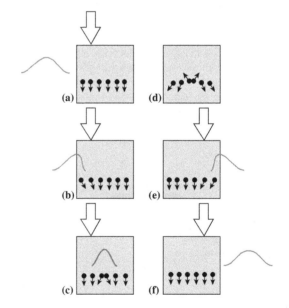

Chapter Summary

Just as it has an effect on a massive particle, any change in potential energy has an effect on a matter wave function. A small particle subject to a force will often manifest its wave nature, behaving as a classical particle would not. It may be reflected by a force that would not classically reflect it, even by a force in the particle's direction of motion. Conversely, its wave function can pass into a region despite a force that classically should cause it to rebound, and a particle may thus escape where classically it should be confined, a process known as tunneling. The probabilities of a particle being reflected or transmitted are governed by the solution $\Psi(x, t)$ of the Schrödinger equation for the given potential energy and the imposition of the physical requirement of smoothness.

To understand the relationship between the motion of a particle and its matter wave, it is useful to represent the particle as a wave group—a sum of plane waves. The speed of an individual plane wave is known as phase velocity and may exceed the speed of light. However, the probability density moves at a different speed, the group velocity, which is the same as the speed of the particle. Speed differences among waves in a group also cause the group to spread with time—the phenomenon of dispersion. Dispersion occurs in matter waves, even in vacuum, and leads to increasing uncertainty in a particle's position.

---

* indicates advanced questions

Conceptual Questions

1. Could the situation depicted in the following diagram represent a particle in a bound state? Explain.

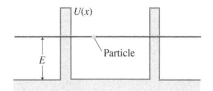

2. For particles incident from the left on the potential energy shown below, what incident energies E would imply a possibility of later being found infinitely far to the right? Does your answer depend on whether the particles behave classically or quantum mechanically?

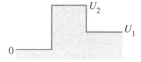

3. Why is the topic of normalization practically absent from Sections 1 and 2?

4. The equations for R and T in the $E > U_0$ barrier are essentially the same as for light passing through a transparent film. It is possible to fabricate a thin film that reflects no light. Is it possible to fabricate one that transmits no light? Why or why not?

5. Your friend has just finished classical physics and can't wait to know what lies ahead. Keeping extraneous ideas and postulates to a minimum, explain the process of quantum-mechanical tunneling.

6. How should you answer someone who asks, "In tunneling through a simple barrier, which way are particles moving in the three regions—before, inside, and after the barrier?"

7. Given the same particle energy and barrier height and width, which would tunnel more readily: a proton or an electron? Is this consistent with the usual rule of thumb governing whether classical or nonclassical behavior should prevail?

8. A ball is thrown straight up at 25 m/s. Someone asks, "Ignoring air resistance, what is the probability of the ball tunneling to a height of 1000 m?" Explain why this is not an example of tunneling as discussed in this chapter, even if the ball were replaced with a small fundamental particle. (The fact that the potential energy varies with position is not the whole answer—passing through nonrectangular barriers is still tunneling.)

9. In the wide-barrier transmission probability of equation (18), the coefficient multiplying the exponential is often omitted. When is this justified, and why?

10. An electron bound in an atom can be modeled as residing in a finite well. Despite the walls, when many regularly spaced atoms are relatively close together—as they are in a solid—all electrons occupy all the atoms. Make a sketch of a plausible multiatom potential energy and electron wave function.

11. The diagram below plots $\omega(k)$ versus wave number for a particular phenomenon. How do the phase and group velocities compare, and does the answer depend on the central value of k under consideration? Explain.

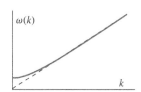

12. The plot below shows the variation of ω with k for electrons in a simple crystal. Where, if anywhere, does the group velocity exceed the phase velocity? (Sketching straight lines from the origin may help.) The trend, indicated by a dashed curve, is parabolic, but it is interrupted by a curious discontinuity, known as a **band gap**, where there are no allowed frequencies/energies. It turns out that the *second* derivative of ω with respect to k is inversely proportional to the effective mass of the electron. Argue that in this crystal, the effective mass is the same for most values of k, but that it is different for some values, and in one region in a very strange way.

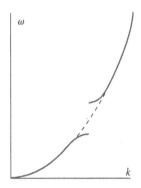

Exercises

Section 1

13. Show that $\psi(x) = A'e^{ikx} + B'e^{-ikx}$ is equivalent to $\psi(x) = A\sin(kx) + B\cos(kx)$, provided that $A' = \frac{1}{2}(B - iA)$ and $B' = \frac{1}{2}(B + iA)$

14. Verify that the transmission and reflection probabilities given in equation (7) add to 1.

15. Calculate the reflection probability for a 5 eV electron encountering a step in which the potential drops by 2 eV.

16. A particle moving in a region of zero force encounters a precipice—a sudden drop in the potential energy to an arbitrarily large negative value. What is the probability that it will "go over the edge"?

17. A beam of particles of energy E and incident upon a potential step of $U_0 = \frac{5}{4}E$ is described by the wave function

$$\psi_{\text{inc}}(x) = 1e^{ikx}$$

(a) Determine completely the reflected wave and the wave inside the step by enforcing the required continuity conditions to obtain their (possibly complex) amplitudes.

(b) Verify by explicit calculation that the ratio of reflected probability density to the incident probability density is 1.

18. A beam of particles of energy E and incident upon a potential step of $U_0 = \frac{3}{4}E$ is described by the wave function

$$\psi_{\text{inc}}(x) = 1e^{ikx}$$

The amplitude of the wave (related to the number incident per unit distance) is arbitrarily chosen as 1. (a) Determine completely the reflected and transmitted waves by enforcing the required continuity conditions to obtain their (possibly complex) amplitudes. (b) Verify that the ratio of reflected probability density to the incident probability density agrees with equations (7).

* 19. It is shown in Section 1 that for the $E < U_0$ potential step, $B = -[(\alpha + ik)/(\alpha - ik)]A$. Use this to calculate the probability density (including both incident and reflected waves) to the left of the step:

$$|\psi_{x<0}|^2 = |Ae^{+ikx} + Be^{-ikx}|^2$$

(a) Show that the result is $4|A|^2\sin^2(kx - \theta)$, where $\theta = \tan^{-1}(k/\alpha)$. Because the reflected wave is of the same amplitude as the incident, this is a typical standing wave pattern, varying periodically between 0 and $4A^*A$.

(b) Determine θ and D (the amplitude of the $x > 0$ wave inside the step) in the limits $k \to 0$ and $\alpha \to 0$, and interpret your results.

20. Particles of energy E are incident from the left, where $U(x) = 0$, and at the origin encounter an abrupt drop in potential energy, whose depth is $-3E$. (a) Classically, what would the particles do, and what would happen to their kinetic energy? (b) Apply quantum mechanics. Assuming an incident wave of the form $\psi_{\text{inc}}(x) = 1e^{ikx}$, where the normalization constant has been given the simple value of 1, determine completely the wave function everywhere, including numeric values for the multiplicative constants. (c) What is the probability that incident particles will be reflected?

Section 2

21. What fraction of a beam of 50 eV electrons would get through a 200 V, 1 nm wide electrostatic barrier?

22. In the $E > U_0$ potential barrier, there should be no reflected wave when the incident wave is at one of the transmission resonances. Prove this by assuming that a beam of particles is incident at the first transmission resonance, $E = U_0 + (\pi^2\hbar^2/2mL^2)$, and combining the continuity conditions to show that $B = 0$. (*Note:* k' is particularly simple in this special case, which should streamline your work.)

23. As we learn in physical optics, thin film interference can cause some wavelengths of light to be strongly reflected while others are not reflected at all. Neglecting absorption, all light has to go one way or the other, so wavelengths not reflected are strongly transmitted. (a) For a film of thickness t surrounded by air, what wavelengths λ (while they are within the film) will be strongly transmitted? (b) What wavelengths (while they are "over" the barrier) of matter waves satisfy condition (14)? (c) Comment on the relationship between the answers in (a) and (b).

24. Consider a potential barrier of height 30 eV. (a) Find a width around 1.000 nm for which there will be no reflection of 35 eV electrons incident upon the barrier. (b) What would be the reflection probability for 36 eV electrons incident upon the same barrier? (*Note:* This corresponds to a difference in speed of less than $1\frac{1}{2}\%$.)

25. A particle of mass m and energy E moving in a region where there is initially no potential energy encounters a potential dip of width L and depth $U = -U_0$.

$$U(x) = \begin{cases} 0 & x \le 0 \\ -U_0 & 0 < x < L \\ 0 & x \ge L \end{cases}$$

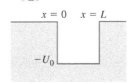

Show that the reflection probability is given by

$$R = \frac{\sin^2\left[\sqrt{2m(E + U_0)}L/\hbar\right]}{\sin^2\left[\sqrt{2m(E + U_0)}L/\hbar\right] + 4(E/U_0)\left[(E/U_0) + 1\right]}$$

(*Hint:* All that is needed is an appropriate substitution in a known probability.)

26. Given the situation of Exercise 25, show that (a) as $U_0 \to \infty$, the reflection probability approaches 1, and (b) as $L \to 0$, the reflection probability approaches 0. (c) Consider the limit in which the well becomes infinitely deep and infinitesimally narrow—that is, $U_0 \to \infty$ and $L \to 0$—but the product U_0L is constant. (This "delta well" model approximates the effect of a narrow but strong

attractive potential, such as that experienced by a free electron encountering a positive ion.) Show that the reflection probability becomes

$$R = \left[1 + \frac{2\hbar^2 E}{m(U_0L)^2}\right]^{-1}$$

* 27. For the $E > U_0$ potential barrier, the reflection and transmission probabilities are the ratios

$$R = \frac{B^*B}{A^*A} \quad \text{and} \quad T = \frac{F^*F}{A^*A}$$

where A, B, and F are the multiplicative coefficients of the incident, reflected, and transmitted waves, respectively. From the four smoothness conditions, solve for B and F in terms of A, insert them in the R and T ratios, and thus derive equations (12).

28. Reflection and transmission probabilities (16) can be obtained from equations (12). The first step is substituting $-i\alpha$ for k'. (a) Why? (b) Make the substitution, then use the definitions of k and α to obtain equations (16).

29. Obtain the smoothness conditions at the boundaries between regions for the $E < U_0$ barrier (i.e., tunneling) case.

* 30. Here we take a direct approach to calculating reflection probability for tunneling, meanwhile obtaining a relationship applied in other exercises.

(a) Write out the smoothness conditions at the boundaries between regions for the $E < U_0$ barrier. From them, show that the coefficient B of the reflected wave is given by

$$B = A\frac{\sinh(\alpha L)}{\sqrt{\sinh^2(\alpha L) + 4\alpha^2 k^2/(k^2 + \alpha^2)^2}}e^{-i\beta}$$

where

$$\beta = \tan^{-1}\left(\frac{2\alpha k}{k^2 - \alpha^2}\coth(\alpha L)\right)$$

(b) Verify that the reflection probability R given in equation (16) follows from this result.

31. Suppose the tunneling probability is 10^{-12} for a wide barrier when E is $\frac{1}{100}U_0$ (a) About how much smaller would it be if E were instead $\frac{1}{1000}U_0$? (b) If this case does not support the general rule that transmission probability is a *very* sensitive function of E, what makes it exceptional?

32. *Jump to Jupiter* The gravitational potential energy of a 1 kg object is plotted versus position from Earth's

surface to the surface of Jupiter. Mostly it is due to the Sun, but there are downturns at each end, due to the attractions to the two planets.

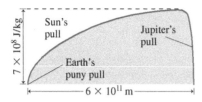

Make the crude approximation that this is a rectangular barrier of width 6×10^{11} m and approximate height 4×10^8 J/kg. Your mass is 65 kg, and you launch yourself from Earth at an impressive 4 m/s. What is the probability that you can jump to Jupiter?

33. Suppose a barrier qualifies as wide, and its height and width are such that $2L\sqrt{2mU_0}/\hbar = 5$. (a) Calculate the transmission probabilities when E/U_0 is 0.4 and when it is 0.6. (b) Repeat part (a), but for the case where $2L\sqrt{2mU_0}/\hbar$ is 50 instead of 5. (c) Repeat part (a), but for $2L\sqrt{2mU_0}/\hbar = 500$. (d) How do your results support the claim that the tunneling probability is a far more sensitive function of E when the tunneling probability is small?

34. Obtain equation (18) from (16) and (17).

Section 3

35. **Fusion in the Sun:** Without tunneling, our Sun would fail us. The source of its energy is nuclear **fusion**, and a crucial step is the fusion of a light-hydrogen nucleus, which is just a proton, and a heavy-hydrogen nucleus, which is of the same charge but twice the mass. When these nuclei get close enough, their short-range attraction via the strong force overcomes their Coulomb repulsion. This allows them to stick together, resulting in a reduced total mass/internal energy and a consequent release of kinetic energy. However, the Sun's temperature is simply too low to ensure that nuclei move fast enough to overcome their repulsion.

   (a) By equating the average thermal kinetic energy that the nuclei would have when distant, $\frac{3}{2}k_BT$, and the Coulomb potential energy they would have when 2 fm apart, roughly the separation at which they stick, show that a temperature of about 10^9 K would be needed.

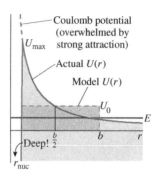

   (b) The Sun's core is only about 10^7 K. If nuclei can't make it "over the top," they must tunnel. Consider the following model, illustrated in the figure: One nucleus is fixed at the origin, while the other approaches from far away with energy E. As r decreases, the Coulomb potential energy increases, until the separation r is roughly the nuclear radius r_{nuc}, whereupon the potential energy is U_{max} and then quickly drops down into a very deep "hole" as the strong-force attraction takes over. Given that $E \ll U_{max}$, the point b, where tunneling must begin, will be very large compared with r_{nuc}, so we approximate the barrier's width L as simply b. Its height, U_0, we approximate by the Coulomb potential evaluated at $b/2$. Finally, for the energy E, which fixes b, let us use $4 \times \frac{3}{2}k_BT$, which is a reasonable limit, given the natural range of speeds in a thermodynamic system. Combining these approximations, show that the exponential factor in the wide-barrier tunneling probability is

$$\exp\left[\frac{-e^2}{(4\pi\varepsilon_0)\hbar}\sqrt{\frac{4m}{3k_BT}}\right]$$

   (c) Using the proton mass for m, evaluate this factor for a temperature of 10^7 K. Then evaluate it at 3000 K, about that of an incandescent filament or hot flame, and rather high by Earth standards. Discuss the consequences.

36. To obtain a rough estimate of the mean time required for uranium-238 to alpha-decay, let us approximate the combined electrostatic and strong nuclear potential energies by a rectangular potential barrier half as high as the actual 35 MeV maximum potential energy. Alpha particles (mass 4 u) of 4.3 MeV kinetic energy are incident. Let us also assume that the barrier extends from the radius of the nucleus, 7.4 fm, to the point where the electrostatic potential drops to 4.3 MeV (i.e., the classically forbidden region). Because $U \propto 1/r$, this

point is 35/4.3 times the radius of the nucleus, the point at which $U(r)$ is 35 MeV.

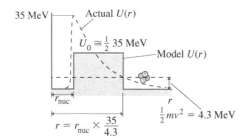

(a) Use these crude approximations, the method suggested in Section 3, and the wide-barrier approximation to obtain a value for the time it takes to decay.

(b) To gain some appreciation of the difficulties in a theoretical prediction, work the exercise "backward." Rather than assuming a value for U_0, use the known value of the mean time to decay for uranium-238 and infer the corresponding value of U_0. Retain all other assumptions.

(c) Comment on the sensitivity of the decay time to the height of the potential barrier.

37. A method for finding tunneling probability for a barrier that is "wide" but whose height varies in an arbitrary way is the so-called WKB approximation.

$$T \cong \exp\left[-\frac{2}{\hbar}\int_1^2 \sqrt{2m(U(x) - E)}\, dx\right]$$

Here $U(x)$ is the height of the arbitrary potential energy barrier, which a particle first penetrates at $x = 0$ and finally exits at $x = L$. Although not entirely rigorous, show that this can be obtained by treating the barrier as a series of rectangular slices, each of width dx (though each is still a "wide" barrier), and by assuming that the probability of tunneling through the total is the product of the probabilities for each slice.

38. The potential energy barrier in field emission is not rectangular, but resembles a ramp, as shown in Figure 16. Here we compare tunneling probability calculated by the crudest approximation to that calculated by a better one. In method 1, calculate T by treating the barrier as an actual ramp in which $U - E$ is initially ϕ, but falls off with a slope of M. Use the formula given in Exercise 37. In method 2, the cruder one, assume a barrier whose height exceeds E by a *constant* $\phi/2$ (the same as the *average* excess for the ramp) and whose width is the

same as the distance the particle tunnels through in the ramp. (a) Show that the ratio T_1/T_2 is $e^{\sqrt{8m\phi^3}/3\hbar M}$. (b) Do the methods differ more when tunneling probability is relatively high or relatively low?

39. **Resonant Tunneling:** Here we investigate the intriguing fact that while a single $E < U_0$ barrier always has a reflected wave, introducing a second barrier can give a reflection probability of *zero*, known as resonant tunneling and important to many modern electronic devices.

Equation (15) gives the wave functions outside a single barrier. (We actually won't need the solutions inside the barrier.) To make room for a second one, we shift this "right barrier" a distance s to the right, so that it extends from $x = s$ to $x = s + L$, which requires that we also shift the wave functions a distance s.

Right barrier: $\psi_{x<+s} = Ae^{+ik(x-s)} + Be^{-ik(x-s)}$

$$\psi_{x>s+L} = Fe^{+ik(x-s)}$$

If we now replace x by $-x$, we obtain solutions of the time-independent Schrödinger equation valid for a "left barrier" extending from $x = -s - L$ to $x = -s$.

$$\psi_{x>-s} = Ae^{+ik(-x-s)} + Be^{-ik(-x-s)}$$

$$\psi_{x<-s-L} = Fe^{+ik(-x-s)}$$

However, note that the complex conjugate of the time-independent Schrödinger equation is the same equation but with ψ^* in place of ψ, because E, $U(x)$, and all other factors are real. In other words, ψ^* is as valid a solution as ψ. Thus, for the left barrier we can instead write

Left barrier: $\psi_{x>-s} = A^*e^{+ik(x+s)} + B^*e^{-ik(x+s)}$

$$\psi_{x<-s-L} = F^*e^{+ik(x+s)}$$

We choose these because the F^*-term represents particles on the left of the left barrier and *moving right*—incident particles. The F-term in the *right*-barrier solutions represents particles transmitted through the right barrier. Together, they imply perfect transmission, for $|F| = |F^*|$. We can satisfy the Schrödinger equation everywhere for both barriers if we can make the solutions compatible in the region between them, $x = -s$ to $x = +s$. By equating the two solutions in this region and using the relationship between B and A given in Exercise 30—a bit messy to derive, but nonetheless true for the $E < U_0$ barrier—show that the width $2s$ of the space between the barriers must obey

$$2s = \beta/k$$

See Exercises 40 and 56 for applications of this result.

40. Exercise 39 gives the condition for resonant tunneling through two barriers separated by a space of width $2s$, expressed in terms of a factor β given in Exercise 30. (a) Suppose that in some system of units, k and α are both 2π. Find two values of $2s$ that give resonant tunneling. What are these distances in terms of wavelengths of ψ? Is the term *resonant tunneling* appropriate? (b) Show that the condition has no solution if $s = 0$, and explain why this must be so. (c) If a *classical* particle wants to surmount a barrier without gaining energy, is adding a second barrier a good solution?

Section 4

41. The matter-wave dispersion relation given in equation (23) is correct only at low speed and when mass/internal energy is ignored.

(a) Using the relativistically correct relationship among energy, momentum, and mass, show that the correct dispersion relation is

$$\omega = \sqrt{k^2 c^2 + \frac{m^2 c^4}{\hbar^2}}$$

(b) Show that in the limit of low speed (small p and k) and ignoring mass/internal energy, this expression agrees with that of equation (23).

42. From equation (33), we concluded that the group velocity of a matter wave group equals the velocity v_0 of the massive particle with which it is associated. However, both the dispersion relation used to show that $v_{\text{group}} = \hbar k_0/m$ and the formula $v_{\text{particle}} = p/m$ used to relate this to the particle velocity are relativistically incorrect. It might be argued that we proved what we wished to prove by making an even number of mistakes.

(a) Using the relativistically correct dispersion relation given in Exercise 41, show that the group velocity of a wave pulse is actually given by

$$v_{\text{group}} = \frac{\hbar k_0 c^2}{\sqrt{(\hbar k_0)^2 c^2 + m^2 c^4}}$$

(b) The fundamental relationship $p = \hbar k$ is universally correct, so $\hbar k_0$ is indeed the particle momentum p. (It is not well defined, but this is its approximate, or central, value.) Making this substitution in the expression for v_{group} from part (a), then using the relativistically correct relationship between momentum p and particle velocity v, show that the group velocity again is equal to the particle velocity.

43. Example 3 gives the refractive index for high-frequency electromagnetic radiation passing through Earth's ionosphere. The constant b, related to the so-called plasma frequency, varies with atmospheric conditions, but a typical value is 8×10^{15} rad^2/s^2. Given a GPS pulse of frequency 1.5 GHz traveling through 8 km of ionosphere, by how much, in meters, would the wave group and a particular wave crest be ahead of or behind (as the case may be) a pulse of light passing through the same distance of vacuum?

44. For a general wave pulse, neither E nor p (i.e., neither ω nor k) are well defined, but they have approximate values E_0 and p_0. Although it comprises many plane waves, the general pulse has an overall phase velocity corresponding to these values.

$$v_{\text{phase}} = \frac{\omega_0}{k_0} = \frac{E_0/\hbar}{p_0/\hbar} = \frac{E_0}{p_0}$$

If the pulse describes a "large" massive particle, the uncertainties are reasonably small, and the particle may be said to have energy E_0 and momentum p_0. Using the relativistically correct expressions for energy and momentum, show that the overall phase velocity is greater than c and given by

$$v_{\text{phase}} = \frac{c^2}{u_{\text{particle}}}$$

Note that the phase velocity is greatest for particles whose speed is least.

45. For wavelengths less than about 1 cm, the dispersion relation for waves on the surface of water is $\omega = \sqrt{(\gamma/\rho)k^3}$, where γ and ρ are the surface tension and density of water. Given $\gamma = 0.072$ N/m and $\rho = 10^3$ kg/m^3, calculate the phase and group velocities for a wave of 5 mm wavelength.

46. For waves on the surface of water, the behavior of long wavelengths is dominated by gravitational effects—a liquid "seeking its own level." Short wavelengths are dominated by surface tension effects. Taking both into account, the dispersion relation is $\omega = \sqrt{gk + (\gamma/\rho)k^3}$, where γ is the surface tension, ρ is the density of water, and g is, of course, the gravitational acceleration.

(a) Make a qualitative sketch of group velocity versus wave number. How does it behave for very large k? For very small k?
(b) Find the minimum possible group velocity and the wavelength at which it occurs. (Use $\gamma = 0.072$ N/m, $\rho = 10^3$ kg/m^3, and $g = 9.8$ m/s^2.)

47. For wavelengths greater than about 20 cm, the dispersion relation for waves on the surface of water is

$\omega = \sqrt{gk}$. (a) Calculate the phase and group velocities for a wave of 5 m wavelength. (b) Will the wave spread as it travels? Justify your answer.

48. From equations (23) and (29) obtain the dispersion coefficient for matter waves (in vacuum), then show that probability density (35) follows from (28).

49. In a Gaussian function of the form $\psi(x) \propto e^{-(x/2\varepsilon)^2}$, ε is the standard deviation, or uncertainty, in position. The probability density for a Gaussian wave function would be proportional to $\psi(x)$ squared: $e^{-(x^2/2\varepsilon^2)}$. Comparing with the time-dependent Gaussian probability of equation (35), we see that the uncertainty in position of the time-evolving Gaussian wave function of a free particle is given by

$$\Delta x = \varepsilon \sqrt{1 + \frac{\hbar^2 t^2}{4m^2\varepsilon^4}}$$

That is, it starts at ε and increases with time. Suppose the wave function of an electron is initially determined to be a Gaussian of 500 nm uncertainty. How long will it take for the uncertainty in the electron's position to reach 5 m, the length of a typical automobile?

* 50. Show that the quite general wave group given in equation (21) is a solution of the free-particle Schrödinger equation, provided that each plane wave's ω does satisfy the matter wave dispersion relation given in (23).

Comprehensive Exercises

51. Solving the potential barrier smoothness conditions for relationships among the coefficients A, B, and F, giving the reflection and transmission probabilities, usually involves rather messy algebra. However, there is a special case that can be done fairly easily, though requiring a slight departure from the standard solutions used in the chapter. Suppose the incident particles' energy E is precisely U_0. (a) Write down solutions to the Schrödinger equation in the three regions. Be especially careful in the region $0 < x < L$. It should have two arbitrary constants, and it isn't difficult—just different. (b) Obtain the smoothness conditions, and from these, find R and T. (c) Do the results make sense in the limit $L \to \infty$?

52. Show that if you attempt to detect a particle while tunneling, your experiment must render its kinetic energy so uncertain that it might well be "over the top." (*Hint*: Apply the uncertainty principle, and note that the particle must be localized within the penetration depth.)

53. A particle experiences a potential energy given by $U(x) = (x^2 - 3)e^{-x^2}$ (in SI units). (a) Make a sketch of $U(x)$, including numerical values at the minima and

maxima. (b) What is the maximum energy the particle could have and yet be bound? (c) What is the maximum energy the particle could have and yet be bound for a considerable length of time? (d) Is it possible for the particle to have an energy greater than that in part (c) and still be "bound" for some period of time? Explain.

54. Consider a particle of mass m inside the well shown. If bound, its lowest energy state would, of course, be the ground state, but would it be bound? Assume that, at least for a while, it occupies its ground state, which is much lower than U_0, and that the barriers qualify as wide. Show that a rough average time it would remain bound is given by $\tau = (mW^4/2000\hbar L^2)\sigma^2 e^\sigma$, where $\sigma \equiv L\sqrt{8mU_0}/\hbar$

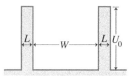

55. Exercise 54 gives a rough lifetime for a trapped particle to escape an enclosure by tunneling. (a) Consider an electron. Given that $W = 100$ nm, $L = 1$ nm, and $U_0 = 5$ eV, first verify that the $E_{ground} \ll U_0$ assumption holds, then evaluate the lifetime. (b) Repeat part (a), but for a 0.1 μg particle, with $W = 1$ mm, $L = 1$ μm, and a barrier height U_0 that equals the energy the particle would have if its speed were just 1 mm per year.

56. Exercise 39 gives the condition for resonant tunneling through two barriers separated by a space of width $2s$, expressed in terms of a factor β given in Exercise 30. Show that in the limit in which the barrier width $L \to \infty$, this condition becomes exactly energy-quantization condition (22) for the finite well. Thus, resonant tunneling occurs at the quantized energies of the intervening well.

Computational Exercises

57. A computer can solve several equations in several unknowns easily, and here we study a particular $E > U_0$ barrier problem, where all the values it needs are real. Once the computer finds the multiplicative constants of all the functions involved, we can verify equations (13) as well as see what is happening when the particles are "over the barrier." Still, it helps to simplify things as much as possible. With length, time, and mass at our disposal, we can choose our units so that the particle mass m and the value of $\hbar$ are both 1 and the barrier width L is exactly π. Suppose that in this system of units, the energy E of the incident particles is 1.125, and the barrier height U_0 is 1. Furthermore, because only ratios are ever

really needed, assume the multiplicative constant A for the incident wave function is 1. (a) Write down solutions to the Schrödinger equation in the three regions, using numerical values wherever possible, then write down the smoothness conditions. (b) You should have four equations in four unknowns. (They should be real—don't forget the Euler formulas.) Use a computer to solve for the unknowns. (c) Do the reflection and transmission probabilities given by your results agree with the general formulas given in (13)? (d) If a particle were located in the region "over the barrier" between $x = 0$ and $x = L$, is it just as likely to be a particle moving left as right? If not, which is more probable, and why?

58. A computer makes solving several equations in several unknowns pretty easy, so provided your computer can handle complex numerical values, finding the multiplicative constants of all the functions in a tunneling problem isn't too bad. Not only can we verify equations (16), but we can also see what the functions inside the barrier are doing. Still, it helps to simplify things as much as possible. With length, time, and mass at our disposal, we can choose our units so that the particle mass m and the value of $\hbar$ are both 1 and the barrier width L is also 1. Suppose that in this system of units, the energy E of the incident particles is 2, and the barrier height U_0 is 4. Furthermore, because only ratios are ever really needed, assume the multiplicative constant A for the incident wave function is 1. (a) Write down solutions to the Schrödinger equation in the three regions, using numerical values wherever possible. Then, write down the smoothness conditions. (b) You should have four equations in four unknowns, with some of the known constants being complex. Use a computer to solve for the unknowns. (c) Do the reflection and transmission probabilities given by your results agree with the general formulas given in (16)? (d) In Section 2, it is said that the coefficient of the exponentially *increasing* function inside the barrier is usually small, implying that the function inside the barrier is essentially a decaying exponential. Do your results agree?

59. Equation (21) is an infinite sum of quantum-mechanical plane waves. Inserting the proper $A(k)$ and carrying out the integral gives a wave function with distinct phase and group velocities. The basic ideas can be illustrated, however, by replacing the integral with a sum of a small number of cosine functions and plotting the results as a function of x at a series of time values. Our simplified function is

$$f(x, t) = \sum_{n=-3}^{n=+3} A\left(1 + \frac{n}{10}\right) \cos\left[\left(1 + \frac{n}{10}\right)x - \omega\left(1 + \frac{n}{10}\right)t\right]$$

Note that parentheses after A and ω indicate function arguments, not multiplication. Where equation (21) has a k, this sum has $(1 + n/10)$, and its seven terms thus correspond to values of k between 0.7 and 1.3. Two functions still need to be specified. Define $A(k)$ as $e^{-25(k-1)^2}$. This says that the cosine function for which $k = 1$ has an amplitude of 1, and the amplitudes of the other cosines fall off. The farther k is from central value 1, the smaller the amplitude. Define $\omega(k)$ as simply k. (a) Plot $f(x, 0)$ from $x = -10$ to $x = 40$. Given that the central value of k is 1.0, does your plot appear to have the correct approximate wavelength? (b) Make a series of plots from $x = -10$ to $x = 40$, with each successive plot incrementing the value of t by 0.5, ending with $t = 20$. Given that you have defined $\omega(k)$ as simply k, what should be the phase and group velocities, and do the crests and envelope indeed move at these speeds? (Animating the series of plots is helpful.) (c) Define $\omega(k)$ as $k^2/2$. Make another series of plots with the same x and t values, and, remembering that your $A(k)$ still makes $k = 1$ the central value, answer the questions in part (b) again. (d) Define $\omega(k)$ as $2k^{1/2}$. Make another series of plots with the same x and t values, and once again answer the questions in part (b).

Answers

15. 0.00704

17. $\left(\frac{3}{5} - \frac{4}{5}i\right)e^{-ikx}$, $\left(\frac{8}{5} - \frac{4}{5}i\right)e^{-\alpha x}$

19. (b) 0, 0°, 2A, 90°

21. 1.1×10^{-54}

23. (a) $2t/m$; (b) $2L/n$

31. (a) about 9% as large

33. (a) 0.080 and 0.16; (b) 5.8×10^{-17} and 7.1×10^{-14}; (c) 2.4×10^{-168} and 1.8×10^{-137}

43. group 36 cm behind, crest 36 cm ahead

45. $v_{\text{phase}} = 0.30$ m/s, $v_{\text{group}} = 0.45$ m/s

47. $v_{\text{phase}} = 2.79$ m/s, $v_{\text{group}} = 1.40$ m/s, yes

49. 0.043 s

51. (b) $R = k^2L^2/(4 + k^2L^2)$, $T = 4/(4 + k^2L^2)$

53. zero, e^{-4}, yes

55. (a) ~33 min; (b) $\gg$ age of universe

Credits

Photograph Credits

19: Digital Instruments; **25:** Peter Sutter, The Colorado School of Mines

Art Credits

26: Courtesy of Dr. Saw-Wai Hla; **27:** Courtesy of Dr. D. F. Phillips

Quantum Mechanics in Three Dimensions and the Hydrogen Atom

Chapter Outline

Perhaps the most profound failure of classical physics is its inability to explain the simplest possible atom: hydrogen—an electron orbiting a proton. According to classical physics, the atom should be unstable. Any time a charged particle accelerates, it emits electromagnetic radiation, so the continuous centripetal acceleration of the hydrogen atom's orbiting electron should cause it to lose energy and spiral into the nucleus. What we observe, however, is that atoms are usually quite stable, emitting no radiation. They can be *induced* to radiate electromagnetic energy, but they do so only at certain frequencies. And while easily demonstrated with a simple diffraction grating, this too defies classical explanation. One of the first great triumphs of quantum mechanics was its explanation of these observations. But before we can understand the hydrogen atom quantum mechanically, we must extend the Schrödinger equation to govern matter waves in real, three-dimensional space.

1 The Schrödinger Equation in Three Dimensions

In one dimension, the Schrödinger equation is

$$-\frac{\hbar^2}{2m}\frac{\partial^2}{\partial x^2}\Psi(x, t) + U(x)\Psi(x, t) = i\hbar\frac{\partial}{\partial t}\Psi(x, t)$$

As we know, this equation is based on an energy accounting of the form KE + $U = E$. In three dimensions, the potential energy is, in general, a function of three spatial coordinates, $U(x, y, z)$, as is the wave function, $\Psi(x, y, z, t)$, leaving only the kinetic energy term on the left to be generalized. This term is $p_x^2/2m$ in operator form. The logical generalization is to replace p_x^2 with $p_x^2 + p_y^2 + p_z^2$ — that is, add terms with y and z in place of x. Thus,

$$-\frac{\hbar^2}{2m}\left(\frac{\partial^2}{\partial x^2} + \frac{\partial^2}{\partial y^2} + \frac{\partial^2}{\partial z^2}\right)\Psi(x, y, z, t) + U(x, y, z)\Psi(x, y, z, t)$$

$$= i\hbar\frac{\partial}{\partial t}\Psi(x, y, z, t)$$

To specify position in three dimensions, we are not required to use rectangular Cartesian coordinates, and they would be particularly awkward for the spherically symmetric hydrogen atom. To avoid bias, the Schrödinger equation is usually expressed in coordinate-independent form. Using the generic symbol $\mathbf{r}$ (boldface) to represent position—Cartesian (x, y, z), spherical polar (r, θ, ϕ), and so on—$U(x, y, z)$ becomes $U(\mathbf{r})$ and $\Psi(x, y, z, t)$ becomes $\Psi(\mathbf{r}, t)$. For the kinetic energy term, we adopt the generic symbol ∇^2 from vector calculus. Expressed in Cartesian coordinates,

$$\nabla^2 = \frac{\partial^2}{\partial x^2} + \frac{\partial^2}{\partial y^2} + \frac{\partial^2}{\partial z^2}$$

Expressed in other coordinate systems, it may have a quite different appearance, but its mathematical function is the same. Altogether, we have

$$-\frac{\hbar^2}{2m}\nabla^2\Psi(\mathbf{r}, t) + U(\mathbf{r})\Psi(\mathbf{r}, t) = i\hbar\frac{\partial}{\partial t}\Psi(\mathbf{r}, t) \tag{1}$$

Now let us briefly discuss other important changes as we move to three dimensions.

Probability Density and Normalization

In one dimension, the complex square of the wave function is the probability per unit length. It is naturally the probability per unit volume in three dimensions. Both are called probability density.

Probability density

$$\text{probability density} = \frac{\text{probability}}{\text{volume}} = \left|\Psi(\mathbf{r}, t)\right|^2$$

We see that the dimensions of the wave function are now $(\text{volume})^{-1/2}$ or $(\text{length})^{-3/2}$.

If a wave function describes a single particle, the total probability of finding it somewhere in three-dimensional space must be 1. In three dimensions, this condition becomes

$$\int_{\text{all space}} |\Psi(\mathbf{r}, t)|^2 \, dV = 1 \qquad (2) \qquad \text{Normalization}$$

The Time-Independent Schrödinger Equation

As in one dimension, we most often consider states in which the energy is well defined and unchanging. This comes from assuming the wave function to be a product of spatial and temporal parts.

$$\Psi(\mathbf{r}, t) = \psi(\mathbf{r})\phi(t)$$

Inserting this product into equation (1) tells us that the temporal part is $\phi(t) = e^{-i(E/\hbar)t}$, exactly as before. It again follows that $\phi(t)^*\phi(t) = 1$ and $|\Psi(\mathbf{r}, t)|^2 = |\psi(\mathbf{r})|^2$. The "spatial side" of the separation of variables then gives us the time-independent Schrödinger equation.

$$-\frac{\hbar^2}{2m}\nabla^2\psi(\mathbf{r}) + U(\mathbf{r})\psi(\mathbf{r}) = E\psi(\mathbf{r}) \qquad (3) \qquad \text{Time-independent Schrödinger equation}$$

This is as far as we can go until we know the potential energy $U(\mathbf{r})$.

Quantum Numbers

We concentrate here on bound states—potential energies capable of confining a particle to a region of space. In one dimension, the physical conditions we imposed on the wave function led to standing waves and quantized energies. Now with conditions in *three* dimensions, we will obtain three-dimensional standing waves, and three **quantum numbers** will arise. These quantum numbers invariably yield quantized energies, but they govern quantization of other physical properties as well, depending on the particular $U(\mathbf{r})$.

2 The 3D Infinite Well

The simplest three-dimensional bound system is the infinite well. It is a good model of the ubiquitous quantum dot, and it highlights several important conclusions in a rather familiar environment, conclusions that can sometimes be obscured in the hydrogen atom's different geometry.

As always, the starting point is the potential energy. In the 3D infinite well, pictured in Figure 1, a particle is bound in a box-shaped region by infinitely

Figure 1 A three-dimensional infinite well.

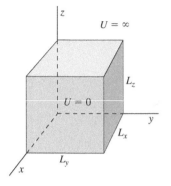

"high" walls at $x = 0$ and L_x, $y = 0$ and L_y, and $z = 0$ and L_z. The potential energy is therefore

$$U(\mathbf{r}) = \begin{cases} 0 & 0 < x < L_x, 0 < y < L_y, 0 < z < L_z \\ \infty & \text{otherwise} \end{cases}$$

As in one dimension, the wave function cannot penetrate outside infinite walls, so we concentrate on the region inside where $U = 0$.

Whenever we face a differential equation involving multiple independent variables, our first step is separation of variables. We assume that the spatial wave function is a product of three functions, each of a different independent variable, and here the obvious choice is Cartesian coordinates.

$$\psi(x, y, z) = F(x)G(y)H(z)$$

Following the usual recipe for separation of variables, we next insert this product into (3), then divide by the product. Expressing ∇^2 in Cartesian coordinates, and noting that U is 0 inside the well, we thus obtain

$$\frac{-\dfrac{\hbar^2}{2m}\left(\dfrac{\partial^2 F(x)G(y)H(z)}{\partial x^2} + \dfrac{\partial^2 F(x)G(y)H(z)}{\partial y^2} + \dfrac{\partial^2 F(x)G(y)H(z)}{\partial z^2} \right)}{F(x)G(y)H(z)}$$

$$= \frac{E\, F(x)G(y)H(z)}{F(x)G(y)H(z)}$$

Canceling top and bottom where possible and multiplying both sides by $-2m/\hbar^2$, we arrive at

$$\frac{1}{F(x)}\frac{\partial^2 F(x)}{\partial x^2} + \frac{1}{G(y)}\frac{\partial^2 G(y)}{\partial y^2} + \frac{1}{H(z)}\frac{\partial^2 H(z)}{\partial z^2} = -\frac{2mE}{\hbar^2} \qquad (4)$$

Each of the spatial variables is now in a separate term, so the usual argument applies: If the equation holds for x_1, y_1, z_1, it can hold for x_2, y_1, z_1 only if the term involving x does not vary with x. *Each* term must be a constant. Thus,

$$\frac{d^2 F(x)}{dx^2} = C_x F(x) \qquad \frac{d^2 G(y)}{dy^2} = C_y G(y) \qquad \frac{d^2 H(z)}{dz^2} = C_z H(z) \qquad (5)$$

Things now look rather familiar. Just as in one dimension, each function must have a second derivative proportional to itself, and because the wave function is 0 *outside* infinite walls, continuity demands that it go to 0 *at* both walls. These are exactly the conditions that gave us standing waves in the 1D infinite well—the solutions are essentially identical.[1]

$$F(x) = A_x \sin\frac{n_x \pi x}{L_x} \qquad G(y) = A_y \sin\frac{n_y \pi y}{L_y} \qquad H(z) = A_z \sin\frac{n_z \pi z}{L_z} \qquad (6)$$

---

[1] One distinction here is that the constants C are not *explicitly* negative. Were they positive, the solutions would be exponential rather than sinusoidal. Exercise 17 demonstrates, however, that exponentials cannot be 0 at both walls.

The only real difference is that each dimension is independent, so the constants n and L need not be the same—thus the subscripts. Inserting solutions (6) back into equation (4) yields

$$-\frac{n_x^2\pi^2}{L_x^2} - \frac{n_y^2\pi^2}{L_y^2} - \frac{n_z^2\pi^2}{L_z^2} = -\frac{2mE}{\hbar^2}$$

or

$$E_{n_x, n_y, n_z} = \left(\frac{n_x^2}{L_x^2} + \frac{n_y^2}{L_y^2} + \frac{n_z^2}{L_z^2}\right)\frac{\pi^2\hbar^2}{2m} \qquad (7)$$

The overall wave function is the product of the individual ones, and using simply A for the product $A_x A_y A_z$ we have

$$\psi_{n_x, n_y, n_z}(x, y, z) = A \sin\frac{n_x\pi x}{L_x}\sin\frac{n_y\pi y}{L_y}\sin\frac{n_z\pi z}{L_z} \qquad (8)$$

Each set of the three quantum numbers (n_x, n_y, n_z) yields a unique wave function, a unique three-dimensional standing wave.

Perhaps the most important lesson here is that whereas boundary conditions in one dimension lead to energy quantization according to the value of a single quantum number, imposing conditions in three dimensions naturally leads to three quantum numbers. In the infinite well, they are n_x, n_y, n_z, but it is true in general that *for each dimension, there is an independent quantum number*.

As in one dimension, there is a ground state. Consider the case $L_x = 1$, $L_y = 2$, and $L_z = 3$ (in arbitrary units). None of the three quantum numbers may be 0, for this would make the wave function 0. The lowest energy is $(n_x, n_y, n_z) = (1, 1, 1)$.

$$E_{1,1,1} = \left(\frac{1^2}{1^2} + \frac{1^2}{2^2} + \frac{1^2}{3^2}\right)\frac{\pi^2\hbar^2}{2m} = \frac{49\pi^2\hbar^2}{72m}$$

The corresponding wave function is

$$\psi_{1,1,1}(x, y, z) = A \sin\frac{1\pi x}{1}\sin\frac{1\pi y}{2}\sin\frac{1\pi z}{3}$$

With three quantum numbers, it isn't quite so obvious what state would have the next-higher energy. It is left as a quick exercise for the reader to verify that it is $(n_x, n_y, n_z) = (1, 1, 2)$.

TABLE 1 States in the 3D well

n_x, n_y, n_z	$E_{n_x,n_y,n_z} / \dfrac{\pi^2\hbar^2}{2mL^2}$
1, 1, 1	3
2, 1, 1	6
1, 2, 1	6
1, 1, 2	6
1, 2, 2	9
2, 1, 2	9
2, 2, 1	9
3, 1, 1	11
1, 3, 1	11
1, 1, 3	11
2, 2, 2	12
1, 2, 3	14
2, 1, 3	14
1, 3, 2	14
2, 3, 1	14
3, 1, 2	14
3, 2, 1	14
3, 2, 2	17
2, 3, 2	17
2, 2, 3	17
4, 1, 1	18
1, 4, 1	18
1, 1, 4	18
1, 3, 3	19
3, 1, 3	19
3, 3, 1	19
1, 2, 4	21
2, 1, 4	21
1, 4, 2	21
2, 4, 1	21
4, 1, 2	21
4, 2, 1	21
2, 3, 3	22
3, 2, 3	22
3, 3, 2	22
4, 2, 2	24
2, 4, 2	24
2, 2, 4	24
1, 3, 4	25
3, 1, 4	25
1, 4, 3	25
3, 4, 1	25
4, 1, 3	25
4, 3, 1	25
3, 3, 3	27
5, 1, 1	27
1, 5, 1	27
1, 1, 5	27

Degeneracy

An idea crucial to many applications in our real three-dimensional world is that multiple states can have the same energy and the *number* of equal-energy states increases with the symmetry of the system.

Suppose the box is as symmetric as possible: a cube.

$$L_x = L_y = L_z \equiv L$$

Energy (7) becomes

$$E_{n_x,n_y,n_z} = (n_x^2 + n_y^2 + n_z^2)\frac{\pi^2\hbar^2}{2mL^2} \qquad (9)$$

Table 1 shows sets of quantum numbers for many allowed energies. Of those shown, only the energies $3(\pi^2\hbar^2/2mL^2)$ and $12(\pi^2\hbar^2/2mL^2)$ correspond to unique sets of quantum numbers, respectively (1, 1, 1) and (2, 2, 2). The energy $27(\pi^2\hbar^2/2mL^2)$, for instance, results from four different sets of quantum numbers. But despite having the same energy, *each set of quantum numbers corresponds to a different wave function.* The wave functions are

$$\psi_{3,3,3} = A\sin\frac{3\pi x}{L}\sin\frac{3\pi y}{L}\sin\frac{3\pi z}{L} \qquad \psi_{5,1,1} = A\sin\frac{5\pi x}{L}\sin\frac{1\pi y}{L}\sin\frac{1\pi z}{L}$$

$$\psi_{1,5,1} = A\sin\frac{1\pi x}{L}\sin\frac{5\pi y}{L}\sin\frac{1\pi z}{L} \qquad \psi_{1,1,5} = A\sin\frac{1\pi x}{L}\sin\frac{1\pi y}{L}\sin\frac{5\pi z}{L}$$

If nothing else, these have their maximum values at different coordinates (x, y, z). The coincidence—different wave functions having the same energy—is called **degeneracy**, and energy levels for which it is true are said to be **degenerate** (implying no moral judgment in this context). The energy $27(\pi^2\hbar^2/2mL^2)$ is said to be 4-fold degenerate. Levels $3(\pi^2\hbar^2/2mL^2)$ and $12(\pi^2\hbar^2/2mL^2)$ are said to be **nondegenerate**—each corresponds to a single wave function.

EXAMPLE 1

An electron is in the $(n_x, n_y, n_z) = (1, 2, 1)$ state of a cubic 3D infinite well of 1 nm side length. (a) Find the electron's energy and wave function. (b) Where is the probability of finding the electron the largest? (c) If there are other states of the same energy, where would an electron most likely be found in each?

SOLUTION

(a) We may use equation (9) for the energy and (8) for the wave function.

$$E_{1,2,1} = (1^2 + 2^2 + 1^2)\frac{\pi^2(1.055 \times 10^{-34}\,\text{J}\cdot\text{s})^2}{2(9.11 \times 10^{-31}\,\text{kg})(10^{-9}\,\text{m})^2}$$

$$= 3.62 \times 10^{-19}\,\text{J} = 2.26\,\text{eV}$$

$$\psi_{1,2,1}(x, y, z) = A\sin\frac{1\pi x}{10^{-9}\text{m}}\sin\frac{2\pi y}{10^{-9}\text{m}}\sin\frac{1\pi z}{10^{-9}\text{m}}$$

Note: To be complete, we would need the normalization constant A. It turns out to be $(2/L)^{3/2}$ and is the same for all sets n_x, n_y, n_z. The proof is left as an exercise.

(b) Where does the probability density have its maximum value?

$$\left|\psi_{1,2,1}(x, y, z)\right|^2 = A^2 \sin^2 \frac{1\pi x}{L} \sin^2 \frac{2\pi y}{L} \sin^2 \frac{1\pi z}{L}$$

The maximum of sine squared is 1, so this product is maximum when $x = \frac{1}{2}L$ and $y = \frac{1}{4}L$ or $\frac{3}{4}L$ and $z = \frac{1}{2}L$. Thus, there are two points (x, y, z) where the electron is most likely to be found.

$$\psi_{1,2,1} \text{ state:} \left(\frac{1}{2}L, \frac{1}{4}L, \frac{1}{2}L\right) \text{ and } \left(\frac{1}{2}L, \frac{3}{4}L, \frac{1}{2}L\right)$$

(c) By symmetry, $E_{2,1,1}$ and $E_{1,1,2}$ equal $E_{1,2,1}$, and the locations of the corresponding functions' maxima follow simply by permuting the coordinates.

$$\psi_{2,1,1} \text{ state:} \left(\frac{1}{4}L, \frac{1}{2}L, \frac{1}{2}L\right) \text{ and } \left(\frac{3}{4}L, \frac{1}{2}L, \frac{1}{2}L\right)$$

$$\psi_{1,1,2} \text{ state:} \left(\frac{1}{2}L, \frac{1}{2}L, \frac{1}{4}L\right) \text{ and } \left(\frac{1}{2}L, \frac{1}{2}L, \frac{3}{4}L\right)$$

Figure 2 represents the probability densities for the three standing waves as density of shading, with two regions of maximum probability for each. They have the same energy, and the shapes of their probability densities are similar, *but they are different states.*

Splitting of Energy Levels

Degeneracy results from symmetry. For example, if instead of a cubic well, we had L_x and L_y equal to L, but L_z equal to $0.9L$, much of the symmetry would be lost, and the result would be **splitting** of formerly degenerate energy levels. For the *cubic* well, equation (9) shows that $E_{2,1,1}$, $E_{1,2,1}$, and $E_{1,1,2}$ are equal.

$$E_{2,1,1} \quad = \quad E_{1,2,1} \quad = \quad E_{1,1,2}$$
$$(2^2 + 1^2 + 1^2)\frac{1}{L^2} = (1^2 + 2^2 + 1^2)\frac{1}{L^2} = (1^2 + 1^2 + 2^2)\frac{1}{L^2}$$

For unequal lengths, equation (7) says that all three levels would rise, but $E_{1,1,2}$ would rise higher.

$$\frac{2^2}{L^2} + \frac{1}{L^2} + \frac{1}{(0.9L)^2} = \frac{1}{L^2} + \frac{2^2}{L^2} + \frac{1}{(0.9L)^2} < \frac{1}{L^2} + \frac{1}{L^2} + \frac{2^2}{(0.9L)^2}$$

$$E_{2,1,1} \quad = \quad E_{1,2,1} \quad < \quad E_{1,1,2}$$

Figure 2 Degeneracy in a cubic infinite well: Equal energy but different states.

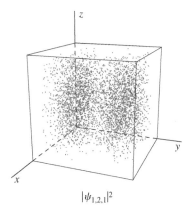

$|\psi_{1,2,1}|^2$

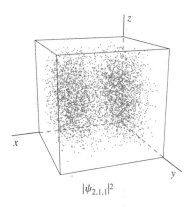

$|\psi_{2,1,1}|^2$

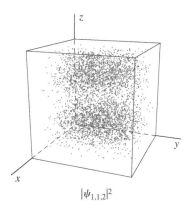

$|\psi_{1,1,2}|^2$

Figure 3 Splitting of formerly degenerate states, caused by the introduction of an asymmetry.

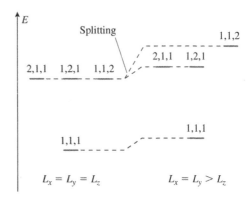

Figure 3 illustrates this energy-level splitting. Many important discoveries in atomic physics have sprung from observations of slight splitting among levels previously thought to be equal.

3 Energy Quantization and Spectral Lines in Hydrogen

Simply put, the hydrogen atom is an electron and a proton moving under the influence of their mutual electrostatic attraction, with insufficient kinetic energy to escape one another. Being about 2000 times as massive, the proton doesn't move much. To a good approximation, it is stationary.[2] Thus, we essentially have just an electron whose point-charge electrostatic potential energy is given by

$$U(r) = -\frac{1}{4\pi\varepsilon_0}\frac{e^2}{r} \tag{10}$$

where e is the fundamental charge and r the distance from the proton at the origin. Figure 4 plots this potential energy in two of the three spatial dimensions. It approaches negative infinity at zero distance and approaches 0 at infinite distance. If the electron is to be bound, it must have a total energy E less than 0, the maximum height of the potential energy "walls." When we apply the Schrödinger equation to hydrogen, we will find "new" properties, besides energy, that are quantized. It is helpful, however, to first study its energy quantization alone and the most obvious experimental evidence—**spectral lines**. Much of this evidence preceded the arrival of quantum mechanics, and we begin with a brief survey of the quest to make sense of it.

[2]Accounting for the proton's motion is not difficult, but it changes things very little. We would simply replace the *electron* mass, wherever it appears, by a *slightly* smaller "reduced mass." (See Comprehensive Exercise 80.)

Figure 4 The hydrogen atom potential energy.

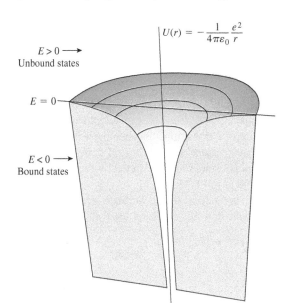

$E > 0 \longrightarrow$
Unbound states

$E = 0$

$E < 0 \longrightarrow$
Bound states

$$U(r) = -\frac{1}{4\pi\varepsilon_0}\frac{e^2}{r}$$

The Spectral Mystery

Spectroscopic observations demonstrate that hydrogen emits only certain wavelengths of light, known as spectral lines.[3] Those in the 400–700 nm visible portion of the spectrum are

656 nm   486 nm   434 nm   410 nm

In 1885, Swiss schoolteacher Johann Balmer found a formula by trial and error that yielded the experimentally observed wavelengths. Although its form suggested a tantalizing pattern, there was no underlying theory; the formula simply worked. The wavelengths obey

$$\frac{1}{\lambda} = 1.097 \times 10^7 \,\mathrm{m}^{-1}\left(\frac{1}{4} - \frac{1}{n^2}\right) \quad \text{where} \quad n = 3, 4, 5, \ldots \quad (11)$$

The constant $1.097 \times 10^7 \,\mathrm{m}^{-1}$, later named the **Rydberg constant**, was merely the value that gave best agreement—and that agreement was excellent!—with the observed wavelengths. Substitution shows that $n = 3$ yields 656 nm, with $n = 4$, 5, and 6 successively yielding the other visible wavelengths. Wavelengths corresponding to $n = 7$ and higher were later observed. Being shorter than the visible, they are in the ultraviolet region of the spectrum.

The path from Balmer's puzzling empirical pattern to the quantum-mechanical explanation took physics through a golden age, with one stunning leap forward following another. An early atomic model, which had the electrons embedded in a diffuse sea of positive charge, was swept away in 1909, when Ernest Rutherford and students Hans Geiger and Ernest Marsden discovered the atomic nucleus. By targeting a thin gold film with alpha particles—positively

[3]Fortunately, a given spectral line is not a perfectly well-defined wavelength, which would be very hard to resolve, but rather a range around a central value. Comprehensive Exercise 86 studies two primary reasons for this "fuzziness."

charged particles lighter than gold atoms but far heavier than electrons—they found that some alphas occasionally bounced *backward*. Only a collision with a heavier, highly concentrated positive core could explain this, and the negative electrons presumably orbited the core as moons orbit a planet. This model's deficiency was that an orbiting electron should lose energy by electromagnetic radiation and spiral into the nucleus. (Exercise 26 estimates that this collapse would take less than a nanosecond.) In 1913, Niels Bohr, addressing the problem with a mixture of classical and early quantum ideas, boldly postulated the existence of stationary states. The electron would not radiate in a stationary state, but it could do so in transitions between these states. Hindsight reveals its flaws, but its stationary states are still a vital feature of quantum mechanics, and its quantized energies are those predicted by the fully quantum-mechanical treatment that arrived in the 1920s.

As we will see in Section 6, the Schrödinger equation predicts that the hydrogen atom's electron is allowed only the following energies:

Hydrogen atom energy levels

$$E_n = -\frac{me^4}{2(4\pi\varepsilon_0)^2\hbar^2}\frac{1}{n^2} \qquad \text{where} \qquad n = 1, 2, 3, \ldots \qquad (12)$$

As expected, the energies are negative, but this is not peculiar to quantum mechanics. A satellite bound to Earth by the negative gravitational potential energy $-Gm_{\text{Earth}}m_{\text{Satellite}}/r$ has negative total mechanical energy. Its kinetic is less than its negative potential, which increases toward 0 as the orbit radius approaches infinity. Energy (12) similarly increases toward 0, but as we move to higher *quantum* levels n. (Exercise 27 obtains quantized energies of this form by a simplified yet instructive approach, sidestepping the complexity of the full Schrödinger route.)

Is Balmer's puzzle solved? In a stationary state, neither the probability density nor the charge density of the electron standing wave would vary with time. But if the electron is in any state above the ground state, a downward transition can occur, during which the probability density does oscillate. In fact, it oscillates at just the right frequency to generate a photon whose energy equals the energy difference between the states. Suppose the electron makes a transition from state n_i to state n_f. The energy given the photon is the electron's initial energy minus its final. Using equation (12), we obtain

$$E_{\text{photon}} = E_{\text{atom, i}} - E_{\text{atom, f}} = -\frac{me^4}{2(4\pi\varepsilon_0)^2\hbar^2}\left(\frac{1}{n_i^2} - \frac{1}{n_f^2}\right)$$

For a photon, $E_{\text{photon}} = hf = hc/\lambda$, so

$$\frac{hc}{\lambda} = \frac{me^4}{2(4\pi\varepsilon_0)^2\hbar^2}\left(\frac{1}{n_f^2} - \frac{1}{n_i^2}\right)$$

or

$$\frac{1}{\lambda} = \frac{me^4}{2(4\pi\varepsilon_0)^2\hbar^2hc}\left(\frac{1}{n_f^2} - \frac{1}{n_i^2}\right) = 1.097 \times 10^7 \text{ m}^{-1}\left(\frac{1}{n_f^2} - \frac{1}{n_i^2}\right) \qquad (13)$$

We infer that the wavelengths given by (11) result from transitions down to the $n_f = 2$ level from the $n_i = 3, 4, 5$ and higher levels—and Balmer's puzzle is solved! Logically, there should be wavelengths corresponding to transitions ending at levels other than $n_f = 2$, and these too have been observed. Those ending at the $n_f = 1$ level, for instance, involve a greater downward energy jump, so they are of relatively short wavelength. All are in the ultraviolet region of the spectrum. Transitions ending at $n_f = 3, 4, \ldots$ involve smaller energy differences and are consequently in the infrared and beyond.

Energies and Wavelengths

Figure 5 illustrates the quantized energies in the hydrogen atom and the transitions possible between them. The combination of constants out front in equation (12) works out to be 13.6 eV, so the energies can be written as

$$E_n = \frac{-13.6 \text{ eV}}{n^2} \qquad n = 1, 2, 3, \ldots \qquad (14)$$

Energy increases, becoming less negative, as n increases, asymptotically approaching 0. In its ground state, the electron is 13.6 eV "deep," a rather famous value. We would need to add 13.6 eV to free it—to reach the lowest unbound energy—which agrees with the well-known **ionization energy** of the hydrogen atom. In Figure 5, arrows signify downward transitions, in which the energy lost by the atom's orbiting electron is emitted in the form of a photon. Transitions are grouped according to the energy level at which they terminate, and each group is named for a pioneer in spectroscopy. The **Balmer series**, for example, comprises all transitions ending at $n_f = 2$. As noted above, hydrogen's four visible wavelengths are due to transitions to this level, so they are members of the Balmer series, the first ($n_i = 3$, $n_f = 2$), the second ($n_i = 4$, $n_f = 2$), and so on.

It is natural to wonder what an electron in an $n_i = 3$ state would do. Would it drop to the $n_f = 2$ state, producing a photon corresponding to the first spectral line in the Balmer series ($n_i = 3 \rightarrow n_f = 2$)? Or would it drop fully to $n_f = 1$, contributing to the second line in the **Lyman series** ($n_i = 3 \rightarrow n_f = 1$)? The answer is that it may do either, governed by probabilities. This issue we take up in Section 10, but there is an even more basic question: If the electron is indeed in a "stationary state," why would it make any transition at all? Our treatment of the hydrogen atom assumes an isolated atom. However, even in what we might consider a vacuum, there are always spontaneously fluctuating electromagnetic fields, known as **vacuum fluctuations**. In effect, these change the all-important potential energy. While we won't go into the underlying theory, known as quantum electrodynamics (QED), vacuum fluctuations perturb the atom so as to cause the electron to seek a lower energy, if there is one. Consequently, an electron not in the ground state will jump down through lower energy levels, producing corresponding photons, and eventually end up there.

An atom may also be induced to jump to a *higher* energy level. Sensibly, the excess energy it sheds in its otherwise inexorable decay to the ground state

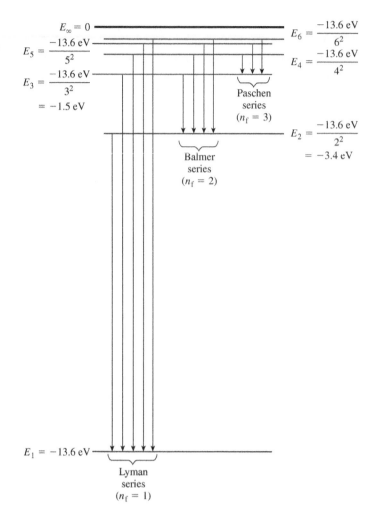

Figure 5 Hydrogen's energies and spectral lines: A photon is emitted when the electron "jumps downward."

must somehow have been given to it in the first place. One way to do this—essentially the reverse of photon emission—is to strike the atom with a photon. To cause the electron cloud to resonate just right, the photon must be precisely the energy difference from one atomic energy level to another, and it is fully absorbed in the process. Another way of increasing an orbiting electron's energy is to strike it with a massive particle. If the colliding particles have sufficient kinetic energy, an atom may absorb a portion of the collision energy and jump to a higher level. The colliding particles naturally depart with reduced kinetic energy after such an inelastic collision.

EXAMPLE 2

The atoms in a sample of hydrogen are all in their ground states, far too cold and slow to bump one another to higher levels. Now a beam of electrons accelerated through a potential difference of 12.3 V is directed at the sample. What wavelengths will the hydrogen atoms emit? (Assume that downward transitions occur so quickly that there is no chance for *multiple* accelerated electrons to combine their energies on an excited atom.)

SOLUTION

All the atoms initially have energy -13.6 eV. Each electron in the beam has kinetic energy of 12.3 eV. So in a collision, it could impart at most 12.3 eV, raising the atom's energy to -13.6 eV $+ 12.3$ eV $= -1.3$ eV. But -1.3 eV is not one of the allowed higher energies. From equation (14), these are

$$\frac{-13.6 \text{ eV}}{2^2} = -3.40 \text{ eV}, \quad \frac{-13.6 \text{ eV}}{3^3} = -1.51 \text{ eV},$$

$$\frac{-13.6 \text{ eV}}{4^2} = -0.85 \text{ eV}, \ldots$$

Thus, a collision has enough energy to raise the atom no higher than the $n = 3$ level. Thereafter, it will emit characteristic photons as its electron drops back to the ground state. Three transitions are possible: It may drop directly from the third to the first energy level, or it may drop from the third to the second, and thereafter it would drop down to the first. In all cases, the photon energy is the difference between the atomic energy levels.

$$E_{3 \rightarrow 1} = E_3 - E_1 = -1.51 \text{ eV} - (-13.6 \text{ eV}) = 12.1 \text{ eV}$$

$$E_{3 \rightarrow 2} = E_3 - E_2 = -1.51 \text{ eV} - (-3.4 \text{ eV}) = 1.9 \text{ eV}$$

$$E_{2 \rightarrow 1} = E_2 - E_1 = -3.4 \text{ eV} - (-13.6 \text{ eV}) = 10.2 \text{ eV}$$

The photon wavelengths follow from $E_{\text{photon}} = hc/\lambda$, or $\lambda = hc/E_{\text{photon}}$. Recalling that the product hc in the present units is 1240 eV $\cdot$ nm, we have

$$\lambda_{3 \rightarrow 1} = \frac{1240 \text{ eV} \cdot \text{nm}}{12.1 \text{ eV}} = 103 \text{ nm}$$

$$\lambda_{3 \rightarrow 2} = \frac{1240 \text{ eV} \cdot \text{nm}}{1.9 \text{ eV}} = 656 \text{ nm}$$

$$\lambda_{2 \rightarrow 1} = \frac{1240 \text{ eV} \cdot \text{nm}}{10.2 \text{ eV}} = 122 \text{ nm}$$

(*Note:* Some values may not appear to work out exactly, but this is due only to round-off error.) The first and third wavelengths are, respectively, the second and first members of the ultraviolet Lyman series. The second wavelength is the first in the Balmer series.

Spectral observations are one of the primary "handles" by which we test the claims of quantum mechanics, but they are also an indispensable tool in chemistry, biology, astronomy, and many other disciplines. For now, we simply note that each element's electrons have different quantized energies and thus emit different wavelengths, a unique spectrum that serves as the element's spectroscopic "fingerprint." Sending an electric discharge through a tube filled with a dilute gas is a common way to reveal such spectra. Another way is simply to heat a gas, although this requires very high temperatures (see Exercise 31). Cold atoms emit no radiation—all electrons are in their ground states and stay there. If the sample is heated, interparticle collisions may become energetic enough to cause the electrons in some atoms to jump to the first state higher

Figure 6 An intervening gas cloud "steals" hydrogen wavelengths from passing starlight.

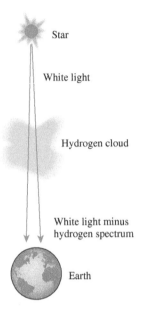

Star

White light

Hydrogen cloud

White light minus hydrogen spectrum

Earth

than the ground state. At this point, the spectrum would be fairly dull, consisting of essentially a single line, corresponding to transitions from the first excited state back down to the ground state. As the temperature is raised, other higher levels become accessible, allowing more wavelengths to be produced in subsequent downward transitions and giving a richer emission spectrum.

Matter may also reveal its composition through what wavelengths it *absorbs*. For example, stars, harboring a high density of charged particles in violent motion, emit essentially a continuous spectrum of wavelengths. This is a blackbody spectrum, and it depends on the star's temperature rather than its composition. However, if this light on its way to Earth passes through a cooler intervening gas, as depicted in Figure 6, wavelengths corresponding to differences in the energy levels of the gas atoms will be absorbed. As the atoms drop back down to the ground state, they reemit these wavelengths in all directions. This reemitted light is so scattered compared with the rest of the light—continuing unaffected on its way from the star to Earth—that it is essentially missing in the light that arrives. Thus, a missing spectrum positively identifies the element that is doing the absorbing. Figure 7 illustrates the phenomenon. The top plot shows an emission spectrum for hydrogen. The bottom plot shows which wavelengths of a continuous spectrum would reach Earth after passing through a cloud of hydrogen. The Balmer series is shown dashed in the absorption spectrum because its presence isn't guaranteed. If the gas is not hot enough, there will be essentially no atoms *initially* in the $n = 2$ state, so photons whose energies correspond to transitions between the $n = 2$ and *higher* levels could not be absorbed. The intervening gas need not be an isolated cloud. Our Sun has absorption lines in its spectrum, because light produced in its interior passes through its cooler atmosphere, where hydrogen, sodium, magnesium, iron, and other elements in a gaseous state absorb their characteristic wavelengths.

Let us now see where hydrogen's quantized energies come from and find out what other quantizations this three-dimensional problem has in store.

Figure 7 Hydrogen's emission spectrum—bright lines at certain wavelengths—and its absorption spectrum—wavelengths missing from a continuum.

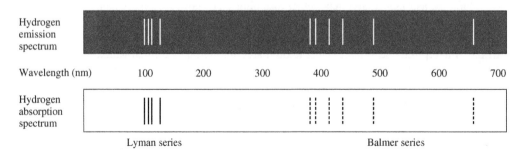

4 The Schrödinger Equation for a Central Force

As noted in Section 3, the potential energy for the hydrogen atom is

$$U(r) = -\frac{1}{4\pi\varepsilon_0}\frac{e^2}{r} \tag{10}$$

Because this depends on r, which is $\sqrt{x^2 + y^2 + z^2}$, solving the Schrödinger equation in Cartesian coordinates would be quite painful. The spherical symmetry of the problem naturally makes spherical polar coordinates the best choice. A brief review of this coordinate system is worthwhile.

In spherical polar coordinates, all of three-dimensional space is represented by values of the three coordinates r, θ, and ϕ, shown in Figure 8. Stretching from the origin to an arbitrary location in space is a position vector **r**. Its length is the coordinate r (the *scalar* distance from the origin and not to be confused with the vector **r**) and is called the **radius**. The coordinate θ is the angle between the position vector and the z-axis and is called the **polar angle**, with the "pole" being the z-axis. The coordinate ϕ is the angle, about the z-axis, between the x-axis and the projection of the position vector in the xy-plane. It is called the **azimuthal angle**.[4] Do they cover all space? For a given radius r and polar angle θ, varying the azimuthal angle ϕ through 2π would inscribe a latitude at angle θ on a spherical surface of radius r. Varying the polar angle θ from 0 to π (not 2π) would then fill in all latitudes from the sphere's north pole to its

Figure 8 Spherical polar coordinates.

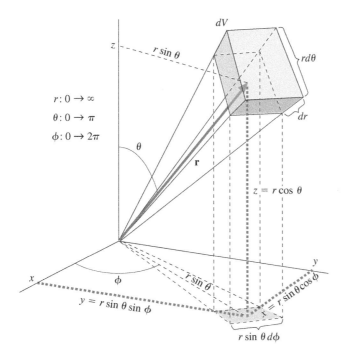

$r: 0 \rightarrow \infty$
$\theta: 0 \rightarrow \pi$
$\phi: 0 \rightarrow 2\pi$

TABLE 2 Cartesian-polar conversions

$x = r \sin \theta \cos \phi$	$r = \sqrt{x^2 + y^2 + z^2}$
$y = r \sin \theta \sin \phi$	$\theta = \cos^{-1} \dfrac{z}{\sqrt{x^2 + y^2 + z^2}}$
$z = r \cos \theta$	$\phi = \tan^{-1} \dfrac{y}{x}$

south pole. Finally, varying r from 0 to infinity would include all concentric spheres—covering all space. The relationships between (x, y, z) and (r, θ, ϕ) are color highlighted in Figure 8 and summarized in Table 2.

To calculate probabilities, such as in normalization integral (2), we need the expression for the infinitesimal volume element dV in spherical polar coordinates. This element is the shaded region in Figure 8. It has one side of length $r d\theta$ (an arc length due to a change in θ), another of length $r \sin \theta \, d\phi$ (an arc length at distance $r \sin \theta$ in the xy-plane due to a change in ϕ), and a thickness dr. The volume is the product.

$$dV = r^2 \sin \theta \, dr \, d\theta \, d\phi$$

In the hydrogen atom, the electron's potential energy depends only on r, the scalar distance from the origin, not on θ or ϕ. Thus, $U(\mathbf{r}) = U(r)$. In general, if the potential energy depends only on r, the force is necessarily along the radial direction and is thus known as a **central force**. For the time being, we will use simply $U(r)$, rather than its specific form (10) for hydrogen, so our results will be valid for any central force.

The only other changes needed to tailor the time-independent Schrödinger equation (3) to a central force are to replace the generic symbol $\mathbf{r}$ with (r, θ, ϕ) in the argument of ψ and to use the appropriate expression for ∇^2. Most analytic geometry texts go through the steps of obtaining ∇^2 in spherical polar coordinates from its Cartesian form. The result is

$$\nabla^2 = \frac{1}{r^2} \left[\frac{\partial}{\partial r} \left(r^2 \frac{\partial}{\partial r} \right) + \csc \theta \frac{\partial}{\partial \theta} \left(\sin \theta \frac{\partial}{\partial \theta} \right) + \csc^2 \theta \frac{\partial}{\partial \phi^2} \right]$$

This hefty expression is the price we pay for simplicity in the potential energy term. Its peculiarity of having factors *between* two derivatives in the r and θ terms may be disconcerting, but it merely gives a more compact form. Each derivative is understood to act on everything to its right—including, of course, ψ, to which the whole thing is applied. Bear in mind that this expression does the same thing as the simpler second partials in Cartesian coordinates. With everything in place, we arrive at the time-independent Schrödinger equation for a central force.

$$-\frac{\hbar^2}{2m} \frac{1}{r^2} \left[\frac{\partial}{\partial r} \left(r^2 \frac{\partial}{\partial r} \right) + \csc \theta \frac{\partial}{\partial \theta} \left(\sin \theta \frac{\partial}{\partial \theta} \right) + \csc^2 \theta \frac{\partial}{\partial \phi^2} \right] \psi(r, \theta, \phi)$$

$$+ U(r) \psi(r, \theta, \phi) = E \psi(r, \theta, \phi) \quad (15)$$

To understand what this tells us, we break it into pieces that we can scrutinize separately. As in the 3D infinite well, we start by writing the wave function as a product of three functions, each of a different independent variable:

$$\psi(r, \theta, \phi) = R(r)\Theta(\theta)\Phi(\phi)$$

Here we introduce some very helpful bookkeeping. The variable is in lower-case, while the corresponding *function* of that variable is in uppercase. When we insert this product function into (15), we obtain a separate differential equation for each variable. The mathematical steps by which the equations come about are outlined in A Closer Look: Separating Variables for a Central Force. In the following sections, we concentrate on what the differential equations tell us.

A Closer Look ## Separating Variables for a Central Force

To aid in separating variables in Schrödinger equation (15), we first rearrange it slightly.

$$\csc\theta\frac{\partial}{\partial\theta}\left(\sin\theta\frac{\partial}{\partial\theta}\right)\psi(r,\theta,\phi) + \csc^2\theta\frac{\partial^2}{\partial\phi^2}\psi(r,\theta,\phi)$$

$$= \left[-\frac{\partial}{\partial r}\left(r^2\frac{\partial}{\partial r}\right) - \frac{2mr^2}{\hbar^2}(E - U(r))\right]\psi(r,\theta,\phi) \quad (16)$$

Now we replace $\psi(r, \theta, \phi)$ by the product of three functions, $R(r)\Theta(\theta)\Phi(\phi)$, and note that the partial derivative in any term acts on only one of these three. Suppressing function arguments for simplicity, we obtain

$$R\Phi\csc\theta\frac{\partial}{\partial\theta}\left(\sin\theta\frac{\partial\Theta}{\partial\theta}\right) + R\Theta\csc^2\theta\frac{\partial^2\Phi}{\partial\phi^2}$$

$$= -\Theta\Phi\frac{\partial}{\partial r}\left(r^2\frac{\partial R}{\partial r}\right) - \frac{2mr^2}{\hbar^2}(E - U(r))R\Theta\Phi$$

The next step, as always, is to divide by the product, $R\Theta\Phi$. This cancels two functions in each term having a derivative, leaving only the one on which the derivative operates. Thus,

$$\frac{1}{\Theta}\csc\theta\frac{\partial}{\partial\theta}\left(\sin\theta\frac{\partial\Theta}{\partial\theta}\right) + \csc^2\theta\frac{1}{\Phi}\frac{\partial^2\Phi}{\partial\phi^2}$$

$$= -\frac{1}{R}\frac{\partial}{\partial r}\left(r^2\frac{\partial R}{\partial r}\right) - \frac{2mr^2}{\hbar^2}(E - U(r)) \quad (17)$$

All dependence on angles θ and ϕ is on the left and all dependence on r is on the right. The usual deduction applies: Because the variables can take on values independently, both sides must equal a constant, for which we choose the symbol C. Setting the right side equal to C, restoring to R its argument, and rearranging a bit yields the **radial equation**.

$$-\frac{d}{dr}\left(r^2\frac{d}{dr}\right)R(r) - \frac{2mr^2}{\hbar^2}ER(r) + \frac{2mr^2}{\hbar^2}U(r)R(r) = CR(r) \quad (18)$$

Setting the left side of (17) to C gives

$$\frac{1}{\Theta}\csc\theta\frac{\partial}{\partial\theta}\left(\sin\theta\frac{\partial\Theta}{\partial\theta}\right) + \csc^2\theta\frac{1}{\Phi}\frac{\partial^2\Phi}{\partial\phi^2} = C \quad (19)$$

To separate Θ from Φ, we multiply both sides of (19) by $\sin^2\theta$, then move the term dependent on ϕ to the right side and the rest to the left.

$$\frac{1}{\Theta}\sin\theta\frac{\partial}{\partial\theta}\left(\sin\theta\frac{\partial\Theta}{\partial\theta}\right) - C\sin^2\theta = -\frac{1}{\Phi}\frac{\partial^2\Phi}{\partial\phi^2} \quad (20)$$

Both sides must be a constant here, too, and we choose the symbol D. Equating the left side to D and rearranging gives the **polar equation**.

$$\sin\theta\frac{\partial}{\partial\theta}\left(\sin\theta\frac{\partial\Theta(\theta)}{\partial\theta}\right) - C\sin^2\theta\Theta(\theta) = D\Theta(\theta) \quad (21)$$

and setting the right side of (20) to D gives the **azimuthal equation**.

$$\frac{\partial^2\Phi(\phi)}{\partial\phi^2} = -D\Phi(\phi) \quad (22)$$

5 Angular Behavior in a Central Force

In this section, we confront some astounding conclusions about the angular motion of an orbiting quantum mechanical particle. It is important to bear in mind that although they apply to the hydrogen atom as a special case, they are applicable in all cases where the force is strictly radial. We take the angular variables one at a time.

The Azimuthal Equation

The equation governing azimuthal motion is

Azimuthal equation

$$\frac{\partial^2 \Phi(\phi)}{\partial \phi^2} = -D\Phi(\phi) \tag{22}$$

Among the differential equations we will encounter, this one is familiar. (Alas, the others are not!) The second derivative of the function is proportional to the function. As we know, this could imply sinusoidal ($D > 0$) or exponential ($D < 0$) solutions, but the latter are ruled out by the particular nature of this spatial coordinate. As the azimuthal angle goes from a given value through 2π about the z-axis, the function $\Phi(\phi)$ *meets itself*, and it must do so smoothly. Exercise 35 shows that no exponential solution can do this. But the requirement restricts even the sinusoidal functions, as we soon see.

A remaining question is whether the solution should be sine, cosine, or some combination. It depends on the application. In chemistry, sine and cosine are used often, as they are well suited to chemical bonding, where one atom reaches out to others along different directions. The function $\cos\phi$ has its largest magnitude when ϕ is 0 or π, along the x-axis, while $\sin\phi$ is largest along the y-axis (see Figure 8). In physics, we usually choose a combination, specifically a complex exponential. (Never forget: $e^{iz} = \cos z + i\sin z$ is sinusoidal!) We discuss the reason for the choice shortly, but let us first consider such a function. Noting that if $\Phi(\phi)$ *is* sinusoidal, then D must be positive, a solution of (22) is

$$\Phi(\phi) = e^{i\sqrt{D}\phi} \tag{23}$$

Exercise 36 shows that if this function is to meet itself smoothly when ϕ changes by 2π, then $\sqrt{D}$ must be an *integer*. The smoothness condition—in this angular situation, a periodicity condition—has therefore given us a quantum number associated with the ϕ coordinate/dimension. We choose the symbol m_ℓ for this integer. Attaching a subscript to distinguish one allowed function from another, we thus have

$$\Phi_{m_\ell}(\phi) = e^{im_\ell\phi} \qquad m_\ell = 0, \pm 1, \pm 2, \pm 3, \ldots \tag{24}$$

For each quantum number that arises—and two dimensions are yet to come—a physical property is quantized. The property quantized according to

Figure 9 Standing waves on the "ϕ-axis."

Re $\Phi_{m_\ell}(\phi)$

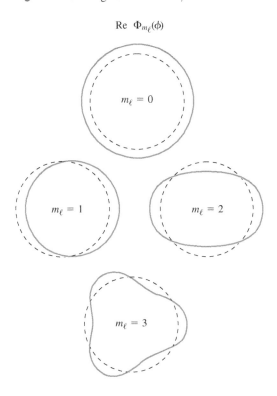

the value of m_ℓ is the z-component of the electron's angular momentum, L_z. This may not strike the reader as even remotely intuitive at first, but consider Figure 9, which crudely pictures the real part of $e^{im_\ell\phi}$. The dashed circle represents a "ϕ-axis." For $m_\ell = 0$, $e^{i0\phi}$ is simply 1 and is thus the same distance "above" the ϕ-axis around the entire circle. For $m_\ell = 1$, $e^{i1\phi}$ is $\cos\phi + i\sin\phi$. Its real part passes through one whole cycle, varying from positive to negative and back, as ϕ goes from 0 to 2π. Similarly, the $m_\ell = 2$ wave, $e^{i2\phi} = \cos 2\phi + i\sin 2\phi$, passes through two cycles in an interval of 2π. In general, the circle's circumference would be an integral number of "wavelengths": $2\pi r = m_\ell\lambda$. If we make the independent argument that a "wavelength around the ϕ-axis" should be inversely related to a tangential momentum mv_t in the usual way ($\lambda = h/p$), we would have $\lambda = h/mv_t$, where m here is the electron mass. Combining these two observations gives us $2\pi r = m_\ell h/mv_t$, which if rearranged becomes $m_\ell\hbar = mv_t r$, and $mv_t r$ is simply the classical expression for angular momentum ($\mathbf{r} \times \mathbf{p}$) in circular orbit. The orbital plane for the azimuthal angle is the xy plane, giving the angular momentum vector a direction along z. Thus,

$$L_z = m_\ell\hbar \qquad m_\ell = 0, \pm 1, \pm 2, \pm 3, \ldots \tag{25}$$

The above argument has several limitations. In particular, it would seem to apply as well to sines or cosines as to complex exponentials, but only the latter represent well-defined quantized L_z. Although the fact that *linear* momentum p is well defined for e^{ikx} but not for $\sin kx$ or $\cos kx$ is some reinforcement for this claim, the more rigorous justification is left to Exercise 40. (It is based on the concept that the complex exponential alone is an eigenfunction of the L_z operator.) In any case, that L_z is *not* well defined for sine and cosine is the main reason physics tends to focus on the complex exponential. Another is that, whereas sine and cosine "stick out" along the x- and y-axes, the complex exponential gives a probability density $(e^{-im_\ell\phi}e^{+im_\ell\phi})$ independent of ϕ. It is the same in all directions, as we expect for an *isolated* atom.

We will discuss the consequences of the quantization of L_z after addressing the polar angle θ, but for now bear in mind the similarities to one-dimensional cases. There we had a quantum number n, which determined the value of the physical quantity energy, and for each n there was a corresponding function. Here the quantum number is m_ℓ, determining the value of the physical quantity L_z, and each has a corresponding function $\Phi_{m_\ell}(\phi)$.

The Polar Equation

Equation (21), governing polar motion, depends on D, and we have just argued that $\sqrt{D}$ has to be an integer, m_ℓ. Making this substitution, we have

Polar equation

$$\sin\theta \frac{\partial}{\partial\theta}\left(\sin\theta \frac{\partial\Theta(\theta)}{\partial\theta}\right) - C\sin^2\theta\,\Theta(\theta) = m_\ell^2\,\Theta(\theta) \tag{26}$$

This is a far more challenging differential equation than others we have seen, and we won't go into the analytical solution (found in any dedicated quantum mechanics text). However, the vital conclusion, which should have a familiar ring from our one-dimensional studies, is this: While there are mathematical solutions $\Theta(\theta)$ for all values of C and m_ℓ, they all violate the physical requirements, diverging at the limits $\theta = 0$ or $\theta = \pi$ or both, unless C and m_ℓ are certain values.[5] It turns out that $C = 0$ and $m_\ell = 0$ give physically acceptable solutions. The values $C = -2$ and $m_\ell = -1$, 0, or $+1$ also work, as do $C = -6$ and $m_\ell = -2$, -1, 0, $+1$, or $+2$. Happily, there is a general way of expressing all the allowed values.

$$C = -\ell(\ell + 1) \qquad \ell = 0, 1, 2, \ldots$$
$$m_\ell = 0, \pm1, \pm2, \ldots, \pm\ell \tag{27}$$

Don't miss the point: The physical requirements have given us standing-wave conditions in our second dimension θ, and our first quantum number m_ℓ has been joined by a second, ℓ. The functions that satisfy equation (26) depend on both quantum numbers and are distinguished by two subscripts, $\Theta_{\ell,m_\ell}(\theta)$. Known collectively as associated Legendre functions, several are given in Table 3. Because we so often need the product of $\Theta_{\ell,m_\ell}(\theta)$ and $\Phi_{m_\ell}(\phi)$, they are usually tabulated together and are known as **spherical harmonics**. What these angular standing waves actually look like we discuss a bit later.

We now address the new physical property that is quantized. As quantum number m_ℓ determines the angular momentum's z-component, L_z,

[5]Computational Exercise 91 lays out a very instructive numerical route to verifying this claim.

quantum number ℓ determines its magnitude, $|L|$. Unfortunately, there isn't a cute and easy way analogous to Figure 9 to justify this claim. Exercise 41 discusses a simplified approach, but the rigorous one is based on the formidable-looking derivatives in equation (19) being proportional to the quantum-mechanical operator for the *square* of the angular momentum. Exercise 42 uses this result to show that equation (19) can be rewritten as

$$\hat{L}^2 \Theta\Phi = -C\hbar^2\Theta\Phi$$

Equation (27) tells us that $C = -\ell(\ell + 1)$, so that

$$\hat{L}^2 \Theta\Phi = \ell(\ell + 1)\hbar^2\Theta\Phi$$

The upshot is that L^2 can take on only the values $\ell(\ell + 1)\hbar^2$. (In the language, the product $\Theta\Phi$ is an eigenfunction of the operator, implying that L^2 has the well-defined values $\ell(\ell + 1)\hbar^2$.) Because the square of a vector is the square of its magnitude, this is equivalent to saying that the magnitude of L obeys the following:

$$|L| = \sqrt{\ell(\ell + 1)}\,\hbar \qquad \ell = 0, 1, 2, \ldots \qquad (28)$$

Due to its relationship to orbital angular momentum, quantum number ℓ is called the **orbital quantum number**, while m_ℓ is known as the **magnetic quantum number**.

The case $\ell = 0$ is troubling. How can a particle orbit without angular momentum? In general, the motion of the orbiting "particle" is a combination of rotational and radial motion. The $\ell = 0$ case is one in which there is no average rotational motion, but there is radial motion. The electron might crudely be pictured as oscillating back and forth through the origin, as would a ball dropped down a tunnel through Earth's center. Still, we must not throw out fundamental principles of quantum mechanics. The electron isn't a particle following a definite path, but rather a diffuse standing wave occupying three dimensions.

Having considered the two angular dimensions of the Schrödinger equation, we have obtained two quantum numbers, ℓ and m_ℓ, which determine two quantized physical properties, $|L|$ and L_z. As noted earlier, until we actually use the specific hydrogen atom potential energy, everything we say applies to any central force. Let us examine these claims of quantized angular momentum more closely.

Quantization of L

The first thing to note is that we should expect some relationship between $|L|$ and L_z—and we have one. Equation (25) gives the allowed values of L_z, *any* integer times $\hbar$, and it arises from the azimuthal part of the Schrödinger equation alone. But the polar part gave us equations (27), which restrict the values of m_ℓ, depending on the value of ℓ. Thus, equation (25) is superseded by the following:

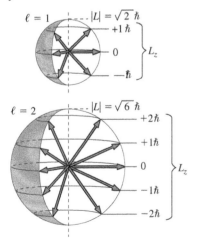

Quantization condition for L_z

$$L_z = m_\ell \hbar \qquad m_\ell = 0, \pm 1, \pm 2, \ldots, \pm \ell \qquad (29)$$

Can we make sense of this dependence? Since a component of a vector may never be greater than its magnitude, L_z must never exceed $|L|$. Equations (28) and (29) agree, for they say that the maximum L_z is $\ell\hbar$, which is strictly less than $\sqrt{\ell(\ell + 1)}\hbar$.

But why not equal? And for that matter, what's so special about the z-direction? The surprising answer to both questions is that it is impossible to know all components of angular momentum at once. What results naturally from the Schrödinger equation for a central force is quantization of $|L|$ and one component of $\mathbf{L}$, which we call the z-component by arbitrary convention. But this is all that *should* result, for knowing additional components would constitute simultaneous knowledge of position and momentum that would violate the uncertainty principle. For $\mathbf{L}$ to point with certainty along a given axis, the wave function would have to be confined to the plane perpendicular to that axis. Calling this the xy-plane, both z and p_z would have to be 0, with zero uncertainty. Impossible! (In effect, this says that the wave function must spread out to some degree in all dimensions open to it.) If, however, only the magnitude and one component are fixed, $\mathbf{L}$ may be in any of an infinite number of directions, though not all directions, as illustrated in Figure 10. That the maximum z-component is *strictly less* than the magnitude of $\mathbf{L}$ guarantees that $\mathbf{L}$ can never point along that axis, in accord with the uncertainty principle.

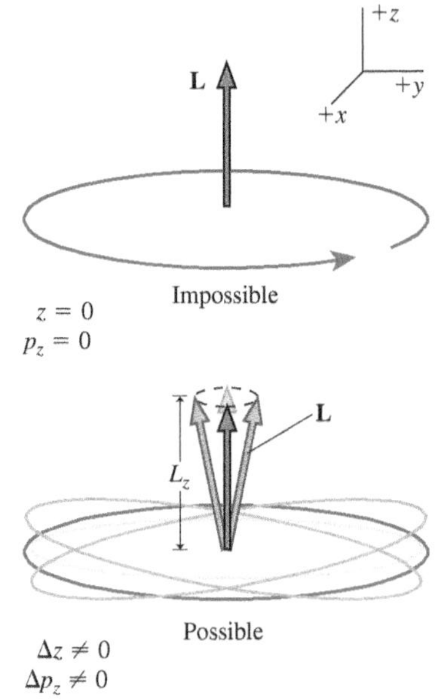

Figure 11 shows the possibilities for $\ell = 1$ and $\ell = 2$. Arrows represent angular momentum vectors, and the sphere's radii are thus $\sqrt{\ell(\ell + 1)}\hbar$. In the $\ell = 2$ case, for instance, all arrows are $\sqrt{6}\hbar$. According to (29), there are five allowed values of m_ℓ ($-2, -1, 0, +1, +2$) and five corresponding values of L_z. With only the one component fixed, $\mathbf{L}$ may point in an infinite number of directions.

Not only is it *theoretically* impossible to know all components of angular momentum simultaneously, but it is also impossible to devise an *experiment* that would determine them all. An experimental apparatus inherently introduces directionality along some axis. That axis becomes the "special" axis, and quantization is demonstrated only along it. It naturally exhibits the peculiarities of the axis we have chosen to call the z-axis. Indeed, without an externally imposed z-axis, it makes little sense to speak of orientations in space.

Figure 10 Planar motion violates the uncertainty principle.

Figure 11 Angular momentum quantization for $\ell = 1$ and $\ell = 2$.

EXAMPLE 3

What is the minimum angle the angular momentum vector may make with the z-axis in the case (a) $\ell = 3$ and (b) $\ell = 1$?

SOLUTION

(a) When $\ell = 3$, the angular momentum is $\sqrt{12}\hbar$, with seven possible z-components. It will be most nearly parallel to the z-axis when its z-component is as large as possible: $3\hbar$. The angle between a vector and its z-component is the polar angle in spherical polar coordinates.

$$\cos\theta = \frac{L_z}{|L|} = \frac{3\hbar}{\sqrt{12}\,\hbar} \quad \Rightarrow \quad \theta = \cos^{-1}\frac{3}{\sqrt{12}} = 30°$$

(b) For $\ell = 1$, $|L| = \sqrt{12}\hbar$, and the largest z-component is $1\hbar$. Thus,

$$\cos\theta = \frac{L_z}{|L|} = \frac{1\hbar}{\sqrt{2}\,\hbar} \quad \Rightarrow \quad \theta = \cos^{-1}\frac{1}{\sqrt{2}} = 45°$$

Figure 12 shows the magnitudes and z-components in both cases.

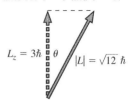

Figure 12 Minimum angles between **L** and z-axis for $\ell = 3$ and $\ell = 1$.

Example 3 shows that the greater the angular momentum, the more nearly parallel it can be to a chosen axis. In the following example, we consider an extreme case.

EXAMPLE 4

A 200 kg satellite orbits Earth at a radius of 42,300 km and a speed of 3.07 km/s. What might be its angular momentum quantum numbers?

SOLUTION

The example may seem absurd. Classical physics is completely adequate for such large objects. Nevertheless, gravity *is* a central force, so our analysis does apply, and we should at least expect to find large quantum numbers—the classical limit.

The angular momentum of a point mass in circular orbit is *mvr*.

$$L = (200\ \text{kg})(3.07 \times 10^3\ \text{m/s})(4.23 \times 10^7\ \text{m}) = 2.60 \times 10^{13}\ \text{kg}\cdot\text{m}^2/\text{s}$$

Thus,

$$L = \sqrt{\ell(\ell+1)}\,\hbar \quad \Rightarrow \quad \frac{2.60 \times 10^{13}\ \text{kg}\cdot\text{m}^2/\text{s}}{1.055 \times 10^{-34}\ \text{J}\cdot\text{s}} = \sqrt{\ell(\ell+1)}$$

$$2.46 \times 10^{47} = \sqrt{\ell(\ell+1)} \cong \ell$$

Clearly, ℓ is a very large number, justifying our replacement of $\ell + 1$ by ℓ, and the satellite is thus in a very high angular momentum state, quantum-mechanically speaking. A unit change in ℓ would represent a negligible fractional change in the angular momentum, whose values would thus seem continuous. According to equation (29), L_z is allowed any value from $-\ell\hbar$ to $+\ell\hbar$, which similarly would seem continuous. In fact, because $\ell \cong \sqrt{\ell(\ell+1)}$, this range is $-|L|$ to $+|L|$, the classical expectation.

Directional Probabilities

Because we have not yet considered the radial aspect of things, we cannot say where in space hydrogen's electron would be found, but we can at least discuss the *angular* whereabouts of a particle experiencing a central force. As always, probability comes from the complex square of the wave function. As noted earlier, the complex square of $\Phi(\phi)$ is 1, giving a probability independent of the azimuthal angle, and $\Theta(\theta)$ is real, so the probability density is just $\Theta^2_{\ell,m_\ell}(\theta)$. But why should it depend on *either* angle? We have spherical symmetry. Shouldn't it be equally likely to find the particle in *any* direction? The answer is that unless an experiment actually determines L_z, it is equally likely to be any of its allowed values, and if we add the probabilities $\Theta^2_{\ell,m_\ell}(\theta)$ for all m_ℓ from $-\ell$ to $+\ell$, the result is indeed independent of θ (see Exercise 50). In short, if we are ignorant of m_ℓ, the probability of finding the particle *is* spherically symmetric. However, in most situations of interest—from chemical reactions to applied electromagnetic fields—there is some kind of external influence that distinguishes the different states, so it is important to have an idea of how they differ.

Figure 13 shows Θ^2_{ℓ,m_ℓ}, from Table 3, plotted versus polar angle for all cases through $\ell = 3$. Several features are noteworthy: First, in the $\ell = 0$ case, the probability is the same in any direction, in contrast to a *particle* without angular momentum, which would oscillate strictly along a line through the origin. Second, in all $\ell \neq 0$ cases, as m_ℓ increases, the probability density changes progressively from mostly along the z-axis to mostly in the xy-plane. An orbiting *particle's* angular momentum would also be more nearly parallel to the z-axis as its orbit plane approaches the xy-plane. The correspondence is

Figure 13 Angular probability densities for a central force.

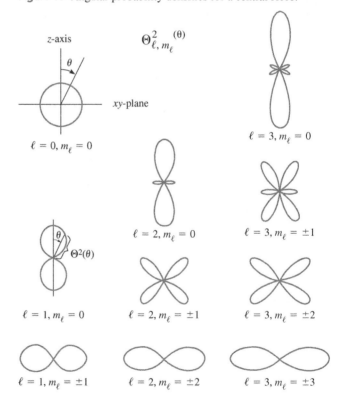

Figure 14 A crude correspondence to orbital motion.

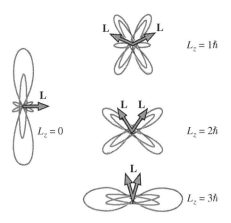

depicted in Figure 14 for the $\ell = 3$ cases, but it is important to note that the separated lobes are typical standing-wave antinodes and are irreconcilable with a particle's strictly planar motion. Third, in all $m_\ell \neq 0$ cases, the probability density is 0 at the z-axis. If a particle is to have nonzero L_z, it must never be found on the z-axis. Lastly, all $m_\ell = \pm\ell$ cases have equatorial lobes, suggesting orbit near the xy-plane, which become flatter as ℓ increases. In Example 3, we found that for large ℓ, the angular momentum vector may point more nearly parallel to the z-axis, suggesting motion more closely restricted to the xy-plane. In the classical limit where ℓ approaches infinity, **L** can be precisely along z, so the probability density *should* become more planar.

6 The Hydrogen Atom

Having dealt with the angular parts of the wave function, we complete our study of the Schrödinger equation for hydrogen by considering its remaining radial part. Radial equation (18) depends on C, which we now know to be $-\ell(\ell + 1)$. Inserting this and then rearranging gives us an enlightening form.

$$\underbrace{\frac{-\hbar^2}{2m}\frac{1}{r^2}\frac{d}{dr}\left(r^2\frac{d}{dr}\right)R(r)}_{\textbf{KE}_{\textbf{rad}}} + \underbrace{\frac{\hbar^2\ell(\ell + 1)}{2mr^2}R(r)}_{\textbf{KE}_{\textbf{rot}}} + \underbrace{U(r)R(r)}_{\textbf{PE}} = E\,R(r) \quad (30)$$

From classical mechanics, we know that rotational kinetic energy may be written $L^2/2I$ and that the moment of inertia I of a point particle is mr^2. Equation (28) tells us that $\hbar^2\ell(\ell + 1) = L^2$, so the second term on the left of (30) accounts for rotational kinetic energy. The third term is, of course, potential, so it seems that the first term must account for radial kinetic energy toward and away from the nucleus. Indeed it does. While we omit the lengthy details, it may be shown that the first term corresponds to $\frac{1}{2}m(dr/dt)^2$. Overall, equation (30) is much like the Schrödinger equation in one dimension. The leading kinetic energy term is a bit more involved, and of course it differs in the rotational energy term, but the latter is merely a scalar function of r, and its effect on the wave function is therefore much like that of an additional potential energy term. ($\text{KE}_{\text{rot}} + \text{PE}$ is sometimes regarded as a single "effective potential.") In particular, the rotational energy term diverges at $r = 0$ whenever ℓ is nonzero, thus excluding all $\ell \neq 0$ wave functions from the origin (see Figure 15 later in this section).

Finally, we insert into (30) the hydrogen atom potential energy (10).

Hydrogen radial equation

$$\frac{-\hbar^2}{2m}\frac{1}{r^2}\frac{d}{dr}\left(r^2\frac{d}{dr}\right)R(r) + \frac{\hbar^2\ell(\ell+1)}{2mr^2}R(r) - \frac{1}{4\pi\varepsilon_0}\frac{e^2}{r}R(r) = E\,R(r) \quad (31)$$

As in the case of polar equation (26), we leave the analytical solution of this intricate differential equation to a higher-level course. But just as in that case, the crucial point is that the solutions are all physically unacceptable, diverging at $r = 0$ or infinity, except when the constants take on certain values. The energy must be one of the values given previously in equation (12):

$$E_n = -\frac{me^4}{2(4\pi\varepsilon_0)^2\hbar^2}\frac{1}{n^2} \qquad n = 1, 2, 3, \ldots$$

and ℓ must obey

$$\ell = 0, 1, 2, \ldots, n - 1 \tag{32}$$

(*Note:* Computational Exercise 92 lays out a numerical approach to these conclusions.) Our third dimension has yielded a third quantum number, n, called the **principal quantum number**, and the corresponding quantized property is energy.

Recall from Section 5 that the solution of the Schrödinger equation's polar part placed a restriction on the quantum number from the preceding azimuthal part—m_ℓ could be no larger than ℓ. We argued that this made sense, for L_z cannot exceed L. Something similar has happened here. Whereas equation (27) said that ℓ could be any nonnegative integer, equation (32) says that it can be no larger than $n - 1$. Again there is a physical reason. The quantum number n specifies the *total* energy, and ℓ is related to the rotational energy, so it is reasonable that ℓ might be limited by the value of n (see Exercise 65). Taking the restriction into account, we must replace equation (28) by the following:

Quantization condition for |L|

$$|L| = \sqrt{\ell(\ell+1)}\hbar \qquad \ell = 0, 1, 2, \ldots, n - 1 \tag{33}$$

For each n and ℓ, equation (31) has a solution $R_{n,\ell}(r)$, known as an associated Laguerre function. Table 4 lists several of these functions, expressed in terms of the **Bohr radius**.

$$a_0 \equiv \frac{(4\pi\varepsilon_0)\hbar^2}{me^2} = 0.0529 \text{ nm} \qquad (34) \qquad \text{Bohr radius}$$

This combination of constants is pervasive in atomic physics, so the definition is very convenient. Moreover, the Bohr radius is a good gauge of atomic dimensions, as we will see.

Our look at the Schrödinger equation for hydrogen is complete. We have found three quantum numbers and three quantized properties, and in Tables 3 and 4 we have the corresponding functions. Let us now turn to two important related topics—degeneracy and normalization.

TABLE 3 Angular solutions: Spherical harmonics

ℓ, m_ℓ	$\Theta_{\ell,m_\ell}(\theta)\Phi_{m_\ell}(\phi)$
0, 0	$\sqrt{\dfrac{1}{4\pi}}$
1, 0	$\sqrt{\dfrac{3}{4\pi}}\cos\theta$
1, ±1	$\sqrt{\dfrac{3}{8\pi}}\sin\theta e^{\pm i\phi}$
2, 0	$\sqrt{\dfrac{5}{16\pi}}(3\cos^2\theta - 1)$
2, ±1	$\sqrt{\dfrac{15}{8\pi}}\cos\theta\sin\theta e^{\pm i\phi}$
2, ±2	$\sqrt{\dfrac{15}{32\pi}}\sin^2\theta e^{\pm 2i\phi}$
3, 0	$\sqrt{\dfrac{7}{16\pi}}(5\cos^3\theta - 3\cos\theta)$
3, ±1	$\sqrt{\dfrac{21}{64\pi}}(5\cos^2\theta - 1)\sin\theta\, e^{\pm i\phi}$
3, ±2	$\sqrt{\dfrac{105}{32\pi}}\cos\theta\sin^2\theta\, e^{\pm 2i\phi}$
3, ±3	$\sqrt{\dfrac{35}{64\pi}}\sin^3\theta\, e^{\pm 3i\phi}$

TABLE 4 Radial solutions of (31)

n, ℓ	$R_{n,\ell}(r)$
1, 0	$\dfrac{1}{(1a_0)^{3/2}}2e^{-r/a_0}$
2, 0	$\dfrac{1}{(2a_0)^{3/2}}2\left(1 - \dfrac{r}{2a_0}\right)e^{-r/2a_0}$
2, 1	$\dfrac{1}{(2a_0)^{3/2}}\dfrac{r}{\sqrt{3}a_0}e^{-r/2a_0}$
3, 0	$\dfrac{1}{(3a_0)^{3/2}}\left(2 - \dfrac{4r}{3a_0} + \dfrac{4r^2}{27a_0^2}\right)e^{-r/3a_0}$
3, 1	$\dfrac{1}{(3a_0)^{3/2}}\dfrac{4\sqrt{2}r}{9a_0}\left(1 - \dfrac{r}{6a_0}\right)e^{-r/3a_0}$
3, 2	$\dfrac{1}{(3a_0)^{3/2}}\dfrac{2\sqrt{2}r^2}{27\sqrt{5}a_0^2}e^{-r/3a_0}$

Degeneracy

The hydrogen atom is spherically symmetric, and there is consequently much degeneracy. Equation (12) tells us that the energy of an electron orbiting a proton depends only on n. But equation (33) tells us that for each value of n, there are states of different angular momentum $|L|$—different ℓ. Equation (29), in turn, tells us that for each ℓ, there are states of different L_z—different m_ℓ. Thus, because each set (n, ℓ, m_ℓ) has a unique wave function $R_{n,\ell}\Theta_{\ell,m_\ell}\Phi_{m_\ell}$, all energy levels except the ground state are degenerate. In fact, as shown in Exercise 46, the degeneracy increases as n^2. Table 5 demonstrates the quickly growing number of states as n increases.

Actually, hydrogen is rather special. Given its spherical symmetry, we do not expect E to depend on m_ℓ. Spatial orientation—a *component* of angular momentum—shouldn't be a factor. But what of ℓ? It appears in equation (31). Shouldn't the allowed energies depend on it? The fact that they do not depend on ℓ is known as **accidental degeneracy**. In general, the allowed energies for equation (30), the radial part of the Schrödinger equation *before* the hydrogen-specific $U(r)$ is inserted, *do* depend on ℓ. It is only in the special case of the simple $1/r$ hydrogen atom potential energy that E "accidentally" does not. *Any* deviation of the potential energy from this simple case would lead to quantum energy levels that depend on ℓ. In particular, additional electrons orbiting the nucleus would alter the potential energy, thus destroying the accidental degeneracy.

Normalization

The probability density is the complex square of the wave function. The temporal part of the wave function drops out in the usual way. As we noted in Section 5, the azimuthal part also drops out, and the polar part is real. Now including the radial, which is also real, we arrive at

Probability density
$$|\Psi(r, \theta, \phi, t)|^2 = R^2(r)\,\Theta^2(\theta) \tag{35}$$

TABLE 5 Degeneracy increasing with n

n	1	2				3								
ℓ	0	0		1		0		1			2			
m_ℓ	0	0	−1	0	+1	0	−1	0	+1	−2	−1	0	+1	+2
Degeneracy: Number of states	1	4				9								

Just as in one dimension, the total probability of finding the electron somewhere in space must be 1. Using the volume element in spherical polar coordinates from Section 4, normalization condition (2) becomes

$$\int_{r=0}^{r=\infty} \int_{\theta=0}^{\theta=\pi} \int_{\phi=0}^{\phi=2\pi} R^2(r)\Theta^2(\theta)r^2 \sin\theta \, dr \, d\theta \, d\phi = 1$$

or

$$\int_{r=0}^{r=\infty} R^2(r)r^2 dr \int_{\theta=0}^{\theta=\pi} \int_{\phi=0}^{\phi=2\pi} \Theta^2(\theta)\sin\theta \, d\theta \, d\phi = 1$$

We could assign a single normalization constant to the entire wave function, but it turns out to be more convenient to consider the overall constant to be a product of two constants—one that is kept with the angular parts and one with the radial part. We choose the constants so that each integral is independently 1.

$$\int_0^\infty R^2(r)r^2 dr = 1 \qquad (7\text{-}36) \qquad \int_0^\pi \Theta^2(\theta)2\pi \sin\theta \, d\theta = 1 \qquad (37)$$

Note that the trivial integration over ϕ has already been carried out. The functions given in Tables 3 and 4 reflect conditions (36) and (37).

EXAMPLE 5

Verify that the Table 3 normalization constant for the spherical harmonic with $\ell = 1, m_\ell = +1$ is correct.

SOLUTION

From the table, we have

$$\Theta_{1,+1}(\theta)\Phi_{+1}(\phi) = \sqrt{\frac{3}{8\pi}} \sin\theta \, e^{+i\phi}$$

whose complex square is

$$\Theta_{1,+1}^2(\theta) = \frac{3}{8\pi} \sin^2\theta$$

Inserting in (37),

$$\int_0^\pi \left(\frac{3}{8\pi} \sin^2\theta\right) 2\pi \sin\theta \, d\theta = \frac{3}{4} \int_0^\pi \sin^3\theta \, d\theta$$

The value of the remaining integral is 4/3, so the normalization constant is correct.

The Electron's Whereabouts

Now we can discuss where hydrogen's electron might be found. Figure 15 represents the probability densities as density of shading for all states through $n = 3$. States are labeled using **spectroscopic notation**, in which the number designates the value of n and the letter the value of ℓ. Table 6 gives the scheme for ℓ (letters advance alphabetically beyond f). Thus, a $3d$ state is one with $n = 3$ and $\ell = 2$. For each (n, ℓ) state, m_ℓ takes on integral values between $-\ell$ and $+\ell$. (The scales are all the same—the light ring in the $2p$ is at $2a_0$ and the light ring in the $3p$ at $6a_0$.)

The surfaces of constant probability density shown in Figure 16 provide an alternative view; in a way, they are the plots of Figure 15 "spun about" the z-axis. (The s states—"boring" spheres—are not shown.) Note that probability densities do not drop to zero abruptly. The surfaces enclose only the vast majority of space where the electron is likely to be found. Exponential tails extend to infinity in all cases.

Figures 15 and 16 paint nice pictures of the probabilities, but several features are especially noteworthy.

1. As always, the probability density is a diffuse cloud spread over space.
2. The probability density extends farther from the origin/proton as n increases.
3. In the s states, where $\ell = 0$ and the kinetic energy is solely radial, the probability density is spherically symmetric. With no orbital motion, there is no hint of an orbital plane. In p states (both the $2p$ and $3p$), three possible approximate orbits are suggested—one with motion roughly along the z-axis ($m_\ell = 0$) and two roughly in the xy-plane ($m_\ell = \pm1$). The d states, $\ell = 2$, suggest five possible orbits, adding two between the z-axis and the xy-plane ($m_\ell = \pm1$) to the extremes of $m_\ell = 0$ and $m_\ell = \pm2$. (See also Figures 13 and 14.) On the other hand, as noted in Section 5, the probability should be spherically symmetric if we are ignorant of m_ℓ, in which case each value of m_ℓ would be equally likely. For any chosen n and ℓ, if the reader imagines adding the probability densities for all values of m_ℓ, a spherically symmetric average should seem quite plausible.
4. In all $\ell \neq 0$ states, the probability density vanishes at the origin. A particle with angular momentum can never be found there.

TABLE 6 Spectroscopic notation

Letter	s	p	d	f	g	h
Value of ℓ	0	1	2	3	4	5

Figure 15 Electron probability densities in the hydrogen atom, through $n = 3$.

$$|\psi(r, \theta, \phi)|^2 = R^2(r)\,\Theta^2(\theta)$$

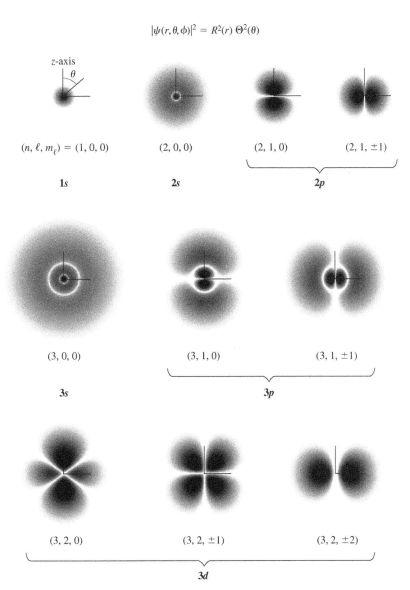

5. If we look at states of a fixed ℓ but increasing n (from $1s$ to $2s$ to $3s$, or from $2p$ to $3p$), we see that the number of radial antinodes increases. Increasing the total energy but not the rotational energy implies greater radial energy, and thus more radial antinodes. By the same token, for fixed n but increasing ℓ ($2s$ to $2p$, or $3s$ to $3p$ to $3d$), the number of radial antinodes decreases, because increasing the rotational energy at a fixed total energy must decrease the radial

Figure 16 Surfaces of constant probability density in the hydrogen atom.

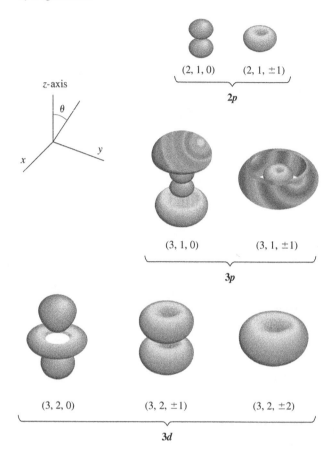

$(2, 1, 0)$ $(2, 1, \pm1)$

$2p$

$(3, 1, 0)$ $(3, 1, \pm1)$

$3p$

$(3, 2, 0)$ $(3, 2, \pm1)$ $(3, 2, \pm2)$

$3d$

energy. Orbits of small ℓ, with more radial antinodes, may be thought of as rather elliptical, with much motion toward and away from the nucleus. On the other hand, states for which ℓ and m_ℓ are both $n - 1$, the largest values allowed, have only one radial antinode and are more like circular orbits at a fixed radius. (The ground state is obviously an exception, with the "largest allowed" angular momentum for $n = 1$ being 0.)

7 Radial Probability

Quite often we are interested only in the electron's radial whereabouts, regardless of direction. A simple example is this question: Typically how far is the electron from the proton in the ground state? Probability integral (36) is the key to any such calculation. Integrating over all space gives a unit total probability, so integrating over a restricted range gives the corresponding fraction.

$$\text{probability of finding particle between } r_1 \text{ and } r_2 = \int_{r_1}^{r_2} R^2(r) r^2 \, dr$$

Moreover, assuming that r_1 and r_2 differ by only dr, the probability dP of finding the electron becomes

$$dP = R^2(r) \, r^2 \, dr$$

Thus, the **radial probability** $P(r)$, a probability *per unit radial distance*, is

$$P(r) = \frac{dP}{dr} = r^2 R^2(r) \qquad\qquad (38) \qquad \text{Radial probability}$$

Note that integrating this from zero to infinity must give 1, as it would merely reproduce (36).

The fact that the radial probability requires an "extra" r^2 with the square of the radial function $R(r)$ is sometimes confusing, but there is a simple argument that (38) should include this factor. Imagine a situation in which the probability *per unit volume* is constant—that is, R, Θ, and Φ are all constant, at least over a considerable portion of space surrounding the origin. Finding the particle somewhere in a thin spherical shell of radius 3 nm would be nine times more likely than finding it in a thin shell of radius 1 nm, simply because the area of the larger shell is nine times as large. (Remember: The area of a sphere is proportional to r^2.) Equation (38) agrees. If R were constant, then r^2 would give the appropriate "area factor" of nine.

Figure 17 shows radial probabilities plotted on axes whose heights are proportional to the hydrogen atom energies. All but the ground state are degenerate, so there are multiple states at the higher energies. Note that all these standing waves extend into the classically forbidden region. Also, as noted in Section 6, at any given n, smaller ℓ implies less rotational energy and thus greater radial energy, resulting in more antinodes and a radial probability that extends farther from the origin. By contrast, the highest angular momentum states, $\ell = n - 1$, have only one antinode and do not extend as far from the origin. They are more like circular orbits at a single well-defined radius. Finally, note that $P(r)$ is 0 at the origin for s states, in which $\ell = 0$, despite the fact that $R(r)$ in such states is nonzero there (refer to Figure 15). While we could simply blame this on the r^2 in $P(r)$, the underlying physics is worth reiterating. Consider the ground state. From Table 4, we see that $R(r)$ for the $1s$ state is a simple decaying exponential, but $P(r)$ starts at 0 and reaches a maximum before falling off. The probability per unit *volume* does fall off monotonically, but the "amount of space" in all directions grows as r increases (the "area factor"), which makes the probability of being found at a given *radius* actually increase for a while. Again we see that if the radial direction is the only concern, $P(r)$ is the better measure.

Figure 17 Radial probabilities and energies in the hydrogen atom. (*Note:* Each higher n adds an ℓ value and a corresponding radial function.)

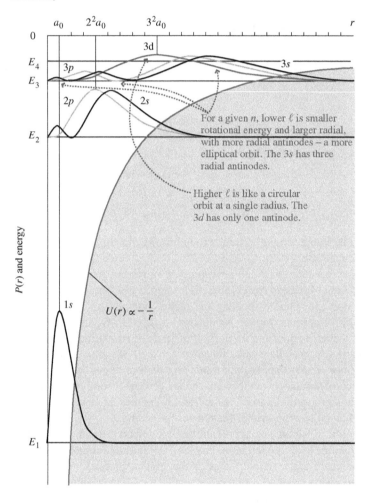

For a given n, lower ℓ is smaller rotational energy and larger radial, with more radial antinodes – a more elliptical orbit. The 3s has three radial antinodes.

Higher ℓ is like a circular orbit at a single radius. The 3d has only one antinode.

$U(r) \propto -\dfrac{1}{r}$

EXAMPLE 6

An electron in a hydrogen atom is in a $3d$ state. What is the most probable radius at which to find it?

SOLUTION

The most probable radius is where the radial probability is maximum. Looking up $R_{3,2}(r)$ in Table 4, we have

$$P(r) = r^2 R_{3,2}^2(r) = r^2 \left(\frac{1}{(3a_0)^{3/2}} \frac{2\sqrt{2}r^2}{27\sqrt{5}a_0^2} e^{-r/3a_0} \right)^2$$

$$= \frac{8}{(3a_0)^3 (27)^2 5 a_0^4} r^6 e^{-2r/3a_0}$$

To find the maximum, we set the derivative to 0. The normalization constant may be ignored.

$$\frac{dP(r)}{dr} = \left(6r^5 + r^6\frac{-2}{3a_0} \right) e^{-2r/3a_0} = 0$$

$$\text{or} \quad r^5\left(6 + r\frac{-2}{3a_0} \right)e^{-2r/3a_0} = 0$$

The equation holds at $r = 0$ and $r = \infty$, but these are obviously minima, where $P(r)$ itself is 0. The maximum occurs where the quantity in parentheses is 0.

$$6 + r\frac{-2}{3a_0} = 0 \quad \Rightarrow \quad r_{\text{most probable}} = 9a_0$$

This agrees with the 3d plot of Figure 17.

In states for which $\ell = n - 1$, the most nearly circular orbits, there is an important pattern to the most probable distance from the proton. According to Table 4,

$$R_{1,0} \propto r^0 e^{-r/1a_0} \qquad R_{2,1} \propto r^1 e^{-r/2a_0} \qquad R_{3,2} \propto r^2 e^{-r/3a_0}$$

In general,

$$R_{n,n-1} \propto r^{(n-1)}e^{-r/na_0}$$

Therefore, the radial probability obeys

$$P(r) = r^2 R^2(r) \propto r^2\left[r^{(n-1)}e^{-r/na_0} \right]^2 = r^{2n}e^{-2r/na_0}$$

It is left as an exercise to show that this function has a maximum given by

$$r_{\text{most probable}} = n^2 a_0 \qquad \text{for} \qquad \ell = n - 1 \tag{39}$$

Note that the 1s, 2p, and 3d plots in Figure 17 all agree. Though $\ell < n - 1$ states are not so easily handled, they follow the rule fairly well. We conclude that *orbit radius increases approximately as the square of n.*

Not only is $P(r)$ useful for finding simple probabilities, but it also allows us to calculate an expectation value of any function of r. As usual, we put the quantity to be averaged in the integral with the probability density and integrate over all possible values.

$$\bar{f} = \int_0^\infty f(r)P(r)dr \tag{40}$$

EXAMPLE 7

What is the expectation value of the radius of an electron in a $3d$ state, and how does it compare with the most probable radius?

SOLUTION

Here, $f(r)$ is just r. With the radial probability found in Example 6, we have

$$\bar{r} = \int_0^\infty rP(r)dr = \int_0^\infty r\left[\frac{8}{(3a_0)^3(27)^2 5a_0^4}r^6 e^{-2r/3a_0}\right]dr$$

$$= \frac{8}{(3a_0)^3(27)^2 5a_0^4}\int_0^\infty r^7 e^{-2r/3a_0}\,dr$$

The integral is given as $\int_0^\infty x^m e^{-bx}\,dx = m!/b^{m+1}$. We have $b = 2/3a_0$ and $m = 7$. Thus,

$$\bar{r} = \frac{8}{(3a_0)^3(27)^2 5a_0^4}7!\left(\frac{3a_0}{2}\right)^8 = 10.5a_0$$

In Example 6, we found the most probable radius of a $3d$ electron to be $9a_0$. An expectation value, on the other hand, is an average of radii we would find if we repeatedly looked for electrons in $3d$ states. The plot of $P(r)$ in Figure 17 has its single maximum at $9a_0$, but while it terminates abruptly at the origin, it extends infinitely far the other way. The average radius certainly appears to be the larger value.

8 Hydrogenlike Atoms

Our solution of the hydrogen atom was based on one all-important piece of information: the potential energy

$$U(r) = -\frac{1}{4\pi\varepsilon_0}\frac{e^2}{r}$$

Any application in which the potential energy is of the same form would follow the same way. **Hydrogenlike** atoms are those with a single electron. Clearly, hydrogen is hydrogenlike, but another example is singly ionized helium. Normally, helium has two electrons orbiting its two-proton nucleus. If one electron is removed, the remaining one has potential energy

$$U(r) = -\frac{1}{4\pi\varepsilon_0}\frac{(2e)(e)}{r} \qquad \text{singly ionized helium}$$

In general, if a single electron orbits a nuclear charge of $+Ze$, the potential energy is

$$U(r) = -\frac{1}{4\pi\varepsilon_0}\frac{Ze^2}{r} \qquad \text{one-electron atom}$$

Thus, all our formulas for hydrogen apply to hydrogenlike atoms if we simply replace e^2, wherever it is found, by Ze^2. In particular, the energy levels follow from equation (12).

$$\text{hydrogen } (Z = 1): E_n = -\frac{me^4}{2(4\pi\varepsilon_0)^2\hbar^2}\frac{1}{n^2} = \frac{-13.6\text{ eV}}{n^2}$$

$$\text{hydrogenlike: } E_n = -\frac{m(Ze^2)^2}{2(4\pi\varepsilon_0)^2\hbar^2}\frac{1}{n^2} = Z^2\frac{-13.6\text{ eV}}{n^2} \quad (41)$$

For $\ell = n-1$, the approximate radii obey

$$\text{hydrogen } (Z = 1): r_n = n^2\frac{(4\pi\varepsilon_0)\hbar^2}{me^2} = n^2a_0$$

$$\text{hydrogenlike: } r_n = n^2\frac{(4\pi\varepsilon_0)\hbar^2}{m(Ze^2)} = \frac{1}{Z}n^2a_0 \quad (42)$$

Bound-state energies are deeper by Z^2, and the orbit radii smaller by $1/Z$.

EXAMPLE 8

What are the ionization energy and the most probable radius of the electron in the ground state of He^+?

SOLUTION

The energy in the ground state is given by (41), with $Z = 2$.

$$E_1 = 2^2\frac{-13.6\text{ eV}}{1^2} = -54.4\text{ eV}$$

An energy of 54.4 eV would be required to remove helium's second electron.
In the $n = 1$ state, ℓ can only be 0 (i.e., $n - 1$), so (42) is applicable.

$$r_1 = \frac{1}{2}1(0.0529\text{ nm}) = 0.026\text{ nm}$$

Singly ionized helium is considerably smaller than hydrogen.

Strange as it might seem, the hydrogenlike, one-electron atom provides an invaluable simple model for understanding behaviors in multielectron atoms.

REAL-WORLD EXAMPLE QUANTUM CONFINEMENT AND TAILORING PHOTON ENERGY

In semiconductors, the fabric of much quantum dot research, an electron can effectively be freed to move about the solid material, but in the process, a free positive charge carrier, called a hole, is also created. These two attract each other just as the proton attracts the electron in hydrogen, forming something like a loosely bound "atom"—called an **exciton**—whose energy and radius are important factors in quantum dot applications. In particular, electrons bound in a quantum dot won't exhibit the tightly controllable energies we desire—**quantum confinement**—if the dot's dimensions are larger than the orbit radius of the exciton. While conditions are of course different in a solid material than in free space, properties of the exciton can be calculated with only a few alterations of hydrogen atom theory. For one thing, dielectric polarization tends to dilute and weaken the Coulomb attraction between electron and hole, and simply dividing the charge Z by the material's dielectric constant accounts for this reasonably well. Another factor, that both the electron and its "nucleus," the hole, move, is handled rather easily by replacing the electron mass with a reduced effective mass, also a property of the semiconducting material.

The orbit radius of the exciton in common semiconductors, fortunately, is much larger than typical atomic dimensions, but it is still submicroscopic, which explains why quantum dot technology took off only after significant advances in our abilities to manipulate materials on a very small scale.

Applying the Physics

The dielectric constant κ and reduced effective mass for a particular semiconductor are roughly 10 and $0.1m_{\text{electron}}$, respectively. (a) Estimate the dimensions necessary for a "dot" of this material to exhibit quantum confinement. (b) The very presence of the hole, actually an *empty* state buried far "below" the electron energy, means that the electron can jump down and produce a photon. In this particular semiconductor, the jump is 1.7 eV, giving a far-red photon wavelength of 730 nm. Confining it to a small dot forces the electron to an energy higher by the dot's ground-state energy, as depicted in Figure 18. Roughly how small a dot would give a 450 nm blue photon?

SOLUTION

(a) Dimensions at least as small as the exciton's orbit radius are needed. This comes from equation (42), replacing the unit value of Z by $1/\kappa$ and m by the reduced effective mass.

$$r_1 = 1^2\frac{(4\pi\varepsilon_0)\hbar^2}{0.1m(1/\kappa)e^2} = \frac{\kappa}{0.1}1^2a_0 = 100a_0$$

100 Bohr radii, 5.3 nm, is indeed an order of magnitude larger than real atoms.

(b) A good model of confinement in three dimensions is the cubic infinite well, whose ground-state energy, from equation (9), is $3(\pi^2\hbar^2/2mL^2)$. We need to "squeeze" the electron higher by the difference between the photon energies.

$$\Delta E = hc\left(\frac{1}{\lambda_{\text{blue}}} - \frac{1}{\lambda_{\text{red}}}\right)$$
$$= 1240\text{ eV}\cdot\text{nm}\left(\frac{1}{450\text{ nm}} - \frac{1}{730\text{ nm}}\right)$$
$$= 1.06\text{ eV}$$

Equating this to the ground-state energy gives

$$1.06\times1.6\times10^{-19}\text{ J} = \frac{3}{2}\frac{\pi^2(1.055\times10^{-34}\text{ J}\cdot\text{s})^2}{(0.1\times9.11\times10^{-31}\text{ kg})L^2}$$

$$\Rightarrow\quad L = 3.3\text{ nm}$$

The calculation assumes, of course, a cube, whereas quantum dots can be of many different shapes. It also overlooks the independent behavior of hole energies when they too are confined, but it is still a good estimate. As we see, control of very small dimensions is essential to tailoring photon energies.

Figure 18 A small dot forces an electron to higher energy.

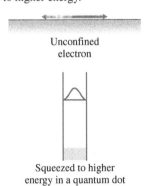

Unconfined electron

Squeezed to higher energy in a quantum dot

9 A Solution Examined

Having skipped the detailed solutions giving us the functions $\Theta(\theta)$ and $R(r)$ in Tables 3 and 4, it would be easy to lose sight of the fact that they do satisfy the Schrödinger equation. Here we demonstrate this fact for a representative wave function, then we study the relationship between the function and the electron's whereabouts.

For our test case, consider the $2p$ state for which $(n, \ell, m_\ell) = (2, 1, +1)$. From Tables 3 and 4, we have

$$R_{2,1}(r)\,\Theta_{1,+1}(\theta)\,\Phi_{+1}(\phi) = \left(\frac{1}{(2a_0)^{3/2}}\frac{r}{\sqrt{3}a_0}e^{-r/2a_0}\right)\left(\sqrt{\frac{3}{8\pi}}\sin\theta\,e^{+i\phi}\right)$$

$$= \frac{1}{8a_0^{5/2}\sqrt{\pi}}re^{-r/2a_0}\sin\theta\,e^{+i\phi}$$

In Section 5, we verified that the complex exponential $e^{im_\ell\phi}$ is a solution of the azimuthal equation, so we move on to polar equation (26). Our $\Theta(\theta)$ is simply $\sin\theta$, so the question is whether the following holds:

$$\sin\theta\frac{\partial}{\partial\theta}\left(\sin\theta\frac{\partial\sin\theta}{\partial\theta}\right) - C\sin^2\theta\sin\theta \overset{?}{=} m_\ell^2\sin\theta$$

In the far-left term, we have one derivative already acting on $\sin\theta$, with the other poised to act on everything to its right. Thus,

$$\sin\theta\frac{\partial}{\partial\theta}(\sin\theta\cos\theta) - C\sin^3\theta \overset{?}{=} m_\ell^2\sin\theta$$

$$\sin\theta\left(\cos^2\theta - \sin^2\theta\right) - C\sin^3\theta \overset{?}{=} m_\ell^2\sin\theta$$

$$\sin\theta(1 - 2\sin^2\theta) - C\sin^3\theta \overset{?}{=} m_\ell^2\sin\theta$$

$$\sin\theta - 2\sin^3\theta - C\sin^3\theta \overset{?}{=} m_\ell^2\sin\theta$$

Our chosen $2p$ state has $m_\ell = +1$, so the $\sin\theta$ terms cancel on the right and the far left, leaving only the $\sin^3\theta$ terms on both sides. The equation holds only if $C = -2$, so our $\ell = 1$ function satisfies (26) for $C = -\ell(\ell+1)$, just as it should.

The radial part of our function, $re^{-r/2a_0}$, should satisfy (31). Does it?

$$\frac{-\hbar^2}{2m}\frac{1}{r^2}\frac{d}{dr}\left(r^2\frac{d}{dr}\right)re^{-r/2a_0} + \frac{\hbar^2\ell(\ell+1)}{2mr^2}re^{-r/2a_0}$$

$$-\frac{1}{4\pi\varepsilon_0}\frac{e^2}{r}re^{-r/2a_0} \overset{?}{=} E\,re^{-r/2a_0} \tag{43}$$

Consider the far-left term.

$$\frac{-\hbar^2}{2m} \frac{1}{r^2} \frac{d}{dr}\left(r^2 \frac{d(re^{-r/2a_0})}{dr}\right)$$

Omitting a few intermediate steps that the reader can easily work out, this becomes

$$\frac{-\hbar^2}{2m} \frac{1}{r^2} \frac{d}{dr}\left[\left(r^2 - \frac{r^3}{2a_0}\right)e^{-r/2a_0}\right] \quad \text{or} \quad \frac{-\hbar^2}{2m}\left(\frac{2}{r^2} - \frac{2}{a_0 r} + \frac{1}{4a_0^2}\right)re^{-r/2a_0}$$

As we reinsert this into (43), note that the function $re^{-r/2a_0}$ appears in each term and cancels. Thus, we have

$$\frac{-\hbar^2}{2m}\left(\frac{2}{r^2} - \frac{2}{a_0 r} + \frac{1}{4a_0^2}\right) + \frac{\hbar^2 \ell(\ell+1)}{2mr^2} - \frac{1}{4\pi\varepsilon_0}\frac{e^2}{r} \overset{?}{=} E$$

Because our state has $\ell = 1$, the two terms with r^2 in the denominator cancel, leaving

$$\left(\frac{\hbar^2}{ma_0} - \frac{e^2}{4\pi\varepsilon_0}\right)\frac{1}{r} - \frac{\hbar^2}{8ma_0^2} \overset{?}{=} E$$

By definition, $a_0 = (4\pi\varepsilon_0)\hbar^2/me^2$, so the term in parentheses is 0, and what remains is

$$-\frac{\hbar^2}{8ma_0^2} = -\frac{me^4}{8(4\pi\varepsilon_0)^2\hbar^2} = E$$

The energy is just what equation (12) says it should be for an $n = 2$ state.

Now let us see if our representative wave function really does correspond to Figures 15 and 16.

EXAMPLE 9

A hydrogen atom electron is in the $(2, 1, +1)$ state. Calculate the probability that it would be found (a) within 30° of the xy-plane, irrespective of radius; (b) between $r = 2a_0$ and $r = 6a_0$, irrespective of angle; and (c) within 30° of the xy-plane *and* between $r = 2a_0$ and $r = 6a_0$.

SOLUTION

(a) The xy-plane is $\theta = 90°$, or $\frac{1}{2}\pi$. We seek the probability for the region within 30°, or $\frac{1}{6}\pi$, of $\frac{1}{2}\pi$. As always, to find a probability over a restricted region, we merely restrict the appropriate normalization integral, in this case (37). Inserting $\Theta(\theta)$ with its normalization constant from Table 3 gives

$$\text{probability} = \int_{\pi/3}^{2\pi/3}\left(\sqrt{\frac{3}{8\pi}}\sin\theta\right)^2 2\pi \sin\theta\, d\theta$$

$$= \frac{3}{4}\int_{\pi/3}^{2\pi/3}\sin^3\theta\, d\theta = \frac{3}{4}\frac{11}{12} = 0.688$$

As it happens, the "solid angle" we have considered, covering $\pi/3 < \theta < 2\pi/3$ and all values of ϕ, is half of space, angularly speaking. (It is 2π steradians out of a total for all space of 4π.) Our probability is considerably greater than $1/2$, so we see that the electron is more likely to be found nearer the xy-plane than the z-axis, which is in agreement with the $\ell = 1$, $m_\ell = \pm 1$ diagrams of Figures 15 and 16.

(b) Inserting $R(r)$ from Table 4 into the restricted radial probability integral (36), we have

$$
\begin{aligned}
\text{probability} &= \int_{2a_0}^{6a_0} R_{2,1}^2(r) r^2 dr \\
&= \int_{2a_0}^{6a_0} \left(\frac{1}{(2a_0)^{3/2}} \frac{r}{\sqrt{3a_0}} e^{-r/2a_0} \right)^2 r^2 dr \\
&= \frac{1}{24a_0^5} \int_{2a_0}^{6a_0} r^4 e^{-r/a_0}\, dr = 0.662
\end{aligned}
$$

(Obtaining the final result involves somewhat tedious integration by parts.) As noted in Section 7, the most probable radius for this state is $4a_0$. Figure 15 appears to agree well, and we now see that indeed the electron is very likely to be found in that vicinity.

(c) The probability if both the radial and the angular ranges are restricted is just the product of the two fractions.

$$
\text{probability} = 0.688 \times 0.662 = 0.455
$$

Although we consider a rather small region of space, the probability is nearly 50%.

10 Photon Emission: Rules and Rates

A D V A N C E D

In Section 3, we noted that photon-producing transitions from one quantum state to another are governed by probabilities. The question of *why* a particle in a "stationary" state would choose to leave it and enter a transitional phase to a lower-energy state has its answer, as noted, in the destabilizing effect of vacuum fluctuations. Our interest here is in *how* a charged particle in a transitional state generates a photon, for it explains why some transitions are highly favored and rapid, while other seemingly plausible transitions essentially do not occur at all.

Allowed Transitions

In a transition from one quantum energy state to another, a particle occupies neither, but rather a combination of the two. As we know, a wave function's temporal part is $e^{-i\omega t} = e^{-iEt/\hbar}$, so if the energies differ, the temporal parts differ.

Because the charge density's time dependence is our main focus here, we need to include each state's temporal part. Accordingly, we crudely represent the transitional state by the following combination:

$$\Psi_{\text{transition}}(\mathbf{r}, t) = \Psi_i(\mathbf{r}, t) + \Psi_f(\mathbf{r}, t)$$

$$= \psi_i(\mathbf{r})e^{-iE_i t/\hbar} + \psi_f(\mathbf{r})e^{-iE_f t/\hbar} \qquad (44)$$

where "i" and "f" are the initial and final states. In general, the proportions of the two states would vary with time, but for simplicity, we pick a simple equal sum of initial and final. The probability density is

$$\Psi_i^*(\mathbf{r}, t)\Psi_f(\mathbf{r}, t)$$

$$= \left(\psi_i(\mathbf{r})e^{-iE_i t/\hbar} + \psi_f(\mathbf{r})e^{-iE_f t/\hbar}\right)^* \left(\psi_i(\mathbf{r})e^{-iE_i t/\hbar} + \psi_f(\mathbf{r})e^{-iE_f t/\hbar}\right) \qquad (45)$$

$$= |\psi_i(\mathbf{r})|^2 + |\psi_f(\mathbf{r})|^2 + \psi_i^*(\mathbf{r})\psi_f(\mathbf{r})e^{-i(E_i - E_f)t/\hbar} + \psi_f^*(\mathbf{r})\psi_i(\mathbf{r})e^{-i(E_f - E_i)t/\hbar}$$

The complex exponentials have angular frequency $\omega = (E_i - E_f)/\hbar$, which is just right to generate a photon whose energy $\hbar\omega$ is $E_i - E_f$ This answers the simple question of how it is even possible to generate a photon—charge density does *not* oscillate in a stationary state—but to quantify the *rate* at which energy is lost, we need to consider the actual process of generating electromagnetic radiation.

Some of the physics we now introduce comes not from quantum mechanics but from classical electromagnetism—namely, the power radiated by an oscillating charge distribution. It turns out that the most efficient radiator is an oscillating electric dipole, depicted in Figure 19, in which positive and negative charges periodically swap locations, producing wavelike oscillations of electromagnetic field. The important quantitative result is

$$\text{power radiated by an oscillating electric dipole} = \frac{p^2\omega^4}{12\varepsilon_0 c^3} \qquad (46)$$

Figure 19 An oscillating dipole is an antenna emitting radiation.

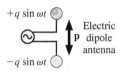

For point charges $+q$ and $-q$ separated by distance d, the electric dipole moment vector is by definition $\mathbf{p} = qd$, the direction being from the negative charge toward the positive. In equation (46), p is the dipole moment's amplitude, and ω is its oscillation frequency.

To be an efficient radiator, a hydrogen atom should have an oscillating dipole moment, but it isn't simply two point charges. Whereas its positive charge, the proton, is compact, its negative charge is an electron cloud. Still, the dipole moment has an expectation value, and this is what we use for $\mathbf{p}$. With charges of $+e$ at the origin and $-e$ at the point $\mathbf{r}$, the dipole moment would be $-e\mathbf{r}$. Multiplying by the probability of finding the electron at $\mathbf{r}$ and integrating over all $\mathbf{r}$ then gives

$$\mathbf{p} = \int\limits_{\text{all space}} (-e\mathbf{r})|\Psi(\mathbf{r},t)|^2 dV \tag{47}$$

Now, if a function changes sign when $\mathbf{r}$ is replaced by $-\mathbf{r}$, we say that it is of odd **parity**. A function of even parity is unchanged by the replacement. If Ψ is of *either* even or odd parity, its square is even parity, and because $\mathbf{r}$ itself is odd, the integrand is of odd parity. Thus, the integral over all space would be 0, as is the integral of any odd function over a one-dimensional interval symmetric about the origin. There would be no net dipole moment. A crucial question, then, is whether Ψ has *any* parity. (A function need not be of either parity, e.g., $1 + x$.)

Let us consider the effect on hydrogen atom wave functions of replacing the position vector $\mathbf{r}$ by $-\mathbf{r}$. In spherical polar coordinates, this involves replacing ϕ with $\phi + \pi$ and θ with $\pi - \theta$. (The radial part $R(r)$ has no bearing on whether a wave function is of even or odd parity. We do *not* replace r with $-r$, because the scalar radius r is the same at $-\mathbf{r}$ as at $\mathbf{r}$.) For all angular solutions $\Theta(\theta)\Phi(\phi)$, the replacement returns the same function for even values of ℓ and the negative of the function for odd values of ℓ. (It is left as an exercise to verify this for the angular solutions in Table 3.) In other words, the wave function $\psi(\mathbf{r}) = R(r)\Theta(\theta)\Phi(\phi)$ is of even parity or odd parity depending on whether ℓ is even or odd. It follows that if the electron is in *any* single stationary state, the probability density $|\Psi|^2$ is even, so the atom has no electric dipole moment at all.

But what of the transitional state? The first two terms of (45) are squares of functions of either even or odd parity, so they are even. For the purpose of calculating dipole moment, they may be ignored. The last two terms are complex conjugates of one another. When added, the result is twice the real part of either. Actually, this factor of 2 is canceled by a multiplicative factor that we need to include in our original transitional state (44) to ensure that it is normalized. (That a sum of normalized functions isn't normalized is addressed in Exercise 78.) With these points in mind, inserting (45) into (47) and using ΔE for $E_f - E_i$ yields

$$\mathbf{p} = -e\,\text{Re}\!\left(e^{i\Delta Et/\hbar} \int\limits_{\text{all space}} \mathbf{r}\psi_f^*(\mathbf{r})\psi_i(\mathbf{r})dV \right) \tag{48}$$

The product $\psi_f^*(\mathbf{r})\psi_i(\mathbf{r})$ will be odd and the dipole moment accordingly nonzero only if the initial and final states are of different parity. Thus, because parity depends on ℓ, we conclude that ℓ must change by an odd number.

Actually, even meeting this restriction does not guarantee that an electric dipole transition can occur. Further restrictions can be deduced from the character of the wave functions, but another crucial factor is the very nature of the photon itself, in particular its spin, which prevents it from carrying away more than a certain amount of angular momentum. Altogether, the various restrictions limit $\Delta\ell$ to ± 1 and Δm_ℓ to 0 or ± 1. These are known as **selection rules**.

EXAMPLE 10

A hydrogen $3p$ electron is in the state $(n, \ell, m_\ell) = (3, 1, +1)$. Which downward transitions are forbidden by the selection rules?

SOLUTION

A transition to the $1s$ state is allowed, as is a transition to the $2s$ state, for both have $\ell = 0$ and $m_\ell = 0$. But a transition to a $2p$ state, regardless of m_ℓ, is forbidden because $\Delta\ell$ would be 0.

Any time the potential energy has great symmetry, selection rules are liable to crop up. For instance, in a diatomic molecule, the interparticle force keeps the oscillating atoms at a certain average separation. For large oscillations, the force is asymmetric, stronger for repulsion than for attraction. But for small oscillations, it behaves essentially as a symmetric simple harmonic oscillator, and by arguments very similar to those above, electric dipole transitions can then occur only between states for which $\Delta n = \pm 1$.

Transition Rate

Equation (46) is the key to estimating how long it should take an electron to drop from one state to another.

$$\frac{\text{energy}}{\text{photon}}\frac{\text{photon}}{\text{time}} \approx \frac{p^2\omega^4}{12\varepsilon_0 c^3} \rightarrow \hbar\omega\frac{\text{photon}}{\text{time}} \approx \frac{p^2\omega^4}{12\varepsilon_0 c^3}$$

$$\Rightarrow \quad \text{transition time} = \frac{\text{time}}{\text{photon}} = \frac{12\varepsilon_0 c^3 \hbar}{p^2\omega^3} \quad (49)$$

The larger the dipole moment or the higher the frequency, the more rapidly we expect the transition to occur.

EXAMPLE 11

A hydrogen atom emits a photon as it drops to the ground state from the $(n,\ell,m_\ell) = (2,1,0)$ state. (a) Calculate the expectation value of the electric dipole moment. (b) Estimate the transition time.

SOLUTION

(a) In equation (48), the final state is $(n,\ell,m_\ell) = (1,0,0)$. Inserting dV in spherical polar coordinates gives

$$\mathbf{p} = -e\,\text{Re}\left(e^{i\Delta E t/\hbar}\int\limits_{\text{all space}}\mathbf{r}\psi^*_{1,0,0}(\mathbf{r})\psi_{2,1,0}(\mathbf{r})r^2\sin\theta\,dr\,d\theta\,d\phi\right)$$

From Tables 3 and 4, the wave functions are

$$\psi^*_{1,0,0}(\mathbf{r})\psi_{2,1,0}(\mathbf{r}) = \left(\frac{1}{a_0^{3/2}}2e^{-r/a_0}\sqrt{\frac{1}{4\pi}}\right)\left(\frac{1}{(2a_0)^{3/2}}\frac{r}{\sqrt{3}a_0}e^{-r/2a_0}\sqrt{\frac{3}{4\pi}}\cos\theta\right)$$

Writing out the $\mathbf{r}$ vector in its Cartesian component form reveals a great simplification.

$$\mathbf{r} = x\,\hat{\mathbf{x}} + y\,\hat{\mathbf{y}} + z\,\hat{\mathbf{z}} = r\sin\theta\cos\phi\,\hat{\mathbf{x}} + r\sin\theta\sin\phi\,\hat{\mathbf{y}} + r\cos\theta\,\hat{\mathbf{z}}$$

Only the z-component survives, for the other two contain $\sin\phi$ or $\cos\phi$, and there is no ϕ elsewhere in the integral—integrating from 0 to 2π gives 0. Moreover, because the wave functions are real, taking the real part of the whole expression merely replaces the complex exponential $e^{i\Delta E t/\hbar}$ with a cosine. Making this replacement, inserting the wave functions and what remains of $\mathbf{r}$, and then factoring out constants, we have

$$\mathbf{p} = \frac{-e}{2^{5/2}\pi a_0^4}\cos\left(\frac{\Delta E t}{\hbar}\right)\int_{\text{all space}}(r\cos\theta\,\hat{\mathbf{z}})\,e^{-r/a_0}\,re^{-r/2a_0}\cos\theta\,r^2\sin\theta\,dr\,d\theta\,d\phi$$

The integral over ϕ gives just 2π, and the separate r and θ integrals are

$$\int_0^\infty r^4 e^{-3r/2a}\,dr = \frac{4!}{(3/2a_0)^5} \qquad \int_0^\pi \cos^2\theta\sin\theta\,d\theta = \frac{2}{3}$$

Thus,

$$\mathbf{p} = \frac{-e}{2^{5/2}\pi a_0^4}\cos\left(\frac{\Delta E t}{\hbar}\right)\frac{4!}{(3/2a_0)^5}\frac{2}{3}2\pi\,\hat{\mathbf{z}}$$

$$= -0.74\,a_0 e\cos\left(\frac{\Delta E t}{\hbar}\right)\hat{\mathbf{z}}$$

Our result is sensible on two accounts. First, the $0.74a_0$ suggests that the charge separation is comparable to a Bohr radius, which is reasonable. Second, the dipole oscillates along the z-axis. Referring to Figures 15 and 16, it is reasonable that oscillation between the spherically symmetric ground state and the $(n,\ell,m_\ell) = (2,1,0)$ state, elongated in the z-direction, should produce a dipole moment along that axis.

(b) To use (49), we need ω. The two energies are -13.6 eV and -13.6 eV$/2^2 = -3.4$ eV, so the photon frequency is

$$\omega = \frac{(13.6 - 3.4)\times 1.6\times 10^{-19}\,\text{J}}{1.055\times 10^{-34}\,\text{J}\cdot\text{s}} = 1.55\times 10^{16}\,\text{s}^{-1}$$

The amplitude of the dipole moment is

$$p = 0.74(0.0529\times 10^{-9}\,\text{m})(1.6\times 10^{-19}\,\text{C}) = 6.3\times 10^{-30}\,\text{C}\cdot\text{m}$$

so that the transition time is approximately

$$\frac{12(8.85\times 10^{-12}\,\text{C}^2/\text{N}\cdot\text{m}^2)(3\times 10^8\,\text{m/s})^3(1.055\times 10^{-34}\,\text{J}\cdot\text{s})}{(6.3\times 10^{-30}\,\text{C}\cdot\text{m})^2(1.55\times 10^{16}\,\text{s}^{-1})^3} \cong 2\,\text{ns}$$

This transition is known to occur in about 1.5 ns, so our estimate is very good. Typical electric dipole transitions occur in the range of 1 to 10 ns.

In conclusion, we note that transitions forbidden as electric dipole transitions may occur by other processes. Charge may, for instance, oscillate as a *magnetic* dipole, where a current loop periodically swaps directions. But such an "antenna" is much less efficient than an electric dipole, so transitions occurring by this process are much slower, typically by a factor of 10^{-4}. Oscillations even more complicated are possible (e.g., electric quadrapole), but these tend to be yet more inefficient and slow. Transitions that can occur only by slow processes cause certain atomic states to be unusually long lived. These are known as **metastable** states and are important to the operation of a laser.

PROGRESS AND APPLICATIONS

High-*n* States: Rydberg Atoms Atoms in which an electron is excited to very high quantum states, typically $n = 40$ and higher, are common topics of discussion nowadays. Known as **Rydberg atoms**, they arise in many active areas of physics research. While the electrons in *ground-state* multielectron atoms interact strongly with each other, if excited to a very high level above the ground state, an electron in *any* atom orbits as though in a hydrogenlike atom, with the nucleus and relatively compact remainder of the electrons constituting an approximately pointlike positive core. With weakly bound electrons orbiting so far from the nucleus, Rydberg atoms are electrostatically malleable and thus well suited to studies of diamagnetism. In many areas of study, Rydberg states of particular interest are those in which ℓ and m_ℓ are the maximum allowed (both $n - 1$), for in these states, the electron's orbit most resembles a classical circle (cf. Figure 16). Owing to the slow means by which they can shed energy, these circular states of high n tend to have very long lifetimes, with important applications in high-energy physics. Furthermore, levels at high n are closely spaced, and each level has a large degeneracy, allowing the electron to occupy a wide range of very interesting *combinations* (superpositions) of states. In fact, Rydberg atoms controlled by external fields have become model systems in which to produce and study wave packets, combinations of quantum states adapted to the particular need. It has been shown that an electron in some combinations of states would behave very much like a stable orbiting classical particle rather than a diffuse wave.

The considerable flexibility allowed a Rydberg wave packet is well illustrated in Figure 20, which depicts how the probability density might, in principle, be tailored to spell out a word. Similar, if less fanciful, **wave packet sculpting** may aid the development of quantum computing, where the ability to control combinations of multiple states is crucial.

Figure 20 At high n, so many states are available that the proper combination could spell out a word!

Antimatter in the Lab Once the subject of theoretical debate alone, **antihydrogen** atoms moving slow enough to allow precise measurements are now being produced in considerable quantities in the lab. All particles have antiparticles, whose mass is the same but whose charge is opposite. The positively charged positron, is the antiparticle of the electron, and the proton's antiparticle is the negatively charged antiproton. That a positron should be able to orbit an antiproton in essentially the same way an electron orbits a proton has long been assumed, but a major hurdle in bringing it about is that antiparticles are very hard to hold. Should an antiparticle meet its particle, the two quickly annihilate. Reducing the odds that antimatter will run into matter, with its dangerous electrons and protons, demands extreme vacuum conditions and containment via matter-free electromagnetic fields. Scientists in the ATRAP (Antihydrogen Trap Collaboration) team at CERN hold antiprotons and positrons in Penning traps—the development of which won the 1989 Nobel Prize in physics—at a vacuum of about 10^{-19} atm! Positrons are cleverly made to do double duty. Not only are they eventually mated to antiprotons, but they are also used to slow the antiprotons to usable speeds beforehand by repeated collisions. So-called hot antihydrogen, produced in collisions more or less direct from a particle accelerator and moving at relativistic speeds, was first observed in small numbers in 1995. However, to allow time for study before the antihydrogen strikes matter and annihilates, production of "cold antihydrogen" was essential. The ATRAP process has been churning out sizable quantities since 2002. These atoms appear to move at speeds less than 10 km/s. Although nonrelativistic, this is still rather fast. They were also in rather high Rydberg states, around $n = 50$. Further studies, using lasers to control the mating of antiproton and positron, promise to yield atoms in less highly excited states and at even lower speeds. The ultimate goal is to hold a sample of ground-state antihydrogen atoms in an atomic trap, where precise spectroscopic measurements can be brought to bear. Then we will see exactly how identical antihydrogen is to hydrogen. Any divergence would be front-page physics news, for symmetry in the behavior of matter and antimatter is at present a fundamental assumption. Another job for antihydrogen is as a test of gravity. While most physicists hold that gravity is attractive for all massive objects—particle or antiparticle—some speculate that antimatter should *repel* matter. A conclusive test with antihydrogen may settle the question.

A Simple "Atom" Without a Nucleus? A very interesting hydrogenlike system increasingly revealed to scrutiny is **positronium**. In hydrogen, the electron orbits a lone positive charge. The "only" difference in positronium is that the positive charge is a positron. In the simplest analysis, characteristics like orbit radius and ground-state energy follow directly from the standard analysis in the chapter (see Comprehensive Exercise 83), but positronium also offers unique insights into fundamental forces. Most important is simply that it contains no proton, a composite of quarks that bring with them the "strong force." In positronium, the electromagnetic force is essentially the only player. Positronium production commonly starts with a positron-emitting radioactive source, followed by slowing of the positrons via collisions, then aiming at a target where some positrons "capture" electrons. Unlike isolated antihydrogen, which can, in principle, live forever, positronium is inherently unstable, for positron and electron annihilate *one another*. Indeed, one of the central questions, and a good test of theories of fundamental forces, has been its survival time. Such are the difficulties of working with this ethereal substance that only in 2003 was experimental confirmation of theoretical predictions obtained. It lives only 142 nanoseconds.

Other recent experiments have investigated the interaction of positronium with "real" atoms. This is important to many fields, for positronium, with its telltale annihilation photons, can be made to form in numerous materials, from gases to semiconductors, in ways that shed new light on their properties. Moreover, beams of positronium may soon serve as a crucial probe in studying the physics of solid surfaces.

Chapter Summary

In three dimensions, the complex square of the wave function, $|\Psi(\mathbf{r}, t)|^2$, is the probability per unit volume of finding the particle in the vicinity of the position $\mathbf{r}$. The spatial part of the wave function must obey the time-independent Schrödinger equation in three dimensions:

$$-\frac{\hbar^2}{2m} \nabla^2 \psi(\mathbf{r}) + U(\mathbf{r})\psi(\mathbf{r}) = E\psi(\mathbf{r}) \qquad (3)$$

In bound systems, the boundary conditions imposed on the wave function in each dimension lead to three quantum numbers, governing quantization of energy and, depending on the system, other physical properties. For each set of three quantum numbers, there is a unique wave function. The more symmetric the potential energy, the larger will be the number of different wave functions with the same energy—that is, the greater the degeneracy.

In the case of the hydrogen atom, the three quantum numbers are the magnetic quantum number m_ℓ, which governs allowed values of the z-component of angular momentum; the orbital quantum number ℓ, which governs the magnitude of the angular momentum; and the principal quantum number n, which governs energy. These values are given by

$$E_n = -\frac{me^4}{2(4\pi\varepsilon_0)^2\hbar^2}\frac{1}{n^2} \qquad n = 1, 2, 3, \ldots \qquad (12)$$

$$|L| = \sqrt{\ell(\ell+1)}\hbar \qquad \ell = 0, 1, 2, \ldots, n-1 \qquad (33)$$

$$L_z = m_\ell\hbar \qquad m_\ell = 0, \pm1, \pm2, \ldots, \pm\ell \qquad (29)$$

For each set (n,ℓ,m_ℓ), there is a unique wave function $\psi(r, \theta, \phi) = R_{n,l}(r)\Theta_{l,m_l}(\theta)\Phi_{m_l}(\phi)$. However, the energy of the hydrogen atom depends only on n. Consequently, the degeneracy grows as n^2.

The probability density in the hydrogen atom varies with r, the distance from the origin/proton, and θ, the polar angle with whatever special axis is established by externally imposed conditions. The radius at which the electron would most likely be found increases with n approximately according to

$$r \cong n^2a_0 \;\; (7\text{-}39) \qquad a_0 \equiv \frac{(4\pi\varepsilon_0)\hbar^2}{me^2} = 0.0529 \text{ nm} \qquad (34)$$

A quantum-mechanical treatment of the hydrogen atom explains observations that cannot be understood classically, including the atom's stability and the discrete wavelengths of light that it emits.

---

* indicates advanced questions

Conceptual Questions

1. What is a quantum number, and how does it arise?
2. Some degeneracies are easy to understand on the basis of symmetry in the physical situation. Others are surprising, or "accidental." In the states given in Table 1, which degeneracies, if any, would you call accidental, and why?
3. Consider a 2D infinite well whose sides are of unequal length. (a) Sketh the probability density—as density of shading—for the ground state. (b) There are two likely choices for the next lowest energy. Sketch the probability density and explain how you know that this must be the next lowest energy. (Focus on the qualitative idea, avoiding unnecessary reference to calculations.)
4. Classically, what happens when a moving object has a head-on elastic collision with a stationary object of exactly equal mass? What if it strikes an object of smaller mass? Of larger mass? How do these ideas relate to Rutherford's conclusion about the nature of the atom?
5. In hydrogen's characteristic spectra, each series—the Lyman, the Balmer, and so on—has a "series limit," where the wavelengths at one end of the series tend to

bunch up, approaching a single limiting value. Is it at the short-wavelength or the long-wavelength end of the series that the series limit occurs, and what is it about hydrogen's allowed energies that leads to this phenomenon? Does the infinite well have series limits?

6. A gas can be too cold to absorb Balmer series lines. Is this also true for the Paschen series? (See Figure 5.) For the Lyman series? Explain.
7. Mathematically, equation (22) is the same differential equation as we had for a particle in a box—the function and its second derivative are proportional. But $\Phi(\phi)$ for $m_\ell = 0$ is a constant and is allowed, whereas such a constant wave function is not allowed for a particle in a box. What physics accounts for this difference?
8. Section 5 argues that knowing all three components of **L** would violate the uncertainty principle. Knowing its magnitude and one component does not. What about knowing its magnitude and *two* components? Would **L** be left any freedom at all, and if so, do you think it would be enough to satisfy the uncertainly principle?
9. Knowing precisely all components of a nonzero **L** would violate the uncertainty principle, but knowing that **L** is precisely *zero* does not. Why not? (*Hint:* For $\ell = 0$ states, the momentum vector **p** is *radial*.)
10. What are the dimensions of the spherical harmonics $\Theta_{\ell,m_\ell}(\theta)\Phi_{m_\ell}(\phi)$ given in Table 3? What are the dimensions of the $R_{n,\ell}(r)$ given in Table 4, and why? What are the dimensions of $P(r)$, and why?
11. Explain to your friend, who has just learned about simple one-dimensional standing waves on a string fixed at its ends, why hydrogen's electron has only certain energies, and why, for some of those energies, the electron can still be in different states.
12. A particle is trapped in a spherical infinite well. The potential energy is 0 for $r < a$ and infinite for $r > a$. Which, if any, quantization conditions would you expect it to share with hydrogen, and why?
13. Taking the $n = 3$ states as representative, explain the relationship between the complexity—numbers of nodes and antinodes—of hydrogen's standing waves in the radial direction and their complexity in the angular direction at a given value of n. Is it a direct or inverse relationship, and why?
14. At heart, momentum conservation is related to the universe being "translationally invariant," meaning that it is the same if you shift your coordinates to the right or left. Angular momentum relates to rotational invariance. Use these ideas to explain at least some of the differences between the physical properties quantized in the cubic three-dimensional box versus the hydrogen atom.

15. (a) For a one-dimensional particle in a box, what is the meaning of n? Specifically, what does knowing n tell us? (b) What is the meaning of n for a hydrogen atom? (c) For a hydrogen atom, what is the meaning of ℓ? Of m_ℓ?

16. Can the transition $2s \rightarrow 1s$ in the hydrogen atom occur by electric dipole radiation? The lifetime of the $2s$ is known to be unusual. Is it unusually short or long?

Exercises

Section 2

17. If the constant C_x in equation (5) were positive, the general mathematical solution would be

$$Ae^{+\sqrt{C_x}\,x} + Be^{-\sqrt{C_x}\,x}$$

Show that this function cannot be 0 at two points. This makes it an unacceptable solution for the infinite well, since it cannot be continuous with the wave functions outside the walls, which are 0.

18. For the cubic 3D infinite well wave function

$$\psi(x, y, z) = A \sin\frac{n_x\pi x}{L} \sin\frac{n_y\pi y}{L} \sin\frac{n_z\pi z}{L}$$

show that the correct normalization constant is $A = (2/L)^{3/2}$.

19. Verify that the solutions given in equations (6) satisfy differential equations (5) as well as the required boundary conditions.

20. An electron is confined to a cubic 3D infinite well 1 nm on a side. (a) What are the three lowest *different* energies possible? (b) To how many different states do these three energies correspond?

21. An electron is trapped in a quantum dot, in which it is confined to a very small region in all three dimensions. If the lowest-energy transition is to produce a photon of 450 nm wavelength, what should be the width of the well (assumed cubic)?

22. Consider a cubic 3D infinite well. (a) How many different wave functions have the same energy as the one for which $(n_x, n_y, n_z) = (5, 1, 1)$? (b) Into how many different energy levels would this level split if the length of one side were increased by 5%? (c) Make a scale diagram, similar to Figure 3, illustrating the energy splitting of the previously degenerate wave functions. (d) Is there any degeneracy left? If so, how might it be "destroyed"?

23. An electron is trapped in a cubic 3D infinite well. In the states $(n_x, n_y, n_z) =$ (a) (2, 1, 1), (b) (1, 2, 1), and (c) (1, 1, 2), what is the probability of finding the electron in

the region $(0 \le x \le L, \frac{1}{3}L \le y \le \frac{2}{3}L, 0 \le z \le L)$? Discuss any differences in the three results.

* **24.** **The 2D Infinite Well:** In two dimensions, the Schrödinger equation is

$$\left(\frac{\partial^2}{\partial x^2} + \frac{\partial^2}{\partial y^2}\right)\psi(x, y) = -\frac{2m(E - U)}{\hbar^2}\psi(x, y)$$

(a) Given that U is a constant, separate variables by trying a solution of the form $\psi(x, y) = f(x)g(y)$, then dividing by $f(x)g(y)$. Call the separation constants C_x and C_y.

(b) For an infinite well,

$$U = \begin{cases} 0 & 0 < x < L, 0 < y < L \\ \infty & \text{otherwise} \end{cases}$$

What should $f(x)$ and $g(y)$ be outside this well? What functions would be acceptable standing-wave solutions for $f(x)$ and $g(y)$ inside the well? Are C_x and C_y positive, negative, or zero? Imposing appropriate conditions, find the allowed values of C_x and C_y.

(c) How many independent quantum numbers are there?

(d) Find the allowed energies E.

(e) Are there energies for which there is not a unique corresponding wave function?

25. Consider a cubic 3D infinite well of side length L. There are 15 identical particles of mass m in the well, but for whatever reason, no more than two particles can have the same wave function. (a) What is the lowest possible *total* energy? (b) In this minimum-total-energy state, at what point(s) would the highest-energy particle most likely be found? (*Note:* Knowing no more than its energy, the highest-energy particle might be in any of multiple wave functions open to it and with equal probability.)

Section 3

26. Classically, an orbiting charged *particle* radiates electromagnetic energy, and for an electron in atomic dimensions, it would lead to collapse in considerably less than the wink of an eye. (a) By equating the centripetal and Coulomb forces, show that for a classical charge $-e$ of mass m held in circular orbit by its attraction to a fixed charge $+e$, the following relationship holds: $\omega = er^{-3/2}/\sqrt{4\pi\varepsilon_0 m}$. (b) Electromagnetism tells us that a charge whose acceleration is a radiates power $P = e^2a^2/6\varepsilon_0c^3$. Show that this can also be expressed in terms of the orbit radius, as $P = e^6/(96\pi^2\varepsilon_0^3mc^3r^4)$. Then calculate the energy lost per orbit in terms of r by multiplying this power by the period $T = 2\pi/\omega$ and using the formula from part (a) to eliminate ω. (c) In such a classical orbit, the total mechanical energy is half the potential energy, or $E_{\text{orbit}} = -e^2/8\pi\varepsilon_0r$. Calculate the change in energy per change in r: dE_{orbit}/dr. From this and the energy lost per orbit from part (b), determine the change in r per orbit and evaluate it for a typical orbit radius of 10^{-10} m. Would the electron's radius change much in a single orbit? (d) Argue that dividing dE_{orbit}/dr by P and multiplying by dr gives the time required for r to change by dr. Then, sum these times for all radii from r_{initial} to a final radius of 0. Evaluate your result for $r_{\text{initial}} = 10^{-10}$ m. (One limitation of this estimate is that the electron would eventually be moving relativistically.)

27. In general, we might say that the wavelengths allowed a bound particle are those of a typical standing wave, $\lambda = 2L/n$, where L is the length of its home. Given that $\lambda = h/p$, we would have $p = nh/2L$, and the kinetic energy, $p^2/2m$, would thus be $n^2h^2/8mL^2$. These are actually the correct infinite well energies, for the argument is perfectly valid when the potential energy is 0 (inside the well) and L is strictly constant. But it is a pretty good guide to how the energies should go in other cases. The length L allowed the wave should be roughly the region classically allowed to the particle, which depends on the "height" of the total energy E relative to the potential energy U (cf. Figure 4). The "wall" is the classical turning point, where there is no kinetic energy left: $E = U$. Treating it as essentially a one-dimensional (radial) problem, apply these arguments to the hydrogen atom potential energy (10). Find the location r of the classical turning point in terms of E, use twice this distance for L (the electron can be on both on sides of the origin), and from this obtain an expression for the expected average kinetic energies in terms of E. For the average potential, use its value at half the distance from the origin to the turning point, again in terms of E. Then write out the expected average total energy and solve for E. What do you obtain for the quantized energies?

28. Show that of hydrogen's spectral series—Lyman, Balmer, Paschen, and so on—only the four Balmer lines of Section 3 are in visible range (400–700 nm).

29. (a) What are the initial and final energy levels for the third (i.e., third-longest wavelength) line in the Paschen series? (See Figure 5.) (b) Determine the wavelength of this line.

30. Calculate the "series limit" of the Lyman series of spectral lines. This is defined as the shortest wavelength possible of a photon emitted in a transition from a higher initial energy level to the $n_f = 1$ final level. (*Note*: In Figure 5, the spectral lines of the series "crowd together" at the short-wavelength end of the series.)

31. The only visible spectral lines of hydrogen are the four Balmer series lines noted at the beginning of Section 3. We wish to cause hydrogen gas to glow with its characteristic visible colors.

    (a) To how high an energy level must the electrons be excited?
    (b) Energy is absorbed in collisions with other particles. Assume that after absorbing energy in one collision, an electron jumps down through lower levels so rapidly that it is in the ground state before another collision occurs. If an electron is to be raised to the level found in part (a), how much energy must be available in a single collision?
    (c) If such energetic collisions are to be effected simply by heating the gas until the average kinetic energy equals the desired upward energy jump, what temperature would be required? (This explains why heating is an impractical way to observe the hydrogen spectrum. Instead, the atoms are ionized by strong electric fields, as is the air when a static electric spark passes through.)

32. A hydrogen atom in an $n = 2$ state absorbs a photon. (a) What should be the photon wavelength to cause the electron to jump to an $n = 4$ state? (b) What wavelength photons might be emitted by the atom following this absorption?

33. To conserve momentum, an atom emitting a photon must recoil, meaning that not all of the energy made available in the downward jump goes to the photon. (a) Find a hydrogen atom's recoil energy when it emits a photon in a $n = 2$ to $n = 1$ transition. (*Note:* The calculation is easiest to carry out if it is assumed that the photon carries essentially all the transition energy, which thus determines its momentum. The result justifies the assumption.) (b) What fraction of the transition energy is the recoil energy?

34. The space between two parallel metal plates is filled with an element in a gaseous state. Electrons leave one plate at negligible speed and are accelerated toward the other by a potential difference ΔV applied between the plates. As ΔV is increased from 0, the electron current increases more or less linearly, but when ΔV reaches 4.9 V, the current drops precipitously. From nearly 0, it builds again roughly linearly as ΔV is increased beyond 4.9 V. (a) How can the presence of the gas explain these

observations? (b) The gas emits a rather pure "light" when ΔV exceeds 4.9 V. What is its wavelength?

Section 5

35. A mathematical solution of the azimuthal equation (22) is $\Phi(\phi) = Ae^{+\sqrt{-D}\phi} + Be^{-\sqrt{-D}\phi}$, which applies when D is negative. (a) Show that this simply cannot meet itself smoothly when it finishes a round trip about the z-axis. The simplest approach is to consider $\phi = 0$ and $\phi = 2\pi$. (b) If D were 0, equation (22) would say simply that the second derivative of $\Phi(\phi)$ is 0. Argue that this too leads to a physically unacceptable solution, except in the special case of $\Phi(\phi)$ being constant, which is covered by the $m_\ell = 0$ case of solutions (24).

36. Prove that if the function $e^{i\sqrt{D}\phi}$ is to meet itself smoothly when ϕ changes by 2π, $\sqrt{D}$ must be an integer.

37. An electron is in an $\ell = 3$ state of the hydrogen atom. What possible angles might the angular momentum vector make with the z-axis?

38. A particle orbiting due to an attractive central force has angular momentum 1.00×10^{-33} kg · m/s. What z-components of angular momentum is it possible to detect?

39. In Section 5, $e^{im_\ell\phi}$ is presented as our preferred solution to the azimuthal equation, but there is a more general one that need not violate the smoothness condition, and that in fact covers not only complex exponentials, but also, with suitable redefinitions of multiplicative constants, sine and cosine:

$$\Phi_{m_\ell}(\phi) = Ae^{+im_\ell\phi} + Be^{-im_\ell\phi}$$

(a) Show that the complex square of this function is not, in general, independent of ϕ. (b) What conditions must be met by A and/or B for the probability density to be rotationally symmetric—that is, independent of ϕ? (This highlights another reason, besides their being of well-defined L_z, why we like our preferred solutions.)

* **40.** Here we pursue the more rigorous approach to the claim that the property quantized according to m_ℓ is L_z. (a) Starting with a straightforward application of the chain rule,

$$\frac{\partial}{\partial\phi} = \frac{\partial x}{\partial\phi}\frac{\partial}{\partial x} + \frac{\partial y}{\partial\phi}\frac{\partial}{\partial y} + \frac{\partial z}{\partial\phi}\frac{\partial}{\partial z}$$

use the transformations given in Table 2 to show that

$$\frac{\partial}{\partial\phi} = -y\frac{\partial}{\partial x} + x\frac{\partial}{\partial y}$$

(b) Recall that $\mathbf{L} \equiv \mathbf{r} \times \mathbf{p}$. From the z-component of this famous formula and the definitions of the operators for p_x and p_y, argue that the operator for L_z is $-i\hbar\,\partial/\partial\phi$. (c) What now allows us to say that our azimuthal solution $e^{im_\ell\phi}$ has a well-defined z-component of angular momentum and that its value is $m_\ell\hbar$?

41. A simplified approach to the question of how ℓ is related to angular momentum—due to P. W. Milonni and Richard Feynman—can be stated as follows: If L_z can take on only those values $m_\ell\hbar$, where $m_\ell = 0, \pm 1, \ldots, \pm\ell$, then its *square* is allowed only the values $m_\ell^2\hbar^2$, and the average of L_z^2 should be the sum of its allowed values divided by the number of values, $2\ell + 1$. Because there really is no preferred direction in space, the averages of L_x^2 and L_y^2 should be the same, and the sum of all three should give the average of L^2. Given the sum $\sum_1^N n^2 = N(N + 1)(2N + 1)/6$, show that by these arguments, the average of L^2 should be $\ell(\ell + 1)\hbar^2$. (Why this is not simply the average but the *well-defined* value of L^2 requires the rigorous approach referred to in Section 5.)

42. The operator for the square of the angular momentum is shown to be

$$\hat{L}^2 = -\hbar^2\left[\csc\theta\frac{\partial}{\partial\theta}\left(\sin\theta\frac{\partial}{\partial\theta}\right) + \csc^2\theta\frac{\partial^2}{\partial\phi^2}\right]$$

Use this to rewrite equation (19) as $\hat{L}^2\Theta\Phi = -C\hbar^2\Theta\Phi$.

Section 6

43. Explicitly verify that the simple function $R(r) = A\,e^{-br}$ can be made to satisfy radial equation (31), and in so doing, demonstrate what its angular momentum and energy must be.

44. How many different $3d$ states are there? What physical property (as opposed to quantum number) distinguishes them, and what different values may this property assume?

45. An electron is in an $n = 4$ state of the hydrogen atom. (a) What is its energy? (b) What properties besides energy are quantized, and what values might be found if these properties were to be measured?

46. In Table 5, the pattern that develops with increasing n suggests that the number of different sets of (ℓ, m_ℓ) values for a given energy level n is n^2. Prove this mathematically by summing the allowed values of m_ℓ for a given ℓ over the allowed values of ℓ for a given n.

47. Show that the angular normalization constant in Table 3 for the case $(\ell, m_\ell) = (1, 0)$ is correct.

48. Show that the normalization constant $\sqrt{15/32\pi}$ given in Table 3 for the angular parts of the $\ell = 2$, $m_\ell = \pm 2$ wave function is correct.

49. Verify the correctness of the normalization constant of the $2p$ radial wave function, given in Table 4 as

$$\frac{1}{(2a_0)^{3/2}\sqrt{3a_0}}$$

50. A hydrogen atom electron is in a $2p$ state. If no experiment has been done to establish a z-component of angular momentum, the atom is equally likely to be found with any allowed value of L_z. Show that if the probability densities for these different possible states are added (with equal weighting), the result is independent of *both* ϕ and θ.

51. A wave function with a noninfinite wavelength—however approximate it might be—has nonzero momentum and thus nonzero kinetic energy. Even a single "bump" has kinetic energy. In either case, we can say that the function has kinetic energy because it has curvature—a second derivative. Indeed, the kinetic energy operator in any coordinate system involves a second derivative. The only function without kinetic energy would be a straight line. As a special case, this includes a constant, which may be thought of as a function with an infinite wavelength. By looking at the curvature *in the appropriate dimension(s)*, answer the following: For a given n, is the kinetic energy solely (a) radial in the state of lowest ℓ—that is, $\ell = 0$; and (b) rotational in the state of highest ℓ—that is, $\ell = n - 1$?

* 52. We have noted that for a given energy, as ℓ increases, the motion is more like a circle at a constant radius, with the rotational energy increasing as the radial energy correspondingly decreases. But is the radial kinetic energy 0 for the largest ℓ values? Calculate the ratio of expectation values, radial energy to rotational energy, for the $(n, \ell, m_\ell) = (2, 1, +1)$ state. Use the operators

$$\hat{KE}_{rad} = \frac{-\hbar^2}{2m}\frac{1}{r^2}\frac{\partial}{\partial r}\left(r^2\frac{\partial}{\partial r}\right)$$

$$\hat{KE}_{rot} = \frac{\hbar^2\ell(\ell + 1)}{2mr^2}$$

which we deduce from equation (30).

Section 7

53. An electron is in the $3d$ state of a hydrogen atom. The most probable distance of the electron from the proton is $9a_0$. What is the probability that the electron would be found between $8a_0$ and $10a_0$?

54. Using the functions given in Table 4, verify that for the more-circular electron orbits in hydrogen (i.e., $\ell = n - 1$), the radial probability is of the form

$$P(r) \propto r^{2n}e^{-2r/na_0}$$

Show that the most probable radius is given by

$$r_{most\ probable} = n^2a_0$$

55. For states where $\ell = n - 1$, the radial probability assumes the general form given in Exercise 54. The proportionality constant that normalizes this radial probability is given in Exercise 64. (a) Show that the expectation value of the hydrogen atom potential energy is exactly twice the total energy. (It turns out that this holds no matter what ℓ may be.) (b) Argue that the expectation value of the kinetic energy must be the negative of the total energy.

56. For a hydrogen atom in the ground state, determine (a) the most probable location at which to find the electron and (b) the most probable radius at which to find the electron. (c) Comment on the relationship between your answers in parts (a) and (b).

57. Consider an electron in the ground state of a hydrogen atom. (a) Sketch plots of E and $U(r)$ on the same axes. (b) Show that, classically, an electron with this energy should not be able to get farther than $2a_0$ from the proton. (c) What is the probability of the electron being found in the classically forbidden region?

58. (a) What is the expectation value of the distance from the proton of an electron in a $3p$ state? (b) How does this compare with the expectation value in the $3d$ state, calculated in Example 7? Discuss any differences.

59. Imagine two classical charges of $-q$, each bound to a central charge of $+q$. One $-q$ charge is in a circular orbit of radius R about its $+q$ charge. The other oscillates in an extreme ellipse, essentially a straight line from its $+q$ charge out to a maximum distance r_{max}. The two orbits have the same energy. (a) Show that $r_{max} = 2R$. (b) Considering the time spent at each orbit radius, in which orbit is the $-q$ charge farther from its $+q$ charge on average?

60. Consider an electron in the ground state of a hydrogen atom. (a) Calculate the expectation value of its potential energy. (b) What is the expectation value of its kinetic energy? (*Hint:* What is the expectation value of the total energy?)

61. Is the potential energy of an electron in a hydrogen atom well defined? Is the kinetic energy well defined? Justify your answers. (You need not actually calculate uncertainties.)

* **62.** Calculate the uncertainties in r for the 2s and 2p states using the formula

$$\Delta r = \sqrt{\overline{r^2} - \overline{r}^2}$$

What insight does the difference between these two uncertainties convey about the nature of the corresponding orbits?

63. The kinetic energy of hydrogen atom wave functions for which ℓ is its minimum value of 0 is all radial. This is the case for the 1s and 2s states. The 2p state has some rotational kinetic energy and some radial. Show that for very large n, the states of largest allowed ℓ have essentially no radial kinetic energy. Exercise 55 notes that the expectation value of the kinetic energy (including both rotational and radial) equals the magnitude of the total energy. Compare this magnitude with the rotational energy alone, $L^2/2mr^2$, assuming that n is large, that ℓ is as large as it can be, and that $r \cong n^2 a_0$.

64. For the more circular orbits, $\ell = n - 1$ and

$$P(r) \propto r^{2n}e^{-2r/na_0}$$

(a) Show that the coefficient that normalizes this probability is

$$\left(\frac{2}{na_0}\right)^{2n+1}\frac{1}{(2n)!}$$

(b) Show that the expectation value of the radius is given by

$$\overline{r} = n\left(n + \frac{1}{2}\right)a_0$$

and the uncertainty by

$$\Delta r = na_0\sqrt{\frac{n}{2} + \frac{1}{4}}$$

(c) What happens to the ratio $\Delta r/\overline{r}$ in the limit of large n? Is this large-n limit what would be expected classically?

65. Here we investigate the link between n and ℓ, reflected in equation (33). (a) Show that if a classical point charge were held in a circular orbit about a fixed point charge by the Coulomb force, its kinetic energy would

be given by $KE = e^2/8\pi\varepsilon_0 r$. (b) According to equation (30), the rotational kinetic energy in hydrogen is $\hbar^2\ell(\ell + 1)/2mr^2$. Of course, r is not well defined for a "cloud," but by using $r \cong n^2 a_0$, argue that the condition that ℓ not exceed n is reasonable.

Section 8

66. Which electron transitions in singly ionized helium yield photons in the 450–500 nm (~blue) portion of the visible range, and what are their wavelengths?

67. Doubly ionized lithium, Li^{2+}, absorbs a photon and jumps from the ground state to its $n = 2$ level. What was the wavelength of the photon?

68. Roughly, how does the size of a triply ionized beryllium ion compare with hydrogen?

Section 9

69. For an electron in the $(n, \ell, m_\ell) = (2, 0, 0)$ state in a hydrogen atom, (a) write the solution of the time-independent Schrödinger equation, and (b) verify explicitly that it is a solution with the expected angular momentum and energy.

70. An electron in a hydrogen atom is in the $(n, \ell, m_\ell) = (2, 1, 0)$ state. (a) Calculate the probability that it would be found within 60° of the z-axis, irrespective of radius. (*Note:* This means within 60° of either the $+z$- or $-z$-direction, solid angles totaling 2π steradians, or "half of space.") (b) Calculate the probability that it would be found between $r = 2a_0$ and $r = 6a_0$, irrespective of angle. (c) What is the probability that it would be found within 60° of the z-axis *and* between $r = 2a_0$ and $r = 6a_0$?

71. Calculate the probability that the electron in a hydrogen atom would be found within 30° of the xy-plane, irrespective of radius, for (a) $\ell = 0$, $m_\ell = 0$; (b) $\ell = 1$, $m_\ell = \pm 1$; and (c) $\ell = 2$, $m_\ell = \pm 2$. (d) As angular momentum increases, what happens to the orbits whose z-components of angular momentum are the maximum allowed?

Section 10

72. Show that a transition where $\Delta m_\ell = \pm 1$ corresponds to a dipole moment in the xy-plane, while $\Delta m_\ell = 0$ corresponds to a moment along the z-axis. (You need consider only the ϕ-parts of ψ_i and ψ_f, which are of the form $e^{im_\ell\phi}$.)

73. Verify for the angular solutions $\Theta(\theta)\Phi(\phi)$ of Table 3 that replacing ϕ with $\phi + \pi$ and θ with $\pi - \theta$ gives the same function when ℓ is even and the negative of the function when ℓ is odd.

74. A particular vibrating diatomic molecule may be treated as a simple harmonic oscillator. Show that a transition from the $n = 2$ state directly to the $n = 0$ ground state cannot occur by electric dipole radiation.

* **75.** Consider a vibrating molecule that behaves as a simple harmonic oscillator of mass 10^{-27} kg, spring constant 10^3 N/m, and charge $+e$. (a) Estimate the transition time from the first excited state to the ground state, assuming that it decays by electric dipole radiation. (b) What is the wavelength of the photon emitted?

76. Calculate the electric dipole moment **p** and estimate the transition time for a hydrogen atom electron making an electric dipole transition from the $(n, \ell, m_\ell) = (2, 1, +1)$ state to the ground state. Comment on the relationship of the result to that in Example 11.

* **77.** Calculate the electric dipole moment **p** and estimate the transition time for a hydrogen atom electron making an electric dipole transition from the $(n, \ell, m_\ell) = (3, 2, 0)$ to the $(2, 1, 0)$ state.

78. When applying quantum mechanics, we often concentrate on states that qualify as "orthonormal." The main point is this: If we evaluate a probability integral over all space of $\psi_1^*\psi_1$ or of $\psi_2^*\psi_2$, we get 1 (unsurprisingly), but if we evaluate such an integral for $\psi_1^*\psi_2$ or $\psi_2^*\psi_1$ we get 0. This happens to be true for all the systems where we have tabulated or actually derived sets of wave functions (e.g., the particle in a box, the harmonic oscillator, and the hydrogen atom). By integrating over all space, show that expression (44) is *not* normalized unless a factor of $\frac{1}{2}$ is included with the probability.

Comprehensive Exercises

79. The $\psi_{2,1,0}$ state—the 2p state in which $m_\ell = 0$—has most of its probability density along the z-axis, and so it is often referred to as a $2p_z$ state. To allow its probability density to stick out in other ways, and thus facilitate various kinds of molecular bonding with other atoms, an atomic electron may assume a wave function that is an algebraic combination of multiple wave functions open to it. One such "hybrid state" is the sum $\psi_{2,1,+1} + \psi_{2,1,-1}$. (*Note:* Because the Schrödinger equation is a linear differential equation, a sum of solutions with the same energy is a solution with that energy. Also, normalization constants may be ignored in the following questions.)

(a) Write this wave function and its probability density in terms of r, θ, and ϕ. (Use the Euler formula to simplify your result.)

(b) In which of the following ways does this state differ from its parts (i.e., $\psi_{2,1,+1}$ and $\psi_{2,1,-1}$) and from the $2p_z$ state: Energy? Radial dependence of

its probability density? Angular dependence of its probability density?

(c) This state is often referred to as the $2p_x$. Why?

(d) How might we produce a $2p_y$ state?

80. Consider two particles that experience a mutual force but no external forces. The classical equation of motion for particle 1 is $\dot{\mathbf{v}}_1 = \mathbf{F}_{2\text{ on }1}/m_1$, and for particle 2 is $\dot{\mathbf{v}}_2 = \mathbf{F}_{1\text{ on }2}/m_2$, where the dot means a time derivative. Show that these are equivalent to

$$\mathbf{v}_{\text{cm}} = \text{constant} \quad \text{and} \quad \dot{\mathbf{v}}_{\text{rel}} = \mathbf{F}_{\text{mutual}}/\mu$$

where $\mathbf{v}_{\text{cm}} \equiv (m_1\mathbf{v}_1 + m_2\mathbf{v}_2)/(m_1 + m_2)$, $\mathbf{F}_{\text{mutual}} \equiv \mathbf{F}_{1\text{ on }2} = -\mathbf{F}_{2\text{ on }1}$, and

$$\mu = \frac{m_1 m_2}{m_1 + m_2}$$

In other words, the motion can be analyzed in two pieces: the center of mass motion, at constant velocity; and the relative motion, but in terms of a one-particle equation where that particle experiences the mutual force and has the "reduced mass" μ.

81. Exercise 80 discusses the idea of reduced mass. When two objects move under the influence of their mutual force alone, we can treat the *relative* motion as a one-particle system of mass $\mu = m_1 m_2/(m_1 + m_2)$. Among other things, this allows us to account for the fact that the nucleus in a hydrogenlike atom isn't perfectly stationary, but in fact also orbits the center of mass. Suppose that due to Coulomb attraction, an object of mass m_2 and charge $-e$ orbits an object of mass m_1 and charge $+Ze$. By appropriate substitutions into formulas given in the chapter, show that (a) the allowed energies are $(Z^2\mu/m)E_1/n^2$, where E_1 is the hydrogen ground state, and (b) the "Bohr radius" for this system is $(m/Z\mu)a_0$, where a_0 is the hydrogen Bohr radius.

82. Exercise 81 obtains formulas for hydrogenlike atoms in which the nucleus is not assumed infinite, as in the chapter, but is of mass m_1, while m_2 is the mass of the orbiting negative charge. (a) What percentage error is introduced in the hydrogen ground-state energy by assuming that the proton is of infinite mass? (b) Deuterium is a form of hydrogen in which a neutron joins the proton in the nucleus, making the nucleus twice as massive. Taking nuclear mass into account, by what percent do the ground-state energies of hydrogen and deuterium differ?

83. Exercise 81 obtains formulas for hydrogenlike atoms in which the nucleus is not assumed infinite, as in the chapter, but is of mass m_1, while m_2 is the mass of the orbiting negative charge. In positronium, an electron orbits a single positive charge, as in hydrogen, but one whose mass is the same as that of the electron—a positron. Obtain numerical values for the ground-state energy and "Bohr radius" of positronium.

84. Classically, it was expected that an orbiting electron would emit radiation of the same frequency as its orbit frequency. We have often noted that classical behavior is observed in the limit of large quantum numbers. Does it work in this case? (a) Show that the photon energy for the smallest possible energy jump at the "low-n end" of the hydrogen energies is $3|E_0|/4$, while that for the smallest jump at the "high-n end" is $2|E_0|/n^3$, where E_0 is hydrogen's ground-state energy. (b) Use $F = ma$ to show that the angular velocity of a classical point charge held in orbit about a fixed point charge by the Coulomb force is given by $\omega = \sqrt{e^2/4\pi\varepsilon_0 mr^3}$. (c) Given that $r \cong n^2 a_0$, is this angular frequency equal to the minimum-jump photon frequency at either end of hydrogen's allowed energies?

85. The expectation value of the electron's kinetic energy in the hydrogen ground state equals the *magnitude* of the total energy (see Exercise 60). What must be the width of a cubic infinite well, in terms of a_0, for its ground state to have this same energy?

86. Spectral lines are fuzzy due to two effects: Doppler broadening and the uncertainty principle. The relative variation in wavelength due to the first effect (see Exercise 2.57) is given by

$$\frac{\Delta\lambda}{\lambda} \cong \frac{\sqrt{3k_BT/m}}{c}$$

where T is the temperature of the sample and m the mass of the particles emitting the light. The variation due to the second effect (see Exercise 4.72) is given by

$$\frac{\Delta\lambda}{\lambda} \cong \frac{\lambda}{4\pi c\,\Delta t}$$

where Δt is the typical transition time.

(a) Suppose the hydrogen in a star has a temperature of 5×10^4 K. Compare the broadening of these two effects for the first line in the Balmer series (i.e., $n_i = 3 \rightarrow n_f = 2$). Assume a transition time of 10^{-8} s. Which effect is more important?

(b) Under what condition(s) might the other effect predominate?

* **87. A Gravitational Analog:** A comet of 10^{14} kg mass describes a very elliptical orbit about a star of mass

3×10^{30} kg, with its minimum orbit radius, known as perihelion, being 10^{11} m and its maximum, or aphelion, 100 times as far. When at these minimum and maximum radii, its radius is, of course, not changing, so its radial kinetic energy is 0, and its kinetic energy is entirely rotational. From classical mechanics, rotational energy is given by $L^2/2I$, where I is the moment of inertia, which for a "point comet" is simply mr^2. (a) The comet's speed at perihelion is 6.2945×10^4 m/s. Calculate its angular momentum. (b) Verify that the sum of the gravitational potential energy and rotational energy are equal at perihelion and aphelion. (*Remember:* Angular momentum is conserved.) (c) Calculate the sum of the gravitational potential energy and rotational energy when the orbit radius is 50 times perihelion. How do you reconcile your answer with energy conservation? (d) If the comet had the same total energy but described a circular orbit, at what radius would it orbit, and how would its angular momentum compare with the value of part (a)? (e) Relate your observations to the division of kinetic energy in hydrogen electron orbits of the same n but different ℓ.

* **88. The Diatomic Molecule:** Exercise 80 discusses the idea of reduced mass μ. Classically or quantum mechanically, we can digest the behavior of a two-particle system into motion *of* the center of mass and motion *relative to* the center of mass. Our interest here is the relative motion, which becomes a one-particle problem if we merely use μ for the mass for that particle. Given this simplification, the quantum-mechanical results we have learned go a long way toward describing the diatomic molecule. To a good approximation, the force between the bound atoms is like an ideal spring whose potential energy is $\frac{1}{2}\kappa x^2$, where x is the *deviation* of the atomic separation r from its equilibrium value, which we designate with an a. Thus, $x = r - a$. Because the force is always along the line connecting the two atoms, it is a central force, so the angular parts of the Schrödinger equation are exactly as for hydrogen. (a) In the remaining radial equation (30), insert the potential energy $\frac{1}{2}\kappa x^2$ and replace the electron mass m with μ. Then, with the definition $f(r) \equiv rR(r)$, show that it can be rewritten as

$$-\frac{\hbar^2}{2\mu}\frac{d^2}{dr^2}f(r) + \frac{\hbar^2\ell(\ell+1)}{2\mu r^2}f(r) + \frac{1}{2}\kappa x^2 f(r) = E f(r)$$

With the further definition $g(x) \equiv f(r)$, show that this becomes

$$-\frac{\hbar^2}{2\mu}\frac{d^2}{dx^2}g(x) + \frac{\hbar^2\ell(\ell+1)}{2\mu(x+a)^2}g(x) + \frac{1}{2}\kappa x^2 g(x) = E g(x)$$

(b) Assume, as is quite often the case, that the deviation of the atoms from their equilibrium separation is very small compared to that separation—that is, x ≪ a. Show that your result from part (a) can be rearranged into a rather familiar form, from which it follows that

$$E = (n + \tfrac{1}{2})\hbar\sqrt{\frac{\kappa}{\mu}} + \frac{\hbar^2 \ell(\ell + 1)}{2\mu a^2} \qquad \begin{array}{l} n = 0, 1, 2, \dots \\ \ell = 0, 1, 2, \dots \end{array}$$

(c) Identify what each of the two terms represents physically.

* **89.** A spherical infinite well has potential energy

$$U(r) = \begin{cases} 0 & r < a \\ +\infty & r > a \end{cases}$$

Since this is a central force, we may use the Schrödinger equation in the form (30)—that is, just before the specific hydrogen atom potential energy is inserted. Show that the following is a solution

$$R(r) = \frac{A \sin br}{r}$$

Now apply the appropriate boundary conditions, and in so doing, find the allowed angular momenta and energies for solutions of this form.

* **90.** Residents of Flatworld—a two-dimensional world far, far away—have it easy. Although quantum mechanics of course applies in their world, the equations they must solve to understand atomic energy levels involve only two dimensions. In particular, the Schrödinger equation for the one-electron flatrogen atom is

$$-\frac{\hbar^2}{2m}\frac{1}{r}\frac{\partial}{\partial r}\left(r\frac{\partial}{\partial r}\right)\psi(r, \theta) - \frac{\hbar^2}{2m}\frac{1}{r^2}\frac{\partial^2}{\partial \theta^2}\psi(r, \theta)$$
$$+ U(r)\psi(r, \theta) = E\psi(r, \theta)$$

(a) Separate variables by trying a solution of the form $\psi(r, \theta) = R(r)\Theta(\theta)$, then dividing by $R(r)\Theta(\theta)$. Show that the θ equation can be written

$$\frac{d^2}{d\theta^2}\Theta(\theta) = C\Theta(\theta)$$

where C is a separation constant.

(b) To be physically acceptable, $\Theta(\theta)$ must be continuous, which, since it involves rotation about an axis, means that it must be periodic. What must be the sign of C?

(c) Show that a complex exponential is an acceptable solution for $\Theta(\theta)$.

(d) Imposing the periodicity condition, find the allowed values of C.

(e) What property is quantized according to the value of C?

(f) Obtain the radial equation.

(g) Given that $U(r) = -b/r$, show that a function of the form $R(r) = e^{-r/a}$ is a solution, but only if C is a certain one of its allowed values.

(h) Determine the value of a, and thus find the ground-state energy and wave function of the flatrogen atom.

Computational Exercises

91. The Polar Equation: Here we verify the claim leading to equations (27) while obtaining plots that agree with the functions $\Theta_{\ell,m_\ell}(\theta)$, given in Table 3. If we expand the derivatives in polar equation (26) and also divide both sides by $\sin^2\theta$, we obtain

$$\frac{\partial^2\Theta(\theta)}{\partial\theta^2} + \cot\theta\frac{\partial\Theta(\theta)}{\partial\theta} - C\Theta(\theta) = m_\ell^2 \csc^2\theta\,\Theta(\theta)$$

The symmetry of the hydrogen atom argues that the probability density should be the same as we move away from the xy-plane in either the positive or negative z-direction. This, in turn, demands that $\Theta_{\ell,m_\ell}(\theta)$ be either an odd or even function *about the xy-plane*, where $\theta = \pi/2$. Therefore, let us change variables, with $\beta \equiv \theta - \pi/2$, so that $\Theta_{\ell,m_\ell}(\beta)$ must either be 0 (odd) or have 0 slope (even) at $\beta = 0$ (i.e., the xy-plane). With this replacement, $\cos\theta = -\sin\beta$ and $\sin\theta = \cos\beta$, and the polar equation becomes

$$\frac{\partial^2\Theta(\beta)}{\partial\beta^2} - \tan\beta\frac{\partial\Theta(\beta)}{\partial\beta} - C\Theta(\beta) = m_\ell^2 \sec^2\beta\,\Theta(\beta)$$

(a) By writing the second derivative in the "finite difference" form and the first derivative similarly as $[\Theta(\beta) - \Theta(\beta - \Delta\beta)]/\Delta\beta$, show that the differential equation can be rewritten as

$$\Theta(\beta + \Delta\beta) = 2\Theta(\beta) - \Theta(\beta - \Delta\beta)$$
$$+ \Delta\beta \tan\beta\,[\Theta(\beta) - \Theta(\beta - \Delta\beta)]$$
$$+ \Delta\beta^2 (C + m_\ell^2 \sec^2\beta)\Theta(\beta)$$

(b) Just as in the one-dimensional linear cases, letting $\beta = \Delta\beta$ and choosing values for $\Theta(\Delta\beta)$ and $\Theta(0)$ would allow calculation of $\Theta(2\Delta\beta)$, then $\Theta(3\Delta\beta)$, then $\Theta(4\Delta\beta)$, and so on. For $\Delta\beta$, use 0.001. Now, choose the simplest values of C and m_ℓ allowed by equations (27), decide whether the corresponding function $\Theta_{\ell,m_\ell}(\theta)$ from Table 3 is an odd or even function of β, choose $\Theta(0)$ and $\Theta(\Delta\beta)$ accordingly, then plot Θ at all positive multiples of $\Delta\beta$ out to $\beta = 1.57$ (i.e., $\pi/2$). Afterward, vary C and m_ℓ by small amounts and describe the effect on Θ. Repeat the process for two other allowed values of C, and all allowed values of m_ℓ for each C, and verify that all these sets give physically acceptable solutions. Note that the symmetries make it unnecessary to plot negative values of β. For each set of C and m_ℓ, discuss how your Θ relates to the functions in Table 3. (*Note:* Plots for larger C may seem to have a slight divergence near the end. This isn't "real." Rather, it is due to the fact that our limited precision fails to accurately "cancel" the $\tan\beta$ and $\sec\beta$, which grow very rapidly near $\pi/2$.)

92. The Radial Equation: Here we verify the claim leading to equations (12) and (32) while obtaining plots with the appropriate radial behavior. Now, let us make some convenient changes of variables.

(a) With the definition $r \equiv a_0 x$, show that radial equation (31) can be rewritten as

$$-\frac{1}{x^2}\frac{d}{dx}\left(x^2\frac{d}{dx}\right)R(a_0x) + \frac{\ell(\ell+1)}{x^2}R(a_0x)$$

$$-\frac{ma_0}{2\pi\varepsilon_0\hbar^2}\frac{e^2}{x}R(a_0x) = \frac{2ma_0^2E}{\hbar^2}R(a_0x)$$

Then, with the definitions $R(a_0x) \equiv f(x)/a_0x$, $\widetilde{E} \equiv 2ma_0^2E/\hbar^2$, and (34), show that this becomes

$$-\frac{d^2f(x)}{dx^2} + \left[\frac{\ell(\ell+1)}{x^2} - \frac{2}{x}\right]f(x) = \widetilde{E}f(x)$$

When expressed in terms of the Bohr radius, the hydrogen ground-state energy of (12) is $-\hbar^2/2ma_0^2$. Thus, we now work in a system of units where the ground-state energy is $\widetilde{E} = -1$, and the definition $r \equiv a_0x$ means that an r of 1 Bohr radius corresponds to $x = 1$. Convenient units! Definitions $r \equiv a_0x$ and $R(a_0x) \equiv f(x)/a_0x$ also say that $f(x)$ is just $rR(r)$. This is important, for it means that $f(x)$ *must be 0 at the origin*.

(b) By writing the second derivative in the "finite difference" form, show that our simplified radial equation can be rewritten as

$$f(x + \Delta x) = 2f(x) - f(x - \Delta x)$$

$$+ \Delta x^2\left[\frac{\ell(\ell+1)}{x^2} - \frac{2}{x} - \widetilde{E}\right]f(x)$$

Letting $x = \Delta x$ and choosing values for $f(\Delta x)$ and $f(0)$ would allow calculation of $f(2\Delta x)$, then $f(3\Delta x)$, then $f(4\Delta x)$, and so on. For Δx, use 0.01. As noted, $f(0)$ has to be 0. Because normalization is not our concern, $f(\Delta x)$ isn't critical. Use 0.01. Now, choose the simplest values allowed by equations (12) and (32)— $\widetilde{E} = -1$ and $\ell = 0$— then plot $f(x)$ at all multiples of Δx out to $x = 10$. (*Note:* This is a numerical technique with limited precision, so even "correct" functions may appear to diverge, which is the reason for limiting x to 10 here.) Afterward, vary $\widetilde{E}$ and ℓ by small amounts, and describe the effect on $f(x)$. Repeat the process for two higher allowed values of $\widetilde{E}$ (remember the system of units!), and for all allowed values of ℓ for each $\widetilde{E}$, and verify that all these sets give physically acceptable solutions. (Here you should plot to higher x, perhaps 20 for the second energy and 30 for the third.) Bearing in mind that Figure 17 plots the *square* of $rR(r)$, discuss how your plots and those in Figure 17 compare.

Answers to Selected Exercises

21. 0.64 nm

23. 0.609, 0.196, 0.609

25. $107 \ \pi^2 \hbar^2 / 2mL^2$, at center

27. $-me^4 / 2\pi^4 \varepsilon_0^2 \hbar^2 n^2$

29. $n_i = 6, n_f = 3, 1.1 \times 10^{-6}$ m

31. $n = 6$, 13.2 eV, 10^5 K

33. 5.5×10^{-8} eV, 5×10^{-9}

37. 150°, 125.3°, 106.8°, 90°, 73.2°, 54.7°, 30°

45. −0.85 eV, magnitude of angular momentum: $0, \sqrt{2}\hbar, \sqrt{6}\hbar,$ $\sqrt{12}\hbar$, z-component of angular momentum: $-3\hbar, -2\hbar, -\hbar,$ $0, +\hbar, +2\hbar, +3\hbar$

51. (a) yes; (b) no

53. 0.212

57. 0.238

59. ellipse

61. no

67. 13.5 nm

71. (a) $\frac{1}{2}$; (b) $\frac{11}{16}$; (c) $\frac{203}{256}$

75. 0.00069 s, 1.9×10^{-6} m

77. $-1.23 \ a_0 e \cos[(1.89 \ \text{eV})t/\hbar]\hat{z}$, 120 ns

79. (a) $(4a_0^{5/2} \sqrt{\pi})^{-1} \ re^{-r/2a_0} \sin\theta \cos\phi,$ $(16a_0^5 \pi)^{-1} \ r^2 e^{-r/a_0} \sin^2\theta \cos^2\phi;$

(b) angular probabilities;

(d) $\psi_{2,1,+1} - \psi_{2,1,-1}$

83. −6.8 eV, 0.106 nm

85. 0.29 nm

87. (a) 6.2945×10^{29} kg · m²/s; (c) 3.9×10^{21} J; (d) 5×10^{12} m and 3.2×10^{30} kg · m²/s or about 5 times

89. $E_n = n^2 \pi^2 \hbar^2 / 2ma^2, L = 0$

Credits

20: C. R. Stroud, Jr., and Michael Noel, University of Rochester

Spin and Atomic Physics

Chapter Outline

It is often said that in quantum mechanics there are only three bound-state problems solvable "in closed form," meaning without numerical approximation techniques: the infinite well, the harmonic oscillator, and the hydrogen atom. Each is basically a one-particle problem—even hydrogen, where the proton contributes to the potential energy but is otherwise ignored. We must now confront the "unsolvable." Most real applications are multiparticle systems, and a logical place to start is an atom with multiple electrons. Still, it is true that once multiple electrons orbit the nucleus, the problem is mathematically unsolvable. It is impossible to solve exactly a Schrödinger equation that takes into account the potential energy shared by each electron with the nucleus *and* that shared between pairs of electrons. The prospect is not as bleak as it might seem. Principles we have already encountered will explain quite a bit. However, the first section of the chapter focuses on a "new" intrinsic property of *individual* particles: spin. Spin must be understood first because, while of little consequence in a one-particle problem, it is vital to understanding multiparticle systems. We introduce this property in the context of a search for evidence of angular momentum quantization in the hydrogen atom.

1   Evidence of Angular Momentum Quantization: A New Property

The claim that angular momentum is quantized, that a component may take on only certain values along an axis established by experiment, is startling. How do we substantiate it? The most famous evidence is based on a

Figure 1 A charge with angular momentum has a magnetic dipole moment.

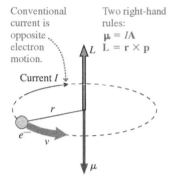

Conventional current is opposite electron motion.

Two right-hand rules:
$\boldsymbol{\mu} = I\mathbf{A}$
$\mathbf{L} = \mathbf{r} \times \mathbf{p}$

Current I

r

e

v

L

μ

simple hypothesis: A charged particle with an angular momentum forms a circulating electric current and thus a magnetic dipole moment, and if an orbiting electron's angular momentum is quantized, its magnetic dipole moment should be too. A magnetic field can exert a force on a magnetic dipole, so shouldn't the magnetic force on the atom in some sense be quantized?

Angular Momentum and Magnetic Dipole Moment

Imagine a classical electron orbiting counterclockwise in a circle of radius r, as depicted in Figure 1. Being negatively charged, it represents a clockwise (conventional) current of magnitude $I = e/T$, where e is the fundamental charge and T the period of revolution. Magnetic dipole moment is given by $\mu = IA$, where A is the area encircled by a current loop, so

$$\mu = IA = \frac{e}{T}\pi r^2 = \frac{e}{2\pi r/v}\pi r^2 = \frac{e}{2}vr = \frac{e}{2m_e}(m_e vr) = \frac{e}{2m_e}L$$

The last step uses the classical formula relating the angular momentum to the mass, speed, and radius of an orbiting point mass, and m_e is the electron mass. By the usual right-hand rules, the electron's angular momentum is up, and its magnetic dipole moment is down. Thus, we may write

$$\boldsymbol{\mu}_\mathbf{L} = -\frac{e}{2m_e}\mathbf{L} \tag{1}$$

(We will address the reason for the subscript on $\boldsymbol{\mu}$ a bit later.) This derivation is entirely classical, treating the electron as a particle. It is meant primarily to illustrate that a charged orbiting particle has a magnetic dipole moment. But it happens that the result is quantum-mechanically correct. It correctly describes the relationship between the angular momentum of an electron matter wave and its magnetic dipole moment.[1] We will soon see how to exploit this relationship to reveal angular momentum quantization via a nonuniform magnetic field, but first we need to understand a peculiar behavior that occurs in *any* magnetic field.

A magnetic dipole in a magnetic field experiences a torque $\boldsymbol{\tau} = \boldsymbol{\mu} \times \mathbf{B}$, and this causes the angular momentum to precess about the B-field line, as does a gyroscope about a gravitational field line. Suppose $\mathbf{B}$ points in the z-direction, as shown in Figure 2. By definition of the cross product, torque $\boldsymbol{\mu}_\mathbf{L} \times \mathbf{B}$ is perpendicular to $\mathbf{B}$ and $\boldsymbol{\mu}_\mathbf{L}$, which, because $\boldsymbol{\mu}_\mathbf{L}$ and $\mathbf{L}$ are opposite, means that it is also perpendicular to $\mathbf{L}$. The *change* in angular momentum $d\mathbf{L}$ by the rotational second law $\boldsymbol{\tau} = d\mathbf{L}/dt$ is in the direction of the torque, so it too is perpendicular to $\mathbf{B}$ and $\mathbf{L}$. Thus, the angular momentum vector maintains the same angle with $\mathbf{B}$, while its point describes a circle—it precesses. We obtain the rate of precession, known as the **Larmor frequency**, from Figure 2 as follows:

$$|\boldsymbol{\tau}| = \left|\boldsymbol{\mu}_\mathbf{L} \times \mathbf{B}\right| \rightarrow \left|\frac{d\mathbf{L}}{dt}\right| = \left|-\frac{e}{2m_e}\mathbf{L} \times \mathbf{B}\right|$$

[1] In the discussions that follow, several references to the angular momentum and magnetic moment really should be to their expectation values, but the conclusions are still valid.

Figure 2   A torque, $\boldsymbol{\mu} \times \mathbf{B}$, perpendicular to $\mathbf{L}$ causes $\mathbf{L}$ to precess.

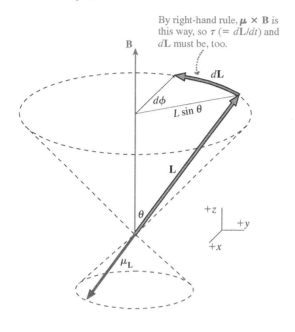

$$\frac{dL}{dt} = \frac{e}{2m_e} LB \sin \theta$$

$$\frac{(L \sin \theta)d\phi}{dt} = \frac{e}{2m_e} LB \sin \theta$$

$$\frac{d\phi}{dt} = \frac{eB}{2m_e} \qquad (2)$$

Overall, we see that while the z-component of $\boldsymbol{\mu}_\mathbf{L}$ is constant, its x- and y-components change continuously at a rate proportional to the B-field strength.

And where does this come into play? Whatever direction $\mathbf{B}$ points becomes a special axis, which we call the z-axis by convention. Only the component of $\boldsymbol{\mu}_\mathbf{L}$ along that axis is fixed, so we cannot simultaneously observe quantization of $\boldsymbol{\mu}_\mathbf{L}$ along another axis. Because $\boldsymbol{\mu}_\mathbf{L}$ and $\mathbf{L}$ are directly related, it follows that we cannot observe quantization of $\mathbf{L}$ along another axis. We have uncovered an intriguing truth: The theoretical conclusion arising from solving the hydrogen atom Schrödinger equation—that only one component of angular momentum is quantized—is in accord with our experimental inability to observe quantization of more than one component. All means of probing possible angular momentum quantization would employ some kind of inherently directional influence, so there is none that does not itself establish a preferred direction—that is, a z-axis.

Figure 3 Stern-Gerlach apparatus: An atom with a magnetic dipole moment passing through a nonuniform magnetic field.

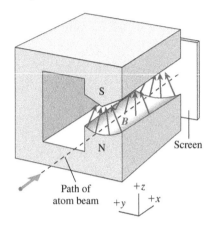

Figure 3 Stern-Gerlach apparatus: An atom with a magnetic dipole moment passing through a nonuniform magnetic field.

The Stern-Gerlach Experiment

In the Stern-Gerlach experiment, illustrated in Figure 3, the poles of a magnet are fashioned to produce a channel along which the field is nonuniform. In hopes of observing a "quantization of force," a beam of atoms is sent through the channel and deposited at a screen beyond. If force may take on only certain discrete values, then the atoms passing through the channel should be deflected to only certain discrete points on the screen.

The origin of the force on a magnetic dipole is illustrated in Figure 4, with the analogous electric case alongside for comparison. As we learn in electricity and magnetism, the net force on a dipole in a *uniform* field is 0, so we see why the Stern-Gerlach setup employs a nonuniform field. The expression for the force comes from the potential energy of a magnetic dipole $\boldsymbol{\mu}$ in an external magnetic field B.

$$U = -\boldsymbol{\mu} \cdot \mathbf{B} \tag{3}$$

In general, force is the negative gradient of the potential energy, so

$$\mathbf{F} = -\nabla(-\boldsymbol{\mu} \cdot \mathbf{B}) \tag{4}$$

Figure 4 Dipoles experience a net force only if the field is nonuniform.

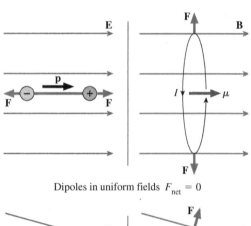

Dipoles in uniform fields $F_{\text{net}} = 0$

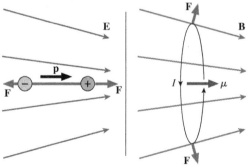

Dipoles in nonuniform fields $F_{\text{net}} \neq 0$

Magnetic dipole moment is an overall property of a current distribution—not a function of position—so again we see that if **B** were constant/uniform, the force would be zero. In the setup of Figure 8, the force reduces to[2]

$$\mathbf{F} = \mu_z \frac{\partial B_z}{\partial z} \hat{\mathbf{z}} \qquad (5)$$

We relate this to angular momentum via equation (1). Note especially, however, that because equation (5) involves only the z-component of $\boldsymbol{\mu}$, we need only the z-component of (1).

$$\mathbf{F} = \left(-\frac{e}{2m_e} L_z\right) \frac{\partial B_z}{\partial z} \hat{\mathbf{z}}$$

Even classically, an orbiting electron would possess a magnetic dipole moment and so should experience a force, but there is no classical reason for quantization along an axis established by the observer. Accordingly, for a given value of L, the z-component L_z could be any of the continuum of values from $-L$ to $+L$, causing atoms to be deflected vertically over a continuous band, as depicted in Figure 5. If L_z is quantized, however, the force should be, too. Using the quantization condition $L_z = m_\ell \hbar$,

$$\mathbf{F} = -\frac{e}{2m_e} m_\ell \hbar \frac{\partial B_z}{\partial z} \hat{\mathbf{z}} \qquad m_\ell = -\ell, \dots, +\ell$$

As we see, m_ℓ is the important factor governing the effect of the magnetic field, which is why it is known as the **magnetic quantum number**.

Now suppose hydrogen atoms whose electrons happen to be in $\ell = 1$ states pass through the channel, precessing as they travel. Because m_ℓ may take on three values, we should expect to see three lines at the screen, corresponding to an upward force ($m_\ell = -1$), a downward force ($m_\ell = +1$), and no force ($m_\ell = 0$), as shown in Figure 6. In general, we should expect to see $2\ell + 1$ lines—an odd number.

When a beam of hydrogen atoms was used with the Stern-Gerlach apparatus, however, *two* lines were seen.[3] Were this not baffling enough, ground-state hydrogen atoms have $\ell = 0$, so we would expect the experiment to show just a

Figure 8 Because a classical dipole might have any orientation in a field, the z-component of force would vary continuously.

Classical expectation
($L \neq 0$)

Figure 6 The force on a magnetic dipole depends on its component along the magnetic field, which is quantized.

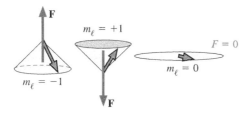

[2]Exercise 26 lays out the steps that obtain this force from orientation energy (3). An important element is that precession averages out lateral forces.

[3]In the original 1922 Stern-Gerlach experiment, two lines were seen, but this was using *silver* atoms. Having one $5s$ electron beyond a closed $n = 4$ shell, they should behave like atoms of $\ell = 0$. Phipps and Taylor repeated the experiment in 1925 using hydrogen to rule out any complication that multiple electrons might introduce.

Figure 7 No orbital motion implies no corresponding magnetic moment, but there is a magnetic moment, with two allowed components.

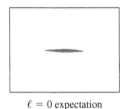

$\ell = 0$ expectation

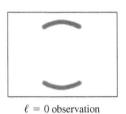

$\ell = 0$ observation

single undeflected line, corresponding to zero force, as in Figure 7. There is no cause for indignation—our deductions thus far are correct. Splitting in the $\ell = 1$ case does occur, but splitting even in the $\ell = 0$ case reveals the effects of a magnetic moment we haven't previously considered.

Spin

Electrons and other particles possess an **intrinsic magnetic dipole moment** and an inextricably related **intrinsic angular momentum**, and it is the quantization of this, rather than of the dipole moment related to the *orbital* angular momentum **L**, that is revealed in Figure 7. Intrinsic angular momentum is given the name **spin** and the symbol **S**. (*Remember:* **S** is an angular momentum.) An **intrinsic property** is one that is fundamental to a particle's nature, that cannot be taken away no matter how we might try. Indeed, intrinsic properties are what distinguish one fundamental particle from another—an electron from a photon, for instance. We are already familiar with two intrinsic properties: mass and charge. To these we now add spin.

Although an experimental fact, the existence of spin is not predicted nor is its nature explained via a nonrelativistic theory. It does arise naturally, but only from a quantum-mechanical theory that adheres to the principles of relativity. In particular, whereas the Schrödinger equation for a free particle rests on $E = p^2/2m$, a relativistically correct generalization must be based on $E^2 = p^2c^2 + m^2c^4$. Relativistic quantum mechanics is beyond the scope of the text, yet we need some quantitative grasp of spin, for it is crucial to understanding much of the world around us, including, notably, most of chemistry. Thus, we must be content with simply accepting the following results of relativistic quantum mechanics.

1. Analogous to the relationship $L = \sqrt{\ell(\ell + 1)}\,\hbar$ between *orbital* angular momentum and the dimensionless value ℓ, the magnitude of a particle's *intrinsic* angular momentum depends on a dimensionless value s.

$$S = \sqrt{s(s + 1)}\,\hbar \qquad (6)$$

Unlike ℓ, however, s is not a quantum number that may take on different values. Instead, it depends on the kind of particle. It is a given fixed value for a given kind of particle.

For the electron, which is our main object of interest, $s = \frac{1}{2}$. The proton also has $s = \frac{1}{2}$. The W^- particle, has $s = 1$. Other examples are given in Table 1. Importantly, it is s that we regard as *the measure* of this new intrinsic property. We say, for instance, that the electron is a spin-$\frac{1}{2}$ particle. This usage is common but rather ambiguous, for we have already called S, the intrinsic angular momentum, "spin," and from (6), its magnitude is $\sqrt{\frac{1}{2}(\frac{1}{2} + 1)}\,\hbar$ or $\frac{\sqrt{3}}{2}\hbar$, not $\frac{1}{2}$. We will find that the ambiguity rarely causes confusion.

2. A given particle's intrinsic magnetic dipole moment is related to its intrinsic angular momentum by

$$\boldsymbol{\mu}_S = g\frac{q}{2m}\mathbf{S} \qquad (7)$$

TABLE 1   Spins of some selected particles

Fermions		Bosons	
(Half-integral spin)		(Integral spin)	
Particle	s	**Particle**	s
Electron, e$^-$	$\frac{1}{2}$	Pion, π^0	0
Proton, p	$\frac{1}{2}$	Alpha particle, α (helium nucleus)	0
Neutron, n	$\frac{1}{2}$	Photon, γ	1
Neutrino, ν	$\frac{1}{2}$	Deuteron, d (bound n-p)	1
Omega, Ω^-	$\frac{3}{2}$	Graviton	2

where q is the particle's charge, m its mass, and g its **gyromagnetic ratio**. The subscript S is very important, for $\boldsymbol{\mu_S}$ is related to *intrinsic* angular momentum S, while $\boldsymbol{\mu_L}$ is related to *orbital* angular momentum L.

For the electron, g_e is 2 (not exactly, but close enough for most uses), and q is of course $-e$, so equation (7) gives

$$\text{electron: } \boldsymbol{\mu_S} = -\frac{e}{m_e}\mathbf{S} \qquad (8)$$

Note that it is only in the factor of 2 that this differs from equation (1) for orbital motion.

For the proton, g_p turns out to be 5.6. Its charge q is $+e$, so its $\boldsymbol{\mu_S}$ and $\mathbf{S}$ are parallel rather than opposite. Moreover, because $m_p \gg m_e$, the proton's magnetic moment is quite small, which is why the predominant effect in the Stern-Gerlach experiment is due to the hydrogen atom's electron.

3. Analogous to $L_z = m_\ell \hbar$, the z-component of intrinsic angular momentum is inherently quantized, taking on only those values given by

$$S_z = m_s \hbar \qquad m_s = -s, -s+1, \ldots, s-1, s \qquad (9)$$

The quantity m_s is a new quantum number, the **spin quantum number**. Its allowed values are from $-s$ to $+s$ in integral steps and are thus dependent on the kind of particle.

The W$^-$ particle has $s = 1$, so m_s may be -1, 0, or $+1$. For an electron, with $s = \frac{1}{2}$, m_s may take on only two values: $-\frac{1}{2}$ or $+\frac{1}{2}$. In another example of seemingly reckless term confusion, m_s is also often referred to as "spin." When m_s is $-\frac{1}{2}$, we say that the electron's spin is minus-one-half or that the electron is "spin down," and when m_s is $+\frac{1}{2}$, its spin is plus-one-half, or it is "spin up." But neither does this further leveling of the terminology cause trouble. These expressions must refer to allowed m_s values, for s and S are fixed—$\frac{1}{2}$ and $\frac{\sqrt{3}}{2}\hbar$, respectively.

Now let us return to the Stern-Gerlach experiment. For $\ell = 0$, the *orbital* magnetic dipole moment $\boldsymbol{\mu_L}$ is 0, so it shouldn't be subject to a force, but there should still be a force on the *intrinsic* magnetic dipole moment. Therefore, in equation (5) we insert (8) rather than (1) and (9) instead of $L_z = m_\ell \hbar$.

$$\mathbf{F} = \left(-\frac{e}{m_e}S_z\right)\frac{\partial B_z}{\partial z}\hat{\mathbf{z}} = -\frac{e}{m_e}m_s\hbar\frac{\partial B_z}{\partial z}\hat{\mathbf{z}} \qquad m_s = -s,\ldots,+s \qquad (10)$$

Because m_s takes on two values for an electron, the force should be restricted to two values. There should indeed be two lines, corresponding to $m_s = -\frac{1}{2}$ and $m_s = +\frac{1}{2}$. (Section 8 discusses the case of $\ell \neq 0$, where *both* orbital and intrinsic magnetic moments come into play and more lines would be seen.)

EXAMPLE 1

Determine the acceleration of a hydrogen atom in a magnetic field whose rate of change is 10 T/m.

SOLUTION

Equation (10) applies, where the electron's spin quantum number m_s may be either of the two values $\pm\frac{1}{2}$.

$$F = -\frac{e}{m_e}m_s\hbar\frac{\partial B_z}{\partial z}$$

$$= -\frac{1.6 \times 10^{-19}\,\text{C}}{9.11 \times 10^{-31}\,\text{kg}}\left(\pm\frac{1}{2}\right)(1.055 \times 10^{-34}\,\text{J}\cdot\text{s})(10\,\text{T/m})$$

$$= \pm 9.3 \times 10^{-23}\,\text{N}$$

Although the force is on the electron's magnetic moment, the entire atom accelerates.

$$a = \frac{F}{m} = \frac{9.3 \times 10^{-23}\,\text{N}}{1.67 \times 10^{-27}\,\text{kg}} = 5.5 \times 10^4\,\text{m/s}^2$$

Exercise 28 investigates the actual distance the atomic beam would be deflected under typical conditions.

The term *spin* suggests that an electron has angular momentum due to spinning on its axis, in addition to that due to its orbit about the nucleus, as does Earth in its orbit of the Sun. Helpful though the spinning sphere notion may be, the intrinsic angular momentum and magnetic dipole moment of an electron cannot be understood on the basis of a spinning charged object. *Spin is nonclassical to its very roots.* No assumptions of mass and charge densities circulating about an axis can explain the observations (see Exercise 25). Spin has nothing whatever to do with spatial motion, something that could presumably be altered—it is truly intrinsic. Indeed, this would seem necessary in view of the strong possibility, suggested by the absence of experimental evidence of a finite radius, that the electron occupies no space!

Even accepting *point* angular momentum—angular momentum without spatial extent—the reader may wonder how such an inherently quantized, non-position-dependent property can be mated to the other aspect of a particle's state that we have thus far represented with a wave function. Although there are alternatives,[4] we will find it sufficient simply to keep these two aspects grouped but separate. For an electron in an atom, the quantum numbers n, ℓ, and m_ℓ are said to specify the electron's **spatial state** (i.e., its wave function), while the quantum number m_s specifies its **spin state**. Its state is then completely specified by the *four* quantum numbers n, ℓ, m_ℓ, and m_s and may be represented as

$$\psi_{n,\,\ell,\,m_\ell,\,m_s} = \psi_{n,\,\ell,\,m_\ell}(r, \theta, \phi)\, m_s \tag{11}$$

Because it can take on only two values, related to two opposite components, we often find it convenient to use an arrow for m_s.

$$\psi_{n,\,\ell,\,m_\ell,\,+\frac{1}{2}} = \psi_{n,\,\ell,\,m_\ell}(r, \theta, \phi)\uparrow \qquad \text{Spin up}$$

$$\psi_{n,\,\ell,\,m_\ell,\,-\frac{1}{2}} = \psi_{n,\,\ell,\,m_\ell}(r, \theta, \phi)\downarrow \qquad \text{Spin down} \tag{12}$$

Neither m_s nor the arrow should be regarded as multiplying $\psi_{n,\,\ell,\,m_\ell}(r, \theta, \phi)$ in the usual sense, because spatial and spin states are of entirely different character. But spin is a necessary part of the overall description of the state, so it is fair to place the symbol alongside the wave function.

Figure 8 illustrates the electron's quantized intrinsic angular momentum and magnetic dipole moment. That it has a dipole moment means that it is, by nature, much like a bar magnet, indicated by the north and south poles. The dipole moment is opposite the intrinsic angular momentum $\mathbf{S}$, whose magnitude is $\frac{\sqrt{3}}{2}\hbar$. And just as the orbital angular momentum $\mathbf{L}$ may be found to make only certain angles with the z-axis in the hydrogen atom an experiment to determine the z-component of $\mathbf{S}$ has only two possible outcomes. Applications that exploit this up-or-down trait of electron spin are countless.

Figure 8   The two possible spin states of an electron.

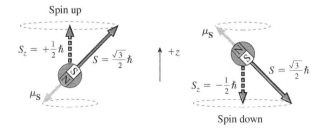

[4]A matrix can replace the wave function, and spin just doubles the number of elements.

REAL-WORLD EXAMPLE ELECTRON SPIN RESONANCE

An effect used as an integrative tool in many sciences is **electron spin resonance** (ESR). In a magnetic field, an electron, with its built-in bar magnet of only two allowed orientations, has two possible energies. A photon of the correct, or "resonant," frequency can excite a transition from the lower-energy orientation to the higher one. In ESR, a material—in particular, a specific atom, ion, or molecule—is subjected to an external magnetic field, electromagnetic radiation in the microwave range is applied, and absorption of the radiation is monitored as either its frequency or the external field is varied. A marked increase in absorption indicates that the photons are of the resonant frequency. This frequency is proportional to the strength of the magnetic field experienced by the material's electrons, which usually includes the external field and fields internal to the material. ESR can be used to study the internal fields, or, for a material in which the effects of these fields are well known, it may be used merely to reveal the presence of that material. To best grasp the basics of ESR, let us analyze a simple case.

Applying the Physics

A magnetic field is applied to a material in which an electron is able to flip its spin orientation and in which internal fields are negligible. (a) If an electron is initially in the low-energy orientation, which way is its spin? (b) Electromagnetic radiation of frequency f is now applied. What magnetic field strength would lead to resonant absorption? (c) Evaluate this field for $f = 9.5$ GHz, a typical ESR frequency.

SOLUTION

(a) The external field establishes the z-axis, so we write $\mathbf{B} = B\,\hat{\mathbf{z}}$. Orientation energy (3) thus becomes

$$U = -\mu_z B$$

As we learn in electricity and magnetism, a dipole is in a low-energy state when it is aligned with a field, which, in this case, is when μ_z is positive. Equation (8) tells us that the spin of an electron is opposite its magnetic dipole moment, so the low-energy state has the spin opposite the field. We say that the electron is spin down, relative to the externally imposed z-axis.

(b) As we did to obtain equation (10), we replace μ_z in the orientation energy of part (a) by $(-e/m_e)S_z$ and use quantization condition (9).

$$U = \frac{e}{m_e} m_s \hbar B$$

Because m_s is restricted to $\pm\frac{1}{2}$, this gives two orientation energies whose difference is $e\hbar B/m_e$. The photon must provide this energy difference.

$$hf = \frac{e}{m_e}\hbar B \quad \Rightarrow \quad B = \frac{2\pi m_e f}{e}$$

(c) Inserting values,

$$B = \frac{2\pi(9.11 \times 10^{-31}\,\text{kg})(9.5 \times 10^9\,\text{Hz})}{(1.6 \times 10^{-19}\,\text{C})} = 0.34\,\text{T}$$

ESR is useful only when the material under study has an unpaired electron. This means that the *spatial* state occupied by the electron is not also occupied by another electron with opposite spin. If it were, then neither electron would be able to flip its spin, for this would put two electrons in the same individual-particle state. As we soon see, this would violate a fundamental principle of quantum mechanics.

Although there are materials in which the internal fields are negligible (useful for apparatus calibration), the real applications of ESR involve internal fields, such as those produced by the electron's own orbit (discussed in Section 6) and those of the atomic nuclei. Analysis is naturally more complicated, but the added detail makes the technique more discriminating. Many of the so-called transition elements (see Section 4) have unpaired electrons and are common targets of ESR in physics and chemistry. Biological applications often target molecules known as free radicals.

Spin and Degeneracy

By simple arguments, spin should increase the degeneracy in the hydrogen atom. Were the energy of the atom independent of m_s, then for each set of n, ℓ, and m_ℓ, there would be two possible values of m_s and thus two different states with the same energy. Doubling the number of states with the same n would increase the degeneracy from n^2 to $2n^2$. However, with spin comes the possibility of new interactions in the atom, which destroy some of the symmetry and so *reduce* the degeneracy. Several sections later in this chapter are devoted to studying these more complex interactions.

Electron Spin: A Two-State System

We have said that an electron can be either spin up or spin down. It is true that an experiment must measure one or the other. But as our acquaintance with the fascinating nature of quantum mechanics tells us, this doesn't mean that the spin *is* either up or down before such a measurement. For example, if an electron's spin is measured as up along the z-axis, then it certainly is up along the z-axis. But a subsequent measurement along, say, the y-axis might find it either up or down along that axis, in fact with equally probability, as the symmetry about z in Figure 8 suggests. In effect, the measurement along the z-axis leaves the electron in a state that is an equal combination/superposition of spin up and spin down along the y-axis. The y-component S_y is *not* 0—that value can *never* be obtained—but the values that are allowed, $+\frac{1}{2}\hbar$ and $-\frac{1}{2}\hbar$, are equally likely.

In general, a spin state may be an arbitrarily weighted superposition of spin up and spin down along an axis, and one promising application is to quantum computing. In conventional digital computing, data bits—zeros and ones—must be stored. Any "two-state device," like a simple on-off switch, might suffice. But quantum computing uses **qubits** (quantum bits), in which the state is an arbitrary superposition of two states. One of the first ways studied to produce a quantum logic gate—a basic element of quantum computing—used the spin of a trapped atom's lone valence electron as a qubit. Yes, a measurement must yield either up or down, but the number of combinations is infinite. While this increase in information makes quantum computing intriguing, it also brings with it a problem. Noise is much more likely to obscure a continuously variable combination than a simple on or off. (See Progress and Applications at the end of this chapter for further discussion.)

The Spin of the Photon

Although the spin-$\frac{1}{2}$ electron is the central player in the chapter, the spin of the photon deserves some attention. Having $s = 1$, the photon is spin-1. A consequence is that if an atom undergoes a transition in which a photon is produced, there is a limit on how much the atom's angular momentum may change—its angular momentum quantum number may change by no more than 1. This restriction manifests itself in the **selection rules** that often arise in discussions of spectral emissions.

2 Identical Particles

As we know, quantum mechanics limits the knowledge we may have of a one-particle system. It places further limitations on our knowledge of multiparticle systems. In Section 3, we will see that these limitations are inextricably linked to spin, but their foundation can be understood without it. To simplify things, we put spin aside for the time being.

Imagine that two identical particles share the same space. Whether we regard them as two particles, two waves, or a single combined wave, it is still reasonable to speak of two "particles," in that we may isolate a system that has twice the intrinsic properties of a known fundamental particle. For instance, a system of two electrons has a charge of $2 \times (-1.6 \times 10^{-19}\,\text{C})$ no matter how we regard it. By "share the same space," we mean that the particles are not physically isolated. There is some region of space in which they "overlap," a region where either particle may be found. By this definition, two electrons rattling around in a box share the same space.

To proceed further we need a two-particle Schrödinger equation. In one dimension, the Schrödinger equation for a single particle depends, of course, on x. To specify kinetic and potential energies in the two-particle case, it is reasonable that we would need an x_1 and an x_2. Still, we seek a true two-particle equation in which the particles are not treated completely independently but are described by a single wave function $\psi(x_1, x_2)$, much as a function describing an electromagnetic wave might represent many photons. The following has passed the experimental test:

$$\left(-\frac{\hbar^2}{2m}\frac{\partial^2}{\partial x_1^2} - \frac{\hbar^2}{2m}\frac{\partial^2}{\partial x_2^2}\right)\psi(x_1, x_2) + U(x_1, x_2)\psi(x_1, x_2) = E\psi(x_1, x_2) \qquad (13)$$

where E is the energy of the entire two-particle system.

As a simple context in which to confront the central point in multiparticle systems, let us consider an infinite well in which the particles exert no forces on each other. (Students interested in the details of separating variables and obtaining solutions in this case should read A Closer Look: Two Particles in a Box.)

A Closer Look **Two Particles in a Box**

To solve equation (13), we apply the trusty separation of variables, assuming that

$$\psi(x_1, x_2) = \psi_a(x_1)\psi_b(x_2) \qquad (14)$$

where ψ_a and ψ_b are in general different functions. As usual, we insert the product into (13), then divide by it.

$$\frac{\left(-\dfrac{\hbar^2}{2m}\psi_b(x_2)\dfrac{\partial^2 \psi_a(x_1)}{\partial x_1^2} - \dfrac{\hbar^2}{2m}\psi_a(x_1)\dfrac{\partial^2 \psi_b(x_2)}{\partial x_2^2}\right)}{\psi_a(x_1)\psi_b(x_2)}$$

$$+ \frac{U(x_1, x_2)\psi_a(x_1)\psi_b(x_2)}{\psi_a(x_1)\psi_b(x_2)} = \frac{E\psi_a(x_1)\psi_b(x_2)}{\psi_a(x_1)\psi_b(x_2)}$$

Now canceling,

$$\frac{-\hbar^2}{2m}\frac{1}{\psi_a(x_1)}\frac{\partial^2 \psi_a(x_1)}{\partial x_1^2} + \frac{-\hbar^2}{2m}\frac{1}{\psi_b(x_2)}\frac{\partial^2 \psi_b(x_2)}{\partial x_2^2}$$
$$+ U(x_1, x_2) = E \qquad (15)$$

As in the one-particle case, the potential energy dictates the solution. Equation (15) as it stands does not have x_1 and x_2 separate, because $U(x_1, x_2)$, in general, need not be a sum of separate functions of x_1 and x_2. The potential energy associated with an internal force between two particles in a system is usually a function of their separation, $|x_1 - x_2|$, and does not separate into a sum. For example, the electrostatic potential energy shared by two electrons is

$$U(x_1, x_2) = \frac{e^2}{(4\pi\varepsilon_0)|x_1 - x_2|} \neq U_1(x_1) + U_2(x_2)$$

If, on the other hand, the particles experience only external forces, the system's potential energy is a sum. (In the case of gravity, for instance, it would be $mgy_1 + mgy_2$.) We consider only external forces here. It is true that this simplification, strictly speaking, precludes applications to charged particles, but it streamlines our investigation of the "new" feature of multiparticle systems most important to us in this section. For two particles exerting no force on one another, experiencing only the external force at infinite walls, equation (15) becomes

$$\frac{-\hbar^2}{2m}\frac{1}{\psi_a(x_1)}\frac{\partial^2 \psi_a(x_1)}{\partial x_1^2} + \frac{-\hbar^2}{2m}\frac{1}{\psi_b(x_2)}\frac{\partial^2 \psi_b(x_2)}{\partial x_2^2}$$
$$+ U(x_1) + U(x_2) = E$$

or

$$\underbrace{\left(\frac{-\hbar^2}{2m}\frac{1}{\psi_a(x_1)}\frac{\partial^2 \psi_a(x_1)}{\partial x_1^2} + U(x_1)\right)}_{C_1}$$

$$+ \underbrace{\left(\frac{-\hbar^2}{2m}\frac{1}{\psi_b(x_2)}\frac{\partial^2 \psi_b(x_2)}{\partial x_2^2} + U(x_2)\right)}_{C_2} = E \qquad (16)$$

where U is the infinite well potential energy. By the usual arguments, each term in parentheses must be a constant, which we have designated C_1 and C_2. Setting each term to its constant yields a differential equation identical to the one-particle infinite well Schrödinger equation, except that E is replaced by C. Therefore, we can simply write down the same solutions, with the corresponding replacements.

$$\psi_n(x_1) = \sqrt{\frac{2}{L}}\sin\frac{n\pi x_1}{L} \qquad C_1 = \frac{n^2\pi^2\hbar^2}{2mL^2}$$

$$\text{and} \qquad \psi_{n'}(x_2) = \sqrt{\frac{2}{L}}\sin\frac{n'\pi x_2}{L}, \qquad C_2 = \frac{n'^2\pi^2\hbar^2}{2mL^2}$$

The quantum numbers need not be the same, so we use an n and an n', and because they serve equally well to distinguish the individual-particle functions, we dispense with the earlier a and b. Wave function (14) becomes

$$\psi(x_1, x_2) = \psi_n(x_1)\psi_{n'}(x_2)$$

and inserting C_1 and C_2 into (16) yields E.

$$\frac{n^2\pi^2\hbar^2}{2mL^2} + \frac{n'^2\pi^2\hbar^2}{2mL^2} = E$$

Perhaps not surprisingly, the total energy of the two-particle system is the sum of the individual infinite well energies in states n and n'.

For two particles in an infinite well, equation (13) is satisfied by a simple product of particle-in-a-box wave functions for each particle, each with its own quantum number.

$$\psi(x_1, x_2) = \psi_n(x_1)\psi_{n'}(x_2) \quad \text{where} \quad \psi_n(x) = \sqrt{\frac{2}{L}}\sin\frac{n\pi x}{L} \qquad (17)$$

Before proceeding, we note some important nomenclature. Because the term *state* can be ambiguous, the term **individual-particle state** is often used for a state occupied by a single particle, such as $\psi_n(x_1)$, while *multiparticle state* usually means the state of the whole system, as in $\psi(x_1, x_2)$.

A Not-So-Small Problem

Let us examine (17) for the case $n = 4$ and $n' = 3$. The system's multiparticle wave function would be

$$\psi(x_1, x_2) = \psi_4(x_1)\psi_3(x_2) = \frac{2}{L}\sin\frac{4\pi x_1}{L}\sin\frac{3\pi x_2}{L}$$

We would expect the square to give us the probability density $P(x_1, x_2)$ for this two-particle system:

$$P(x_1, x_2) = \psi^2(x_1, x_2) = \frac{4}{L^2}\sin^2\frac{4\pi x_1}{L}\sin^2\frac{3\pi x_2}{L} \qquad (18)$$

Figure 9 Probability densities of the third and fourth infinite well states.

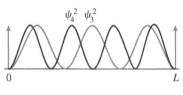

Probability densities

As a logical generalization of its meaning in the one-particle case, this would be the probability of simultaneously finding particle 1 within a unit distance at x_1 and particle 2 within a unit distance at x_2—that is, probability/(distance$_1$ · distance$_2$). If we integrate (18) over both x_1 and x_2 between limits 0 and L, we obtain a sensible result: The probability of finding both particles *somewhere* within the box is 1.

Figure 9 shows the *individual* probability densities for the fourth and third particle-in-a-box energy levels, and Figure 10 shows the total probability

Figure 10 An asymmetric probability density.

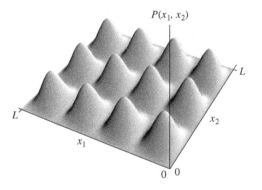

density (18) as a function of the two variables x_1 and x_2. (The box is not two dimensional. Perpendicular axes for x_1 and x_2 allow us to distinguish them, but they are really parallel.) Note how the behaviors with respect to x_1 and x_2 differ. There are four bumps as a function of x_1 but only three as a function of x_2. In particular, we see that, independent of the value of x_2, the probability of finding particle 1 at the center of the box is 0. Equation (18) agrees. Inserting $x_1 = \frac{1}{2}L$,

$$P(\tfrac{1}{2}L, x_2) = \frac{4}{L^2} \sin^2 \frac{4\pi(\frac{1}{2}L)}{L} \sin^2 \frac{3\pi x_2}{L} = 0$$

The probability of finding particle 2 at the center is nonzero in general, depending on the value of x_1.

$$P(x_1, \tfrac{1}{2}L) = \frac{4}{L^2} \sin^2 \frac{4\pi x_1}{L} \sin^2 \frac{3\pi(\frac{1}{2}L)}{L} = \frac{4}{L^2} \sin^2 \frac{4\pi x_1}{L} \neq 0$$

This cannot be! To claim that particle 2 may be found at a given location but that Particle 1 may never be found there is to claim what cannot be known! Particles 1 and 2 are *identical*. They bear no distinctive label, they cannot be watched to keep track of them separately, and their wave functions share the same space. Identical particles sharing the same space are said to be **indistinguishable**. If an experiment is performed and a particle found, we simply cannot know which particle it is. Because it is impossible to verify any asymmetry in the behaviors of the two particles, we demand that the probability density obey the following restriction:

> Probability density must be unchanged if the labels of indistinguishable particles are switched.

The reader may be uneasy with this restriction. It is one thing to alter a theory because it renders predictions that can be experimentally verified as *false*, but it is quite another to alter it merely because it renders predictions that *cannot be verified* experimentally (because we can't know which particle we've found). However, the restriction is necessary. The far-reaching and verifiable consequences we soon discuss cannot be explained otherwise.

How might we alter $P(x_1, x_2)$ so that switching particle labels 1 and 2 leaves it unchanged? We might try adding the same function with the 1 and 2 switched.

$$P(x_1, x_2) \stackrel{?}{=} \frac{4}{L^2} \sin^2 \frac{4\pi x_1}{L} \sin^2 \frac{3\pi x_2}{L} + \frac{4}{L^2} \sin^2 \frac{4\pi x_2}{L} \sin^2 \frac{3\pi x_1}{L}$$

This is indeed symmetric—the same function—under interchange of the particle labels. But it is unacceptable because, quite simply, it isn't the square of a solution of the Schrödinger equation. To produce a symmetric probability density, we must start with the wave function. There are two ways of modifying the product solution in equation (17) to meet the requirement:

$$\psi_S(x_1, x_2) \equiv \psi_n(x_1)\psi_{n'}(x_2) + \psi_{n'}(x_1)\psi_n(x_2) \qquad \text{Symmetric} \quad (19)$$

$$\psi_A(x_1, x_2) \equiv \psi_n(x_1)\psi_{n'}(x_2) - \psi_{n'}(x_1)\psi_n(x_2) \qquad \text{Antisymmetric} \quad (20)$$

Because the Schrödinger equation is a *linear* differential equation (for which sums and differences of solutions are also solutions), both of these are as valid mathematically as (17). But in solutions (19) and (20), the notion that one of the particles occupies state n and the other state n' is abandoned. Both are *combinations* of particle 1 in state n, particle 2 in state n' and of particle 1 in state n', particle 2 in state n. Our immediate concern is whether wave functions (19) and (20) lead to a symmetric probability density. A simple argument shows that they do. If we switch the particle labels, the symmetric wave function is unchanged, while the antisymmetric switches sign—hence their names. In neither case would the *square* change. Writing out the probability densities clarifies the point.

$$P_S(x_1, x_2) = \psi_S^2(x_1, x_2) = \psi_n^2(x_1)\psi_{n'}^2(x_2)$$
$$+ \psi_{n'}^2(x_1)\psi_n^2(x_2) + 2\psi_n(x_1)\psi_{n'}(x_2)\psi_{n'}(x_1)\psi_n(x_2)$$
$$P_A(x_1, x_2) = \psi_A^2(x_1, x_2) = \psi_n^2(x_1)\psi_{n'}^2(x_2)$$
$$+ \psi_{n'}^2(x_1)\psi_n^2(x_2) - 2\psi_n(x_1)\psi_{n'}(x_2)\psi_{n'}(x_1)\psi_n(x_2)$$

Interchanging particle labels 1 and 2 leaves both expressions unchanged. For convenience, we refer to these probability densities as "symmetric" or "antisymmetric"—that is, according to the corresponding *wave function*—but both probability densities are symmetric. Note that only the probability density is required to be symmetric, for, as always, the wave functions themselves cannot be observed.

Both the symmetric and antisymmetric probability densities preserve certain features of the *un*symmetrized probability density (18). When properly normalized, they yield 1 when integrated over all values of x_1 and x_2, and they may be interpreted as a probability of finding particle 1 within a unit distance at x_1 and particle 2 within a unit distance at x_2. Now, however, the probability is the same if 1 and 2 are switched.

To illustrate similarities and differences, Figure 11 shows $P_S(x_1, x_2)$ and $P_A(x_1, x_2)$ for our special case $n = 4$, $n' = 3$. Like the unsymmetrized probability

Figure 11 Symmetric and antisymmetric probability densities when $n = 3$ and $n = 4$ states are occupied.

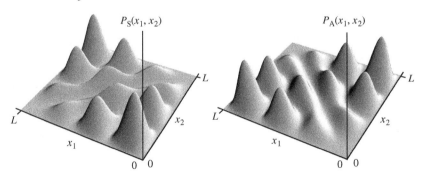

density of Figure 10, they have 12 bumps, but in both P_S and P_A, they are divided symmetrically between x_1 and x_2. Nevertheless, there is a crucial distinction between P_S and P_A. The largest values of P_S occur where the particles are close together, near the line $x_1 = x_2$. On the other hand, P_A has its largest bumps when x_1 is near L and x_2 near 0 and when x_1 is near 0 and x_2 near L. It is *identically zero* when $x_1 = x_2$. It may be said that the particles are, on average, farther apart in an antisymmetric spatial state than in a symmetric one.

EXAMPLE 2

Two particles in a box occupy the $n = 4$ and $n' = 3$ states. Equations (19) and (20) say that the symmetric and antisymmetric wave functions are of the form

$$\psi_S(x_1, x_2) = \frac{\sqrt{2}}{L} \left(\sin\frac{4\pi x_1}{L} \sin\frac{3\pi x_2}{L} + \sin\frac{3\pi x_1}{L} \sin\frac{4\pi x_2}{L} \right)$$

$$\psi_A(x_1, x_2) = \frac{\sqrt{2}}{L} \left(\sin\frac{4\pi x_1}{L} \sin\frac{3\pi x_2}{L} - \sin\frac{3\pi x_1}{L} \sin\frac{4\pi x_2}{L} \right)$$

The normalization constant $\frac{\sqrt{2}}{L}$ ensures that the total probability of finding both particles somewhere in the box is 1. (Verification is left as an exercise.) For both ψ_S and ψ_A, calculate the probability that both particles would be found in the left half of the box, between 0 and $\frac{1}{2}L$. Then, compare with the case where the symmetrization requirement is ignored—that is, where the particles are treated completely independently. The following integrals will be helpful (j and k are integers):

$$\int_0^{L/2} \sin^2\frac{j\pi x}{L}\,dx = \frac{L}{4}$$

$$\int_0^{L/2} \sin\frac{k\pi x}{L}\sin\frac{j\pi x}{L}\,dx = \frac{L}{2\pi}\left(\frac{\sin[\pi(k-j)/2]}{k-j} - \frac{\sin[\pi(k+j)/2]}{k+j} \right)$$

SOLUTION

We integrate the square of the wave function only over values of x_1 and x_2 between 0 and $\frac{1}{2}L$. Using a $\pm$ to treat both cases at once, we have

$$\text{probability} = \int_0^{L/2}\left[\frac{\sqrt{2}}{L}\left(\sin\frac{4\pi x_1}{L}\sin\frac{3\pi x_2}{L} \pm \sin\frac{3\pi x_1}{L}\sin\frac{4\pi x_2}{L} \right) \right]^2 dx_1\,dx_2$$

$$= \frac{2}{L^2}\int_0^{L/2}\sin^2\frac{4\pi x_1}{L}dx_1 \int_0^{L/2}\sin^2\frac{3\pi x_2}{L}dx_2 + \frac{2}{L^2}\int_0^{L/2}\sin^2\frac{3\pi x_1}{L}dx_1 \int_0^{L/2}\sin^2\frac{4\pi x_2}{L}dx_2$$

$$\pm\,2\frac{2}{L^2}\int_0^{L/2}\sin\frac{4\pi x_1}{L}\sin\frac{3\pi x_1}{L}dx_1 \int_0^{L/2}\sin\frac{3\pi x_2}{L}\sin\frac{4\pi x_2}{L}dx_2$$

The first four integrals evaluate to $L/4$, and the last two evaluate to $4L/7\pi$. Thus

$$\text{probability} = \frac{2}{L^2}\frac{L}{4}\frac{L}{4} + \frac{2}{L^2}\frac{L}{4}\frac{L}{4} \pm \frac{4}{L^2}\frac{4L}{7\pi}\frac{4L}{7\pi}$$

$$= \frac{1}{4} \pm 0.132 = \begin{cases} 0.382 & \text{Symmetric} \\ 0.118 & \text{Antisymmetric} \end{cases}$$

Ignoring symmetrization, the probability of either particle individually being found in the box's left half would be $\frac{1}{2}$, so the probability of both being there would be $\frac{1}{4}$. The symmetrization requirement yields two states: the symmetric, in which the probability is greater than $\frac{1}{4}$, and the antisymmetric, in which it is less. Note that the calculated probabilities agree qualitatively with Figure 11.

Before moving on, we note that ψ_S and ψ_A have equal energy, the same as that of the unsymmetrized wave function (see Exercise 34). Accordingly, it would seem equally likely to find the system in the antisymmetric state as in the symmetric. But this wouldn't be the case if the particles exerted forces on one another. Were the two particles electrons, the antisymmetric state would be of lower energy, because, as Example 2 verifies, particles in such a state are less likely to be found close together—the repulsive energy would be reduced. This argument holds even though the interparticle potential energy renders the Schrödinger equation unsolvable except by numerical methods.

Including Spin

To ensure a symmetric probability density, it is not sufficient to consider just the spatial state, related to particles being found at given *locations*. We must ensure that the probability of finding them at given locations *and in given spin states* is symmetric under exchange of labels. Equations (19) and (20) may be generalized as follows:

$$\psi_S \equiv \psi_n(1)\psi_{n'}(2) + \psi_{n'}(1)\psi_n(2) \qquad \text{Symmetric} \qquad (21)$$

$$\psi_A \equiv \psi_n(1)\psi_{n'}(2) - \psi_{n'}(1)\psi_n(2) \qquad \text{Antisymmetric} \qquad (22)$$

Here, n represents all quantum numbers needed to specify the individual-particle state, and the arguments of the functions are the particles' labels, standing in for coordinates in whatever coordinate system is appropriate. For example, to represent an electron with spin up in a hydrogen's ground state, n is actually the set $\{n, \ell, m_\ell, m_s\} = \{1, 0, 0, +\frac{1}{2}\}$, and, in accord with equations (12), $\psi_n(2)$ would mean $\psi_{1,0,0}(r_2, \theta_2, \phi_2)\uparrow$.

We use the term **exchange symmetry** to refer to the character of a state when particle labels are exchanged. If it doesn't change sign when labels are switched, its exchange symmetry is symmetric; if it changes sign, its exchange symmetry is antisymmetric.

3 The Exclusion Principle

We are now ready for one of the central ideas of the chapter: Why is spin so crucial to the behavior of multiparticle systems? It is fundamental to nature that a system of multiple indistinguishable particles will be in a multiparticle state of definite exchange symmetry, and *whether it is symmetric or antisymmetric depends on the spin of the system's particles*. All fundamental particles have spin s that is either integral or half-integral, and this divides them into two categories. Theory predicts and experiment verifies that:

> **Bosons** Particles for which $s = 0, 1, 2, \ldots$ manifest a symmetric multiparticle state
> **Fermions** Particles for which $s = \frac{1}{2}, \frac{3}{2}, \frac{5}{2}, \ldots$ manifest an antisymmetric multiparticle state

Table 1 in Section 1 gives several examples of bosons and fermions. It also reveals that all the familiar building blocks of nature—electrons, protons, and neutrons—are spin-$\frac{1}{2}$. Being thus fermions, they always assume antisymmetric multiparticle states. This fact may seem innocuous, but the consequences are resounding. Let us investigate the most far reaching.

Fermions: The Exclusion Principle

Consider a system of two fermions occupying individual-particle states n and n'. If n and n' are equal, the antisymmetric two-particle state, equation (22), is identically 0.

$$\psi_n(1)\psi_n(2) - \psi_n(1)\psi_n(2) = 0$$

We conclude that two fermions cannot have the same quantum numbers—their spatial state or their spin state or both must differ. This is known as the **exclusion principle**:

> No two indistinguishable fermions may occupy the same individual-particle state.

Exclusion principle

To specify a particle's full set of quantum numbers is to specify its state, so an equivalent way of expressing the exclusion principle is that no two indistinguishable fermions may have the same set of quantum numbers. Although we have considered only the simple case of two fermions, the exclusion principle holds for any number.[5] It was discovered by Wolfgang Pauli in 1924, and the achievement won him the 1945 Nobel Prize.

The exclusion principle applies only to *indistinguishable* fermions. As noted earlier, this means that they must (1) be of the same kind and (2) share the same space. Of course, all electrons are identical and all protons are identical, but we can tell electrons from protons. Their charge and mass serve as labels. We don't demand exchange symmetry for particles that can be distinguished, so the exclusion principle does not apply to a system of different

[5]Several end-of-chapter exercises discuss a generalization of equation (22) applicable to any number of particles and leading to the same conclusion. It is known as the Slater determinant.

kinds of fermions, such as hydrogen's proton and electron. The second condition is a more delicate issue. Inasmuch as wave functions in real situations do not end abruptly in space, tending instead to fall off exponentially, we might argue that everything in the universe shares the same space, that the wave functions of all things overlap. This being the case, there should be a multiparticle state for all the electrons in the universe, antisymmetric under exchange of any two labels, with no two occupying the same state. However, for all practical purposes, electrons far apart, whose wave functions overlap only negligibly, do not share the same space, so the requirement of exchange symmetry can be ignored. (See Exercise 40 for further discussion.) Thus, the exclusion principle can be restated as: No two identical fermions may occupy the same individual-particle state *in a separated atom or other nearly isolated system.*

The importance of the exclusion principle cannot be overstated. As we shall soon see, were there no exclusion principle, nature would be profoundly different. It is the foundation of chemistry.

Bosons

The exclusion principle arises directly from the nature of an antisymmetric multiparticle state, specifically the minus sign that causes (22) to be 0 if n and n' are equal. However, bosons manifest the symmetric state (21), which is *not* 0, so occupation of the same individual-particle state is perfectly acceptable. *The exclusion principle does not apply to bosons.*

Composite Particles and Pairing

Fundamental particles are either fermions or bosons, but composite particles can also be one or the other. In fact, most of the particles listed in Table 1 are composites, even the familiar proton and neutron, which are composed of quarks. The quantitative rules of angular-momentum addition are discussed in detail in Section 7, but an important result is this: Integers must always add to integers, so when bosons are "glued" together into a composite unit—they need not even be identical—that unit is a boson; and half-integers can add to integers or half-integers, so an even number of fermions forms a boson, and an odd number a fermion. For example, the proton, comprising three spin-$\frac{1}{2}$ quarks, is a fermion. There is a short-lived subatomic particle containing the same three quarks that is a spin-$\frac{3}{2}$ fermion, but the spins inside the proton combine to give the next smaller allowed total (the details of which are still the subject of active research). In no case can the three spin-$\frac{1}{2}$ constituents form an integer-spin boson.

Some of the hottest topics (figuratively speaking) in physics research focus on exotic, tenuously bound composites. In particular, pairs of fermions are center stage in superconductivity and certain kinds of superfluids and Bose-Einstein condensates. These topics are discussed further but all involve fermions **pairing** to form bosons (electrons in the case of super-conductivity, whole fermion atoms in the other cases). Accordingly, they are no longer constrained by an exclusion principle. In fact, bosons, ever the counterpoint to fermions, actually "prefer" to be in the same state, and this is what gives rise to the classically weird properties exhibited in these systems: zero resistance, zero viscosity, monolithic behavior. The mechanism by which pairing occurs is rarely obvious, and it is often destroyed by thermal agitation even at very low temperatures, but the more we learn about such mechanisms, the more opportunities there will be to put characteristically quantum behaviors to use in everyday technology.

4 Multielectron Atoms and the Periodic Table

To grasp the basics of quantum mechanics in three dimensions, the hydrogen atom is a splendid object of study. But isolated hydrogen atoms are rare on Earth, so if we are to understand our surroundings, we must understand multielectron atoms. The exclusion principle is of prime importance: No two electrons may be in the same individual-particle state. Thus, the lowest energy state of an atom with Z protons in its nucleus would have its Z electrons fill up the Z lowest-energy quantum states, one electron per state. It may fairly be said that the whole of chemistry is a consequence. Before we explore this claim, however, we need to discuss a "new" factor in energy quantization.

The Dependence of Energy on ℓ

The presence of multiple electrons in an atom brings with it many changes. For one, the spatial states are not the same functions as in the hydrogen atom. Nonetheless, they have much the same character and are again distinguished by quantum numbers n, ℓ, and m_ℓ. Another change has to do with the quantized energies and merits a bit more attention.

We found that the energy in hydrogen depends only on the principal quantum number n. We noted that this "accidental degeneracy" is due to the potential energy in the Schrödinger equation having a simple $1/r$ dependence and that any deviation would cause the energy to depend also on ℓ. Repulsive forces between electrons are a deviation. How does the energy vary with ℓ as a result? The key is where we observed that a smaller ℓ may be thought of as a more elliptical orbit. For instance, a $3s$ ($\ell = 0$) electron might be found either near or far from the origin, while in a $3d$ ($\ell = 2$) state, its radius is more nearly uniform, more circular, as depicted in Figure 12. In a circular/large-ℓ orbit, an electron orbits not only the nucleus but also all electrons closer to the nucleus than itself. We say that the inner electrons **screen** the outer ones from the nucleus. In effect, electrons in circular/large-ℓ states orbit a smaller positive charge and thus have a smaller *negative* potential energy than they would without the other electrons. They are in a relatively high energy state. On the other hand, an elliptical/small-ℓ orbit of the same average radius—that is, the same n—brings the electron closer to the nucleus, which, therefore, is not screened as effectively, resulting in a larger negative potential energy. Of course, an elliptical orbit also extends *farther* from the origin than does a circular one, but the screening "cloud" is close to the

Figure 12 Small-ℓ states approach closer to the nucleus than do large-ℓ states.

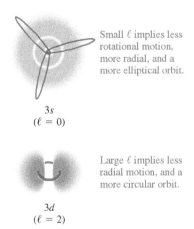

Small ℓ implies less rotational motion, more radial, and a more elliptical orbit.

$3s$
($\ell = 0$)

Large ℓ implies less radial motion, and a more circular orbit.

$3d$
($\ell = 2$)

TABLE 2 Subshell ordering and capacity

Subshell $n\ell$	1s	2s	2p	3s	3p	4s	3d	4p	5s	4d	5p	6s	4f	5d	6p	7s	5f	6d
$n + \ell$	1	2	3	3	4	4	5	5	5	6	6	6	7	7	7	7	8	8
Number of electrons $2(2\ell + 1)$	2	2	6	2	6	2	10	6	2	10	6	2	14	10	6	2	14	10

nucleus, so the energy-lowering effect at small radii dominates. Although the multielectron atom cannot be solved exactly, approximation techniques verify the claim: *For a given n, energy is lower for more-elliptical/lower-ℓ orbits.* (See Exercises 48 and Computational Excercise 86.)

Approximation techniques also provide the support for an important rule of thumb: As electrons fill states in an atom, they do so according to the lowest value of $n + \ell$, the state of lowest n being lower energy in cases of equal $n + \ell$. We refer to electrons with a given value of n as being in the nth **shell** and the subset with a given value of ℓ as being in the $n\ell$-**subshell**. Thus, the $1s$ shell fills first, and the $2s$ subshell ($n + \ell = 2$) fills before the $2p$ subshell ($n + \ell = 3$), which in turn fills before the $3s$ subshell ($n + \ell$ is also 3, but n is lower in the $2p$). The $3p$ is next, but the $4s$ subshell ($n + \ell = 4$) fills before the $3d$ ($n + \ell = 5$). Table 2 illustrates this schedule, as well as the number of electrons able to fit into each subshell—the product of the number of allowed m_s values and m_ℓ values, $2(2\ell + 1)$.

As *outer* subshells fill, however, the complex electron interactions cause the ordering of *inner* subshells to change. For instance, if only the $1s$, $2s$, and $2p$ subshells are full, the $4s$ is of lower energy than the $3d$, and so it is the next subshell to fill. But if subshells are filled out to $n = 4$ or more, the $3d$ is of lower energy than the $4s$. In fact, as more and more electrons orbit the nucleus, the tendency is for inner-shell energies *not* to intermingle. A lower n is a lower energy, whereas a lower ℓ is still a lower energy *within* a shell. Figure 13 schematically depicts this progressive change in subshell ordering. (It does not reflect the lowering of *all* energies with Z, a point we will discuss soon.)

Figure 13   The energy ordering of electron states varies with Z.

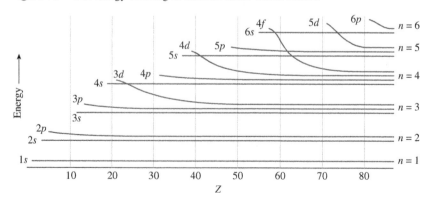

Chemical Behavior: The Periodic Table

Nothing is as fundamental to chemistry as the periodic table. The periodicity is that of the elements' chemical behaviors, which depend almost entirely on the number and binding energies of each element's **valence electrons—** weakly bound electrons, dangling at the periphery of the electron cloud. Quantum mechanics and the exclusion principle play the central role. Without the exclusion principle, the ground states of *all* atoms would have all electrons bound very tightly in the $1s$ state. They would have compact, spherically symmetric probability/charge densities, would not produce external electric fields (as asymmetric densities would) to interact with other atoms, and would thus be chemically inert. The exclusion principle tells us that there is room for only two electrons in the $n = 1$ level, eight in the $n = 2$, and so on, so most elements have an unfilled shell with electrons "sticking out."

A chemical reaction involves exchange or rearrangement of electrons between atoms. Hydrogen has one electron, which is naturally all it has to offer in a chemical reaction. It has one $1s$ valence electron. Having an energy of -13.6 eV, the energy required to free this electron from its nucleus is 13.6 eV.

Let us now look at the other elements. As we do, keep in mind that each time we imagine adding another electron, *we also add a proton* to the nucleus. We study chemical behaviors of neutral atoms, not weird cases of many electrons orbiting one proton. Adding protons to the nucleus lowers the energy of a *single* orbiting electron. Even though things are more complex in multielectron atoms, each proton's attraction to orbiting electrons still tends to lower the energies of all levels. Figure 14 depicts this trend and guides the following discussion. Note that it is schematic only and not intended to be quantitatively accurate.

Helium in its ground energy state has its two electrons in the $1s$ level, with spins opposite to satisfy the exclusion principle. Its valence would be 2, except that these two complete the $n = 1$ shell and are at relatively low energy. Being in the same *spatial* state, they aren't very effectively screened from the nucleus by one another, and they feel an attractive force to a nuclear charge twice that of hydrogen's. Ignoring their mutual repulsion, each would behave as a lone electron orbiting a nucleus of $Z = 2$, with an energy of -54.4 eV. Their repulsion raises this only to about -40 eV. Compared with hydrogen, then, helium's electrons are very tightly bound and thus extremely reluctant to engage in chemical reactions. Helium is accordingly known as a **noble gas** (noble and aloof), and its valence is said to be 0. By convention, we indicate the occupation of an element's atomic levels via its ground-state **electronic configuration**. These are shown in the margin for hydrogen and helium. The superscripts indicate the number of electrons in each subshell.

H: $1s^1$
He: $1s^2$

Beyond helium, additional electrons must go into the next-lowest energy levels. Electrons in $n = 2$ are considerably less tightly bound than $n = 1$ electrons. Not only are they farther from the nucleus, but they are also screened by the $1s$ electrons from the full nuclear charge of $+Ze$. Consequently, it is the $n = 2$ electrons that participate in chemical reactions—the $1s$ electrons are *not* part of the valence. First is $Z = 3$ lithium, with a single $2s$ valence electron.

It is chemically quite active, for this high-energy electron is easily lost. With $Z = 4$ beryllium, the $2s$ subshell is full, opposite spins allowing room for two. From $Z = 5$ to $Z = 10$, the $2p$ fills, with the three m_ℓ and two m_s values providing room for six electrons. The valence of elements beyond helium thus progresses from 1 for $Z = 3$ lithium to 8 for $Z = 10$ neon.

With the filling of the p states, a question arises: Now that there is freedom to occupy different *spatial* states—different m_ℓ values—within the subshell, how indeed do they fill? Because energy is independent of m_ℓ, one value is just as likely as another to be "chosen" by the first $2p$ electron in $Z = 5$ boron. But there is a correlation once other electrons are added, beginning with $Z = 6$ carbon. As noted in Section 2, the repulsive energy between electrons is lowered if the *spatial* state is antisymmetric, which requires that the m_ℓ values be different. For reasons discussed in Section 9, the antisymmetric spatial state in turn requires the spins to be aligned, a consequence known as **Hund's rule**. The trend continues with $Z = 7$ nitrogen. Each of its three $2p$ electrons has a different m_ℓ value, and their spins are all aligned.

As the $n = 2$ shell nears completion, the outer electrons, being all at about the same radius, are not screened much by one another; meanwhile they "see" an ever larger nuclear charge Z. Thus, they become increasingly tightly bound to the nucleus, reflected in the downward trend in Figure 14. By $Z = 10$, the $n = 2$ shell is complete.

The abrupt change in chemical behavior near a complete shell is a pivotal feature of the periodic table. Sodium has $Z = 11$. Its last electron cannot fit into the $n = 2$ shell and must go into the $3s$. Rarely do tightly bound, inner-shell electrons participate in chemical reactions, so sodium has only this lone valence electron, which is far from the nucleus and weakly bound. Accordingly, sodium exhibits enthusiastic chemical activity in the same way as lithium. Fluorine, on the other hand, for which $Z = 9$, lacks one electron to complete its low-energy $n = 2$ shell, so it prefers to capture a weakly bound electron of *another* atom rather than give up any of its many tightly bound outer electrons. Like sodium, fluorine is quite chemically active, but in the opposite sense—it is the taker rather than the giver and is thus said to be of valence -1. (Likewise, $Z = 8$ oxygen, two electrons short of a complete shell, is said to be valence -2. There is no real distinction between a valence of -2 and one of $+6$, nor between -1 and $+7$. Valences are specified simply according to whether the atom usually tends to receive or donate electrons in a chemical reaction.) If a sodium atom and fluorine atom are brought together, the fluorine atom will seize sodium's dangling, weakly bound valence electron, completing its more tightly bound $n = 2$ shell. Although pulling the electron from sodium requires energy, the "hole" in fluorine's $n = 2$ shell is deep, and the net result is a lower-energy state. An **ionic bond** is formed, in which the ions are held together by electrostatic attraction. Completing the comparison, $Z = 10$ neon differs by just one electron from sodium and fluorine, but its behavior is vastly different from both. Its $n = 2$ shell is full. It has no valence electrons to offer, as does sodium, and no holes to fill, as does fluorine. It thus joins helium as a zero-valence noble gas, only grudgingly participating in chemical reactions with other elements.

As Z increases beyond 10, the $3s$ and then the $3p$ states fill, and the valence (now excluding both full $n = 1$ and $n = 2$ shells) increases exactly as it

C: $1s^2 2s^2 2p^2$

F: $1s^2 2s^2 2p^5$
Ne: $1s^2 2s^2 2p^6$
Na: $1s^2 2s^2 2p^6 3s^1$

Figure 14 Increasingly higher filled shells combine with lowering of all levels to produce periodic chemical behavior.

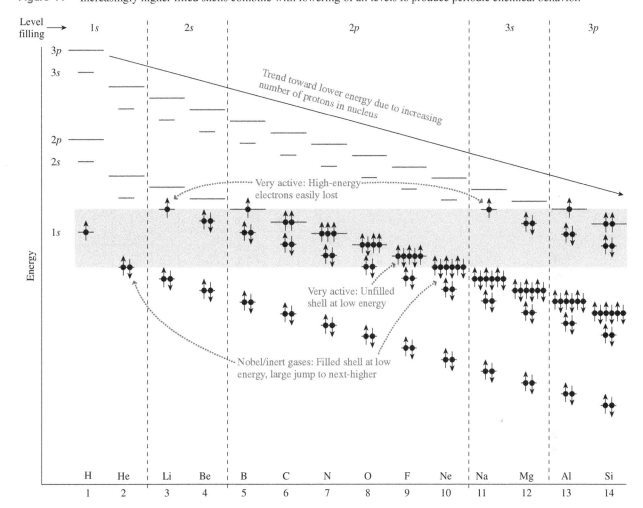

does during the filling of the $n = 2$ levels. And just as the chemical behaviors of $Z = 11$ sodium and $Z = 3$ lithium are similar—each having one electron beyond a filled shell—so too are the behaviors of $Z = 12$ magnesium and $Z = 4$ beryllium, each with two valence electrons. This is the *periodicity* of the periodic table! Shown in Figure 15, its first column is valence 1, containing $Z = 1$, $Z = 3$, and $Z = 11$; the second column is valence 2, containing $Z = 4$ and $Z = 12$. The eighth and last column does *not* correspond to a filled $n = 3$ shell. The $3p$ states are full, but the $3d$ states remain. Furthermore, as Table 2 indicates, the $3d$ states fill only after the $4s$. However, the energy jump from the $3p$ to the $4s$ level is large. Thus although $Z = 18$ argon does not have a full $n = 3$ shell, it is relatively tightly bound, so in common with $Z = 10$ and $Z = 2$, it behaves as a noble gas of valence 0. By these same arguments, $Z = 17$ chlorine, in the seventh column, is chemically similar to $Z = 9$ fluorine. Both are valence -1.

Periodic Table of the Elements

Symbol — **He** — 2 — Atomic number Z
4.0026 — Atomic mass*
$1s^2$ — Electronic configuration (if different from pattern)

Spin and Atomic Physics

Subshell → Typical valence →	ns^1 +1	ns^2 +2	$(n-1)d^1$	$(n-1)d^2$	$(n-1)d^3$	$(n-1)d^4$	$(n-1)d^5$	$(n-1)d^6$	$(n-1)d^7$	$(n-1)d^8$	$(n-1)d^9$	$(n-1)d^{10}$	np^1 +3	np^2 +4	np^3 +5	np^4 -2	np^5 -1	np^6 0
Shell n ↓ 1	**H** 1 1.00794																	**He** 2 4.0026 $1s^2$
2	**Li** 3 6.941	**Be** 4 9.01218											**B** 5 10.811	**C** 6 12.011	**N** 7 14.0067	**O** 8 15.9994	**F** 9 18.9984	**Ne** 10 20.1797
3	**Na** 11 22.9898	**Mg** 12 24.3050											**Al** 13 26.9815	**Si** 14 28.0855	**P** 15 30.9738	**S** 16 32.066	**Cl** 17 35.4527	**Ar** 18 39.948
4	**K** 19 39.0983	**Ca** 20 40.078	**Sc** 21 44.9559	**Ti** 22 47.88	**V** 23 50.9415	**Cr** 24 51.9961 $3d^54s^1$	**Mn** 25 54.9381	**Fe** 26 55.847	**Co** 27 58.9332	**Ni** 28 58.6934	**Cu** 29 63.546 $3d^{10}4s^1$	**Zn** 30 65.39	**Ga** 31 69.723	**Ge** 32 72.61	**As** 33 74.9216	**Se** 34 78.96	**Br** 35 79.904	**Kr**
5	**Rb** 37 85.4678	**Sr** 38 87.62	**Y** 39 88.9059	**Zr** 40 91.224	**Nb** 41 92.9064 $4d^45s^1$	**Mo** 42 95.94 $4d^55s^1$	**Tc** 43 (98)	**Ru** 44 101.07 $4d^75s^1$	**Rh** 45 102.906 $4d^85s^1$	**Pd** 46 106.42 $4d^{10}5s^0$	**Ag** 47 107.868 $4d^{10}5s^1$	**Cd** 48 112.411	**In** 49 114.82	**Sn** 50 118.710	**Sb** 51 121.757	**Te** 52 127.60	**I** 53 126.904	**Xe**
6	**Cs** 55 132.905	**Ba** 56 137.327	**Lu** 71 174.967	**Hf** 72 178.49	**Ta** 73 180.948	**W** 74 183.85	**Re** 75 186.207	**Os** 76 190.2	**Ir** 77 192.22	**Pt** 78 195.08 $5d^96s^1$	**Au** 79 196.967 $5d^{10}6s^1$	**Hg** 80 200.59	**Tl** 81 204.383	**Pb** 82 207.2	**Bi** 83 208.980	**Po** 84 (209)	**At** 85 (210)	**Rn**
7	**Fr** 87 (223)	**Ra** 88 (226)	**Lr** 103 (262)	**Rf** 104 (261)	**Db** 105 (262)	**Sg** 106 (263)	**Bh** 107 (262)	**Hs** 108 (265)	**Mt** 109 (266)	**Ds** 110 (281)	**Rg** 111 (280)	**Uub** 112 (285)	**Uut** 113 (284)	**Uuq** 114 (289)	**Uup** 115 (288)	**Uuh** 116 (293)		

$(n-2)f$ subshell:

	f^1	f^2	f^3	f^4	f^5	f^6	f^7	f^8	f^9	f^{10}	f^{11}	f^{12}	f^{13}	f^{14}
Lanthanides	**La** 57 138.906 $5d^16s^2$	**Ce** 58 140.115 $4f^15d^16s^2$	**Pr** 59 140.908	**Nd** 60 144.24	**Pm** 61 (145)	**Sm** 62 150.38	**Eu** 63 151.965	**Gd** 64 157.25 $4f^75d^16s^2$	**Tb** 65 158.925 $4f^95d^06s^2$	**Dy** 66 162.50	**Ho** 67 164.930	**Er** 68 167.26	**Tm** 69 168.934	**Yb** 70 173.04
Actinides	**Ac** 89 (227) $6d^17s^2$	**Th** 90 232.038 $6d^27s^2$	**Pa** 91 (231) $5f^26d^17s^2$	**U** 92 238.029 $5f^36d^17s^2$	**Np** 93 (237) $5f^46d^17s^2$	**Pu** 94 (244)	**Am** 95 (243)	**Cm** 96 (247) $5f^76d^17s^2$	**Bk** 97 (247)	**Cf** 98 (251)	**Es** 99 (252)	**Fm** 100 (257)	**Md** 101 (258)	**No** 102 (259)

* In atomic mass units, u. Averaged over naturally occurring isotopes. Values in parentheses are mass numbers of most stable known isotopes.

Figure 15 Periodic table of the elements.

After the $3p$ subshell, the $4s$ fills. Because of the large energy jump involved, this begins a new sequence with valences 1 and 2, $Z = 19$ and $Z = 20$. There is a break, however, between valences 2 and 3—between the completion of the $4s$ subshell and the start of the $4p$—where we find the **transition elements**, which involve filling of d subshells after the shell of higher n has already begun to fill. As the ten $3d$ states fill, the electronic configuration does not always vary consistently with Z. The first deviation is $Z = 24$ chromium, in which the $3d$ level increases by 2 over $Z = 23$, while the $4s$ level loses an electron. The energy levels are relatively close, and such "exceptional" behavior is not uncommon. Although there are various arguments to explain deviations from consistent filling, the forces in multielectron atoms are complicated, and ground-state configurations ultimately rest on experiment.

By $Z = 30$, the $3d$ has filled completely, beyond which the $4p$ fills in a consistent way, adding a third period of elements of valence 3 to valence 8. As does completion of the $3p$, completion of the $4p$ level—but neither the $4d$ nor the $4f$—yields a noble gas. The complete $4p$ is fairly tightly bound, and the jump to the $5s$ is large.

The next row in the periodic table, beginning with $Z = 37$ rubidium, is very similar to the previous. The $5s$ fills; then a lower-n subshell, the $4d$; then the $5p$. The row beginning with $Z = 55$ cesium exhibits an expansion similar to the one accommodating the transition elements, caused by an increase in the number of lower-n subshells filling "late." The $6s$ fills, then in turn the $4f$, $5d$, and $6p$. The elements involved in filling the $4f$ subshell are the 14 **lanthanides**, $Z = 57-70$, also known as the **rare earths** (a misnomer, as many are quite abundant in nature). The row beginning with $Z = 87$ francium mirrors the previous row. The $7s$ fills, then the $5f$, comprising the 14 **actinides**, $Z = 89-102$, then the $6d$. The $7p$ fills next, adding yet another valence 3 to valence 8 period, though not all of these elements have yet been identified.

The periodicity of electron energies is also apparent in the experimentally determined first ionization energies shown in Figure 16. The first ionization energy is the energy needed to remove the first electron from the atom. Local maxima occur at the noble gases—He, Ne, Ar, Kr, Xe, and Rn—in which electrons are tightly bound. In the elements immediately after the noble gases—Li,

Figure 16   First ionization energies of the elements.

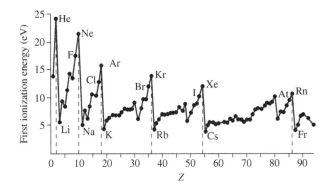

Na, K, Rb, Cs, and Fr—the energy needed to remove the single valence electron drops precipitously. It is easily stolen by an electron-hungry atom. Elements immediately before the noble gases—F, Cl, Br, I, and At—have their electrons fairly tightly bound, and their having room for one more explains their appetite.

EXAMPLE 3

$r_n = n^2 a_0/Z$ for the approximate orbit radii in a hydrogenlike atom, in which an electron orbits a nuclear charge of $+Ze$. A larger nuclear charge pulls an orbiting electron closer. By one experimental method of defining atomic radius (a difficult task when it is a "cloud" that orbits), the radii of fluorine and sodium are quoted as, respectively, 0.050 nm and 0.180 nm. As noted early in this section, wave functions in multielectron atoms are not exactly hydrogenlike, due to electron interactions, but they provide a good basis for approximations. Estimate an effective nuclear charge "seen" by the valence electrons in sodium and fluorine and discuss the results. The Bohr radius a_0 is 0.053 nm.

SOLUTION

The valence electrons in fluorine are in $n = 2$ states.

$$0.050 \text{ nm} = 4(0.053 \text{ nm})/Z_{eff} \qquad \Rightarrow \qquad Z_{eff} = 4.2$$

Sodium's lone valence electron has $n = 3$.

$$0.180 \text{ nm} = 9(0.053 \text{ nm})/Z_{eff} \qquad \Rightarrow \qquad Z_{eff} = 2.7$$

Fluorine has $Z = 9$. (Note that fluorine is nevertheless about the same size as $Z = 1$ hydrogen.) According to our estimate, each of fluorine's $n = 2$ valence electrons would see a charge of only 4.2, so 4.8 are screened. We would expect the intervening $n = 1$ electrons to screen roughly two charges, but the seven $n = 2$ electrons should also screen each other to some extent. Each has six others orbiting in the same range of radii, so an effective screening of about 3 is reasonable.

If sodium's $n = 3$ electrons were completely screened by all lower-n electrons, it should see an effective Z of only 1. An s-state, however, is a highly elliptical orbit, giving this electron considerable presence inside the inner clouds, increasing its effective Z.

In hydrogen, an $n = 3$ orbit radius is approximately $3^2/2^2 = 2.25$ times an $n = 2$ radius. The sodium radius is more than three times that of fluorine because sodium's valence electron, besides being in a higher n, also orbits an effectively smaller charge.

---

5 Characteristic X-Rays

In ground-state atoms, electrons completely fill the lowest-energy states up to some maximum energy. Excited valence electrons can jump around among higher unfilled levels. Downward jumps involve no more than tens of electronvolts, as Figure 16 indicates, producing photons in the ultraviolet range. However, atoms can be made to emit much shorter wavelengths.

Figure 17 Characteristic X-rays are produced when an inner-shell hole is made.

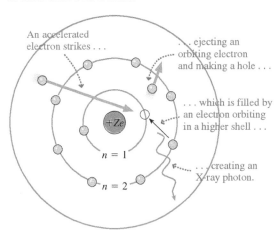

we learned that electrons smashed into a target produce a *continuous* spectrum of X-rays via bremsstrahlung—but something else also happens. As Figure 17 illustrates schematically, if an accelerated electron knocks an orbiting electron out of an atom's *inner* shell, a "hole" remains. An electron in a higher energy state can then jump down into the hole, producing a photon. Of course, this leaves another hole, so the process can repeat. Inner-shell energies are often thousands of electronvolts, and photons produced in transitions between them are therefore in the energy range of X-rays, $10^3 - 10^5$ eV, with corresponding wavelengths of 10 nm to 10^{-2} nm.

Because atomic energy levels are quantized, only certain X-rays can be emitted by a given element, and each element is different, so these **characteristic X-rays** serve as fingerprints by which we can distinguish the elements. Figure 18 depicts the X-ray spectrum for a particular target element. Superimposed on the continuous bremsstrahlung spectrum are some of the target's characteristic X-rays. We use distinctive notation to refer to the X-ray photons generated in inner-shell transitions. The $n = 1$ shell we refer to as the K-shell, the $n = 2$ as the L-shell, the $n = 3$ as the M-shell, and so on. These letters are also used to indicate the shell at which a transition *terminates*. A subscript advancing from α on through the Greek alphabet designates how many shells higher the transition began. An α transition begins one shell higher, a β two shells higher, and so forth. Thus, a transition beginning at the L-shell ($n = 2$) and ending at the K-shell ($n = 1$) produces a K_α line. An L_β line is from the N-shell ($n = 4$) down to the L-shell. (Transitions *within* a given shell are not energetic enough to be part of an element's X-ray spectrum.) Inner-shell electronic structure is largely independent of the behavior of the valence electrons, with their temperamental periodicities, so the variation of characteristic X-ray wavelengths with Z is relatively smooth. Figure 19 illustrates the smooth variation of K_α lines.

Figure 18 An X-ray spectrum.

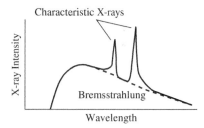

Figure 19 K_α X-rays.

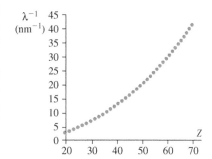

EXAMPLE 4

The energies for an electron orbiting a charge of Z are given as $-13.6\,\text{eV} \times Z^2/n^2$. Estimate the wavelength of a K_α X-ray in $Z = 60$ neodymium. Assume that after the transition, the K-shell electron orbits a charge of 59, due to screening by its fellow K-shell electron and small contributions from other clouds, and that before the transition, it orbits a charge of 55, as about half of the L-shell clouds add to the screening.

SOLUTION

The photon energy is the electron's initial energy minus its final.

$$\frac{hc}{\lambda} = -13.6\,\text{eV}\left[\frac{55^2}{2^2} - \frac{59^2}{1^2}\right] = 3.71 \times 10^4\,\text{eV}$$

Using $1240\,\text{eV} \cdot \text{nm}$ for hc gives

$$\lambda = \frac{1240\,\text{eV} \cdot \text{nm}}{3.71 \times 10^4\,\text{eV}} = 0.033\,\text{nm}$$

Actual neodymium K_α X-rays are between 0.033 nm and 0.034 nm wavelength. Exercise 59 estimates K_α wavelengths for many elements using similar approximations and shows just how well the model fits the data of Figure 19.

Characteristic X-rays are used many ways. Those produced by a known target material are a common X-ray source for crystallography. Conversely, those coaxed from samples somewhat *unknown* are also very useful. By matching characteristic X-rays with tabulated values and measuring relative intensities, we learn much about the sample's elemental composition and concentration. An accelerated electron is not the only way to excite characteristic X-rays. Protons and helium nuclei (alpha particles) are also commonly used, and the technique is then known as particle-induced X-ray emission (PIXE). The primary advantage of this technique is its sensitivity, due to a lower background level of bremsstrahlung X-rays. The continuous bremsstrahlung spectrum is caused by deceleration of the charged particles and has nothing to do with the specific target. Given comparable kinetic energies, a proton, with a much larger mass than an electron, has a correspondingly smaller acceleration, so it emits less "braking radiation."

A D V A N C E D 6 The Spin-Orbit Interaction

In this section and several that follow, we will study some of the ways in which the atom's various angular momenta interact. We start with the simplest case, returning to the one-electron hydrogen atom.

In an atom, the electron, with its intrinsic magnetic dipole moment, is essentially an orbiting magnet, so it should interact with any magnetic fields present. Our simple solution to the hydrogen atom assumed that the only potential energy in the atom is due to the Coulomb attraction between nucleus and electron. This is certainly oversimplified if there is any magnetic field present.

We need look no further than the atom itself. Moving charges produce magnetic fields. Because it orbits, the electron produces a magnetic field, and from its perspective, pictured in Figure 20, the *nucleus* is in orbit, producing a field in which the electron's intrinsic magnetic dipole moment has an orientation energy.

A detailed study of this interaction is beyond the scope of the text. But with fairly simple considerations, we gain a good qualitative understanding and a reasonable idea of how much the interaction might alter the atomic energy levels. Strictly speaking, this "new" interaction invalidates our naive hydrogen atom solution. However, we will see that the interaction energy is small, so the effect can be considered a minor perturbation on an essentially correct description.

The orientation energy of a dipole $\boldsymbol{\mu}$ in a magnetic field $\mathbf{B}$ is $U = -\boldsymbol{\mu} \cdot \mathbf{B}$. Here the dipole moment is the electron's intrinsic $\boldsymbol{\mu}_S$, related to its spin, and the field is due to orbital motion—hence the name spin-orbit interaction. Thus we write

$$U = -\boldsymbol{\mu}_S \cdot \mathbf{B}_{\text{due to } \mathbf{L}} \tag{23}$$

To obtain a rough idea of $\mathbf{B}$, we assume that the electron "sees" the proton orbiting it in a circle, as in Figure 20. The field at the center of a current loop is given by $B = \mu_0 I / 2r$, and the current I we relate to L as follows:

$$I = \frac{e}{T} = \frac{e}{2\pi r / v} = \frac{e}{2\pi m_e r^2} m_e v r = \frac{e}{2\pi m_e r^2} L$$

Here we have assumed that whether the motion is viewed as proton orbiting electron or vice versa, the orbit radius and speed are the same. Therefore, by multiplying and dividing by the *electron* mass, we relate I to the electron's orbital angular momentum. As Figure 20 shows, the $\mathbf{B}$ felt by the electron is in the same direction as $\mathbf{L}$, by the usual right-hand rules, so we have

$$B = \frac{\mu_0 I}{2r} = \frac{\mu_0}{2r} \frac{e}{2\pi m_e r^2} L \quad \rightarrow \quad \mathbf{B} = \frac{\mu_0 e}{4\pi m_e r^3} \mathbf{L} \tag{24}$$

Finally, inserting this and equation (8) into (23), the orientation energy is

$$U = -\boldsymbol{\mu}_S \cdot \mathbf{B}_{\text{due to } \mathbf{L}}$$

$$= -\left(-\frac{e}{m_e} \mathbf{S}\right) \cdot \left(\frac{\mu_0 e}{4\pi m_e r^3} \mathbf{L}\right) = \frac{\mu_0 e^2}{4\pi m_e^2 r^3} \mathbf{S} \cdot \mathbf{L} \tag{25}$$

The energy is high/positive when the two angular momenta are aligned and low/negative when antialigned. This makes sense, for if $\mathbf{S}$ were aligned with $\mathbf{L}$, $\boldsymbol{\mu}_S$ would be opposite $\mathbf{L}$ and thus $\mathbf{B}$, and we know that a dipole's highest energy is when it is opposite the field. As we might expect from Section 1, the spin has only two possible components along the internal field. However, the values,

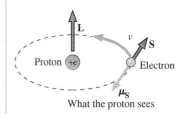

Figure 20 The electron feels a magnetic field, due to the "orbiting" proton, in the same direction as $\mathbf{L}$.

What the proton sees

What the electron sees

Figure 21 The electron's two possible orientation energies.

A high-energy state: $\boldsymbol{\mu}_S$ opposite **B**, **S** parallel to **L**

A low-energy state: $\boldsymbol{\mu}_S$ parallel to **B**, **S** opposite **L**

$\pm\frac{1}{2}\hbar$, do not correspond to *perfect* alignment. Figure 21 illustrates the point (see also Figure 8).

To give us an order-of-magnitude idea of the energy involved in the spin-orbit interaction, the product of μ_{S_z} and B will suffice. The dipole moment is straightforward.

$$\mu_{S_z} = \frac{e}{m_e}S_z \cong \frac{e}{m_e}\frac{1}{2}\hbar = \frac{1.6 \times 10^{-19}\,\text{C}}{9.11 \times 10^{-31}\,\text{kg}}\frac{1}{2}(1.055 \times 10^{-34}\,\text{J}\cdot\text{s})$$

$$= 9.3 \times 10^{-24}\,\text{A}\cdot\text{m}^2$$

Determining B via (24), itself a rough approximation, requires reasonable assumptions about r and ℓ. First, we note that a state with $\mathbf{L} = 0$ should have no orientation energy at all. There is no magnetic field if no charge has any consistent circulating motion. Thus, the interaction comes into play only when ℓ is 1 or larger, which, in turn, requires n to be 2 or larger. Choosing the simplest case, a $2p$ state, $L = \sqrt{\ell(\ell+1)}\hbar = \sqrt{2}\hbar$ and $r = n^2 a_0 = 4a_0$.

$$B = \frac{\mu_0 e}{4\pi m_e (4a_0)^3}\sqrt{2}\hbar$$

$$= \frac{(4\pi \times 10^{-7}\,\text{T}\cdot\text{m/A})(1.6 \times 10^{-19}\,\text{C})}{4\pi(9.11 \times 10^{-31}\,\text{kg})(4 \times 0.0529 \times 10^{-9}\,\text{m})^3}\sqrt{2}(1.055 \times 10^{-34}\,\text{J}\cdot\text{s})$$

$$= 0.28\,\text{T}$$

Considering the size of the particles involved, this is a strong field, thousands of times Earth's field at its surface. Now completing our calculation,

$$U \cong \mu_{S_z}B = (9.3 \times 10^{-24}\,\text{A}\cdot\text{m}^2)(0.28\,\text{T}) \cong 3 \times 10^{-24}\,\text{J} \sim 2 \times 10^{-5}\,\text{eV}$$

Electron energies in hydrogen are on the order of electronvolts, so we see that the spin-orbit energy is very small. Nonetheless, the interaction is clearly discernible in the **fine structure** of hydrogen's spectral lines. Energy levels predicted in ignorance of spin to be degenerate are split according to the orientation of **L** and **S**. States in which **L** and **S** are aligned are of slightly higher energy than those in which they are antialigned, so photons produced in transitions to or from these states are of slightly different energies.

ⒶD V A N C E D   7 Adding Angular Momenta

Angular momentum vectors do not add in an arbitrary way, but rather by strict quantum-mechanical rules. In this section, we discuss these rules mostly in the context of adding **S** and **L**, but *the same addition rules apply in all cases* in which various angular momenta interact within a system—spin angular momentum with orbital angular momentum, spin with spin, and orbital with orbital.

The angular momenta **S** and **L** in an atom are not independent. The whole idea of the spin-orbit interaction is that spin and orbital angular momenta affect each other through a magnetic field internal to the atom. One result of this coupling of **S** and **L** is that if quantization is probed with a weak *external* *B*-field—much weaker than the internal, so as not to overwhelm the internal interaction—we do not observe independent quantization of each, but rather of the vector sum: the **total angular momentum J**.

$$\mathbf{J} = \mathbf{L} + \mathbf{S} \qquad (26)$$

The individual magnitudes L and S are not altered. Both follow the usual form: $L = \sqrt{\ell(\ell + 1)}\,\hbar$ and $S = \sqrt{s(s + 1)}\,\hbar$. But the vectors **L** and **S** may add in only certain ways—the angle θ in Figure 22 can take on only certain values. We have some reason to expect this. Recall from the discussion of the Stern-Gerlach experiment that if spin could somehow be ignored, **L** could make only certain angles—corresponding to $2\ell + 1$ allowed values of m_ℓ— with the z-axis of the *external B*-field. We now know that orbital motion produces an *internal B*-field parallel to **L**—an "internal z-axis"—so it is certainly plausible that the intrinsic angular momentum **S** should make only certain angles with **L**. Indeed, we might expect $2s + 1$ such angles, corresponding to the $2s + 1$ allowed values of m_s.

And this is exactly what we find. The magnitude J and the z-component J_z of the total angular momentum are restricted to the following values:

$$J = \sqrt{j(j + 1)}\,\hbar, \quad j = |\ell - s|, |\ell - s| + 1, \ldots, \ell + s - 1, \ell + s \quad (27)$$

$$J_z = m_j\hbar, \quad m_j = -j, -j + 1, \ldots, j - 1, j \quad (28)$$

Each allowed j gives a different magnitude J, which in turn implies a different angle θ between **L** and **S**. The number of j-values is the number of values from $|\ell - s|$ to $\ell + s$ in integral steps, which is indeed $2s + 1$, the same as from $-s$ to $+s$. Of course, in applying this rule to hydrogen with its lone electron, s is $\frac{1}{2}$, so j may take on only the two values $\ell + \frac{1}{2}$ and $\ell - \frac{1}{2}$, corresponding respectively to **L** and **S** being aligned and antialigned. In multielectron atoms, discussed in Section 9, total spin can be greater, and j may take on more values.

In some sense, equation (27) resembles standard rules for vector addition. As Figure 23 demonstrates, given vectors **A** and **B**, the magnitude of the vector sum $\mathbf{C} = \mathbf{A} + \mathbf{B}$ cannot be greater than $A + B$ nor less than $|A - B|$. However, the angular momentum magnitudes L, S, and J aren't simply proportional to the values ℓ, s, and j. Each is proportional to $\sqrt{i(i + 1)}$, where i stands for ℓ, s, or j. Let us see what this implies.

Figure 22 Quantum-mechanical rules allow **L** and **S** to add only at certain orientations.

Figure 23 The maximum and minimum sums of two vectors.

The maximum value of j allowed by (27) is $\ell + s$, and the corresponding total angular momentum is

$$J_{max} = \sqrt{(\ell + s)(\ell + s + 1)}\,\hbar$$

If **L** and **S** *were* parallel, the magnitude of the vector sum would be

$$L + S = \sqrt{\ell + (\ell + 1)}\,\hbar + \sqrt{s(s + 1)}\,\hbar$$

Squaring both of these, we have

$$J_{max}^2 = (\ell^2 + \ell + s^2 + s + 2\ell s)\hbar^2$$

$$(L + S)^2 = (\ell^2 + \ell + s^2 + s + 2\sqrt{\ell^2 s^2 + \ell^2 s + s^2\ell + \ell s})\hbar^2$$

By inspection, $J_{max} < L + S$, and we conclude that rule (27) forbids **L** and **S** to be exactly parallel. It is left as an exercise to show that $J_{min} > |L - S|$, which tells us that the vectors also cannot be exactly opposite. (An exception is $\ell = s$, in which J_{min} is identically 0.) We see that the terms *aligned* and *antialigned* must not be taken literally.

Summarizing, the atom's internal B-field causes **L** and **S** to be "locked together" at one of certain allowed angles, corresponding to the $2s + 1$ values of J allowed by (27). If we probe angular momentum quantization by applying a weak *external* B-field, it is quantization of J_z that we observe. For atoms with a given allowed value of J, we would find J_z to be one of the $2j + 1$ values allowed by equation (28). (*Note:* The Stern-Gerlach experiment of Section 1 is a special case: $\ell = 0$, implying that $j = s = \frac{1}{2}$ and correctly giving just two components.) Figure 24 illustrates the relationships for the case $\ell = 2, s = \frac{1}{2}$. Given ℓ and s, the magnitudes L and S are fixed, but there are

Figure 24 Possibilities for total angular momentum **J** for case $\ell = 2, s = \frac{1}{2}$.

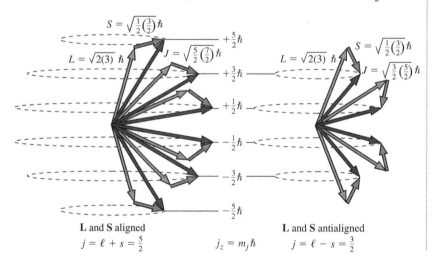

two possible angles between **L** and **S**: an aligned state where $j = \ell + s = \frac{5}{2}$ and an antialigned one where $j = \ell - s = \frac{3}{2}$. Each **J** can make $2j + 1$ possible angles with the externally imposed z-axis, but with only its z-component fixed/quantized, it may point in an infinite number of directions *about* that axis, leaving J_x and J_y uncertain. Vectors **L** and **S** have similar freedom to revolve as a unit about **J**.

Good Quantum Numbers

Given that an external field reveals quantization of J_z, related to m_j, it may seem that m_ℓ and m_s are now quantum numbers of no relevance. Indeed, with the spin-orbit interaction coupling **L** and **S** into a total **J**, we regard $n, \ell, j,$ and m_j as the relevant, or "good," quantum numbers. It is reassuring, however, that the total number of states is the same whether m_ℓ and m_s or j and m_j are truly relevant. Consider again the case $\ell = 2, s = \frac{1}{2}$. Ignoring any coupling of **S** and **L**, $L_z = m_\ell \hbar$ could take on five (i.e., $2\ell + 1$) values, and for each, there would be two possible values of m_s, for a total of ten states. The coupling in Figure 24 gives six allowed m_j values for $j = \frac{5}{2}$ and four for $\frac{3}{2}$, which also add to ten. If no strong external B-field is present, the latter view is correct—the states form groups according to j. But a strong enough external field can overwhelm and break the coupling of intrinsic angular momentum to the atom's internal B-field. In that case, both **L** and **S** are *independently* quantized. Each precesses with a fixed component along the external field/z-axis, and m_ℓ and m_s again become relevant indicators of the system's state—good quantum numbers. Section 8 further discusses these different behaviors in an external field.

EXAMPLE 5

Identify the different total angular momentum states possible for the case $\ell = 3, s = \frac{1}{2}$.

SOLUTION

If we ignore any coupling of **L** and **S**, the number of states is simply the product of the number of allowed values of m_ℓ and m_s: $(2\ell + 1) \times 2 = 14$. According to (27), j is allowed two values. These and the corresponding values of m_j are

$$j_{max} = \ell + s = \frac{7}{2} \qquad m_j = -\frac{7}{2}, -\frac{5}{2}, -\frac{3}{2}, -\frac{1}{2}, +\frac{1}{2}, +\frac{3}{2}, +\frac{5}{2}, +\frac{7}{2}$$

$$j_{min} = \ell - s = \frac{5}{2} \qquad m_j = -\frac{5}{2}, -\frac{3}{2}, -\frac{1}{2}, +\frac{1}{2}, +\frac{3}{2}, +\frac{5}{2}$$

As noted, the number of states should be the same whether or not the spin-orbit interaction is a factor, and again we have 14. The actual physical properties are

$$J_{max} = \sqrt{\frac{7}{2}\left(\frac{7}{2} + 1\right)}\,\hbar = \frac{\sqrt{63}}{2}\hbar \qquad J_z = \pm\frac{7}{2}\hbar, \pm\frac{5}{2}\hbar, \pm\frac{3}{2}\hbar, \pm\frac{1}{2}\hbar$$

$$J_{min} = \sqrt{\frac{5}{2}\left(\frac{5}{2} + 1\right)}\,\hbar = \frac{\sqrt{35}}{2}\hbar \qquad J_z = \pm\frac{5}{2}\hbar, \pm\frac{3}{2}\hbar, \pm\frac{1}{2}\hbar$$

Relativity and Hydrogen Atom Energy Levels

Because spin is relativistic in origin, the spin-orbit interaction may be viewed as a relativistic effect. It destroys some of the symmetry in the hydrogen atom and reduces the degeneracy. The energy is higher when **L** and **S** are aligned ($j = \ell + \frac{1}{2}$) than when they are antialigned ($j = \ell - \frac{1}{2}$). However, the spin-orbit interaction is not the only relativistic cause of discrepancy between the naive energy levels and those we actually observe. Another involves the ellipticity of orbits.

Recall that for a given n, a wave function of *smaller* ℓ has comparatively less rotational energy and greater radial energy—its orbit is more elliptical. We noted that energy being independent of ℓ is "accidental," a consequence of the simplicity of the Coulomb potential energy, and that any mathematical alteration of the problem destroys this degeneracy. Although too involved to quantify here, the more complicated relativistic dependence of energy on speed is such an alteration, and we find that a more elliptic orbit is of lower energy than a large-ℓ orbit of the same n. Unlike the spin-orbit interaction, this relativistic factor affects even the $n=1$, $\ell = 0$ state. It too is of lower energy than we would otherwise expect. Of course, the two effects—the spin-orbit interaction and the dependence of energy on ellipticity—coexist. Taking both into account, theory predicts and experiment confirms that (1) the energies in the hydrogen atom are all slightly lower than expected nonrelativistically, and (2) the deviation depends on the total angular momentum. The smaller the value of J, the lower the energy. Consequently, to specify states of different energy, we incorporate into the spectroscopic notation a subscript for the total angular momentum quantum number j. A $3d$ state in which **L** and **S** are antialigned ($j = \ell - s = 2 - \frac{1}{2} = \frac{3}{2}$) is a $3d_{3/2}$ state, and it is slightly lower energy than the $3d_{5/2}$ state, in which they are aligned.

Figure 25 illustrates the relativistic splitting of hydrogen atom energy levels. States that by nonrelativistic theory should be degenerate are shifted downward and split according to the total angular momentum. Note that the $3d_{3/2}$ and $3p_{3/2}$ states, of equal j, are of equal energy. The ellipticity effect argues that a $3p$ state—the more elliptic—should be of lower energy. But the $3p_{3/2}$ state has **L** and **S** aligned ($j = \frac{3}{2} = 1 + \frac{1}{2} = \ell + s$), while in the $3d_{3/2}$ state, they are antialigned ($j = \frac{3}{2} = 2 - \frac{1}{2} = \ell - s$). So the spin-orbit effect argues that the $3p_{3/2}$ should be higher. As it turns out, the two effects balance. Still, the figure reflects each effect independently. For **LS**-aligned states, larger ℓ corresponds to higher energy, and for a given ℓ, aligned states are higher energy than antialigned ones.

Figure 25 greatly exaggerates the splitting. The spacing of the nonrelativistic energies is correct, but the slopes showing how the true energies deviate are all much steeper than they should be, specifically by the constant value $1/\alpha^2$. Called the **fine-structure constant**, α is defined as

$$\alpha \equiv \frac{e^2}{4\pi\varepsilon_0 \hbar c} \cong \frac{1}{137} \tag{29}$$

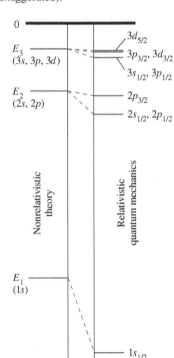

Figure 25 Relativistic splitting of hydrogen atom energies (greatly exaggerated).

This combination of factors often appears in a relativistic treatment of the hydrogen atom, and its square, ~5×10^{-5}, is a fair measure of the deviations from nonrelativistic expectation. (Exercise 69 suggests how to find this factor in the spin-orbit energy, whose value of about 10^{-5} times hydrogen atom energies is not coincidental.) The relativistic splitting of the hydrogen atom energy levels is obviously small, but it doesn't escape our notice. Precise spectroscopic equipment can discern the slight wavelength differences of photons produced in transitions expected *non*relativistically to be of the same energy. For instance, a transition from the $3d_{3/2}$ state to the $2p_{1/2}$ yields a photon of slightly higher energy than does a transition from the $3s_{1/2}$ state to the $2p_{3/2}$. Explanation of the **fine structure** of hydrogen's spectral lines was one of the great early triumphs of relativistic quantum mechanics.

Even fine structure doesn't tell the whole story of hydrogen's spectral lines. There are several smaller effects. The Lamb shift, an interaction between electromagnetic vacuum fluctuations and the electron, splits states of a given n and j according to the value of ℓ. Another interaction, between the electron and the proton's small magnetic moment—responsible for the so-called hyperfine structure—splits each (n, j, ℓ) level into a doublet, higher energy when electron and proton spins are aligned, lower when antialigned. Comprehensive Exercise 85 discusses a famous aspect of the latter effect: the so-called 21 cm line. We leave further study of these topics to a higher-level course.

8 External Magnetic Fields and the Z-Axis

A D V A N C E D

In the simple hydrogen atom, energy depended only on the principle quantum number n. In Sections 6 and 7, we learned that spin and other relativistic factors complicate matters. Energy also depends on total angular momentum, the quantum number j. Still, without an external influence such as an experimental observation, there is no preferred direction in space, and thus no dependence on m_ℓ, m_s, or m_j. A z-component is meaningless without a z-axis. But what happens if we introduce an external influence?

Given the atom's magnetic dipole moments, an external magnetic field is an obvious influence to consider. States that are otherwise degenerate should split into different energies depending on the orientation of the dipoles in that field. As it turns out, it is easiest to analyze cases at opposite extremes: where the external field is considerably stronger than the atom's internal field and where it is considerably weaker. We use hydrogen as an example in this section, but we will see in Section 9 that the results are applicable to valence electrons in multielectron atoms as well.

Weak Field: The Zeeman Effect

In a weak external B-field, **S** and **L** are coupled by the atom's internal magnetic field into a total angular momentum **J**. Consequently, $\boldsymbol{\mu}_S$ and $\boldsymbol{\mu}_L$ are also coupled into a total magnetic dipole moment $\boldsymbol{\mu}_J$, and different orientations of $\boldsymbol{\mu}_J$

with $\mathbf{B}_{ext}$ have different energies. Fundamental relationships (1) and (8) reveal a factor-of-two difference that is crucial to quantifying these energies.

$$\boldsymbol{\mu}_{\mathbf{L}} = -\frac{e}{2m_e}\mathbf{L} \qquad \boldsymbol{\mu}_{\mathbf{S}} = -\frac{e}{m_e}\mathbf{S} \qquad (30)$$

No analogous fundamental relationship relates $\boldsymbol{\mu}_{\mathbf{J}}$ to $\mathbf{J}$. It is merely the vector sum of $\boldsymbol{\mu}_{\mathbf{L}}$ and $\boldsymbol{\mu}_{\mathbf{S}}$.

$$\boldsymbol{\mu}_{\mathbf{J}} = \boldsymbol{\mu}_{\mathbf{L}} + \boldsymbol{\mu}_{\mathbf{S}} = -\frac{e}{2m_e}(\mathbf{L} + 2\mathbf{S}) \qquad (31)$$

Figure 26 illustrates the relationships. Because $\mathbf{L} + \mathbf{S}$ (equal to $\mathbf{J}$) is obviously not $\mathbf{L} + 2\mathbf{S}$ (to which $\boldsymbol{\mu}_{\mathbf{J}}$ is opposite), $\boldsymbol{\mu}_{\mathbf{J}}$ and $\mathbf{J}$ are not collinear. It is $\mathbf{J}$ that precesses at a fixed angle about the z-axis, the *external* field, but $\boldsymbol{\mu}_{\mathbf{J}}$ has an additional precession about an axis through $\mathbf{J}$, arising from the other field. The atom's *internal* field locks $\mathbf{S}$ into a fixed angle with $\mathbf{L}$, while still allowing them to precess as a unit about $\mathbf{J}$, twirling the captive $\boldsymbol{\mu}_{\mathbf{J}}$ around as they do. The internal field being much stronger than the external simplifies what would otherwise be a very difficult analysis. From equation (2), we know that precessional frequency is proportional to the field strength. The spinning of $\mathbf{S}$, $\mathbf{L}$, and $\boldsymbol{\mu}_{\mathbf{J}}$ about $\mathbf{J}$ is much faster than the precession of $\mathbf{J}$ about the external field, so for the orientation energy of $\boldsymbol{\mu}_{\mathbf{J}}$ in the external field, we simply use its average value as it twirls—its component opposite $\mathbf{J}$.

Figure 26 In a weak external field, $\mathbf{J}$ precesses slowly about $\mathbf{B}_{ext}$, with J_z fixed/quantized, while $\mathbf{L}$ and $\mathbf{S}$ precess rapidly about $\mathbf{J}$.

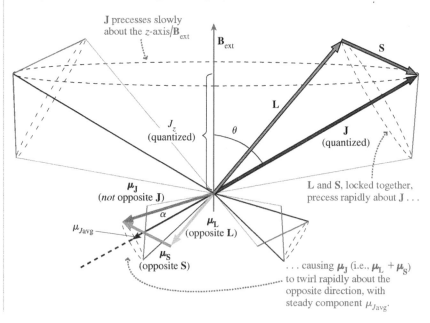

Even so, several steps are needed before we obtain a usable expression. From Figure 26 we see that

$$\mu_{J\mathrm{avg}} = \mu_J \cos \alpha$$

Angle α is between $\boldsymbol{\mu}_{\mathbf{J}}$ and the direction opposite $\mathbf{J}$, so that $\boldsymbol{\mu}_{\mathbf{J}} \cdot (-\mathbf{J}) = \mu_J J \cos \alpha$, and we may write

$$\mu_{J\mathrm{avg}} = \mu_J \frac{-\boldsymbol{\mu}_{\mathbf{J}} \cdot \mathbf{J}}{\mu_J J} = -\frac{\boldsymbol{\mu}_{\mathbf{J}} \cdot \mathbf{J}}{J}$$

Now inserting relationship (31) and $\mathbf{J} = \mathbf{L} + \mathbf{S}$,

$$\mu_{J\mathrm{avg}} = \frac{e}{2m_{\mathrm{e}}} \frac{(\mathbf{L} + 2\mathbf{S}) \cdot (\mathbf{L} + \mathbf{S})}{J} = \frac{e}{2m_{\mathrm{e}}} \frac{L^2 + 2S^2 + 3\mathbf{L} \cdot \mathbf{S}}{J}$$

Using $J^2 = (\mathbf{L} + \mathbf{S}) \cdot (\mathbf{L} + \mathbf{S}) = L^2 + S^2 + 2\mathbf{L} \cdot \mathbf{S}$, we can put $\mathbf{L} \cdot \mathbf{S}$ is terms of the magnitudes J, L, and S, and thus in terms of j, ℓ, and s. Straightforward algebra, left as an exercise, then gives

$$\mu_{J\mathrm{avg}} = \frac{e}{2m_{\mathrm{e}}} \frac{3j(j + 1) - \ell(\ell + 1) + s(s + 1)}{2\sqrt{j(j + 1)}} \hbar \tag{32}$$

Now returning to Figure 26, the angle between this average dipole moment and the external field is $180 - \theta$, so the orientation energy is

$$U = -\mu_{J\mathrm{avg}} B_{\mathrm{ext}} \cos(180 - \theta) = \mu_{J\mathrm{avg}} B_{\mathrm{ext}} \cos\theta$$

Using $J_z = J \cos\theta$ and $J = \sqrt{j(j + 1)}\hbar$, we obtain

$$U = \mu_{J\mathrm{avg}} B_{\mathrm{ext}} \frac{J_z}{\sqrt{j(j + 1)}\hbar}$$

and inserting (32), we have

$$U = g_{\mathrm{Lande}} \frac{e}{2m_{\mathrm{e}}} J_z B_{\mathrm{ext}} \tag{33}$$

where we define the **Lande g-factor** as

$$g_{\mathrm{Lande}} \equiv \frac{3j(j + 1) - \ell(\ell + 1) + s(s + 1)}{2j(j + 1)} \tag{34}$$

Note that the *coefficient* of B_{ext} in orientation energy (33) is exactly where we expect to find the z-component of a dipole moment, and it resembles the

z-components of expressions (30) for **L** and **S** alone. In fact it covers both. Simple substitution shows that in the $s = 0, j = \ell$ case, g_{Lande} is 1, and in the $\ell = 0, j = s$ case, it is 2.

Finally, using equation (28), $J_z = m_j, \hbar$ (34)   may be rewritten

$$U = g_{\text{Lande}} \frac{e}{2m_e} m_j \hbar B_{\text{ext}} \tag{35}$$

It is worth reiterating that it is impossible to solve the hydrogen atom without approximation while taking into account the effects of the spin-orbit interaction and external fields. But when these effects are small, merely adding their energies to those of the simple hydrogen atom gives the correct energies.

$$E_{\text{weak external field}} = E_{\text{zero field}} + \frac{e}{2m_e} g_{\text{Lande}} m_j \hbar B_{\text{ext}} \tag{36}$$

In a weak external magnetic field, energy depends on n, ℓ, j, and m_j.

In summary, a weak external magnetic field splits otherwise degenerate atomic states into $2j + 1$ states about the zero-field level according to m_j, and the degree of splitting depends, through g_{Lande}, on j, ℓ, and s. By the arguments of Section 1, we conclude that if the field were nonuniform, it would exert different force on states of different m_j, so a Stern-Gerlach-type experiment would break one beam of atoms into $2j + 1$ separate ones. But even a uniform external field makes its presence known. As we now see, it can split one spectral line into many.

EXAMPLE 6

Hydrogen atoms are subjected to a 0.05 T external magnetic field (weak compared to the 0.3 T internal field estimated in Section 6). (a) Into how many levels are the $1s_{1/2}$ and $2p_{3/2}$ states split? (b) In each case, how large is the splitting? (c) The photon's spin is 1, yielding a selection rule that m_j cannot change by more than 1 in a photon-producing transition between states. Into how many lines is the $2p_{3/2}$ to $1s_{1/2}$ spectral line split by the field? (d) What is the energy spacing between the lines? (e) By about how much is the wavelength of a spectral line shifted?

SOLUTION

(a) Because $j = \frac{1}{2}$ in the $1s_{1/2}$ state, m_j is restricted to $\pm\frac{1}{2}$. Different dipole orientations thus split the level into two energies. Similarly, for $j = \frac{3}{2}$, m_j can be any of the four values, $\pm\frac{3}{2}$ and $\pm\frac{1}{2}$, giving four energies.

(b) First we calculate g_{Lande} for the two states.

$$g_{\text{Lande}, 1s_{1/2}} = \frac{3\frac{1}{2}(\frac{1}{2} + 1) - 0 + \frac{1}{2}(\frac{1}{2} + 1)}{2\frac{1}{2}(\frac{1}{2} + 1)} = 2$$

$$g_{\text{Lande}, 2p_{3/2}} = \frac{3\frac{3}{2}(\frac{3}{2} + 1) - 1(1 + 1) + \frac{1}{2}(\frac{1}{2} + 1)}{2\frac{3}{2}(\frac{3}{2} + 1)} = \frac{4}{3}$$

We see that the splitting of the $2p_{3/2}$ states is only two-thirds that of the $1s_{1/2}$. Figure 27 illustrates the relative spacing. Now using (35),

$$U_{1s_{1/2}} = 2 \frac{1.6 \times 10^{-19}\,\text{C}}{2(9.11 \times 10^{-31}\,\text{kg})} \left\{ \pm \tfrac{1}{2} \right\} (1.055 \times 10^{-34}\,\text{J} \cdot \text{s})(0.05\,\text{T})$$

$$= \left\{ \pm \tfrac{1}{2} \right\} 9.3 \times 10^{-25}\,\text{J} = \left\{ \pm \tfrac{1}{2} \right\} 5.8 \times 10^{-6}\,\text{eV}$$

and

$$U_{2p_{3/2}} = \frac{4}{3} \frac{1.6 \times 10^{-19}\,\text{C}}{2(9.11 \times 10^{-31}\,\text{kg})} \left\{ \begin{matrix} \pm \tfrac{3}{2} \\ \pm \tfrac{1}{2} \end{matrix} \right\} (1.055 \times 10^{-34}\,\text{J} \cdot \text{s})(0.05\,\text{T})$$

$$= \left\{ \begin{matrix} \pm \tfrac{3}{2} \\ \pm \tfrac{1}{2} \end{matrix} \right\} 6.2 \times 10^{-25}\,\text{J} = \left\{ \begin{matrix} \pm \tfrac{3}{2} \\ \pm \tfrac{1}{2} \end{matrix} \right\} 3.9 \times 10^{-6}\,\text{eV}$$

The splitting in the $1s_{1/2}$ is 5.8×10^{-6} eV, and in the $2p_{3/2}$, is 3.9×10^{-6} eV. Given the external field's weakness relative to the internal, it isn't surprising that these shifts are smaller than the spin-orbit energy of Section 6.

(c) Using (36), with $E_{1s_{1/2}}$ and $E_{2p_{3/2}}$ representing the zero-field energies, a transition from a $2p_{3/2}$ state to a $1s_{1/2}$ state would involve an energy difference of

$$\Delta E = \left(E_{2p_{3/2}} + \frac{e}{2m_e} \frac{4}{3} \left\{ \begin{matrix} \pm \tfrac{3}{2} \\ \pm \tfrac{1}{2} \end{matrix} \right\} \hbar B_{\text{ext}} \right) - \left(E_{1s_{3/2}} + \frac{e}{2m_e} 2 \left\{ \pm \tfrac{1}{2} \right\} \hbar B_{\text{ext}} \right)$$

Of eight possible transitions from the $2p_{3/2}$ to the $1s_{1/2}$, the selection rule forbids two, indicated in Figure 27. As the reader may verify, the energy differences can be written as

$$\Delta E = (E_{2p_{3/2}} - E_{1s_{1/2}}) + \frac{e}{2m_e} \hbar B_{\text{ext}} \left\{ \begin{matrix} \pm \tfrac{5}{3} \\ \pm \tfrac{3}{3} \\ \pm \tfrac{3}{3} \\ \pm \tfrac{1}{3} \end{matrix} \right\}$$

There are six equally spaced photon energies.

(d) We see that the spacing is

$$\frac{e\hbar}{2m_e} B_{\text{ext}} \frac{2}{3} = \frac{(1.6 \times 10^{-19}\,\text{C})(1.055 \times 10^{-34}\,\text{J} \cdot \text{s})}{2(9.11 \times 10^{-31}\,\text{kg})} (0.05\,\text{T}) \frac{2}{3}$$

$$= 3.1 \times 10^{-25}\,\text{J} = 1.9 \times 10^{-6}\,\text{eV}$$

(e) The splitting is very small. The transition energy is still essentially

$$E_2 - E_1 = \frac{-13.6\,\text{eV}}{2^2} - \frac{-13.6\,\text{eV}}{1^2} = 10.2\,\text{eV} = 1.6 \times 10^{-18}\,\text{J}$$

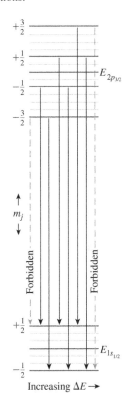

Figure 27 In a weak magnetic field, there are six allowed $2p_{3/2}$ to $1s$ transitions.

Increasing $\Delta E \rightarrow$

Thus, the ratio of the energy shift to the total energy is about $1.9 \times 10^{-6}/10.2 \cong 2 \times 10^{-7}$, causing a similar shift in the wavelength. This first line in the Lyman series is about 122 nm, so the external field splits it into six spectral lines spaced about 2.4×10^{-5} nm apart.

Strong Field: The Paschen-Back Effect

Analyzing the splitting of degenerate levels is much easier if B_{ext} is strong—on the order of several tesla. So strong a field overwhelms the internal field that would otherwise couple **L** and **S** together, and each is then quantized independently along B_{ext}, as depicted in Figure 28. Using (30), the orientation energies are

$$U_L = -\boldsymbol{\mu}_\mathbf{L} \cdot \mathbf{B}_{\text{ext}} = -\mu_{Lz} B_{\text{ext}} = -\left(-\frac{e}{2m_{\text{e}}} L_z\right) B_{\text{ext}} = \frac{e}{2m_{\text{e}}} m_\ell \hbar B_{\text{ext}}$$

and

$$U_S = -\boldsymbol{\mu}_\mathbf{S} \cdot \mathbf{B}_{\text{ext}} = -\mu_{Sz} B_{\text{ext}} = -\left(-\frac{e}{m_{\text{e}}} S_z\right) B_{\text{ext}} = \frac{e}{m_{\text{e}}} m_s \hbar B_{\text{ext}}$$

Although a strong field can break the spin-orbit coupling, its effect is still usually small enough that the overall energies are once again obtained by merely adding these perturbations to the zero-field energies.

$$E_{\text{strong external field}} = E_{\text{zero field}} + \frac{e}{2m_{\text{e}}}(m_\ell + 2m_s)\hbar B_{\text{ext}} \qquad (37)$$

In a strong external magnetic field, energy depends on n, ℓ, m_ℓ, and m_s.

Figure 28 A strong external field forces both **L** and **S** to precess independently about **B**.

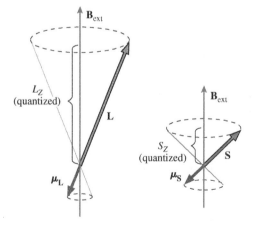

336

The reader is encouraged to compare this result with the corresponding weak-field result (36) and to compare Figures 26 and 28. This should help clarify why, besides n and ℓ, the good quantum numbers are j and m_j in the weak-field case, but m_ℓ and m_s in a strong field.

9 Excitation Spectra   A D V A N C E D

In Section 5, we learned about characteristic X-rays—spectral emissions caused by holes "under" the valence electrons. Here we take a look at photon emission due to the excitation of valence electrons above their ground state.

As we know, to understand the richness of spectral lines, we need to know how the various angular momenta interact. We have studied the spin-orbit interaction in the one-electron hydrogen atom. In multielectron atoms, the many spin and orbital angular momenta give rise to more complex interactions. To begin, let us consider **total spin**.

Total Spin

As noted in Section 7, the quantum rules are the same when adding any angular momenta. Just as $\mathbf{L}$ and $\mathbf{S}$ can add to a total angular momentum of magnitude $J = \sqrt{j(j+1)}\hbar$, where j may take on any integral value between $\ell + s$ and $|\ell - s|$, two equal-magnitude spin angular momenta can add to a total spin $\mathbf{S}_T$ of magnitude $S_T = \sqrt{s_T(s_T + \ell)}\hbar$, where s_T takes on integral values between $s + s$ and $|s - s|$. For two spin-$\frac{1}{2}$ particles, s_T can be only 1 or 0, corresponding to $S_T = \sqrt{2}\hbar$ and $S_T = 0$. The z-component S_{Tz} obeys the usual quantization rules, so for $s_T = 1$, there are three possible z-components, $+\hbar$, 0, $-\hbar$, known as a **triplet** of spin states. Naturally, for $s_T = 0$, the z-component can only be 0, and this loner is known as a **singlet** state.

Figure 29 depicts how the two spins add to form the triplet states. In all three, the angle between the spins is the same. They are as aligned as the

Figure 29 Formation of triplet states.

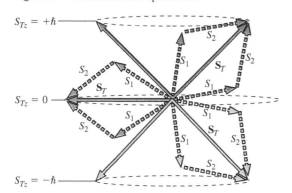

337

quantum addition rules allow, and the total spin is of magnitude $\sqrt{2}\hbar$. As usual, though this angular momentum makes a fixed angle with the z-axis, it may point in any direction in the xy-plane. Note that the $s_{Tz} = +\hbar$ state has both spins up, more or less, and the $s_{Tz} = -\hbar$ state has both down. The $S_{Tz} = 0$ state has one up and one down, but even though *z-components* add to 0, the *spins* are just as aligned as in the other two states, giving $\mathbf{S}_T$ the same magnitude. In the singlet state (not shown), the *spins*—not just the z-components— are truly opposite, perfectly antialigned, giving $S_T = 0$.

Let us now consider the exchange symmetry of the total spin states, resorting to a simpler representation. With the left arrow representing m_s for particle 1 and the right arrow m_s for particle 2, we might expect the following four possible spin combinations:

$$\uparrow\uparrow \quad \uparrow\downarrow \quad \downarrow\uparrow \quad \downarrow\downarrow$$

The second and third do not treat the particles symmetrically. Swapping the arrows on the second gives a different state, the third. But equivalent to these four are three symmetric combinations and one antisymmetric combination, not coincidentally the number of triplet and singlet states.

$$\left. \begin{matrix} \uparrow\uparrow \\ \uparrow\downarrow + \downarrow\uparrow \\ \downarrow\downarrow \end{matrix} \right\} \quad \begin{matrix} \text{Triplet} \\ \text{symmetric} \\ s_T = 1 \end{matrix} \qquad\qquad \begin{matrix} \text{Singlet} \\ \uparrow\downarrow - \downarrow\uparrow \quad \text{antisymmetric} \\ s_T = 0 \end{matrix} \qquad (38)$$

Note the correspondences between this representation of the triplet states and that in Figure 29. Each shows one state with both spins up, one with both down, and one with opposite z-components. Recall also the claim made in Section 4 in connection with Hund's rule: An antisymmetric spatial state, which lowers the repulsive energy between electrons in an atom, implies aligned spins. The full argument is that an antisymmetric *spatial* state, where swapping particle labels on the wave functions *alone* gives a sign change, will give the required antisymmetric *multiparticle* state only if the *spin* state is symmetric (no sign change), and this implies aligned spins, as in the triplet states. (Exercises 45 and 46 investigate separating spatial and spin exchange symmetries.)

LS Coupling

For lighter atoms, the usual interaction among the various angular momenta is as follows: The valence electrons' orbital angular momenta interact to form a quantized total orbital angular momentum $\mathbf{L}_T$; the spins interact to form a quantized total spin angular momentum $\mathbf{S}_T$; then these two engage in an overall spin-orbit interaction, giving a quantized "grand total" angular momentum $\mathbf{J}_T$. Each angular momentum addition follows the standard rules we have discussed. This kind of interaction is known as *LS* coupling—the "final step" is coupling of L and S. At its root is the tendency for the electron repulsion to enforce correlation in the spatial states, including, of course, ℓ-values, which in turn, because the *multiparticle* state must be antisymmetric, demands correlation between the spin states. Only "after" these two correlations does a relatively weak overall spin-orbit interaction come into play.

The character of excited energy levels in monovalent atoms is much the same as in hydrogen, for the predominant effect of the inner-shell electrons is simply to screen the valence electron from almost all the positive charge in the nucleus. To sort out the effects of true multielectron interactions, let us examine the simplest case of interaction between two valence electrons: a helium atom in which one electron is excited while the other remains in the 1s. (Raising *both* out of the 1s would take more energy than liberating one *completely* and ionizing the atom.) Suppose the excited level is the 2p. By the angular momentum addition rules, the quantum number ℓ_T for the total orbital angular momentum may be anywhere from $|\ell_2 - \ell_1|$ to $(\ell_2 + \ell_1)$ in integral steps. Because ℓ is 0 for the 1s and 1 for the 2p, ℓ_T can be only 1. The spins couple to form a total spin s_T of 0 or 1—the singlet (antialigned) and triplet (aligned) states discussed above. Finally, $\mathbf{L}_T$ and $\mathbf{S}_T$ couple via a spin-orbit interaction to form a total angular momentum $\mathbf{J}_T$, where j_T may take on any value between $|\ell_T - s_T|$ and $(\ell_T + s_T)$ in integral steps. For $s_T = 0$, this is the single value ℓ_T, which is 1, while for $s_T = 1$, it may be 0, 1, or 2. Thus, we see that the excited electron has open to it many different 2p states. The conventional notation is given in the margin, where ℓ_T follows the same lettered scheme as for single electrons, except uppercase. Thus, the $(\ell_T, s_T, j_T) = (1, 0, 1)$ state is the singlet 2^1P_1 state, the $(1, 1, 1)$ state is the triplet 2^3P_1 state, and so on. In this notation, the *ground* state is the singlet 1^1S_0. There is no triplet 1^3S_1 state, for the spin state must be antisymmetric when two electrons are in the same spatial state. Table 3 summarizes how LS coupling governs states in helium with one electron excited.

Multielectron spectroscopic notation:
$n^{s_T+1}\ell_{T_{j_T}}$

In general, different LS coupled states are of different energy. Of the many factors competing to determine lowest energy, the major ones are the following: (1) The preference for an antisymmetric spatial state favors a symmetric spin state—a *larger* s_T. (2) The reduction in electrostatic repulsion afforded by having multiple $\ell \neq 0$ electrons orbit in the same direction, "passing one another" less often than if counterrevolving, favors a *larger* ℓ_T. (3) The spin-orbit interaction favors a *smaller* j_T. (A complete analysis can be found in any dedicated atomic physics text.)

With so many states split in so many ways, it should not be surprising that spectra can be quite rich. Figure 30, though not to scale, illustrates the wealth of spectral lines in excited helium just through $n = 3$. Some transitions are forbidden by selection rules:

$$\Delta\ell_T = \pm 1 \qquad \Delta s_T = 0 \qquad \Delta j_T = 0, \pm 1 \ (j_T = 0 \nleftrightarrow j_T = 0)$$

As usual, these are based on angular momentum conservation—the emitted photon has unit spin—and the ability of the atom in transition to oscillate as an electric dipole. Because Δs_T must be 0, the lines naturally divide into those among the $s_T = 0$ singlet states and those among the $s_T = 1$ triplet states. Interestingly, from the triplet 2^3S_1 state, a jump to the

TABLE 3 LS coupling in helium (one electron excited)

$n_1 \ell_1 n_2 \ell_2$	ℓ_T $\lvert \ell_2 - \ell_1 \rvert$ to $(\ell_2 + \ell_1)$	s_T $\lvert s_2 - s_1 \rvert$ to $(s_2 + s_1)$	j_T $\lvert \ell_T - s_T \rvert$ to $(\ell_T + s_T)$	State
$1s1s$	0	0	0	1^1S_0
$1s2s$	0	0	0	2^1S_0
		1	1	2^3S_1
$1s2p$	1	0	1	2^1P_1
		1	0	2^3P_0
			1	2^3P_1
			2	2^3P_2
$1s3s$	0	0	0	3^1S_0
		1	1	3^3S_1
$1s3p$	1	0	1	3^1P_1
		1	0	3^3P_0
			1	3^3P_1
			2	3^3P_2
$1s3d$	2	0	2	3^1D_2
		1	1	3^3D_1
			2	3^3D_2
			3	3^3D_3

ground state is not allowed. This is a good example of a **metastable state**. Transitions to the ground state can occur only by means other than electric dipole photon generation, such as interatomic collisions, which are invariably slow. Metastable states are central to the operation of lasers, and this particular one in helium is exploited in the common helium-neon laser.

It is worth noting that if an element is subjected to a weak external magnetic field, its spectral lines are further enriched, split according to m_{j_T} by the Zeeman effect. In fact, equations (33) to (35) may be used directly, with ℓ_T, s_T, and j_T replacing ℓ, s, and j. Somewhat misleading nomenclature from the early days of atomic physics persists. In the "normal" Zeeman effect, levels are split according to the z-component of *orbital* angular momentum alone, giving an odd number of levels, as noted in Section 1. Before spin was understood, splitting into an even number, as in Example 6, was inexplicable and known as the anomalous Zeeman effect. We now know that the "normal" behaviors merely involve multivalent atoms whose total spin is 0.

Figure 30 Helium's rich spectrum.

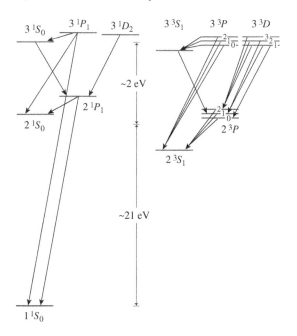

We won't delve deeper into multielectron-atom excitation spectra, except to identify an important alternative to LS coupling. It involves a spin-orbit coupling between *each* electron's **S** and **L**, yielding a quantized **J** for each, followed by a coupling of all these individual **J** vectors into a quantized grand total angular momentum $\mathbf{J_T}$. As the final step is coupling of individual **J** vectors, rather than $\mathbf{S}_T$ and $\mathbf{L}_T$, this kind of interaction is known as *jj*-coupling. It predominates in high-Z atoms, where the intense magnetic field of the highly charged "orbiting" nucleus favors an "immediate" spin-orbit interaction for each electron. Left until last is a **J** coupling that reduces the relatively weak electron repulsion.

PROGRESS AND APPLICATIONS

Controlling Quantum Coherence in Spin It is impossible to overstate the role of spin in modern technologies, and the developing field of quantum computing is an excellent example of its utility. Most schemes for building the basic units of a quantum computer rely in some way on spin—of electrons or of whole atoms or of nuclei. Many exploit both spin and the convenience of the quantum dot formed in a semiconducting solid. In quantum computing, however, preventing random external factors from altering the quantum state is crucial, and in some semiconductor quantum dots, the nuclear spins of the surrounding atoms

can perturb the confined electrons. A recent advance by a team at Harvard essentially neutralized these effects by using two nearby dots and two electrons (Petta, et al., *Science*, 30 September 2005, 2180–2184). In this system, the two qubit states, which can combine/superpose in an infinite number of ways, are those in which the electron spins are opposite and in which they are aligned—the singlet and (middle) triplet states of Section 9. To demonstrate the protection of the pure singlet state, the two electrons are begun in one dot in the same spatial state, requiring, of course, opposite spins. Via external controls, the potential energy is altered, and one electron is nudged to an adjacent dot separated by a barrier through which wave functions can pass/tunnel as depicted in Figure 31. The semiconductor nuclear spins affect the separated electrons differently, adding a random amount of triplet state pollution and destroying the previously coherent singlet state in only about 10 ns. However, by a clever and well-timed application of external voltages, the individual electrons' spins are swapped, effectively averaging out the asymmetries between the dots and returning the pair to a relatively pure singlet state as much as a microsecond later.

Passing Entangled Information to Photon Spin In the symmetric and antisymmetric combinations discussed in Section 2, the states of two particles are **entangled**. We don't say which is in state n and which in state n', but this fuzziness has a solid core, for if a subsequent measurement finds one to be in n, then the other is in n'. (The particles can be far apart when the measurement is carried out, but it doesn't represent instantaneous information transmission, so cause and effect is safe!) Numerous entangled systems of photons alone and atoms alone have been achieved in recent years, but entanglement between these two very different kinds of particles has now also been demonstrated, and it may one day be exploited to communicate quantum information from one place to another. In a University of Michigan experiment (Blinov, et al., *Nature*, 11 March 2004, 153–157), a single cadmium ion emits a photon as it deexcites. Two equally likely transitions are possible, depending on the alignment or antialignment of the cadmium electron's final state spin and the spin of the cadmium nucleus (the hyperfine interaction referred to in Section 7). Like electrons, photons have just two possible spin states, and angular momentum conservation demands that the photon's spin be one value for electron-nucleus antialignment and the other value for alignment. However, until a measurement is

made, either outcome might result, with equal probability. The atom is a two-state qubit (aligned or antialigned electron and nuclear spins) and so is the photon (spin states), and these qubits are entangled. The experiment detected photon spin state and final atomic (electron-nucleus) alignment and was repeated with many different orientations chosen as "up." It found excellent correlation between the atom and photon qubits, verifying the entanglement. A stationary atom seems a good place to store information, and a moving photon a good messenger. Hurdles in practical application lie ahead, but successfully passing the quantum baton from one to the other is an important advance.

Spintronics Today's electronic devices rely on electrons (and holes in semiconductors), and the vital characteristic exploited is their charge. As we know, electrons also possess spin, but electric current ordinarily flows in a state of random spin orientation, so spin is of little consequence. However, in this age of increasing control over material properties and microscopic structures, the possibility of exploiting this distinct trait has led to the field of study known as **spintronics**, short for spin electronics. An early success was the development of giant magnetoresistance (GMR) devices. The most famous, the **spin valve**, is the "eye" by which modern personal computers read the information stored on their hard disks. In the spin valve, two layers of metal qualifying as ferromagnetic (possessing a large, permanent internal magnetic field) sandwich a nonmagnetic conducting layer. If the outer layers' magnetizations are aligned, electrons of one spin orientation—intrinsic bar magnets that they are—flow easily between them, but if antialigned, electrons flow poorly. A passing data bit (magnetic region) on the spinning disk temporarily changes the magnetization direction of one layer, causing an unusually prominent change in resistance, hence the word magnetoresistance. In the late 1990s, this spin-based technology ushered in a considerable increase in information storage density over its predecessor (which, employing feebler non-spin-based magnetoresistance, was not "giant").

While this benefit has already made its mark, more applications are foreseen for spintronics. Control of one circuit by another, the essence of amplification and switching, is a primary element in essentially all of our existing electronics, and control of spin-polarized current in an operating circuit is a key goal in spintronics. An early proposal, the Datta-Das spin field effect transistor (SFET), was to sandwich a semiconductor between ferromagnets whose magnetizations are aligned, as illustrated in Figure 32. A potential difference would coax electrons from the source ferromagnet whose spins are aligned with its magnetization. Without

Figure 31 Two electrons with opposite spins in separate dots. The clusters represent semiconductor nuclei, which perturb the electron spins.

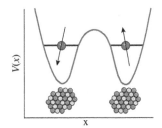

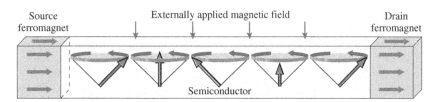

Figure 32 A proposed spintronic device, where spin precession in an external magnetic field controls electron flow from one ferromagnet to another.

external influences, these electrons would arrive aligned with the drain ferromagnet and be accepted. However, an applied magnetic field in the semiconducting region would impose a controllable precessional frequency and would thus control the degree of acceptance at the drain. Alas, such a device has yet to be made workable. Other methods of controlling spin current are being pursued, and there is no shortage of innovative proposals. Practical problems loom, however. Efficiently injecting a spin-polarized current into a semiconductor (the dominant fabric of modern circuits) and preserving its polarization, particularly at interfaces between materials, are major hurdles.

Chapter Summary

Fundamental particles possess intrinsic angular momentum, called spin, that is inherently quantized. The measure of this property is the value of s, a characteristic of a given kind of particle. The relationship between this numerical value and the particle's intrinsic angular momentum S is

$$S = \sqrt{s(s + 1)}\hbar \qquad (6)$$

The z-component of a particle's intrinsic angular momentum is quantized according to the value of a new quantum number, m_s.

$$S_z = m_s\hbar \qquad m_s = -s, -s + 1, \ldots, s - 1, s \qquad (9)$$

The electron is said to be a spin-$\frac{1}{2}$ particle, because $s = \frac{1}{2}$, and it follows that S is $\frac{\sqrt{3}}{2}\hbar$, $m_s = \pm\frac{1}{2}$, and $S_z = \pm\frac{1}{2}\hbar$. Inextricably related to spin is intrinsic magnetic dipole moment, and the relationship for the electron is $\boldsymbol{\mu_S} = -(e/m_e)\mathbf{S}$. With S_z and thus μ_{S_z} restricted to two values, the electron is much like a bar magnet with only two possible orientations along a given axis.

For an electron in an atom, the quantum numbers n, ℓ, and m_ℓ are said to specify the spatial state, while m_s specifies the spin state, up or down.

For a multiparticle system, the probability density must be unchanged if any two particle labels are exchanged. Solutions of the Schrödinger equation not violating this requirement are symmetric or antisymmetric combinations of products of individual-particle states. For two particles, these are

$$\psi_S \equiv \psi_n(1)\psi_{n'}(2) + \psi_{n'}(1)\psi_n(2) \qquad \text{Symmetric} \qquad (21)$$

$$\psi_A \equiv \psi_n(1)\psi_{n'}(2) - \psi_{n'}(1)\psi_n(2) \qquad \text{Antisymmetric} \qquad (22)$$

Although both give symmetric probability densities when squared, they are of different character. Particles are more likely to be found close together in the symmetric state and far apart in the antisymmetric.

A system of indistinguishable particles will form a multiparticle state of definite exchange symmetry—symmetric versus antisymmetric—depending on the particle spin. Particles whose spin s is an integer form symmetric multiparticle states and are known as bosons. Particles whose spin s is half-integral form antisymmetric multiparticle states and are known as fermions.

Because the antisymmetric combination of two states with the same full set of quantum numbers is identically 0, no two indistinguishable fermions may occupy the same individual-particle state. Electrons are fermions, so no two electrons in the same atom may possess the same set of quantum numbers. This is the exclusion principle.

Complete characterization of the multielectron atom is problematic. The Schrödinger equation cannot be solved exactly when multiple interparticle forces are involved. Nevertheless, understanding of much atomic behavior follows from one-particle quantum mechanics and application of the exclusion principle. Only two electrons may occupy the lowest-energy spatial state $n, \ell, m_\ell = 1, 0, 0$, one with $m_s = +\frac{1}{2}$ and one with $m_s = -\frac{1}{2}$. The greater the number of electrons, the higher must be the values of n they occupy. Consequently, many electrons may be far from the nucleus and screened from its attractive force by intervening lower-energy electrons. The number of valence electrons—weakly bound outer electrons—available to participate in chemical reactions with other atoms depends intimately on the number allowed in the various shells and subshells (n- and ℓ-values).

---

* indicates advanced questions

Conceptual Questions

1. A dipole *without* angular momentum can simply rotate to align with the field (though it would oscillate unless it could shed energy). One with angular momentum cannot. Why?

2. Does circulating charge require *both* angular momentum and magnetic moment? Consider positive and negative charges simultaneously circulating and countercirculating.

3. Summarize the connection between angular momentum quantization and the Stern-Gerlach experiment.

4. Compare and contrast the angular momentum and magnetic moment related to *orbital* motion with those that are *intrinsic*.

5. The neutron comprises multiple charged quarks. Can a particle that is electrically neutral but really composed of charged constituents have a magnetic dipole moment? Explain your answer.

6. Suppose that at the channel's outgoing end in the hydrogen ($\ell = 0$) Stern-Gerlach apparatus of Figure 3, you place a second such apparatus whose channel is aligned with the first but rotated 90° about the x-axis, so that its B-field lines point roughly in the y-direction instead of the z. What would you see emerging at the end of your added apparatus? Consider the behavior of the spin-up and spin-down beams separately. Assume that when these beams are separated in the first

apparatus, we can choose to block one or the other for study, but also assume that neither is deviated too far from the center of the channel.

7. Your friend asks: "Why is there an exclusion principle?" Explain in the simplest terms.

8. Imagine two indistinguishable particles that share an attraction. All other things being equal, would you expect their multiparticle spatial state to be symmetric, antisymmetric, or neither? Explain.

9. Whether a neutral whole atom behaves as a boson or a fermion is independent of Z, instead depending entirely on the number of neutrons in its nucleus. Why? What is it about this number that determines whether the atom is a boson or a fermion?

10. In nature, lithium exists in two isotopes: lithium-6, with three neutrons in its nucleus, and lithium-7, with four. As individual atoms, would these behave as bosons or as fermions? Might a gas of either behave as a gas of bosons? Explain.

11. The "radius of an atom" is a debatable quantity. Why?

12. Solving (or attempting to solve!) a 4-electron problem is not twice as hard as solving a 2-electron problem. Would you guess it to be more or less than twice as hard? Why?

13. Concisely, why is the table periodic?

14. A good electron thief needs a trap at low energy to entice its prey. A poor electron shepherd will have at least some of its flock dangling out at high energy. Consider rows 2 and 5 in the periodic table. Why should fluorine, in row 2, be more reactive than iodine, in row 5, while lithium, in row 2, is less reactive than rubidium, in row 5?

15. Discuss what is right or wrong about the following statement: Noble gases correspond to full shells.

16. Lithium is chemically reactive. What if electrons were spin-$\frac{3}{2}$ instead of spin-$\frac{1}{2}$. What value of Z would result in an element reactive in roughly the same way as lithium? What if electrons were instead spin-1?

17. What if electrons were spin-$\frac{3}{2}$ instead of spin-$\frac{1}{2}$. What would be Z for the first noble gas?

18. As indicated in Figure 16, to remove one of helium's electrons requires 24.6 eV of energy. Is its energy when orbiting -24.6 eV? Why or why not?

19. Early on, the lanthanides were found to be quite uncooperative when attempts were made to chemically separate them from one another. One reason can be seen in Figure 16. Explain.

20. Figure 16 shows that in the $Z = 3$ to 10 filling of the $n = 2$ shell (lithium to neon), there is an upward trend in elements' first ionization energies. Why is there a *drop* as Z goes from 4 to 5, from beryllium to boron?

21. As the $2p$ levels fill, from $Z = 5$ to 10, the elements' first ionization energies tend to increase. But, as Figure 16 clearly indicates, it is slightly *easier* to remove an electron from $Z = 8$ oxygen than from $Z = 7$ nitrogen. What might explain this?

22. Huge tables of characteristic X-rays start at lithium. Why not hydrogen or helium?

23. Bearing in mind its limiting cases of 1 and 2 mentioned in Section 8, how would you describe the significance of the Lande g-factor.

24. The total-spin singlet state for two electrons has one spin up and one down, but one of the triplet states does, too. What is the difference?

Exercises

Section 1

25. The electron is known to have a radius no larger than 10^{-18} m. If actually produced by circulating mass, its intrinsic angular momentum of roughly $\hbar$ would imply very high speed, even if all that mass were as far from the axis as possible. (a) Using simply rp (from $|\mathbf{r} \times \mathbf{p}|$) for the angular momentum of a mass at radius r, obtain a rough value of p and show that it would imply highly relativistic speed. (b) At such speeds, $E = \gamma mc^2$ and $p = \gamma mu$ combine to give $E \cong pc$ (just as for the speedy photon). How does this energy compare with the known internal energy of the electron?

26. In classical electromagnetism, the simplest magnetic dipole is a circular current loop, which behaves in a magnetic field just as an electric dipole does in an electric field. Both experience torques and thus have orientation energies, $-\mathbf{p} \cdot \mathbf{E}$ and $-\boldsymbol{\mu} \cdot \mathbf{B}$. (a) The designation "orientation energy" can be misleading. Of the four cases shown in Figure 4, in which would work have to be done to move the dipole horizontally *without* reorienting it? Briefly explain. (b) In the magnetic case, using B and μ for the magnitudes of the field and the dipole moment, respectively, how much work would be required to move the dipole a distance dx to the left? (c) Having shown that a rate of change of the "orientation energy" can give a force, now consider equation (4). Assuming that $\mathbf{B}$ and $\boldsymbol{\mu}$ are general, write $-\boldsymbol{\mu} \cdot \mathbf{B}$ in component form. Then, noting that $\boldsymbol{\mu}$ is not a function of position, take the negative gradient. (d) Now, referring to the *specific* magnetic field pictured in Figure 3, which term of your part (c) result can be discarded immediately? (e) Assuming that μ_x and μ_y vary periodically at a high rate due to precession about the z-axis, what else may be discarded as averaging to 0? (f) Finally, argue that what you have left reduces to equation (5).

27. Show that the frequency at which an electron's intrinsic magnetic dipole moment would precess in a magnetic field is given by $\omega \cong eB/m_e$. Calculate this frequency for a field of 1.0 T.

28. In the Stern-Gerlach experiment, how much would a hydrogen atom emanating from a 500 K oven $\left(\text{KE} = \frac{3}{2}k_B T\right)$ be deflected in traveling 1 m through a magnetic field whose rate of change is 10 T/m?

29. What angles might the intrinsic angular momentum vector make with the z-axis for a deuteron? (See Table 1.)

30. A hydrogen atom in its ground state is subjected to an external magnetic field of 1.0 T. What is the energy difference between the spin-up and spin-down states?

31. The subatomic omega particle has spin $s = \frac{3}{2}$. What angles might its intrinsic angular momentum vector make with the z-axis?

32. Is intrinsic angular momentum "real" angular momentum? The famous **Einstein-de Haas effect** demonstrates it. Although it actually requires rather involved techniques and high precision, consider a simplified case. Suppose you have a cylinder 2 cm in diameter hanging motionless from a thread connected at the very center of its circular top. A representative atom in the cylinder has atomic mass 60 and one electron free to respond to an external field. Initially, spin orientations are as likely to be up as down, but a strong magnetic field in the upward direction is suddenly applied, causing the magnetic moments of all free electrons to align with the field. (a) Viewed from above, which way would the cylinder rotate? (b) What would be the initial rotation rate?

33. Figure 3 shows the Stern-Gerlach apparatus. It reveals that spin-$\frac{1}{2}$ particles have just two possible spin states. Assume that when these two beams are separated inside the channel (though still near its centerline), we can choose to block one or the other for study. Now a second such apparatus is added after the first. Their channels are aligned, but the second one is rotated about the x-axis by an angle ϕ from the first. Suppose we block the spin-down beam in the first apparatus, allowing only the spin-up beam into the second. There is no wave function for spin, but we can still talk of a probability amplitude, which we square to give a probability. After the first apparatus' spin-up beam passes through the second apparatus, the probability amplitude is $\cos(\phi/2) \uparrow_{\text{2nd}} + \sin(\phi/2) \downarrow_{\text{2nd}}$, where the arrows indicate the two possible findings for spin in the second apparatus. (a) What is the probability of finding the particle spin up in the second apparatus? Of finding it spin down? Argue that these probabilities make sense individually for representative values of ϕ and that their sum is also sensible. (b) By contrasting this spin probability amplitude with a *spatial* probability amplitude, such as $\psi(x) = A e^{-bx^2}$, argue that although the arbitrariness of ϕ gives the spin case an infinite number of values, it is still justified to refer to it as a "two-state system," while the spatial case is an infinite-state system.

Section 2

34. Show that the symmetric and antisymmetric combinations of (19) and (20) are solutions of the two-particle Schrödinger equation (13) of the same energy as $\psi_n(x_1)\psi_{n'}(x_2)$, the unsymmetrized product (17).

35. Two particles in a box occupy the $n = 1$ and $n' = 2$ individual-particle states. Given that the normalization constant is the same as in Example 2 (see Exercise 36), calculate for both the symmetric and antisymmetric states the probability that both particles would be found in the left side of the box (i.e., between 0 and $\frac{1}{2}L$).

36. Verify that the normalization constant given in Example 8.2 is correct for both symmetric and antisymmetric states and is independent of n and n'.

37. The general form for symmetric and antisymmetric wave functions is $\psi_n(x_1)\psi_{n'}(x_2) \pm \psi_{n'}(x_1)\psi_n(x_2)$, but it is not normalized. (a) In applying quantum mechanics, we usually deal with quantum states that are "orthonormal." That is, if we integrate over all space the square of any individual-particle function, such as $\psi_n^*(x)\psi_n(x)$ or $\psi_{n'}^*(x)\psi_{n'}(x)$, we get 1, but for the product of *different* individual-particle functions, such as $\psi_n^*(x)\psi_{n'}(x)$, we get 0. This happens to be true for all the systems in which we have obtained or tabulated sets of wave functions (e.g., the particle in a box, the harmonic oscillator, and the hydrogen atom). Assuming that this holds, what multiplicative constant would normalize the symmetric and antisymmetric functions? (b) What value A gives the vector $\mathbf{V} = A(\hat{\mathbf{x}} \pm \hat{\mathbf{y}})$ unit

length? (c) Discuss the relationship between your answers in (a) and (b).

38. Two particles in a box have a total energy $5\pi^2\hbar^2/2mL^2$. (a) Which states are occupied? (b) Make a sketch of $P_S(x_1, x_2)$ versus x_1 for points along the line $x_2 = x_1$. (c) Make a similar sketch of $P_A(x_1, x_2)$. (d) Repeat parts (b) and (c) but for points on the line $x_2 = L - x_1$. (*Note:* $\sin[m\pi(L - x)/L] = (-1)^{m+1} \sin(m\pi x/L)$.)

* **39.** The wave functions for the ground and first excited states of a simple harmonic oscillator are $A e^{-bx^2/2}$ and $B x e^{-bx^2/2}$. Suppose you have two particles occupying these two states. (a) If distinguishable, an acceptable wave function would be $A e^{-bx_1^2/2}B x_2 e^{-bx_2^2/2}$. Calculate the probability that both particles would be on the positive side of the origin and divide by the total probability for both being found over all values of x_1 and x_2. (This kind of normalizing-as-we-go will streamline things.) (b) Suppose now that the particles are indistinguishable. Using the $\pm$ symbol to reduce your work, calculate the same probability ratio, but assuming that their multiparticle wave function is either symmetric or antisymmetric. Comment on your results.

Section 3

40. Here we consider adding two electrons to two "atoms," represented as finite wells, and investigate when the exclusion principle must be taken into account. In the accompanying figure, diagram (a) shows the four lowest-energy wave functions for a double finite well that represents atoms close together. To yield the lowest energy, the first electron added to this system must have wave function A and is shared equally between the atoms. The second would also have function A and be equally shared, but it would have to be opposite spin. A third would have function B. Now consider atoms far apart. As diagram (b) shows, the bumps do not extend much beyond the atoms—they don't

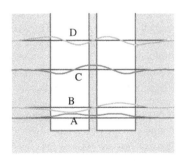

(a)

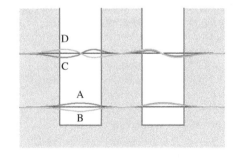

(b)

overlap—and functions A and B approach equal energy, as do functions C and D. Wave functions A and B in diagram (b) describe essentially identical shapes in the right well, while being opposite in the left well. Because they *are* of equal energy, sums or differences of A and B are now a valid alternative. An electron in a sum or difference would have the same energy as in either alone, so it would be just as "happy" in A, B, A + B, or A − B. Argue that in this spread-out situation, electrons can be put in one atom without violating the exclusion principle, no matter what states electrons occupy in the other atom.

41. What is the minimum possible energy for five (noninteracting) spin-$\frac{1}{2}$ particles of mass m in a one-dimensional box of length L? What if the particles were spin-1? What if the particles were spin-$\frac{3}{2}$?

42. **Slater Determinant:** A convenient and compact way of expressing multiparticle states of antisymmetric character for many fermions is the Slater determinant:

$$\begin{vmatrix} \psi_{n_1}(x_1)m_{s1} & \psi_{n_2}(x_1)m_{s2} & \psi_{n_3}(x_1)m_{s3} & \ldots & \psi_{n_N}(x_1)m_{sN} \\ \psi_{n_1}(x_2)m_{s1} & \psi_{n_2}(x_2)m_{s2} & \psi_{n_3}(x_2)m_{s3} & \ldots & \psi_{n_N}(x_2)m_{sN} \\ \psi_{n_1}(x_3)m_{s1} & \psi_{n_2}(x_3)m_{s2} & \psi_{n_3}(x_3)m_{s3} & \ldots & \psi_{n_N}(x_3)m_{sN} \\ \ldots & \ldots & \ldots & \ldots & \ldots \\ \psi_{n_1}(x_N)m_{s1} & \psi_{n_2}(x_N)m_{s2} & \psi_{n_3}(x_N)m_{s3} & \ldots & \psi_{n_N}(x_N)m_{sN} \end{vmatrix}$$

It is based on the fact that for N fermions there must be N different individual-particle states, or sets of quantum numbers. The ith state has *spatial* quantum numbers (which might be n_i, ℓ_i, and $m_{\ell i}$) represented simply by n_i, and spin quantum number m_{si}. Were it occupied by the jth particle, the state would be $\psi_{n_i}(x_j)m_{si}$. A column corresponds to a given state and a row to a given particle. For instance, the first column corresponds to individual-particle state $\psi_{n_1}(x_j)m_{s1}$, where j progresses (through the rows) from particle 1 to particle N. The first row corresponds to particle 1, which successively occupies all individual-particle states (progressing through the columns).

(a) What property of determinants ensures that the multiparticle state is 0 if any two individual-particle states are identical?

(b) What property of determinants ensures that switching the labels on any two particles switches the sign of the multiparticle state?

43. The Slater determinant is introduced in Exercise 42. Show that if states n and n' of the infinite well are occupied and both spins are up, the Slater determinant yields the antisymmetric multiparticle state:

$$\psi_n(x_1)\uparrow\psi_{n'}(x_2)\uparrow - \psi_{n'}(x_1)\uparrow\psi_n(x_2)\uparrow$$

44. The Slater determinant is introduced in Exercise 42. Show that if states n and n' of the infinite well are occupied, with the particle in state n being spin up and the one in n' being spin down, then the Slater determinant yields the antisymmetric multiparticle state:

$$\psi_n(x_1)\uparrow\psi_{n'}(x_2)\downarrow - \psi_{n'}(x_1)\downarrow\psi_n(x_2)\uparrow$$

45. Exercise 44 gives an antisymmetric multiparticle state for two particles in a box with opposite spins. Another antisymmetric state with spins opposite and the same quantum numbers is

$$\psi_n(x_1)\downarrow\psi_{n'}(x_2)\uparrow - \psi_{n'}(x_1)\uparrow\psi_n(x_2)\downarrow$$

Refer to these states as I and II. We have tended to characterize exchange symmetry as to whether the state's sign changes when we swap particle *labels*, but we could achieve the same result by instead swapping the particles' *states*, specifically the n and n' in equation (22). In this exercise, we look at swapping only *parts* of the state—spatial or spin. (a) What is the exchange symmetry—symmetric (unchanged), antisymmetric (switching sign), or neither—of multiparticle states I and II with respect to swapping *spatial* states alone? (b) Answer the same question, but with respect to swapping *spin* states/arrows alone. (c) Show that the algebraic sum of states I and II may be written

$$\left(\psi_n(x_1)\psi_{n'}(x_2) - \psi_{n'}(x_1)\psi_n(x_2)\right)\left(\downarrow\uparrow + \uparrow\downarrow\right)$$

where the left arrow in any couple represents the spin of particle 1 and the right arrow that of particle 2. (d) Answer the same questions as in parts (a) and (b), but for this algebraic sum. (e) Is the sum of states I and II still antisymmetric if we swap the particles' total—spatial plus spin—states? (f) If the two particles repel each other, would any of the three multiparticle states—I, II, and the sum—be preferred? Explain.

46. Exercise 45 refers to states I and II and puts their algebraic sum in a simple form. (a) Put the algebraic difference between these states in a similarly simple form. (b) Repeat parts (d) and (e) of Exercise 45 but for the algebraic difference.

47. A lithium atom has three electrons. These occupy individual-particle states corresponding to the sets of four quantum numbers given by (n, ℓ, m_ℓ, m_s) $= \left(1, 0, 0, +\frac{1}{2}\right)$, $\left(1, 0, 0, -\frac{1}{2}\right)$, and $\left(2, 0, 0, +\frac{1}{2}\right)$. Using

$\psi_{1,0,0}(\mathbf{r}_j)\uparrow$, $\psi_{1,0,0}(\mathbf{r}_j)\downarrow$, and $\psi_{2,0,0}(\mathbf{r}_j)\uparrow$ to represent the individual-particle states when occupied by particle j, apply the Slater determinant discussed in Exercise 42 to find an expression for an antisymmetric multiparticle state. Your answer should be *sums* of terms like

$$\psi_{1,0,0}(\mathbf{r}_1)\uparrow\psi_{1,0,0}(\mathbf{r}_2)\downarrow\psi_{2,0,0}(\mathbf{r}_3)\uparrow$$

Section 4

48. To investigate the claim that lower ℓ implies lower energy, consider a simple case: lithium, which has two $n = 1$ electrons and a lone $n = 2$ valence electron. (a) First find the approximate orbit radius, in terms of a_0, of an $n = 1$ electron orbiting three protons. (b) Assuming the $n = 1$ electrons shield/cancel out two of the protons in lithium's nucleus, find the orbit radius of an $n = 2$ electron orbiting a net charge of just $+e$. (c) Argue that lithium's valence electron should certainly have lower energy in a $2s$ state than in a $2p$ state.

49. Write the electronic configurations for phosphorus, germanium, and cesium.

50. Element 117 has never been found, but what would we expect its valence to be?

51. Were it to follow the standard pattern, what would be the electronic configuration of element 119?

52. The radius of cesium is roughly 0.26 nm. (a) From this, estimate the effective charge its valence electron orbits. (b) Given the nature of the electron's orbit, is this effective nuclear charge reasonable? (c) Compare this effective Z with that obtained for sodium in Example 3. Are the values at odds with the evidence given in Figure 16 that it takes less energy to remove an electron from cesium than from sodium? Explain.

53. Consider row 4 of the periodic table. The trend is that the $4s$ subshell fills, then the $3d$, then the $4p$. (a) Judging by adherence to and deviation from this trend, what might be said of the energy difference between the $4s$ and $3d$ relative to that between the $3d$ and $4p$? (b) Is this also true of row 5? (c) Are these observations in qualitative agreement with Figure 13? Explain.

54. A Simple Model: The multielectron atom is unsolvable, but simple models go a long way. Let us see how useful these are by considering lithium. (a) Treat one of lithium's $n = 1$ electrons as a single electron in a one-electron atom of $Z = 3$. Find the energy and orbit radius. (b) The other $n = 1$ electron, being in the same spatial state, must have the same energy and radius, but we must account for the repulsion between these electrons. Assuming they are roughly one orbit diameter apart, what repulsive energy would they share, and if each claims half this energy, what would be the energies of these two electrons? (c) Approximately what charge does lithium's lone valence electron orbit, and what radius and energy would it have? (d) Is it reasonable to dismiss the role of the $n = 1$ electrons in chemical reactions? (e) The actual energies of lithium's electrons are about -98 eV (twice, of course) and -5.4 eV. How good is the model? (f) Why should the model's prediction for the valence electron's energy differ in the direction it does from the actual value?

55. Consider $Z = 19$ potassium. As a rough approximation, assume that each of its $n = 1$ electrons orbits 19 protons and half an electron—that is, on average, half its fellow $n = 1$ electron. Assume that each of its $n = 2$ electrons orbits 19 protons, two $1s$ electrons, and half of the seven other $n = 2$ electrons. Continue the process, assuming that electrons at each n orbit a correspondingly reduced positive charge. (At each n, an electron also orbits some of the electron clouds of higher n, but we ignore this in our rough approximation.) (a) Calculate in terms of a_0 the orbit radii of hydrogenlike atoms of these effective Z. (b) The radius of potassium is often quoted at around 0.22 nm. In view of this, are your $n = 1$ through $n = 3$ radii reasonable? (c) About how many more protons would have to be "unscreened" to the $n = 4$ electron to agree with the quoted radius of potassium? Considering the shape of its orbit, should potassium's $n = 4$ electron orbit entirely outside all the lower-n electrons?

Section 5

56. Rank the following lines according to increasing wavelength: K_α, K_β, and L_α. Explain your answer.

57. The K_α line in copper is a very common one to use in X-ray crystallography. To produce it, electrons are accelerated through a potential difference and smashed into a copper target. The energies in a hydrogenlike atom as $Z^2(-13.6 \text{ eV}/n^2)$. Making the reasonable approximation that an $n = 1$ electron in copper orbits the nucleus and *half* of its fellow $n = 1$ electron, being unaffected by the roughly spherical cloud of other electrons around it, estimate the minimum accelerating potential needed to make a hole in copper's K shell.

58. Using a beam of electrons accelerated in an X-ray tube, we wish to knock an electron out of the K shell of a given element in a target. The energies in a hydrogenlike atom as $Z^2(-13.6\text{ eV}/n^2)$. Assume that for fairly high Z, a K-shell electron can be treated as orbiting the nucleus alone. (a) A typical accelerating potential in an X-ray tube is 50 kV. In roughly how high a Z could a hole in the K-shell be produced? (b) Could a hole be produced in elements of higher Z?

59. Estimate K_α characteristic X-ray wavelengths: A hole has already been produced in the $n = 1$ shell, and an $n = 2$ electron is poised to jump in. Assume that the electron behaves as though in a "hydrogenlike" atom, with energy given by $Z_{\text{eff}}^2(-13.6\text{ eV}/n^2)$. Before the jump, it orbits Z protons, one remaining $n = 1$ electron, and (on average) half its seven fellow $n = 2$ electrons, for a Z_{eff} of $Z - 4.5$. After the jump, it orbits Z protons and half of its fellow $n = 1$ electron, for a Z_{eff} of $Z - 0.5$. Obtain a formula for $1/\lambda$ versus Z. Compare the predictions of this model with the experimental data given in Figure 19 and Table 4.

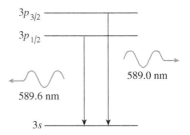

(the 3s having no orbital angular momentum to lead to spin-orbit interaction), there are two different wavelengths possible for the emitted photon. Calculate the difference in energy between the two photons. From this, obtain a rough value of the average strength of the internal magnetic field experienced by sodium's valence electron.

61. All other things being equal, should the spin-orbit interaction be a larger or smaller effect in hydrogen as n increases? Justify your answer.

TABLE 4	K_α X-rays
Z	$\lambda^{-1}(\text{nm}^{-1})$
20 (Ca)	3.0
30 (Zn)	7.0
40 (Zr)	12.7
50 (Sn)	20.3
60 (Nd)	29.9
70 (Yb)	41.8

Section 6

60. The well-known **sodium doublet** is two yellow spectral lines of very close wavelength, 589.0 nm and 589.6 nm. It is caused by splitting of the 3p energy level, due to the spin-orbit interaction. In its ground state, sodium's single valence electron is in the 3s level. It may be excited to the next higher level, the 3p, then emit a photon as it drops back to the 3s. However, the 3p is actually two levels, in which $\mathbf{L}$ and $\mathbf{S}$ are aligned and antialigned. (In the notation of Section 7 these are, respectively, the $3p_{3/2}$ and the $3p_{1/2}$.) Because the transitions start from slightly different initial energies yet have identical final energies

Section 7

62. Identify the different total angular momentum states (j, m_j) allowed a 3d electron in a hydrogen atom.

63. Show that unless $\ell = s$, $\mathbf{L}$ and $\mathbf{S}$ cannot be exactly opposite; that is, show that at its minimum possible value, for which $j = \ell - s$, the magnitude J of the total angular momentum is strictly greater than the difference $|L - S|$ between the magnitudes of the orbital and intrinsic angular momentum vectors.

64. Assuming that the spin-orbit interaction is not overwhelmed by an external magnetic field, what is the minimum angle the *total* angular momentum vector $\mathbf{J}$ may make with the z-axis in a 3d state of hydrogen?

65. What is the angle between $\mathbf{L}$ and $\mathbf{S}$ in a (a) $2p_{3/2}$ and (b) $2p_{1/2}$ state of hydrogen?

* 66. Whether adding spins to get total spin, spin and orbit to get total angular momentum, or total angular momenta to get a "grand total" angular momentum, addition rules are always the same: Given $J_1 = \hbar\sqrt{j_1(j_1 + 1)}$ and $J_2 = \hbar\sqrt{j_2(j_2 + 1)}$, where J is an angular momentum (orbital, spin, or total) and j a quantum number, the total is $J_T = \hbar\sqrt{j_T(j_T + 1)}$, where j_T may take on any value between $|j_1 - j_2|$ and $j_1 + j_2$ in integral steps; and for each value of J_T, $J_{Tz} = m_{jT}\hbar$, where m_{jT} may take on any of $2j_T + 1$ possible values in integral steps from $-j_T$ to $+j_T$. Since separately there would be $2j_1 + 1$

possible values for m_{j1} and $2j_2 + 1$ for m_{j2}, the total number of states should be $(2j_1 + 1)(2j_2 + 1)$. Prove it; that is, show that the sum of the $2j_T + 1$ values for m_{jT} over all the allowed values for j_T is $(2j_1 + 1)(2j_2 + 1)$. (*Note:* Here we prove in general what we verified in Example 5 for the special case $j_1 = 3, j_2 = \frac{1}{2}$.)

67. The general rule for adding angular momenta is given in Exercise 66. When adding angular momenta with $j_1 = 2$ and $j_2 = \frac{3}{2}$, (a) what are the possible values of the quantum number j_T and the total angular momentum J_T, (b) how many different states are possible, and (c) what are the (j_T, m_{jT}) values for each of these states?

68. Using the general rule for adding angular momenta discussed in Section 7 and further in Exercise 66, find the allowed values of j_T for *three* spin-$\frac{1}{2}$ fermions. First add two, then add the third.

69. The hydrogen spin-orbit interaction energy given in equation (25) is $(\mu_0 e^2/4\pi m\ r_e^2)^3 \mathbf{S} \cdot \mathbf{L}$. Using a reasonable value for r in terms of a_0 and the relationships $S = \frac{\sqrt{3}}{2}$ and $L = \sqrt{\ell(\ell + 1)}\hbar$, show that this energy is proportional to a typical hydrogen atom energy by the factor α^2, where α is the fine structure constant.

70. Angular momenta $\mathbf{J}_1$ and $\mathbf{J}_2$ interact so that they obey the strict quantum mechanical rules for angular momentum addition. If $j_1 = 1$ and $j_2 = \frac{3}{2}$, what angles between $\mathbf{J}_1$ and $\mathbf{J}_2$ are allowed?

Section 8

71. Repeat Example 6, but assume that the upper state is the $2p_{1/2}$ rather than the $2p_{3/2}$.

72. The spin-orbit interaction splits the hydrogen $4f$ state into many. (a) Identify these states and rank them in order of increasing energy. (b) If a weak external magnetic field were now introduced (weak enough that it does not disturb the spin-orbit coupling), into how many different energies would each of these states be split?

73. The angles between $\mathbf{S}$ and $\boldsymbol{\mu}_\mathbf{S}$ and between $\mathbf{L}$ and $\boldsymbol{\mu}_\mathbf{L}$ are 180°. What is the angle between $\mathbf{J}$ and $\boldsymbol{\mu}_\mathbf{J}$ in a $2p_{3/2}$ state of hydrogen?

74. The Zeeman effect occurs in sodium just as in hydrogen—sodium's lone $3s$ valence electron behaves much as hydrogen's $1s$. Suppose sodium atoms are immersed in a 0.1 T magnetic field.

(a) Into how many levels is the $3p_{1/2}$ level split?
(b) Determine the energy spacing between these states.
(c) Into how many lines is the $3p_{1/2}$ to $3s_{1/2}$ spectral line split by the field?
(d) Describe quantitatively the spacing of these lines.
(e) The sodium doublet (589.0 nm and 589.6 nm) is two spectral lines, $3p_{3/2} \rightarrow 3s_{1/2}$ and $3p_{1/2} \rightarrow 3s_{1/2}$, which are split according to the two different

possible spin-orbit energies in the $3p$ state (see Exercise 60). Determine the splitting of the sodium doublet (the energy difference between the two photons). How does it compare with the line splitting of part (d), and why?

75. Using $J^2 = L^2 + S^2 + 2\,\mathbf{L} \cdot \mathbf{S}$ to eliminate $\mathbf{L} \cdot \mathbf{S}$, as well as $L = \sqrt{\ell(\ell + 1)}\hbar$, $S = \sqrt{s(s + 1)}\hbar$, and $J = \sqrt{j(j + 1)}\hbar$, obtain equation (32) from the equation that precedes it.

76. A hydrogen atom is subjected to a magnetic field B strong enough to completely overwhelm the spin-orbit coupling. Into how many levels would the $2p$ level split, and what would be the spacing between them?

Section 9

77. What is the angle between the spins in a triplet state?

78. In its ground state, carbon's $2p$ electrons interact to produce $j_T = 0$. Given Hund's rule, what does this say about the total *orbital* angular momentum of these electrons?

79. In its ground state, nitrogen's $2p$ electrons interact to produce $j_T = \frac{3}{2}$. Given Hund's rule, how might the *orbital* angular momenta of these three electrons combine?

80. A beam of identical atoms in their ground state is sent through a Stern-Gerlach apparatus and splits into three lines. Identify possible sets $\{s_T, \ell_T\}$ of their total spin and total orbital angular momentum? Ignore possibilities in which s_T is 2 or higher.

81. (a) Show that, taking into account the possible z-components of J, there are a total of 12 *LS*-coupled states corresponding to $1s2p$ in Table 3. (b) Show that this is the same number of states available to two electrons occupying the $1s$ and $2p$ if *LS* coupling were ignored.

82. As is done for helium in Table 3, determine for a carbon atom the various states allowed according to *LS* coupling. The coupling is between carbon's two $2p$ electrons (its filled $2s$ subshell not participating), one of which always remains in the $2p$ state. Consider cases in which the other is as high as the $3d$ level. (*Note:* When both electrons are in the $2p$, the exclusion principle restricts the number of states. The only allowed states are those in which s_T and ℓ_T are both even or both odd.)

Comprehensive Exercises

83. Relativistic effects are rather small in the hydrogen atom, but not so in higher-Z atoms. Estimate at what value of Z relativistic effects might alter energies by about a percent and whether it applies equally to all orbiting electrons or to some more than others. For this crude guess, it is acceptable to combine quantum-mechanical results you have learned, related to energy, angular momentum, and/or probable radii, with some classical relationships.

84. (a) Estimate the repulsive energy between helium's electrons. Do this by comparing the energy required to remove the first electron, 24.6 eV (see Figure 16), then the second from the remaining hydrogenlike atom, to the energy required to remove both if there were no repulsion—that is, if both electrons behaved simply as though in a hydrogenlike atom. (b) How far apart would two electrons have to be to produce such a repulsive energy? (c) How does this distance compare with the approximate orbit radius in the $Z = 2$ hydrogenlike atom?

85. The 21 cm Line: One of the most important windows to the mysteries of the cosmos is the **21 cm line**. With it, astronomers map hydrogen throughout the universe. An important trait is that it involves a highly forbidden transition that is, accordingly, quite long-lived. But it is also an excellent example of the coupling of angular momenta. Hydrogen's ground state has no spin-orbit interaction—for $\ell = 0$, there is no orbit. However, the proton and electron magnetic moments do interact. Consider the following simple model. (a) The proton sees itself surrounded by a spherically symmetric cloud of $1s$ electron, which has an intrinsic magnetic dipole moment/spin that, of course, has a direction. For the purpose of investigating its effect on the proton, treat this dispersed magnetic moment as behaving effectively like a single loop of current whose radius is a_0, then find the magnetic field at the middle of the loop in terms of e, $\hbar$, m_e, μ_0, and a_0. (b) The proton sits right in the middle of the electron's magnetic moment. Like the electron, the proton is a spin-$\frac{1}{2}$ particle, with only two possible orientations in a magnetic field. Noting, however, that its spin and magnetic moment are parallel rather than opposite, would the interaction energy be lower with the proton's spin aligned or antialigned with that of the electron? (c) For the proton, g_p is 5.6. Obtain a rough value for the energy difference between the two orientations. (d) What would be the wavelength of a photon that carries away this energy difference?

Computational Exercises

86. Screening and Energy Dependence on ℓ: In Section 4, we claimed that the effects of screening by inner electrons were such that for outer electrons, a lower ℓ would have lower energy, given the same n. Here we investigate the claim. We begin with a form of the Schrödinger equation already adapted to the task. Computational Exercise lays out the steps that

transform the hydrogen atom radial equation to the following:

$$-\frac{d^2f(x)}{dx^2} + \left[\frac{\ell(\ell + 1)}{x^2} - \frac{2}{x}\right]f(x) = \widetilde{E}f(x)$$

The function $f(x)$ is actually $rR(r)$, and the transformation gives us a system of units where $x = 1$ is one Bohr radius and an energy $\widetilde{E} = -1$ is the hydrogen ground-state energy -13.6 eV. Computational Exercise solves the equation numerically and verifies that physically acceptable solutions occur when $(\widetilde{E}, \ell) = (-1, 0)$, $\left(-\frac{1}{4}, 0\right)$, $\left(-\frac{1}{4}, 1\right)$, $\left(-\frac{1}{9}, 0\right)$, $\left(-\frac{1}{9}, 1\right)$, and $\left(-\frac{1}{9}, 2\right)$; that is, the $1s$, $2s$, $2p$, $3s$, $3p$, and $3d$. Notably, energy depends *only* on n. A common way of attacking multielectron atoms is to assume that a given electron orbits the nucleus plus a rather inert cloud of other electrons. The second term in brackets in the above differential equation is the electrostatic potential energy term. To handle a diffuse charge cloud, we need only insert a $Z(x)$ in this term, accounting for the potential energy "felt" by an electron at a certain distance from the origin. Actually, we insert it in a form that further adapts the differential equation to a numerical solution.

$$f(x + \Delta x) = 2f(x) - f(x - \Delta x) +$$

$$\Delta x^2 \left[\frac{\ell(\ell + 1)}{x^2} - \frac{2Z(x)}{x} - \widetilde{E}\right]f(x)$$

We study lithium's lone $n = 2$ valence electron. To a good approximation, the effective Z produced by its three nuclear protons and the roughly fixed cloud from its two $n = 1$ electrons is given by

$$Z(x) = 7.5\exp(-1.26x) - 5.5\exp(-1.11x) + 1$$

(a) Plot $Z(x)$ from $x = 0$ to 10. Does it make sense at the limits? (b) Lithium's valence electron is not allowed in the full $1s$ level, whose two electrons have energies of roughly -100 eV, or about -7 in the units of this exercise. Which plots the *square* of $rR(r)$, as a guide, try values of $\widetilde{E}$ and ℓ until you find physically acceptable solutions whose shape is what we expect of $2s$ and $2p$ states. (Plotting out to $x = 15$ is sufficient.) Do these $n = 2$ states have equal energy? Can you explain the first ionization energy shown for lithium in Figure 16?

Answers to Selected Exercises

29. $45°$, $90°$, $135°$

31. $39.2°$, $75°$, $105°$, $140.8°$

33. spin up, $\cos^2(\phi/2)$

35. symmetric 0.43, antisymmetric 0.07

37. $1/\sqrt{2}$

39. (a) 0.25; (b) symmetric 0.409, antisymmetric 0.091

41. $19\ \pi^2\hbar^2/2mL^2$, $5\ \pi^2\hbar^2/2mL^2$, $8\ \pi^2\hbar^2/2mL^2$

45. (a) neither; (b) neither; (d) antisymmetric; symmetric; (e) yes; (f) sum

47. $\psi_{1,0,0}(\mathbf{r}_1)\uparrow \psi_{1,0,0}(\mathbf{r}_2)\downarrow \psi_{2,0,0}(\mathbf{r}_3)\uparrow$
$-\ \psi_{1,0,0}(\mathbf{r}_1)\uparrow \psi_{2,0,0}(\mathbf{r}_2)\uparrow \psi_{1,0,0}(\mathbf{r}_3)\downarrow$
$+\ \psi_{1,0,0}(\mathbf{r}_1)\downarrow \psi_{2,0,0}(\mathbf{r}_2)\uparrow \psi_{1,0,0}(\mathbf{r}_3)\uparrow$
$-\ \psi_{1,0,0}(\mathbf{r}_1)\downarrow \psi_{1,0,0}(\mathbf{r}_2)\uparrow \psi_{2,0,0}(\mathbf{r}_3)\uparrow$
$+\ \psi_{2,0,0}(\mathbf{r}_1)\uparrow \psi_{1,0,0}(\mathbf{r}_2)\uparrow \psi_{1,0,0}(\mathbf{r}_3)\downarrow$
$-\ \psi_{2,0,0}(\mathbf{r}_1)\uparrow \psi_{1,0,0}(\mathbf{r}_2)\downarrow \psi_{1,0,0}(\mathbf{r}_3)\uparrow$

49. phosphorus: $1s^2\ 2s^2\ 2p^6\ 3s^2\ 3p^3$; germanium: $1s^2\ 2s^2\ 2p^6$ $3s^2\ 3p^6\ 3d^{10}\ 4s^2\ 4p^2$; cesium: $1s^2\ 2s^2\ 2p^6\ 3s^2\ 3p^6\ 3d^{10}\ 4s^2$ $4p^6\ 4d^{10}\ 5s^2\ 5p^6\ 6s^1$

51. $1s^2\ 2s^2\ 2p^6\ 3s^2\ 3p^6\ 3d^{10}\ 4s^2\ 4p^6\ 4d^{10}\ 4f^{14}\ 5s^2\ 5p^6\ 5d^{10}$ $5f^{14}\ 6s^2\ 6p^6\ 6d^{10}\ 7s^2\ 7p^6\ 8s^1$

53. (a) $4s \rightarrow 3d$ is smaller; (b) yes; (c) yes

55. $0.054a_0$, $0.30a_0$, $1.64a_0$, $16a_0$; (b) yes; (c) ~3.8, no

57. 11 kV

59. $3.4\ \text{eV}/hc\ (3Z^2 + 5Z - 19.25)$

65. (a) $66°$; (b) $145°$

67. (a) $\frac{\sqrt{63}}{2}\hbar$, $\frac{\sqrt{35}}{2}\hbar$, $\frac{\sqrt{15}}{2}\hbar$, $\frac{\sqrt{3}}{2}\hbar$; (b) 20; (c) $(\frac{7}{2}, +\frac{7}{2})$, $(\frac{7}{2}, +\frac{5}{2})$, $(\frac{7}{2}, +\frac{3}{2})$, $(\frac{7}{2}, +\frac{1}{2})$, $(\frac{7}{2}, -\frac{1}{2})$, $(\frac{7}{2}, -\frac{3}{2})$, $(\frac{7}{2}, -\frac{5}{2})$, $(\frac{7}{2}, -\frac{7}{2})$, $(\frac{5}{2}, +\frac{5}{2})$, $(\frac{5}{2}, +\frac{3}{2})$, $(\frac{5}{2}, +\frac{1}{2})$, $(\frac{5}{2}, -\frac{1}{2})$, $(\frac{5}{2}, -\frac{3}{2})$, $(\frac{5}{2}, -\frac{5}{2})$, $(\frac{3}{2}, +\frac{3}{2})$, $(\frac{3}{2}, +\frac{1}{2})$, $(\frac{3}{2}, -\frac{1}{2})$, $(\frac{3}{2}, -\frac{3}{2})$, $(\frac{1}{2}, +\frac{1}{2})$, $(\frac{1}{2}, -\frac{1}{2})$

73. $167°$

77. $70.5°$

83. $Z \sim 20$ or higher, and smaller n

Statistical Mechanics

Chapter Outline

Think of it! We're surrounded by countless air molecules, whose velocities we cannot know, much less control. If they all moved in the same direction, we would be in trouble. Why don't they? Whenever there are countless particles free to move about, the answer is always the same—probabilities.

In statistical mechanics, our concern is making predictions about properties and behaviors in systems where the number of particles is huge—typically Avogadro's number. We cannot be absolutely certain about things, simply because it is impossible to know what each particle is doing. Faced with incomplete knowledge, we make *statistical* predictions based on the applicable laws of *mechanics*—classical or quantum. Necessarily, our prediction of what will be observed is the average of all the things that might possibly occur. Air pressure, for instance, a smooth effect according to human senses, we find to be perfectly explained as an average of forces exerted in isolated microscopic collisions.

Though it may seem ironic, since increasing the number of particles would appear to increase the amount of information that we *don't* know, statistical mechanics is able to make successful predictions, indeed *because* the number of particles is large. Averages over very large numbers are much more precise than those over small numbers. The average force per unit area exerted on our skin by the countless air molecules in a room is so extraordinarily predictable as to seem constant. If rooms contained "only" thousands of particles exerting the same average force per area by colliding more energetically, the effect would be a terrifying series of sporadic blows. Consider another example: an experiment in which a lone volunteer is placed in the center of a long hallway. What will be the location of the "particle" later? Obviously, a prediction is almost certain to be wrong. There are many things the subject might choose to do: walk one way, run the other, stop to think. But if Avogadro's number of volunteers were somehow available and released in the hallway, a prediction of the *average* location of the "particles" at a later time would be accurate. If they moved independently—that is, they didn't decide to stick together—their average location would be precisely where they were released. Just as many would go one way down the hall at a given speed as would go down the other. Even if they didn't move independently, there might be some way to model the correlation and still produce an accurate prediction.

A system in which the number of particles is large enough that predictions become very precise is known as a **thermodynamic system**. It is only in such macroscopic systems that the average properties of pressure, temperature, and density (or concentration) have real meaning. The molecules of air in a room, the electrons in a conducting wire, the photons within a bed of glowing coals—each constitutes a thermodynamic system. Two colliding electrons do not.

Thermodynamic system: Countless particles; precise average behaviors

Statistical mechanics is not nonclassical, or "modern," physics in the same sense that special relativity and quantum mechanics are. Rather, it is a distinct area of physics that applies to many others, classical as well as quantum. The answer to the obvious question "Why study it now?" is that we will soon encounter branches of modern physics that require it. A gas laser is a thermodynamic system of gas molecules, and a semiconductor is a thermodynamic system of atoms bound in a solid lattice.

In this chapter, we will be concerned mostly with understanding energy distributions. An energy distribution specifies the fraction of a system's particles that will be in a given energy state. Generally speaking, the higher the energy of a state, the smaller will be the number of particles in that state. To show how large numbers lead to reliable predictions, however, let us begin with another kind of distribution in one of the simplest thermodynamic systems imaginable.

1 A Simple Thermodynamic System

N = Total number of particles

Consider a box divided in half by an imaginary line, as depicted in Figure 1, and containing *N* point particles that are free to move back and forth. An example would be the air molecules in a room that is divided into right and left halves, which we refer to as the "two-sided room." The distribution we consider here is not an *energy* distribution, but a simpler one: the *number* of particles on a given side. The reader may wonder why we bother with so "trivial" a case. The obvious answer is that, on average, half the particles should be on each side. It isn't the simple answer that is important here, but the ease with which we can show that deviations from the expected distribution are negligible when *N* is large. The basic idea is this: There are only two possible "states" of a given air molecule—being on the right side and being on the left—and the probability of being in either of these states is $\frac{1}{2}$. But if the room contained only four molecules, it would not be safe to say that half are on each side—the probability of all being on one side is, in fact, 12.5%. It *would* be safe to say this, however, if the room contained a truly *macroscopic* number of molecules.

Being statistical predictions, distributions rest upon probabilities, and probabilities rest upon numbers of ways of doing something (e.g., arranging

Figure 1 A two-sided room.

Left   Right

20 apples in 5 baskets). For our two-sided room, the number of ways $W^N_{N_R}$ of arranging N air molecules so that N_R are on the right side is given by the **binomial coefficient:**

$$W^N_{N_R} = \binom{N}{N_R} \equiv \frac{N!}{N_R!(N-N_R)!} \tag{1}$$

For instance, if N were 4, there would be only one way of obtaining no molecules on the right side ($N_R = 0$)—that is, all four on the left, as shown at the top of Figure 2. Equation (1) agrees:

$$W^4_0 = \binom{4}{0} \equiv \frac{4!}{0!\,4!} = 1$$

The number of ways of obtaining one molecule on the right ($N_R = 1$) should be four, since any of the particles might be on that side.

$$W^4_1 = \binom{4}{1} \equiv \frac{4!}{1!\,3!} = 4$$

And there are six ways of obtaining two on one side.

$$W^4_2 = \binom{4}{2} \equiv \frac{4!}{2!\,2!} = 6$$

Now a point fundamental to statistical mechanics: All ways of arranging *specific* particles on given sides are equally probable.[1] But a state in which the distribution of particles is uniform, regardless of which specific particles are on which side, is the most probable, simply because there is a greater *number* of ways of obtaining it.

To see how large numbers lead to a precise average, consider cases of increasing N. For the case $N = 4$, the numbers of ways of obtaining the five distributions with different N_R are plotted in Figure 3(a). The total number of ways is $1 + 4 + 6 + 4 + 1 = 16$ and is approximately the area under the curve. Figure 3(b) plots numbers of ways of arranging 40 molecules. Of the 41 possible distributions, the maximum still occurs at $N_R = \frac{1}{2}N$, but it is *much* larger—10^{11} rather than 6. Even more important, the distributions in which N_R is far from $\frac{1}{2}N$ constitute a smaller *fraction* of the total number of ways of distributing molecules—again, the area under the curve. In other words, the curve is peaked more sharply at $N_R = \frac{1}{2}N$ than in the $N = 4$ case. The trend continues for $N = 400$. Only a tiny fraction of the total number of ways is far from the $N_R = \frac{1}{2}N$ distribution, so the probability of finding a significantly nonuniform distribution is very small. For the macroscopic case of 10^{23}, shown in Figure 3(d), the total number of ways occupies a minuscule region

Figure 2 Number of ways of distributing four particles on two sides.

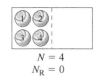

$$N = 4$$
$$N_R = 0$$

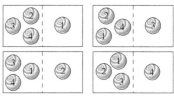

$$N = 4$$
$$N_R = 1$$

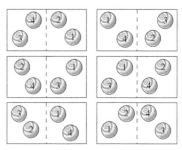

$$N = 4$$
$$N_R = 2$$

[1]Each way occurs with a probability of $\frac{1}{2} \times \frac{1}{2} \times \cdots = \frac{1}{2}N$ because the probability of a given particle being on a given side is $\frac{1}{2}$ and the total probability is the product, since particles, by assumption, move independently.

Figure 3 Number of ways of distributing particles on two sides of a room—variation as total number of particles increases from 4 to 10^{23}.

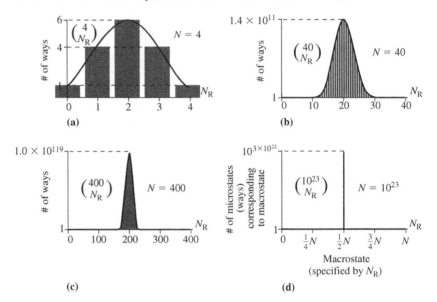

(a)

(b)

(c)

(d)

around $N_R = \frac{1}{2}N$. True, there is a *possibility* of the air in a room being predominantly on one side, but it is so extremely unlikely as to be dismissed. We have reached our conclusion: Each *individual particle* has a probability of $\frac{1}{2}$ of being in either of its two possible "states," left or right, and the *distribution* of particles will indeed have half in each state if it is a truly thermodynamic system.

Microstates and Macrostates

The two-sided room provides a good framework for learning some important terminology that helps us keep in mind the crucial distinction between the microscopic and the macroscopic. As shown in Figure 3(d), in the $N = 10^{23}$ case, there are $10^{3\times10^{22}}$ ways of obtaining the distribution in which $N_R = \frac{1}{2}N$. Each "way" is a different **microstate**. The microstate is the *state* of the system, given complete *micro*scopic knowledge of the states of the individual particles. In the two-sided room, the individual-particle states are simply "left" and "right." (For classical cases in general, as discussed in Section 4, the state may also encompass velocity, which we ignore here. For quantum cases, the individual-particle state is naturally a quantum state.)

Realistically, however, such microscopic information is unknowable. No real observer could keep track of molecules crossing the room and know which ones are on which side. The $10^{3\times10^{22}}$ microstates corresponding to $N_R = \frac{1}{2}N$ would be utterly indistinguishable. We assume that it is plausible to know at least the *number*, or concentration, of molecules on the two sides, but this constitutes knowledge of only the **macrostate**. To know the macrostate of a system is to know the properties that do not depend on the exact microscopic states of every individual particle: the overall properties of number, energy, and volume and the average local properties of pressure, temperature, and particle concentration. In the two-sided room, the $N_R = \frac{1}{4}N$ macrostate is that in which the particle concentration is three times as large on the left side as on the right—a ratio of $\frac{3}{4}$ to $\frac{1}{4}$. In the $N = 4$ case, four microstates correspond to this macrostate. The $N_R = 0$ macrostate has a vacuum on the right. There is only one way to do this; only one microstate corresponds to this macrostate. The $N_R = \frac{1}{2}N$ macrostate has equal particle concentrations on the two sides and is the one obtainable in the greatest number of microscopic ways: 6 for $N = 4$, and $10^{3 \times 10^{22}}$ for $N = 10^{23}$. Because it corresponds to the greatest *number* of microstates, all of which are assumed equally probable, it is the most probable macrostate. The most probable macrostate is what we know as the **equilibrium state**.[2]

Equilibrium

If left alone, thermodynamic systems eventually reach **equilibrium**, a macrostate whose macroscopic properties of pressure, temperature, and particle concentration do not change with time. Begun in a *nonequilibrium* macrostate, one for which the number of ways/microstates is relatively small, a thermodynamic system will pass through other macrostates, its macroscopic properties varying in space and time, while inexorably approaching its unchanging equilibrium state. In the two-sided room, for example, if air were released on one side and allowed to undergo free expansion, *both* the microstate and the macrostate would change—individual molecules would move from one side to the other and an observer would certainly detect the macroscopic wind. But the air eventually attains a macrostate of unchanging uniform distribution, because it is extremely unlikely that it would not sometime later, and for all time thereafter, be in one of the huge preponderance of microstates corresponding to that most probable macrostate. When this equilibrium point is reached, the *microstate* still changes—molecules still move about the room—but the macrostate does not. And if the system's macrostate is the same forever, so are its macroscopic properties. This unchanging, overwhelmingly most probable macrostate defines the equilibrium state.

In a more general system, where individual particles have available to them many different *energy* states, we might initially distribute the total energy in a strange way, perhaps putting half the particles in their ground states and half in their 37th quantum levels. But, in time, the system would assume its most probable state, with a predictable fraction of the particles in each individual-particle state. It is such equilibrium energy distributions that we study beginning in Section 3.

[2]The word *way* nearly always refers to a microstate. Expressions such as "microscopic ways" are thus redundant but are often used for clarity. The ambiguous term *state*, when applied to a system, usually refers to the macrostate. When applied to a particle, it refers to the individual-particle state, and if we knew *all* particles' "states," we would know the microstate.

2 Entropy and Temperature

O P T I O N A L

Everyone has some idea of what temperature means, but it may be somewhat disturbing when it suddenly appears *in an equation*. Because temperature does appear in all the energy distributions we consider, it is helpful to see how the idea becomes a quantifiable property. It begins with entropy.

The second law of thermodynamics says that the disorder—that is, the entropy—of an isolated system will not decrease. In contrast to other basic laws of physics, this law has a reason: *A more disordered state is a more probable state*, and thermodynamic systems invariably move toward more probable states. In the $N = 4$ case of the two-sided room, for instance, the $N_R = 2$ macrostate is more probable than the $N_R = 0$, and it is more disordered—a state with two molecules on each side is less ordered than one in which all are on one side. Given that disorder increases with probability, and probability with number of microscopic ways, we may give the concept of disorder a logical quantitative definition by relating it to the number of ways of obtaining the macrostate. For several reasons, we choose to define entropy S as proportional to the natural logarithm of the number of ways:

$$S \equiv k_B \ln W \tag{2}$$

where k_B is the Boltzmann constant. Because the equilibrium macrostate corresponds to the greatest number of microscopic ways, (2) says that *entropy is maximum at equilibrium*.

Why the choice of natural logarithm? First, numbers of ways tend to be proportional to numerical factors to the Nth power (e.g., $\frac{1}{2}^N$), so this definition gives an entropy proportional to the number of particles in the system. Consider the two-sided room with $N = 10^{23}$: In the $N_R = \frac{1}{2}N$ macrostate, $W = 10^{3 \times 10^{22}}$ and $S = k_B \ln W = k_B 7 \times 10^{22}$. It is no coincidence that the factor multiplying the Boltzmann constant is of the same order of magnitude as N. Second, it makes entropy additive. The total number of ways of arranging two independent systems is the product of the separate numbers of ways, $W_a \times W_b$, and the log of a product is the sum of the logs, so the total entropy is then the sum. Finally, by this definition, a state so completely ordered that it can be obtained in just one way has zero entropy, as in the totally ordered $N_R = 0$ macrostate of the two-sided room.

Relating entropy to number of ways is fairly easy in the two-sided room. In more complex, realistic cases, it is, of course, more difficult. Nevertheless, if W could somehow be calculated, the change in entropy according to (2) would be

$$\Delta S = S_f - S_i = k_B (\ln W_f - \ln W_i) = k_B \ln \frac{W_f}{W_i} \tag{3}$$

Fortunately, there is another way to calculate entropy changes that is, in most cases, easier to use and with which the reader is probably already familiar. Before we see how it fits in, let us investigate the link between entropy and temperature.

Temperature

In thermodynamics, temperature is given a clear, logical definition. Identified by layperson and scientist alike as the measure of the ability to transfer thermal energy, temperature's definition naturally involves the phenomenon of heat transfer.

Imagine two thermodynamic systems of fixed volume, perhaps two rigid containers of gas. The two systems cannot exchange *mechanical* energy by doing work on one another, but they are in "thermal contact," as in Figure 4, so that *thermal* energy can flow via microscopic collisions. Suppose heat is flowing slowly from system 1 to system 2. (We might say that system 1 is higher temperature, but this is not yet part of our vocabulary.) Slow heat flow between the two allows each individual system time to assume a new equilibrium state and entropy at each step of the process. Now consider a short time interval during which an infinitesimal amount of heat flows from system 1 to system 2. The total change in entropy is the sum of the changes:

$$dS_{total} = dS_1 + dS_2$$

Energy exchange alone causes the entropy change, so dS may be expressed as $(\partial S/\partial E)\, dE$. The partial derivative keeps other things constant that might affect the entropy.[3]

$$dS_{total} = \left(\frac{\partial S}{\partial E}\right)_2 dE_2 + \left(\frac{\partial S}{\partial E}\right)_1 dE_1$$

System 2 gains the energy lost by system 1, so we must have $dE_1 = -dE_2$:

$$dS_{total} = \left[\left(\frac{\partial S}{\partial E}\right)_2 - \left(\frac{\partial S}{\partial E}\right)_1 \right] dE_2$$

Now if systems 1 and 2 are far from being in equilibrium with one another, the entropy change of the total two-container system must be nonzero as it moves toward its maximum. Thus, $\partial S/\partial E$ would have to be *different* for system 1 than for system 2. But suppose that only an infinitesimal amount of heat remains to be transferred from 1 to 2 for the total system to attain equilibrium. Think of the entropy of the total system as a function of this small energy. If transferring it in one "direction" causes the entropy to increase to its maximum value, further energy transfer in the *same* direction must cause it to decrease, so dS_{total} would have to be 0 at this point. (A process carried out infinitesimally close to equilibrium is known as a "reversible" process. Entropy does not change in reversible processes.) Accordingly, $\partial S/\partial E$ would have to be the *same* for both. Thus, systems 1 and 2 will be in equilibrium with one another if and only if $\partial S/\partial E$ is the same for both. *This is exactly the property we ascribe to temperature.* For several reasons,[4] we define temperature as inversely proportional to $\partial S/\partial E$.

$$\frac{\partial S}{\partial E} \equiv \frac{1}{T} \tag{4}$$

A glance at equations (2) and (4) raises an obvious question: How on Earth do we take a derivative with respect to E of a number of ways? We

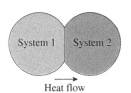

Figure 4 Two systems in "thermal contact."

Heat flow

[3]In general, entropy depends not only on a system's internal energy but also on its volume and the numbers of different kinds of particles/chemical species. It might be increased by heating at constant volume ($\Delta E > 0$, $\Delta V = 0$), by free expansion ($\Delta E = 0$, $\Delta V > 0$), or in a chemical reaction that changes neither the volume nor the internal energy.

[4]In heat transfer from system 1 to system 2, the disorder of system 2 must increase by more than the disorder of system 1 decreases; that is, $\partial S_2/\partial E > |\partial S_1/\partial E|$. A definition involving a reciprocal properly assigns to system 1 the larger value of T. The definition also agrees with the ideal gas law.

won't actually need the answer, and it is unfortunately rather involved, but it is worthwhile to proceed a bit beyond equation (4) to a relationship likely familiar and show a clear connection to "numbers of ways" in at least one simple case.

Equation (4), with its partial derivative, relates temperature to a change in entropy on the assumption of constant volume. In such a zero-work case, it would be valid to write $dS = (1/T) \, dE$. But because dE would then equal the heat dQ added to the system, we might as well write $dS = (1/T) \, dQ$. That this relationship is correct even when two systems are allowed to exchange energy via work follows from a straightforward generalization (see Exercise 24) of the earlier thermal-contact arguments. Integrating gives a rather famous result:

$$\Delta S = S_f - S_i = \int_i^f \frac{dQ}{T} \tag{5}$$

Note that while a system's entropy change depends only on its initial and final states, this way of calculating it requires a process in which the system is at each step infinitesimally close to equilibrium with its surroundings—a so-called reversible process. Now let us look at a simple application.

EXAMPLE 1

An ideal gas containing 10^{23} molecules is initially confined to one side of a room, then expands to fill the whole room. Its internal energy does not change. (a) Calculate its entropy change using equation (3). Stirling's approximation, $J! \cong \sqrt{2\pi J} J^J e^{-J}$, will be helpful. It is correct within $\frac{1}{10}\%$ for $J > 100$, becoming even more accurate as J increases. (b) Entropy/disorder should change by the same amount, no matter how the constant-energy expansion from initial to final state occurs. Assume that the air is kept always close to equilibrium by doing work against a slow-moving piston, while heat is constantly added to maintain the internal energy. Calculate its entropy change using equation (5).

SOLUTION

(a) Equation (3) tells us that $\Delta S = k_B \ln(W_f/W_i)$. In our simple two-sided room, there is only *one* way of having all particles on one side, and the number of ways of having $\frac{1}{2}N$ on each side is $N! / \left[\left(\frac{1}{2}N \right)! \right] \left[\left(\frac{1}{2}N \right)! \right]$. Thus,[5]

$$\frac{W_f}{W_i} = \frac{N! \left/ \left[\left(\frac{1}{2}N \right)! \right] \left[\left(\frac{1}{2}N \right)! \right] \right.}{1} = \frac{N!}{\left[\left(\frac{1}{2}N \right)! \right]^2}$$

Because N is so large, the approximation is valid.

$$\frac{W_f}{W_i} = \frac{\sqrt{2\pi N}\, N^N \, e^{-N}}{\left[\sqrt{2\pi \frac{1}{2}N} \left(\frac{1}{2}N \right)^{N/2} e^{-N/2} \right]^2} = \frac{\sqrt{2\pi N}}{\pi N} \frac{N^N}{\left(\frac{1}{2}N \right)^N} \frac{e^{-N}}{e^{-N}} = \sqrt{\frac{2}{\pi N}} 2^N$$

[5]Having narrowed the question to simply "Is it on the right or the left?" we are *defining* the initial entropy to be zero. We wouldn't ordinarily think of the disorder of air confined to half a room as zero, but the *change* in entropy/disorder is the same so long as we are consistent in ignoring the particles' *unchanging* thermal energy.

Now using a property of logarithms,

$$\Delta S = k_B \ln \left(\sqrt{\frac{2}{\pi N}} 2^N \right) = k_B \left(\ln 2^N + \ln \sqrt{\frac{2}{\pi N}} \right)$$

For $N = 10^{23}$, the second term in parentheses is negligible; the factor 2^N dominates the ratio of the numbers of ways. Thus,

$$\Delta S = k_B \ln 2^N = N k_B \ln 2$$

Inserting numerical values,

$$\Delta S = 10^{23}(1.38 \times 10^{-23} \, \text{J/K}) \ln 2 = 0.96 \, \text{J/K}$$

(b) Because the heat added equals the work done, we may replace dQ with $dW = PdV$. Using $PV = N k_B T$, this becomes $dW = (N k_B T/V) \, dV$. Thus,

$$\Delta S = \int_i^f \frac{(N k_B T/V) \, dV}{T} = N k_B \int_i^f \frac{dV}{V} = N k_B \ln \frac{V_f}{V_i} = N k_B \ln 2$$

The result is the same! While this, of course, does not prove that (3) and (5) are equivalent, they nevertheless are. It is interesting to reflect that by calculating an entropy change through such familiar properties as heat and temperature in equation (5), we are, by its equivalence to (3), determining a ratio of numbers of ways, final to initial.

The example reiterates a fundamental idea. Unconfined air expands and its entropy increases because the state in which the air is evenly distributed is a vastly more probable state than one in which it is unevenly distributed—the ratio of numbers of ways goes as 2^N! Thus, it would be extremely unlikely for the system to move away from equilibrium. The second law of thermodynamics boldly makes it official: It *will not* move away from equilibrium.

3 The Boltzmann Distribution

One of the most important and useful predictions of statistical mechanics is how energy will be distributed among a large number of identical particles that are able to exchange energy and thus reach a common equilibrium state (but are otherwise weakly interacting, with no explicit correlation in their behaviors). In the following sections, we study several such **equilibrium energy distributions** and their applications. Each gives the number of particles in a state of a given energy; that is, how many will be in their $n = 1$ states, how many in their $n = 2$, and so on. Although the word *equilibrium* may suggest uniformity, it is the most disordered state microscopically. Energy is constantly being exchanged randomly between particles; some will have less than the average energy, others more. It is one of the wonders of physics that knowing only whether the particles are bosons, fermions, or "classically distinguishable" particles, we can say

Figure 5 Harmonic oscillators exchanging energy.

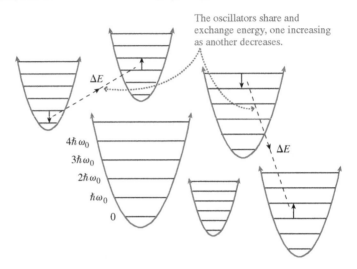

how many will be in each state. Once again, the simple reason is that average behaviors become quite predictable when N approaches Avogadro's number.

We begin with the **Boltzmann distribution**, a special case that applies when particles are so spread out that the indistinguishability of identical bosons or fermions may be ignored. A good example is a gas under ordinary conditions. The gas molecules, though identical, are so far apart as to not share the same space. Their wave functions don't significantly overlap; they can be distinguished.

A rigorous derivation of the Boltzmann distribution from principles of statistics is fairly involved. Since it reveals as clearly as possible how and why energy is distributed as it is, let us first consider a simple special case. Figure 5 represents a system of N identical but separately identifiable (i.e., distinguishable) harmonic oscillators, exchanging energy in some unspecified way—one oscillator jumps to a higher level as another drops to a lower. We choose the harmonic oscillator because its energy depends in a simple way on a single quantum number: $E = \left(n + \frac{1}{2}\right)\hbar\omega_0$. We simplify things further by shifting the potential energy (as is always allowed) by $-\frac{1}{2}\hbar\omega_0$ so that the ground-state energy is 0. The energy of the ith oscillator in its n_ith energy level is thus

$$E_{n_i} = n_i\hbar\omega_0 \qquad (n_i = 0, 1, 2, \dots) \qquad (6)$$

and the total energy of the N oscillators is

$$E = \sum_{i=1}^{N} n_i\hbar\omega_0 = M\hbar\omega_0 \qquad \text{where} \qquad M \equiv \sum_{i=1}^{N} n_i \qquad (7)$$

Note that the integer M, the sum of the quantum numbers of all oscillators, is directly proportional to the total energy.

To find the probability of a given particle/oscillator being in a given energy state, we must use some elementary probability and statistics. An axiom of statistics is that, given numerous equally likely possibilities, the probability that a particular subset will occur is the number of ways the subset might occur divided by the total number of ways of obtaining all possibilities. The probability of obtaining subset a is thus

$$P_a = \frac{\text{number of ways of obtaining subset } a}{\text{total number of ways of obtaining all possibilities}}$$

Applying this to our case, the probability that particle i will possess energy E_{n_i}— that its quantum number will be n_i— is

$$P_{n_i} = \frac{\text{number of ways energy can be distributed with } n_i \text{ fixed}}{\text{total number of ways energy can be distributed}} \qquad (8)$$

Here we are invoking the same postulate of statistical mechanics used in the two-sided room of Section 1: All microscopic ways of distributing a given total energy are assumed equally likely, so the probability depends merely on relative *numbers* of ways/microstates.

Now, the number of ways N integers—the particles' quantum numbers—can be added to give the integer M (see Exercise 34) is

$$\text{number of ways } N \text{ integers can add to } M = \frac{(M + N - 1)!}{M!(N - 1)!}$$
$$= \binom{M + N - 1}{M}$$

This would be the total number of ways the energy could be distributed among the N quantum numbers. The smaller number of ways energy can be distributed with n_i fixed is the number of ways the $N - 1$ *other* quantum numbers can be added to give $M - n_i$, which is proportional to the *remainder* of the energy. This would be the same expression, except with $N - 1$ replacing N and $M - n_i$ replacing M. Thus, the ratio in (8) becomes

$$P_{n_i} = \binom{(M - n_i) + (N - 1) - 1}{(M - n_i)} \Big/ \binom{M + N - 1}{M} \qquad (9)$$

Suppose now that $N = 10$ and $M = 50$. That is, there are ten particles/oscillators, and the sum of their quantum numbers is 50. The average energy per particle is

$$\overline{E} = \frac{E}{N} = \frac{M\hbar\omega_0}{N} = 5\hbar\omega_0 \qquad (10)$$

Figure 6 Probabilities of a given oscillator being in its n_i state, and Boltzmann probability.

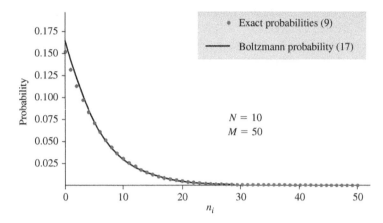

An average oscillator occupies its fifth energy level. The probability that particle i has the average energy—that $n_i = 5$ and the remaining nine particles' quantum numbers add to 45—would be

$$P_{n_i=5} = \left(\begin{array}{c} 45 + 9 - 1 \\ 45 \end{array} \right) \Big/ \left(\begin{array}{c} 50 + 10 - 1 \\ 50 \end{array} \right)$$

$$= 8.86 \times 10^8 / 1.26 \times 10^{10} = 0.0705$$

The probabilities given by (9) for all values of n_i are shown in Figure 6. The curve drops sharply as n_i increases, which leads to an important conclusion:

> Varying the energy of just one particle causes a sharp change in the number of ways of distributing the remaining energy among the other particles. The greatest freedom to distribute the remaining energy occurs when that one particle has the least energy. Therefore, the more probable state for a given particle, the state in which the number of ways of distributing the energy among all particles is greatest, is one of lower energy.

Equation (9) is cumbersome and limited to the special case of harmonic oscillators. In a system of infinite wells, for instance, E_n is proportional to n *squared*, and the expression would be entirely different. However, it may be shown that in the limit of large systems of distinguishable particles, *all* cases converge to the Boltzmann probability.

Boltzmann probability

$$P(E_n) = Ae^{-E_n/k_\mathrm{B}T} \tag{11}$$

This is the probability that in a large system at temperature T, an individual particle will be in state n of energy E_n, where n stands for the set of quantum numbers necessary to specify the individual-particle state (e.g., n, ℓ, m_ℓ, m_s). Probability drops exponentially with energy.

It is important to note that the Boltzmann probability and all the distributions yet to come can be applied to subsystems of larger systems. In small subsystems, there might be significant fluctuations, but the prediction still holds on average, becoming more precise as the subsystem grows. The large remainder of the overall system is what we call a **reservoir**. The temperature, appearing in all the distributions we discuss, is a well-defined property of the overall macroscopic system. (See Section 2.)

While the exponential in (11) obviously drops off qualitatively like the exact probabilities of Figure 6, a quantitative comparison might be more convincing. Doing so requires a diversion, but a very important one, for it spotlights one of the most basic tasks in statistical mechanics: finding an average.

We begin by noting that the probability summed over all individual-particle states n must be 1.

$$\Sigma\, P(E_n) = \sum_n A e^{-E_n/k_\text{B}T} = 1 \quad \Rightarrow \quad A = \frac{1}{\displaystyle\sum_n A e^{-E_n/k_\text{B}T}}$$

This step enables us to eliminate the multiplicative constant A and write the Boltzmann probability as

$$P(E_n) = \frac{e^{-E_n/k_\text{B}T}}{\displaystyle\sum_n e^{-E_n/k_\text{B}T}} \tag{12}$$

As always, the average of a quantity is the sum of the quantity's possible values times the probabilities for each. So the average energy of a particle is

$$\overline{E} = \Sigma\, E_n P(E_n) = \sum_n E_n \frac{e^{-E_n/k_\text{B}T}}{\displaystyle\sum_n e^{-E_n/k_\text{B}T}} = \frac{\displaystyle\sum_n E_n\, e^{-E_n/k_\text{B}T}}{\displaystyle\sum_n e^{-E_n/k_\text{B}T}} \tag{13}$$

A quotient like this is a very common form in which to express an average.

Now returning to the comparison of equations (9) and (11), if we insert equation (6) into (13), we have[6]

$$\overline{E} = \frac{\displaystyle\sum_{n=0}^{\infty} n\hbar\omega_0\, e^{-n\hbar\omega_0/k_\text{B}T}}{\displaystyle\sum_{n=0}^{\infty} e^{-n\hbar\omega_0/k_\text{B}T}} \tag{14}$$

The sums can then be carried out fairly easily (see Exercise 30), yielding

$$\overline{E} = \frac{\hbar\omega_0}{e^{\hbar\omega_0/k_\text{B}T} - 1} \tag{15}$$

[6] The average energy is the same for any particle, so we omit the subscript i on n. Also, while the particle cannot have more than the *total* energy—n cannot exceed M—the exponential probability drops to essentially 0 long before this point is reached, and the convenience of extending the sum to infinity introduces no error.

This result, important in its own right, we'll discuss again later, but for now it provides the link between temperature, found in the Boltzmann probability (11), and the integers M and N of the exact probability (9). We merely ensure that the average energies agree. The average energy in the exact approach is given in equation (10), $M\hbar\omega_0/N$. Substituting this for $\overline{E}$ in (15) and solving gives us the link.

$$k_{\mathrm{B}}T = \frac{\hbar\omega_0}{\ln(1 + N/M)} \qquad (16)$$

(See Exercises 31 and 32.) Inserting this and equation (6) back into (12) then gives the Boltzmann probability in terms of M, N, and n.

$$P(E_n) = \frac{N}{M + N}e^{-n\ln(1+N/M)} \qquad (17)$$

As shown in Figure 6, the exponential Boltzmann probability agrees quite well with the exact probabilities of (9). The slight deviation is due only to the fact that the N we have considered is so small. In a realistic macroscopic limit, the messy factorials and smooth Boltzmann function coincide precisely (see Exercise 33).

In the case depicted in Figure 6, where $M/N = 5$, equation (16) gives $k_{\mathrm{B}}T = \hbar\omega_0/\ln(1.2) \cong 5\hbar\omega_0$. Figure 7 shows the Boltzmann probability plotted versus energy for three different cases: $k_{\mathrm{B}}T/\hbar\omega_0 = \frac{1}{5}$, 1, and 5. Temperature is related to average particle energy, and $1\hbar\omega_0$ is the first energy above the zero-energy ground state. Therefore, the curves represent cases in which the average particle energy is less than, comparable to, and greater than the first excited-state energy. Sensibly, at the low temperature, we see that it is quite unlikely for a given particle to be in any energy level higher than the ground state, while at the high temperature, occupation of the ground state is not much more likely than occupation of the second, the third, and so forth.

Figure 7 Variation of Boltzmann probability from $k_{\mathrm{B}}T < \hbar\omega_0$ to $k_{\mathrm{B}}T > \hbar\omega_0$.

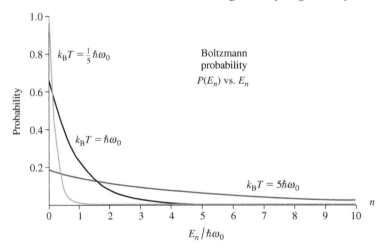

Often we are interested not so much in the *probability* of occupying a given state as in the *number* of particles expected to occupy that state, referred to as the **occupation number**, $\mathcal{N}$. (This symbol is chosen with care. It is a number, but we must not confuse it with the system's total number of particles, N, nor with a quantum number, often represented with an n.) The relationship is a simple one: The number expected in a given state is just the probability of occupying that state times the total number of particles N. Thus, the Boltzmann (occupation number) distribution follows directly from (11):

$$\mathcal{N}(E_n)_{\text{Boltz}} = NAe^{-E_n/k_{\text{B}}T} \qquad (18)$$

Boltzmann distribution

(Here again, n represents the full set of quantum numbers needed to specify the state.) Logically, given that summing probability (11) gives 1, summing (18) must give N. Though we omit the justification, the principle of Section 1 still applies: As the numbers occupying the various states become large, they also become precise. A thermodynamic system started with any odd distribution of energy would progress inexorably toward a vastly most probable equilibrium macrostate in which occupation number drops exponentially with energy (see Exercise 40).

Before going any further with the Boltzmann distribution, we call attention to a distinction often overlooked but crucial to applying all energy distributions. From their derivations, we find that they give a number of particles *in a given state* of energy E, not the number of a given energy E. These two things sound dangerously similar, but here is how they differ: If there are *multiple states of the same energy*, then the number of particles of energy E_n is the number in a given state of that energy—the occupation number $\mathcal{N}(E_n)$—times the number of states with that energy. This principle is so important in statistical mechanics as to merit memorization!

$$\begin{pmatrix} \text{number of} \\ \text{particles of} \\ \text{energy } E \end{pmatrix} = \begin{pmatrix} \mathcal{N}, \text{ number of} \\ \text{particles in a given} \\ \text{state of energy } E \end{pmatrix} \times \begin{pmatrix} \text{number of} \\ \text{states of} \\ \text{energy } E \end{pmatrix} \qquad (19)$$

EXAMPLE 2

Consider a sample of hydrogen atoms at a temperature of 300 K. (Ordinarily, hydrogen exists as diatomic molecules. We consider individual atoms for the sake of simplicity.) (a) What is the ratio of the number of atoms in $n = 2$ energy levels to those in $n = 1$? (b) At what temperature would the ratio be $\frac{1}{10}$?

SOLUTION

(a) Hydrogen's degeneracy (ignoring small effects like the spin-orbit interaction) is $2n^2$—the n^2 due to different ℓ and m_ℓ values and the 2 due to the lone electron's two allowed values of spin, m_s. Thus, the $n = 2$ level has eight different states with the same energy. Equation (18) says that the number of atoms in, for instance, the state $\{n, \ell, m_\ell, m_s\} = \{2, 1, +1, +\frac{1}{2}\}$, is

$$\mathcal{N}(E_{2,1,+1,+\frac{1}{2}}) = NA \exp\left(-\frac{E_{2,1,+1,+\frac{1}{2}}}{k_B T}\right)$$

Having the same energy, E_2, the $\{2, 0, 0, -\frac{1}{2}\}$, the $\{2, 1, -1, +\frac{1}{2}\}$, and all other $n = 2$ states have the same number. Similarly, there are two $n = 1$ states, $\{1, 0, 0, +\frac{1}{2}\}$ and $\{1, 0, 0, -\frac{1}{2}\}$, of energy E_1. So the ratio of the number of atoms in $n = 2$ states to those in $n = 1$ states is

$$\frac{\text{number with energy } E_2}{\text{number with energy } E_1} = \frac{\mathcal{N}(E_2) \times 8}{\mathcal{N}(E_1) \times 2}$$

$$= 4\frac{NAe^{-E_2/k_B T}}{NAe^{-E_1/k_B T}} = 4e^{-(E_2-E_1)/k_B T} \tag{20}$$

The hydrogen atom energies are $-13.6 \text{ eV}/n^2$, so that

$$E_2 - E_1 = \frac{-13.6 \text{ eV}}{2^2} - \frac{-13.6 \text{ eV}}{1^2} = 10.2 \text{ eV}$$

and at 300 K,

$$k_B T = (1.38 \times 10^{-23} \text{ J/K})(300 \text{ K}) = 4.14 \times 10^{-21} \text{ J} = 0.0259 \text{ eV}$$

Therefore,

$$\frac{\text{number with energy } E_2}{\text{number with energy } E_1} = 4e^{-10.2/0.0259} \cong 10^{-171}$$

At room temperature, the probability of finding even a single hydrogen atom in an excited state is practically zero.[7]

(b) Inserting in (20),

$$0.1 = 4e^{-10.2 \text{ eV}/k_B T} \quad \Rightarrow \quad T \cong 32{,}000 \text{ K}$$

The Sun's surface is about 6000 K, giving a ratio of about 10^{-8}. We conclude that except at extremely high temperatures, the overwhelming majority of hydrogen atoms are in their ground states.

For the sake of consistency with things to come, let us reexpress the average in (13) in terms of the occupation number (18) and leave off the subscript on $\mathcal{N}$ to allow for other distributions later. Thus,

$$\overline{E} = \frac{\displaystyle\sum_n E_n \mathcal{N}(E_n)}{\displaystyle\sum_n \mathcal{N}(E_n)} \tag{21}$$

Average energy (summation)

[7]Note that degeneracy increases but the energy difference is at most 13.6 eV. Might the number at a higher energy be greater? See Exercise 36.

This says that the average energy is the energy E_n of a given state times the number of particles in that state, summed over all states and then divided by the total number of particles in all states.

From a Sum to an Integral

Often in statistical mechanics, the spacing of the quantum levels is much smaller than typical particle energies. This is certainly the case classically, where discrete quantum levels are unresolvable, but is also true in many quantum thermodynamic systems. If quantum levels are indeed closely spaced, a sum over states may be replaced by an integral. As justification, consider the ratio of the Boltzmann probability at energy E_n to its value at the next higher energy, E_{n+1}.

$$\frac{e^{-E_n/k_BT}}{e^{-E_{n+1}/k_BT}} = e^{(E_{n+1}-E_n)/k_BT}$$

If $E_{n+1} - E_n$ is much smaller than k_BT—our definition of "closely spaced"—the ratio is nearly 1. In a sum, such as in equation (13), the summand would vary quite slowly with n, so replacing the sum by an integral should introduce little error.

However, a quantum number is rarely the most convenient integration variable (i.e., $\Delta n \rightarrow dn$). Energy is a logical alternative, but here we must be careful. Consider a simple case: Suppose we wish to calculate an average energy in a collection of hydrogen atoms via equation (21). In the numerator, the sum written out would begin

$$\sum_n E_n \mathcal{N}(E_n) = \sum_n E_n \, NAe^{-E_n/k_BT}$$

$$= E_{1,0,0,+\frac{1}{2}} \, NA \exp\left(-E_{1,0,0,+\frac{1}{2}}/k_BT\right) + E_{1,0,0,-\frac{1}{2}} \, NA \exp\left(-E_{1,0,0,-\frac{1}{2}}/k_BT\right)$$

$$+ E_{2,0,0,+\frac{1}{2}} \, NA \exp\left(-E_{2,0,0,+\frac{1}{2}}/k_BT\right) + E_{2,0,0,-\frac{1}{2}} \, NA \exp\left(-E_{2,0,0,-\frac{1}{2}}/k_BT\right)$$

$$+ E_{2,1,+1,+\frac{1}{2}} \, NA \exp\left(-E_{2,1,+1,+\frac{1}{2}}/k_BT\right) \cdots + \qquad (22)$$

Since the energy actually depends only on quantum number n, this sum over *states*, $\{1,0,0,+\frac{1}{2}\}$, $\{1,0,0,-\frac{1}{2}\}$, $\{2,0,0,+\frac{1}{2}\}$, ..., can be written instead as a sum over *energies* (a vital point!), $E_1, E_2, \ldots$, as follows:

$$E_1 NAe^{-E_1/k_BT} \times 2 + E_2 NAe^{-E_2/k_BT} \times 8 + \cdots$$

$$= \sum_{E_n} E_n \, NAe^{-E_n/k_BT} \times (\text{number of states of energy } E_n)$$

$$= \sum_{E_n} E_n \left[\mathcal{N}(E_n) \times (\text{number of states of energy } E_n)\right] \qquad (23)$$

To proceed to an integral, we would replace the discrete E_n by a continuous variable E, but, as we see, we still need to include the number of states at the given energy. In fact, this just restates the principle in (19). An average energy should involve multiplying a specific energy value times the number of particles with that energy, which, according to (19), is exactly the quantity in brackets in (23).

The final step in going from the sum in (21) to an integral must somehow give us a dE in the integrand. It arises naturally. If E indeed becomes a continuous variable, the number of states at a *particular* energy is differentially small, and we naturally account for this through the number of states *per range of energy*. The following rather tautological relationship expresses the idea:

differential number of states within range dE of E

$$= \frac{\text{differential number of states within range } dE \text{ of } E}{dE} dE \qquad (24)$$

The left side of (24) is what appears in brackets in (23), but we will instead insert the right side. In this way, we avoid choosing a new symbol for the left side, which could possibly be confusing—it is a number (of states), but not a total number of particles (N), nor a number occupying a given state ($\mathcal{N}$). More important, the noninfinitesimal quotient multiplying the dE on the right side contains the truly important information, as we will see. It is given the symbol $D(E)$ and the descriptive name **density of states**.

Density of states, defined

$$\frac{\text{differential number of states within range } dE \text{ of } E}{dE} \equiv D(E) \qquad (25)$$

Note that density of states has dimensions "one over energy."

Thus, applying (22) through (25), average (21) in the limit of closely spaced energy levels becomes

Average energy (integration)

$$\overline{E} = \frac{\int E \, \mathcal{N}(E) D(E) dE}{\int \mathcal{N}(E) D(E) dE} \qquad (26)$$

This form, which serves as our model of an average via integration, says that the average energy is a possible energy, E, times the number of particles in a state of that energy, $\mathcal{N}$, times the number of states per energy range at that energy, $D(E)$, times a range of energy, dE, summed over all energies, then divided by the total number of particles.

Actually determining densities of states can be complicated and depends on the system under study. As a first example, however, consider the simplest case, our trusty system of oscillators, ignoring spin. Where do we start? What relates allowed states to energy? The answer is the quantization condition special to the system:

$$E = n\hbar\omega_0$$

How many allowed states/quantum numbers are there in an energy range dE? As n changes by 1, E changes by $\hbar\omega_0$, so the ratio of the number of states covered per change in energy is just $1/\hbar\omega_0$. More formally,

$$dn = d\left(\frac{E}{\hbar\omega_0}\right) = \frac{1}{\hbar\omega_0}dE \quad \text{so} \quad \frac{\text{differential number of states}}{dE} = \frac{1}{\hbar\omega_0}$$

$$D(E) = \frac{1}{\hbar\omega_0} \qquad (27)$$

Density of states: Oscillators (spin ignored)

This density of states calculation may seem too cute and easy to be true, but it is correct. Because others later will be quite a bit more involved, it is helpful to consider briefly a case only slightly different. What if our system were, say, a collection of particles in a box? In this case, E would again be proportional to a single quantum number n, but *squared*. Contrary to the oscillator's equally spaced energies, the levels get farther apart as n increases. Shouldn't a "density of states" decrease as energy increases? It is left as an exercise to show, by the same procedure as above, that if $E \propto n^2$, then $D(E) \propto E^{-1/2}$. It does decrease as energy increases.

We close the section with a basic question: What would be the average energy in a system of oscillators if the temperature were high enough that the quantum levels could be considered "closely spaced"? This is the limit for which we have tailored (26). Inserting (18) and (27),

$$\overline{E} = \frac{\int E\, NAe^{-E/k_BT}\,(1/\hbar\omega_0)dE}{\int NAe^{-E/k_BT}\,(1/\hbar\omega_0)dE}$$

Several things cancel top and bottom: the multiplicative constant A, the total number of particles N, and, perhaps surprisingly, the density of states. While $D(E)$ always cancels this way when it doesn't actually depend on E, we are careful to put it where it belongs, for in several cases to come, it *will* depend on E. Now integration (see Exercise 38) over all energies from 0 to infinity gives a very simple result:

$$\overline{E} = k_BT \qquad (28)$$

Is our switch to integration valid? We obtained equation (15) via summation:

$$\overline{E} = \frac{\hbar\omega_0}{e^{\hbar\omega_0/k_BT} - 1}$$

It is left as an exercise to verify that in the limit of closely spaced energy levels, $\hbar\omega_0 \ll k_BT$, equation (15) becomes (28). It fits!

4 Classical Averages

The Boltzmann distribution is applicable only when indistinguishability of identical particles may be ignored. There are quantum thermodynamic systems in which the particles are distinguishable, but the Boltzmann distribution is often said to be a classical distribution, because it is the correct one in all systems in the limit where quantum mechanical behaviors converge to the classical.

Classical averages naturally involve not summation over allowed quantum states but integration over the continuum of "classical states"— that is, particle positions and velocities. In Cartesian coordinates, $dx\,dy\,dz\,dv_x\,dv_y\,dv_z$ is our infinitesimal element, and the energy E_n becomes $E(x, y, z, v_x, v_y, v_z)$, because kinetic energy depends on velocity and potential energies depend on position. Because we integrate over "states" rather than energies, we do not need a density of states, but the fact that we assume infinitely many states raises an interesting and subtle question. The uncertainty principle tells us that position and velocity/momentum cannot be known simultaneously with absolute precision, so it really makes no sense to speak of a continuum of such states. There is an inescapable granularity, a spacing between position and velocity values that can be declared truly distinct. Nevertheless, it can be shown that there is a one-to-one correspondence between quantum mechanical states and these "distinguishable" position-velocity states, so that accounting for the granularity would just introduce a proportionality constant that in calculating an average would cancel top and bottom.

In classical systems, it is quite common to calculate averages of quantities other than energy—location or speed, for instance. Fortunately we need no new apparatus. Equation (26) is a model for all averages. To average an arbitrary quantity Q, just put it in the integral with the exponential Boltzmann probability factor. (Note the analogy to expectation value in quantum mechanics, where knowing the probability density, $|\psi(x)|^2$, we find the average of any function of x simply by putting it in the integral with the probability.) The following example illustrates the point.

EXAMPLE 3

By approximating the atmosphere as a column of classical particles of mass m at temperature T in a uniform gravitational field g, calculate the average height of an air molecule above Earth's surface.

SOLUTION

Probability depends on energy, and in this example, we have

$$E = \text{KE} + U_{\text{grav}} = \frac{1}{2}m(v_x^2 + v_y^2 + v_z^2) + mgy \equiv \frac{1}{2}mv^2 + mgy$$

We may use (26) with two simple changes: We average y rather than E, and, as noted, there is no need for a density of states.

$$\bar{y} = \frac{\int y \, NA \, \exp\left[-(\frac{1}{2}mv^2 + mgy)/k_B T\right] dx \, dy \, dz \, dv_x \, dv_y \, dv_z}{\int NA \, \exp\left[-(\frac{1}{2}mv^2 + mgy)/k_B T\right] dx \, dy \, dz \, dv_x \, dv_y \, dv_z}$$

The constant NA cancels top and bottom, leaving the all-important exponential Boltzmann factor. Furthermore, integrations over all variables but y separate and cancel top and bottom. Carrying out the remaining integrations, we obtain

$$\bar{y} = \frac{\int_0^\infty y e^{-(mgy/k_B T)} dy}{\int_0^\infty e^{-(mgy/k_B T)} dy} = \frac{k_B T}{mg}$$

The result makes sense qualitatively. At a higher temperature, particles are more energetic and so should rise to greater heights. Conversely, if either m or g were larger, we wouldn't expect particles to rise as high. Inserting the mass of an N_2 molecule, $m = 4.7 \times 10^{-26}$ kg, and assuming a uniform temperature of 273 K (although the atmosphere is *not* of uniform temperature, nor is it all nitrogen), the result is 8.2 km, a bit less than the elevation of Mount Everest—a fair approximate value.

The Maxwell Speed Distribution

The distribution of speeds in an ideal gas is an important topic in classical thermodynamics. Known as the Maxwell speed distribution, it is just one of the many faces of the Boltzmann distribution.

We begin by considering the average of a yet unspecified property $f(v)$ that depends only on the gas particle's speed, v. Examples would be the speed itself and kinetic energy. The energy is assumed to be solely translational kinetic energy, dependent, of course, on v.[8]

$$E = \frac{1}{2}m(v_x^2 + v_y^2 + v_z^2) \equiv \frac{1}{2}mv^2$$

We now average, as in Example 3, but in this case the *spatial* integrations over the volume V cancel.

$$\overline{f(v)} = \frac{\int f(v) e^{-\frac{1}{2}mv^2/k_B T} \, dV dv_x dv_y dv_z}{\int e^{-\frac{1}{2}mv^2/k_B T} \, dV dv_x dv_y dv_z} = \frac{\int f(v) e^{-\frac{1}{2}mv^2/k_B T} \, dv_x dv_y dv_z}{\int e^{-\frac{1}{2}mv^2/k_B T} \, dv_x dv_y dv_z}$$

Since $f(v)$ depends only on speed, rather than on velocity, we further simplify things by using not rectangular velocity components but spherical polar coordinates: $v_x, v_y, v_z \rightarrow v, \theta, \phi$. By analogy with $dV = r^2 \sin\theta \, dr \, d\theta \, d\phi$ in *spatial* coordinates, the "volume" element in *velocity* coordinates is $dv_x \, dv_y \, dv_z \rightarrow v^2 \sin\theta \, dv \, d\theta \, d\phi$. With this replacement, the angular integrals cancel, and integration over speed v alone remains:

[8] Polyatomic ideal gases have internal degrees of freedom, rotational and vibrational, which depend on *relative* positions and velocities of atoms in the molecule. But these variables would separate and cancel, because $f(v)$ is a function of only the molecule's overall *translational* speed.

$$\overline{f(v)} = \frac{\int f(v)\, e^{-\frac{1}{2}mv^2/k_{\rm B}T}\, v^2 \sin\theta\, dv\, d\theta\, d\phi}{\int e^{-\frac{1}{2}mv^2/k_{\rm B}T}\, v^2 \sin\theta\, dv\, d\theta\, d\phi} = \frac{\int_0^\infty f(v)\, e^{-\frac{1}{2}mv^2/k_{\rm B}T}\, v^2\, dv}{\int_0^\infty e^{-\frac{1}{2}mv^2/k_{\rm B}T}\, v^2\, dv}$$

The denominator is a standard Gaussian integral, whose value works out to be $\sqrt{\pi}/2\,(k_{\rm B}\,T/m)^{3/2}$. Rearranging a bit, we arrive at

$$\overline{f(v)} = \int_0^\infty f(v)\left[\sqrt{\frac{2}{\pi}}\left(\frac{m}{k_{\rm B}T}\right)^{3/2} v^2 e^{-\frac{1}{2}mv^2/k_{\rm B}T}\right]dv \qquad (29)$$

Viewing (29) as $\overline{f(v)} = \int f(v)\, dP = \int f(v)\,(dP/dv)dv$, where P is probability, we see that the quantity in brackets is a probability per unit speed.

$$P(v)_{\rm Maxwell} = \frac{dP}{dv} = \sqrt{\frac{2}{\pi}}\left(\frac{m}{k_{\rm B}T}\right)^{3/2} v^2 e^{-\frac{1}{2}mv^2/k_{\rm B}T}$$

Often, the number per unit volume per unit speed is of greater interest, which follows simply by multiplying the probability per unit speed by N/V. The result is the **Maxwell speed distribution**:

Maxwell speed distribution

$$n(v)_{\rm Maxwell} = \frac{N}{V}\sqrt{\frac{2}{\pi}}\left(\frac{m}{k_{\rm B}T}\right)^{3/2} v^2 e^{-\frac{1}{2}mv^2/k_{\rm B}T} \qquad (30)$$

Figure 8 plots the distribution. As a reference, it indicates $v_{\rm rms}$, the **rms speed**. This is a very useful quantity, closely related to the average kinetic energy in a gas, and is an excellent example of a speed-dependent quantity one may calculate from the distribution. It is defined as $v_{\rm rms} \equiv \sqrt{\overline{v^2}}$—the square root of the mean of the square of the speed—hence, rms. In Exercise 41, it is shown to be $\sqrt{3k_{\rm B}T/m}$.

Because the plot of $n(v)_{\rm Maxwell}$ increases from 0 before decreasing, it might be tempting to conclude that probability does not strictly decrease with energy. On the contrary, the probability of occupation of a *given state/velocity* does drop exponentially with energy, but the *number of states*—velocity vectors—at a given speed increases as the square of the speed. Consider an analogy: The set of position vectors of a fixed magnitude describes a sphere of radius r centered at the origin. Doubling r would quadruple the area of the sphere. In effect, the "number of position vectors" of magnitude r increases as the area of a sphere, proportional to r^2. The same may be said of velocity. The "number of velocity vectors" of fixed speed v increases as v^2. It is the three-dimensional velocity element $dv_x dv_y dv_z = v^2 \sin\theta\, dv\, d\theta\, d\phi$ that introduces this factor, which should not be surprising, for this differential element accounts for the "number of states" in our classical sum/integral. Although the number of states/velocities increases with speed, causing the Maxwell distribution to increase initially, the exponentially decaying probability does eventually win out, bringing the distribution to 0.

Figure 8 Maxwell speed distribution.

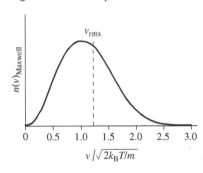

5 Quantum Distributions

In the ten-oscillator example of Section 3, we said that the number of ways of distributing energy with one particle fixed at energy E_{n_i} was the number of ways the other particles' quantum numbers could add up to account for the system's remaining energy. We implicitly assumed that switching the labels of any two particles yielded a *different* way of distributing energy. For instance, if $n_j = 5$ and $n_k = 2$ for particles j and k was one way, then $n_j = 2$ and $n_k = 5$ was a different way. However, if the particles are indistinguishable, then these are *not* different ways, and if numbers of ways are different quantum-mechanically than classically, then probabilities will also be different. From these ideas, perhaps seeming of little practical interest, arise many startling and far-reaching consequences.

Recall that there are two very different types of indistinguishable particles: bosons (integral spin) and fermions (half-integral spin). We now investigate how and why the distributions of energy in systems of these two should differ from the Boltzmann distribution and from each other. To see the basic distinctions most easily, we consider a simple case: four particles, a, b, c, and d, bound by a harmonic oscillator potential energy. It is convenient to define the ground-state energy as 0 and the spacing between levels as δE.

$$E_i = n_i \hbar \omega_0 \equiv n_i \, \delta E \qquad (n_i = 0, 1, 2, \dots)$$

Now suppose that the system has total energy $2\delta E$, that is,

$$n_a + n_b + n_c + n_d = 2$$

Given this constraint, how may the energy be distributed among the particles? Table 1 shows all possible ways/microstates for distinguishable particles. We see that the smallest quantum number is most common; the largest, least.

TABLE 1 Ways of distributing energy $2\delta E$ among distinguishable particles a, b, c, d

n	Ways	Number of times n appears (#)	Probability P (#/40)	Probable number of particles ($P \times 4$)
2	a b c d	4	0.1	0.4
1	ab ac ad bc bd cd	12	0.3	1.2
0	bcd acd abd abc cd bd bc ad ac ab	24	0.6	2.4
	Totals	40	1.0	4.0

TABLE 2 Ways of distributing energy $2\delta E$ among four indistinguishable bosons and spin-$\frac{1}{2}$ fermions

n	Ways	Bosons			Ways	Fermions $\left(s = \frac{1}{2}\right)$		
		Number of times n appears (#)	Probability P (#/8)	Probable number of particles ($P \times 4$)		Number of times n appears (#)	Probability P (#/4)	Probable number of particles ($P \times 4$)
2	X	1	0.125	0.5		0	0.0	0
1	XX	2	0.250	1.0	XX	2	0.5	2
0	XXX XX	5	0.625	2.5	XX	2	0.5	2
	Totals	8	1.000	4.0	Totals	4	1.0	4

Figure 9 The probable number of particles at the allowed energies depends on whether the particles are bosons, fermions, or distinguishable.

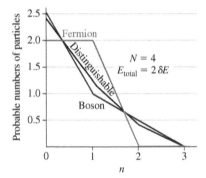

As always, *the probable number of particles in a given state decreases with increasing energy.*

If the particles are indistinguishable bosons, however, *there are no labels*, and truly different states are distinguished only by having different *numbers* of particles at different levels. Table 2 shows how the energy may be distributed in this case. Again, the probable number of particles drops with increasing energy, but in a different way. It would seem that bosons "like" being together in the ground state more than classical particles do. Yet another way is exhibited by indistinguishable $s = \frac{1}{2}$ fermions, for which any distribution with more than two particles in the same n is strictly forbidden by the exclusion principle. Plotting the tabulated data, Figure 9 illustrates these curious differences. (See Exercise 50 for a closer look at how indistinguishability and the exclusion principle should lead to the plots' distinctive shapes.)

It may be hard to accept that *physical* consequences arise merely from our inability to distinguish identical particles. (Why should the particles abide by these probabilities? How do *they* know we can't distinguish them?) As always, however, the answer is that the resulting predictions agree with the experimental evidence. As we will soon see, there is a sensible limit in which both bosons and fermions behave just as we would expect distinguishable particles to behave. But, in general, they behave in their own special ways *by nature*.

Now let us move on from our simple four-particle case to truly thermodynamic systems. For distinguishable particles, detailed, case-specific probabilities converge to the Boltzmann distribution. For quantum-mechanically indistinguishable particles, they converge to two different distributions: the **Bose-Einstein** for bosons and the **Fermi-Dirac** for fermions. Although introducing no new principles, they are rather involved.

Here we merely present the distributions and study how they compare.

$$\text{case-specific} \xrightarrow{\text{large } N} \mathcal{N}(E) = \begin{cases} \dfrac{1}{Be^{E/k_B T}} & \begin{array}{l} \text{Boltzmann} \\ \text{(distinguishable)} \end{array} & (31) \\[2ex] \dfrac{1}{Be^{E/k_B T} - 1} & \begin{array}{l} \text{Bose-Einstein} \\ \text{(bosons)} \end{array} & (32) \\[2ex] \dfrac{1}{Be^{E/k_B T} + 1} & \begin{array}{l} \text{Fermi-Dirac} \\ \text{(fermions)} \end{array} & (33) \end{cases}$$

Boltzmann and the two quantum distributions

Each is a probable number of particles occupying a given state. All are decreasing functions of E—the higher the state's energy, the fewer will be the particles occupying it. And in all cases, B is related to the total number of particles N. The most conspicuous difference is whether -1, 0, or $+1$ is added to the exponential in the denominator. The consequences can be drastic.

Demonstrating this quantitatively involves a determination of B, for although it is independent of E, B does in general depend on T, sometimes in a complicated way. Exercises 52 and 53 calculate $B(T)$ for the three distributions in a simple system of one-dimensional oscillators. The results are shown in Figure 10. Whether the temperature qualifies as high or low is measured relative to a constant $\mathcal{E}$ (discussed further shortly), defined as the topmost energy level that would be occupied *if* particles filled all individual-particle states, one particle per state, "upward" from the ground state. Of course, only fermions obey an exclusion principle, but $\mathcal{E}$ nonetheless serves as a good indicator of how spread out among energies we expect particles to be. If $k_B T$ is much greater than $\mathcal{E}$, we would expect particles to be spread out so diffusely among energy levels that there would be little chance of any two occupying the same state. So it shouldn't matter whether the particles are bosons, fermions, or classically distinguishable. But if $k_B T$ is much less than $\mathcal{E}$, suggesting that particles might tend to "pile up," bosons should show their enhanced tendency to crowd together into the ground state, while fermions should scrupulously avoid occupying the same state. Figure 10 bears out these expectations perfectly. At high temperature, $k_B T = 5\mathcal{E}$, the occupation number is much less than 1 for states at all energies, and the distributions nearly coincide. In the low-temperature plots, $k_B T = \frac{1}{5}\mathcal{E}$, the Bose-Einstein lies below the classical Boltzmann at intermediate energy levels but is higher at the smallest E values. The Fermi-Dirac, on the other hand, lies above the classical at intermediate energies and below at small values of E. The lower the temperature, the more pronounced will be the fermion curve's low-energy bulge, reflecting a packing of particles as "close" as the exclusion principle allows. Note the qualitative agreement between the $k_B T = \frac{1}{5}\mathcal{E}$ plots of Figure 10 and those in Figure 9, also a low-temperature case. (In fact, $2\delta E$ is the lowest energy possible for fermions in the four-particle case. Also note that the fermion data in Figure 9 plateaus at 2 instead of 1 only because it includes both spins at each energy, while Figure 10 applies to either up or down spin separately.)

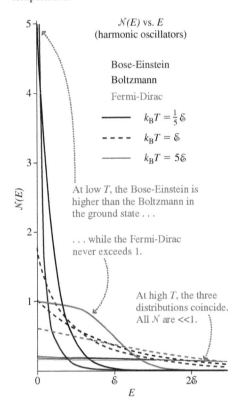

Figure 10 The three distributions for oscillators at low, intermediate, and high temperature.

$\mathcal{N}(E)$ vs. E
(harmonic oscillators)

Bose-Einstein
Boltzmann
Fermi-Dirac

$k_B T = \frac{1}{5}\mathcal{E}$

$k_B T = \mathcal{E}$

$k_B T = 5\mathcal{E}$

At low T, the Bose-Einstein is higher than the Boltzmann in the ground state . . .

. . . while the Fermi-Dirac never exceeds 1.

At high T, the three distributions coincide. All $\mathcal{N}$ are $\ll 1$.

Summarizing:

At high temperatures, particles are spread out sparsely over individual-particle states. With occupation numbers much less than 1, it is irrelevant whether the particles are bosons, fermions, or classically distinguishable, and the quantum distributions thus agree with the classical. At low temperatures, bosons tend to congregate in the lowest-energy individual-particle state, while fermions tend to fill states, one particle per state, up to some maximum energy.

Figure 11 Average oscillator energy versus temperature for the three types of particles.

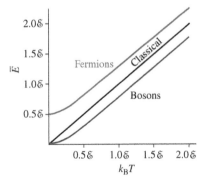

Plots of average particle energy, shown in Figure 11, are also illuminating. (The task of obtaining them is left to Computational Exercise 94.) At high temperatures, $k_B T \gg \mathcal{E}$, both boson and fermion cases are essentially plots of a linear relationship $\overline{E} = k_B T$, the same as the classical result (28). The particles are spread so diffusely among states that indistinguishability is unimportant. Even so, the energy is somewhat lower for bosons, which tend to congregate at lower levels more than would be expected classically, and is somewhat higher for fermions, which avoid already-occupied lower energy states. At lower temperatures, the average energy for bosons approaches 0, while that for fermions approaches $\frac{1}{2}\mathcal{E}$, the logical average when equally spaced levels fill uniformly from 0 to a maximum of $\mathcal{E}$.

The smooth curves in Figure 11 rely on the assumption that integration is valid—that k_BT is comparable to $\mathcal{E}$, which is a fairly high quantum level. But at *very* low temperatures, where k_BT is comparable to the spacing $\hbar\omega_0$ between individual levels, summation would be required. The boson case is particularly sensitive; the minus sign in the denominator of (32) causes a pronounced increase in $\mathcal{N}(E)$ near $E = 0$. One result is that the vast majority of particles in a boson gas may drop into the ground state, leading to "superfluid" behavior. We discuss this amazing phenomenon in Section 6, where we also introduce the electron gas, one of the most important *fermion* systems. But let us first take a look at an aspect of the Fermi-Dirac distribution that has nothing to do with the specific system.

The Fermi Energy

As Figure 10 shows, at low temperature, the Fermi-Dirac occupation number is nearly 1 out to a certain energy, where it quickly drops to nearly 0. This energy is known as the **Fermi energy** E_F. Strictly speaking, the Fermi energy is defined as the energy at which the occupation number is $\frac{1}{2}$. The convenience of this definition is that the constant B in (33) may be written in terms of E_F, no matter what the system might be. Given that $\mathcal{N}(E)_{FD} = \frac{1}{2}$ at $E = E_F$, we have

$$\mathcal{N}(E_F)_{FD} = \frac{1}{Be^{+E_F/k_BT} + 1} = \frac{1}{2} \quad \Rightarrow \quad B = e^{-E_F/k_BT}$$

Thus,

$$\mathcal{N}(E)_{FD} = \frac{1}{e^{(E-E_F)/k_BT} + 1} \tag{34}$$

In this form, it is easy to see that in the limit $T \to 0$, the Fermi-Dirac distribution is a "step function": 1 for $E < E_F$ and 0 for $E > E_F$. Figure 12 illustrates this all-or-nothing filling of states at $T = 0$ in the oscillator case.

Since it is really just another way of writing B, which is, in general, temperature dependent, the Fermi energy does vary with temperature, but its value at $T = 0$ is most important. Figure 13 for the oscillator case shows why. At $T = 0$, the occupation number drops to zero abruptly at E_{F0}. When k_BT is *not* 0 but still small compared with E_{F0}, the plot passes through $\frac{1}{2}$ at nearly the same energy—the Fermi energy is essentially constant. Moreover, it deviates from a true step function nearly symmetrically about the Fermi energy. Only when k_BT becomes comparable to E_{F0} is the bulge significantly depleted and the plot passes through $\frac{1}{2}$ at significantly lower energy. When we speak of a Fermi energy, we are usually referring to very low temperature, so it is justifiable to refer to "the" Fermi energy as if it were constant.

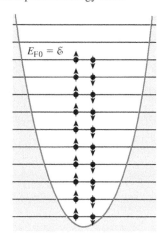

Figure 12 Fermion oscillators in the lowest possible energy state.

$E_{F0} = \mathcal{E}$

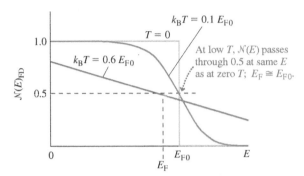

Figure 13 The Fermi-Dirac distribution at $T = 0$ and above. For low temperatures, the Fermi energy E_F differs little from its $T = 0$ value.

Exercise 56 derives the expression for E_F as a function of T on which Figure 13 is based and also verifies that its $T = 0$ limit, E_{F0}, is what it should be: the ε of Figures 10 and 11, the highest occupied energy in one-per-state filling. Although our observations here have been based mostly on a system of simple oscillators, the qualitative features are common to all systems of fermions.

6 The Quantum Gas

We now apply the quantum distributions to a situation more realistic than oscillators attracted to a common origin. As we do, we enter an area of physics that, since the 1990s, has been one of the most active in research, involving behaviors that a "classical physicist" would find completely baffling.

The system we consider is one in which N massive particles are free to move in three dimensions, as are molecules in a classical gas. (The massless photon is treated in Section 7.) However, we are not considering ordinary gases, but systems in which particle concentration is high enough that quantum indistinguishability must be taken into account. It may be a gas of bosons, such as spin-0 helium atoms, or a gas of fermions, such as spin-$\frac{1}{2}$ electrons in a metal. The particles are assumed to be moving freely, yet they are still bound to some region, so that they occupy discrete quantum states. The logical model is the infinite well, in which particles experience no force except at the confining walls. Of course, to allow for motion in three dimensions, we must use the 3D well.

Before looking at the quantitative side, a crude yet useful picture summarizes what we might expect to find. Figure 14(a) depicts a relatively high temperature, with speedy, short-wavelength particles bouncing about their well and enjoying their distinct individuality. Whether they are bosons or fermions matters little, for they are spread out over many, many states. Indeed, with such freedom, each might "cover" a range of wavelengths and behave like a well-localized particle, in keeping with the uncertainty principle. When things get cold, however, wavelengths get longer, freedom is restricted, and the line between boson and fermion becomes clear. Each fermion claims its own state, while bosons indulge their preference for piling together in the same lowest state.

Figure 14 Classical distinguishable particles at high T, and two different low-T behaviors. (Adapted from Nobel lecture by Wolfgang Ketterle, *Rev. Mod. Phys. 74*, October 2002.)

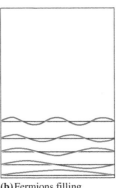

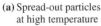

(a) Spread-out particles at high temperature

(b) Fermions filling lowest levels allowed

(c) Bosons all in the lowest possible level

So far as calculations go, we will mostly consider circumstances where quantum states are closely spaced and integration is valid, so we will need the density of states for our new system. The allowed energies in a 3D infinite well are shown to be

$$E_{n_x, n_y, n_z} = (n_x^2 + n_y^2 + n_z^2)\frac{\pi^2 \hbar^2}{2mL^2} \tag{35}$$

Computing the density of states is fairly simple for one-dimensional oscillators, because E is directly proportional to the lone quantum number n. How do we determine the number of quantum states in an energy interval dE now? This is one of those junctures in physics where we learn that the best resort is a trick: Picture the set (n_x, n_y, n_z) as coordinates in three-dimensional "quantum-number space," depicted in Figure 15, with each point representing a quantum state and a *unit volume* thus enclosing one state. The radial "distance" n from the origin in this space would be given by

$$n = \sqrt{n_x^2 + n_y^2 + n_z^2}$$

Thus,

$$E = \frac{\pi^2 \hbar^2}{2mL^2} n^2 \quad \text{or} \quad n = \sqrt{\frac{2mL^2 E}{\pi^2 \hbar^2}} \tag{36}$$

Sensibly, the "radius" increases with energy. Now, if the energy increases by dE, the radius increases by a corresponding dn, so an energy *interval* of dE encloses a "volume" in quantum-number space of $\frac{1}{8}4\pi n^2 \, dn$ (i.e., a one-eighth section of a spherical shell of thickness dn). But a *volume* in quantum-number space is a *number* of quantum states, so we may write

differential number of states in range $dE = \frac{1}{8}4\pi n^2 \, dn$

Figure 15 Allowed states in a 3D infinite well. The shell encloses all states in range dn at "radius" n—in this case, 5.

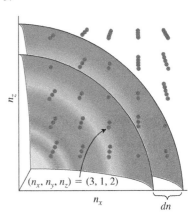

n_z

$(n_x, n_y, n_z) = (3, 1, 2)$

n_x

dn

Thus, by definition,

$$D(E) = \frac{\text{differential number of states in range } dE}{dE} = \tfrac{1}{8} 4\pi n^2 \frac{dn}{dE} \quad (37)$$

Of course, $D(E)$ should be a function of E, and what we have depends on n. It is left as an exercise to show that, using relationship (36) between n and E, n may be eliminated, leaving

$$D(E) = \frac{m^{3/2} L^3}{\pi^2 \, \hbar^3 \, \sqrt{2}} E^{1/2} \quad (38)$$

Finally, it is more convenient to express this in terms not of the box's side length L but of the volume $V = L^3$. We must also multiply by $2s + 1$ to account for the multiple allowed spin states.

$$D(E) = \frac{(2s + 1) \, m^{3/2} V}{\pi^2 \, \hbar^3 \, \sqrt{2}} E^{1/2} \quad (39)$$

Density of states: Gas in a 3D well
(massive particles)

A good starting calculation would be the familiar average particle energy. Unfortunately, the parameter B in the quantum distributions (32) and (33) depends on the system, and the complexity of these formulas and $D(E)$ prevents a closed-form calculation of B and, therefore, of $\bar{E}(T)$ for the quantum gas. However, even an approximate solution is revealing. Exercise 72 outlines the steps that give $\bar{E}(T)$ as a series in powers of the particle density N/V. The result is

$$\bar{E} \cong \frac{3}{2} k_{\mathrm{B}} T \left[1 \mp \frac{\pi^3 \, \hbar^3 \, \sqrt{2}}{(2s + 1)(2\pi m k_{\mathrm{B}} T)^{3/2}} \left(\frac{N}{V} \right)^1 + \cdots \right] \quad (40)$$

In contrast to our oscillators system, in which volume was not even a consideration, the average energy in a quantum gas depends on both temperature *and* particle density N/V. Squeeze the particles together—increase N/V—and the average fermion (bottom sign) energy increases, while for bosons it decreases. Note that this approximation is good only when T is not too low and the particle density not too high.

Let us look closer. The first term in (40) is sensible, being the famous average energy of a classical gas particle. It would seem, then, that the effects of quantum indistinguishability must arise in the second term. Actually, we can confirm this in two ways, each relying on ideas already introduced. First, as depicted in Figure 14(a), we claim that classical particle behavior should prevail if particles have *short* wavelengths and *large* separations. Wavelength depends on speed, and the rms speed (Section 4) of a gas particle is $\sqrt{3k_{\mathrm{B}} T/m}$. Therefore,

$$\lambda = \frac{h}{p} = \frac{h}{mv} = \frac{h}{m\sqrt{3k_{\mathrm{B}} T/m}} \propto \frac{h}{\sqrt{m k_{\mathrm{B}} T}}$$

The linear distance d between particles is roughly the cube root of the volume per particle—that is, $d \propto (V/N)^{1/3}$. Thus, the second term in equation (40) is proportional to $(\lambda/d)^3$. It is small when particles' wavelengths are much smaller than interparticle separations (the classical case), becoming large when particles' wave functions begin to overlap.

The second path is more roundabout but takes us through a result that has many applications. It is based on how diffusely the particles are spread out among the energy levels. To begin, we calculate the Fermi energy at $T = 0$. Strictly speaking, the Fermi energy applies only to a gas of fermions, for only they obey the exclusion principle. But for now we view it simply as a one-particle-per-state standard. If the energy of a system, no matter what kind of particle, is much greater than this standard, it is unlikely that multiple particles inhabit any state, and classical behavior should prevail. The starting point is an expression for the total number of particles:

$$N = \int_0^\infty \mathcal{N}(E)_{FD}\, D(E)\, dE \qquad (41)$$

(Remember: Number = number per state $\times$ states per $dE \times dE$.) A great simplification is that we consider $T = 0$, where $\mathcal{N}$ is simply a step function: 1 for $E < E_F$ and 0 for $E > E_F$. Thus, we simply integrate the number of states per energy $D(E)$ from 0 to E_F and solve for E_F.

$$N = \int_0^{E_F} \frac{(2s+1)m^{3/2}\,V}{\pi^2\,\hbar^3\,\sqrt{2}} E^{1/2}\, dE = \frac{(2s+1)m^{3/2}\,V}{\pi^2\,\hbar^3\,\sqrt{2}}\left(\frac{2}{3}E_F^{3/2}\right)$$

or

$$E_F = \frac{\pi^2\hbar^2}{m}\left[\frac{3}{(2s+1)\pi\sqrt{2}}\frac{N}{V}\right]^{2/3} \qquad (42)$$

This important result says that *even at zero temperature*, the greater the density of fermions, the higher will be their energies. We will have more to say about this shortly, but let us first show how it figures into (40). If we rearrange (42) a bit, we have

$$\frac{\hbar^3}{(2s+1)m^{3/2}}\frac{N}{V} \propto E_F^{3/2}$$

Thus, we see that the second term in (40) is proportional to $(E_F/k_BT)^{3/2}$. If $k_BT \gg E_F$, only the classical first term survives. The particles are spread so diffusely among states that quantum indistinguishability can be ignored.

Summarizing, a gas will behave classically so long as the "quantum term" in (40) is small, which can be expressed two ways:

$$\left(\frac{\lambda}{d}\right)^3 \ll 1 \quad \text{or} \quad \frac{N}{V}\frac{\hbar^3}{(mk_BT)^{3/2}} \ll 1 \qquad \text{Classical limit} \qquad (43)$$

When quantum effects do begin to arise, the average energy in a boson gas is lower than in a classical one (as was true for oscillators in Figure 11). Being related to average energy, the pressure is also lower. Conversely, the average energy and pressure in a fermion gas are higher than in a classical gas.

EXAMPLE 4

Show that the nitrogen molecules in the air around us need not be treated as indistinguishable particles.

SOLUTION

Equation (43) should provide the answer. If air does indeed behave classically, the ideal gas law allows us to replace N/V by $P/k_B T$.

$$\frac{P}{k_B T} \frac{\hbar^3}{(mk_B T)^{3/2}} = \frac{P \hbar^3}{m^{3/2}(k_B T)^{5/2}}$$

Now inserting 80%—nitrogen's share—of atmospheric pressure, a plausible room temperature of 300 K, and the molecular mass of diatomic nitrogen, we arrive at

$$\frac{(0.8 \times 1.01 \times 10^5 \, \text{Pa})(1.055 \times 10^{-34} \, \text{J} \cdot \text{s})^3}{(28 \times 1.66 \times 10^{-27} \, \text{kg})^{3/2}(k_B \times 300 \, \text{K})^{5/2}} \approx 9 \times 10^{-9}$$

The ratio is much less than 1, as it would clearly also be for oxygen and for any other temperatures naturally occurring, so the criterion for classical behavior is met.

Figure 16 Packing in more positive ions takes the single-atom potential energy to that of a finite well.

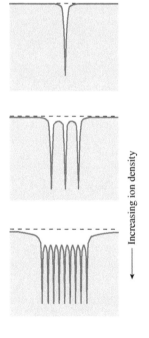

Increasing ion density

From the example, we see that our atmosphere is "classical," but in the many important bound systems where quantum indistinguishability *cannot* be ignored, our 3D infinite well model yields excellent predictions. One application arises in cosmology. By treating them as systems of gravitationally bound fermions and using result (42), we may predict the radii of so-called white dwarf stars and neutron stars. The conclusions are startling: A typical radius for a neutron star whose mass is somewhat larger than our Sun's is only about 10 km! Exercises 89 and 90 lay out the calculations step-by-step. Another very common application is that of the electrostatically bound conduction electrons in a metal.

Conduction Electron Energy Levels

In metals, some of each atom's valence electrons are shared among all atoms, moving essentially freely in three dimensions through the solid. They are known as **conduction electrons** and are a good example of a fermion gas. This "gas" is confined in a potential well whose origin, illustrated in Figure 16, is the net effect of the potential energies of the positive ions spaced regularly throughout the solid. The top diagram shows the potential energy of an electron in the presence of a single positive ion—a simple Coulomb potential energy. Three ions, of course, make the potential energy more complex, but as more ions are added, the net potential energy begins to assume the form of a finite well. In a crystalline solid, the density of positive ions is so great that a finite well becomes an excellent approximation. Often the even simpler *infinite* well model we have developed is valid. Accepting this, let us investigate whether the electron gas in a typical metal must indeed be treated as a quantum gas.

EXAMPLE 5

Assume that the conduction electrons in a piece of silver behave as a fermion gas, with each atom contributing one electron. Calculate the Fermi energy, then compare it with the energy that might be expected classically at room temperature. (The density of silver is 10.5×10^3 kg/m^3.)

SOLUTION

Equation (42) gives the Fermi energy in terms of properties easily determined. We know the mass and spin of electrons, but we must also determine the number of conduction electrons per unit volume. At one conduction electron per atom, this is equivalently the number of silver atoms per unit volume.

$$\frac{N}{V} = \frac{\text{mass/volume}}{\text{mass/atom}} = \frac{10.5 \times 10^3 \text{ kg/m}^3}{107.9 \text{ u} \times 1.66 \times 10^{-27} \text{ kg/u}} = 5.86 \times 10^{28} \text{ m}^{-3}$$

Thus,

$$E_F = \frac{\pi^2 \hbar^2}{9.11 \times 10^{-31} \text{ kg}} \left(\frac{3}{2\pi\sqrt{2}} 5.86 \times 10^{28} \text{ m}^{-3} \right)^{2/3}$$

$$= 8.8 \times 10^{-19} \text{ J} = 5.5 \text{ eV}$$

Were we to apply classical physics to the conduction electron gas, the average energy would be $\frac{3}{2} k_B T$. At a room temperature of 300 K, this is only about 0.04 eV, and we have shown that even at *zero* temperature, electrons in silver must fill states up to 5.5 eV! Here we have an excellent example of $k_B T \ll E_F$, where (40) would be an awful approximation, its "quantum term" much larger than its classical first term. Because $k_B T$ at room temperature is only about $\frac{1}{100} E_F$, the occupation number distribution would resemble the extreme nonclassical $T = 0$ plot of Figure 13. To electrons in a metal, room temperature is very cold. Temperatures hundreds of times higher would be needed before they could spread out among higher energy levels, and because such temperatures would vaporize most metals, we conclude that conduction electron behavior is a decidedly quantum-mechanical affair.

That the exclusion principle forces conduction electrons to fill up states unusually high by classical standards has a famous consequence, one that puzzled physicists terribly before quantum mechanics matured. The electrons' freedom to move about in a metal was obvious, and if behaving as a classical gas, that freedom should increase the heat capacity of metals relative to nonmetals. But the electrons' contribution is, in fact, very small, and the reason is that most of them, sandwiched between states already occupied by others, simply cannot gain energy from a modest increase in temperature. Only those few at the top near the Fermi energy, with some "room" to spread out, can gain energy. Thus, the large majority of electrons contribute nothing to the energy storage. (See Section 9.)

Other properties of metals also come into clearer focus. Work function, the minimum energy required to remove an electron from a metal, is simply the energy difference between the Fermi energy and the top of the finite well in which the conduction electrons are bound, pictured in Figure 17.

$$\phi = U_0 - E_F$$

Figure 17 Electron energies in a "cold" metal.

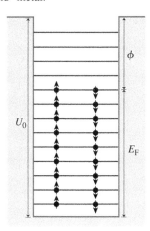

Figure 18 Contact potential arises from unequal work functions.

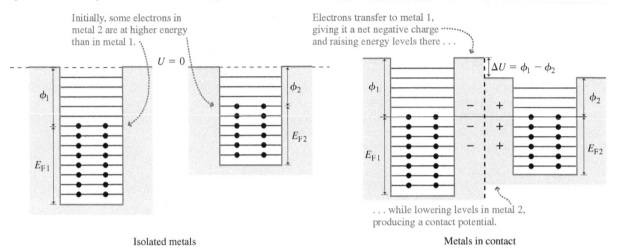

Initially, some electrons in metal 2 are at higher energy than in metal 1.

$U = 0$

Electrons transfer to metal 1, giving it a net negative charge and raising energy levels there . . .

$\Delta U = \phi_1 - \phi_2$

. . . while lowering levels in metal 2, producing a contact potential.

Isolated metals

Metals in contact

Moreover, it is the difference in the work functions of different metals that is responsible for the phenomenon of **contact potential**, the potential difference that develops when different kinds of metal come into contact. Suppose that two kinds of metal are electrically isolated and at the same electric potential, arbitrarily designated $V = 0$, and that the work function of metal 1 is greater than that of metal 2, as shown in Figure 18. When they are put in contact, the most energetic electrons in metal 2—that is, those ϕ_2 below the top of their finite well—are of greater energy than the most energetic in metal 1. Seeking a lower energy state, electrons from metal 2 move to metal 1. This effectively shifts the energy levels of metal 1 upward, through an increase in electrostatic repulsion, while correspondingly shifting the energy levels in metal 2 downward. The transfer of electrons stops when the two Fermi energies are at the same level.[9] At this point, metal 1 has a net negative charge, and the potential difference is $V_1 - V_2 = (\phi_1 - \phi_2)/(-e) = (\phi_2 - \phi_1)/e$.

While contact potential between dissimilar metals can have obvious effects—such as promoting corrosion—it alone does not make a battery. An equilibrium is, after all, established in which electrons cross the junction in equal numbers both ways, with no net transport. In fact, a voltmeter, which actually measures the "electrochemical" potential difference, would read 0. However, when combined with nonuniform heating—different temperatures at different places—calling into play another property in electron transport, a "battery" does result. The dependences on the various properties are too involved to discuss here, but they produce a reliable temperature-dependent potential difference. A bimetallic device that exploits the effect to measure temperature is known as a **thermocouple**, and it can operate over temperature ranges too extreme for conventional thermometers.

The conduction electron quantum gas is obviously important. But other systems of fermions should exhibit the same low-temperature characteristics.

[9] Only a minute fraction of the conduction electrons need to transfer to shift energy levels by the few electronvolts needed. See Exercise 69 for an order-of-magnitude estimate.

Even whole atoms, so long as they are fermions, should fill states one-by-one from the bottom. See Progress and Applications for a discussion of recent experimental verification that this is indeed true.

The Bose Gas and Bose-Einstein Condensation

Interest in the low-temperature behavior of quantum gases has multiplied enormously in recent years, since the achievement in the mid-1990s of the first true Bose-Einstein condensate. At very low temperatures, the minus sign in the denominator makes the Bose-Einstein distribution (32) very large near $E = 0$. The physical consequence in a boson gas is a decidedly nonsmooth dropping of particles into the lowest-energy quantum state—and amazing behavior! Helium-4 was the first example. As noted, under normal conditions, gases are so diffuse that it is irrelevant whether the particles are bosons or fermions. However, the helium-4 atom is a spin-0 boson; the total spin of its nucleus is 0 and its two $1s$ electrons also add to 0 spin. (By contrast, the helium-3 atom, with an odd number of spin-$\frac{1}{2}$ fermions in its nucleus, is a fermion. In the present discussion, "helium" means helium-4, the vastly more abundant form.) Reluctant to solidify, helium atoms move as a fluid down to very low temperatures. At some point, of course, interparticle forces become large, and the fluid is no longer a simple gas, as we have assumed, but becomes a liquid. Nevertheless, at very low temperatures, about 10%—a considerable fraction!—of its atoms "condense" into the same lowest-energy individual-particle state. If there are cases where quantum effects should be perceptible, this certainly qualifies.

Indeed, liquid helium exhibits so-called **superfluid** characteristics: negligible viscosity and near-perfect thermal conductivity. Both are consequences of the extreme order that reigns in a system where many of the particles move essentially as one. Where motion is disordered, viscosity and resistance to heat flow follow, but ordered motion implies streamlined collective behaviors. In liquid helium, the transition to the unusually ordered state occurs at about 2.2 K. Exercise 63 obtains an order-of-magnitude prediction of this temperature from the criteria of (43).

Superfluid properties are responsible for a remarkable phenomenon, shown in Figure 19. If, at very low temperature, a bowl is lowered into liquid helium and then raised above the surface, the liquid will crawl up the sides, seemingly defying gravity, and spill over the edge until the bowl is empty. The mechanism is capillarity combined with negligible viscosity and perfect thermal conductivity. Helium adheres to the inside surface of the bowl, creeping in a film up the side, similar to ordinary water in a capillary tube. In an ordinary liquid, a height limit is reached, due to temperature variations between liquid and bowl. When the bowl is hotter, the film evaporates; when colder, vapor condenses back to the liquid below. This, however, cannot occur in liquid helium, with its near-perfect thermal conductivity. Additional helium moves upward in the film, unimpeded by viscosity, to grasp the bowl at ever greater heights until the top edge is reached.

Because the interactions between particles are so strong in liquid helium-4, it doesn't demonstrate Bose-Einstein condensation as simply as we might

Figure 19 Superfluid liquid helium creeping out of its quarters. (Courtesy of A. Leitner, Rensselaer Polytechnic Institute.)

like. It is referred to as a two-component fluid—one a superfluid and the other normal. But advances in "holding" particles have led to the production of true Bose-Einstein condensates in numerous dilute gases, as well as in several other surprising systems, such as gases of paired fermions. These recent breakthroughs are discussed in Progress and Applications.

7 Massless Bosons: The Photon Gas

Photons, being spin-1, are bosons, but to study a gas of photons, we need a new density of states. The quantum gas density of states (39) isn't applicable, for it is based on energy quantization condition (35) for *massive* particles. It is expressed, however, not in terms of energy, but frequency.

$$\frac{\text{differential number of states in range } df}{df} = \frac{8\pi V}{c^3} f^2$$

Using $E = hf$, we convert this to the usual number per unit energy

$$\frac{\text{differential number of states in range } dE}{dE/h} = \frac{8\pi V}{c^3} (E/h)^2$$

so that

$$D(E) = \frac{8\pi V}{h^3 c^3} E^2 \qquad (44)$$

Density of states: Photon gas

    The photon application differs in another important way. Whereas situations abound in which a fixed number of massive objects is confined to some volume, this isn't the case for photons. A bowl containing liquid helium does not emit and absorb helium atoms; we might say it reflects them. All objects, however, are constantly emitting and absorbing photons. The point is that in a photon gas, the number isn't "chosen" beforehand; rather, it is determined by whatever conditions lead to equilibrium between the photons and the surrounding matter. It may seem strange to think of a gas of photons having a temperature and being in equilibrium with matter. But we can certainly imagine a nonequilibrium overall state where one is hotter than the other, where energy on average is transferred from photons to matter or vice versa. If they exchange energy but are otherwise isolated, a most probable/disordered state of uniform temperature must result.

    But this would seem to lead to a difficulty: How do we use the Bose-Einstein distribution if the number N is not fixed, for we have said that the distribution's parameter B is related to the total number of particles? For now, we just accept the happily simple conclusion: $B = 1$.

    Distribution in hand, we are ready to use the tools we have developed.

EXAMPLE 6

Internal energy in the form of electromagnetic radiation permeates all matter, since all matter contains oscillating charged particles. How do the energies of the radiation and matter compare? (a) First calculate the total photon energy in a volume V, calling it U_{photon}. (*Note:* To avoid overuse of symbols, we will henceforth tend to use U for the total internal energy of a macroscopic *system* of many particles, a "large" quantity, reserving E for the energy or average energy of a particle, a "small" quantity.) The following integral will be useful:

$$\int_0^\infty \frac{x^3}{e^x - 1} dx = \frac{\pi^4}{15}$$

(b) Assume that an ideal monatomic gas at STP (273 K, 1 atm) is in equilibrium with electromagnetic radiation. Find the ratio of the photon internal energy to the internal kinetic energy U_{matter} of the gas.

SOLUTION

(a) As noted earlier, the denominator in (26) is the total number of particles. The numerator is the total energy, and to calculate it, we need $\mathcal{N}(E)$ and $D(E)$—equations (32) and (44), respectively—with $B = 1$.

$$U_{photon} = \int E \frac{1}{1 \ e^{E/k_B T} - 1} \frac{8\pi V}{h^3 c^3} E^2 \, dE \tag{45}$$

We allow for all possible energies from 0 to infinity, so we may use the integral provided if we make the definition: $E \equiv k_B Tx$. Thus,

$$U_{photon} = \frac{8\pi V}{h^3 c^3} \int_0^\infty k_B Tx \frac{1}{e^x - 1} (k_B Tx)^2 k_B T dx = \frac{8\pi V k_B^4 T^4}{h^3 c^3} \int_0^\infty \frac{x^3}{e^x - 1} dx$$

or

$$U_{photon} = \frac{8\pi V k_B^4 T^4}{h^3 c^3} \frac{\pi^4}{15} = \frac{8\pi^5 V k_B^4 T^4}{15 \ h^3 c^3} \tag{46}$$

We see that the energy in a photon gas grows as temperature to the *fourth* power. As a rule, we expect *average* particle energies to be proportional to T to the first power, and this is indeed the case for the photon gas. The total grows so quickly because the *number* of particles/photons grows as T to the third (see Exercise 74).

(b) For electromagnetic radiation,

$$U_{photon} = \frac{8\pi^5 V k_B^4 (300 \, \text{K})^4}{15 \ h^3 c^3} = 6.1 \times 10^{-6} \, \text{J/m}^3 \times V$$

The kinetic energy of the atoms is N times the average energy of $\frac{3}{2} k_B T$. Using the ideal gas law,

$$U_{matter} = N \times \tfrac{3}{2} k_B T = \tfrac{3}{2} PV = \tfrac{3}{2}(1.013 \times 10^5 \, \text{Pa}) \times V$$

The ratio is

$$\frac{U_{photon}}{U_{matter}} = \frac{6.1 \times 10^{-6}}{\frac{3}{2}(1.013 \times 10^5)} = 4 \times 10^{-11}$$

We conclude that under ordinary conditions, the fraction of a thermodynamic system's total energy in the form of electromagnetic radiation is very small.

Thermodynamics and Light: Blackbody Radiation

Quantum statistical mechanics provides the crucial link between temperature and electromagnetic radiation. Previously, the nature of the electromagnetic radiation coming from an object of a given temperature was mostly a matter of observation. For example, the **Stefan-Boltzmann law** originated as merely a statement of the experimental observation that the radiation's intensity depends on T^4. The law is very important because it governs heat transfer via electromagnetic radiation, yet it lacked theoretical justification. Accordingly, equation (46), from which the law follows (see Exercise 78), was one of statistical mechanics' more celebrated early achievements.

To gain further insight, let us examine the integrand in (45). It is the contribution to the total electromagnetic energy of those photons whose energies lie in a small range dE around E.

$$dU_{\text{photon}} = E \frac{1}{e^{E/k_{\text{B}}T} - 1} \frac{8\pi V}{h^3\, c^3} E^2\, dE$$

Using $E = hf$, we may reexpress this in terms of f, giving the contribution due to the photons in the frequency range df around f:

$$dU_{\text{photon}} = \frac{hf^3}{e^{hf/k_{\text{B}}T} - 1} \frac{8\pi V}{c^3}\, df \tag{47}$$

Plotted in Figure 20, this is Planck's **spectral energy density**, or blackbody radiation law. Clearly, the total photon energy has a maximum, and it can be shown that the frequency at which this maximum occurs is directly proportional to the temperature. This is the essence of **Wien's law**, which, like Stefan-Boltzmann, was originally put forth without theoretical justification. (See Exercise 79 for the derivation.) The proportionality is reflected in Figure 20. The 2300 K curve has a maximum at a frequency of 238 THz; the 4600 K curve, at 476 THz. The T^4 dependence of the Stefan-Boltzmann law is also borne out, for the total energy in the 4600 K case (the area under the curve)

Figure 20 Electromagnetic energy radiated by an object versus frequency at two different temperatures.

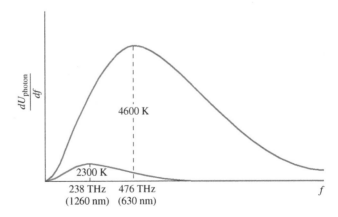

is 2^4 times that in the 2300 K case. Extrapolating to still lower temperatures, we can easily see why something at near room temperature, such as a human body, emits relatively little electromagnetic radiation, and essentially all of it at wavelengths longer than the 400–700 nm visible range. "Red hot" is very hot!

8 The Laser

Few modern scientific discoveries have attracted more attention than the laser. Eye surgery, communication, nuclear fusion, information storage and retrieval, product bar code readers, precision alignment, and holography are but a few of its applications. The heart of its utility is its production of **coherent** light. Light is coherent when it travels in only one direction, is of a single wavelength, and is in phase, meaning there are definite wave fronts where the oscillating electromagnetic field is at a maximum at a given instant—depicted in Figure 21. By contrast, light from an incandescent lightbulb diverges in all directions, contains a broad spectrum of wavelengths, and comprises disjoint pieces of waves produced by countless *independent* oscillating sources in the hot filament. While ordinary light can be focused with lenses or mirrors into a near-unidirectional beam, and gas vapor lights may produce reasonably well-defined wavelengths, a laser does these things better automatically. Above all, the "in phase" nature of its light cannot be well duplicated with ordinary sources. How is all this accomplished?

Light from ordinary sources is produced chiefly by **spontaneous emission**, one of the photon-atom interactions shown in Figure 22. Suppose the light-producing material is a gas, such as in a fluorescent bulb or sodium streetlight. An electron in a higher atomic energy level drops to a lower level in a short but unpredictable time, producing a photon. Transitions between the same levels in the material's many atoms produce photons that are of the same wavelength but uncoordinated, moving in arbitrary directions and not in phase with each other. Another possible photon-atom interaction occurs when an electron is promoted to a *higher* atomic energy level by *absorbing* a photon of precisely the correct wavelength. A third interaction is **stimulated emission**. An electron in one energy level, if influenced by a passing photon whose energy is precisely the difference between that level and a lower one, may be induced to drop to the lower level. In essence, the first photon stimulates the emission of a second photon of precisely the same wavelength. Moreover, the second photon moves in the same direction as and in phase with the first; they are coherent. The word *laser* stands for "light amplification by the stimulated emission of radiation."

To understand how we exploit stimulated emission to produce a coherent light source of *many* photons, we need to consider the exchange and balance of energy between matter and the electromagnetic radiation with which it interacts. As we do so, an intriguing conclusion arises.

Figure 21 Coherent versus incoherent light.

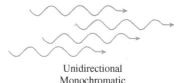

Unidirectional
Monochromatic
Not in phase
Not coherent

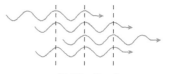

Unidirectional
Monochromatic
In phase
Coherent

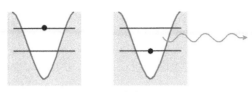

Figure 22 Three different photon-atom interactions.

Spontaneous emission

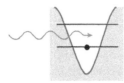
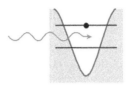

Absorption

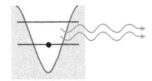

Stimulated emission

Let us assume that the matter is a gas of atoms and restrict our attention to transitions between just two of their energy states, as in Figure 22. The lower state we refer to as level 1 and the upper as level 2. It is reasonable that the rate of spontaneous emission, R_{spon}, should be proportional to the number of atoms poised to drop down from the upper level, N_2. We use A_{spon} for this proportionality constant.

$$R_{spon} = A_{spon} N_2$$

Similarly, the rate of absorption should be proportional to the number of particles in the lower level that are poised to be promoted, but it must also depend on the number of nearby photons that are of just the right energy to promote them. This energy would naturally be $E_2 - E_1 \equiv \Delta E$. For the number of photons of this energy, let us temporarily use the simple symbol $Y(\Delta E)$.

$$R_{abs} = B_{abs} N_1 Y(\Delta E)$$

Here we use B_{abs} for the proportionality constant. It was Einstein who first charted the course we follow, and the coefficients are known universally as the **Einstein A and B coefficients**. Finally, the rate of stimulated emission should depend on the number at the *upper* level, available for emission, and a*gain* on the number of photons of just the right energy.

$$R_{stim} = B_{stim} N_2 Y(\Delta E)$$

Now, assuming *equilibrium* between atoms and photons, the rate at which atoms make upward transitions from level 1 to level 2 must equal the downward transition rate. This is known as the "principle of detailed balance." Simply put, the two emission rates must add to the absorption rate.

$$A_{\text{spon}} N_2 + B_{\text{stim}} N_2 \, Y(\Delta E) = B_{\text{abs}} N_1 \, Y(\Delta E)$$

Solving for $Y(\Delta E)$,

$$Y(\Delta E) = \frac{A_{\text{spon}}/B_{\text{abs}}}{\dfrac{N_1}{N_2} - \dfrac{B_{\text{stim}}}{B_{\text{abs}}}}$$

The gas atoms, being diffuse, obey the Boltzmann distribution, so the ratio N_1/N_2 is $e^{-E_1/k_{\text{B}}T}/e^{-E_2/k_{\text{B}}T} = e^{\Delta E/k_{\text{B}}T}$. Thus,

$$Y(\Delta E) = \frac{A_{\text{spon}}/B_{\text{abs}}}{e^{\Delta E/k_{\text{B}}T} - \dfrac{B_{\text{stim}}}{B_{\text{abs}}}}$$

Here is where the "intriguing conclusion" arises. We defined the quantity $Y(\Delta E)$ as the number of photons of energy ΔE, but we know what this must be! It is the photon gas spectral energy density (47), with ΔE (i.e., the photon energy; not one of the atomic energies E_1 and E_2) replacing hf in that formula. The $e^{\Delta E/k_{\text{B}}T}$ is in place where it needs to be, and the only way the rest of the denominator can be correct is if $B_{\text{stim}} = B_{\text{abs}}$. This means that if the numbers of atoms occupying the two levels happened to be equal, a stray photon of the proper frequency is just as likely to induce absorption as stimulated emission! Of course, in a laser, we don't want these rates equal. We want stimulated emission to predominate, but how?

As the reader might have guessed, simply making $N_2 \gg N_1$ would do it—R_{stim} would be much larger than R_{abs}—but such a situation is certainly not the way things are in equilibrium, where number *drops* with energy. (*Note:* We assumed equilibrium to prove that $B_{\text{stim}} = B_{\text{abs}}$, but they are indeed constants, so they are equal even when the situation is far from equilibrium.) In fact, such an overpopulation of higher levels is crucial to laser operation and is known as a **population inversion**. Being unnatural, it must be established by some external means. But so long as it exists, one photon of the proper frequency, perhaps the result of spontaneous emission, may become two, which become four, and so on, very quickly resulting in a large number of coherent photons.

Before investigating how a population inversion might be established, let us take a look at the basic elements of a laser, shown in Figure 23. Because spontaneous emissions could initiate separate "outbreaks" of coherence in different directions, the medium is tuned to amplify the coherent light in just one. Parallel mirrors are placed at the medium's two ends. Photons not parallel to the axis have relatively few opportunities to induce stimulated emission, while those parallel reflect back and forth, providing many opportunities. The length along the axis is tuned to a standing-wave condition $L = n\lambda/2$, so that waves moving in opposite directions constructively interfere. In the resulting **resonant cavity**, the radiation parallel to the axis is greatly amplified, and off-axis radiation is diminished. In fact, this resonance is so selective in its tuning that the variation in the laser wavelength is typically several orders of magnitude narrower than the natural "line width" of the spontaneous atomic transition that gets the process started. (Accordingly, simultaneous output of multiple closely spaced wavelengths within the line width is possible; see

Figure 23 Basic components of a laser.

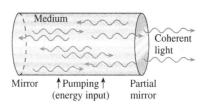

Figure 24 The original laser, with spiral flashtube surrounding resonant cavity of ruby.

Exercise 80.) By making the mirror at one end only partially reflecting, a fraction of coherent light is allowed to exit the cavity.

There are several ways of adding the external energy needed to promote electrons to the higher levels. One is **optical pumping**, used most often in solid-state lasers, where the laser medium is a transparent solid. The medium is subjected to a very intense light of broad spectrum, of which at least a fraction is of the required frequency. Although much of the input energy is dissipated as heat, a significant amount becomes coherent light. Usually, optical pumping in a solid-state laser is pulsed to allow time for cooling. Figures 24 and 25 show two examples of optical pumping. The first is the original ruby laser, whose optical pump is a flashtube wound around a ruby crystal, the "lasing" material. Figure 25 shows a one-pass laser amplifier, in which a bank of high-intensity lamps "charges up" neodymium glass plates just prior to a laser beam's entry. When the beam enters, atoms in the glass deexcite and a much more powerful beam emerges. (The beam is polarized, and light is passed without reflection by orienting the plates at Brewster's angle.)

Another means of energy input is **electric discharge pumping**, used in gas lasers. Atoms are raised to higher energy levels as the discharge ionizes some atoms and produces generally violent motion. Because excess heat dissipation is less of a problem in a gas, it is usually possible to sustain continuous, as opposed to pulsed, operation.

A vexing problem remains: Optical pumping can increase the population of a higher energy level only when the number of electrons at the lower level

Figure 25 A one-pass laser amplifier. An LRU is a replaceable unit of neodymium glass plates.

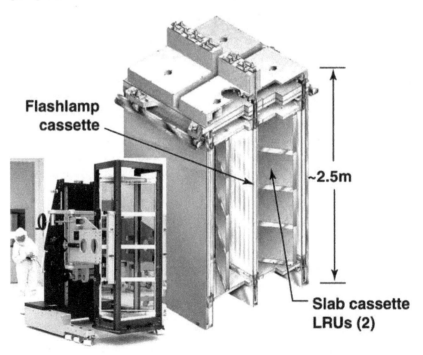

is greater. No matter how intense, it cannot increase a higher level's population beyond the point where the numbers in the two levels are equal, for at this point, absorption is no more probable than is stimulated emission. (Remember: $B_{stim} = B_{abs}$.) Nor would this stimulated emission be useful, since it would be induced by the incoherent photons from the optical pumping source. Electric discharge alone is also incapable of establishing a population inversion. Then how can it be done? The problem is solved by using a medium with a **metastable state**. Most downward atomic transitions occur spontaneously within about 10^{-8} s. A few, occurring via relatively inefficient mechanisms, take much longer, typically 10^{-3} s. The upper level in such a transition is known as a metastable—nearly stable—state.

To see how this solves the problem, consider the simplified model in Figure 26—a collection of atoms with only three energy levels: the ground state E_1, an excited metastable state E_2, and a yet higher, nonmetastable state E_3, from which electrons drop preferentially to E_2 rather than fully down to E_1. The temperature is low ($k_B T < E_2 - E_1$), so that essentially all atoms are in the ground state. Very intense optical pumping is now applied, so intense that a point of equal absorption and stimulated emission is reached between all levels: $N_1 \cong N_2 \cong N_3$. Then the pumping is stopped. After about 10^{-8} s, all electrons will have dropped from the "fast" E_3 state, but more to E_2 than to E_1. For the next $\sim 10^{-3}$ s, N_2 is greater than N_1, and the situation is ripe for a cascade of stimulated emissions between E_2 and E_1. In practice, pumping need not be stopped, and output is continuous as long as pumping keeps ahead of the stimulated emission, which would otherwise quickly deplete E_2.

What we have just described is the **three-level laser**. A way of increasing efficiency is the **four-level laser**, depicted in Figure 27, in which another "fast" level is employed, above the ground state but below the metastable one. Let us call this the near-ground state. Its energy is E_1, and we redefine the ground state as E_0. The benefit of this arrangement is that in the first $\sim 10^{-8}$ s after pumping, all excited states but the metastable one depopulate. Thus, rather than dropping to a nonempty ground state, electrons in the metastable state may drop to the essentially empty near-ground state. The four-level laser is more efficient simply because the ground state is not the terminal state for

Figure 26 Energy transitions in the three-level laser.

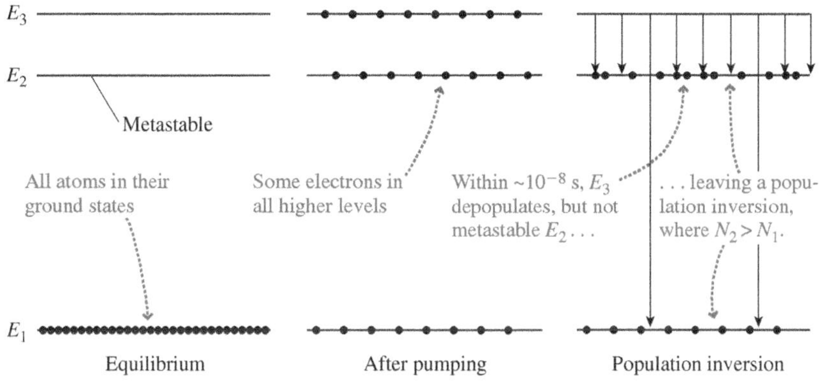

Figure 27 Four-level laser.

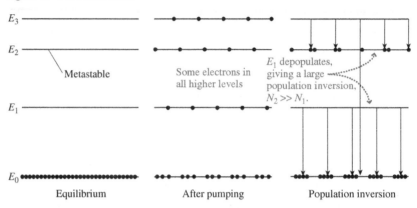

stimulated emission. A virtually complete population inversion between E_2 and E_1 is obtained without having to pump the ground state so near empty as in the three-level laser. In practice, lasers often employ even more than four energy levels, but the basis of the four-level laser still applies. (The semiconductor diode laser is different. A population inversion is still needed, but it has some interesting twists, including a completely different pumping mechanism.)

No matter how many levels are employed, only certain substances meet the criteria required for laser operation. As noted earlier, the first laser used a ruby crystal as the medium. Three-level and optically pumped, ruby lasers produce 694.3 nm light. Four-level neodymium glass lasers, used in laser fusion experiments, produce 1060 nm infrared light. The most common gas laser is the helium-neon, producing red-orange 632.8 nm light. It establishes a population inversion in neon by a roundabout path. Energy passes first from electric discharge to metastable helium states, then via helium-neon collisions to neon states at essentially the same energies as those in the helium, followed by stimulated emission to lower neon states. Driven by rapidly expanding applications, exciting advances are constantly being made in finding new laser materials with improved capabilities.

A D V A N C E D 9 **Specific Heats**

The ability of a substance to store energy internally is of great concern in many fields. At heart, it is a macroscopic average of microscopic energy storage, and thus it is an excellent example of the utility of statistical mechanics.

A basis for understanding specific heats is the **equipartition theorem**. When derived using *classical* statistical mechanics, it is as follows:

Equipartition theorem

> A particle in a thermodynamic system at equilibrium will have, on average, $\frac{1}{2}k_B T$ of energy for each independent variable, or degree of freedom, on which its energy depends quadratically.

Examples of independent variables and quadratic dependence are a one-dimensional oscillator, $E = \frac{1}{2}mv^2 + \frac{1}{2}\kappa x^2$, which has 2 degrees of freedom; an atom in a monatomic ideal gas, $E = \frac{1}{2}mv_x^2 + \frac{1}{2}mv_y^2 + \frac{1}{2}mv_z^2$, which has 3; and an object rotating about a single fixed axis, $E = \frac{1}{2}I\omega^2$, which has 1. We won't prove the theorem; rather, we will investigate the circumstances in which quantum mechanics limits the theorem's application. As we shall see, low temperatures are the problem. First, though, let us see why the theorem is so important.

According to the equipartition theorem, for each degree of freedom,

$$\overline{E}_{\text{one particle}} = \frac{1}{2}k_{\text{B}}T \quad \text{per degree of freedom}$$

Since the total internal energy is just the average energy times the number, the internal energy of a mole of particles (Avogadro's number N_{A}) would be

$$U_{\text{per mole}} = N_{\text{A}}\frac{1}{2}k_{\text{B}}T = \frac{1}{2}RT \quad \text{per degree of freedom}$$

where we have used $R \equiv N_{\text{A}} k_{\text{B}}$. Although specific heat is usually defined as the amount of heat required to warm a unit *mass* per degree of temperature, measured in J/kg·K, we will study the related but more revealing **molar heat capacity**, an energy per *mole* per degree, in J/mol·K. At constant volume, when no mechanical work is involved, this is defined as

$R \equiv N_{\text{A}} k_{\text{B}} = 8.315 \text{ J/mol·K}$

$$C_V = \frac{\partial U_{\text{per mole}}}{\partial T}$$

Thus, we see the utility of the equipartition theorem: Yielding the coefficient relating U and T, it is the route to heat capacity.

Gases

The equipartition theorem says that the internal energy per mole of a monatomic gas is $\frac{3}{2}RT$ (degrees of freedom: v_x, v_y, v_z), so the molar heat capacity is $\frac{3}{2}R$. A diatomic gas molecule, however, may also possess energy associated with rotation about the two axes perpendicular to the axis through the atoms. Calling the latter the x-axis, this adds 2 degrees of freedom: ω_y and ω_z, the angular velocities about y and z. (There is no rotational energy about the x-axis, because all the mass lies along that axis.) A diatomic molecule may also vibrate along its x-axis, adding the 2 degrees of freedom of a one-dimensional oscillator: v_{relative} and x_{relative}. According to classical statistical mechanics, then, a gas of diatomic molecules, with 7 degrees of freedom, should have $U_{\text{per mole}} = \frac{7}{2}RT$ and $C_V = \frac{7}{2}R$.

Diatomic hydrogen's molar heat capacity does approach $\frac{7}{2}R$, but only at more than 1000 K! As Figure 28 shows, it is $\frac{5}{2}R$ at room temperature. It doesn't appear to store energy in vibrational motion. The reason is that, so far as quantum oscillator states are concerned, room temperature is very cold.

Figure 28 Variation of hydrogen's molar heat capacity with temperature. (*Note:* The H_2 molecule dissociates before the vibrational plateau is reached.)

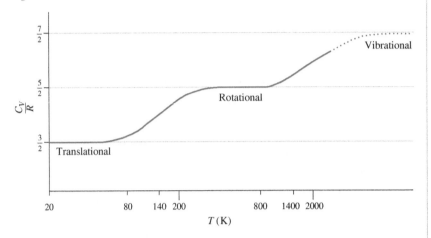

That is, $k_B T$ is much less than $\hbar\omega_0$, the energy jump to the first excited state. Consequently, if we wish to determine the vibrational specific heat contribution by calculating the average oscillator energy, even though the Boltzmann distribution is correct for a diffuse gas of molecules, *integration* is invalid. We integrated to obtain (28), $\overline{E} = k_B T$, and it clearly won't do. $U_{\text{per mole}}$ would be RT, and the vibrational contribution to C_V would be the *constant R*—it would not suddenly "kick in" at any particular temperature. Equation (15), obtained via summation, is the correct route:

$$\overline{E} = \frac{\hbar\omega_0}{e^{\hbar\omega_0/k_B T} - 1}$$

As shown in Figure 29(a) and noted in Section 3, at high temperature, where $k_B T \gg \hbar\omega_0$, this vibrational energy approaches the expected linear increase with temperature $k_B T$. This agrees with the classical equipartition theorem: 2 degrees of freedom gives $2 \times \frac{1}{2}k_B T$. But at low temperature, $k_B T \ll \hbar\omega_0$, the average energy increases only very slowly, because few of the molecules would be energetic enough to occupy any state other than the ground.

Let us now see how this affects the heat capacity. For a mole of oscillators, the internal energy due solely to vibrational motion would be

$$U_{\text{per mole, vib.}} = N_A \frac{\hbar\omega_0}{e^{\hbar\omega_0/k_B T} - 1}$$

Differentiation then gives the vibrational contribution to C_V.

$$C_{V,\text{ vib.}} = \frac{\partial U_{\text{per mole, vib.}}}{\partial T} = N_A k_B \frac{(\hbar\omega_0)^2\, e^{\hbar\omega_0/k_B T}}{(k_B T)^2 (e^{\hbar\omega_0/k_B T} - 1)^2}$$

Figure 29 Average energy and molar heat capacity of a system of oscillators at temperatures where $k_B T \sim \hbar\omega_0$.

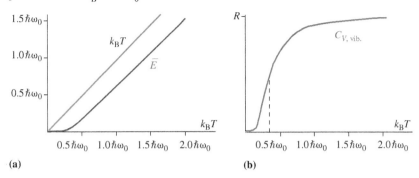

(a)　　　　　　　　　　　　　　　　　(b)

Figure 29(b), essentially the slope of 29(a), plots $C_{V, \text{vib.}}$. Its resemblance to the vibrational jump in Figure 28 is conspicuous. From 0, it jumps to practically R at $k_B T \cong 0.3\,\hbar\omega_0$. At around this temperature, translational kinetic energies should be great enough to begin an interchange with vibrational energies. Given that ω_0 is 8.28×10^{14} rad/s for the hydrogen molecule, the corresponding temperature works out to be 1900 K, which is in good agreement with Figure 28.

The other jump in hydrogen's heat capacity, around 200 K, is due to the beginnings of energy exchange with *rotational* quantum states. The basic idea is the same. Unless the temperature is at least comparable to the jump to the first excited rotational state, rotational states cannot participate in energy exchange. Here we simply note that it is because hydrogen's rotational level spacing is much smaller than its vibrational spacing that the rotational jump occurs at a lower temperature.

In summary, we see that the spacing between quantum energy levels must be taken into account when applying the equipartition theorem to predict heat capacity. At low temperatures, certain degrees of freedom are "frozen out," effectively storing no energy.

Solids

In a solid, atoms can't move freely. They oscillate about fixed locations and do not have rotational degrees of freedom. They may be thought of as being held in place by "springs," due to interatomic forces in the three spatial dimensions. Because a one-dimensional oscillator has 2 degrees of freedom, we should expect an atom oscillating in three dimensions to have 6: x, y, z, v_x, v_y, and v_z. Accordingly, the internal energy per mole should be $\frac{6}{2}RT$ and the molar heat capacity $3R$. In a metal, however, the conduction electrons do not oscillate with the individual atoms, but move freely about the material. They constitute a gas coexisting with the solid, and with no vibrational or rotational energies (being "monatomic"), they should add a factor of $\frac{3}{2}R$ to the molar heat capacity of the solid. Classically, then, the molar heat capacities of solids should obey

$$
\begin{aligned}
&\text{Insulator: } C_V = 3R \\
&\text{Conductor: } C_V = 4.5R
\end{aligned}
\qquad \text{Classical expectation}
$$

By now, it shouldn't be surprising that classical arguments break down at low temperatures. In particular, even at room temperature, the molar heat capacities of conductors don't differ much from those of insulators—and we already have the reason. At $T = 0$, electrons in a metal fill the lowest energy states possible up to a maximum E_F. But at ordinary temperatures, $k_B T$ is so much less than E_F that it might as well be 0 (cf. Example 5). A modest temperature *change* would still have the electrons packed into essentially the same energy levels, and if their average energy changes very little with temperature, their heat capacity is very small. (It increases from zero linearly with T, however, as Exercise 84 shows.) If we accept that the electrons shouldn't be much of a factor, Table 3 shows just how well classical statistical mechanics predicts heat capacity for certain crystalline solids near room temperature. For both insulators and conductors, it is very near $3R$. Still, the prediction fails for many solids, specifically those whose vibrating atoms find room temperature too cold.

To investigate how the heat capacity of the atoms in a solid behaves at low temperature, we might be tempted to apply the same analysis as for vibrating gas molecules, though without allowance for free translation or rotation. But the situation isn't so simple. Gas molecules interact very weakly. Although they do exchange energy, they do so only one collision at a time. They are essentially free and separate particles whose vibrational motions are independent. In a solid, however, atomic vibrations are strongly *interdependent*. The motion of one affects all those around it, the motions of which affect all those around them, and so on, in a wavelike fashion. How do we analyze the *collective* motions of the atoms?

There are two different but equivalent approaches, the same two used to analyze electromagnetic radiation bound in some region: the standing-wave approach, used to derive Planck's spectral energy density the boson gas approach of Section 7. There are great similarities between vibrations bound in a solid object and electromagnetic "vibrations" bound in a cavity. In either case, the standing-wave approach treats the oscillations as

TABLE 3 Properties of selected solids

Solid	c_V (J/g · K)	m (g/mol)	C_V (J/mol · K)
Li	3.51	6.9	24.2
Al	0.90	27.0	24.3
P	0.77	31.0	23.8
S	0.71	32.1	22.6
Fe	0.45	55.8	25.1
Ag	0.23	107.9	24.8
			$3R = 24.9$

distinguishable standing waves of different energies and uses the Boltzmann distribution. The boson gas approach, on the other hand, treats the energy as a gas of indistinguishable boson particles. In the case of electromagnetic radiation, the particles are, of course, photons. We now assert that mechanical vibrations in a solid may also be treated as a gas of free bosons, known as **phonons**. A phonon—a quantum of vibration—has zero spin, and it may travel from one point in a solid to another, carrying an energy hf. The reader may be suspicious about phonons. Are they *real* particles? The answer is no, not in the same sense as photons or electrons. They have no existence apart from the medium of propagation. However, whether one takes the standing-wave approach or the boson gas approach, the predictions come out the same, and this is strong evidence that *vibrations in a solid may be treated as comprising an integral number of discrete phonons rather than diffuse waves.*

The Debye Model

Whichever approach is taken, the steps to finding the heat capacity of a crystalline solid coincide at many points and are generally referred to as the **Debye model**. Because it most closely parallels the treatment of photons in Section 7, we use the boson gas approach and begin with the internal energy of a phonon gas, analogous to the photon expression (45). To adapt this equation to phonons, we need only modify it to account for three principal differences.

Maximum Phonon Energy While photons of arbitrarily short wavelength are possible, if improbable, in a cavity, there is an absolute lower limit on the wavelength of vibrations in a crystal. Figure 30 illustrates the reason. In a vibrational wave, adjacent atoms oscillate at the same frequency but are at different points in their cycles. A long wavelength involves a small phase difference between adjacent atoms, as shown in Figure 30(a). Figure 30(b) shows a short wavelength, in which adjacent atoms are one-half cycle and thus one-half wavelength apart. Let us refer to this as λ_{min}. As suggested in Figure 30(c), it may be shown that for any wavelength shorter than λ_{min}, there is a wavelength longer than λ_{min} for which the atoms would be at the same points in their cycles. (The proof is left as an exercise.) Thus, it makes no sense to speak of a wave for which $\frac{1}{2}\lambda$ is less than the spacing between adjacent atoms, because it is physically identical to one for which $\frac{1}{2}\lambda$ is greater than the spacing—the sine waves coincide at all discrete atoms. Accordingly, the minimum wavelength is $2a$, twice the atomic spacing.[10] A minimum wavelength implies a maximum frequency and thus a maximum phonon energy E_{max}. The integration in (45) must be terminated at E_{max}.

Propagation Speed All photons move at c in a vacuum. Vibrational waves in a solid, however, not only don't travel at c, they don't all travel at the *same* speed. But we assume that as an approximation they *do* move at the same speed—the speed of sound v_s characteristic of the material. We replace c by v_s.

[10]Because the sine waves do not coincide at all points *in space*, the argument applies only when discrete points alone are "real." Electromagnetic waves don't propagate via the motion of discrete atoms—we might say that the spacing of points in *vacuum* is 0—so they don't obey such a restriction.

Figure 30 In a crystal, only vibrational wavelengths greater than 2a make sense.

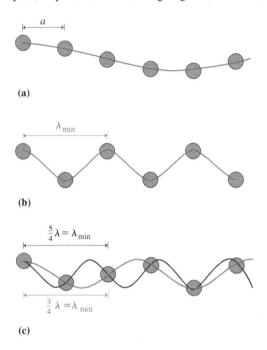

(a)

(b)

(c)

Figure 31 Atoms in a crystalline solid.

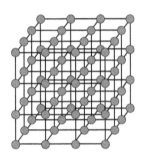

Figure 32 A cube of allowed wave numbers and a spherical octant of equal "volume."

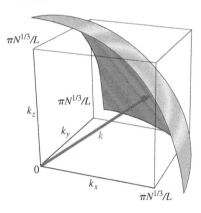

Longitudinal Oscillation Density of states (44), includes a factor of 2 for light's two independent transverse polarizations. In a solid, *longitudinal* vibration is also allowed. Assuming equal speeds for transverse and longitudinal waves, the net effect is simply to multiply (44) by $\frac{3}{2}$.

Taking the three factors into account, equation (45) becomes

$$U_{\text{phonon}} = \int_0^{E_{\text{max}}} E \frac{1}{e^{E/k_B T} - 1} \frac{12\pi V}{h^3 v_s^3} E^2 \, dE \qquad (48)$$

Still, we have yet to link E_{max} to the minimum wavelength 2a.

In one dimension, atomic spacing a would be the length of the solid divided by number, L/N, and the minimum phonon wavelength would thus be $2L/N$. In three dimensions, determining the minimum wavelength is a bit more involved. Consider a crystalline solid with atoms at the corners of cubes, as in Figure 31. The number along one side is not N but $N^{1/3}$. Thus, the spacing between atoms is $L/N^{1/3}$, and the minimum wavelength "along one axis" would be $2L/N^{1/3}$. Wavelength isn't a vector, but there is something related to it that *is*: wave number. (Remember: $\mathbf{p} = \hbar\mathbf{k}$ is a vector form of $p = h/\lambda = hk$.) Using $k = 2\pi/\lambda$, the corresponding *maximum* wave-number component k_x would be $\pi N^{1/3}/L$. In three dimensions, the wave-number vector may point anywhere within a cube in wave-number space, depicted in Figure 32, that has one corner at 0 and is of side length $\pi N^{1/3}/L$. Its maximum magnitude would obviously depend on its direction (it would be greatest when pointing toward the far corner). But by finding a spherical octant that encloses the same "volume," we obtain a reasonable average maximum—the "radius" of the sphere would be k_{max}. Equating the volumes of the cube and spherical octant,

$$\left(\frac{\pi N^{1/3}}{L}\right)^3 = \frac{1}{8}\left(\frac{4}{3}\pi k_{max}^3\right) \quad\Rightarrow\quad k_{max} = \left(\frac{6\pi^2 N}{L^3}\right)^{1/3} = \left(\frac{6\pi^2 N}{V}\right)^{1/3}$$

We now need only relate k to E. For a simple plane wave, $k = 2\pi/\lambda = 2\pi f/v$, so that $E = hf = hvk/2\pi$. Thus, with our assumption that all waves move at the same speed v_s, we have

$$E_{max} = \frac{hv_s k_{max}}{2\pi} = hv_s\left(\frac{3N}{4\pi V}\right)^{1/3}$$

Before inserting this in (48), we streamline things with the following definition:

$$T_D \equiv \frac{E_{max}}{k_B} = \frac{hv_s}{k_B}\left(\frac{3N}{4\pi V}\right)^{1/3} \tag{49}$$

Being an energy divided by the Boltzmann constant (in J/K), T_D has units of temperature. It is known as the **Debye temperature** and depends on properties of the given material, N/V and v_s. Equation (48) thus becomes

$$U_{phonon} = \int_0^{k_B T_D} E\frac{1}{e^{E/k_B T} - 1}\frac{9N}{(k_B T_D)^3}E^2\,dE \tag{50}$$

We simplify this by redefining the dummy variable of integration.

$$E/k_B T \equiv x$$

Therefore,

$$U_{phonon} = 9k_B N\frac{T^4}{T_D^3}\int_0^{T_D/T}\frac{x^3}{e^x - 1}dx$$

Finally, assuming 1 mol, that is, $N = N_A$, and using $k_B N_A \equiv R$, we obtain for the internal vibrational energy of a solid

$$U_{per\,mole} = 9R\frac{T^4}{T_D^3}\int_0^{T_D/T}\frac{x^3}{e^x - 1}dx \tag{51}$$

Alas, after all this work, the integral cannot be done in closed form. Figure 33(a) shows the result of a numerical evaluation. As expected, the molar internal energy approaches the classical $3RT$ at high temperature, but we also see that "high" temperature for a solid is judged relative to its Debye temperature. This makes sense, for T_D is proportional to the speed of sound v_s, which increases with the strength of interatomic forces, and stronger "springs"

Figure 33 Debye model average energy and molar heat capacity, and actual heat capacities of solids at low temperature.

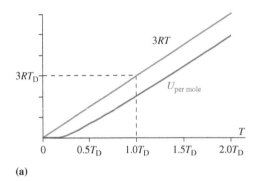

(a)

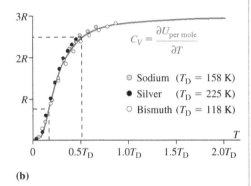

(b)

imply larger jumps between quantum levels. Figure 33(b) shows the molar heat capacity. At high temperature, it approaches the classical $3R$, but it drops to 0 at very low T. Plotted with the theoretically predicted heat capacity are measured heat capacities of several crystalline solids of different Debye temperatures. Even given the approximations we've made along the way—uniform speed for longitudinal and transverse waves, geometry-dependent averaging, and so on—agreement is excellent and greatly strengthens the case for treating the vibrational energy in a crystalline solid as a phonon gas. (The theory fails for amorphous solids such as glasses, in which the atoms are not arranged in a regular pattern. Liquids are similarly difficult to analyze.)

EXAMPLE 7

The molar heat capacity of diamond at 293 K is 6.0 J/mol · K, or about $0.73R$. (a) According to the Debye model, at what temperature would the molar heat capacity be $2.5R$? (b) What is the "cutoff" (maximum) phonon frequency for diamond?

SOLUTION

(a) From Figure 33(b), we see that a heat capacity of $0.73R$ occurs at around $T = 0.16T_D$. Therefore,

$$T_D \cong \frac{293 \text{ K}}{0.16} = 1830 \text{ K}$$

The value $2.5R$ occurs at around $0.51T_D = 0.51(1830 \text{ K}) \cong 930 \text{ K}$, which happens to agree well with experiment.

(b) Using (49), the maximum phonon energy is

$$E_{max} = k_B T_D = (1.38 \times 10^{-23} \text{ J/K})(1830 \text{ K}) = 2.5 \times 10^{-20} \text{ J}$$

Thus,

$$f_{max} = \frac{E_{max}}{h} = 3.8 \times 10^{13} \text{ Hz}$$

PROGRESS AND APPLICATIONS

BEC: Many Acting as One   Studied for most of a century, liquid helium, with its two components—superfluid and normal—and strong interactions is an imperfect Bose-Einstein condensate (BEC). But in 1995, after years of slow progress, the quest for the first true BEC ended (Nobel Prize, 2001, Cornell, Ketterle & Wieman), and a huge upsurge in BEC research began. The first success was in a dilute gas of several thousand rubidium-87 atoms. Rubidium-87 has 37 electrons, 37 protons, and 50 neutrons—an even number of fermions—making the collection a boson. Magnetic traps confined the atoms, while laser cooling and simple evaporative cooling, the mechanism that cools the human body, combined to lower the temperature to less than 0.1 μK. A major hurdle was keeping the atoms in a gaseous state where evaporative cooling is efficient, overcoming their tendency to bond. Figure 34 documents the achievement. The spike shows a large preponderance of atoms in the same state. Even its shape confirmed the success. "Normal" atoms would spread symmetrically after the nonuniform confining fields were switched off, but the condensed atoms undergo dispersion as a single wave function, which "remembers" that field and thus spreads at different rates in different directions. True BECs have now been produced in numerous different gases of bosons.

Whole Atoms as Fermions   The celebrity of the low-temperature quantum gas that began in 1995 has been magnified by numerous related breakthroughs. In 1999, researchers at the National Institute of Standards and Technology (NIST) produced the first system of whole atoms behaving as a degenerate gas of fermions. The term *degenerate* here means that the particles' wavelengths are long and overlapping, as in Figure 14(b), so they should exhibit quantum behavior. For a fermion, this means a tendency toward filling states, one per particle, to a maximum level—the Fermi energy. Atoms containing an odd number of fermions should themselves be fermions and so should fill states this way, but demonstrating this required surmounting not only the same challenges as in the BEC but also a challenge special to fermions. The goal was reached in a gas of potassium-40 (19 electrons, 19 protons, and 21 neutrons). As in the BEC case, the atoms were held in magneto-optical traps (MOTs), and final evaporative cooling lowered the sample to about 0.3 μK. The "new" hurdle was the reluctance of these fermions to collide! Evaporative cooling requires collisions to reestablish

Figure 34 Number of rubidium atoms, plotted vertically, versus velocity in two dimensions before (left), near (middle), and at achievement of an essentially pure BEC (right).

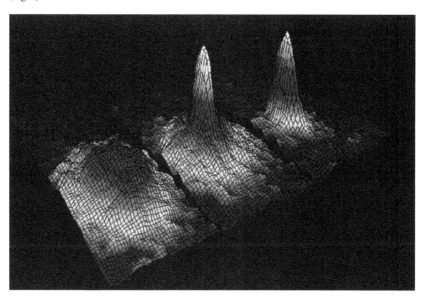

equilibrium after fast particles are lost, but magnetic traps tend to sift particles according to spin state—"spin" here meaning the combined orbital and intrinsic angular momentum of all the atom's constituents—and two fermions in the same spin state can't "touch." (Aligned spins implies an antisymmetric spatial state, which is 0 when particle locations coincide). A clever solution trapped two gases of different spins, which can collide, before banishing one with a microwave broom and studying the other. The lowest energy levels in the final state were approximately 60% occupied. Although this is not complete degeneracy, it is far greater than in a normal gas and is sufficient to show "abnormal" behaviors special to fermions, including a precipitous drop in the efficiency of the evaporative cooling process in the single-spin system (DeMarco & Jin, *Science*, 10 September 1999).

Fermions Pairing to Form Bosons Yet another player in the expanding ultracold gas drama is a system of fermions exhibiting behaviors traditionally attributed to bosons: superfluidity and condensation to a single state. To the natural question "What business do fermions have condensing as bosons?" the answer is pairing. That a pair of fermions may behave as a boson is interesting enough, but perhaps even more important is how the pairing comes about, a multifaceted question in itself and a hot research topic that bears on many other exciting areas of physics, from cosmology to superconductivity. While pairing of electrons in superconductivity had been studied for decades, the first evidence of fermion atom pairing was the discovery in 1972 (Nobel Prize, 1996, Lee, Osheroff & Richardson) of superfluidity in liquid helium-3, comprising 2 electrons, 2 protons, and 1 neutron. The subsequent theoretical explanation (Nobel Prize, 2003, Leggett) was that relatively distant atoms formed pairs by a fairly weak interaction, very much like that between electrons in superconducting metallic elements, but involving a more complex relative motion. A qualitatively different pairing mechanism seemed to be at play when, following the 1995 watershed, experiments first produced BECs in gases of fermion atoms. Here, the interaction between atoms was short range and strong enough to produce a gas of paired two-atom molecules, which condense as bosons and were later shown to exhibit the hallmark trait of Bose-Einstein condensation already seen in liquid helium-3: superfluidity. A bridge between the mechanisms was formed when it was shown possible, by manipulating the external magnetic fields, to "tune" the interaction to an intermediate state.
The work continues, spurred by the belief that a better understanding of fermion pairing might lead to revolutionary applications, such as a room-temperature superconductor.

Single-Atom Laser As lasers attract new applications, their characteristics come under closer scrutiny. One much-studied trait of the conventional laser is the fluctuation in its photon production rate. Of no significance in many applications, such "noise" can pose quite a problem in others. In the promising field of quantum computing, for instance, the ability of certain simple systems to manipulate quantum information is hindered by fluctuations in photon output. In an ironic twist, given that large numbers usually imply small fluctuations, fluctuations in laser light can be suppressed by *decreasing* the number of atoms involved. Starting in the late 1980s, numerous experiments produced laser operation via just a few atoms, and in 2003, the logical limit was reached in which a single indefatigable cesium atom bore the whole weight of photon production (McKeever, Boca, Boozer, Buck & Kimble, *Nature*, 18 September 2003). A special optical trap imposes the "strong coupling" required when spontaneous misfires cannot be tolerated. Naturally, output is low, and this **single-atom laser**, depicted in Figure 35, differs in several fundamental ways from the conventional laser (an inversion in a population of one?) but its importance is the precision with which it can produce photons. In the field of quantum cryptography, the ability to produce a single photon on demand is very important. The single-atom laser is one of several routes that may provide the solution.

High Power from Wiggling Electrons An entirely different way of producing coherent light, and one at the opposite end in terms of power, is the **free-electron laser** (FEL). In this device, whose components are shown in Figure 36, the "lasing medium" consists of a relativistic beam of free electrons sent through a series of magnets, which cause the electrons to "wiggle" along their paths.

Figure 35 In a single-atom laser, a lone cesium atom (black dot) trapped between mirrors M_1 and M_2 is pumped by external source Ω_3, yielding very precise photon output in transition g. Source Ω_4 drives a roundabout return to the starting level.

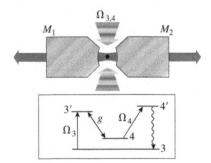

Figure 36 Free-electron laser: Electrons "wiggled" by a series of magnets produce coherent, high-power light.

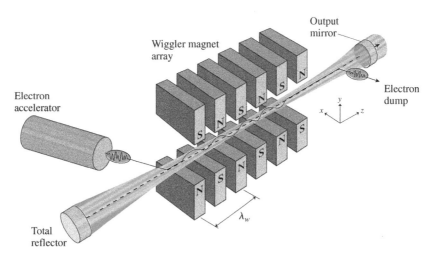

All accelerating (i.e., wiggling) charges emit electromagnetic radiation, and in the FEL, the interplay with the electromagnetic fields causes the beam of wiggling electrons to bunch up in a periodic way at the laser output wavelength and generate coherent light along the axis of the beam. The chief disadvantage of the FEL is that it is not a tabletop device but a massive facility relying on a high-energy electron accelerator, explaining why FELs tend to be found at large universities and other research laboratories. Their great advantages are very high power, typically more than 1 kW and in some cases much higher, and easily tunable wavelength, often by a factor of 3 about the design wavelength, which may range from far infrared to ultraviolet and beyond. These capabilities make the FEL attractive for applications in biology, medicine, nuclear fusion, and materials science, among others.

Chaos While we have concentrated on thermodynamic systems in which the behavior is predictable, the scientific community has only fairly recently recognized in many systems a special kind of unpredictability: **chaos**. It arises in nearly every physical and biological science, in many seemingly unrelated situations. The unifying thread is that these situations all involve a phenomenon governed by a differential equation that is nonlinear. The differential equations we encounter in this text are linear, depending on a function and its derivatives to only the first power. Dependence on any other power makes a differential equation nonlinear. Quite often there is no mathematical technique able to solve it, so we must fall back on numerical approximations. But then we run into another quirk of nonlinear differential equations: Extremely small changes in the conditions at one point may result in extremely large differences later. What actually happens may thus appear completely unpredictable. (The atmosphere's behavior is governed by nonlinear fluid dynamics, and it is often mused that the weather at one place may hinge on the earlier flap of a butterfly's wing on the other side of the world.)

A common example is a nonlinear (non–Hooke's law) oscillator driven by a periodic force. For certain values of the force's amplitude, the oscillator's period is that of the driving force. However, if the amplitude is changed even slightly, although the *driving* period has not changed, the *system* oscillates at a period larger by a factor of 2. Further change may reveal another abrupt doubling of the period. At some point, a small change may produce *aperiodic* behavior! It may seem random; it may seem like noise; but it isn't, for it is governed by a mathematical relationship—however intractable. Such deterministic but seemingly unpredictable behavior is what we call chaos and is found in mechanical oscillators, electrical circuits, fluid flow, optics, chemistry, population systems, biological development, heart fibrillation, the weather, and on and on. Much work is now being done on controlling the onset of chaos in cases where it is unwanted or on extracting some kind of sense from it in cases where it is either uncontrollable or a natural characteristic of the system under study. Chaos is a huge and expanding field. The interested reader is encouraged to consult the literature and the Internet.

Chapter Summary

Statistical mechanics is the area of physics in which probabilities and statistics are used to predict the average properties and behaviors of thermodynamic systems. A thermodynamic system is one where the number of particles is so large that deviations from statistically predicted average behavior are very small. Relationships between entropy and the statistical idea of numbers of ways and between entropy and temperature are two of the most fundamental.

$$S \equiv k_B \ln W \qquad (2)$$

$$\frac{\partial S}{\partial E} \equiv \frac{1}{T} \qquad (4)$$

In a thermodynamic system in equilibrium, the number of particles in a given individual-particle state—the occupation number $\mathcal{N}(E)$—obeys a distribution that depends only on the kind of particle. Distinguishable particles obey the Boltzmann distribution; bosons, the Bose-Einstein; and fermions, the Fermi-Dirac.

$$\mathcal{N}(E)_{\text{Boltz}} = \frac{1}{Be^{E/k_B T}} \qquad (31)$$

$$\mathcal{N}(E)_{\text{BE}} = \frac{1}{Be^{E/k_B T} - 1} \qquad (32)$$

$$\mathcal{N}(E)_{\text{FD}} = \frac{1}{Be^{E/k_B T} + 1} \qquad (33)$$

Occupation number decreases with increasing energy in all three cases, and the quantum distributions converge to the "classical" Boltzmann distribution whenever quantum indistinguishability may be ignored, or whenever the occupation number is much less than 1. An important special case of the Boltzmann distribution is the Maxwell distribution of speeds in a classical gas. The quantum distributions differ most at low temperature and/or high density. The Bose-Einstein tends more toward having all particles congregating in the lowest-energy quantum state, while the Fermi-Dirac tends toward an occupation number of 1—one particle per state—up to the Fermi energy, at which the occupation number drops abruptly to 0.

Calculations, such as an average, often involve a sum over possible states, and if the spacing between individual-particle states is much less than $k_B T$, the sum over states may be replaced by an integral over energies. The integrand must then include the density of states $D(E)$—the number of quantum states per energy range dE—whose form depends on the system.

Among the things quantum statistical mechanics explains are the energies of conduction electrons in a metal, a fermion gas; the unusual properties of liquid helium, a boson gas; the relationship between temperature and frequency in an electromagnetic gas of photons; and specific heats of materials at various temperatures.

The laser is a device that produces coherent light via stimulated emission. A nonequilibrium population inversion is established in the light-producing medium, in which the number of electrons in a higher-energy state is greater than that in a lower-energy state. If the higher state is metastable, electrons promoted to it by external optical pumping or electric discharge are prevented from quickly returning and reestablishing equilibrium. A passing photon whose energy equals the difference between the higher and lower states then precipitates stimulated emission, in which the newly produced photon is coherent with the first. With a population inversion, the process quickly multiplies—one producing two, two producing four, and so on—and a powerful coherent beam results.

---

* indicates advanced questions

Conceptual Questions

1. Consider a system of two identical objects heading straight toward each other. What would qualify and what would disqualify the system as a *thermodynamic* system, and how, if at all, would this relate to the elasticity of the collision?

2. What information would you need in order to specify the macrostate of the air in a room? What information would you need to specify the microstate?

3. Given an arbitrary thermodynamic system, which is larger: the number of possible macrostates, or the number of possible microstates, or is it impossible to say? Explain your answer. (For most systems, both are *infinite*, but it is still possible to answer the question.)

4. A scientifically untrained but curious friend asks, "When I walk into a room, is there a chance that all the air will be on the other side?" How do you answer this question?

5. Defend or refute the following claim: An energy distribution, such as the Boltzmann distribution, specifies the microstate of a thermodynamic system.

6. Not surprisingly, in a collection of oscillators, as in other thermodynamic systems, raising the temperature causes particles' energies to increase. Why shouldn't a point be reached where there are more particles in some high energy state than in a lower energy state? (The fundamental idea, not a formula that might arise from it, is the object.)

7. When would a density of states be needed: in a sum over states? in a sum over energies? in an integral over energies? in an integral over states?

8. Suppose we have a system of identical particles moving in just one dimension and for which the energy quantization relationship is $E = bn^{2/3}$, where b is a

constant and n an integer quantum number. Discuss whether the density of states should be independent of E, an increasing function of E, or a decreasing function of E.

9. By considering its constituents, determine the dimensions (e.g., length, distance over time, etc.) of the denominator in equation (26). Why is the result sensible?

10. There are more permutations of particle labels when two particles have energy 0 and two have energy 1 than when three particles have energy 0 and one has energy 2. (The total energies are the same.) From this observation alone argue that the Boltzmann distribution should be lower than the Bose-Einstein at the lowest energy level.

11. The Fermi energy in a quantum gas depends inversely on the volume. Basing your answer on simple type quantum mechanics (not such quaint notions as squeezing classical particles of finite volume into a container too small), explain why.

12. A block has a cavity inside, occupied by a photon gas. Briefly explain what the characteristics of this gas should have to do with the temperature of the block.

13. Consider a gas of atoms that might serve as a laser medium but that is in equilibrium, with no population inversions. A photon gas coexists with the atoms. Would a photon whose energy is precisely the difference between two atomic energy states be more likely to be absorbed or to induce a stimulated emission or neither? We expect that in equilibrium the numbers of atoms at different levels and the number of photons of a given energy should be *stable*. Is your answer compatible?

14. What is special about a metastable state, and why is it so useful in a laser? Why wouldn't a nonmetastable state at the same energy work?

15. In a certain design of helium-neon laser, the chamber containing these gases has a perfect mirror at one end, as usual, but only a window at the other. Beyond the window is a region of free air space and then the second mirror, which is partially reflecting, allowing the beam to exit. The resonant cavity between the mirrors thus has a region free of the helium-neon gas—the "lasing material"—in which you can insert something. If you insert a sheet of clear plastic at any orientation in this region between the mirrors, the laser beam disappears. If the same sheet is placed in the beam *outside* the partially reflecting mirror, the beam passes through it, regardless of the orientation. Why?

16. Suppose that in Figure 27, the level labeled E_1, rather than the one labeled E_2, were metastable. Might the material still function as a laser? Explain.

17. Classically, what would be the average energy of a particle in a system of particles free to move in the xy-plane while rotating about the z-axis?

18. At high temperature, the average energy of a classical one-dimensional oscillator is $k_B T$, and for an atom in a monatomic ideal gas, it is $\frac{3}{2} k_B T$. Explain the difference, using the equipartition theorem.

Exercises

Section 1

19. Consider the two-sided room. (a) Which is more likely to have an imbalance of five particles (i.e., $N_R = \frac{1}{2} N + 5$): a room with $N = 20$ or a room with $N = 60$? (*Note:* The total number of ways of distributing particles, the sum of $W_{N_R}^N$ from 0 to N, is 2^N.) (b) Which is more likely to have an imbalance of 5% (i.e., $N_R = \frac{1}{2} N + 0.05 N$)? (c) An average-size room is quite likely to have a trillion more air molecules on one side than on the other. Why may we say that precisely half will be on each side?

20. A two-sided room contains six particles, a, b, c, d, e, and f, with two on the left and four on the right. (a) Describe the macrostate. (b) Identify the possible microstates. (*Note:* With only six particles, this isn't a thermodynamic system, but the general idea still applies, and the number of combinations is tractable.)

21. Consider a room divided by imaginary lines into three equal parts. Sketch a two-axis plot of the number of ways of arranging particles versus N_{left} and N_{right} for the case $N = 10^{23}$. Note that N_{middle} is not independent, being of course $N - N_{right} - N_{left}$. Your axes should be N_{left} and N_{right}, and the number of ways should be represented by density of shading.

22. The Stirling approximation, $J! \cong \sqrt{2\pi} \, J^{J+1/2} e^{-J}$, is very handy when dealing with numbers larger than about 100. Consider the following ratio: the number of ways N particles can be evenly divided between two halves of a room to the number of ways they can be divided with 60% on the right and 40% on the left. (a) Show, using the Stirling approximation, that the ratio is approximately $(4^{0.4} 6^{0.6}/5)^N$ for large N. (b) Explain how this fits with the claim that average behaviors become more predictable in large systems.

Section 2

23. The entropy of an ideal monatomic gas is $(3/2) N k_B \ln E + N k_B \ln V - N k_B \ln N$, to within an additive constant. Show that this implies the correct relationship between internal energy E and temperature.

24. The diagram shows two systems that may exchange both thermal and mechanical energy via a movable, heat-conducting partition. Because both E and V may change, we consider the entropy of each system to be a function of both: $S\,(E,\,V)$. Considering the exchange of thermal energy only, we argued in Section 2 that it was reasonable to define $1/T$ as $\partial S/\partial E$. In the more general case, P/T is also defined as something. (a) Why should pressure come into play, and to what might P/T be equated? (*Note:* Check to see whether the units make sense.) (b) Given this relationship, show that $dS = dQ/T$. (Remember the first law of thermodynamics.)

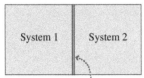

Movable heat-conducting partition

25. A "cold" object, $T_1 = 300$ K, is briefly put in contact with a "hot" object, $T_2 = 400$ K, and 60 J of heat flows from the hot object to the cold one. The objects are then separated, their temperatures having changed negligibly due to their large sizes. (a) What are the changes in entropy of each object and the system as a whole? (b) Knowing only that these objects are in contact and at the given temperatures, what is the ratio of the probabilities of their being found in the second (final) state to that of their being found in the first (initial) state? What does this result suggest?

Section 3

26. We based the exact probabilities of equation (9) on the claim that the number of ways of adding N distinct nonnegative integers/quantum numbers to give a total of M is $(M + N - 1)!/[M!(N - 1)!]$. Verify this claim (a) for the case $N = 2$, $M = 5$ and (b) for the case $N = 5$, $M = 2$.

27. Four distinguishable harmonic oscillators a, b, c, and d may exchange energy. The energies allowed particle a are $E_a = n_a \hbar \omega_0$; those allowed particle b are $E_b = n_b \hbar \omega_0$; and so on. Consider an overall state (macrostate) in which the total energy is $3\hbar\omega_0$. One possible microstate would have particles a, b, and c in their $n = 0$ states and particle d in its $n = 3$ state; that is, $(n_a, n_b, n_c, n_d) = (0, 0, 0, 3)$. (a) List *all* possible microstates. (b) What is the probability that a given particle will be in its $n = 0$ state? (c) Answer part (b) for all other possible values of n. (d) Plot the probability versus n.

28. In a large system of distinguishable harmonic oscillators, how high does the temperature have to be for the probability of occupying the ground state to be less than $\frac{1}{2}$?

29. In a large system of distinguishable harmonic oscillators, how high does the temperature have to be for the probable number of particles occupying the ground state to be less than 1?

30. Obtain equation (15) from (14). Make use of the following sums, correct when $|x| < 1$:

$$\sum_{n=0}^{\infty} x^n = \frac{1}{1 - x}$$

$$\sum_{n=0}^{\infty} n x^n = \frac{x}{(1 - x)^2}$$

31. Show that equation (16) follows from (15) and (10).

32. Using the relationship between temperature and M and N given in (16) and that between E and n in (6), obtain equation (17) from (12). The first sum given in Exercise 30 will be useful.

33. Show that in the limit of large numbers, the exact probability of equation (9) becomes the Boltzmann probability of (17). Use the fact that $K!/(K - k)! \equiv K^k$, which holds when $k \ll K$.

34. The exact probabilities of equation (9) rest on the claim that the number of ways of adding N distinct nonnegative integers to give a total of M is $(M + N - 1)!/[M!(N - 1)!]$. One way to prove it involves the following trick. It represents two ways that N distinct integers can add to M—9 and 5, respectively, in this special case.

1	X	X	X	I	I	X	I	I	I	I	X	I	I
2	I	X	X	I	I	I	I	X	I	I	I	X	X

The X's represent the total of the integers, M—each row has 5. The I's represent "dividers" between the distinct integers, of which there will of course be $N - 1$—each row has 8. The first row says that n_1 is 3 (three X's before the divider between it and n_2), n_2 is 0 (no X's between its left divider with n_1 and its right divider with n_3), n_3 is 1, n_4 through n_6 are 0, n_7 is 1, and n_8 and n_9 are 0. The second row says that n_2 is 2, n_6 is 1, n_9 is 2, and all other n are 0. Further rows could account for all possible ways that the integers can add to M. Argue that, properly applied, the binomial coefficient can be invoked to give the correct total number of ways for any N and M.

35. Consider a simple thermodynamic system in which particles can occupy only two states: a lower state, whose energy we define as 0, and an upper state, energy E_u.

(a) Carry out the sum (with only two states, integration is certainly not valid) giving the average particle energy $\overline{E}$, and plot your result as a function of temperature.

(b) Explain qualitatively why it should behave as it does.

(c) This system can be used as a model of paramagnetism, where individual atoms' magnetic moments can either be aligned or antialigned with an external magnetic field, giving a low or high energy, respectively. Describe how the average alignment or antialignment depends on temperature. Does it make sense?

36. Example 2 obtains a ratio of the number of particles expected in the $n = 2$ state to that in the ground state. Rather than the $n = 2$ state, consider arbitrary n.

(a) Show that the ratio is

$$\frac{\text{number of energy } E_n}{\text{number of energy } E_1} = n^2 e^{-13.6 \text{ eV}(1-n^{-2})/k_B T}$$

Note that hydrogen atom energies are $E_n = -13.6 \text{ eV}/n^2$.

(b) What is the limit of this ratio as n becomes very large? Can it exceed 1? If so, under what condition(s)?

(c) In Example 2, we found that even at the temperature of the Sun's surface (~ 6000 K), the ratio for $n = 2$ is only 10^{-8}. For what value of n would the ratio be 0.01?

(d) Is it realistic that the number of atoms with high n could be greater than the number with low n?

37. Consider a system of one-dimensional spinless particles in a box somehow exchanging energy. Through steps similar to those giving equation (27), show that

$$D(E) = \frac{m^{1/2}L}{\hbar\pi\sqrt{2}}\frac{1}{E^{1/2}}$$

38. By carrying out the integration suggested just before equation (28), show that the average energy of a one-dimensional oscillator in the limit $k_B T \gg \hbar\omega_0$ is $k_B T$.

39. Show that in the limit $\hbar\omega_0 \ll k_B T$, equation (15) becomes (28).

40. We claim that the famous exponential decrease of probability with energy is natural, the vastly most probable and disordered state given the constraints on total energy and number of particles. It should be a state of maximum entropy! The proof involves mathematical techniques beyond the scope of the text, but finding support is good exercise and not difficult. Consider a system of 11 oscillators sharing a total energy of just $5\hbar\omega_0$. In the symbols of Section 3, $N = 11$ and $M = 5$.

(a) Using equation (9), calculate the probabilities of n_i being 0, 1, 2, and 3.

(b) How many particles, N_n, would be expected in each level? Round each to the nearest integer. (Happily, the number is still 11, and the energy still $5\hbar\omega_0$.) What you have is a distribution of the energy that is as close to expectations as possible, given that numbers at each level in a real case are integers.

(c) Entropy is related to the number of microscopic ways the macrostate can be obtained, and the number of ways of permuting particle labels with N_0, N_1, N_2, and N_3 fixed and totaling 11 is $11!/(N_0! N_1! N_2! N_3!)$. Calculate the number of ways for your distribution.

(d) Calculate the number of ways if there were 6 particles in $n = 0$, 5 in $n = 1$, and none higher. Note that this also has the same total energy.

(e) Find at least one other distribution in which the 11 oscillators share the same energy, and calculate the number of ways.

(f) What do your findings suggest?

Section 4

41. Show that the rms speed of a gas molecule, defined as $v_{rms} \equiv \sqrt{\overline{v^2}}$, is given by $\sqrt{3k_B T/m}$.

42. (a) Calculate the average speed of a gas molecule in a classical ideal gas. (b) What is the average velocity of a gas molecule?

43. (a) Using the Maxwell speed distribution, determine the most probable speed of a particle of mass m in a gas at temperature T. (b) How does this compare with v_{rms}? Explain.

44. Determine the relative probability of a gas molecule being within a small range of speeds around $2v_{rms}$ to being in the same range of speeds around v_{rms}.

45. Figure 8 cannot do justice to values at the very high-speed end of the plot. This exercise investigates how small it really gets. However, although integrating the Maxwell speed distribution over the *full* range of speeds from 0 to infinity can be carried out (the so-called Gaussian integrals), over any restricted range, it is one of those integrals that, unfortunately, cannot be done in closed form. Using a computational aid of your choice, show that the fraction of molecules moving faster than $2v_{rms}$ is $\sim 10^{-2}$; faster than $6v_{rms}$ is $\sim 10^{-23}$; and faster than $10v_{rms}$ is $\sim 10^{-64}$, where v_{rms}, from Exercise 41, is $\sqrt{3k_B T/m}$. (Exercise 48 uses these values in an interesting application.)

46. For a room 3.0 m tall, by roughly what percent does the probability of an air molecule being found at the ceiling differ from that of an equal-speed molecule being found at the floor? Ignore any variation in temperature from floor to ceiling.

47. To obtain the Maxwell speed distribution, we assumed a uniform temperature, a kinetic-only energy of $E = \frac{1}{2}m(v_x^2 + v_y^2 + v_z^2)$, and we assumed that we wished to find the average of an arbitrary function of v. Along the way, we obtained a probability per unit speed, $P(v)$. (a) Assuming a uniform temperature and an energy of $E = \frac{1}{2}m(v_x^2 + v_y^2 + v_z^2) + mgy$ and assuming we wish to find the average of an arbitrary function of y, obtain a probability per unit height, $P(y)$. (b) Assuming a temperature of 300 K, how much less is the density of the atmosphere's N_2 at an altitude of 800 m (about 3000 ft) than at sea level? (c) What of the O_2 in the atmosphere?

48. A particle subject to a planet's gravitational pull has a total mechanical energy given by $E_{mechanical} = \frac{1}{2}mv^2 - GMm/r$, where m is the particle's mass, M the planet's mass, and G the gravitational constant 6.67×10^{-11} N·m ^{2}/kg^2. It may escape if its energy is *zero*—that is, if its positive KE is equal in magnitude to the negative PE holding it to the surface. Suppose the particle is a gas molecule in an atmosphere. (a) Temperatures in Earth's atmosphere may reach 1000 K. Referring to the values obtained in Exercise 45 and given that $R_{Earth} = 6.37 \times 10^6$ m and $M_{Earth} = 5.98 \times 10^{24}$ kg, should Earth be able to "hold on" to hydrogen (1 g/mol)? to nitrogen (28 g/mol)? (*Note:* An upper limit on the number of molecules in Earth's atmosphere is about 10^{48}.) (b) The moon's mass is 0.0123 times Earth's, its radius 0.26 times Earth's, and its surface temperatures rise to 370 K. Should it be able to hold on to these gases?

Section 5

49. Verify that the probabilities shown in Table 1 for four distinguishable oscillators sharing energy $2\delta E$ agree with the exact probabilities given by equation (9).

50. You have six shelves, one above the other and all above the floor, and six volumes of an encyclopedia, A, B, C, D, E, and F.

    (a) List all the ways you can arrange the volumes with five on the floor and one on the sixth/top shelf. One way might be {ABCDE, –, –, –, –, F}.
    (b) List all the ways you can arrange them with four on the floor and two on the third shelf.
    (c) Show that there are many more ways, relative to parts (a) and (b), to arrange the six volumes with two on the floor and two each on the first and second shelves. (There are several ways to answer

this, but even listing them all won't take forever—it's fewer than 100.)

    (d) Suddenly, a fantastic change! All six volumes are volume X—it's impossible to tell them apart. For each of the three distributions described in parts (a), (b), and (c), how many different (distinguishable) ways are there now?
    (e) If the energy you expend to lift a volume from the floor is proportional to a shelf's height, how do the total energies of distributions (a), (b), and (c) compare?
    (f) Use these ideas to argue that the relative probabilities of occupying the lowest energy states *should* be higher for bosons than for classically distinguishable particles.
    (g) Combine these ideas with a famous principle to argue that the relative probabilities of occupying the lowest states should be lower for fermions than for classically distinguishable particles

51. There is a simple argument, practically by inspection, that distributions (31), (32), and (33) should agree whenever occupation number is much less than 1. Provide the argument.

52. Equation (27) gives the density of states for a system of oscillators but ignores spin. The result, simply one state per energy change of $\hbar\omega_0$ between levels, is incorrect if particles are allowed different spin states at each level, but modification to include spin is easy. We know that a particle of spin s is allowed $2s + 1$ spin orientations, so the number of states at each level is simply multiplied by this factor. Thus, $D(E) = (2s + 1)/\hbar\omega_0$.

    (a) Using this density of states, the definition $N\hbar\omega_0/(2s + 1) \equiv \mathcal{E}$, and

$$N = \int_0^\infty \mathcal{N}(E)D(E)dE$$

    calculate the parameter B in the Boltzmann distribution (31) and show that the distribution can thus be rewritten as

$$\mathcal{N}(E)_{Boltz} = \frac{\mathcal{E}}{k_B T} \frac{1}{e^{E/k_B T}}$$

    (b) Argue that if $k_B T \gg \mathcal{E}$, the occupation number is much less than 1 for all E.

53. Using density of states $D(E) = (2s + 1)/\hbar\omega_0$, which generalizes equation (27) to account for multiple

allowed spin states (see Exercise 52), the definition $N\hbar\omega_0/(2s + 1) \equiv \mathcal{E}$, and

$$N = \int_0^\infty \mathcal{N}(E)D(E)dE$$

solve for B in distributions (32) and (33)—careful use of $\pm$ will cut your work by about half. Then plug back in and show that for a system of simple harmonic oscillators, the distributions become

$$\mathcal{N}(E)_{BE} = \cfrac{1}{\cfrac{e^{E/k_BT}}{1 - e^{-\mathcal{E}/k_BT}} - 1} \quad \text{and} \quad \mathcal{N}(E)_{FD} = \cfrac{1}{\cfrac{e^{E/k_BT}}{e^{+\mathcal{E}/k_BT} - 1} + 1}$$

You will need the following integral: $\int_0^\infty (Be^z \pm 1)^{-1} dz = \pm \ln(1 \pm 1/B)$.

54. Exercise 52 gives the Boltzmann distribution for the special case of simple harmonic oscillators, expressed in terms of the constant $\mathcal{E} \equiv N\hbar\omega_0/(2s + 1)$. Exercise 53 gives the Bose-Einstein and Fermi-Dirac distributions in that case. Consider a temperature low enough that we might expect multiple particles to crowd into lower energy states: $k_BT = \frac{1}{5}\mathcal{E}$. How many oscillators would be expected in a state of the lowest energy, $E = 0$? Consider all three—classically distinguishable, boson, and fermion oscillators—and comment on the differences.

55. Exercise 52 gives the Boltzmann distribution for the special case of simple harmonic oscillators, expressed in terms of the constant $\mathcal{E} \equiv N\hbar\omega_0/(2s + 1)$, and Exercise 53 gives the two quantum distributions in that case. Show that both quantum distributions converge to the Boltzmann in the limit $k_BT \gg \mathcal{E}$.

56. (a) From equation (34) and the Fermi-Dirac distribution given in Exercise 53, obtain an expression for $E_F(T)$, the Fermi temperature for a collection of fermion oscillators. (b) Show that $E_{F0} = \mathcal{E}$. (c) Plot $E_F(T)$ versus $k_BT/\mathcal{E}$ from 0 to $k_BT/\mathcal{E} = 1.5$. (d) By what percent does the Fermi energy drop from its maximum $T = 0$ value when k_BT rises to 25% of $\mathcal{E}$?

57. Exercise 54 calculates the three oscillator distributions' $E = 0$ values in the special case where k_BT is $\frac{1}{5}\mathcal{E}$. Using a very common approximation technique, show that in the more general low-temperature limit, $k_BT \ll \mathcal{E}$, the occupation numbers become $\mathcal{E}/k_BT$, $e^{\mathcal{E}/k_BT}$, and 1, for the distinguishable, boson, and fermion cases, respectively. Comment on these results. (*Note:* Although we assume that $k_BT \ll N\hbar\omega_0/(2s + 1)$, we also still assume that levels are closely spaced—that is, $k_BT \gg \hbar\omega_0$.)

Section 6

58. Show that, using equation (36), density of states (38) follows from (37).

59. Density of states (39) does not depend on N, the total number of particles in the system; neither does the density of states in equation (27). Why not?

60. For a particle in a one-dimensional (1D) box, E_n is proportional to a single quantum number n. Let us simplify things by ignoring the proportionality factor: $E_n = n^2$. For a 3D box, $E_{n_x, n_y, n_z} = n_x^2 + n_y^2 + n_z^2$, and the 2D box is fairly obvious. (a) The table shows a start on accounting for allowed states. Complete the table, stopping after the 10th state (state, not energy) for all three cases. (b) Find the number of states per energy difference for the first five states and the last five states for all three cases. For instance, for the first five in the 1D case, it is 5 states per energy difference of 24, or 5/24. (c) Overlooking the obviously crude aspects of this accounting, does the "density of states" seem to increase with energy, decrease with energy, or stay about the same?

1D		2D		3D	
State	**E**	**State**	**E**	**State**	**E**
1	1	...	...	1,1,1	3
2	4			2,1,1	6
3	9			...	...
4	16				
5	25				
...	...				

61. Calculate the Fermi energy for copper, which has a density of 8.9×10^3 kg/m^3 and one conduction electron per atom. Is room temperature "cold"?

62. Copper has one conduction electron per atom and a density of 8.9×10^3 kg/m^3. By the criteria of equation (43), show that at room temperature (300 K), the conduction electron gas must be treated as a quantum gas of indistinguishable particles.

63. Obtain an order-of-magnitude value for the temperature at which helium might begin to exhibit quantum/superfluid behavior. See equation (43). (Helium's specific gravity is about 0.12.)

64. Determine the density of states $D(E)$ for a 2D infinite well (ignoring spin) in which

$$E_{n_x, n_y} = (n_x^2 + n_y^2)\frac{\pi^2\hbar^2}{2mL^2}$$

65. Example 4 investigated one criterion for quantum indistinguishability with reference to atmospheric nitrogen. Here we investigate the other. (a) Calculate the average separation between nitrogen molecules in the air. Assume a temperature of 300 K, a pressure of 1 atm, and air that is 80% nitrogen. (b) Calculate the wavelength of a typical nitrogen molecule in the air. (c) How do your results relate to Example 4?

66. The **Fermi velocity** v_F is defined by $E_F = \frac{1}{2}mv_F^2$, where E_F is the Fermi energy. The Fermi energy for conduction electrons in sodium is 3.1 eV. (a) Calculate the Fermi velocity. (b) What would be the wavelength of an electron with this velocity? (c) If each sodium atom contributes one conduction electron to the electron gas and sodium atoms are spaced roughly 0.37 nm apart, is it necessary, by the criteria of equation (43), to treat the conduction electron gas as a *quantum* gas?

67. To obtain equation (42), we calculated a total number of fermions N as a function of E_F, assuming $T = 0$, starting with equation (41). But note that (41) is the denominator of our model for calculating average particle energy, equation (26). Its numerator is the total (as opposed to average particle) energy, which we'll call U_{total} here. (In other words, the total system energy U is the average particle energy $\overline{E}$ times the total number of particles N.) Calculate U_{total} as a function of E_F and use this to show that the minimum ($T = 0$) energy of a gas of spin-$\frac{1}{2}$ fermions may be written

$$U_{total} = \frac{3}{10}\left(\frac{3\pi^2\hbar^3}{m^{3/2}V}\right)^{2/3} N^{5/3}$$

68. Exercise 67 calculates the minimum *total* energy in a system of spin-$\frac{1}{2}$ fermions and is applicable to conduction electrons in a metal. The *average* particle energy is the total energy divided by the number of particles N. Show that the average particle energy $\overline{E}$ of a conduction electron at low temperature ($T \cong 0$) is $(3/5)E_F$. This form is convenient, being rather simple, and it can easily be put in terms of N, V, and m via equation (42).

69. This problem investigates what fraction of the available charge must be transferred from one conductor to another to produce a typical contact potential. (a) As a rough approximation, treat the conductors as 10 cm × 10 cm square plates 2 cm apart—a parallel-plate capacitor—so that $q = CV$, where $C = \varepsilon_0 (0.01 \text{ m}^2/0.02 \text{ m})$. How much charge must be transferred from one plate to the other to produce a potential difference of 2 V? (b) Approximately what fraction would this be of the total number of conduction electrons in a 100 g piece of copper, which has one conduction electron per atom?

70. The maximum wavelength light that will eject electrons from metal 1 via the photoelectric effect is 410 nm. For metal 2, it is 280 nm. What would be the potential difference if these two metals were put in contact?

71. Copper has a density of 8.9×10^3 kg/m³, and no photoelectrons are ejected from it if the wavelength of the incident light is greater than 275 nm (in the ultraviolet range). How deep is the well in which its conduction electrons—one per atom—are bound?

* **72.** Derivation of equation (40): Our model for calculating $\overline{E}$ is equation (26), whose denominator is the total number of particles N and whose numerator is the total energy of the system, which we here call U_{total}. Start with the denominator:

$$N = \int_0^\infty \mathcal{N}(E)D(E)dE$$

Insert the quantum gas density of states and an expression for the distribution, using ± to distinguish the Bose-Einstein from the Fermi-Dirac. Then change variables: $E = y^2$, and factor Be^{+y^2/k_BT} out of the denominator. In the integrand will be a factor

$$\left(1 \mp \frac{1}{B}e^{-y^2/k_BT}\right)^{-1}$$

Using $(1 \mp \varepsilon)^{-1} \cong 1 \pm \varepsilon$, a sum of two integrals results, each of Gaussian form. The integral thus becomes two terms in powers of $1/B$. Repeat the process, but instead find an expression for U_{total} in terms of $1/B$, using

$$U_{total} = \int_0^\infty E\mathcal{N}(E)D(E)dE$$

Divide your expression for U_{total} by that for N, both in terms of $1/B$. Now $1/B$ can safely be eliminated by using the lowest-order expression for N in terms of $1/B$.

Section 7

73. Heat capacity (at constant volume) is defined as $\partial U/\partial T$. (a) Using a result derived in Example 6, obtain an expression for the heat capacity per unit volume, in J/K · m³, of a photon gas. (b) What is its value at 300 K?

74. (a) Show that the number of photons per unit volume in a photon gas of temperature T is approximately $(2 \times 10^7$ K⁻³m⁻³$)T^3$. (*Note:* $\int_0^\infty x^2(e^x - 1)^{-1} dx \cong 2.40$.)

(b) Combine this with a result derived in Example 6 to show that the average photon energy in a cavity at temperature T is given by $\bar{E} \cong 2.7\, k_B T$.

75. Using the result of part (a) in Exercise 74, determine the number of photons per unit volume in outer space, whose temperature—the so-called **cosmic background temperature**—is 2.7 K.

76. The temperature of our Sun's surface is ~6000 K. (a) At what wavelength is the spectral emission of the Sun a maximum? (Refer to Exercise 79) (b) Is there something conspicuous about this wavelength?

77. At what wavelength does the human body emit the maximum electromagnetic radiation? Use Wien's law from Exercise 79 and assume a skin temperature of 70°F.

78. The electromagnetic intensity thermally radiated by a body of temperature T is given by

$$I = \sigma T^4 \quad \text{where} \quad \sigma = 5.67 \times 10^{-8}\, \text{W/m}^2 \cdot \text{K}^4$$

This is known as the **Stefan-Boltzmann law**. Show that this law follows from equation (46). (*Note:* Intensity, or power per unit area, is the product of the energy per unit volume and distance per unit time. But because intensity is a flow in a given direction away from the blackbody, the correct speed is not c. For radiation moving uniformly in all directions, the average *component* of velocity in a given direction is $\frac{1}{4}c$.)

79. According to **Wien's law**, the wavelength λ_{max} at which the thermal emission of electromagnetic energy from a body of temperature T is maximum obeys

$$\lambda_{max} T = 2.898 \times 10^{-3}\, \text{m} \cdot \text{K}$$

Show that this law follows from equation (47). To do this, use $f = c/\lambda$ to reexpress (47) in terms of λ rather than f, then obtain an expression that, when solved, would yield the wavelength at which this function is maximum. The transcendental equation cannot be solved exactly, so it is enough to show that $\lambda = (2.898 \times 10^{-3}\, \text{m} \cdot \text{K})/T$ solves it to a reasonable degree of precision.

Section 8

80. The fact that a laser's resonant cavity so effectively sharpens the wavelength can lead to the output of several closely spaced laser wavelengths, called **longitudinal modes**. Here we see how. Suppose the spontaneous emission serving as the seed for stimulated emission is of wavelength 633 nm, but somewhat fuzzy, with a line width of roughly 0.001 nm

either side of the central value. The resonant cavity is exactly 60 cm long. (a) How many wavelengths fit the standing-wave condition? (b) If only a single wavelength were desired, would changing the length of the cavity help? Explain.

Section 9

81. Somehow you have a two-dimensional solid, a sheet of atoms in a square lattice, each atom linked to its four closest neighbors by four springs oriented along the two perpendicular axes. (a) What would you expect the molar heat capacity to be at very low temperature and at very high temperature? (b) What quantity would determine, roughly, the line between low and high?

82. The Debye temperature of copper is 345 K. (a) Estimate its molar heat capacity at 100 K, using the plot in Figure 33(b). (b) Determine its corresponding specific heat and compare it with the experimental value of 0.254 J/g·K.

83. From equation (51), show that the specific heat (per mole) of a crystalline solid varies as T^3 for $T \ll T_D$.

84. The electrons' contribution to the heat capacity of a metal is small and goes to 0 as $T \to 0$. We might try to calculate it via the total internal energy, $U = \int E\, \mathcal{N}(E) D(E)\, dE$, but it is one of those integrals impossible to do in closed form, and $\mathcal{N}(E)_{FD}$ is the culprit. Still, we can explain why the heat capacity should go to zero and obtain a rough value. (a) Starting with $\mathcal{N}(E)_{FD}$ expressed as in equation (34), show that the slope $d\mathcal{N}(E)_{FD}/dE$ at $E = E_F$ is $-1/(4k_B T)$. (b) Based on part (a), the accompanying figure is a good approximation to $N(E)_{FD}$ when T is small. In a *normal* gas, such as air, when T is raised a little, *all* molecules, on average, gain a little energy, proportional to $k_B T$. Thus, the internal energy U increases linearly with T, and the heat capacity, $\partial U/\partial T$, is roughly constant. Argue on the basis of the figure that in this *fermion* gas, as the temperature increases from 0 to a small value T, while some particles gain energy of roughly $k_B T$, not all do, and the number doing so is also roughly proportional to T. What effect does this have on the heat capacity? (c) Viewing the total energy increase as simply $\Delta U =$ (number of particles whose energy increases) $\times$ (energy change per particle) and assuming the density of states is simply a constant D over the entire range of particle energies, show that the heat capacity under these lowest-temperature conditions should be proportional to $(k_B R/E_F)T$. (Trying to be more precise is not

really worthwhile, for the proportionality constant is subject to several corrections from effects we ignore.)

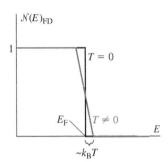

85. In Exercise 35, a simple two-state system is studied. Assume that the particles are distinguishable. Determine the molar specific heat C_V of this material and plot it versus T. Explain qualitatively why it should behave as it does.

* **86.** Prove that for any sine function $\sin(kx + \phi)$ of wavelength shorter than $2a$, where a is the atomic spacing, there is a sine function with a wavelength longer than $2a$ that has the same values at the points $x = a$, $2a$, $3a$, and so on. (*Note:* It is probably easier to work with wave number than with wavelength. We seek to show that for every wave number *greater* than π/a there is an equivalent one less than π/a.)

Comprehensive Exercises

87. Nuclear density is approximately 10^{17} kg/m³. (a) Treating them as a gas of fermions bound together by the (nonelectrostatic) "strong internucleon attraction," calculate E_F for the neutrons in lead-206 (82 protons and 124 neutrons). (b) Treating them the same way, what would E_F be for the protons? (c) In fact, the energies of the most energetic neutrons and protons, those at the Fermi energy, are essentially equal in lead-206. What has been left out of parts (a) or (b) that might account for this?

88. From elementary electrostatics, the total electrostatic potential energy in a sphere of uniform charge Q and radius R is given by

$$U = \frac{3}{5}\frac{1}{4\pi\varepsilon_0}\frac{Q^2}{R}$$

(a) What would be the energy per charge in a lead nucleus if it could be treated as 82 protons

distributed uniformly throughout a sphere of radius 7×10^{-15} m?

(b) How does this result fit with Exercise 87?

89. When a star has nearly burned up its internal fuel, it may become a **white dwarf**. It is crushed under its own enormous gravitational forces to the point at which the exclusion principle for the electrons becomes a factor. A smaller size would decrease the gravitational potential energy, but assuming the electrons to be packed into the lowest energy states consistent with the exclusion principle, "squeezing" the potential well necessarily increases the energies of all the electrons (by shortening their wavelengths). If gravitation and the electron exclusion principle are the only factors, there is a minimum total energy and corresponding equilibrium radius.

(a) Treat the electrons in a white dwarf as a quantum gas. The minimum energy allowed by the exclusion principle (see Exercise 67) is

$$U_{\text{electrons}} = \frac{3}{10}\left(\frac{3\pi^2\hbar^3}{m_e^{3/2}V}\right)^{2/3} N^{5/3}$$

Note that as the volume V is decreased, the energy does increase. For a neutral star, the number of electrons, N, equals the number of protons. Assuming that protons account for half of the white dwarf's mass M (neutrons accounting for the other half), show that the minimum electron energy may be written

$$U_{\text{electrons}} = \frac{9\hbar^2}{80m_e}\left(\frac{3\pi^2 M^5}{m_p^5}\right)^{1/3}\frac{1}{R^2}$$

where R is the star's radius.

(b) The gravitational potential energy of a sphere of mass M and radius R is given by

$$U_{\text{grav}} = -\frac{3}{5}\frac{GM^2}{R}$$

Taking both factors into account, show that the minimum total energy occurs when

$$R = \frac{3\hbar^2}{8G}\left(\frac{3\pi^2}{m_e^3 m_p^5 M}\right)^{1/3}$$

(c) Evaluate this radius for a star whose mass is equal to that of our Sun, $\sim 2 \times 10^{30}$ kg.

(d) White dwarfs are comparable to the size of Earth. Does the value in part (c) agree?

90. Exercise 89 discusses the energy balance in a white dwarf. The tendency to contract due to gravitational attraction is balanced by a kind of incompressibility of the electrons due to the exclusion principle.

(a) Matter contains protons and neutrons, which are also fermions. Why do the electrons become a hindrance to compression before the protons and neutrons do?

(b) Stars several times our Sun's mass have sufficient gravitational potential energy to collapse further than a white dwarf; they are able to force essentially all their matter to become neutrons (formed when electrons and protons combine). When they cool off, an energy balance is reached similar to that in the white dwarf but with the neutrons filling the role of the incompressible fermions. The result is a **neutron star**. Repeat the process of Exercise 89, but assume a body consisting solely of neutrons. Show that the equilibrium radius is given by

$$R = \frac{3\hbar^2}{2G}\left(\frac{3\pi^2}{2m_n^8 M}\right)^{1/3}$$

(c) Show that the radius of a neutron star whose mass is twice that of our Sun is only about 10 km.

Computational Exercises

91. Referring to Exercise 40, write a computer program to find *all* possible distributions (i.e., sets of N_0, N_1, N_2, N_3, etc.) in which 11 oscillators share an energy of $5\hbar\omega_0$. Calculate the number of ways in which each distribution can be obtained, and comment on your results.

92. Defining temperature through a derivative of a log of a number of ways—equations (2) and (3)—may be hard to embrace, but it's built into the Boltzmann distribution and all others. We can at least verify it in the oscillator case. Equation (16) comes from equating the average energy $M\hbar\omega_0/N$ of a collection of oscillators to the average predicted by the Boltzmann distribution. According to equation (4), the temperature it gives should be $(\partial S/\partial E)^{-1}$. Is it? Reasonable precision demands a fairly large system. Assume the number of particles N is 10,000 and the total energy E is 49,000 $\hbar\omega_0$. It's easiest to choose energy units in which $\hbar\omega_0 \equiv 1$, so that, according to equation (7), E and M are both 49,000. (a) Calculate the number of particles, N_n, at each level by multiplying N by the exact probabilities of equation (9)—using n instead of n_i, since

our interest is the total number at a given level, not a specific particle. Note that with $\hbar\omega_0 \equiv 1$, n is the level's energy. Round each N_n to the nearest integer, then determine the total energy simply by multiplying N_n by n—the number times the energy at each level—and summing over all levels. It might seem that the total should be 49,000. Due to rounding, it won't be, but it should differ by less than 1%. Entropy is fairly easy to calculate here. The number of ways of rearranging particle labels when N particles are distributed in different boxes/levels is $N!/\Pi_n(N_n)!$ Use this to calculate the entropy via equation (2). (b) Repeat part (a), changing only M, making it 51,000 instead of 49,000. (c) Calculate the quotient: change in entropy over change in energy. Bearing in mind that we consider a system of $N = 10,000$ and $M \cong 50,000$, how does it compare with equation (16)?

93. Write a computer program to determine the probable numbers of particles occupying oscillator levels for distinguishable, boson, and fermion particles, as plotted in Figure 9, but with the following changes: Assume six particles, and for the total energy, assume first that it is $6\delta E$ (the lowest possible for fermions) and then $12\delta E$. Comment on your results. Here is some help: Call the particles' energies e(1), e(2), e(3), and so on. If the total energy were, say, 6, let e(1) range from 0 to 6, e(2) from e(1) to 6, e(3) from e(2) to 6, and so forth. By making each particle's energy greater than or equal to the previous, we exclude distributions that differ only by a permutation of particle labels.. This is perfect for bosons and fermions, which *don't* have labels, and it saves *a lot* of computational time. Run through all the possibilities. If the sum of all particles' energies isn't 6, go to the next. If it is, count the number of particles in each level and save this *set* with a "serial number" for later retrieval. But if the number at any level is greater than 2, designate the set as unacceptable for fermions. Afterward, for bosons and fermions, add the numbers at each level for all acceptable sets, then divide by the number of sets, thus giving average numbers at each level. The "trick" for the distinguishable case is to multiply the numbers at each level for each acceptable set by the number of permutations of particle labels, $6!/\Pi_n(N_n)!$, where n runs from 0 to 6 (and later 12), and afterward divide not by the number of sets but by the sum of all these numbers of permutations.

94. Exercise 53 gives the Bose-Einstein and Fermi-Dirac distributions for the special case of simple harmonic oscillators, expressed in terms of a constant ε. (a) With equation (26) as a guide, write a formal expression—not actually attempting to carry out integrals—for the average particle energy for boson and fermion oscillators. Use of $\pm$ and/or $\mp$ allows one compact expression for both. (b) Because integration is over E, your result is a function of T alone, but unfortunately the integrals cannot be done in closed form. Assume a system of units in which $\mathcal{E}/k_B$ is 1, then invoke your computer's

numerical integration routine to obtain results for the ten values of T from 0.05 to 1.0 in increments of 0.05. Afterward, make scatter plots—one for bosons, one for fermions—of $\overline{E}$ versus T. Do your results agree with Figure 11?

Answers to Selected Exercises

19. (a) 60; (b) 20
25. ΔS_1: 0.20 J/K, ΔS_2: -0.15 J/K, $+0.05$ J/K, $e^{3.6 \times 10^{21}}$
27. (a) (3, 0, 0, 0), (0, 3, 0, 0), (0, 0, 3, 0), (0, 0, 0, 3), (2, 1, 0, 0), (2, 0, 1, 0), (2, 0, 0, 1), (1, 2, 0, 0), (1, 0, 2, 0), (1, 0, 0, 2), (0, 2, 1, 0), (0, 2, 0, 1), (0, 1, 2, 0), (0, 1, 0, 2), (0, 0, 2, 1), (0, 0, 1, 2), (1, 1, 1, 0), (1, 1, 0, 1), (1, 0, 1, 1), (0, 1, 1, 1); (b) 0.5
29. $N\hbar\omega/k_B$
43. (a) $\sqrt{2k_B T/m}$; (b) smaller
47. (a) $(mg/k_B T)e^{-mgy/k_B T}$; (b) 8.4% less; (c) 9.6% less
61. 7.0 eV

63. 1 K
65. (a) 3.71×10^{-9} m; (b) 2.76×10^{-11} m; (c) classically
69. 10^{-11} C, 10^{-16}
71. 11.5 eV
73. $(32\pi^5 k_B^4/15h^3 c^3)T^3$, 8.12×10^{-8} J/K $\cdot$ m^3
75. 3.9×10^8 m^{-3}
77. 9.85×10^{-6} m
81. (a) $2R$ at high T, 0 at low T.
85. $R(E_u/k_B T)^2 e^{E_u/k_B T}\left(1 + e^{E_u/k_B T}\right)^{-2}$
87. (a) 21.8 MeV; (b) 16.5 MeV
89. 7.17×10^6 m

Credits

Photographs Credits

Art Credits

Bonding: Molecules and Solids

Chapter Outline

The topics we study in this chapter are the foundation of a large part of science today—in particular, novel materials and modern electronics. Our focus is how atoms bond together to form molecules and solids and what characteristics and behaviors arise when they do. As in the case of multielectron atoms, it is impossible to analyze multiatom bonding solely from first principles—to solve the Schrödinger equation. On the other hand, physics would not have advanced far had physicists tackled only those problems that could be solved with pencil and paper. Thus, it is of great importance that we learn to combine first principles with simple models and qualitative arguments, if found to agree with the experimental evidence.

1 When Atoms Come Together

Underlying much of this chapter is the idea that when isolated atoms approach one another, electrons are influenced by more than "their own" atom. Our concern is no longer isolated atom wave functions, but those of a more complex multiatom potential energy. Even so, the resulting multiatom states are often recognizable as closely related to, or combinations of, isolated atom states.

Fortunately, we can grasp the main ideas in a simple, one-dimensional system. Consider the possible quantum states of a single electron in the presence of two "atoms," represented by one-dimensional finite wells of width L and separation a. We choose the finite well as a model because it is capable of holding an electron bound, as is an atom, and it allows wave functions to wander through the classically forbidden region, as the unrealistic infinite well would not. We must allow for mingling of wave functions among atoms.

From Chapter 10 of *Modern Physics*, Second Edition. Randy Harris. Copyright © 2008 by Pearson Education, Inc.
Published by Pearson Addison-Wesley. All rights reserved.

Figure 1 Two close "atoms" have pairs of molecular states, which at large separation converge to sums and differences of isolated atomic states.

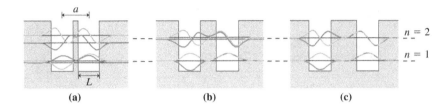

(a) (b) (c)

Figure 1(a) shows wave functions and energies for the four lowest energy states in wells/atoms whose separation is small. They somewhat resemble the four lowest energy wave functions of a *single* finite well. (The top light red one has four antinodes, the dark red below it has three, the light red below it has two, and the bottom dark red one has only one badly distorted antinode.) However, these states form pairs at high and low energy. At a larger separation, Figure 1(b), the energies of the lower pair are essentially equal, and their wave functions are very similar, virtually coincident in the right atom and opposite in the left atom. The energies of the upper pair have also become closer. At still larger separation, Figure 1(c), each pair converges to a single energy.

It is no coincidence that *pairs* approach equal energy. The low-energy pair converges at large separation to two states that if algebraically added and subtracted are the $n = 1$ states of the *two* isolated "atoms." In other words, the two molecular states are different linear combinations of the two $n = 1$ atomic states. Similarly, the upper pair converges to states that are combinations of the two $n = 2$ isolated-atom states. Were there three wells, there would be three $n = 1$ molecular states, which at large separation would converge to three isolated-atom $n = 1$ states. In general, when N atoms come together, their $n = 1$ isolated-atom states combine to form a set, or band, of N related molecular states; their $n = 2$ atomic states form another N-state molecular band; and so on. A given band's energies cluster around the energy of the isolated-atom state and spread apart as the atomic separation decreases. Figure 2 illustrates schematically the combining of atomic states of N wells/atoms to produce N-state molecular bands. While electrons can and do belong to separate atoms when those atoms are far apart (see Exercise 26), we concentrate in this chapter on true multiatom states that are shared by the whole.

2 Molecules

Atoms form molecules when the molecular state is of lower energy than the separated atoms. The behavior of the atoms' valence electrons is crucial. As they rearrange, relative to their separated-atom orbits, a lower energy may result. But how? We begin by considering the simplest possible case: the H_2^+ molecule, two protons and one electron, depicted in Figure 3. The total energy may be divided into two parts: (1) the electron's energy—its kinetic energy plus the negative, attractive potential energy it shares with the protons—and (2) the positive, repulsive potential energy shared by the two protons. Consider first the electron's

Figure 2 At small separations, each atomic state becomes an N-state band.

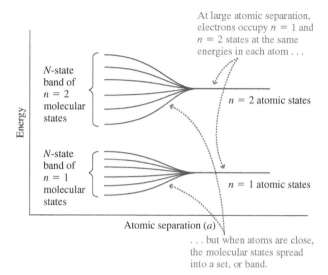

At large atomic separation, electrons occupy $n = 1$ and $n = 2$ states at the same energies in each atom . . .

N-state band of $n = 2$ molecular states

N-state band of $n = 1$ molecular states

$n = 2$ atomic states

$n = 1$ atomic states

Energy

Atomic separation (a)

. . . but when atoms are close, the molecular states spread into a set, or band.

Figure 3 A simple molecule, $H_2{}^+$—an electron shared by two protons a distance a apart.

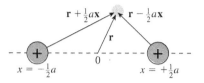

$\mathbf{r} + \frac{1}{2}a\mathbf{x}$ $\mathbf{r} - \frac{1}{2}a\mathbf{x}$

$\mathbf{r}$

$x = -\frac{1}{2}a$ 0 $x = +\frac{1}{2}a$

energy. If the proton separation a were very large, the lowest possible energy would have the electron simply bound to one proton or the other, with an energy of -13.6 eV. Putting it somewhere *between* the distant protons would yield a free electron of zero energy. At the other extreme, were the protons fused, we would essentially have helium, but with only one electron, which is also easily analyzed. The electron's energy would be -54.4 eV. Thus, we expect the electron's lowest-possible energy to decrease with decreasing proton separation. However, the positive electrostatic potential energy shared by the protons increases as their separation decreases. At large separations, it is zero, and at negligible separation, it is arbitrarily large and positive. Altogether, the *total* energy is -13.6 eV at large proton separation and arbitrarily large at negligible separation.[1] Now the important question: Is there a minimum, less than -13.6 eV? If the protons' repulsive energy were to increase faster than the electron's energy decreases, there would be no advantage to forming a molecular bond. Since it is an experimental fact that $H_2{}^+$ does form a stable molecule, the answer must be yes.

Of course, we might be interested in proving this via the Schrödinger equation. As always, we would begin with the potential energy. Given the positions shown in Figure 3, the electron's potential energy is

$$U(\mathbf{r}) = \frac{1}{4\pi\varepsilon_0}\left(\frac{-e^2}{|\mathbf{r} - \frac{1}{2}a\hat{\mathbf{x}}|} + \frac{-e^2}{|\mathbf{r} + \frac{1}{2}a\hat{\mathbf{x}}|}\right)$$

Unfortunately, even for this simplest of cases, the Schrödinger equation is solvable only by numerical techniques. When such a solution is carried out, we find that the electron's energy does vary from -13.6 eV for large a to -54.4 eV for

[1]Helium does not have infinite energy. As we will see protons actually attract via the strong force when in the same nucleus, but the $H_2{}^+$ molecule attains a minimum energy long before this point is reached.

$a = 0$ and that when the protons' repulsive energy is added, there is a minimum in the total energy. Its value is -16.3 eV, and it occurs at a proton separation of $a \cong 0.11$ nm, in agreement with experiment.

And what of the wave function? A separation of 0.11 nm is only about twice the Bohr radius of the hydrogen atom, so the electron in H_2^+ should be strongly influenced by both protons. Indeed, we find that the ground state is an even function of x, symmetric about the midpoint between the protons, and that the majority of its probability/charge density is in the region between them. The attraction both protons share with the intervening electron cloud is the root of the molecular bond's lower energy.

Adding a second electron would, of course, yield the neutral H_2 molecule, but just as for multielectron *atoms*, this drastically complicates the potential energy. As we might guess, however, the ground state has both electrons in the same lowest energy spatial state. This energy-minimizing sharing of a pair of valence electrons of opposite spin is known as a **covalent bond**. Its strength derives from the electron pair's spatial state being centrally located and thus attracted to both positive ions. Loosely speaking, both atoms in H_2 lay claim to two electrons, so we see behavior somewhat like helium—more stable and less chemically reactive than separated atoms would be. Taking the idea further, valence -1 elements should also attain greater stability by sharing a pair of electrons in a covalently bonded diatomic molecule. Fluorine ($Z = 9$), with seven electrons in the $n = 2$ shell, becomes somewhat neonlike ($Z = 10$) by forming diatomic F_2, with each atom donating an electron to an equally shared pair. The covalent molecules Cl_2, Br_2, and I_2 form in a corresponding way. With only six electrons in the $n = 2$ shell, oxygen atoms must share two electron pairs to form the stable molecule O_2. Similarly, three pairs are shared in N_2. This triple sharing makes nitrogen unusually inert for a non-noble gas.

Bonding and Antibonding States

Useful though it is, the portrayal of covalent bonding as atoms acquiring noble gas character by sharing specific pairs of valence electrons is oversimplified. First, the quantum states of a molecule are inherently different from those of isolated noble gas atoms. Second, "nonbonding" electrons may also be shared.

Consider Figure 4, which depicts states of an electron bound to two protons. Much like the finite well "atoms" of Figure 1, if the protons are far apart, then there are two atomic $1s$ states, and adding or subtracting them gives two equal-energy molecular states that are even or odd functions of position. At the small separation in a real molecule, however, the electron's wave function is affected by both protons at once. While qualitatively similar to the sums and differences of atomic states, the molecular states are the truly valid ones, and they no longer have equal energy. The even one is given the symbol $\sigma 1s$ and is known as a **sigma bonding orbital**. It is of low energy because both protons are close to the bulk of the electron cloud in the center. The odd one, given the symbol σ^*1s and called a **sigma antibonding orbital**, is of higher energy— higher even than the atomic state—because the wave function node keeps the electron away from the central region. Despite the node, this wave function is also "shared" by both protons.

Figure 4 Reducing atomic separation yields high- and low-energy molecular 1s states.

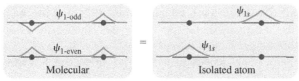

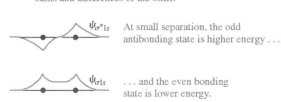

At large proton separation, atomic and molecular states are equivalent pairs, each being sums and differences of the other.

ψ_{σ^*1s} At small separation, the odd antibonding state is higher energy . . .

$\psi_{\sigma 1s}$ . . . and the even bonding state is lower energy.

Figure 5 Formation of 1s bonding and antibonding states. Plus and minus refer to signs of the wave function at an instant in time, not to charge.

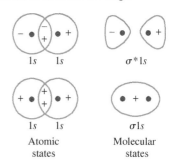

Figure 5 illustrates in a different way how 1s molecular wave functions arise from 1s atomic ones. The plus and minus signs do *not* represent the sign of a charge, but rather that of a wave function. Remember that all wave functions contain an oscillatory temporal part and thus change sign periodically. The even $\sigma 1s$ state results from the isolated-atom states combining in phase; in the odd σ^*1s, they combine a half cycle out of phase. Of course, plus and minus are irrelevant to the probability/charge density, the *square* of the net wave function.

In the spirit of Figure 2, the energy-level diagram of Figure 6 shows the separation-dependent link between the 1s atomic states and the corresponding molecular states. It is the $\sigma 1s$ molecular state that is occupied by the lone electron in H_2^+ and by the spins-opposite pair in neutral H_2. Figure 7 further illustrates the point. A molecular bond forms because it is of lower energy than an isolated-atom 1s state. On the other hand, Figure 7 also shows that although the σ^*1s state is of *higher* energy than the atomic 1s state, it is still possible for an "antibonding" state to be occupied in a *bound* molecule. While helium doesn't form an He_2 molecule, the ion He_2^+ is bound.[2] Two electrons in the $\sigma 1s$ state and one in the σ^*1s state give a lower average energy than three electrons in atomic 1s states (i.e., isolated He and He^+).

Figure 6 Atomic 1s energy levels form bonding and antibonding molecular 1s levels at small separation.

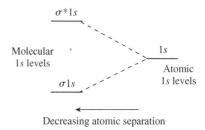

Figure 7 Filling of the 1s levels in molecular hydrogen and helium.

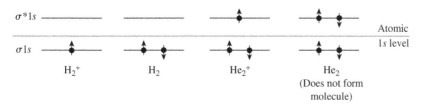

[2]At very low temperature, He_2 does form a "dimer," an extremely weakly bound pair of atoms.

Figure 8 Three perpendicular $2p$ atomic states.

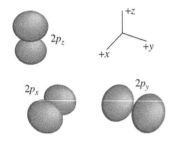

Bond Types and Hybrid States

Naturally, molecular states exhibit richer detail in atoms with occupied $n = 2$ levels. Atomic $2s$ states form a high-energy $\sigma*2s$ and low-energy $\sigma 2s$ in essentially the same way as for the $1s$. To understand how $2p$ atomic states combine, a brief digression is helpful.

The angular dependences of hydrogen's three equal-energy $2p$ spatial states are given in as

$$\psi_{2,1,0} \propto \cos \theta \qquad \psi_{2,1,\pm 1} \propto \sin \theta \, e^{\pm i\phi}$$

They may be combined to yield the three equivalent states depicted in Figure 8 as follows:

$$\psi_{2p_z} = \psi_{2,1,0} \propto \cos \theta$$

$$\psi_{2p_x} = \psi_{2,1,+1} + \psi_{2,1,-1} \propto \sin \theta \cos \phi \qquad (1)$$

$$\psi_{2p_y} = \psi_{2,1,+1} - \psi_{2,1,-1} \propto \sin \theta \sin \phi$$

The states ψ_{2p_x} and ψ_{2p_y} are the same shapes as the ψ_{2p_z}; they are just oriented differently. The impetus for the states to combine this way is to form low-energy bonds with other atoms along different directions.

For *two* identical atoms, there are six $2p$ spatial states, which form six molecular states. Figure 9 depicts these states, with the x-axis arbitrarily chosen as the molecular axis. (Again, plus and minus refer to the wave function. For instance, ψ_{2p_x} is $+\sin \theta$ when $\phi = 0$ and $-\sin \theta$ when $\phi = 180°$.) The $2p_x$ orbitals combine as do the $1s$ and $2s$ states to form bonding and antibonding states in which charge density is largest along the molecular axis, qualifying them as **σ-bonds**. The $2p_y$ and $2p_z$ also form bonding (centrally shared) and antibonding (divided) states but with the charge density largest off-axis, known as **π-bonds**. By symmetry, the energies of the $\pi 2p_y$ and $\pi 2p_z$ are equal, as are those of the $\pi*2p_y$ and $\pi*2p_z$.

Figure 10 shows the filling of molecular levels in the covalent N_2, O_2, and F_2. Several features are noteworthy. First, at these values of Z, the $1s$ electrons are confined to their respective atoms. Second, as occurs in atomic energy levels, the ordering of levels can vary from one element to another. The $\sigma 2p$, for instance, is higher than the $\pi 2p$ in N_2, but lower in O_2 and F_2. Third, oxygen's two $\pi*2p$ electrons occupy different states, for the same reason that electrons in an individual atom's unfilled subshell tend to spread out among the m_ℓ values: to lower their repulsive energy (requiring an antisymmetric spatial state). Lastly, while all $n = 2$ electrons are shared, we might say that only electrons in low-energy bonding states *in excess* of those in high-energy antibonding states contribute to a *net* lowering of energy. For instance, O_2 has six bonding and two antibonding $2p$ electrons, or a net two pairs of bonding electrons. N_2 is particularly inert because none of its $2p$ electrons is required to occupy an antibonding state.

Figure 9 Formation of $2p$ bonding and antibonding states.

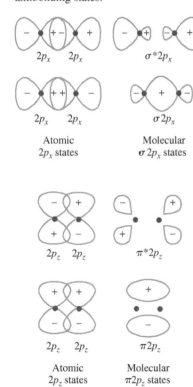

Atomic $2p_x$ states   Molecular $\sigma 2p_x$ states

Atomic $2p_z$ states   Molecular $\pi 2p_z$ states

Figure 10 Molecular energy levels in nitrogen, oxygen, and fluorine.

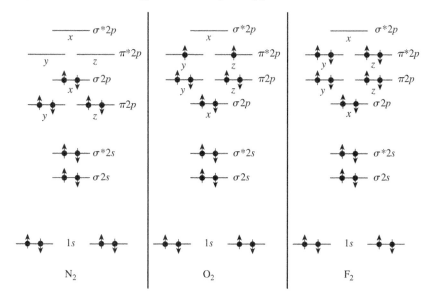

N₂   O₂   F₂

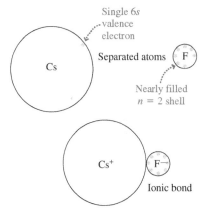

Figure 11 In an ionic bond, an electron is transferred, and the resulting ions attract electrostatically.

Being symmetric, molecules comprising two identical atoms have no electric dipole moment. In bonds between atoms of different elements, however, electrons are not shared equally, resulting in **polar covalent** bonds. For instance, when HF forms, hydrogen's $n = 1$ and fluorine's $n = 2$ electrons are shared asymmetrically. The fluorine end has a significant excess of negative, leaving an equal positive excess at the hydrogen end.

The asymmetry is most pronounced when a compact atom that is one electron short of noble gas structure meets a large, spongy atom with a lone valence electron far from its nucleus. In an extreme case like CsF, depicted in Figure 11, the fluorine does not *share* cesium's valence electron; instead, it wholly appropriates it. The fluorine ion assumes a stable, spherically symmetric neon structure, and the cesium ion is left with a stable xenon structure. Such a bond is not *co*valent, but is known as an **ionic bond**. It is true that energy must be expended to produce the positive ion by detaching its valence electron, but the final overall energy is lowered as this electron completes the low-energy outer shell of the negative ion and the ions draw together by electrostatic attraction. In general, molecular bonds exhibit characteristics somewhere between purely covalent and purely ionic.

Atomic states may **hybridize** in many ways to form bonds of the lowest possible energy. Let us consider an important example that leads to the tetrahedral geometry common in carbon compounds. When surrounded by electron-hungry atoms, carbon often shares all four of its $n = 2$ electrons. Just as the $\psi_{2,1,0}$, $\psi_{2,1,+1}$, and $\psi_{2,1,-1}$ may form the ψ_{2p_x}, ψ_{2p_y}, and ψ_{2p_z}, all four of carbon's $n = 2$ states may combine to form four equal-energy atomic states that stick out toward vertices of a tetrahedron, as shown in Figure 12. (As we know, atomic s and p states are not of equal energy, but external influences, such as nearby atoms, can

Figure 12 Carbon's sp^3 tetrahedral lobes.

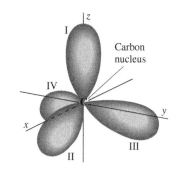

alter the relationships.) Known as **hybrid sp^3** states, the combinations that yield these four identical lobes are

Hybrid sp^3 states

$$\psi_{\text{I}} = \psi_{2s} - \psi_{2p_z} \qquad \psi_{\text{II}} = \psi_{2s} + \tfrac{1}{3}\psi_{2p_z} - \tfrac{\sqrt{8}}{3}\psi_{2p_x}$$

$$\psi_{\text{III}} = \psi_{2s} + \tfrac{1}{3}\psi_{2p_z} + \tfrac{\sqrt{2}}{3}\psi_{2p_x} - \tfrac{\sqrt{6}}{3}\psi_{2p_y} \tag{2}$$

$$\psi_{\text{IV}} = \psi_{2s} + \tfrac{1}{3}\psi_{2p_z} + \tfrac{\sqrt{2}}{3}\psi_{2p_x} + \tfrac{\sqrt{6}}{3}\psi_{2p_y}$$

Figure 13 The crystalline structure of diamond.

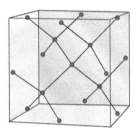

Figure 13 shows one example of tetrahedral bonding: diamond, a pure carbon solid in which each atom bonds covalently to four others. Each bond is a pair of electrons sharing the same molecular spatial state, the bonding combination of sp^3 lobes from the participating atoms, as illustrated in Figure 14. Because the lobe is along the line connecting the atoms, each is a σ bond. The presence of four covalent bonds per atom makes diamond a very strong crystalline structure. A typical *compound* in the tetrahedral configuration is methane (CH_4), in which each lobe shares a hydrogen electron and one of the carbon's four. Although the sharing is unequal, with the hydrogen being slightly positive, the arrangement of the lobes at the 109.5° tetrahedral angle (see Exercise 31) is symmetric and leaves methane with no electric dipole moment.

As Figure 15 shows, elements near carbon in the periodic table often assume a similar geometry. In ammonia (NH_3), one of nitrogen's five $n = 2$ electrons takes the place of the "missing" hydrogen electron. With the proton also missing, this lobe has a negative charge, giving ammonia an electric dipole moment and accounting for many of its properties as a solvent. One step further removed, water (H_2O) has oxygen's two extra $n = 2$ electrons replacing hydrogen electrons at two lobes. Naturally, it too has an electric dipole moment. The angles between the nitrogen-hydrogen bonds in ammonia and oxygen-hydrogen bonds in water are found to be 107.3° and 104.5°, respectively, which are very close to the tetrahedral angle. (That they are not equal is due to some mixing with the 90° p_x, p_y, p_z hybridization.)

Figure 14 The sp^3 carbon-carbon bond.

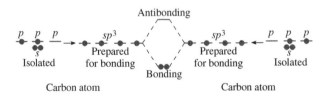

Figure 15 Similar electron orbits.

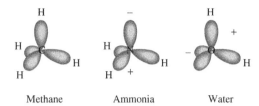

Methane   Ammonia   Water

EXAMPLE 1

Another hybridization common in carbon bonding is the sp^2, which combines only three of its $n = 2$ electrons. It can be represented as follows:

$$\psi_I = \psi_{2s} + \sqrt{2}\,\psi_{2p_x} \qquad \psi_{II} = \psi_{2s} - \sqrt{\tfrac{1}{2}}\,\psi_{2p_x} + \sqrt{\tfrac{3}{2}}\,\psi_{2p_y}$$

$$\psi_{III} = \psi_{2s} - \sqrt{\tfrac{1}{2}}\,\psi_{2p_x} - \sqrt{\tfrac{3}{2}}\,\psi_{2p_y}$$

One way of demonstrating angles between lobes is to regard the $2p_x$ and $2p_y$ states as vectors along x and y, whose lengths are the coefficients of the states. (a) Why do we not make a similar assignment for the $2s$ state? (b) Find the angles between the three $2sp^2$ states. (c) Relative to these three lobes, where does the remaining $2p$ state stick out?

SOLUTION

(a) Like all s-states, the $2s$ is spherically symmetric. It has no direction.

(b) We find the angle between vectors by the definition of the dot product, $\mathbf{A} \cdot \mathbf{B} = AB \cos \theta$. Ignoring the s-state contribution, the squares of the lengths of our "vectors" are

$$|\psi_I|^2 = (\sqrt{2})^2 = 2 \qquad |\psi_{II\ or\ III}|^2 = \left(\frac{1}{\sqrt{2}}\right)^2 + \left(\sqrt{\frac{3}{2}}\right)^2 = 2$$

and the dot products are

$$\psi_I \cdot \psi_{II\ or\ III} = (\sqrt{2}, 0) \cdot \left(\frac{-1}{\sqrt{2}}, \pm\sqrt{\frac{3}{2}}\right) = -1$$

$$\psi_{II} \cdot \psi_{III} = \left(\frac{-1}{\sqrt{2}}, \sqrt{\frac{3}{2}}\right) \cdot \left(\frac{-1}{\sqrt{2}}, -\sqrt{\frac{3}{2}}\right) = -1$$

In all cases, $\mathbf{A} \cdot \mathbf{B} = -1$ and AB is 2. Therefore, $\cos \theta = -1/2$, so θ is 120°. Thus, the three lobes are evenly spaced in the xy-plane. This is the geometry that gives graphite and benzene their planar hexagonal patterns. Each lobe forms a σ-bond with an adjacent atom. Section 10 and Progress and Applications discuss important examples of sp^2 hybridization in carbon and other elements.

(c) The lobes of the $2p_z$ state lie along z and are therefore perpendicular to the other three.

3 Rotation and Vibration

In addition to the different energy levels its electrons may occupy, a molecule may store energy in the rotational and vibrational motions of its atoms. Not only are these forms of energy storage important to the molecule's heat capacity, but the fact that these energies are quantized also leads to spectral "fingerprints" that aid in determining identity and concentration. Let us consider a simple case.

Diatomic Molecules

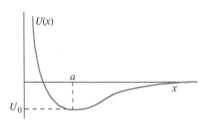

Figure 16 Potential energy in a diatomic molecule.

Figure 16 depicts the diatomic molecule potential energy. A given molecule has a particular equilibrium separation between its atoms, labeled as a. If the atoms—nuclei plus nonvalence electrons—are pulled farther apart, the potential energy increases due to a less favorable arrangement of the valence electron cloud between them, and it ultimately levels off as all forces diminish. If the atoms are pushed together, not only does nuclear repulsion increase, but also the nonvalence electrons begin to occupy the same space and are forced to higher energies by the exclusion principle. (Atomic motion doesn't bump electrons to different quantum states; rather, it modifies the existing clouds.) We see that a bound state is possible, we know that bound particles must oscillate. Although it may seem that we know very little about this potential energy, if the oscillatory motion is small, we can explain quite a bit based on only two characteristics: its equilibrium separation a and its "spring constant" κ.

Near a local minimum, any smooth potential energy "looks" like an ideal spring—a parabola. It is left as an exercise to show that for small oscillations about its equilibrium separation, the potential energy of Figure 16 can be replaced by

$$U(x_{\mathrm{r}}) \cong U_0 + \frac{1}{2}\kappa x_{\mathrm{r}}^2$$

where $x_{\mathrm{r}} \equiv x - a$ (i.e., the amount by which the actual atomic separation x differs from a) and

$$\kappa \equiv \left. \frac{d^2 U(x)}{dx^2} \right|_a \tag{3}$$

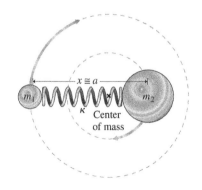

Figure 17 A simplified diatomic molecule, free to rotate about its center of mass and to vibrate along the molecular axis.

The constant value U_0 is irrelevant to energy *changes*, our main focus. Thus, we model a diatomic molecule as in Figure 17: two masses an average distance of a apart, free to rotate as a whole and to oscillate along their axis as though connected by an ideal spring.

Although we omit the quantitative details it should not be surprising that when both are present, the molecular energy levels depend on two quantum numbers n and ℓ, related to vibrational and rotational energy, respectively. The vibrational part in particular is identical to the one-dimensional case.

$$E_{n,\ell} = E_{\text{vib}} + E_{\text{rot}} = \left(n + \frac{1}{2}\right)\hbar\sqrt{\frac{\kappa}{\mu}} + \frac{\hbar^2\ell(\ell+1)}{2\mu a^2} \quad \begin{matrix} n = 0, 1, 2, \ldots \\ \ell = 0, 1, 2, \ldots \end{matrix} \quad (4)$$

Vibration-rotation energy levels

Though arising from a similar differential equation, the ℓ here relates *not* to electron orbital motion, as in hydrogen, but to rotation of the molecule. Like hydrogen, however, different rotational orientations are allowed, governed by a quantum number obeying $m_\ell = 0, \pm 1, \ldots, \pm\ell$. The mass in equation (4) is that of the equivalent single particle. It is given by

$$\mu \equiv \frac{m_1 m_2}{m_1 + m_2} \quad (5)$$

and is known as the **reduced mass**. Were one particle of overwhelming mass, the reduced mass would be simply that of the other ($m_2 \gg m_1 \Rightarrow \mu = m_1$). This makes sense. With an essentially infinite mass at one end of a spring, the only thing moving, vibrationally or rotationally, would be the small particle at the other end. In general, however, the reduced mass is less than both m_1 and m_2.

EXAMPLE 2

The diatomic HD molecule comprises an ordinary hydrogen atom and a deuterium atom, a form of hydrogen in which a neutron joins the proton in the nucleus. Their masses are 1.007 u and 2.013 u, and the bond length is 0.074 nm. Using the Boltzmann distribution, determine the temperature at which the ratio of molecules in $\ell = 1$ rotational states to those with no rotational energy would be 1/10. Jumps to higher *vibrational* levels require more energy and thus occur at higher temperature (as we soon see), so assume that all molecules are in their ground vibrational states.

SOLUTION

Taking into account the three different rotational orientations (values of m_ℓ) allowed for $\ell = 1$ and just one for $\ell = 0$, the ratio is

$$\frac{\text{number with energy } E_{0,1}}{\text{number with energy } E_{0,0}} = 3 \times \frac{e^{-E_{0,1}/k_B T}}{e^{-E_{0,0}/k_B T}} = 3e^{-(E_{0,1} - E_{0,0})/k_B T}$$

To calculate energies, we need the reduced mass. Using (5),

$$\mu = \frac{(1.007 \text{ u})(2.013 \text{ u})}{1.007 \text{ u} + 2.013 \text{ u}} = 0.671 \text{ u}$$

As noted, the reduced mass is less than either individual mass. With no vibrational change, the energy difference given by (4) is

$$E_{0,1} - E_{0,0} = \frac{\hbar^2 1(1+1)}{2\mu a^2} - \frac{\hbar^2 0(0+1)}{2\mu a^2} = \frac{\hbar^2}{\mu a^2}$$

$$= \frac{(1.055 \times 10^{-34} \, \text{J} \cdot \text{s})^2}{(0.671 \times 1.66 \times 10^{-27} \, \text{kg})(0.074 \times 10^{-9} \, \text{m})^2}$$
$$= 1.82 \times 10^{-21} \, \text{J} = 0.011 \, \text{eV}$$

Now setting the ratio to one-tenth, we arrive at

$$\frac{1}{10} = 3 \exp\left[\frac{-1.82 \times 10^{-21} \, \text{J}}{(1.38 \times 10^{-23} \, \text{J/K})T}\right] \implies T \cong 40 \, \text{K}$$

Odd though it may seem, at temperatures much below 40 K, the vast majority of the molecules are simply incapable of rotating. There is insufficient translational kinetic energy to bump them to nonzero rotational levels.

Example 2 explains hydrogen's rotational heat capacity jump, shown in Figure 18. Rotation should begin to contribute to energy storage as soon as levels *above* the ground state become accessible, and the choice of a one-tenth probability is a fair measure. Ordinary H_2 has the same bond length as HD, though it has a somewhat smaller reduced mass ($\sim$0.5 u), so we should expect the jump to begin somewhat above 40 K, as Figure 18 clearly demonstrates.

Spectra

If the vibrational and rotational energies of molecules are indeed restricted to only certain discrete values, we might expect to see evidence in the light they emit and absorb. Spectral data should therefore be a good test of our model.

Clearly, if some of the molecule's vibrational/rotational energy is given to a photon, n or ℓ or both must decrease, but the possible transitions are restricted

Figure 18 Variation of hydrogen's molar heat capacity with temperature. (*Note:* The H_2 molecule dissociates before the vibrational plateau is reached.)

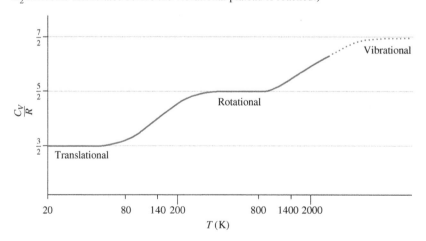

by selection rules. First, because the photon is spin-1, the system's total angular momentum before emission can equal that afterward only if ℓ for the molecule changes by 1, leading to the selection rule $\Delta\ell = \pm 1$. Second, electromagnetic radiation is emitted or absorbed most effectively by a charge distribution when it oscillates as an electric dipole. Although charge density in a *stationary* state produces no electromagnetic radiation, it does oscillate in a *transition* between vibrational states. It may be shown that a charged harmonic oscillator oscillates as an electric dipole only in transitions between energy states whose quantum numbers differ by 1, so the selection rule for vibrational levels is $\Delta n = \pm 1$. (The rule is valid only so long as the oscillation energy is low enough to make the parabolic approximation a good one.)

To lose vibrational energy, the molecule must, of course, jump to the next lower n, but the vibrational energy spacing is usually so much larger than the rotational spacing that the energy decreases whether ℓ decreases or increases. By subtracting the molecule's final energy from its initial for both cases, $\Delta\ell = \pm 1$ (see Exercise 40), we obtain from equation (4) the possible energies of the emitted photon.

$$E_{\text{photon}} = \hbar\sqrt{\frac{\kappa}{\mu}} \pm I\frac{\hbar^2}{\mu a^2} \quad I = 1, 2, 3, \ldots \tag{6}$$

Photons will be observed whose energies are spaced equally on either side of the vibrational jump $\hbar\sqrt{\kappa/\mu}$. The energy $\hbar\sqrt{\kappa/\mu}$ itself is conspicuously absent because angular-momentum conservation requires that any transition involve a (unit) change in ℓ. The same formula gives the energies of photons *absorbed* by the molecule.

Guided by equation (4), Figure 19 plots molecular vibrational levels for $n = 0$ and $n = 1$, and the much closer-spaced rotational levels $\ell = 0, 1, 2,$ and 3. It also indicates the transitions allowed in photon emission and absorption, which obey equation (6). Only six transitions occur between the states shown, each differing from the next by $\hbar^2/\mu a^2$. The "hole" in the middle is due to the forbidden $\Delta\ell = 0$ transition. We say that the photon energies constitute a **vibration-rotation band**, and Figure 20 shows how well the theory agrees with experiment. The figure plots intensity of light absorbed by diatomic HCl versus frequency (i.e., E_{photon}/h). Each spike represents *missing* transmitted light, because photons of that frequency are readily absorbed. The spacing isn't quite equal. As ℓ increases, the interatomic spring must stretch slightly farther to hold the atoms in their mutual orbit, and a larger separation a implies a slightly smaller rotational energy than otherwise expected. Thus, $\Delta\ell = +1$ absorptions are somewhat less energetic than the formula suggests, and $\Delta\ell = -1$ absorptions are more energetic. Still, the spacing is fairly regular and the hole in the middle quite apparent. Note that each spike is split because chlorine in nature comprises two isotopes of slightly different mass, giving two slightly different sets of data.

Our simple model seems to fit the experimental curve well qualitatively. Let us see what the quantitative side can tell us.

Figure 19 Vibrational and rotational energy levels, and photon-producing transitions between them, restricted by selection rules, $\Delta n = \pm 1$ and $\Delta \ell = \pm 1$.

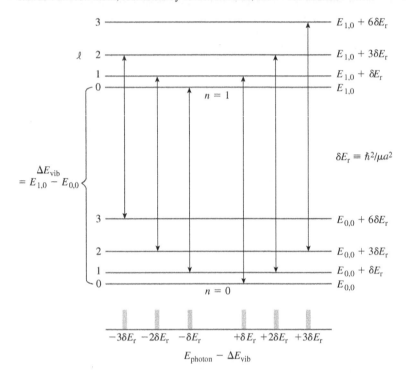

Figure 20 Vibration/rotation absorption spectrum of HCl. The "hole" in the middle is due to the forbidden $\Delta \ell = 0$ transition.

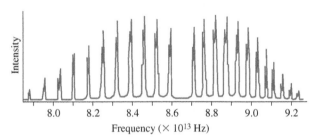

EXAMPLE 3

From the data given in Figure 20, determine (a) the approximate bond length and (b) the effective force constant in an HCl molecule.

SOLUTION

(a) From the tenth line to the left of the hole to the tenth to the right (20 steps) is a frequency range of 1.2×10^{13} Hz, giving an average spacing of 6.0×10^{11} Hz. Thus, the photons represented by these lines differ in energy by $(6.63 \times 10^{-34} \text{ J} \cdot \text{s})$

$(6.0 \times 10^{11} \text{ Hz}) = 4.0 \times 10^{-22} \text{ J} = 0.0025 \text{ eV}$. This must equal the energy spacing $\hbar^2/\mu a^2$ indicated in equation (6). To find μ, we use data from the periodic table which is averaged over naturally occurring isotopes:

$$m_H = 1.01 \text{ u} \quad m_{Cl} = 35.5 \text{ u}$$

$$\mu = \frac{(1.01 \text{ u})(35.5 \text{ u})}{1.01 \text{ u} + 35.5 \text{ u}} = 0.982 \text{ u} = 1.63 \times 10^{-27} \text{ kg}$$

Thus,

$$4.0 \times 10^{-22} \text{ J} = \frac{(1.055 \times 10^{-34} \text{ J} \cdot \text{s})^2}{(1.63 \times 10^{-27} \text{ kg})a^2} \quad \Rightarrow \quad a = 1.3 \times 10^{-10} \text{ m}$$

(b) The hole falls at 8.65×10^{13} Hz, or a photon energy hf of

$$(6.63 \times 10^{-34} \text{ J} \cdot \text{s})(8.65 \times 10^{13} \text{ Hz}) = 5.73 \times 10^{-20} \text{ J} = 0.358 \text{ eV}$$

According to equation (6), this feature corresponds to the vibrational energy spacing of $\hbar\sqrt{\kappa/\mu}$. As noted earlier, we see that it is much larger than the rotational spacing. Plugging in,

$$5.73 \times 10^{-20} \text{ J} = (1.055 \times 10^{-34} \text{ J} \cdot \text{s})\sqrt{\frac{\kappa}{1.63 \times 10^{-27} \text{ kg}}} \quad \Rightarrow \quad \kappa = 482 \text{ N/m}$$

Thus far we have discussed only the molecule's rotational and vibrational energies. Generally speaking, transitions where *electrons* change states (e.g., the Balmer series in hydrogen) involve much greater energy differences (>1 eV) than those involving molecular vibrational transitions (>0.1 eV), which are in turn more energetic than molecular rotational energy differences (<0.1 eV). Although not to proper scale, Figure 21 illustrates the relationships. The curves represent two different electron states—perhaps the ground state and the first excited state. When an electron is in an excited state, the atoms are still bound to each other but are farther apart on average, and the interatomic potential energy well is wider and shallower. Even so, for each electronic state, there are closely spaced vibrational levels and even more closely spaced rotational levels. Thus, while we might expect a molecule to produce a simple spectral line when an electron jumps from one of its allowed energies to another, vibrational and rotational energy changes break each line into many, yielding a much richer structure. Note that *symmetric* molecules, such as H_2 and N_2, lack an electric dipole moment, so they do not produce spectra due to pure vibration-rotation transitions. However, the distinctive structure of these levels is superimposed on spectral lines arising from transitions between electron states. (The oscillating electron cloud provides the necessary dipole moment in these cases.)

Figure 21 Molecular vibrational and rotational levels for two different electron levels.

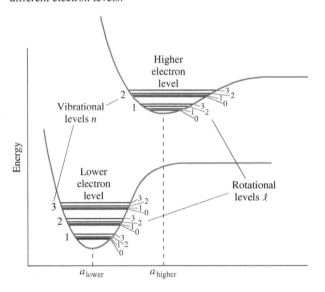

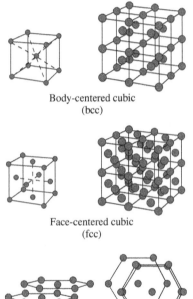

Figure 22 Some crystal lattices.

Body-centered cubic
(bcc)

Face-centered cubic
(fcc)

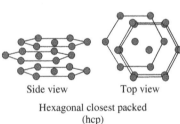

Side view   Top view

Hexagonal closest packed
(hcp)

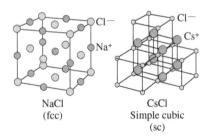

NaCl   CsCl
(fcc)   Simple cubic
              (sc)

4 Crystalline Solids

Let us now turn from molecules, the bonding of a relatively small number of atoms into somewhat larger units, to cases in which a huge number of atoms bond to form structures of macroscopic size. This takes us into the field known as **condensed matter**, by far the most active area of physics research today. Condensed matter includes studies of solids, liquids, and other systems in which the behaviors of many atoms together must be understood (such as Bose-Einstein condensates. In the following sections, we restrict our attention to crystalline solids.

All elements and compounds form solids at sufficiently low temperature and/or high pressure, most often as a **crystal lattice**, in which certain atoms are found at specific locations in a microscopic unit that is repeated identically countless times in all dimensions. (Some materials form amorphous solids, in which angles and bond lengths are so irregular that the location of one atom is essentially unrelated to that of another only a few atoms away. Familiar examples are glass and rubber.) Typical atomic spacing in a crystal is 0.25 nm to 0.5 nm, or 5 to 10 Bohr radii.

Geometrical considerations show that in three dimensions there are only 14 possible **lattice types**, or ways in which atoms can be arranged in a regular geometric pattern. (Exercise 45 gives a simple example of "geometrical considerations" in two dimensions.) Figure 22 shows several of the most common. The **body-centered cubic** is a repetition of cubes with atoms at the corners and center. It is found in the solid forms of the periodic table's first-column elements, as well as in a number of transition metals, such as iron, chromium, and tungsten. The **face-centered cubic** is also a repetitive cubic structure, but with atoms at the centers of the cubic *faces* instead of at the center of the cube. The noble gases (except helium) solidify in this structure, as do many transition elements, including copper, silver, and gold. The **hexagonal closest-packed** structure has a six-sided symmetry and shares with the face-centered cubic the distinction of resulting in the smallest volume per atom for a lattice of identical spheres. Elements with this structure are found throughout the periodic table—helium, magnesium, zinc, titanium, osmium, and many rare earths. Compounds form in the same crystalline structures as elements. For instance, sodium chloride is a face-centered cubic structure in which a sodium-chlorine pair replaces the individual atom. In fact, the sodium and chlorine ions each independently form a face-centered cubic arrangement, because the atoms of one are a fixed displacement from those of the other. Cesium chloride, though resembling the body-centered cubic, is an example of a **simple cubic** structure, formed by each ionic type independently.

Besides their lattice geometry, crystalline solids are often categorized according to how the valence electrons are bound in the solid. Four categories are generally recognized.

Covalent Solid

In a **covalent solid**, such as diamond, each atom shares covalent bonds with those surrounding it, resulting in an unbroken network of strong bonds. Such solids are relatively hard, due to the inherent strength of the covalent bond, and have high melting points. They are poor electrical conductors because all valence electrons are locked into bonds between adjacent atoms. The crystal lattice assumes a geometry determined by the directionality of the covalent bonds. In the case of diamond, it is face-centered cubic.

Ionic Solid

When atoms with nearly filled shells meet atoms with weakly bound valence electrons, the former may seize electrons from the latter, producing an **ionic solid**. The solid is held together by the strong electrostatic attraction between the ions. Thus, ionic solids are relatively hard, with high melting points. Because the transfer of electrons leaves both positive and negative ions with noble gas electronic structure, electrons are not free to respond to electric fields, so ionic solids are poor electrical conductors. The ionic bond lacks directionality, and the lattice geometry is therefore determined by whatever arrangement leads to the lowest electrostatic energy, which depends on the relative sizes of the ions. In any case, lowest energy results when signs alternate—that is, the closest neighbor of an ion of one sign is an ion of the other. Because ionic solids depend on asymmetry between atoms, *elements* do not form ionic solids.

Metallic Solid

Except for noble gases, all elements have valence electrons. But in most cases, no arrangement of covalent bonds can join all of a given atom's valence electrons to those of the atoms surrounding it. An element or compound with "leftover" valence electrons forms a **metallic solid**.

When bound to their isolated atoms, valence electrons have relatively high energy. In a metallic solid, however, the atomic valence states mix, much as in a diatomic covalent bond but encompassing all the atoms in the crystal. This mixing produces a virtual continuum of states whose energies are lower than those in isolated atoms. Shared by all atoms, the valence electrons occupying these states move rather unfettered about the crystal lattice, forming an electron gas, a distinguishing feature of the metallic solid.

The attraction that holds a metallic solid together is between the positive ions and the pervasive electron gas, and the ions assume whatever spacing leads to the lowest energy of the whole system. Because the cohesive forces are not in the form of covalent bonds *between the ions* forming the lattice, metals are often malleable and possess lower melting points than covalent solids. The valence electrons that are free to move among the continuum of states, the **conduction electrons**, readily respond to an external electric field. Accordingly, metallic solids are usually excellent conductors of electricity.

Molecular Solid

It would seem that noble gases should not form crystalline solids in any of the above ways. Their electrons are already so tightly bound that there is no incentive to share, either with neighboring atoms (covalent) or the whole crystal (metallic). But the same should be true of *molecules* whose bonding is so tight as to result in near noble gas stability, such as the covalent molecules H_2, N_2, O_2, F_2, CH_4, NH_3, and H_2O. Nevertheless, "noble molecules" can form a crystalline solid, known fittingly as a **molecular solid**. When atoms are close together, even when disinclined to share electrons, the charge distributions as a whole still interact. For noble gas atoms and symmetric covalent molecules (e.g., H_2, N_2) with no *permanent* electric dipole moment, a given atom/molecule may have the effect of an electric dipole upon its neighbor *at any instant*. This, in turn, causes its neighbor's charge distribution also to assume an instantaneous *induced* electric dipole moment. Although the molecules' dipole moments fluctuate about zero, the fluctuations are always correlated so as to produce a net attraction and a lower energy. The induced dipole-dipole attraction is known as the **London force**. Compared with the electron sharing in covalent solids and the (monopole-monopole) electrostatic attraction in ionic solids, the London force is very weak. Accordingly, the temperature must be low for such solids to form, and even then they are fairly soft.

If the molecules have permanent electric dipole moments (e.g., NH_3 and H_2O), an additional, somewhat stronger dipole-dipole attraction comes into play. It is particularly strong in the case of water and accounts for the unusually high melting point of this molecular solid.

Molecular solids assume a lattice geometry dependent on the size and shape of the atoms/molecules. Composed of "noble" particles, they lack free electrons and are poor electrical conductors.

EXAMPLE 4

What kind of solid should be formed by potassium alone, by chlorine alone, and by potassium and chlorine together?

SOLUTION

Potassium is valence $+1$ and chlorine valence -1. When together, chlorine will seize potassium's lone valence electron, producing complete-shell positive and negative ions. The ions should then form an ionic potassium-chloride solid. Individually, neither chlorine nor potassium can form an ionic solid, as identical atoms will not share electrons asymmetrically. Potassium has a single $3s$ electron in a spherically symmetric orbit, so it will not tend to bond covalently with multiple others surrounding it in a lattice. With leftover electrons, potassium should form a metallic solid. Chlorine, like fluorine in Figure 10, should form covalent molecules, and thus should form a molecular solid.

Just as for individual molecules, bonding in solids can be complex and is often a combination of the various types. For instance, there are always London forces between atoms, and bonds in compounds are often partly covalent, partly ionic. A good example of the complexity of bonding in solids is the progressive change in character among the tetravalent elements: carbon ($Z = 6$), silicon ($Z = 14$), germanium ($Z = 32$), and tin ($Z = 50$). Although at $0°C$, all four solids exhibit the covalent diamond structure, electrical conductivity increases progressively from diamond, an insulator, to tin, a fair conductor. Apparently, electrons are not free to move about the solid in diamond, but they are free to do so in tin.[3] How can this be explained? The somewhat unsatisfying answer is that even covalent and ionic solids must often be treated as though all the valence electrons are shared by all atoms, just as in a metallic solid. Different electrical properties are then based on the fact that the electronic states do not form an unbroken continuum of energies from which the electrons may choose—they separate into energy bands.

5 Energy Bands and Electrical Conduction

If all of a metal's valence electrons are released to the solid as a whole, why do we find that the number of *conduction* electrons per atom—those actually free to respond to an electric field—often does not equal the number of *valence* electrons per atom? And if even nonmetals must be treated as though they freely share electrons throughout the solid, how can they be electrical insulators? The answers rest upon the fact that the well into which the valence electrons are entrusted is not a simple well. It restricts the electrons to **energy bands**.

In reference to the double finite well of Figure 1, we noted that the wave functions resemble states of a single large well, but they also form pairs centered on the energies of the individual "atoms." Figure 23 demonstrates the same ideas in a four-atom "crystal." Electrons are attracted to each positive ion in a crystal, and we model this attraction with a simple finite well, giving low potential energy *at* each ion (center of a well) and high potential energy at the points *between* them. (The functions and energies shown in Figure 23 follow from numerical solution of the Schrödinger equation. See Computational Exercise 80.)

With four wells, the states naturally divide into four bands. To see why, consider the state at the top of the $n = 2$ band. The wave function, with eight antinodes, is of just the right wavelength to be zero at points halfway between the "positive ions," where the periodic ionic potential energy is maximum. This state's potential energy (expectation value) is thus relatively low. Its total energy, including kinetic, differs little from what it would be *without* any periodic variation due to the positive ions, represented by the single large well on

[3]At around 23°C, tin undergoes a transformation, abandoning the diamond structure for a more characteristically metallic one.

437

Figure 23 In a crystal, the periodic ionic potential energy breaks states into bands—one per single-atom state.

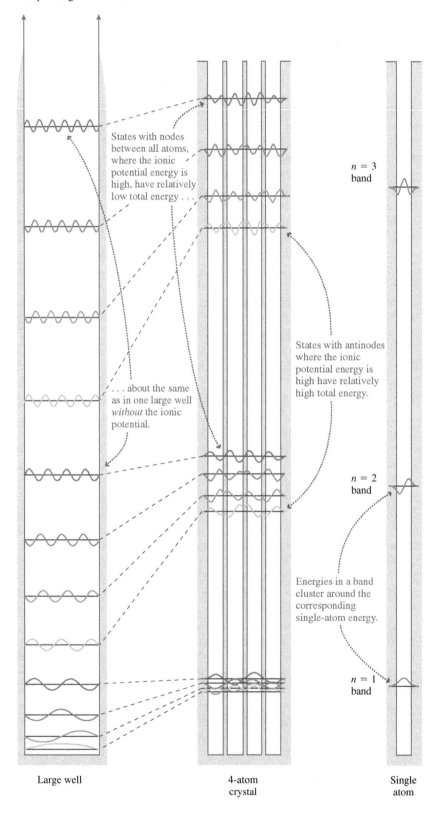

States with nodes between all atoms, where the ionic potential energy is high, have relatively low total energy . . .

. . . about the same as in one large well *without* the ionic potential.

States with antinodes where the ionic potential energy is high have relatively high total energy.

Energies in a band cluster around the corresponding single-atom energy.

$n = 3$ band

$n = 2$ band

$n = 1$ band

Large well

4-atom crystal

Single atom

the left. The next-lower wave function has seven (somewhat misshapen) anti-nodes. This gives it a *kinetic* energy, $\hbar^2 k^2/2m$, somewhat lower, but it also makes it the wrong wavelength to be zero between all ions. Its *potential* energy is *higher*. Thus, its total energy is not much lower than the top-of-the-band state. The next-lower state, six antinodes, is lower still in kinetic but higher again in potential, and so again is only slightly lower in total energy. The bottom-of-the-band state, with five antinodes, is nearly at its *maximum* at all interatomic points. Thus, while of still lower kinetic energy, it is of very high potential, again resulting in only a slight decrease in the total. The situation changes drastically at the next-lower energy state, the top of the $n = 1$ band, for it returns to a situation in which nodes fall exactly between the ions. Besides a somewhat lower kinetic energy, it has a *much* lower potential, so the total energy drops greatly. There is an **energy gap**, or **band gap**.

On the right in Figure 23 are plotted the wave functions and energies of a single "atom" of the same width as in the four-atom crystal. Note the similarities between these wave functions and the top-of-the-band functions in the crystal. There are three antinodes per atom at the top of the $n = 3$ band, two at the top of the $n = 2$, and one at the top of the $n = 1$. Not coincidentally, the bands' energies cluster around the single-atom energies. Thus, we see that each band is related to an individual-atom state.

Figure 24, which plots energy versus wave number, further illustrates the effect of the ionic potential. In one large well of width L, the allowed wave numbers k would be multiples of π/L, and the energy would be purely

Figure 24 The periodic ionic potential groups the large-well states into bands.

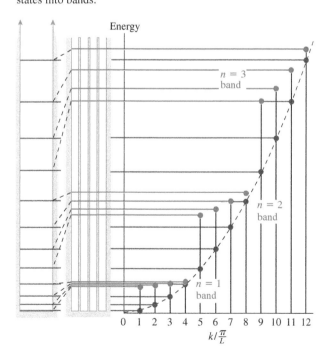

kinetic, $\hbar^2 k^2/2m$, giving the dashed parabola. The four-atom crystal has the same wavelengths (though misshapen) and thus the same kinetic energies. So in its E-versus-k plot we clearly see the grouping caused by the ionic potential. Bottom-of-the-band states have unusually high potential energy.

When N Becomes Large

Figure 25 shows features that allow us to draw two important conclusions applicable no matter how many atoms make up the crystal. As in Figure 23, at the top of each band is a state where nodes fall exactly between atoms. Each atom in band n "holds" exactly n antinodes, so the atomic spacing a is n half-wavelengths: $a = n\lambda/2$ or $k = n\pi/a$. The state just above each—the bottom of the next band—is a state of high potential energy. It adds one more antinode to the *whole crystal*. In the four-atom case, this is significant, but for a macroscopic number of atoms N, this is essentially the same number of antinodes *per atom*. Thus, although representing a high potential energy with *antinodes* between atoms, a bottom-of-the-band state has essentially the same wavelength as the top of the band below. Our first conclusion is

The jump between bands n and $n + 1$ occurs sharply at $k = n\pi/a$.

Figure 25 Band gaps occur when $a = n\lambda/2$ or $k = n\pi/a$. Top-of-the-band states are zero between atoms, where the potential energy is high, whereas bottom-of-the-band states are large there.

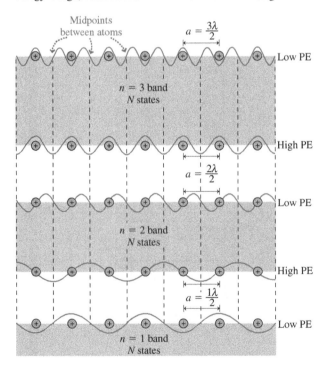

Now, if the top of band n has n antinodes per atom and there are N atoms overall, then this state has a total of nN antinodes. The top of band $n + 1$ will have $(n + 1)N$ antinodes, so the number of states from the top of one band to the top of the next is N. Our second conclusion is thus

> Each band consists of N states.

Because N is so large, a band is essentially a *continuum* of energies. When a is not too small, they spread above and below the single-atom energies, as in Figure 26. The extent of spreading depends on how much overlap there would be between the wave functions of *adjacent* atoms. (See again Figure 1.) Consequently, the **band width** depends not on the *number* of atoms but on the atomic *spacing*, increasing as a decreases. (See Exercise 48.) At very small separations, the repulsion of the positive ions, ignored in our four-atom model, leads to a rapid rise in overall energy. The crystal forms with a spacing at which the overall energy is minimum.

In summary, from the *macroscopic* crystal arises a continuum of energies, but the *microscopic* ionic potential energy divides the continuum into bands related to the individual-atom states. Figure 27 plots allowed energies versus wave number in a one-dimensional crystal where N is large and k may be of either sign, as electrons may move in either direction. The general parabolic shape shows that allowed energies are the virtual continuum of kinetic energies available to an electron roaming freely in a macroscopic infinite well, $\hbar^2 k^2/2m$. Exceptions arise only near $k = n\pi/a$, where the alignment of wave function nodes and antinodes with the ionic potential leads to a jump from an unusually low energy at the top of one band to an unusually high energy at the bottom of the next.

Thus far, we have discussed only the nature of states *available* to an electron in a crystal. We have not addressed the question of how many electrons might be present to *fill* those states, and it is this point that governs whether a material will be a conductor or an insulator.

Electrical Conduction

Before we study the relationship between energy bands and conductivity, it is worthwhile to review aspects of electrical conduction that may be understood from a classical point of view and to identify those that require a quantum-mechanical approach.

Figure 26 Behavior of allowed electron states as atomic spacing varies.

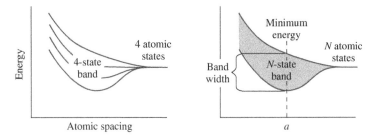

Figure 27 Bands and gaps in a one-dimensional crystal.

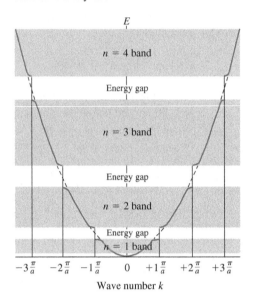

In the classical picture, electrons are free to move about in a conductor, but they may suffer collisions with the positive ions. This is a necessary ingredient in understanding why the electrical current is proportional to the applied field rather than being an increasing function of time. Were there no collisions, electrons subject to a constant electric field would constantly accelerate, producing a steadily increasing current. Collisions represent a retarding force. In essence, electrons almost instantaneously attain terminal speed in which a balance is reached between the accelerating field and the decelerating effect of collisions.

Classically, a typical electron moves randomly with an average speed $\bar{v}$ characteristic of the temperature. After a collision with a positive ion, it is just as likely to be moving in one direction as another. With no external electric field, the average velocity of all the electrons is zero. But when an electric field is present, the electrons gain, in the time between collisions, a component of velocity opposite the field. Let us define τ as the average time between collisions, or **collision time**. At any instant in time, a given electron may have been freely accelerating for an arbitrary span of time, but an average electron will have been accelerating for a time τ. It will thus have acquired an added velocity component of magnitude $(eE/m_e)\tau$, where e is the fundamental charge, E the electric field strength, and m_e the electron mass. Superimposed on the much faster random thermal motion, this slight shift toward velocities opposite the field is known as **drift velocity**. The resulting current density j is found as follows:

$$j \equiv \frac{\text{charge}}{\text{time} \cdot \text{area}} = \frac{\text{charge}}{\text{distance} \cdot \text{area}} \frac{\text{distance}}{\text{time}} = \frac{e \times \text{number}}{\text{volume}} \frac{\text{distance}}{\text{time}}$$

Thus,

$$j = e\eta v_{\text{drift}} = e\eta \frac{eE}{m_e} \tau = \frac{e^2 \eta \tau}{m_e} E$$

where η is the number of free charge carriers per unit volume. We see that the effect, a current density, is proportional to the cause, an electric field, which is Ohm's law. The proportionality constant is known as the **conductivity** of the material—the reciprocal of its **resistivity** ρ—and is given the symbol σ.

$$j = \sigma E \quad \text{where } \sigma = \frac{e^2 \eta \tau}{m_e} \tag{7}$$

Classically, conductivity decreases as the collision time τ decreases. One way to decrease the collision time is to increase the temperature, for faster-moving particles collide more frequently with obstructions around them. Thus, the conductivity of conductors decreases as temperature increases.

Much of the classical view of electrical conductivity is valid quantum mechanically. Collisions are still viewed as the origin of electrical resistance. However, we find that in metals, though Ohm's law still holds, the collision time is much larger than can be explained by a theory in which electrons may collide with all positive ions. The quantum-mechanical explanation is that (except near edges of bands) the states allowed an electron in a periodic crystal are essentially those of a free particle. The electron is a *wave*, upon which the positive ions have little effect. It is not the regular array of positive ions that upsets the otherwise free electrons. Rather, *deviations* from regularity perturb the electron wave and thus determine resistance. The most important deviations at ordinary temperatures are vibrations of the positive ions. These increase with temperature, contributing to an increase in resistance. (The fact that conductivity in metals tends to vary as T to the first power is further evidence that ionic *motion*, not mere *presence*, is key. See Comprehensive Exercise 77.) At temperatures below about 10 K, vibrational motion is so diminished that the predominant sources of collisions are microscopic **lattice imperfections**. These may be either point defects, due to atomic vacancies or impurities, or more widespread disruptions of crystal regularity. In any case, the quantum wells at certain locations are altered, and the electron wave is perturbed. Unlike ionic vibrations, the abundance of lattice imperfections is largely independent of temperature, and so is the resistance they cause.

In all solids, electrons fill bands from low to high energy in accord with the exclusion principle. In a conductor, the topmost band is only partially filled; this band is where the conduction electrons reside. (Lower full bands do not participate in conduction, as we see in Section 6.) To a good approximation, the conduction electrons behave as though moving freely inside a macroscopic well (the entire crystal) with no ionic potential. Their energies are those of an electron gas, and the energy of the highest-occupied state, measured from the bottom of the band, is the Fermi energy, E_F. As depicted in Figure 28, with no external electric field, as many electrons

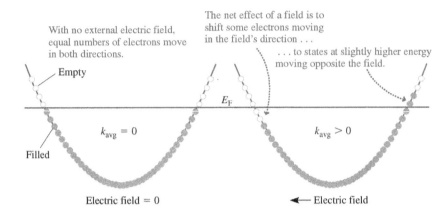

Figure 28 Conduction electrons occupy states of a large well. An external electric field shifts their momenta.

With no external electric field, equal numbers of electrons move in both directions.

The net effect of a field is to shift some electrons moving in the field's direction . . .

. . . to states at slightly higher energy moving opposite the field.

Empty

E_F

Filled

$k_{avg} = 0$

$k_{avg} > 0$

Electric field $= 0$

Electric field

would be moving in one direction as in the opposite direction. The effect of an external field is to shift electron momenta toward those in which k ($= p/\hbar$) is opposite the field. Although the momenta of all the conduction electrons are shifted, we see that it is a *net* shift only among the highest-energy states, from states slightly below E_F, where the momentum is in the direction of the field, to those slightly above E_F, where it is opposite. Classically or quantum mechanically, however, electrons do not continue to climb to higher energy levels—they do not accelerate indefinitely. The retarding effect of collisions invariably produces a balance, so that a given electric field results in a given net momentum and corresponding current density.

EXAMPLE 5

The density of silver is 5×10^3 kg/m^3. (a) What is the approximate atomic separation? (b) The Fermi energy in silver is 5.5 eV (more than 200 times the average thermal energy of classical particles at room temperature). Determine the velocity corresponding to this energy, and use it to estimate the collision time if electrons collided with every lattice ion. (c) Compare the conductivity predicted by this model with the actual room temperature value of $6.3 \times 10^7 \ \Omega^{-1} \cdot$ m^{-1}. Silver has one conduction electron per atom.

SOLUTION

(a) From the periodic table, we find the atomic mass of silver to be 107.9 u. The number of atoms per unit volume is therefore

$$\frac{10.5 \times 10^3 \text{ kg/m}^3}{(107.9 \text{ u/atom})(1.66 \times 10^{-27} \text{ kg/u})} = 5.86 \times 10^{28} \text{ atom/m}^3$$

The volume per atom is the reciprocal of this value, and the cube root of the volume is approximately the linear separation.

$$(5.86 \times 10^{28} \text{ atom/m}^3)^{-1/3} = 2.57 \times 10^{-10} \text{ m} \cong 0.26 \text{ nm}$$

(b) Using $KE = \frac{1}{2}mv^2$,

$$v = \sqrt{\frac{2(5.5 \times 1.6 \times 10^{-19}\,\text{J})}{9.11 \times 10^{-31}\,\text{kg}}} = 1.39 \times 10^6\,\text{m/s}$$

so that

$$\tau = \frac{2.57 \times 10^{-10}\,\text{m}}{1.39 \times 10^6\,\text{m/s}} = 1.85 \times 10^{-16}\,\text{s}$$

(c) Applying equation (7),

$$\sigma = \frac{(1.6 \times 10^{-19}\,\text{C})^2\,(5.86 \times 10^{28}\ \text{electrons/m}^3)(1.85 \times 10^{-16}\,\text{s})}{9.11 \times 10^{-31}\,\text{kg}}$$

$$= 3.0 \times 10^5\,\Omega^{-1}\cdot\text{m}^{-1}$$

This predicted conductivity is less than 1/100 of the actual value. All our assumptions are reasonable, except one. We conclude that an electron passes a great many lattice ions before suffering a collision.

6 Conductors, Insulators, and Semiconductors

The fundamental difference between an insulator and a conductor is whether the highest band occupied by electrons is completely or only partially full. We introduced bands in the context of a simple finite well model, but a more realistic potential energy wouldn't change the most important conclusions. Figure 29 depicts an isolated atom with a Coulomb-type well, and the result when many atoms are brought together. The main difference is that the atoms are still effectively far apart for low energy states, so these states do not form a band. Higher states, where the key valence electrons reside, are again broken into bands by the ionic potential.

Figure 29 When atoms form a crystal, low-lying nonvalence levels still belong to each atom, while higher levels become bands.

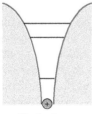

Single atom

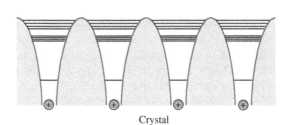

Crystal

Figure 30 Lithium's partially filled band, and beryllium's full one?

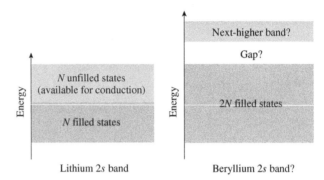

Lithium 2s band

Beryllium 2s band?

Band Occupation and Conductivity

By the simplest argument, lithium ($Z = 3$) should be a conductor and beryllium ($Z = 4$) an insulator.[4] As we know, energy bands comprise N *spatial* states, or wave functions, where N is the number of atoms in the crystal. Therefore, including spin, each band can hold $2N$ electrons. In a solid of N atoms, monovalent lithium would have N valence electrons. It follows that because the $2s$ state in the lithium *atom* is only half full, the $2s$ band in *solid* lithium is only half full. Thus, as shown in Figure 30, there is still half a band of unfilled energy levels available to its $2s$ electrons. When an external electric field is applied, they are free to enter these states and thus participate in electrical conduction. A beryllium atom, on the other hand, has a full $2s$ level, so the solid, with $2N$ valence electrons, should have a full $2s$ band. Assuming a significant energy gap to the next-higher band, electrons in beryllium should be unable to freely absorb energy or to change states in any way in response to an external field. Beryllium should be an insulator.

Beryllium is a conductor. It is the last assumption that is incorrect. Given the close spacing of some atomic energy levels, it should not be surprising that the corresponding bands might overlap, leaving no gap. As depicted schematically in Figure 31, we find that the $2s$ and $2p$ bands overlap significantly in beryllium. Accordingly, the system's ground state will have electrons occupying the lower energies of the $2p$ band rather than filling the $2s$. Thus, beryllium's electrons also have a continuum of unfilled states available just "above" them, making beryllium a conductor.

Relating atomic states (n, ℓ, m_ℓ) to bands in a solid can be rather complicated. Fortunately, we can grasp the essentials of conductivity without this complication by simply regarding overlapping bands as one band and considering how electrons fill these combined bands. The highest-energy band that would be completely full at zero temperature is defined as the **valence band**, and the band just above it is the **conduction band**. Figure 32 illustrates the features that distinguish insulators, conductors, and semiconductors. (Plotted alongside the bands is the Fermi-Dirac distribution at $T = 0$, the number of electrons per state drops abruptly to zero at E_F, while at low nonzero temperature, it falls off less steeply.) A material will be a

Figure 31 Overlap may change full and empty bands into one partially filled band.

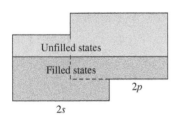

[4]These are the simplest cases of interest, since hydrogen and helium form molecular solids (the latter only at pressures above about 25 atm).

Figure 32 Band filling for an insulator, a conductor, and a semiconductor at zero and nonzero temperature. When $T > 0$, a semiconductor will have some electrons in the conduction band.

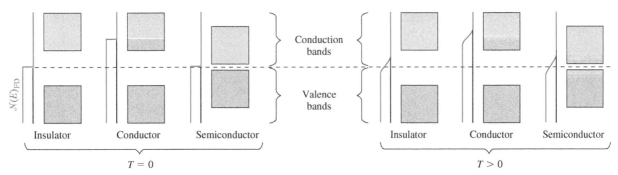

conductor if the band occupied by the highest-energy electrons is not full, making it, by definition, the conduction band. Even at zero temperature, electrons in this band will be free to absorb even a small amount of energy from an external field, so there will always be a response. A material will be an insulator if electrons happen to fill states just to the top of a band that is separated from the band above—the empty conduction band—by a large gap. The next-higher allowed energy is so high that ordinary electric fields simply cannot bump electrons up there. The electrons cannot occupy any states they were not already occupying, so there is essentially no response to the field. Even at rather high temperatures, the number of electrons energetic enough to occupy a state in the conduction band is negligible.

The term **semiconductor** is applied to materials that are insulators at zero temperature but in which the gap between the valence and conduction bands is small. By somewhat arbitrary definition, an insulator with a band gap smaller than about 2 eV is considered a semiconductor. With such a small gap, the temperature does not have to be very high to produce significant occupation of the conduction band.

Semiconducting elements commonly used in electronic devices are silicon and, to a lesser extent, germanium. Both are "covalent" solids with the same lattice geometry as diamond (Figure 13). Nevertheless, they are properly treated via band theory, as though all atoms share all valence electrons. The relevant states are the four tetrahedral states. Four spatial states and two spins could form a band of $8N$ states, which four valence electrons per atom would fill halfway. But this band splits in two, just as the bonding and antibonding atomic states split in the carbon-carbon bond of Figure 14. The lower band of $4N$ states is the full valence band, and the higher is the empty conduction band. The bands are separated by an energy gap of 1.1 eV in silicon and 0.7 eV in germanium. Diamond shares the same band structure in its $n = 2$ states, but its 5.4 eV gap qualifies it as an insulator.

The Conductivity Gap

By applying some statistical physics, let us investigate more closely the link between temperature and conductivity in insulators and semiconductors.

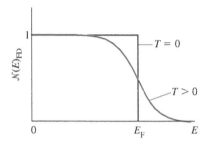

The number of electrons expected in a state of energy E obeys the Fermi-Dirac distribution.

$$\mathcal{N}(E)_{FD} = \frac{1}{e^{(E-E_F)/k_B T} + 1} \tag{8}$$

Plotted in Figure 33, it is always less than or equal to 1, as the exclusion principle demands. At $T = 0$, electrons fill all states up to E_F, the Fermi energy. At higher T, some are thermally excited to higher energies. We will use (8) to find the number of electrons thermally excited from the valence band to the conduction band. However, to go from a number in a given *state*, which the distribution gives us, to a number in energy range dE, we need to multiply by the number of allowed states in that range—the density of states. This quantity can vary with E, but we will assume that it is simply a constant D. This leads to a further simplification. In an insulator or semiconductor, the Fermi energy, by definition, falls between the valence and conduction bands, because the former is full and the latter empty. At nonzero temperature, the Fermi-Dirac distribution deviates from a step function *symmetrically* about the Fermi energy, as Figure 33 shows. We conclude that, because the number of electrons appearing in the valence band due to the thermal excitation must exactly equal the number disappearing from the valence band, the Fermi energy is right in the *middle* of the gap.

Figure 34 illustrates these points. The vertical axes are the number of electrons per energy range dE; that is, $\mathcal{N}(E)_{FD} \times D$, the number of electrons per state times the number of states per dE. Thus, an "area" is a number of

Figure 34 Number of electrons at a given energy in a semiconductor versus energy at $T = 0$ and $T > 0$.

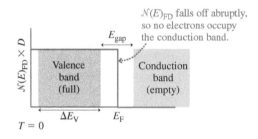

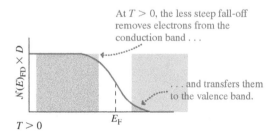

electrons. Calculating the number in the valence band at $T = 0$ is easy, for $\mathcal{N}(E)_{\text{FD}}$ is 1 everywhere within it. Using ΔE_V for the band's width, we have

$$N_V = \int_{E_{V,\text{bottom}}}^{E_{V,\text{top}}} \mathcal{N}(E)_{\text{FD}} D\, dE = \int_{E_{V,\text{bottom}}}^{E_{V,\text{top}}} 1\, D\, dE = D\Delta E_V \qquad (9)$$

To find the number excited to the conduction band at $T > 0$, we integrate from the bottom of that band, which is $\frac{1}{2}E_{\text{gap}}$ higher than E_F.

$$N_{\text{excited}} = \int_{E_F + \frac{1}{2}E_{\text{gap}}}^{\infty} \frac{1}{e^{(E-E_F)/k_B T} + 1} D\, dE = Dk_B T \ln\left(1 + e^{-E_{\text{gap}}/2k_B T}\right) \qquad (10)$$

(Because $\mathcal{N}(E)_{\text{FD}}$ falls off quickly, extending the upper limit to infinity introduces no error. The integration is left as an exercise.) Given that the gap for insulators and semiconductors is on the order of 1 eV and that $k_B T$ is about $\frac{1}{40}$ eV at room temperature, the factor $e^{-E_{\text{gap}}/2k_B T}$ will be quite small in all relevant conditions. We may therefore use the approximation $\ln(1 + \varepsilon) \cong \varepsilon$ for $\varepsilon \ll 1$. Equation (10) becomes

$$N_{\text{excited}} = Dk_B T\, e^{-E_{\text{gap}}/2k_B T}$$

Thus, the ratio of electrons excited at $T > 0$ to the total number in the valence band at $T = 0$ is

$$\frac{N_{\text{excited}}}{N_V} = \frac{k_B T}{\Delta E_V} e^{-E_{\text{gap}}/2k_B T} \qquad (11)$$

Equation (11) is a very useful relationship. Bands tend to be of order 10 eV in width (see Exercise 50), and with $k_B T_{\text{room}} \cong \frac{1}{40}$ eV, we see that the multiplicative factor is roughly of order 10^{-3}. However, it is the exponential factor that dominates. (A realistically varying density of states would change only the less-important multiplicative factor.) The difference in conductivity between conductors and insulators is one of the most stark contrasts in nature and was baffling to early physicists. The energy gap is the key. Given a typical 5 eV band gap for an insulator, the exponential factor at room temperature would be $\sim 10^{-42}$! Because N_V is "only" of order 10^{23}, we should expect no electrons at all in the conduction band, and thus no current in response to an external electric field. For a semiconductor, on the other hand, with a gap of 1 eV, the exponential factor is roughly 10^{-8}—higher by 30 orders of magnitude from a mere factor of 5 in E_{gap}.

EXAMPLE 6

Near room temperature, an increase of 1 K decreases the conductivity of copper by only about 0.4%. For a particular semiconductor, it *increases* the conductivity by 4.8%. Estimate the semiconductor's band gap.

SOLUTION

If we attribute the increased conductivity solely to an increase in charge carriers—that is, those excited into the conduction band—we need only find a ratio of (11) at the two temperatures.

$$\frac{N_{\text{excited},f}}{N_{\text{excited},i}} = \frac{T_f}{T_i} e^{-(E_{\text{gap}}/2k_B T_f) + (E_{\text{gap}}/2k_B T_i)}$$

Multiplying both sides by T_i/T_f and then taking logs gives

$$\ln\left(\frac{T_i}{T_f}\frac{N_{\text{excited},f}}{N_{\text{excited},i}}\right) = \frac{E_{\text{gap}}}{2k_B}\frac{T_f - T_i}{T_f T_i}$$

Thus, given a 4.8% increase and taking T_i to be 300 K, we arrive at

$$\ln\left(\frac{300 \text{ K}}{301 \text{ K}} 1.048\right) = \frac{E_{\text{gap}}}{2(1.38 \times 10^{-23} \text{ J/K})} \frac{1\text{K}}{(301 \text{ K})(300 \text{ K})}$$

$$\Rightarrow E_{\text{gap}} = 1.09 \times 10^{-19} \text{ J} = 0.68 \text{ eV}$$

The 4.8% quoted happens to be that for germanium. Our band gap estimate is quite good.

7 Semiconductor Theory

The simple circuits of resistors, capacitors, and inductors we study in introductory electricity and magnetism are of limited utility. Without a means of amplification, electronic communication—public address systems, long-distance telephone, radio, television—would be impossible. Related to amplification is electronic switching; that is, the ability of one thing to change the state of another from off to on, which is the heart of the digital computing that pervades our civilization. (A switch is merely an amplifier that knows no middle ground.) And why are electronics and semiconductors so inextricably related? The answer is that semiconductors are the simplest route to the basic devices of amplification and switching. The most fundamental device, which we discuss in detail in the next section, is the diode, through which current may flow only one way, distinguishing it entirely from resistors, capacitors, and inductors. The key to this remarkable property is that the diode controls the interaction of charge carriers of *both* positive and negative sign. It is true that the positive ions in a solid do not move about freely, but in semiconductors, the net response of the electrons to an external field can be precisely the same as freely moving positive charges. These effective positive charge carriers are known as **holes**.

Figure 35 Thermal excitation creating a pair of charge carriers.

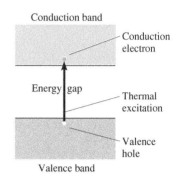

Holes

The identification of effective electron behavior with the motion of positive charges is much deeper than the simple notion of "conventional current." In introductory circuits, we often treat negative charges moving opposite an electric field as a conventional current of positive charges moving in the field direction. For most purposes, the two are indistinguishable. Nevertheless, it is easily demonstrated that the charge carriers in copper are not positive. The simplest way involves the Hall effect, in which positive-carrier and negative-carrier currents behave differently in an external *magnetic* field. Holes, on the other hand, behave precisely as positive charges whether the field is electric or magnetic. For all practical purposes, positive charge carriers do exist. Let us investigate holes and see why they are found in semiconductors but not in ordinary conductors.

At zero temperature, the full valence band and empty conduction band leave a semiconductor's electrons no freedom to respond to an electric field, just like an insulator. When thermal excitation at nonzero T promotes an electron across the gap, a "hole" at the top of the valence band remains, as depicted in Figure 35. Not only is there now an electron free to move in the conduction band, but the empty state it leaves behind also represents a certain freedom in the valence band. Suppose the promoted electron had occupied state n in the valence band—the hole is in state n. Now a valence band electron in state n' may jump into state n, creating a vacancy in state n'. The hole has changed from state n to state n'. Thus, while valence *electrons* are not free—constrained to move only into the one unoccupied state—that *unoccupied state* is as free to move in the otherwise full valence band as would be an electron in an empty band.

The special nature of holes relies on two further ingredients. First, a *lower* energy state results when a hole is *higher* in the band. Figure 36 illustrates the useful analogy of an air bubble rising through water. The system's energy decreases whether we view it as the sinking of the water (sea of electrons) or the rising of a bubble (hole). As an electron tends to sink to the lowest energy state open, a hole tends to "float" as high as possible. In moving among states in a band, a hole's energy varies in the opposite sense from that of an electron.

The second ingredient is **effective mass**. By definition, this is the ratio not of the *net* force on an electron to its acceleration but of the *external* force to the acceleration. This is a more useful quantity than mass, because it is the external force that we control via the applied field. For the derivation showing how effective mass relates to electron energy, refer to A Closer Look: Effective Mass at the end of this section. We find that

$$m_{\text{eff}} = \hbar^2 \left(\frac{d^2E}{dk^2} \right)^{-1}$$

(12)   Effective mass

Although this result is not intuitively obvious, a special case is reassuring. A free particle has only kinetic energy, so $E = \hbar^2 k^2 / 2m$. It is left as an exercise to verify that in this zero-force case, the effective mass is just m. To show how equation (12) applies in our system of interest, Figure 37 plots energy versus wave number for electrons in a crystalline solid. As noted in connection

Figure 36 Holes float.

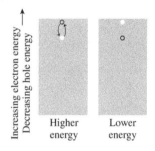

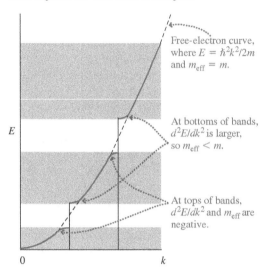

Figure 37 Energy versus wave number for electrons in a one-dimensional crystal. An electron's effective mass depends on what state it occupies.

Free-electron curve, where $E = \hbar^2 k^2 / 2m$ and $m_{eff} = m$.

At bottoms of bands, d^2E/dk^2 is larger, so $m_{eff} < m$.

At tops of bands, d^2E/dk^2 and m_{eff} are negative.

Figure 38 In a semiconductor at $T > 0$, both holes and electrons contribute to current in the direction of an applied electric field.

Conduction electrons

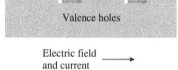

Valence holes

Electric field and current

with Figure 27, in most regions, it is a plot of a free particle in a macroscopic well, with $E = \hbar^2 k^2 / 2m$ and thus an effective mass of m. The positive ions have little effect on electrons at these energies. Only near the band gaps is the curvature different. At the bottoms of the bands, the effective mass is less than m (the curvature d^2E/dk^2 is larger). At the tops of the bands, it is negative.[5] Here the forces internal to the crystal are such that the electron's acceleration is opposite the external force. (See Comprehensive Exercise 78 for an instructive mechanical analog of negative effective mass.)

Now let us put the ingredients together. In an ordinary conductor like copper, electrons fill states to around the *middle* of a band, where they are essentially free particles of mass m. In a semiconductor, however, electrons fill states to the *top* of the valence band, where the effective mass is negative. Because hole energy varies in the opposite sense, we might imagine Figure 37 flipped upside down, with opposite curvature. Therefore, at the top of a band, and only there, a hole has positive effective mass, and thus it moves in the direction of the external field. Figure 38 illustrates how conduction electrons and valence holes respond to a field.

Doping

The semiconductors we have considered thus far are referred to as **intrinsic semiconductors**. In these pure materials, the number of electrons thermally excited to the conduction band necessarily equals the number of holes left behind in the valence band. By **doping**—addition of small amounts of impurity elements—we produce **extrinsic** semiconductors. These have a large majority of either conduction electrons or valence holes and, in either case, a much greater concentration of charge carriers than the pure intrinsic semiconductor. In the following discussion, we assume the intrinsic semiconductor to be the

[5]Note that Figure 37 has inflection points, where $d^2E/dk^2 = 0$. The effective mass of an electron in such a state is infinite! The explanation of this surprising conclusion is that the particularly strong internal forces between the solid and the electron in such a state convey the external force to the solid as a whole. Clearly, the electron would seem very massive.

most common type: a covalent lattice of tetravalent atoms, such as silicon or germanium.

An **n-type** extrinsic semiconductor is produced by interspersing a small fraction of **impurity** atoms of a pentavalent element, such as phosphorus or arsenic. Typical doping would have one of every 10^5 atoms of the intrinsic material replaced by an impurity. The valence band in the intrinsic semiconductor is completely full, and each impurity atom adds an extra electron for which there is no room, as only four of its electrons can share in the solid's tetrahedral structure. This does not automatically put the extra electron in the conduction band, however, for each impurity atom also has an extra *positive* charge. The net effect is that each impurity atom creates a new electron state slightly *below* the conduction band, known as a **donor state**. This may be thought of as a state in which the extra electron is bound to the extra positive charge at the impurity site, and the energy needed to free it is the amount by which the donor state lies below the conduction band. As shown in Figure 39, a typical value is only 0.05 eV. Accordingly, even fairly low temperatures readily excite electrons from donor states to the conduction band. Because the impurity atoms are sparse and isolated, donor states do not form a band, so the earlier arguments about holes do not apply. Vacated donor states don't behave as free positive charge carriers, but the electrons vacating these states do become free negative charge carriers in the conduction band. They are far more abundant than any electron-hole pairs that might be created by thermal excitation across the *entire* gap (see Exercise 62). Therefore, in an n-type (negative) semiconductor, the vast majority of charge carriers are conduction band electrons.

By complementary arguments, a **p-type** (positive) extrinsic semiconductor adds impurity atoms of a trivalent element, such as aluminum or gallium. Although it seems that the missing valence electrons should produce holes in the valence band, the missing *positive* charges in the atoms again alter the structure, pushing these unfilled states slightly above the valence band. They are known as **acceptor states** and are illustrated in Figure 40. (Using a system of seven finite wells, Computational Exercise 81 shows how an impurity can be modeled as simply an increase or a decrease in the depth of a well, producing a donor or

Figure 39 At $T = 0$, extra electrons in an n-type semiconductor occupy donor states. At $T > 0$, they easily become conduction electrons.

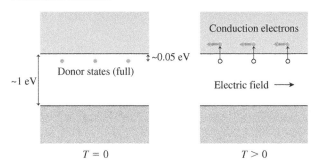

Figure 40 At $T = 0$, a p-type semiconductor has empty acceptor states, which at $T > 0$ are filled by electrons from the valence band, freeing holes.

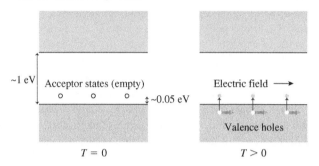

$T = 0$

$T > 0$

acceptor state.) Thermal excitation readily bumps electrons from the valence band to acceptor states, leaving freely moving holes.

Again, there is always some thermal excitation across the entire valence-to-conduction gap, creating electron-hole pairs in both n-type and p-type semiconductors. Both thus harbor charge carriers of the "wrong" sign (i.e., valence holes in n-type and conduction electrons in p-type), known as **minority carriers**. But far more abundant are the **majority carriers**: valence holes in p-type and conduction electrons in n-type. What makes doped semiconductors unique is the ease with which we can vary the sign and abundance of the carriers via impurity type and concentration. As we see in the next section, this is central to modern electronics.

A Closer Look **Effective Mass**

The velocity of a particle, called group velocity, is related to its matter wave properties ω and k by

$$v_{\text{particle}} = v_{\text{group}} = \frac{d\omega}{dk}$$

The dispersion relation that gives ω as a function of k accounts for the effects of a medium on a particle moving through it. Thus, we may write the acceleration of a particle in any medium, including a crystalline solid, as

$$a = \frac{d}{dt}v_{\text{particle}} = \frac{d}{dt}\left(\frac{d\omega}{dk}\right) = \frac{d^2\omega}{dk^2}\frac{dk}{dt}$$

Effective mass is defined as the ratio of the external force to this acceleration. Ignoring losses due to frictional forces, it is the external force alone that does the net work on

a particle moving through a medium, and the force times the particle's velocity is the work per unit time (power).

$$F_{\text{ext}}v_{\text{particle}} = \frac{dE}{dt}$$

Using $E = \hbar\omega$, we then have

$$F_{\text{ext}}v_{\text{particle}} = \hbar\frac{d\omega}{dt} = \hbar\frac{d\omega}{dk}\frac{dk}{dt} = \hbar v_{\text{particle}}\frac{dk}{dt}$$

or, canceling v_{particle} on both sides,

$$F_{\text{ext}} = \hbar\frac{dk}{dt}$$

Thus,

$$m_{\text{eff}} \equiv \frac{F_{\text{ext}}}{a} = \frac{\hbar\dfrac{dk}{dt}}{\dfrac{d^2\omega}{dk^2}\dfrac{dk}{dt}} = \frac{\hbar}{\dfrac{d^2\omega}{dk^2}} = \hbar^2\left(\frac{d^2E}{dk^2}\right)^{-1}$$

8 Semiconductor Devices

Let us now study how doped semiconductors may be exploited to produce two of the most important circuit elements.

The Diode

In many applications, we wish to allow current to flow only one way. The most basic is a rectifier, which converts the sinusoidally varying (alternating) current supplied to homes into the direct current needed by most electronic circuitry. Actually building a device that does this automatically, known as a **diode**, requires some ingenuity. The primitive solution used evacuated glass tubes housing bulky electrodes and heaters. The advent of doped semiconductors brought a revolution. Asymmetric current flow can be achieved through a simple *physical* asymmetry: charge carriers of different sign in different regions. We produce a diode by joining an n-type semiconductor to a p-type semiconductor. The area of contact is known as a **p-n junction**. As shown in Figure 41, if we apply a potential difference with the p-type at higher potential, known as a **forward-biased** condition, free holes in the p-type region and free electrons in the n-type flow toward the junction. When they meet there, as we discuss below, they annihilate, or **recombine**. Current flows continuously as electrons are added at the low-potential side and holes are added (valence electrons removed) at the high potential side. On the other hand, if the n-type is at the higher potential—a **reverse-biased** condition—both holes and electrons move away from the junction. A region devoid of free charge carriers quickly forms, and current stops almost instantly.

Energy-level diagrams help clarify the behaviors. Figure 42(a) shows an **unbiased** condition. If we simply join a p-type and an n-type, without an external potential difference, electrons "high" in the n-type conduction band cross to the p-type side, raising all electron energies there by repulsion, while correspondingly lowering them in the n-type. Few electrons need actually cross before an equilibrium is reached in which the highest occupied levels—the

Figure 41 The motion of the charge carriers in forward and reverse biased p-n junctions.

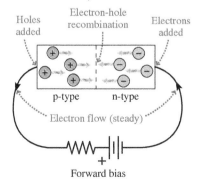
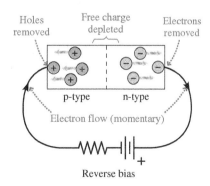

Figure 42 Bands in a diode. (a) With no external bias, the highest-energy electrons are at the same level in both p-type (left) and n-type (right) regions. (b) An externally applied reverse bias exacerbates the dogleg in the bands. (c) A forward bias evens it out and current flows.

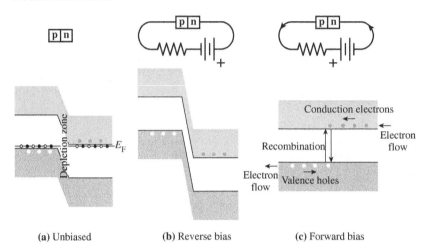

(a) Unbiased   **(b)** Reverse bias   **(c)** Forward bias

Fermi energies—on both sides are equal. Because electrons fill states to approximately the donor levels in the n-type and to the acceptor levels in the p-type, these are the energies that equalize, resulting in a characteristic dogleg in the conduction and valence bands from one side to the other. The immediate region of the junction, called the **depletion zone**, has no free charge carriers. It is too wide to tunnel through (the tunnel diode, discussed in Exercise 68, is an exception), and conduction electrons in the n-type no longer have reason to cross, for they would have to "climb" the conduction band hill. Similarly, valence holes in the p-type refuse to "dive" to the lower valence band in the n-type.

Omitting donor and acceptor states for simplicity, Figure 42(b) shows that a reverse bias—applying a lower potential on the p-type side—exaggerates the dogleg in the energy bands, shifting the p-type energies still higher relative to the n-type. (Remember: Low potential is high potential *energy* for a negative electron.) Note that *minority* carriers would very much like to cross the junction in a reverse-biased condition. Conduction electrons in the p-type would readily slide downward to the n-type conduction band, while valence holes in the n-type would float upward to the p-type valence band. But in normal diode operation, minority carriers are scarce, so the reverse current is negligible.

Forward-biasing the diode, as shown in Figure 42(c), shifts the n-type conduction band upward relative to that of the p-type. Conduction electrons near the junction readily wander, or diffuse, across as soon as the unevenness is eliminated. Holes do the same, and once in the same physical region, the two recombine; that is, the conduction electrons jump down to fill the valence holes. Energy is, of course, conserved, and the energy lost in the jump across the gap can go to heat (some diodes incorporate large heat-sinks) or to light. In fact, this transition is how the LED (light-emitting diode) produces its light, and we see that the photon energy equals the gap energy. We also see that the gap energy is the amount by which the external potential must shift the bands to even them out. Thus, a diode of 1 eV band gap would need a forward bias of 1 V before turning on.

REAL-WORLD EXAMPLE THE PHOTODIODE

Ways of exploiting the diode's band gap and its two types of charge carrier are endless. One important application is essentially the reverse of the LED. In an LED, the electrical energy of conduction electrons and valence holes becomes light energy of photons. What if we deliberately shine light at a diode?

Applying the Physics

Consider an unbiased diode whose band gap is 1.0 eV. Suppose that photons whose energy slightly exceeds the band gap strike all regions—p-type, n-type, and the junction. (a) Describe the behavior of electrons and holes. Will a potential difference develop? (b) At approximately what wavelength would this device become effective?

SOLUTION

(a) Just as an *atom* can emit or absorb a photon of the proper wavelength, with an electron jumping down or up in the process, the transition in which electrons and holes recombine and give off a photon can be driven the other way. In whatever region it may strike, a photon can create an electron in the conduction band and a hole in the valence, as shown in Figure 43. A conduction electron in the p-type, where it is a minority carrier, would be delighted to "slide" down to the lower conduction band in the n-type, as would conduction electrons created in the depletion zone around the junction. Similarly, holes created in either the depletion zone or n-type valence would happily float up to the p-type valence. If the light were switched off, the diode would, of course, return to its unbiased state. But as long as it shines, the light drives negative charges to the n-type and positive ones to the p-type, thus establishing a potential difference. The device becomes a battery!

(b) The photon energy must be at least the gap energy.

$$\lambda = \frac{hc}{E_{\text{gap}}} = \frac{1240 \text{ eV} \cdot \text{nm}}{1 \text{ eV}} = 1240 \text{ nm}$$

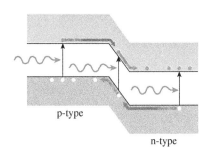

Figure 43 Photons create electron-hole pairs in an unbiased diode. Conduction electrons slide down to the n-type, and valence holes float up to the p side.

In reference to Figure 41, one might ask why, if pairs of charge carriers "disappear" at the junction in a forward-bias case, they cannot appear in the reverse-bias case and thereby also allow current to flow. As we see in this example, an energy *input* would be needed for each pair created—in fact, quite a bit of energy, far greater than $k_B T$. What we have here is the essence of the photovoltaic cell, which turns light into electricity. Naturally, many refinements have been applied. A common one adds a layer of intrinsic semiconductor between the n- and p-type regions, widening the depletion zone where electron-hole pairs are sorted quickly and contributing to improved efficiency in high-frequency applications. Another, used in solar cells, stacks semiconductors of various band gaps, each "picking off" the wavelengths it most effectively absorbs and producing a more efficient overall conversion of natural light.

Another application of the diode deserves mention: the **diode laser**. As in the LED, the energy given up in electron-hole recombination is the source of light in a laser diode. Large concentrations of electrons and holes at the junction produce the required population inversion. As in other laser types, a resonant cavity is needed to amplify the desired wavelength; in a diode laser, it can be formed simply by cleaving the ends of the crystal parallel to each other. (Semiconductors' high refractive index gives sufficiently complete reflection.) Because it too often gives up its recombination energy in forms other than light, silicon is a poor choice for diode lasers. A material producing photons with much higher efficiency is gallium arsenide, a compound lattice formed of trivalent and pentavalent atoms. Other combinations symmetric about column IV of the periodic table (both III–V and II–VI) have also been used. Diode lasers typically have efficiencies—electrical power to light power—greater then 50% and are found in CD players, bar code scanners, laser pointers, and a host of other applications.

The Transistor

Although opening up a whole new world, the transistor is actually a fairly simple extension of ideas we have already discussed. If we join in succession three alternating extrinsic semiconductors, with certain refinements, we have a transistor. It can be either a pnp or npn. Because the two are complementary, we restrict our attention to the npn.

The p-type center region of an npn transistor is called the **base**, and the n-type regions are the **emitter** and **collector**. (While seemingly interchangeable, the latter two are biased differently and are of different size and doping level, tailoring them to the respective roles.) In operation, as depicted in Figure 44, the emitter-base diode is forward biased, so conduction electrons flow from the emitter into the base. They are discouraged from recombining with holes there by making the base of small size and of very light doping. The beauty of the transistor is that these conduction electrons are *minority* carriers in the base and the collector-base diode is reverse biased. Consequently, while a small fraction of the electrons do recombine and pass out the base, the rest are quite happy to slide down to the collector's conduction band. Here is the essence of amplification: The fraction that flows out the collector (eventually returning to the emitter through the output circuit) is *proportional to and typically 100 times greater than* that which flows out the base (returning through the input circuit). For their 1948 discovery of the transistor, John Bardeen, Walter Brattain, and William Shockley were awarded the 1956 Nobel Prize in physics.

Figure 45 shows the rudiments of a transistor amplifier. The input, perhaps a microphone, introduces minute voltage variations in the emitter-base bias, with proportional variations in the rate at which electrons flow into the base from the emitter. A tiny fraction of this current leaves the base and circulates as a varying current in the input (emitter-base) circuit; the overwhelming remainder constitutes a proportional varying current in the output (emitter-collector) circuit.

Figure 44 Bands and charge flow in a npn transistor.

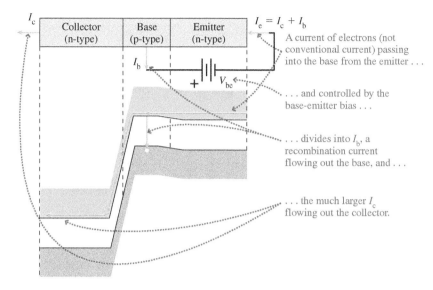

A current of electrons (not conventional current) passing into the base from the emitter . . .

. . . and controlled by the base-emitter bias . . .

. . . divides into I_b, a recombination current flowing out the base, and . . .

. . . the much larger I_c flowing out the collector.

Figure 45 The elements of a transistor amplifier.

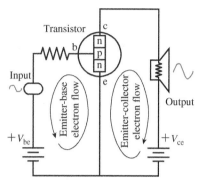

The **bipolar** transistor discussed above is just one of many semiconductor amplification devices. Another is the field effect transistor (FET), one type of which is the **MOSFET**, depicted in Figure 46 and discussed in Exercise 71. Its electrical properties and ease of fabrication make it one of the most common switching devices in **integrated circuits**—the heart of today's ubiquitous microchip electronics. A silicon chip can be modified so that doping is arbitrarily n-type or p-type in successive minuscule regions, creating transistors smaller than 1 μm^2 in area. By appropriate doping level in single n-type or p-type regions, either resistors or highly conducting "wires" can be incorporated—hence the name integrated circuit. By the early 2000s, circuits of a billion transistors could be "written" into a single chip. Figure 47 exhibits a typical transistor density. Densities continue to multiply every few years.

9 Superconductivity

Some materials at low temperature lose all electrical resistance. Figure 48 shows resistivity versus temperature for tin and copper. While copper retains resistance down to the lowest measurable temperatures, tin's resistivity plummets to zero at its **critical temperature** T_c, a characteristic of the material. In such a state, the material is known as a **superconductor**. About 40% of the natural elemental metals are known to become superconductors at low temperature. In this section, we discuss features common to superconducting materials and the mechanism by which superconductivity occurs.

With no resistance, an electric current established in a superconducting material should persist indefinitely, without an applied voltage. Indeed, many experiments have been done testing this very prediction, one indicating a minimum time for significant current decay of 100,000 years!

Figure 46 A MOSFET is well suited to integrated circuits. The gate, separated from the semiconductor by an insulating layer, controls electron flow from the source to the drain.

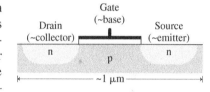

Figure 47 A modern computer processor. The small chip in the center, only 143 mm^2 in area, contains about 300 million transistors.

Figure 48 Copper always has electrical resistance, while tin becomes a superconductor.

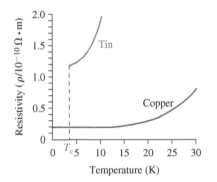

Figure 49 When it drops below its critical temperature, a superconductor expels magnetic field lines.

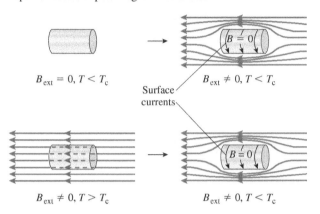

Another feature of superconductors is that they exclude magnetic field lines, as depicted in Figure 49. If a material is below its critical temperature (i.e., in a superconducting state) in a region of zero magnetic field, and an external magnetic field is introduced, then the field lines will curve around the object, never passing through. We might expect this on the basis of Faraday's law. Any change in magnetic flux through a cross section would induce an emf, and if there is no resistance, an arbitrarily large surface current is possible, able to produce an internal field that cancels the external. However, it can be shown that even perfect conductivity would allow an external field to creep slowly from the surface into the material. Moreover, a complete lack of resistance is insufficient to explain another behavior. If a superconducting material *above* its critical temperature is *initially* permeated by a magnetic field and *then* cooled, the magnetic field lines will be expelled as it drops below its critical temperature. The result is the same—a superconducting state that excludes magnetic field lines. Because the external field is not varied, we would not expect currents to be induced that might cancel that field, but surface currents do arise, and they persist indefinitely.

To explain magnetic effects, we must attribute to superconductors not only perfect conductivity but also perfect diamagnetism. This being the case, a superconductor always repels a magnet. A vivid example is shown in Figure 50, in which a small magnet hovers above a disk of superconducting material. Liquid nitrogen (77 K) surrounding the disk keeps it below its critical temperature, so that the disk pushes away on the magnet and its field. Exclusion of magnetic field lines by a superconductor is known as the **Meissner effect**.

For all superconducting materials, there is a limit on the strength of the external field they can exclude. If the field is too strong, superconductivity is destroyed, and the field penetrates the material in the normal way. The field strength at which this occurs is known as the **critical field** B_c. It is temperature dependent, being highest at $T = 0$ and dropping to zero at the critical temperature. It is natural to wonder what uses we make of superconductors. This inevitably

Figure 50 To exclude the field lines of the permanent magnet (above), a superconducting disk (below) becomes an opposing magnet. Note the vapor from the liquid nitrogen, needed to keep the ceramic YBCO below its critical temperature.

leads to the reason why so much emphasis is placed on their magnetic properties. According to Ampere's law, electrical current is always accompanied by magnetic fields, and if there is a limit on the magnetic field that a material can bear, then there will be a limit on its ability to carry current. Let us now study two types of superconductors and their important magnetic properties.

Type-I and Type-II Superconductors

The discovery of superconductivity won the 1913 Nobel Prize for Heike Kamerlingh-Onnes. The first elements found to exhibit the effect are now known as Type-I superconductors. Figure 51(a) shows how the critical field B_c varies with temperature. Type-I superconductors are characterized by a sharp transition as the external magnetic field increases, from field-excluding superconducting state to field-penetrating normal (nonsuperconducting) state. Figure 51(b) illustrates how the net and induced fields vary with the external field at a given $T < T_c$. Up to B_c, the net field inside is zero. The external field is perfectly canceled by the field due to currents induced at the sample's surface. Beyond B_c, the material is normal, and the external field passes through freely. Superconducting elements tend to be Type I. Their critical fields and temperatures are relatively low, typically 0.01–0.1 T and 1–9 K, so their usefulness is limited.

Type-II superconductors are distinguished by their tendency to spontaneously form microscopic **vortices**. Depicted in Figure 52, vortices are superconducting regions of circulating current surrounding "tubes," known as

Figure 51 A Type-I superconductor. (a) The critical field B_c decreases as $T \rightarrow T_c$. (b) When it is superconducting, the induced field perfectly opposes the external—the net field inside is 0.

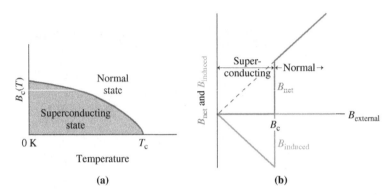

(a)

(b)

normal cores, in which the material is in the nonsuperconducting state and through which field lines pass. As the external field increases, vortices become more dense, as in Figure 53, allowing more field lines to pass through. Figure 54(a) shows that the behavior of vortices is tied to the existence of *two* critical fields. At external field strengths below B_{c1}, a Type II behaves just like a Type I. Above B_{c1}, the **vortex state** begins. Field lines begin to pass through normal cores while the surrounding regions remain superconducting. Increasing flux penetration in the vortex state is demonstrated clearly in Figure 54(b). By the time B_{c2} is reached, all of the external field lines pass through, so that $B_{induced} = 0$ and $B_{net} = B_{external}$, and the entire sample is normal.

Metallic compounds and alloys tend to be Type-II superconductors. They typically have critical temperatures more than twice as high, in the 20 K range, and critical fields 2–3 *orders of magnitude* higher than Type I, giving them much wider practical application.

Figure 52 Magnetic field lines passing through vortices in a type-II superconductor.

Figure 53 Vortices become more dense as field strength increases. (Both represent $B_{c1} < B_{external} < B_{c2}$. See Figure 54.)

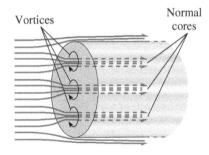

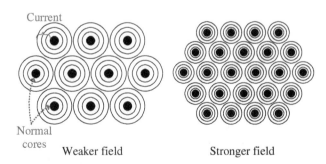

Weaker field

Stronger field

Figure 54 In a Type-II superconductor, an external field increasing from B_{c1} would penetrate through an increasing density of vortices, until at B_{c2} the material is normal.

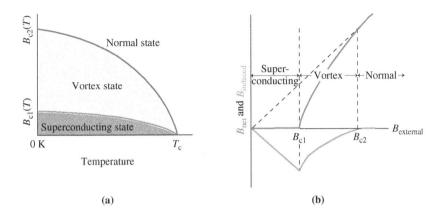

(a)

(b)

BCS Theory

Although there are obvious differences between Type-I and Type-II superconductors, the mechanism by which superconductivity occurs is the same for both: the ordered motion of the electrons in pairs, known as **Cooper pairs**. The motions of all pairs are so strongly correlated and ordered that they respond to an external electric field as one; thus, they are unable to scatter individually in ways that ordinarily result in electrical resistance.

Superconductivity via Cooper pairs depends intimately on interactions between the conduction electrons and the lattice of positive ions, and there are two important clues. First, a given material's critical temperature varies with the average mass M of the positive ions according to $T_c \propto M^{-1/2}$. This is known as the **isotope effect**. Atoms of the same element but differing numbers of neutrons in the nucleus, and thus differing masses, are referred to as different isotopes. That the atomic mass affects T_c certainly suggests that the positive ions are somehow involved in the process. Second, elements that superconduct at low temperatures usually make poor conductors at room temperature, and vice versa. This suggests that strong interactions/collisions between electrons and the lattice—the bane of conductivity at room temperature—are a *requirement* for superconductivity at low temperature.

The logical next question is how the electron-lattice interaction can form a Cooper pair. At low temperatures, two electrons in a solid can experience a net attraction, mediated by a phonon. As shown in Figure 55, an electron moving through a solid causes a local distortion of the lattice, attracting the positive ions and thus creating a region of unusually high positive charge concentration. This distortion pulls on the electron as the two go their separate ways through the lattice. We say that the electron has emitted a phonon. When the phonon/distortion approaches another electron, the positive charge concentration pulls on it—the second electron absorbs the phonon. The net effect is that the electrons experience equal

Figure 55 A phonon-mediated attraction between electrons. A lattice deformation caused by one electron propagates as a particle of vibration—a phonon—that conveys a force to another electron. The electrons are pulled toward each other.

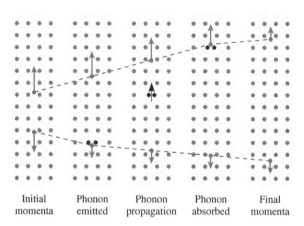

| Initial momenta | Phonon emitted | Phonon propagation | Phonon absorbed | Final momenta |

Figure 56 All Cooper pairs have the same momentum: zero when current is zero; nonzero otherwise.

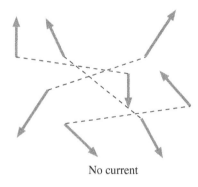

No current

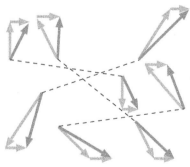

Electron current

momentum changes toward one another, just as would particles sharing an attractive force. Under the proper conditions, this phonon-mediated attraction is stronger than the electrons' Coulomb repulsion, producing a bond. Even so, the binding energy is small, typically 10^{-3} eV, and the electron separation is fairly large, on the order of 1 μm. Because this is much larger than atomic spacing in a lattice, a great many Cooper pairs overlap one another.

The explanation of superconductivity involves not just a possible binding attraction between pairs of electrons, but also correlations in the system as a whole. It is known as **BCS theory**, after its discoverers, Bardeen, Cooper, and Schrieffer, who received the 1972 Nobel Prize for their work of 15 years earlier. The theory encompasses essentially all behaviors common to Type-I and Type-II superconductors: perfect conductivity, the Meissner effect, the existence of a critical temperature, and so on. Let us look at a few of its more important points.

According to BCS theory, an overall state of lowest energy occurs when the most energetic conduction electrons, those near E_F, form opposite-spin Cooper pairs, with all pairs having the same net momentum. As illustrated in Figure 56, in the state of zero current, each pair has zero net momentum; when current flows, the momentum common to all pairs is nonzero. The result in any case is a very ordered state. Although members of a pair experience changes in their *relative* momentum, the centers of mass of all pairs have precisely the same momentum. To engage in the attraction at all, electrons must have some freedom to change their relative momentum. There is no such freedom in the electron states completely filled up to E_F, so those electrons that form Cooper pairs must actually occupy states slightly above E_F. Nevertheless, the attraction results in an overall state that is lower in energy. Only electrons near E_F participate in the superconducting state. Raising "deeper" electrons to free states near E_F would increase the energy more than the weak attraction could lower it.

Although lattice vibrations (i.e., phonons) are actually an integral part of the superconducting state, electrical resistance is zero because *random* vibrations and lattice imperfections effectively cannot scatter electrons. To disrupt the collective, ordered motion would require breaking apart Cooper pairs. BCS theory shows that at zero temperature, the binding energy of a pair is $3.5k_BT_c$, and, as noted above, a typical value is 10^{-3} eV. Small though this may be, it is still larger than the thermal energy available in a collision with the lattice at low temperature, so such collisions essentially cannot occur! Thus, the lowest-energy ordered state of current flow persists. The minimum jump from the superconducting state to an excited normal state is somewhat similar to the jump between bands in a semiconductor, and it is also referred to as a gap.

The distinction between Type-I and Type-II superconductors lies in the material's **mean free path**, the average distance its electrons travel before undergoing a collision. A material in which the mean free path is large will have Cooper pairs interlocked in a coherent, orderly way over a vast region. Thus, they tend to assume states homogeneous throughout the sample, completely excluding magnetic fields. Type-I superconductors fit this description. Type-II superconductors, on the other hand, have a relatively short mean free path, so order can be much shorter range, allowing for a microscopic network of flux-carrying normal cores within an otherwise superconducting region.

Another interesting conclusion of BCS theory is **flux quantization**. The magnetic flux passing through any region encircled by a supercurrent, whether in a microscopic vortex or a macroscopic ring, must be an integer times $\pi\hbar/e$.

High-T_c Superconductors

The year 1986 ushered in an extended field day for experimental physicists and a challenge for theoretical physicists. A new variety of superconductor was discovered: the **high-T_c superconductor**. The materials were compounds of copper and oxygen with other elements, and they qualified as ceramics. The discovery was astonishing because ceramics are excellent *insulators* at ordinary temperatures. The first one found was $La_{2-x}Ba_xCuO_4$, for which Bednorz and Müller won the 1987 Nobel Prize in physics. The x means that the compound is basically La_2CuO_4 but with barium atoms replacing lanthanum atoms at random locations. The most startling thing was that the critical temperature, 30 K, was more than 5 K higher than that of any metallic material discovered in seven prior decades of research. A frenzied hunt ensued. A milestone was reached in 1987 when YBCO ($YBa_2Cu_3O_7$) was found to have a critical temperature of 92 K, exceeding the 77 K boiling point of liquid nitrogen. Previous work on superconductivity required the materials to be cooled with liquid helium, a precious commodity. The new material could be cooled using relatively plentiful liquid nitrogen. The early 1990s brought the record to around 135 K, followed by a stall of about a dozen years, until in 2006, a copper-oxide compound was reported with a critical temperature near 150 K.

These high-T_c superconductors, generally referred to as **cuprates**, possess the Type-II traits of forming vortices and having two critical field values.

However, the mechanism of superconductivity differs in significant ways from the standard BCS behavior of the Type I and Type II. For one thing, high-T_c superconductors do not, as a rule, exhibit the isotope effect. Electron pairs still play a role, but the interaction with the bulk material is different. The fact that all high-T_c superconductors have alternating planes of copper and oxygen atoms has led to an understanding of the basic electron/lattice interaction, but a comprehensive theory has yet to emerge.

Owing to the great convenience of using liquid nitrogen as a coolant, high-T_c superconductors have spawned an industry in superconducting wires and cables, and numerous other uses have been found. However, much of the early fever has subsided, as promise has dimmed that these types of materials will produce a room-temperature superconductor—the Holy Grail of superconductivity.

Uses

One current use of superconducting materials is in superconducting magnets for particle accelerators. Because current flows without resistance, little heat is generated and little power wasted. Strong magnetic fields can be sustained while incurring only the expense of maintaining the coolant, necessary simply to prevent the material from rising above its critical temperature. Obviously, with a room-temperature superconductor, even this expense could be eliminated. Other proposed uses of room-temperature superconductors include computers, where the ever-decreasing size of microchip circuitry has led to an increasing heat dissipation problem; power lines, where resistance heating wastes power and mandates high-voltage/low-current transmission and unwieldy transformers; and rail transportation, in which friction can be practically eliminated by exploiting the repulsion between magnets and superconductors to suspend the vehicle without physical contact. If workable, very-high-temperature superconductors can be found, uses will multiply enormously, bringing a revolution in technology.

10 Fullerenes

Nothing could be more fitting to discuss now than **fullerenes**, perhaps the most actively studied novel materials in science today. To enumerate their characteristics is to recount essentially every topic in this chapter—and a host of others.

The story began in 1985 with the discovery of the **buckyball**,[6] now designated C60, a hollow spherical molecule about 1 nm in diameter and composed entirely of carbon atoms arranged in an interesting pattern of pentagons and hexagons. As shown in Figure 57, each carbon atom bonds to three others. In Example 1, we noted that a common hybridization in carbon is sp^2, which produces a planar, three-lobed pattern and allows σ bonds in three directions. Graphite forms in flat sheets of regular hexagons in this pattern. Although bonding *between* sheets is weak—allowing them to slide easily along each other and making graphite slippery—the sheets themselves are very strong, due

[6]The names *buckyball* and *fullerene* developed from the observation that these structures resembled dome-shaped buildings popularized by Buckminster "Bucky" Fuller.

Figure 57 The buckyball—a single molecule of 60 carbon atoms.

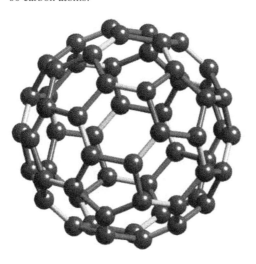

to the great strength of the sp^2 bond. Fullerenes share this trait. Curl, Kroto, and Smalley were awarded the 1996 Nobel Prize in chemistry for their discovery of fullerenes.

Buckyballs and similar ellipsoidal structures, such as C70 and C240, are studied in many fields. Although practical applications have been slow to appear, some of the proposed uses of buckyballs are as molecular ball bearings and efficient microscopic strainers. Molecular solids of buckyballs have been doped with impurities to produce conductors and even superconductors, though, as yet, their critical temperatures are much lower than in the high-T_c cuprates. (A famous claim of 117 K became infamous when it was later revealed to be a case of gross scientific misconduct.) Buckyballs with various atoms, ions, or small molecules trapped inside—so-called endohedral fullerenes—are studied for their interesting chemical and electronic properties. They have also been shown capable of slightly accelerating radioactive decay.

The carbon nanotube, **CNT**, has emerged as even more versatile than the buckyball and is seemingly able to fill just about every role we might imagine in modern technology. The prototype CNT is a graphite sheet (more properly known as graphene) rolled into a cylinder and topped with a fullerene half sphere. The tensile strength of a CNT—the pressure at which pulling its ends would fracture it—is typically 100 times higher than steel, while its density is much less. Accordingly, CNTs are expected to take on an important role as a high-strength structural element. Among the first uses have been sports equipment and protective clothing made of CNT yarn.

A delightful characteristic of CNTs is that the graphite sheets can form cylinders in different ways, which determine the conducting behavior of the material. Figure 58 shows a CNT in which the geometry changes from the so-called **armchair** configuration at the top, where adjacent hexagons line up vertically, to the **zigzag** configuration at the bottom, where they line up in

Figure 58 A carbon nanotube in which the configuration changes from arm-chair at top to zigzag at the bottom. The top is metallic and the bottom is semi-conducting.

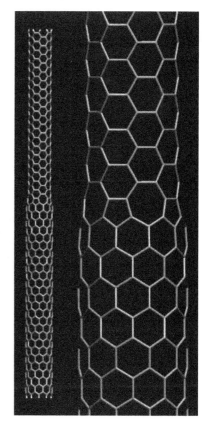

rings around the cylinder. Any configuration between these two is known as **chiral** and is characterized by a helical twist. Armchair configurations are always metallic, while zigzag and chiral ones can be metallic or semiconducting, depending on the number of hexagons around the cylinder and the degree of twist.

Conducting nanotubes are of great interest. The filamentary nature of CNTs, their small diameter, and their thermal and chemical stability make them very well suited to the role of emitters in the field emission display, FED. Several variations are being tried. Figure 59 shows an electron microscope image of a bundle of CNTs that may one day serve as an FED electron source/cathode. (The electrons exit through the hole to an anode not shown. See Figure 6.17.) The bundle's conical shape appears to offer several advantages over earlier less-manicured bundles (Moon, et al., *Journal of Vacuum Science and Technology B*, September/October 2005, 1964–1969). CNT-FEDs may soon be major contenders in the flat-screen display market. The CNT has also been applied to the basic element of modern electronics—the transistor. In 1998, IBM produced a field-effect transistor in which a CNT provided the conductive path from the source to the drain. Figure 60 depicts a typical design. (Note the resemblance to Figure 46.) With recent advances in uniform fabrication and positioning of CNTs, these microelectronic devices may soon make significant inroads on the reigning silicon chip. An unusual CNT application is as a light antenna. As we know, light and radio are the same phenomenon, and an array of CNTs has now been shown to detect light waves in much the same way that an antenna receives radio waves (Wang, et al., *Applied Physics Letters*, 27

Figure 59 CNTs in a cone-shaped bundle approximately 3 μm in diameter, serving as an electron source, or cathode. Electrons pass through the hole to an anode (not shown). FEDs comprise two-dimensional arrays of such cathodes.

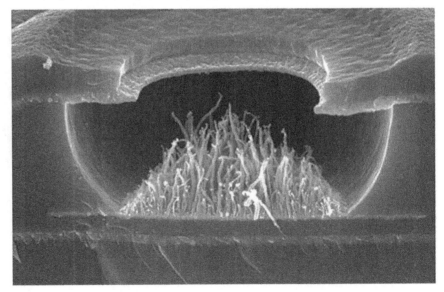

September 2004, 2607–2609). If the antenna/CNT length is not the correct multiple of the light wavelength, or if its orientation is perpendicular to the light polarization, the reception becomes inefficient. Rounding out their résumé, CNTs superconduct, though again at fairly low temperatures.

Many of the applications noted above employ so-called multiwalled CNTs, depicted in Figure 61, of which combinations are endless. Discoveries of properties and uses of CNTs are multiplying at a dizzying pace, and the reader is encouraged to search the Internet as the knowledge unfolds.

Finally, it is worth mentioning a few variations on the theme. Just as silicon can be replaced by quadravalent germanium in some semiconductor applications and by trivalent/pentavalent (III,V) mixtures in others, nanotubes have been fabricated from silicon and from boron-nitride (III,V). The latter should stand up better to high temperatures and exhibit superior resistance to oxidation than CNTs, but it is too early to say what role either of these newcomers will eventually play.

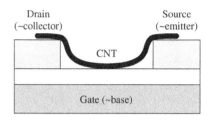

Figure 60 The design of a typical CNT FET (field effect transistor).

Figure 61 A multiwalled carbon nanotube.

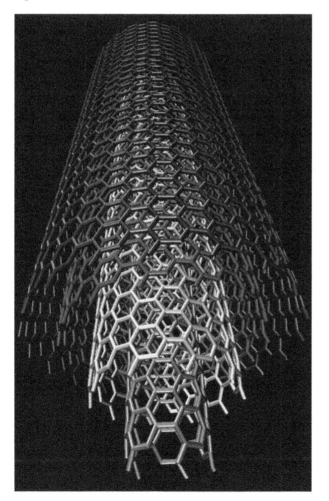

PROGRESS AND APPLICATIONS

Light Detection and Energy Gaps Photon detection is vital in many areas of science. Astronomy is perhaps the best example. While the abilities of telescopes to *collect* light (and other parts of the electromagnetic spectrum) have improved modestly over the years, means of light *detection* have taken great leaps in recent decades, and super-conductivity may be involved in the next big jump. The leader today, a tremendous advance over early photographic techniques, is the **CCD**, or charge coupled device, based on the trusty silicon semiconductor. In a single CCD pixel, each arriving photon excites an electron across the gap (efficiency can approach 100% in the visible). The conduction electrons are trapped in an electrostatic potential well created by charged external electrodes, while the oppositely charged holes are repelled from the well, preventing recombination. The number of electrons accumulating in each pixel across a 2D grid is read immediately after the exposure. Besides being a workhorse in astronomy, this is the type of light sensor in today's digital cameras. A promising alternative to the CCD for some applications is the superconducting tunnel junction (STJ) detector, depicted in Figure 62. In this device, still in development, an insulating region separates two superconductors, and a slight potential bias is applied across the entire stack. As in a semiconductor, electrons in a superconductor "see" a gap, the energy required to free them from their Cooper pairs. But it is much smaller, measured in meV rather than eV. When a visible photon, in the eV range, strikes the superconductor on the high energy side, it doesn't promote *an* electron across the gap; instead,

it breaks *thousands* of Cooper pairs. The liberated electrons are promoted "upward" across the gap, then tunnel through the insulator to the other superconductor, resulting in a measurable charge transfer. (Tunneling of electrons still in Cooper pairs is suppressed by an external magnetic field.) One of the primary advantages offered by the STJ is that because the number of electrons promoted is proportional to the photon energy, it can discriminate different wavelengths of incident light. A disadvantage of the STJ detector is the extreme low temperatures needed. To prevent thermally excited electron-hole pairs, CCDs in the most sensitive applications must be kept cold with liquid nitrogen, 77 K, but the critical temperatures of the superconducting metals used in STJs are so low that liquid helium cooling is required.

New Light-Emitting Devices The light-emitting diode has been around since the 1960s. However, progress toward shorter wavelengths was rather slow. It was not until the mid-1990s that bright blue LEDs became available. The main difficulty was fabricating a semiconductor that produced photons efficiently and had the appropriate large band gap. Success came with gallium-nitride, a III-V semiconductor. While the visible spectrum was thus covered, the LED has recently gone well into the ultra-violet. By innovative techniques, scientists at the NTT Basic Research Laboratories in Japan have fabricated aluminum nitride LEDs that emit at 210 nm (Taniyasu, et al., *Nature*, 18 May 2006, 325–328). The achievement is an important step in the quest to replace less-efficient sources, such as vapor lights, over a range of wavelengths. The researchers speculate that the new device may be useful in high-density information storage and in air and water purification and sterilization.

Another recent breakthrough with enormous potential is the light-emitting *transistor* (Feng, et al., *Applied Physics Letters*, 5 January 2004, 151–153). In a transistor, while most of the electrons that flow from the emitter into the base slide down to the collector, a fraction engage in electron-hole recombination in the base, constituting the base-emitter input current. Ordinarily, the recombination energy simply produces heat, but a research team at the University of Illinois has found a way to divert it to infrared light. In effect, the bipolar transistor's standard electrical input and output channels are joined by a third channel: light output, proportional to the other two. This photon generation can be controlled at far higher frequencies than in an LED and opens up the revolutionary possibility of replacing the electron currents that flow through an integrated circuit's tiny wires with light signals.

Figure 62 In an STJ (superconducting tunnel junction), a photon breaks a Cooper pair, and the excited electrons tunnel through an insulating barrier.

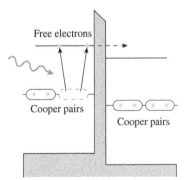

Free electrons

Cooper pairs

Cooper pairs

Superconducting MgB$_2$ Coming as quite a surprise when it was discovered in 2001 was the superconductivity of magnesium diboride, MgB$_2$ (Nagamatsu, et al., *Nature*, 1 March 2001, 63–64). With attention focused on the cuprates and their critical temperatures over 100 K, a T_c of only 39 K did not dominate headlines in the popular press, but this critical temperature was nearly twice as high as in any all-metal superconductor previously known (though boron qualifies as a "metalloid"). Furthermore, the fact that MgB$_2$ exhibited the isotope effect suggested that the superconductivity mechanism was more like that in conventional superconductors than in the mysterious cuprates. On the other hand, MgB$_2$ was found to have a unique property: *two* gap energies. Both theory and experiment soon attributed this to certain characteristics of the MgB$_2$ structure. As illustrated in Figure 63, the boron atoms form hexagonal sheets like graphite, with σ-bonds in the plane of the sheets and π-bonds perpendicular. The larger of the two gaps is the result of electrons in the σ states being more strongly coupled to the lattice. The stronger the coupling between electron and phonon, the higher the binding energy of the Cooper pair. The weaker coupling in π states makes the gap energy for these electrons only about one-fourth that of the σ electrons. A particularly interesting feature of MgB$_2$ is that

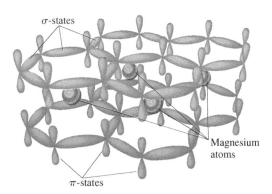

Figure 63 The structure of MgB$_2$. Graphitelike hexagonal planes of boron, with magnesium atoms between.

σ-states

Magnesium atoms

π-states

alloying and doping with various other elements has produced extremely high upper critical fields B_{c2}, even surpassing those of the cuprates. The interplay between the two superconducting modes in MgB$_2$ is still not fully understood, but its investigation is already adding considerably to our understanding of superconductivity, and who can say what might be around the corner.

Summary

Bonding between atoms involves rearrangement of the atoms' valence electrons. Molecules and solids form whenever the states that the electrons occupy result in a lower energy than for isolated atoms. These many-atom states may be thought of as combinations of single-atom states. When N atoms bond, the nth single-atom state becomes an N-state band.

In molecules, a covalent bond occurs when two electrons, one from each atom, occupy a molecular spatial state centered between the atoms. The energy is low because both atoms attract both electrons. If the atoms are not identical, the electrons are not shared equally. The extreme case, where a -1 valence atom wholly appropriates the valence electron of a $+1$ valence atom, is known as an ionic bond, and the attraction is simply between negative and positive ions. The character of most molecular bonds is between purely covalent and purely ionic.

Pure solids usually form in a regular arrangement of atoms known as a crystal lattice, of which there are many geometrical types. Regardless of the lattice type, bonding is usually categorized as one of four different kinds: covalent, ionic, metallic, and molecular. The bonding in the first two is as in individual molecules. A metallic solid's valence electrons are shared by all atoms. They move freely through the solid, giving metals high electrical conductivity. Noble gas atoms and tightly bound molecules do not share electrons, but form molecular solids via relatively weak dipole-dipole attractions.

Even in covalent and ionic solids, valence electrons must often be treated as being bound not to individual atoms but to the solid as a whole. The potential energy is essentially that of one macroscopic potential well, but with a superimposed periodic variation due to regularly spaced positive ions. Because N is so large, each N-state energy band is a virtual continuum of allowed energies. The range of forbidden energies between bands is known as a band gap.

The electrical conductivity of a solid is related to filling of its bands. The topmost band that is full at $T = 0$ is known as the valence band. If electrons fill part of the next-higher band, known as the conduction band, the material will be an electrical conductor. The highest-energy electrons may enter immediately higher states and thus respond to an external electric field. If electrons fill states only to the top of the valence band, the material will be an insulator. Having no easily accessible states, the electrons have no freedom to respond.

An insulator with a small valence-conduction band gap is called a semiconductor. Common examples are silicon and germanium. With a small band gap, thermal excitation can promote a significant number of electrons from the valence band to the otherwise empty conduction band. These respond to an external field just as do electrons in a conductor. The resulting valence band vacancies also contribute to electrical conductivity. They are known as holes and respond to an external field as positive charge carriers.

The numbers of conduction band electrons and valence band holes can be varied freely by doping, or introducing into the lattice a small fraction of impurity atoms. Trivalent impurity atoms yield a p-type semiconductor, in which valence holes far outnumber conduction electrons, while an n-type semiconductor, where conduction electrons predominate, results from pentavalent impurity atoms. Important devices are made by assembling various combinations of n-type and p-type semiconductors. Joining one of each type in a p-n junction yields a diode, which allows electrical current to pass only one way. Three together form a transistor, a basic element of amplification.

Many metals and a growing number of novel materials lose all resistance below a material-dependent critical temperature, becoming superconductors. Current is carried by electrons bound in Cooper pairs, the result of an attraction mediated by the crystal lattice, and all pairs move as one. The effect is broken by high temperature and/or a strong magnetic field.

* indicates advanced questions

Conceptual Questions

1. The left diagram in Figure 1 might represent a two-atom crystal with two bands. Basing your argument on the kinetic energy inside either individual well, explain why both energies in the lower band should be roughly equal to that of the $n = 1$ atomic state and why both energies in the upper should roughly equal that of the $n = 2$ atomic state.

2. Upon what definitions do we base the claim that the ψ_{2p_x} and ψ_{2p_y} states of equations (1) are related to x and y just as ψ_{2p_z} is to z?

3. Section 2 discusses σ-bonds and π-bonds for p-states and σ-bonds for s-states, but not π-bonds for s-states. Why not?

4. Of N_2, O_2, and F_2, none has an electric dipole moment, but one does have a magnetic dipole moment. Which one, and why? (Refer to Figure 10.)

5. It takes less energy to dissociate a diatomic fluorine molecule than a diatomic oxygen molecule (in fact, less than one-third as much). Why is it easier to dissociate fluorine?

6. Why is covalent bonding directional, while ionic bonding is not?

7. For the four kinds of crystal binding—covalent, ionic, metallic, and molecular—how would the density of valence electrons vary throughout the solid? Would it be constant, centered on the atoms, or largest between the atoms? Or would it alternate, with a net charge density positive at one atom and negative at the next?

8. Why should magnesium form a metallic solid?

9. The energy necessary to break the ionic bond between a sodium ion and a fluorine ion is 4.99 eV. The energy necessary to separate the sodium and fluorine ions that form the ionic NaF crystal is 9.30 eV per ion pair. Explain the difference qualitatively.

10. Brass is a metal consisting principally of copper alloyed with a smaller amount of zinc, whose atoms do not alternate in a regular pattern in the crystal lattice but are somewhat randomly scattered about. The resistivity of brass is higher than that of either copper or zinc at room temperature, and it drops much slower as the temperature is lowered. What do these behaviors tell us about electrical conductivity in general?

11. Explain the dependence of conductivity on temperature for conductors and for semiconductors.

12. In the boron *atom*, the single 2p electron does not completely fill any 2p spatial state, yet *solid* boron is not a conductor. What might explain this? (It may be helpful to consider again why beryllium is not an insulator.)

13. The bonding of silicon in molecules and solids is qualitatively the same as that of carbon. Silicon atomic states become *molecular* states analogous to those in Figure 14, and in a solid, these effectively form the valence and conduction *bands*. Which of silicon's atomic states are the relevant ones, and which molecular state corresponds to which band?

14. What factors decrease the conductivity of a conductor as temperature increases? Are these factors also present in a semiconductor, and if so, how can its conductivity vary with temperature in the *opposite* sense?

15. Based only on the desire to limit minority carriers, why would silicon be preferable to germanium as a fabric for doped semiconductors?

16. Why does the small current flowing through a *reverse*-biased diode depend much more strongly on temperature than on the applied (reverse) voltage?

17. In a concise yet fairly comprehensive way, explain why doped semiconductors are so pervasive in modern technology.

18. It is often said that the transistor is the basic element of amplification, yet it supplies no energy of its own. Exactly what is its role in amplification?

19. The "floating magnet trick" is shown in Figure 50. If the disk on the bottom were a permanent magnet, rather than a superconductor, the trick wouldn't work. The superconductor does produce an external field very similar to that of a permanent magnet. What other characteristic is necessary to explain the effect? (*Hint:* What happens when you hold two ordinary magnets so that they repel, and then you release one of them?)

20. The isotope effect says that the critical temperature for superconductivity decreases as the mass of the positive ions increases. Can you argue why it should *decrease*?

21. What is a Cooper pair, and what role does it play in superconductivity?

22. Describe the similarities and differences between Type-I and Type-II superconductors.

23. In a buckyball, three of the bonds around each hexagon are so-called double bonds. They result from adjacent atoms sharing a state that does *not* participate in the sp^2 bonding. Which state is it, and is this extra bond a σ-bond or a π-bond? Explain.

24. What are some of the properties of fullerenes that make them potentially so useful?

Exercises

Section 1

25. Formulate an argument explaining why the even wave functions in Figure 1 should be lower in energy than their odd partners.

26. The accompanying diagrams represent the three lowest energy wave functions for three "atoms." As in all truly molecular states we consider, these states are shared among the atoms. At such large atomic separation, however, the energies are practically equal, so an

electron would be just as happy occupying any combination. (a) Identify algebraic combinations of the states (for instance, I + II/2 + III/2) that would place the electron in each of the three atoms. (b) Were the atoms closer together, the energies of states I, II, and III would spread out and an electron would occupy the lowest energy one. Rank them in order of increasing energy as the atoms draw closer together. Explain your reasoning.

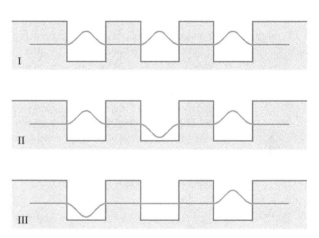

Section 2

27. Section 2 gives the energy and approximate proton separation of the H_2^+ molecule. What is the energy of the electron alone?

28. From the diagrams in Figure 7.15 and the qualitative behavior of the wave functions they represent, argue that a combination of the $2p_z$ (i.e., $m_\ell = 0$) and the negative of the $2s$ would produce a function that sticks out preferentially in the *positive z* direction. This is known as a **hybrid** *sp* state.

29. Electron affinity is a property specifying the "appetite" of an element for gaining electrons. Elements, such as fluorine and oxygen, that lack only one or two electrons to complete shells can achieve a lower energy state by absorbing an external electron. For instance, in uniting an electron with a neutral chlorine atom, completing its $n = 3$ shell and forming a Cl^- ion, 3.61 eV of energy is liberated. Suppose an electron is detached from a sodium atom, whose ionization energy is 5.14 eV, then transferred to a (faraway) chlorine atom. (a) Must energy on balance be put in by an external agent, or is some energy actually liberated? If so, how much? (b) The transfer leaves the sodium with a positive charge and the chlorine with a negative. Energy can now be extracted by allowing these ions to draw close, forming a molecule. How close must they approach to recover the energy expended in part (a)? (c) The actual separation of the atoms in a NaCl molecule is 0.24 nm. How much lower in energy is the molecule than the separated neutral atoms?

30. Exercise 29 outlines how energy may be extracted by transferring an electron from an atom that easily loses an electron to one with a large appetite for electrons, then allowing the two to approach, forming an ionic bond.

(a) Consider separately the cases of hydrogen bonding with fluorine and sodium bonding with fluorine. In each case, how close must the ions approach to reach "break even," where the energy needed to transfer the electron between the separated atoms is balanced by the electrostatic potential energy of attraction? The ionization energy of hydrogen is 13.6 eV, that of sodium is 5.1 eV, and the electron affinity of fluorine is 3.40 eV.

(b) Of HF and NaF, one is considered to be an ionic bond and the other a covalent bond. Which is which, and why?

31. The vertices of a tetrahedron are four vertices of a cube symmetrically chosen so that no two are adjacent. Show that the angle between the vertices of a tetrahedron is 109.5°.

32. By the "vector" technique of Example 1, show that the angles between all lobes of the hybrid sp^3 states are 109.5°.

* **33.** In Section 2, we discussed two-lobed p_x, p_y, and p_z states and four-lobed hybrid sp^3 states. Another kind of hybrid state that sticks out in just one direction is the sp, formed from a single p state and an s state. Consider an arbitrary combination of the $2s$ state with the $2p_z$ state. Let us represent this by $\cos\tau\,\psi_{2,0,0} + \sin\tau\,\psi_{2,1,0}$. (The trig factors ensure normalization. In carrying out the integral, cross terms integrate to 0, leaving

$$\cos^2\tau \int |\psi_{2,0,0}|^2 dV + \sin^2\tau \int |\psi_{2,1,0}|^2 dV, \text{ which is 1.)}$$

(a) Calculate the probability that an electron in such a state would be in the $+z$-hemisphere. (*Note:* Here, the cross terms do *not* integrate to 0.)

(b) What value of τ leads to the maximum probability, what is the value of the maximum probability, and what is the corresponding ratio of $\psi_{2,0,0}$ to $\psi_{2,1,0}$?

(c) Using a computer, make a density (shading) plot of the probability density—density versus r and θ—for the τ-value found in part (b).

* **34.** Referring to equations (2), lobe I of the hybrid sp^3 states combines the spherically symmetric s state with

the p state that is oriented along the z-axis, and thus sticks out in the $+z$ direction (see Exercises 28 and 33). If Figure 12 is a true picture, then in a coordinate system rotated counterclockwise about the y-axis by the tetrahedral angle, lobe II should become lobe I. In the new frame, y-values are unaffected, but what had been values in the zx-plane become values in the $z'x'$-plane, according to $x = x'\cos\alpha + z'\sin\alpha$ and $z = z'\cos\alpha - x'\sin\alpha$, where α is 109.5°, or $\cos^{-1}\left(-\frac{1}{3}\right)$.

(a) Show that lobe II becomes lobe I. Note that since neither the $2s$ state nor the *radial* part of the p states is affected by a rotation, only the angular parts given in equations (1) need be considered.

(b) Show that if lobe II is instead rotated about the z-axis by simply shifting ϕ by $\pm 120°$, it becomes lobes III and IV.

Section 3

35. By expanding an arbitrary $U(x)$ in a power series about a local minimum assumed to be at $x = a$, prove that the effective spring constant is given by equation (3).

36. The interatomic potential energy in a diatomic molecule (Figure 16) has many features: a minimum energy, an equilibrium separation, a curvature, and so on. (a) Upon what features do the rotational energy levels depend? (b) Upon what features do the vibrational levels depend?

37. The bond length of the N_2 molecule is 0.11 nm, and its effective spring constant is 2.3×10^3 N/m. At room temperature, (a) what would be the ratio of molecules with rotational quantum number $\ell = 1$ to those with $\ell = 0$ (at the same vibrational level), and (b) what would be the ratio of molecules with vibrational quantum number $n = 1$ to those with $n = 0$ (with the same rotational energy)?

38. The bond length of the N_2 molecule is 0.11 nm, and its effective spring constant is 2.3×10^3 N/m. (a) From the size of the energy jumps for rotation and vibration, determine whether either of these modes of energy storage should be active at 300 K. (b) According to the equipartition theorem, the heat capacity of a diatomic molecule storing energy in rotations but not vibrations should be $\frac{5}{2}R$ (3 translational + 2 rotational degrees of freedom). If it is also storing energy in vibrations, it should be $\frac{7}{2}R$ (adding 2 vibrational degrees). Nitrogen's molar heat capacity is 20.8 J/mol · K at 300 K. Does this agree with your findings in part (a)?

39. The effective force constant of the molecular "spring" in HCl is 480 N/m, and the bond length is 0.13 nm.

(a) Determine the energies of the two lowest-energy vibrational states.

(b) For these energies, determine the amplitude of vibration if the atoms could be treated as oscillating *classical* particles.

(c) For these energies, by what percentage does the atomic separation fluctuate?

(d) Calculate the classical vibrational frequency $\omega_{vib} = \sqrt{\kappa/\mu}$ and the rotational frequency $\omega_{rot} = L/I$. For the rotational frequency, assume that L is its lowest nonzero value, $\sqrt{1(1 + 1)}\,\hbar$, and that the moment of inertia I is μa^2.

(e) Is it valid to treat the atomic separation as fixed for rotational motion while changing for vibrational?

40. Starting with equation (4), show that if Δn is -1 as a photon is emitted by a diatomic molecule in a transition among rotation-vibration states, but $\Delta \ell$ can be ± 1, then the allowed photon energies obey equation (6).

41. Vibration-rotation spectra are rich! For the CO molecule (data are given in Exercise 42), roughly how many rotational levels would there be between the ground vibrational state and the first excited vibrational state?

42. The carbon monoxide molecule CO has an effective spring constant of 1860 N/m and a bond length of 0.113 nm. Determine four wavelengths of light that CO might absorb in vibration-rotation transitions.

43. From the qualitative shapes of the interatomic potential energies in Figure 21, would you expect the vibrational levels in the excited electronic state to be spaced the same, farther apart, or closer together than those in the lower-energy electronic state? Explain. What about the rotational levels?

44. As noted in Example 2, the HD molecule differs from H_2 in that a deuterium atom replaces a hydrogen atom. (a) What effect, if any, does the replacement have on the bond length and force constant? Explain. (b) What effect does it have on the rotational energy levels? (c) And what effect does it have on the vibrational energy levels?

Section 4

45. Two-dimensional lattices with three- or four-sided symmetries are possible, but there is none with a five-sided symmetry. To see why, consider the following: A piece of paper can be cut into identical equilateral triangles or squares with no excess. Prove that this is not the case for equilateral pentagons.

* 46. Exercise 29 notes that more energy is required to ionize sodium than is retrieved by adding that electron to an isolated chlorine atom, but the NaCl bond represents a lower energy because the attracting ions draw close

together. Quantifying the energy-lowering effect of having alternating plus and minus charges can be rather involved for a 3D lattice, but a one-dimensional calculation is instructive. Consider an infinite line of point charges alternating between $+e$ and $-e$, with a uniform spacing between adjacent (opposite) charges of a. (a) The electrostatic potential energy per ion is the same for a given positive ion as for a given negative ion. Why? (b) Calculate the electrostatic potential energy per ion. For simplicity, assume that a positive charge is at the origin. The following power series expansion will be helpful: $\ln(1 + x) = -\sum_{n=1}^{\infty}(-x)^n/n$.

Section 5

47. Make rough sketches of the wave functions at the top of the $n = 2$ band and the bottom of the $n = 3$ band for a one-dimensional "crystal" consisting of seven finite wells. Explain why these two states of roughly equal wave number have vastly different energies.

48. As we see in Figures 23, in a one-dimensional crystal of finite wells, top-of-the-band states closely resemble infinite well states. In fact, the famous particle-in-a-box energy formula gives a fair value for the energies of these states and thus the energies of the bands to which they belong. (a) If for n in that formula you use the number of antinodes in the whole wave function, what would you use for the box length L? (b) If, instead, the n in the formula were taken to refer to *band n*, could you still use the formula? If so, what would you use for L? (c) Explain why the energies in a band do or do not depend on the size of the crystal as a whole.

49. In Figure 24, the $n = 1$ band ends at $k = 4\pi/L$, while in Figure 27 it ends at π/a. Are these compatible? If so, how?

50. Assuming an interatomic spacing of 0.15 nm, obtain a rough value for the width (in eV) of the $n = 2$ band in a one-dimensional crystal.

51. The density of copper is 8.9×10^3 kg/m³, its Fermi energy is 7.0 eV, and it has one conduction electron per atom. At liquid nitrogen temperature (77 K), its resistivity is about $4 \times 10^{-9}\ \Omega \cdot$ m. Estimate how far a conduction electron would travel before colliding and how many copper ions it would pass.

Section 6

52. Carbon (diamond) and silicon have the same covalent crystal structure, yet diamond is transparent while silicon is opaque to visible light. Argue that this should be the case based only on the difference in band gaps— roughly 5 eV for diamond and 1 eV for silicon.

53. In diamond, carbon's four full (bonding) s and p spatial states become a band, and the four empty (antibonding) ones become a higher-energy band. Considering the trend in the band gaps of diamond, silicon, and germanium, explain why it might not be surprising that "covalent" tin behaves as a conducting metallic solid.

54. Section 6 notes that as causes of resistance, ionic vibrations give way to lattice imperfections at around 10 K. A typical spring constant between atoms in a solid is of order of magnitude 10^3 N/m, and typical spacing is nominally 10^{-10} m. Estimate how much the vibrating atoms' locations might deviate, as a fraction of their nominal separation, at 10 K.

55. Carry out the integration indicated in equation (10).

56. The resistivity of silver is $1.6 \times 10^{-8}\ \Omega \cdot$ m at room temperature (300 K), while that of silicon is about $10\ \Omega \cdot$ m. (a) Show that this disparity follows, at least to a rough order of magnitude, from the approximate 1 eV band gap in silicon. (b) What would you expect for the room-temperature resistivity of diamond, which has a band gap of about 5 eV?

57. Show that for a room-temperature semiconductor with a band gap of 1 eV, a temperature rise of 4 K would raise the conductivity by about 30%.

58. The Fermi velocity v_F is defined by $E_F = \frac{1}{2} m v_F^2$, where E_F is the Fermi energy. The Fermi energy for silver is 5.5 eV. (a) Calculate the Fermi velocity. (b) What would be the wavelength of an electron with this velocity? (c) How does this compare with the lattice spacing of 0.41 nm? Does the order of magnitude make sense?

59. For a small temperature change dT, a material's resistivity (reciprocal of conductivity) will change linearly according to

$$\rho(dT) = \rho_0 + d\rho = \rho_0(1 + \alpha dT)$$

The fractional change in resistivity, α, also known as the temperature coefficient, is thus

$$\alpha = \frac{1}{\rho_0} \frac{d\rho}{dT}$$

Estimate α for silicon at room temperature. Assume a band gap of 1.1 eV.

Section 7

60. A **semimetal** (e.g., antimony, bismuth) is a material in which electrons would fill states to the top of a band—the valence band—except for the fact that the top of this band overlaps very slightly with the bottom of the next-higher band. Explain why such a material, unlike the

"real" metal copper, will have true positive charge carriers and equal numbers of negative ones, even at zero temperature.

61. Verify using equation (12) that the effective mass of a free particle is m.

62. (a) Compare equation (11) evaluated at room temperature for a silicon band gap of 1.1 eV and for a typical donor-state/conduction band gap of 0.05 eV. (b) Assuming only one impurity atom for every 10^5 silicon atoms, do your results suggest that majority carriers, bumped up from donor levels, should outnumber minority carriers created by thermal excitation across the whole 1.1 eV gap? (The calculation ignores the difference in density of states between donor levels and bands, which actually strengthens the argument.)

63. As a crude approximation, an impurity pentavalent atom in a (tetravalent) silicon lattice can be treated as a one-electron atom, in which the extra electron orbits a net positive charge of 1. Because this "atom" is not in free space, however, the permitivity of free space, ε_0, must be replaced by $\kappa \varepsilon_0$, where κ is the dielectric constant of the surrounding material. The hydrogen atom ground-state energies would thus become

$$E = -\frac{me^4}{2(4\pi\kappa\varepsilon_0)^2\ \hbar^2} \frac{1}{n^2} = \frac{-13.6\ \text{eV}}{\kappa^2 n^2}$$

Given $\kappa = 12$ for silicon, how much energy is needed to free a donor electron in its ground state? (Actually, the effective mass of the donor electron is less than m_e, so this prediction is somewhat high.)

Section 8

64. The photons emitted by an LED arise from the energy given up in electron-hole recombinations across the energy gap. How large should the energy gap be to give photons at the red end of the visible spectrum (700 nm)?

65. When electrons cross from the n-type to the p-type to equalize the Fermi energy on both sides in an unbiased diode, they leave the n-type side with an excess of positive charge and give the p-type side an excess of negative. Charge layers oppose one another on either side of the depletion zone, producing, in essence, a capacitor, which harbors the so-called **built-in electric field**. The crossing of the electrons to equalize the Fermi energy produces the dogleg in the bands of roughly E_{gap}, and the corresponding potential difference is E_{gap}/e. The depletion zone in a typical diode is 1 μm wide, and the band gap is 1.0 eV. How large is the built-in electric field?

66. In a diode laser, electrons dropping from the conduction band, across the gap, and into the valence band produce the photons that add to the coherent light. The ZnTe laser has a band gap of 2.25 eV. About what wavelength laser light would you expect it to produce?

67. An LED is connected in series with a resistor and a power supply of variable voltage. The supply voltage starts from -5 V and increases linearly with time to a maximum of $+5$ V. The figure shows the supply voltage, the voltage across the diode, and the current in the circuit as functions of time. The LED does not glow for the whole time shown. (a) Explain the plots, and identify the period when the LED glows. (b) Approximately what color is the light produced by the LED?

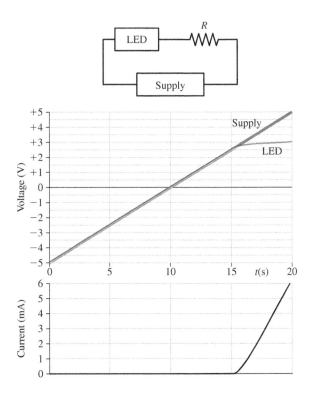

68. The diagram shows the energy bands of a **tunnel diode** as the potential difference is increased. In this device, high-impurity atom density causes the occupied donor and unoccupied acceptor levels to spread into **impurity bands**, which overlap, respectively, the n-type conduction and the p-type valence bands. In all unbiased diodes, the depletion zone between the n-type and p-type bands constitutes a potential barrier, but in the tunnel diode, it is so thin that significant tunneling occurs. The current versus voltage plot shows that unlike a normal diode, significant current begins to flow as soon as there is an applied voltage—before the bias voltage is E_{gap}/e. It then *decreases* (so-called negative resistance), before again increasing in the normal way. Explain this behavior.

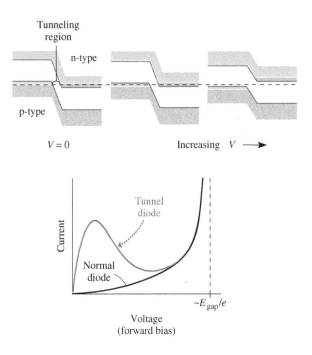

69. Volumes have been written on transistor biasing, but Figure 45 gets at the main idea. Suppose that $V_{be} = 1.5$ V and that the "input" produces its own voltage, 0.1 V $\sin(\omega t)$. The total resistance is 10 kΩ in the input loop, which goes clockwise from the emitter through the various components to the base, then back to the emitter through the base-emitter diode. This diode is forward biased, with the base at all times 0.7 V higher than the emitter. Suppose also that $V_{ce} = 12$ V and that the "output" is 350 Ω. Now, given that for every 201 electrons entering the emitter, 1 passes out the base and 200 out the collector, calculate the maximum and minimum in the sinusoidally varying (a) current in the base-emitter (input) circuit, (b) power delivered by the "input," (c) power delivered to the "output," and (d) power delivered by V_{ce}. (e) What does most of the work?

70. Sketch an energy-versus-position diagram, complementary to Figure 44, showing valence hole motion and conduction electron participation in an operating pnp transistor.

71. In many kinds of integrated circuits, the preferred element of amplification/switching is not the bipolar transistor discussed in the chapter, but the MOSFET (metal oxide semiconductor field effect transistor). The accompanying diagram shows one in its "normally off" state: Conduction electrons cannot flow from the n-type **source**, which is analogous to the emitter, "over the bump" in the p-type region to the n-type **drain**, analogous to the collector. (An npn arrangement is shown, but just as for the bipolar transistor, a pnp would yield the complementary device.) The important difference is that rather than a direct electrical contact to the p-type region, as in the base of the bipolar, the center lead, the **gate**, is a conductor bonded to the p-type region but separated by a thin insulating layer.

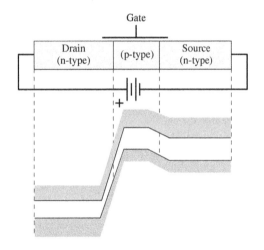

(a) Explain how applying a bias to the gate can cause this device to turn on. Should the gate bias voltage be positive or negative (relative to the source)? Why is the control mechanism referred to as "field effect"?

(b) The MOSFET is often said to be a "unipolar" device because valence holes (conduction electrons in the pnp device) do not play the important role that they do in the bipolar. Explain. Would you expect a significant current through the gate due to electron-hole recombination in the p-type region? Why or why not?

(c) A low-input-impedance device is one in which there are large oscillations in input current for small oscillations in input voltage. Correspondingly, a high-input-impedance device has a small input current

for a large input voltage. Bearing in mind that the voltage across the forward-biased base-emitter diode of a bipolar transistor is always about E_{gap}/e, while the input current is proportional to the output current, would you say that the bipolar transistor has low or high input impedance? What about the MOSFET?

72. The diagram shows a bridge rectifier circuit. A sinusoidal input voltage is fed into four identical diodes, each represented by the standard diode circuit symbol. The symbol indicates the direction of conventional current flow through the diode. The plots show input and output voltages versus time. Note that the output voltage is strictly in one direction. Explain (a) how this circuit produces the unidirectional output voltage it does, and (b) what features in the output plot indicate that the band gap of the diodes is about half an electronvolt. (It might seem that about one volt is correct, but consider how many diodes are on and in series at any given instant. In fact, although not the usual habit, it might be more accurate to plot the output voltage shifted upward relative to the input.)

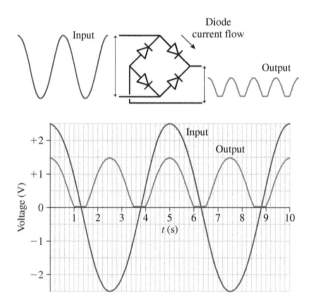

Section 9

73. The diagram shows an idealization of the "floating magnet trick" of Figure 50. Before it is cooled, the superconducting disk on the bottom supports the small permanent magnet simply by contact. After cooling, the magnet floats. Make a sketch, showing what new magnetic fields arise. Where are the currents that produce them?

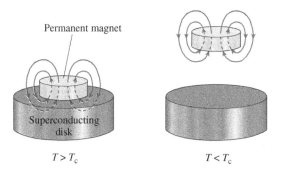

$T > T_c$ $T < T_c$

74. The critical temperature of lead is 7.2 K. What is the binding energy of its Cooper pairs at zero temperature?

75. The magnetic field at the surface of a long wire of radius R and carrying a current I is $\mu_0 I / 2\pi R$. How large a current could a 0.1 mm diameter niobium wire carry without exceeding its 0.2 T critical field?

76. We learned that the uncertainty principle is a powerful tool. Here we use it to estimate the size of a Cooper pair from its binding energy. Due to their phonon-borne attraction, each electron in a pair (if not the pair's center of mass) has changing momentum and kinetic energy. Simple differentiation will relate uncertainty in kinetic energy to uncertainty in momentum, and a rough numerical measure of the uncertainty in the kinetic energy is the Cooper-pair binding energy. Obtain a rough estimate of the physical extent of the electron's (unknown!) wave function. In addition to the binding energy, you will need to know the Fermi energy. (As noted in Section 9, each electron in the pair has an energy of about E_F.) Use 10^{-3} eV and 9.4 eV, respectively, values appropriate for indium.

Comprehensive Exercises

77. If electrical conductivity were determined by the mere static presence of positive ions, rather than by their motion, the collision time would be inversely proportional to the electron's average speed. If, however, it were dominated by the motion of the ions, it should be inversely proportional to the "area" presented by a jiggling ion, which is, in turn, proportional to the square of its amplitude as an oscillator. Argue that only the latter view gives the correct temperature dependence in conductors of $\sigma \propto T^{-1}$. Use the equipartition theorem (usually covered in introductory thermodynamics.

78. A string wrapped around a hub of radius R pulls with force F_T on an object that rolls without slipping along horizontal rails on "wheels" of radius $r < R$. Assume a mass m and rotational inertia I. (a) Prove that the ratio of F_T to the object's acceleration is negative. (*Note:* This object can't roll without slipping unless there is friction.) You can do this by actually calculating the acceleration from the translational and rotational second laws of motion, but it is possible to answer this part without such a "real" calculation. (b) Verify that F_T times the speed at which the string moves in the direction of F_T (i.e., the power delivered by F_T) equals the rate at which the translational and rotational kinetic energies increase. That is, F_T does all the work in this system, while the "internal" force does none. (c) Briefly discuss how parts (a) and (b) correspond to behaviors when an external electric field is applied to a semiconductor.

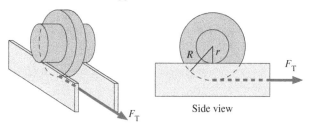

Side view

79. The accompanying diagram shows resistivity (reciprocal of conductivity) data for four solid materials from 77 K to 273 K, scaled so that the maximum value plotted for each material is 1. Two are metals, one of which undergoes a transition between ordered and disordered spins in this temperature range. Speculate as to which plots correspond to these two metals and what the other two materials might be. Explain your reasoning.

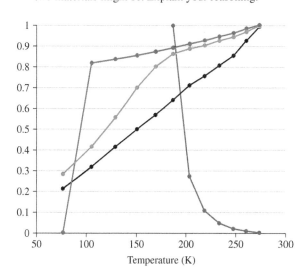

Computational Exercises

Before working Exercises 80 and 81, discuss the Schrödinger equation adapted to numerical solution, with m and $\hbar$ both defined as 1. Choosing only $\psi(0)$ and $\psi(\Delta x)$, the following relationship gives $\psi(2\Delta x)$, then, by reapplication, ψ at every multiple of Δx.

$$\psi(2\Delta x) = 2\psi(\Delta x) - \psi(0) + 2\Delta x^2(U(\Delta x) - E)\psi(\Delta x)$$

Here we consider only $U(x)$ that are symmetric about $x = 0$, so that $\psi(x)$ must be either an odd or even function of x. Our potential energy will model a one-dimensional crystal as an array of finite wells. A flexible (though not terribly elegant) way to define this $U(x)$ starts by defining a "single well function" that is 1 everywhere except in a unit-width region centered on X, where it is B, standing for bottom.

$$sw(x, X, B) = (B + 1)/2 + \text{sign}[1/4 - (X - x)^2]*(B - 1)/2$$

If x differs from X by less than 1/2, this function is B, and if by more than 1/2, it is 1. Now we can define a $U(x)$ that is U_0 everywhere but in wells centered on $x = 0$, X_1, X_2, and X_3, where it is 0.

$$U(x) = U_0 \, sw(x, 0, 0) \, sw(x, X_1, 0) \, sw(x, X_2, 0) \, sw(x, X_3, 0)$$

The *assumption* of symmetric $U(x)$ allows us to plot ψ for positive x only (we know it is odd or even), but it also means that, in effect, our crystal has three more wells at negative x, so it has seven atoms. (*Note:* Many further studies are possible within the framework provided. Exercise 80, for example, can investigate various atomic spacings, showing the effect on band width. The number of atoms can also easily be varied.)

80. **Formation of Bands:** Define $U(x)$ with X_1, X_2, and X_3 equal to 1, 2, and 3, respectively. This gives unit-width wells separated by walls of zero width—that is, one large well 7 units wide. For U_0, use 20, and for Δx, use 0.001. (a) Following the guidelines on choosing $\psi(0)$ and $\psi(\Delta x)$, test both odd and even functions at different trial values of E by finding ψ at all multiples of Δx and plotting the results from $x = 0$ to $x = 5$. Find 14 allowed energies. Note that the indicator of having passed an allowed energy is the flip of the diverging large-x tail. The lowest energy or two will take the most work. Except for these, there is no need to exceed three significant figures. (b) With m and $\hbar$ both defined as 1, particle-in-a-box energies are simply $n^2\pi^2/2L^2$. How do your energies compare, and why do some agree better

than others? (c) Change X_1, X_2, and X_3 to 1.2, 2.4, and 3.6, respectively, which gives seven equally spaced wells separated by walls of width 0.2. Again find 14 energies. Afterward, make a scatter plot of E_n versus n, where n goes from 1 to 14. Also make one of your part (a) results, then describe the main difference. (d) Consider the wave functions at the top of the first band and the bottom of the second. Kinetic energy depends on momentum, and thus on the function's wavelength (misshapen though it may be). Potential energy depends on the amplitude of the wave function in the walls, because these are the only places where our $U(x)$ is nonzero. (If a wave function were always zero whenever $U(x)$ is nonzero, the expectation value of U would be zero.) Compare the approximate kinetic energies of these two states, then discuss quantitatively their potential energies. Argue that there should be a relatively large energy jump from one state to the other.

81. **Donor and Acceptor Levels:** Define $U(x)$ with X_1, X_2, and X_3 set to 1.2, 2.4, and 3.6, respectively, which gives seven equally spaced wells separated by walls of width 0.2. For U_0, use 20, and for Δx, use 0.001. (a) (*Note:* This part can be skipped if also working Exercise 80.) Following the guidelines on choosing $\psi(0)$ and $\psi(\Delta x)$, test both odd and even functions at different trial values of E by finding ψ at all multiples of Δx and plotting the results from $x = 0$ to $x = 5$. Find 14 allowed energies. Note that the indicator of having passed an allowed energy is the flip of the diverging large-x tail. The lowest energy or two will take the most work. Except for these, there is no need to exceed three significant figures. Afterward, make a scatter plot of E_n versus n, where n goes from 1 to 14. (b) Now replace two atoms with impurity atoms as follows: For either the well at 1.2 or the well at 2.4, change B from 0 to 0.1. (*Note:* Changing one well automatically changes the corresponding well at negative x. We avoid changing the outermost wells simply because it doesn't work as nicely.) This puts the bottom of the altered well at $0.1U_0$, or 2 units. Again find 14 energies, and make another scatter plot. (c) Repeat part (b), but choosing -0.1 for B in the "impurity" atom, putting its bottom at -2 units. (d) Discuss how the impurities added in parts (b) and (c) correspond to atoms whose valence differs from that of the intrinsic atoms. (e) If each intrinsic atom comes with two electrons, and the impurities come with one and three, respectively, which states would be filled in parts (b) and (c)? Remember that there are two spin states. (f) Discuss the overall result of adding the impurities.

Answers to Selected Exercises

27. -29.4 eV

29. 1.53 eV must be put in, 0.94 nm, 4.46 eV lower

33. $\frac{1}{2} - \frac{3}{8}\sin(2\tau)$, $-1, \frac{7}{8}$

37. 2.94, 1.2×10^{-5}

39. (a) 0.179 eV, 0.537 eV; (b) 0.011 nm, 0.019 nm; (c) 8.5%, 14.6%; (d) 5.4×10^{14} s^{-1}, 5.4×10^{12} s^{-1}

41. 33

43. vibrational levels would be spaced more closely, rotational levels more closely spaced

51. 0.17 μm, ~700

59. -0.07 K^{-1}

63. ~$\frac{1}{10}$ eV

65. 10^{-6}V

69. (a) 90 μA, 70 μA; (b) 9 μW, -7 μW; (c) 113 mW, 69 mW; (d) 220 mW, 168 mW

71. positive bias, bipolar: low-input impedance, MOSFET: high-input impedance

75. 100 A

Credits

47: Intel Corporation; **50:** Courtesy Author; **58:** Alain Rochefort, Assistant Professor, Engineering Physics Department, Nanostructure Group, Center for Research on Computation and Its Applications (CERCA); **59:** *J. Vac. Sci. Technol.* B 23(5) Sep/Oct 2005, p. 1964; **62:** Alain Rochefort, Assistant Professor, Engineering Physics Department, Nanostructure Group, Center for Research on Computation and Its Applications (CERCA)

Fundamental Particles and Interactions

Chapter Outline

The search to find the fundamental building blocks of nature has been going on for a long time. Ancient philosophers postulated that the world comprised simply air, water, earth, and fire. Scientific study later revealed a more diverse fabric. It came to be accepted that the world was composed of atoms, of which there seemed to be dozens of distinct types: the "elements." A brief return to a simpler view followed the discovery that all the elements appeared to be built of the same three "fundamental" particles: protons, neutrons, and electrons. However, as technology advanced and physicists probed deeper, a host of new subatomic particles appeared, named after Greek letters—the pion, the sigma, the rho—and allowing room for expansion. Even more recently, research has again reduced the number of particles suspected of being fundamental. Protons, neutrons, and many of the new particles have internal structure and appear to be merely different combinations of a limited number of more-basic constituents, now called quarks. In this chapter, we discuss the prevailing theory of the building blocks of nature and the inseparable question of how they interact.

1 How Forces Act

In the most basic view, the physical universe consists of elementary particles that interact in only a few distinct ways. But this simple outlook is the result of an evolution of understanding much like the path taken by each student of physics.

In introductory classical mechanics, we tend to concentrate on forces that require physical contact, such as tension, normal forces, and friction. A curious exception is gravity, which appears to act through a vacuum. Later, in a deeper study of gravitation and electromagnetism, we learn that force without physical contact is more the rule than the exception. Tension, for instance, is

From Chapter 12 of *Modern Physics*, Second Edition. Randy Harris. Copyright © 2008 by Pearson Education, Inc.
Published by Pearson Addison-Wesley. All rights reserved.

Figure 1 A force between students conveyed by exchange of a snowball.

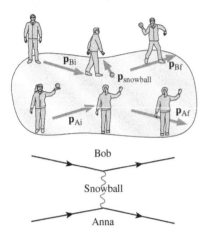

actually a coarse manifestation of microscopic electromagnetic forces. However, we are taught that particles do not exert forces on one another at a distance. Force is really conveyed by a pervasive field, gravitational or electromagnetic as the case may be. We now take the idea one step further.

The modern view is that a fundamental force between particles is conveyed by the exchange of a **mediating particle** whose role is special to that force. The mediating particle is also known as a **field quantum**—a particle of field—which gives the theory its name, **quantum field theory**. Thus, there are two classes of particles: those that experience the force, and those that are exchanged to convey it. (As we will see later, this is a bit too restrictive, as the particle exchanged is in some cases capable of experiencing the force it conveys.) Consider the following analogy: Physics students Anna and Bob slide along a frictionless frozen pond. Each is unable to change velocity without engaging in a mutual force with some other object. As shown in Figure 1, Anna has a snowball that she can throw to Bob. The exchange of the snowball has the effect of a mutual repulsive force between them. Anna's momentum is changed by $-\mathbf{p}_{\text{snowball}}$ as she throws the snowball, and Bob's is changed by $+\mathbf{p}_{\text{snowball}}$ as he catches it. We might term this the "snowball-mediated force": a force between physics students (the particles experiencing the force) mediated by a snowball (the particle conveying it). The lower diagram in Figure 1 represents the net effect. The exchange of the mediating particle is the cause of the momentum changes experienced by the particles engaging in the force. Diagrams of this sort are known as Feynman diagrams. We will see them again in Section 5.

The snowball example clarifies how the exchange of a particle might convey a force, but as an analogy to the workings of a fundamental force, it has several shortcomings. One is that it would seem capable of conveying only a *repulsive* force. Both Anna and Bob experience momentum changes *away* from the mediating particle. To convey an attraction, the throwing of the snowball would have to force Anna *toward* the snowball, and the catching of the snowball would have to cause Bob to move in the direction from which the snowball came. The total momentum after the catch might indeed equal the total momentum before the throw, but momentum conservation would seem to be violated *during* the mediating particle's exchange. Another deficiency in the analogy is that for a real fundamental force, the mediating particle exists only during its exchange. The "snowball" is created solely for the occasion, disappearing just as mysteriously afterward. This raises concerns about energy conservation. Although energy might be the same at the end as at the beginning, what about the interval during which the mediating particle performs its task?

Mediating particles do not obey the usual momentum and energy rules in the way that "real" particles do, and for this reason, the particles exchanged to convey force are known as **virtual particles**. In fact, they differ from the corresponding real particles only in their lack of adherence to those rules and in being undetectable in such a state, which the physics of quantum fields tells us is fleeting. In many ways, the phenomenon is like tunneling, in which kinetic energy is negative and the probability of its occurrence drops off rapidly with separation.

Although not rigorous, one way of relating the range of the force to a property of the mediating particle is via the energy-time uncertainty principle. Considered for an interval of time Δt, there is an inherent uncertainty ΔE in the energy of a system, governed by

$$\Delta t \Delta E \approx \hbar$$

A particle of energy ΔE could appear and disappear without verifiably upsetting energy conservation so long as it existed for no longer than $\Delta t \approx \hbar/\Delta E$. (This also covers the temporary problem with momentum conservation.) By this argument, a force whose mediating particle has mass must be a short-range force. If a massive particle must be created, there is a lower limit on the amount by which the total energy could deviate: the mass/internal energy of that particle. This, in turn, implies that the maximum time the particle could survive is $\Delta t \approx \hbar/mc^2$. Even at the speed of light, the particle could travel at most

$$\Delta x \approx c\Delta t \approx \frac{\hbar}{mc}$$

or

$$\text{range} \approx \frac{\hbar}{c}\frac{1}{m} \tag{1}$$

If the mediating particle has mass, the range of the force is limited.

Conversely, a force whose mediating particle is massless could have infinite range. With no mass, there would be no lower limit on the energy of the mediating particle. Its strictly kinetic energy could be arbitrarily small, so the time and range could be arbitrarily large. Consider the electromagnetic force. Although it does fall off with distance, it nevertheless reaches infinitely far, so it would have to be conveyed by massless particles. Indeed, electromagnetic forces are conveyed by the exchange of massless photons. An electrostatic repulsion between electrons, for instance, is conveyed when one electron emits a virtual photon that is absorbed by the second electron.

We will return to equation (1) when we discuss specific fundamental forces in Section 3. Here, we merely note that it has been used in several instances to predict fairly accurately the mediating particle mass from knowledge of the force's range *before* the mediating particle was first detected. This is one of the most convincing arguments for treating forces as the exchange of particles.

2 Antiparticles

Before delving further into fundamental interactions between particles, we must understand antiparticles. For each kind of particle, there is an antiparticle that shares essentially all the properties of the particle except that it is of opposite charge. The positron has the same mass and spin as an electron but is of positive charge. An electron and positron can be created in the process of pair production. When they meet, pair annihilation may follow, in which they disappear and their mass energy is converted to photon energy. Many other antiparticles have been found, such as the antiproton (negatively charged) and antineutron (uncharged). It might seem that an uncharged neutron has no property to distinguish it from its antiparticle. However, the antineutron's distinct identity is confirmed by the fact that it does annihilate with the neutron, whereas two neutrons do not annihilate. Actually, as we will see in Section 3, the neutron is not fundamental—nor is the proton—and its internal structure distinguishes particle from antiparticle. (Some uncharged particles, such as the π^0, lack such distinguishing structure and are their own antiparticles.)

The conventional symbol for an antiparticle is the same as for the particle but with an overbar. The antiproton is thus $\bar{p}$ and the antineutron $\bar{n}$. An alternative convention is often used for charged particles. The positron is usually represented e^+ rather than $\overline{e^-}$, and the antiproton is sometimes written p^-. Similarly, the μ^+ and μ^- are antiparticles of one another.

The existence of antiparticles is an experimental fact, but there is a theoretical basis: relativistic quantum mechanics. Let us pursue just enough of this advanced theory to gain some idea of how combining relativity with quantum mechanics might suggest the existence of antiparticles.

The Schrödinger equation for a free particle in one dimension is

$$-\frac{\hbar^2}{2m}\frac{\partial^2}{\partial x^2}\Psi(x,t) = i\hbar\frac{\partial}{\partial t}\Psi(x,t) \tag{2}$$

Expressed in terms of operators, where $\hat{p} = -i\hbar(\partial/\partial x)$ and $\hat{E} = i\hbar(\partial/\partial t)$, it becomes

$$\frac{1}{2m}\hat{p}^2\Psi(x,t) = \hat{E}\Psi(x,t)$$

As we know, this equation is based on energy. In the absence of external potential energies, the kinetic energy of a particle, $p^2/2m$, equals its total energy E. However, because $p^2/2m$ is not the relativistically correct expression for kinetic energy, $p^2/2m = E$ cannot serve as the basis of a relativistic replacement for the Schrödinger equation. A logical basis is the relativistically correct expression:

$$p^2c^2 + m^2c^4 = E^2 \tag{3}$$

To obtain a relativistic matter wave equation, we might try inserting the appropriate operators and then have each term operate on a wave function:

$$c^2\hat{p}^2\Psi(x,t) + m^2c^4\Psi(x,t) = \hat{E}^2\Psi(x,t)$$

or

$$-c^2\hbar^2\frac{\partial^2}{\partial x^2}\Psi(x,\,t)\,+\,m^2c^4\Psi(x,\,t)\,=\,-\hbar^2\frac{\partial^2}{\partial t^2}\Psi(x,\,t) \qquad (4)$$

Known as the **Klein-Gordon equation**, this has been shown to yield correct predictions about the behavior of spinless massive particles at all speeds. Particles with spin obey the related **Dirac equation**. In nonrelativistic quantum mechanics, we work with spatial states that are solutions of the Schrödinger equation, and we treat spin states separately. In the Dirac equation, spin is incorporated as an integral part of the overall state from the outset. We leave study of the Dirac equation to a higher-level course. The most important point here is that both it and the Klein-Gordon equation are based on (3) and thus share a "problem."

The main difficulty with basing a relativistic matter wave equation on equation (3) is that it involves E *squared*. If $E = p^2/2m$, then E is positive. Solutions to the Schrödinger equation are thus always of positive energy. But equation (3) is equally well satisfied whether E is positive or negative. There are perfectly valid mathematical solutions of (4) for which the total energy is negative. The question is how to interpret these mathematical solutions physically.

There is another difficulty with (4). It can be shown that the integral $\int\Psi^*\Psi dV$ does not change with time if Ψ is a solution of the *Schrödinger* equation. This is reassuring, for we have always interpreted this integral as the sum of the probability density $\Psi^*\Psi$ over all space—the total probability of finding the particle—and we claim that it must always be 1. However, the integral may change with time if Ψ is instead a solution of the Klein-Gordon equation. Were we to interpret it in the usual way, the particle might either appear or disappear as time passes! We *can* form a density that doesn't change in time from solutions of the Klein-Gordon equation (see Exercise 15), but we cannot interpret it as a probability density, for it can be either positive or negative.

A conspicuous link between the problems of negative energy and negative density is that the sign of the density is correlated with the sign of the energy. Positive-energy solutions correspond to a density of one sign and negative-energy solutions to a density of the opposite sign. This clue serves as the basis for the following interpretation: The new density is *charge* density, whose integral over space must indeed be a constant in time but may be of either positive or negative sign. A negative-energy solution describes a particle identical to that described by the positive-energy solution, except that its charge is of the opposite sign—the antiparticle.

The idea of negative energy is still troubling. Without going too deeply into relativistic quantum mechanics, it might be said that an *antiparticle* state is a "hole" in a sea of allowed but usually filled negative-energy states of the *particle*, as depicted in Figure 2. A *uniform* "Dirac sea" of charged negative-energy particles would be undetectable. A particle may fall into a hole and thus disappear, but only if the hole already exists—that is, only if an antiparticle is present. In filling the hole, the particle surrenders an energy equal to the

Figure 2 Whether a positive-energy particle drops into an empty negative-energy state, or two positive-energy particles annihilate, the result is the same.

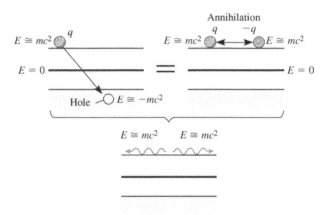

difference between the positive initial and negative final energies—twice the particle's energy. This lost energy goes to photons, two of which are needed to conserve momentum. Because equal energy would be released in either view, we see that it is equivalent to regard the filling of the hole as the annihilation of two particles, each of positive energy mc^2.

3 Forces and Particles: How Many?

Efforts to demonstrate the essential equivalence of seemingly diverse forces have been very successful in the past century or so. For instance, electric and magnetic phenomena had been once thought to be completely distinct, but by the early 20th century, they were conclusively shown to be simply different faces of the single electromagnetic interaction. Electromagnetism was, in fact, the first force to be successfully married to the quantum-mechanical idea of force being conveyed by the exchange of particles. Known as quantum electrodynamics, or **QED**, the theory was worked out independently by Tomonaga, Schwinger, and Feynman in the 1940s and 1950s (Nobel Prize, 1965). Our present knowledge indicates that all forces are manifestations of three distinct fundamental interactions: the **gravitational**, the **electroweak**, and the **strong**. Four had been accepted until the 1960s, when theoretical advances by Sheldon Glashow, Abdus Salam, and Steven Weinberg, working independently, showed that the weak and electromagnetic interactions are really just two aspects of the same electroweak interaction (Nobel Prize, 1979). Nevertheless, the two forces are still often referred to separately because the "weak part" is manifest only in certain reactions among subatomic particles. It is not revealed in ordinary electromagnetic phenomena.

Much research continues to be devoted to showing the equivalence of the three remaining interactions. A theory in which all interactions appear as

TABLE 12.1 Fundamental forces and particles

Force	Gravitation	Electroweak			Strong	Residual
Property	Mass/energy	Charge/weak charge			Color charge	
Strength	$\sim 10^{-39}$	$\sim 10^{-2}$	$\sim 10^{-6}$		1	
Range	$1/r^2$	$1/r^2$	10^{-3} fm		short	1 fm
Mediating Bosons	Graviton?	Photon, γ	W^+, W^-	Z^0	Gluon	$\pi^\pm, \pi^0$
Spin	2?	1	1	1	1	0
Mass	0?	$< 6 \times 10^{-22}$	80.4×10^3	91.2×10^3	< 10	140, 135
Charge	—	0	$+1, -1$	0	0	$\pm 1, 0$
Color charge	—	—	—	—	r, g, or b + $\bar{r}, \bar{g},$ or $\bar{b}$	Neutral

Leptons
Participants in gravitation and electroweak

	Spin	Mass	Charge
Electron, e	$\frac{1}{2}$	0.511	-1
e-neutrino, ν_e	$\frac{1}{2}$	$< 10^{-5}$	0
Muon, μ	$\frac{1}{2}$	106	-1
μ-neutrino, ν_μ	$\frac{1}{2}$	< 0.2	0
Tauon, τ	$\frac{1}{2}$	1.78×10^3	-1
τ-neutrino, ν_τ	$\frac{1}{2}$	< 20	0

Quarks
Participants in gravitation, electroweak, and strong

	Spin	Mass	Charge	Color charge
Up, u	$\frac{1}{2}$	~ 5	$+\frac{2}{3}$	r, g, b
Down, d	$\frac{1}{2}$	~ 10	$-\frac{1}{3}$	r, g, b
Strange, s	$\frac{1}{2}$	~ 100	$-\frac{1}{3}$	r, g, b
Charm, c	$\frac{1}{2}$	$\sim 1.3 \times 10^3$	$+\frac{2}{3}$	r, g, b
Bottom, b	$\frac{1}{2}$	$\sim 4.5 \times 10^3$	$-\frac{1}{3}$	r, g, b
Top, t	$\frac{1}{2}$	$\sim 180 \times 10^3$	$+\frac{2}{3}$	r, g, b

Spins given in units of $\hbar$, masses in units of MeV/c^2, and charges in units of e. All particles have antiparticles of opposite charge and color charge.

merely different aspects of a single fundamental interaction would be the ultimate **unified theory**. Alas, such a theory has eluded many of the brightest minds in physics to this day. Unified theories are discussed in Section 7.

Adding to our suspicions that the fundamental forces are somehow related are two characteristics they share. First, the fundamental particles experiencing the force are fermions, and they engage in the force by exchanging mediating particles that are bosons. Second, for a fermion to engage in a force, it must possess the property associated with that force. These properties are mass/energy, for gravitation; charge or weak charge, for the electroweak; and color charge, for the strong interaction. Table 1 summarizes the state-of-the-art in fundamental particles and interactions. As we proceed, we will see how the pieces fit together. Let us now study qualitatively the presently accepted fundamental interactions and introduce the particles that engage in them.

Figure 3 The proton and neutron are not fundamental. They contain quarks.

The Strong Force

Neither the proton nor the neutron is fundamental. As depicted in Figure 3, each is a combination of more-basic particles, called **quarks**, that are bound together by a mutual attraction, the strong force. As far as we know, quarks are the fundamental fermions that engage in the strong force, and there appear to

Proton

Neutron

be six types. As each was identified or proposed, it was given a fanciful name, and the names have stuck: up, down, strange, charm, top, and bottom. Their properties are summarized in Table 1. The proton and the neutron comprise three quarks each, with **quark content** uud and udd, respectively. From the tabulated charges of these quarks—$+\frac{2}{3}$ for the up and $-\frac{1}{3}$ for the down—we obtain the proper charges of the proton and neutron: $+\frac{2}{3} + \frac{2}{3} - \frac{1}{3} = +1$ and $-\frac{1}{3} - \frac{1}{3} + \frac{2}{3} = 0$. Particles composed of quarks are known by the generic name **hadrons**. We discuss other hadrons later.

Perhaps the most remarkable property of quarks is that they have nonintegral charge. This would appear to dash our time-honored belief that any amount of charge is always an integral multiple of the "fundamental charge" $e = 1.6 \times 10^{-19}$ C. But the belief is safe for the time being, for no way has yet been found of isolating a quark. Moreover, there is reason to believe that it will never be done. Because the electrostatic force falls off as $1/r^2$, the energy required to pull opposite charges apart, even infinitely far, is finite. The strong force, on the other hand, actually gets stronger with separation. (The force holding nucleons together in the nucleus, discussed later in the section, is an *aspect* of the strong force that does decrease with separation.) Consequently, infinite energy would be required to separate quarks. **Quark confinement** is the term used to describe the refusal of quarks to be separated. Certainly the attempt can be made, but what we invariably find is that the energy expended is sufficient, even at very small separations, to create quark-antiquark pairs. We end up not with *separated* quarks, but simply with a greater *number* of quarks, which form multiquark hadrons of integral charge. Even so, this explanation would seem to raise more questions than it answers. If quarks cannot be isolated, how do we know they are of nonintegral charge? Indeed, how do we know they even exist?

Rutherford discovered the atomic nucleus by probing gold foil with high-energy alpha particles. In a very similar way, much of our information about the internal structure of hadrons has come from experiments in which they are struck by high-energy electrons. Fundamental point electrons are sent in to probe for other fundamental point particles (i.e., quarks). In **deep inelastic scattering experiments**, electrons of energy greater than 20 GeV and momentum 20 GeV/c have been smashed into nucleons. The corresponding wavelength of the electrons is on the order of 10^{-16} m. Because this is only about a $\frac{1}{10}$ the nucleon radius, the electron should indeed be able to resolve structural details within a nucleon. These experiments have provided unmistakable evidence that the nucleon contains three particles of fractional charge. (The experiments are "inelastic" because some the electron's kinetic energy creates additional hadrons.)

The mediating boson of the strong force is the **gluon**. Thus, hadrons may be thought of as quarks bound together by continuous exchange of gluons. Gluons are spin-1 and massless. According to equation (1), this would seem to imply an infinite range, which fits with the observation that the strong force actually increases with quark separation. However, the effective range is very short. As noted above, attempting to pull quarks apart, even small distances, simply generates more hadrons.

The property a particle must possess to engage in the strong force is known as color charge, or simply **color**. While similar in some respects, it is distinct from electric charge. Whereas electric charge can be of two kinds, color can be of three, styled red, green, and blue. (They aren't actual colors of light.) Quarks may be any of the three colors, while antiquarks may be antired, antigreen, or antiblue. Quarks are the only fundamental *fermions* that possess color and are thus able to engage in the strong force. However, gluons themselves carry color. (For reasons discussed in Section 5, they carry a color-anticolor pair, e.g., blue-antigreen.) This is one reason the character of the strong force differs so much from that of the electromagnetic. Photons, the mediating particles of the electromagnetic interaction, do not themselves possess electric charge. Thus, whereas photon exchange is how charged fundamental fermions interact, photons do not interact electrostatically with photons. Gluons, on the other hand, not only are emitted and absorbed by colored fundamental fermions—that is, quarks—but they also interact strongly with one another. Thus, we see that it is not quite general to say that fundamental forces are conveyed by the exchange of mediating bosons *between fermions*.

A rationale for the term *color* is that red, green, and blue light add to neutral light, and all evidence indicates that hadrons must be color neutral. Electrostatics tells us that two electrons, constituting a nonzero net *electric* charge, repel one another, but there is a net *attraction* in a charge-neutral system, such as a hydrogen atom. Similarly, zero net color leads to attraction. To be color neutral, hadrons can be bound states of three quarks, one of each color (red + green + blue = neutral), or bound states of two quarks, comprising a quark of one color and an antiquark of its anticolor (red + antired = neutral).

Just as for quarks, it has not been possible to isolate gluons or color charge, but there is ample evidence of their existence. High-energy collisions often produce **jets** (isolated sectors) of "extra" hadrons streaming away from the collision point. Analysis of certain collisions verifies that some of these jets are the decay products of individual gluons emitted immediately after the collision. As to color, the Δ^{++} and Δ^- hadrons comprise three identical quarks (uuu and ddd, respectively) in the same ground spatial state, and they are spin-$\frac{3}{2}$, meaning that all three quarks are in the same spin state. Without another property to distinguish their quarks, these hadrons would violate the exclusion principle. Different colors make the quarks distinguishable. Indicating the importance of color, the theory of the strong interaction is known as **quantum chromodynamics** (*chroma* is Greek for "color"), or **QCD**.

A glance at Table 1 shows that the masses of the up and down quarks are far too small to account for the mass of a three-quark nucleon, which is roughly 940 MeV/c^2. The masses given are often called bare masses and are at best only rough values. Scattering experiments have established that the nucleon is definitely not three quarks alone. The quarks are surrounded by a sizable cloud of energetic gluons and virtual quark-antiquark pairs constantly undergoing creation and annihilation. This cloud constitutes the majority of the nucleon mass and makes assigning definite values to quark masses problematic.

Categories of Hadrons

With six quarks and six antiquarks, a great number of different hadrons are possible. Many of the possible combinations have been produced in high-energy, inelastic collisions in which kinetic energy is converted to mass (explaining why the terms *particle physics* and *high-energy physics* are used interchangeably). Table 2 lists some commonly produced hadrons, along with their quark content, masses, and other properties. All have antiparticles in which each quark is replaced by its antiquark. Three-quark hadrons are known as **baryons** (from the Greek for "heavy") and two-quark hadrons as **mesons** (intermediate). The neutron, for instance, is a baryon. As noted earlier, color neutrality demands that it have one quark of each color. An example of a meson is the pion, which comes in three varieties. The π^+ is of quark content $u\bar{d}$. Its $+1$ charge is accounted for by the $+\frac{2}{3}$ charge of the up quark and the $+\frac{1}{3}$ charge of the antidown, the antiparticle of the down quark. The up and antidown quarks might be red and antired, green and antigreen, or blue and antiblue. The antiparticle of the π^+ is the π^-, of quark content $\bar{u}d$ and therefore of charge -1. The π^0 has no electric charge. It is a mixture of the charge- and color-neutral quark combinations $\bar{u}u$ and $\bar{d}d$.

From Table 2, we see that many hadrons are much heavier than nucleons. Greater mass output requires greater kinetic energy input, so heavier ones tend to be more recent discoveries using higher-energy accelerators. From the average lifetime data, we see that all non-nucleon hadrons are fairly short lived. In cases of very short-lived particles, it is common to specify an energy **width** rather than a lifetime. According to the uncertainty principle, a particle's energy can be known to no greater precision than $\Delta E \cong \hbar/\tau$, where τ is the time interval during which the particle exists. The lifetime corresponding to a width of 50 MeV is about 10^{-23} s.

Intrinsic Properties

All quarks are spin-$\frac{1}{2}$ fermions. By the rules of angular momentum addition, three-quark baryons should be fermions that are either spin-$\frac{3}{2}$ or spin-$\frac{1}{2}$, as Table 2 reflects. (Actually, it isn't quite so easy. See Progress and Applications for a note on the spin crisis.) Similarly, two-quark mesons are spin-0 or spin-1 bosons. In general, when we apply the term *spin* to a hadron, we really mean total angular momentum, which includes any orbital angular momentum its constituents might have.

Table 2 shows that some hadrons have the same quark content and spin, yet are different particles. For instance, the Λ^0 and Σ^0 are both uds and spin-$\frac{1}{2}$. The distinction lies in the intrinsic property called **isospin**, I. It is not an angular momentum, as is spin, but it does have a similarly quantized "third component" I_3 and obeys the same addition rules—hence, the name. The up and down quark each have isospin $I = \frac{1}{2}$, while the strange quark has isospin $I = 0$. In the Σ^0, the isospins of the up and down quarks are aligned, giving a total isospin $I = 1$, while in the Λ^0, they are antialigned, yielding $I = 0$. The distinction between the K_S^0 and K_L^0 (the subscripts refer to short and long lifetimes) is not based on isospin, but on an unusual mixing of the K^0 particle and

TABLE 12.2 Commonly produced hadrons

Baryons	Mass (MeV/c^2)	Spin	Strange-ness	I, I_3	Lifetime, τ (or width $\hbar/\tau$)	Mesons	Mass (MeV/c^2)	Spin	Strange-ness	I, I_3	Lifetime, τ (or width $\hbar/\tau$)
p (uud)	938	$\frac{1}{2}$	0	$\frac{1}{2}, +\frac{1}{2}$	$>10^{32}$ yr	π^+ (u$\bar{\text{d}}$)	140	0	0	$1, +1$	2.6×10^{-8} s
n (udd)	940	$\frac{1}{2}$	0	$\frac{1}{2}, -\frac{1}{2}$	889 s	π^0 (u$\bar{\text{u}}$ + d$\bar{\text{d}}$)	135	0	0	$1, 0$	8.4×10^{-17} s
Σ^+ (uus)	1189	$\frac{1}{2}$	-1	$1, +1$	8.0×10^{-11} s	π^- (d$\bar{\text{u}}$)	140	0	0	$1, -1$	2.6×10^{-8} s
Σ^0 (uds)	1193	$\frac{1}{2}$	-1	$1, 0$	7.4×10^{-20} s	K^+ (u$\bar{\text{s}}$)	494	0	$+1$	$\frac{1}{2}, +\frac{1}{2}$	1.2×10^{-8} s
Λ^0 (uds)	1116	$\frac{1}{2}$	-1	$0, 0$	2.6×10^{-10} s	K_S^0 (d$\bar{\text{s}}$, s$\bar{\text{d}}$)	498	0	mix	$\frac{1}{2}$, mix	8.9×10^{-11} s
Σ^- (dds)	1197	$\frac{1}{2}$	-1	$1, -1$	1.5×10^{-10} s	K_L^0 (d$\bar{\text{s}}$, s$\bar{\text{d}}$)	498	0	mix	$\frac{1}{2}$, mix	5.2×10^{-8} s
Ξ^0 (uss)	1315	$\frac{1}{2}$	-2	$\frac{1}{2}, -\frac{1}{2}$	2.9×10^{-10} s	K^- (s$\bar{\text{u}}$)	494	0	-1	$\frac{1}{2}, -\frac{1}{2}$	1.2×10^{-8} s
Ξ^- (dss)	1321	$\frac{1}{2}$	-2	$\frac{1}{2}, -\frac{1}{2}$	1.6×10^{-10} s	ρ^+ (u$\bar{\text{d}}$)	769	1	0	$1, +1$	151 MeV
Δ^{++} (uuu)	1232	$\frac{3}{2}$	0	$\frac{3}{2}, +\frac{3}{2}$	120 MeV	ρ^0 (u$\bar{\text{u}}$ + d$\bar{\text{d}}$)	769	1	0	$1, 0$	151 MeV
Δ^+ (uud)	1232	$\frac{3}{2}$	0	$\frac{3}{2}, +\frac{1}{2}$	120 MeV	ρ^- (d$\bar{\text{u}}$)	769	1	0	$1, -1$	151 MeV
Δ^0 (udd)	1232	$\frac{3}{2}$	0	$\frac{3}{2}, -\frac{1}{2}$	120 MeV	K^{*+} (u$\bar{\text{s}}$)	892	1	$+1$	$\frac{1}{2}, +\frac{1}{2}$	50 MeV
Δ^- (ddd)	1232	$\frac{3}{2}$	0	$\frac{3}{2}, -\frac{3}{2}$	120 MeV	K^{*0} (d$\bar{\text{s}}$)	896	1	$+1$	$\frac{1}{2}, -\frac{1}{2}$	51 MeV
Σ^{*+} (uus)	1383	$\frac{3}{2}$	-1	$1, +1$	~40 MeV	$\overline{K^{*0}}$ (s$\bar{\text{d}}$)	896	1	-1	$\frac{1}{2}, +\frac{1}{2}$	51 MeV
Σ^{*0} (uds)	1384	$\frac{3}{2}$	-1	$1, 0$	~40 MeV	K^{*-} (s$\bar{\text{u}}$)	892	1	-1	$\frac{1}{2}, -\frac{1}{2}$	50 MeV
Σ^{*-} (dds)	1387	$\frac{3}{2}$	-1	$1, -1$	~40 MeV	Heavy mesons—containing quarks beyond the strange					
Ξ^{*0} (uss)	1532	$\frac{3}{2}$	-2	$\frac{1}{2}, +\frac{1}{2}$	~10 MeV	J/ψ (c$\bar{\text{c}}$)	3100	1	0	$0, 0$	87 keV
Ξ^{*-} (dss)	1535	$\frac{3}{2}$	-2	$\frac{1}{2}, -\frac{1}{2}$	~10 MeV	Υ (b$\bar{\text{b}}$)	9460	1	0	$0, 0$	~50 keV
Ω^- (sss)	1672	$\frac{3}{2}$	-3	$0, 0$	8.2×10^{-11} s						

its antiparticle $\overline{K^0}$. A discussion of this mixing may be found in higher-level texts on particle physics.

Yet another intrinsic property given in Table 2 is **strangeness**. Sensibly, it is the strange quark that endows a particle with strangeness. By arbitrary sign choice, possession of one strange quark gives a strangeness of -1; of two, a strangeness -2; of an antistrange, a strangeness $+1$; and so forth. We discuss strangeness further in Section 5. For now, we note simply that the hadrons containing only u, d, and s quarks can be grouped into several related multiplets according to spin, and that an individual member of a multiplet is distinguished by its strangeness and isospin. (Four such groups are set apart in the table.)

The Residual Strong Force

Neutral atoms may attract each other electrostatically. Each may have an electric dipole moment (permanent or induced), and if the moments are properly oriented, a net attraction results. Tenuous though it may seem, this attraction is how some substances, notably water, form solids. In a similar effect, color-neutral particles may attract each other via the strong interaction. It is this attraction that holds the nucleons together in the nucleus. Called the **residual strong force**, it is not a distinct force, but rather a coarse manifestation of the true strong interaction. Still, it too can be viewed as being conveyed by the exchange of a particle. Color-neutral uud protons and udd neutrons may exchange a two-quark, color-neutral combination of u, d, $\bar{u}$, and $\bar{d}$ quarks—a pion. Although the lightest of hadrons, the pion does have mass, which explains why the residual strong force is short range. In fact, rough knowledge of the force's range led, through equation (1), to a reasonably accurate prediction of the pion's mass before it was ever detected (see Exercise 9).

The Electroweak Force

Particles that possess charge or **weak charge** can engage in the electroweak force. Besides quarks, this includes the class of particles known as **leptons** (from the Greek for "light"), which lack color charge and are therefore blind to the strong force. As shown in Table 1, there are six known leptons in three pairs: the electron and electron-neutrino; the muon and mu-neutrino; and the tauon and tau-neutrino. (All also have antiparticles, but whether those of the neutrinos are actually distinct particles is not settled. See Section 6.) Despite their different masses, the electron, muon, and tauon are very much alike, and one of the open questions in high-energy physics is why we "need" to have all three.

Although earlier work had unified the electromagnetic and weak forces, electroweak theory received a great boost from the contributions of Gerardus 't Hooft and Martinus Veltman around 1970 (Nobel Prize, 1999). Their new mathematical framework made excellent predictions of the masses of multiple mediating particles a decade before these particles were discovered. It is now confirmed that the electroweak force is conveyed by the exchange of any of four mediating bosons: the photon and the **weak bosons** W^+, W^-, and Z^0. A glance at their properties quickly reveals the complexity of the electroweak interaction. The photon, exchanged in the "electromagnetic part" of the interaction, is massless, while the $W^\pm$ and Z^0 particles, exchanged in the "weak part," are among the heaviest fundamental particles yet detected. If there is indeed only one underlying interaction, these four are all field quanta of the *same* field. But how?

The schism is known as a **spontaneously broken symmetry**. The asymmetry is the different behaviors of the electromagnetic and weak forces, and it occurs at low particle energies. A toy top provides a useful mechanical analogy: If spinning at high rotational energy, it will be oriented symmetrically relative to the ground, but at low energy, it spontaneously drops to an asymmetric repose on its side. The true underlying symmetry of the electroweak interaction becomes apparent only at particle energies much higher than those presently accessible to observation. A value of about 1 TeV is a common guess. At very high energies, the intrinsic mass of a particle becomes irrelevant. The massive particle momentum–energy relation, $E^2 = p^2c^2 + m^2c^4$, becomes that for a massless particle, $E = pc$, and the behaviors of the mediating particles converge.

All leptons are spin-$\frac{1}{2}$ fermions. Neutrinos are uncharged and therefore do not engage in strictly electromagnetic interactions, but all leptons engage in weak interactions—all possess weak charge. We won't study the relationship between charge and weak charge, except to note that the greater strength of the electromagnetic force relative to the weak force is not because weak *charge* is weaker than electric charge, but rather because of the mysterious mass difference between the mediating bosons. Nonzero mass is an impediment responsible for both the weakness and the short range of the weak force relative to the electromagnetic.

The theories of the strong and electroweak forces together form what is known as the **Standard Model**. It exhibits a pleasing symmetry: six quarks and six leptons occurring in three increasingly massive tiers, or **generations**, each comprising charges of $(+\frac{2}{3}e, -\frac{1}{3}e)$ and $(-e, 0)$. The lightest generation comprises the (u, d) and (e$^-$, v_e); next is the (c, s) and (μ^-, v_μ); and the heaviest is the (t, b) and (τ^-, v_τ). In many ways the Standard Model is a very harmonious theory that explains much of our observations. However, the picture is still incomplete. A relatively new "problem" is neutrino mass, discussed in Section 5. But the riddle that has been center stage for decades is the spontaneously broken symmetry of the electroweak force. The answer may lie with the one particle conspicuously missing in the Standard Model, the most sought after in high-energy physics: the **Higgs boson**. It is difficult to overstate the importance of the Higgs boson, for it is believed to be what is responsible for the masses of all particles! In short, space is thought to be permeated by a field, called the Higgs field, through which all particles naturally must pass. This field governs the behavior of particles passing through it in much the same way that a solid governs the behavior of conduction electrons passing through it, producing an effective mass. At the relative low energies of particles we can observe today, an asymmetry in the Higgs field leads to a hard way and an easy way to travel through. Moving the hard way produces the characteristic of mass. Photons move the easy way and are thus massless, while the W and Z move the hard way. The particle associated with the field is the Higgs boson. Predictions vary, but its mass is expected to be in the general vicinity of 200 GeV/c^2. Energies available at upgraded and new colliders in the next few years should either confirm its existence and support the Standard Model—or hasten searches in new directions.

The Gravitational Force

General relativity tells us that all particles with mass or any other form of energy attract one another via the gravitational force. Obviously, this broad categorization includes all the fundamental particles, for even massless particles move at c and thus have kinetic energy. However, to date, no quantum aspects of the gravitational force have been observed. A major difficulty is its relative weakness. By analogy with the two other interactions, we assume that things attract one another gravitationally via the exchange of a field quantum, which should be massless because the force is of infinite range. Moreover, given gravity's attractive-only nature, the theory of gravitation suggests that this mediating boson should be of spin 2. It has even been given a name—**graviton**. Yet it has never been detected. We will return to this quantum-mechanically intransigent force when we discuss unified theories.

4 Particle Production and Detection

As noted earlier, our view of which particles are truly fundamental has changed quite a bit over the years. We will now briefly survey the progress and experimental means that have brought us to where we are.

A Brief Chronology

Perhaps not surprisingly, the first subatomic particle to be discovered was the electron, in 1897. Proof of a compact, positively charged nucleus came in 1909, followed in 1919 by the discovery of the proton. Despite mounting interest and rapidly advancing technology, the neutron was not discovered until 1932. This gives some idea of the difficulty of detecting uncharged particles. Even most of today's particle detectors detect uncharged particles only indirectly, by analyzing the behavior of the charged particles with which they interact.

The first source of high energy for particle creation was natural: cosmic rays reaching Earth from space. Cosmic-ray particles—mostly protons—often have kinetic energies greater than 1 GeV, so they are energetic enough to produce other particles whose mass energies are comparable to the nucleon's ~ 1 GeV. Besides the positron, cosmic rays served as the source for the discovery in the 1930s and 1940s of the muon ($m_\mu = 0.11$ GeV), the pion ($m_\pi = 0.14$ GeV), and the kaon ($m_K = 0.49$ GeV). After the kaon, or K-meson, a great many other hadrons were identified. But cosmic rays were soon no longer the best energy source. The particle accelerator had arrived.

Although not realized at the time, the discovery of the kaon had brought to three the number of quarks subject to study. The first hadrons discovered were merely different combinations of the same three quarks: the up, the down, and the strange. Indeed, after a decade or so of finding recurring patterns, strong suspicions arose that the known hadrons were composed of a smaller number of more fundamental particles. The three-quark theory that came to be accepted is due to Murray Gell-Mann, who was awarded the 1969 Nobel Prize for his work of 1964 (and by whom the name *quark* was chosen). The theory was widely embraced, but it was not until the deep inelastic scattering experiments (Section 3) of Friedman, Kendall, and Taylor in 1967 that the first direct experimental evidence of quarks was obtained. Still, other more massive quarks lay undiscovered.

As the energy available to us has increased, so has our ability to produce massive particles. The appearance of much more powerful accelerators since the 1970s led to regular successes in the production of many theoretically predicted particles. Consider a few examples of the progression: In 1974, the 3.1 GeV J/ψ particle, a $\bar{c}c$ meson, was discovered, adding a fourth quark. Discovery of the 1.8 GeV tauon, the third massive lepton (joining the electron and muon), came in 1975. The bottom quark, the fifth, was identified in 1977 via production of the 9.5 GeV Υ meson, a bound $b\bar{b}$. The weak bosons, $W^\pm$ (80 GeV) and Z^0 (91 GeV), were found in 1983. And in 1994, the sixth quark, the 180 GeV top, was positively identified.

TABLE 3 Some particle accelerators

Facility	Location	Type	Energy
SLC	Stanford, CA USA	Linear e^+e^-	50 GeV ($\times$2)
TEVATRON—Fermilab	Batavia, IL USA	Synchrotron $\bar{p}p$	1 TeV ($\times$2)
LHC—CERN (est. 2007)	Geneva, Switzerland	Synchrotron pp	7 TeV ($\times$2)
		Synchrotron PbPb	575 TeV ($\times$2)

Accelerators and Detectors

Today's accelerators may be categorized in several ways: (1) They may have two colliding beams, or one beam and a stationary target. A collider is inherently more difficult to align, but technology has surmounted this problem, making its advantages decisive in many applications (see Exercise 25). Accordingly, most accelerators nowadays are colliders. (2) The accelerated particles are often protons or electrons, including the $\bar{p}$ and e^+, but heavy ions are also used. (3) The particles may be linearly accelerated, or they may follow a circular path. In all cases, electric fields speed up the particles, while turning is done by magnetic fields. Data on a few of the many colliding-beam facilities are given in Table 3. In a **synchrotron**, the magnetic field is constantly adjusted so that while being "kicked" by electric fields the particles still move in a circle of constant radius inside a narrow tube. Figures 4 through 7 show features of several of the larger accelerators.

Of course, it does no good to produce a particle if we can't verify it. Reliable detectors are crucial. Of the many types, a few of the more important are the scintillation counter, the multiwire proportional counter, the Cerenkov detector, the silicon detector, and the calorimeter.

The **scintillation counter** houses one of many substances known to produce a flash of light when struck by a charged particle, a common example

Figure 4 The accelerator chain at CERN, covering about 70 km^2 in Switzerland and France. The largest black oval is the Large Hadron Collider (LHC). Linear accelerators (linacs) are the sources for various particles.

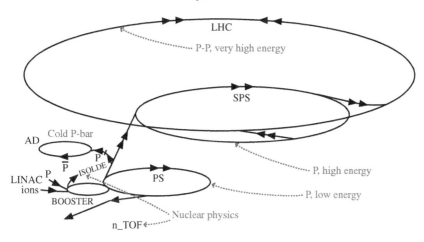

Figure 5 The beam line for the Large Hadron Collider.

Figure 6 At the Stanford Linear Accelerator Center (SLAC), electrons and positrons from a 3-km-long linear accelerator (existing injector) are used for various experiments. The BaBar detector studies CP violation in the decay of B mesons (Section 6).

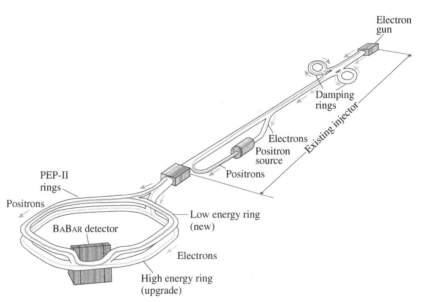

Figure 7 The $1\frac{1}{4}$-mile diameter Tevatron studies collisions of high-energy protons and antiprotons.

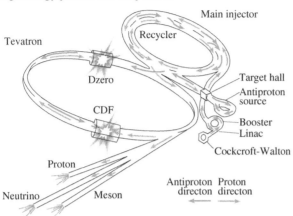

being a thallium-doped NaI crystal. The flash is amplified in a photomultiplier tube. Efficiency is high and response time short. A **multiwire proportional counter** contains a grid of conductors at alternating electric potential within a gas-filled region. When a charged particle enters the region, it ionizes the gas around it, which then causes a brief current between nearby conductors. Determining which conductors are conducting at a given time establishes the particle's location, and computer analysis of the signals provides an excellent picture of the particle's motion. "Proportional" refers to the proportion between the energy deposited by the particle and the electric response of the detector. Simpler gas discharge detectors, like the Geiger counter, give only a "yes" or "no" response and do not track a moving particle. In a **Cerenkov detector**, a charged particle enters a medium at a speed greater than light moves in the medium. (Of course, it never travels faster than light moves through a vacuum.) The particle emits electromagnetic radiation called Cerenkov radiation. In much the same way that an object moving through air at supersonic speed produces a shock cone, Cerenkov radiation forms a distinctive cone whose angle determines the particle speed. **Silicon detectors** are grids of p-n junctions. A charged particle excites electron-hole pairs in proportion to the energy it deposits in the region through which it passes, and the electrical signals at different points in the grid map out the particle's path. When a particle enters a **calorimeter**, it adds energy, which is then shed in numerous ways—creating showers of other particles, for instance. Analysis of these secondary occurrences determines the incoming particle's energy.

5 Decay Modes and Conservation Rules in the Standard Model

Accelerators produce many particles for us to study. Almost all the ones of interest are unstable. Indeed, it might be argued that there are few stable particles. The μ and τ leptons are unstable, and all hadrons but the proton are known to decay. Some particles decay so quickly that we can study them only indirectly, through the particles that result from their decay. Thus, it is very important to understand decay processes. Decays are classified as strong, electromagnetic, or weak, depending on whether the interaction involves the exchange of gluons, photons, or weak bosons, respectively.

From mechanics, we know that momentum and energy conservation constrain the possible outcome of all processes. Energy conservation, for instance, tells us that a spontaneous decay, in which kinetic energy increases, must be accompanied by a decrease in mass. This alone might suggest that *all* massive particles should be liable to decay to the lightest stable particle. In particle physics, however, other conservation rules come into play.

New Rules

Historically, it has often come to the attention of scientists that one quantity or another seems to be conserved. After standing the test of laborious scrutiny, some of these are officially proclaimed conserved quantities and their conservation accepted as a law of nature. Mistakes have been made. Mass was once thought to be conserved, but we now know that it is merely one kind of energy and that it may change while total energy is still conserved. As we discuss various decays, we will refer to the rules summarized in Table 4. Bear in mind that just as for "mass conservation," some of these rules are based on nothing more than a pattern that has not *yet* been violated. They undergo continual reassessment. In many cases, a conservation rule has been found to be obeyed only for a particular type of decay. For instance, strangeness is conserved in strong and electromagnetic interactions but not in weak ones (another example of the asymmetry in the electroweak interaction).

The standard conservation laws of classical physics appear to be safe. Momentum, energy, angular momentum, and charge are always conserved. And all interactions seem to conserve color. Another quantity apparently conserved in all cases is **baryon number**. Baryon number B is $+1$ for baryons, -1 for antibaryons, and 0 for nonbaryons.

Until fairly recently, **lepton number** was also believed to be universally conserved. It is common to define one number for each generation. The electron lepton number L_e is $+1$ for the electron and the electron neutrino, -1 for their antiparticles, and 0 for all other particles. The muon lepton number L_μ and tau lepton number L_τ are defined analogously. In 1998,

TABLE 4 Some conservation rules

Conserved? Interaction	Momentum, Energy, Angular Momentum, Charge, Color	Baryon Number (B)	Lepton Numbers* (L_e, L_μ, L_τ)	Strangeness	Parity (P)	Charge Conjugation (C)	Time Reversal (T)
Strong	Yes	Yes	Yes	Yes	Yes	Yes	Yes
Electromagnetic	Yes	Yes	Yes	Yes	Yes	Yes	Yes
Weak	Yes	Yes	Yes	No	No	No	No

* Recent evidence indicates some exceptions.

evidence was obtained that one type of neutrino can change into another (called neutrino oscillation and discussed further in Section 6). When this occurs, one lepton number must decrease as another increases. Recent studies of some highly unusual decays (see Progress and Applications) also suggest that conservation of lepton number may not be a universal rule. Nonetheless, almost all processes conserve the three lepton numbers independently.

Let us now study particle decays and conservation rules[1] by considering interactions on the simplest possible level: the interaction of a mediating boson and a fundamental fermion. We do this via **Feynman diagrams**. These are very convenient devices, for they show what is occurring without going through a complex calculation.

Feynman Diagrams

The basic element of a Feynman diagram is a **vertex** representing the interaction of a fundamental fermion with a mediating boson. Figure 8 shows the vertices for emission of a boson by a fermion. The horizontal axis is time, advancing from left to right, and the vertical axis stands in for all spatial dimensions. (Feynman diagrams do not really represent spatial motion.) Fermions and mediating bosons are represented by straight and wavy lines, respectively. Only particles possessing color can engage in the strong force, so the only fermions involved in the strong vertex are quarks. Note that in this vertex, the quark may change color. To conserve color in the interaction, the gluon carries a color-anticolor charge. The electromagnetic vertex shows that all fundamental particles can interact electromagnetically, except neutrinos, which are uncharged. Their strictly weak interaction makes them very difficult to detect. The weak vertices reflect the fact that all fundamental fermions may interact via the Z^0 and $W^\pm$ bosons. In the $W^\pm$ case, the charge of the fermion is changed, and a transmutation of particles takes place. Thus, W^+ emission changes a $+\frac{2}{3}$-charge quark (u, c, or t) to a $-\frac{1}{3}$-charge quark (d, s, or b), or a neutrino to the other member of its lepton pair. Emission of a W^- has the opposite effect.

To obtain the vertices for absorption, we would draw the boson as coming into the vertex rather than leaving it and switch its charge or color charge.

[1]The rules pertaining to parity, charge conjugation, and time reversal are deferred to Section 6.

Figure 8 Emission vertices for strong, electromagnetic, and weak processes. Time advances horizontally to the right. A fermion (straight) emits a boson (wavy) and leaves a fermion.

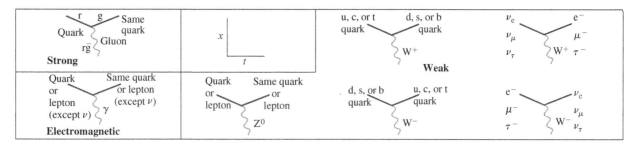

501

Figure 9 Representative destruction and creation vertices.

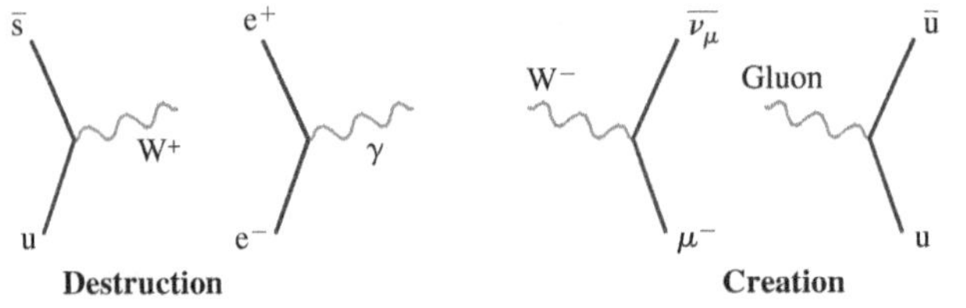

Destruction   **Creation**

(If emission of a positive conserves charge, so would the absorption of a negative.) Replacing all particles with their antiparticles would give the antiparticle vertices.

With just a few other changes, the vertices can represent other processes. Figure 9 shows some examples. If the final fermion of an emission vertex is replaced with its antiparticle and the diagram is rotated 90° counterclockwise, a diagram for the destruction of a particle and an antiparticle results. Reversal along the time axis represents the creation of such a pair.

We represent whole processes by putting vertices together. Figure 10 is the prototype Feynman diagram of an interaction between fundamental fermions. One electron emits a photon, and the other absorbs it. Note the similarity to the snowball-mediated force of Figure 1.

Figure 11 shows diagrams representing various types of spontaneous decay. Diagram (a) shows the β decay of a free neutron—a weak decay because it involves the exchange of a weak boson. Diagram (b) depicts the weak π^- decay. Its lifetime of 2.6×10^{-8} s is typical for a weak decay. (The neutron's 15 min. lifetime is unusually long.) Diagrams (c) and (d) show weak Σ^- and μ^+ decays. An example of an electromagnetic decay is the decay of the Σ^0 in diagram (e). Involving the stronger part of the electroweak force, electromagnetic decays occur in a much shorter time than weak ones, typically 10^{-17} s. A gluon-mediated strong decay is the K^{*0} decay, shown in diagram (f). Involving a yet stronger force, strong decay lifetimes are typically only 10^{-23} s. Once created, a particle able to decay strongly does not survive long. Indeed, such a short-lived entity is often called a **resonance** rather than a particle. Its constituents "stay in tune" for scarcely longer than it takes them to pass one another at high speed.

Diagrams (c), (e), and (f) in Figure 11 bear out the conservation rule for strangeness. While conserved in electromagnetic and strong decays, (e) and (f), strangeness is not conserved in weak decay (c). The W emission changes the strange quark to one of another kind. The values given in the shaded rectangles illustrate conservation of other properties. The final mass is always less than the initial, as it must be for a spontaneous release of kinetic energy. Baryon and lepton numbers are conserved in all of these decays. By the angular momentum addition rules, the final angular momenta are able to add to the initial. Note that the *spins* don't add up in the K^{*0} decay of diagram (f), in which a spin-1 particle becomes two spinless particles. But the decay is allowed because the kaon and pion depart in a state of unit *orbital* angular momentum. Total angular momentum is still conserved.

Figure 10 Electrons interact by exchanging a photon.

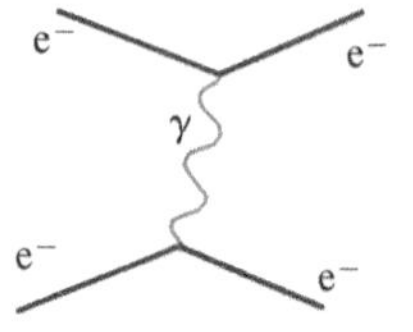

Figure 11 Feynman diagrams for various spontaneous decays.

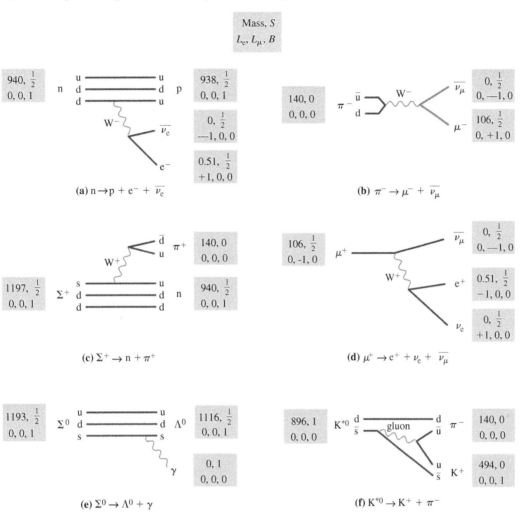

EXAMPLE 1

By considering the conservation of charge, energy (i.e., mass decrease), angular momentum, strangeness, and baryon and lepton numbers, indicate whether each of the proposed decays is possible. If it is not possible, indicate which rules are violated. If it is possible, indicate whether it is a strong, electromagnetic, or weak decay, and sketch a Feynman diagram. Use data from Tables 1 and 2.

(a) $\tau^- \rightarrow \mu^- + v_\tau + \overline{v_\mu}$

(b) $\Xi^0 \rightarrow K^+ + K^-$

(c) $\Delta^+ \rightarrow n + K^+$

(d) $\overline{\Lambda^0} \rightarrow \overline{p} + \pi^+$

Figure 12 Feynman diagrams for τ^- and $\overline{\Lambda^0}$ decay.

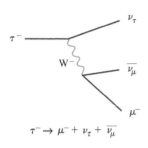

$$\tau^- \rightarrow \mu^- + \nu_\tau + \overline{\nu_\mu}$$

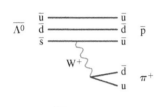

$$\overline{\Lambda^0} \rightarrow \overline{p} + \pi^+$$

SOLUTION

Charge is conserved in all the decays.

(a) The initial mass is 1.78×10^3 MeV, the final is 106 MeV, and no baryons are involved. The initial lepton numbers are $(L_e, L_\mu, L_\tau) = (0, 0, +1)$, and those of the product particles are $(0, +1, 0)$, $(0, 0, +1)$, and $(0, -1, 0)$. Lepton numbers are conserved. Three spin-$\frac{1}{2}$ particles may add up to a spin of $\frac{1}{2}$, so angular momentum may be conserved. The decay is allowed. Because neutrinos interact only via the weak force, this must be a weak decay. The Feynman diagram is shown in Figure 12. The boson must be a W, for a Z couldn't "erase" the τ^-.

(b) This is forbidden on two accounts. First, although the final mass of 2×494 MeV is less than the initial 1315 MeV and no leptons are involved, it begins with a baryon number of $+1$ and ends with no baryons. Second, angular momentum cannot be conserved. The initial spin is $\frac{1}{2}$, while the product particles are spinless. Orbital angular momentum, which comes in integral steps, can't make up the difference.

(c) Since the Δ and n are both baryons and the kaon is a meson, this decay would conserve baryon number. No leptons are involved. A final orbital angular momentum might allow the spin-$\frac{3}{2}$ particle to decay to a spin-$\frac{1}{2}$ and a spinless pion. However, because the final mass of 940 MeV + 494 MeV is greater than the initial 1232 MeV, the Δ^+ cannot decay this way.

(d) The initial and final masses are 1116 MeV and 938 MeV + 140 MeV. The $\overline{\Lambda^0}$ and antiproton are both of baryon number -1, and the pion has baryon number 0, so baryon number is conserved. The $\overline{\Lambda^0}$ and antiproton are spin-$\frac{1}{2}$, while the pion is spinless. This decay is allowed and does occur. Because the $\overline{\Lambda^0}$ contains a strange quark, which is absent in the products, strangeness is not conserved, so this must be a weak decay. Figure 12 shows the Feynman diagram. A W boson changes the strange quark to a $\overline{u}$.

Note that there is a guiding principle in particle physics that says that if a decay *can* occur—if it violates no conservation rules—then it *must* occur. For many hadrons and leptons, there are multiple avenues of decay that obey all the required conservation rules and therefore do occur. For example, the τ^- may decay via $\tau^- \rightarrow e^- + \overline{\nu_e} + \nu_\tau$ and the $\overline{\Lambda^0}$ via $\overline{\Lambda^0} \rightarrow \overline{p} + e^+ + \nu_e$.

The conservation rules we have discussed govern not only spontaneous decays of fundamental particles and hadrons but also other interactions between them.

EXAMPLE 2

Many of today's colliders smash protons together. Consider the two proposed reactions shown below. (a) Does either violate any of the conservation rules in Table 4 (excluding P, C, and T)? If so, which rules? (b) If not, what minimum kinetic energy must the two initial particles have for the reaction to occur?

$$1{:}\ p + p \rightarrow p + \overline{p} + \pi^+ + \pi^+ \qquad\qquad 2{:}\ p + p \rightarrow p + p + \pi^+ + \pi^-$$

SOLUTION

(a) Reaction 1 conserves charge because the final proton and antiproton cancel. Energy can be conserved if the initial kinetic energy is high enough. Pions are spinless, so the two spin-$\frac{1}{2}$ particles before and after the reaction can conserve angular momentum. No leptons or strange quarks are involved. However, the initial baryon number is $1 + 1$, and the final is $1 - 1 + 0 + 0$, so it is not conserved. Reaction 2 *does* conserve baryon number and all the earlier rules by similar arguments.

(b) The energy of the final state in reaction 2 exceeds that of the initial by at least the mass energy of the two pions. Therefore, the initial protons must have kinetic energy of at least $2 \times 140 \text{ MeV} = 280 \text{ MeV}$.

6 Parity, Charge Conjugation, and Time Reversal

Let us take a look at the remaining conservation rules of Table 4, parity inversion, charge conjugation, and time reversal. They touch upon fundamental ideas of space and time, while raising difficult questions.

Parity inversion changes the sign of all spatial coordinates: $(x, y, z) \rightarrow (-x, -y, -z)$. Strong and electromagnetic interactions appear identical from a parity-inverted view, but the weak interaction does not. The simplest example is β decay. To see this, we first note that if a point particle were orbiting in a clockwise direction about the z-axis and we change its coordinates according to $(x, y, z) \rightarrow (-x, -y, -z)$, it would still orbit clockwise, as depicted in Figure 13. By the same token, the direction of spin (intrinsic angular momentum) is unaffected by a parity inversion. Now consider the β^+ decay in Figure 14(a). The neutrino and positron move in opposite directions and carry away from the nucleus 1 unit of angular momentum (their spins are aligned). What happens if we change parity? The spins of the nucleus, neutrino, and positron are unchanged, and the neutrino and positron move opposite their previous directions, as shown in Figure 14(b). If nature were always the same under a parity inversion, this process should occur with equal probability—but it doesn't. We say that the weak interaction is not invariant under a parity inversion.

Just as parity inversion replaces all spatial coordinates with their opposite, **charge conjugation** replaces all particles with their antiparticles. For example, the diagrams of Figure 14 would become those of Figure 15. In the β^+ decay of Figure 14(a), a proton in the nucleus emits a positron. In Figure 15(a) an antiproton emits an electron. Actually doing the latter experiment would require antiatoms. (Only recently has even the simplest one, antihydrogen, become readily available.) However, for reasons discussed shortly, we expect the process in Figure 15(a) to be just as unlikely as the one in Figure 14(b). We say that the weak interaction is not invariant under charge conjugation. On the other hand, the *combined* operation of parity inversion and charge conjugation produces the decay in Figure 15(b), which we *would* expect to see. With some rare exceptions, to be discussed later in the section, the weak interaction seems to be invariant under the product of the two transformations, referred to as a *CP* transformation (*C* for charge conjugation, *P* for parity).

Figure 13 If all points on an arrow are redrawn at points on the opposite side of the origin, the rotation direction is unchanged. Parity inversion does not change the direction of angular momentum.

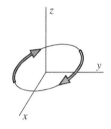

Figure 14 (a) A nucleus losing 1 unit of spin in β^+ decay. (b) The process viewed with parity reversed. Angular momenta are unchanged, but velocities are opposite.

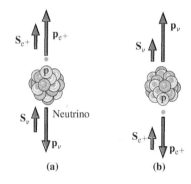

Figure 15 (a) The β^+ decay of Figure 14 under charge conjugation, all particles changed to antiparticles. (b) The same process viewed with parity reversed.

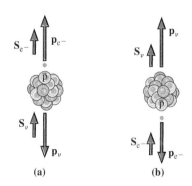

A common way of explaining the asymmetry of the weak force is to appeal to the **helicity** of the neutrino. Helicity refers to the orientation of a particle's spin relative to its momentum. Electrons do not have a definite helicity. Suppose an electron moves in the $+z$ direction at 500 m/s with spin up; that is, spin and momentum aligned. In a frame moving at 1000 m/s in the $+z$ direction relative to the first, the electron is moving at 500 m/s in the *negative* direction and is spin up, so that its spin and momentum are antialigned. The spin and momentum of the same electron can be either aligned or antialigned, depending on the frame of reference. A massless particle, on the other hand, moves at c in any frame. Because it cannot be overtaken, if its spin and momentum are aligned in one frame, they must be aligned in all frames. In the Standard Model, neutrinos are massless, so they would have definite helicities. The neutrino would always have its spin opposite its momentum—referred to as left-handed—which explains why the decay in Figure 14(b) would not occur. The neutrino would have an antiparticle—the antineutrino—which would be right-handed, with its spin parallel to its momentum. In Figure 15, in which particles have been changed to antiparticles, the particle produced with the electron would have to be the antineutrino. Thus, Figure 15(a) would not be observed, and Figure 15(b) would be.

One problem with the explanation is that neutrinos apparently do have mass. The evidence comes from **neutrino oscillations**, the ability of one kind of neutrino to change into another. This phenomenon was first documented at the Super Kamiokande facility, located in Japan and operated jointly with the United States. As noted earlier, the neutrino interacts only via the weak force, which makes it extremely difficult to catch (see Exercise 49). Located 1 km underground to shield it from cosmic rays, the Super Kamiokande is essentially a huge water tank, as shown in Figure 16. Thousands of Cerenkov detectors, each employing a photomultiplier tube, watch for the light generated by charged particles scattered by rare neutrino interactions. Research at another immense facility, the Sudbury Neutrino Observatory in Canada, has recently confirmed that a long irksome shortfall in the observed neutrino flux from the sun relative to the predicted flux is due to neutrino oscillations. Unfortunately, neutrino oscillations tell us only the *differences* in neutrino masses, not what those masses actually are. Another factor related to neutrino mass has great bearing on the explanation of parity violation. Considerable doubt has arisen lately on the question of whether there really is a difference between a neutrino and an antineutrino. Obviously, a full understanding of the weak interactions will have to await the answers to these questions. The neutrino has become one of the most active research topics in physics.

As noted above, the weak interaction is not always invariant even under the combined *CP* transformation. The first violation was discovered in 1964 by James Cronin and Val Fitch (Nobel Prize, 1980), who found that in 0.3% of instances, the K_L^0 meson decays weakly in a way that is not invariant under *CP*. Decades of intense study did little to shed light on this enigmatic phenomenon. With higher-energy accelerators producing heavier particles, attention shifted to decays of B^0 ($b\bar{d}$) and $\overline{B^0}$ mesons, which should behave much the same as the K mesons but with fewer unrelated decays to obscure the results. Finally in 2001, conclusive evidence of *CP* violation in these decays was

Figure 16 The 1 km deep Super Kamiokande neutrino detector in Japan, 40 m in diameter and over 50 m tall. In the inset, workers in an inflatable boat (center) make an inspection as refilling goes on. The globes are photomultiplier tubes—thousands of eyes to watch for light.

found. Much has yet to be learned, and it is of great importance, for *CP* violation is thought to hold the key to another asymmetry: the apparent imbalance between matter and antimatter in the universe.

Finally, **time reversal** replaces t with $-t$. In effect, to view the time-reversed result of a given process would be to view a motion picture of the process run backward. Almost without exception, microscopic processes are time-reversal invariant. They obey the same laws of physics whether time moves forward or backward. A general result of quantum field theory is the **CPT theorem**, which states that under the combined operations of charge conjugation (*C*), parity inversion (*P*), and time reversal (*T*), all interactions are invariant. Absolutely no exceptions to this symmetry of nature have ever been found. It follows that if processes are invariant under the combined operation *CP*, they *must* be invariant under *T*. On the other hand, if a process is not invariant under *CP*, it cannot be under *T*, so all *CP* violations are automatically exceptions to microscopic time-reversal invariance. It has often been taken for granted in physics that laws governing microscopic processes should be obeyed equally well backward as forward in time, so these violations are intriguing indeed.

7 Unified Theories and Cosmology

In recent years, the areas of high-energy physics and cosmology have been drawing ever closer. The primary reason is that the study of the universe and its history may be one of the best ways to understand fundamental interactions, for it seems that the ultimate high-energy experiment was the Big Bang. In this section, after briefly surveying some of the most promising unified theories, we resume the study of cosmology and tie in some of the physics we have learned since.

The low-energy symmetry breaking that is responsible for the schism in the electroweak force may shed light on the pattern for the unification of *all* forces. Many physicists believe that the strong and electroweak interactions are really asymmetric manifestations of the same interaction, and that their equivalence becomes apparent only at particle energies even higher than the level at which the electromagnetic and weak converge. Similarly, this unified interaction may converge with the gravitational interaction at yet higher energies.

A theory in which the strong and electroweak forces appear as one is known as a **grand unified theory**, or **GUT**. At present, various competing theories are being pursued. To establish its validity, a new theory must, of course, agree with existing evidence, but it must also either explain the previously unexplainable or make new predictions that can be experimentally verified. Present GUTs have not been particularly successful in either regard, so they remain "mere" theories.

One of the most provocative predictions of GUTs is proton decay. As we know, conservation of baryon number is presently accepted as applying to all decays. If true, the proton must be stable, for there is no lighter baryon into which it might decay. But in GUTs, the barrier between quark and lepton is broken down, and the proton is liable to decay into electrons plus pions, photons, or other light particles. However, the predicted lifetime is invariably greater than 10^{30} s, or 10^{22} years. To put this in perspective, cosmologists speculate that the age of the universe is 10^{10} years. Thus, to have any hope of succeeding, experiments dedicated to finding proton decay have employed gigantic quantities of matter, are maintained for many years, and are buried deep below the ground to reduce cosmic-ray noise. Several facilities throughout the world have been in continuous operation since the early 1980s. Despite the hopes of theorists and vigilance of experimentalists, no proton decay has yet been substantiated. Rather, the value for the minimum possible lifetime of the proton has progressively increased. It is now known to be greater than 10^{32} s.

Another prediction of GUTs is the existence of magnetic monopoles, which should be very massive. Efforts to find these have also failed. On the bright side, GUTs, unlike the Standard Model, predict nonzero neutrino mass, which is now established. The quest to unify the strong and electroweak forces continues. As the yet mysterious asymmetry that breaks the electroweak into electromagnetic and weak parts is expected to disappear at particle energies above about 1 TeV, it is speculated that the strong and electroweak forces might converge at around 10^{12} TeV. Note that this is a fantastically high energy—a megajoule (a car at 100 mph) per elementary particle!

The prospect of unifying gravity with the other forces was gloomy for a long time. Gravity is a very tough problem. To give some measure of the difficulty, Einstein himself, driven by tantalizing similarities; spent much of his later years attempting to unify gravitation with electromagnetism—without success. However, although quantum gravity still lacks experimental evidence such as the graviton, recent theoretical advances offer reasonable hope for the future. A promising direction for the unification of all forces is **superstring theory**, in which the fundamental particles of the universe are one-dimensional "strings" of extraordinarily small size, on the order of 10^{-33} m, the so-called **Planck length**. What makes the theory "super" is that it incorporates **supersymmetry**, in which each fundamental fermion would have a bosonic supersymmetric partner, and vice versa. For the electron, there would be the (boson) selectron; for each quark, a (boson) squark; for the photon, the (fermion) photino; for the graviton, the (fermion) gravitino; and so forth. There would also be multiple Higgs particles. Space would consist of 10 dimensions rather than just 4, with the extra ones "curled up" and largely hidden from view. Alas, no supersymmetric partners have been detected, and there is as yet no experimental verification of superstring theory. A theory that goes beyond a GUT, by also incorporating gravity, is often referred to as a theory of everything (TOE). At what particle energies might gravitation unite with the strong-electroweak force? Who knows!

Back to Cosmology

Because gravity is the only fundamental interaction that is both long range and of one sign (attractive only), it is by far the most important force in the motion of the things we see in the heavens today. But things would have been quite different in the early moments following a Big Bang. At such an unimaginably high energy density and temperature, one superunified force may have governed all. Only later, with decreasing density and lower average particle energy, could asymmetries creep into the picture and the one force manifest itself as many. Before we discuss conditions near the Big Bang, which are necessarily the most speculative, let us take a look at more recent events.

The Universe Expands

A watershed event was the decoupling of light from matter, for it has left us a very revealing sign. When particle energies were higher than typical atomic binding energies, matter would have consisted not of neutral atoms, but of a plasma of electrons and positive ions. These charged particles would have interacted strongly with the electromagnetic energy permeating the universe, and an equilibrium would have existed. However, when the temperature of the universe dropped to about 3000 K, at which $k_B T$ approaches atomic binding energies, so much matter formed neutral atoms that the infrequent remaining interactions were no longer able to keep photons in equilibrium with the matter. It is said that the photons were "frozen out." They embarked upon their random, independent journeys, contributing to the universe a blackbody spectrum characteristic of the 3000 K temperature at which they ceased to interact. Such radiation seen today was produced in equilibrium with the plasma very far away, very long ago. But the universe was expanding even then, and this distant plasma would have been receding from Earth at a significant fraction of c. Accordingly, the radiation received now is redshifted, so that it corresponds to a blackbody spectrum of much lower temperature. Confirmation of this scenario came in 1964, when A. A. Penzias and R. W. Wilson (Nobel Prize, 1978) discovered what we now know as the **cosmic microwave background** (CMB). Its 2.7 K temperature is famous, and the agreement with the theory of a universe expanding from a Big Bang is excellent.

Still, there are many unknowns in the expansion of the universe. We can begin to grasp some of the factors with a simple model: Consider a projectile of mass m launched straight upward from the surface of a planet of mass M. Its energy could be written as

$$E = \frac{1}{2}m\left(\frac{dr}{dt}\right)^2 - \frac{GMm}{r}$$

where r is its distance from the planet's center. If E is positive, the projectile escapes, for it has kinetic energy remaining when r is infinite—when the potential energy is zero. If E is negative, then r must still be finite when the kinetic energy drops to zero. The projectile would return. Zero energy is the dividing line. (This is the condition of escape velocity from classical mechanics.) Now suppose the planet explodes, expanding as a sphere of uniform but decreasing density in such a way that its outer edge is always at the very radius $r(t)$ of the projectile. The projectile's behavior would be exactly the same (by Gauss' law of gravitation), but we could replace M by density times volume.

$$E = \frac{1}{2}m\left(\frac{dr}{dt}\right)^2 - \frac{Gm\rho}{r}\frac{4}{3}\pi r^3$$

or, after rearranging a bit,

$$\left(\frac{dr/dt}{r}\right)^2 = \frac{8\pi G\rho}{3} + \frac{2E/m}{r^2} \tag{5}$$

This form is more general than it might seem. It would govern the behavior of every chunk of the exploding planet, provided no fragment ever overtakes another.

A conspicuously similar expression governing the expansion of the universe can be derived from Einstein's equations of general relativity. It is known as the **Friedmann equation**:

$$\left(\frac{dR/dt}{R}\right)^2 = \frac{8\pi G\rho}{3} - \frac{K}{R^2} \tag{6}$$

The quantity $R(t)$ is called the **scale factor** and is a measure of the size of the universe. The constant K is analogous to the projectile energy, but in general relativity, we refer to the overall curvature of space. If $K > 0$, space is positively curved, like the surface of a sphere, and the universe cannot spread out forever. It must eventually return to $R = 0$, much like a projectile with negative energy. If $K < 0$, giving space a negative curvature, like a saddle, expansion can continue indefinitely.

The density of matter decreases as the universe expands. An easy way to account for this is to define R as 1 at the present age of the universe, in which case the density of matter is ρ_M/R^3, where ρ_M is the matter density now. As we make this change to the Friedmann equation, we add one other density, ρ_Λ. We will have more to say about this later. For now, we simply note that it is a constant, independent of R, and thus has the weird property of not dissipating as the universe expands.

$$\left(\frac{dR/dt}{R}\right)^2 = \frac{8\pi G\rho_M}{3R^3} + \frac{8\pi G\rho_\Lambda}{3} - \frac{K}{R^2}$$

To put the Friedmann equation in a final convenient form, we redefine our mass and time units to absorb some constants and set dR/dt to 1 at the present age.

$$\left(\frac{dR/dt}{R}\right)^2 = \frac{\Omega_M}{R^3} + \Omega_\Lambda - \frac{K'}{R^2} \qquad R_{\text{present}} = 1 \qquad (dR/dt)_{\text{present}} = 1 \qquad \text{Friedmann equation}$$

$$\tag{7}$$

This equation suggests vastly different behaviors depending on the three parameters Ω_M, Ω_Λ, and K'. The universe appears to be flat, meaning that $K' = 0$. But even this allows great variation. Suppose we dispense with Ω_Λ. If we simply evaluate equation (7) at the present age, we see that $\Omega_M = 1$. In the units we have adopted, the matter density for which the universe is flat—the **critical density**—is conveniently 1. It is left as an exercise to show that in this case, if we choose the present time to be 1, the actual solution is $R(t) = \left[\frac{3}{2}(t - \frac{1}{3})\right]^{2/3}$. The universe would expand forever, though at an ever-diminishing rate, as illustrated by curve A in Figure 17. The figure also plots t alone. This would represent a simple case in which the expansion rate was always what it is now and the "age of the universe" would be 1. Curve A shows that the actual age would be less, due to the backward gravitational pull.

The Friedmann equation has a fairly simple solution in the case just discussed. Although it is more difficult for nonzero Ω_Λ, this case cannot

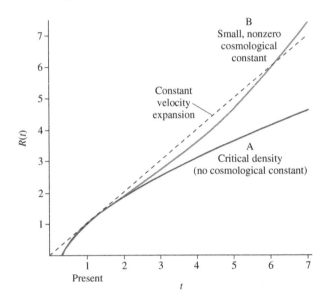

Figure 17 A critical universe of mass alone, curve A, would expand forever. Its beginning would be later than a constant-speed expansion at today's rate would suggest. A cosmological constant, curve B, can accelerate expansion.

be ignored. This weird density is the **cosmological constant** attached to space itself and undiluted as the universe spreads. As just one example of the possibilities, curve B in Figure 17 shows what would happen if the density at present were again critical, but with 1% being due to Ω_Λ. The curve looks very similar at early times, but Ω_Λ causes the universe later to expand *more* rapidly. In fact, it would eventually grow exponentially (see Exercise 52). Computational Exercise 54 lays out a method of solving the Friedmann equation numerically and looks at several interesting cases. The value of the cosmological constant is unknown, but it could explain a peculiar feature of the early universe—inflation.

Early Times

Although there will continue to be lively debate about many of the steps, there is some consensus on a rough chronology of events beginning with the Big Bang. Figure 18 illustrates the story. Immediately after $t = 0$, the universe was likely a firestorm of high-energy fundamental particles interacting at a feverish pace via their lone unified interaction. It would have been unimaginably small—orders of magnitude smaller than a nucleon. Very soon, however, a quick, tremendous expansion occurred, called **inflation**. This is the prevailing explanation for a "problem" in *today's* universe. The universe is actually very homogenous, suggesting an equilibrium. But its parts are much too far apart to have communicated, *unless* they were once in closer contact before undergoing a drastic expansion. We aren't sure what caused inflation, but a flareup in the cosmological constant is one possibility. Somewhere in this early period, spontaneous symmetry breaking would occur. First, gravity would sever its relationship with the

Figure 18 The genealogy of particles?

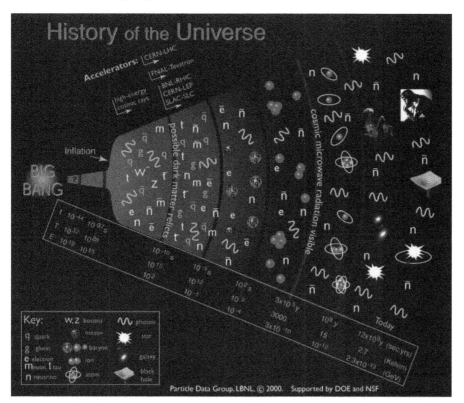

grand unified strong-electroweak force, striking out on its own at an early age. The next rebel would be the strong, splitting off from the electroweak. Cooling would continue, but so long as particle energies remained above about 1 TeV (10^3 GeV), there would still be plenty of energy to ensure an abundance of all three generations of fundamental fermions: the least massive tier (u, d, e, v_e), the middle (s, c, μ, v_μ), and the heaviest (b, t, τ, v_τ), along with their antiparticles. This hot mixture is sometimes called the quark-lepton soup.

By perhaps 10^{-12} s, average energies would have dropped to approximately 1 TeV, whereupon the electromagnetic and weak forces would part company, thus beginning the four-force, asymmetric behavior we observe today. This is roughly at the limit of experimentally attainable energies. At around $1-10$ μs and $1-0.1$ GeV, the heavier fermions would have become increasingly scarce, for they are liable to decay to lighter particles, and available energies would be insufficient to renew the supply. Below this limit, the universe would consist mostly of nucleons and light leptons. After several minutes, average energy would have dropped to ~1 MeV. This is roughly the binding energy per nucleon in the atomic nucleus, so nuclei would form. At around a million years and a temperature of 3000 K, as noted above, atoms would form. Heavenly bodies arrive on the scene much later.

Conclusion

At present, we have a fairly pleasing view of fundamental particles and interactions: six quarks, six leptons, and three forces. But many questions remain: Just how does the asymmetry in the electroweak interaction come about? Will the Higgs be found? Does it explain mass? Will a theory encompassing all forces be established, and what will it tell us about the universe? What really happened right after the Big Bang? Was a united force shared by particles more fundamental than quarks and leptons? Are there other fundamental forces? Exciting discoveries lie ahead.

PROGRESS AND APPLICATIONS

Producing a Quark-Gluon Plasma Presently the world's most-powerful accelerator of ions is the Relativistic Heavy Ion Collider (RHIC) at Brookhaven National Laboratory. It smashes gold ions together at a tremendous 100 GeV per nucleon. Such a ferocious impact of many nucleons is said to "melt" neutrons and protons for an instant into a quark-gluon plasma, much like conditions in the early universe. A very interesting phenomenon observed at RHIC is jet quenching, in which jets produced in fairly simple collisions appear to be smothered by a swarm of subsequent collisions in the furious mass of quarks and gluons. Further study should tell us much about these constituents of the nucleons. RHIC may also help solve the **spin crisis**, a persistent puzzle in high-energy physics. Although its three spin-$\frac{1}{2}$ quarks contribute to the overall spin of the proton, experimental evidence in the 1980s showed that they account for less than a third. Plausible candidates for making up the difference include orbital motion, angular momenta of the spin-1 gluons, and the quark-antiquark pairs appearing and disappearing within the proton's lively interior.

A Conservation Law Hangs in the Balance A rare form of radioactive decay is double beta decay. In a peculiar leapfrog, a nucleus that cannot beta decay, because the would-be daughter is *heavier*, can emit two beta particles at once if the daughter at the end of the double process is lighter than the original parent. Just as a neutrino is produced in ordinary beta decay, double beta decay produces two neutrinos. However, one of the hottest quests in high-energy physics today is *neutrinoless* double beta decay. The traditional view of beta decay, in harmony with conservation of lepton number, is that when a nucleus undergoes β^- decay, the electron, of $L_e = +1$, must be joined by an *anti*neutrino of $L_e = -1$. But so far as we know, the neutrino *may* be its own antiparticle, and if it is, the accounting fails. Moreover, the neutrino produced in the "first" decay of a double beta decay could, in effect, annihilate with the neutrino from the second, leaving just two electrons to be ejected from the nucleus. A report of neutrinoless double beta decay has been published, but the evidence is not yet considered conclusive. If it can be substantiated, an actual value for neutrino mass—vexingly unavailable from neutrino oscillation studies—may follow, as well as substantial rethinking of the Standard Model.

Dark Energy The term **dark energy** is heard much nowadays and refers to the deficit between the critical density and the matter density of the universe. The universe appears to be critical, or flat, but matter density, both luminous and dark, appears to account for only about 35% of the critical value. What about the other 65%? Little is known, but theories abound. One proposed candidate is "quintessence," an unseen form of energy that could vary with position and time. However, the more common view is that dark energy is synonymous with the cosmological constant, which still doesn't provide much help. This constant wouldn't stretch thinner with the growing universe, but would be something special to the very vacuum of space itself. Theories of electromagnetic vacuum fluctuations have been quite successful in explaining Earthly behaviors. But calculations of the cosmological constant based in part on similar assumptions are a bit off—too large by more than 100 orders of magnitude. String theory, which hopes to unify all the forces, is also chiming in on this problem. Some versions of string theory offer a possible explanation, though accompanied by legions of other dimensions and alternative universes. Dark energy is one of the biggest mysteries in modern physics today.

Chapter Summary

The study of fundamental particles and their interactions, known as particle physics or high-energy physics, is the quest to understand the physical universe on the most basic level possible. At this level, interactions between particles occur in discrete events. Fundamental fermions share a force by exchanging a mediating boson, or field quantum.

Each fundamental particle has an antiparticle with the same mass and spin as the particle but of opposite charge. Antiparticles are predicted by relativistic quantum mechanics.

At present, physics recognizes three fundamental forces. Each involves a property required to engage in that force, and each has its own mediating boson(s). In order of decreasing strength, they are the strong force, the electroweak force, and the gravitational force.

The strong force requires the property of color charge, which can be red, green, or blue. The fundamental fermions with this property, called quarks, come in three pairs: the u and d, the c and s, and the t and b. The mediating boson is the gluon. Separated individual quarks have never been found. The smallest gluon-bound units are quark-antiquark mesons and three-quark baryons, known collectively as hadrons. The proton and neutron are baryons of quark content uud and udd, respectively. In a nucleus, all nucleons attract each other via a coarse manifestation of the strong force known as the residual strong force. The property required for the electroweak force is charge/weak charge. Besides quarks, leptons possess this property. There are three pairs of leptons: (e^-, ν_e), (μ^-, ν_μ), and (τ^-, ν_τ). The mediating bosons are the massless photon, associated with the electromagnetic part, and three very massive weak bosons $W^\pm$ and Z^0, associated with the weak part. The asymmetry between the two parts is not fully understood. Gravitation is an attractive force that pulls on all energy and so is felt by all particles. The presumed mediating boson, the graviton, has not yet been found.

Decays and other interactions between particles are governed by numerous conservation rules. Some rules are obeyed in only certain kinds of decays.

Many physicists believe that today's three forces will one day be revealed as merely different aspects of one fundamental interaction. The unification is expected to be apparent only at extremely high particle energies. Advances in cosmology may clarify the picture, for it is believed that the universe began with a Big Bang, in which all forces were one.

---

* indicates advanced questions

Conceptual Questions

1. Explain to your friend, who has just completed a study of classical electromagnetism, the term *field quantum*.

2. The increase in potential energy as two atoms in a diatomic molecule get closer is partly due to the core electrons being forced by the exclusion principle to higher energies. Can you argue why the residual strong force—the internucleon attraction should have a "hard core"?

3. Why could it be argued that the range of the strong force should be infinite, and why isn't it?

4. We have noted that photons don't interact with photons electrostatically but that gluons can interact with gluons. Should gravitons self-interact? Explain.

5. What does color neutrality have to do with quark confinement?

6. Does the requirement of color neutrality for a real particle prohibit the existence of hadrons containing four quarks? Five quarks? Any number? If so, why? If not, what rules would apply?

7. Identify a process that exhibits *CT* violation and explain how you know that it does. Is violation of time-reversal invariance (*T*) in any way strange for a *macroscopic* process?

8. Equation (5) would apply to any given chunk of an expanding spherical mass, provided that no chunks overtake any others—if, for instance, speed increases with distance from the origin. Why? (Think of Gauss' law from electrostatics.)

Exercises

Section 1

9. From the experimental evidence that the force between nucleons has a range of about 1 fm, obtain a rough value (in MeV/c^2) for the mass of the particle exchanged to convey this force, the pion.

10. From the masses of the weak bosons given in Table 1, show that the range of the weak part of the electroweak force should be about 10^{-3} fm.

11. Someone proposes the existence of a new force whose range is 10^{-20} m. We found that accelerators turn kinetic energy into mass. About how much energy do you estimate an accelerator would need to create the mediating particle for such a force?

Section 2

12. As in electron-positron annihilation, when a proton and antiproton annihilate, two photons can be produced. Of what wavelength are these photons? (Assume that the pair is initially at rest.)

13. To show that the Klein-Gordon equation has valid solutions for negative values of E, verify that equation (4) is satisfied by a wave function of the form

$$\Psi(x, t) = Ae^{\pm ipx/\hbar \pm iEt/\hbar}$$

* **14.** (a) Show that $\Psi_1(x, t) = Ae^{ikx-i\omega t}$ is a solution of both the Klein-Gordon and the Schrödinger equations.

(b) Show that $\Psi_2(x, t) = Ae^{ikx} \cos \omega t$ is a solution of the Klein-Gordon but not of the Schrödinger equation.

(c) Show that Ψ_2 is a combination of positive and negative energy solutions of the Klein-Gordon equation (see Exercise 13).

(d) Compare the time dependence of $|\Psi|^2$ for Ψ_1 and Ψ_2.

15. For solutions of the Klein-Gordon equation, the quantity

$$i\Psi * \frac{\partial}{\partial t} \Psi - i\Psi \frac{\partial}{\partial t} \Psi *$$

is interpreted as charge density. Show that for a positive-energy plane-wave solution (see Exercise 13), it is a real constant, and for the negative-energy solution, it is the negative of that constant.

* **16.** In nonrelativistic quantum mechanics, governed by the Schrödinger equation, the total probability of finding a particle does not change with time.

(a) Prove it. Begin with the time derivative of the total probability:

$$\frac{d}{dt} \int \Psi * (x, t) \Psi(x, t) \, dx$$

$$= \int \left(\Psi(x, t) \frac{\partial}{\partial t} \Psi * (x, t) \right.$$

$$\left. + \Psi*(x, t) \frac{\partial}{\partial t} \Psi(x, t) \right) dx$$

Then use the Schrödinger equation to eliminate the partial time derivatives in favor of partial spatial derivatives, integrate by parts, and show that the result is 0. Assume that the particle is reasonably well localized, so that Ψ and $\partial \Psi/\partial x$ are 0 when evaluated at $\pm\infty$.

(b) Does this procedure lead to the same conclusion if the wave function must obey the Klein-Gordon rather than the Schrödinger equation? Why or why not?

Section 3

17. The electron energy mentioned in Section 3 for deep inelastic scattering experiments is 20 GeV, and the momentum is given as 20 GeV/c. Why so simple a conversion?

18. Approximately what energy would electrons need to have to be useful as probes that could reveal features as small as 10^{-18} m, the approximate range of the weak force?

19. Suppose a force between two particles decreases with distance according to $F = k/r^b$. What is the limit on b if the energy required to separate the particles infinitely far is not to be infinite?

20. Trying to pull two quarks apart would produce more quarks in groups, or hadrons. Suppose that when the separation reaches 1 fm (the approximate radius of a nucleon), the lightest hadron, a π^0, is created.

(a) Roughly how much force is involved? (b) Compare this with the electrostatic force between two fundamental charges the same distance apart. Does your result agree with the strengths in Table 1?

21. For which particles does Table 2 show both particle and antiparticle? Which particles are their own antiparticle?

22. Symmetries are compelling in physics. The properties of the particles in Table 2 show some interesting ones. (a) Make a two-dimensional plot, with strangeness along the vertical axis and the third component of isospin I_3 on the horizontal. Add spots representing the Δ^{++} and the nine other baryons below it in Table 2. (b) Are properties other than strangeness and I_3 correlated?

Section 4

23. To produce new particles, accelerators often smash two equal-mass objects together—proton and proton or electron and positron. The threshold energy is the kinetic energy before the collision needed simply to produce the final particles—their mass/internal energy alone, with no leftover kinetic energy. Consider a colliding-beam accelerator in which two initial particles of mass m are moving at the same speed relative to the lab. Assume that the total mass of the (stationary) particles after the collision is M. Show that the threshold energy is $(M - 2m)c^2$.

24. Exercise 23 discusses the threshold energy for two particles of mass m in a colliding-beam accelerator to produce a final stationary mass M. If the accelerator is instead a stationary-target type, more initial kinetic energy is needed to produce the same final mass. Show that the threshold energy is $(M^2/2m - 2m)c^2$. The calculation is greatly streamlined by using the momentum-energy invariant.

The main point is that the quantity $(E_{\text{total}}/c)^2 - P_{\text{total}}^2$ must be the same not only before and after the collision but also in any reference frame. The quick approach is to equate this quantity *after* the collision in the center-of-mass frame, where the final mass is stationary, to its value *before* the collision in the lab frame, where the target is stationary. You will need to use $E^2 = p^2c^2 + m^2c^4$ to eliminate the moving particle's momentum in the lab frame.

25. Exercises 23 and 24 give the threshold energies for which two particles of mass m can produce a given mass M in colliding-beam and stationary-target accelerators, respectively. Evaluate the two for a collision in which two protons become three protons and one antiproton. How much more energy is needed for the stationary target?

26. A lead nucleus at rest is roughly 10^{-14} m in diameter. If moving through the laboratory with a kinetic energy of 600 TeV, how thick would the nucleus be in the direction of motion?

27. The classical magnetic force formula $F = qvB$ is correct relativistically. But if a magnetic field is to keep a high-energy charged particle moving in a circle, it must satisfy the relativistically correct relationship between force and centripetal acceleration, $F = \gamma_v m(v^2/r)$. (a) To keep a 1 TeV proton in a 1 km radius circle, as is done at the Tevatron, how strong must the magnetic field be? (b) How large would the radius have to be for magnets of the same strength to keep a 20 TeV proton in a circle?

Section 5

28. Although not truly fundamental, the residual strong force shared by nucleons can also be represented by a Feynman diagram, with the pion filling the role of mediating boson. The accompanying diagram represents a force between a neutron and a proton mediated by a π^0 boson. Suggest a diagram in which they exchange a π^- particle. (We demand that there be a neutron and a proton only at the start and finish.)

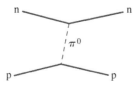

29. Table 2 gives the "width" of the K^{*0} meson. (a) Approximately what is its lifetime? (b) This meson's actual radius is on the order of 1 fm. Would its constituents have time to "bounce around inside" a great deal?

30. Sketch a Feynman vertex for the creation of a $\overline{d}$ quark and c quark.

31. Sketch a Feynman vertex for the annihilation of a b quark and $\overline{u}$.

32. (a) What is the quark content of the antineutron? (b) Sketch the Feynman diagram for its β decay.

In the following exercises, indicate whether the proposed decay is possible. If it is not possible, indicate which rules are violated. Consider only charge, energy, angular momentum, strangeness, and lepton and baryon numbers. If the decay is possible, indicate whether it is a strong, electromagnetic, or weak decay, and sketch a Feynman diagram.

33. $\tau^+ \rightarrow e^+ + \nu_e + \overline{\nu}_\tau$
34. $\mu^+ \rightarrow e^+ + \nu_e$
35. $\overline{n} \rightarrow p + e^- + \overline{\nu}_e$
36. $\Xi^- \rightarrow \Lambda^0 + \pi^-$
37. $\Xi^{*-} \rightarrow \Sigma^0 + e^- + \nu_e$
38. $\Lambda^0 \rightarrow p + \pi^-$
39. $K^+ \rightarrow \mu^+ + \overline{\nu}_\mu$
40. $\Omega^- \rightarrow \Xi^0 + \pi^-$
41. $\Delta^+ \rightarrow \Sigma^+ + \pi^0 + \gamma$
42. $\pi^0 \rightarrow \mu^- + \overline{\nu}_\mu$

In the following exercises, two protons are smashed together in an attempt to convert kinetic energy into mass and new particles. Indicate whether the proposed reaction is possible. If not, indicate which rules are violated. Consider only those for charge, angular momentum, and baryon number. If the reaction is possible, calculate the minimum kinetic energy required of the colliding protons.

43. $p + p \rightarrow p + p + p + \overline{p}$
44. $p + p \rightarrow p + \overline{p} + n + \overline{n}$
45. $p + p \rightarrow p + p + n + \overline{n}$
46. $p + p \rightarrow p + K^+$
47. $p + p \rightarrow p + K^+ + \Lambda^0$
48. $p + p \rightarrow p + \Sigma^+ + K^0$

Section 6

49. If a neutrino interacted with a quark every time their separation was within the 10^{-18} m range generally accepted for the weak force, then the cross section of a neutron or proton "seen" by a neutrino would be on the order of 10^{-36} m^2. Even at such separation, however, the probability of interaction is quite small. The nucleon appears to have an effective cross section of only about 10^{-48} m^2. (a) About how many nucleons are there in a column through Earth's center of 1 m^2 cross-sectional area? (b) What is the probability that a given neutrino passing through space and encountering Earth will actually "hit"?

Section 7

50. Verify that if the universe were critical ($\Omega_M = 1$), "flat" ($K' = 0$), and free of a cosmological constant ($\Omega_\Lambda = 0$), then equation (7) would be satisfied by a scale factor $R(t)$ of $\left[\frac{3}{2}\left(t - \frac{1}{3}\right)\right]^{2/3}$.

51. Equation (7) assumes a matter-dominated universe, in which the energy density of radiation is insignificant. This situation prevails today and has to do with the different rates at which the densities of matter and radiation vary with the size of the universe. Matter density is simply inversely proportional to the volume, obeying ρ_M/R^3, where ρ_M is the matter density now. Radiation density, however, would be proportional to $1/R^4$. (Not only does the volume increase, but also all wavelengths are stretched in proportion to R, lowering the energy density by the extra factor.) This density drops faster as the universe grows, but it also grows more quickly in the backward time direction. In other words, long ago, the universe would have been radiation dominated. Show that if the function used for matter density in equation (7) is replaced by one appropriate to radiation, but retaining the assumption that K' and Ω_Λ are both 0, then the scale factor R would grow as $t^{1/2}$.

52. Show that the presence of a positive cosmological constant in Friedmann equation (7) must, as R becomes very large, lead to an exponential expansion of the universe.

53. You are a promising theoretical physicist who does not believe that gravity is a distinct fundamental force but is instead related to the other forces by an all-encompassing relativistic, quantum-mechanical theory. In particular, you do not believe that the universal gravitational constant G is really one of nature's elite set of fundamental constants. You believe that G can be *derived* from more-basic constants: the fundamental constant of quantum mechanics, Planck's constant h; the fundamental speed limiting the propagation of any force, the speed of light c; and one other—a fundamental length l, important to the one unified force. Using simply dimensional analysis, find a formula for G, then an order-of-magnitude value for the fundamental length.

Computational Exercises

54. Here we solve the Friedmann equation numerically and look at some interesting special cases. The first step is to convert the Friedmann equation to a second-order differential equation. If we multiply both sides of equation (7) by $R^2(t)$, take a time derivative of the whole equation, then cancel $dR(t)/dt$, the result is

$$\frac{d^2 R(r)}{dt^2} = -\frac{\Omega_M}{2R^2(t)} + \Omega_\Lambda R(t)$$

Equation comes from the Schrödinger equation, which says that

$$\frac{d^2\psi(x)}{dx^2} = -\frac{2m(E - U(x))}{\hbar^2}\psi(x)$$

Adapting to our problem thus gives

$$R(t + \Delta t)$$
$$= 2R(t) - R(t - \Delta t) + \left(\frac{\Omega_M}{2R^2(t)} - \Omega_\Lambda R(t)\right)\Delta t^2$$

This would allow us to plot all values of $R(t)$ from a starting point at the present age, whose time we choose as 1. We would also like to look backward in time, and the modification is straightforward.

$$R(t - \Delta t)$$
$$= 2R(t) - R(t + \Delta t) + \left(\frac{\Omega_M}{2R^2(t)} - \Omega_\Lambda R(t)\right)\Delta t^2$$

Let us use 0.001 for Δt. Together with our choices in Section 7 that both R and its time rate of change are 1 at present, we thus have $R(1) = 1$, $R(1 + \Delta t) = 1.001$, and $R(1 - \Delta t) = 0.999$. Now we have everything needed to plot $R(t)$ both forward and backward from $t = 1$. However, with an $R(t)$ in the denominator above, a 0 value could cause trouble. So incorporate into your program instructions that (1) will assign 0 to any "new" value of $R(t)$ that the equation might cause to be *less* than 0, and (2) will check to see if a *previous* value is 0, and if so, simply assign 0 to the new value. With these instructions, your computer will never actually try to divide by 0. If your universe ever shrinks to 0, it will just stay there.

The values we now input and check are those of Ω_M and Ω_Λ. Plotting from $t = 1$ to $t = -2$ and from $t = 1$ to $t = 18$ (except as noted), consider the following values of $[\Omega_M, \Omega_\Lambda]$, and in each case discuss your findings. (a) [1, 0] (b) [0.6, 0] (c) [1.4, 0] (d) [0, 1], with an upper limit of $t = 4$ (e) [0.95, 0.05], with an upper limit of $t = 8$ (f) [0.6, 0.01] (g) [1.4, 0.01] (h) [0.5, 2], with an upper limit of $t = 3$.

Answers to Selected Exercises

9. $197 \text{ MeV}/c^2$

11. ~20 TeV

19. $b > 1$

21. mesons, π^0 and ρ^0

25. colliding beam $2m_p c^2$, stationary target $6m_p c^2$

27. 3.4 T, 20 km

29. $\sim 10^{-23}$ s

33. weak

35. baryon number not conserved

37. lepton number not conserved

39. lepton number not conserved

41. energy conservation would be violated

43. 1876 MeV

45. 1880 MeV

47. 672 MeV

49. (a) $\sim 4 \times 10^{37}$; (b) $\sim 4 \times 10^{-11}$

53. $c^3 l^2 / h$, 4×10^{-35} m

Credits

Photograph Credits

5: CERN; **6:** Stanford Linear Accelerator Center; **7:** Fermilab National Accelarator Laboratory; **16:** Kamioka Observatory, ICRR (Institute for Cosmic Ray Research), The University of Tokyo; **18:** Lawrence Berkeley National Laboratory

Art Credits

4: Courtesy of Kevin McClean, CERN High School Teachers Program; **18:** Courtesy of the Particle Data Group at Lawrence Berkeley National Laboratory

Nuclear Physics

Chapter Outline

Although all atoms contain nuclei, studying the "atom" usually means focusing on the behavior of its orbiting electrons. The nuclei are assumed to be essentially inert. But nuclei are not always inert. For one thing, they can fragment, spontaneously or otherwise, and such nuclear reactions release enormous amounts of energy compared to chemical reactions. In nuclear physics, it is the orbiting electrons that are of little concern. It is true that they are bound to the nuclei, but compared with the energies within the nucleus, electron binding energies are usually negligible. The nucleus is the focus. Unfortunately, it is a hard problem to solve. While much has been learned, nuclear physics continues to be an active area of research.

The importance of nuclear physics cannot be overstated. It explains the operation of nuclear reactors and nuclear weapons; nuclear magnetic resonance is routinely used to produce images of the body's interior; and radioactivity—energetic particles emanating from nuclei—is both a useful diagnostic tool, via radioactive tracing and dating, and a mounting disposal problem, as we continue to unearth and artificially produce more radioactive materials. Moreover, the study of nuclear physics is an essential step in our quest to unravel the fundamental structure of the physical universe.

1 Basic Structure

All nuclei consist of protons and neutrons, known collectively as **nucleons**. Masses are given in Table 1. Introducing important symbols, Figure 1 depicts a helium atom—two electrons orbiting a nucleus of two protons and two neutrons. We use the symbol N for the number of neutrons and Z, the

From Chapter 11 of *Modern Physics*, Second Edition. Randy Harris. Copyright © 2008 by Pearson Education, Inc.
Published by Pearson Addison-Wesley. All rights reserved.

Figure 1 A crude picture of helium.

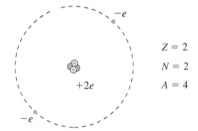

$Z = 2$
$N = 2$
$A = 4$

TABLE 1 Basic masses

	Charge	Mass
Proton	$+e$	$1.6726217 \times 10^{-27}$ kg $= 1.007276$ u
Neutron	0	$1.6749273 \times 10^{-27}$ kg $= 1.008665$ u
Electron	$-e$	9.109×10^{-31} kg $= 5.486 \times 10^{-4}$ u

atomic number, for the number of protons. The symbol A, called the **mass number**, is the total number of nucleons.

An element's chemical behavior depends only on the number of electrons orbiting its nucleus, equal to Z. But *nuclei* of the same element rarely behave alike if they have different numbers of neutrons. For instance, while the nucleus of ordinary hydrogen is simply a proton, about 0.015% of hydrogen atoms in nature have nuclei consisting of a proton plus a neutron. Known as deuterium, or heavy hydrogen, this atom is roughly twice as massive as ordinary hydrogen. Deuterium participates in chemical reactions—rearrangements of orbiting electrons—precisely like ordinary hydrogen, making chemical separation of the two problematic. However, it participates in *nuclear* reactions—rearrangements of nucleons—in vastly different ways.

Nuclei with the same number of protons but different numbers of neutrons are said to be **isotopes** of the same element. Thus, we say that there are two naturally occurring isotopes of hydrogen—ordinary hydrogen and deuterium, depicted in Figure 2. Both are **stable**, remaining unchanged indefinitely. Hydrogen has a third isotope, tritium, with one proton and two neutrons in the nucleus. While it can be produced artificially, it is essentially absent in nature because it is **unstable**, meaning that it is subject to a spontaneous nuclear reaction that changes it to a different element, known as radioactive decay. We often use the convention element-A to refer to different isotopes, but hydrogen is a special case. Although we could speak of hydrogen-1, hydrogen-2, and hydrogen-3, we usually use the names hydrogen (understood to be $A = 1$), deuterium, and tritium.

Helium has two naturally occurring isotopes: helium-3 (two protons, one neutron) and the more abundant helium-4 (two protons, two neutrons).

Figure 2 Isotopes of hydrogen.

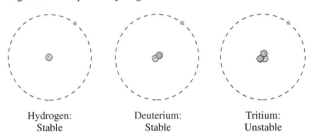

Hydrogen:
Stable

Deuterium:
Stable

Tritium:
Unstable

Carbon-12 (six protons, six neutrons), the most abundant carbon isotope in nature, is the basis of a standard measure of mass. The **atomic mass unit** u is defined to be one-twelfth the mass of the carbon-12 atom, including electrons. Some elements have a host of naturally occurring isotopes. For example, tin has 10. Many, such as aluminum, have only one. Some have none; they aren't found in nature. Nonetheless, they may be produced artificially, or they may appear fleetingly from the radioactive decay of other nuclei. While no isotopes *absent* in nature are stable—at least, none has yet been artificially produced—some isotopes *present* in nature are unstable. For instance, uranium-238 and thorium-232 are both more abundant in nature than silver and do undergo radioactive decay, but they will be around a long time, for their half-lives are billions of years.

1 u = 1.660559 × 10^{-27} kg

Size

The first experiments to probe the nucleus, carried out by Ernest Rutherford and his colleagues fired α particles toward a thin foil of gold. (An α particle is the nucleus remaining when helium's electrons are stripped away.) The vast majority of α particles passed through the foil undeflected. They missed! A few bounced backward. Evidently, these had encountered a compact, heavy, positively charged object—the nucleus. The size of the nucleus was determined by increasing the α particle's speed. In short, the idea is that an α particle approaching a nucleus loses kinetic energy to electrostatic potential energy, and a head-on trajectory, as in Figure 3, would enable it to approach closest. At high enough initial speed, its closest approach would breach the nuclear surface, and the scattering would change in an obvious way, for the force would no longer be simply electrostatic repulsion.

Scattering experiments indicate that nuclei are roughly spherical, with radii obeying the approximate relation

Figure 3 Probing for the radius of the nucleus.

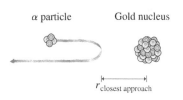

$$r = A^{1/3} \times R_0 \tag{1}$$

where A is the mass number and R_0 is 1.2×10^{-15} m. A femtometer (fm), 10^{-15} m, is thus a good measure of nuclear size. Typical *atomic* dimensions, defined by electron orbits, are 5 orders of magnitude larger. If the atom with its electron cloud were the size of a football stadium, its nucleus would be a bit smaller than a ladybug.

The dependence of radius on A in equation (1) is conspicuous. The nuclear volume is

Scale of nuclear dimensions:
1 fm = 10^{-15} m

$$V_{\text{total}} = \frac{4}{3}\pi r^3 = \frac{4}{3}\pi \left(A^{1/3}R_0\right)^3 = A \times \frac{4}{3}\pi R_0^3 \tag{2}$$

Because neutrons and protons have nearly equal mass, the fact that the volume is proportional to the number of nucleons means that it is proportional to the total mass. All nuclei have about the same density!

$$\rho = \frac{\text{mass}}{\text{volume}} = \frac{A \times m_{\text{nucleon}}}{A \times \frac{4}{3}\pi R_0^3}$$

$$\cong \frac{1.67 \times 10^{-27}\,\text{kg}}{\frac{4}{3}\pi(1.2 \times 10^{-15}\,\text{m})^3} \cong 10^{17}\,\text{kg/m}^3$$

(3)

Constant density, in turn, suggests that nucleons behave as incompressible objects packed as close together as possible. Although this view is oversimplified, experimental evidence confirms that nucleons have a strongly repulsive hard core. The volume allowed each nucleon in a close-packed arrangement would be the total volume divided by the total number A—that is, $\frac{4}{3}\pi R_0^3$. So we see that the effective radius of an individual nucleon is R_0, or about 1 fm.

2 Binding

If it is indeed true that the nucleus contains many protons close together, then it is natural to wonder what prevents it from exploding. To this there is a simple, if smug, answer: Another force is at play, an attractive force that holds the nucleons together. It certainly isn't gravitation. Simple calculations show that this attraction is woefully inadequate to hold protons so close together against their electrostatic repulsion. The "new" force is aptly named the **strong force**. Just as all particles endowed with mass attract one another gravitationally and those with charge attract or repel electromagnetically, all nucleons possess a property that causes them to attract one another via the strong force.

The strong force is one of nature's fundamental forces: gravitational, electromagnetic-weak, and strong. Actually, what we refer to in this chapter as the strong force is only an aspect of the strong force, for which we often use the descriptive term *internucleon attraction*. Table 2 compares the relative strengths of the fundamental forces, based on assumptions of typical charge, mass, separation, and so on. The strong force is not as easily characterized as the more-familiar forces. For one thing, it does not diminish gradually with particle separation, as do the $1/r^2$ forces. It is strong only for nucleon separations less than about 2 fm; that is, only when nucleons are not much farther apart than the effective nucleon diameter. At larger separations, the strong force is negligible. As we shall see, this plays an important role in the stability of the nucleus. Electrostatic repulsion, although weaker than the strong force at close range, becomes a significant destabilizing effect in larger nuclei, where protons are too far apart to attract via the strong force. (In no ordinary circumstance is gravitation significant. Weird, unearthly cases, such as neutron stars and black holes, are discussed elsewhere in the text.)

It might seem reasonable to *claim* that because the nucleus would otherwise explode, there must be another force hidden from our senses, but where is the proof? Much of our evidence comes from scattering experiments in which one nucleon is fired at another in all possible combinations: proton–proton, proton–neutron, neutron–neutron. The details of how they scatter

TABLE 2 Forces compared

Force	Relative Strength	Range
Strong	1	∼1 fm
Electromagnetic-Weak	∼10^{-2} ∼10^{-6}	Long: ∝ $1/r^2$ ∼10^{-3} fm
Gravitational	∼10^{-39}	Long: ∝ $1/r^2$

give us information about the nature of the force they share. Figure 4 depicts the strong-force potential energy shared by a nucleon at the origin and another at an arbitrary distance r, and it illustrates some of what we have learned. The strong force is attractive, though with an incompressible hard core, and it is short ranged and strong. We also find that whether it is between two protons, two neutrons, or a proton and a neutron, the attraction is very nearly identical. It does, however, depend on the orientation of the nucleon spins. Perhaps not surprisingly, there is no simple formula for this force, which indeed has yet to be fully characterized. Nonetheless, we can explain quite a bit from what we do know about it.

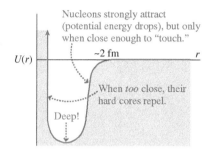

Figure 4 The basic elements of the internucleon (strong force) potential energy—a strong, short-range attraction with a repulsive hard core.

Stability: A Theoretical Model

With all nucleons engaging in an extremely strong attraction, we might imagine that we could bring together any combination and have a stable nucleus. However, the vast majority would be unstable, disintegrating in a time span ranging from an instant to an eon. A few would be stable.

The following discussion of nuclear stability may seem rather speculative, but the complex forces in the nucleus have defied formulation of a comprehensive theory, so we must resort to a model—well-informed but simplified guesswork. In a later section, we discuss well-established models that refine the one we begin here, but it is good to gain a qualitative understanding of the various factors first. As we do, we won't speculate whether any particular combination of nucleons should actually be stable; we will simply argue whether a given factor should *tend* to make the combination more stable or less stable. A nucleus is more stable when its constituents are bound in a state of lower energy, requiring a greater expenditure of energy to extract a representative nucleon. Energy is all-important.

Two-Nucleon Nuclei

The simplest possible combinations of nucleons are two protons (p–p), two neutrons (n–n), and a proton–neutron pair (p–n). Which should be most stable? Let us look at the factors. The short-range strong attraction should create something like a narrow but deep potential energy well, and if the force doesn't "care" whether the particles are protons or neutrons, the well should be the same for all three combinations. This condition is no guarantee that any would hold together—wells can be too shallow to have any bound states —but at least they should all be the same. On the other hand, the p–p combination would include Coulomb repulsion between the protons, which would raise the energy, and this argues that it should be somewhat less stable than the other two.

These arguments are valid, but the truth is that only the p–n, known as a **deuteron**, forms a bound nucleus (that of the stable deuterium atom discussed earlier). The n–n and p–p don't stick together at all. Why? The internucleon attraction is spin-dependent, and it is stronger when spins are aligned. We will find that this dependence is less significant in larger nuclei, but here it calls into play another factor that is crucial in *all* nuclei: the exclusion principle.

Figure 5 The deuteron's neutron and proton bound in a well resulting from their attractive potential energy.

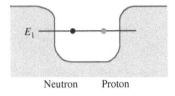

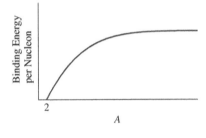

Figure 6 Binding energy per nucleon due to the strong internucleon attraction only. The smallest nuclei have few bonds per nucleon. In large nuclei, many nucleons are surrounded.

Figure 7 Coulomb repulsion raises proton energies.

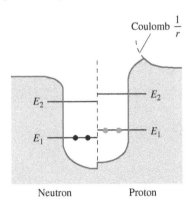

Protons and neutrons are spin-$\frac{1}{2}$ fermions, so they cannot occupy the same state in the same system. The lowest energy possible for two nucleons in a well should have both in the ground spatial state with their spins aligned (the orientation of stronger attraction), but such a state is forbidden to the p–p and n–n by the exclusion principle. Is this indeed why the p–n forms, but the p–p and n–n do not? Experimental evidence verifies that the deuteron is only barely bound; its potential well has no excited bound states, just the one ground state. Moreover, the neutron and proton spins *are* aligned (its total spin is 1). If the p–n cannot bind any other way—with spins opposite or with one nucleon in a higher spatial state—then the other two should *not* bind at all. The energy in the deuteron is depicted in Figure 5. (The repulsive nucleon cores are ignored.) Two nucleons occupy the lone bound state in a well that arises from their mutual attraction.

Arbitrary Nucleon Number

We now consider nuclei comprising any number of nucleons, addressing in turn the effects of the three main factors: the strong force, Coulomb repulsion, and the exclusion principle.

Strong Internucleon Attraction A two-nucleon nucleus has only one bond, but a three-nucleon nucleus has three. Thus, the former has half a bond *per nucleon* and the latter one bond per nucleon. A four-nucleon nucleus would have six bonds, or one-and-a-half bonds per nucleon, so a representative nucleon would be harder to extract than in a three-nucleon nucleus. This increasing trend in bonds per nucleon does not continue indefinitely, however. Nucleons attract, but they also have a hard core that causes the nucleus to grow like a collection of hard spheres stuck together. The internucleon attraction is so short range that a given nucleon attracts only those immediately surrounding it, so each surrounded nucleon will have the same maximum number of bonds. (We say that the force saturates.) Of course, nucleons at the surface are *not* completely surrounded, but as the nuclear sphere grows, the number at the surface is a diminishing fraction of the total. The ratio is essentially area/volume $= 4\pi r^2 / \frac{4}{3}\pi r^3 \propto 1/r$. Thus, the average number of bonds per nucleon should initially increase fairly rapidly as the nucleus grows, then gradually approach a constant, as more nucleons become surrounded. Figure 6 shows the trend. Rather than bonds per nucleon, however, we now speak of binding energy per nucleon. **Binding energy** is the energy that would be required to pull all nucleons apart, and binding energy per nucleon is the fraction required for a representative nucleon.

Coulomb Repulsion All pairs of protons in the nucleus repel. In effect, this positive potential energy shifts all proton energies closer to the top of the finite well in which all nucleons are bound, as depicted in Figure 7 for the case of helium-4. In such small nuclei, all nucleons are "touching," so there is still a strong *net* attraction between all pairs. But in large nuclei, pairs of protons can be too far apart to attract via the strong force, and these pairs add to the nucleus an uncompensated net repulsion. Thus, while under control in small

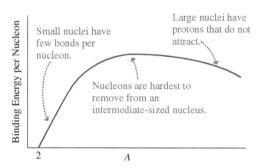

Figure 8 Binding energy per nucleon due to both the strong internucleon attraction and Coulomb repulsion.

Large nuclei have protons that do not attract.

Small nuclei have few bonds per nucleon.

Nucleons are hardest to remove from an intermediate-sized nucleus.

nuclei, Coulomb repulsion should be an increasingly destabilizing factor in larger ones. The energy needed to extract an "average" nucleon becomes progressively smaller. Combining this with our previous arguments, we should expect the binding energy per nucleon to vary as in Figure 8. Accordingly, somewhere between the extremes, there should be a mass number more stable than all others, for which the nucleons are the most tightly bound possible.

The Exclusion Principle To this point, it would seem that the best way to produce a stable nucleus is to build it of essentially all neutrons, for only protons repel. This argument overlooks the fact that protons and neutrons in the same nucleus must obey the exclusion principle, each independently. Putting Coulomb repulsion temporarily aside, the most important consequence of the exclusion principle is that for a given A, the state of lowest energy would have equal numbers of protons and neutrons. Why?

Suppose that Z does equal N, as illustrated on the left in Figure 9. The lowest energy state consistent with the exclusion principle would have all the neu-

Figure 9 Ignoring Coulomb repulsion, the exclusion principle argues that for a given number of nucleons, the lowest energy should have $N = Z$.

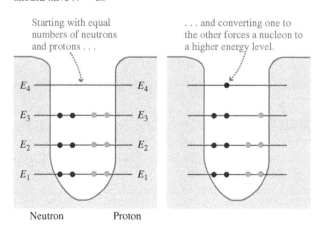

Starting with equal numbers of neutrons and protons . . .

. . . and converting one to the other forces a nucleon to a higher energy level.

Figure 10 In large nuclei, when Coulomb repulsion becomes significant, the lowest energy should have $N > Z$.

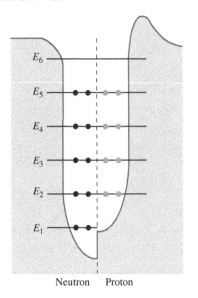

Neutron   Proton

tron energy levels filled, each with an opposite-spins pair, up to some maximum energy. Considering only the internucleon attraction, protons would occupy an identical well and would fill levels to the same maximum energy. Now, keeping A fixed, a decrease by 1 in the proton number would mean an increase by 1 in the neutron number. Because all lower energy levels are filled, the new neutron would have to occupy an energy level higher than the previously occupied proton level, and the total energy would increase. The argument applies just as well if we change a neutron to a proton. Thus, the state $Z = N$ is of lowest energy. (If either top level initially had only one neutron or proton, we might have to change a second particle before the energy increased.)

Let us now factor in Coulomb repulsion. In small nuclei, where essentially all nucleons touch, all proton repulsions are overwhelmed by the strong attraction, so $Z \cong N$ should be the more stable state. In large nuclei, uncompensated Coulomb repulsions may shift the proton energies upward enough to align with different neutron levels, as depicted in Figure 10. The lowest energy state—with the tops of the proton and neutron levels roughly equal—should then have more neutrons than protons. A balance is struck between having extra neutrons serve as nonrepulsive "glue" and forcing them into higher-energy states by the exclusion principle.

Overall, our model suggests that a representative nucleon should be most tightly bound—in a lowest energy state—in a nucleus of intermediate mass number, but it is not a function of A alone. The binding energy per nucleon should have a *relative* maximum at $Z \cong N$ for small A and at $N > Z$ for large A.

Stability: The Experimental Truth

The validity of any theory rests on its agreement with experimental evidence. Obtaining evidence to support our model of binding might seem to involve pulling a nucleus apart while measuring forces, but it is much simpler than that. All we need to know are nuclear masses. If we *were* to pull a stationary nucleus apart into separate stationary nucleons, we would have to expend our own energy, which would increase the system's internal energy and therefore its mass. The mass of the parts must be greater than that of the whole bound nucleus. Figure 11 bears this out for our simplest nucleus.

$$\text{deuteron mass} = 2.013553 \text{ u}$$

$$\text{proton mass} + \text{neutron mass} = 1.007276 \text{ u} + 1.008665 \text{ u} = 2.015941 \text{ u}$$

$$\text{mass of parts} - \text{mass of whole} = 2.015941 \text{ u} - 2.013553 \text{ u} = 0.002388 \text{ u}$$

Figure 11 A deuteron weighs less than the sum of its parts.

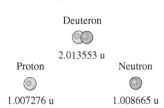

Deuteron

2.013553 u

Proton   Neutron

1.007276 u   1.008665 u

We see that we must do work to pull the deuteron apart. For an arbitrary nucleus, the energy required to pull all the nucleons apart—the total binding energy BE—is the difference between the final and the initial energies, which follows simply from the mass difference.

$$\text{BE} = m_f c^2 - m_i c^2 = (\text{mass of parts} - \text{mass of whole})c^2 \qquad (4)$$

Applying this to the deuteron, we obtain

$$\begin{aligned} \text{BE} &= (0.002388 \text{ u} \times 1.661 \times 10^{-27} \text{ kg/u})\,(3 \times 10^{8} \text{ m/s})^{2} \\ &= 3.57 \times 10^{-13} \text{ J} = 2.22 \text{ MeV} \end{aligned}$$

The atomic nucleus isn't special in this regard. The same arguments hold for the bound electron–proton system that we know as the hydrogen atom. Given that 13.6 eV must be added to pull the atom apart, equation (4) shows that the atom should be less massive than the sum of the electron and proton masses by 2.4×10^{-35} kg. The important difference is in the *fractional* mass change. It is very small for the hydrogen atom: $(2.4 \times 10^{-35} \text{ kg})/(1.67 \times 10^{-27} \text{ kg}) \cong 10^{-8}$. For the deuteron, it is $(0.002388 \text{ u})/(2.013553 \text{ u}) \cong 10^{-3}$. Although $\frac{1}{10}\%$ may not sound like much, as a mass-energy conversion it is huge. The 5 orders of magnitude difference between electronic and nuclear binding energies is typical, and the simple reason is that nuclear binding involves much stronger forces.

Our theoretical model looked at binding energy *per nucleon,* so to judge its merit, we need to divide total binding energy by total number. For the deuteron, this is (2.22 MeV)/2, or 1.11 MeV per nucleon. For arbitrary nuclei, equation (4) would suffice for BE, but because tables invariably list atomic rather than nuclear masses, we will find it convenient to use an alternative form.

$$\text{BE} = \left(Zm_{\text{H}} + Nm_{\text{n}} - M_{^{A}_{Z}X}\right)c^{2} \qquad (5)$$

Binding energy, calculated from masses

Here, the mass of the parts has the neutron number N multiplying the neutron mass m_{n}, as it should. The proton number Z, on the other hand, multiplies not the proton mass m_{p}, but the hydrogen *atomic* mass m_{H}. Therefore, this term is too large by the mass of Z electrons. However, $M_{^{A}_{Z}X}$ stands for the *atomic* mass of the isotope of element X with Z protons (and electrons) and A nucleons, and thus subtracts the proper number of electron masses. (Actually, this form is not perfectly accurate, for it ignores *electron* binding energies, but they are *very* small in comparison. See Exercise 18.) The hydrogen mass is given in the margin, along with a conversion factor very handy in nuclear physics.

$m_{\text{H}} = 1.007825$ u

$1 \text{ u} \times c^{2} = 931.5$ MeV

EXAMPLE 1

Calculate the binding energy per nucleon of an iron-56 nucleus.

SOLUTION

From the atomic mass data we find the mass of iron-56:

$$^{56}_{26}\text{Fe} = 55.934939 \text{ u}$$

The neutron number N is $A - Z = 56 - 26 = 30$. Using (5),

$$\text{BE} = (26 \times 1.007825 \text{ u} + 30 \times 1.008665 \text{ u} - 55.934939 \text{ u})c^{2}$$

$$= (0.528461 \text{ u})c^{2}$$

The iron nucleus is less massive than the sum of its parts by more than half a nucleon mass! The conversion factor may be used to express c^2 in MeV/u.

$$(0.528461 \text{ u}) \times 931.5 \text{ MeV/u} = 492.3 \text{ MeV}$$

There are 56 nucleons, so the binding energy per nucleon is

$$\frac{\text{BE}}{\text{nucleon}} = \frac{492.3 \text{ MeV}}{56} = 8.79 \text{ MeV}$$

Figure 12 plots BE/nucleon for the naturally occurring isotopes. We see how it validates our model by considering different views. Figure 13 is a top view that shows the locations of naturally occurring isotopes in the ZN-plane. They describe a path known as the **curve of stability**. As our model predicted, for small A, the greatest stability occurs at $N = Z$, but it tends toward $N > Z$ as A increases. Figure 14 is a cross section of Figure 12 taken roughly along the curve of stability. Because BE/nucleon varies with both N and Z, no two-axes plot can represent it for all isotopes. However, Figure 14 shows the general trend with nuclear size, and it looks conspicuously similar to Figure 8. From the deuteron's 1.11 MeV, it rises to a maximum at about $A = 60$ of 8.79 MeV, shared by iron-56, iron-58, and nickel-62. Of all elements, these have the most stable, tightly bound nuclei. Thereafter, the BE/nucleon plot falls slowly to 7.57 MeV for uranium-238, owing to the growth in Coulomb repulsion between protons too distant to engage in the internucleon attraction.

Figure 12 Binding energy per nucleon versus Z and N.

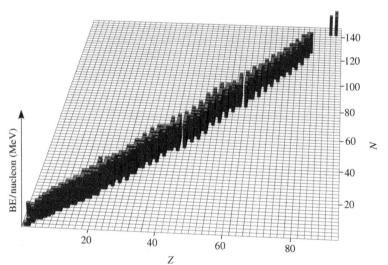

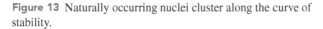

Figure 13 Naturally occurring nuclei cluster along the curve of stability.

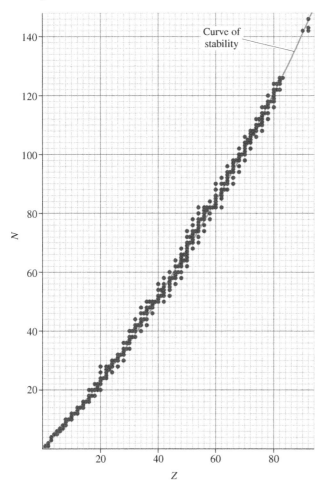

We stress binding energy *per nucleon* because of its importance to releasing nuclear energy. Binding energy alone increases rather consistently with A. For instance, it is 2.22 MeV for the deuteron, 492 MeV for iron-56, and 1802 MeV for uranium-238. This occurs because the number of nucleons increases, and each nucleon is bound by some net attraction to its nucleus. However, if we wished to find a minimum-energy state for a fixed amount of nuclear matter, we would not group nucleons into nuclei of the largest A. Given J total nucleons divided into nuclei of A nucleons each, the total binding energy would be the number of nuclei J/A times the binding energy of each nucleus: $(J/A) \cdot BE$ or $J \cdot (BE/A)$. We see that for fixed J, nuclei with the highest binding energy *per nucleon* would give the highest total binding energy—the lowest energy state—and would enable us to extract the greatest amount of energy for other purposes. We will return to these ideas in Section 7.

Figure 14 Binding energy per nucleon versus A.

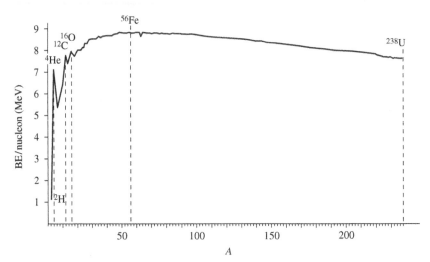

3 Nuclear Models

We now discuss two of the most useful theoretical models of the nucleus. Each has its emphasis. Although they agree in some ways, each rests upon unique assumptions and simplifications and makes its own predictions. Until and unless the nucleus is "completely understood," there will always be room for complementary models.

The Liquid Drop Model

The force between the molecules in a drop of water is strongly repulsive at very small separations but attractive at greater separations. In fact, the potential energy qualitatively resembles Figure 4. This explains why water is essentially incompressible while nonetheless exhibiting a reluctance to be pulled apart. To move a water molecule to the surface, we must pull it away from those that would otherwise attract it on all sides. This takes energy. Thus, the lowest energy state of a water droplet is one in which the surface area is minimum—a sphere.

Similarities between the energies in a liquid drop and those in the nucleus give the **liquid drop model** its name. In both cases, interior particles are attracted to all particles in the immediate vicinity. Were all particles interior, the total binding energy would be directly proportional to the number of particles. Particles at the surface, however, share fewer bonds with others, which reduces the total binding energy.

The centerpiece of the liquid drop model is an expression for nuclear binding energies. To know binding energy is to know mass, so it may also be said that the model yields nuclear masses. We have already discussed the governing factors, and the quantitative expression we now obtain is a sum of terms arising from each.

Volume Term

If we consider only the internucleon attraction and ignore the fact that not all nucleons are surrounded in the nuclear interior, then the total binding energy should be directly proportional to the number of nucleons. Thus, we begin our sum with the term shown in the margin.

$$BE = c_1 A + \cdots$$

While the proportionality constant c_1 has been theoretically predicted, the terms yet to come include similar constants, and all the constants are usually chosen so as to give the best overall agreement with experimentally determined values. The question might then arise: Is this really a theory, or just a way of codifying experimental findings? The answer is that it is a model of a very complex system *guided* by experimental knowledge. The known binding energies per nucleon describe a certain shape as a function of Z and N, and as Figure 12 shows, it is not a simple shape. For most functions with arbitrary constants (e.g., $c_1 Z^2 + c_2 N + c_3$), it would simply be impossible to fit the known shape. That the functional form of the liquid drop model can be made to do so as well as it does is strong evidence that the assumptions upon which it is based are valid. Furthermore, as we would expect for a good model, it may be used to predict binding energies of isotopes yet unknown.

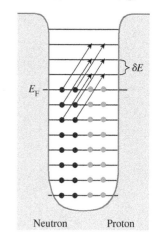

Figure 15 If j neutrons become protons, the energy increases by $\frac{1}{2}j^2\delta E$.

Surface Term

The binding energy of *surface* nucleons is lower. They should be easier to extract, because fewer other nucleons are around to attract them. Accordingly, the total binding energy should be *reduced* by a factor proportional to the surface area, which is in turn proportional to volume to the two-thirds power. We know that the volume is proportional to the number of nucleons, so we obtain the term given in the margin.

$$-c_2 A^{2/3}$$

Coulomb Term

Coulomb repulsion raises the overall potential energy, *reducing* the binding energy. The electrostatic potential energy shared by two protons separated by r is proportional to e^2/r. In a nucleus of Z protons, there are $Z(Z-1)$ pairs, and typical proton separation is of the order of the nuclear radius, which equation (1) tells us is proportional to $A^{1/3}$. Thus, we arrive at the term shown in the margin.

$$-c_3 \frac{Z(Z-1)}{A^{1/3}}$$

Asymmetry Term

Coulomb repulsion aside, a lower-energy state occurs when $N \cong Z$, due to the exclusion principle. To quantify this effect, we first note that neutron and proton energy levels due to the internucleon attraction alone should be nearly identical. Suppose they are filled to equal heights, E_F, and that the levels are roughly equally spaced, δE apart, as depicted in Figure 15. If j neutrons are now changed to protons (or vice versa), the top neutrons must go from neutron level E_F to proton level $E_F + (j/2)\delta E$. The others must make an equal jump. If the energy of each of j particles increases by $(j/2)\delta E$, the total energy increases by $(j^2/2)\delta E$. We can easily express j in terms of Z and N. If we start with $Z = N$, then gain j protons and lose j neutrons, $Z - N$ must now be $2j$, giving $j = \frac{1}{2}(Z - N)$. Thus, an asymmetry between Z and N should decrease the binding energy (increase the overall energy) by a factor proportional to $(N - Z)^2 \delta E$. Exercise 33 applies a result to argue that the level spacing δE should be proportional to $1/A$. Factoring this in gives us the term in the margin. As expected, it is zero if $Z = N$, and it reduces the binding energy as the asymmetry between N and Z increases.

$$-c_4 \frac{(N - Z)^2}{A}$$

Semiempirical Binding Energy Formula

Taking all four terms together, we have an expression for the binding energy of an arbitrary nucleus.

Semiempirical binding energy formula

$$\text{BE} = c_1 A - c_2 A^{2/3} - c_3 \frac{Z(Z - 1)}{A^{1/3}} - c_4 \frac{(N - Z)^2}{A} \tag{6}$$

Trial and error has shown that the sum best fits experimentally determined binding energies with the following values, all in MeV:

$$c_1 = 15.8 \qquad c_2 = 17.8 \qquad c_3 = 0.71 \qquad c_4 = 23.7$$

Because the forms of the terms are based on theoretical arguments but the coefficients are chosen to fit experimental data, equation (6) is known as the **semiempirical binding energy formula**.

EXAMPLE 2

What binding energy per nucleon does the liquid drop model predict for iron-56?

SOLUTION

Using (6) and the coefficients provided,

$$\text{BE} = 15.8(56) - 17.8(56)^{2/3} - 0.71 \frac{26(25)}{(56)^{1/3}} - 23.7 \frac{(30 - 26)^2}{56}$$

$$= 496.9 \text{ MeV}$$

$$\frac{\text{BE}}{\text{nucleon}} = \frac{496.9 \text{ MeV}}{56} = 8.87 \text{ MeV}$$

This differs from the true experimental value of Example 1 by less than 1%.

Figure 16 shows the predictions of the semiempirical binding energy formula plotted against the known values of BE/nucleon from Figure 14. For most nuclei, the curves are quite close. Predicted less well are the binding energies of very light nuclei, in which we might expect the average behaviors assumed in the model to be poor approximations. Helium, in particular, is much more tightly bound than the model predicts. The reason is that both N and Z are even numbers and so-called magic numbers. Terms to account for

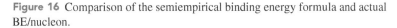

Figure 16 Comparison of the semiempirical binding energy formula and actual BE/nucleon.

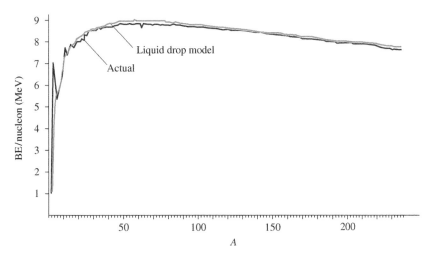

these effects are often appended to the semiempirical binding energy formula, but in most cases (helium being a notable exception) introduce only small corrections. Their explanation really belongs to the shell model.

The Shell Model

An indication of the complexities of the strong force is that the two most useful nuclear models are so vastly different. Except for the asymmetry term's use of the exclusion principle, the liquid drop model is classical, while the shell model is thoroughly quantum mechanical. In the liquid drop model, essentially classical particles interact via strong interparticle forces, and total binding energy is predicted. In the shell model, particles are treated as occupying quantum states in an average potential well that largely ignores specific interparticle forces. The shell model's unique successes are predictions of nuclear angular momenta and the tendencies for both N and Z to be magic numbers or at least even numbers.

As electrons in an atom orbit in a potential well resulting from their attraction to the nucleus, the nucleons in the shell model "orbit" in a potential well that is the net effect of all the forces they experience. After our having repeatedly pictured the nucleus as hard spheres stuck together, this may seem absurd. Wouldn't collisions preclude the possibility of a given nucleon roaming about the nucleus? Actually, the idea that motion might be rather free quantum mechanically when classical physics would suggest otherwise is nothing new. As we saw electrons in a conducting solid move rather freely despite the countless positive ions around them, and their wave functions spread throughout the volume of the solid. Nucleon wave functions must also permeate their enclosure. Moreover, if they assume a lowest-energy overall state consistent with the exclusion principle, they would fill all individual states to a maximum level—the Fermi energy—and this would prevent most nucleons from changing states at all. They could not undergo the momentum changes characteristic of a collision. Only nucleons near the "top" have much freedom. The real challenge in the shell model of the nucleus is that the forces are far more complex than the Coulomb force experienced by electrons in the atom. The form of the potential energy is rather speculative. A starting assumption is that the nucleons orbit independently of each other in one large spherically symmetric potential well. A rounded finite well has been most widely used. Let us see if an even simpler choice is useful.

EXAMPLE 3

Nuclei in excited states can lower their energy by gamma emission, in which a photon carries away the excess energy. As a rough approximation, assume that the nucleons behave as though trapped in an infinite well. Make a reasonable estimate of the energy of the photon emitted as a nucleon makes a transition from one energy level to another.

SOLUTION

The energy levels in the 1D infinite well are

$$E = \frac{\hbar^2 \pi^2 n^2}{2mL^2}$$

A cubic infinite well might be more realistic, but this would merely replace n^2 by $n_x^2 + n_y^2 + n_z^2$ and would not change our conclusion. For L, we use a typical nuclear diameter. Suppose $A = 100$. Using equation (1),

$$2r = 2(100)^{1/3} \times 1.2 \times 10^{-15} \text{ m} \cong 10^{-14} \text{ m}$$

The mass of a nucleon is about 1.67×10^{-27} kg. Thus,

$$E = \frac{(1.055 \times 10^{-34} \text{ J} \cdot \text{s})^2 \pi^2 n^2}{2(1.67 \times 10^{-27} \text{ kg})(10^{-14} \text{ m})^2} = (3.3 \times 10^{-13} \text{ J})n^2 \cong (2 \text{ MeV})n^2$$

We might expect energy jumps to be of several MeV. Although this is certainly a crude approximation, it is no coincidence that typical gamma energies are on the order of 1 MeV.

The shell model was proposed when it was found that nuclear stability exhibited some periodicity. Careful inspection of Figure 13 reveals a disproportionate number of nuclei with either N or Z or both equal to one of the **magic numbers**: 2, 8, 20, 28, 50, 82, 126. Apparently, great stability accompanies these values. Because it was known that atoms of atomic number 2, 10, 18, 36, 54, . . . are unusually stable because they possess complete shells or subshells, it was natural to attribute magic numbers to similar behavior in nuclei. After allowance for a strong nuclear spin-orbit interaction, this hypothesis was confirmed.

Another success of the shell model is that when expanded slightly to allow for specific interparticle forces, it explains the **pairing effect**—the tendency for Z or N to be simply even numbers. This is also apparent in Figure 13 in the clustering of stable nuclei along lines of even N and Z. Finally, the shell model predicts nuclear angular momenta, which agree well with experimental observation. This should not be too surprising, for we know that solution of the Schrödinger equation for a spherically symmetric potential energy (central force) yields quantized angular momentum states.

4 Nuclear Magnetic Resonance and MRI ◉ P.T I O N A L

Angular momentum is quantized in the nucleus, and so is its inevitable companion: magnetic dipole moment. **Magnetic resonance imaging** (MRI), a popular term for imaging by **nuclear magnetic resonance**, exploits this quantized magnetic moment to produce images of the body's interior.

The most important requirements in producing such an image are getting whatever one uses for a probe into the body, interacting in different ways with different features once inside, and detecting the interaction from the outside—all without damage to the tissues. Light fails as a probe because its penetration of the body is very short ranged. The requirements are met reasonably well by X-rays. They pass easily into the body, they are absorbed at different rates as they interact with electron clouds in different regions, and the portion that passes through unabsorbed is easily detected. In a simple X-ray, the transmitted intensity registers on photographic film and yields an image of average density. The intensity is different, for instance, where X-rays pass through skin, muscle, and bone than where they pass through skin and muscle only. However, X-ray photons typically have energies measured in keV—easily enough to tear ions apart—and thus carry with them a degree of biological hazard.

To produce an image using nuclear magnetic resonance, electromagnetic radiation is sent into the body to interact not with the electron charge densities, but directly with the nuclei. The body is immersed in an external magnetic field so that the magnetic moments of the nuclei have quantized orientation energies along that axis. To cause a flip to a higher orientation energy, only photons of a certain frequency will work—only these meet the resonance condition. (Electron spin resonance is very similar, though it exploits electron spin rather than nuclear spin.) As the nuclei jump back down, or relax, the absorbed energy is reradiated in all directions and easily detected.

The size of the energy jump is proportional to the strength of the external magnetic field (see Exercise 35). In MRI studies of the human body, the field is chosen so that photons in the radio frequency range have the proper energy to excite jumps. Such radiation passes easily into the body; however, with

Figure 17 A healthy, living human brain, as seen by MRI.

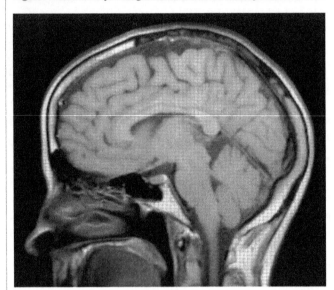

photon energies far less than chemical bond energies or ionization energies, it poses no biological threat. MRI has further advantages:

1. Because it uses an external magnetic field that is nonuniform, MRI is better able to "look" at specific locations within the body. The resonant frequency is different in a plane where the field has one value than in a plane where it has another.
2. The absorption and relaxation process is more detailed. It varies with time in a way that depends on the nature of the surrounding nuclei and atoms. This time dependence thus serves as additional information that distinguishes one material or tissue from another.
3. While the most common target nucleus is hydrogen, the incoming radiation can be tuned to resonant frequencies of different nuclei, which can provide an important alternative "view."

Figure 17 shows a nicely detailed image of a human brain. Although its medical applications are best known, nuclear magnetic resonance is used in many areas of scientific research. Its ability to "see" the structure of complex molecules is indispensable in chemistry.

5 Radioactivity

A nucleus may be bound yet still in a relatively high energy state, and if it can attain a lower energy, it will eventually do so. Nuclei fitting this description are termed unstable, or radioactive, and the process is known as **radioactive decay**. Radioactive decay usually takes the form of the spontaneous emission of a small energetic particle, as in the gamma decay of Example 3. Of course, energy is conserved. Kinetic energy increases as mass/internal energy decreases. We use the symbol Q for the kinetic energy released.

$$\Delta KE = -\Delta mc^2 = -(m_f - m_i)c^2$$
$$Q = (m_i - m_f)c^2 \tag{7}$$

Let us take a look at the various forms of radioactive decay.

Figure 18 Alpha decay.

Parent

Daughter α particle

Alpha Decay

α decay noted that its classically baffling traits can be understood by assuming that the α particle (helium nucleus) quantum-mechanically tunnels out of a large nucleus. But it is natural to ask what makes an α particle so effective at lowering the energy of such a nucleus. Figure 14 shows that helium is unusually tightly bound for its size; that is, its mass is less than the sum of its parts by an unusually large amount. The figure also shows that the heaviest nuclei tend to be less tightly bound than those of somewhat smaller mass number. Thus, it shouldn't be terribly surprising that a large nucleus, called a **parent nucleus**, might split into a lighter, more tightly bound one, called a **daughter nucleus**, plus a tightly bound α particle. Figure 18 depicts the process. Because the α particle takes away two neutrons and two protons, the daughter nucleus in α decay has two fewer of each than the parent.

EXAMPLE 4

Uranium-238, one of the most abundant radioactive isotopes in nature, attains a lower energy state by α decay. What is the daughter nucleus, and how much kinetic energy is released?

SOLUTION

Uranium-238 has 92 protons, and $238 - 92 = 146$ neutrons, so the daughter has 90 protons and 144 neutrons, identifying it as thorium-234. The reaction is thus

$$^{238}_{92}U \rightarrow {}^{234}_{90}Th + {}^{4}_{2}He$$

Obtaining the masses the change in kinetic energy is

$$Q = (m_i - m_f)c^2$$
$$= [238.050784\ u - (234.043593\ u + 4.002603\ u)]\ 931.5\ MeV/u$$
$$= 4.27\ MeV$$

Note that, just as we do in calculating binding energies, we use atomic rather than nuclear masses. The "extra" electrons included in the initial mass are subtracted in the final, $92 = 90 + 2$.

Strictly speaking, the α particle and daughter share the energy released in α decay. However, when a massive object splits into two (nonrelativistic) pieces, momentum conservation tells us that the ratio of their kinetic energies is the *inverse* of the ratio of their masses. Thus, the α particle gets almost all the kinetic energy.

Beta Decay

Electrostatic attraction cannot trap an electron in the nucleus, yet we find that electrons are *emitted* by some nuclei. We conclude that they are spontaneously created, then immediately depart. When created and emitted in this way, an electron is called a **β^- particle**, and the process is known as **β^- decay**.

The phenomenon of β^- decay is certainly curious. If charge is to be conserved, what must be happening in the nucleus? We find that after β^- decay, the remaining nucleus, again known as a daughter, has one more proton and one less neutron than the parent had. In effect, a neutron in the parent spontaneously changes into a proton and an electron. Charge is conserved.

But this is not the whole story. As in α decay, if the parent were to decay into only a daughter and a β particle, the tiny β particle would carry off essentially all the available kinetic energy Q. This would make Figure 19 alarming indeed. It shows β particle energies found in a large number of β decays. They vary widely and are often essentially *zero*. A β decay with only two product particles violates energy conservation![1]

Things get even worse. The simplest example of β decay is neutron decay. While neutrons inside stable nuclei live forever, a *free* neutron is unstable. Because a free proton is significantly less massive than a free neutron, a neutron may attain a lower energy/mass via β^- decay into a proton. However, if a spin-$\frac{1}{2}$ neutron were to become *only* a spin-$\frac{1}{2}$ proton and a spin-$\frac{1}{2}$ electron, the final total spin would be an integer, either 1 or 0. Angular momentum could not be conserved. Allowance for the creation of photons (spin-1) would not solve the problem, for the total spin would still be an integer. All other β^- decays share the same problem.

This seeming violation of fundamental laws of physics caused much consternation among early nuclear physicists. Wolfgang Pauli postulated a solution: The decay produces an unseen particle, which carries away angular momentum and variable portions of the available kinetic energy. Charge and angular momentum could be conserved if it were uncharged and spin-$\frac{1}{2}$. (By the rules of angular momentum addition, *three* final spins of $\frac{1}{2}$ can add to the neutron's initial $\frac{1}{2}$.) Moreover, the β particle does sometimes acquire a kinetic energy nearly equal to the Q calculated by assuming a final mass of *only* daughter and β, so it would seem that the mystery particle has negligible mass. After much effort, Pauli's unseen particle was found, and the fundamental laws saved.

We call this new kind of particle the **neutrino**. Its discovery lagged its prediction because the neutrino is extremely difficult to detect. Having no charge, neutrinos do not interact electrostatically, nor do they experience the strong force. They interact only by the so-called weak force, which is so feeble that most neutrinos traveling through space and encountering Earth pass right through it. Perhaps it isn't surprising that

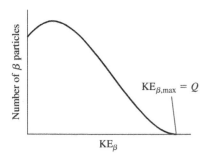

Figure 19 The mysterious variation in β particle energies.

Number of β particles

$KE_{\beta,\text{max}} = Q$

KE_β

[1]If sufficient energy were released to produce relativistic motion, the kinetic energy ratio would no longer be simply the inverse of the mass ratio, but each particle would still get an unvarying fraction of the available energy.

we still have much to learn about neutrinos. Recent experiments suggest that the neutrino has mass, but the most we can say is that it is very much less than that of the electron. It certainly can be neglected in a calculation of Q. We leave further discussion of the neutrino with the following exception: The particle produced in β^- decay has traditionally been referred to as the *anti*neutrino, symbol $\bar{\nu}$, with the term *neutrino* and symbol ν applied to a complementary kind of decay soon to be discussed. Physicists aren't even sure if these are different particles. While we uphold the tradition, the distinction will never come into play.

Figure 20 depicts a β^- decay. An important question is how β^- decay allows a nucleus to decrease its energy. Consider the case of boron-12, $^{12}_{5}\text{B}$, which has five protons and seven neutrons. If a neutron changes into a proton and an electron, the daughter nucleus has six protons and six neutrons. Lighter nuclei tend to be more tightly bound when $N = Z$, and when both N and Z are even numbers, so it is reasonable that boron-12 might attain a lower energy via β^- decay.

Simply to account for nucleon number and charge, the β^- particle is often represented as $^{0}_{-1}\beta^-$, meaning that it has no nucleons but carries a charge opposite that of a proton. Thus, we express the β^- decay of boron-12 as

$$^{12}_{5}\text{B} \rightarrow \,^{12}_{6}\text{C} + \,^{0}_{-1}\beta^- + \bar{\nu}$$

The energy released in this reaction is again $-\Delta m c^2$. However, because there are five electrons in boron-12 and six in carbon-12, using *atomic* masses would include an extra electron in the final mass. We circumvent the difficulty by allowing this extra electron mass to account for the mass of the β^- particle. Thus,

$$\beta^- \text{ decay:} \quad Q = (m_{\text{parent}} - m_{\text{daughter}})c^2 \qquad (8)$$

Applying this to the boron-12 decay and using atomic masses, we have

$$Q = (12.014352 \text{ u} - 12 \text{ u})\, 931.5 \text{ MeV/u} = 13.4 \text{ MeV}$$

Complementary to β^- decay is **β^+ decay**. Consider $^{12}_{7}\text{N}$, which has five neutronsand seven protons. It could become $^{12}_{6}\text{C}$, with six each, if only it could change a proton to a neutron. This is effectively what happens in β^+ decay, depicted in Figure 21. Charge is conserved by the emission of a *positively* charged electron. The neutrino again ensures conservation of angular momentum. Thus, nitrogen-12 β^+ decays according to

$$^{12}_{7}\text{N} \rightarrow \,^{12}_{6}\text{C} + \,^{0}_{+1}\beta^+ + \nu$$

The *atomic* mass of the daughter would be one electron mass too small to cancel the number of electrons included in the parent atomic mass, so to find the

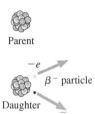

Figure 20 β^- decay. A neutron becomes a proton, and an electron and antineutrino are emitted.

Parent

Daughter

$-e$

β^- particle

$\bar{\nu}$

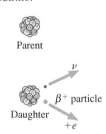

Figure 21 β^+ decay. A proton becomes a neutron, a positron, and a neutrino.

Parent

Daughter

ν

β^+ particle

$+e$

Figure 22 Electron capture, in which an orbiting electron combines with a proton to form a neutron and neutrino.

Parent

Daughter

energy released, we must include *two* electron masses with the final mass—one to cancel the extra parent electron and one for the β^+.

$$\beta^+ \text{ decay: } Q = \left(m_{\text{parent}} - m_{\text{daughter}} - 2m_e\right)c^2 \tag{9}$$

For nitrogen-7, this gives

$$Q = (12.018613 \text{ u} - 12 \text{ u} - 2 \times 5.486 \times 10^{-4} \text{ u})$$
$$931.5 \text{ MeV/u} = 16.3 \text{ MeV}$$

As in all forms of radioactive decay, the final mass is less than the initial.

Interestingly, although a free neutron is liable to β^- decay to a proton, a free proton cannot β^+ decay to a neutron, for mass would *increase*. In a nucleus, however, a proton can decay to a "more massive" neutron, because factors such as decreased Coulomb repulsion can still result in a lower total mass/internal energy. Although free proton decay is predicted in unified theories, it cannot occur by β^+ decay.

Figure 22 depicts a third form of β decay: **electron capture**. A nucleus with too many protons, the type that might tend to β^+ decay, may approach $N = Z$ another way. It may seize an orbiting electron and effectively convert it and a proton into a neutron in the nucleus, meanwhile emitting a neutrino. Thus, as in β^+ decay, Z decreases by 1, and N increases by 1. Many nuclei that β^+ decay also engage in electron capture. Often, electron capture is "energetically preferred." In β^+ decay, the mass of the parent nucleus must be at least one electron mass *greater* than the daughter, for a positron is created. In electron capture, however, the electron already exists, so the parent's mass can be as small as one electron mass *less* than the daughter. Carbon-11, though able to become boron-11 by both processes, "prefers" electron capture approximately 100 to 1.

$$^{11}_{6}\text{C} + ^{\ 0}_{-1}\beta^- \rightarrow ^{11}_{5}\text{B} + \nu$$

The energy released in electron capture depends simply on the difference in the *atomic* masses of parent and daughter.

$$\text{Electron capture: } Q = \left(m_{\text{parent}} - m_{\text{daughter}}\right)c^2 \tag{10}$$

The "extra" electron in the parent atomic mass accounts for the mass of the captured electron.

Figure 23 shows the effect on Z and N of the decays we have discussed. By altering Z and N differently, they constitute different ways of approaching the curve of stability. Heavy nuclei with too many protons often α decay (Z and N both reduced by 2), light nuclei with too many protons β^+ decay or engage in electron capture (Z reduced by 1, N increased by 1), and nuclei with too many neutrons β^- decay (Z increased by 1, N reduced by 1).

Also shown in Figure 23 are the **decay series** of thorium-232 and uranium-238, two radioactive but reasonably abundant naturally occurring

Figure 23 The "directions" of α and β decays, and the decay series of uranium-238 and thorium-232.

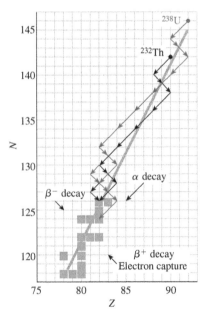

isotopes. A decay need not result in a stable state; many daughter nuclei are themselves radioactive. Thus, one decay can be followed by a series of other α and β decays. Moreover, many unstable isotopes decay in more than one way, so a decay series may **branch**, governed by probabilities. Even so, a stable nucleus will eventually be reached. Thorium-232 ends up as lead-208, and uranium-238 as lead-206. It is true that lead is not one of the most stable nuclei. (As we know, the most tightly bound are around $A = 60$.) But these lead isotopes are still stable simply because there is no form of radioactive decay available that can take them to a state any lower in energy/mass. Conversely, there are isotopes that appear to be on the curve of stability but that are unstable because there *is* a form of decay that leads to an even lower mass. A good example is potassium-40, discussed in Exercise 43.

Gamma Decay

Figure 24 Gamma decay.

An atom in an excited state may lower its energy by emitting a photon, and so may a nucleus. When emitted from the nucleus, a photon is called a γ particle. In α and β decay, one element becomes another, because α and β particles carry charge, but in γ decay, pictured in Figure 24, neither Z nor N change. Gamma decay often accompanies other forms. In many decays, the daughter nucleus is not left in its lowest energy state, and it may continue to lower its energy by emitting a photon. We learn much about excited states of nuclei by studying their gamma emissions. Moreover, gamma energies are characteristic of a given isotope—a spectral "fingerprint"—and thus serve to identify it. (See Progress and Applications.)

Spontaneous Fission

A somewhat rare form of radioactive decay exhibited by a few of the heavier nuclei is **spontaneous fission**, illustrated in Figure 25. Unlike other decays, which produce one fairly large daughter and a small particle or two, in this decay, a nucleus fissions (splits) into two nuclei of intermediate mass number. The driving force behind spontaneous fission is the reduction of the destabilizing effect of Coulomb repulsion. It is true that fission increases the total surface area. This alone would *raise* the overall energy, requiring more nucleons to be pulled to the surface against their mutual attraction. But splitting the whole into two smaller nuclei also decreases the number of protons that are too far apart to attract each other, so the number exhibiting a net repulsion is reduced, which more than compensates for the increased "surface energy."

As Figure 25 suggests, spontaneous fission also releases neutrons. Heavy nuclei have many more neutrons than protons, but intermediate-mass nuclei are most tightly bound when Z and N are more nearly equal. Thus, when a heavy nucleus breaks up, the fragments tend to have too many neutrons. A lower energy results if the excess neutrons are simply freed. This freeing of multiple neutrons in fission is a very important factor in the release of nuclear energy. We will return to it in Section 7.

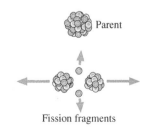

Figure 25 Spontaneous fission, in which a nucleus splits into two smaller ones. Neutrons are also freed.

Radioactive Identification

Mixing a radioactive isotope with a nonradioactive material gives the material an unmistakable signature, recognizable by the energy of the particle emitted. Scientific research exploits this in numerous ways. To trace how some nonradioactive materials move about or how they stick to one another, radioactive atoms are introduced, either as a loose mixture or by being bonded to specific molecular groups. The subsequent behavior of the material is then easily followed by the telltale decays of the radioactive tracer. In one of many biological research applications, a steroid molecule is tagged (covalently bonded) with tritium, a β emitter, and then mixed with a protein. The *steroid's* ability to bind to the protein is clearly indicated by how much *tritium* ends up stuck to the protein. Let us now look at another characteristic of radioactive decay that is also much exploited in scientific investigation.

6 The Radioactive Decay Law

All forms of radioactive decay fundamentally change the parent nucleus, and the nucleus may decay in a particular way only once. A good analogy is a lightbulb, which can burn out only once, after which it is fundamentally different from a working lightbulb. Furthermore, decays are governed by probabilities. It is impossible to know exactly when specific nuclei in a sample will decay. One nucleus may decay right away and another after a very long time. In a large sample, however, there should be a predictable *average* time, characteristic of the particular decay; it may be long for the α decay of isotope X and short for the β^+ decay of isotope Y. The lightbulb analogy is again helpful. One never knows when a lightbulb will burn out, but in a huge office building with thousands of lightbulb X, there would be a predictable number burning out per day. A reliable average lifetime would be apparent. In a similar building with thousands of lightbulb Y—a competitor's lower-quality unit—a predictable average lifetime would also be apparent, though it might be much shorter.

No matter what value the lifetime might be, if we increase the size of the sample (building), the number decaying (burning out) per unit time should increase proportionally. In other words, the *change* per unit time in the number of nuclei present should be directly proportional to the number present.

$$\frac{dN}{dt} \propto N \tag{11}$$

We make this an equation by using the symbol λ for the proportionality constant. (*Note:* In this section, N stands for the number of nuclei, rather than the number of neutrons in a given nucleus.) Because the number of radioactive nuclei that are present is constantly decreasing ($dN/dt < 0$), the equation requires a minus sign.

$$\frac{dN}{dt} = -\lambda N \tag{12}$$

Differential equations in which a quantity diminishes at a rate proportional to its instantaneous value are very common in science. (A familiar example is a capacitor discharging through a resistor. The current, which is the negative of the rate of change of the capacitor's charge, $-dQ/dt$, is proportional to the voltage across the capacitor, Q/C.) The inevitable result is an exponential decay. To show this, we separate variables.

$$\frac{dN}{N} = -\lambda\, dt$$

Integrating time from 0 to t as the number of nuclei goes from N_0 to N, we have

$$\int_{N_0}^{N} \frac{dN'}{N'} = -\lambda \int_{0}^{t} dt' \qquad \text{or} \qquad \ln\left(\frac{N}{N_0}\right) = -\lambda t$$

Thus,

$$N = N_0 e^{-\lambda t} \tag{13}$$

Radioactive decay law

The number of nuclei falls exponentially with time. It is worth reiterating that equation (11), on which (13) is based, is valid only if the number of parent nuclei yet to decay is large. Only then will the exponential decay be smooth. If the number is small (the office building is small or most lightbulbs are already burnt out), decays will be sporadic, and the number remaining will fluctuate considerably about an exponentially decreasing trend.

The constant λ is called the **decay constant**. (It is not a wavelength!) Equation (13) says that the larger the value of λ, the more rapidly the number N decreases. Equation (12) agrees. When we speak of decay rate, however, we usually mean an absolute value, R, in decays per second. Accordingly, (12) is often written as

$$R = \lambda N \tag{14}$$

We conclude that the rate decreases exponentially with time, just as the number of nuclei present does.

A property of exponential functions is that they decrease by the same fraction in equal successive intervals of time. If in time interval 1, the number drops to half its initial value, in interval 2, it will drop to half of this value, or one-quarter of the initial value; in interval 3, it will drop to half this value, or one-eighth the initial. The time required for the number to fall to half its initial value is the characteristic by which decay rates are usually categorized. It is called the **half-life** and is given the symbol $T_{1/2}$. Figure 26 shows the decrease of N in terms of half-lives. The connection to the decay constant is straightforward. By definition, t is $T_{1/2}$ when N is $\frac{1}{2}N_0$. Thus,

$$\frac{1}{2}N_0 = N_0 e^{-\lambda T_{1/2}}$$

Figure 26 Exponential decay.

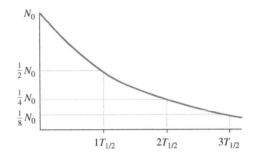

TABLE 3 Selected decays

Isotope	Decay Mode	Half-Life
$^{35}_{20}\text{Ca}$	β^+	50 ms
$^{3}_{1}\text{H}$	β^-	12.3 yr
$^{238}_{92}\text{U}$	α	4.5×10^9 yr

Canceling N_0, taking natural logs, and rearranging, we have

$$\lambda = \frac{\ln 2}{T_{1/2}} \tag{15}$$

Sensibly, the decay constant is large when the half-life is small, and vice versa.

Given the complexities of nuclear binding and the possibility of multiple decay modes, it is not a simple matter to predict half-lives. Many have been measured, however, covering a range from about 10^{-22} s to 10^{17} yr. Table 3 gives a few examples.

EXAMPLE 5

A vessel holds 2 μg of tritium. (a) What is its initial decay rate? (b) How much time will elapse before the decay rate falls to 1% of its initial value?

SOLUTION

(a) Decay rate is proportional to the number of radioactive nuclei present, which we find in the usual way. Using the atomic mass,

$$N = \frac{2 \times 10^{-9} \text{ kg}}{3.02 \text{ u} \times 1.66 \times 10^{-27} \text{ kg/u}} = 4.0 \times 10^{17}$$

The decay constant we find from equation (15), and the half-life from Table 3.

$$\lambda = \frac{\ln 2}{12.3 \text{ yr}} \times \frac{1 \text{ yr}}{3.16 \times 10^7 \text{ s}} = 1.78 \times 10^{-9} \text{ s}^{-1}$$

Now using (14),

$$R = \lambda N = (1.78 \times 10^{-9} \text{ s}^{-1})\,(4 \times 10^{17}) = 7.1 \times 10^8 \text{ decays/s}$$

Although the number decaying each second is large, it is still a very small fraction of the total number.

(b) Because $R = \lambda N$ holds at all times, the decay rate drops to 1% when the number of tritium nuclei present does. Inserting $N = \frac{1}{100}N_0$ in equation (13),

$$\frac{1}{100}N_0 = N_0 e^{-\lambda t} \quad \rightarrow \quad \ln\frac{1}{100} = -\lambda t$$

$$t = \frac{-\ln\dfrac{1}{100}}{1.78 \times 10^{-9}\,\text{s}^{-1}} = 2.6 \times 10^9\,\text{s} = 81.7\,\text{yr}$$

An alternative route is $\left(\frac{1}{2}\right)^n = \frac{1}{100}$, which gives $n = 6.64$, and 6.64 half-lives is 81.7 years.

Radioactive Dating

An important use of the radioactive decay law is radioactive dating, in which we attempt to determine the age of something old, such as a fossil, a rock, or an artifact. There are several methods, using different radioactive isotopes. All rely on assumptions about the abundance of certain isotopes in the past. If both the initial number and the final number of nuclei in a sample are known, a simple calculation gives the time elapsed.

REAL-WORLD EXAMPLE CARBON-14 DATING

The most famous technique of radioactive dating relies on the isotope carbon-14, which β^- decays with a half-life of 5730 years. The assumption in this technique is that the abundance of carbon-14 in the biosphere, the part of our world inhabited by and interacting with biological organisms, was the same in the past as it is now. Although carbon-14 does decay, it is continuously replenished by the action of cosmic rays, high-energy particles from space. When these particles strike nitrogen in the upper atmosphere, they initiate a nuclear reaction that produces the isotope, which then spreads throughout the biosphere, maintaining a constant ratio of carbon-14 to stable carbon nuclei. Factors such as atmospheric nuclear testing and industrialization have had effects, but the ratio is usually taken to be about 1.3×10^{-12}. Carbon-14 dating works only for (formerly) living organisms. While a plant or animal lives, it exchanges carbon with the environment through its food supply and the atmosphere. Because isotopes of the same element are chemically identical, a living organism should take in a fraction of carbon-14 atoms equal to the fraction in the environment. When it dies, it ceases to exchange carbon with the environment, and from that point onward, the amount of carbon-14 decays exponentially.

Applying the Physics

What is the age of a fossil sample that contains 6 g of carbon and has a decay rate of 30 decays per minute?

SOLUTION

At 12 g/mol, the fossil contains $\frac{1}{2}$ mol of carbon, or 3.01×10^{23} carbon atoms, nearly all of which would be the stable carbon-12. The fraction that would initially have been carbon-14 is

$$N_0 = (1.3 \times 10^{-12})(3.01 \times 10^{23}) = 3.9 \times 10^{11}$$

We will need the decay constant

$$\lambda = \frac{\ln 2}{T_{1/2}} = \frac{\ln 2}{5730 \times 3.16 \times 10^7 \text{ s}} = 3.83 \times 10^{-12} \text{ s}^{-1}$$

We may find the present number via (14).

$$\frac{30 \text{ decays}}{60 \text{ s}} = 3.83 \times 10^{-12} \text{ s}^{-1} \times N \quad \Rightarrow \quad N = 1.31 \times 10^{11}$$

Thus,

$$1.31 \times 10^{11} = 3.9 \times 10^{11} \, e^{-(3.83 \times 10^{-12} \text{ s}^{-1})t}$$
$$\Rightarrow \quad t = 2.86 \times 10^{11} \text{ s} \cong 9000 \text{ yr}$$

To give a sufficiently high β^- decay count rate, the traditional method of carbon-14 dating requires a large amount of carbon, measured in grams. Retrieving this much from the bone of a valuable archaeological specimen may be out of the question. An increasingly common method (see Progress and Applications) determines the present amount of carbon-14 by mass spectroscopy and can get by with a sample size on the order of a milligram. In any case, carbon-14 dating, like all dating techniques, has limits. It is most reliable for time scales within about an order of magnitude of the half-life.

To determine the ages of rocks and other things that do not exchange carbon with the biosphere, other methods of radioactive dating must be used. The "age" of a rock is the time that has passed since it formed a solid. One technique for determining ages of rocks uses the decay of potassium-40 to argon-40. The assumption is that when the rock formed, it contained no argon at all. Argon is an inert gas, so it does not form compounds, and it easily passes out of a molten mass. Thus, any Ar-40 atoms present now should be the result of radioactive decay since the solid formed. A slight difficulty arises in determining the number of K-40 decays. It is not simply the number of Ar-40 atoms present, for K-40 also decays to calcium-40, and the rock might well have been "contaminated" with Ca-40 when it formed. However, decays to Ca-40 and Ar-40 occur in a fixed ratio, so the total number of K-40 decays is directly proportional to the number of Ar-40 atoms. Adding the number of K-40 atoms decayed and the number present gives the initial number, and with the initial number, present number, and half-life, we can calculate the age. Other radioactive isotopes found in various types of rock and commonly used for dating are uranium-238, decaying to lead-206; thorium-232, decaying to lead-208; and rubidium-86, decaying to strontium-86.

7 Nuclear Reactions

The term **nuclear reaction** refers to any occurrence in which nucleons are changed or exchanged between nuclei, much as electrons are exchanged between atoms in a chemical reaction. Radioactivity is a form of nuclear reaction, but a spontaneous one. We now study nuclear reactions that are *induced* by striking a nucleus with another particle. An example is

$$_{5}^{10}\text{B} + _{0}^{1}\text{n} \rightarrow _{3}^{7}\text{Li} + _{2}^{4}\text{He}$$

Boron-10 is stable, but the neutron destabilizes its nucleus, which then breaks into two pieces. The change in kinetic energy is again given by equation (7).

$$(10.012937 \text{ u} + 1.008665 \text{ u} - 7.016003 \text{ u} - 4.002603 \text{ u}) \times 931.5 \text{ MeV/u}$$
$$= 2.79 \text{ MeV}$$

Once again, kinetic energy increases as mass decreases. In chemistry, we would call this an exothermic reaction. Of course, endothermic reactions are possible. If the reactants have kinetic energy before the reaction, it is quite possible for the products to have less kinetic energy and therefore more mass. Mass increases in the following reaction, commonly used to produce monoenergetic neutrons:

$$_{3}^{7}\text{Li} + _{1}^{1}\text{H} \rightarrow _{4}^{7}\text{Be} + _{0}^{1}\text{n}$$

It is left as an exercise to show that $Q = -1.64$ MeV.

Exothermic reactions are of particular interest. To release kinetic energy, mass must decrease, which means that the products must be more tightly bound than the reactants. There are two essentially opposite ways to do this. Because binding energy per nucleon peaks at around $A = 60$, a given number of nucleons would be in a lowest energy state if grouped into sets of 60. In nature, of course, nucleons are not all grouped this way. Therefore, energy can be released by breaking heavier nuclei apart or by putting lighter nuclei together. These are the processes of fission and fusion.

Fission

Heavy nuclei have less binding energy per nucleon than do those of intermediate mass number. We can exploit this, as illustrated in Figure 27, by breaking a heavy nucleus into intermediate-sized pieces in which the nucleons end up in a lower energy state. Lower internal energy means smaller mass and a release of kinetic energy. As noted in connection with spontaneous fission, the driving force is the reduction of Coulomb repulsion.

Few isotopes spontaneously fission, and even these few usually decay other ways. Of greater practical use is **induced fission**, in which we stimulate release

Figure 27 Decreasing BE/nucleon via fission.

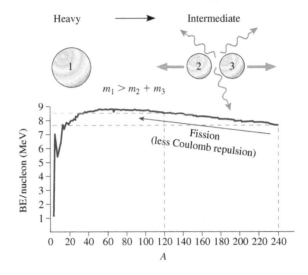

of energy at a time of our choosing. Certain nuclei are particularly susceptible to fission induced by a neutron, an important example being uranium-235.

$$\begin{aligned}
{}^{235}_{92}\text{U} + {}^{1}_{0}\text{n} &\rightarrow {}^{141}_{56}\text{Ba} + {}^{92}_{36}\text{Kr} + 3\,{}^{1}_{0}\text{n} \\
{}^{235}_{92}\text{U} + {}^{1}_{0}\text{n} &\rightarrow {}^{140}_{54}\text{Xe} + {}^{94}_{38}\text{Sr} + 2\,{}^{1}_{0}\text{n} \qquad (16)\\
{}^{235}_{92}\text{U} + {}^{1}_{0}\text{n} &\rightarrow {}^{132}_{50}\text{Sn} + {}^{101}_{42}\text{Mo} + 3\,{}^{1}_{0}\text{n}
\end{aligned}$$

As depicted in Figure 28, a U-235 nucleus absorbs a neutron, becoming briefly an excited state of U-236, then fissions in one of a host of possible ways. (We discuss uranium-235, but there are other nuclei that behave similarly, notably plutonium-239.) The final kinetic energy is shared by the fission fragments—barium and krypton in the first reaction—freed neutrons, and γ particles. Furthermore, the fission fragments tend to be radioactive, and they release more energy in the form of β particles and neutrinos. Because the energy release is rather complicated, a simple calculation of Q is not possible, but we can estimate its value. According to Figure 27, from mass numbers near 240 to those near 120 (a rough average of the product nuclei), binding energy per nucleon increases by slightly less than 1 MeV. Thus, in a reaction in which about 240 uranium nucleons end up near $A = 120$, binding energy should increase by about 200 MeV.

All the reactions in (16) have free neutrons among the products. As noted in Section 5 in connection with spontaneous fission, the reason is that heavy nuclei have a higher neutron-to-proton ratio than do lighter ones. The presence of *multiple* neutrons among the products of induced fission is fateful, for if we collect many nuclei together, a **chain reaction** is possible. Suppose that each reaction liberates n product neutrons. If a neutron is required to initiate a reaction and each reaction produces n neutrons, then each reaction may

Figure 28 Neutron-induced fission, freeing more neutrons.

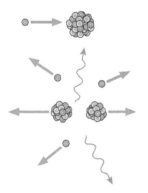

initiate n other reactions; each of these may initiate n others, and so on, with each successive generation releasing n times the energy of the previous. Using E_0 for the energy released in each fission, the energy released in the jth generation would be

$$E_j = E_0\, n^j \qquad (17)$$

It would increase exponentially with time.

Given that uranium-235 nuclei do exist on Earth and that a spontaneous fission might get the process started, it is reasonable to wonder why we don't stumble onto chain reactions in nature. It is one thing for multiple neutrons to be *produced*, but quite another for all of them to be *absorbed* by other uranium-235 nuclei thereafter. Uranium-235 nuclei are extremely rarefied in nature, so the chance of any reaction setting off another is remote. To ensure that a chain reaction will be self sustaining, the fissionable material must be arranged in the proper size and shape—into a **critical assembly**. The reader may have heard the term *critical mass*. It is true that there is a minimum *mass* for a chain reaction to be self sustaining, but it is the minimum only for a completely pure sample arranged in a sphere. Geometry and impurities are factors. One of the ways of losing neutrons is through the surface area. A mass of uranium-235 that would be critical if arranged in a sphere would not be critical if formed into a flat sheet, for there would be too much area from which to lose neutrons. A sphere has the minimum surface area to volume ratio. However, even for a sphere, there is a minimum size, because the ratio increases as the size of the sphere decreases. Impurities come into play because they may absorb free neutrons without fissioning. To compensate, the assembly would have to be larger.

Whether an assembly is critical is determined by the **multiplication constant** k, the average number of reactions set off by a given reaction. If three neutrons were liberated in each reaction and each induced another reaction, the number of reactions in each generation would be 3 times the number in the previous generation, and k would be its maximum possible value of 3. However, the reactions in (16) show that some fissions liberate fewer neutrons. Losses at the surface and absorptions by impurities would further reduce the multiplication constant. Thus, to give the true energy released for a given generation, we replace n in equation (17) by k.

$$E_j = E_0\, k^j$$

A sustained chain reaction requires a multiplication constant of at least 1. If $k > 1$, the energy released increases exponentially with time. If $k = 1$, successive generations would all release the same amount of energy, giving a steady chain reaction. If $k < 1$, the energy per generation *decreases* exponentially with time. The chain reaction—however it may have started—would die out.

An **uncontrolled chain reaction** is the basis of the "atomic bomb."[2] Subcritical ($k < 1$) parts are brought quickly together to form a supercritical assembly ($k > 1$), and the rapid exponential increase in energy results in an explosion, releasing 5–6 orders of magnitude more energy per kilogram than explosives based on chemical reactions.

[2]Early in the nuclear age, breaking the *nucleus* apart was popularly referred to as "splitting the atom," even though ordinary ionization splits an atom. Early fission weapons were thus termed "atomic bombs," and the name stuck. Later weapons involving fusion of hydrogen isotopes were termed "hydrogen bombs." Both are "nuclear bombs."

The Fission Reactor

A steady unchanging generation of energy requires a multiplication factor of 1. In a fission reactor, an assembly in which k is capable of *exceeding* 1 is controlled so as to keep k *at* 1. **Control rods** are made of materials that readily absorb neutrons, remaining otherwise inert. Boron and cadmium are commonly used. If introduced into a region where a chain reaction is occurring, control rods reduce the multiplication factor. Because they can only *decrease* k, which must be maintained at 1, a fission reactor must have a potential multiplication constant greater than 1.

Given the close proximity of fissioning nuclei, it might seem that if k somehow began to exceed 1, things would get out of control almost instantly, leaving no time for corrective measures. Fortunately, some neutrons come from decay of the fission products and therefore lag behind the fission by many seconds. Though less than 1% of the free neutrons, the delayed neutrons are purposely relied upon in a reactor to keep k at 1. Without these neutrons, the reaction would die out; with them, it builds slowly enough to permit control rods to be readjusted.

Uranium-235 is the most common fuel in today's fission reactors, yet it is very difficult to concentrate. Natural uranium is 99.3% U-238, which absorbs neutrons but rarely fissions. Because they are the same element, the two cannot be separated by ordinary chemical methods. The alternatives are tedious, relying only on the small mass difference between U-235 and U-238. Common methods include (1) deflecting the ions at different radii in a magnetic field—the cyclotron method; (2) establishing different concentration gradients in a high-speed centrifuge; and (3) exploiting different diffusion rates in a gaseous state through a porous barrier. In any event, reactors do not use pure U-235. Some operate with only the small fraction of U-235 present in natural uranium, while others use uranium in which the component of U-235 has been enriched. How much the uranium must be enriched depends on the effectiveness of the **moderator**. Neutrons produced in fission—"fast" neutrons—tend to have kinetic energies of about 1 MeV, but U-235 is more likely to absorb slow, or "thermal," neutrons, whose kinetic energy is characteristic of the ambient temperature: $\overline{\text{KE}} = \frac{3}{2} k_B T \ll 0.1$ MeV. It is the moderator's task to slow the neutrons and thus increase the likelihood that they will induce a U-235 fission. Simple mechanics shows that the best way to slow a particle is via a head-on collision with an equal-mass particle. Because protons and neutrons have about the same mass, ordinary water, with single-proton hydrogen nuclei, would seem to be a good choice for a moderator. Unfortunately, hydrogen readily absorbs neutrons, becoming stable deuterium. Thus, the requirements for a moderator are small nuclear size *and* no appetite for absorbing neutrons. These requirements are adequately met by graphite (carbon), helium, and "heavy water," in which the deuterium atoms already contain one neutron and do not readily absorb another. Even so, most reactors in the United States get by with ordinary water, because their fuel is sufficiently enriched in U-235 to more than compensate for hydrogen's parasitic neutron absorption.

Plutonium-239 behaves very much like U-235, so it is also useful as a fission fuel. Although it is not found in nature, it may be produced in a **breeder**

Figure 29 The elements of a pressurized water reactor employing nuclear fission. Energy from fission heats water, which enters a steam generator, creating steam to run a turbine.

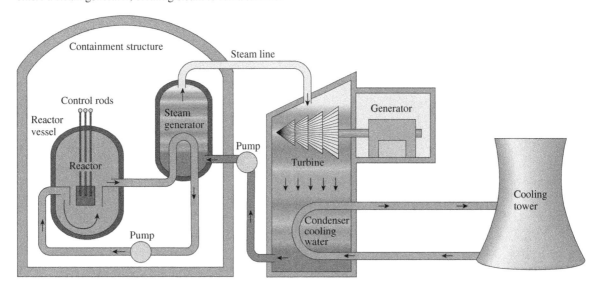

reactor, in which the presence of U-238 is actually desirable. When U-238 absorbs a neutron, it briefly becomes uranium-239, then β^- decays twice, becoming Pu-239, which then serves as fuel for the reactor.

All nuclear reactors currently producing commercial power are fission (as opposed to fusion) reactors. Figure 29 illustrates one of the most common types, a **pressurized water reactor**, in which heat from the reactor transfers first to water, then to a heat exchanger in a steam generator. From this point, it operates just like a fossil fuel power plant, with the steam driving a turbine that runs an electricity generator.

Fusion

Light nuclei, like heavy ones, are less tightly bound than those of intermediate mass number. Thus, as Figure 30 shows, if light nuclei are thrust together to form somewhat heavier ones, the total mass should decrease and kinetic energy should increase. This is fusion. A typical reaction is

$$\underset{2.0141\,u}{{}_1^2\text{H}} + \underset{1.0078\,u}{{}_1^1\text{H}} \rightarrow \underset{3.0160\,u}{{}_2^3\text{He}} + \gamma \qquad Q = 5.48\,\text{MeV}$$

As we see, helium-3 is less massive than hydrogen and deuterium combined. Despite crowding two protons into the same nucleus, this process decreases the internal energy, because the number of attractive, energy-lowering strong bonds triples, from one in the deuterium to three in the helium.

Fusion is the means by which stars generate energy. The most abundant element in stars is hydrogen, and a series of fusion reactions, known as the

Figure 30 Decreasing BE/nucleon via fusion.

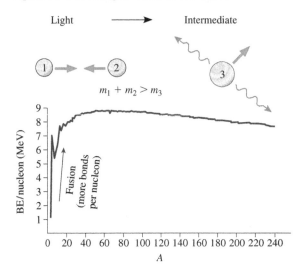

proton–proton cycle, leads it inexorably toward the tightly bound helium-4. Illustrated in Figure 31, the cycle begins with two protons uniting to form a deuteron.

$$\textbf{1:}\ {}_1^1\text{H} + {}_1^1\text{H} \rightarrow {}_1^2\text{H} + {}_{+1}^{0}\beta + \nu \qquad Q = 0.42\ \text{MeV}$$

As we know, there is no bound state of two protons. For this fusion to occur, a proton must first be induced to become a neutron plus a positron and a neutrino. Because this involves the weak force, the process is relatively slow. In the next fusion, the deuteron combines with another proton to form helium-3.

Figure 31 The proton-proton fusion cycle. Protons are shown in light red; neutrons in dark gray.

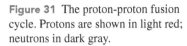
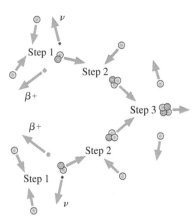

$$\textbf{2:}\ {}_1^2\text{H} + {}_1^1\text{H} \rightarrow {}_2^3\text{He} \qquad Q = 5.48\ \text{MeV}$$

In the final step, two helium-3 nuclei fuse to form helium-4.

$$\textbf{3:}\ {}_2^3\text{He} + {}_2^3\text{He} \rightarrow {}_2^4\text{He} + {}_1^1\text{H} + {}_1^1\text{H} \qquad Q = 12.9\ \text{MeV}$$

This step must be preceded by two of steps 1 and 2. Altogether, the process results in four protons (six from steps 1 and 2 minus two from step 3) becoming helium-4 plus positrons and neutrinos. Meanwhile, 24.7 MeV of energy is released, which is further increased by pair annihilation of the positrons.

While the proton–proton cycle is the primary energy source in our Sun, in stars where the temperature and helium concentration are high enough, another process occurs. Two ${}_2^4\text{He}$ nuclei fuse to form ${}_4^8\text{Be}$, which is unstable and would naturally decay back to two helium-4 nuclei. However, if enough fast-moving helium-4 nuclei are around, another will fuse before the decay can occur, resulting in tightly bound $^{12}_{6}\text{C}$. With this nucleus begins the **carbon cycle**, a much more rapid way of "burning" hydrogen. The steps are as follows:

1: $^{12}_{6}\text{C} + {}^{1}_{1}\text{H} \rightarrow {}^{13}_{7}\text{N}$ **2:** $^{13}_{7}\text{N} \rightarrow {}^{13}_{6}\text{C} + {}^{0}_{+1}\beta + \nu$

3: $^{13}_{6}\text{C} + {}^{1}_{1}\text{H} \rightarrow {}^{14}_{7}\text{N}$ **4:** $^{14}_{7}\text{N} + {}^{1}_{1}\text{H} \rightarrow {}^{15}_{8}\text{O}$

5: $^{15}_{8}\text{O} \rightarrow {}^{15}_{7}\text{N} + {}^{0}_{+1}\beta + \nu$ **6:** $^{15}_{7}\text{N} + {}^{1}_{1}\text{H} \rightarrow {}^{12}_{6}\text{C} + {}^{4}_{2}\text{He}$

In this cycle, carbon-12 is merely a catalyst. It is necessary to initiate the process, but it is not used up, for it reappears at the end. The net effect is the same as in the proton–proton cycle: four protons becoming helium-4 plus two positrons and two neutrinos. But it proceeds much faster, because at no point does it require a proton to become a neutron *before* fusion can occur.

At high enough temperatures and particle concentrations, elements of even higher Z than carbon may be formed in stars. Beyond about $A = 60$, nuclei become *less* tightly bound, so elements beyond the corresponding Z are much less likely to be formed by fusion. However, capture of neutrons freed in other reactions can occur and, when followed by β^{-} decay, leads to the production of elements of higher Z. A similar but quicker process in supernovae is thought to be the primary source of the heaviest elements in the universe.

Whereas fission may occur spontaneously, there is no such thing as spontaneous fusion. Nuclei are positively charged and must be *forced* together. They may well be capable of fusing via the short-range internucleon attraction, but only if their long-range Coulomb repulsion can be surmounted. Figure 32 depicts an analogy: Imagine trying to roll a boulder up the side

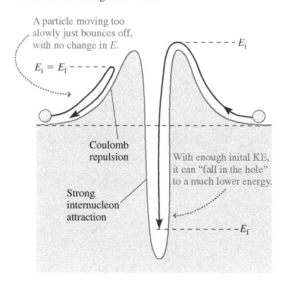

Figure 32 Nuclear fusion: over the Coulomb hurdle, then into the strong force well.

of a volcano so that it falls into a deep hole at the top. If the boulder (one nucleus) is not headed directly toward the center of the volcano (another nucleus) at sufficient speed, it will be deflected to the side or will simply roll back down. Only if initially moving fast enough in the proper direction can it settle into the low-energy hole, whose bottom is *very* far below "ground level." Even if a particle cheats near the finish line by tunneling through the top of the classically forbidden hill, the large available energy, $E_f - E_i$, cannot be released without enough initial energy to make tunneling likely.

We conclude that high density and temperature should favor fusion. A greater density of nuclei implies more frequent collisions, and a higher temperature means that a greater fraction will have enough energy to surmount the Coulomb barrier. The conditions are easily met in a star but not so easily on Earth. The first success was the hydrogen bomb. The high density and temperature were produced by setting off a fission device, or atomic bomb. If properly arranged near the fissioning materials, hydrogen isotopes will fuse in abundance. Pound for pound, fusion explosions are more energetic than fission explosions for the simple reason that, as Figure 14 shows, the binding energy per nucleon increases more steeply from light toward intermediate than from heavy toward intermediate.

The Fusion Reactor

The greater their charge, the greater becomes the difficulty in forcing two nuclei close enough to fuse. Therefore, to achieve significant fusion under conditions not so impractical as detonation of a fission device, the following reactions of $Z = 1$ nuclei are most promising. (D stands for deuterium and T for tritium.)

$$
{}_{1}^{2}\text{D} + {}_{1}^{2}\text{D} \rightarrow
\begin{cases}
{}_{1}^{3}\text{T} + {}_{1}^{1}\text{H} & Q = 4.0\ \text{MeV} \\
{}_{2}^{3}\text{He} + {}_{0}^{1}\text{n} & Q = 3.3\ \text{MeV}
\end{cases}
\tag{18}
$$

$$
{}_{1}^{2}\text{D} + {}_{1}^{3}\text{T} \rightarrow {}_{2}^{4}\text{He} + {}_{0}^{1}\text{n} \quad Q = 17.6\ \text{MeV}
$$

The two D–D reactions occur with about equal probability.

Even these best hopes, however, require conditions of extreme density and temperature that have thus far prevented civilization from exploiting fusion as a viable power source. To gain some idea of the difficulty, let us set the average thermal kinetic energy equal to the electrostatic potential energy that two $+e$ charges would have when separated by the rough nucleon diameter of 2 fm:

$$
\frac{1}{4\pi\varepsilon_0}\frac{q_1 q_2}{r} = \frac{3}{2}k_\text{B}T
$$

$$
9 \times 10^9\ \frac{\text{N} \cdot \text{m}}{\text{C}^2}\frac{(1.6 \times 10^{-19}\ \text{C})^2}{2 \times 10^{-15}\ \text{m}} = \frac{3}{2}(1.38 \times 10^{-23}\ \text{J/K})T
$$

$$
\Rightarrow \quad T \cong 6 \times 10^9\ \text{K}
$$

This overestimates the temperature required. Speeds naturally vary over a range, and particles can quantum-mechanically tunnel through the top of the barrier. Our Sun is thus able to continue burning its fuel at "only" about 10^7 K. Still, even this temperature would vaporize any part of a solid structure it touches. Therefore, to avoid contamination, the fuel in a fusion reactor has to be confined without solid structures! Two methods have received the most attention: magnetic confinement and inertial confinement.

Magnetic Confinement

In a magnetic field, a charged particle is compelled to describe a spiral path along and about the field lines, and this may be exploited to confine nuclei. The most promising magnetic confinement scheme is based on a toroidal magnetic field, as shown in Figure 33(a). A gas of deuterium or deuterium-tritium is heated sufficiently to produce an ionized **plasma** of electrons and positive nuclei. These ions spiral about and along the circular field lines inside the toroid. However, the field weakens near the outside of a toroid, causing charges to drift along the direction of the toroid's axis (opposite ways for opposite charges) and thus escape confinement. To solve this problem, the **tokamak** design includes another set of coils that use electromagnetic induction to produce a huge current in the plasma, which produces its own field perpendicular to the toroidal field. The net field, depicted in Figure 33(b), spirals as it circles the toroid and averages out drift along the axis.

Nevertheless, confinement alone does not ensure pressure or temperature high enough to produce significant fusion. Several heating methods have been tried. One squeezes the plasma with additional magnetic fields; another injects high-energy neutral particles, which are unaffected by the fields and thus can be easily directed for most-effective heating. Unfortunately, other problems arise. Not only do random collisions scatter ions, but all heating methods also tend to destabilize the fuel. Trying to hold a plasma in a magnetic field while "squeezing" it can be very frustrating. The harder we squeeze at one place, the quicker it squirts out elsewhere.

A relatively new magnetic-confinement research facility in the United States is the National Spherical Torus Experiment (NSTX), a collaboration involving several laboratories and universities and located at the Princeton Plasma Physics Laboratory. As the name suggests, the plasma in this device is confined in a region more spherical than donutlike, though still with a hole in the middle. Figure 34 shows the configuration. This shape appears to have several advantages over the conventional tokamak in securing high pressures with fewer instabilities, but much work lies ahead to demonstrate its ultimate potential.

A criterion by which magnetic confinement is judged is **power amplification**, or the ratio of energy released from fusion to energy needed simply to provide heating—notably excluding energy needed for confinement. Established tokamak facilities in Europe and Japan have achieved values approaching 1 in recent years, though a practical breakeven still appears some ways off. Nevertheless, optimism about our abilities to surmount many current hurdles has led to an undertaking much larger than anything presently in operation—the ITER. This proposed facility has the pledged support of many countries worldwide

Figure 33 Magnetic confinement. (a) Charged particles in a toroid follow helical paths along field lines. (b) A tokamak adds a spiral field that averages out drift along the axis.

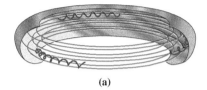

(a)

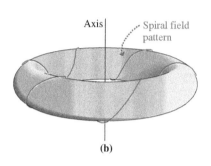

(b)

Figure 34 The National Spherical Torus Experiment and its interesting field pattern.

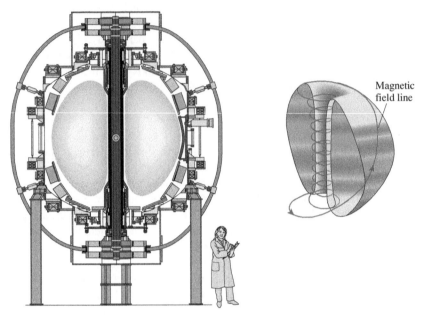

Magnetic
field line

and is expressly dedicated to producing, in essence, a first-generation fusion power plant. Depicted in Figure 35, it is intended to sustain a power amplification of 5. The plan calls for construction to be completed in France in time for plasma testing in 2016.

Inertial Confinement

Inertial confinement involves merely delivering simultaneous blows to a quantity of fuel from many sides so quickly that it has no time to slip away, as shown in Figure 36. The blow can be struck by high-speed heavy ions or by laser pulses.

In the forefront of inertial confinement research is the Omega Laser Facility at the University of Rochester. Here, a target containing deuterium and tritium is struck simultaneously from all sides by 60 beams of 351 nm wavelength laser light. In an instant, the target is vaporized and the fuel transformed into a high-pressure, high-temperature plasma. While studies at this facility continue, with an expansion in the works, the approaching leader in inertial confinement is the National Ignition Facility (NIF) at Lawrence Livermore National Laboratory. Still under construction, though already in partial operation, NIF, depicted in Figure 37, will eventually have 192 laser beams directed at the target. Although direct impact on a deuterium–tritium fuel capsule is possible, the method expected to yield best results is indirect drive, in which the beams strike a heavy-metal (gold or lead) vessel containing the capsule. The metal vessel serves as an intermediary, converting the laser energy to X-rays, which then compress the fuel. Although its primary goal is to demonstrate net energy gain in inertial confinement, NIF is intended to have a number of applications in the field of plasmas and fusion.

Figure 35 ITER (proposed). The first fusion power plant? (Note man near bottom left for scale.)

Figure 36 In inertial confinement fusion, beams of laser light or heavy ions strike a quantity of fuel at once from different directions.

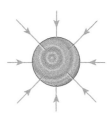

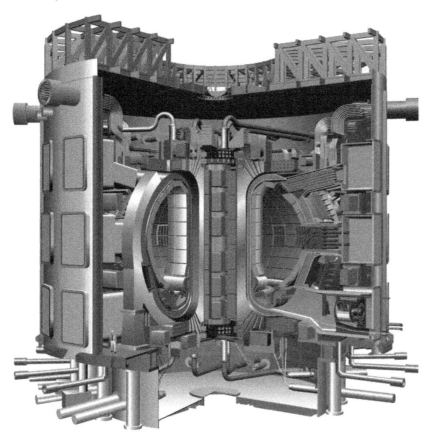

Figure 37 The National Ignition Facility. The insert depicts indirect drive, in which the laser beams are incident at the ends of a metal vessel, producing X-rays that compress the enclosed D-T fuel capsule.

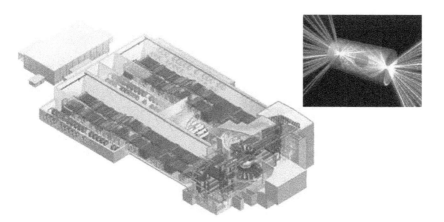

Fission and Fusion: A Comparison

As sources or potential sources of power, fission and fusion share certain characteristics. Because both exploit the energy associated with the strong force, rather than the relatively weak electromagnetic forces of "chemical reactors," they do not use much fuel. Neither requires the huge volumes of fuel needed by conventional fossil fuel power plants. Moreover, they do not produce carbon dioxide gas, an inevitable product of fossil fuel burning that is suspected of contributing to global warming. On the down side, both fission and fusion cause the structures that confine the fuel to become radioactive. The useful lives of these structures are limited, and disposal of such "hot" materials is a problem.

In other aspects, fission and fusion differ in very important ways. First is the nature of the fuel. While rather abundant, uranium and thorium (a promising breeder fuel) are mildly radioactive and, of course, require mining—a costly and sometimes contentious process. Breeding of Pu-239 from U-238 makes very efficient use of natural uranium, but plutonium is highly toxic chemically and must be handled with great care. Deuterium, the future fusion fuel, is chemically harmless hydrogen and is fairly easily distilled from natural water. As a fuel source, it would be practically inexhaustible. Second, and far more important, are the "combustion" products. Fission products tend to be fairly heavy elements that are themselves highly radioactive, often with long half-lives. Disposal of this waste is therefore a serious concern. Fusion products, mostly helium isotopes and tritium, are much less hazardous. Helium is harmless. Tritium *is* radioactive, but its half-life is relatively short, and it is not chemically poisonous. It is far less "dirty" than typical fission products. Finally, fusion does not involve a chain reaction, with its delicate exponential dependence and controls; instead, it "burns" its fuel in a way completely analogous to the chemical fires of conventional power plants. The advantages offered by fusion certainly merit further effort to make it a commercially viable power source.

REAL-WORLD EXAMPLE EXPLOITING AN ABUNDANT ENERGY SOURCE

Unlike earlier ones, our final Real-World Example involves physics not *yet* put into practical application. However, amid growing concerns about reliance on fossil fuels, the subject is attracting increasing scrutiny. If the technical hurdles can be surmounted, the availability, relative clean burning, and power per kilogram of tomorrow's fusion fuel may answer the energy needs of our advancing civilization. Let us see how its energy potential compares with that of the reigning king.

Applying the Physics

The energy available in a barrel of crude oil, released via "chemical fire," is roughly 6 million BTU. About how many barrels of crude oil would be needed to equal the energy that could be extracted from a barrel of seawater by fusion of its deuterium nuclei? (*Note:* 1 barrel = 158 L and 1 BTU = 1055 J.)

SOLUTION

To begin, we find the approximate number of water molecules in a barrel. The molecular mass of water is 18 u. For our estimate, the density of water is a sufficiently good approximation for seawater.

$$\frac{\text{density} \cdot \text{volume}}{\text{mass/molecule}} = \frac{(10^3 \text{ kg/m}^3)(158 \times 10^{-3} \text{ m}^3)}{18 \times 1.66 \times 10^{-27} \text{ kg/molecule}}$$

$$= 5.3 \times 10^{27} \text{ molecules}$$

The number of hydrogen atoms, at two per water molecule, would be twice this number. As noted earlier in the chapter, the percent natural abundance of deuterium is 0.015 %. Thus,

$$\text{number of deuterium atoms} = 2 \times 5.3 \times 10^{27} \times 0.00015$$

$$= 1.6 \times 10^{24}$$

Equation (18) gives fusion reactions of two deuterons, which occur with roughly equal probability, so *each atom's* share of the energy released should be about half the average of two Q values, or about 1.8 MeV. The energy released by complete fusion of the deuterium is therefore

$$\text{total energy} = (1.6 \times 10^{24})(1.8 \times 10^6 \text{ eV})(1.6 \times 10^{-19} \text{ J/eV})$$

$$= 4.6 \times 10^{11} \text{ J} \cong 4 \times 10^8 \text{ BTU}$$

The ratio of the energy available from the deuterium to that from burning the same volume of crude oil is $(4 \times 10^8)/(6 \times 10^6) \cong 70$. About 70 barrels of crude oil would equal 1 barrel of seawater burned by "fusion fire."

Inefficiencies in the standard methods of converting heat energy to electrical energy would reduce the usable power in both processes. But even allowing for efficiency differences at other stages, the availability of seawater relative to crude oil makes our result worthy of consideration.

PROGRESS AND APPLICATIONS

Altering a Half-Life In reference books, we find hundreds of half-lives tabulated, suggesting that they are not subject to variation. For the most part, half-lives do appear to be impervious to external influences, but the possibility of exceptions has been studied for some time. Of the various forms of radioactive decay, electron capture might seem most susceptible, as it depends not only on events within the nucleus but also on the electron orbiting outside. Actually, it is important that the electron is not *always* outside, and as we know (Figure 7.15), wave functions of s-state electrons are nonzero at the origin. Still, even this form of decay has, until recently, appeared largely inert. However, the ubiquitous buckyball has now entered the picture. Since the discovery of fullerenes, science journals have been abuzz with novel ways of getting various atoms or small molecules inside these all-carbon cages and then studying the effects. A team of researchers in Japan has succeeded in stuffing C60 molecules with $^7_3$Be atoms, which decay by electron capture with a half-life of about

53 days (Ohtsuki, et al., *Physical Review Letters*, 26 February 2001). While other environments showed half-life variations of no more than 0.2%, inside the C60 it dropped by nearly 1%. Ideas of substantially altering half-lives to aid with radioactive waste disposal are fanciful, but this new result is certainly of interest, shedding light on radioactivity and the unique environment inside the buckyball.

Pyroelectric Fusion As shown in Section 7, if thermal motion alone is to drive fusion, setting the electrostatic potential energy barrier to the average thermal energy implies a very high temperature. However, setting it equal to $q\Delta V$ shows that a deuterium nucleus need only be accelerated through about 1 MV to fuse with another, even unaided by tunneling. Although not an obviously practical route to fusion power, this alternative method of sticking deuterons together has recently been demonstrated in a surprisingly convenient way that may find numerous

Figure 38 The electric field around a pyroelectric crystal and a sharp tip ionizes deuterium and drives it toward a deuterated target, where nuclear fission occurs.

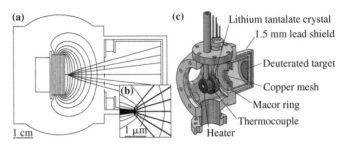

(a)

(b)

1 cm

1 μm

(c)

Lithium tantalate crystal

1.5 mm lead shield

Deuterated target

Copper mesh

Macor ring

Thermocouple

Heater

important applications. A pyroelectric crystal is one that causes charge to separate when it is heated. Researchers at UCLA used this effect to produce deuterons and to accelerate them toward other deuterons (B Naranjo, et al., *Science*, 28 April 2005, 115–117). Figure 38 illustrates the apparatus. Positive charge from one face of the crystal collected at a sharp tungsten tip. Heating the crystal by just 25 K produced an electric field at the tip greater than 25 GV/m, sufficiently high to ionize nearby atoms in a surrounding gas of deuterium. This field and that of the crystal itself then drove the resulting ions away violently, imparting kinetic energies in excess of 80 keV. The ions then struck a target of deuterated erbium and, aided by tunneling, fused in great numbers. The evidence was a flux of 2.45 MeV neutrons from the reaction $D + D \rightarrow {}_2^3He + n$, which was far in excess of the background level and proportional to the ion current. Although the actual energy output in this setup was rather modest, the researchers anticipate that larger tips or arrays of tips combined with operation at cryogenic temperatures can scale the effect by a factor of 1000. This may lead to a reliable, handheld neutron source, and one day might even power thrusters in miniature spacecraft.

Medical Imaging: Turning on Gammas with a Neutron Beam Medical imaging has seen the establishment of a number of new techniques in recent decades, among them the CT scan, which employs X-rays, and MRI, which uses radio-frequency electromagnetic radiation and an external magnetic field. All imaging methods have their strengths and weaknesses, so the search for new ones continues. A promising technique in early development is neutron stimulated emission computed tomography, or NSECT (Floyd Jr., et al., *Physics in Medicine and Biology*, 23 June 2006, 3375–3390). This method uses relatively high-energy neutrons, produced in the same fusion reaction noted in

connection with pyroelectric fusion, $D + D \rightarrow {}_2^3He + n$. As presently implemented, the deuterons emerge from an accelerator with a kinetic energy of 2.8 MeV, giving 6 MeV neutrons. Leaving the helium nuclei behind, the neutrons pass through a collimator, producing a narrow beam, then to the target. Here they scatter inelastically from nuclei, raising the nuclei to excited states from which they deexcite by gamma decay.

As noted in Section 5, gamma energies are like fingerprints, distinguishing one element from another, and this is one of the great potential advantages of the new technique. While X-rays respond simply to electron density and MRI images work best for only certain isotopes (in ways dependent on and potentially obscured by the local electromagnetic environment), NSECT can lay bare the presence of all elements. The only exceptions are hydrogen, whose nucleus has no excited states, and helium, whose excitation energies are above 6 MeV. (Helium isn't of much concern in the body, anyway.) Because neutrons, being uncharged, penetrate the body quite well, the technique has the potential for true 3D imaging, and the ability to distinguish all elements would be a great advantage. For reasons not yet fully understood, cancers in the early stages cause changes in ratios of certain trace elements. Thus, by comparing gamma intensities, NSECT might identify regions of concern by a noninvasive scan long before present scanning techniques would notice anything unusual and without the tissue extraction required by other methods. Of course, it is natural to ask what hazards the high-energy neutrons themselves might pose. Investigation of this aspect continues, but the belief is that the radiation dosage per volume would ultimately be less than that in a standard chest X-ray. Besides early cancer detection, the technique could provide a vital new way to track movements of metabolic tracers—both stable and unstable—within the body.

Chapter Summary

The constituents of the nucleus—protons and neutrons—are known collectively as nucleons. The mass number A is the number of nucleons, and the atomic number Z, which identifies the element, is the number of protons. Nuclei of the same atomic number but different numbers of neutrons are called isotopes of the given element. Nuclear radii are in the range of femtometers (1 fm $= 10^{-15}$ m), about 5 orders of magnitude smaller than radii typical of electron orbits in atoms. All nuclei have about the same density, suggesting a closest-packed arrangement of incompressible spheres.

The predominant forces in the nucleus are the strong force, a strong, short-range attraction between all nucleons but with a central hard core; and the electrostatic force, a weaker but more far-reaching repulsion between all protons. Along with the exclusion principle, these forces cause nuclei of intermediate mass number to be most stable. For nuclei around $A = 60$, the greatest energy per nucleon would have to be expended to separate the nucleons. Furthermore, light nuclei are most stable when the numbers of protons and neutrons are about equal, while in heavy nuclei, the most tightly bound arrangement has more neutrons than protons, reducing the destabilizing effect of Coulomb repulsion.

The energies binding nucleons to their nuclei are about 5 orders of magnitude larger than those binding electrons to their atoms. Thus, much more so than the atom, the nucleus has a mass significantly less than that of its separated parts. Binding energy may be calculated directly from this mass difference.

$$BE = \left(Zm_H + Nm_n - M_{Z}^{A}X\right)c^2 \qquad (5)$$

Because of our incomplete knowledge of the strong force, the nuclear "problem" cannot be solved exactly. Models must be used. The liquid drop model and shell model have been particularly successful.

Unstable nuclei attain a lower energy state via radioactive decay. Forms include α decay, in which the nucleus expels a bound two-proton–two-neutron particle; β decay, in which a neutron becomes a proton, or vice versa, and an electron or positron is created; electron capture, in which an orbiting electron is seized and combined with a proton, producing a neutron; and γ decay, in which a photon carries away excess nuclear energy.

Radioactive decay is probabilistic. Consequently, the number of radioactive nuclei present in a sample drops exponentially with time. The most common measure of the decay rate is half-life, $T_{1/2}$, or the time required for the number of nuclei present to decay to half its initial value.

$$N = N_0 e^{-\lambda t} \qquad (13) \qquad\qquad \lambda = \frac{\ln 2}{T_{1/2}} \qquad (15)$$

A nuclear reaction occurs when nucleons are changed or exchanged among nuclei. Reactions may be either endothermic or exothermic, depending on whether the mass increases or decreases, and the kinetic energy released is given by

$$Q = (m_i - m_f)c^2 \qquad (7)$$

Particularly important exothermic reactions are fission and fusion, which exploit the very tight binding of intermediate-mass nuclei. In fission, heavy nuclei are split, and in fusion, light nuclei are brought together. In either case, the lost mass energy becomes the kinetic energy of the products.

---

* indicates advanced questions

Conceptual Questions

1. Explain to your perplexed friend how you can bring together twelve objects of mass 1.01 and end up with one object of mass 12.00.
2. How is it that a high binding energy is a low energy?
3. In Section 2, it is said that iron and nickel represent maximum stability. Chemistry emphasizes that helium is the most stable element? How can these claims be reconciled?
4. Why might a flat-bottom finite well be a better approximation of the potential well confining nucleons than a Coulomb well, tapering to a lowest energy in the middle?
5. The semiempirical binding energy formula has four terms. Suppose we have a nucleus with 18 protons and 22 neutrons. For each term in the formula, indicate (without calculation) whether adding one more proton would cause an increase or a decrease, and explain why it should have this effect. Focus on the underlying idea.
6. The vast majority of measured nuclear spins are fairly small, between zero and nine times $\frac{1}{2}\hbar$. More to the point, nuclear spin does not uniformly increase with A. Argue that if the assumptions in the shell model are valid, then these observations are not unexpected.
7. Using Figure 14 as a guide, explain why the heaviest of naturally occurring nuclei might be inclined to emit α particles but not to emit other small groups of nucleons.
8. Certain nuclei with half-lives between days and a few years are found in nature in small abundances that do not change at all over many, many years. How is this possible? (*Hint:* Natural uranium and thorium have *very* long half-lives.)
9. Why does fission of heavy nuclei tend to produce free neutrons?
10. In both D–D reactions in equation (18), two deuterons fuse to produce *two* particles, a nucleus of $A = 3$ and a free nucleon. Mass decreases because the

binding energy of the $A = 3$ nucleus is greater than the combined binding energies of the two deuterons. The binding energy of helium-4 is even greater still. Why can't the deuterons simply fuse into a helium-4 nucleus and nothing else? Why must multiple particles be produced?

11. Thorium-232 is rather abundant on Earth and is now coming into use as a breeder fuel. It behaves almost exactly like uranium-238, merely shifted by even numbers of protons and neutrons, which means that it is not the actual fission fuel. What isotope is?

12. An untrained but perceptive friend exclaims, "They say that nuclear energy can be released by sticking nuclei together and by breaking them apart. That doesn't make sense!" Straighten out your friend's confusion.

Exercises

Section 1

13. What fraction of space is actually occupied by iron nuclei in a "solid" piece of iron? (The density of iron is 7.87×10^3 kg/m^3.)

14. At what speed would α particles have to be directed at gold foil if some are to contact gold nuclei?

15. From the abundances and atomic masses given of the two naturally occurring isotopes of boron, determine the average atomic mass of natural boron. Compare this with the value given in the periodic table.

16. Determine the approximate ratio of the diameter of a uranium nucleus ($A = 238$) to that of a beryllium nucleus ($A = 9$).

Section 2

17. (a) For a nucleus of $A = 220$, estimate very roughly how many nucleons would be at the surface. (b) If the binding energy of an *interior* nucleon due to the internucleon attraction were E_1 and if *all* nucleons were as tightly bound, the total binding energy would be AE_1. Taking into account the different binding of surface nucleons, roughly what would be the total binding energy?

18. To remove one electron from helium requires 24.6 eV, and removing its second takes 54.5 eV. The ionization energy of hydrogen is 13.6 eV. When applied to helium-4, by what percentage is equation (5) in error due to its ignoring of electronic binding energies?

19. Show that the energy required to remove a neutron from helium-4 is 20.6 MeV.

20. By classical, hard-sphere assumptions, what smallest value of A would make one nucleon surrounded? Relate your answer to Figure 14.

21. By considering how many other spheres could be put in contact with a given sphere, calculate the maximum possible number of strong bonds per nucleon for a surrounded nucleon. (*Note:* Because nucleons share a bond, each nucleon "owns" only half a given bond.) Recalling that the deuteron, ^{2}H, has half a bond per nucleon, how does your calculated maximum number correspond to Figure 14?

22. Calculate the binding energy per nucleon of technetium-98.

23. Calculate the binding energy per nucleon of carbon-12.

Section 3

24. Using the semiempirical binding energy formula, estimate the mass of a europium-152 atom.

25. According to the semiempirical binding energy formula, what should be the binding energy per nucleon of technetium-98?

26. Nuclei of the same mass number but different Z are known as **isobars**. Oxygen-15 and nitrogen-15 are isobars. (a) In which of the factors considered in nuclear binding (represented by terms in the semiempirical binding energy formula) do these two isobars differ? (b) Which of the isobars should be more tightly bound? (c) Is your conclusion in part (b) supported by the decay mode information? Explain. (d) Calculate the binding energies of oxygen-15 and nitrogen-15. By how much do they differ? (e) Repeat part (d) but use the semiempirical binding energy formula rather than the known atomic masses.

27. (a) Calculate the binding energies per nucleon of the isobars (defined in Exercise 26) boron-12, carbon-12, and nitrogen-12. (b) In which of the terms of the semiempirical binding energy formula do these binding energies differ, and how should these differences affect the binding energies per nucleon? (c) Determine the binding energies per nucleon using the semiempirical binding energy formula, and discuss the results.

28. What does the semiempirical binding energy formula predict for the mass of a carbon-12 atom? Comment on your answer.

29. The first two terms in the semiempirical binding energy formula deal solely with the internucleon attraction. (a) Calculate the ratio of the second term to the first term for $A = 20$. What does it say about the surface nucleons? (b) Repeat part (a), but for $A = 220$.

30. The semiempirical binding energy formula predicts the binding energies of neon-20, iron-56, and uranium-238 within about 1%. Make a 3×9 table whose rows are the three isotopes, whose first four columns are numerical values of the four terms in the formula, whose next four columns are each of these terms *divided by A*, and whose final column is the sum of the preceding four. Discuss in some detail what the table reveals.

31. Exercise 19 notes that the energy needed to remove a neutron from helium-4 is 20.6 MeV. (a) Show that the energy required to remove a proton is 19.8 MeV. (b) Why do these values disagree with the BE/nucleon value shown for helium-4 in Figure 14? (*Hint:* Consider nuclei around helium-4 in the figure.)

32. Obtain a semiempirical binding energy *per nucleon* formula. Using this as a guide, explain why the Coulomb force, which is only about $\frac{1}{100}$ as strong as the internucleon attraction for two protons "in contact" (cf. Table 2), would eventually *have to become* a dominant factor in large nuclei. Assume that Z, N, and A increase in rough proportion to one another.

* **33.** Gives the Fermi energy for a collection of identical fermions packed into the lowest energies allowed by the exclusion principle. Argue that if applied to neutrons or protons (ignoring their repulsion) in a nucleus, the equation suggests that the Fermi energy is roughly the same for all nuclei. Making the rough approximation that the spacing between quantum levels is a constant in a given nucleus, argue that this spacing should vary from one nucleus to another in proportion to A^{-1}.

Section 4

34. All target nuclei used in MRI have an odd number of protons or neutrons or both. What does this suggest about nuclear spins? (*Note:* Both the proton and the neutron have gyromagnetic ratios.)

35. In electron spin resonance, incoming electromagnetic radiation of the proper (resonant) frequency causes the electron's magnetic moment to go from its lower-energy, or "relaxed," orientation, aligned with the external field, to its higher-energy antialigned state. MRI is analogous. A quantity commonly discussed in MRI is the ratio of the frequency of the incoming radiation to the external magnetic field. Calculate this ratio for hydrogen. Note that the proton gyromagnetic ratio, g_p, is 5.6.

36. MRI relies on only a tiny majority of the nuclear magnetic moments aligning with the external field. Consider the common target nucleus hydrogen. The difference between the aligned and antialigned states of a dipole in a magnetic field is $2\mu_z B$. Using the Boltzmann distribution, show that for a 1.0 T field and a reasonable temperature, the number aligned exceeds the number antialigned by less than $\frac{1}{1000}\%$.

Section 5

37. As noted in Section 5, carbon-11 decays to boron-11. How do the various factors involved in nuclear stability argue that such a decay is favorable?

38. Calculate Q for neutron decay.

39. How much kinetic energy is released and what is the daughter nucleus in the α decay of polonium-210?

40. How much kinetic energy is released and what is the daughter nucleus in the β^+ decay of nitrogen-13?

41. Oxygen-19 β^- decays. What is the daughter nucleus, and what may be said of the kinetic energy of the emitted β^- particle?

42. Polonium-207 may undergo three kinds of radioactive decay: β^+, α, and electron capture. But it does not β^- decay. Given its position relative to the curve of stability, explain why this is not unexpected.

43. Potassium-40 ($Z = 19$, $N = 21$) is a radioactive isotope that is rare but not unknown in nature. It is particularly interesting in that it lies along the curve of stability yet decays by *both* β^+ and β^-—that is, in both directions *away* from the curve of stability. (a) Identify the daughter nuclei for both decays. (b) Many factors governing nuclear stability are discussed in the chapter (e.g., those in the semiempirical binding energy formula, magic numbers, and even numbers). Identify those that would argue *only* for β^- decay. (c) Which factors argue *only* for β^+ decay? (d) Which argue for either β^- or β^+ decay?

44. Find Q for the decay of beryllium-10.

45. Calcium-41 decays by electron capture. (a) Find Q for the decay. (b) Show that calcium-41 cannot decay by β^+ emission.

* **46.** Using the semiempirical binding energy formula to determine whether energy would likely be released, would you expect the hypothetical nucleus $^{288}_{119}X$ to (a) α decay, (b) β^+ decay, or (c) β^- decay?

47. The total kinetic energy carried by the products of the spontaneous fission of plutonium-240 is typically about 180 MeV. Use this to argue that reduction in Coulomb repulsion is the main impetus behind the process. Assume for simplicity that the two fragment nuclei are of equal Z.

48. Glancing at the binding energy per nucleon plot of Figure 14—with its maximum around iron, $Z = 26$—it might naively be argued that fission would be favorable for any nucleus of about $Z = 52$ or higher. Show that if tellurium-130 broke into two iron-56 nuclei, freeing the excess neutrons, the total binding energy would actually *decrease*. Explain what is wrong with the naïve argument.

49. What is the recoil speed of the daughter nucleus when $^{152}_{67}\text{Ho}$ α decays? (Treat all motion as nonrelativistic.)

Section 6

50. Given initially 100 g of plutonium-239, how much time must pass for the amount to drop to 1 g?

51. The initial decay rate of a sample of a certain radioactive isotope is 2.00×10^{11} s^{-1}. After half an hour, the decay rate is 6.42×10^{10} s^{-1}. Determine the half-life of the isotope.

52. The half-life $T_{1/2}$ is not the average lifetime τ of a radioactive nucleus. We find the average lifetime by multiplying t by the probability per unit time $P(t)$ that the nucleus will "live" that long, then integrating over all time. (a) Show that $P(t)$ should be given by $\lambda e^{-\lambda t}$. (*Hint:* What must be the *total* probability?) (b) Show that $\tau = T_{1/2}/\ln 2$.

53. Eighty centuries after its death, what will be the decay rate of 1 g of carbon from the thigh bone of an animal?

54. A fossil specimen has a carbon-14 decay rate of 3.0 s^{-1}. (a) How many carbon-14 nuclei are present? (b) If this number is $\frac{1}{10}$ the number that must have been present when the animal died, how old is the fossil?

55. A fossil specimen has a ^{14}C decay rate of 5.0 s^{-1}. (a) How many carbon-14 nuclei are present? (b) If the specimen is 20,000 years old, how many carbon-14 nuclei were present when the animal died? (c) How much kinetic energy (in MeV) is released in each β decay, and what is the total amount released in all β decays since the animal died?

56. A bone of an animal contains $\frac{1}{10}$ mol of carbon when it dies. (a) How many carbon-14 atoms would be left after 200,000 yr? (b) Is carbon-14 dating useful to predict the age of such an old bone? Explain.

57. Potassium-40 has a half-life of 1.26×10^9 yr, decaying to calcium-40 and argon-40 in a ratio of 8.54 to 1. If a rock sample contained no argon when it formed a solid but now contains one argon-40 atom for every potassium-40 atom, how old is the rock?

58. (a) Determine the total amount of energy released in the complete decay of 1 mg of tritium. (b) According to the law of radioactive decay, how much time would this release of energy span? (c) In a practical sense, how much time will it span?

59. Given initially 40 mg of radium-226 (one of the decay products of uranium-238), determine (a) the amount that will be left after 500 yr, (b) the number of α particles the radium will have emitted during this time, and (c) the amount of kinetic energy that will have been released. (d) Find the decay rate of the radium at the end of the 500 yr.

60. Ten milligrams of pure polonium-210 is placed in 500 g of water. If no heat is allowed to escape to the surroundings, how much will the temperature rise in 1 hr?

Section 7

61. Determine Q for the reaction

$$^{7}_{3}\text{Li} + ^{1}_{1}\text{H} \rightarrow ^{7}_{4}\text{Be} + ^{1}_{0}\text{n}$$

62. Calculate the net amount of energy released in the deuterium-tritium reaction

$$^{2}_{1}\text{D} + ^{3}_{1}\text{T} \rightarrow ^{4}_{2}\text{He} + ^{1}_{0}\text{n}$$

63. In an assembly of fissionable material, the larger the surface area per fissioning nucleus (i.e., per unit volume), the more likely is the escape of valuable neutrons. (a) What is the surface-to-volume ratio of a sphere of radius r_0? (b) What is the surface-to-volume ratio of a cube of the same volume? (c) What is the surface-to-volume ratio of a sphere of twice the volume?

64. If all the nuclei in a pure sample of uranium-235 were to fission, yielding about 200 MeV each, what is the kinetic energy yield in joules per kilogram of fuel?

65. (a) To release 100 MW of power, approximately how many uranium fissions must occur every second? (b) How many kilograms of U-235 would have to fission in 1 yr?

66. Two deuterons can fuse to form different products. Although not the most probable outcome, one possibility is helium-4 plus a gamma particle (see Conceptual Question 10). Calculate the net energy released in this process.

67. Consider equal numbers of deuterium and tritium nuclei fusing to form helium-4 nuclei, as given in equation (18). (a) What is the yield in joules of kinetic energy liberated per kilogram of fuel? (b) How does this compare with a typical yield of 10^6 J/kg for chemical fuels?

68. For the carbon cycle to become established, helium-4 nuclei must fuse to form beryllium-8. Calculate Q for this reaction.

69. Ignoring annihilation energies of the positrons, how much total kinetic energy is released in the six-step carbon cycle? (There is a quick way to answer this, and a much slower way.)

70. (a) How much energy can be extracted by deuterium fusion from a gallon of sea water? Assume that an average D–D fusion yield is about 2 MeV per atom.

(b) A modern supertanker can hold 9×10^7 gallons. How many "water tankers" would be needed to supply the energy needs of greater Los Angeles, consuming electricity at a rate of about 20 GW, for 1 yr? Assume that only 20% of the available energy actually becomes electrical energy.

71. A fusion reaction used to produce neutron beams (see Progress and Applications) is

$$^2_1D + {}^2_1D \rightarrow {}^3_2He + {}^1_0n$$

Assuming that the kinetic energy before the fusion is negligible compared with the energy released, calculate the neutron kinetic energy after the fusion.

Comprehensive Exercises

72. The binding energy per nucleon in helium-3 is 2.57 MeV/nucleon. Assuming a nucleon separation of 2.5 fm, determine (a) the gravitational potential energy *per nucleon* and (b) the electrostatic energy *per proton* between the protons. (c) What is the approximate value of the internucleon potential energy per nucleon? (d) Do these results agree qualitatively with Table 2?

73. For the lightest of nuclei, binding energy per nucleon is not a very reliable gauge of stability. There is no nucleon binding at all for a single proton or neutron,

yet one is stable (so far as we know) and the other is not. (a) Helium-3 and hydrogen-3 (tritium) differ only in the switch of a nucleon. Which has the higher binding energy per nucleon? (b) Helium-3 is stable, while tritium, in fact, decays into helium-3. Does this somehow violate laws?

74. You occupy a one-dimensional world in which beads—of mass m_0 when isolated—attract each other if and only if in contact. Were the beads to interact solely by this attraction, it would take energy H to break the contact. Consequently, we could extract this much energy by sticking two together. However, they also share a repulsive force, no matter what their separation, for which the potential energy is $U(r) = 0.85Ha/r$, where a is a bead's radius and r is center-to-center separation. The closer the beads, the higher is this energy. (a) For one stationary bead, by how much does the energy differ from m_0c^2? (b) For two stationary beads in contact, by how much does the energy differ from $2m_0c^2$? (c) For three beads in contact (in a line, of course, since this world is one-dimensional), by how much does the energy differ from $3m_0c^2$? (d) For four beads in contact, by how much does the energy differ from $4m_0c^2$? (e) If you had 12 isolated beads and wished to extract the most energy by sticking them together (in linear groupings), into sets of what number would you group them? (f) Sets of what number would be suitable fuel for the release of fusion energy? Of fission energy?

Answers to Selected Exercises

13. 3×10^{-14}

15. 10.811 u

17. ~ 145, $\sim 150E_I$

21. 6

23. 7.68 MeV/nuc

25. 8.75 MeV/nuc

27. (a) 6.63 MeV/nuc, 7.68 MeV/nuc, 6.17 MeV/nuc; (c) 6.85 MeV/nuc, 7.25 MeV/nuc, 6.28 MeV/nuc

29. (a) 0.42; (b) 0.19

35. 43 MHz/T

37. reduced Coulomb repulsion

39. lead-206, 5.41 MeV

41. fluorine-19, 4.82 MeV, a maximum KE, since shared with antineutrino

43. (a) Ar-40, Ca-40; (b) magic numbers, asymmetry; (c) Coulomb repulsion; (d) even numbers

45. 0.713 MeV

49. 3.94×10^5 m/s

51. 18.3 min

53. 5.7 per min

55. 1.30×10^{12}, 1.47×10^{13}, 0.156 MeV, 0.332 J

57. 4.28×10^9 yr

59. 32.2 mg, 2.1×10^{19}, 1.6×10^7 J, 1.2×10^9 s^{-1}

61. -1.64 MeV

63. (a) $3/r_0$; (b) $3.72/r_0$; (c) $2.38/r_0$

65. 3.13×10^{18} fissions/s, 38.5 kg/yr

67. 3.4×10^{14} J/kg, about eight orders of magnitude larger

69. 24.7 MeV

71. 2.45 MeV

73. hydrogen-3

Credits

Photograph Credits

17: Donna Beeler/Shutterstock; **35:** ITER International Fusion Energy Organization (IIFEO); **37:** National Ignition Facility

Art Credits

29: Courtesy of the Tennessee Valley Authority; **34:** Courtesy of the Princeton Plasma Physics Laboratory; **38:** Courtesy of *Nature* magazine

Appendix:

Solving for the Fourier Transform

Here we derive equation extracting $A(k)$ from below equation.

$$\psi(x) = \int\limits_{-\infty}^{+\infty} A(k)\, e^{ikx}\, dk$$

The trick is to multiply by $e^{-ik'x}$, then integrate over x from $-b$ to $+b$ on both sides. After some rearranging on the right side, the result is

$$\int\limits_{-b}^{+b} \psi(x)\, e^{-ik'x}\, dx = \int\limits_{-\infty}^{+\infty} A(k)\left[\int\limits_{-b}^{+b} e^{i(k-k')x}\, dx \right] dk \qquad (1)$$

Let us concentrate on the integral in brackets.

$$\int\limits_{-b}^{+b} e^{i(k-k')x}\, dx = \frac{e^{i(k-k')b} + e^{-i(k-k')b}}{i(k-k')} = \frac{2\sin[(k-k')b]}{k-k'} \qquad (2)$$

Note that we have used the relationship $\sin z = (e^{+iz} - e^{-iz})/2i$ that follows from the Euler formula.

To obtain our final result, we will let b approach infinity, but the behavior of the function on the right side of (2) is a bit peculiar. Figure 1 shows this function plotted versus k for two different values of b. In either case, it is just $2/(k-k')$ times a sine that oscillates back and forth between $+1$ and -1; but the larger the b, the faster the oscillation. Also note that as b increases, the function becomes more sharply peaked at $k = k'$. In fact, by l'Hopital's rule, its value at $k = k'$ is $2b$, as indicated in the figure, so it becomes infinitely tall there as b approaches ∞. Now, it happens that the *integral* of the right side of (2) over all k—the area under the curve—is always 2π, independent of b or k' (changing k' just "slides" it right or left). Thus, the infinitely tall peak at $k = k'$ must effectively become infinitesimally narrow. At all other regions on the k-axis, it oscillates infinitely rapidly between $+1$ and -1. When multiplying any reasonably smooth but otherwise arbitrary function—such as $A(k)$—it would cause the product to average to zero. In other words, in equation (1), it really doesn't matter what $A(k)$ is anywhere but at $k = k'$—its values elsewhere will be

Figure 1 An arbitrary smooth function $A(k)$, and one sharply peaked at $k = k'$. As b becomes large, $2 \sin[(k - k')b]/(k - k')$ becomes a narrow but tall peak, with rapidly oscillating "wings."

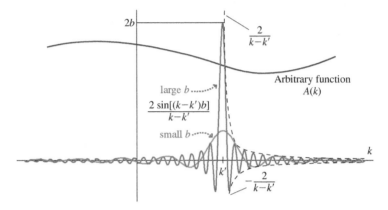

averaged to zero. It might as well be just the constant value $A(k')$, which can be pulled out of the integral! Therefore, in the limit $b \to \infty$ the *right* side of (1) becomes

$$\int_{-\infty}^{+\infty} A(k) \lim_{b \to \infty} \frac{2 \sin\left[(k - k')b\right]}{k - k'} \, dk = A(k') \lim_{b \to \infty} \int_{-\infty}^{+\infty} \frac{2 \sin\left[(k - k')b\right]}{k - k'} \, dk$$

$$= A(k')2\pi \tag{3}$$

where we have used the fact, as noted, that the integral is 2π. Having allowed b to go to infinity on the right side of (1), we do the same on the left side, arriving at

$$\int_{-\infty}^{+\infty} \psi(x)e^{-ik'x} \, dx = 2\pi A(k') \quad \text{or} \quad A(k') = \frac{1}{2\pi} \int_{-\infty}^{+\infty} \psi(x)e^{-ik'x} \, dx \tag{4}$$

Now that the earlier k is gone, we can choose to omit the prime, giving us equation (22).

Having shown what we set out to show, it is worthwhile to take a second look at our "peculiar" function. In equation (3), it might be a function of any arbitrary variable—for instance, z rather than k—and the function it accompanies in the integral would also be a function of z. Dividing both sides of (3) by 2π, we can thus say that

$$\int_{-\infty}^{+\infty} A(z) \left\{ \lim_{b \to \infty} \frac{\sin\left[(z - z')b\right]}{\pi(z - z')} \right\} dz = A(z') \tag{5}$$

The function in braces has an unusual property—it "sifts" out the value of $A(z)$ at the point z' only. It does this because it goes to infinity at $z = z'$ but is zero everywhere else. This may sound rather pathological, and indeed it is, but it is much used in physics and is in fact the way we represent a particle whose position is known precisely— nonzero only at the point $z = z'$. It is called the **Dirac delta function**. We leave further study of this weird function to a higher-level course.

Appendix:
The Momentum Operator

The derivation of the momentum operator rests on the assertion that the Fourier transform $A(k)$ is to wave number k what $\psi(x)$ is to position x: a probability amplitude of finding a value—of either x or k. The symmetry in the way x and k appear in equations (21) and (22) is certainly suggestive.

$$\psi(x) = \int\limits_{-\infty}^{+\infty} A(k)e^{ikx}\,dk \quad (21) \qquad A(k) = \frac{1}{2\pi}\int\limits_{-\infty}^{+\infty} \psi(x)e^{-ikx}\,dx \quad (22)$$

In particular, a Gaussian function that progressively changes from a spiky function of well-defined x in the bottom plot to a very broad plane wave of well-defined wave number/momentum in the top plot, whose Fourier transform is a spiky function of k. Just as $|\psi(x)|^2$ is the probability per distance of finding the particle at x, $|A(k)|^2$ is the probability per wave number of finding the particle to have wave number k. It follows that if we write

$$\overline{x} = \int\limits_{-\infty}^{+\infty} x|\psi(x)|^2\,dx$$

then we must write

$$\overline{k} = 2\pi \int\limits_{-\infty}^{+\infty} k|A(k)|^2\,dk \quad (1)$$

(We take up the 2π later.) Because $p = \hbar k$, to know $\overline{k}$ is to know $\overline{p}$.

However, we wish to calculate $\overline{k}$ using $\psi(x)$, not its Fourier transform, so we eliminate $A(k)$ by inserting and its complex conjugate into (1).

$$\overline{k} = \frac{1}{2\pi}\int\limits_{-\infty}^{+\infty} k\left(\int\limits_{-\infty}^{+\infty} \psi(x')e^{-ikx'}\,dx'\right)^*\left(\int\limits_{-\infty}^{+\infty} \psi(x)e^{-ikx}\,dx\right)dk$$

or, rearranging a bit,

$$\overline{k} = \frac{1}{2\pi}\int\limits_{-\infty}^{+\infty}\int\limits_{-\infty}^{+\infty}\int\limits_{-\infty}^{+\infty} k\,\psi^*(x')e^{+ikx'}\left(\psi(x)e^{-ikx}\right)dx\,dx'\,dk \quad (2)$$

Let us integrate by parts the term in parentheses involving x.

$$\int\limits_{-\infty}^{+\infty} \psi(x)e^{-ikx}\,dx = \int\limits_{-\infty}^{+\infty} \psi(x)\,d\left(\frac{i}{k}e^{-ikx}\right)$$

$$= \psi(x)\frac{i}{k}e^{-ikx}\bigg|_{-\infty}^{+\infty} - \int\limits_{-\infty}^{+\infty} \frac{d\psi(x)}{dx}\frac{i}{k}e^{-ikx}\,dx$$

Assuming that $\psi(x)$ is well behaved, falling to 0 at $x = \pm\infty$, the first term on the right is 0. When we reinsert the second term into (2), we see that k cancels.

$$\bar{k} = \frac{1}{2\pi}\int\limits_{-\infty}^{+\infty}\int\limits_{-\infty}^{+\infty}\int\limits_{-\infty}^{+\infty} \psi^*(x')e^{+ikx'}(-i)\frac{d\psi(x)}{dx}e^{-ikx}\,dx\,dx'\,dk$$

or

$$\bar{k} = \frac{1}{2\pi}\int\limits_{-\infty}^{+\infty}\int\limits_{-\infty}^{+\infty} \psi^*(x')\left[\int\limits_{-\infty}^{+\infty} e^{+ik(x'-x)}\,dk\right](-i)\frac{d\psi(x)}{dx}\,dx\,dx' \tag{3}$$

Now the integration over k may be carried out, but here we must be careful. Writing it explicitly as a limit, we have

$$\lim_{b\to\infty}\int\limits_{-b}^{+b} e^{+ik(x'-x)}\,dk = \lim_{b\to\infty}\frac{e^{+ib(x'-x)} - e^{-ib(x'-x)}}{i(x'-x)} = \lim_{b\to\infty}\frac{2\sin[(x'-x)b]}{x'-x}$$

Thus, (3) becomes

$$\bar{k} = \frac{1}{2\pi}\int\limits_{-\infty}^{+\infty}\int\limits_{-\infty}^{+\infty} \psi^*(x')\left\{\lim_{b\to\infty}\frac{2\sin[(x'-x)b]}{x'-x}\right\}(-i)\frac{d\psi(x)}{dx}\,dx'\,dx$$

Grouping together the functions of x' and moving the 2π into the integral then gives

$$\bar{k} = \int\limits_{-\infty}^{+\infty}\left[\int\limits_{-\infty}^{+\infty} \psi^*(x')\left\{\lim_{b\to\infty}\frac{\sin[(x'-x)b]}{\pi(x'-x)}\right\}dx'\right](-i)\frac{d\psi(x)}{dx}\,dx \tag{4}$$

Integrals having the form of the x' integration in brackets. Using equation (5), we arrive at

$$\bar{k} = \int\limits_{-\infty}^{+\infty} \psi^*(x)(-i)\frac{d\psi(x)}{dx}\,dx \tag{5}$$

Now, regarding the factor of 2π in (1), for that formula to make sense, the average of 1 must be 1.

$$2\pi \int_{-\infty}^{+\infty} 1 \, |A(k)|^2 \, dk = 1 \qquad (6)$$

To carry out this integral, we would follow the same course as before, skipping only the integration by parts that cancels to the k—equation (6) doesn't have one—and replaces $\psi(x)$ by $-i$ times its derivative. Thus, in place of (5), we would have

$$1 = \int_{-\infty}^{+\infty} \psi^*(x)\psi(x) \, dx$$

Because this must hold, equation (6) must also hold, so we see that equation (1) "needs" the 2π to satisfy normalization.

Finally, multiplying both sides of (5) by $\hbar$ and using $p = \hbar k$, we have

$$\overline{p} = \int_{-\infty}^{+\infty} \psi^*(x)(-i\hbar)\frac{d\psi(x)}{dx} dx$$

We conclude that to calculate the expectation value of the momentum, we must apply the operator $-i\hbar(d/dx)$ to the wave function $\psi(x)$ in the probability integral. (*Note:* Had we considered the full $\Psi(x, t)$, we would have employed partial derivatives with respect to x, and to be general, the operator is usually written in that form.)

Appendix:

Time Evolution of a Gaussian Wave Packet

Starting from a general wave group—a sum of quantum-mechanical plane waves—our goals here are (1) to determine what coefficients of the waves produce a group that is initially Gaussian in shape and (2) to determine the time evolution of that Gaussian group. Our general wave group is given in equation.

$$\Psi(x, t) = \int_{-\infty}^{+\infty} A(k) e^{i(kx - \omega t)} \, dk \tag{21}$$

Equation (27) is the Gaussian form we wish it to have at $t = 0$

$$\Psi(x, 0) = C \, e^{-(x/2\varepsilon)^2} e^{ik_0 x} \tag{27}$$

The first step is simply to evaluate both sides of (21) at $t = 0$, with (27) inserted on the left.

$$C \, e^{-(x/2\varepsilon)^2} e^{ik_0 x} = \int_{-\infty}^{+\infty} A(k) e^{ikx} \, dk \tag{1}$$

The task of solving this equation for $A(k)$ is carried out and the conclusion is

$$\psi(x) = C \, e^{-(x/2\varepsilon)^2} e^{ik_0 x} \quad (23) \qquad \Leftrightarrow \qquad A(k) = \frac{C\varepsilon}{\sqrt{\pi}} e^{-\varepsilon^2(k - k_0)^2} \quad (24)$$

We conclude that inserting this $A(k)$ into (21) ensures the correct form at $t = 0$ and describes, at least formally, how the Gaussian wave group evolves in time.

$$\Psi(x, t) = \int_{-\infty}^{+\infty} \frac{C\varepsilon}{\sqrt{\pi}} e^{-\varepsilon^2(k - k_0)^2} e^{i(kx - \omega t)} \, dk \tag{2}$$

ω depends on k differently for different wave phenomenon, and, strictly speaking, without knowing that dependence, we can go no further. However, our wave pulse has a reasonably well-defined

From Appendix F of *Modern Physics*, Second Edition. Randy Harris. Copyright © 2008 by Pearson Education, Inc. Published by Pearson Addison-Wesley. All rights reserved.

wave number/momentum. Being itself a Gaussian, $A(k)$ is a peaked function, with its maximum occurring at k_0. Accordingly, most of the contribution to the integral occurs near k_0, and if we replace $\omega(k)$ with a power series expanded about the point k_0, we introduce little error. Thus, we write

$$\omega(k) \cong \omega(k_0) + s(k - k_0) + \tfrac{1}{2}D(k - k_0)^2 \tag{3}$$

$$\text{where} \quad s \equiv \left. \frac{d\omega(k)}{dk} \right|_{k_0} \quad \text{and} \quad D \equiv \left. \frac{d^2\omega(k)}{dk^2} \right|_{k_0} \tag{4}$$

Inserting (3) back into (2) yields

$$\Psi(x, t) = \int_{-\infty}^{+\infty} \frac{C\varepsilon}{\sqrt{\pi}} e^{-\varepsilon^2(k - k_0)^2} e^{i[kx - \omega(k_0)t - s(k - k_0)t - \frac{1}{2}D(k - k_0)^2 t]} \, dk$$

A change of variables, $z \equiv k - k_0$, simplifies this expression considerably.

$$\Psi(x, t) = \int_{-\infty}^{+\infty} \frac{C\varepsilon}{\sqrt{\pi}} e^{-\varepsilon^2 z^2} e^{i(zx + k_0 x - \omega(k_0)t - szt - \frac{1}{2}Dz^2 t)} \, dz$$

$$= \frac{C\varepsilon}{\sqrt{\pi}} e^{i(k_0 x - \omega(k_0)t)} \int_{-\infty}^{+\infty} e^{-\varepsilon^2 z^2} e^{i(zx - szt - \frac{1}{2}Dz^2 t)} \, dz$$

$$= \frac{C\varepsilon}{\sqrt{\pi}} e^{i(k_0 x - \omega(k_0)t)} \int_{-\infty}^{+\infty} e^{-(\varepsilon^2 + \frac{1}{2}iDt)z^2} e^{(ix - ist)z} \, dz$$

The remaining integral is a standard Gaussian integral.

$$\Psi(x, t) = \frac{C\varepsilon}{\sqrt{\pi}} e^{i(k_0 x - \omega(k_0)t)} \exp\left[\frac{(ix - ist)^2}{4(\varepsilon^2 + \frac{1}{2}iDt)}\right] \sqrt{\frac{\pi}{(\varepsilon^2 + \frac{1}{2}iDt)}}$$

Rearranging and using simply ω_0 for the frequency corresponding to the central wave number k_0, we have

$$\Psi(x, t) = \frac{C}{\sqrt{1 + iDt/2\varepsilon^2}} \exp\left[\frac{-(x - st)^2}{4\varepsilon^2(1 + iDt/2\varepsilon^2)}\right] e^{i(k_0 x - \omega_0 t)} \tag{5}$$

Note that at $t = 0$, this function is indeed the Gaussian wave pulse of (23) and (27), but now we see how it propagates in time. The complex exponential on the right is its "oscillatory part," including explicit time dependence. It is a plane wave of the pulse's approximate wave number k_0 and frequency ω_0, and it moves at the corresponding phase velocity ω_0/k_0. The other exponential is the "Gaussian part," which modulates the plane wave.

Its maximum occurs at the point $x = st$, so it moves at the speed s, the group velocity. Note that what we have is essentially. The oscillatory crests (light red) move at one speed—the phase velocity—and the simple Gaussian envelope (dark red) moves at quite another.

To calculate the probability density, we note that

$$\frac{1}{1 + iDt/2\varepsilon^2} \frac{1}{1 - iDt/2\varepsilon^2} = \frac{1}{1 + D^2t^2/4\varepsilon^4}$$

and

$$\frac{1}{1 + iDt/2\varepsilon^2} + \frac{1}{1 - iDt/2\varepsilon^2} = \frac{2}{1 + D^2t^2/4\varepsilon^4}$$

From these the reader can show that the probability density for wave function (5) works out to be

$$|\Psi(x, t)|^2 = \frac{C^2}{\sqrt{1 + D^2t^2/4\varepsilon^4}} \exp\left[\frac{-(x - st)^2}{2\varepsilon^2(1 + D^2t^2/4\varepsilon^4)}\right]$$

The oscillatory part and its phase velocity have vanished, irrelevant to the propagation of the particle. Only the group/particle velocity s remains.

Appendix:

The Operator for L^2

To derive the operator for the square of the angular momentum, $\hat{L}^2$, we begin with $\mathbf{L} = \mathbf{r} \times \mathbf{p}$, whose components are

$$L_x = yp_z - zp_y \qquad L_y = zp_x - xp_z \qquad L_z = xp_y - yp_x$$

We determine the operators for these quantities by inserting the basic momentum and position operators. Exercise 40 carries out the steps for L_z. Expressed in spherical polar coordinates, the result is

$$\hat{L}_z = -i\hbar \frac{\partial}{\partial \phi}$$

Let us do the same for L_x and L_y.

$$\hat{L}_x = y\left(-i\hbar \frac{\partial}{\partial z}\right) - z\left(-i\hbar \frac{\partial}{\partial y}\right) \quad \hat{L}_y = z\left(-i\hbar \frac{\partial}{\partial x}\right) - x\left(-i\hbar \frac{\partial}{\partial z}\right)$$

To express these in spherical polar coordinates, we transform the partial derivatives using standard rules of partial differentiation.

$$\hat{L}_x = -i\hbar \left[y\frac{\partial}{\partial z} - z\frac{\partial}{\partial y} \right]$$

$$= -i\hbar \left[y\left(\frac{\partial r}{\partial z}\frac{\partial}{\partial r} + \frac{\partial \theta}{\partial z}\frac{\partial}{\partial \theta} + \frac{\partial \phi}{\partial z}\frac{\partial}{\partial \phi} \right) - z\left(\frac{\partial r}{\partial y}\frac{\partial}{\partial r} + \frac{\partial \theta}{\partial y}\frac{\partial}{\partial \theta} + \frac{\partial \phi}{\partial y}\frac{\partial}{\partial \phi} \right) \right]$$

$$\hat{L}_y = -i\hbar \left[z\frac{\partial}{\partial x} - x\frac{\partial}{\partial z} \right] \tag{1}$$

$$= -i\hbar \left[z\left(\frac{\partial r}{\partial x}\frac{\partial}{\partial r} + \frac{\partial \theta}{\partial x}\frac{\partial}{\partial \theta} + \frac{\partial \phi}{\partial x}\frac{\partial}{\partial \phi} \right) - x\left(\frac{\partial r}{\partial z}\frac{\partial}{\partial r} + \frac{\partial \theta}{\partial z}\frac{\partial}{\partial \theta} + \frac{\partial \phi}{\partial z}\frac{\partial}{\partial \phi} \right) \right]$$

From Appendix G of *Modern Physics*, Second Edition. Randy Harris. Copyright © 2008 by Pearson Education, Inc. Published by Pearson Addison-Wesley. All rights reserved.

TABLE 1 Rectangular-polar transformation

$x = r \sin \theta \cos \phi$	$r = \sqrt{x^2 + y^2 + z^2}$
$y = r \sin \theta \sin \phi$	$\theta = \cos^{-1} \dfrac{z}{\sqrt{x^2 + y^2 + z^2}}$
$z = r \cos \theta$	$\phi = \tan^{-1} \dfrac{y}{x}$

We now need partial derivatives such as $\partial r/\partial z$ and $\partial\theta/\partial z$ in terms of spherical polar coordinates. These we find by implicit differentiation of the formulas for r, θ, and ϕ (see Table 1) with respect to x, y, and z, followed by reexpression of all coefficients in terms of r, θ, and ϕ. For example, in the first instance in equations (2) below, $\partial r/\partial x$ is $\partial \sqrt{x^2 + y^2 + z^2}/\partial x = x/\sqrt{x^2 + y^2 + z^2} = x/r = \sin \theta \cos \phi$. The others are left to the concerned reader. The complete results are

$$\frac{\partial r}{\partial x} = \sin \theta \cos \phi \qquad \frac{\partial r}{\partial y} = \sin \theta \sin \phi \qquad \frac{\partial r}{\partial z} = \cos \theta$$

$$\frac{\partial \theta}{\partial x} = \frac{\cos \theta \cos \phi}{r} \qquad \frac{\partial \theta}{\partial y} = \frac{\cos \theta \sin \phi}{r} \qquad \frac{\partial \theta}{\partial z} = -\frac{\sin \theta}{r} \qquad (2)$$

$$\frac{\partial \phi}{\partial x} = -\frac{\sin \phi}{r \sin \theta} \qquad \frac{\partial \phi}{\partial y} = \frac{\cos \phi}{r \sin \theta} \qquad \frac{\partial \phi}{\partial z} = 0$$

Inserting the coefficients from equations (2) into equations (1) gives

$$\hat{L}_x = -i\hbar \left[r \sin \theta \sin \phi \left(\cos \theta \frac{\partial}{\partial r} - \frac{\sin \theta}{r} \frac{\partial}{\partial \theta} + 0 \frac{\partial}{\partial \phi} \right) \right.$$

$$\left. - r \cos \theta \left(\sin \theta \sin \phi \frac{\partial}{\partial r} + \frac{\cos \theta \sin \phi}{r} \frac{\partial}{\partial \theta} + \frac{\cos \phi}{r \sin \theta} \frac{\partial}{\partial \phi} \right) \right]$$

$$= -i\hbar \left[-\sin \phi \frac{\partial}{\partial \theta} - \cot \theta \cos \phi \frac{\partial}{\partial \phi} \right]$$

$$\hat{L}_y = -i\hbar \left[r \cos \theta \left(\sin \theta \cos \phi \frac{\partial}{\partial r} + \frac{\cos \theta \cos \phi}{r} \frac{\partial}{\partial \theta} - \frac{\sin \phi}{r \sin \theta} \frac{\partial}{\partial \phi} \right) \right.$$

$$\left. - r \sin \theta \cos \phi \left(\cos \theta \frac{\partial}{\partial r} - \frac{\sin \theta}{r} \frac{\partial}{\partial \theta} + 0 \frac{\partial}{\partial \phi} \right) \right]$$

$$= -i\hbar \left[\cos \phi \frac{\partial}{\partial \theta} - \cot \theta \sin \phi \frac{\partial}{\partial \phi} \right]$$

Now squaring, we obtain

$$\hat{L}_x^2 = -\hbar^2\left(-\sin\phi\frac{\partial}{\partial\theta} - \cot\theta\cos\phi\frac{\partial}{\partial\phi}\right)\left(-\sin\phi\frac{\partial}{\partial\theta} - \cot\theta\cos\phi\frac{\partial}{\partial\phi}\right)$$

$$= -\hbar^2\left[\sin^2\phi\frac{\partial^2}{\partial\theta^2} + \cot\theta\cos\phi\frac{\partial}{\partial\phi}\left(\sin\phi\frac{\partial}{\partial\theta}\right)\right.$$

$$\left. + \sin\phi\cos\phi\frac{\partial}{\partial\theta}\left(\cot\theta\frac{\partial}{\partial\phi}\right) + \cot^2\theta\cos\phi\frac{\partial}{\partial\phi}\left(\cos\phi\frac{\partial}{\partial\phi}\right)\right]$$

$$\hat{L}_y^2 = -\hbar^2\left(\cos\phi\frac{\partial}{\partial\theta} - \cot\theta\sin\phi\frac{\partial}{\partial\phi}\right)\left(\cos\phi\frac{\partial}{\partial\theta} - \cot\theta\sin\phi\frac{\partial}{\partial\phi}\right)$$

$$= -\hbar^2\left[\cos^2\phi\frac{\partial^2}{\partial\theta^2} - \cot\theta\sin\phi\frac{\partial}{\partial\phi}\left(\cos\phi\frac{\partial}{\partial\theta}\right)\right.$$

$$\left. - \cos\phi\sin\phi\frac{\partial}{\partial\theta}\left(\cot\theta\frac{\partial}{\partial\phi}\right) + \cot^2\theta\sin\phi\frac{\partial}{\partial\phi}\left(\sin\phi\frac{\partial}{\partial\phi}\right)\right]$$

When these are added, the first terms add to $-\hbar^2(\partial^2/\partial\theta^2)$ and the third terms add to 0. Using the product rule on the quantities in parentheses shows that the second terms add to $-\hbar^2\cot\theta(\partial/\partial\theta)$ and the fourth to $-\hbar^2\cot^2\theta(\partial^2/\partial\phi^2)$. Thus,

$$\hat{L}_x^2 + \hat{L}_y^2 = -\hbar^2\left[\frac{\partial^2}{\partial\theta^2} + \cot\theta\frac{\partial}{\partial\theta} + \cot^2\theta\frac{\partial^2}{\partial\phi^2}\right]$$

Together with $\hat{L}_z^2 = -\hbar^2(\partial^2/\partial\phi^2)$, we then have

$$\hat{L}^2 = \hat{L}_x^2 + \hat{L}_y^2 + \hat{L}_z^2 = -\hbar^2\left[\frac{\partial^2}{\partial\theta^2} + \cot\theta\frac{\partial}{\partial\theta} + \cot^2\theta\frac{\partial^2}{\partial\phi^2}\right] - \hbar^2\frac{\partial^2}{\partial\phi^2}$$

$$= -\hbar^2\left[\frac{\partial^2}{\partial\theta^2} + \cot\theta\frac{\partial}{\partial\theta} + (\cot^2\theta + 1)\frac{\partial^2}{\partial\phi^2}\right]$$

$$= -\hbar^2\left[\frac{\partial^2}{\partial\theta^2} + \cot\theta\frac{\partial}{\partial\theta} + \csc^2\theta\frac{\partial^2}{\partial\phi^2}\right]$$

or

$$\hat{L}^2 = -\hbar^2\left[\csc\theta\frac{\partial}{\partial\theta}\left(\sin\theta\frac{\partial}{\partial\theta}\right) + \csc^2\theta\frac{\partial^2}{\partial\phi^2}\right]$$

Appendix:

Energy Distributions

Our goal here is to determine, for a thermodynamic system in which N particles share a total energy E, the number of particles, N_n, expected to occupy individual-particle state n whose energy is E_n. We start with a statement similar to equation (9):

$$\text{probability of } N_n \text{ particles} \atop \text{being in state } n = \frac{W(N - N_n, E - E_n N_n)}{\displaystyle\sum_{N_n} W(N - N_n, E - E_n N_n)}$$

The numerator in equation (9) was the number of ways of distributing the remaining energy $M - n_i$ among the remaining $N - 1$ oscillators. Here, the numerator is the number of ways of distributing the remaining energy $E - N_n E_n$ among the remaining $N - N_n$ particles *not* in state n. It naturally has two arguments, but we assume no explicit form. The denominator, as always, is the total number of ways—a sum over all possible values of N_n of the number of ways with N_n restricted. For now, we assume the particles to be indistinguishable; we have not concerned ourselves with *which* particles are in state n. And we leave the limits on the sums unspecified, deferring until later concerns about what values N_n is allowed to take on.

The average number of particles in state n follows the usual rule:

$$\text{average number of} \atop \text{particles in state } n = \frac{\displaystyle\sum_{N_n} N_n W(N - N_n, E - E_n N_n)}{\displaystyle\sum_{N_n} W(N - N_n, E - E_n N_n)} \qquad (1)$$

We assume that $N_n \ll N$, so that the $N - N_n$ other particles constitute the **reservoir**, or the vastly larger part of the system.[1] Given that W is unknown, it is not obvious how to proceed, but a power series in the "small" N_n is the key.

First we take a brief mathematical aside. Suppose we have a function of two arguments, each of which is a function of x: $f[a(x), b(x)]$. Consider the power series expansion.

$$f\big[a(x), b(x)\big] = f\big[a(0), b(0)\big]$$

$$+ \left(\frac{d}{dx} f\big[a(x), b(x)\big]\right)\bigg|_{x=0} x + \frac{1}{2}\left(\frac{d^2}{dx^2} f\big[a(x), b(x)\big]\right)\bigg|_{x=0} x^2 + \cdots$$

[1] It would seem that in many cases $N - N_n$ is surely *not* larger. In room-temperature hydrogen gas, for instance, if state N is the ground *vibrational* state, then $N - N_n$ would be nearly 0, for nearly all molecules are in their ground vibrational state. But *translational* energy states may be viewed as the "vastly larger part of the system" with which energy is exchanged and whose unchanging properties define the common temperature. Any change in the number of particles in a given state of vibration *and translation* is an opposite change in the vast number in all *other* vibrational/translational states. Though the actual energy in this larger part of the system remains essentially unchanged, the number of ways of *distributing* it changes significantly.

If x is small, we may truncate this series after the second term. Using the chain rule on the quantity in parentheses in that term, we thus have

$$f\big[a(x), b(x)\big] \cong f\big[a(0), b(0)\big] + \left(\frac{\partial f}{\partial a}\frac{\partial a}{\partial x} + \frac{\partial f}{\partial b}\frac{\partial b}{\partial x}\right)\bigg|_{x=0} x \tag{2}$$

To apply this result, we make the following replacements:

$$f \equiv \ln\big[W(N - N_n, E - E_n N_n)\big]$$

$$x \equiv N_n \qquad a \equiv N - N_n \qquad b \equiv E - E_n N_n \tag{3}$$

The choice $x \equiv N_n$ is logical, for it is the small thing. The definitions of a and b are also sensible, being the arguments of W in equation (1) and functions of the small thing. The perhaps surprising choice is the *logarithm* of W. The reason is that numbers of ways always involve combinatorial factors, such as $\frac{1}{2}^N$ and $N!$, and when N is replaced by $N - N_n$, where $N_n \ll N$, such factors tend to vary *exponentially* with N_n.[2] An exponential is, of course, not linear, so to expand it in powers of N_n and stop at the linear term would be an awful approximation. But the logarithm of an exponential *is* linear. Replacing in equation (2),

$$\ln\big[W(N - N_n, E - E_n N_n)\big] \cong \ln\big[W(N, E)\big] \tag{4}$$

$$+ \left(\frac{\partial \ln\big[W(N, E)\big]}{\partial N}(-1) + \frac{\partial \ln\big[W(N, E)\big]}{\partial E}(-E_n)\right)N_n$$

Having been evaluated at $N_n = 0$, the two remaining partial derivatives depend on the full N and E, so they are properties of the overall system, or reservoir. From definition, we have $\ln W = S/k_B$, so these terms are partial derivatives of the overall system's entropy. To the first we give the symbol α.

$$\frac{\partial \ln\big[W(N, E)\big]}{\partial N} = \frac{\partial(S/k_B)}{\partial N} = \alpha \tag{5}$$

Although we will not study it, α is proportional to the **chemical potential** of the system. The other property, however, is quite familiar.

$$\frac{\partial \ln\big[W(N, E)\big]}{\partial E} = \frac{\partial(S/k_B)}{\partial E} \equiv \frac{1}{k_B T} \tag{6}$$

Do not overlook this important step. Energy distributions depend on temperature, and it is here that temperature enters the picture. Substituting into (4),

$$\ln\big[W(N - N_n, E - E_n N_n)\big] \equiv \ln\big[W(N, E)\big] - \left(\alpha + \frac{E_n}{k_B T}\right)N_n$$

[2]The reader may verify that $(X - x)! \cong X! e^{-x \ln X}$ by plotting the two functions versus x, using a large value, perhaps 100, for X. Note also that $\frac{1}{2}^{X-x} = \frac{1}{2}^X \frac{1}{2}^{-x} = \frac{1}{2}^X e^{-x \ln \frac{1}{2}}$.

or

$$W(N - N_n, E - E_n N_n) = W(N, E)e^{-\alpha N_n - E_n N_n/k_B T}$$

Having finished our power series expansion and invoked some important relationships, we may now insert this back into (1):

$$\begin{aligned}\text{average number of} \atop \text{particles in state } n &= \frac{\displaystyle\sum_{N_n} N_n W(N, E)e^{-\alpha N_n - E_n N_n/k_B T}}{\displaystyle\sum_{N_n} W(N, E)e^{-\alpha N_n - E_n N_n/k_B T}} \\[2em] &= \frac{\displaystyle\sum_{N_n} N_n e^{-\alpha N_n - E_n N_n/k_B T}}{\displaystyle\sum_{N_n} e^{-\alpha N_n - E_n N_n/k_B T}}\end{aligned} \qquad (7)$$

Note that $W(N, E)$, which is independent of the summation index N_n, has canceled. This step is also easily overlooked but of great importance, for $W(N, E)$ contains all the messy factorials and other factors related to distributing energy in the overall system. That it need not even be known means that *the Bose-Einstein and Fermi-Dirac distributions are applicable regardless of the specific system involved.*

We simplify the work ahead with a standard mathematical trick. That (7) leads to the following is left as a mental exercise:

$$\text{average number of} \atop \text{particles in state } n = -\frac{\partial}{\partial \alpha} \ln\left(\sum_{N_n} e^{-\alpha N_n - E_n N_n/k_B T}\right)$$

What we have thus far referred to as "the average number of particles in state n" is in fact the occupation number. Naturally, it is subject to fluctuations, but it becomes increasingly precise as numbers grow.

$$\mathcal{N}(E_n) = -\frac{\partial}{\partial \alpha} \ln\left(\sum_{N_n} e^{-\alpha N_n - E_n N_n/k_B T}\right) \qquad (8)$$

Only now must we distinguish between fermions and bosons. For bosons, N_n is unrestricted. The sum is of the form Σz^{N_n}, where z is $e^{-\alpha - E_n/k_B T}$, and is thus a geometric series. Terms get small very quickly, so it will introduce little error to extend the sum to infinity, enabling us to use the well-known result: $\Sigma_{m=0}^{\infty} z^m = 1/(1 - z)$. Thus,

$$\mathcal{N}(E_n)_{BE} = -\frac{\partial}{\partial \alpha} \ln\left(\sum_{N_n=0}^{\infty} \left(e^{-\alpha - E_n/k_B T}\right)^{N_n}\right) = -\frac{\partial}{\partial \alpha} \ln\left(\frac{1}{1 - e^{-\alpha - E_n/k_B T}}\right)$$

$$= \frac{\partial}{\partial \alpha} \ln\left(1 - e^{-\alpha - E_n/k_B T}\right)$$

or, after differentiating and some rearranging,

$$\mathscr{N}(E_n)_{\mathrm{BE}} = \frac{1}{e^{\alpha + E_n/k_{\mathrm{B}}T} - 1}$$

For fermions, N_n is restricted to the values 0 and 1, so the sum has just two terms.

$$\mathscr{N}(E_n)_{\mathrm{FD}} = -\frac{\partial}{\partial \alpha} \ln\left(\sum_{N_n=0}^{1} \left(e^{-\alpha - E_n/k_{\mathrm{B}}T}\right)^{N_n} \right) = -\frac{\partial}{\partial \alpha} \ln\left(1 + e^{-\alpha - E_n/k_{\mathrm{B}}T}\right)$$

or

$$\mathscr{N}(E_n)_{\mathrm{FD}} = \frac{1}{e^{\alpha + E_n/k_{\mathrm{B}}T} + 1}$$

With $e^{\alpha} \equiv B$, these are expressions.

The Boltzmann Distribution

The foregoing derivation assumed indistinguishable particles. *Which* particles occupied state n never entered the picture. However, there are $N!/N_n!$ ways of switching specific particle labels between state n and the rest of the states without actually changing N_n, and these are indeed different ways *if (but only if) the particles are distinguishable*. We may account for the increased permutations of particle labels simply by including $N!/N_n!$ in all sums over N_n. It carries through to (7), whereupon $N!$ cancels top and bottom, so that (8) becomes

$$\mathscr{N}(E_n)_{\mathrm{Boltz}} = -\frac{\partial}{\partial \alpha} \ln\left(\sum_{N_n} \frac{\left(e^{-\alpha - E_n/k_{\mathrm{B}}T}\right)^{N_n}}{N_n!} \right)$$

If we again allow N_n to extend to infinity, we see that the sum is of the form $\sum_{m=0}^{\infty} z^m/m! = e^z$, where z is $e^{-\alpha - E_n/k_{\mathrm{B}}T}$. Thus,

$$\mathscr{N}(E_n)_{\mathrm{Boltz}} = -\frac{\partial}{\partial \alpha} \ln\left(\exp(e^{-\alpha - E_n/k_{\mathrm{B}}T}) \right) = -\frac{\partial}{\partial \alpha} e^{-\alpha - E_n/k_{\mathrm{B}}T}$$

or

$$\mathscr{N}(E_n)_{\mathrm{Boltz}} = \frac{1}{e^{\alpha + E_n/k_{\mathrm{B}}T}}$$

With $e^{\alpha} \equiv B$, this is Boltzmann distribution.

$B = 1$ for the Photon Gas

A photon gas in which the number of photons is not preset, but rather determined solely by the condition of equilibrium between it and the matter with which it interacts. Although the photon *energy* is tied to the energy of the matter by energy conservation, the photon *number* is not similarly dependent. This means that the total *number* of photons must be that which maximizes the photon gas entropy; that is, $\partial S/\partial N$ must be 0. By the definition of α in (5), we conclude that $B = e^{\alpha} = 1$ for the photon gas.

Appendix:
Properties of Isotopes

Z	Element	Symbol	A	Atomic Mass	% Natural Abundance*	Half-Life (Decay Modes)†
1	Hydrogen	H	1	1.007825	99.985	
			2	2.014102	0.015	
			3	3.016049		12.32 yr (β^-)
2	Helium	He	3	3.016029	1.37×10^{-6}	
			4	4.002603	≈ 100	
3	Lithium	Li	6	6.015121	7.5	
			7	7.016003	92.5	
4	Beryllium	Be	7	7.016928		53.28 d (EC)
			8	8.005305		≈ 0.07 fs (2α)
			9	9.012182	100	
			10	10.013534		1.52 Myr (β^-)
5	Boron	B	10	10.012937	19.9	
			11	11.009305	80.1	
			12	12.014352		20.2 ms (β^-)
6	Carbon	C	11	11.01143		20.3 min (EC, β^+)
			12	12	98.9	
			13	13.003355	1.1	
			14	14.003241		5730 yr (β^-)
7	Nitrogen	N	12	12.018613		11.00 ms (β^-)
			13	13.005738		9.97 min (β^+)
			14	14.003074	99.63	
			15	15.000108	0.37	
8	Oxygen	O	15	15.003065		122.2 s (β^+)
			16	15.994915	99.76	
			17	16.999131	0.04	
			18	17.99916	0.30	
			19	19.003577		26.9 s (β^-)
9	Fluorine	F	19	18.998403	100	
10	Neon	Ne	20	19.992435	90.48	
			21	20.993843	0.27	
			22	21.991383	0.25	
11	Sodium	Na	23	22.989767	100	
12	Magnesium	Mg	24	23.985042	78.99	
			25	24.98537	10.00	
			26	25.982593	11.01	
13	Aluminum	Al	27	26.981539	100	

* Usually, having a percent natural abundance and being unstable—having a half-life—are mutually exclusive. Potassium-40, thorium-232, and uranium-234, -235, and -238 are exceptions.

† EC stands for electron capture. SF stands for spontaneous fission.

Z	Element	Symbol	A	Atomic Mass	% Natural Abundance*	Half-Life (Decay Modes)†
14	Silicon	Si	28	27.976927	92.23	
			29	28.976495	4.67	
			30	29.97377	3.10	
15	Phosphorus	P	31	30.973762	100	
			32	31.973907		14.28 d (β^-)
16	Sulfur	S	32	31.97207	95.02	
			33	32.97146	0.75	
			34	33.967866	4.21	
			35	34.969031		87.2 d (β^-)
			36	35.96708	0.02	
17	Chlorine	Cl	35	34.968852	75.77	
			37	36.965903	24.23	
18	Argon	Ar	36	35.967545	0.337	
			38	37.962732	0.063	
			40	39.962384	99.600	
19	Potassium	K	39	38.963707	93.2581	
			40	39.963999	0.0117	1.26 Gyr (β^-, β^+, EC)
			41	40.961825	6.7302	
20	Calcium	Ca	35	34.99523		50 ms (β^+)
			40	39.962591	96.941	
			41	40.962278		0.103 Myr (EC)
			42	41.958618	0.647	
			43	42.958766	0.135	
			44	43.95548	2.086	
			46	45.953689	0.004	
			48	47.952533	0.187	
21	Scandium	Sc	45	44.95591	100	
22	Titanium	Ti	46	45.952629	8.0	
			47	46.951764	7.3	
			48	47.947947	73.8	
			49	48.947871	5.5	
			50	49.944792	5.4	
23	Vanadium	V	50	49.947161	0.250	
			51	50.943962	99.750	
24	Chromium	Cr	50	49.946046	4.345	
			52	51.940509	83.79	
			53	52.940651	9.50	
			54	53.938882	2.365	
25	Manganese	Mn	55	54.938047	100	
26	Iron	Fe	54	53.939612	5.9	
			56	55.934939	91.72	
			57	56.935396	2.1	
			58	57.933277	0.28	
27	Cobalt	Co	59	58.933198	100	
			60	59.933819		5.271 yr (β^-)

Z	Element	Symbol	A	Atomic Mass	% Natural Abundance*	Half-Life (Decay Modes)†
28	Nickel	Ni	58	57.935346	68.077	
			60	59.930788	26.223	
			61	60.931058	1.140	
			62	61.928346	3.634	
			64	63.927968	0.926	
29	Copper	Cu	63	62.939598	69.17	
			65	64.927793	30.83	
30	Zinc	Zn	64	63.929145	48.6	
			66	65.926304	27.9	
			67	66.927129	4.1	
			68	67.924846	18.8	
			70	69.925325	0.6	
31	Gallium	Ga	69	68.92558	60.108	
			71	70.9247	39.892	
32	Germanium	Ge	70	69.92425	21.24	
			72	71.922079	27.66	
			73	72.923463	7.72	
			74	73.921177	35.94	
			76	75.921401	7.44	
33	Arsenic	As	75	74.921594	100	
34	Selenium	Se	74	73.922475	0.89	
			76	75.919212	9.36	
			77	76.919912	7.63	
			78	77.917308	23.77	
			80	79.91625	49.61	
			82	81.916698	8.74	
35	Bromine	Br	79	78.918336	50.69	
			81	80.916289	49.61	
36	Krypton	Kr	78	77.9204	0.35	
			80	79.91638	2.25	
			82	81.913482	11.6	
			83	82.914135	11.5	
			84	83.911507	57.0	
			86	85.910616	17.3	
			92	91.926270		1.84 s (β^-)
37	Rubidium	Rb	85	84.911794	72.17	
			87	86.909187	27.83	
38	Strontium	Sr	84	83.91343	0.56	
			86	85.909267	9.86	
			87	86.908884	7.00	
			88	87.905619	82.58	
			94	93.915367		1.27 min (β^-)
39	Yttrium	Y	89	88.905849	100	
40	Zirconium	Zr	90	89.904703	51.45	
			91	90.905644	11.22	
			92	91.905039	17.15	

Z	Element	Symbol	A	Atomic Mass	% Natural Abundance*	Half-Life (Decay Modes)†
			94	93.906314	17.38	
			96	95.908275	2.80	
41	Niobium	Nb	93	92.906377	100	
42	Molybdenum	Mo	92	91.906808	14.84	
			94	93.905085	9.25	
			95	94.90584	15.92	
			96	95.904678	16.68	
			97	96.90602	9.55	
			98	97.905406	24.13	
			100	99.907477	9.63	
			101	100.910345		14.6 min (β^-)
43	Technetium	Tc	98	97.907215		4.2 Myr (β^-)
44	Ruthenium	Ru	96	95.907599	5.54	
			98	97.905287	1.86	
			99	98.905939	12.7	
			100	99.904219	12.6	
			101	100.905582	17.1	
			102	101.904348	31.6	
			104	103.905424	18.6	
45	Rhodium	Rh	103	102.9055	100	
46	Palladium	Pd	102	101.905634	1.02	
			104	103.904029	11.14	
			105	104.905079	22.33	
			106	105.903478	27.33	
			108	107.903895	26.46	
			110	109.905167	11.72	
47	Silver	Ag	107	106.905092	51.839	
			109	108.904757	48.161	
48	Cadmium	Cd	106	105.906461	1.25	
			108	107.90418	0.89	
			110	109.903005	12.49	
			111	110.904182	12.8	
			112	111.902758	24.13	
			113	112.9044	12.22	
			114	113.903357	28.73	
			116	115.904754	7.49	
49	Indium	In	113	112.904061	4.3	
			115	114.90388	95.7	
50	Tin	Sn	112	111.904826	0.97	
			114	113.902784	0.65	
			115	114.903348	0.36	
			116	115.901747	14.53	
			117	116.902956	7.68	
			118	117.901609	24.22	
			119	118.90331	8.58	
			120	119.9022	32.59	
			122	121.90344	4.63	
			124	123.905274	5.79	
			132	131.917760		40 s (β^-)

Z	Element	Symbol	A	Atomic Mass	% Natural Abundance*	Half-Life (Decay Modes)†
51	Antimony	Sb	121	120.903821	57.36	
			123	122.904216	42.64	
52	Tellurium	Te	120	119.904048	0.095	
			122	121.903504	2.59	
			123	122.904271	0.905	
			124	123.902823	4.79	
			125	124.904433	7.12	
			126	125.903314	18.93	
			128	127.904463	31.70	
			130	129.906229	33.87	
53	Iodine	I	125	124.90462		59.4 d (EC)
			127	126.904473	100	
54	Xenon	Xe	124	123.905894	0.10	
			126	125.904281	0.09	
			128	127.903531	1.91	
			129	128.90478	26.4	
			130	129.903509	4.1	
			131	130.905072	21.2	
			132	131.904144	26.9	
			134	133.905395	10.4	
			136	135.907214	8.9	
			140	139.921620		13.6 s (β^-)
55	Cesium	Cs	133	132.905429	100	
			135	134.905885		2.3 Myr (β^-)
56	Barium	Ba	130	129.906282	0.106	
			132	131.905042	0.101	
			134	133.904486	2.42	
			135	134.905665	6.593	
			136	135.904553	7.85	
			137	136.905812	11.23	
			138	137.905232	71.70	
			141	140.914363		18.3 min (β^-)
57	Lanthanum	La	138	137.90711	0.0902	
			139	138.906347	99.9098	
58	Cerium	Ce	136	135.90714	0.19	
			138	137.905985	0.25	
			140	139.905433	88.43	
			142	141.909241	11.13	
59	Praseodymium	Pr	141	140.907647	100	
60	Neodymium	Nd	142	141.907719	27.13	
			143	142.90981	12.18	
			144	143.910083	23.80	
			145	144.91257	8.30	
			146	145.913113	17.19	
			148	147.916889	5.76	
			150	149.920887	5.64	
61	Promethium	Pm	145	144.912743		5.98 h (β^-)

Z	Element	Symbol	A	Atomic Mass	% Natural Abundance*	Half-Life (Decay Modes)†
62	Samarium	Sm	144	143.911998	3.1	
			147	146.914895	15.0	
			148	147.91482	11.3	
			149	148.917181	13.8	
			150	149.917273	7.4	
			152	151.919729	26.7	
			154	153.922206	22.7	
63	Europium	Eu	151	150.919847	47.8	
			153	152.921225	52.2	
64	Gadolinium	Gd	152	151.919786	0.20	
			154	153.920861	2.18	
			155	154.922618	14.80	
			156	155.922118	20.47	
			157	156.923956	15.65	
			158	157.924099	24.84	
			160	159.927049	21.86	
65	Terbium	Tb	148	147.924140		1.0 h (β^+, EC)
			159	158.925342	100	
66	Dysprosium	Dy	152	151.924716		2.37 h (EC, α)
			156	155.925277	0.06	
			158	157.924403	0.10	
			160	159.925193	2.34	
			161	160.92693	18.9	
			162	161.926795	25.5	
			163	162.928728	24.9	
			164	163.929171	28.2	
67	Holmium	Ho	152	151.931580		2.4 min (β^+, α)
			165	164.930319	100	
68	Erbium	Er	162	161.928775	0.14	
			164	163.929198	1.61	
			166	165.93029	33.6	
			167	166.932046	22.95	
			168	167.932368	26.8	
			170	169.935461	14.9	
69	Thulium	Tm	169	168.934212	100	
70	Ytterbium	Yb	168	167.933894	0.13	
			170	169.934759	3.05	
			171	170.936323	14.3	
			172	171.936378	21.9	
			173	172.938208	16.12	
			174	173.938859	31.8	
			176	175.942564	12.7	
71	Lutetium	Lu	175	174.94077	97.41	
			176	175.942679	2.59	
72	Hafnium	Hf	174	173.940044	0.162	
			176	175.941406	5.206	
			177	176.943217	18.606	
			178	177.943696	27.297	

Z	Element	Symbol	A	Atomic Mass	% Natural Abundance*	Half-Life (Decay Modes)†
			179	178.945812	13.629	
			180	179.946545	35.100	
73	Tantalum	Ta	180	179.947462	0.012	
			181	180.947992	99.988	
74	Tungsten	W	180	179.946701	0.12	
			182	181.948202	26.3	
			183	182.95022	14.28	
			184	183.950928	30.7	
			186	185.954357	28.6	
75	Rhenium	Re	185	184.952951	37.40	
			187	186.955744	62.60	
76	Osmium	Os	184	183.952488	0.02	
			186	185.95383	1.58	
			187	186.955741	1.6	
			188	187.95586	13.3	
			189	188.958137	16.1	
			190	189.958436	26.4	
			192	191.961467	41.0	
77	Iridium	Ir	191	190.960584	37.3	
			193	192.962917	62.7	
78	Platinum	Pt	190	189.959917	0.01	
			192	191.961019	0.79	
			194	193.962655	32.9	
			195	194.964766	33.8	
			196	195.964926	25.3	
			198	197.967869	7.2	
79	Gold	Au	197	196.966543	100	
80	Mercury	Hg	196	195.965807	0.15	
			198	197.966743	9.97	
			199	198.968254	16.87	
			200	199.9683	23.10	
			201	200.970277	13.18	
			202	201.970617	29.86	
			204	203.973467	6.87	
81	Thallium	Tl	203	202.97232	29.524	
			205	204.974401	70.476	
			208	207.981988		3.053 min (β^-)
82	Lead	Pb	204	203.97302	1.4	
			206	205.97444	24.1	
			207	206.975872	22.1	
			208	207.976627	52.4	
			210	209.984163		22.6 yr (β^-)
			212	211.991871		10.64 h (β^-)
			214	213.999798		27 min (β^-)
83	Bismuth	Bi	209	208.980374	100	
			210	209.984095		5.01 d (β^-)

Z	Element	Symbol	A	Atomic Mass	% Natural Abundance*	Half-Life (Decay Modes)†
			212	211.991255		1.009 h (β^-)
			214	213.998691		19.9 min (β^-)
84	Polonium	Po	209	208.982404		102 yr (α)
			210	209.982848		138.38 d (α)
			212	211.988842		298 ns (α)
			214	213.995176		163.7 μs (α)
			216	216.001889		145 ms (α)
85	Astatine	At	210	209.987126		8.1 h (EC, α)
86	Radon	Rn	220	220.017570		55.6 s (α)
			222	222.01757		3.8235 d (α, β^-)
87	Francium	Fr	223	223.019733		21.8 min (β^-)
88	Radium	Ra	224	224.020186		3.66 d (α)
			226	226.025402		1599 yr (α)
			228	228.031064		5.76 yr (β^-)
89	Actinium	Ac	227	227.02775		21.77 yr (β^-, α)
			228	228.031015		6.15 h (β^-)
			229	229.032980		1.04 h (β^-)
			230	230.038550		7.5 min (β^-)
90	Thorium	Th	232	232.038054	100	14 Gyr (α)
			234	234.043593		24.1 d (β^-)
91	Protactinium	Pa	231	231.03588		32.5 kyr (α)
92	Uranium	U	234	234.040946	0.0055	245 kyr (α)
			235	235.043924	0.720	704 Myr (α)
			238	238.050784	99.2745	4.46 Gyr (α)
93	Neptunium	Np	234	234.042888		4.4 d (β^+, EC)
			237	237.048167		214 Myr (α)
			238	238.050941		2.117 d (β^-)
94	Plutonium	Pu	239	239.052157		24.11 kyr (α)
			244	244.064199		82 Myr (α, SF)
95	Americium	Am	243	243.061375		7.37 kyr (α)
96	Curium	Cm	247	247.070347		15.6 Myr (α)
97	Berkelium	Bk	247	247.070300		1.4 kyr (α)
98	Californium	Cf	251	251.079580		0.90 kyr (α)
99	Einsteinium	Es	252	252.082944		1.29 yr (α, EC)
100	Fermium	Fm	257	257.075099		100.5 d (α, SF)
101	Mendelevium	Md	258	258.098570		51.5 d (α)
102	Nobelium	No	259	259.100931		58 min (α, EC)
103	Lawrencium	Lr	260	260.105320		3 min (α)
104	Rutherfordium	Rf	261	261.108690		65 s (α)
105	Dubnium	Db	262	262.113760		34 s (SF, α)

Z	Element	Symbol	A	Atomic Mass	% Natural Abundance*	Half-Life (Decay Modes)†
106	Seaborgium	Sg	263	263.1182		0.8 s (SF, α)
107	Bohrium	Bh	262	262.1231		0.10 s (α)
108	Hassium	Hs	265	265.1300		2 ms (α)
109	Meitnerium	Mt	266	266.1378		$\approx$3.4 ms (α)

Appendix:

Probability, Mean, Standard Deviation, and Numbers of Ways

Here we highlight the main ideas arising whenever we speak of probabilities in modern physics. Note that most equation numbers have an a, b, c, or d. The reason is not to sneak in more equations, but to emphasize the fact that, despite the seemingly endless ways of reexpressing things, we really deal with only a few basic concepts.

The first concept is probability itself. A quantity Q is the focus, and it can take on various possible values—Q_1, Q_2, Q_3, and so on—each with its probability—P_1, P_2, P_3, and so on. For example, the quantity Q might be the location of a pet house cat. At an arbitrary instant, it may be at a window, Q_1; its favorite sleeping location, Q_2; or its food dish, Q_3, each with a probability. For instance, $P_1 = 0.040$, $P_2 = 0.780$, $P_3 = 0.065$. And there may be some locations where the probability is 0 unless an external agent intervenes, such as the pet washtub. We might have a theory that predicts the probabilities, or they may rest on experimental observation, but in either case, one thing is certain: The sum of *all* the probabilities—the total probability of finding the cat *somewhere* in the house—must be 1.

$$\Sigma_i P_i = 1 \tag{1a}$$

Often probabilities are based on a collection of data, such as N exams, where the quantity Q is the score, or N repetitions of an air-quality experiment, where Q is a fluctuating pollutant level. If value Q_i turns up N_i times out of a total of N, then the probability is simply

$$P_i = \frac{N_i}{N}$$

which fits perfectly.

$$\Sigma_i P_i = \Sigma_i \frac{N_i}{N} = \frac{1}{N}\Sigma_i N_i = \frac{1}{N}N = 1$$

On the other hand, N_i is often a theoretical number of ways of obtaining a particular value. For example, suppose we have an office with four identical cubicles and four workers. We define Q as the number of workers in cubicle 1. As Figure 1 shows, of all the possible ways of distributing the workers, one subset has three workers in cubicle 1, which we designate Q_3, and can be done

Figure 1 Ways of arranging workers a, b, c, and d in four cubicles.

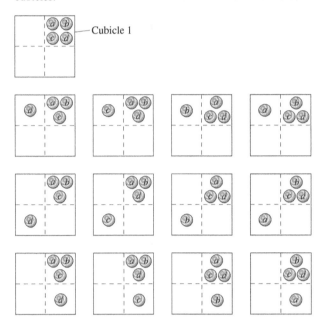

12 ways. Another subset has all four there, designated Q_4, and this can be done only one way. What are the probabilities? We need a bit more to go on. The most common additional assumption is that any way of arranging specific objects in specific locations is equally likely. If this were to apply to the workers (a dubious assumption for real coworkers), then all 13 ways shown in Figure 1 and all the other ways not shown are equally likely. If we were to do an experiment, each way should turn up as often as any other. Therefore, Q_3, in which three workers (independent of their identities) occupy cubicle 1, should turn up 12 times as often as Q_4, simply because there are 12 times as many ways to do it. It happens that the total number of ways is 256 (that is, 4^4), so the probabilities are 12/256 and 1/256. Again, $P_i = N_i/N$, where N is now a number of ways.

Mean

No matter how probability arises, the concept of a **mean**, or average, is always the same. Suppose a quantity can take on only two values, $Q_1 = -60$ and $Q_2 = +60$, and that P_1 is 2/3, so that P_2 is 1/3. With twice the probability, it is logical that we should give Q_1 twice the weighting. A mean of -20 would indeed be half as far from -60 as from $+60$ and would follow from the general prescription: To find the mean $\overline{Q}$, multiply each value by its probability and add.

$$\overline{Q} = \Sigma_i Q_i P_i \tag{2a}$$

If we use $P_i = N_i/N$, this assumes a common form that may be familiar:

$$\overline{Q} = \Sigma_i Q_i \frac{N_i}{N} = \frac{\Sigma_i Q_i N_i}{N} \tag{2b}$$

This says that the mean is a possible value Q_i times the number of times/ways the quantity is obtained, summed over all values, then divided by the total number of times/ways.

Quite often it is relatively easy to obtain something that is *proportional* to probability, but actually expressing the proportionality constant is difficult or messy. In these cases, it is common to write the mean differently. Suppose P' is proportional to the actual probability P:

$$P_i = A P'_i$$

where A is a constant. The total probability must be 1, so

$$\Sigma_i P_i = 1 \implies \Sigma_i A P'_i = A \Sigma_i P'_i = 1 \implies A = \frac{1}{\Sigma_i P'_i}$$

Thus

$$\overline{Q} = \Sigma_i Q_i A P'_i = A \Sigma_i Q_i P'_i = \frac{\Sigma_i Q_i P'_i}{\Sigma_i P'_i} \tag{2c}$$

Again, in this form, P' need only be proportional to P and the proportionality constant disappears.

Finally, if we wish to average something that is a *function* of Q, the probability of obtaining $f(Q_i)$ is the same as obtaining Q_i, and the probabilities still add to 1, so the mean is

$$\overline{f(Q)} = \Sigma_i f(Q_i) P_i \tag{3a}$$

Standard Deviation

Our next concept is a way of quantifying how much the values of Q deviate from the mean. Many recipes are possible, but the most common is the **standard deviation**. How do we come to choose it?

A given value deviates from the mean by

$$\text{deviation: } Q_i - \overline{Q}$$

Some values of Q_i will be above the mean, some below. The deviation is a function of Q_i, which we can average via (3a). The result of the average is logical, but not very helpful.

mean of deviation: $\Sigma_i(Q_i - \overline{Q})P_i = \Sigma_i Q_i P_i - \overline{Q}\,\Sigma_i P_i = \overline{Q} - \overline{Q}\,1 = 0$

So we don't average the deviation! However, if we average its *square*, the sum can have no negative values, and the farther that Q_i values stray from the mean, the larger the average should be.

mean of the square of the deviation: $\Sigma_i\left(Q_i - \overline{Q}\right)^2 P_i$

To yield something that has the same dimensions as Q, we take the square root, giving us the root-mean-square deviation, known as the standard deviation. Of the many symbols used for this important concept, we choose a delta.

$$\Delta Q \equiv \sqrt{\Sigma_i\left(Q_i - \overline{Q}\right)^2 P_i} \tag{4a}$$

Note that this can be *zero* only if P_i is zero whenever $Q_i - \overline{Q}$ is nonzero. Mathematically expressed, $Q_i \neq \overline{Q} \Rightarrow P_i = 0$ In other words, the value $Q_i = \overline{Q}$ is the only one ever obtained. Combined with the fact that ΔQ does spread as deviations increase, we see that standard deviation is a very logical definition.

Standard deviation is often not presented or calculated in form (4a), but instead in a closely related form, whose derivation is a good exercise in sorting out the various quantities we have discussed thus far.

$$\begin{aligned}
\Delta Q &= \sqrt{\Sigma_i\left(Q_i - \overline{Q}\right)^2 P_i} \\
&= \sqrt{\Sigma_i\left(Q_i^2 - 2Q_i\overline{Q} + \overline{Q}^2\right)P_i} \\
&= \sqrt{\Sigma_i Q_i^2 P_i - 2\overline{Q}\,\Sigma_i Q_i P_i + \overline{Q}^2\Sigma_i P_i}
\end{aligned}$$

We have used the fact that $\overline{Q}$ is not a function of summation index i, but simply a number that can be brought outside a summation. In the second term inside the radical, we now recognize the definition of $\overline{Q}$, and in the third, a unit total probability. In the first, we have the mean of the *square* of Q.

$$\Delta Q = \sqrt{\overline{Q^2} - 2\overline{Q}\,\overline{Q} + \overline{Q}^2}$$

or

$$\Delta Q = \sqrt{\overline{Q^2} - \overline{Q}^2} \tag{4b}$$

While obscuring the fact that the radical's argument is necessarily nonnegative, this form makes a simple point: To calculate standard deviation, we need only find the mean of the square, $\overline{Q^2}$, and the square of the mean, $\overline{Q}^2$.

Just as equation (2b) follows from (2a), an alternative form for standard deviation follows from (4a).

$$\Delta Q = \sqrt{\Sigma_i\left(Q_i - \overline{Q}\right)^2\frac{N_i}{N}} = \sqrt{\frac{\Sigma_i\left(Q_i - \overline{Q}\right)^2 N_i}{N}} \tag{4c}$$

A Different Route

Mean and standard deviation can be expressed in a seemingly different form that is really just a matter of redefinition. If the sums are not over possible *values* of the quantity Q but instead over all "trials"—all individual instances of all values, for which we will use j rather than i—then a sum over i with an N_i in the sum is the same as a sum over j alone. For example, if in a series of six trials/experiments we obtain only three values—$Q_1 = 1.2$, $Q_2 = 1.5$, and $Q_3 = 1.8$—in sequence 1.2, 1.8, 1.5, 1.2, 1.2, 1.8, the following are equivalent:

$$\overline{Q} = \frac{\sum_{i=1}^{3} Q_i N_i}{N} = \frac{1.2 \cdot 3 + 1.5 \cdot 1 + 1.8 \cdot 2}{6}$$

$$\overline{Q} = \frac{\sum_{j=1}^{6} Q_i}{N} = \frac{1.2 + 1.8 + 1.5 + 1.2 + 1.2 + 1.8}{6}$$

With this redefinition, all N_i would disappear from sums, and (2b) and (4c) would appear as

$$\overline{Q} = \frac{\sum_{j\,(\text{trials})} Q_j}{N} \qquad \qquad \Delta Q = \sqrt{\frac{\sum_{j\,(\text{trials})} \left(Q_j - \overline{Q}\right)^2}{N}}$$

We avoid this route because it tends to obscure the role of probability and clutters the otherwise seamless transition to continuous quantities.

Continuous Quantities

The number of workers in cubicles is a discrete quantity, its values being restricted to nonnegative integers. Except on average, we don't obtain 1.3 workers in a cubicle. Some quantities are inherently continuous, meaning that from one value to the next is an infinitesimal change. An example would be the locations of a swinging pendulum. In such a case, a sum naturally becomes an integral, and the probabilities of being at particular point locations must become infinitesimal; otherwise, summing over the infinity of locations could not yield a unit total probability. The basic formulas translate in a straightforward way.

$$\sum_i P_i = 1 \qquad \rightarrow \qquad \int dP(Q) = 1$$

$$\overline{Q} = \sum_i Q_i P_i \qquad \rightarrow \qquad \overline{Q} = \int Q \, dP(Q)$$

$$\overline{f(Q)} = \sum_i f(Q_i) P_i \qquad \rightarrow \qquad \overline{f(Q)} = \int f(Q) dP(Q)$$

$$\Delta Q \equiv \sqrt{\sum_i \left(Q_i - \overline{Q}\right)^2 P_i} \qquad \rightarrow \qquad \Delta Q = \sqrt{\int \left(Q - \overline{Q}\right)^2 dP(Q)}$$

Note that equation (4b) is unchanged, as its form is independent of whether a sum or integral is involved.

Finally, for continuous variables, it is usually more convenient to deal not with a differential probability but with a **probability density**, a probability per unit Q, defined as follows:

$$D(Q) \equiv \frac{dP(Q)}{dQ} \quad \text{so that} \quad dP(Q) = D(Q)dQ$$

With this definition, formulas (1a), (2a), (3a), and (4a) become

$$\int D(Q)dQ = 1 \tag{1b}$$

$$\overline{Q} = \int Q\, D(Q)dQ \tag{2d}$$

$$\overline{f(Q)} = \int f(Q)\, D(Q)dQ \tag{3b}$$

$$\Delta Q = \sqrt{\int \left(Q - \overline{Q}\right)^2 D(Q)dQ} \tag{4d}$$

Note that in quantum mechanics, the quantity Q might be location x and the probability density comes from the wave function, $D(x) = |\psi(x)|^2$.

EXAMPLE 1

A quantity Q is measured 40 times, giving the following results:

Value Q_i	1	2	3	4	5	6	7
Number of Times N_i	1	4	9	12	9	4	1

What are the mean and standard deviation?

SOLUTION

The way in which the data are given makes (2b) quickest for the mean.

$$\overline{Q} = \frac{1\cdot 1 + 2\cdot 4 + 3\cdot 9 + 4\cdot 12 + 5\cdot 9 + 6\cdot 4 + 7\cdot 1}{40} = 4$$

For the standard deviation, we can use (4c) directly.

$$\Delta Q = \sqrt{\frac{(1-4)^2 1 + (2-4)^2 4 + (3-4)^2 9 + \cdots + (7-4)^2 1}{40}} = 1.30$$

Another way is equation (4b). This requires calculating the mean of the square, for which equation (3a) is appropriate, the "function" being just the square. Equation (3a) is expressed in terms of probability, but $P_i = N_i/N$ puts it in the form

$$\overline{f(Q)} = \frac{\Sigma_i f(Q_i)N_i}{N}$$

Thus,

$$\overline{Q^2} = \frac{1^2\cdot 1 + 2^2\cdot 4 + 3^2\cdot 9 + 4^2\cdot 12 + 5^2\cdot 9 + 6^2\cdot 4 + 7^2\cdot 1}{40} = 17.7$$

Now using (4b)

$$\Delta Q = \sqrt{17.7 - (4)^2} = 1.30$$

We see that 30 of the 40 values are within 1 standard deviation of the mean. Standard deviation usually covers the majority of values.

EXAMPLE 2

The probability density—probability per unit height— for finding a given object at height y is given by

$$D(y) = A\,e^{-by}$$

and applies to all values of y from 0 to $+\infty$. Find the mean and standard deviation of y in terms of the constant b. The following integral will be useful:

$$\int_0^\infty y^m e^{-by} dy = m!/b^{m+1}$$

SOLUTION

Apparently our result should not depend on A. We can use (1b) to determine it, naturally using y in place of Q.

$$\int_0^\infty A\,e^{-by} dy = 1 \;\; \rightarrow \;\; A \int_0^\infty e^{-by} dy = 1 \;\; \rightarrow \;\; A(1/b) = 1 \;\; \Rightarrow \;\; A = b$$

Thus,

$$D(y) = be^{-by}$$

(*Note:* In quantum mechanics, the process of ensuring unit probability is called normalization.) Now using (2d),

$$\bar{y} = \int_0^\infty y\,be^{-by} dy = b \int_0^\infty y\,e^{-by} dy = b(1!/b^2) = 1/b$$

The result is sensible. If b increases, the exponential falls off faster, and we would expect the average height to be smaller. Moreover, its dimensions are correct. The argument of the exponential must be dimensionless, so the dimensions of b must be one over length.

For the standard deviation, we could use (4d) directly, but let us instead use (4b) after finding the mean of the square via (3b). As in Example 1, the function here is just the square.

$$\overline{y^2} = \int_0^\infty y^2\,be^{-by} dy = b \int_0^\infty y^2 e^{-by} dy = b\left(2!/b^3\right) = 2/b^2$$

Now inserting in (4b)

$$\Delta y = \sqrt{\left(2/b^2\right) - (1/b)^2} = 1/b$$

Not only does this have the correct dimensions of length, but it also happens to equal the mean. We conclude that most values obtained should be in the range of heights between zero to twice the mean.

Figure 2 Ways of parking two of three cars in two parking spaces.

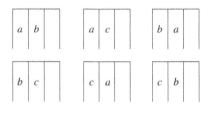

Factorials—Numbers of Ways

Suppose we have N different cars and N individual parking spaces. How many different ways can we arrange the cars in the spaces? Any of the N cars could be in the first space, and any of the remaining $N - 1$ could be in the second space. Thus, filling just the first two spaces, there are $N(N - 1)$ ways. In the special case of three cars, a, b, and c, and three spaces, these six possible ways are shown in Figure 2. Continuing, any of the remaining $N - 2$ cars might be in the third space, so to this point we would have $N(N - 1)(N - 2)$ ways. Of course, in the three-car case, $N - 2$ is 1, and no more ways are added, as there is only one choice for the last car. For arbitrary N, the number of ways would be multiplied by $N - 2$, then $N - 3$, and so on, until again there is only one car left. So the total number of ways is $N\cdot(N - 1)\cdot(N - 2) \cdots 3\cdot2\cdot1$, which is the definition of $N!$ and is referred to as "N factorial."

Figure 3 A region within which rearrangement of objects is declared irrelevant.

Region i

Now let us designate a group of N_i parking spaces as region i, as depicted in Figure 3. By the above arguments, there are $N_i!$ ways of rearranging cars among these spaces *alone*, without affecting cars elsewhere. What happens if we now declare that it doesn't matter where the N_i cars are in this region, and we will consider it as only one way of arranging all N cars? *For any* previous single way of parking all cars in all individual spaces, there *would have been* $N_i!$ different ways (including that single way) that would leave the cars *not* in region i exactly where they were before, and we have now declared these $N_i!$ formerly different ways as just one way. Thus, the previous total number of ways, $N!$, is simply divided by $N_i!$, the number of rearrangements within region i that change nothing outside. Repeating the process, we choose another group of parking spaces from the $N - N_i$ not in region i, calling this new group of N_j spaces region j, and again declaring that rearrangements within it are irrelevant. By the same arguments, we must divide the existing number of ways by $N_j!$ to obtain the new number of ways. If in the end we have broken the line of N spaces into M regions, the number of ways W to park cars in spaces, where rearrangement within any given region is not considered a different way, is

$$W = \frac{N!}{\prod_{i=1}^{M} N_i!} \tag{5}$$

Consider the limits. If each space were a "region," there would be N regions, each with one car—so that $N_i = 1$ for all i—and W would be simply $N!$ (divided by 1! to the power N), as we expect. At the other extreme, if there were just one region encompassing all N spaces, W would be 1, which is also sensible.

We have used cars and parking spaces as the framework, but the arguments are general. Formula (5) gives the number of ways of arranging N objects among M separate categories (regions, boxes, energy levels, etc.), where N_1 particles are in category 1—rearrangements within being irrelevant—N_2 in category 2, and so on.

The most common special case is just two categories, one with n objects, leaving the other with $N - n$ objects, in which case we have

$$W = \frac{N!}{n!(N - n)!}$$

This factor is known as the **binomial coefficient** and is so common that it has been given its own special symbol.

$$W = \frac{N!}{n!(N - n)!} \equiv \binom{N}{n} \tag{6}$$

Appendix:

Some Important Math

In this appendix, we touch on several mathematical topics of particular importance in modern physics.

Complex Numbers

A complex number has two parts: a real number, and another real number multiplied by i, where i is defined by $i^2 = -1$. For example, in $X = 3 + i4$, the **real part** is 3, and the **imaginary part** (which is a real number) is 4. These two parts are sometimes referred to by the notation Re and Im. Thus, Re $X = 3$ and Im $X = 4$. Complex numbers include real numbers as a subset— that is, when the imaginary part is 0—and may be thought of as a compact way of conveying twice the information of a real number. However, they also obey special rules of arithmetic, based on keeping i (to the first power) separate, while i^2 becomes -1. Thus, given $U = u_1 + i\,u_2$ and $V = v_1 + i\,v_2$,

$$U + V = (u_1 + i\,u_2) + (v_1 + i\,v_2) = (u_1 + v_1) + i(u_2 + v_2)$$

$$UV = (u_1 + i\,u_2)(v_1 + i\,v_2) = u_1 v_1 + i\,u_1 v_2 + i\,u_2 v_1 + i^2 u_2 v_2$$
$$= (u_1 v_1 - u_2 v_2) + i(u_1 v_2 + u_2 v_1)$$

The two parts of a complex number may each be functions, for example, $U(x) = u_1(x) + i\,u_2(x)$.

A function whose *argument* is complex may often be broken into its real and imaginary parts. A common example is the exponential. Consider first an exponential whose argument has no real part: e^{ix}, where x is real. The power series $e^b = \sum_{n=0}^{\infty} b^n/n!$ enables us to write

$$e^{ix} = \sum_{0}^{\infty} \frac{(ix)^n}{n!}$$

$$= 1 + ix + i^2\frac{x^2}{2!} + i^3\frac{x^3}{3!} + i^4\frac{x^4}{4!} + i^5\frac{x^5}{5!} + i^6\frac{x^6}{6!} + i^7\frac{x^7}{7!} + i^8\frac{x^8}{8!} + \cdots$$

Using $i^3 = i^2 i = -i$, $i^4 = i^3 i = 1$, $i^5 = i^4 i = i$, and so on, this naturally breaks into two series.

$$e^{ix} = \left(1 - \frac{x^2}{2!} + \frac{x^4}{4!} - \frac{x^6}{6!} + \frac{x^8}{8!} - \cdots\right) + i\left(x - \frac{x^3}{3!} + \frac{x^5}{5!} - \frac{x^7}{7!} + \cdots\right)$$

The sums in parentheses are the power series for cosine and sine, and the result is an identity used very often in physics, known as the **Euler formula**.

Euler formula

$$e^{ix} = \cos x + i \sin x \tag{1}$$

If the argument also has a real part, then $e^{x_1 + ix_2} = e^{x_1} e^{ix_2} = (e^{x_1} \cos x_2) + i(e^{x_1} \sin x_2)$. Useful formulas following directly from the Euler formula are

$$\cos x = \frac{e^{+ix} + e^{-ix}}{2} \qquad \sin x = \frac{e^{+ix} - e^{-ix}}{2i} \tag{2}$$

In the same way as a two-dimensional vector, a complex number has a real, positive magnitude defined as the square root of the sum of the squares of its two parts.

$$|U| = \sqrt{u_1^2 + u_2^2}$$

Given a complex number or function X, its **complex conjugate**, denoted X^*, is obtained by replacing i by $-i$ wherever it occurs. Examples:

$$U = u_1 + iu_2 \implies U^* = u_1 - iu_2$$

$$f(x) = \cos x - i \sin x \implies f^*(x) = \cos x + i \sin x$$

$$f(x) = e^{-x^2} e^{+ix} \implies f^*(x) = e^{x^2} e^{-ix}$$

$$f = \tanh^{-1}(3 - i4) \implies f^* = \tanh^{-1}(3 + i4)$$

The product of a quantity and its complex conjugate gives the square of the quantity's magnitude.

$$U^* U = (u_1 - iu_2)(u_1 + iu_2) = u_1^2 + u_2^2 = |U|^2 \tag{3}$$

Figure 1 The complex exponential e^{ikx} has unit magnitude and "rotates" in the real-complex plane at frequency k.

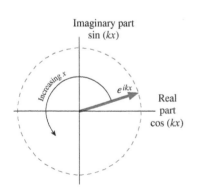

An important special function is the **complex exponential**, $e^{ikx} = \cos(kx) + i \sin(kx)$, whose behavior is represented in Figure 1. It is oscillatory because both its real and imaginary parts are oscillatory, of angular frequency k, and k must have dimensions rad/m or simply m^{-1}. Moreover, the magnitude of e^{ikx} is 1.

$$f(x) = e^{ikx} \implies f^*(x)f(x) = e^{-ikx} e^{+ikx} = e^{-ikx + ikx} = e^0 = 1$$

or, equivalently

$$f^*(x)f(x) = [\cos(kx) - i \sin(kx)][\cos(kx) + i \sin(kx)]$$
$$= \cos^2(kx) + \sin^2(kx) = 1$$

The complex exponential e^{ikx} "rotates" in the real-imaginary plane at frequency k while maintaining unit length.

Differential Equations

A differential equation is one involving derivatives of a function. To be ***mth-order*** is to involve derivatives as high as the mth. A **partial**, as opposed to an **ordinary**, differential equation is one in which the function has multiple independent variables and the derivatives are partial derivatives with respect to those variables. A **linear**, as opposed to **nonlinear**, differential equation is one in which each term involves either the function or one of its derivatives to the *first* power only. Following are some examples:

$$\frac{df(x)}{dx} = bf(x)$$ First-order, ordinary, linear

$$\frac{d^2 f(t)}{dt^2} = bf(t)$$ Second-order, ordinary, linear

$$\frac{\partial^2 f(x, y, z)}{\partial x^2} + \frac{\partial^2 f(x, y, z)}{\partial y^2} + \frac{\partial^2 f(x, y, z)}{\partial z^2} = bf(x, y, z)$$ Second-order, partial, linear

$$\frac{\partial^2 f(x, t)}{\partial x^2} = b\frac{\partial f(x, t)}{\partial t}$$ Second-order, partial, linear

$$\frac{df(t)}{dt} = bf^2(t)$$ First-order, ordinary, nonlinear

Different kinds of differential equations demand different techniques to solve for f. The easiest to solve are the ordinary, linear ones. Partial differential equations are often converted to separate ordinary differential equations, one for each independent variable, by **separation of variables**. To apply this technique to a function such as $f(x, y, z)$, we substitute in the differential equation a product of separate functions of the independent variables: $f_1(x)f_2(y)f_3(z)$. The differential equation is then rearranged so that dependence on each variable is isolated, resulting in three separate ordinary differential equations, which, when solved, give $f_1(x)$, $f_2(y)$, and $f_3(z)$. For many differential equations, particularly nonlinear ones, no technique exists to find a closed-form solution. Numerical approximation techniques are required.

In this text, the reader need become familiar with only two differential equations, summarized below. (Separation of variables will be used to convert any partial differential equations to ordinary ones.) Readers unfamiliar with the techniques by which the function f is actually obtained in these cases are encouraged to consult a math text. Our interest is in the results. Nevertheless, the reader is encouraged at least to *verify* by substitution that the functions f given below do indeed solve their corresponding differential equations.

First-Order Linear

$$\frac{df(x)}{dx} = bf(x) \quad \Rightarrow \quad f(x) = Ae^{bx} \tag{4}$$

Solution of a first-order equation yields one arbitrary constant, essentially a constant of integration, which, in the above result, is A. It can take on any value while still solving the equation. The methodical technique of solving this basic differential equation is to rearrange it to $df/f = b\,dx$, then integrate both sides.

Second-Order Linear

$$\frac{d^2f(x)}{dx^2} = bf(x) \quad \Rightarrow \quad f(x) = \tag{5}$$

$$\begin{cases} A\sin\left(\sqrt{|b|}x\right) + B\cos\left(\sqrt{|b|}x\right) \text{ or } Ae^{+i\sqrt{|b|}x} + Be^{-i\sqrt{|b|}x} & b < 0 \\ Ae^{+\sqrt{b}x} + Be^{-\sqrt{b}x} \text{ or } A\sinh\left(\sqrt{b}x\right) + B\cosh\left(\sqrt{b}x\right) & b > 0 \\ Ax + B & b = 0 \end{cases}$$

A second-order equation yields two arbitrary constants (of integration). Note that the sign of the constant b is *crucial*, for different signs lead to functions whose behaviors are entirely different. If b is negative, the function f is oscillatory; if b is positive, f is exponential, growing or decaying or some combination thereof; and if b is 0, f is a straight line.

Useful Integrals

Below is a short list of integrals most often needed in the text.

$$\int \sin^2\left(\frac{n\pi x}{L}\right) dx = \frac{x}{2} - \frac{L}{4n\pi}\sin\left(\frac{2n\pi x}{L}\right)$$

$$\int x\sin^2\left(\frac{n\pi x}{L}\right) dx = \frac{x^2}{4} - \frac{Lx}{4n\pi}\sin\left(\frac{2n\pi x}{L}\right) - \frac{L^2}{8n^2\pi^2}\cos\left(\frac{2n\pi x}{L}\right)$$

$$\int x^2\sin^2\left(\frac{n\pi x}{L}\right) dx = \frac{x^3}{6} - \frac{Lx^2}{4n\pi}\sin\left(\frac{2n\pi x}{L}\right)$$

$$- \frac{L^2x}{4n^2\pi^2}\cos\left(\frac{2n\pi x}{L}\right) + \frac{L^3}{8n^3\pi^3}\sin\left(\frac{2n\pi x}{L}\right)$$

$$\int_0^\infty x^m e^{-bx}\,dx = \frac{m!}{b^{m+1}}$$

Gaussian Integrals

$$\int_{-\infty}^{+\infty} e^{-a(z-b)^2} dz = \sqrt{\frac{\pi}{a}} \qquad\qquad \int_{-\infty}^{+\infty} e^{-az^2+bz} dz = e^{b^2/4a} \sqrt{\frac{\pi}{a}}$$

$$\int_{-\infty}^{+\infty} z e^{-a(z-b)^2} dz = b\sqrt{\frac{\pi}{a}} \qquad\qquad \int_{-\infty}^{+\infty} z^2 e^{-az^2} dz = \frac{1}{2}\sqrt{\frac{\pi}{a^3}}$$

$$\int_{-\infty}^{+\infty} z^2 e^{-a(z-b)^2} dz = \left(\frac{1}{2a} + b^2\right)\sqrt{\frac{\pi}{a}}$$

Physical Constants and Useful Values

Speed of light	c	2.99792458×10^8 m/s
Gravitational constant	G	6.67×10^{-11} N·m²/kg²
Planck's constant	h	$6.6260690 \times 10^{-34}$ J·s
	$\hbar$	1.054572×10^{-34} J·s
Boltzmann constant	k_B	1.380650×10^{-23} J/K
Avogadro's number	N_A	6.0221418×10^{23} mol^{-1}
Fundamental charge	e	$1.60217649 \times 10^{-19}$ C
Permitivity of free space	ε_0	$8.854187817 \times 10^{-12}$ C²/N·m²
Permeability of free space	μ_0	$4\pi \times 10^{-7}$ N/A²
Coulomb constant	$1/4\pi\varepsilon_0$	8.987552×10^9 N·m²/C²
Electron mass	m_e	$9.1093822 \times 10^{-31}$ kg
Proton mass	m_p	$1.6726217 \times 10^{-27}$ kg
Neutron mass	m_n	$1.6749273 \times 10^{-27}$ kg
Atomic mass unit	u	$1.6605389 \times 10^{-27}$ kg $= 931.4941$ MeV/c^2

From *Modern Physics*, Second Edition. Randy Harris. Copyright © 2008 by Pearson Education, Inc. Published by Pearson Addison-Wesley. All rights reserved.

Useful Integrals

$$\int \sin^2\left(\frac{n\pi x}{L}\right)dx = \frac{x}{2} - \frac{L}{4n\pi}\sin\left(\frac{2n\pi x}{L}\right)$$

$$\int x\sin^2\left(\frac{n\pi x}{L}\right)dx = \frac{x^2}{4} - \frac{Lx}{4n\pi}\sin\left(\frac{2n\pi x}{L}\right) - \frac{L^2}{8n^2\pi^2}\cos\left(\frac{2n\pi x}{L}\right)$$

$$\int x^2\sin^2\left(\frac{n\pi x}{L}\right)dx = \frac{x^3}{6} - \frac{Lx^2}{4n\pi}\sin\left(\frac{2n\pi x}{L}\right)$$

$$- \frac{L^2 x}{4n^2\pi^2}\cos\left(\frac{2n\pi x}{L}\right) + \frac{L^3}{8n^3\pi^3}\sin\left(\frac{2n\pi x}{L}\right)$$

$$\int_0^\infty x^m e^{-bx}dx = \frac{m!}{b^{m+1}}$$

Gaussian Integrals

$$\int_{-\infty}^{+\infty} e^{-a(z-b)^2}dz = \sqrt{\frac{\pi}{a}} \qquad \int_{-\infty}^{+\infty} e^{-az^2+bz}dz = e^{b^2/4a}\sqrt{\frac{\pi}{a}}$$

$$\int_{-\infty}^{+\infty} ze^{-a(z-b)^2}dz = b\sqrt{\frac{\pi}{a}} \qquad \int_{-\infty}^{+\infty} z^2 e^{-az^2}dz = \frac{1}{2}\sqrt{\frac{\pi}{a^3}}$$

$$\int_{-\infty}^{+\infty} z^2 e^{-a(z-b)^2}dz = \left(\frac{1}{2a} + b^2\right)\sqrt{\frac{\pi}{a}}$$

Useful Equations

Complex Numbers

$$e^{+ix} = \cos x + i \sin x$$

$$\cos x = \frac{e^{ix} + e^{-ix}}{2} \quad \sin x = \frac{e^{ix} - e^{-ix}}{2i}$$

$$U^*U = (u_1 - iu_2)(u_1 + iu_2) = u_1^2 + u_2^2 = |U|^2$$

$$f(x) = e^{ikx} \quad \Rightarrow \quad f^*(x)f(x) = e^{-ikx}e^{+ikx} = e^{-ikx+ikx} = e^0 = 1$$

$$|U| = \sqrt{u_1^2 + u_2^2}$$

Differential Equations

$$\frac{df(x)}{dx} = bf(x) \quad \Rightarrow \quad f(x) = Ae^{bx}$$

$$\frac{d^2f(x)}{dx^2} = bf(x)$$

$$\Rightarrow \quad f(x) = \begin{cases} A \sin\left(\sqrt{|b|}x\right) + B \cos\left(\sqrt{|b|}x\right) \text{ or } Ae^{+i\sqrt{|b|}x} + Be^{-i\sqrt{|b|}x} & b < 0 \\ Ae^{+\sqrt{b}x} + Be^{-\sqrt{b}x} \text{ or } A \sinh\left(\sqrt{b}x\right) + B \cosh\left(\sqrt{b}x\right) & b > 0 \\ Ax + B & b = 0 \end{cases}$$

Periodic Table of the Elements

Key:

Symbol	**He** — Atomic number Z — 2
	4.0026 — Atomic mass*
Electronic configuration (if different from pattern)	$1s^2$

Shell n \ Subshell	ns^1	ns^2	$(n-2)f$	$(n-1)d^1$	$(n-1)d^2$	$(n-1)d^3$	$(n-1)d^4$	$(n-1)d^5$	$(n-1)d^6$	$(n-1)d^7$	$(n-1)d^8$	$(n-1)d^9$	$(n-1)d^{10}$	np^1	np^2	np^3	np^4	np^5	np^6
Typical valence	+1	+2		+3	+4	+5								+3	+4	+5	−2	−1	0
1	**H** 1 / 1.00794																		**He** 2 / 4.0026 / $1s^2$
2	**Li** 3 / 6.941	**Be** 4 / 9.01218												**B** 5 / 10.811	**C** 6 / 12.011	**N** 7 / 14.0067	**O** 8 / 15.9994	**F** 9 / 18.9984	**Ne** 10 / 20.1797
3	**Na** 11 / 22.9898	**Mg** 12 / 24.3050												**Al** 13 / 26.9815	**Si** 14 / 28.0855	**P** 15 / 30.9738	**S** 16 / 32.066	**Cl** 17 / 35.4527	**Ar** 18 / 39.948
4	**K** 19 / 39.0983	**Ca** 20 / 40.078		**Sc** 21 / 44.9559	**Ti** 22 / 47.88	**V** 23 / 50.9415	**Cr** 24 / 51.9961 / $3d^54s^1$	**Mn** 25 / 54.9381	**Fe** 26 / 55.847	**Co** 27 / 58.9332	**Ni** 28 / 58.6934	**Cu** 29 / 63.546 / $3d^{10}4s^1$	**Zn** 30 / 65.39	**Ga** 31 / 69.723	**Ge** 32 / 72.61	**As** 33 / 74.9216	**Se** 34 / 78.96	**Br** 35 / 79.904	**Kr** 36 / 83.80
5	**Rb** 37 / 85.4678	**Sr** 38 / 87.62		**Y** 39 / 88.9059	**Zr** 40 / 91.224	**Nb** 41 / 92.9064 / $4d^45s^1$	**Mo** 42 / 95.94 / $4d^55s^1$	**Tc** 43 / (98)	**Ru** 44 / 101.07 / $4d^75s^1$	**Rh** 45 / 102.906 / $4d^85s^1$	**Pd** 46 / 106.42 / $4d^{10}5s^0$	**Ag** 47 / 107.868 / $4d^{10}5s^1$	**Cd** 48 / 112.411	**In** 49 / 114.82	**Sn** 50 / 118.710	**Sb** 51 / 121.757	**Te** 52 / 127.60	**I** 53 / 126.904	**Xe** 54 / 131.29
6	**Cs** 55 / 132.905	**Ba** 56 / 137.327	La–Yb	**Lu** 71 / 174.967	**Hf** 72 / 178.49	**Ta** 73 / 180.948	**W** 74 / 183.85	**Re** 75 / 186.207	**Os** 76 / 190.2	**Ir** 77 / 192.22	**Pt** 78 / 195.08 / $5d^96s^1$	**Au** 79 / 196.967 / $5d^{10}6s^1$	**Hg** 80 / 200.59	**Tl** 81 / 204.383	**Pb** 82 / 207.2	**Bi** 83 / 208.980	**Po** 84 / (209)	**At** 85 / (210)	**Rn** 86 / (222)
7	**Fr** 87 / (223)	**Ra** 88 / (226)	Ac–No	**Lr** 103 / (262)	**Rf** 104 / (261)	**Db** 105 / (262)	**Sg** 106 / (263)	**Bh** 107 / (262)	**Hs** 108 / (265)	**Mt** 109 / (266)	**Ds** 110 / (281)	**Rg** 111 / (280)	**Uub** 112 / (285)	**Uut** 113 / (284)	**Uuq** 114 / (289)	**Uup** 115 / (288)	**Uuh** 116 / (293)		

Lanthanides

f^1	f^2	f^3	f^4	f^5	f^6	f^7	f^8	f^9	f^{10}	f^{11}	f^{12}	f^{13}	f^{14}
La 57 / 138.906 / $5d^16s^2$	**Ce** 58 / 140.115 / $4f^15d^16s^2$	**Pr** 59 / 140.908	**Nd** 60 / 144.24	**Pm** 61 / (145)	**Sm** 62 / 150.38	**Eu** 63 / 151.965	**Gd** 64 / 157.25 / $4f^75d^16s^2$	**Tb** 65 / 158.925 / $4f^95d^16s^2$	**Dy** 66 / 162.50	**Ho** 67 / 164.930	**Er** 68 / 167.26	**Tm** 69 / 168.934	**Yb** 70 / 173.04

Actinides

f^1	f^2	f^3	f^4	f^5	f^6	f^7	f^8	f^9	f^{10}	f^{11}	f^{12}	f^{13}	f^{14}
Ac 89 / (227) / $6d^17s^2$	**Th** 90 / 232.038 / $6d^27s^2$	**Pa** 91 / (231) / $5f^26d^17s^2$	**U** 92 / 238.029 / $5f^36d^17s^2$	**Np** 93 / (237) / $5f^46d^17s^2$	**Pu** 94 / (244)	**Am** 95 / (243)	**Cm** 96 / (247) / $5f^76d^17s^2$	**Bk** 97 / (247)	**Cf** 98 / (251)	**Es** 99 / (252)	**Fm** 100 / (257)	**Md** 101 / (258)	**No** 102 / (259)

* In atomic mass units, u. Averaged over naturally occurring isotopes. Values in parentheses are mass numbers of most stable known isotopes.

From *Modern Physics*, Second Edition. Randy Harris. Copyright © 2008 by Pearson Education, Inc.
Published by Pearson Addison-Wesley. All rights reserved.

Index

631